LIFE
IN
SOCIETY

Introductory Readings in Sociology

LIFE IN SOCIETY

Thomas E. Lasswell, University of Southern California
John H. Burma, Grinnell College
Sidney H. Aronson, New York University

Scott, Foresman and Company   Chicago   Atlanta   Dallas   Palo Alto   Fair Lawn, N.J.

Library of Congress Catalog No. 65-17726
Copyright © 1965 by Scott, Foresman and Company
Printed in the United States of America
All Rights Reserved

Preface

Sociology is the study of interpersonal relations. As is true of any scholarly discipline, it rises above the development of a skill or the learning of a technique and focuses instead upon the orderly effort to discover and to understand the most general principles of its special perspective of human existence.

The orderly study of any phenomenon involves three basic operations: (1) the definition of concepts, (2) the observation of phenomena, and (3) the formulation of general statements. There is no "proper" sequence for these operations; they may even occur simultaneously (and perhaps spontaneously) in a student's mind as a "flash of insight" that encompasses instantaneous sensation, perception, comprehension, and cognitive integration. Such a flash of insight may come at first acquaintance with an object, event, or process, or it may come after years of the most patient search, or it may never come.

With these thoughts in mind, the editors of this book set about to supplement the regular textbooks in sociology with a collection of readings designed to increase the probability that a beginning student will have an adequate cognitive schema for intellectual insight into interpersonal relations. The readings were selected according to several criteria. First of all, bearing in mind that many students will be undergoing their initiation into the behavioral sciences as they read this book, the editors made an effort to choose readings that did not assume the completion of any advanced course in the behavioral sciences; if they were successful, any intelligent college freshman should be able to understand each selection.

Second, an effort was made to choose readings dealing with sociological concepts that are consensual rather than controversial among sociologists. Generally accepted definitions and illustrations were sought to strengthen rather than to challenge the concepts in orthodox introductory texts, in order to develop the student's critical abilities with respect to a relatively few "standard" concepts rather than to extend them into a great variety of specialized areas.

Third, although care was taken not to assume sophistication in methods and statistics on the part of the readers, an effort was made to include in each section of the book at least one reading that presents or illustrates some form of controlled empirical observation.

Fourth, articles and excerpts were sought whose general statements have remained valid and reliable through time. As a rule, the editors chose well-established validity over current sociological fashion. Certainly every teacher will want to add a few readings from new books and journals to those reproduced here. This volume is not intended to compete with the current journal literature but rather to provide a background for understanding it more fully.

Fifth, our general goal was to provide sound education for beginning sociology students rather than to win the accolade of our colleagues for unusual or clever selections. Some readings that seem to have made a point well year in and year out have been included for precisely that reason. We admit to including a few selections experimentally on the grounds of logical choice, but no effort at all was made to produce an experimental volume.

Finally, where there was a choice between articles about the phenomenal world and articles about mathematical models, we chose the former. The editors are in accord that the beginning student should relate sociology to society, with abstractions kept at as low a level as possible.

Each part begins with an introductory note that discusses the concepts to be treated within it and shows how the articles are related to these concepts and to each other. The introductory notes are continued as headnotes for each selection throughout the part, so that each part may be read as an integrated unit. A recognized specialist was selected to write an original report on current trends in sociological research in the subject area of the part. These Recent Research notes at the end of each part are intended particularly to guide highly motivated students into specialized independent study; some teachers may wish each of their students to make an independent investigation of one suggested area.

Although the editors worked together to plan the volume as a whole, each one assumed detailed responsibility for specific sections: Lasswell, Parts I, II, VI, and VIII; Burma, Parts V, VII, and IX; Aronson, Parts III and IV, although Aronson and Lasswell collaborated on the introduction to Part IV.

In addition to the many teachers, colleagues, and students who have given us general guidance through the years, we owe a special debt for the very real and specific contributions of Edward C. McDonagh, H. Laurence Ross, Ruth M. Talley, Dorothy Lepire, Linda Norris, Charles Mulford, Robert A. Feldmesser, Fred Knell, and Sharon Baumgartner.

Thomas E. Lasswell
John H. Burma
Sidney H. Aronson

Contents

Part I

INTRODUCTION: SOCIOLOGY AS A
BEHAVIORAL SCIENCE

Sociology is defined as the study of interpersonal relations, including the "structure" and function of human society. Relationships between persons range from an individual's understandings and expectations about the specific behaviors of others to his understanding of and behaviors in complex social systems of all sizes and kinds—even to his understanding of societies and civilizations—as frameworks in which his behaviors and those of others have significance.

A number of aspects of interpersonal relations are studied by sociologists. A few of them should be defined as a point of departure.

Interaction is a part of interpersonal relations by definition, since it occurs whenever one person provides a stimulus to which another person responds.

Social organization comprises the recurring and interrelated patterns of interaction among the members of social entities. The referent for social organization is the actual behavior of persons involved in interpersonal relations.

Social groups are persons in interaction. In its most restricted use, the term *social group* refers to any number of persons from whose interpersonal relations emerge an enduring pattern of interrelated roles and statuses, a set of shared beliefs and values, and a feeling of common identity.

Culture is the complex whole which includes knowledge, beliefs, art, morals, laws, customs, and any other capabilities and habits acquired by man as a member of a society. Descriptions of a given culture usually stress the ideal standards or "designs for living" which the members of a society believe must or should be used to guide their behavior. Interpersonal relations can be partially understood, explained, and predicted in terms of the cultural prescriptions enacted by the participants.

Social institutions are the broad complexes of cultural prescriptions which are associated with important segments of interpersonal relations (e.g., political, economic, and religious) and which are recognized and sanctioned by society generally.

Socialization refers to the learning processes through which the individual is prepared to participate in interpersonal relations by incorporating societal sentiments, knowledge, beliefs, and standards into his personality.

Demography is the numerical and statistical analysis of the human population—its gross physical and social characteristics and its changes with respect to time and space. The demographic composition of a social aggregate, especially at the community or society level, may be influential in determining the nature of interpersonal relations.

Human *ecologists* study the relationships of human beings with their environments and the resulting spatial and temporal patterning of populations, services, and structures.

Social problems are significant discrepancies between cultural standards and actual social conditions which the members of social groups believe can and should be eliminated or reduced. Social problems either disrupt the expected patterns of human interaction or are the subject of widespread disapproval as "social evils."

While among the behavioral sciences sociology emphasizes interpersonal relationships, *psychology* is primarily concerned with the individual's responses to internal and external stimuli as reflected in his intelligence, motivations, fears, aspirations, and other behavioral dimensions, and in the mechanisms which mediate such stimuli and responses.

Social psychology, a subdivision of both sociology and psychology, focuses on the way in which the individual interacts in social groups, and on the social and cultural influences in personality development.

Anthropology, literally defined as the science of man, embraces two distinct areas of study: *Physical anthropology* deals with the biological characteristics of men related to their temporal, spatial, and social distributions; *archaeology*, *ethnology*, *ethnography*, *linguistics*, and *social* and *cultural anthropology* are concerned with the material and nonmaterial traits of human societies and societal subdivisions.

In many ways, accumulating and ordering knowledge about human behavior can be more difficult than studying nonhuman objects, which may be less complex and less subject to rapid change. It is necessary for sociologists to use extremely stringent methods for arriving at conclusions.

Most sociologists believe that valid and reliable knowledge is most likely to be acquired by using the scientific method. It can be shown, of course, that valid and reliable knowledge occasionally has been gained by unscientific means in all scholarly fields, but sociologists have come to look upon the scientific method as the final test for verifying the validity and reliability of their research. The rigorous methods of science do not imply that originality of approach or creativity can be sacrificed. On the contrary, these qualities are fully as important as they are in letters or in arts. Scientific procedure is most productive when it is executed by highly motivated, imaginative men operating within an expanding cultural base.

Using sociological methods, men can discover, classify, and predict social phenomena, but sociology does not *create* truth. Since many "truths" that were accepted in the past have been modified or even refuted by more recent findings, scholars avoid making claims of having discovered truth for more reasons than modesty. Nevertheless, some of the knowledge of human interpersonal relations that has been accrued seems sufficiently valid and reliable to be useful both in explaining social phenomena and in helping solve problems of human interrelationships.

No sociologist would be foolish enough to claim that everything written in sociology books is either entirely accurate or completely scientific. New information constantly supersedes old information, as in any expanding field of study. Sociology has the disadvantage of being a young science, of having a relatively short (half a century or so) period of academic development and hence a relatively small "cultural base," but it also has the promise and excitement of a frontier of inquiry in an area certain to be a focus of intellectual interest for centuries to come.

Although the basic task of sociological research is to answer questions, it also performs the important function of raising new questions. In order to provide a storehouse of information for present and future research, it is necessary for the sociologist to discover, identify, and record observations about people and their interactions. To insure the usefulness of these observations, it is necessary to classify them—to separate them into categories and relate them to concepts.

Funds have always been more easily acquired where there was evidence that proposed research might contribute to the solution or alleviation of an immediate social problem; it has been more difficult to obtain funds simply for the purpose of securing knowledge. Ironically, however, many scholars believe that more problems are solved and more progress is made through basic than through applied research.

The sources of research questions are many. They may arise from the statement of problems, they may arise from the efforts to explain something in the classroom, they may arise from idle speculation or from the observation of people in interaction. When existing sociological theory demands the answer to a question or the verification of a speculation, the "guessed" answer or the speculation to be verified is called a *hypothesis*. Any part of a theory for which sufficient evidence has not been collected and found in support is *hypothetical*; it is a tentative explanation rather than a verified one.

Some typical sociological research questions are: Is there a higher rate of delinquency among children who come from broken homes than among children who come from unbroken homes? Does the rate of mental illness increase as population becomes more dense? Is the length of time a couple is engaged to be married related to their chances of divorce? So far, research on these three questions has led to answers involving statistical probabilities; but it is even more important that the initial answers have raised more sophisticated questions, which have in turn made new and more sophisticated research possible.

The ideal of all sociological research is to develop such definitive and explicit concepts for use in fully testable hypotheses (which are derived from emerging theory) that controlled empirical observations, which will precisely confirm or deny the hypotheses, can be made. For example, from the general theoretical principle that culture is acquired through interaction one may derive the hypothesis that an infant deprived of verbal interaction will not exhibit the language (cultural behavior) of his parents. All of the concepts used are specific and the hypothesis is testable. No child known to be deprived of verbal interaction since infancy has ever been observed upon discovery to exhibit the language behavior of his parents. The hypothesis is confirmed to date. The evidence supports the more general theoretical principle. It is clear that an important part of research lies in asking the right questions. As new knowledge is found, more sophisticated questions become possible. Science will have been perfected on that probably impossible day when every question will have a known answer in which complete confidence can be placed.

After a research question has been formulated, three distinct steps are involved in the research process.

First, the question or problem to be studied must be carefully identified; this involves classifying the incidents or cases upon which the research is being conducted. Conceptual and taxonomic factors are obviously of the essence at this point. If no absolute or arbitrary definitions are available and accepted—and they most often are not—an *operational definition,* which establishes the exact diacritica for identifying objects or categories in the study at hand, must be set down for each important factor. A "child," for example, might be variously defined as any person eighteen years of age or under, as any *unmarried* person eighteen years of age or under, or as any person who has not yet reached the physical state of puberty, and so forth. To be fully operational, a term must refer to something that can be observed objectively.

All of the incidents or cases in a category or aggregation being studied sociologically constitute a *universe* or *population.* Such a universe must be located in space, time, and relevant taxonomic contexts and often in cultural and social contexts.

If an entire universe is not studied, the researcher must state how many cases were studied and how the cases were selected. Any number of cases fewer than the total is called a *sample.* Great care must be taken that the cases in the sample are both categorically and proportionately identical to the universe; if they do not correctly represent every category of the universe, the conclusions from the findings may be overgeneralized if not wholly inaccurate.

The size of the sample is important. It should constitute a convincingly large fraction of the universe if conclusions are to be drawn directly from the data, as they sometimes are in medical research and in census studies. If conclusions are to be drawn on the basis of mathematical probability, which is more often the case, the sample must be large enough to meet all the requirements of the statistical procedures used.

The second step in the research process is the accumulation of information which may support, refute, or bear in some other way on the validity of possible answers to the research question. This step usually involves both primary and secondary research methods. *Secondary research* involves classifying, analyzing, correlating, or interpreting data which the researcher did not obtain for himself but which he is willing to accept as accurate and representative. Such information is acquired from previous documents or studies—surveys, censuses, monographs, theses, dissertations, research reports, etc. *Primary research,* on the other hand, involves the direct acquisition of information by the researcher. It should not be inferred that primary research is always superior to secondary research; few of us, for example, could hope to gather population data as completely and accurately as does the United States Census Bureau. Some of the techniques commonly used in primary research are listed and briefly described below.

Surveys are made by gathering many kinds of information about a region or a community or a particular phase of social life in either, using, perhaps, both primary and secondary research methods.

Polls are taken by asking a question or set of questions of the members (or a sample of the members) of a population. Polls may be conducted by personal interviews, by telephone, or by mail. If several questions are asked by the researcher, he usually arranges the answers in order on a *schedule.* A *questionnaire,* by contrast, is a sheet (or sheets) of questions which is given or sent to a person so that he can give his answers to the researcher in written form.

Personal interviews always involve direct contact with the person from whom or about whom information is sought. Polls and surveys may include personal interviews. Successful interviewing requires skill both in conducting an interview and in preparing a report of it. This is particularly true when the questions on the schedule are *open-ended*—that is, when they have no fixed, factual answers (such as yes, no, age, occupation) but are designed to draw out unrestricted statements of feeling or opinion. An example of an open-ended question is: How do you feel desegregation should be carried out? If the interviewer has no schedule but wishes to gain information about a particular topic through a flexible line of questioning (or listening), which he adapts to the course of the interview, he is conducting a *focused interview*.

Experimental and control group studies are usually conducted by taking two matched samples. Matched samples might be found, for example, in two twelfth-grade English classes in the same high school, provided that the ratio of boys to girls, the distribution of ages, the distribution of intelligence, and as many other factors as might be of importance to the study are the same or nearly the same. When the samples have been selected, the groups are compared for their likeness in the trait or quality in question. Then, after only one of the two groups is given a particular experience, the groups are compared a second time and the effects of the experience are deduced from the differences found between the two comparisons. This technique was used when the Salk poliomyelitis vaccine was first tried in schools. Some children were given Salk vaccine and others were given injections of distilled water; neither the children nor their parents were told into which category they fell. After a time the number of cases of polio that occurred in each category subsequent to the injections was counted, and it was found that a decidedly smaller number of those who had been given the vaccine (the experimental group) contracted polio than of those who had been given distilled water (the control group). Since there was no reason to believe that cases of polio prior to the experiment had occurred more frequently among persons who had been given injections of distilled water or less frequently among persons who had not, the researchers concluded that administration of the Salk vaccine was a significant variable in reducing the incidence of polio in the experimental group.

Personal documents, such as letters, diaries, or specially prepared papers, may be used by a researcher to obtain information about his subjects. This method of research is necessarily limited in its use to subjects who are capable of expressing themselves in writing. Terman's famous *Genetic Studies of Genius* made extensive use of personal documents, as did Thomas and Znaniecki's *The Polish Peasant in Europe and America.*

Life histories may be useful in research. This technique usually involves both personal interviews and personal documents. It frequently gives insight not only into the behavior of the individual but also into the nature and culture of the society in which he lives and may therefore be especially helpful in formulating new research questions. Life histories are a form of *longitudinal research* (unless done *ex post facto*), continuous studies over a relatively long period of time. Such studies are expensive and time-consuming; they often involve long-term commitments to which researchers prefer not to tie themselves. As every researcher knows, "acts of God" often occur which impair or destroy the value of a research project, and this risk is unusually great in longitudinal research because of the time involved. Further, few researchers want to defer the publication of their major contribution until their old age (or until after their death), and few research foundations and universities care to employ untried scholars on the promise that they will produce something significant in a quarter of a century or so. Researchers themselves may be deterred from such long-term projects by fear of indeterminate results after years of thoughtful research. Hence, it is not surprising that there is a dearth of longitudinal research, even though such studies are virtually indispensable to psychiatry and clinical psychology.

Case studies may take the form of life histories, but more often they are studies of an individual's behavior in a single situation. The criminologist frequently turns to this form of research. For example, in order to understand murder better, he may review a large number of murder cases; after he develops a tentative explanation, he continues to compare each new case with that explanation. The method of perfecting a tentative explanation by continually verifying or revising it according to information from new cases is called *analytic induction.*

The third step in the research process takes place when as much evidence has been collected as is possible or feasible, or when the sample shows signs of being statistically satisfactory: the researcher must report his findings. The increase of knowledge is dependent upon communication; research which is not reported can be useful only to the researcher. He must show how the data he has gathered serve to answer his original question.

Principles and general statements are made on the basis of evidence gathered through research. From one point of view, a principle is always tentative, for if all subsequent research in the same area does not support the principle, it must be modified or rejected. Verification is never considered final; each new case is a test.

The development of principles is abetted by constructive criticism from informed persons, but even the most authoritative opinions should never be substituted for direct research. Research may be directed by speculations, but speculations are not research. Neither is logic (and hence mathematics) research, although it may be of real help to the researcher. Every morning when the sun "rises" we put to test the principles which have been developed about the movement of the earth with respect to other heavenly bodies. No logic, no reasoning, no opinion, no authority is as relevant to those principles as is the actual rising of the sun at the predicted time. However, these principles have been observed to be valid in such a great number of cases that should the sun be reported to have risen a few minutes late, we would suspect either an error on the part of the reporter or an inaccuracy in his information.

When principles, general statements, or laws relating to an idea or concept are gathered, they may be incorporated into a *theory.* Basically, a theory is an explanation of how something works. In practice, theories often contain a certain amount of speculation and some untested hypotheses. Theories in every scientific field are continually questioned, constantly rephrased or reoriented; it is thus realistic to think of them as *emergent,* always subject to modification. Some explanations of phenomena, particularly very new or radically different explanations, originate as almost entirely intuitive or speculative "guesses" or shifts in perspective. Even though such explanations cannot be considered valid or reliable until they are supported by empirical research, they do provide the necessary framework for such research and hence are sometimes loosely referred to as theories, although exacting scientists may object to this use of the term.

Social theory is still in its infancy and contains a disproportionate amount of speculation. Most sociological principles are still in the early stages of verification. Social scientists themselves are among the first to admit how little is known about the nature of human interaction—known, that is, in the form of carefully described phenomena, verified principles, and replicated findings that are universally accepted by objective students.

In developing a general theory of interpersonal relations, it seems convenient presently to relegate the *kinds* of causes involved to special areas. Social phenomena cannot be believed to "just happen" for no reason, if we have any hope of deriving valid and reliable principles about them. The very essence of prediction assumes an orderly sequence of events antecedent to any predictable phenomenon, unless we wish to include occult and metaphysical forecasts in the concept of prediction.

The kinds of antecedent events or conditions with which we can deal by means of objective descriptions, measurements, and some kind of theoretical framework for interpreting them fall into seven broad areas of inquiry. Every social phenomenon involves factors which have been studied in each of these areas, and potential explanations of the phenomenon should always take each into account.

The areas of inquiry and examples of the kinds of questions asked in each are as follows:

1. *Genetic:* Is one of the persons involved a hemophiliac? Blue-eyed? Rh negative? Color-blind? Caucasian? Is the social situation affected by it?
2. *Physiological:* Is one of the persons involved senile? Diabetic? Menstruating? Physically exhausted? Hungry? Feverish? Sterile? Newly-born? Is the social situation affected by it?
3. *Psychological:* Is one of the persons involved highly intelligent? Paranoid? Conditioned to respond in special ways to special stimuli? Mentally well balanced? Is the social situation affected by it?
4. *Cultural:* Was one of the persons involved reared in a society where only Icelandic was spoken? Where polygyny was common? Where there was a well-established aristocracy? Where whale blubber was the principal dietary item? Where there was no private property? Is the social situation affected by it?
5. *Social:* Are the persons involved married? To each other? Is one the mother of another? Have they met before? Will the social situation be affected by the presence of an observer?
6. *Ecological:* What kinds of relationships do the people involved have with other forms of life in the area? Are they competing for survival? With tigers? With microbes? With corn-borers? Can plant life survive the year round? Is the indigenous plant life easily perishable? Is the social situation affected by it?
7. *Geophysical:* Is it winter? Is it raining? At what altitude is the situation occurring? At what latitude? At what phase of the moon? What kind of tide is there? What is the barometric pressure? What is the wind velocity? Are there any geological faults in the vicinity? What minerals are accessible? Is the social situation affected by it?

Although a change in any of the above kinds of factors may alter a given social phenomenon, sociologists are especially concerned with the cultural and social areas of inquiry.

The collection of readings which follows emphasizes the cultural and social areas, but there is a good deal of dipping into other areas and many references to them. Part II deals with culture change, as well as with the concept of culture itself. Parts III, IV, and V are concerned primarily with more strictly social phenomena. Part III, for example, discusses the social aspects of personality development and interpersonal relationships. While groups are always comprised of persons, the perspective from which the group is viewed here necessitates a change in the students' frame of reference. Part IV focuses on this group perspective, and Part V presents materials related to the recognizable interaction patterns in social behavior.

In the last three parts, cultural and social phenomena are inextricably interwoven. Institutions, the subject matter of Part VII, have been called "ideas (usually cultural in origin) plus a structure (usually social)." That categories of people are differentially valued also has both social and cultural implications and is discussed in Part VIII. Social problems, the topic for Part IX, are of course social phenomena, but they can be defined only in a cultural context.

Factors in any one area thus have concomitants in other areas; barometric pressure, for example, affects physiology, and psychological interpretations of symbols are undeniably related to the cultural frame of reference. Similarly, requisite to the understanding of the last three parts are certain demographic and ecological concepts, which have been introduced in Part VI.

The principal effort in this collection, then, is to extend and enrich the student's conceptual background for dealing with and understanding the principles and general statements that sociologists today are setting forth about interpersonal relationships. Some of the articles were selected to show socio-logical methods at work; some report research findings; some provide "cases"; some deal with emergent sociological theory; many simply work toward a conceptual clarification of what must be studied. Every selection—whether its approach is methodological or whether it is concerned with findings or with explanations—has as its focus the study of the patterns and dynamics of human interrelationships.   *T.E.L.*

Selection *1*

The Proper Study of Mankind
Stuart Chase

Although man has devoted enormous time and energy to the study of his *physical* environment, for many centuries he has been largely content to inter-pret his *human* environment through sentiment and emotion on the one hand and through myth and tradition on the other. Man has been slow to undertake the objective study of mankind, even though he attaches extreme importance to his relationships with others—an importance of such magnitude that he has allowed emotional factors to almost completely overshadow unbiased observa-tion of these relationships. Paradoxically, a subject of such importance would be expected logically to demand the most effective study methods.

Stuart Chase's sincere, thoughtful survey of the goals, methods, and accom-plishments of social science provides a setting for this book of readings. Chase tells us that the task of the social scientist consists of "watching . . . people behave, and searching out the laws that govern that behavior." The "watchers" and the "searchers" are cultural anthropologists, social psychologists, sociologists, economists, and political scientists. Chase has compiled an impressive list of their accomplishments, including the discovery of certain laws governing human behavior, but he follows the list with a criticism of the techniques for discovery as having been developed more by trial and error or common sense than by the scientific method.

Chase's points are amplified in the selections that follow. Samuel A. Stouffer presents the basic scheme for sociological research; Talcott Parsons briefly sketches the history of sociology; and Robert K. Merton describes the current state of sociology.

This first selection leaves unanswered many questions concerning the hows and whys and whether-we-shoulds that creep through Chase's optimistic view of the future of social science. The reader will find some more or less satisfying answers in subsequent readings; but, more important, it is the hope of the editors that these readings will stimulate the reader to join the social scientist in his search for knowledge about human relations.

Because there is a long-honored term, "social science," it is natural to believe that out there in the world somewhere is an entity which corresponds to the term. There is no such entity out there, and we must beware of constructing one in our heads. What *is* to be found in the space-time world?

A television camera would show a number of professors lecturing to more or less bored students in more or less stuffy classrooms; experiments being performed in psychological laboratories; clinical studies in factories and offices; teams of investigators taking notes in communities like Middletown; social workers making records on their rounds and in clinics; a battery of Hollerith machines clicking away while they sort cards for social security or opinion polls; sunburned persons in pith helmets asking questions of slightly puzzled natives in New Guinea. . . . Finally, the camera would focus on shelf after shelf of books. Many of the volumes are famous; many of them contain prose as good as the advice is bad—for instance, Plato's recipe for bringing up children.

Out there in America, 145 million people scattered over 3 million square miles of plain, valley, and hillside form and re-form into numberless groups and organizations, with loyalties and sentiments clustered about each. In Newburyport, Massachusetts, a recent study showed more than 800 organizations among 17,000 people. The camera indicates the many curious methods by which Americans earn their living, or seek to mitigate the boredom of earning a living under machine age conditions.

Here then is the field of the social scientist: watching these people behave, and searching out the laws which govern that behavior. Kurt Lewin believed that the laboratory of the social scientist is living society, that observations must have a date put on them, for society is always changing, and that a small *controlled* change can be made to provide a scale for measurement and comparison.

THE MAJOR DISCIPLINES

The consensus of professional opinion . . . recognizes five disciplines as the hard core of social science:

(1) Cultural anthropology, (2) social psychology, (3) sociology, (4) economics, (5) political science. The order corresponds inversely with their age, for anthropology and psychology are the youngest of the disciplines, while political science is the oldest. Aristotle as the author of *Politics* might be nominated as the father of political science.

Economics, which once was called "political economy," became a formal discipline with the work of Adam Smith in the late eighteenth century. Sociology was launched in the nineteenth century with such sponsors as Durkheim, Hobhouse, Giddings, and Ward. A little later social psychology gathered impetus from William James. Cultural anthropology was born with Morgan's work on the family systems of Seneca Indians, and began to be prominent after the turn of the century. A landmark was the publication of Sumner's *Folkways* in 1906. "Physical" anthropology as a science was much older, but it dealt with the measurement of skulls, rather than with human societies.

In addition to the Big Five, various other disciplines have been offered as candidates in the course of my study. *History* receives almost as many votes as political science, but usually with a reservation. Because it deals with events which have gone into limbo, history can never hope to measure living phenomena or use the full scientific method, and must therefore remain a kind of accessory discipline. *Legal science* receives a number of votes, and so do *educational methods, social*

From "Knowledge in the Storehouse" from *The Proper Study of Mankind* by Stuart Chase, pp. 47-56. Copyright 1948 by Stuart Chase. Reprinted with permission of Harper & Row, Publishers, Incorporated.

work, demography, human geography, public administration.

There are a few scattering votes for *philosophy, comparative religion,* and *ethics* but without much conviction behind them. These studies are now generally classed, not with social science, but with the *humanities,* where one sits in an armchair and reads the Great Books . . . , and where scientific research has no place. The humanities are noble studies; they elevate the mind and often produce great psychological certitude, but they put little in the storehouse. The problems they solve do not stay solved.

One of my correspondents, however, is prepared to battle for the inclusion of *ethics* with social science—at least as he defines ethics. He says:

". . . The major problems of ethics can be formulated in scientific terms: If A, then B; if you increase the police, then there will be x per cent decrease in crime. . . . Many such predictions can be made and checked . . . instead of being argued about. 'Ethics' as a philosophical discipline may disappear with the establishment of enough such statements predicting human behavior under a variety of conditions, but actual ethics may then be realizable. 'Ethics' now is simply an area in which we don't know enough. That's why cultural anthropology is so important—it has vastly increased the number of statements about human nature that can be verified. . . . I have been giving a course 'Philosophy 123: Ethics,' and all I teach is cultural anthropology. I see no other way of teaching ethics that makes sense to me— in other words, it should be taught as *applied social science.*"

The Big Five, anthropology, psychology, sociology, economics, and political science, stand out above the others, with the qualification that the lines between them are beginning to melt. Like railroads or steel companies the social disciplines have a tendency to merge. The Social Science Research Council is itself a kind of clearing house.

Assisting them are four tools: mathematics, statistics, logic, and semantics. Each of these tools is a formidable discipline in its own right; each is useful if not mandatory where problems are to be solved. The scientific method would be stillborn without mathematics and statistics. It could make no hypotheses and theories without logic. Increasingly we are realizing that people often do not know what they are talking about without some functional understanding of language and its pitfalls—which is the domain of the young discipline of semantics.

Between social science and natural science is a broad zone where various disciplines and studies cut across both fields. Is fingerprinting social science or anatomy? What about Mr. Sherlock Holmes and all his professional descendants? How about Dr. Yerkes's revealing studies on the habits of chimpanzees? A very strong case can be made for *psychiatry* as a bridge between the two fields. Not only has it contributed enormously to social science, but it draws on it as well. "Psychiatry," says Dr. William C. Menninger, of the famous Topeka clinic, "is a medical science but it is also a social science. The psychiatrist, more than the physician in any other medical discipline, must concern himself with the social situation of his patients." Dr. Menninger names race prejudice and involuntary unemployment as especially detrimental to mental health. "These social ills should be among our very special concerns."

SOME OUTSTANDING ACCOMPLISHMENTS

With the help of the questionnaires, interviews, visits to universities, and the reading of many monographs, I have accumulated a list of more than one hundred outstanding accomplishments in the social sciences. Some are brilliant individual research findings, some cover whole groups of studies.

Generally accepted as most important is what we may call the *culture concept* in anthropology and sociology. This label covers a body of principles derived from field studies, all revolving around the basic idea that an individual cannot be understood apart from the culture which contains him; or, to put it in a more familiar way, that man is a social animal. It is a broad and general concept, on the scale of Darwin's theory of evolution, and perhaps even more important. The anthropologists, by studying living cultures around the world and checking with the records of past cultures, have worked out some of the laws which govern all human societies everywhere.

Other accomplishments which have received high ratings are the following:

The Army Air Force program [in the behavioral sciences].

The studies in race relations of Boas, Benedict, Myrdal, Young, Klineberg, and others. There is as yet no proof of racial inequality that will meet the test of science. The real problem today is how to transmit these scientific conclusions to the front line—where a lynching may be in the making.

Ogburn's intensive work on the laws of social change.

The Cross-Cultural Index at Yale—a kind of Rosetta Stone of anthropology.

Leighton's work with interned Japanese-Americans during the war. He discovered some fundamental principles of administration, and the governing of men.

Sampling theory and its applications to census figures, population, insurance, and the remarkable techniques of the Social Security Board.

The polls of public opinion—also founded on sampling theory. They are at present enjoying a great vogue, and constitute a lively and important addition to the science of human relations.

Elton Mayo's scientific approach to labor-management relations, combining anthropology, psychology, sociology, and economics, which is now spreading all over the country.

The "Middletown" surveys and techniques, especially the Yankee City studies.

Seashore, IQ, and other testing techniques. A culture-free IQ is needed, however, to compare people of different cultures.

Learning theory, especially the work of Dollard and Miller at Yale.

New light and new techniques on crime and punishment.

Area studies by social scientists during the war. Studies of Japanese morale by remote control. Surveys to assist the armed services in their dealing with native cultures, especially the preparation for the Okinawa landing.

Manpower analysis for recruiting soldiers and war workers—an outstanding statistical achievement.

Development of Gross National Product and other statistical techniques during the war by the War Production Board, OPA, Bureau of Agricultural Economics, Bureau of Labor Statistics, the Treasury, and other agencies.

Wesley Mitchell's work on business cycles.

The Keynesian approach in economics, especially for handling problems of depression, and of war finance.

Dr. Kinsey's analysis of the sexual life of American males. His goal is 100,000 case histories.

New techniques in public administration—city-manager plans, the TVA, traffic controls and traffic statistics, etc.

New techniques in social work, now increasingly influenced by the culture concept and social psychology.

The development of semantics by Ogden and Richards, Korzybski, Hayakawa, Johnson, and many more.

. . . The bare list is presented here to give the reader an idea of the breadth of the field. Some of the projects I knew well; some, like Dr. Kinsey's work, I had heard mentioned; many were a complete surprise. I had had no notion that so much knowledge was already gathered. Most social scientists, I find, have little idea of the richness of their total field.

THE MAJOR CLASSES

Can we give the list a more orderly classification? To classify by disciplines is almost useless, as many of the achievements embrace two or more disciplines. The Middletown surveys and the Okinawa project, for instance, were the work of *teams*. Perhaps the following classification will do to begin with:

1. *Social science theory.* Generalizations and laws which have been verified and which hold good under similar conditions in any society. Examples: the "universals" in the culture concept, sampling theory, the reproductive index for population. The test of sound theory is its ability to predict. . . .*

2. *Applied social science,* sometimes called social engineering. Here theory is taken off the shelf and put to work in actual human situations. Examples: conducting a public opinion poll, conducting a Middletown survey, giving a million foremen in war industry the Training Within Industry program. It should be noted, however, that sometimes theory and engineering become hopelessly entangled. Flanagan had to stop work and develop theory from time to time in order to get on with his work of selecting pilots. The Manhattan project had to do likewise, according to the Smyth report. Lancelot Hogben has pointed out that with deep shaft mining in the sixteenth century, questions of air pressure, ventilation, and explosives became urgent. Lacking this practical urge, he says, chemistry including pure theory would have remained at the level the Greeks left it.

3. *Social techniques* developed more by trial and error and common sense than by the scientific method. Many apply only to our own culture, many are very useful, but for the long run they badly need more research and theoretical foundation. Examples: city-manager plans, managed currency devices, compensatory economy plans. . . .

---

* Editors' note: For a somewhat more operational definition of *theory,* see p. 6.

WASTED KNOWLEDGE

I asked a number of social scientists this question: *Do you recall any regrettable examples where accredited knowledge was available and not used?* It brought a lively list of grievances, of which the most frequent was against the high brass in Army and Navy who refused to let the scientists have enough scope in helping to run the war. Among the complaints:

"'Military government' did not really apply social science.

"Race data was not sufficiently employed in dealing with Negroes in the armed services.

"Social science was not adequately used even in psychological warfare—where it was obviously a natural.

"Army chiefs did not realize that 1942 draftees were a different type of youngster from those of 1917. 'We tried to tell the chiefs what had happened to America in twenty-five years but they would not listen.'"

Not all the generals disregarded social science by any means. Great strides were made in its application during the war; witness the pilot-testing work. If an admiral or a general had his share of intelligence, he soon realized that here was a powerful new weapon. So powerful indeed was the final effect on top echelons that now, long after V-J Day, the services are financing large research projects on human relations, still strictly "classified." Among other benefits, this could lead to better communication lines between the officers and the rank and file. . . .

THE GREAT UNANSWERED QUESTIONS

Unsolved questions are always in the agenda of any developing science, and our survey has disclosed plenty of them. The scientists who helped me were, for the most part, frank about the things which had been left undone. There was little self-congratulation to be found but rather the contrary. . . . "We have been at it so long, and worked so hard, and produced so little. . . ." This is a better foundation to build on, however, than the mood: "We know all the answers."

The storehouse of social science has many empty shelves. How to contain atomic energy is, of course, the most immediately ominous problem, but plenty more are crowding right behind it. Here is a sample lot:

What are the interrelations between individual personality and culture?

How large can a society grow before its members lose touch with one another, and so begin to lose essential social functions—in a sense their very humanity?

What is the effect of a high energy culture on human beings, especially workers in mass production industries? Are mental diseases on the increase from this cause?

How can workers in western civilization again find interest in their work?

What kind of social structure can provide both freedom and economic security? . . .

How can leaders be protected from the demoralizing effects of their own power?

What techniques in communication will help bring out more agreement?

What kind of education does a high energy culture demand? How many child-years per pupil are wasted by present methods?

How can we *apply* more widely the knowledge already available?

Such is the type of inquiry which awaits more research. I asked Dr. Louis Wirth, of Chicago University, among others, to give me a list of what he considered to be the "great unanswered questions." He did so, and ended with a statement so fine that I would like to put it in the record:

"The great unanswered questions of the social sciences are the great unanswered questions of mankind. How can we get peace, freedom, order, prosperity and progress under different conditions of existence? How can we establish the conditions of human well-being that have been attained in some parts of the world, or by certain groups, so that they will apply to other groups, and to other parts of the world? How can we achieve consensus in a mass democracy? How can we get the advantages of a rapidly developing technology without destroying the other values which we cherish?

"I know these are general and cosmic questions, but until social scientists make a usable answer to the ways and means of achieving such ends, they will be playing a game which may be interesting enough to themselves, but one which they have no right to expect society to support."

The accomplishments listed earlier . . . show that Dr. Wirth's injunction has been taken seriously by many in the field. . . . I hope the reader will be as impressed as I have been with the work already done.

Selection 2

Some Observations on Study Design
Samuel A. Stouffer

It seems self-evident to say that modern physicians can cure more human ills than can preliterate shamans. You and I *believe* that this is true. We would probably be subjected to ridicule, if not censure, by our friends and neighbors if we acted as if this belief were not true. But suppose that we (or they) should be called upon to *prove* the truth of this belief. How would we proceed? We might appeal to some authority and say that it is true because wise or old or holy or sick or healed people *say* that it is true. We might angrily state that common sense tells us that it is true and refuse to investigate it.

Social scientists are often accused of investigating that which is obvious to anyone with common sense; yet it is frequently common-sense knowledge that needs the most investigation. People knew, for example, that heavy objects fell toward the earth long before Sir Isaac Newton made his noted study of gravity and falling bodies. But think how much the world has gained from Newton's investigation of the obvious.

Careful scientific investigation often leads to the correction of erroneous common-sense ideas. For centuries, common sense reassured even the most learned scholars that the earth was flat and that the sun revolved around the earth. Common sense may tell us that a preliterate man cannot be as intelligent as a literate man. Nevertheless, through scientific research these and many other common-sense ideas have been proved false.

The battle against the intrusion of untested common sense into research is particularly important in the social sciences, because so many bits of knowledge and so many ideas about people are accompanied by emotions and feelings. One of the most powerful weapons in this battle is good *study design*. In the following article, Stouffer presents some elementary principles of study design. He recommends that such common-sense techniques as "figuring things out" be abandoned for planned observation or testing. The four-cell scheme he presents is an extremely simple procedure for assuring the researcher that it is *possible* for his study to yield valid results. If the student can determine whether such research designs have been used to produce the conclusions reached in the articles and books he reads, he will be better able to distinguish between common-sense statements and the results of social research.

As a youth I read a series of vigorous essays in the *Century Magazine* by its editor, the late Glenn Frank. His theme was that the natural sciences had remade the face of the earth; now had arrived the age of the social sciences. The same techniques which had worked their miracles in physics, chemistry, and biology should, in competent hands, achieve equally dazzling miracles in economics, political science, and sociology. That was a long time ago. The disconcerting fact is that people are writing essays just like that today. Of course, the last two decades have seen considerable progress in social science—in theory, in technique, and in the accumulation of data. It is true that the number of practitioners is pitifully few; only a few hundred research studies are reported annually in sociology, for example,

"Some Observations on Study Design" by Samuel A. Stouffer. Reprinted from *The American Journal of Sociology*, Vol. LV (1950), 335-361, by permission of The University of Chicago Press.

as compared with more than twenty thousand studies summarized annually in *Biological Abstracts*. But the bright promise of the period when Frank was writing has not been fulfilled.

Two of the most common reasons alleged for slow progress are cogent, indeed.

The data of social science are awfully complex, it is said. And they involve values which sometimes put a strain on the objectivity of the investigator even when they do not incur resistance from the vested interests of our society. However, an important part of the trouble has very little to do with the subject matter of social science as such but, rather, is a product of our own bad work habits. That is why this paper on the subject of study design may be relevant. So much has been spoken and written on this topic that I make no pretense to originality. But in the course of a little experience, especially in an effort during the war to apply social psychology to military problems, and in an undertaking to nurture a new program of research in my university, I have encountered some frustrations which perhaps can be examined with profit.

A basic problem—perhaps *the* basic problem—lies deeply imbedded in the thoughtways of our culture. This is the implicit assumption that anybody with a little common sense and a few facts can come up at once with the correct answer on any subject. Thus the newspaper editor or columnist, faced with a column of empty space to fill with readable English in an hour, can speak with finality and authority on any social topic, however complex. He might not attempt to diagnose what is wrong with his sick cat; he would call a veterinarian. But he knows precisely what is wrong with any social institution and the remedies.

In a society which rewards quick and confident answers and does not worry about how the answers are arrived at, the social scientist is hardly to be blamed if he conforms to the norms. Hence, much social science is merely rather dull and obscure journalism; a few data and a lot of "interpretation." The fact that the so-called "interpretation" bears little or no relation to the data is often obscured by academic jargon. If the stuff is hard to read, it has a chance of being acclaimed as profound. The rewards are for the answers, however tediously expressed, and not for rigorously marshaled evidence.

In the army no one would think of adopting a new type of weapon without trying it out exhaustively on the firing range. But a new idea about handling personnel fared very differently. The last thing anybody ever thought about was trying out the idea experimentally. I recall several times when we had schemes for running an experi-

mental tryout of an idea in the sociopsychological field. Usually one of two things would happen: the idea would be rejected as stupid without a tryout (it may have been stupid, too) or it would be seized on and applied generally and at once. When the provost marshal wanted us to look into the very low morale of the MP's, our attitude surveys suggested that there was room for very much better selectivity in job assignment. There were routine jobs like guarding prisoners which could be given to the duller MP's, and there were a good many jobs calling for intelligence, discretion, and skill in public relations. We thought that the smarter men might be assigned to these jobs and that the prestige of these jobs would be raised further if a sprinkling of returned veterans with plenty of ribbons and no current assignment could be included among them. We proposed a trial program of a reassignment system in a dozen MP outfits for the purpose of comparing the resulting morale with that in a dozen matched outfits which were left untouched. Did we get anywhere? No. Instead, several of our ideas were put into effect immediately throughout the army without any prior testing at all.

The army cannot be blamed for behavior like that. In social relations it is not the habit in our culture to demand evidence for an idea; plausibility is enough.

To alter the folkways, social science itself must take the initiative. We must be clear in our own minds what proof consists of, and we must, if possible, provide dramatic examples of the advantages of relying on something more than plausibility. And the heart of our problem lies in study design *in advance*, such that the evidence is not capable of a dozen alternative interpretations.

Basically, I think it is essential that we always keep in mind the model of a controlled experiment, even if in practice we may have to deviate from an ideal model. Take the simple accompanying diagram. The test of whether a difference

	BEFORE	AFTER	
EXPERIMENTAL GROUP	x_1	x_2	$d = x_2 - x_1$
CONTROL GROUP	x_1'	x_2'	$d' = x_2' - x_1'$

d is attributable to what we think it is attributable to is whether d is significantly larger than d'.

We used this model over and over again during the war to measure the effectiveness of orientation films in changing soldiers' attitudes. . . .

One of the troubles with using this careful design was that the effectiveness of a single film when thus measured turned out to be so slight. If, instead of using the complete experimental design, we simply took an unselected sample of men and compared the attitudes of those who said they had seen a film with those who said they had not, we got much more impressive differences. This was more rewarding to us, too, for the management wanted to believe the films were powerful medicine. The gimmick was the selective fallibility of memory. Men who correctly remembered seeing the films were likely to be those most sensitized to their message. Men who were bored or indifferent may have actually seen them but slept through them or just forgot.

Most of the time we are not able or not patient enough to design studies containing all four cells as in the diagram above. Sometimes we have only the top two cells, as in the accompanying diagram.

In this situation we have two observations of the same individuals or groups taken at different times. This is often a very useful design. In the army, for example, we would take a group of recruits, ascertain their attitudes, and restudy the same men later. From this we could tell whose attitudes changed and in what direction (it was almost always for the worse, which did not endear us to the army!). But exactly what factors in the early training period were most responsible for deterioration of attitudes could only be inferred indirectly.

The panel study is usually more informative than a more frequent design, which might be pictured thus:

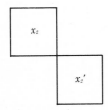

Here at one point in time we have one sample, and at a later point in time we have another sample. We observe that our measure, say, the mean, is greater for the recent sample than for the earlier one. But we are precluded from observing which men or what type of men shifted. Moreover, there is always the disturbing possibility that the populations in our two samples were initially different; hence the differences might not be attributable to conditions taking place in the time interval between the two observations. Thus we would study a group of soldiers in the United States and later ask the same questions of a group of soldiers overseas. Having matched the two groups of men carefully by branch of service, length of time in the army, rank, etc., we hoped that the results of the study would approximate what would be found if the same men could have been studied twice. But this could be no more than a hope. Some important factors could not be adequately controlled, for example, physical conditions. Men who went overseas were initially in better shape on the average than men who had been kept behind; but, if the follow-up study was in the tropics, there was a chance that unfavorable climate already had begun to take its toll. And so it went. How much men overseas changed called for a panel study as a minimum if we were to have much confidence in the findings.

A very common attempt to get the results of a controlled experiment without paying the price is with the design that might be as shown in the accompanying diagram. This is usually what

we get with correlation analysis. We have two or more groups of men whom we study at the same point in time. Thus we have men in the infantry and men in the air corps and compare their attitudes. How much of the difference between x'_2 and x_2 we can attribute to experience in a given branch of service and how much is a function of attributes of the men selected for each branch we cannot know assuredly. True, we can try to rule out various possibilities by matching; we can compare men from the two branches with the same age and education, for example. But there is all too often a wide-open gate through which other uncontrolled variables can march.

Sometimes, believe it or not, we have only one cell:

When this happens, we do not know much of anything. But we can still fill pages of social science journals with "brilliant analysis" if we use plausible conjecture in supplying missing cells from our imagination. Thus we may find that the adolescent today has wild ideas and conclude that society is going to the dogs. We fill in the dotted cell representing our own yesterdays with hypothetical data, where x_1 represents us and x_2

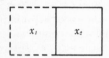

our offspring. The tragicomic part is that most of the public, including, I fear, many social scientists, are so acculturated that they ask for no better data.

I do not intend to disparage all research not conforming to the canons of the controlled experiment. I think that we will see more of full experimental design in sociology and social psychology in the future than in the past. But I am well aware of the practical difficulties of its execution, and I know that there are numberless important situations in which it is not feasible at all. What I am arguing for is awareness of the limitations of a design in which crucial cells are missing.

Sometimes by forethought and patchwork we can get approximations which are useful if we are careful to avoid overinterpretation. Let me cite an example:

In Europe during the war the army tested the idea of putting an entire platoon of Negro soldiers into a white infantry outfit. This was done in several companies. The Negroes fought beside white soldiers. After several months we were asked to find out what the white troops thought about the innovation. We found that only 7 per cent of the white soldiers in companies with Negro platoons said that they disliked the idea very much, whereas 62 per cent of the white soldiers in divisions without Negro troops said they would dislike the idea very much if it were tried in their outfits. We have:

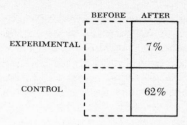

Now, were these white soldiers who fought beside Negroes men who were naturally more favorable to Negroes than the cross-section of white infantrymen? We did not think so, since, for example, they contained about the same proportion of southerners. The point was of some importance, however, if we were to make the inference that actual experience with Negroes reduced hostility from 62 to 7 per cent. As a second-best substitute, we asked the white soldiers in companies with Negro platoons if they could recall how they felt when the innovation was first proposed. It happens that 67 per cent said they were initially opposed to the idea. Thus we could tentatively fill in a missing cell and conclude that, under the conditions obtaining, there probably had been a marked change in attitude.

Even if this had been a perfectly controlled experiment, there was still plenty of chance to draw erroneous inferences. The conclusions apply only to situations closely approximating those of the study. It happens, for example, that the Negroes involved were men who volunteered to leave rear-area jobs for combat duty. If other Negroes had been involved, the situation might have been different. Moreover, they had white officers. One army colonel who saw this study and whom I expected to ridicule it because he usually opposed innovations, surprised me by offering congratulations. "This proves," he said, "what I have been arguing in all my thirty years in the army—that niggers will do all right if you give 'em white officers!" Moreover, the study applied only to combat experience. Other studies would be needed to justify extending the findings to noncombat or garrison duty. In other words, one lone study, however well designed, can be a very dangerous thing if it is exploited beyond its immediate implications.

Now experiments take time and money, and there is no use denying that we in social science cannot be as prodigal with the replications as the biologist who can run a hundred experiments simultaneously by growing plants in all kinds of soils and conditions. The relative ease of experimentation in much—not all—of natural science goes far to account for the difference in quality of proof demanded by physical and biological sciences, on the one hand, and social scientists, on the other.

Though we cannot always design neat experiments when we want to, we can at least keep the experimental model in front of our eyes and behave cautiously when we fill in missing cells with dotted lines. But there is a further and even more important operation we can perform in the interest of economy. That lies in our choice of the initial problem.

Professor W. F. Ogburn always told his students to apply to a reported research conclusion the test, "How do you know it?" To this wise advice I should like to add a further question: "What of it?" I suspect that if before designing a study we asked ourselves, more conscientiously than we do, whether or not the study really is important, we would economize our energies for the few studies which are worth the expense and trouble of the kind of design I have been discussing.

Can anything be said about guides for selecting problems? I certainly think so. That is where theory comes in and where we social scientists have gone woefully astray.

Theory has not often been designed with research operations in mind. Theory as we have it in social science serves indispensably as a very broad frame of reference or general orientation. Thus modern theories of culture tell us that it is usually more profitable to focus on the learning process and the content of what is learned rather than on innate or hereditary traits. But they do not provide us with sets of interrelated propositions which can be put in the form: If x_1, given x_2 and x_3, then there is strong probability that we get x_4. Most of our propositions of that form, sometimes called "theory," are likely to be *ad hoc* common-sense observations which are not deducible from more general considerations and which are of the same quality as the observation, "If you stick your hand in a fire and hold it there, you will get burned."

Now in view of the tremendous cost in time and money of the ideal kind of strict empirical research operations, it is obvious that we cannot afford the luxury of conducting them as isolated fact-finding enterprises. Each should seek to be some sort of *experimentum crucis*, and, with rare exceptions, that will only happen if we see its place *beforehand* in a more general scheme of things. Especially, we need to look for situations where two equally plausible hypotheses deducible from more general theory lead to the expectation of different consequences. Then, if our evidence supports one and knocks out the other, we have accomplished something.

The best work of this sort in our field is probably being done today in laboratory studies of learning and of perception. I do not know of very good sociological examples. Yet in sociology experiments are possible. One of the most exciting, for example, was that initiated long before the war by Shaw and McKay to see whether co-operative effort by adult role models within a delinquent neighborhood would reduce juvenile delinquency. So many variables are involved in a single study like that that it is not easy to determine which were crucial. But there was theory behind the study, and the experimental design provided for controlling at least some variables.

It may be that in sociology we will need much more thinking and many more descriptive studies involving random ratlike movements on the part of the researcher before we can even begin to state our problems so that they are in decent shape for fitting into an ideal design. However, I think that we can reduce to some extent the waste motion of the exploratory period if we try to act as if we have some a priori ideas and keep our eyes on the possible relevance of data to these ideas. This is easier said than done. So many interesting rabbit tracks are likely to be uncovered in the exploratory stages of research that one is tempted to chase rabbits all over the woods and forget what his initial quarry was.

Exploratory research is of necessity fumbling, but I think that the waste motion can be reduced by the self-denying ordinance of deliberately limiting ourselves to a few variables at a time. Recently two of my colleagues and myself have been doing a little exploratory work on a problem in the general area of social mobility. We started by tabulating some school records of fifty boys in the ninth grade of one junior high school and then having members of our seminar conduct three or four interviews with each boy and his parents. We had all the interviews written up in detail, and we had enough data to fill a book—with rather interesting reading, too. But it was a very wasteful process because there were just too many intriguing ideas. We took a couple of ideas which were deducible from current general theory and tried to make some simple fourfold tables. It was obvious that, with a dozen variables uncontrolled, such tables meant little or nothing. But that led us to a second step. Now we are trying to collect school records and a short questionnaire on two thousand boys. We will not interview all these boys and their parents in detail. But, with two thousand cases to start with, we hope to take a variable in which we are interested and find fifty boys who are plus on it and fifty who are minus, yet who are approximately alike on a lot of other things. A table based on such matched comparisons should be relatively unambiguous. We can take off from there and interview those selected cases intensively to push further our exploration of the nexus between theory and observation. This, we think, will be economical, though still exploratory. Experimental manipulation is far in the future in our problem, but we do hope we can conclude the first stage with a statement of some hypotheses susceptible to experimental verification.

I am not in the least deprecating exploratory work. But I do think that some orderliness is indicated even in the bright dawn of a youthful enterprise.

One reason why we are not more orderly in our exploratory work is that all too often what is missing is a sharp definition of a given variable, such that, if we wanted to take a number of cases and even throw them into a simple fourfold table, we could.

Suppose we are studying a problem in which one of the variables we are looking for is over-protection or overindulgence of a child by his mother. We have a number of case histories or questionnaires. Now how do we know whether we are sorting them according to this variable or not? The first step, it would seem, is to have some way of knowing whether we are sorting them along any single continuum, applying the same criteria to each case. But to know this we need to have built into the study the ingredients of a scale. Unless we have some such ingredients in our data, we are defeated from the start. This is why I think the new interest social scientists are taking in scaling techniques is so crucially important to progress. . . .

Trying to conduct a social science investigation without good criteria for knowing whether a particular variable may be treated as a single dimension is like trying to fly without a motor in the plane. Students of the history of invention point out that one reason why the airplane, whose properties had been pretty well thought out by Leonardo da Vinci, was so late in development was the unavailability of a light-weight power plant, which had to await the invention of the

internal combustion motor. We are learning more and more how to make our light-weight motors in social science, and that augurs well for the future. But much work is ahead of us. In particular, we desperately need better projective techniques and better ways of getting respondents to reveal attitudes which are too emotionally charged to be accessible to direct questioning. . . .

I have tried to set forth the model of the controlled experiment as an ideal to keep in the forefront of our minds even when by necessity some cells are missing from our design. I have also tried to suggest that more economy and orderliness are made possible, even in designing the exploratory stages of a piece of research—by using theory in advance to help us decide whether a particular inquiry would be important if we made it; by narrowing down the number of variables; and by making sure that we can classify our data along a particular continuum, even if only provisionally. And a central, brooding hope is that we will have the modesty to recognize the difference between a promising idea and proof.

Oh, how we need that modesty! The public expects us to deal with great problems like international peace, full employment, maximization of industrial efficiency. As pundits we can pronounce on such matters; as citizens we have a duty to be concerned with them; but as social scientists our greatest achievement now will be to provide a few small dramatic examples that hypotheses in our field can be stated operationally and tested crucially. And we will not accomplish that by spending most of our time writing or reading papers like this one. We will accomplish it best by rolling up our sleeves and working at the intricacies of design of studies which, though scientifically strategic, seem to laymen trivial compared with the global concerns of the atomic age. Thereby, and only thereby, I believe, can we some day have the thrilling sense of having contributed to the structure of a social science which is cumulative.

Selection 3

The Development of Sociology as a Discipline
Talcott Parsons

Of all the academic disciplines taught around the world, none is more completely dominated by American leadership than sociology. Many American sociologists believe that Talcott Parsons is the outstanding figure in contemporary sociology, and almost all of them would surely rank him among the top few. In the following selection, Parsons presents a genetic account of American sociology as an academic discipline and a short history of the profession which has developed about it.

Of particular importance is the emergence of a clear distinction of sociology from social welfare—a distinction which many uninformed persons fail to make. In some respects the differentiation is analogous to that between physiology and medicine. The welfare worker—like the physician—focuses on the survival and well-being of his client; the sociologist—like the physiologist—focuses on the observation of facts and principles and the development and verification of theories.

Parsons observes that sociology as a science has not been completely distinguished from social philosophy and "social problems." We have noted in the preceding selections the difficulty of making such distinctions. On the surface, it would appear that social scientists need only decide to restrict their activities to answering questions objectively and constructing theories with a minimum of hypothetical principles and hypothetical "facts." Those who are unwilling to so restrict themselves could then be called "unscientific," and sociology would emerge as a pure science. Unfortunately, such a conclusion would be quite superficial. It is true that the distinction between social problems and questions about society is conceptually simple, but this is not where the difficulty lies. Nor is the problem really about whether it is worth while to gain knowledge simply for the sake of gaining knowledge; most philosophers accept the value of "pure" knowledge as readily as do their scientific colleagues. Part of the problem lies in the magnitude of the study; part of it lies in the inadequate development of a philosophy of science; part of it lies in the demand for "practical" knowledge; part of it lies in the lack of a social mathematics; and part of it lies in the use of unproved analogies with other scientific disciplines.

The reader of Parsons' article cannot fail to be impressed by the newness of the discipline of sociology. Many living Americans were born before the first course in sociology was taught under that name in an American university. The first professional journal in sociology, *The American Journal of Sociology,* began publication in 1896, and the American Sociological Society was not founded until 1905.

In the perspective of history, any high-level scientific knowledge of human social behavior is a very recent phenomenon, having been achieved, with such antecedent developments as those in economic theory and in statistics, largely in the present century. In this brief period, sociology has advanced with seemingly great rapidity. But cultural growth is so complex and the time so short that it almost goes without saying that the development of sociology stands at present in an early stage.

Given this situation, it is not surprising that the differentiation between social science, on the one hand, and the most closely related non- or partially-scientific components of the general culture, on the other hand, is recent, incomplete, and unstable. I refer to the differentiation of social science from both "social philosophy" and "social problems." A field of science cannot be institutionalized until a relatively clear orientation to its own investigative problems has been worked out which is not dominated by either of these two socially important but predominantly non-scientific bases of concern. The third problem of differentiation, then, refers to the place of sociology within the corpus of scientific disciplines, above all those dealing with human behavior. A brief discussion of each of these three problems of differentiation seems to be in order.

First, with respect to the most general differentiation of social science from the philosophical

From the *American Sociological Review*, Vol. 24 (1959), 547-559. Reprinted by permission of the American Sociological Association.

matrix in which it had earlier been embedded, we may speak of a religious, a philosophical, and a more generally scientific aspect of this matrix. The relative predominance of these aspects partly corresponds with principal phases of Western intellectual history.

In the earliest of these phases, the differentiation of secular social thought from religious apologetics was brought about, becoming a considerable movement only in the 17th century. The primary emphasis in this first major secular phase was political in a broad and diffuse sense, dealing with secular society as a politically organized "state" contrasting with the church. Once this step had been taken, a differentiation of substantive specialties within the field could gradually develop.

Not until the late 18th century did the field of economics begin clearly to emerge from this diffuse political matrix, with Adam Smith as the first highly eminent writer leading up to the classical economics. The focus of political theory tended to become considerably narrower, centering on the phenomena of government in the increasingly differentiated type of society of the time. Thus, along with history, which refused to identify itself with any particular focus of substantive interest, in the 19th century the broad frames of reference were laid out for political science and for economics.

This intellectual situation provided the main setting for the emergence of sociology along one of its main paths, namely the treatment of those more macroscopic aspects of society that were not adequately accounted for in the utilitarian tradition which had gained such prominence in political theory and in economics. With Comte as the most important precursor and Marx pointing up the problem of the status of "economic factors," Durkheim and Weber in Europe were the great theoretical tone-setters of the new sociological approach, being greatly preoccupied with the assessment of the institutional framework within which modern economic processes took place, and which were independent in certain ways of the operations of political organization. They were also oriented to the "collectivist" mode of thought stemming from Rousseau and from German idealism, which provided the major point of reference for their critiques of utilitarianism. In general, they looked to the "ideal" as contrasted with "material" factors for the key concepts—such as values and institutionalized norms—of their analyses.

Within the "scientific" aspect of the philosophical matrix of social thought, referred to above, the phase given impetus by Darwinian biology in the second half of the 19th century had particular relevance to sociology. Spencer and the American evolutionists Sumner and Ward in particular derive from this background and its complex interrelations with utilitarianism and positivistic rationalism. But in addition to their influence on the emergence of sociology, the concept of evolution and the broad framework of the relation between competition and cooperation, laissez faire and planning, also provided the intellectual matrix from which grew anthropology in Great Britain, and which underlies much of the development of modern psychology. Of course, psychology, by way of Freud, also traces back in a complex manner to medical biology; and anthropology, especially as influenced in this country by Franz Boas, was infused by German idealist-historicist thinking. In the United States the "social psychology" of C. H. Cooley and G. H. Mead was an important bridge between these intellectual currents.

In very schematic terms, these are the main Western intellectual trends in the developmental background of the present social sciences. It can be readily seen that the lines which distinguish them from each other are far from being very sharply drawn. From the viewpoint of the more macroscopic disciplines like political science and economics, sociology has often been treated as a residual category or as a more or less "imperialistic" summation of all knowledge about society. In Germany in particular it has tended to be identified with the philosophy of history, the main difference being sociology's greater claim to empirical standing. There has been an increasingly clear focus, however, on phenomena of values and norms and their relation to personality, independently of technical concerns, particularly of economics.

Within the complex more closely associated with Darwinian biology, there are also difficult borderline problems *vis-à-vis* both anthropology and psychology. The earlier anthropological concentration on the study of nonliterate peoples helped to postpone consideration of such questions, but more recently the distinction between sociology and anthropology has become less conspicuous. It is not an easy question whether the relative emphases on "culture," as made by many American anthropologists, and on social systems, as stressed by at least some sociologists, is an adequate working basis for a differentiation of the two disciplines. Psychology, however, seems clearly to focus on the study of analytically distinct components of behavior imputable to the "individual." But since virtually all human behavior is concretely both individual and social (and also cultural), here there are also formidable difficulties in drawing clear analytical lines; hence the ambiguous position of social psychology.

It seems to be in the nature of such a complex of scientific disciplines that, first, in studying empirical phenomena, any analytical classification crosscuts common sense classifications. Thus economics cannot be the theory of "business" in a simple sense, political theory the theory of "government," nor psychology the theory of individual behavior, any more than physiology studies living organisms only and chemistry only lifeless matter. Secondly, the line cannot be drawn altogether clearly between the scientific components of this complex of disciplines and their non-scientific philosophical matrix. Such issues as positivism and the possible ontological status of the individual in the utilitarian frame of reference, for example, cannot be fully excluded from theoretical discussion in the social sciences.

These intellectual problems, which are unlikely to be easily and quickly settled, have an important bearing on the position and behavior of the professional groups involved in them. They are sources of strain both within and between disciplines. The social sciences have come to form a "family" which is well enough structured for certain working purposes, but which still leaves many areas of indeterminacy and of potential and sometimes open conflict. It may well be that only a minority of members of the relevant professional groups actively concern themselves with these problems at any given time—undoubtedly a desirable situation—but this does not justify treating the problems themselves as trivial in their implications for the professional situation.

I have suggested that the historical process by which the social science disciplines have come to be differentiated is so closely intertwined with the process by which they have gradually emerged from a more philosophical matrix that a single treatment of both trends has been necessary. Turning to the third problem of differentiation, between scientific disciplines and prescriptions for practical action, perhaps the most striking fact is the very near recency of any clear differentiation. Both political and economic theory throughout their formative periods were directly concerned with prescribing public policy and did not seriously attempt to separate even conceptually the bases of empirical generalization from the evaluative basis of policy recommendation. Marxism is a particularly important example of an economic theory that attempts no such distinction, and indeed denies its legitimacy. Max Weber was probably the first major theorist to assert the fundamental importance of carefully distinguishing between problems of scientific generalization and those of evaluation and policy, and to work out a clear methodological basis for the distinction.

It is virtually only within the last generation that acceptance of this distinction has come to be generally diffused within the social science professions, and it is still quite incomplete. . . .

One feature of the history of American sociology, which differs from the European (especially Continental), is important in the present-day situation. European social sciences generally and sociology in particular had been primarily concerned with a highly macroscopic interpretation of society's development. Hence the prominence of such general rubrics as capitalism and socialism. In the United States, however, there was considerably less concern with macroscopic interpretation. The broad outline of the society and its major values were more apt to be taken for granted, with the emphasis given to particular "social problems." There was a deep concern with how actual situations deviated from values, which were above all the values of liberal Protestantism in the era when the "social gospel" was particularly prominent. Here problems associated with slums, rural life, immigration, and Negro-White relations were at the center of attention.

This kind of interest helps to explain why American sociology has been far less concerned with the borderline of philosophy than has European. It could become separated from political theory and economics more readily since these two disciplines tended to take a macroscopic view of society. Under these circumstances, the most serious problem of differentiation for American sociology has stemmed from its applied interests. In its earlier period sociology was closely identified with religiously defined ethical obligations and with philanthropy, which became institutionalized in certain aspects of community service and social work. Thus many early American sociologists were trained in the ministry, and several university departments combined sociology and social work. However, a rather early and sometimes sharp reaction developed against the latter association, often resulting in the separation of the two fields, notably at the University of Chicago and later at Harvard.

Although the problem of differentiation from applied interests was particularly acute in the American case, concentration on less macroscopic problems had a special advantage. This emphasis encouraged the development of a variety of techniques for empirical research, for example, participant observation, the use of personal documents, interviewing, and questionnaire methods. That this rapid technical development coincided with a similar growth in statistics was highly important. In the general American climate of interest in empirical matters, this technical emphasis, much more pronounced than in Europe, helped significantly to speed the development of sociology as an empirical science.

It is also important that the more microscopic emphasis of American sociology brought it into relatively close touch with psychology, particularly in the overlapping field of social psychology, and with anthropology, particularly in the study of small communities, which were the first major objects in modern society of anthropological study. Both psychology and anthropology were fields which, in different ways, were very active in developing detailed empirical research. The Continental European type of sociology would have had much more difficulty in becoming an integral part of the more general trend of empirical research than this has actually been the case in the United States. It would be hard to exaggerate the importance of a strong tradition of empirical research in bringing about the differentiation between sociology as a scientific discipline and its application to social policy.

In sum, within the last generation or so sociology has reached what is, perhaps, a first level of maturity as a scientific discipline. Although the process of differentiation is far from complete and there remain many indistinct borderline areas, sociology, along with the other social sciences, has become relatively differentiated from the philosophical matrix. It has, again with a good deal of indistinctness, achieved a fairly clearly defined place in the general cluster of scientific disciplines which deal with human behavior. It has also been disentangled from the earlier simple identification with specific practical goals in the society, to become an independent, relatively "pure" discipline with a research and theoretical tradition of its own. As we have seen, however, each of these borderlines is still highly problematical, and the unclarity of the cultural lines is a focus of strain at each point. I would say that the problem of ideological contamination is the most urgent one *vis-à-vis* the philosophical background; that of interdisciplinary imperialisms and conflict in relations with sister disciplines; and the problem of full commitment to pure research and training, not the formulation of social policy, *vis-à-vis* the applied front.

THE INSTITUTIONALIZATION OF
SOCIOLOGY IN THE UNIVERSITIES

. . . Now for the first time, sociology has come to be recognized as one of the regular disciplines in every major university in the United States—with Johns Hopkins finally completing the roster. Only in a few elite colleges of liberal arts—for example, Amherst, Williams, and Swarthmore—has this development still failed to occur. This situation stands in sharp contrast to that in Europe, where the total number of chairs constitutes a rather small fraction of the American, with as yet only minimal recognition of sociology at Oxford and Cambridge and, on the Continent, with only about one half of the universities north of the Alps showing some interest.

If the conception of sociology as a profession organized about a scientific discipline be accepted, the importance of the broad development in the United States can scarcely be exaggerated. A secure position in university faculties of course is the structural base from which a scientifically oriented profession can most effectively operate. Sociology is thus completely involved in the situation confronting the scientific professions generally, and the social sciences particularly, in American society. Yet no other base of operations could be so advantageous for sociology's further development as a discipline and its eventual influence in the society. . . .

Sociology's central operating base in university faculties raises the important problem of the place of sociology relative to its sister disciplines in these faculties. As noted above, there are many points at which, in terms of intellectual content, the borderlines are unclear. Although many of these borderline problems lack clear substantive and organizational definition, the situation seems to be fairly satisfactory. From the point of view of the profession's institutionalization in the academic community, there are two conspicuous encouraging facts about the current situation. First, sociology as a "subject" has gained generally acknowledged academic "citizenship," as we have seen. Second, although there are cases in which sociology is organizationally combined with other disciplines—sometimes with the economics-political science complex, sometimes with psychology or anthropology or both—there is no threatening uniformity of the pattern in which this occurs.

Sociology's middle position in relation to the other "behavioral sciences" is clearly a highly strategic one. The professional group is in no danger of being absorbed into any of its neighbors; moreover it offers something essential to each of them. To economists and political scientists, for instance, it provides a better understanding of "institutional" factors than their own disciplines make readily available. To psychologists it contributes a focus on "social" factors not readily reducible to individual terms. *Vis-à-vis* anthropology, the line is not so clear, but perhaps without seeming invidious one may say that anthropologists, having derived so much of their experience from the study of relatively undifferentiated societies, can use some help in the analysis of structurally complex modern societies, a field in which sociologists have a certain "head start." . . .

A final point concerning the relation of sociology to its sister disciplines concerns the increasing participation of sociologists in interdisciplinary research projects. One major type of interdisciplinary venture is the "area" study, but there is a variety of other types such as studies of organizations and local community situations. These projects provide an important setting in which the nature of the participating disciplines can become better defined.

I have briefly outlined the general strengthening of sociology's position as a scientific discipline, its establishment in university faculties, and the development of its research and training functions; and touched upon the contributions it can make to its sister disciplines. Two other main developments remain to be reviewed. Anticipating the subsequent discussion somewhat, it may first be said that sociology's contribution to our society's ideological "definition of the situation" has greatly increased in importance in recent years. The frequency with which the term "sociology" appears in popular discussions, albeit often with dubious technical justification, is an index of this situation. Secondly, although sociologists are still well behind their economist, political scientist, and psychologist colleagues, the change over the past twenty years in the extent to which they have won a place in the world of practical affairs is unmistakable. The upshot of this whole shift, to which no one factor has predominantly contributed, is that sociology may perhaps be said to have graduated from being the least respectable of the social science disciplines to being the most controversial.

SOCIOLOGY'S CONTRIBUTION TO CONTEMPORARY IDEOLOGY

An important index of the relationship which has been developing between changes in the society itself and the place of the social science professions within it is that the term sociology is coming increasingly to be a central symbol in the popular ideological preoccupations of our time. In this respect, perhaps we may say that, ideologically, a "sociological era" has begun to emerge, following an "economic" and, more recently, a "psychological" era.

Not only was the industrial economy the great new phenomenon from the latter 19th well into this century; intellectually economic theory of varying kinds provided the terms for defining the character of that period. Schools of thought ranged from the most orthodox laissez-faire capitalism through varying shades of liberalism and reformism to radical socialism, eventually crystallizing in Marxism; but underlying all these views was a common set of assumptions about the critical character of "economic factors." This ideological era, the last major phase of which was the New Deal period, was undoubtedly intimately connected with the process by which economics as a science came to be established in the academic world. The salience of economics as an ideological focus has now greatly subsided, although of course it continues to play an important role in various issues of public policy. The economic era was succeeded, in a considerably less "massive" form, by the psychological era. This shift, which came to a head in the 1930s, was signalled by the growing concern with the role of rational *versus* "irrational" factors in the motivation of the individual. Similarly, it was closely associated with the rapid development of psychology as a scientific discipline.

While the economic era of ideology was related to the *fact* of industrialization, the psychological era has been related to industrialization's *consequences* for the individual. If the psychological movement challenged the adequacy of simpler-minded economic interpretations of human behavior, however, it became apparent that the understanding of the complexities and changes of our large-scale society and its "mass" phenomena require more than analysis of individual conduct. The new ideological era, which has overlapped with the psychological one, can be described as a kind of dialectic between a psychological focus of interest in the individual and a sociological focus of interest in the society. Inevitably the problem of constraints on individual freedom is a central theme in this complex. This seems to be the background of contemporary concern with the problem of "conformity." Note the striking difference between the emphasis in this case and what it was in the era of economic ideological primacy, when the essential problem—often posed as productivity *versus* equality—was to find a basis for adequate "satisfaction of wants." Certainly, in a sense, the conformity problem is peculiar to an "affluent society."

The emergence of this broad ideological preoccupation has affected the status of the sociological profession because now the sociologist is beginning to be defined by a much broader public as an expert on intellectual problems of public concern. The fact that his expertise is viewed with a large measure of ambivalence does not detract from the significance of this point. . . .

THE APPLIED FUNCTION

[Another] principal area of the profession's involvement in the structure of the society I have called the applied function. As noted, this interest was particularly prominent in sociology's early phase, especially in the social problems field, but was followed by a rather sharp withdrawal in favor of building up the central academic core of the discipline. More recently, however, there has been a notable return to applied interests over a far broader front than before. The turning point probably lay in the attempt to mobilize social science talent for military purposes in World War II, a movement in which sociology played an appreciable though far from leading part. Developments in such fields as industrial sociology and market research have also given impetus to the steady expansion of the applied function.

During the early development of a new discipline having practical possibilities, it is common for its own professional personnel directly to undertake these practical functions, and in some professions this pattern continues and expands. Chemistry perhaps is the profession in which this pattern is most prominent; a large proportion of those with Ph.D.s in chemistry do applied technological work for industry and government, probably outnumbering the chemical engineers. A similar pattern marks the recent growth of sociology and will probably continue to do so, most importantly perhaps in industrial organization, governmental organization, especially the armed services; opinion and attitude research; and various types of social agencies concerned with criminology, health, and the like. As yet, however, by far the largest proportion of sociologists with the Ph.D.—about 86 per cent—are employed by colleges and universities, exceeded in this respect only by history, literature, and other humanities, while a significantly smaller proportion of holders of the Ph.D. in political science and economics are so employed (76 and 69 per cent, respectively).[1]

An important and rapidly expanding bridge between non-academic and academic employment is the consultant role in various non-academic organizations. This ranges from a relatively individualized service to particular clients to a considerable amount of "conferencing" where groups of professionals, often interdisciplinary in composition, are called on to help clarify a practical problem area.

A critical difference between the development of applied functions in sociology and psychology is the lesser importance in the former of anything like "practice," in the sense of individual service for a fee. The employers of sociologists, on both full time and consulting bases, are more likely to be organizations such as business firms, governmental units, social agencies, and research offices, which as such are unlikely to need the same kind of protection against charlatanism or other exploitation needed by an individual employing professional services. Hence the sociological profession is more likely to be able to minimize the complicated problems of legal certification, licensing, or both, in which the psychologists have recently become heavily involved.[2]

A new pattern of application has recently emerged, however, in which sociologists participate along with specialists in other "basic sciences" in research and training for a range of applied professions. Historically the closest affiliation of sociology with an applied profession was that with social work. When sociology withdrew from this activity social work formed a primary alliance

---

[1] According to a 1952 survey reported in "Personnel Resources in the Social Sciences and Humanities," U.S. Bureau of Labor Statistics Bulletin #1169, Table A-17, pp. 94-96. The differences are even more striking among those holding a Master's degree: of sociology Masters, 69.1 per cent were employed in colleges or universities, but only 36.8 per cent of those in political science and 46.3 per cent of those in economics were so employed. It is suggestive in this connection that a more up-to-date survey of graduate students, not yet published by N.O.R.C., shows a smaller proportion (68 per cent) of sociologist-anthropologist Ph.D. candidates intending to enter academic life. By comparison, the proportions of candidates with this intention in some other fields are: English, 82 per cent; political science, 49 per cent; economics, 48 per cent; psychology, 42 per cent; chemistry, 39 per cent. (Personal communication from James A. Davis, National Opinion Research Center.)

[2] In this case the problem stems mainly from the rapid expansion of practice in clinical psychology and the ambiguities of its relation to the practice of psychiatry. As a defense against the medical claim to a monopoly on legitimate psychotherapy, the psychologists have adopted a policy in favor of legal certification, to be implemented by certifying not functions as such but the use of the title "psychologist." This has impinged on the interests of sociologists because the certification of the title in the terms spelled out in some statutes would exclude social psychologists with sociological training and affiliation from certification and hence from performing various applied functions. This issue is currently the object of complex negotiation between the two professional associations. But it is clear that certification of the title of an academic discipline in order to define legitimate applied practice seems to involve serious complications both for the discipline itself and for those closely related to it in the scientific community.

with psychiatry. Only recently has the relationship been reestablished, primarily through the participation of sociologists both in the training of graduate social work students and in research bearing on social work.

The primary break-through of the new pattern has occurred in the field of health, especially mental health. After the overwhelming predominance, during the first quarter of the century, of the definition of "scientific" medicine as "organic" medicine, the emergence of concern with psychological and social factors in illness and health has been a dramatic development. Within this framework, sociologists perhaps have come to take the lead more than any other "behavioral" scientists, in collaboration and friendly rivalry with the anthropologists, and apparently drawing ahead of the psychologists, although the latter constitute numerically and organizationally a more powerful group. This seems to be largely because sociology is uninvolved in claims to control the therapy of individual patients. The sociologist helps with problems that impinge on medicine and public health, but his functions cannot be seen as practice in the traditional medical sense. Hence sociology is not viewed as a threat to the psychiatric treatment of patients in the same way as is clinical psychology.

It is now well known that appointments in medical and public health organizations of various sorts constitute one of the major fields of employment for sociologists, probably the largest single field except for the central teaching-research occupation. The character of these openings varies greatly, perhaps qualitatively the most important type being appointment to faculty posts in medical schools and schools of public health. The trend is certainly toward the inclusion of sociology among the basic sciences underlying the practice of medicine, and thus toward the incorporation of sociologists, along with other behavioral scientists, in an organizational status parallel to that of physiologists, biochemists, biophysicists, bacteriologists, and so on.

The health field, however, is only one of several applied areas in which this new pattern is emerging. Although not as yet on so large a scale, the same trend is observable in the relation of the social sciences generally, and sociology in particular, to schools of business and public administration, of education, of law, and even of divinity. Perhaps the furthest advancement along these lines so far is in business schools—the most important precursor of this development having been the linkage between rural sociology and colleges of agriculture. The two most important

branches of sociology to business schools are of course industrial sociology and survey research. Probably the field in which sociology's role is most likely to grow rapidly in the near future is education, not least because of our society's present urgent need for expansion and improvement of educational facilities. The penetration of the social sciences into the field of law has been rather slow—notwithstanding such assertions as Dean Griswold's that law itself is a social science;[3] but it may be expected to accelerate and to be substantial in the long run. . . .

SUMMARY AND CONCLUSION

This review yields a fairly clear picture. Sociology is a profession centered about a growing scientific discipline which, within the last decade or so, has reached a new level of maturity and has come to occupy an increasingly strategic place in the cluster of social sciences. The latter have acquired in this century a position in the society never before accorded to them. The technical basis of sociology has developed enormously in the last generation, with a far deeper and broader battery of research technology than before and a substantial improvement of its theory. The output of superior research results has greatly expanded at the same time that its average quality has substantially improved.

As a profession, its central working base in the universities has been greatly extended and consolidated; now every major American university has made a place for sociology. The number of professionally trained new personnel is about three times the figure of twenty years ago, and will certainly increase. Sociology has moved into a central place in current broad intellectual preoccupations. The involvement of sociologists in practical functions has greatly expanded. At least prominent beginnings have been made in establishing it as a basic science underlying a whole range of applied professions. The various professional associations have been greatly expanded and strengthened. On every essential front there has been growth and, I think, improvement.

---

[3] Erwin N. Griswold, "Law Schools and Human Relations," Tyrrell Williams Lecture delivered at the Law School of Washington University, St. Louis, April 19, 1955 (mimeo.), p. 6.

Selection *4*
_____

The Case for Sociology
Robert K. Merton

In *The New York Times Magazine,* June 25, 1961, Professor Russell Kirk, a political scientist, published an article contending that: (1) sociology is doubtfully scientific; (2) no science can deal scientifically with "living and erratic man"; (3) many sociologists are infatuated with jargon and meaningless statistics; (4) sociologists believe that they will be able to predict and control human behavior and thus will become the engineers of a new social order; and (5) only poets, theologians, political theorists, and other "men of imagination" can have a true knowledge of man.

Merton's reply to Kirk's attack provides a review of some of the ideas, purposes, methods, and problems of sociology discussed in the preceding selections. The student may wish to re-examine the readings in terms of Merton's comments in órder to place them in context. The chapter from Chase's book, for example, indicates the practical need for knowledge about human society and about the nature of human interrelationships. Although Parsons would probably call Chase's work a problem approach rather than a scientific approach, Chase does show how scientific questions emerge from social problems. Stouffer is concerned with the methods of producing sociological knowledge: how, indeed, can we extract facts from observations, and how can we convert facts to meaningful knowledge?

With Parsons' brief historical sketch of sociology's emergence as a discipline, the mortar has been prepared for the introduction of selected pebbles into our sociological mosaic. Whether social scientists could, let alone should, predict and control the course of society is treated by Merton as an issue basically irrelevant to the present-day discipline of sociology. But here again we observe a crossing of the paths of science and philosophy and are forced to note the complexity of their interrelationships.

Once again the season of the anti-sociologists is upon us. The academic year has ended and professors are ready to turn from talking to writing. A self-selected few will dust off and publish yet again the litany that fiercely imprecates sociology and all its works. This year, the avowed conservative professor of political science, Russell Kirk, got in first. His version will serve to exhibit the curious admixture of illogic and sentiment that makes up the creed and canons of anti-sociology.

Some sociologists find these assaults tiresome. To me, they have the peculiar charm of testifying to the need for the very kind of sociological inquiry they caricature. For each jaded version reads as though it were written by a sociologist-*manqué.* Each purports to describe the behavior of sociologists, to explain that behavior and, even more ambitiously, to describe and explain the responses to it.

With practiced ease, for example, Mr. Kirk reviews the work of thousands of social scientists and promulgates the first canon that "the representative" specimen is an "empiricist of the positivist variety; emotionally, he is often a secular evangelist." Had Mr. Kirk allowed himself to profit from the introductory course in sociology he so deplores, he might have learned of the danger of creating out of his private impressions a sterotype of the aims and behavior of large numbers of people, all the while pretending to have caught hold of the representative reality. But amateur sociologizing has no place for disciplined inquiry. Rather, it assumes that statements become authoritative simply by being put into the black and white magic of print.

The second canon declares the absurdity and impiety of statistics dealing with the behavior of men in society. For nothing significant about man's behavior can be counted. If it could be counted, it would be immoral to do so. Everyone knows that no good can come of it.

To support this canon, Mr. Kirk cites Carlyle, who knew little about the primitive statistical methods of his own day and nothing, obviously, about the mathematical bases of modern statistics. As further proof, he quotes the attack by the sociologist Pitirim A. Sorokin on "quantophrenia" or an uncritical devotion to faulty statistics. Unlike myself, Mr. Kirk has not had the benefit of having been Professor Sorokin's student, and so does not know, apparently, that Sorokin used vast arrays of social statistics in every one of his major works and, in "Social and Cultural Dynamics," states that "quantitative judgments . . . in verbal form" are inevitable in any substantial work of history.

No doubt it is more inviting to assume statistics of human behavior. The amateur sociologist will explain, for example, why it is that we have such high rates of mental illness in what Mr. Kirk feels free to describe as our age of "twentieth-century social disintegration." But while the amateur sociologist explains *why* this is so, the disciplined sociologist proceeds first to find out whether it really *is* so. Only through painstaking analysis of the statistics of mental illness—as in the work of Herbert Goldhamer and Andrew Marshall—do we find that we had best postpone our ready-to-hand explanations, if only because it now seems probable that the rate of confinement for mental illness is no higher today than it was during the past century.

Turning up like death and taxes, the third canon of the anti-sociologists declares the sociologists to be both perpetrators and victims of jargon. Here, the anti-sociologist knows himself to be on altogether safe ground, for just about everyone can be counted on to be "against jargon" in the same penetrating sense that President Coolidge's minister declared himself against sin.

Perhaps it is time to distinguish between jargon and that essential of all disciplined thought, technical language. Technical language is a more precise and condensed form of thought and communication than colloquial language. It is designed to fix definite meanings in which each word has ideally only one denotation and is deliberately deprived of connotations. Jargon, in contrast, is a muddled and wordy imitation of technical language.

The mere unfamiliarity or unesthetic quality of language is no criterion. Jargon and technical language sound alike to someone untrained in the discipline where the language is employed.

All this is only prologue to the pair of canons central to the anti-sociologists' creed. Briefly put, these hold, first, that sociological truths cannot be discovered, for there are no detectable uniformities in human behavior, since man is incorrigibly unpredictable. And second, that sociologists constitute a danger to society, for they provide the knowledge through which men can be molded to fit a new and obnoxious social order. I need not burlesque the logic of the anti-sociologists, for they have preceded me here. I need only review it.

It would seem clear that, if there are no discoverable uniformities about man in society, there can be no sociological knowledge employed to regiment him. Should anti-sociologists admit that there are such uniformities, they can scarcely argue that these uniformities can be discovered by the defective sociology of today, with its inapplicable statistics, its tattered jargon, and its total misunderstanding of human nature.

Forced to acknowledge that there are discoverable uniformities in social life and that modern sociology, for all its limitations, discovers some of them, would they then propose to exercise this knowledge for fear that it might be used to violate civilized values? On this last line of retreat, the anti-sociologists would join forces with the anti-intellectuals and totalitarian regimenters of thought they ostensibly combat. They would declare themselves guardians of us all, alone able to distinguish dangerous from undangerous knowledge.

The remaining canons of the anti-sociologists are transparently trivial. Criticism among sociologists, for example, is described by the anti-sociologists in the militant metaphors of "warring camps" and "internecine warfare." Perhaps they should pause before advocating monolithic agreement on intellectual issues. It would be a curious reading of the history of thought to suggest that the absence of disagreement testifies to a developing discipline.

As for the anti-sociologists' canon that gives them alone access to the recorded wisdom of the past—from Plato to Montesquieu and Burke—this need only be stated to refute itself.

Since the anti-sociologists impose their grotesque versions of the methods of sociological inquiry upon a public too busy to look for themselves, a few words should be said about those methods. Social scientists believe it no longer sufficient to describe the behavior, attitudes, values and social relations obtaining in a complex society simply on the basis of a large but scattered array of documents, both public and private, and on educated guesses about what people are thinking and feeling. Studies of the historical past, of course, have no alternative. But in the study of present-day societies, these procedures are giving way to systematic, though far from perfected, methods.

One such method is the "sample survey," which sounds out the practices and attitudes of a group selected as representative of the larger population from which they are drawn. This type of survey is now part of the intellectual landscape. However, the "opinion polls" in the popular press do not begin to reproduce the analytical uses to which such surveys are put by academic sociologists.

Furthermore, it is with this instrument as with the rest: the most devastating criticisms of its misuse have come, not from the anti-sociologists who know about it only through casual inspection, but from the professional sociologists who are prepared to study their sometimes disappointing experience with it. For they, at least the best of them, know that, whatever the worth of one or another tool of inquiry, it is the questions put into the inquiry that determine the significance of the results. If the questions are trivial, then the answers will be trivial.

For sociology as for most other scientific disciplines, the electronic computer has emerged as a new resource. Contrary to the imagery of the anti-sociologists, this machine is not the universal mind of our day. It must be told what to do. But, as with most technical creations, the computer has a capacity for deflecting men from the pursuit of purposes that genuinely matter. It tempts its tenders to cast all manner of raw data into its maw and wait for the thoroughly digested product that will itself be senseless if the thought of its managers is without sense. The potential victims, by their professional training, are best qualified to recognize and to counter this danger.

With or without the computer, today's sociology makes no attempt to substitute science for ethics and esthetics or to displace humanism with scientism. Every responsible sociologist, and there are not a few, knows that his knowledge is no substitute for artistic thought.

The thinking humanist, for his part, recognizes that the social scientist who knows his business seeks only to provide an understanding of certain, not all, aspects of the behavior of men and the organization of human society. The intellectual gulf between humanist and social scientist has begun to be bridged. The late Gilbert Murray, critic and classical scholar, said that sociology is "destined to bear abundant and ever-increasing fruit." The political journalist Richard Rovere, has observed that "those of us who have been educated in the twentieth century habitually think in sociological terms, whether or not we have had any training in sociology."

After all this, it is only natural to ask: what is going on in sociology and what does it all amount to? It would be foolish to answer this question by staking out the boundaries of sociology, as though it were a piece of real estate. That is not the character of intellectual property. But we can, in this short space, at least hint at the answer.

In the large, sociology is engaged in finding out how man's behavior and fate are affected, if not minutely governed, by his place within particular kinds, and changing kinds, of social structure and of culture. This means that sociology moves across a wide, varied and, to the layman, often bewildering range of topics and problems.

In doing so, one of its principal functions is to subject popular beliefs about man and his works to responsible investigation. As I have implied, the sociologist asks about many of these beliefs, "Is it really so?" The popular assumption, for example, that the rate of social mobility in America has recently declined has been put in question by systematically assembled data.

The alleged breakdown of the American family, with obsequies read regularly over the remains by those who should know better, has been found to be specious; thorough analyses of data on divorce and death find American marriages remaining intact more often now than they once did. Or, to tackle one last widespread assumption, people who reject orthodox religious beliefs are not more apt to engage in crime than people who hold fast to such beliefs.

Some of the findings of sociology take a considerable time to enter the public domain. For more than a generation, sociologists have found that complex organizations of widely different kinds—economic, political, military, educational—exhibit the same tendencies. These tendencies make for the "bureaucratic man," who is shaped by organizationally induced pressures to conform to the rules even when this means that conformity gets in the way of doing the job effectively. How far this is inevitable remains to be seen, and inquiries are now under way to find out how these tendencies can be counteracted.

Basic to sociology is the premise that, in the course of social interaction, men create new conditions that were not part of their intent. Short-run rationality often produces long-run irrationality. Public health measures may go awry; financial incentives may lead to a decline rather than an increase in production; intensified punishment may aggravate rather than curb crime. Growing recognition of this has become one of the sources of an enlarged use of sociological research in such fields as medicine and public health, social work, law, education, the ministry, architecture and city planning, business, organized labor and agriculture.

Yet it must be added, that sociologists, perhaps better than the anti-sociologists, know they are just beginning to acquire the knowledge needed to cope with the many social ills man has the inveterate capacity to contract.

We sociologists need to be saved from the anti-sociologists only in respect to the exaggerated claims they make for our prowess and accomplishments. It is they, not we, who say that "sociology is a power in the land." It is they, not we, who make the absurd claim that sociology has the power and the intent to turn men into robots and to construct a new social order. The men and women at work in sociological inquiry have more modest and less sadistic hopes. Like their colleagues in other scholarly and scientific disciplines, they recognize that this "very new science of an ancient subject" has still a long way to go. And undisturbed by the cannonades of the anti-sociologists, they are methodically proceeding on their way.

Part II

CULTURE

In Part I it was noted that sociology is the study of interpersonal relations. The understanding of human interrelationships requires some understanding of the concept of culture.

The term *culture* denotes the storehouse of *ways* of believing and behaving, learned through contact with other human beings rather than inherited genetically, that characterize a particular society. The culture of a people is an indefinitely large, unpublished code made up of their answers to such questions as: "What should I do in this situation?" "How shall I do it?" "With what shall I do it?" "How will my behavior be judged by others?" "How can I expect others to behave toward me and toward each other?" Culture also includes beliefs about what foods taste best, what personal adornments are most attractive, what girls are marriageable, and what "rights" a woman has.

People *have* a culture—they do not constitute a culture. Students should be careful to distinguish between a society and its culture. A society is comprised of *people;* a culture is comprised of *ways.* To speak of the Chinese people is a substantively different thing from speaking of Chinese ways.

The case for culture should be neither overstated nor understated. Cultural principles unquestionably provide an understanding of a wide range of behaviors in any society, but no very large aggregation of people conforms exactly to a single set of rules. There are regional variations on the cultural themes of geographically diffuse societies, and there are class variations in most societies. In Selection 5, Evon Z. Vogt and Thomas F. O'Dea show how the different culturally learned values of the members of two different communities produced two observably different patterns of community behavior. William Graham Sumner's classic presentation in Selection 7 shows that no culture is so rigid that it does not include many alternative ways of believing and behaving nor so flexible as to be entirely without prescriptions and taboos.

Objects, events, symbols, beliefs, and behaviors that are meaningful in a society and characteristic of it are called *culture traits.* Some culture traits are peculiar to a single society; others are used with different meanings in different societies; and still others have similar meanings in many societies. It is quite safe to say that no contemporary society has a culture that is unique in all its traits—probably not even in an appreciable percentage of its traits. On the other hand, the *configuration* of traits in every culture *is* unique. It is impossible to grasp the full significance of any trait apart from its cultural context, since it will inevitably have special relationships to certain other traits and to the total configuration. One cannot speak of wedding rings without speaking of weddings, of weddings without speaking of marriage, and so forth.

In order to grasp something of the concept of culture as anthropologists of Sumner's day understood it, it may be helpful to review one of the early classifications of culture traits. In 1881, E. B. Tylor wrote about cultures under the following headings:

1. Language (ways of speaking, writing, gesturing, etc.)
2. Arts of life (ways of getting food, making and using tools, providing shelter and warmth, cooking, making and using clothing and ornaments, and exchanging goods)
3. Arts of pleasure (ways of dancing, drawing, carving, modeling, singing, reciting poetry, and presenting drama)
4. Science (ways of counting, measuring, reasoning, performing magic, and dealing systematically with the physical world)
5. The spirit-world (ways of believing and behaving with respect to the supernatural, including religious forms)
6. History and mythology (ways of recounting the social heritage, ancestry, ideals and dream-myths, and origins of the society)
7. Society (ways in which people interact and relate themselves to one another)

Since Sumner's day there have been other schemes for categorizing cultural traits. The most famous and most comprehensive is the Cross-Cultural Survey done at Yale University under the leadership of George P. Murdock.

Most of us assume that when the first earthling sets foot on another planet inhabited by intelligent beings, he will find those beings able to communicate with one another. We also assume that the strangers will have created distinctive styles in their manufactured goods, that they will enjoy special kinds of food (perhaps even earthlings!), that they will have some explanation—mythological or scientific—for their relationship to the universe, and that they will have a system for differentiating among and relating themselves to one another. In short, we cannot conceive of intelligent beings existing anywhere without some kind of culture.

Culture is limited by definition to *learned* ways of believing and behaving. Man's purely biological functions (breathing, digesting, and the like) distinguish him as a biological species but do not link him to any particular society. Cultural characteristics are not transmitted genetically; if a characteristic is inherited genetically, it cannot be properly classed as cultural. Many biological needs are, however, gratified in learned, cultural ways. Hunger, a biological need universally inherited by humans, is gratified by eating—but what a person eats, how he prepares it, and the manner in which he eats it are generally culturally determined. In Selection 6, Marston Bates indicates some of the culturally derived sentiments regarding food and sex that are learned, not inherent in the biological human. Although cultural phenomena are readily separable from biological phenomena, no general statement can be made about their relative influence on human behavior. We can readily appreciate that fear of embarrassment may be a more powerful motivation than biological discomfort. For example, the "need" to conceal certain body areas is not always justified by lack of protection or of warmth; it is more often a reflection of cultural sentiment than the fulfillment of a biological need that keeps us "properly" clothed.

Sumner's *Folkways* is concerned with the regulative and prescriptive effects on social behavior of customary ways of doing things. Interpersonal behavior is rarely so primitive that it is entirely without cultural prescription; in every society there is a "proper" time, place, and way to engage in almost any behavior. Also, almost any behavior is subject to cultural interpretation: dipping one's fingers into the gravy to find a choice morsel has a vastly different social significance in Nigeria from that which it has in the United States.

As Sumner observes, ideas of good and bad are usually cultural, and the doers of good and bad deeds are respectively rewarded and punished in cultural ways. However, it is not correct to say that the culture gives the reward or punishment; culture, a set of ways, can be enacted only through the minds and bodies of people. People, not cultures, reward or punish, accept or reject. As noted in Vogt and O'Dea's work, culture may be superindividual, but it is definitely not superhuman.

The culture of every society includes some ideas and attitudes which are so pervasive and are involved in so many behaviors and thoughts that they not only affect that society's entire way of living but also become means by which members of that society are recognized by those of other societies. In the United States today, for example, most people are oriented toward success and happiness. These two values are so much a part of most of us that we cannot believe people normal if they have no aspirations toward their achievement. The German love for neatness and order and the calm and patience of the Japanese are characteristic of the beliefs, behaviors, and feelings of those people.

Ingrained cultural beliefs and feelings become incorporated into a people's language; language, in turn, affects beliefs and feelings by providing names for the concepts by which man deals with his world socially as well as intellectually. It is impossible to separate the study of personality and language from the study of culture.

The infant learns to define, classify, relate, and think abstractly about his environment—as Vogt and O'Dea indicate—under the tutelage of persons who are already participating in social interaction according to cultural patterns. Elements of an individual's own culture seem normal and natural to him. He tends to judge all behaviors, ideas, and artifacts in terms of his own cultural background as he adopts its ways of thinking, feeling, and behaving. He must adapt exotic culture traits to the configuration of his own culture before they "make sense" or "feel right" to him. Sumner calls this condition *ethnocentrism*. In extreme ethnocentrism, one may identify emotionally with his own culture to such an extent that he believes his culture provides the *only* normal and natural ways of behaving and believing. Usually, however, ethnocentrism results merely in misunderstanding, confusion, and the general avoidance of unfamiliar traits.

While ethnocentrism may be declining as our shrinking world becomes culturally more homogeneous, we do not have to look far back into social history to find practices that twentieth-century Americans cannot accept, even in their proper contexts. Cannibalism, female infanticide, human sacrifice, and human slavery are very difficult for us to understand because we have deeply ingrained sentiments against them. On the other hand, Moslems of a few generations ago would have been shocked to see American women eating in public with men, and some Orientals still consider the idea of kissing on the mouth not only unsanitary but highly indecent.

All human culture, whether primitive African or modern American, is the result of a long, slow, complex process of change and development, as George P. Murdock shows in Selection 8, and the process is never complete. A culture remains always in an emergent state, its configurations never finished. A culture is thus always unstable in the sense that its pattern never endures long enough to be described in all its details. Yet every cultural element can be related in some way to previously existing elements; no part of the most recent space capsule, for example, is without a cultural antecedent. In Selection 10, W. Fred Cottrell describes several aspects of the emergence of nuclear energy as a culture trait in modern society.

Social change takes place as rapidly or slowly and as inevitably as cultural change, and often the two kinds of change are closely interwoven. If cultural habits are at all satisfactory, they tend to persist; as a result, there are constant pressures to *adjust* old traits to new patterns and new traits to old patterns. Relationships between persons change in the same way—satisfactory relationships tend to persist, but there are constant pressures to change them. New people are born, people marry, people grow up and age and die; new leaders emerge as people are caught up in industrial, economic, and political trends and are transformed from bicycle makers to billionaires, from emperors to exiles, from platoon leaders to presidents.

Ideas change, too. Education, once a privilege of only a few, has changed from a private prerogative to a public obligation, most states requiring by law school attendance of all persons between the ages of six and sixteen. Husband-wife and parent-child relationships reflect conceptions of family life that are inextricably interwoven with economic and political change. Matters of morality become matters of law. The sacred becomes secular. A basic characteristic of life is change.

Several processes can be identified in the emergence of a culture. The tendency for people to resist change, to retain the ways of thinking, behaving, and believing to which they have become accustomed, is called *cultural conservatism.* Opposed to cultural conservatism are the processes of *invention* and *culture borrowing.*

Invention is the development of new uses for, or new combinations of, existing traits and resources. An invention may be simple in nature, such as using a brick for a doorstop, or it may be extremely complex, such as sending a man into outer space. Even in an invention as complex as a space rocket, however, the newest elements are the ideas and behaviors made possible by it, and even they are modifications of previously existing ideas and behaviors. Culture borrowing takes place when traits of one society are adopted by another society, but because cultural contexts are different, the borrowed traits may undergo modification in either form or significance.

Both inventions and borrowed traits by definition effect some change in the way a society lives. Every change in turn creates a degree of social disorganization. As we have learned in aiding underdeveloped countries, for example, improved medical care may increase population to the point of famine, and education may create discontent and rebellion. To maintain its stability, a society must be sufficiently flexible to reorganize after experiencing the disorganizing effects of cultural and social change. In Selection 11, William F. Ogburn points out how particular culture elements which fail to change become incongruous in a generally changing culture.

The following selections are not intended to treat the subjects of culture and culture change exhaustively—it would not be possible to do so in many whole libraries. They have been chosen, rather, because each one links the study of culture to the study of interpersonal relations.   *T.E.L.*

Selection 5

Cultural Differences in Two Ecologically Similar Communities

Evon Z. Vogt and Thomas F. O'Dea

Man's ability to accomplish as much as he does in a short lifetime lies partly in his ability to organize his world—to place specific objects into general categories and to devise or adopt satisfactory ways of dealing with all objects in the category. For example, when one has identified an object as a chair, one knows (i.e., has a preconception about) how to use it most satisfactorily or most efficiently. Every individual develops his own system for dealing with various situations. Obviously, he has neither the time nor the ingenuity to develop all of his methods logically, so most of them are learned or copied from other people. But even if he could develop a completely unique system, it would have many disadvantages and pose many problems. If each man used chairs that no one else recognized as chairs, played music that no one else knew was music, or spoke a language that no one else understood, we would certainly have a world so different from the present one that we cannot comprehend what it would be like.

Personal systems of adjusting to the universe are not independent of social systems. People who are thrown into frequent contact with one another assume or establish devices for meaningfully relating themselves to each other—devices which allow them to attain a tolerable degree of satisfaction for their personal needs and wants. When a number of people are involved in a pattern of such relationships, the pattern is called a *social system*. Every family evolves enduring —and yet constantly changing—definitions of its members and their relationships to each other. So, in fact, does every town, every city, and every nation.

It is easy to understand how the members of a family might evolve a mutually satisfactory social system, even without learning patterns from other persons. But consider the behavior that takes place at a metropolitan airport, where large numbers of people who have never before seen each other interact predictably and efficiently. It is evident that there are principles of organization at work which transcend spontaneous, individual systems. We may rule out the possibility that these principles are instinctive, for there are times and places (as demonstrated, perhaps, by a few people present at the airport) where they are not known. We must conclude that much of the behavior that we see consists of responses to ideas and feelings learned from other people in other places. Each person carries the potential for that behavior in his own body, and a sufficient number of people accomplish their purposes that airports remain a part of our culture.

Selections 5 through 7 deal with aspects of culture—that collection of ways of dealing with the environment that is characteristic of a society. Bates observes how shared sentiments about food and sex seem to be present in every society. Sumner discusses the empirical fact of shared ways of doing things and classifies them in terms of the importance that the society or group attaches to them. By comparing the different cultural values in two communities, Vogt and O'Dea show how feelings of rightness, wrongness, goodness, repulsion, anger, etc., toward objects and ideas affect actions. In other words, they offer an explanation of how *persons* are related to *culture*.

It is one of the central hypotheses of the Values Study Project that value-orientations play an important part in the shaping of social institutions and in influencing the forms of observed social action. By value-orientations are understood those views of the world, often implicitly held, which define the meaning of human life or the "life situation of man" and thereby provide the context in which day-to-day problems are solved. The present article is an outgrowth of one phase of the field research carried out in western New Mexico. It presents the record of two communities composed of people with a similar cultural background and living in the same general ecological setting.

The responses of these two communities to similar problems were found to be quite different. Since the physical setting of the two villages is remarkably similar, the explanation for the differences was sought in the manner in which each group viewed the situation and the kind of social relationships and legitimate expectations which each felt appropriate in meeting situational challenges. In this sphere of value-orientations a marked difference was found. Moreover, the differences in response to situation in the two cases were found to be related to the differences between the value-orientations central to these communities.

We do not deny the importance of situational factors. Nor do we intend to disparage the importance of historical convergence of value-orientations with concrete situations in explaining the centrality of some values as against others and in leading to the deep internalization of the values we discuss. But the importance of value-orientations as an element in understanding the situation of action is inescapably clear. . . .

FOCUS OF THE INQUIRY

The inquiry is focused upon a comparison of the Mormon community of *Rimrock* with the Texan community of *Homestead*, both having populations of approximately 250 and both located (forty miles apart) on the southern portion of the Colorado Plateau in western New Mexico. The natural environmental setting is virtually the same for the two villages: the prevailing elevations stand at 7,000 feet; the landscapes are characterized by mesa and canyon country; the

flora and fauna are typical of the Upper Sonoran Life Zone with stands of pinyon, juniper, sagebrush, and blue gramma grass and some intrusions of Ponderosa pine, Douglas fir, Englemann spruce and Gambel oak from a higher life zone; the region has a steppe climate with an average annual precipitation of 14 inches (which varies greatly from year to year) and with killing frosts occurring late in the spring and early in the autumn. The single important environmental difference between the two communities is that Rimrock is located near the base of a mountain range which has elevations rising to 9,000 feet, and a storage reservoir (fed by melting snow packs from these higher elevations) has made irrigation agriculture possible in Rimrock, while in Homestead there is only dry-land farming. Today both villages have subsistence patterns based upon combinations of farming (mainly irrigated crops of alfalfa and wheat in Rimrock, and dry-land crops of pinto beans in Homestead) and livestock raising (mainly Hereford beef cattle in both villages).

Rimrock was settled by Mormon missionaries in the 1870's as part of a larger project to plant settlements in the area of northern Arizona. Rimrock itself, unlike the Arizona sites, was established as a missionary outpost and the intention of the settlers was the conversion of the Indians, a task conceived in terms of the *Book of Mormon*, which defines the American Indian as "a remnant of Israel."

The early settlers were "called" by the Church, that is, they were selected and sent out by the Church authorities. The early years were exceedingly difficult and only the discipline of the Church and the loyalty of the settlers to its gospel kept them at the task. Drought, crop diseases, and the breaking of the earth and rock dam which they had constructed for the storage of irrigation water added to their difficulties, as did the fact that they had merely squatted on the land and were forced to purchase it at an exorbitant price to avoid eviction. The purchase money was given by the Church authorities in Salt Lake City, who also supplied 5,000 pounds of seed wheat in another period of dearth. The original settlers were largely from northern Utah although there

From the *American Sociological Review*, Vol. 18 (1953), 645-654. Reprinted by permission of the American Sociological Association.

were also some converts from the southern states who had been involved in unsuccessful Arizona settlements a few years earlier.

As the emphasis shifted from missionary activities to farming, Rimrock developed into a not unusual Mormon village, despite its peripheral position to the rest of Mormondom. Irrigation farming was supplemented by cattle raising on the open range. In the early 1930's the Mormons began to buy range land, and Rimrock's economy shifted to a focus upon cattle raising. Today villagers own a total of 149 sections of range land and about four sections of irrigated or irrigable land devoted to gardens and some irrigated pastures in the immediate vicinity of the village. The family farm is still the basic economic unit, although partnerships formed upon a kinship basis and devoted to cattle raising have been important in raising the economic level of the village as a whole. In recent years some of the villagers—also on the basis of a kinship partnership—purchased the local trading post which is engaged in trading with the Indians as well as local village business. In addition to 12 family partnerships which own 111 sections of land, there is a village cooperative which owns 38 sections. Privately-owned commercial facilities in the village include two stores, a boarding house, two garages, a saddle and leather shop, and a small restaurant. With this economic variety there is considerable difference in the distribution of wealth.

The Church is the central core of the village and its complex hierarchical structure, including the auxiliary organizations which activate women, youth, and young children, involves a large portion of the villagers in active participation. The church structure is backed up and impenetrated by the kinship structure. Moreover, church organization and kinship not only unify Rimrock into a social unit, they also integrate it into the larger structure of the Mormon Church and relate it by affinity and consanguinity to the rest of Mormondom.

Rimrock has been less affected by secularization than most Mormon villages in Utah and is less assimilated into generalized American patterns. Its relative isolation has both kept such pressures from impinging upon it with full force and enhanced its formal and informal ties with the Church, preserving many of the characteristics of a Mormon village of a generation ago.

Homestead was settled by migrants from the South Plains area of western Texas and Oklahoma in the early 1930's. The migration represented a small aspect of that vast movement of people westward to California which was popularized in Steinbeck's *Grapes of Wrath* and which was the subject of investigation by many governmental agencies in the 1930's and 1940's. Instead of going on to California, these homesteaders settled in a number of semi-arid farming areas in northern and western New Mexico and proceeded to develop an economy centered around the production of pinto beans. The migration coincided with the period of national depression and was due in part to severe economic conditions on the South Plains which forced families to leave their Texas and Oklahoma communities, in part to the attraction of land available for homesteading which held out the promise of family-owned farms for families who had previously owned little or no land or who had lost their land during the depression. The land base controlled by the homesteaders comprises approximately 100 sections. Each farm unit is operated by a nuclear family; there are no partnerships. Farms now average two sections in size and are scattered as far as twenty miles from the crossroads center of the community which contains the two stores, the school, the post office, two garages, a filling station, a small restaurant, a bean warehouse, a small bar, and two church buildings. Through the years, farming technology has shifted almost completely from horse-drawn implements to mechanized equipment.

With the hazardous farming conditions (periodic droughts and early killing frosts) out-migration from Homestead has been relatively high. A few of these families have gone on to California, but more of them have moved to irrigated farms in the middle Rio Grande Valley and entered an agricultural situation which in its physical environmental aspects is similar to the situation in the Mormon community of Rimrock.

THE MORMON CASE

In broad perspective these two villages present local variations of generalized American culture. They share the common American value-orientations which emphasize the importance of achievement and success, progress and optimism, and rational mastery over nature. In the Mormon case, these were taken over from the 19th century American milieu in western New York where the Church was founded, and reinterpreted in terms of an elaborate theological conception of the universe as a dynamic process in which God and men are active collaborators in an eternal progression to greater power through increasing mastery. The present life was and is conceived as a single episode in an infinity of work and mastery. The result was the heightening for the Mormons of convictions shared with most other Americans. Moreover, this conception was closely related to the belief in the reopening of divine revelation through the agency first of Joseph Smith, the original Mormon prophet, and later through the institutionalized channels of the Mormon Church. The Mormons conceived of themselves as a covenant people especially chosen for a divine task. This task was the building of the kingdom of God on earth and in this project—attempted four times unsuccessfully before the eventual migration to the west—much of the religious and secular socialism of the early 19th century found a profound reflection. The Mormon prophet proposed the "Law of Consecration" in an attempt to reconcile private initiative with cooperative endeavor. Contention led to its abandonment in 1838 after some five years of unsuccessful experiment. Yet this withdrawal did not limit, but indeed rather enhanced, its future influence in Mormon settlement. The "Law of Consecration" was no longer interpreted as a blueprint prescribing social institutions of a definite sort, but its values lent a strong cooperative bias to much of later Mormon activity. In the context of the notion of peculiarity and reinforced by out-group antagonism and persecution, these values became deeply embedded in Mormon orientations. The preference for agriculture combined with an emphasis upon community and lay participation in church activities resulted in the formation of compact villages rather than isolated family farmsteads as the typical Mormon settlement pattern.

While Rimrock and Homestead share most of the central value-orientations of general American culture, they differ significantly in the values governing social relationships. Rimrock, with a stress upon community cooperation, an ethnocentrism resulting from the notion of their own peculiarity, and a village pattern of settlement, is more like the other Mormon villages of the West than it is like Homestead.

The stress upon *community cooperation* in Rimrock contrasts markedly with the stress upon *individual independence* found in Homestead. This contrast is one of emphasis, for individual initiative is important in Rimrock, especially in family farming and cattle raising, whereas cooperative activity does occur in Homestead. In Rimrock, however, the expectations are such that one must show his fellows or at least convince himself that he has good cause for *not* committing his time and resources to community efforts while in Homestead cooperative action takes place *only* after certainty has been reached that the claims of other individuals upon one's time and resources are legitimate.

Rimrock was a cooperative venture from the start, and very early the irrigation company, a mutual non-profit corporation chartered under state law, emerged from the early water association informally developed around—and in a sense within—the Church. In all situations which transcend the capacities of individual families or family combinations, Rimrock Mormons have recourse to cooperative techniques. Let us examine four examples.

The "tight" land situation

Rimrock Mormons, feeling themselves "gathered," dislike having to migrate to non-Mormon areas. However, after World War II the 32 returned veterans faced a choice between poverty and under-employment or leaving the community. This situation became the concern of the Church and was discussed in its upper lay priesthood bodies in the village. It was decided to buy land to enable the veterans to remain. The possibilities of land purchase in the area were almost nonexistent and it appeared that nothing could be done, when unexpectedly the opportunity to buy some 38 sections presented itself. At the time, the village did not have the needed 10,000 dollars for the down payment, so the sum was borrowed from the Cooperative Security Corporation, a Church Welfare Plan agency, and the land was purchased. The patterns revealed here—community concern over a community problem, and appeal to and reception of aid from the general authorities of the Church—are typically Mormon. However, Mormon cooperation did not end here. Instead of breaking up the purchased land into plots to be individually owned and farmed, the parcel was kept as a unit, and a cooperative Rimrock Land and Cattle Company was formed. The company copied and adapted the form of the mutual irrigation company. Shares were sold in the village, each member being limited to two. A quota of cattle per share per year to be run on the land and a quota of bulls relative to cows were established. The cattle are privately owned, but the land is owned and managed cooperatively. The calves are the property of the owners of the cows. The project, which has not been limited to veterans, supplements other earnings sufficiently to keep most of the veterans in the village.

The graveling of the village streets

The streets of Rimrock were in bad repair in the fall of 1950. That summer a construction company had brought much large equipment into the area to build and gravel a section of a state highway which runs through the village. Before this company left, taking its equipment with it, villagers, again acting through the Church organization, decided that the village should avail itself of the opportunity and have the town's streets graveled. This was discussed in the Sunday priesthood meeting and announced at the Sunday sacrament meeting. A meeting was called for Monday evening, and each household was asked to send a representative. The meeting was well attended, and although not every family had a member present, practically all were represented at least by proxy. There was considerable discussion, and it was finally decided to pay 800 dollars for the job which meant a 20 dollar donation from each family. The local trader paid a larger amount, and, within a few days after the meeting, the total amount was collected. Only one villager raised objections to the proceedings. Although he was a man of importance locally, he was soon silenced by a much poorer man who invoked Mormon values of progress and cooperation and pledged to give 25 dollars which was 5 dollars above the norm.

The construction of a high school gymnasium

In 1951 a plan for the construction of a high school gymnasium was presented to the Rimrock villagers. Funds for materials and for certain skilled labor would be provided from state school appropriations, providing that the local residents would contribute the labor for construction. The plan was discussed in a Sunday priesthood meeting in the church, and later meetings were held both in the church and in the schoolhouse. Under the leadership of the principal of the school (who is also a member of the higher priesthood), arrangements were made whereby each able-bodied man in the community would either contribute at least 50 hours of labor or 50 dollars (the latter to be used to hire outside laborers) toward the construction. The original blueprint was extended to include a row of classrooms for the high school around the large central gymnasium.

Work on the new building began in late 1951, continued through 1952, and is now (in 1953) nearing completion. The enterprise was not carried through without difficulties. A few families were sympathetic at first but failed to contribute full amounts of either labor or cash, and some were unsympathetic toward the operation from the start. The high school principal had to keep reminding the villagers about their pledges to support the enterprise. But in the end the project was successful, and it represented an important cooperative effort on the part of the majority.

The community dances

The Mormons have always considered dancing to be an important form of recreation—in fact a particularly Mormon form of recreation. Almost every Friday evening a dance is held in the village church house. These dances are family affairs and are opened and closed with prayer. They are part of the general Church recreation program and are paid for by what is called locally "the budget." The budget refers to the plan under which villagers pay 15 dollars per family per year to cover a large number of entertainments, all sponsored by the Church auxiliary organization for youth, the Young Men's Mutual Improvement Association, and the Young Women's Mutual Improvement Association. The budget payment admits all members of the family to such entertainments.

Observation of these dances over a six months period did not reveal any tension or fighting. Smoking and drinking are forbidden to loyal Mormons, and those who smoked did so outside and away from the building. At dances held in the local school there has been evidence of drinking, and at times fighting has resulted from the presence of non-villagers. But on the whole the Rimrock dances are peaceful family affairs.

Rimrock reveals itself responding to group problems *as a group*. The economic ethic set forth by Joseph Smith in the Law of Consecration is seen in the dual commitment to private individual initiative (family farms and family partnerships in business and agriculture) and to cooperative endeavor in larger communal problems (irrigation company, land and cattle company, graveling the streets, and construction of school gymnasium). For the Mormons, cooperation has become second nature. It has become part of the institutionalized structure of expectations, reinforced by religious conviction and social control.

THE HOMESTEADER CASE

The value-stress upon individual independence of action has deep roots in the history of the homesteader group. The homesteaders were part of the westward migration from the hill country of the Southern Appalachians to the Panhandle country of Texas and Oklahoma and from there to the Southwest and California. Throughout their historical experience there has been an emphasis upon a rough and ready self-reliance and individualism, the Jacksonianism of the frontier West. The move to western New Mexico from the South Plains was made predominantly by isolated nuclear families, and Homestead became a community of scattered, individually-owned farmsteads—a geographical situation and a settlement pattern which reinforced the stress upon individualism.

Let us now examine the influence of this individualistic value-orientation upon a series of situations comparable to those that were described for Rimrock.

The "tight" land situation

In 1934 the Federal Security Administration, working in conjunction with the Land Use Division of the Department of Agriculture, proposed a "unit re-organization plan." This plan would have enabled the homesteaders to acquire additional tracts of land and permit them to run more livestock and hence depend less upon the more hazardous economic pursuit of dry-land pinto bean farming. It called for the use of government funds to purchase large ranches near the Homestead area which would be managed cooperatively by a board of directors selected by the community. The scheme collapsed while it was still in the planning stages, because it was clear that each family expected to acquire its own private holdings on the range and that a cooperative would not work in Homestead.

The graveling of the village streets

During the winter of 1949-50 the construction company which was building the highway through Rimrock was also building a small section of highway north of Homestead. The construction company offered to gravel the streets of Homestead center if the residents who lived in the village would cooperatively contribute enough funds for the purpose. This community plan was rejected by the homesteaders, and an alternative plan was followed. Each of the operators of several of the service institutions—including the two stores, the bar, and the post office—independently hired the construction company truck drivers to haul a few loads of gravel to be placed in front of his own place of business, which still left the rest of the village streets a sea of mud in rainy weather.

The construction of a high school gymnasium

In 1950 the same plan for the construction of a new gymnasium was presented to the homesteaders as was presented to the Mormon village of Rimrock. As noted above, this plan was accepted by the community of Rimrock, and the new building is now nearing completion. But the plan was rejected by the residents of Homestead at a meeting in the summer of 1950, and there were long speeches to the effect that "I've got to look after my own farm and my own family first; I can't be up here in town building a gymnasium." Later in the summer additional funds were provided for labor; and with these funds adobe bricks were made, the foundation was dug, and construction was started—the homesteaders being willing to work on the gymnasium on a purely business basis at a dollar an hour. But as soon as the funds were exhausted, construction stopped. Today a partially completed gymnasium, and stacks of some 10,000 adobe bricks disintegrating slowly with the rains, stand as monuments to the individualism of the homesteaders.

The community dances

As in Rimrock, the village dances in Homestead are important focal points for community activity. These affairs take place several times a year in the schoolhouse and are always well-attended. But while the dances in Rimrock are well-coordinated activities which carry through the evening, the dances in Homestead often end when tensions between rival families result in fistfights. And there is always the expectation in Homestead that a dance (or other cooperative activity such as a picnic or rodeo) may end at any moment and the level of activity reduced to the component nuclear families which form the only solid core of social organization within the community.

The individualistic value-orientation of the homesteaders also has important functional relationships to the religious organization of the community. With the exception of two men who are professed atheists, all of the homesteaders define themselves as Christians. But denominationalism is rife, there being ten different denominations represented in the village: Baptist, Presbyterian, Methodist, Nazarene, Campbellite, Holiness, 7th Day Adventist, Mormon, Catholic, and Present Day Disciples.

In the most general terms, this religious differentiation in Homestead can be interpreted as a function of the individualistic and factionalizing tendencies in the social system. In a culture with a value-stress upon independent individual action combined with a "freedom of religion" ideology, adhering to one's own denomination becomes an important means of expressing individualism and of focusing factional disputes around a doctrine and a concrete institutional framework. In turn, the doctrinal differences promote additional factionalizing tendencies, with the result that competing churches become the battleground for a cumulative and circularly reinforcing struggle between rival small factions within the community.

To sum up, we may say that the strong commitment to an individualistic value-orientation has resulted in a social system in which inter-personal relations are strongly colored by a kind of factionalism and in which persons and groups become related to one another in a competitive, feuding relationship. The homesteaders do not live on their widely separated farms and ignore one another, as it might be possible to do. On the other hand, they do not cooperate in community affairs as closely as does a hive of bees. They interact, but a constant feuding tone permeates the economic, social and religious structure of the community.

RELATIONSHIP BETWEEN THE TWO COMMUNITIES

Although there is some trading in livestock, feed, and other crops, the most important contacts between the two communities are not economic but are social and recreational. The village baseball teams have scheduled games with one another for the past two decades, and there is almost always joint participation in the community dances and in the summer rodeos in the two communities. Despite Mormon objections to close associations with "gentiles," there is also considerable inter-dating between the two communities among the teen-age groups, and three intermarriages have taken place.

In general, the homesteaders envy and admire the Mormons' economic organization, their irrigated land, and more promising prospects for good crops each year. On the other hand, they regard the Mormons as cliquish and unfriendly and fail completely to understand why anyone "wants to live all bunched up the way the Mormons do." They feel that the Mormons are inbred and think they should be glad to get "new blood" from inter-marriages with homesteaders. They add, "That Mormon religion is something we can't understand at all." Finally, the homesteaders say that Mormons "used to have more than one wife, and some probably still do; they dance in the church, they're against liquor, coffee, and tobacco, and they always talk about Joseph Smith and the *Book of Mormon.*"

The Mormons consider their own way of life distinctly superior to that of the homesteaders in every way. Some will admit that the homesteaders have the virtue of being more friendly and of "mixing more with others," and their efforts in the face of farming hazards are admired, but Homestead is generally regarded as a rough and in some ways immoral community, especially because of the drinking, smoking, and fighting (particularly at dances) that takes place. They also feel that Homestead is disorganized and that the churches are not doing what they should for the community. For the past few years they have been making regular missionary trips to Homestead, but to date they have made no conversions.

COMPARISONS AND CONCLUSIONS

In the case of Rimrock and Homestead, we are dealing with two communities which are comparable in population, in ecological setting, and which are variants of the same general culture. The two outstanding differences are: (a) irrigation versus dry-land farming and associated differences in settlement pattern, compact village versus isolated farmstead type; (b) a value stress upon cooperative community action versus a stress upon individual action. The important question here involves the relationship (if any) between these two sets of variables. Is the cooperation in Rimrock directly a function of an irrigation agriculture situation with a compact village settlement pattern, the rugged individualism in Homestead a function of a dry-land farming situation with a scattered settlement pattern? Or did these value-orientations arise out of earlier historical experience in each case, influence the types of communities which were established in western New Mexico, and later persist in the face of changed economic situations? We shall attempt to demonstrate that the second proposition is more in accord with the historical facts as we now know them.

Nelson has recently shown that the general pattern of the Mormon village is neither a direct function (in its beginnings) of the requirements of irrigation agriculture, nor of the need for protection against Indians on the frontier. Rather, the basic pattern was a social invention of the Mormons, motivated by a sense of urgent need to prepare a dwelling place for the "Savior" at "His Second Coming." The "Plat of the City of Zion" was invented by Joseph Smith, Sidney Rigdon, and Frederick G. Williams in 1833 and has formed the basis for the laying out of most Mormon villages, even those established in the Middle West before the Mormons migrated to Utah.

It is very clear that both the compact village pattern and the cooperative social arrangements centered around the church existed before the Mormons engaged in irrigation agriculture and had a strong influence upon the development of community structure not only in Utah but in the Mormon settlements like Rimrock on the periphery of the Mormon culture area. There is no objective reason in the Rimrock ecological and cultural setting (the local Navahos and Zunis did not pose a threat to pioneer settlements in the 1880's) why the Mormons could not have set up a community which conformed more to the isolated farmstead type with a greater stress upon individualistic social relations. Once the Mormon community was established, it is clear that the cooperation required by irrigation agriculture of the Mormon type and the general organization of the church strongly reinforced the value stress upon communal social action.

It is of further significance that as the population expanded and the Rimrock Mormons shifted from irrigation agricultural pursuits to dry-land ranching in the region outside of the Rimrock valley, the earlier cooperative patterns modeled on the mutual irrigation company were applied to the solution of economic problems that are identical to those faced by the Homesteaders. Moreover, in midwestern and eastern cities to which Mormons have recently moved, church wards have purchased and cooperatively worked church welfare plan farms.

In Homestead, on the other hand, our evidence indicates that the first settlers were drawn from a westward-moving population which stressed a frontier-type of self-reliance and individualism. They were searching for a place where each man could "own his own farm and be his own boss." Each family settled on its isolated homestead claim, and there emerged from the beginning an isolated farmstead type of settlement pattern in which the nuclear family was the solidary unit. The service center which was built up later simply occupied lots that were sold to storekeepers, filling station operators, the bartender, and others, by the four families who owned the four sections which joined at a crossroads. Only two of these four family homes were located near the service center at the crossroads. The other two families continued to maintain their homes in other quarters of their sections and lived almost a mile from "town." In 1952 one of the former families built a new home located over a mile from the center of town, and commented that they had always looked forward to "getting out of town."

There is no objective reason in the Homestead ecological setting why there could not be more clustering of houses into a compact village and more community cooperation than actually exists. One would not expect those farmers whose farms are located 15 or 20 miles from the service center to live in "town" and travel out to work each day. But there is no reason why those families living within 2 or 3 miles of the village center could not live in town and work their fields from there.

In typical Mormon villages a large percentage of the farms are located more than three miles from the farm homes. For example, in Rimrock over 31 per cent, in Escalante over 38 per cent, and in Ephriam over 30 per cent of the farms are located from three to eight or more miles from the center of the villages.

It is clear that the homesteaders were operating with a set of individualistic property arrangements (drawn, of course, from our generalized American culture) and that their strong stress upon individualism led to a quite different utilization of these property patterns (than was the case with the Mormons) and to the establishment of a highly scattered type of community. Once Homestead was established, the individualism permitted by the scattered dry-land farming pattern, and encouraged by the emphasis upon the small nuclear family unit and upon multi-denominationalism in church affiliation reacted on and strongly reinforced the value stress upon individual independence. It is evident that the homesteaders continue to prefer this way of life, as shown by their remarks concerning the "bunched up" character of a Mormon village and the fact that a number of families have recently moved "out of town" when they built new houses.

Of further interest is the fact that when homesteader families move to irrigated farms in the middle Rio Grande Valley, the stress upon individual action tends to persist strongly. They do not readily develop cooperative patterns to deal with this new setting which is similar to the situation in the irrigated valley of the Mormons at Rimrock. Indeed, one of the principal innovations they have been promoting in one region along the Rio Grande where they are replacing Spanish-Americans on the irrigated farming land is a system of meters on irrigation ditches. These meters will measure the water flowing into each individual farmer's ditches, and effectively eliminate the need for more highly organized cooperative arrangements for distributing the available supply of water.

In conclusion, we should like to reiterate that we are strongly cognizant of situational factors. If the Rimrock Mormons had not been able to settle in a valley which was watered by melting snow packs from a nearby mountain and which provided the possibilities for the construction of a storage reservoir, they certainly could not have developed an irrigation agricultural system at all. In the case of Rimrock, however, the actual site of settlement was selected from among several possible sites in a larger situation. The selection was largely influenced by Mormon preconceptions of the type of village they wished to establish.

In fact, Mormons chose the irrigable valleys throughout the inter-montane west. On the other hand, the physical environmental features for the development of irrigation were simply not present in the Homestead setting, and the people had no alternative to dry-land farming. There is no evidence to suggest that had they found an irrigable valley, they would have developed it along Mormon lines. In fact, the homesteaders' activities in the Rio Grande Valley suggest just the opposite. It is clear that the situational facts did not *determine* in any simple sense the contrasting community structures which emerged. Rather, the situations set certain limits, but within these limits contrasting value-orientations influenced the development of two quite different community types. It would appear that solutions to problems of community settlement pattern and the type of concrete social action which ensues are set within a value framework which importantly influences the selections made with the range of possibilities existing within an objective situation.

Selection *6*

Man, Food and Sex
Marston Bates

In the previous selection, Vogt and O'Dea offered an explanation of how people who are in frequent interaction with each other devise or assume patterns of social organization. Due to various overlapping intercultural associations, elements of local social systems are often established by a sort of chain reaction on a national or international scale. However, certain barriers—ecological or geographical, perhaps—limit interaction and adaptation; hence, social systems around the world differ greatly, and variant beliefs and practices can be noted even within small villages.

Most of us will sometime come into contact with an individual from a society other than our own who cannot seem to keep from making continual reference to the superior way in which things were done in his community of origin. He does not feel comfortable or even secure in the different social and cultural organizations of a new community; his sentimental preference for familiar systems and patterns is called *ethnocentrism.*

In the following selection Bates discusses various means of gratifying two biological needs that are common to all human societies—nutrition and reproduction. He shows how ethnocentric sentiments—feelings about ideas—are learned from society, how they affect the individual, and how cultural peculiarities persist through the inculcation of sentiments in individuals.

Bates' observation that humans do not treat food rationally supports a sentiment theory of human social organization quite as readily as it might support an instinct theory. Observed societal differences in the definitions of sexual propriety and perversity also fit a sentiment theory, but they are inconsistent with an instinct theory (unless one should argue that there are different species of humans).

Food and sex are different—almost any adult can tell them apart. But they are curiously parallel in many ways, and they may even sometimes blend. In a few species of insects and spiders, the female eats the male—after copulation—and food exchange of some sort is a part of courtship behavior in many groups of animals. In human behavior, the parallels are shown in the use and meanings of a whole list of words that can pass back and forth between the contexts of food and sex: *appetite, hunger, satiated, starved.*

It is hardly extraordinary that there should be

Reprinted from *The American Scholar,* Volume 27, Number 4 (Autumn, 1958), 449-458. Copyright © 1958 by the United Chapters of Phi Beta Kappa. By permission of the publishers.

parallels because food and sex—nutrition and reproduction—are two basic needs or drives of all organisms. In the special case of human behavior, these biological needs have come under strong cultural control, and the cultural control has often modified them, restricted them, twisted them, in comparable ways.

Before looking at human behavior, we might briefly consider the biological roles of food and sex. From this point of view, we have to deal with three levels of organization—the individual, the population and the community. It is only when we look at individual behavior that we find parallels. Populations, as the biologist sees them, are defined in terms of sex, of reproductive behavior; communities, in terms of food. One could say that in studying the community, the biologist is concerned with who eats whom; in studying a population, with who sleeps with whom.

A biological species is defined as a population of individuals that form, actually or potentially, an interbreeding aggregation, separated from other similar populations by barriers to breeding, either behavioral or physiological. . . . [T]he problem of the origin of species becomes the problem of the origin of breeding barriers within populations— the problem of the ways in which an interbreeding aggregation may become subdivided into two or more reproductively isolated populations, no longer capable of exchanging gene material, and hence subject to independent evolutionary developments.

The biological community—a quite different concept from that of the social community—is most easily described in terms of food chains or food webs. A forest, a pond, a coral reef, any biological community, is composed of the green plants that store up energy from the sun, of the key industry animals that live directly off the plants, of the secondary consumers that live off the key industry animals, and so ad infinitum, to the molds and bacteria that reduce the animal corpses to dust again. Food is thus the cement of the biological community, sex the cement of the species population.

Every individual animal, then, must deal with sex in relation to his species or population, and with food in relation to his biotic community; and there must be satisfactory adjustments of both food and sex relations if the species is to survive. Man is an animal and thus, in theory at least, subject to biological laws. But he is unique in being a cultured animal, and this culture does odd things to biological regularities. This is nowhere more apparent than when we try to interpret human sex habits or food habits in biological terms.

In general, throughout nature, sexual behavior can be studied in terms of reproduction. Mating occurs, for instance, only when the eggs of the female are ready for fertilization, and there are elaborate mechanisms to insure the proper timing of events in the two sexes of a particular species. But in cultured man, reproduction seems to be an incidental or even accidental consequence of sex. Food behavior, similarly, can generally be studied in terms of nutrition, and food still serves man for nutrition. But it would be difficult to explain salad dressings, wine sauces or soufflés purely in terms of either protein or vitamin needs.

It is a commonplace comment on Freudian psychology that its emphasis on sex comes from its basis in Western culture where sex is scarce— or at least strictly controlled—while food is reasonably abundant and generally available. British anthropologist Audrey Richards, in rebellion against this, set out some years ago to study human relations in an African tribe where sex was abundant and food restricted. She found, as expected, that in that society food dominated the subconscious as well as the conscious life of the people. In her book *Hunger and Work in a Savage Tribe,* she maintains that food behavior in man is far more basically and extensively governed by cultural or traditional considerations than is sexual behavior, and she is probably right. In our own society, food behavior is subject to all sorts of taboos and controls, which provide endless opportunity for psychological exploration.

I think one could safely say that there is no human society that deals rationally with the food in its environment, that eats according to the availability, edibility and nutritional value of the possible food materials within its reach. Very primitive, food-gathering cultures, like those of the Australian aborigines, probably come closest since they have to eat almost everything available and edible in order to survive; but even in such cultures we find special restrictions in regard to things like totem animals.

Our own food habits are certainly under strong cultural control, which may be inconvenient even though it does not involve the strong conscious and subconscious frustrations of sexual controls. Some patterns of food behavior are shared by all Western peoples, some are national, and some are more narrowly restricted. None of us, however, can afford to look down our noses at other people because of their food habits.

I became acutely conscious of this some years ago when asking a Hindu houseguest about his food requirements. He explained that he did not really have any deep religious convictions about food, but that he had rather not be expected to eat cow—that he supposed he felt about eating cows the way I would about eating dogs. The Hindu attitude toward cows is clearly uneconomical; but so is our attitude toward dogs. Maybe we can afford the prejudice better than they, but I suspect this is irrelevant. After all, dogs are specifically raised as food in some cultures, and eaten as opportunity affords in many others; they are said to be quite tasty. I still have not eaten dog, but I think I have a better understanding of the Hindu problem from this explanation.

A dog taboo appears to be universal in European civilization. A similar horse prejudice is much more local, but still powerful. The Harvard Faculty Club started serving horse steaks during the last war, and as far as I know still serves them on certain days. My wife, eating a horse steak, thought this was a fine idea, and when she got home tried to buy horse meat from our butcher. But she discovered that in our community horse meat could not be bought through the regular channels; it was sold only as a preparation for dog and cat food. We made one experiment with the stuff sold as dog food, only to discover that dog requirements in tenderness apparently differed from ours.

Even though repugnance to a particular food may have a cultural rather than physiological basis, it can still be very strong. The big lizards called iguanas are a highly prized article of food in all parts of tropical America where they occur; the meat has a delicate, chicken-like flavor. But in Europe and North America, lizards are not eaten for some reason, probably because we do not have any suitable species. I remember serving iguana at a dinner party in South America. The subject had been thoroughly discussed, and we thought everyone understood what they were eating; certainly they all ate with gusto. But as the conversation continued during the meal, a French lady who was present suddenly realized from the talk that the iguana she had been eating *était un lézard* and became violently nauseated, although a few minutes before she had considered the meat delicious.

I remember once, in the llanos of Colombia, sharing a dish of toasted ants at a remote farmhouse. This was my first voluntary experience with ants—I had eaten lots of them involuntarily, raw, when they just tasted sour—and soon we were talking about the general question of what people eat and do not eat. I remarked that in my country people ate the legs of frogs, the very thought of which horrified my ant-eating friends. It was rather as though we had been talking about repulsive sexual habits.

The question of what is repulsive and what is accepted or gratifying is certainly under strong cultural control with both food and sex. Look at the varying cultural attitudes toward kissing, for instance. What would a Micronesian think of the display near a girls' dormitory at an American university just before check-in time? Or how could one explain to a Micronesian the attitude of the American male toward the breasts of the female of the species?

The anthropologists have explained that the kinds of sexual behavior regarded as "perverse" vary greatly from culture to culture, but neither they nor the psychologists have bothered much about food perversions. Maybe we are surrounded by food perverts, undetected and unclassified, undermining the fiber of our civilization, infiltrating our diplomatic service, influencing our mass media, corrupting our youth. We need a Havelock Ellis to survey the field and a Kinsey to quantify it. Who knows how many people in this country put sugar in their salad dressings, make strawberry shortcake with sweet biscuit, use rice for dessert, or engage in similar abominable and unwholesome practices?

But one must not be culture-bound. Rice pudding is no crime against nature; it is merely a crime against the culture of people who believe that rice should be the basic starch of a meal rather than the dessert. If we tried to deal with such cultural traits as perverse we would get into endless trouble. We would be better off, I think, to define food perversion as food behavior not directed toward nutrition. The alleged custom of some ancient Romans taking an emetic so that they could feast again on the tongues of larks would thus truly be perverse.

Dirt-eating, since it seems often to be related to a mineral deficiency in the ordinary diet, would not be perverse by this definition. But the whole catalogue of substances that man takes for stimulation or hallucination or relaxation would represent perverse behavior. These substances may serve a greatly felt need, but the need can hardly be called nutritional. In many cases, the substances are clearly antinutritional: the chronic alcoholic suffers, it appears, mostly from nutritional deficiencies, and tobacco notoriously cuts down the desire for food.

It is curious how widely these nonnutritional substances are taken by man. It cannot be said that every culture has some drug to help its members escape from reality, but I would guess that the vast majority have, and of the most diverse sorts. The virtues of alcohol have been discovered independently by many peoples, and they have found many ways of producing the alcohol: through allowing the sweet sap of palms and other plants to ferment, through fermenting grains or fruits, through chewing starches (like manihot) and fermenting the saliva-mixed product. And primitive man ransacked the plant kingdom to find substances that could be drunk, chewed or inhaled for a lift, or for a temporary escape into the world of dreams.

These "perversities" may be accepted and institutionalized by the culture, or they may be suppressed or hidden or deplored—just as are the unreproductive sexual customs. Our own culture is quite confused in the matter, with every possible attitude represented somewhere. A few consistent extremists would suppress everything— tea, chocolate, coffee and the like. Tobacco and alcohol are subjects of eternal debate. Many of us still have vivid memories of our national experiment in the prohibition of alcohol. "Drugs" from marijuana to heroin are still prohibited, though a vocal minority maintains that prohibition is not the proper way to deal with the problem of drug addiction.

We can call all of these things, by definition, "perverse," but that still leaves open the question of whether they are "good" or "bad." There seems to be no way of arriving at opinion on this outside of the cultural context. We could, of course, equate "good" with "healthy," but we are still left with problems. All of these non-nutritional food substances could probably be shown to be unhealthy in a physiological sense, or at best harmless. But physiology isn't everything. The Andean Indian apparently needs the lift from chewing his coca leaves to help him get through the arduous days of his bleak environment. I seem to need the lift of tobacco to get through my days, even though I am not exposed to the physical discomfort of the Indian. How do we balance the physiological loss against the psychological gain?

There are similar problems in the evaluation of sex habits. If we define as perverse all sexual behavior not directed toward reproduction, we include masturbation, homosexuality, bestiality, voyeurism and the like; but we also necessarily include all contraceptive practices. Again there is an extreme but consistent view that would regard all of these as "bad" and another extreme that would regard none as bad except where innocent individuals are hurt.

In both sex and food it is clear that adult human behavior is largely a result of a conditioning or learning process. There must be basic, underlying drives for sex outlet—to use Kinsey's term—and for food intake, but it is hard to dissect away the cultural overlay to demonstrate this biological basis. In the case of sex, experiments with chimpanzees at the Yerkes Laboratory show that the adult behavior patterns of individuals are learned. It is possible to make a nice sequence from animals like rats and mice, where learning is only of slight importance in copulatory behavior, through dogs and monkeys, where learning is more important, to the great apes, where learning is necessary for successful copulation.

Food behavior probably shows a similar sequence in the importance of learning, though I do not know of much good experimental evidence. I suspect that even in man there is left over an "instinctive" aversion to very bitter things, a reaction that would be of value in avoiding poisons. But we put bitters in our Old Fashioneds! There seems also to be a general aversion to some kinds of smells in association with food; yet some very nasty-smelling cheeses are eaten, as well as certain stinking fruits like the famous durian of tropical Asia.

Interesting individual and cultural differences are shown in whether particular foodstuffs are eaten raw or cooked, alive or dead. In general, only mute things are eaten alive—plants and invertebrates. If oysters shrieked as they were pried open, or squealed when jabbed with a fork, they would never be eaten alive. As it is, thoughtful people quite callously look for the muscular twitch as they drop lemon juice on a poor oyster to be sure that it is alive before they eat it.

The moral problem of killing for food leads many people to vegetarianism. But as Samuel Butler long ago pointed out, vegetables should have rights, too. The Erewhonians reached the logical end of the moral argument when they were reduced to eating cabbages certified to have died a natural death.

There are numerous vegetarian subcultures, especially in Indian civilization and in our own, but voluntary avoidance of meat seems to be limited to groups within such "high" cultures. A goodly proportion of mankind lives on a largely vegetarian diet, but this is perforce because meat is scarce or too expensive. At the other extreme, Eskimos eat meat exclusively. The primates—the monkeys and apes—are generally vegetarian or, at most, eaters of insects and similar small prey. The adoption of the carnivorous habit was probably one of the major steps in human evolution, especially since hunting, by such a feeble creature as man, must have at the same time involved tool-using and group-cooperation, providing a base for man's social evolution.

Vegetarianism now is frequently linked with religious considerations of one kind or another. It is curious how frequently food habits or food restrictions are associated with religion. This provides another of the parallels between food and sex, since sex also gets involved with religion in the most diverse sorts of ways. There is an elemental difference between food and sex, in that an individual can refrain completely from sexual activity and still live. Chastity can thus be a lifetime preoccupation, while fasting is necessarily either of short duration or intermittent.

I suspect that lifetime chastity, the cult of virginity, is a characteristic of the sophisticated and complex cultures that we call civilizations: it would hardly seem either possible or worth while to the more primitive cultures closer to nature. Yet such cultures do have a variety of religious controls over sexual behavior. Sex may be taboo before or during special activities such as fishing, hunting or war. Sex may be required in relation to ceremonies to insure fertility of crops. Either food or sex may get involved in ideas of sacrifice, and the sacrifice may involve either abstention or indulgence. Thus we find cults of temple prostitution on the one hand, and of chastity on the other; ceremonies which require that no food be eaten, and others at which participants must eat.

In sophisticated situations, at least, one can understand social and religious control of sexual and food behavior in terms of man's efforts to master his appetites, and thus to master himself. Neither the glutton nor the libertine cuts a very admirable figure in terms of the moral or aesthetic values of most high cultures. European culture in particular has kept the Greek ideal of moderation, of temperance, though sometimes carrying temperance itself to an unaesthetic excess in the puritan or the prude.

In religious and social control of food and sex, we are dealing with deliberate, in a sense voluntary, abstentions and indulgences. There may also be involuntary controls, perhaps more frequently with food than with sex. We have chronic undernourishment and malnutrition in many human situations simply because food is not available. And there is, through history, a long succession of famines, of epidemic, involuntary fasting on the part of large segments of mankind. It is more difficult to find examples of epidemic, involuntary chastity; although, as a friend pointed out to me, this has occurred in certain situations like the gold rush to the western United States in the last century. The prostitution that builds up under such circumstances could be regarded as only a partial alleviation, such as the hoarding and black markets accompanying famines.

This makes me wonder whether the selling of sex or the selling of food is the older profession. It is a meaningless sort of question, of course,

since both food and sex were commonly exchanged long before any idea of "sale" developed. From the accounts of the European explorers who first encountered the primitive peoples of the modern world, I judge that the ideas of selling either fruits and vegetables or the services of women were taken up with about equal alacrity—or reluctance. Where the natives were reluctant, these civilized Europeans seem to have had little compunction about commandeering either the food or the women.

On the other hand, both food and sex are widely linked with the idea of hospitality: the welcomed stranger is offered something to eat and someone to sleep with. This can be embarrassing in both cases if he is a fussy feeder and finds the proffered food repugnant, or if, for cultural or aesthetic reasons, he is fussy about his women. Still, sharing a hard-won food supply or a treasured wife is surely the ultimate in friendly gestures.

In general, the question of who eats with whom and who sleeps with whom can become quite complicated, subject to all sorts of different kinds of cultural restrictions. There seems to be one cultural universal in sex that has no universal parallel in food—the presence of some kind of an incest taboo. But I suspect that food restriction or regulation is more elaborate and more rigid than sex regulation. This is apparent in our own culture: the stereotyped Southerner would hardly be able to force himself to the indignity of eating with a colored woman; but often he seems to have had no compunction about sleeping with one.

Perhaps this is a consequence of the fact that sex is secret in our culture and eating is open. The Southerner would not marry a Negro any more than he would eat with her; and perhaps he would not mind sharing grits and salt pork with her if he were sure he would not be caught. On the other hand, there may be public consequences of the sexual communion, in the form of offspring, which seem to carry no particular stigma for the male concerned.

In some cultures, eating is a secret act. Many years ago A. E. Crawley, in *The Mystic Rose*, developed a theory that it is a sort of basic element of human nature to carry out all of the primary biological functions—eating, copulating, excreting—in solitude. If this is so, then eating has certainly come out into the open more generally than either the copulatory or excretory functions, but it is still rather rigidly controlled. Often men are prohibited from eating with women; different social castes and social classes are very generally prohibited from eating together; children, in some subcultures of our civilization, may not be allowed to eat with grownups until they have reached adolescence.

And then there is the endlessly complicated matter of the etiquette of eating: what is eaten, how it is eaten, when it is eaten, what clothes are worn for the eating, whether talk is prohibited or required while eating. When one looks at all of the complications, it is a wonder that man has been able to feed himself at all; but it is also a wonder, in view of the complications, that he has been able to reproduce. In general, man seems to have gotten along fairly well on both counts, although it may be only in terms of a certain psychic cost.

Selection 7
_____

Folkways and Mores
William Graham Sumner

Bates recorded in the previous selection that at least two basic human needs can be met in a variety of ways. Societies are concerned with a great deal more than the satisfaction of biological needs, however. Men living together on a consensual or shared basis develop languages, social systems, games, technologies, religions, and arts, to name only a few, each of which is a part of their total environment. Just as people establish or assume various devices for relating themselves to one another, so they also establish or assume various devices for adapting to their environment.

From studies of how people with different ways of life adjust to the same natural environment, we know that there are many ways of successfully adapting to group life in a given environment. For example, the past and present inhabitants of the banks of the Hudson River, studied and compared by Sumner, bear little cultural resemblance to each other, but both made an adaptation that was for them satisfactory.

Some of the devices for adapting are far less emotionally charged than the ways of getting food and sex mentioned by Bates, yet they are definitely a part of group life. Sumner coined the term *folkways* for such devices—the normal, characteristic forms of behavior and usage that become established in a society and hence are part of its culture. A contemporary American folkway, for example, is the practice of manufacturing men's clothing with buttons on the right side of the openings and women's clothing with buttons on the left side of the openings. No law requires this pattern, and it would not be immoral to change it. It is simply the current way of doing things, and it is easier and less disrupting to conform to the established pattern than to make a separate decision each time one makes or dons clothing.

Mores are folkways that a society considers extremely important. One of the mores in the United States directs that a father should provide as many advantages for his immature children as possible without damaging his own physical or mental health. Another *mos* (the singular, rarely used form of *mores*) is that children should love their parents. A negative mos is called a *taboo*. The use of marihuana as an intoxicant is an example of a taboo in our society.

The passages reproduced here present Sumner's concept of folkways, mores, and taboos. They are part of one of the early classics in the literature of American sociology.

If we put together all that we have learned from anthropology and ethnography about primitive men and primitive society, we perceive that the first task of life is to live. Men begin with acts, not with thoughts. Every moment brings necessities which must be satisfied at once. Need was the first experience, and it was followed at once by a blundering effort to satisfy it. It is generally taken for granted that men inherited some guiding instincts from their beast ancestry, and it may be true, although it has never been proved. If there were such inheritances, they controlled and aided the first efforts to satisfy needs. Analogy makes it easy to assume that the ways of beasts had produced channels of habit and predisposition along which dexterities and other psychophysical activities would run easily. Experiments with newborn animals show that in the absence of any experience of the relation of means to ends, efforts to satisfy needs are clumsy and blundering. The method is that of trial and failure, which produces repeated pain, loss, and disappointments. Nevertheless, it is a method of rude experiment and selection. The earliest efforts of men were of this kind. Need was the impelling force. Pleasure and pain, on the one side and the other, were the rude constraints which defined the line on which efforts must proceed. The ability to distinguish between pleasure and pain is the only psychical power which is to be assumed. Thus ways of doing things were selected, which were expedient. They answered the purpose better than other ways, or with less toil and pain. Along the course on which efforts were compelled to go, habit, routine, and skill were developed. The struggle to maintain existence was carried on, not individually, but in groups. Each profited by the other's experience; hence there was concurrence towards that which proved to be most expedient. All at last adopted the same way for the same purpose; hence the ways turned into customs and became mass phenomena. . . . In this way folkways arise. The young learn them by tradition, imitation, and authority. The folkways, at a time, provide for all the needs of life then and there. They are uniform, universal in the group, imperative, and invariable. As time goes on, the folkways become more and more arbitrary, positive, and imperative. If asked why they act in a certain way in certain cases, primitive people always answer that it is because they and their ancestors always have done so. A sanction also arises from ghost fear. The ghosts of ancestors would be angry if the living should change the ancient folkways.

The operation by which folkways are produced consists in the frequent repetition of petty acts, often by great numbers acting in concert or, at least, acting in the same way when face to face with the same need. . . . Out of the unconscious experiment which every repetition of the ways includes, there issues pleasure or pain, and then, so far as the men are capable of reflection, convictions that the ways are conducive to societal welfare. These two experiences are not the same. The most uncivilized men, both in the food quest and in war, do things which are painful, but which have been found to be expedient. Perhaps these cases teach the sense of social welfare better than those which are pleasurable and favorable to welfare. The former cases call for some intelligent reflection on experience. When this conviction as to the relation to welfare is added to the folkways they are converted into mores, and, by virtue of the philosophical and ethical element added to them, they win utility and importance and become the source of the science and the art of living.

It is of the first importance to notice that, from the first acts by which men try to satisfy needs, each act stands by itself, and looks no further than the immediate satisfaction. From recurrent needs arise habits for the individual and customs for the group, but these results are consequences which were never conscious, and never foreseen or intended. They are not noticed until they have long existed, and it is still longer before they are appreciated. Another long time must pass, and a higher stage of mental development must be reached, before they can be used as a basis from which to deduce rules for meeting, in the future, problems whose pressure can be foreseen. The folkways, therefore, are not creations of human purpose and wit. They are like products of natural forces which men unconsciously set in operation. . . . [T]he life of human beings, in all ages and stages of culture, is primarily controlled by a vast mass of folkways handed down from the earliest existence of the race. . . . We are told of savages that "It is difficult to exhaust the customs and small ceremonial usages of a savage people. Custom regulates the whole of a man's actions,—his bathing, washing, cutting his hair, eating, drinking, and fasting. From his cradle to his grave he is the slave of ancient usage. In his life there is nothing free, nothing original, nothing spontaneous, no progress towards a higher and better life, and no attempt to improve his condition, mentally, morally, or spiritually." All men act in this way with only a little wider margin of voluntary variation. . . .

From *Folkways* by W. G. Sumner (Boston: Ginn and Company, 1940), pp. 17-20, 27-28, 40-44, 46-47, 65-67.

Ethnocentrism is the technical name for [the] view of things in which one's own group is the center of everything, and all others are scaled and rated with reference to it. . . . Each group nourishes its own pride and vanity, boasts itself superior, exalts its own divinities, and looks with contempt on outsiders. Each group thinks its own folkways the only right ones, and if it observes that other groups have other folkways, these excite its scorn. Opprobrious epithets are derived from these differences. "Pig-eater," "cow-eater," "uncircumcised," "jabberers," are epithets of contempt and abomination. The Tupis called the Portuguese by a derisive epithet descriptive of birds which have feathers around their feet, on account of trousers. For our present purpose the most important fact is that ethnocentrism leads a people to exaggerate and intensify everything in their own folkways which is peculiar and which differentiates them from others. It therefore strengthens the folkways.

The Papuans on New Guinea are broken up into village units which are kept separate by hostility, cannibalism, head hunting, and divergences of language and religion. Each village is integrated by its own language, religion, and interests. A group of villages is sometimes united into a limited unity by connubium. A wife taken inside of this group unit has full status; one taken outside of it has not. The petty group units are peace groups within and are hostile to all outsiders. The Mbayas of South America believed that their deity had bidden them live by making war on others, taking their wives and property, and killing their men.

When Caribs were asked whence they came, they answered, "We alone are people." The meaning of the name Kiowa is "real or principal people." The Lapps call themselves "men," or "human beings." The Greenland Eskimo think that Europeans have been sent to Greenland to learn virtue and good manners from the Greenlanders. Their highest form of praise for a European is that he is, or soon will be, as good as a Greenlander. The Tunguses call themselves "men." As a rule it is found that nature peoples call themselves "men." Others are something else—perhaps not defined—but not real men. In myths the origin of their own tribe is that of the real human race. They do not account for the others. The Ainos derive their name from that of the first man, whom they worship as a god. Evidently the name of the god is derived from the tribe name. When the tribal name has another sense, it is always boastful or proud. The Ovambo name is a corruption of the name of the tribe for themselves, which means "the wealthy." Amongst the most remarkable people in the world for ethnocentrism are the Seri of Lower California. They observe an attitude of suspicion and hostility to all outsiders, and strictly forbid marriage with outsiders.

The Jews divided all mankind into themselves and Gentiles. They were the "chosen people." The Greeks and Romans called all outsiders "barbarians." In Euripides' tragedy of *Iphigenia in Aulis* Iphigenia says that it is fitting that Greeks should rule over barbarians, but not contrariwise, because Greeks are free, and barbarians are slaves. The Arabs regarded themselves as the noblest nation and all others as more or less barbarous. In 1896, the Chinese minister of education and his counselors edited a manual in which this statement occurs: "How grand and glorious is the Empire of China, the middle kingdom! She is the largest and richest in the world. The grandest men in the world have all come from the middle empire." In all the literature of all the states equivalent statements occur, although they are not so naïvely expressed. In Russian books and newspapers the civilizing mission of Russia is talked about, just as, in the books and journals of France, Germany, and the United States, the civilizing mission of those countries is assumed and referred to as well understood. Each state now regards itself as the leader of civilization, the best, the freest, and the wisest, and all others as inferior. Within a few years our own man-on-the-curbstone has learned to class all foreigners of the Latin peoples as "dagos," and "dago" has become an epithet of contempt. These are all cases of ethnocentrism.

. . . All the practical and direct element in [one's own] folkways seems to be due to common sense, natural reason, intuition, or some other original mental endowment. It seems rational (or rationalistic) and utilitarian. Often in the mythologies this ultimate rational element was ascribed to the teaching of a god or a culture hero. In modern mythology it is accounted for as "natural."

Although the ways adopted must always be really "true" and "right" in relation to facts, for otherwise they could not answer their purpose, such is not the primitive notion of true and right.

The folkways are the "right" ways to satisfy all interests, because they are traditional, and exist in fact. They extend over the whole of life. There is a right way to catch game, to win a wife, to make one's self appear, to cure disease, to honor ghosts, to treat comrades or strangers, to behave when a child is born, on the warpath, in council, and so on in all cases which can arise. The ways are defined on the negative side, that is, by taboos. The "right" way is the way which the ancestors used and which has been handed down. The tradition is its own warrant. It is not held subject to verification by experience. . . . In the folkways, whatever is, is right. This is because they are traditional, and therefore contain in themselves the authority of the ancestral ghosts. . . . The notion of right and ought is the same in regard to all the folkways, but the degree of it varies with the importance of the interest at stake. . . . Some usages contain only a slight element of right and ought. It may well be believed that notions of right and duty, and of social welfare, were first developed in connection with ghost fear and other-worldliness, and therefore that, in that field also, folkways were first raised to mores. "Rights" are the rules of mutual give and take in the competition of life which are imposed on comrades in the in-group, in order that the peace may prevail there which is essential to the group strength. Therefore rights can never be "natural" or "God-given," or absolute in any sense. The morality of a group at a time is the sum of the taboos and prescriptions in the folkways by which right conduct is defined. Therefore morals can never be intuitive. They are historical, institutional, and empirical.

World philosophy, life policy, right, rights, and morality are all products of the folkways. They are reflections on, and generalizations from, the experience of pleasure and pain which is won in efforts to carry on the struggle for existence under actual life conditions. The generalizations are very crude and vague in their germinal forms. They are all embodied in folklore, and all our philosophy and science have been developed out of them. . . .

When the elements of truth and right are developed into doctrines of welfare, the folkways are raised to another plane. They then become capable of producing inferences, developing into new forms, and extending their constructive influence over men and society. Then we call them the mores. The mores are the folkways, including the philosophical and ethical generalizations as to societal welfare which are suggested by them, and inherent in them, as they grow.

The mores necessarily consist, in a large part, of taboos, which indicate the things which must not be done. In part these are dictated by mystic dread of ghosts who might be offended by certain acts, but they also include such acts as have been found by experience to produce unwelcome results, especially in the food quest, in war, in health, or in increase or decrease of population. These taboos always contain a greater element of philosophy than the positive rules, because the taboos contain reference to a reason, as, for instance, that the act would displease the ghosts.

The primitive taboos correspond to the fact that the life of man is environed by perils. His food quest must be limited by shunning poisonous plants. His appetite must be restrained from excess. His physical strength and health must be guarded from dangers. The taboos carry on the accumulated wisdom of generations, which has almost always been purchased by pain, loss, disease, and death. Other taboos contain inhibitions of what will be injurious to the group. The laws about the sexes, about property, about war, and about ghosts, have this character. They always include some social philosophy. They are both mystic and utilitarian, or compounded of the two.

Taboos may be divided into two classes, (1) protective and (2) destructive. Some of them aim to protect and secure, while others aim to repress or exterminate. Women are subject to some taboos which are directed against them as sources of possible harm or danger to men, and they are subject to other taboos which put them outside of the duties or risks of men. On account of this difference in taboos, taboos act selectively, and thus affect the course of civilization. They contain judgments as to societal welfare.

It is not to be understood that primitive men philosophize about their experience of life. That is our way; it was not theirs. They did not formulate any propositions about the causes, significance, or ultimate relations of things. They made myths, however, in which they often presented conceptions which are deeply philosophical, but they represented them in concrete, personal, dramatic and graphic ways. They feared pain and ill, and they produced folkways by their devices for warding off pain and ill. Those devices were acts of ritual which were planned upon their vague and crude faiths about ghosts and the other world. We develop the connection between the devices and the faiths, and we reduce it to propositions of a philosophic form, but the primitive men never did that. . . .

In the present work the proposition to be maintained is that the folkways are the widest, most fundamental, and most important operation by which the interests of men in groups are served, and that the process by which folkways are made is the chief one to which elementary societal or group phenomena are due. The life of society consists in making folkways and applying them. The science of society might be construed as the study of them. The relations of men to each other, when they are carrying on the struggle for existence near each other, consist in mutual reactions (antagonisms, rivalries, alliances, coercions, and coöperations), from which result societal concatenations and concretions, that is, more or less fixed positions of individuals and subgroups towards each other, and more or less established sequences and methods of interaction between them, by which the interests of all members of the group are served. . . . The societal concretions are due to the folkways in this way,—that the men, each struggling to carry on existence, unconsciously coöperate to build up associations, organization, customs, and institutions which, after a time, appear full grown and actual, although no one intended, or planned, or understood them in advance. They stand there as produced by "ancestors." These concretions of relation and act in war, labor, religion, amusement, family life, and civil institutions are attended by faiths, doctrines of philosophy (myths, folklore), and by precepts of right conduct and duty (taboos). The making of folkways is not trivial, although the acts are minute. Every act of each man fixes an atom in a structure, both fulfilling a duty derived from what preceded and conditioning what is to come afterwards by the authority of traditional custom. The structure thus built up is not physical, but societal and institutional, that is to say, it belongs to a category which must be defined and studied by itself. It is a category in which custom produces continuity, coherence, and consistency, so that the word "structure" may properly be applied to the fabric of relations and prescribed positions with which societal functions are permanently connected. The process of making folkways is never superseded or changed. It goes on now just as it did at the beginning of civilization. "Use and wont" exert their force on all men always. They produce familiarity, and mass acts become unconscious. The same effect is produced by customary acts repeated at all recurring occasions. The range of societal activity may be greatly enlarged, interests may be extended and multiplied, the materials by which needs can be supplied may become far more numerous, the processes of societal coöperation may become more complicated, and contract or artifice may take the place of custom for many interests; but, if the case is one which touches the ways or interests of the masses, folkways will develop on and around it by the same process as that which has been described as taking place from the beginning of civilization. The ways of carrying on war have grown into folkways of commanding range and importance. The factory system of handicrafts has produced a body of folkways in which artisans live, and which distinguish factory towns from commercial cities or agricultural villages. The use of cotton instead of linen has greatly affected modern folkways. The applica-

tions of power and machinery have changed the standards of comfort of all classes. The folkways, however, have kept their character and authority through all the changes of form which they have undergone. . . .

It is most important to notice that, for the people of a time and place, their own mores are always good, or rather that for them there can be no question of the goodness or badness of their mores. The reason is because the standards of good and right are in the mores. If the life conditions change, the traditional folkways may produce pain and loss, or fail to produce the same good as formerly. Then the loss of comfort and ease brings doubt into the judgment of welfare (causing doubt of the pleasure of the gods, or of war power, or of health), and thus disturbs the unconscious philosophy of the mores. . . . Another society may . . . pass judgment on the mores. In our literary and historical study of the mores we want to get from them their educational value, which consists in the stimulus or warning as to what is, in its effects, societally good or bad. This may lead us to reject or neglect a phenomenon like infanticide, slavery, or witchcraft, as an old "abuse" and "evil," or to pass by the crusades as a folly which cannot recur. Such a course would be a great error. Everything in the mores of a time and place must be regarded as justified with regard to that time and place. "Good" mores are those which are well adapted to the situation. "Bad" mores are those which are not so adapted. The mores are not so stereotyped and changeless as might appear, because they are forever moving towards more complete adaptation to conditions and interests, and also towards more complete adjustment to each other. People in mass have never made or kept up a custom in order to hurt their own interests. They have made innumerable errors as to what their interests were and how to satisfy them, but they have always aimed to serve their interests as well as they could. This gives the standpoint for the student of the mores. All things in them come before him on the same plane. They all bring instruction and warning. They all have the same relation to power and welfare. The mistakes in them are component parts of them. We do not study them in order to approve some of them and condemn others. They are all equally worthy of attention from the fact that they existed and were used. The chief object of study in them is their adjustment to interests, their relation to welfare, and their coördination in a harmonious system of the life policy. For the men of the time there are no "bad" mores. What is traditional and current is the standard of what ought to be.

The masses never raise any question about such things. If a few raise doubts and questions, this proves that the folkways have already begun to lose firmness and the regulative element in the mores has begun to lose authority. This indicates that the folkways are on their way to a new adjustment. The extreme of folly, wickedness, and absurdity in the mores is witch persecutions, but the best men of the seventeenth century had no doubt that witches existed, and that they ought to be burned. The religion, statecraft, jurisprudence, philosophy, and social system of that age all contributed to maintain that belief. It was rather a culmination than a contradiction of the current faiths and convictions, just as the dogma that all men are equal and that one ought to have as much political power in the state as another was the culmination of the political dogmatism and social philosophy of the nineteenth century. Hence our judgments of the good or evil consequences of folkways are to be kept separate from our study of the historical phenomena of them, and of their strength and the reasons for it. The judgments have their place in plans and doctrines for the future, not in a retrospect.

We may now formulate a more complete definition of the mores. They are the ways of doing things which are current in a society to satisfy human needs and desires, together with the faiths, notions, codes, and standards of well living which inhere in those ways, having a genetic connection with them. By virtue of the latter element the mores are traits in the specific character . . . of a society or a period. They pervade and control the ways of thinking in all the exigencies of life, returning from the world of abstractions to the world of action, to give guidance and to win revivification. "The mores . . . are, before any beginning of reflection, the regulators of the political, social, and religious behavior of the individual. Conscious reflection is the worst enemy of the mores, because mores begin unconsciously and pursue unconscious purposes, which are recognized by reflection often only after long and circuitous processes, and because their expediency often depends on the assumption that they will have general acceptance and currency, uninterfered with by reflection." "The mores are usage in any group, in so far as it, on the one hand, is not the expression or fulfillment of an absolute natural necessity [e.g. eating or sleeping], and, on the other hand, is independent of the arbitrary will of the individual, and is generally accepted as good and proper, appropriate and worthy."

The process by which mores are developed and established is ritual. Ritual is so foreign to our mores that we do not recognize its power. In primitive society it is the prevailing method of activity, and primitive religion is entirely a matter of ritual. Ritual is the perfect form of drill and of the regulated habit which comes from drill. Acts which are ordained by authority and are repeated mechanically without intelligence run into ritual. If infants and children are subjected to ritual they never escape from its effects through life. Galton says that he was, in early youth, in contact with the Mohammedan ritual idea that the left hand is less worthy than the right, and that he never overcame it. We see the effect of ritual in breeding, courtesy, politeness, and all forms of prescribed behavior. Etiquette is social ritual. Ritual is not easy compliance with usage; it is strict compliance with detailed and punctilious rule. It admits of no exception or deviation. The stricter the discipline, the greater the power of ritual over action and character. In the training of animals and the education of children it is the perfection, inevitableness, invariableness, and relentlessness of routine which tells. They should never experience any exception or irregularity. Ritual is connected with words, gestures, symbols, and signs.

Selection *8*

How Culture Changes
George P. Murdock

An object or a behavior cannot be called cultural unless it is recognized by, and is significant to, a large number of persons in its host society. Cultural change is always preceded by novelties in individual or group artifacts, ideas, or activities. Cultural change is sometimes studied longitudinally, by tracing the sequence of social and cultural antecedents of particular ideas, activities, and artifacts; it is also studied as a phenomenon produced by general principles and processes that can be abstracted from particular events and patterns. Murdock refers to the former method as the historical approach, to the latter as the scientific approach. The two methods are complementary; both are valuable in the study of cultural change.

In the reading presented here, Murdock describes the general processes that have been abstracted from the histories and observations of cultures around the world. He defines the processes of innovation, social acceptance, selective elimination, and integration; he outlines their component processes; and through the total configuration, he explains the general process of cultural change.

One change in a cultural trait inevitably produces changes in other elements related to its use, manufacture, execution, or social significance, and it frequently produces changes in related traits as well. The gross cultural significance of some of the changes likely to result from the introduction of nuclear reactors, for example, will be considered in Selection 10; a few of these cultural changes have already been accomplished. The meaning of warfare has changed, and so has the meaning of national defense. The idea of fallout shelters as distinct from bomb (blast) shelters is now understood. Knowledge of the dangers of radiation has increased; a symbol for radiation warning has been devised. The discipline of physics has become more prestigious, and physicists can obtain higher incomes as a result of the increasing demand for their services. And, in addition to the countless secondary reactions to these and other changes, we are experiencing an overall change in the style and meaning of life for individuals, families, and society as a whole. One might speculate that the very first innovation made in human culture set in motion a chain reaction that has not yet stopped.

Murdock is an optimist. He believes that cultural change generally is overwhelmingly in the direction of better adaptation to the natural and social environment, since the principle of "survival of the fittest" may be applied to culture traits as well as to biological species.

It is a fundamental characteristic of culture that, despite its essentially conservative nature, it does change over time and from place to place. Herein it differs strikingly from the social behavior of animals other than man. Among ants, for example, colonies of the same species differ little in behavior from one another and even, so far as we can judge from specimens embedded in amber, from their ancestors of fifty million years ago. In less than one million years man, by contrast, has advanced from the rawest savagery to civilization and has proliferated at least three thousand distinctive cultures.

The processes by which culture changes are by now reasonably well known to science. . . .

. . . Whenever social behavior persistently deviates from established cultural habits in any direction, it results in modifications first in social expectations, and then in customs, beliefs, and rules. Gradually, in this way, collective habits are altered and the culture comes to accord better with the new norms of actual behavior.

Changes in social behavior, and hence in culture, normally have their origin in some significant alteration in the life conditions of a society. Any event which changes the situations under which collective behavior occurs, so that habitual actions are discouraged and new responses are favored, may lead to cultural innovations. Among the classes of events that are known to be especially influential in producing cultural change are increases or decreases in population, changes in the geographical environment, migrations into new environments, contacts with peoples of differing culture, natural and social catastrophes such as floods, crop failures, epidemics, wars, and economic depressions, accidental discoveries, and even such biographical events as the death or rise to power of a strong political leader.

From *Man, Culture, and Society,* edited by Harry L. Shapiro, pp. 247-260. © Oxford University Press, Inc., 1956. Reprinted by permission.

The events which produce cultural change by altering the conditions under which social behavior proves adaptive, i.e. is or is not rewarded, are invariably historical, i.e. specific with respect to time and place. Events occurring at different places and times may resemble one another, however, and exert parallel influences upon different cultures. It is thus possible to view changes in culture either in relation to their spatial and temporal setting or in relation to comparable events wherever and whenever they have occurred. The former or 'historical' approach answers such questions as what? when? and where? The latter or 'scientific' approach, by illuminating the processes by which change occurs, answers the question how? Both approaches are valid and completely complementary.

Historical anthropologists commonly discuss particular traits of culture, such as the use of tobacco, the wheel, the domesticated horse, the alphabet, or money, treating of their 'invention' at specific times and places and of their 'diffusion' from the points of origin to other parts of the world. Since our problem is to describe *how* culture changes, we must abandon the bird's-eye view of the historian and examine the processes within societies by which all changes, and not merely particular ones, take place. These processes may be conveniently grouped under the terms 'innovation,' 'social acceptance,' 'selective elimination,' and 'integration.'

Cultural change begins with the process of *innovation,* the formation of a new habit by a single individual which is subsequently accepted or learned by other members of his society. An innovation originates through the ordinary psychological mechanism of learning, and differs from purely individual habits only in the fact that it comes to be socially shared. It is nevertheless useful to distinguish several important variants of the process.

An innovation may be called a *variation* when it represents a slight modification of pre-existing habitual behavior under the pressure of gradually changing circumstances. The slow evolution in the forms of manufactured objects over time usually represents an accumulation of variations. In the same manner, tattooing can be extended over a wider area of the body, additional barbs may be added to a harpoon, skirts may be lengthened or shortened, folk tales may grow by accretion, or ceremonial may become increasingly elaborate and formalized. Variation occurs in all cultures at all times. The individual increments of change are often so slight as to be almost imperceptible, but their cumulative effect over long periods may be immense.

When innovation involves the transfer of elements of habitual behavior from one situational context to another, or their combination into new syntheses, it is called *invention*. At least some degree of creativeness is always present. Most of the important technological innovations are of this type. Thus the invention of the airplane involved the synthesis of such elements as the wings of a glider, an internal-combustion engine from an automobile, and an adaptation of a ship's propeller. Though less well known, inventions are equally common in the non-material aspects of culture. The city-manager plan, for example, represents an obvious transfer of techniques of business management to the sphere of local government, and most forms of religious worship are modeled on behavior toward persons of high social status, e.g. sacrifice upon bribery, prayer upon petitions, laudation upon flattery, ritual upon etiquette.

Since invention always involves a new synthesis of old habits, it is dependent upon the existing content of the culture. A synthesis cannot occur if the elements which it combines are not present in the culture. It is for this reason that parallel inventions so rarely occur among unconnected peoples of differing culture. With the exception of such simple and obvious combinations as the hafting of tools, anthropologists know of only a handful of genuine inventions that have been arrived at independently by historically unrelated peoples. Among them perhaps the most famous are the fire piston, invented by the Malays and a French physicist, and the dome, developed by the ancient Romans from the arch and independently invented by the Eskimos for their snow igloos.

Among peoples of the same or related cultures, on the other hand, parallel inventions are extraordinarily common. The culture provides the same constituent elements to many people, and if one person does not achieve the synthesis others are likely to do so. The Patent Office furnishes thousands of examples. In one famous instance, the telephone, applications for a patent were received on the same day from two independent inventors, Bell and Gray. Another noted case is the independent formulation of the theory of natural selection by Darwin and Wallace. So common is this phenomenon that scientists often live in dread of the anticipation of their discoveries by rivals. Parallel invention thus appears to be frequent and almost inevitable among peoples of similar culture, though so rare as to be almost non-existent among peoples of different culture.

A third type of innovation may be called *tentation.* Unlike the previous types, which merely modify or recombine elements of habit already in existence, tentation may give rise to elements that show little or no continuity with the past. The mechanism by which these are acquired is that which psychologists call 'trial-and-error learning.' Tentation may occur in any situation in which established habits prove ineffective and individuals are so strongly motivated that they try out other modes of behavior in a search for an adequate solution to their problems. They will ordinarily try out first a number of variations and recombinations of existing habitual responses, but if all of these fail they will resort to 'random behavior,' in the course of which they may accidentally hit upon some novel response which solves the problem and thereby becomes established as a new cultural element.

Crises are particularly conducive to tentation. In a famine, for instance, people try out all sorts of things that they have never eaten before, and if some of them prove nutritious and tasty they may be added to the normal diet. An epidemic similarly leads to a search for new medicines, and both primitive and civilized peoples have discovered useful remedies in this way. War also leads to improvisation, as do economic crises. The New Deal in the recent history of the United States, for example, reveals numerous instances of tentation. Scientific experimentation, it should be pointed out, is often a form of controlled tentation, as when a new series of chemical compounds are systematically put to test. The saying that 'necessity is the mother of invention' applies more forcefully to tentation than to invention proper.

When accidental discoveries lead to cultural innovations, the process is commonly that of tentation. The origin of the boomerang in aboriginal Australia will serve as an example. Over much of that continent the natives used curved throwing sticks to kill or stun small animals, and in a limited part of the area the true boomerang was used for this purpose. Almost certainly the first boomerang was produced by sheer accident in the attempt to fashion an ordinary throwing stick. Observing the unique behavior of the particular stick in flight, the maker and his fellows doubtless attempted to duplicate it. They must have resorted to tentation, or trial-and-error behavior, until they eventually succeeded, and thereby established boomerang manufacture as a habit. The history of modern 'inventions' is full of such instances, the discovery of the photographic plate by Daguerre being one of the most familiar examples.

Tentation also accounts for a type of cultural parallel which is distinct from genuine independent invention. There are certain universal problems which every people must solve and for which there are a limited number of easy and obvious solutions, so that peoples in different parts of the world have often hit upon the same solution quite independently. Rules of descent provide a good illustration. In all societies, each individual must be affiliated with a group of relatives to whom he regards himself as most closely akin and to whom he can turn for aid in time of need. There are only three possibilities: patrilineal descent, which relates an individual to kinsmen in the male line; matrilineal descent, which affiliates him with relatives through females; and bilateral descent, which associates him with a group of his closest relatives irrespective of their line of descent. Every society must choose one of these alternatives or some combination thereof, and, since the possibilities are limited to three, many peoples have, of necessity, arrived independently at the same cultural solution. Funeral customs present another example, since there are only a limited number of feasible ways of disposing of a dead body. In all such instances, if a society is compelled for any reason to abandon its previous custom it will inevitably, through tentation, arrive at an alternative solution which other peoples have independently adopted.

The fourth and last type of innovation is *cultural borrowing*, which is what the historical anthropologist, with his bird's-eye view, calls 'diffusion.' In this case the innovator is not the originator of a new habit, but its introducer. The habit has previously been part of the culture of another society; the innovator is merely the first member of his social group to adopt it. From the point of view of psychology, cultural borrowing is merely a special case of the learning process known as 'imitation.' The innovator, faced with a situation in which the shared habits of his own society are not fully satisfactory, copies behavior which he has observed in members of another society, instead of resorting to variation, invention, or tentation to solve his problem.

Of all forms of innovation, cultural borrowing is by far the most common and important. The overwhelming majority of the elements in any culture are the result of borrowing. Modern American culture provides a good illustration, as can be shown by a few random examples. Our language comes from England, our alphabet from the Phoenicians, our numerical system from India, and paper and printing from China. Our family organization and system of real property derive from medieval Europe. Our religion is a composite of elements largely assembled from the ancient Hebrews, Egyptians, Babylonians, and Persians. Metal coinage comes from Lydia, paper money from China, checks from Persia. Our system of banking, credit, loans, discounts, mortgages, et cetera, is derived in its essentials from ancient Babylonia, with modern elaborations from Italy and England. Our architecture is still largely Greek, Gothic, Georgian, et cetera. Our favorite flavors in ice creams, vanilla and chocolate, are both borrowed from the Aztecs of Mexico and were unknown to Europeans before the conquest by Cortez. Tea comes from China, coffee from Ethiopia, tobacco from the American Indians. Our domesticated animals and plants, virtually without exception, are borrowed. If the reader were to make a list of absolutely everything he eats during the next week, analysis would probably show that one third are products that were already cultivated in Neolithic times and that at least two thirds were being raised at the time of Christ, and it would be surprising if the list contained any item that was not cultivated for food somewhere in the world when Columbus sailed for America.

Our own culture is not unique in this respect, for it is doubtful whether there is a single culture known to history or anthropology that has not owed at least ninety per cent of its constituent elements to cultural borrowing. The reason is not far to seek. Any habit that has become established in a culture has been tried out by many people and found satisfactory. When a society finds itself in a dilemma, therefore, the chances that an element already present in the culture of another people will turn out to be an adequate solution to its own problem are vastly greater than those of any random and untested innovation of another type. Cultural borrowing is thus highly economical, and most peoples tend to ransack the cultural resources of their neighbors for adaptive practices before they resort to invention or tentation.

Cultural borrowing depends upon contact. Obviously the opportunity for borrowing is lacking in the case of a completely isolated society. Other factors being equal, the extent to which one culture will borrow from another is proportionate to the intensity and duration of the social intercourse between their bearers. Contact need not always be face-to-face, however, for there are numerous instances of cultural borrowing at a distance through the medium of written language or through copying of articles received by trade. By and large, however, societies borrow mainly from their immediate neighbors, with the result that the products of diffusion are ordinarily clustered in geographically contiguous areas.

Trade, missionary enterprise, and political conquest create conditions conducive to cultural borrowing. Peculiarly important, however, is inter-marriage, for this brings individuals of differing culture together within the family, where children can learn from both parents. Diffusion then proceeds through the socialization process, which produces far more perfect copying than does cultural borrowing on the adult level. The American 'melting pot' operates largely through this mechanism. Primitive peoples practicing local exogamy, i.e. requiring individuals to obtain spouses from another village or band, commonly reveal considerable cultural uniformity over wide areas, as in aboriginal Australia and among the Indians of the Northwest Coast. By contrast, in areas like Melanesia and Central California where marriage normally takes place within the community, even villages a few miles apart may differ strikingly in dialect and customs. In the one case culture is diffused through the same process by which it is transmitted; in the other, even adult contacts tend to be restricted to a minimum.

Incentive—a need or drive—is as essential in cultural borrowing as in other types of innovation. A people rarely borrows an alien cultural element when they already possess a trait which satisfactorily fills the same need. Thus the blubber lamp of the Eskimos was not borrowed by the Indians to the south, who had plenty of wood for fires to heat and light their dwellings. On the other hand, the extraordinarily rapid diffusion of tobacco over the earth after the discovery of America reflected the general absence of competing traits. It has been observed that the first individuals in a society to borrow alien customs are likely to be the discontented, underprivileged, and maladjusted. Thus in India Christian missionaries have made many more converts among the 'untouchables' than in the higher strata of society, and in our own country fascism and communism attract an unduly high proportion of unsuccessful and neurotic people.

The presence in a receiving society of some of the habit elements involved in a new trait greatly facilitates borrowing. It is for this reason that diffusion occurs most readily among peoples of similar culture, who already share many elements of habit. Thus Englishmen and Americans borrow more frequently and easily from each other than from Russians, Chinese, or Hottentots. Conversely, aboriginal peoples are greatly handicapped in taking over the complex technology of modern civilization. They cannot, for example, begin to manufacture the steel products which they want without also taking over such things as blast furnaces and rolling mills.

Cultural borrowing will occur only if the new habit is demonstrably rewarding. The native quickly adopts steel knives and axes from the white man because their superiority to his former stone implements becomes immediately apparent. On the other hand, Europeans were slow to borrow paper manufacture from the Chinese because the advantages of paper over parchment appeared very slight at first. The Chinese and Japanese have not yet adopted the alphabet from western civilization because, however great its ultimate advantages, it would impose heavy burdens and discomforts upon all literate persons during the necessary period of readjustment. Geographic and climatic factors may prevent diffusion by withholding or reducing the possibilities of reward, and social prejudices such as ingrained conservatism may counterbalance potential advantages by inflicting disapprobation upon innovators.

Borrowing need not be exact. Oftentimes, indeed, all that is borrowed is the external 'form' of a custom and not its 'meaning,' i.e. the collective ideas associated with it. The familiar caricature of the cannibal chief wearing a silk hat provides a good illustration. Frequently an imperfect copy is quite adequate. Thus when the Plains Indians took over horses and riding equipment from the Spaniards they omitted the horseshoe, which was quite unnecessary on the prairie. Sometimes changes are imposed by the conditions of the geographical environment. When the Iroquois Indians adopted the birchbark canoe from their Algonkian neighbors, for example, they altered the material to elm bark because of the scarcity of birch trees in their habitat. Frequently cultural factors favor a modification. The original Phoenician alphabet lacked characters for vowels, the nature of their language being such that consonant signs sufficed for the identification of words. Since this was not true of the Greek language, when the Greeks borrowed the Phoenician alphabet they converted characters for which they had no need into symbols for vowels.

Modifications are so common in cultural borrowing that authorities like Malinowski have regarded the process as scarcely less creative than other forms of innovation. Often, indeed, it is inextricably blended with invention or tentation. This is well illustrated in instances of 'stimulus diffusion,' in which only the general idea of an alien cultural trait is borrowed, the specific form being supplied by improvisation. Thus a famous Cherokee chief named Sequoyah, though an illiterate man, had noticed that white men could somehow understand messages from pieces of paper on which peculiar marks were inscribed, and he came to the conclusion that this would be a useful skill for his own people to acquire. He therefore set himself the task of devising a system of marks by which the Cherokee language could be written. Inventing some signs of his own and copying some from pieces of printed matter—numbers and punctuation marks as well as letters, upside down or on their sides as often as upright—he produced a novel form of writing, a syllabary rather than an alphabet, which his tribesmen learned and still use to this day. (See Fig. 1.)

Courtesy of Mr. Tom B. Underwood,
Museum of The Cherokee Indian, and The Stephens Press.

Fig. 1. Sequoyah, the famous Cherokee Indian chief, invented this syllabary for recording his native language by giving syllabic values to alphabetic letters and typographical signs arbitrarily chosen and arranged from English and German type.

The second major process in cultural change is *social acceptance*. So long as an innovation, whether original or borrowed, is practiced by the innovator alone in his society, it is an individual habit and not an element of culture. To become the latter it must be accepted by others; it must be socially shared. Social acceptance begins with the adoption of a new habit by a small number of individuals. From this point it may spread until it becomes part of the sub-culture of a family, clan, local community, or other sub-group, or until it becomes a 'specialty' characteristic of persons belonging to a particular occupational, kinship, age-graded, or other status category, or until it becomes an 'alternative' widely but optionally practiced. Eventually it may even become a 'universal,' shared by all members of the society. The term 'degrees of cultural saturation' has been proposed for the various steps in social acceptance.

The learning mechanism involved in social acceptance is imitation, as in the case of cultural borrowing, but the model whose behavior is copied is a member of one's own rather than another society. So similar are the two processes that the term 'diffusion' is often applied to both; social acceptance is called 'internal' or 'vertical' diffusion to differentiate it from cultural borrowing, which is termed 'external' or 'horizontal' diffusion. With minor exceptions, most of what has previously been stated about the latter process applies equally to the former. Since close contact and similarity of culture can be taken for granted, however, copying is usually far more exact, and this is accentuated by social control.

A factor of considerable importance in social acceptance is the prestige of the innovator and of the group who are first to imitate him. Changes advocated by an admired political or religious leader are readily adopted, whereas few will follow an unpopular or despised innovator. Clothing styles accepted by 'the four hundred' quickly diffuse throughout the masses, but the 'zoot suit' does not spread from the taxi dance hall to the ballroom. Women imitate men more readily than *vice versa*. In our own society, for example, many women have adopted masculine garments, smoking and drinking habits, and occupations, but there appears to be no concerted movement among men to wear skirts, use cosmetics, or apply for positions as nurses, governesses, or baby-sitters.

Selective elimination constitutes a third major process of cultural change. Every innovation that has been socially accepted enters, as it were, into a competition for survival. So long as it proves more rewarding than its alternatives a cultural habit will endure, but when it ceases to bring comparable satisfactions it dwindles and eventually disappears. The process superficially resembles that of natural selection in organic evolution. It should be noted, however, that cultural traits do not compete directly with one another but are competitively tested in the experience of those who practice them. Oftentimes the competition is carried on between organized groups of people with contrasting customs and beliefs, as between nations, political parties, religious sects, or social and economic classes, and the issue is decided indirectly by the victory of one group over the other. By and large, the cultural elements that are eliminated through trial and error or social competition are the less adaptive ones, so that the process is as definitely one of the survival of the fittest as is that of natural selection.

Few of the genuine gains of culture history— the achievements of technology, of science, of man's control over nature—have ever been lost. The so-called 'lost arts of antiquity' are largely mythical. To be sure, particular peoples have declined in civilization, but not until they have passed on their contributions to others. What man has lost, in the main, is a mass of maladaptive and barbarous practices, inefficient techniques, and outworn superstitions. New errors arise, of course, in each generation, but it is comforting to realize that the mortality of error is vastly greater than that of truth.

It is the genuine achievements of man that anthropologists have in mind when they say that culture is cumulative, comparing culture history to the growth of a snowball as it is rolled down a hill. Even achievements that are superseded rarely disappear. Today the electric light has proved superior to earlier methods of lighting, but the gas mantle, the kerosene lamp, and the tallow candle still survive in out-of-the-way places or under special conditions. Survival is often assured through a change in function. The use of outmoded weapons has been preserved, for example, in athletic sports like fencing and archery and in boyhood toys such as the sling and the peashooter. Other ancient usages survive in legal, religious, and academic ceremonial. Written records, of course, preserve much of the culture of the past from oblivion. Our libraries bulge with the puerilities as well as the achievements of history.

The fourth and last important process of cultural change is that of *integration*. The shared habits that constitute a culture not only fluctuate in their degree of social acceptance, and compete for survival, but they also become progressively adapted to one another so that they tend to form an integrated whole. They exhibit what Sumner has called 'a strain toward consistency.' Every innovation alters in some respect the situations under which certain other forms of habitual behavior occur, and leads to adaptive changes in the latter. Similarly it must, in its turn, be adjusted to modifications elsewhere in the culture. While each such change is in itself, of course, an innovation, their reciprocal interaction and cumulative effect deserve special recognition as an integrative process.

The history of the automobile during the present century in our own culture provides an excellent example. . . . A similar story could be told for other modern innovations such as the telephone, the airplane, the radio, and electrical household gadgets, and all of them pale before the potentialities of atomic energy.

Certain anthropologists have erroneously assumed that the elements of any culture are in a state of nearly perfect integration, or equilibrium, at all times. Actually, however, perfect equilibrium is never achieved or even approached. The adjustment of other elements of culture to an innovation, and of it to them, requires time—often years or even generations. In the meantime other innovations have appeared and set in motion new processes of integration. At any given time, therefore, a culture exhibits numerous instances of uncompleted integrative processes as well as examples of others which have been carried through to relatively satisfactory completion. What we always encounter is a strain toward internal adaptation, never its full realization.

The period of time which must elapse between the acceptance of an innovation and the completion of the integrative readjustments which follow in its train Ogburn has aptly called 'cultural lag.' During such a period of lag people attempt, through variation, invention, tentation, and cultural borrowing, to modify old customs and ideas to accord with the new, and to adjust the new to the old, so as to eliminate inconsist-encies and sources of friction and irritation. In a modern democratic society, politics is a major scene of such efforts.

The net effect of the various processes of cultural change is to adapt the collective habits of human societies progressively over time to the changing conditions of existence. Change is always uncomfortable and often painful, and people frequently become discouraged with its slowness or even despair of achieving any genuine improvement. Neither history nor anthropology, however, gives grounds for pessimism. However halting or harsh it may appear to participants, cultural change is always adaptive and usually progressive. It is also inevitable, and will endure as long as the earth can support human life. Nothing—not even an atomic war—can destroy civilization.

Selection 9

The Sociology of the Bicycle

Sidney H. Aronson

In the preceding selection, Murdock described a type of innovation called *tentation*. Elements of tentation are found in the popularization of the bicycle in the United States, since a variety of experimental models were tried and rejected before the "safety" bicycle finally won acceptance by the American people. The "necessity" for a conveyance of this sort can probably be reckoned by (1) the number of attempts made to introduce a satisfactory model, (2) the number of years that elapsed between the initial conceptualization and mass production of the first acceptable model, and (3) the number of people who began to use the invention when it appeared.

The introduction of the bicycle into the United States is also an example of cultural borrowing, insofar as the cultures of England and the United States are distinct. The cultural base for the bicycle was present, in that the wheel, the chain drive, the sprocket, and the English saddle—as well as the wish (or "need") to travel widely and rapidly—were all to be found here.

Aronson calls attention to cultural changes that resulted from the introduction of the bicycle into American life. Some of the changes, such as modifications of clothing styles and the disappearance of the chaperone, might have occurred even if the bicycle had not appeared when it did. Other changes, however, such as traffic laws and road improvements, seem to have been direct results of the bicycle's introduction. Further, laws and road improvements designed for the bicycle literally paved the way for the automobile; both the invention and the rapid adoption of the automobile, Aronson points out, were hastened by wide acceptance of the bicycle.

The concept of emergent culture is well illustrated in this selection, and the continuity of cultural change—the appearance and disappearance of cultural elements—can be appreciated by noting the number of specific modifications, inventions, and selective eliminations that accompanied the innovation of the bicycle.

The bicycle came to America three times. The first two models, of 1819 and 1869, were duds, but the third, brought here in 1879, was the real thing, and brought an explosion which can only be—and, indeed, was—called a "bicycle boom."

Perhaps the primary reason for this phenomenon was a mechanical one: the 1879 "bike" was the best made. The 1819 model, known first as the "dandy-horse" and later as the velocipede, was brought to this country from England. It consisted of two wheels of equal size connected by a long wooden bar; the operator straddled this bar and propelled the machine by walking or running along the ground. Once the rider built up some speed he would lift up his legs and glide until the force petered out. Going downhill, the cyclist did not have to do anything but coast and hope that he would not run into anything—for the machine had no brakes. There was a brief flutter of excitement over this vehicle, centering in Boston and Philadelphia where riding schools opened; but soon the novelty wore off and the machine disappeared from sight.

With the 1869 model, the rider's foot power was used somewhat more subtly; cranks were placed on the front wheel. This machine had wooden wheels with iron tires; it was heavy and cumbersome, and did not ride smoothly, especially over the roads of the seventies. For these reasons the machine was called, not too affectionately, the "bone crusher." By 1871 it, too, passed from the American scene.

But in 1879 came the first successful wheel, again from England, and soon afterward, Colonel Albert A. Pope, the father of the American bicycle, began to manufacture it in Boston. This machine, known as the ordinary or high bicycle, made good speed, and its solid rubber tires gave a smoother ride. But it was awkward to mount because the seat was perched on top of the front wheel, which was four to five feet in diameter. Balance, too, was very difficult and a quick stop or the slightest roughness on the road would throw the driver in a fall which, in the popular jargon, became known as a "header." The vehicle was propelled by pedals on the front wheel, another factor which made smooth braking a rarity. This bicycle became only moderately popular and mostly among young and athletic males. It lingers on today as a favorite prop of clowns and vaudevillians.

Finally, in 1885 the safety bicycle, which made cycling possible for young and old of both sexes, was developed in England. Several factors made this machine simpler and safer to ride. The two wheels were each about two feet in diameter and hence the vehicle was easier to mount; a saddle rested on an iron frame between the wheels. The machine was driven by a sprocket and chain attached to the rear wheel and moved by pedals below the saddle. In 1890 the invention of the pneumatic tire assured its success by greatly increasing its speed, comfort, and ease of propulsion. It was in fact substantially the same bicycle that we use today.

This is not to say that the adoption of the bicycle came spontaneously and without the opposition that so often accompanies social innovation. As has been shown above, the first group of cyclists in the eighties was an eager and athletic one, which gave little regard to the rights of others as they "scorched" over the highways training for record-breaking attempts. Later cyclists, though tamer, inherited the antagonism of horsemen and teamsters. The latter, accustomed to having the roads to themselves, resented the intrusion, especially because the newcomers frightened horses and caused runaways. The hostility between the two groups took various forms. Often the horsemen and teamsters deliberately turned on the cyclists and ran them down. Fist-fighting between wheelmen and draymen was frequent and fierce.

Sometimes pedestrians, who were irked by the cyclists, teamed up with the horsemen and passed laws prohibiting the riding of bicycles in public parks and drives. But in 1879 wheelmen won an important victory when a Massachusetts court ruled that "bicycles cannot be deemed as nuisances but are entitled to the reasonable use of the highways." A few years later the Treasury Department classified bicycles as carriages rather than as steel products, which meant a ten percent reduction in the tariff.

To further this legal struggle as well as for other reasons, the League of American Wheelmen was formed on May 31, 1880. American cyclists were fortunate in having the aggressive and influential League to protect their interests. Throughout its history, the L.A.W. kept its pledge "to

"The Sociology of the Bicycle" by Sidney Aronson from *Social Forces*, Vol. 30 (1951-1952), 305-312. Reprinted by permission of the University of North Carolina Press.

promote the general interests of bicycling; to ascertain, defend, and protect the rights of wheelmen." It was through the League's efforts in several test cases that the laws which were applied to carriages came to be applied to bicycles as well.

Another group was not so much opposed to cycling as it was to using the "bike" on Sundays. Perhaps it would not have been so terrible to break the Sabbath if the offense had consisted in carrying the riders to church instead of to the country. On the contrary, according to a New Haven clergyman, the road of the cyclists led "to a place where there is no mud on the streets because of its high temperature." Such admonitions were of no avail, and one writer cleverly noted that "one curious effect which should afford some consolation to Sabbatarians is that theatres in certain cities which were formerly open on Sundays have been closed permanently."

Not all men of religion opposed the bicycle, however. Henry Ward Beecher, as early as 1869, when asked about the coming man and how he would come, answered, "I think he is coming on a velocipede. I shall not be at all surprised," he continued, "to see in a short time a thousand velocipedists wheeling their machines to Plymouth Church." Clergymen themselves started to take up the exercise—Beecher was among the first—and the editor of the *Spectator* wrote that it was proper for a bishop to cycle provided, of course, he didn't "coast downhill on his bicycle with his legs up." And by 1896 the *Boston Daily Advertiser* could write, "It seems to be settled that the majority of the clergymen are in favor of Sunday cycling."

The bicycle was the subject not only of religious but also of medical dispute. In this debate both sides made extravagant claims. The anti-bicyclists said that the cycle path led straight to the hospital or the grave. They discovered all sorts of new ailments which the cyclist was heir to, including kyphosis bicyclistarum, or bicycle stoop, which was acquired by pedalling in a bent-over position. Cyclist's sore throat was found to occur after a long ride on a dusty road. Perhaps worst of all was bicycle face, a result of the wheelman's continuous worrying about keeping his equilibrium while he rode. The *Christian Intelligence* added that another cause of bicycle face was the habitual violation of the law of the Sabbath by cyclists. Many more "normal" diseases were also laid to the exercise.

The proponents of the bicycle, on the other hand, likened its effects to that of a wonder drug. Among the more important illnesses that it could cure were rheumatism, indigestion, alcoholism, anaemia, gout, liver trouble, and "nerves." At the same time, though not altogether denying the existence of such ills as bicycle face or bicycle stoop, the advocates of the wheel minimized their danger or told how to avoid them. At a meeting of the Academy of Medicine in 1895, doctors advised the average American cyclist that he would not be troubled by bicyclist's stoop if he sat erect. Indeed, Dr. Graeme M. Hammond, in a paper before the same academy, reported that detailed physical examinations of cyclists revealed them to be unusually healthy. An article in the *New York Daily Tribune* [July 14, 1895] maintained that bicycle face was not an illness to be avoided but to be sought after and that

". . . anybody who rides every day on a wheel and does not acquire the bicycle face lacks character, and is a menace to himself and everybody else when on the road or on the track. The bicycle face denotes strength of mind in the persons who possess it. It means alertness, quick perception and prompt action in emergencies. The idiotic grin of some of the cigarette smoking fellows who make fun of bicycling can never be mistaken for the bicycle face."

There were saner elements among medical authorities, and most of these agreed that cycling for the normal person was a healthful form of exercise. It was especially good because, unlike many forms of athletics, the cyclist did not have to be phenomenally muscular or robust. Of course, these doctors warned, if carried to excess, cycling, like any physical activity, could be harmful. Most people came to accept this view. An editorial in the *Literary Digest* expressed the common feeling when it said, "The notion has been exploded, happily, that wheeling is a panacea for all ailing folks and for all ailments."

Having thus reviewed the mechanical, legal, religious, and medical skirmishes which preceded the full acceptance of the bicycle, what were the consequences of this acceptance in certain areas of social life? Perhaps the bicycle's greatest impact was upon the American woman. As soon as the safety and drop frame made it easier for the fair sex to mount and ride, women seized upon the vehicle as a new means of defying tradition. This was the period, it must be remembered, of the suffragettes, when the genteel female was on her way out and women were demanding every form of equality with men. Thus for example, probably because of the reluctance of elderly ladies to learn to ride, it became socially proper for a boy and girl to go cycling without a third party. (Or was it because the bicycle built-for-two had no room for a chaperone?)

For the sake of both comfort and safety, women's

clothing was drastically changed. As one female cyclist put it, "On the [bicycle] excursion a special adaptation of dress is absolutely necessary, for skirts, while they have not hindered women from climbing to the topmost branches of higher education, may prove fatal in down-hill coasting." Some of the bolder among the sex easily adapted their dress to cycling by shortening their skirts, shockingly exposing their ankles to view. The courage of some yet more daring women gave America the famous bloomer girl. "Skirts," as one advocate of dress reform was quoted in the [*New York Daily*] *Tribune* [July 7, 1895], "long or short . . . are bound to go. It is merely a question of time when an unadulterated man's suit . . . will be the universal garb for women, and all this talk and agitation of the question will be forgotten." And bloomers did resemble men's knickerbockers, though they were wider and more flowing. Despite the censure and ridicule directed at them, the women stuck doggedly to the new fashion. "The time for a woman to faint if a man caught sight of her ankle," said the new woman, "has passed."

Public opinion was not entirely unfavorable to this new turn in women's fashion. An editorial in the *Philadelphia Item* was perhaps typical of some of the more tolerant comments. "Let the women alone," it began; "they can work out their own salvation, if they desire to wear bloomers why let them bloom."

The effect of the bicycle on women's clothing was truly revolutionary—within a period of two or three years the bicycle gave the American woman the liberty of dress which reformers had been seeking for generations.

Because women rode bicycles, new problems of etiquette presented themselves. One difficulty which appeared for the first time—and which still plagues us today—was whether it was a man's duty to fix a flat tire for a woman. An editorial in *Harper's Weekly* [October 3, 1896] tried to resolve this problem:

"It is recognized as befitting a gentleman to offer his services in repairing a punctured tire, adjusting a nut, or arranging something that has gone astray with a woman's wheel, and it is not considered improper for a woman to accept his politely proffered services for the mending of a wheel, which he can do better than herself."

But this friendliness and familiarity of the road should not be carried too far; the same editorial frowned on the practice of a male cyclist tipping his hat to a woman rider he did not know. The rule of the right of way at an intersection was a problem, in those days as in ours. But this maga-zine's solution was simple and gallant. "A woman," wrote *Harper's*, "should always have the right of way."

Yet, as late as 1896, there continued to be opposition to these newly won freedoms for women. The dissent was led by the Woman's Rescue League of Washington, D.C. This organization claimed that cycling prevented married women from having children, that the new dress was shocking and indecent, and that the new familiarity and companionship with men led to immorality. "Bicycling by young women," a spokesman for the League wrote, "has helped more than any other medium to swell the ranks of reckless girls, who finally drift into the army of outcast women of the United States." But this was definitely a minority opinion; many more of the fair sex considered cycling a step toward even greater freedom. "Many a woman," wrote Mrs. Elizabeth Cady Stanton, "is riding to the suffrage on a bicycle."

As would be expected, the bicycle was an innovation of considerable importance for the American economy. In 1880 the manufacture of bicycles and tricycles was not even listed as a separate industry in the census reports on manufacturing. We may adduce here another reason for the failure of the old ordinary. Every cyclist required a different size of driving wheel, so that this vehicle was not easily adaptable to mass-production techniques. The invention of the safety, however, with its pedals in a position which could be reached by any cyclist, allowed the use of factory methods in bicycle production. In 1889 the volume of orders received by wheel manufacturers and jobbers in Boston, which was then the center of the industry, was unprecedented. And in 1890 the census reports listed the manufacture, as well as the repair of bicycles and tricycles, as separate industries.

A few statistics will show the phenomenal expansion of the cycling industry after the introduction of the safety bicycle. In 1890 there were 27 establishments making bicycles and tricycles. By 1900 this number had risen to 312. The total capital investment in 1890 was $2,058,072; in 1900 it was $29,783,659. In 1890 establishments manufacturing bicycles employed 1,797 people and paid them a total of $1,105,728. In 1900 they hired 17,525 and the wage bill had risen to $9,358,904. Reliable estimates put the total number of bicycles in use during the nineties at ten million in a population approaching seventy-six million. Cycle repairing underwent a similar growth. Furthermore, many companies began to turn out bicycle accessories and found a lucrative market for them. Bicycle lamps, bells, saddles, tools, tires, trouser-clips, rear-view mirrors are typical of the extras of the nineties. All sorts of bicycle clothing were manufactured: bloomers, bicycle stockings, bicycle caps, bicycle shoes, bicycle pants—with reinforced seats, even bicycle corsets were sold. Employment opportunities were offered in riding schools to which thousands flocked. Jordan Marsh and Company of Boston converted one of its floors into a riding academy and offered free lessons to anyone who purchased a wheel there.

At the same time the price of the safety dropped to about $60 compared to the $150 for the ordinary, and by 1900 new bicycles could be purchased for as little as $18. In addition, the fashion of trading the machine in every year or two had already been established, so that a second-hand "bike" was within the reach of all.

Some industries actually suffered adverse effects from the bicycle boom. Fortunately, many retailers were able to bolster their sagging sales by taking in a stock of roadsters (another name for bicycles). Soon jewelry, shoe, gun, hardware, and department stores were all selling wheels.

The bicycle had its effect on the United States Army, too. Some military men predicted bicyclized warfare. "It is in rapidly moving considerable bodies of infantry," wrote one officer, "that the bicycle will find its highest function in time of war." Military maneuvers were held in which the bicycle was used. The Colt Automatic Rifle was mounted on the handle bars of a wheel. The Medical Corps received training in evacuating men on the bicycle. And in 1896, 200 wheels were shipped to Cuba and were probably used in the fighting there.

It was to be expected that bicycling would make its mark in the world of sports. Because of limited space only the slightest summary will be made here of the bicycle's impact on the American sporting scene. Race tracks cropped up throughout the country and thousands of tournaments enabled amateurs and professionals to vie for honor and reward. Many colleges had bicycle teams which engaged in school meets. The six-day bicycle race attracted thousands to Madison Square Garden each year. Arthur A. Zimmerman was the Di Maggio of bicycle racing and the idol of a considerable segment of American youth. His speed on the wheel earned him $40,000 annually. To help keep the sport honest, the League of American Wheelmen took charge of professional racing in 1895.

But easily the greatest significance of the bicycle was the interference it ran for the automobile. The bicycle did the dirty work for its mechanized successor in a variety of ways. We may first mention the adoption in cycle manufac-

turing of assembly-line techniques. Standardization had been perfected to such a degree that the manufacturing company no longer constructed the entire bicycle under its own roof, but had merely to assemble the parts which smaller companies had contracted to make. The importance of this method for automobile manufacture is obvious. As a matter of fact, the census of 1900 noted that 56 automobiles had in that year been made in bicycle factories. The census report even classified the auto under the general heading of bicycle.

The abundance of repair shops—there were 6,328 of them in 1900—was another of the bicycle's gifts to the automobile. Not only did these become the logical repair places for the auto, but they were the training schools for a group of mechanics who could easily turn from the bicycle when the new vehicle became popular. Charles and Frank Duryea owned such a bicycle repair shop in Springfield, Massachusetts, and it was here that they built the first American automobile.

By carrying on effective agitation for road repairs and construction, the cyclists rendered still another inestimable service to future autoists. Without good roads the automobile could never have succeeded: the earliest autos had had to be put on tracks because they could not be made to run effectively on the English highways of their day; hence they became locomotives, with all the limitations that tracks entailed. Privately built and operated turnpikes, which had once given the United States good roads, had become unprofitable because of the railroads. Furthermore, road construction and maintenance were the responsibilities of the cities and towns and not of the federal or state governments. As a result, the roads were rough and rutted, muddy in the spring, sandy and dusty all summer.

To the League of American Wheelmen goes most of the credit for road reform in the eighties and nineties. Under its direction, pamphlets and books—including the *Good Roads* magazine—urging reform were written and distributed. In Washington the League lobbied unsuccessfully for a federal highway, but did succeed in 1893 in getting the national government to create the Office of Public Roads Inquiries. Other returns for this effort began to roll in. By 1896, 16 states appropriated money to improve their roads. Several states—Massachusetts and New Jersey were the first—also established state control of roads through a central highway commission. In Massachusetts, all the members of the State Highway Commission belonged to the L.A.W. In Iowa and Kentucky, the custom was begun of putting convicts to building and repairing roads.

In still other ways the League of American Wheelmen sought to improve roads. The League backed legislation for lighted streets and for erecting guideposts at intersections with the names of streets. This remarkable organization even built signs on the road marking the danger spots; these signs would be sent free to any place in the country by the Committee on Danger Signs. In like manner, the League constructed signposts with important travel information, such as direction and distances of neighboring cities. League members were asked to record their mileage on cycling trips, so that this information would be available. These services were important not only to cyclists but also to riders of the new horse-less carriages.

The pressure of millions of wheels on the road during the nineties compelled the passage of a new series of laws regulating their use. Many states required cyclists to purchase licenses for their wheels; in some cases the money derived from this source was used to keep roads in repair. New Jersey was the first state to require bicycles to be lighted at night and also be equipped with a bell to give a warning signal. Riding on sidewalks was prohibited in virtually all states. Successful lobbying on the part of the League of American Wheelmen brought about statutes requiring that names and addresses be exchanged in case of accidents. Wheelmen in Massachusetts, Michigan, and New Hampshire were obliged to keep to the right side of the road except when passing. Though not yet a matter of law many cyclists voluntarily began the practice of passing on the left and giving hand signals when turning. Speed limits were set at ten miles per hour on the highways and eight miles in the public parks, but these laws were apparently frequently violated and the phrase "fined for scorching" became a familiar one.

Along with these laws and practices and their infractions, the system of enforcement was part of the legacy which the bicycle bequeathed to the automobile when the latter began its reign in the twentieth century. For the speed demon, so familiar to the modern American scene, dates back to the coming of the bicycle and jeopardized the lives of pedestrians and other wheelmen. So many accidents occurred that a new obituary column entitled "Death by the Wheel," appeared in newspapers. Cyclists boasted about the close shaves they experienced on the road. Since the scorchers could outdistance police on horseback, police methods had to be modernized.

Many cities coped with this problem by equipping squadrons of bicycle cops. Daring races between bicycle policemen and scorchers became common; the public enjoyed these free contests and, more often than not, cheered the speedster—especially a female one—and hissed the officer. Not only was the wheel effective in combating scorchers, but policemen also found it an efficient instrument when covering their beats—a fore-shadowing of the patrol car.

It was the bicycle which gave rise in the nineties to that new type of mobility which became so characteristic of the twentieth century. In the earlier part of the century, horses and carriages were only for the more well-to-do. The average city worker and his family, except for an occasional railroad trip, rarely left their place of residence. But the wheel made it possible for Americans to visit the country-side and neighboring towns. Despite the inadequacy of the roads, the cyclist thought little of covering twenty-five to fifty miles in the course of a Sunday. Often the whole family participated in these outings; the children all had bicycles of their own, and the parents might have had a convertible—a tandem bicycle which could also be used as a single safety. The wayside inn, so much a part of the American scene today, was rescued from oblivion by the bicycle. The hostelry, because of the railroads, had been on the point of extinction, until hordes of hungry and thirsty wheelmen in the nineties thronged the country roads.

In the summer time many people went on bicycle journeys in much the same way as we today go on automobile trips. Of course, they didn't cover as much mileage as we do, but these hardy Americans did cover several hundred miles. The League of American Wheelmen provided its two hundred thousand members with maps which marked out the best roads and listed hotels at which members received discounts, and even took the trouble of advising members not to disclose their League affiliation until their stay was over lest they be put in poorer accommodations because of the rebate. "Unlike the steam car," wrote one cycling vacationist, "the bicycle takes one to the out-of-the-way places and scenes; unlike the horse, it is not a source of care and anxiety, or liable to serious ills on the way."

But not only were many Americans enabled to visit the country, but many also found it possible to live on the outskirts of the city and cycle into and home from work. Many could afford to make this change because suburban rents were still as low as tenement rents.

Thus it can be concluded that the bicycle provided a preview on a miniature scale of much of the social phenomena which the automobile enlarged upon. Of course, the automobile, for the most part, displaced the bicycle as a means of transportation, but made full use of the institutions which accompanied the two-wheeled vehicle. At any rate, an early cyclist hardly realized how right he was when he said, with the bicycle in mind, "Walking is now on its last legs."

Selection 10

Nuclear Fission and Cultural Change

W. Fred Cottrell

In Selection 8, Murdock indicated the pervasiveness of the effects of cultural change. Selection 10 deals at some length with the ability of a host society to accept a major cultural change without undergoing intolerable social disorganization. As previously noted, any cultural change produces changes in many cultural traits. The number, speed, and magnitude of the accommodative changes that occur in response to a given change vary from one society to another, as does the extent of social reorganization necessary to adapt to those changes.

The announcement of the first conversion of matter to energy by means of nuclear fission came as a surprise to most Americans because of the cloak of military secrecy which surrounded its intended use. The vast majority of the population still have little understanding of its implications for their personal lives other than that it brought a close to World War II and that it could cause large-scale destruction in another war. Probably not more than 1 or 2 per cent of the people of the United States are aware of the total economic, political, and cultural potential resulting from the harnessing of nuclear fission devices for peaceful energy converters—at least, not aware of that potential to the extent to which Cottrell deals with it here.

The following article may be viewed as a study in cultural relativism as well as a study of cultural change. Certainly the meaning of nuclear energy conversion is dramatically different in different cultures.

Among the most significant questions about effects the atom will have on the future is "What will happen to cities?" Will they have to be abandoned in the face of the threat of the bombs? Will they be relocated to serve the new age of costless energy? Will they be organized so that their functions and population will continue to be distributed as in the past? There is no way to answer these questions accurately. There is, in fact, no generally accepted theory as to the specific effects which given energy sources have had or may have on civilization. We cannot assume that the arrangements in the past which were thought to be a part of human nature may not have been the result of adjustments to physical conditions which can now be altered. So the uses of history are limited. Nor can we reason accurately from recent experience either, for it is too soon to know what man will be able to do with his new inventions.

. . . What is primary and most apparent is the fact that it is now possible to destroy urban civilization. This is not, however, a new thing in human history. Pestilence and starvation resulting from conflicts which could not be resolved have laid waste to cities before. . . . As men become accustomed to the idea that it is possible to destroy the urban world they come also to believe that it will not, in fact, be destroyed. . . .

This is not to say that the threat of bombing will have little effect on our way of life. The cost of building new atomic weapons and the cost of a defense against similar weapons is tremendous and alters greatly the uses to which resources might otherwise be put. But military threat also requires the maintenance and extension of total physical production. For this reason, moves which seem likely to greatly reduce it, such as the relocation or deconcentration of cities, are not likely to persist. Assuming then that cities are not likely to be changed much by the threat of bombing—just how will the atom affect them otherwise? There are no presently visible changes in cities which can be traced back to the use, or putative use, of atomic power. So, if we are to do anything more than speculate we will have to examine the way which other sources of energy have affected the past development of cities and see how atomic energy compares with them.

Let us start with the proposition that men will shift from one fuel source with which they have been making a living to another only as they see some advantage in so doing. The new source may be less costly to them than the old. Perhaps they can expand its production more rapidly and to a much greater total. It may be more convenient or less costly to convert it into other forms than those in which it is found naturally. It may be quieter, cleaner, or more dependable. On the other hand, if a new fuel is adopted, some new social arrangements must be made. These may result in the shift of wealth, power, and prestige from one group or region to another, or they may make it easier to promote one set of values over another. A new energy source is thus as likely to be opposed by those whose values or position it changes adversely as it is to be supported by those to whom it promises advantage. Therefore, to anticipate how and where atomic energy is to affect cities it must be compared with other fuels in all those respects which influenced city people to use or reject them. Namely, the fuel cost, cost of conversion, the values enhanced and those degraded, groups aided and those who suffered loss.

What is a city? However we describe it, we will note that not all the food consumed there is raised within its borders. Now food is the energy source for all work done by the bodies of men, and since the city does not supply its own food, no city exists except as it is supplied energy from elsewhere. The outside limit on the size of its population, then, is set by the amount of food which its suppliers are able to produce regularly in excess of their own biological needs, minus the food which must be consumed by those who transport it. Early cities grew up where men had learned to grow the grains which yield considerably more food than that consumed in their cultivation and harvest, and which could be transported and stored without excessive spoilage. Sometimes there was no way of getting the surplus to the city without consuming most of it in transport. For this and other reasons not all grain-growing people contributed to city growth.

Most of the early cities were located on rivers where the energy of the flowing stream used in transport could be added to that gained from the grain, though some, through the development of roads and wheeled vehicles, were able to concentrate and control the surplus of fairly large regions.

Many of today's cities are located at sites selected under such conditions, obtaining the larger part of the energy they use from plants, men, and animals, plus some from down stream transportation. To them the flow of food must continue and, if the city is to grow, must increase. If anything threatens to diminish this flow the people of the city must either intervene to prevent the decrease or see the local population reduced. One way atomic power might affect cities in the future is to alter the pattern of food production and distribution upon which they depend. When we have laid adequate groundwork we will return to see whether, in fact, it is likely to do so.

. . . At various periods when social conditions permitted or encouraged trade, the growth of cities based on the use of the sail was rapid. The maximum size of a particular city was no longer set by the energy of the food produced in and the stream flow of its hinterland. It could be expanded as the ability of the trader to bring food and raw materials from overseas was established. The size and location of cities still depended upon the energy available but that now included the power of wind on sail.

The trading cities of the West were developed with this aid. Many hitherto "underdeveloped" areas in other parts of the world were, by military, economic, and political means, forced into a pattern of regional and occupational specialization which would serve these cities. In turn the competition between local and distant sources of food and raw material greatly altered the relative power and wealth of traders and others in the city. There was a resultant shift in Western ideology and social structure which was necessary for the continued dominance of Western cities. However, in the eighteenth century the trading city began to feel the effects of the use of a new fuel—coal. The rise of industrial towns based on the exploitation of this fuel disturbed the pattern which was developing with the use of sail-borne trade. Some of the urban world began to undergo changes resulting from this new source of power, but no clear pattern emerged before the use of electricity and petroleum created a different set of alternatives from those previously possible. Thus, atomic power will potentially come into use in many areas where people have still to discover the most effective means to exploit other fuels.

The relative advantages and disadvantages of using atomic power will thus be varied. It will not everywhere compete in a society well-adjusted to the use of fuels already at hand. Often it will be but one of the alternatives which individuals and groups striving for various objectives may seize upon to achieve their purposes. Many of the people of the world have never used extensively coal, petroleum, natural gas, and hydro-electricity. For those who seek to maintain a way of life based on the self-contained village community, the threat offered by any of these power sources leaves little choice among them. However, for those seeking to industrialize and urbanize, the advantage one fuel offers must be compared with that of the others. Our first concern, then, will be to discover in the most general terms the advantages each offers to those who would use it.

A great deal has been made of the fact that the atom offers so much "free" energy. A point difficult for many people to grasp is that all energy in the form in which man first deals with it is "free." What is significant is the size of the free gift *after* it has been put into the form sought by a consumer. The only costs of energy are those of converting it from the form found in nature to the form in which it is consumed. . . . [H]ourly wages represent costs to an industrial manager; so a reduction in the man-hours means less cost to him. The fact that the time required to perform a task can often be reduced by increasing the energy used provides for managers a compelling incentive to make use of fuels which provide the largest energy surpluses. They are thus able to replace costly human time with the "free gift of nature."

Those who decide whether or not to use a new fuel, then, will consider whether the time saved by using it will reduce costs to them in terms of valued goods, services and social position below those of providing the additional energy which permits that time saving. . . .

The first cost of securing energy is that of changing it from the form found in nature to fuel. Sunlight, wind, and the flowing stream cost nothing in fuel form. To secure all other fuels the expenditure of some time and energy is required. For example, a Japanese farmer produces in the form of rice about twelve and a half times the energy he expends in raising it. This is a very high average for hoe farmers. In comparison, a clipper ship delivered at maximum efficiency about two hundred times the energy consumed by its crew. Contrast this with the surplus energy produced by the coal miner in the United States last year, which was about eighteen thousand times the energy consumed by his body in mining it. Those engaged in mining petroleum in the United States in that year produced almost seventy thousand times the energy produced by their bodies each day. . . .

For comparison we should also know the energy costs of atomic fuel. But while the potential *yield* from uranium has been ascertained, its costs are not known nor is the *per-man-hour surplus* to be gotten from it. . . . Because of the secrecy involved and because those proposing to develop reactors estimate their cost in money, it is not possible at present to compare the energy or man-hour costs of atomic fuel with those of coal or petroleum.

. . . Since the AEC now plans to retain ownership in all of the fuel in use, its monetary costs will be subordinated to military and other political consideration and thus remain unknown.

What evidence there is points to the proposition that atomic fuel costs at least as much money per unit of recoverable energy as does much of the coal and petroleum known to exist in the United States. . . .

. . . The exact calculation of the costs of converting various fuels is a highly complicated scientific and economic procedure, but we *can* state some very general propositions about them, and something of the order of such costs.

During most of man's history he was himself the primary converter of fuel to mechanical energy, so there was no particular need to calculate his cost as a converter nor was it important to consider the cost of the tools he could use since they were not very expensive in terms of time and energy. The picture changed somewhat with the development of the ship, for it required that a large amount of energy be devoted to the production of a good which was not used primarily for human satisfaction but for further production. The energy exerted on its sails in a single voyage was often greater than that which went into the ship's production, and in the early days at least the monetary gains from its use resulted in a quick recovery of its money costs. Limits on the use to which it could be put were probably more significant than costs of the ship. It could be used only on water over which winds regularly blew; so the ship contributed to the building of cities only at sites on such water. Other cities remained dependent for their energy on plants, animals, and men, and were affected by the sailing ship only as competition between cities that used it and those that did not changed the relations between cities and their hinterlands. Within trading cities the use of the ship led to modified patterns of development. Competition for dock space was not often intense since most harbors provided adequate room for new quays to be built as the volume of trade increased. Ship suppliers and dock laborers claimed the immediately adjacent areas for residence and service trades in a ribbon-like pattern paralleling the shore, and the more opulent who could afford the time and energy to carry them there chose the high ground for their residences and accompanying services. This pattern still characterizes many port cities.

The development of coal-burning steam engines involved a quite different order of costs. Steam engines are quite expensive and even from the great surplus energy gained from the mining of coal could return their investment only with considerable use over a fairly long time. Thus, for example, a railroad could pay for itself only within or between areas of rather high population density among people with fairly high productivity-and a culture which permitted them to trade. Thus city dwellers determined where the new fuel and its converters were to be used. They were influenced in their decision as to the location of new industry not only by the values which guided them in the use of the new machines but also by the physical facts which affected the efficiency with which those values could be achieved. The first of those physical facts was the geographic location of coal. Coal which could be used near the mines required less expenditure for transportation; that is particularly important in such operations as the production of steel and iron where large amounts of coke are used both for heat and as a reducing agent. So steel cities and others producing goods that used large amounts of coal in production were located near the coal fields. A second fact was involved in the means of transmitting steam power, which in the early days was very wasteful. So the location of men and machines near the boilers increased their physical efficiency. This concentration of jobs led workers to concentrate their residence within walking distance of the plants, which were in turn located on arteries of cheap freight transportation. The coal-fueled railroad provided a carrier far less costly in terms of human time and energy than any previous overland conveyance; so it came into wide use, but while doing so it imposed its own characteristic use patterns. The fact that coal-burning engines are very heavy in relation to their power, and up to a point more efficient as they are increased in size, encouraged the use of large and heavy trains. Since most of the energy required to move a mass is expended in starting and stopping it, the efficient use of the steam train called for a pattern of infrequent stops. For example, a number of people all getting on and

off the train together can be moved a given distance at far less energy and time cost than could half that number if they embarked and disembarked from a heavy train at frequent intervals along the track. The pattern of the city which could use the steam locomotive efficiently was set by these facts. This pattern was even more accentuated as related to freight trains. Most people get on and off trains without assistance, but freight must be handled. The cost of loading and unloading less than car-load lots is very high, for the railroad must delay the train, supply a crew adequate to rapidly unload at any given station along the line, or set out the cars to be unloaded, again reducing the efficiency with which they can be used. Thus, intervals between freight stations grew longer and short-distance hauling comparatively more expensive. Once it left the rails freight had to be handled by men and teams of horses; so industries concentrated near the widely scattered railroad terminals to reduce their transportation costs. Cities developing out of the use of the railroad show the effects of this pattern.

The use of electricity led to a new modification. Electric power costs more to produce than direct steam power, but electricity is much more easily and cheaply transmitted, divided, combined, and converted into other forms of energy than is steam. Because of the low transmission costs of electric power, concentration lost many of its previous advantages for large power users. Industries not using heavy and bulky materials could escape competition for scarce trackside space with those that did, since power costs were little higher within a few miles from rail terminals than at them. Electrification also made possible a new cheap pattern of passenger transportation. Electromotive power which carries only the motor to propel it can have a very high power-to-weight ratio. This permits rapid acceleration and frequent stops at low cost. Thus passengers can be distributed at regular intervals along the tracks, permitting very wide spread residence without prohibitive costs in time or money.

The spread and differential segregation of industry began to manifest itself under the influence of these facts. In many cases this resulted in political devices designed to protect residence and other property values against industrial invasion; the observable patterns show both economic and political influences at work. Then this pattern of usage came under the influence of a new converter, using still another fuel before it took on a typical form. The petroleum-burning automobile, truck and tractor permit far more flexibility than either steam or electricity, and the growth of many new cities demonstrates how differently space may be used where they are adopted. In contrast with steam and electricity, which put a considerable penalty on the use of small and mobile generators, the great advantage of the internal combustion engine is that it is as efficient in even fractional horsepower motors as in larger ones. The fuel it uses is very low in cost, is more easily transported and more concentrated than is coal, and can more cheaply be refined into other fuels having the special qualities needed for a particular operation. Small internal combustion engines may be used without being attached through expensive transmission lines to central power stations. Thus they are suitable for mobile power and for individual use. It is impossible to show here the many ways this converter has modified the pattern of city growth, but perhaps some of its past effects may be emphasized by discussing briefly what would happen if we were to return in American cities to the use of steam engines or electrical power systems operating in fairly large units—say five thousand horsepower or so, such as are required for atomic power. Within the central city it would quickly become apparent that the even spread of land use in one-story buildings would not be desirable. Having to walk farther from a trolley stop to one shop or office than to another sets up quite a different kind of competition for space than that which prevails when most persons move by automobile. As distance from the central city increased it would again become clear that because of the long walk required to get to such local services as schools and churches, cleaners, barbers, grocers, and drug and hardware stores, the ribbon-like pattern of spacing residences along a road was less efficient than a circular pattern centered upon an interurban station and surrounding shops and offices. In the absence of automobiles and trucks many businesses located as they are in modern cities would be faced with hopeless odds in competing for retail trade. For example, supermarkets, which are built for use with the automobile, would be at great disadvantage in competing with more centrally located stores if everybody rode trolley busses. The old tendency toward sky scrapers found in American cities like New York and to a lesser degree in the cities of Europe where the elevator is less commonly used, would probably reassert itself. Dozens of similar influences could be illustrated. The structure of modern cities, particularly those in the western part of the United States in whose growth the automobile, truck and automotive bus were an original component, shows clearly the significance of petroleum converters. These would suffer most from high cost individual transporta-

tion. There are, however, many cities in the world which could survive without much change were there no automotive transportation supplied by liquid fuel. Since many American cities could also fairly quickly be adapted to trolley, bus, and truck transportation, too much emphasis should not be placed on the difference between the pattern which internal combustion engines have produced within the cities themselves and that required to use atomic power efficiently.

When we come to consider the urban world as a whole, with the connections it must maintain with rural regions, this change would appear to be crucial. Not many areas of the world produce agricultural surpluses greatly in excess of their own needs. Most of those which do have made very extensive use of petroleum-fueled power. Before the use of the steam railroad and the tractor, the great plains of the Americas and Australia supplied very little food for the rest of the world. The steam railroad made it possible to concentrate in distant cities the product of men using horses to increase greatly the area one man could farm and the surplus food he could produce. Most of it went by rail and ship to feed the cities of Europe and America, which grew enormously. The output per man-hour on the farms was still quite small because of the limited power a horse can deliver and the amount of land which is required to feed it. During World War I the tractor came into widespread use. With its use it was possible to increase greatly the area one family could cultivate and harvest. In turn, the truck brought land distant from the rails into economical reach of cheap transportation. The combination—truck, tractor, and railroad—permitted constant rises in food production accompanied by constant reduction in farm dwellers. Distance between farmsteads and farm villages grew, and the wasteful use of small stores and churches, half empty one-room schools and other local services was decreased by abandoning inefficient sites. It is only when we ask what would happen if there were no substitute for liquid fuel for use in internal combustion engines that we realize how dependent is the future of cities upon a means which will economically replace petroleum when the tar sands and shales and the conversion of coal can no longer do so. As we shall see later, atomic power hardly fills these specifications.

In general, it can be presumed that the atom will be first used where it is most immediately advantageous. Much wood, peat, coal, natural gas, and petroleum are now used for space heating. The converter for this purpose is relatively cheap, consisting of a stove or simple furnace. Because its converter costs so much, atomic energy is not competitive in this way now. Much coal and gas are also used in heat processing in such industries as ceramics and cement. So far the difficulty of transferring energy at high temperatures without dangerous radiation makes the use of atomic energy in these areas difficult and expensive. To replace coal in iron smelting atomic energy would probably have first to be converted into electricity to produce hydrogen for use as a reducing agent. The cost of building the generating equipment would be added to that of the fuel itself. Their sum would be much larger than the amount now paid for coke. It is, then, as electricity that atomic power is likely to be importantly competitive in the foreseeable future. . . .

. . . Once atomic power exists in the form of electricity it is, of course, indistinguishable from that derived from other fuels. It will not, therefore, introduce new changes because of the pattern required for its use. The introduction of atomic fuel for use within cities in the immediate future thus involves no revolutionary change.

It is in its use for mobile power, particularly outside the city, that atomic power differs so greatly from conventional fuels. Now a very large part of the power used in the United States is consumed in mobile form. Some of this is provided as electricity delivered by trolley, but for the most part mobile power is automotive. For efficient use this requires a converter no larger than that needed for the particular task involved. The commonly used medium-sized tractor needs about fifty kilowatts and the automobile engine about one hundred to two hundred kilowatts. Compare this with five thousand that even a small atomic reactor will produce. Because of the great weight of the necessary shielding it is obvious that it is not feasible to mount a reactor for use on the highways or in the fields. To be used widely, then, atomic power will have to be distributed by electric transmission lines. Battery-powered tractors and trucks for farm and farm-to-market use might be charged from a power grid, but at the moment, at least, the most efficient batteries weigh about twenty times as much per power unit developed as do diesels, spark-ignited engines, or gas turbines. Field use for battery-powered tractors is thus likely to be limited. It is possible to supply an electric tractor through a trailing cable, but this is clumsy and would impose very great costs for the necessary transmission lines to fields where power might be used on a given piece of land less than fifty hours a year.

But assuming that electricity were to become the power source for agriculture, what would the consequences be? To the high costs for trans-mission of power to the fields would be added costs for electric freight lines to carry the product to the city. To amortize such costs efficiently, agriculture would have to be concentrated and intensified. It is possible to increase greatly agricultural productivity per man-hour and per acre by irrigation and heavy use of fertilizer, both of which can be achieved with the use of electric power. But to get adequate moisture to permit larger crops, farming would become concentrated in well-watered areas such as the great river basins. The semi-arid regions such as western Kansas, the Dakotas, and Oklahoma, bereft of cheap field power and road transportation would probably turn to herding. In fact, there are present trends which lead to this kind of land use without much change in power or transportation costs. The rising productivity of urban industrial workers has been reflected in a demand for beef at prices which sometimes offer greater return from land used for grazing than for its use in cultivated crops to be sold at world prices. A part of the advantage gained by the growing of grass is the great decline in needed man power and machinery. Thus, where once cultivated land is returned to grass there should be an exodus of farm hands. This is taking place in many counties of the United States. There the existing villages have become too numerous to be supported by a declining population. In fact, in many cases it is desirable to wipe out completely any permanent residence with its attendant requirement of roads, schools, medical practitioners, and similar services. Increasing costs for mobile power for cultivation and transportation which would accompany the use of atomic power would accelerate this trend. Thus the cities would receive large increases in population from rural areas. Such surplus man power has, until quite recently, been considered an asset by many urban regions. Previously, conditions in cities were such that urban people did not reproduce themselves, so the maintenance and growth of cities depended upon people raised in the country. Today, a large number of cities are producing more than enough children to maintain their growth. However, it costs a great deal more to raise a child in an urban environment with a high standard of living than in low standard rural places. It also costs a great deal more to create a new job opportunity which will permit its holder to use large amounts of cheap energy than it did to supply a man with a hoe. Thus the enlarging city populations put great strain on the flow of available energy in the form of demand for consumers goods and services for the growing child and for converters with which he can work when mature.

Furthermore, the rising productivity of the farmers which permits them to raise food enough for an increasing number of urban residents, is also secured by increased use of machines and cheap energy. For example, it costs more than fifty thousand dollars to supply one Middle Western farm family with the equipment it needs to produce the expected standard of living for that family. This necessary equipment must be produced in addition to that demanded by urbanites. Thus, unless the existing stock of converters is greatly enlarged or is much more efficiently used than now, the growth of population will lead to declining productivity per manhour. The period when cities will welcome large numbers of people from rural areas would seem to be coming to a close. What is sought from these areas is specific goods, raw materials, and food. While the shift to efficient production of those goods may result in depriving many rural workers of the opportunity to work locally, that is not the end sought, nor is there necessarily any reason to believe that such workers will find a place in the urban system. Thus, the introduction of "more efficient" labor saving farm practices may pose the threat of precipitous decline in the level of living of many rural families. Even if they offer their bodies at no more than the cost of bare survival they cannot successfully compete with converters which can use cheap fuel.

This brings us to the question of the relation between already urbanized areas and those presently undeveloped. In spite of great efforts in the past, using an ideology which encouraged the export of much of the capital it produced, England and the West were not able to supply converters fast enough to increase significantly the productivity per man hour of the undeveloped but densely populated world. In the face of explosive population growth, is it possible that with the use of atomic power the West and the USSR can, and will, supply the means to do so? Perhaps if we summarize the necessary conditions the answer may become a little more apparent.

The initial costs of producing the means to make atomic fuel are very high. To build the first atom bomb, the United States spent over two billion dollars. Not all of these costs had to be duplicated to double the output of atomic fuel, but it is obvious that multiplication has been extremely costly. Since under these conditions no underdeveloped country could hope to supply the means to produce its original stock of fuel, the decision to supply atomic energy or not lies with already urbanized areas.

Second, the investment in fuel itself, as compared with that required by other sources, is very large. The amount of fuel in a reactor must be great enough from the outset to maintain a critical mass, even while some fuel is being reprocessed. Thus, a larger initial outlay for fuel is called for than that which is required by the use of petroleum or coal, which can be supplied as they are used. Moreover, if the undeveloped areas were to attempt to supply their own atomic fuel and reactors they would first have to produce or secure a large number of converters such as trucks, tractors, earthmovers, pumps, and machine tools, which could be used instead to provide them with consumer goods or services more directly. Even if atomic fuels were used, when delivered they would frequently have a higher cost per unit than most of the fuels obtainable directly from existing sources near them.

Perhaps most crucial is not the provision of fuel but the capital outlay for the reactor and generator and the necessary transmission equipment. This is very large even in highly urbanized nations such as the United States. To build it in the wilderness would be fantastically expensive. Also, most of the energy delivered would be in the form of electricity, which while extremely useful in cities can do only a very few of the tasks involved in farming and herding, the present sources of livelihood for most of those in the underdeveloped areas. Even the use of tractors is frequently uneconomical in such areas. The Japanese get as much product per acre using their bodies, without additional investment, as do American rice farmers with tractors, trucks, and electric pumps, which are, to the Japanese farmer, enormously costly equipment. Moreover, the threat of dislocation and unemployment, which "labor-saving" machinery is to the millions of men who have nothing to offer in return for their keep but their own labor, often makes it necessary to impose on them a whole new social order to get their assent to the necessary changes. In the light of these facts it hardly seems likely that atomic power will increase food production to the point that the pressure of growing rural populations can be disregarded. Nor does it appear likely that the regions which have been unable to accumulate the capital to build bus lines, buy trucks, and use small gasoline motors in their work will find the means to build cities for themselves out of the surplus energy supplied by the atom.

The use of the atom as a power source, then, is likely only as an adjunct to existing sources for urban societies which can supply the prerequisites and wish to do so. Investment of capital in present food producing regions must compete with the immediate claims of city dwellers for both consumers and producers goods and with military needs which continually demand more and more energy for the protection of the already urbanized world. Under these conditions there would seem to be little likelihood of any renewed outpouring of capital such as characterized the relation between European states and their empires in the nineteenth century.

Some observers expect that there will be a great relocation of cities at points which presently suffer from a scarcity of energy. The economics and sociology involved in predictions of this kind are certainly not definitive. Perhaps another illustration might serve to indicate some of the considerations involved. Since it is now possible by using atomic power to save the cost of delivering coal there, it is thought by some that a steel city is likely to be built near the Labrador iron mines. The energy saved in this process would be that involved in transporting ore to the present steel centers as is now done, or coal from the nearest coal fields to the iron mines. The steel produced would, however, have to be shipped to the places where it will be used. Existing steel plants are now located near the largest markets for steel, so the saving would actually consist of the difference between the energy involved in shipping the ore from Labrador to present mills and that of shipping finished steel to approximately the same place. To offset this saving in energy, however, a number of additional costs would ensue. In the first place, there would have to be a very large investment in atomic reactors to produce the power which would be needed to secure hydrogen as a reducing agent. Generating equipment adequate to furnish the space heating required by the added population would also have to be built. Large amounts of heat would be required to obtain the very large amounts of water used, in a climate where the streams are frozen for a considerable part of the year. All of the population required over and above that which would otherwise have to be there simply to get the ore out would put in a claim for transportation of the materials required to supply food, clothing, housing, schooling, and recreation. This would presumably be furnished by atom-powered electric rail facilities, which might equally well have been used delivering the ore to existing mills. A little calculation would probably reduce enthusiasm for a northern steel city. In fact, since atomic power can probably be used as effectively in rail transportation as in almost any other way, its use is likely to reduce the advantage of moving populations away from existing centers as much as or more than it is to increase it. In most cases, the local transporta-

tion costs of workers and their families, and of supplying their needs in the form of housing, food, clothing, education, and recreation are as large as or larger than the costs of transporting the fuel they use. Space heating uses up about a third of the energy produced in the United States. For this purpose electricity is comparatively expensive. On the other hand, it is in this use that solar heating offers its greatest promise. Thus, an industry can often save enough on space heating by moving to a temperate climate to more than compensate for the energy used in transporting fuel and raw material to those sites. It does not seem likely that the use of atomic power will reverse the present flow of population to the south and to coastal areas.

There are unquestionably special uses to which atomic power can be put which will permit the use of natural resources now too remote to be used in competition with existing sources. Canada, Australia, and similarly sparsely settled but already urbanized states will undoubtedly make effective use of this power in remote places. Apparently the populations at those places will be kept to a minimum, the product being made available in distant cities rather than fostering local ones; for if that population becomes at all large the costs of transportation of their consumer supplies will equal that of shipping the product to places where men otherwise can live more cheaply. Atomic power was not developed because it is cheap. It was developed because in the form of an explosion it can deliver so much more energy in a given period than any previously known source. Only a few uses need or can use such characteristics. For example, the navy can, by using atomic power, greatly reduce the size of its naval train with attendant costs for its protection. This offers such advantages that all naval ships large enough to use atomic power will probably be built to do so. In most other cases, however, military needs move in another direction.

As we have seen, the use of atomic power involves an extremely costly roundabout process of accumulating converters and fuel. Moreover, the cold war demands a constant stream of energy to produce the rapidly obsolescing power-in-being or the "foreign aid" supplies which it calls for. Expansion of production by using coal and petroleum is much faster than by atomic power. The demand for immediate physical productivity meets head on the demand for expanded atomic refining plants and reactors. The same or more intense need exists beyond the iron curtain. On neither side can any extensive development of atomic power be looked to for immediate salvation.

On the other hand, there is pressure in the West for increased productivity which grows not only from military but from economic necessity. So far, the potential of the West has remained larger than that of Asia and Africa simply because the Western worker could and did produce more. A large part of his high productivity came from the use of power from coal, oil, hydro-electricity and natural gas. The worker became more productive as he was supplied with converters which could make use of those fuels instead of the food and animal products on which his competitors so largely depended. This is one basis for the success of "capitalism." Since wages are to the "capitalist" costs which could not in our culture be continuously reduced by pressure on the worker, increased physical productivity was the most effective way to reduce costs and increase profits. It was found that by using part of the energy delivered to the machine to control some of its operations man power could be greatly reduced. Automation is no more than the most recent step in this process. Feedback was built in the form of a governor into even very early steam engines. It was a basic component of the continuous rolling mill and has been widely used in other industries. Its chief recent progress comes from the introduction of electronic controls that are much more delicate and accurate than any mechanical ones could be—and more flexible. However, automation is like atom power—it is an even more roundabout process than that which preceded it. To carry it out many entire new industries such as electronics and instrumentation had to be built and manned. These call for large amounts of man power and energy, devoted for a comparatively long time to their own creation before they show results in added consumer goods and services. Thus, the demand of one industry for the capital required for automation increases the costs of all competing uses. Atomic power and automation are both in competition with less roundabout methods of production and with the demand for consumers goods now. The growing population which clamors for more housing, schools, roads, hospitals, automobiles, etc., is in a position in the West to make its wishes manifest both through the market and the polling places. Here, it is likely that except when confronted by an overwhelming felt need for national military purposes or national policy, increasing costs of converters will slow up both automation and the development of atomic power. Where "humane" considerations govern, the children and old people now living will not be sacrificed to provide future increased productivity.

In the USSR and its satellites the pressures do not take the same form, but they are there. Workers and peasants have so far successfully been denied any large share of their rising productivity. Two sets of reasons are given them. The first is the ideological proposition, also propagated in capitalist countries, that only in such a way can converters be created to increase productivity per man-hour. The second points to an ever-present threat of military invasion by a hostile world. Just to what extent each is a component cannot presently be determined. But certainly if fear of invasion were lessened it would be more and more difficult to preserve a system which diverts so much energy to the production of prime movers and machine tools and so little to consumers goods. There are many elements of the system of values taught behind the iron curtain which would permit a faction to rise to power supported by those who do not wish to grow old or die before they share the abundance for which they have sacrificed so much. When to this pressure is added that of the peasant who knows and can demonstrate that he will eat better than now if allowed to till the fields by hand, rather than use some of his output to build tractors, the difficulties encountered behind the iron curtain in expanding the production of converters can certainly not be said to be less than those of the West.

Cultural Lag as Theory

William F. Ogburn

It has been frequently noted throughout Part II that specific cultural elements are not independent of a general cultural system that has a high degree of integrity. Murdock observed that each cultural system has a metabolism capable of both the intussusception of new elements and the sloughing off of old elements. In order for integrity to be preserved among the elements of a culture and for its host society to be organized and functional, a major cultural change must invariably be followed by a series of changes in related elements—with the relationship sometimes being obscure to the trained student as well as to the people involved. Ogburn calls this series of changes *adjustment* when it produces a general effect in the direction of societal goals and when the integrity of the society and its culture is promoted.

No dynamic culture can be expected to be comprised of completely congruous elements. When a culture undergoes changes, elements are affected in a variety of ways. Some elements continue to be quite functional (like corn meal, the sledge hammer, the needle, the clay brick, and other items which have changed little or not at all through several centuries of use in our culture). Some elements lose their relevance to the culture (like the spinning wheel). Some elements become symbolic (like the military sword and the academic cap and gown). Some elements are so maladaptive that they threaten to create widespread social disorganization (like the idea that there can be full sovereignty among nations armed with nuclear weapons).

When elements remain in a culture even though they are maladaptive to the emergent cultural system, Ogburn calls them *cultural lags*. By no means is every element that fails to change a cultural lag. Corn meal is just as adaptive to thermostatically controlled electric ovens as it was to hand-stoked mud ones. On the other hand, whether the electoral college adapts as well to twentieth-century democracy as it did to eighteenth-century democracy is doubtful. A definite cultural lag was seen in the French dependence upon the Maginot line (a system of underground defenses against invasion by foot soldiers and artillery) as protection against the mechanized, air-borne German *blitzkrieg* of World War II.

The readings in Part II have been devoted to illustrating the interrelatedness of society, culture, and the person. Selections 5-7 stressed how man binds himself to society by feeling, thinking, behaving, believing, and speaking in cultural ways, and how his feelings, thoughts, beliefs, behaviors, and words would be meaningless—even to himself in most instances—without a cultural basis. Selections 8-11 showed how culture and society are living, changing entities and suggested some of the ways in which society, culture, and the person emerge as dynamic yet stable, changing yet persistent.

I shall begin with a definition. A cultural lag occurs when one of two parts of culture which are correlated changes before or in greater degree than the other part does, thereby causing less adjustment between the two parts than existed previously.

An illustration is the lag in the construction of highways for automobile traffic. The two parts in this illustration are the automobile and the highway. These two parts of culture were in good adjustment in, say, 1910, when the automobile was slow and the highways were narrow country roads with curves and bends over which had been laid a hard surface. The automobile traveled at not a great rate of speed and could take the turns without too much trouble or danger. It was essentially for local transportation. But as time went on, this first part, the automobile, which

is called an independent variable, underwent many changes, particularly the engine, which developed speeds capable of 60, 70, 80 miles an hour, with brakes that could stop the car relatively quickly. But the narrow highways with sharp bends did not change as soon as did the automobile. On these roads the driver must slow up or have accidents. A decade or more later we are building a few broad highways with no sharp curves, which will make the automobile a vehicle for long-distance travel. The old highways, the dependent variable, are not adapted to the new automobiles, so that there is a maladjustment between the highways and the automobile. The adjustment, as measured by speeds, was better

From *Sociology and Social Research,* Vol. 41 (1957), 167-174.

for local travel around 1910 than it is for long-distance travel in these roads at present. The adjustment will be better on the new express highways. Since the adjustment is made by the dependent variable, it is that part of culture which adapts and is called adaptive culture.

The concept of cultural lag, just defined and illustrated, was first published in 1922 in a chapter of a book on social change which carried this title, "The Hypothesis of Cultural Lag." Since I was not sure whether this term would be understood, I asked my colleague Lee McBain, then Dean of the Faculty of Political Science at Columbia University, whether he thought it was an appropriate title. He advised me not to use it, because, he said with a twinkle in his eye, it might be mistaken for a dance step. This was in the 1920's, when new types of dances in the night clubs of the prohibition era were very popular. However, I did use the term, and I note with interest that it now appears in the dictionary and is in use in several countries in different parts of the world and has, in the United States, been found particularly useful by historians.

. . . I do not consider all delays in taking up a new idea as being a lag. For instance, I have been told that Queen Mary of England, who died in 1953, had never used a telephone. Well, she certainly delayed adopting a new invention; however, the failure to adopt a new invention is a delay—not a cultural lag. The theory of the cultural lag is somewhat more complex. It calls for the following steps: (1) the identification of at least two variables; (2) the demonstration that these two variables were in adjustment; (3) the determination by dates that one variable has changed while the other has not changed or one has changed in greater degree than the other; and (4) that when one variable has changed earlier or in greater degree than the other, there is a less satisfactory adjustment than existed before.

I call attention to this series of steps in the formulation of the theory of cultural lag because it has sometimes been commented that the cultural lag is merely a concept. It is surely a much more elaborate concept than that, for instance, of primary group. I think it better to say that, since it is a concept of a relationship, it is a theory. It is therefore more than merely a new term in the language.

. . . In order to prove a theory, one must set it up in a form that can be proved, with places for the relevant data. Thus, for proof, a theory evolves into a hypothesis. But the war came along, and it was only after the war that I took up the verification of this hypothesis by considering the adjustment of law to industrial accidents, which were increasing because of the introduction of whirling machinery with rapidly moving wheels. In this case, the independent variable was technology, the machinery of which, before the factory system, had been simple tools such as those on early farms to which the common law of accidents was very well suited. But after the coming of the factories in the United States around 1870, accidents continued to be dealt with by the old common law and with much maladjustment, for, where workers suffered loss of life or an injury to a limb, there was little compensation and long delay in paying for these disasters to the individual or his family. It was not until around 1910 that employers' liability and workmen's compensation were adopted in this country. So that there was a lag of about 30 or 40 years when the maladjustment could be measured by inadequate provision for several hundred thousand injuries and deaths to which there would have been a better adjustment if we had had laws of employers' liability or workmen's compensation.

I still considered it a hypothesis because we needed more proof than one particular case. I attempted, though, to cite many hypotheses of cultural lag, and in nearly all cases the independent variable proved to be a scientific discovery or mechanical invention. For instance, the invention of the steam engine led to the factory, and only afterwards to the change in the legal rights of women. Most of the illustrations given at this time were initiated by technological changes and scientific discoveries, and the lagging adaptive culture was generally some social organization or ideology. These illustrations led to a characterization, by some, of the theory of cultural lag as a technological interpretation of history. I stated, however, at the time the hypothesis of cultural lag was published that the independent variable could very well be an ideology or a nontechnological variable. For instance, changes in the law of primogeniture, an independent variable, constituted a change in the legal system and not in technology. Changes in the law of primogeniture were accompanied, after a lag, by a change in the economic system related to agriculture and household production. So the fact that the technological change came first was simple observation of a temporal nature, and not inherent in the theory as such. For instance, it is quite probable that religion and not technology was the cause of most social changes in India 2,500 years ago at about the time of Buddha. Also students of stone age techniques have pointed out the essential conservative nature of stone technology, that it was very resistant to change and that probably the causes of changes then were ideological or social. But in our times in the Western world, technology and science are the great prime movers of social change. That this is so is an almost universal observation.

I did attempt to generalize the theory. It is this: A cultural lag is independent of the nature of the initiating part or of the lagging part, provided that they are interconnected. The independent variable may be technological, economic, political, ideological, or anything else. But when the unequal time or degree of change produces a strain on the interconnected parts, or is expressed differently when the correlation is lessened, then it is called a cultural lag. The extent of the generalized applicability of the theory rests on how much interconnection exists among the parts of culture. That many connections exist is obvious. Religion is interrelated with science. Family is correlated with education. Education and industry have connections. Highways are necessary for automobiles. On the other hand, some interrelations are slight or do not exist at all between other parts. . . . To the extent that culture is like a machine with parts that fit, cultural lag is widespread. If, however, cultural parts are no more related than pebbles strewn on the beach, then cultural lags are rare. There must, of course, be change occurring at unequal time intervals. . . .

. . . It has been said that the hypothesis of cultural lag is not a scientific instrument, because, it is claimed, it cannot be scientifically demonstrated. The reason why, critics claim, maladjustments (and presumably adjustments) cannot be objectively determined is that there is a subjective factor which exists because of a value judgment, and value judgments are not subject to measurement.

Values are truly difficult to rank or to measure. We can measure the temperature by a thermometer, but it is said we cannot measure the goodness in morals. This observation does not invalidate the hypothesis of cultural lag. It only concerns the difficulty of determining degrees of maladjustment. But, of course, many maladjustments are quite demonstrable irrespective of the variation in value systems. Maladjustment was an essential factor in Darwin's theory of evolution and he had no difficulty in proving maladjustment. He used death as a test. But there are other tests. Sickness is another. So is insanity. Furthermore, maladjustment may be conceived as a deviation from a social norm. Certainly norms can be described and measured and hence deviations also. Even though maladjustment be difficult to demonstrate, and even though we fail to show it in some cases, it can be proved in many

cases, and the hypothesis of cultural lag is not invalidated.

The application of the theory to modern times suggests a possible appendix to the theory which runs like this: The number of patents, discoveries in applied science, and inventions has been increasing in something like an exponential curve. Most of these are minor; but important ones have been coming very rapidly, as, for instance, the magnifying of light or the putting of vision on tape or the isotopes from nuclear fission. As these discoveries and inventions are adopted, we must adjust to them, we must adapt ourselves to this changing environment, but we do it with a certain amount of lag. So an addendum to the theory of cultural lags is that lags accumulate because of the great rapidity and volume of technological change.

However, there are certain events that tend to cause cultural lags to crumble. One of these, I pointed out in my book *Social Change*, is revolution; and the reports we get from . . . China . . . indicate that there are many lags having to do with the family and rural life and Confucianism that have been toppled over by the revolution. For instance, women are less in bondage since the revolution. Also, feudalism has been overthrown. An observation closer to home is that war causes a decline in the pile of accumulated lags. For instance, the war has taken more women out of the home and put more of them into industry, offices, and stores, where they tend to remain after the war is over. Similarly, the position of Negroes has been changed by war. As Negroes have been differentiated into upper classes, middle classes, professional groups, it becomes obvious that the whites cannot treat these upper-class educated Negroes in the same way that they formerly treated Negro field hands or domestic servants. Yet many Negroes in the twentieth century cities with their middle and upper classes are being treated as they were in villages of the South when they emerged from slavery shortly after the Civil War. The war, however, broke some of the old lags down because it put Negroes into association on the basis of equality with the whites of the armed forces and the Negroes were drawn into the cities of the North. So war tends to break down cultural lags. It may preserve a few too. This is a matter for empirical observation.

Even though war and revolution are breaking down cultural lags, there are many that persist. For instance, one such lag that is clearly demonstrable regards our foreign policy. In the eighteenth century the advice of President Washington to avoid entangling alliances with foreign powers was very appropriate because of our isolation, because of the abundance of our natural resources, and because of slow transportation. But in the twentieth century there have come the airplane, the fast steamboat, the radio, telephone, and also the search for raw materials which are needed for our industries and which are widely but universally distributed over the world. The old foreign policy of isolationism is a maladjustment to the changed technological situation. Isolationism however is diminishing. How long it may persist is a question. . . . [N]onisolationists are the most influential in guiding our foreign policy. Yet for a large part of the twentieth century, isolationism in foreign policy was a lag.

Another illustration which, I think, is clearly demonstrable has to do with the death rate and the birth rate in their relation to the increase in population, particularly in South East Asia. Throughout the great period of written history, the birth rate and the death rate have tended to be the same except for intermittent periods when the death rate fell and the birth rate stayed high. When that occurred, there was, of course, an increase in population. Such is occurring now in India, where the birth rate is probably around 35 per 1,000 and where the death rate is about 25 per 1,000. The result is the increase in the population of India of 4 million per year. Occurring in an agricultural country where the farms have an acreage of about 3 acres, this pressure of population upon the food supply will bring hardships and may result in great human tragedies and will certainly make it very difficult for the standard of living to be raised.

This imbalance of births and deaths produces a maladjustment in other countries also, as for instance in Egypt and probably, if we had the figures, in China. The adjustment could be restored by raising the death rate, which of course we do not wish to do, or by lowering the birth rate, which is resisted by some moral and religious groups and by customs. However, the imbalance in the birth and death rate represents a cultural lag in some densely populated countries.

A long-continuing lag is in the adjustment to cities which were produced in great numbers and in large sizes by the factory and the railroad. In many ways we were better adjusted to rural life. For instance, a greater death rate exists in cities than in the rural districts. There is also more crime in cities. Thus in several respects we have not adjusted well to this urban environment.

I have time to mention only one other lag, the lag in adjusting to the atomic bomb. The atomic bomb brought the possibility of great destruction to cities in a war. The atomic bomb was produced in 2½ years. And yet a decade later we have developed no defense against the atomic bomb, nor have we made an adjustment either in the dispersion of urban populations or in controlling atomic energy or in agreeing to ban the atomic bomb. Possibly many decades may pass before we will adjust to the atomic bomb—a lag of great danger.

. . . Cultural lags are one characteristic of the process of social evolution which occurs in a closely integrated society in periods of rapid change. In the long perspective of history, though, lags are not visible because they have been caught up. They are visible phenomena largely at the present time.

Recent Research

Ralph A. Luebben

The word *culture* can be traced back to the classic or perhaps preclassic Latin verb *colere* or *cultura,* which originally conveyed a meaning of "tending" or "being cultivated." Linking the word to man's history and his way of life was apparently a post-1750 development which appeared first in Germany. Tylor[1] presumably borrowed the word from the German *Kultur* or *Cultur* and introduced it, with its modern meaning, into the English language. In Tylor's early and still often quoted definition, culture is conceptualized as the totality of man's specifically human activity.

"Culture . . . is that complex whole which includes knowledge, belief, art, law, morals, custom, and any other capabilities and habits acquired by man as a member of a society."

Today, when *culture* is used in an academic, technical manner, the word suggests the distinctive way of life followed by an aggregate of people called a society, rather than the more popular connotation of sophistication. Few social scientists would deny that culture, in a technical sense, is one of the key concepts of contemporary social scientific thought; yet the concept has diffused slowly to society in general. The 1929 edition of *Webster's New International Dictionary* first acknowledged the existence of a scientific meaning, but it was not until the 1949 edition that an adequate English definition focused on custom was presented.

The concept of culture has been examined from varying points of view, and definitions emphasizing culture content, social heritage, tradition as a rule or way of life, ideals or values, learning, habit patterning or organization, symbols, and other aspects have all had their vogue. Prior to 1952, theoretical development of the culture concept had been sporadic, and there had been no all-inclusive, synthesizing statement made about it. In that year, however, Kroeber and Kluckhohn published a monograph, *Culture: A Critical Review of Concepts and Definitions*,[2] which took a hard look at culture. The authors exhaustively explored the general history of the word, definitions of the concept, and its nature, components, properties, and relationships. Not all of the most recent trends in the study of culture are new. In fact, some current ideas represent revitalizations of earlier thinking.

The culture concept is constantly being reviewed, reappraised, and refined. Consider, for example, the structuring or organization of culture. Tylor's definition made no reference to the relationship of the various interdependent traits and complexes included in a specific way of life. Culture is organized, men like Opler[3] began to point out, but not so tightly as had been previously believed. This trend of thought prevails today,[4] but comments by various persons on Hoyt's article, "Integration of Culture: A Review of Concepts,"[5] convince the reader that the last word on integration of traits and complexes has not been written.

A trend toward less conceptual rigidity is also observable in culture and personality studies. The individual is no longer viewed as a standardized, cultural by-product of conditioned learning, with emphasis on a single facet like toilet training or breast feeding. Instead, cultural effects are considered in the light of multiple causation, the affective or emotional state of the individual, and the manner in which the learning situations were structured.[4] Earlier theories of basic, modal, or normative personalities, originally derived from research in small nonliterate societies, were useful bases on which to build complementary theories of personality structuring in complex, modern cultures like Russia.[6] A flurry of national character studies, each bearing political and military overtones, appeared in the literature of the early 1950's.

Small, nonliterate cultures have been most often selected for description; however, since the appearance in 1941 of Warner and Lunt's *Yankee City Series*,[7] the culture concept has been increasingly utilized as a tool for examining complex societies or, more often, one facet of such societies. In 1955, for example, almost an entire issue of the *American Anthropologist*[8] was devoted to American culture. The periodical *Human Organization*, once titled *Applied Anthropology*, presents a consistently excellent record of data from modern situations. Recently, attention has also been directed toward subcultures such as European village communities within highly complex cultures[9] and to peasant cultures lying on the periphery of more advanced ones.[10, 11, 12] Applying methods and approaches developed for dealing with nonliterate cultures to more complex cultures creates certain problems, however.[13]

In defining culture as an associated complex of "ideas," Ward[14] first emphasized the importance of covert, concealed, or mental components of culture. Each separate cultural system is built on a set of premises, develops a system of logic, assigns meanings to traits and complexes, and evolves a set of cultural values which are usually defined as the motivating sentiments behind overt or manifest components like personal action, interaction between people, and man-made artifacts. Recently, cultural values have been singled out for intensive study by a number of theorists.[15] Researchers like Faron[16] have attempted to relate values to the social order. Just prior to his death, Clyde Kluckhohn revived interest in universal or fundamental human values.[17] His interest was triggered by data collected by students of various disciplines in The Comparative Study of Value in Five Cultures Project, which involved Zuni and Navaho Indians, Spanish-speaking Americans, Texas homesteaders, and Mormons who resided in the same ecological setting.

Within the last ten years, there have been numerous attempts to examine cultural ecology. Steward,[18] who has written most extensively on the theoretical aspects of human ecology, also uses an ecological approach to explain specific problems of culture change. In a series of articles entitled "Ecology and Anthropology: A Symposium," Baker[19] and other authors explore the latest thinking on culture's relationship to man's biology and to his physical-biotic environment. All men demonstrate certain universal qualities which are rooted partly in biological processes and partly in psychic potentialities. In a very interesting article, Livingston[20] demonstrated what can be done with an ecological approach; he related habitat, malaria, and sickle celling of certain blood types to the distribution and diffusion of Negroid people in west Africa. Studies like these present a very profitable approach to some human problems, particularly those of change.

Documentation of culture changes which were occurring or supposedly had already occurred began in earnest in the middle of the eighteenth century. Throughout the nineteenth century, over-ambitious reconstructions of the supposed evolution of a particular institution, like marriage,[21] or of culture history[22] were published. These long-range universal histories viewed man's progress through a set series of evolutionary stages: from savagery, to barbarism, and finally to civilization. Moreover, during the last four decades of the nineteenth century, man's progress was described as the product of similar psychic processes and experiences shared by all men.

During the first half of the twentieth century, many students of culture repudiated this kind of evolutionary approach. Recently, however, there has been a resurgence of modified evolutionary thinking[23] in which evolutionary changes are no longer considered the end products of psychic responses and processes. Some of the interest in cultural evolution may have been fostered by the Darwin centennial, but independent gains in the popularity and respectability of modified evolutionism mark it as once again a viable force in cultural research.

Twentieth-century scholars have tended to abandon grand schemes of reconstruction and to restrict their attention to changes which take place over a shorter period of time. Invention and discovery, subsequent contact between individuals, and the ultimate diffusion of specific traits and complexes have become the foci of study. After 1940, the diffusion of traits and complexes began to receive less emphasis,[24] and scholars favored descriptions of change. They examined the conditions under which change is most likely to occur or to be restricted, analyzed the acculturation processes which are involved in change, and attempted to determine causality. Spicer's book, *Perspectives in American Indian Culture Change*,[25] is an excellent example of this trend.

When specific nonliterate cultures were first documented by field researchers, notations of change were usually either accidental or only incidental to *status quo* descriptions. Today culture change is often the principal object of field studies; the author,[26] for example, recently had a Social Science Research Training Fellowship for extended field investigation of the changing culture of the Navaho Indians in a Colorado mining community. Observation over an extended period of time yields new insights into the attendant situation, and once the groundwork has been laid, a second, later description reveals changes which have taken place within a culture. For example, in 1936 *We, The Tikopia*,[27] an ethnographic study of a primitive Polynesian society, joined the growing number of descriptive works. Then, using the earlier work as a baseline, *Social Change In Tikopia*[28] compared the same culture more than twenty years later and under pressure of outside influences. However, neither cultural description nor comparisons of a culture at two points in time provide a sound basis for process analysis.

While much can be learned by observing uncontrolled change, experimental situations in which the deliberate introduction of change is possible provide a new kind of opportunity to increase our knowledge of the process of change and to improve our ability to control and predict change. A notable experiment has been carried out by Cornell University and the Peruvian government in the Indian community of Vicos high in the Andes. The various innovations which were successfully introduced there and an appraisal of the whole project are considered in articles by John and Mary Collier in the *Scientific American*,[29] by Fried in the *American Anthropologist*,[30] and by a number of authors in a series appearing in *Human Organization*.[31, 32, 33, 34, 35, 36]

As members of our own culture, in groups like the Peace Corps, begin to engage in programs for modernizing underdeveloped areas of the world, the need for an understanding of the problems inherent in a changing situation and the desirability of using our accumulated knowledge of culture change are apparent. Even given a thorough knowledge of change theory, however, the manipulator of culture has been less successful than the engineer in working out solutions to practical problems. A machine gives a single, built-in response to a situation, but each society presents its members with several acceptable, alternative solutions to problems.

While the student of culture often considers himself a scientist, some doubt exists about the extent to which he uses the scientific method. The scholarly approach to culture has been essentially clinical, because the bulk of cultural data is descriptive and has been collected in most cases with little regard for theory and hypothesis. Moreover, a humanistic attitude toward the data prevailed. Until very recently, most descriptions tended to single out a modal construct, but today there is an increased effort to describe the whole range of both real and ideal cultural patterns, to notice the frequency of occurrence of various elements, and to suggest correlations of items and deviations from the norms. Murdock's *Social Structure*[37] marked the beginning of a new trend in the use of statistics and of the postulate method of scientific inquiry in making cross-cultural comparisons. Factor analysis[38] is another technique among those being explored today as possible tools in the study of culture.

The concept of culture, in a technical sense, is but one approach to the ultimate understanding of man and his behavior. The above remarks concerning recent trends in the study of culture represent a personally selected sample of some aspects of the new cultural frontier. They are not all-inclusive, and the references are merely suggestions for additional reading.

References

1. E. B. Tylor, *Primitive Culture* (New York: G. P. Putnam, 1871).
2. A. L. Kroeber and Clyde Kluckhohn, "Culture: A Critical Review of Concepts and Definitions," *Papers of the Peabody Museum of American Archaeology and Ethnology, Harvard University*, XLVII, No. 1 (Cambridge, Mass.: 1952).
3. M. E. Opler, "Themes as Dynamic Forces in Culture," *American Journal of Sociology*, 51 (1945), 198-206.
4. Fred W. Voget, "Man and Culture: An Essay in Changing Anthropological Interpretation," *American Anthropologist*, 62 (1960), 943-965.
5. Elizabeth E. Hoyt, "Integration of Culture: A Review of Concepts (with comments)," *Cultural Anthropology*, 2 (1961), 407-426.
6. Margaret Mead, "What Makes Soviet Character?" *Natural History*, LX: 7 (1951), 296-303.
7. W. L. Warner and P. S. Lunt, "The Social Life of a Modern Community," *Yankee City Series*, Vol. 1 (New Haven: Yale University Press, 1941).
8. Margaret Lantis (ed.), "The USA as Anthropologists See It," *American Anthropologist*, 57 (1955), 1113-1279.
9. Leonard W. Moss and Stephen C. Cappannari, "Estate and Class in a South Italian Hill Village," *American Anthropologist*, 64 (1962), 287-300.
10. Eric R. Wolf, "Types of Latin American Peasantry: A Preliminary Discussion," *American Anthropologist*, 57 (1955), 452-471.
11. George M. Foster, "The Dyadic Contract: A Model for the Social Structure of a Mexican Peasant Village," *American Anthropologist*, 63 (1961), 1173-1192.
12. Arnold Strickson, "Class and Kinship in Argentina," *Ethnology*, I (1962), 500-515.
13. S. N. Eisenstadt, "Anthropological Studies of Complex Societies (with comments)," *Current Anthropology*, 2 (1961), 201-222.
14. Lester F. Ward, *Pure Sociology* (New York: The Macmillan Co., 1963).
15. David Bidney and A. L. Kroeber (eds.), "The Concept of Value in Modern Anthropology," in *Anthropology Today* (Chicago: University of Chicago Press, 1953), pp. 682-699.
16. Louis C. Faron, "Symbolic Values and the Integration of Society Among the Mapuche of Chile," *American Anthropologist*, 64 (1962), 1151-1164.
17. Florence R. Kluckhohn, *Variations in Value Orientations* (Evanston, Ill.: Row, Peterson & Co., 1961).
18. Julian Steward, *Theory of Culture Change: The Methodology of Multilinear Evolution* (Urbana, Ill.: University of Illinois Press, 1955).
19. Paul T. Baker *et al.*, "Ecology and Anthropology: A Symposium," *American Anthropologist*, 64 (1962), 15-59.
20. Frank Livingston, "Anthropological Implications of Sickle Cell Gene Distribution in West Africa," *American Anthropologist*, 60 (1958), 533-553.
21. J. F. McLennan, *Primitive Marriage* (London: 1865).
22. Lewis H. Morgan, *Ancient Society* (Chicago: Charles H. Kerr & Co., 1877).
23. Marshall D. Sahlins and Elman R. Service, *Evolution and Culture* (Ann Arbor, Mich.: University of Michigan Press, 1960).
24. Munro S. Edmonson, "Neolithic Diffusion Rates," *Current Anthropology*, 2 (1961), 71-102.

25. Edward H. Spicer (ed.), *Perspectives in American Indian Culture Change* (Chicago: University of Chicago Press, 1961).
26. Ralph A. Luebben, "The Navaho Dilemma: A Question of Necessity," *American Indian*, 8:2 (1958), 6-16.
27. Raymond Firth, *We, The Tikopia* (London: American Book Co., 1936).
28. Raymond Firth, *Social Change in Tikopia* (New York: The Macmillan Co., 1959).
29. John and Mary Collier, "An Experiment in Applied Anthropology," *Scientific American*, January 1957, 38-45.
30. Jacob Fried, "Social Organization and Personal Security in a Peruvian Hacienda Indian Community: Vicos," *American Anthropologist*, 64 (1962), 711-780.
31. Jacob Fried, "The Indian and Mestizaje in Peru," *Human Organization*, 20 (1961), 23-26.
32. Allan R. Holmberg, "Participant Intervention in the Field," *Human Organization*, 14:1 (1955), 23-26.
33. Allan R. Holmberg, "The Research and Development Approach to the Study of Change," *Human Organization*, 17 (1958), 12-16.
34. Allan R. Holmberg, "Land Tenure and Planned Social Change," *Human Organization*, 18 (1959), 7-9.
35. Allan R. Holmberg, "Community and Regional Development: The Joint Cornell-Peru Experiment," *Human Organization*, 21 (1962), 107-124.
36. William F. Whyte and Allan R. Holmberg, "From Paternalism to Democracy: The Cornell-Peru Project," *Human Organization*, 15:3 (1956), 15-18.
37. George P. Murdock, *Social Structure* (New York: The Macmillan Co., 1949).
38. Harold E. Driver and Karl F. Schuessler, "Factor Analysis of Ethnographic Data," *American Anthropologist*, 59 (1957), 655-663.

Part III

PERSONALITY AND

INTERPERSONAL RELATIONS

It has become commonplace in the social sciences to state that man is not born human, that he is born with the capacity to attain qualities adjudged to be human, but that he must struggle to achieve those qualities. For example, the newborn infant brings into the world a potential for speech—that is a biological "given"—but the child will never utter an intelligible sound unless he is taught to speak. Similarly, he is born with the capacity to make an amazing variety of noises, but the particular pattern of words he makes—that is, the language he will speak—is determined by the culture into which he is born. It will be demonstrated by Erwin H. Ackerknecht in Selection 12 that a person who moves from one society to another may, if the change occurs early enough in his life, completely learn the ways, including the language, of the new culture. It has even been said that human infants can develop animal-like personalities, and although cases of "wolf-boys" have never been documented to the satisfaction of scientists, they do in principle illustrate man's dependence on learning in order to become human.

The process by which man realizes his potentiality for human nature is referred to as the *socialization of personality*. Perhaps the term should be written "social-ization" to emphasize properly the social nature of the process. The very process of realizing that one is a person distinct from all other persons—the development of self-awareness—is impossible apart from social interaction. One of the pioneers of American social science, George Herbert Mead, described the process by which self-awareness is acquired as "taking the role of the other." That is, the child gradually gains self-consciousness by taking, in his imagination, a position outside himself and looking at himself as though he were some other person. Self-conceptions are thus always based on how an individual imagines that other people evaluate his behavior and his personal qualities; in other words, the self is always a social self.

The socialization of personality may be validly approached from many angles. The physiologically oriented psychologist may focus on the biological or constitutional determinants of personality, such as energy level, temperament, drive, and the like. Freudian psychoanalysts are also concerned with internal stimuli, which they label "instincts" or the "id," and especially with the struggle between the id and what Freudians regard as a repressive society. In the psychoanalytic view, discussed at greater length by Harold Orlansky in

Selection 13, personality emerges as the result of this encounter. The social psychologist—whose approach is closest to that of the sociologist—is interested in the social determinants of perception, of emotion, and especially of the sentiments or attitudes the individual develops toward certain value-laden objects. And these examples by no means exhaust the variety of approaches to personality study.

The sociological focus deals with the way the individual learns to fulfill the requirements of the various social roles he is called upon to play during his lifetime. If the key concept of personality in social psychology is the attitude, in sociology it is the *norm*—the social rule—since norms define the way a person is supposed to behave and help determine his attitudes toward social objects.

How important norms—that is, culture—are to the development of personality is illustrated by the great variety of personality types found not only throughout the world but also within a society. Since physiology, biology, and psychology uphold the idea of the basic similarity and unity of mankind, variations in personality types must be largely determined by cultural and subcultural differences. Although very little systematic work has been done on the change of personality from one historical period to another, it is reasonable to assume that personality types vary through time, that personality changes as culture changes—a topic elaborated upon by Urie Bronfenbrenner in Selection 14.

Thus one *learns* to be a typical American—he is not born one. One learns to be a full-fledged member of any social system, whether it be a small group or a large society, by developing his personality according to its culture—the complex of norms and values which directs the actions of its members. Another way of stating this is that the human infant cannot survive unless he *learns* how to satisfy his needs; he cannot do so automatically or instinctively. He learns how to gratify his needs by adopting the solutions or norms made available to him by those responsible for humanizing him, the members of an ongoing sociocultural system. So dependent is the individual on pre-existing norms to deal with problems posed by his physical and social environment that he is pressed to invent a norm where none is available. So dependent is the individual on the solutions of others that he feels constrained to accept group norms no matter how "fantastic" they may be. It has been experimentally illustrated that group pressures frequently force subjects to accept norms that are contrary to their perceptions. And if conformity to group standards prevails over individual reason even in situations that are clearly perceived by the individual, what must be the power of group norms in situations that lack perceptual precision—those which involve race relations, anti-Semitism, the economic and political organization of society, the cold war, and so on? Selections 17 and 18, by Solomon E. Asch and Robert J. Lifton respectively, are devoted to discussions of the power of groups to enforce conformity to their norms.

There are many ways of analyzing social rules. The most familiar classification in the history of sociology is that made by William Graham Sumner, who distinguished between folkways and mores (see Selection 7). A major distinction between them lies in the degree of punishment invoked against transgressors. Mores are regarded as of central importance to the group, and their violation incurs the group's wrath. Deviation from a folkway arouses a less extreme group response, but conformity to both types of norm is essential to the survival of the group. *Values* are more abstract, general standards for behavior and qualities; it is the function of folkways and mores to define and implement the values of a group. Since values are the most general kind of guide to behavior, they tend to be more universally shared than folkways and mores.

All cultures are complex—witness the intricate kinship structure of the "simplest" society—and it is impossible for an individual to know all the values and norms of any culture. Furthermore, it is not necessary, possible, or even useful for all members of a society to learn all its norms. It would not be efficient, for example, in a society living at the subsistence level to give all the males time out from the task of producing food to enable them to learn the norms governing religious beliefs, ritual, and medicine—frequently the responsibilities of medicine men in primitive society. Norms dealing with the practice of religion are essential to the survival of society, but it would nevertheless be wasteful and detrimental to train all men to be religious practitioners. Thus a few men specialize in learning the norms dealing with the supernatural, and the others concentrate on raising food.

Universally, there is specialization in mastering culture. Each person need not learn all the norms of society, only those norms appropriate for his particular social situation. The term *role* designates the norms governing the behavior of an individual in a given situation. Father, mother, sister, brother, student, and instructor are some familiar roles.

The concept of role was, obviously, borrowed from the theatre. Similarly, it has become customary in the vocabulary of sociology to refer to members of society, as they enact their roles, as actors. But the term *role* has a double referent, society as well as the individual. The individual acts in accordance with the requirements of his role, and it is through role-playing that he comes to know who he is—that is, to acquire his social identity. But the content of each role is predetermined for the individual actor by the social groups of his society. Role-expectations are socially determined.

It is clear that society is not simply actors learning and playing roles; there is often a gap between required and actual behavior. And the term *role* is used to refer to the way an actor does in fact behave, as well as to the way he is supposed to act. Daniel J. Levinson, in Selection 19, suggests one way to resolve this confusion of the term.

One of the major problems in sociology is to identify the source of the assignment of roles. Ralph Linton, an American anthropologist and one of the "discoverers" of the concept, distinguished between *ascribed* and *achieved* roles. Ascribed roles are assigned without reference to individual choice but, rather, according to reference points deemed important in society—age, sex, and kinship relationships, for example. Achieved roles, as the label implies, are those left open to individual choice and competition. In American society, familial roles are ascribed and occupational roles are largely achieved. Yet ascriptive factors are also relevant to occupational achievement in the United States—indeed, in any society which includes the institution of the family—since family background always determines the opportunities for achieving the skills or, in the terminology utilized here, for learning the norms necessary to attain high-ranking occupational roles.

The differences in role-assignments between men and women seem to be largely determined by the biological factor of sex. Women bear children, and for most of human history (since bottle feeding is a relatively recent innovation) only women could feed infants. Thus the female role tended to be primarily associated with child rearing, and men were involved in a wider range of economic and political activities. Yet there has been from time to time in the West, especially among intellectuals, a yearning to free women from the "biological imperatives" of their role. It was a hope and promise of Marxist philosophy to liberate the housewife, who was seen as little more than a domestic slave as the result of her confining existence. The ideology of the early collective settlements of Israel challenged traditional ways of treating women. With the sole exception of childbearing, a hard biological fact, roles were assigned without reference to sex differences. Early results of the continuing struggle between the new ideology and traditional female roles are discussed by Yonina Talmon in Selection 20.

As Linton pointed out in his early discussion of the concept of role, every individual fills more than one role at a time (a fact that contributes to personality diversity within society). This is one reason for the discrepancy between the way a person ought to behave and the way he actually does behave. Violation of one role-requirement often occurs in the course of conformity to another. Modern society is full of conflicting role-demands. For example, military and familial roles seem to be inherently incompatible. One of the factors contributing to the demoralization of the Polish army in the face of the Nazi onslaught in the early days of World War II was that soldiers serving on the frontier were allowed to have their families nearby. The Polish soldiers were prevented from fulfilling the obligations associated with their military role because that role conflicted with their family loyalties. In contrast, the men of certain subcastes of the Nayar of the Malabar Coast of India were required to be on active military duty during most of their youth. In this society, the inherent conflict between loyalty to the state and to the conjugal family was obviated by permitting Nayar soldiers to have several wives and, of course, children with each. The system prevented strong affectional ties from existing between a man and his many wives and children—whose paternity may have been in doubt because Nayar women were also permitted several spouses—and primary loyalty thus went to the military. Some of the mechanisms by which society contains role-conflict are suggested by Samuel A. Stouffer in Selection 21.

The stress placed here on the concepts of norm and role illustrates the sociological approach to the socialization of personality. A person becomes human by internalizing the expectations about behavior of the people with whom he interacts. The term *expectation* is the same as *norm;* the complex of norms associated with a social situation is a *role,* and *personality* consists of the complex of roles the individual is called upon to play.   S. H. A.

Selection 12
_____

White Indians

Erwin H. Ackerknecht

Not so long ago, social scientists believed that the characteristic behavior patterns of an individual could be traced to hereditary factors. Further, since culture reflected the personalities of the members of a society, cultural differences were thought to be the result of biological differences in people. The differences between the culture and behavior of Negroes in Africa and whites in America were, according to this view, the result of genetic differences. With the development of the field of psychology, however, it became apparent that what had been regarded as caused by innate characteristics was in fact the result of learning, and that variations in personality and culture from one society to another could be better accounted for by differences in what was taught in each society than by genetics. Socialization of personality, then, is synonymous with the term *learning*; during socialization, a person learns the behavior that is appropriate for him in varying social situations.

The people who take on the responsibility for teaching a child to realize his potential for learning correct behavior are socializing agents. With few exceptions the first socializing agents are the child's relatives, especially his mother. But anyone who teaches is a socializing agent, and socialization does not end with childhood.

What a person learns from others, then, is what transforms "original nature" into "human nature." It has even been stated that infants can learn how to act like animals. Although the "wolf-boy" cases, as previously mentioned, have never been satisfactorily proven, they are plausible because human qualities do not develop inevitably along with physiological maturation. This fact has been amply illustrated by cases of neglected children, whose mothers gave them only enough attention to keep them alive; when later discovered, these isolated children could not talk, walk, or show other human qualities.

The importance of learning in the development of personality is also illustrated in Ackerknecht's fascinating account of the experiences of American children who were kidnaped and raised by Indians during the eighteenth and nineteenth centuries. These well-documented cases support the stress psychologists place on learning as the key to personality development. It had always been believed that resistance to disease, physical stamina, trances, and so on were hereditary Indian traits. Yet the stolen children came to "look like" Indians, to grow so accustomed to their new way of life that they were no longer comfortable in a white man's house or bed, and to display the immunities to certain illnesses and the vigor and vitality of the red men.

Psychologically, these "white Indians" regarded themselves as Indians. They experienced the same kind of dreams and visions thought to be peculiar to Indians. Despite the fact that during the eighteenth and nineteenth centuries the red men were being persecuted and exterminated by the whites, most of the stolen children turned down opportunities to return to their old homesteads. Those who did go back suffered from the experience of most immigrants; they became "marginal men," torn between their Indian nature and the demands of the culture of the whites. They had learned to be Indians as others learn the cluster of traits referred to by the word *American*. As Ackerknecht concludes, ". . . it is a fact that people, once they are put upon them in their youth, must run along these cultural rails for the rest of their lives."

The abduction and adoption of children of a "civilized" nation by savage neighbors is by no means a rare phenomenon and has at all times made a deep impression on popular imagination. In India children grow up with the fable of "wolf children," most probably a mythological transformation of real events; European children to this day are told stories of children stolen by Gypsies, and American youngsters (and not youngsters alone) for generations have shed tears over the poor Indian captives.

It has hardly ever been noticed that these fascinating happenings, no less than the stories of the wild boy of Aveyron or of Caspar Hauser, constitute a unique biological, psychological, and sociological experiment, spontaneously performed by history, and thus merit not only human sympathy but scientific analysis. In most parts of the world authentic documents concerning these events are, of course, relatively scarce, for in such cases the child of literate people disappears forever among non-literates. Therefore it seemed to us of some interest to collect the evidence for that group of abducted children for whom, on account of certain historical reasons, we have

From *Bulletin of the History of Medicine*, Vol. 15 (1944), 15-35. Reprinted by permission of The Johns Hopkins Press.

relatively numerous and extensive reports: the children of Anglo-Saxon parentage abducted by North American Indians during the 18th and 19th centuries. To be sure, even in this instance the accounts are rare compared to the frequency of the phenomenon. While there is an entire literature on adult captives, and while children must have been abducted by the hundreds, we have been unable to collect more than eight fairly well recorded life histories of such stolen children.

LIFE HISTORIES

Eunice Williams was born in 1696, the sixth of the eleven children of a fanatical New England minister. In 1704, at the age of 7, she was abducted in Deerfield, Mass., by a war party of Canadian Mohawks. Her sick mother and two younger children were killed on this occasion. The Indians used to kill the unfit in such circumstances, not from cruelty, but from necessity. Eunice was rebaptized "Margaret" by French Jesuits and married a young Indian. In 1713 she had already forgotten her English and when interviewed by J. Schuyler she refused to leave the tribe. In the same year she refused to go with her father. It was not until 1740, at the age of 43, that she paid an incidental visit to her old home in the company of her Indian family. She died among the Indians at the age of 90.

Mary Jemison was born the child of Irish parents aboard ship during their journey to North America in 1743. Captured in 1758, at the age of 15, near Franklin township, Adams County, Pa., by a party of Shawnees, she and a little boy were spared while her mother, three brothers and two other children were killed during the flight. She was adopted into a Seneca family and was married in 1760, when she was 17, to a Delaware to whom she bore a son, Thomas, in 1762 (Thomas became a chief and was killed in 1811 by his step-brother, John). After the death of her first husband she married Hiakatoo, a famous Delaware chief and warrior. Free to leave in 1760, and again in 1783, she emphatically refused. With Hiakatoo she had the following children: John (1766-1817), Nancy (1773-1839), Betsy (1776-1839), Polly (1779-1839), Jesse (1784-1812—also killed by John in a drunken brawl). In 1811 Hiakatoo died, at the age of 103, after 50 years of happy married life with Mary. In 1831 Mary and her family were removed to the Buffalo reservation where she died in 1833, having reached the age of 90. She was an outspoken heathen, but shortly before her death she suddenly remembered the injunc-

tions of her dying mother to say the Lord's prayer and asked the missionary, Mrs. Wright, to do so for her. Her son, John, was a medicine man and was suspected of witchcraft; so was Mary herself. One of her grandsons, James Shongo (son of Polly, born in 1821), was an "Indian doctor," practicing among reds and whites alike at Allegheny Reservation. Her grandson, Jacob Jemison (a son of Thomas), who received a liberal education, was a highly respected surgeon in the U.S. Navy. Another son of Thomas, Buffalo Tom, later became the head of the family and a very prosperous man.

Old White Chief, also called "Old White Boy" or "White Boy," could remember neither his name nor his mother tongue nor the place from which he had been stolen. All he knew was that he was about 4 years old when he was abducted. His abduction must have taken place around 1760. In his boyhood he was very strongly attached to his Indian mother and, incited by the mockery of his playmates, he decided to make himself respected in spite of his white skin. He fully succeeded. Not only he himself but all his sons (White Seneca, Seneca White, John Seneca) became famous Seneca chiefs. When his youngest son was elected chief, he feared that the jealousy of the Indians might be aroused by his continuous success and therefore he wanted to leave; but they begged him to stay, so he did. On his deathbed, although now converted to Christianity like many of his fellow tribesmen, he declared: "I have never had any reason to regret my decision." He died around 1833 at Buffalo Reservation as a very old man.

Frances Slocum was born in 1773 as one of the 10 children of a Quaker family. She was captured in 1778 by Delawares near Wyoming, Pa. Her brothers made numerous searching expeditions throughout the Indian country in 1784, 1788, 1793, 1797 and 1798, but it was only in 1837 that she was rediscovered, by chance, near Peru, Indiana. She was then more than 60 years old, a "respectable Indian," the wealthy widow of the Miami chief, She-pon-can-ah, living with two adult daughters and their offspring (her two sons had died). All she remembered was that her father was a Quaker and that her second name was Slocum. Her two aged brothers and a sister identified her by a scar on her finger. She refused to leave her living children and the graves of her Indian relatives. It was particularly the murder of the converted Moravian Indians in 1782 that had set her against the whites and Christianity. In 1845 her relatives obtained from Congress the assurance that she would not be deported like the other Miamis. Her white nephew George, a missionary, came to live with her and to protect her against horse stealing pioneer neighbors. She died in 1849, 76 years of age, and was buried with her Indian family.

Eleanor Lytle, in 1770, at the age of 9, was captured in the Allegheny Valley together with her mother, a 7 year old brother, and an infant who was killed. The abductors, a party of Senecas, were led by "Big White Man." (It is quite possible that "Big White Man" was identical with the above mentioned "Old White Boy." Mrs. John Kinzie, Jr., who later became Eleanor Lytle's daughter-in-law, maintains that the leader of the party was the famous Cornplanter. But how could she have known better than the victim herself?) The chief sent the mother and the brother back, but he adopted her as his sister under the name of "The-ship-under-full-sail." She loved her Indian mother and brother dearly, but was given back to her own white mother by the compassionate Indians in 1783. In later life she became the wife of John Kinzie, the first citizen of Chicago. In 1832 she consulted the famous Dr. Beaumont at Prairie du Chien. Although this case does not properly belong to our group because her stay with the Indians was not a lifetime experience, we have mentioned it on account of the conspicuous role of Eleanor Lytle Kinzie in pioneer history. Eleanor Lytle was of great vigor and strength and still rode on horseback when she was 60 years old. It is perhaps not purely incidental that, returning from the Indians, she had the gift of "second sight."

John Tanner was born around 1780. At the age of 6 he was stolen near the mouth of the Big Miami in Kentucky by a party of Saginaw Chippewas to take the place of an Indian child who had died. The male members of his first foster family treated him badly, but soon he was adopted by a woman chief of the Ottawa, an imposing woman whom he always respected greatly, even though she was ruining herself with alcohol. He became a good hunter, stronger and more resistant even than the average Indian. When still a boy he always had had to provide for a family of 4 to 6. The Ottawas led a life of extreme hardship, being on the verge of starvation every winter; but he felt unable to give up the Indian way of life and to return to the whites. He married twice. His first wife left him

because one of the then numerous "prophets," whom he fought, told her that Tanner had killed her brothers and sisters by sorcery. Therefore he had to bring up his children by himself. When an attempt was made on his life, he discovered that his second wife had betrayed him and he drove her away. In 1819 he renewed his contacts with the whites. In this year he visited his surviving relatives in Ohio and in 1820, some others in Kentucky. But he had no desire to remain with them. He went back to the Great Lakes and chose a position between the two cultures, working first as the employee of a trader, then as a government interpreter at Mackinac, and after 1828 at Sault Ste. Marie where Schoolcraft was the agent. Many visitors to the place mention him; the famous Dr. Daniel Drake met him there in 1842. When Tanner dictated his autobiography he had recovered his three young children and was still fighting for the return of two older daughters. One of his sons wanted to stay with the Indians and he left him there.

Tanner lived for 18 years at Sault Ste. Marie. Around 1830 he married a white girl, but this marriage also soon ended in divorce. We ignore the story of his fourth marriage with a baptized Indian girl which took place in 1837. Tanner suspected that Schoolcraft had been instrumental in his third wife's escape. The deep enmity between the best known "white Indian" and the best known Indian specialist of this period perhaps dates from this time. Schoolcraft contradicts himself in this respect, at one time claiming that the conflict dates from 1831, another time saying that it goes back to 1838, while up to that time (that would be for 10 years) he had thought him "to be a brave man." However that may be, in 1846 Schoolcraft's brother, the trader James L. Schoolcraft, was shot; Tanner was accused of the murder and of several other crimes (even Schoolcraft calls him "half-crazed" at this time), and fled back to the Indians; he seems to have died soon afterwards (in 1847). One of his sons, James, became a Unitarian missionary.

Thomas Armstrong was stolen as a small child during the War of Independence. In 1789 he decided to stay with the Indians. He had forgotten his name, but the Indians told him later on that his father's name was Thomas Armstrong. He married a woman who as a young girl had also been captured and never again learned English. When he was 20, he visited his only surviving white sister, but he returned to the Indians without even revealing his identity to her, realizing the utter futility of such an act. Allen met him in 1820 when he was an interpreter at

Buffalo Creek Reservation. At that time he was in his sixties.

Cynthia Ann Parker, when 9 years old, together with her brother John, 6 years old, were captured by Comanches in the Massacre of Parkers Fort, Limestone County, Texas, in 1836. John became a famous Comanche warrior but, for love of a Mexican girl, later became Mexican. He had a ranch across the Rio Grande and never visited any of his relatives in Texas. At the age of 14, and again at 24, Cynthia refused to return to her family. She married the famous war chief, Peta Nacona. In 1860 one of her daughters and her husband were killed by the whites in the battle of "Pease River." But her young sons escaped and one of them, Quanah, was to become, like his father, a famous Comanche chief. Cynthia was recaptured. She had forgotten everything "white" but her name. She was restored to her relatives but had to be watched closely since she tried to escape. She died in white captivity in 1864 when she was 38 years old, shortly after her baby daughter who had been captured with her.

William Filley was stolen at Jackson, Mich., in 1837 when 5 years old. He lived among the Sioux, Big Crows and Comanches until 1866. He returned to his family—it is not clear whether his return was permanent or temporary—yet in his book he says "we Indians," and "we Comanches." With the Comanches he had risen to the position of a medicine man and second chief. On his return home after 29 years he too was identified by a scar. His mother had died; but his father who, partially deranged after the disappearance of his eldest son, had given up his business and for many years had led a roving life in search of his son, visiting without success Indian tribes in Michigan, Ohio, Canada, fortunately was still alive.

OTHER CAPTIVE CHILDREN

It is true that many of the captive white children, especially those taken during the French and Indian War and the War of Independence, were given back after a short time, before the Indian environment could operate fundamental changes upon them. Nevertheless it seems certain that the number of white children growing up with the Indians and staying with them was quite considerable. In the life histories of our 8 cases we have found mention of several others, and to corroborate our assumption we shall adduce in the following some more facts, collected at random and without any intention of completeness.

In 1789, at the request of the U.S. Government, a great gathering of Indians took place at Tioga Point (now Athens, Pa.). There the Indians had to exhibit all children captured during the past war, and parents came from all over the land to look for their lost offspring (poor Mother Slocum, too, made the strenuous journey, without success). A white woman who had grown up among the Indians and had forgotten her name once came to see Mrs. Slocum to find out whether she might be her daughter. A Wyandot chief of this period was married to such a "white" woman. *Cole,* the father-in-law of the famous Miami chief, Godfroy, was a captured and Indianized white child. Another Miami chief, *Captain Wells,* who was a mature man around 1812, had also been stolen in Kentucky while still a boy, and refused to return to his own race.

Around 1810, in Northern Precinct, Williamson County (Illinois), a certain *John Dunlap* practised as an "Indian Doctor" (the "Indian Doctor" apparently was quite a common figure among the pioneers of this period). He had been raised as a captive by the Indians, and the Indian herb doctor's instruction had constituted his whole academic course. Medicine was only one of the many vocations of *Dr. B. Greenwood* of Springfield. Born in 1810, he was captured at the age of 4; he was ransomed by the government in 1824 and employed as an interpreter. Also a good carpenter, he was a still better businessman and one of the friends of Abraham Lincoln. *James Pratt Plummer,* captured, like Cynthia Ann Parker, in 1836 at the age of 2, and redeemed in 1842 at the age of 8, became a respected citizen in Texas. On the battlefield of Wichita in 1858 the whites recaptured a completely Indianized small white girl whom they baptized "*Lizzie Ross.*" In 1845 a white boy of about 10 years of age was taken from the Indians near Albany; he was first thought to be William Filley. These few facts testifying to the frequent occurrence of abductions could easily be multiplied.

This is not the place to dwell on the emotional side of our problem, the less so since to stress this particular aspect has become an abuse. Yet it should not be overlooked. In a time when thousands of children are again being torn from their parents by a pitiless enemy or the misfortunes of war, the problem has regained painful actuality, and we are more acutely aware of the human tragedies hidden in these short life-stories than were previous generations. Parents and brothers going out year after year to look for their lost ones, never to discover them! Or when they did find them, to find total strangers, unwilling to return, Indians in spite of the scar left from youthful play, of the white skin or the auburn hair! They were not mistreated as their parents feared, yet were victims of another, a greater tragedy, which overshadows all these petty personal fates: the extermination of the red man.

THE RESULTS OF CAPTIVITY

Now the question arises, what were the consequences of captivity on these white children. Ballard, the brother-in-law and biographer of Filley, by no means a very sophisticated man, states bluntly: *"In fact, his long residence among the Indians has made him an Indian."* And indeed the same could have been said of Eunice Williams, Mary Jemison, Old White Chief, Frances Slocum, John Tanner or Cynthia Ann Parker. In spite of their race these whites had become Indianized to such an extent that they may properly be called "White Indians." That these people had become Indianized was first of all made obvious by external traits. *All* but one of our 8 examples—they were all captured between the age of 4 and 9—*forgot their mother tongue;* the only one to retain it, Mary Jemison, was captured at 15. Some of them, like Thomas Armstrong and Old White Chief, forgot even their names. Those who ever spoke English again (Tanner, Filley, Thomas Armstrong, C. A. Parker) had to learn it slowly and painfully from the beginning. Furthermore, all of them acquired that outward impassibility of the Indian which was so often mistaken for dullness or insensibility. Mary Jemison was "grave and serious after the manner of the Indians." Schoolcraft says of Tanner: "He entered on the duties [of an interpreter] faithfully, but with the dignity and reserve of an Indian chief . . . he seldom or never smiled." Whereas the aged brothers and the sister of Frances Slocum at that first meeting after 59 years wept bitterly, she remained externally dispassionate. These whites had so accustomed their bodies to harsh conditions that *most of them could no longer sleep in a "white" house or bed.* This fact is expressly recorded regarding Eunice Williams, Frances Slocum, John Tanner, and William Filley.

Many comments have been made as to the Indians' ability to stand unheard of degrees of starvation, exposure and all kinds of exertions, to survive the most terrible wounds from war or religious torture, very often without secondary infection. Since the time of Catlin and the miserable Timothy Flint, the theory persists that the Indian possesses a special racial immunity towards secondary infection, a special racial insensi-

bility (Flint even alleged that the Indian's nerves did not shrink in amputations) or *special recuperative powers.* Even Max Bartels, a serious student of the problem, attributed these phenomena mainly to the influence of race, and we, ourselves, in dealing with Grinnell's Cheyenne material, have hesitated to dismiss such a theory altogether. But some observations on our "captives," it seems, entitle us to look elsewhere for an explanation. *It is noteworthy that most of our "white Indians" displayed these "Indian" traits of resistance no less than did the Indians themselves.* Tanner, for instance, was able to sustain hunger of an almost incredible degree; he survived a severe fall from a tree. In his forties he passed through the following experience: While traveling in his canoe he was shot by a young Indian. The bullet passed through the right humerus, which of course was broken, and entered the wall of his chest. He saved himself by climbing onto a bare rock in midstream where he lay exposed a whole day long, bleeding continuously. During the night he swam to shore. When picked up by traders the next morning he himself set the bone fragments and then extracted the bullet from his chest, breaking two knives in his muscle before he succeeded with the third knife. When hardly healed, he slipped on the ice and broke his arm again, but he recovered without permanent disablement. Filley survived severe wounds inflicted by a "lion." The bodily vigor of these "white Indians" is generally emphasized (Frances Slocum still rode well when 64). Most of them were also of a remarkable longevity.

Now there is no doubt that heredity had not conferred these recuperative powers upon our subjects. These individuals, unlike many adults who turned Indian from some "affinity," had not even themselves chosen the Indian's life. But they had been submitted to a process of rigorous selection. The Indians having a relatively low reproduction rate sometimes stole children to replace one of their own who had died, and naturally selected children who seemed to them the fittest. When children were adopted out of the mass of war prisoners a selection also took place; those whom they judged unfit for adoption they either killed or sent back. Then these white children were brought up under extremely primitive circumstances and it may reasonably be assumed that many of them died, as did many of the red children who were unfit for the Indian way of life, especially under the trying conditions of the 19th century. It is hardly surprising, therefore, that these whites, if they succeeded at all to reach adulthood, showed the same physical stamina as did the Indians. On the other hand it seems more likely that the resistance of the Indians was the effect of continuous natural selection and nurture rather than that of true racial heredity. A human child of any race whatever, if brought up this way and surviving, would probably show these biological peculiarities.

How far selection also accounts for the strange fact that *most of our white Indians assumed a rather dominating role in Indian life* is difficult to decide. We have little doubt that this factor as well as the stimulus of a certain "inferiority complex" had influence and played a role in individual cases (as, for instance, the life of Old White Chief graphically shows), yet generally speaking we think they were of secondary importance. To us the decisive point seems to be that these children, on account of their being "strange" (different skin, hair), already enjoyed a certain respect and for this reason were usually adopted into the families of chiefs or at least into those of good standing, and that thereby their further success was to a large extent prepared.

The fact that these children became Indians mentally, and, as we have already seen, to a certain extent even physically, appears most clearly in their own mental orientation. They regarded themselves as Indians and, as brought out in our life histories and in other cases, *the overwhelming majority of them never returned to the white community.* It is remarkable that their not returning was in all instances due not to lack of opportunity but to conscious choice. *Most of them expressly refused to return,* some of them only a few years after their capture (Eunice Williams, Mary Jemison, Thomas Armstrong). Cynthia Ann Parker when recaptured even had to be watched to make her escape impossible.

The few who did return seem never to have become real whites again but rather appear to have paid dearly for this step; for indeed they became "marginal men," in profession and mentality living between the two cultures in a state of great unhappiness. The description which Schoolcraft gives of Tanner, although its content is tinged with hatred, brings out this fact rather well:

"He is now a gray-headed, hard featured old man whose feelings are at war with every one on earth, white and red. Every attempt to meliorate his manners and Indian notions, has failed. He has invariably misapprehended them and is more suspicious, revengeful, and bad tempered than any Indian I ever knew."

Nor could Schoolcraft, his enmity notwithstanding, deny that Tanner "excites commiseration by the very isolation of his position."

Our "white Indians," in so far as they ever became articulate, in spite of the most harassing experiences are *unanimous in their praise of the Indian character and of Indian morals.*

"The vices of the Indians she [Mary Jemison] appeared not to aggravate and seemed to take pride in extoling their virtues."

"There are more honest Indians according to their numbers than there are whites."

The "white Indians," although most of them came from very devout Christian families, also adopted the Indian's religion. Of Mary Jemison it is reported that "she was as strong a pagan in her feelings as any Indian." "Her ideas of religion correspond in every respect to those of the great mass of the Senecas. The doctrine taught in the Christian religion she is a stranger to." It was Mary who coined one of the bitterest indictments ever made by an Indian concerning white culture as it presented itself to the Indian:

"The use of ardent spirits among the Indians and the attempts which have been made to civilize and Christianize them has constantly made them worse and worse."

It is true, Mary, on her deathbed, asked for Christian prayers, but this can hardly be called a conversion. It is true, Old White Boy became converted to Christianity—so did other Indians. But it is more significant that even after their "return" to white culture Tanner and Filley continued to believe fervently in the "Great Spirit." Frances Slocum died a heathen despite the presence of her beloved missionary nephew George.

Tanner is the only one to tell us more of the religious experiences of his Indian life. He not only prayed in all difficulties to the Great Spirit —and generally was helped, he not only had his Indian medicine bag and opposed the change of its contents when it was ordered by one of the new prophets (in religious matters he seems to have been something of an Indian conservative), *he also had the typical dream visitations and visions which for such a long time have been thought to be a peculiar "racial" trait of the Indians.* It is interesting that the first one came to him when at twenty he tried to defy an Indian superstition by sleeping in a place where two dead brethren used to appear; they appeared to him too and showed him a spot where he would find a horse. Although very suspicious of those dreams which his Indian mother related to him, he nevertheless describes in detail three visitations of his own guardian spirit who in the time of starvation pointed out to him the location of deer. Tanner also successfully used magic images for hunting. In his last dream, shortly before his return to the whites, his guardian spirit warned him that his wife was about to take part in an attempt against his life—the one mentioned above —and told him that he would never visit him again.

It is extremely regrettable that none of the other captives dared to speak of such experiences to their white interviewers. That they also had them is most likely. But even taken alone, Tanner's case is one more proof that dreams of this kind are by no means "pathological" or "racial." They are "cultural." Some hundred years ago they were as widespread among our forefathers as they still are among the Indians, and since we lack them they were obviously no racial trait with our ancestors. It seems to follow that a child of any race whatever, brought up in a culture where visions are considered normal and necessary, will have visions.

Now, how are we to explain the fact that these whites became so strongly attached to the Indian community which, after all, they had entered against their will? This phenomenon is by no means so self-evident as it may seem at a first glance. Although our heroes generally were well treated in a culture which apparently was unfamiliar with the notion of the hereditary evil of the white race, even here some individuals could certainly be found who clothed their personal envy and animosity or their persecutionary drives in the convenient ideology of race prejudice. The white stranger naturally attracted accusations of sorcery, which were numerous in most Indian cultures anyhow (see Mary Jemison, Tanner). In the period in which our "experiment" took place, Indian society was being shaken by its death crisis. The Indians were morally degraded by alcohol and cheated in trading; they were constantly persecuted and chased from their hunting grounds by the wave of white immigrants. Food became scarce. The white pressure resulted in a terrible increase in intertribal warfare. It seems natural that under such conditions persons who by nature belonged to the stronger, wealthier, more secure and victorious party, should take the easy step of returning to their race. But no, they chose the Indian side with its persecution and misery. Why?

Frances Slocum, when found in 1837, told her brothers: "It is very easy to make an Indian out of a white man, but you cannot make a white man out of an Indian." But this is a contention, not an explanation.

Hunter, whoever he may have been, is one of the few to have given some thought to our problem. He has spoken of the mystic "fascination" of Indian life and has tried to define the elements which are responsible for this fascination as *"love of ease and indolence, unrestrained freedom, supine and indolent life."* Tanner gives as his reason for not returning his passion for hunting, which made every other activity irksome. Filley in his clumsy manner explained his attitude in the following manner:

"I dislike work as I have never been taught to labor, nor brought up to do any kind of business; but I am always willing and ready to help anyone who is sick and suffering. Thus I have been accustomed many years. . . . I do not eat salt with my food, as I see others do at every meal. I can get along without water or other drink. I sleep in my blanket on the floor or carpet, although it makes my friends more trouble."

These men, then, seem to attribute their attachment to the Indians to their dislike of systematic work, to love for roving and hunting (which was magnified to its greatest extent only after and by the contact with the white fur trade), and to their desire for independence—other "racial traits" of the Indians very easily acquired by their white pupils. While it is possible that these factors constitute elements of the answer, they certainly are not the fundamental ones. After all, not only the Indians, but many of the pioneers too, led fairly indolent, roving and independent lives. And when we ponder over the actual life histories of these very three men, as told by themselves, and the story of continuous exacting exertions, starvation, persecution and suppression which they relate, their finding "ease, indolence and unrestrained freedom" in Indian life seems like a bitter joke.

The fundamental element seems to be indicated quite naively by Filley, when he writes:

"Some people here may think me very tenacious in my habits. I am, and well I might be, as I was raised, except the first five years of my life, among the redmen of the mountains. I hold to just the same principles and dispositions as the red men and squaws who raised me."

Indian education, quite independent of the incidental color of their hair, eyes and skin, had cast them into a certain form, had pressed upon them a certain culture pattern; and one cannot throw away, like an old shoe, a firmly acquired culture pattern at a moment arbitrarily chosen. Whether good or bad, it is a fact that people, once they are put upon them in their youth, must run along these cultural rails for the rest of their lives.

In addition the history of our captives brings out other important reasons for their attachment. The "culture pattern" was not a pale abstraction for them; *they were tied to the Indian community by the strongest family ties.* Although there was no common "blood," the families which had adopted them became their own families. The one or the other Indian might scorn them—their family stuck to them in good and bad days, it was always willing to help, to defend, to avenge them. It is remarkable with how deep a love and devotion they all speak of these families: Mary Jemison of her Indian sisters and brothers, Old White Chief and John Tanner, of the *gentle Indian mothers.* Later on, when married, the women of course stuck to their children and their husbands (e.g. Mary Jemison, Frances Slocum, Cynthia Ann Parker were full of praise for their husbands). Of the experience of the men who took Indian wives we hear nothing except for Tanner whose marital misfortunes seem atypical and caused by his own peculiar character, since his marriage to a white woman was a failure too.

From the above described attitude of the "white Indians" toward Indian morals and religion it becomes clear that *they found a kind of unity of thought and action and a kind of social cohesion* which deeply appealed to them, and which they did not find with the whites, especially not with the pioneers. There is no doubt that this fact largely contributed to their staying with the Indians. This Indian characteristic, so naively formulated by Filley—"I am always willing and ready to help anyone. . . . Thus I have been accustomed many years"—was also of great material consequences. Tanner, when 14, argued quite logically that, all his close relatives probably being

dead, there would be nobody among the whites to take care of him in his helplessness. While living with the Indians he would have something to eat as long as any of them would have something to eat. The husband of Eunice Williams answered the messenger of her father, who asked her to return, in these few words which reveal the same reasoning: "She no go. Her father marry twice times. He no have marry, she go."

At a very advanced age, Mrs. Caswell, a former Indian missionary who was by no means uncritical of her flock, wrote the following lines on the problem of our captured children:

"A faithful history of all the captives who have been taken by the various Indian tribes, and adopted and grown up among them, would form a very interesting volume. And if such a record could be placed by the side of Indian wrongs faithfully delineated, it may be doubted, whether the comparison would not be greatly in favor of the Indians so far as humanity is concerned, notwithstanding all that has been said and written of the cruelty of savages."

Unfortunately we have been unable to write this book Mrs. Caswell speaks of and which is truly to be desired. But indeed, even our short article which, apart from some characteristic mental and physiological changes in these children, points out their deep attachment to the Indians gives evidence "in favor of the Indians." It shows that in its downfall and persecution this culture still retained values which could make it worthwhile even for white people to stay within its orbit.

Selection *13*

Destiny in the Nursery

Harold Orlansky

As the Ackerknecht selection illustrated, much of personality consists of behavior patterns learned in a particular culture: white boys and girls brought up as Indians act like Indians. But this fact raises many questions about personality development which have not yet been satisfactorily answered. What are the crucial experiences of childhood? Which teaching methods, for example, resulted in a white boy's developing the courage of the Indian? A child does not become brave simply because bravery is urged upon him. Social science has not yet established the links between what is taught, the methods used, and the personality traits that follow.

One of the most important theories in answer to this problem was advanced by the psychoanalytic school founded by Sigmund Freud. Freudians seek to explain personality largely in terms of the child's psychosexual development—the way the child learns to control his infantile erotic drives. The initial drive, an oral one, is gratified by sucking. After a year or so, the child moves to the next phase, the anal period, in which his primary pleasure comes from activities associated with the anus, such as eliminating, playing with excrement, and so on. The final stage is labeled the genital period because, as the name implies, gratification is directly associated with the genitalia.

In the following selection, Orlansky reviews the Freudian "oral-anal" theory. According to the psychoanalytic school, the way that parents or other socializing agents teach the child to cope with each psychosexual stage determines to a large extent the type of adult personality that develops. If, for example, the child is forced to develop "clean" toilet habits before he is "ready," and if he is severely punished for any "accidents," he will develop what the Freudians regard as negative traits—compulsive cleanliness, frugality, punctuality, and obedience. Freudians also see unfavorable consequences for personality in abrupt, harsh weaning from the breast or (even worse) the bottle. On the other hand, the child who receives gentle, generous treatment during the oral period will grow up with a kindly, optimistic disposition. According to this view, many Americans display anal personality characteristics because they are subjected to similar coercive toilet-training methods.

If the oral-anal theory of child development is accepted, it is possible to generalize about adult societies on the grounds that because methods of handling children tend to be shared in any given society, the adults in that society will tend to be alike. Such reasoning has led psychoanalytically oriented anthropologists to correlate the behavior of the Nazis, Japanese, and Russians with the ways these peoples are taught to channel infantile drives.

Orlansky examines this hypothesis. If social science is to be legitimately called a science, he implies, it must conform to scientific methodology, testing its hypotheses according to scientific procedures. In his own investigations, Orlansky found few studies designed to test the oral-anal theory and many of those he did find were poorly conceived and the data from the better ones were not convincing.

Orlansky challenges other assumptions of Freudian theory, one of which brings to mind the selection by Ackerknecht. Freud and his followers were convinced that the first two or three years of life are the period in which personality is "irrevocably structured" and that adult personality is a "mere projection of the infant's personality." It is true that what a child learns influences his later learning and hence his adult personality, but learning does not end in childhood. Ackerknecht's study of "white Indians" showed that seven of the eight captured children quite completely adopted the Indian way of life; they had been taken between the ages of four and nine. True, the oldest child, fifteen at the time of her capture, retained her knowledge of English and remembered her Christian upbringing, but she nevertheless became an Indian.

Orlansky does not, of course, deny the importance of learning in the early years of life, but he does challenge the view that learning to deal with oral and anal drives is the most crucial learning experience of infancy. The way the child is taught to handle these drives is likely to be consistent with the way he is taught to cope with other problems. As Orlansky points out, if stress is placed on early toilet training and on a strict regimen in eating, stress is likely to be placed on obedience, frugality, and punctuality as well, because these are the values of middle-class American society. Furthermore, Freudians see unfortunate consequences in early toilet training and abrupt weaning no matter what the quality of the relationship between mother and child; a more fruitful hypothesis relates the personality of the child to the mother's attitude toward her child during socialization.

In recent years there has grown up a new theory of human behavior, based principally on certain aspects of psychoanalytic theory. The "oral-anal" view of personality and culture, as it may be called, holds that the infant's early experiences in feeding and toilet training determine his adult character, and that this character, in turn, determines the nature of his culture, since most adults in any culture have received similar training during childhood. On the basis of this theory, an increasing number of pediatricians have been instructing mothers in methods of infant care, and some anthropologists have been conducting investigations of foreign cultures.

The tenor of these investigations may, perhaps, be suggested by an earlier study—Geoffrey Gorer's analysis of Japanese culture. It attributes the "overwhelming brutality and sadism of the Japanese at war," their type of ethics, their famous Tea Ceremony, and their landscape gardening to the early bowel training of Japanese infants. Gorer has also analyzed the "national character" of Andean Indians, Russians, Burmese, and Americans in terms of their mechanisms of infant rearing —how long and how often infants are breast-fed, when toilet training is instituted, and whether or not the infant is swaddled or cradled after birth. Some social scientists, following in his footsteps, seem engaged in the creation of a new science of history in which war, Nazism, Stalinism, free enterprise, and other manifestations of "national character" are explained by such infant disciplines.

Considering the theory's popularity and importance, one must regret that it has so far been subjected to little intensive criticism. My own analysis is here restricted to the effect upon personality of nursing and sphincter disciplines in *infancy*—i.e., the first year or two of life, excluding other aspects of infant experience and the entire world of later childhood. It should also be stressed at the outset that the oral-anal theory in its extreme form (which attributes personality formation to a few mechanical features of infant care) is held only by a small group of writers most of whom are mentioned in this article. (Other students of personality and culture—Harry Stack Sullivan and Erich Fromm, for example—ex-

plain the formation of character in terms of the total social situation in which children are reared; with this approach the writer is in agreement.)

Let us first present the core of the theory in somewhat greater detail, by quoting one of its proponents, Lawrence Frank:

". . . it appears that the infant who has had generous breast feeding and a benevolent weaning will face life with a benign, generous and optimistic attitude or disposition, while the infant who has been denied adequate nursing and mothering, and has been abruptly weaned will feel deprived, suspicious and fearful and bear resentment that may be crystallized into active hostility and aggression.

"Again it appears that the child who has been trained in continence of urine and faeces slowly and without pressure or punishment will yield control over his elimination without anxiety or resentment, learning to release without conflict; but a precocious or harshly coercive training . . . will set up resistance . . . and focus the child's behavior upon acquisitive or compensatory outlets for the denial of possession of his own eliminations."[1]

It will be clear to anyone acquainted with psychoanalysis that this view stems directly from the "oral-anal-genital" characterology initially formulated by Freud and later elaborated by Karl Abraham, Edward Glover, and Ernest Jones. According to this analysis, the infant whose oral eroticism (pleasure in feeding, especially through satisfaction of the sucking function) is gratified by adequate nursing tends to develop an optimistic, confident adult personality; whereas inadequate nursing produces a sadistic or pessimistic adult who remains basically dependent upon others, attempting in all his important relationships, by force or supplication, to obtain again the love of which he was deprived during infancy. The infant whose anal eroticism (pleasure in free bowel movement) is frustrated by early and severe sphincter training will tend in his adult life to exhibit

From *Commentary*, Vol. 5 (1948), 563-569. Copyright 1948 by the American Jewish Committee.
[1] *Psychiatry*, 2 (1939), 22.

exaggerated and compulsive traits of cleanliness, orderliness, obstinacy, frugality, punctuality, etc. Where the infant is permitted to complete his "natural" cycle of growth, he develops beyond the stages of oral and anal eroticism into a normal or "genital" character.

Now psychoanalytic literature affords considerable documentation as to the existence of these three character types among adults—though there is a good deal of ambiguity in definition, especially with the "oral" and "genital" characters. But it offers almost no empirical evidence on the origin of these character-types in infancy; clearly, adult reconstructions of infantile experience derived from the analytic couch do not constitute empirical findings on the *infantile* situation. Melanie Klein and Anna Freud have added something to our direct knowledge of infant psychology, but they have generally been more interested in applying psychoanalytic theory than in testing it. We must turn to the literature of medicine, psychology, and anthropology for scientific data which, though deficient in many ways, can provide at least a partial test.

According to the theory, infants nursed at the breast for a long time and weaned late should be less frustrated than infants weaned early or those bottle-fed on a strict feeding schedule, and early bowel training should be more frustrating than late. Do the objective facts verify these hypotheses?

Two London physicians, B. C. F. and C. H. Rogerson, studied 109 children who had been infants in their clinic seven years previously; those children who had been artificially fed in infancy showed a higher frequency of feeding and sleeping problems, bed-wetting, fear, nervousness, etc., than those who had been breast-fed. This investigation made no effort to equate the groups studied for factors other than method of feeding during infancy. The physical and psychological difficulties found among the artificially fed children can be accepted as accurate for these children, but the inference that artificial feeding was the cause of these difficulties is not warranted; indeed, the authors themselves expressly point this out. (To the social scientist, who almost daily encounters hypotheses of fundamental and universal import "verified" by the investigation of anywhere from ten to a hundred accidentally assembled "cases," there is always something refreshing about a study that makes no final claims.)

Our suggestion that the difficulties of the bottle-fed children in the above study were probably due to factors other than the manner of feeding is supported by another study which comes somewhat closer to the scientific ideal of controlled experiment. At the Stanford University clinic, Drs. Harold Faber and Leonard Sutton compared forty-two babies who had been breast-fed less than six weeks and thereafter fed from bottles, with an equal number of babies who had been breast-fed for an average of forty weeks. In other respects than the type of milk, the diets of both groups were alike; twenty-six members of each group were paired for weight at birth, and all babies received excellent care. It was found that the breast-fed babies gained more weight than the bottle-fed babies during the first quarter-year, but that this relationship was reversed during the rest of the year. The significance of these findings lies in the fact that weight, physical maturation, and bodily health are generally accepted as indices of psychological development in early infancy.

In the light of present data, it does not appear possible to establish the desirability of breast or bottle feeding without consideration of the entire home environment and the psychological condition of the mother. Where nursing conditions are hectic and the mother's health poor, as is frequently the situation in the lower-class home, bottle-feeding is certainly preferable, though the norm for lower-class families in England and America probably entails breast feeding in a greater proportion of cases than among middle-class families. Similarly, a middle-class mother who disliked breast-feeding would be ill-advised to institute it, or the child might pay the psychological penalty for the pediatrician's obstinacy. I have seen no evidence that breast-feeding is inevitably more advantageous to the child's emotional development than artificial feeding.

At least five studies have examined the possibility of a correlation between the duration of breast feeding in infancy and the psychological characteristics of the child or adult. All findings I have read agree that no direct correlation can be observed between the duration of breast feeding and any major aspect of personality; this is the only definitive conclusion that present evidence seems to permit. On the basis of two studies, one might presume that a medial duration of breast feeding is more likely than either brief or prolonged nursing to be associated with "normal" personality development in our society, but this hypothesis is flatly contradicted by another study which found the highest degree of emotional security in adults "who were breast-fed little or not at all and . . . [in] those who were fed at the breast for over a year." Leaving aside questions as to the validity of the personality tests and the methodological procedures employed, it is clear that extreme caution is necessary in making any generalization applying to large populations from the very inadequate samples upon which all of these studies were based.

The widespread opinion in modern pediatric and psychiatric circles is that "self-demand" feeding—in which the infant is nursed whenever it cries—is more likely to produce a confident and unneurotic personality than is scheduled feeding. As O. H. Mowrer and Clyde Kluckhohn have expressed this thesis, "The parent who responds to a clock rather than to the behavior of the child is, from the child's point of view, not responsive at all. . . . An apathetic or an anxious or a hostile individual is likely to result [from scheduled feeding]."[2]

Clearly, such statements must be regarded as mere hypotheses, and there is evident in them a great deal of reading-in of adult emotion into the infant situation. Only a few years ago the "best scientific opinion" favored scheduled feeding to promote healthy personality development in the child. Certainly, even very young infants quickly learn to adjust their sleeping and eating habits to a schedule of regular feeding, and it would seem that this imposed regularity might contribute to a sense of security and confidence just as much as to a feeling of apathy or hostility.

I know of only two studies that have subjected the self-demand hypothesis to empirical test, and the published account of these studies is such a specimen of social science inadequacies that it is worth quoting at some length:

"Miss Trainham . . . reported on a study begun at the Merrill-Palmer school. Two groups of children were chosen, one group on self-regulating feeding regimes, and the other not self-regulated. The parents of both groups were quite similar. . . . One group consisted of ten subjects and the other twelve. . . . The results suggested in a very striking way that the self-regulated children are in all categories of the tests more advanced in their development. . . .

"Dr. Escalona had conducted similar studies . . . and had arrived at opposite results. She, too, had only worked with small groups. One group consisted of babies on self-regulated feeding regimes, and the other group consisted of babies who were on the conventional rigid feeding schedules. The group of babies who were more frustrated [i.e., those fed on time schedules] . . . showed more rapid maturation [read, "were more advanced in their development"—H. O.] by test scores. Until she had heard Miss Trainham's report, she had explained her findings by the theory that the frustrated babies are forced to recognize the environment earlier."[3]

It is easy to manufacture a theory to "explain" a particular empirical finding. To explain *all* the relevant findings is not so easy, and I have no simple solution to offer here.

Means of measuring personality at present available are not very adequate; our knowledge of its genesis is even less adequate. But surely we may ask of the social scientist that minimum of historical and cultural sophistication which would enable him to give thought to the position that the human groups he studies occupy in the *real* social world to which they—and the social scientist—belong (as contrasted to the position the social scientist ascribes to them in the artificial world of his "control" laboratory). The scientist's observations might then at least have the validity of descriptive statements about a designated portion of the real world; ultimately, after enough such statements had been accumulated, a fairly complete description of the real social world might be obtained. To generalize about psychological or social laws on the basis of limited observations of small, unrepresentative groups, can lead only to such predicaments as that of the unfortunate Miss Trainham and Dr. Escalona.

In summary, it must be conceded that social scientists—because of a general lack of historical sophistication, the difficulty of isolating single factors for study, and the difficulty of establishing the validity of the personality measurements employed—have failed to produce a definitive answer to the question of the relation between nursing disciplines and character development. Accepting the sparse experimental findings as tentative markers, however, it appears reasonable to reject the thesis that specific nursing disciplines have a specific and unvarying psychological effect upon the child. Instead, the hypothesis may be proposed that the emotional effect of a particular discipline will vary in accordance with the parental attitudes associated with its administration, the organic constitution of the child, and the entire social situation of which the discipline is a part. Erich Fromm has made a similar formulation: "For an infant who has confidence in the unconditional love of his mother, the sudden interruption of breast-feeding will not have any grave characterological consequences; the infant who experiences a lack of reliability in the mother's love may acquire 'oral' traits even though the feeding process went on without any particular disturbances."[4] In short, personality is to be viewed not as the product of instinctual infantile

---

[2] McV. Hunt, ed., *Personality and the Behavior Disorders*, I, p. 90.
[3] M. J. Senn, ed., *Problems of Early Infancy*, p. 33.
[4] *Escape from Freedom*, p. 293.

erotic drives mechanically channeled by parental disciplines, but rather as the product of a complex interaction of a unique organism undergoing maturation and a unique socio-cultural environment.

The anal erotic, anal sadistic, or compulsive character is the most clearly-drawn picture in Freud's album of characterology. So widespread is the anal character in Western society that Geza Róheim has argued that the entire culture is "based on sublimations or reaction formations of anal trends." However, when one looks for empirical verification of the influence of sphincter training upon personality, the data are not very imposing.

Mabel Huschka, after studying 213 problem children at a New York hospital, concludes that children who were subjected to "coercive" bowel training manifested "undesirable" responses—such as constipation, fear, and rage—more frequently than children who were "adequately" trained; but no attempt is made to correlate these responses with any permanent effects upon personality, and no normal children were used for comparison with the problem children. In a similar study, the same author secured comparable data on the reaction of 215 problem children to the institution of bladder training. G. V. Hamilton, comparing a group of adults who recalled constipation or other anal traits in childhood with a group who did not, found some evidence in favor of Freud's theory of the anal origin of such adult personality traits as stinginess, sadism, masochism, and concern for clothes.

These inadequate studies are all that I have been able to discover in the psychological literature. Ardent believers in psychoanalysis have shown a tendency to regard these and even less substantial data as confirmatory of their hypotheses, but a reading of the original studies does not incline an impartial student to such optimism. Thus one writer, reviewing a series of studies by Margaret Fries, states that the direct influence of bowel training on personality "was proved beyond doubt." Dr. Fries herself, however, had explicitly drawn a contrary inference from her work, stating that "any attempt to correlate age at which habit training was started with later personality traits, without consideration of the mother's personality type, would involve a large factor of error."[5]

In opposition to the orthodox Freudian's emphasis upon rigid bowel training as the cause of the anal character, it is possible to explain all elements of the anal character—obedience, punctuality, cleanliness, hoarding, etc.—*and* early bowel training as well—as traits inculcated in the child by middle-class parents in capitalist society: we recognize this pattern of character traits as being historically associated with the Protestant virtues that were economically so well rewarded during the rise of capitalism. The origin of the "anal" character can be understood as an adjustment of the individual, on the level of personality, to specific economic and social conditions. The contrary contention, advanced by Róheim, that these very economic and social conditions are the results of severe anal training, is historically and logically unsatisfactory: was money invented so that we might hoard it, or clocks so that we might be compulsively punctual? (One is reminded of the dialectic of Voltaire's Dr. Pangloss: the nose was made to hold spectacles; therefore we have spectacles.)

Otto Fenichel, outstanding among psychoanalysts for his recognition of the importance of social conditions in the development of personality, argues persuasively against Róheim's position on just this point. But even Fenichel holds that "anal eroticism produces the desire to collect something," although he adds that "what is collected is determined by reality." To speak of a libidinal "desire to collect something" as existing apart from the demands of a specific cultural situation is, however, to invoke a factor for which no independent evidence can be advanced. The more economical theory would appear to be to explain "anal" traits solely in terms of the cultural situation which gives rise to them.

If the confirmatory evidence is so weak, what are the reasons for the popularity of the oral-anal theory?

The pediatrician cannot change the nature of the child's home environment or the personality of its parents, but he can modify the type of discipline to which it is subjected. As Arnold Gesell and Frances Ilg have remarked, "In America the adoption and duration of breast feeding depends to a surprising degree on more or less fortuitous cultural influences. We know of a pediatrician with a wide metropolitan practice who . . . has induced three-fourths of his maternal clients to adopt breast feeding in preference to bottle feeding. In many other instances this ratio is reversed."[6] One may surmise that acceptance of the oral-anal theory gives some pediatricians a gratifying, if illusory, sense of power.

Again, the liberal psychiatrist, keenly aware of the prevalence of psychological difficulties in our society, may seize upon the oral-anal theory as offering a simple mechanism for the prevention of neurosis and a "safe" program of social reform—

[5] *Psychoanalytic Study of the Child*, 2 (1946), 92.
[6] *Infant and Child in the Culture of Today*, p. 86.

safe in the sense that it does not involve difficult and controversial political action. (And what *efficacious* program of reform is ever personally safe?) Illustrative of this tendency is the Cornelian Corner, a national organization of psychiatrists which energetically propagates the view that "a psychologically healthy race of Americans could be produced by . . . consistently loving care to the pre-conscious child," and that "through the scientific application of correct mothering . . . a new form of mature collectivization could be established." [7]

In anthropology, similarly, the oral-anal theory offers an attractively simple solution to complex cultural problems. In the work of writers like Róheim, Gorer, Weston La Barre, and Erik Erikson, the psychology of infant discipline performs the role of monistic simplification once filled by racial or geographical explanations of culture. Thus we find a long list of cultural phenomena—trade, gardening, the plow, domestication of cattle, money, etc.—explained by one or another of these authors as originating in infantile erotic experience.

The psychological interpreters of culture would profit by reading Leslie White's article on "Culturological *vs.* Psychological Interpretations of Human Behavior." [8] White points out that psychological "explanations" of cultural phenomena—such as that war results from man's "warlike" propensities, mother-in-law avoidance from a "horror of incest," or a taboo on eating pork from an innate "loathing" of pigs—are virtually meaningless, since they do not explain why the phenomena occur in some times and places but not in others. If the psychological factor is "innate" or "universal," it can obviously not account for variable events; an adequate explanation can only be given in cultural or historical terms; indeed, analysis of the cultural situation often shows that presumed psychological "causes" are rather the effects of this very situation—thus it is closer to the truth to say that war produces "warlike" qualities, and that Jews loathe pork because their culture places a taboo upon it, rather than the reverse.

The main strength of the oral-anal theory, however, as has been indicated, derives from its psychoanalytic roots, and before passing ultimate judgment on the theory one must evaluate these roots. It is obviously beyond my province to attempt any criticism of psychoanalytic theory as a whole, but it should be useful to summarize, all too briefly, certain aspects of the psychoanalytic view of infancy upon which the oral-anal theory of personality rests, and to criticize this view in the light of the empirical evidence.

1. The infant is generally regarded as a *miniature adult* who experiences adult emotions of anger, fear, anxiety, and love in response to maternal treatment. "When a child comes into this world, he comes in lonely and he is afraid," one psychoanalyst writes. The psychoanalyst interprets infant experience in terms of what it would mean *to him* if he were an infant. But this view is intensely colored by the cultural bias of the adult and fails to acknowledge the fact that no infant shares this bias—i.e., infants are culturally "neutral." Thus, when Freud states that little children "cannot help conceiving the sexual act as a kind of maltreating or overpowering, that is, it impresses them in a sadistic sense," he may be giving us insight into the Viennese, but not the infantile mind; and when Otto Rank writes of the "trauma of birth" he is anthropomorphizing and not observing the animal-fetal state. Direct observation reveals only that the newborn infant is an immature organism, mainly capable of generalized responses, in which a stable conditioned reflex cannot readily be established; indeed, many child psychologists have abandoned use of the word "emotion" to describe the physical states of this organism during its first three months.

2. What is frustrating to the adult is conceived to be frustrating to the infant, and aggression (direct or disguised) is considered the automatic and invariable consequence of frustration. But both halves of this formula are very questionable. The evidence indicates that what is frustrating to a person is determined by his previous experience, and the infant has not had the adult's experience. Thus, restraint of motion is frustrating to an adult, but it is not necessarily frustrating to an infant who has been strapped into a cradle from birth and has never experienced freedom of motion. Nor is aggression a necessary consequence of infantile frustration, as David M. Levy has observed: "There are any number of frustrations that do not evoke aggressive response in the sense of discharging hostility against a social object or its surrogates. There are, for example, a number of experiments in which animals are frustrated and in which such aggression does not occur. The sucking frustrations in infancy cause finger sucking or sucking other objects . . . rather than increased aggression. There is no proof that the so-called weaning traumas of infancy cause more aggression or even more phantasies of hostility . . . than in other children. The same may be said of all those frustrations that have to do with bowel and bladder control." [9]

---

[7] See *Psychiatric Quarterly*, 20 (1946), 603-609.
[8] *American Sociological Review*, December 1947.
[9] Newcomb and Hartley, eds., *Readings in Social Psychology*, p. 264.

3. Infancy (the first year or two of life) is considered the period in which personality is irrevocably structured; the initial mold into which the infant libido is cast cannot be recast by later experience. This conclusion derives from Freud's biological and instinctual orientation, and one may say it represents a mechanical rather than a dialectical view of personality development. But the personality of the adult cannot legitimately be regarded as a mere projection of the infant's personality. Although the experience of later years often reinforces the character structure laid down in infancy, this is not invariably the case. Thus, Navaho infants receive ideally indulgent and unfrustrating care according to the oral-anal theory, with unlimited breast feeding and no interference with free bowel movements; nevertheless, they grow into anxiety-ridden adults because of the nature of their post-infant experience. As Lois Murphy has written, "a satisfying infancy does not necessarily compensate for economic deprivation in the next ten years, and there is increasing evidence that later gratification may go far toward offsetting the effects of early frustration."

Are we, then, to assert that infant disciplines bear no relation whatsoever to the development of personality? Obviously not. I can do no better here than quote an admirable statement by Gerald Pearson, summarizing his conclusions from a study of personality development in seventy-two children: "There is no question that the physical situations of a child's life bear a definite relation to the formulation of his personality, but the number of associated etiological factors renders it impossible to consider any single situation as causative. This study does indicate, however, the marked importance of parental attitudes. . . . The child forms most of his ideas about the world of humanity from his impressions of his parents, and their attitude to him . . . must affect the formation of his personality to a far greater degree than the length of [labor at] his birth or the duration of his breast feeding. The events of a child's life enhance and crystallize the parental attitude toward him . . . and the child reacts to the parental attitude through its association with the events of his life rather than to the events themselves."[10]

But how are "attitudes" communicated to the infant if not by physical behavior?

Obviously, emotion must be communicated to the child by bodily actions—but this does not mean that some *simple* prescription for parental behavior can automatically create a beneficent atmosphere for child rearing. In the last analysis, the oral-anal theory is an attempt to make things simple, reducing the complex problem of infant care to a few clear "duties" easily defined by pediatricians and easily carried out by parents. But simplification distorts reality. The infant's awareness of those who care for him is surely far more complex than the oral-anal theory would have it.

Some students write of the infant's sensing the mother's attitude to it by a process of "empathy." This concept is dangerously similar to Margarethe Ribble's semi-mystical concept of "mothering," but it may have objective validity when reduced to certain motor indicators by which the infant learns to distinguish emotions which the mother feels as anxiety, anger, or love. After the first six months of life, the infant becomes increasingly sensitive to forms of parental emotional expression —as Margaret Fries has expressed it, he is bathed in "a twenty-four hour emotional atmosphere." And it is by this atmosphere—the entire mother-family-society environment of infancy *and childhood*—that the personality is presumably shaped, rather than by the mechanical disciplines of infancy. Thus, the *consistency* with which a discipline is enforced by the mother may be a more important factor that the nature of the particular discipline itself; for example, the infant may be able to adjust contentedly to a wide range of feeding regimes, but a stable emotional adjustment would be difficult if his regime were repeatedly altered.

From this point of view, the efforts of an organization like the Cornelian Corner to reform American society by having mothers breast-feed their infants are misguided. And similar efforts to produce decisive alterations in German and Japanese society by changing certain techniques of infant discipline would be equally ineffective. A much wider range of childhood experience—not to mention the surrounding adult environment— would have to be changed before any significant change in "national character" or culture could be effected.

No theory of personality formation can be simple and yet fit all the facts. Lest we slip into another oversimplified theory that would explain the genesis of personality solely in terms of the personality of parents or the social environment of the home, it would be well to bear in mind the following genealogy which Thomas Fuller has derived from a well-known journal:

"Roboan begat Abia; that is a bad father begat a bad son; Abia begat Asa; that is a bad father begat a good son; Asa begat Josephat; that is a good father begat a good son; Josephat begat Joam; that is a good father begat a bad son."

---

[10]*American Journal of Orthopsychiatry*, I (1931), 289-290.

Selection *14*

The Changing American Child— A Speculative Analysis

Urie Bronfenbrenner

The specific techniques used to train (i.e., socialize) small children, according to Orlansky, as well as the interaction between parents and children, derive their importance from the fact that it is during the training period that parental ideas about the world and the child are communicated to the child. Two mothers may use the same training techniques but express very different attitudes, and the more important variable in child development is not the actions but the attitudes which accompany them.

It follows that a change in actions and attitudes—in parental style—will result in a change in personality. Bronfenbrenner's and others' research on the changes in child-rearing patterns shows that during the past few decades parents have become more permissive, more affectionate, and more likely to use compelling psychological techniques of discipline—the threat of love-withdrawal, for example. Although social class differences in approach still exist, the gap between classes is closing. Fathers and mothers have become less specialized in their roles and tend to act alike toward their children. There are still some differences in the treatment of boys and girls—girls get more love but also more love-oriented discipline, while boys receive less affection and more physical punishment—but even these differences are disappearing.

Early assessments of the consequences of the new approach to child rearing showed that it has successfully developed "favorable" qualities in children, but Bronfenbrenner's research suggests that there have been losses as well. The new style has had the effect of "undermining capacities for initiative and independence," particularly in boys. But the most striking finding deals with the effects of the obscured distinction between fathers and mothers: equalitarian parents who share responsibility and authority beget adolescents who tend to be "most dependent and least dependable." Consider, with this finding, the fact that much recent social criticism deals with the overconformist, the person who is afraid to entertain norms that may deviate from those of his superiors or of his peers lest social approval be withheld.

Why do styles in child rearing change? Although this question involves many variables, Bronfenbrenner's analysis shows that family and personality are related not only to each other but also to the wider society; there is a continuity between socialization patterns in the family and the kinds of personalities "required" by society. As societies develop and change, new problems appear which are best solved by new personality types.

The personality type characteristic of modern society is the result of vast changes in the social system. Industrialization, urbanization, a highly complex division of labor with specialization of function have made the large bureaucratic organization—as embodied in the business corporation, the large university, the government agency—a major form for organizing social relationships. In these organizations, the problem is to integrate masses of people who perform many different but interdependent tasks. Orlansky pointed out that the host of characteristics associated with an anal personality were the "Protestant virtues" and were important during the rise of capitalism. Can it not be similarly argued that the present-day "democratic" family, by producing the type of person who can get along with others, is providing the type of individual needed in a bureaucratic society?

Bronfenbrenner suggests that changes in socialization patterns are already taking place in response to new problems in American life. The cold-war competition between the United States and the Soviet Union has led Americans to be concerned with excellence and leadership. To compete successfully against this external threat, American families will have to produce children with strong motivations for achievement. A shift away from permissiveness is already discernible. But just as overconformity was the price paid for the bureaucratic personality, so Bronfenbrenner believes that social costs will have to be paid for children with strong achievement drives.

A word of caution should be injected, however. The "findings" Bronfenbrenner presents can only be regarded as tentative; he himself calls his discussion "speculative." That relationships exist between personality, the family, and the wider society is not disputed, but how personality traits are formed and how society's needs are mediated through the family and other socializing agents are largely unknown. Personality types have not even been clearly delineated, and measuring social relationships by methods that only faintly approximate the classical experiment leaves too much to uncontrolled variables.

It is now a matter of scientific record that patterns of child rearing in the United States have changed appreciably over the past twenty-five years. At the same time, the gap between social classes in their goals and methods of child rearing appears to be narrowing, with working-class parents beginning to adopt both the values and techniques of the middle class. Finally, there is dramatic correspondence between these observed shifts in parental values and behavior and the changing character of attitudes and practices advocated in successive editions of such widely read manuals as the Children's Bureau bulletin on *Infant Care* and Dr. Spock's *Baby and Child Care.* Such correspondence should not be taken to mean that the expert has now become the principal instigator and instrument of social change, since the ideas of scientists and professional workers themselves reflect in part the operation of deep-rooted cultural processes. Nevertheless, the fact remains that changes in values and practices advocated by prestigeful professional figures can be substantially accelerated by rapid and widespread dissemination through mass media of communication and public discussion.

Given these facts, it becomes especially important to gauge the effect of the changes that are advocated and adopted. We must ask whether the changes that have occurred in the attitudes and actions of parents over the past twenty-five years have been such as to affect the personality development of their children, so that the boys and girls of today are somewhat different in character structure from those of a decade or more ago. Or, to put the question more succinctly: Has the changing American parent produced a changing American child?

A STRATEGY OF INFERENCE

Do we have any basis for answering this intriguing question? Do we have any evidence of changes in the behavior of children in successive decades analogous to the evidence we have already been able to find for parents?

Unfortunately, the present writer has, to date, been unable to locate enough instances in which comparable methods of behavioral assessment have been employed over an extended period of time with different groups of children of similar ages. Although the absence of such material precludes any direct and unequivocal approach to the question at hand, it is nevertheless possible, through a series of inferences from facts already known, to arrive at some estimate of the effects on children of changing parental attitudes and actions.

From the *Merrill-Palmer Quarterly of Behavior and Development,* Vol. 7 (1961), 73-84.

Specifically, although as yet we have no comparable data on the relation between parental and child behavior for different families at successive points in time, we do have facts on the influence of parental treatment on child behavior at a given point in time; that is, we know that certain variations in parental behavior tend to be accompanied by systematic differences in the personality characteristics of children. If we are willing to assume that these same relationships obtain not only at a given moment but across different points in time, we are in a position to infer the possible effects on children of changing patterns of child rearing over the years. It is this strategy that we propose to follow.

THE CHANGING AMERICAN PARENT

[The major changes in parental behavior over a twenty-five-year period] may be summarized as follows: (a) greater permissiveness toward the child's spontaneous desires; (b) freer expression of affection; (c) increased reliance on indirect "psychological" techniques of discipline (such as reasoning or appeals to guilt) *vs.* direct methods (such as physical punishment, scolding, or threats); (d) in consequence of the above shifts in the direction of what are predominantly middle-class values and techniques, a narrowing of the gap between social classes in their patterns of child rearing.

. . . [A] new study has documented an additional trend. Bronson, Katten, and Livson[1] have compared patterns of paternal and maternal authority and affection in two generations of families from the California Guidance Study. Unfortunately, the time span surveyed in their study overlaps only partially with the twenty-five-year period covered in our own analysis, the first California generation having been raised in the early 1900's and the second in the late 1920's and early 1930's. Accordingly, if we are to consider the California results along with the others cited above, we must make the somewhat risky assumption that a trend discerned in the first three decades of the century has continued in the same direction [until the present].

With this important qualification, an examination of the data cited by Bronson *et al.* points to a shift over the years in the pattern of parental role differentiation within the family. Specifically, in succeeding generations the relative position of the father vis-a-vis the mother is shifting with the former becoming increasingly more affectionate and less authoritarian and the latter becoming relatively more important as the agent of discipline, especially for boys.

"PSYCHOLOGICAL" TECHNIQUES OF DISCIPLINE AND THEIR EFFECTS

In pursuing our analytic strategy, we seek next for evidence of the effects on the behavior of children of the changes in parental treatment noted in our inventory. We may begin by noting that the variables involved in the first three secular trends listed above constitute a complex that has received considerable attention in recent research on parent-child relations.

Within the last three years, two sets of investigators, working independently, have called attention to the greater efficacy of "love-oriented" or "psychological" techniques in bringing about desired behavior in the child. The present writer, noting that such methods are especially favored by middle-class parents, has offered the following analysis of the nature of these techniques and the reasons for their effectiveness.

"Such parents are, in the first place, more likely to overlook offenses, and when they do punish, they are less likely to ridicule or inflict physical pain. Instead, they reason with the youngster, isolate him, appeal to guilt, show disappointment—in short, convey in a variety of ways, on the one hand, the kind of behavior that is expected of the child; on the other, the realization that transgression means the interruption of a mutually valued relationship. . . .

"These findings mean that middle class parents, though in one sense more lenient in their discipline techniques, are using methods that are actually more compelling. Moreover, the compelling power of these practices is probably enhanced by the more permissive treatment accorded to middle class children in the early years of life. The successful use of withdrawal of love as a discipline technique implies the prior existence of a gratifying relationship; the more love present in the first instance, the greater the threat implied in its withdrawal."

It is now a well-established fact that children from middle-class families tend to excel those from lower-class families in many characteristics ordinarily regarded as desirable, such as self-control, achievement, responsibility, leadership, popularity, and adjustment in general. If, as seems plausible, such differences in behavior are attributable at least in part to class-linked variations in parental treatment, the strategy of infer-

---

[1] W. C. Bronson, E. S. Katten, and N. Livson, "Patterns of Authority and Affection in Two Generations, *Journal of Abnormal Psychology*, 58 (1959), 143-152.

ence we have adopted would appear on first blush to lead to a rather optimistic conclusion.

Since, over the years, increasing numbers of parents have been adopting the more effective socialization techniques typically employed by the middle class, does it not follow that successive generations of children should show gains in the development of effective behavior and desirable personality characteristics?

Unfortunately, this welcome conclusion, however logical, is premature, for it fails to take into account all of the available facts.

SEX, SOCIALIZATION, AND SOCIAL CLASS

To begin with, the parental behaviors we have been discussing are differentially distributed not only by socioeconomic status but also by sex. . . . [G]irls are exposed to more affection and less punishment than boys but at the same time are more likely to be subjected to love-oriented discipline of the type which encourages the development of internalized controls. And, consistent with our line of reasoning, girls are found repeatedly to be "more obedient, cooperative, and in general better socialized than boys at comparable age levels." But this is not the whole story.

". . . At the same time, the research results indicate that girls tend to be more anxious, timid, dependent, and sensitive to rejection. If these differences are a function of differential treatment by parents, then it would seem that the more 'efficient' methods of child rearing employed with girls involve some risk of what might be called 'oversocialization.'"[2]

One could argue, of course, that the contrasting behaviors of boys and girls have less to do with differential parental treatment than with genetically based maturational influences. Nevertheless, two independent lines of evidence suggest that socialization techniques do contribute to individual differences, *within the same sex*, precisely in the types of personality characteristics noted above.

In the first place, variations in child behavior and parental treatment strikingly similar to those we have cited for the two sexes are reported in a recent comprehensive study of differences between first- and later-born children. Like girls, first children receive more attention, are more likely to be exposed to psychological discipline, and end up more anxious and dependent, whereas later children, like boys, are more aggressive and self-confident.

A second line of evidence comes from our own current research. We have been concerned with the role of parents in the development of such constructive personality characteristics as responsibility and leadership among adolescent boys and girls. Our findings reveal not only the usual differences in adolescents' and parents' behaviors associated with the sex of the child but also a striking contrast in the relationship between parental and child behaviors for the two sexes.

As we expected, girls were rated by their teachers as more responsible than boys, whereas the latter obtained higher scores on leadership. Expected differences similarly appeared in the realm of parental behavior: Girls received more affection, praise, and companionship; boys were subjected to more physical punishment and achievement demands.

Quite unanticipated, however, at least by us, was the finding that both parental affection and discipline appeared to facilitate effective psychological functioning in boys but to impede the development of such constructive behavior in girls. Closer examination of our data indicated that both extremes of either affection or discipline were deleterious for all children, but that the process of socialization entailed somewhat different risks for the two sexes. Girls were especially susceptible to the detrimental influence of overprotection; boys, to the ill effects of insufficient parental discipline and support. Or, to put it in more colloquial terms: Boys suffered more often from too little taming; girls, from too much.

In an attempt to account for this contrasting pattern of relationships, we proposed the notion of differential optimal levels of affection and authority for the two sexes.

"The qualities of independence, initiative, and self-sufficiency, which are especially valued for boys in our culture, apparently require for their development a somewhat different balance of authority and affection than is found in the 'love-oriented' strategy characteristically applied with girls. While an affectional context is important for the socialization of boys, it must evidently be accompanied by and be compatible with a strong component of parental discipline. Otherwise, the boy finds himself in the same situation as the girl, who, having received greater affection, is more sensitive to its withdrawal, with the result that a little discipline goes a long way and strong authority is constricting rather than constructive."[3]

---

[2] Urie Bronfenbrenner, "Some Familial Antecedents of Responsibility and Leadership in Adolescents," in L. Petrullo and B. M. Bass, eds., *Leadership and Interpersonal Behavior* (New York: Holt, Rinehart, and Winston, Inc., 1961), p. 260.
[3] *Ibid.*

Available data suggest that this process may already be operating for boys from upper middle-class homes. To begin with, differential treatment of the sexes is at a minimum for these families. Contrasting parental attitudes and behaviors toward boys and girls are pronounced only at lower-class levels and decrease as one moves up the socioeconomic scale. Our own results show that it is primarily at lower middle-class levels that boys get more punishment than girls, and the latter receive greater warmth and attention. With an increase in the family's social position, direct discipline drops off, especially for boys, and indulgence and protectiveness decrease for girls. As a result, patterns of parental treatment for the two sexes begin to converge. In like manner, we find that the differential effects of parental behavior on the two sexes are marked only in the lower middle class. It is here that girls are at special risk of being overprotected and boys of not receiving sufficient discipline and support. In the upper middle class the picture changes. Girls are not as readily debilitated by parental affection and power, nor is parental discipline as effective in fostering the development of responsibility and leadership in boys.

All these trends point to the conclusion that the risks experienced by each sex during the process of socialization tend to be somewhat different at different social class levels. Thus the danger of overprotection for girls is especially great in lower-class families, but less in the upper middle class. Analogously, boys are in greater danger of suffering from inadequate discipline and support in the lower middle than in the upper middle class. But the upper middle-class boy, unlike the girl, exchanges one hazard for another. Since at this upper level the more potent psychological techniques of discipline are likely to be employed with both sexes, the boy presumably now too runs the risk of being over-socialized, of losing some of his capacity for independent aggressive accomplishment.

Accordingly, if our line of reasoning is correct, we should expect a changing pattern of sex differences at successive socioeconomic levels. Specifically, aspects of effective psychological functioning favoring girls should be most pronounced in the upper middle class; those favoring boys, in the lower middle class. A recent analysis of some of our data bears out this expectation. Girls excel boys on such variables as responsibility and social acceptance primarily at the higher socioeconomic levels. In contrast, boys surpass girls on such traits as leadership, level of aspiration, and competitiveness almost exclusively in the lower middle class. Indeed, with a rise in family social position, the differences tend to reverse themselves with girls now excelling boys.

The implications for our original line of inquiry are clear. We are suggesting that the love-oriented socialization techniques, which over the past twenty-five years have been employed in increasing degree by American middle-class families, may have negative as well as constructive aspects. While fostering the internalization of adult standards and the development of socialized behavior, they may also have the effect of undermining capacities for initiative and independence, particularly in boys. Males exposed to this "modern" pattern of child rearing might be expected to differ from their counterparts of a quarter century ago in being somewhat more conforming and anxious, less enterprising and self-sufficient, and, in general, possessing more of the virtues and liabilities commonly associated with feminine character structure.

At long last, then, our strategy of inference has led us to a first major conclusion. The term "major" is appropriate since the conclusion takes as its points of departure and return four of the secular trends which served as the impetus for our inquiry. Specifically, through a series of empirical links and theoretical extrapolations, we have arrived at an estimate of the effects on children of the tendency of successive generations of parents to become progressively more permissive, to express affection more freely, to utilize psychological techniques of discipline, and, by moving in these directions, to narrow the gap between the social classes in their patterns of child rearing.

But one other secular trend remains to be considered: What of the changing pattern of parental role differentiation during the first three decades of the century? If our extrapolation is correct, the balance of power within the family has continued to shift, with fathers yielding parental authority to mothers and taking on some of the nurturant and affectional functions traditionally associated with the maternal role. Again we have no direct evidence of the effects of this change on successive generations of children and must look to analogous data on contemporary relationships.

We may begin by considering the contribution of each parent to the socialization processes we have examined thus far. Our data indicate that it is primarily mothers who tend to employ love-oriented techniques of discipline and fathers who rely on more direct methods like physical punishment. The above statement must be qualified, however, by reference to the sex of the child, for it is only in relation to boys that fathers use direct punishment more than mothers. More generally:

". . . the results reveal a tendency for each parent to be somewhat more active, firm, and demanding with a child of the same sex, more lenient and indulgent with a child of the opposite sex. The reversal is most complete with respect to discipline, with fathers being stricter with boys, mothers with girls. In the spheres of affection and overprotectiveness, there is no actual shift in preference, but the tendency to be especially warm and solicitous with girls is much more pronounced among fathers than among mothers. In fact, generally speaking, it is the father who is especially likely to treat children of the two sexes differently."[4]

Consistent with this pattern of results, it is primarily the behavior of fathers that accounts for the differential effects of parental behavior on the two sexes and for the individual differences within each sex. In other words, it is paternal authority and affection that tend especially to be salutary for sons but detrimental for daughters.

But as might be anticipated from what we already know, these trends are pronounced only in the lower middle class; with a rise in the family's social status, both parents tend to have similar effects on their children, both within and across sexes. Such a trend is entirely to be expected since parental role differentiation tends to decrease markedly as one ascends the socioeconomic ladder. It is almost exclusively in lower middle-class homes that fathers are stricter with boys, and mothers with girls. To the extent that direct discipline is employed in upper middle-class families, it tends to be exercised by both parents equally. Here again we see a parallelism between shifts in parental behavior across time and social class in the direction of forms (in this instance of family structure) favored by the upper middle-class group.

What kinds of children, then, can we expect to develop in families in which the father plays a predominantly affectionate role, and a relatively low level of discipline is exercised equally by both parents? A tentative answer to this question is supplied by a preliminary analysis of our data in which the relation between parental role structure and adolescent behavior was examined with controls for the family's social position. The results of this analysis are summarized as follows:

". . . Both responsibility and leadership are fostered by the relatively greater salience of the parent of the same sex. . . . Boys tend to be more responsible when the father rather than the mother is the principal disciplinarian; girls are more dependable when the mother is the major authority figure. . . . In short, boys thrive in a patriarchal context, girls in a matriarchal. . . . The most dependent and least dependable adolescents describe family arrangements that are neither patriarchal nor matriarchal, but equalitarian. To state the issue in more provocative form, our data suggest that the democratic, family, which for so many years has been held up and aspired to as a model by professionals and enlightened laymen, tends to produce young people who 'do not take initiative,' 'look to others for direction and decision,' and 'cannot be counted on to fulfill obligations.' "[5]

In the wake of so sweeping a conclusion, it is important to call attention to the tentative, if not tenuous, character of our findings. The results were based on a single study employing crude questionnaire methods and rating scales. Also, our interpretation is limited by the somewhat attenuated character of most of the families classified as patriarchal or matriarchal in our sample. Extreme concentrations of power in one or the other parent were comparatively rare. Had they been more frequent, we suspect the data would have shown that such extreme asymmetrical patterns of authority are detrimental rather than salutary for effective psychological development, perhaps even more disorganizing than equalitarian forms.

Nevertheless, our findings do receive some peripheral support in the work of others. A number of investigations, for example, point to the special importance of the father in the socialization of boys. Further corroborative evidence appears in studies of the effects of paternal absence. The absence of the father apparently not only

---

[4] *Ibid.*, p. 240.
[5] *Ibid.*, p. 267.

affects the behavior of the child directly but also influences the mother in the direction of greater overprotectiveness. The effect of both these tendencies is especially critical for male children; boys from father-absent homes tend to be markedly more submissive and dependent. Studies dealing explicitly with the influence of parental role structure in intact families are few and far between.

Papanek, in an unpublished doctoral dissertation, reports greater sex role differentiation among children from homes in which the parental roles were differentiated.[6] And in a carefully controlled study, Kohn and Clausen find that "schizophrenic patients more frequently than normal persons . . . report that their mothers played a very strong authority role and their fathers a very weak authority role."[7]

Finally, what might best be called complementary evidence for our inferences regarding trends in family structure and their effects comes from the work of Miller and Swanson[8] and their associates on the differing patterns of behavior exhibited by families from *bureaucratic* and *entrepreneurial* work settings. These investigators argue that the bureaucratic-entrepreneurial dichotomy represents a new cleavage in American social structure that cuts across and overrides social class influences and carries with it its own characteristic patterns of family structure and socialization. Thus one investigation contrasts the exercise of power in families of husbands employed in two kinds of job situations: (a) those working in large organizations with three or more levels of supervision; and (b) those self-employed or working in small organizations with few levels of supervision. With appropriate controls for social class, equalitarian families were found more frequently in the bureaucratic group; patriarchal and, to a lesser extent, matriarchal, in the entrepreneurial setting.

Miller and Swanson[9] show that parents from these same two groups tend to favor rather different means and ends of socialization, with entrepreneurial families putting considerably more emphasis on the use of psychological techniques of discipline. These differences appear at both upper and lower middle-class levels but are less pronounced in higher socioeconomic strata. It is Miller and Swanson's belief, however, that the trend is toward the bureaucratic way of life, with its less structured patterns of family organization and child rearing. The evidence we have cited on secular changes in family structure and the inferences we have drawn regarding their possible effects on personality development are on the whole consistent with their views.

If Miller and Swanson are correct in the prediction that America is moving toward a bureaucratic society that emphasizes, to put it colloquially, "getting along" rather than "getting ahead," then presumably we can look forward to ever increasing numbers of equalitarian families who, in turn, will produce successive generations of ever more adaptable but unaggressive "organization men." But recent signs do not all point in this direction. In our review of secular trends in child-rearing practices, we detected in the data from the more recent studies a slowing up in the headlong rush toward greater permissiveness and toward reliance on indirect methods of discipline. We pointed out also that if the most recent editions of well-thumbed guidebooks on child care are as reliable harbingers of the future as they have been in the past, we can anticipate something of a return to the more explicit techniques of an earlier era.

Perhaps the most important forces acting to redirect both the aims and methods of child rearing in America emanate from behind the Iron Curtain. With the firing of the first sputnik, achievement began to replace adjustment as the highest goal of the American way of life. We have become concerned, perhaps even obsessed, with "education for excellence" and the maximal utilization of our intellectual resources. Already, ability grouping and the guidance counselor who is its prophet have moved down from the junior high to the elementary school, and parents can be counted on to do their part in preparing their youngsters for survival in the new competitive world of applications and achievement tests.

But if a new trend in parental behavior is to develop, it must do so in the context of changes already under way. And if the focus of parental authority is shifting from husband to wife, then perhaps we should anticipate that pressures for achievement will be imposed primarily by mothers rather than fathers. Moreover, the mother's continuing strong emotional investment in the child should provide her with a powerful lever for evoking desired performance. It is noteworthy in this connection that recent studies of the familial

[6] M. Papanek, "Authority and Interpersonal Relations in the Family," unpublished doctoral dissertation, Radcliffe College, 1957.

[7] M. L. Kohn and J. A. Clausen, "Parental Authority Behavior and Schizophrenia," *American Journal of Orthopsychiatry*, 26 (1956), 309.

[8] D. R. Miller and G. E. Swanson, *The Changing American Parent* (New York: John Wiley & Sons, Inc., 1958).

[9] *Ibid.*

origins of need-achievement point to the matri-archy as the optimal context for development of the motive to excel.

The prospect of a society in which socializa-tion techniques are directed toward maximizing achievement drive is not altogether a pleasant one. As a number of investigators have shown, high achievement motivation appears to flourish in a family atmosphere of "cold democracy" in which initial high levels of maternal involvement are followed by pressures for independence and accomplishment. Nor does the product of this process give ground for reassurance. True, chil-dren from achievement-oriented homes excel in planning ability and performance, but they are also more aggressive, tense, domineering, and cruel. It would appear that education for excel-lence, if pursued single-mindedly, may entail some sobering social costs.

But by now we are in danger of having stretched our chain of inference beyond the strength of its weakest link. Our speculative analysis has become far more speculative than

analytic and to pursue it further would bring us past the bounds of science into the realms of science fiction. In concluding our discussion, we would re-emphasize that speculations should, by their very nature, be held suspect. It is for good reason that, like "damn Yankees," they too carry their almost inseparable sobriquets: Speculations are either *idle* or *wild*. Given the scientific and social importance of the issues we have raised, we would dismiss the first of these labels out of hand, but the second cannot be disposed of so easily. Like the impetuous child, the wild specula-tion responds best to the sobering influence of friendly but firm discipline, in this instance from the hand of the behavioral scientist.

As we look ahead to the next twenty-five years of human socialization, let us hope that the opti-mal levels of involvement and discipline can be achieved not only by the parent who is unavoid-ably engaged in the process but also by the scientist who attempts to understand its working and who, also unavoidably, contributes to shaping its course.

Selection 15

Social Norms

W. J. H. Sprott

Socialization may be viewed as the process of learning rules about proper and improper behavior in various social situations. The rules or standards of behavior —what Sumner called folkways and mores—shared by members of a society are called *social norms*. The *normative order* consists of all the norms of a group or a society. We have already seen how important these norms are to the develop-ment of personality. Learning and acting in accordance with the norms of society is the core of personality and is much more important than racial inheritance, as Ackerknecht's study of "white Indians" demonstrated. As social norms change, so do personality types within the society.

Norms are as indispensable for a society as a whole as for personality, however. As Sprott demonstrates in the following selection, orderly social inter-action could not long continue without mutually accepted standards, or what he also calls *systems of morality*, for humans cannot perform instinctively the actions necessary for their own and their group's survival. Certain norms, such as the need to control the aggressive tendencies of group members, are conditions for the survival of the group. The content of the norms that control hostility, as well as of those that deal with other needs, may be changed, but unless members of the social system agree on a specific alternative, peaceful relationships are impossible. Norms also produce predictability in the human environment. As Sprott puts it, the significance of shared norms can be seen in the sentence, "You never know what he will do next." A man knows that his next-door neighbor will smile and offer to drive him to work in the morning rather than swear and run him down, because both men share "common rules of politeness"— i.e., norms. Groups cannot exist, then, without norms.

Of special importance is Sprott's discussion of the origin of norms. He challenges the notion that the source of norms is outside the group and that social rules thus have a coercive quality. Norms may seem to have such an exterior quality, especially to an individual who joins a group that has had a long history. But, Sprott contends, "The having of standards springs out of social intercourse; it is not imposed from outside upon it." Norms are the product of a group's history and originate in the group's efforts to deal with its problems. However, not all group-evolved norms deal effectively with problems; indeed, some norms contravene the interests of the group.

Yet it is never enough to know just the norms of a society in order to predict how its members will behave. Kinsey, for instance, would not have learned much about the sex lives of Americans by investigating only sexual norms. For one thing, there is often a difference between what ought to be and what is. For another, social relationships are always dynamic—rules change, not all people are capable of meeting the requirements of the norms, some norms are in conflict with others, and many norms are evaded. An understanding of society thus requires knowledge of actual social relationships in addition to that of social norms.

While not subscribing to Freud's account of the nature of groups, as expounded in his *Group Psychology*, we must accept his view that in all groups there is a moral element, there are standards or 'norms' of conduct incumbent upon its members to obey. We must, too, accept Deutsch's insistence on the fact that groups, in our sense, have purposes which are collectively pursued. Such purposes may be the furtherance of some interest, the solution of a task, even quite a small one, or the purpose of sheer survival. What these standards will be will vary from group to group, partly in terms of their past histories and vicissitudes, partly in terms of the particular task to be done, partly in terms of the dangers, if any, that threaten them from within or from without.

Thus we must think of groups as dynamic entities, and not as mere collections of people, haphazardly thrown together. Of course the urgency of their collective purposiveness will vary from situation to situation. The purposive unity of a village or a town may lie dormant for a considerable time, and it may affect individual villagers and citizens to different degrees, but it may be aroused in time of danger or when something that affects the unit as a whole presents itself. The threat of destruction from the air may lead to collective action, or to collective inaction if it is thought that nothing of a useful nature can be accomplished. The hopes of a drainage scheme or the death of the Rector may lead to collective action or shared distress. But whether the members of a group are overtly engaged in the pursuit of a goal or not, their interactions are in part controlled by the standards of conduct current in the group.

The presence of standards of conduct is an essential feature of group interaction because interaction itself cannot go on for long without mutually accepted standards emerging. Standards have two aspects; they are frameworks of expectation and measures of esteem. If two people interact with one another, each has to adapt his response to the other, and so to behave that he can foresee what the other will do in response to his response. Theoretically speaking, each of the interacting parties has an enormous repertoire of behaviour, any one item of which he can call on at will, but it is obvious that if the behaviour of each were entirely random, they could never

From *Human Groups* by W. J. H. Sprott (Harmondsworth, Middlesex, England: Penguin Books, Ltd., 1958), pp. 11–15.

be said to *inter*-act. So it comes about that A will behave in a certain way calculated to elicit a certain range of responses from B, and B will, if he wishes the interaction to continue, respond to fit in with A's expectation more or less and to prompt A to respond in an appropriate fashion . . . and so on.

Of course, if you consider two people who belong to any culture—a system of standards accepted by the wide community of which they are members—meeting for the first time, it is perfectly true that they will be equipped already with expectations about each other. They will have learnt to deal with strangers, according to the rules of their larger group; that among other things is what 'manners' are for. Their initial contact, if they have been adequately trained, will be smooth enough; they will not have to develop standards of their own for the purposes of superficial or temporary interchange. If, however, they go on meeting, and form a group of two, each will have to respect the 'little ways' of the other; they will have common interests, in the arts, in sport, in financial enterprises or in anything else. Gradually mutual customs peculiar to themselves will be accepted by each, and form a set of mutually harboured expectations which form the standards of their interacting, over and above what one would call the 'common rules of politeness'. In addition, action in accordance with these standards will be regarded as 'right', and unexpected action, where an expectation is present, is something which has to be explained—it is somehow inappropriate and threatens the harmonious existence of the group. The significance of a framework of expectations can be seen when we reflect on the sentence: 'I can't get on with him, you never know how to take him', or 'you never know what he will do next'.

If standards of conduct, forming a framework of expectations, are required for the persistence of a 'friendship', it is clear that larger groups cannot do without them. There the situation is far more complicated. In a group of four, A has expectations about B, C, and D, and each of these has expectations about A, and each has to shape his conduct so as to fit in with the expectations of the others, and to elicit responses which will fit in with the expectations of all. The point is that they cannot keep together if each person behaves at random with respect to the others.

All this sounds very complicated, and of course complex mechanisms are at work, but in experience it is not complicated at all. What happens is that, without the participants noticing it, a set of customs becomes established which are regarded as 'right' within the context in which

the group operates, and they are felt by each member as being in some sense outside himself. He does not think: 'I must do so and so because of B's expectation, C's expectation, and D's expectation'; he thinks, if he thinks about the matter at all: 'I must do so and so because it is *our* way of behaving'; or, 'because, if I do not, I shall let the group down', or 'because, if I do not, I shall get black looks'. The group, if it has been in being for a time, assumes a kind of independent existence in the minds of its members, and the rules are ascribed to it.

This is a somewhat sketchy account of the origination of norms of conduct in groups, as emerging from the prerequisites of persistent interaction. . . . It is also true that groups vary in the 'tightness' of their standards; some are more 'free and easy' than others, and some members may be tolerated by a group even though they behave, from the point of view of the group, very 'oddly'. All that is necessary at this stage is to realize that every group has some standards characteristic of it, and that it could not continue to exist unless this were so.

This point about groups having to have standards, and spontaneously generating them in the course of the interacting which is the basis of their existing at all, is important from another point of view. Because members of groups conceive of the standards of their groups as outside of them individually, because they can be put into words and communicated to a stranger or to a new member, and because they can be a matter of reflection and discussion, one easily gets the idea that they really do come somehow or other from outside. The individual may have intentions of his own which conflict with the standards of his group and he feels 'coerced'. The standards may, indeed, arouse such reverence that their origin is attributed to some supernatural being. This, of course, does not happen in the case of the smaller groups, . . . but it does happen in the larger inclusive groups of which we are all members. When group standards are thought of as something apart from the interacting of the group members, we tend to think of them as somehow 'imposed' upon them. This gives rise to the notion that man is naturally unsocial, and that law-givers or moralists must come along and rescue him from his nasty brutish ways. This is nonsense. The generation of, and acceptance of, standards which regulate conduct and preclude randomness is, as we have already said, a prerequisite of social intercourse. The having of standards springs out of social intercourse; it is not imposed from outside upon it.

To say that all systems of morality spring out

of social intercourse may, indeed, be going too far, but not so much 'too far' as might at first appear. Systems of morality involve two things: the obligation to control one's conduct in some way or other, both positively and negatively, and the obligation to do this particular kind of thing, and refrain from doing other particular kinds of things. The first element, the having of rules at all, springs from the necessities of persistent social intercourse. The second element, what the rules shall be, springs partly from social intercourse, and partly from reflection. Certain rules, such as the obligation to keep hostility by any members of a group down to a minimum, are required for the very existence of groups. Other rules which go beyond the mere survival of groups, and which may even prejudice their interests, derive from reflection. But the moral teacher, it must be remembered, does not teach in a vacuum. He can assume the idea of obligation as already there in the minds of his audience; what he sets out to do is to modify the content of the standards that have emerged out of the very nature of persistent living together.

Selection 16

Effects of Group Pressures upon the Modification and Distortion of Judgments

Solomon E. Asch

Social norms make society possible by providing order and predictability in the human environment. Man does not react instinctually to the diverse circumstances which confront him; instead, he requires normative direction in order to survive. Life would be impossible if each person had to invent a response for every new situation he faced; the fact is that most situations are defined by group-evolved norms. Preceding selections have demonstrated that the core of the process of personality socialization, from the sociological point of view, consists of learning the norms that define proper behavior in various social situations.

Man's dependence on norms has been vividly illustrated in two rigorously and ingeniously designed experiments, one by Muzafer Sherif[1] and the other, presented below, by Solomon E. Asch. Sherif investigated (1) the individual's need for norms by which to orient his behavior and (2) the group-determined property of norms. To study the first problem, Sherif placed his subjects in a vague, "objectively unstable" situation—one that lacked any meaning or guiding norm. The experimental situation produced an *autokinetic effect:* a single, small, stationary light surrounded by complete darkness appeared to move because it had no external frame of reference. At no time during the experiment did the light actually move, but college-student subjects were asked to report the distance the light "moved" each time it was shown.

When a solitary individual was exposed to the autokinetic effect, he did not present a "hodgepodge of erratic judgments"—a possibility, provided subjects

---

[1] Muzafer Sherif, "Group Influences Upon the Formation of Norms and Attitudes," in Eleanor E. Maccoby, Theodore M. Newcomb, and Eugene L. Hartley, eds., *Readings in Social Psychology* (New York: Henry Holt and Co., 1958), pp. 219-232.

could react to this unstable situation normlessly. Instead, each subject established his own norm, including a definite range of distances within which the light was perceived to move and a central tendency within that range. Each individually determined norm differed from those established by other individuals. Once he had established it, each subject held to his norm on subsequent exposures. When persons were introduced to the experiment in two- and three-member groups, the same result emerged: each group established its own peculiar norm and held to it through later trials. Sherif thus demonstrated that, far from experiencing norms as constraining, man evolves norms when they are lacking.

The next step in Sherif's experiment was to measure the influence of group-evolved norms on individual behavior. When a subject who had developed his norm alone was placed in a group that had already developed its distinctive norms, the norm of the individual changed in the direction of the group norm. When the same individual again faced the test alone, he perceived the light the way he had learned to do in the group, even though he was then free of the physical presence of the group. Thus, Sherif illustrated that group norms take precedence over individually evolved standards. Furthermore, there need not be any relationship between the group's standard and any "objective" standard: remember that although the group members agreed that the light moved and that it moved a characteristic distance, it did not actually move at all.

The power of the group in defining reality is even more dramatically demonstrated by Asch's brilliant experiment. Unlike Sherif's, Asch's subjects were not presented with a vague situation. Instead, students were asked to match in length an unmarked line that clearly corresponded to one of three different labeled lines. When answers were written anonymously, the students—the control group—matched the unmarked line to the labeled one with almost complete accuracy. However, when "naive" subjects were asked to match the lines publicly after other "instructed" subjects had purposely given incorrect answers, a significant number of naive subjects also gave incorrect answers. If the group says black is white, then, indeed, black is likely to be perceived as white by the individual.

The reaction of the naive subjects to group pressure is illuminating. So great was the influence of the group that some subjects actually did perceive the line to be as the group said it was. Others felt that the group was wrong but agreed with it anyway. Many subjects who refused to conform experienced great discomfort as they challenged the group. When we remember that Asch's instructed subjects could wield only expressions of disbelief and ridicule to enforce their norms, the stronger means of ensuring conformity that are available to societal groups—beating, imprisonment, ostracism, execution, etc.—would seem to give such groups great power indeed.

In a sense, even those naive subjects who refused to agree with the instructed subjects were conforming to a norm—not the norm established by Asch but a norm that had been developed by other groups prior to the experiment. Why some persons conformed to the norm of the experimental group while others maintained their allegiance to norms established by groups outside the room is a problem raised by Asch in his discussion of nonconformity. Asch believes that it was more virtuous to have deviated from the group in the experimental room, but whether such deviation really represented nonconformity is an important and puzzling question.

It seems appropriate to ask the student to predict how he would react as a naive subject in what has come to be known as the "Asch situation." For a most exciting demonstration of group power, the reader is invited to replicate Asch's experiment in the classroom.

We shall here describe in summary form the conception and first findings of a program of investigation into the conditions of independence and submission to group pressure.[1]

Our immediate object was to study the social and personal conditions that induce individuals to resist or to yield to group pressures when the latter are perceived to be *contrary to fact.* The issues which this problem raises are of obvious consequence for society; it can be of decisive importance whether or not a group will, under certain conditions, submit to existing pressures. Equally direct are the consequences for individuals and our understanding of them, since it is a decisive fact about a person whether he possesses the freedom to act independently, or whether he characteristically submits to group pressures.

The problem under investigation requires the direct observation of certain basic processes in the interaction between individuals, and between individuals and groups. To clarify these seems necessary if we are to make fundamental advances in the understanding of the formation and reorganization of attitudes, of the functioning of public opinion, and of the operation of propaganda. Today we do not possess an adequate theory of these central psycho-social processes. Empirical investigation has been predominantly controlled by general propositions concerning group influence which have as a rule been assumed but not tested. With few exceptions investigation has relied upon descriptive formulations concerning the operation of suggestion and prestige, the inadequacy of which is becoming increasingly obvious, and upon schematic applications of stimulus-response theory.

Basic to the current approach has been the axiom that group pressures characteristically induce psychological changes *arbitrarily,* in far-reaching disregard of the material properties of the given conditions. This mode of thinking has almost exclusively stressed the slavish submission of individuals to group forces, has neglected to inquire into their possibilities for independence and for productive relations with the human environment, and has virtually denied the capacity of men under certain conditions to rise above group passion and prejudice. It was our aim to contribute to a clarification of these questions, important both for theory and for their human implications, by means of direct observation of the effects of groups upon the decisions and evaluations of individuals.

THE EXPERIMENT AND FIRST RESULTS

To this end we developed an experimental technique which has served as the basis for the present series of studies. We employed the procedure of placing an individual in a relation of radical conflict with all the other members of a group, of measuring its effect upon him in quantitative terms, and of describing its psychological consequences. A group of eight individuals was instructed to judge a series of simple, clearly structured perceptual relations—to match the length of a given line with one of three unequal lines. Each member of the group announced his judgments publicly. In the midst of this monotonous "test" one individual found himself suddenly contradicted by the entire group, and this contradiction was repeated again and again in the course of the experiment. The group in question had, with the exception of one member, previously met with the experimenter and received instructions to respond at certain points with wrong—and unanimous—judgments. The errors of the majority were large (ranging between ½″ and 1¾″) and of an order not encountered under control conditions. The outstanding person—the critical subject —whom we had placed in the position of a *minority of one* in the midst of a *unanimous majority*— was the object of investigation. He faced, possibly for the first time in his life, a situation in which a group unanimously contradicted the evidence of his senses.

This procedure was the starting point of the investigation and the point of departure for the study of further problems. Its main features were the following: (1) The critical subject was submitted to two contradictory and irreconcilable forces—the evidence of his own experience of a clearly perceived relation, and the unanimous evidence of a group of equals. (2) Both forces were part of the immediate situation; the majority was concretely present, surrounding the subject physically. (3) The critical subject, who was re-

From *Readings in Social Psychology,* Third Edition, edited by Eleanor E. Maccoby, Theodore M. Newcomb, and Eugene L. Hartley, pp. 174-183. Copyright © 1947, 1952, 1958, Holt, Rinehart and Winston, Inc. By permission. Some portions reprinted by permission of Carnegie Press.
[1] The earlier experiments out of which the present work developed and the theoretical issues which prompted it are discussed in S. E. Asch, *Social Psychology* (New York: Prentice-Hall, Inc., 1952), Ch. 16.

quested together with all others to state his judgments publicly, was obliged to declare himself and to take a definite stand *vis-à-vis* the group. (4) The situation possessed a self-contained character. The critical subject could not avoid or evade the dilemma by reference to conditions external to the experimental situation. (It may be mentioned at this point that the forces generated by the given conditions acted so quickly upon the critical subjects that instances of suspicion were infrequent.)

The technique employed permitted a simple quantitative measure of the "majority effect" in terms of the frequency of errors in the direction of the distorted estimates of the majority. At the same time we were concerned to obtain evidence of the ways in which the subjects perceived the group, to establish whether they became doubtful, whether they were tempted to join the majority. Most important, it was our object to establish the grounds of the subject's independence or yielding—whether, for example, the yielding subject was aware of the effect of the majority upon him, whether he abandoned his judgment deliberately or compulsively. To this end we constructed a comprehensive set of questions which served as the basis of an individual interview immediately following the experimental period. Toward the

conclusion of the interview each subject was informed fully of the purpose of the experiment, of his role and of that of the majority. The reactions to the disclosure of the purpose of the experiment became in fact an integral part of the procedure. The information derived from the interview became an indispensable source of evidence and insight into the psychological structure of the experimental situation, and in particular, of the nature of the individual differences. It should be added that it is not justified or advisable to allow the subject to leave without giving him a full explanation of the experimental conditions. The experimenter has a responsibility to the subject to clarify his doubts and to state the reasons for placing him in the experimental situation. When this is done most subjects react with interest, and some express gratification at having lived through a striking situation which has some bearing on them personally and on wider human issues.

Both the members of the majority and the critical subjects were male college students. We shall report the results for a total of fifty critical subjects in this experiment. In Table 1 we summarize the successive comparison trials and the majority estimates. The reader will note that on certain trials the majority responded correctly; these were the "neutral" trials. There were twelve

TABLE 1: Lengths of Standard and Comparison Lines

TRIAL	LENGTH OF STANDARD LINE (IN INCHES)	COMPARISON LINES (IN INCHES)			CORRECT RESPONSE	GROUP RESPONSE	MAJORITY ERROR (IN INCHES)
		1	2	3			
1	10	8¾	10	8	2	2	—
2	2	2	1	1½	1	1	—
3	3	3¾	4¼	3	3	1 *	+¾
4	5	5	4	6½	1	2 *	−1.0
5	4	3	5	4	3	3	—
6	3	3¾	4¼	3	3	2 *	+1¼
7	8	6¼	8	6¾	2	3 *	−1¼
8	5	5	4	6½	1	3 *	+1½
9	8	6¼	8	6¾	2	1 *	−1¾
10	10	8¾	10	8	2	2	—
11	2	2	1	1½	1	1	—
12	3	3¾	4¼	3	3	1 *	+¾
13	5	5	4	6½	1	2 *	−1.0
14	4	3	5	4	3	3	—
15	3	3¾	4¼	3	3	2 *	+1¼
16	8	6¼	8	6¾	2	3 *	−1¼
17	5	5	4	6½	1	3 *	+1½
18	8	6¼	8	6¾	2	1 *	−1¾

* *Starred figures designate the erroneous estimates by the majority.*

critical trials on which the responses of the majority responded incorrectly.

The quantitative results are clear and unambiguous.

1. There was a marked movement toward the majority. One third of all the estimates in the critical group were errors identical with or in the direction of the distorted estimates of the majority. The significance of this finding becomes clear in the light of the virtual absence of errors in the control group, the members of which recorded their estimates in writing. The relevant data of the critical and control groups are summarized in Table 2.

TABLE 2: Distribution of Errors in Experimental and Control Groups

NUMBER OF CRITICAL ERRORS	CRITICAL GROUP * (N = 50)	CONTROL GROUP (N = 37)
	F	F
0	13	35
1	4	1
2	5	1
3	6	
4	3	
5	4	
6	1	
7	2	
8	5	
9	3	
10	3	
11	1	
12	0	
Total	50	37
Mean	3.84	0.08

All errors in the critical group were in the direction of the majority estimates.

2. At the same time the effect of the majority was far from complete. The preponderance of estimates in the critical group (68 percent) was correct despite the pressure of the majority.

3. We found evidence of extreme individual differences. There were in the critical group subjects who remained independent without exception, and there were those who went nearly all the time with the majority. (The maximum possible number of errors was 12, while the actual range of errors was 0–11.) One fourth of the critical subjects was completely independent; at the other extreme, one third of the group displaced the estimates toward the majority in one half or more of the trials.

The differences between the critical subjects in their reactions to the given conditions were equally striking. There were subjects who remained completely confident throughout. At the other extreme were those who became disoriented, doubt-ridden, and experienced a powerful impulse not to appear different from the majority.

For purposes of illustration we include a brief description of one independent and one yielding subject.

Independent. After a few trials he appeared puzzled, hesitant. He announced all disagreeing answers in the form of "Three, sir; two, sir"; not so with the unanimous answers on the neutral trials. At Trial 4 he answered immediately after the first member of the group, shook his head, blinked, and whispered to his neighbor: "Can't help it, that's one." His later answers came in a whispered voice, accompanied by a deprecating smile. At one point he grinned embarrassedly, and whispered explosively to his neighbor: "I always disagree—darn it!" During the questioning, this subject's constant refrain was: "I called them as I saw them, sir." He insisted that his estimates were right without, however, committing himself as to whether the others were wrong, remarking that "that's the way I see them and that's the way they see them." If he had to make a practical decision under similar circumstances, he declared, "I would follow my own view, though part of my reason would tell me that I might be wrong." Immediately following the experiment the majority engaged this subject in a brief discussion. When they pressed him to say whether the entire group was wrong and he alone right, he turned upon them defiantly, exclaiming: "You're *probably* right, but you *may* be wrong!" To the disclosure of the experiment this subject reacted with the statement that he felt "exultant and relieved," adding, "I do not deny that at times I had the feeling: 'to heck with it, I'll go along with the rest.'"

Yielding. This subject went with the majority in 11 out of 12 trials. He appeared nervous and somewhat confused, but he did not attempt to evade discussion; on the contrary, he was helpful and tried to answer to the best of his ability. He opened the discussion with the statement: "If I'd been first I probably would have responded differently"; this was his way of stating that he had adopted the majority estimates. The primary factor in his case was loss of confidence. He perceived the majority as a decided group, acting without hesitation: "If they had been doubtful I probably would have changed, but they answered with such confidence." Certain of his errors, he explained, were due to the doubtful nature of the comparisons; in such instances he went with the majority. When the object of the experiment was explained, the subject volunteered: "I suspected about the middle—but tried to push it out of my mind." It is of interest that his suspicion did not restore his confidence or diminish the power of the majority. Equally striking is his report that he assumed the experiment to involve an "illusion" to which the others, but not he, were subject. This assumption too did not help to free him; on the contrary, he acted as if his divergence from the majority was a sign of defect. The principal impression this subject produced was of one so caught up by immediate difficulties that he lost clear reasons for his actions, and could make no reasonable decisions.

A FIRST ANALYSIS OF
INDIVIDUAL DIFFERENCES

On the basis of the interview data described earlier, we undertook to differentiate and describe the major forms of reaction to the experimental situation, which we shall now briefly summarize.

Among the *independent* subjects we distinguished the following main categories:

(1) Independence based on *confidence* in one's perception and experience. The most striking characteristic of these subjects is the vigor with which they withstand the group opposition. Though they are sensitive to the group, and experience the conflict, they show a resilience in coping with it, which is expressed in their continuing reliance on their perception and the effectiveness with which they shake off the oppressive group opposition.

(2) Quite different are those subjects who are independent and *withdrawn*. These do not react in a spontaneously emotional way, but rather on the basis of explicit principles concerning the necessity of being an individual.

(3) A third group of independent subjects manifests considerable tension and doubt, but adhere to their judgment on the basis of a felt necessity to deal adequately with the task.

The following were the main categories of reaction among the *yielding* subjects, or those who went with the majority during one half or more of the trials.

(1) *Distortion of perception* under the stress of group pressure. In this category belong a very few subjects who yield completely, but are not aware that their estimates have been displaced or distorted by the majority. These subjects report that they came to perceive the majority estimates as correct.

(2) *Distortion of judgment.* Most submitting subjects belong to this category. The factor of greatest importance in this group is a decision the subjects reach that their perceptions are inaccurate, and that those of the majority are correct. These subjects suffer from primary doubt and lack of confidence; on this basis they feel a strong tendency to join the majority.

(3) *Distortion of action.* The subjects in this group do not suffer a modification of perception nor do they conclude that they are wrong. They yield because of an overmastering need not to appear different from or inferior to others, because of an inability to tolerate the appearance of defectiveness in the eyes of the group. These subjects suppress their observations and voice the majority position with awareness of what they are doing.

The results are sufficient to establish that independence and yielding are not psychologically homogeneous, that submission to group pressure and freedom from pressure can be the result of different psychological conditions. It should also be noted that the categories described above, being based exclusively on the subjects' reactions to the experimental conditions, are descriptive, not presuming to explain why a given individual responded in one way rather than another. The further exploration of the basis for the individual differences is a separate task.

EXPERIMENTAL VARIATIONS

The results described are clearly a joint function of two broadly different sets of conditions. They are determined first by the specific external conditions, by the particular character of the relation between social evidence and one's own experience. Second, the presence of pronounced individual differences points to the important role of personal factors, or factors connected with the individual's character structure. We reasoned that there are group conditions which would produce independence in all subjects, and that there probably are group conditions which would induce intensified yielding in many, though not in all. Secondly, we deemed it reasonable to assume that behavior under the experimental social pressure is significantly related to certain characteristics of the individual. The present account will be limited to the effect of the surrounding conditions upon independence and submission. To this end we followed the procedure of experimental variation, systematically altering the quality of social evidence by means of systematic variation of the group conditions and of the task.

The Effect of Nonunanimous Majorities. Evidence obtained from the basic experiment suggested that the condition of being exposed *alone* to the opposition of a "compact majority" may have played a decisive role in determining the course and strength of the effects observed. Accordingly we undertook to investigate in a series of successive variations the effects of *nonunanimous* majorities. The technical problem of altering the uniformity of a majority is, in terms of our procedure, relatively simple. In most instances we merely directed one or more members of the instructed group to deviate from the majority in prescribed ways. It is obvious that we cannot hope to compare the performance of the same individual in two situations on the assumption that they remain independent of one another; at best we can investigate the effect of an earlier upon a later experimental condition. The comparison of different experimental situations therefore requires the use of different but comparable groups of critical subjects. This is the procedure we have followed. In the variations to be described we have maintained the conditions of the basic experiment (e.g., the sex of the subjects, the size of the majority, the content of the task, and so on) save for the specific factor that was varied. The following were some of the variations studied:

The presence of a "true partner"

(a) In the midst of the majority were *two* naïve, critical subjects. The subjects were separated spatially, being seated in the fourth and eighth positions, respectively. Each therefore heard his judgments confirmed by one other person (provided the other person remained independent), one prior to, the other after announcing his own judgment. In addition, each experienced a break in the unanimity of the majority. There were six pairs of critical subjects. (b) In a further variation the "partner" to the critical subject was a member of the group who had been instructed to respond correctly throughout. This procedure permits the exact control of the partner's responses. The partner was always seated in the fourth position; he therefore announced his estimates in each case before the critical subject.

The results clearly demonstrate that a disturbance of the unanimity of the majority markedly increased the independence of the critical subjects. The frequency of promajority errors dropped to 10.4 percent of the total number of estimates in variation (a), and to 5.5 percent in variation (b). These results are to be compared with the frequency of yielding to the unanimous majorities in the basic experiment, which was 32 percent of the total number of estimates. It is clear that the presence in the field of *one other* individual who responded correctly was sufficient to deplete the power of the majority, and in some cases to destroy it. This finding is all the more striking in the light of other variations which demonstrate the effect of even small minorities provided they are unanimous. Indeed, we have been able to show that a unanimous majority of 3 is, under the given conditions, far more effective than a majority of 8 containing 1 dissenter. That critical subjects will under these conditions free themselves of a majority of 7 and join forces with one other person in the minority is, we believe, a result significant for theory. It points to a fundamental psychological difference between the condition of being alone and having a minimum of human support. It further demonstrates that the effects obtained are not the result of a summation of influences proceeding from each member of the group; it is necessary to conceive the results as being relationally determined.

Withdrawal of a "true partner"

What will be the effect of providing the critical subject with a partner who responds correctly and then withdrawing him? The critical subject started with a partner who responded correctly. The partner was a member of the majority who had been instructed to respond correctly and to "desert" to the majority in the middle of the experiment. This procedure permits the observation of the same subject in the course of the transition from one condition to another. The withdrawal of the partner produced a powerful and unexpected result. We had assumed that the critical subject, having gone through the experience of opposing the majority with a minimum of support, would maintain his independence when alone. Contrary to this expectation, we found that the experience of having had and then lost a partner restored the majority effect to its full force, the proportion of errors rising to 28.5 percent of all judgments, in contrast to the preceding level of 5.5 percent. Further experimentation is needed to establish whether the critical subjects were responding to the sheer fact of being alone, or to the fact that the partner abandoned them.

Late arrival of a "true partner"

The critical subject started as a minority of 1 in the midst of a unanimous majority. Toward the conclusion of the experiment one member of the majority "broke" away and began announcing correct estimates. This procedure, which reverses the order of conditions of the preceding experiment, permits the observation of the transition from being alone to being a member of a pair against a majority. It is obvious that those critical subjects who were independent when alone would continue to be so when joined by a partner. The variation is therefore of significance primarily for those subjects who yielded during the first phase of the experiment. The appearance of the late partner exerts a freeing effect, reducing the level of yielding to 8.7 percent. Those who had previously yielded also became markedly more independent, but not completely so, continuing to yield more than previously independent subjects. The reports of the subjects do not cast much light on the factors responsible for the result. It is our impression that some subjects, having once committed themselves to yielding, find it difficult to change their direction completely. To do so is tantamount to a public admission that they had not acted rightly. They therefore follow to an extent the precarious course they had chosen in order to maintain an outward semblance of consistency and conviction.

The presence of a "compromise partner"

The majority was consistently extremist, always matching the standard with the most unequal line. One instructed subject (who, as in the other variations, preceded the critical subject) also responded incorrectly, but his estimates were always intermediate between the truth and the majority position. The critical subject therefore faced an extremist majority whose unanimity was broken by one more moderately erring person. Under these conditions the frequency of errors was reduced but not significantly. However, the lack of unanimity determined in a strikingly consistent way the *direction* of the errors. The preponderance of the errors, 75.7 percent of the total, was moderate, whereas in a parallel experiment in which the majority was unanimously extremist (i.e., with the "compromise" partner excluded), the incidence of moderate errors was 42

percent of the total. As might be expected, in a unanimously moderate majority, the errors of the critical subjects were without exception moderate.

The Role of Majority Size. To gain further understanding of the majority effect, we varied the size of the majority in several different variations. The majorities, which were in each case unanimous, consisted of 2, 3, 4, 8, and 10–15 persons, respectively. In addition, we studied the limiting case in which the critical subject was opposed by one instructed subject. Table 3 contains the mean and the range of errors under each condition.

With the opposition reduced to 1, the majority effect all but disappeared. When the opposition proceeded from a group of 2, it produced a measurable though small distortion, the errors being 12.8 percent of the total number of estimates. The effect appeared in full force with a majority of 3. Larger majorities did not produce effects greater than a majority of 3.

The effect of a majority is often silent, revealing little of its operation to the subject, and often hiding it from the experimenter. To examine the range of effects it is capable of inducing, decisive variations of conditions are necessary. An indication of one effect is furnished by the following variation in which the conditions of the basic experiment were simply reversed. Here the majority, consisting of a group of 16, was naïve; in the midst of it we placed a single individual who responded wrongly according to instructions. Under these conditions the members of the naïve majority reacted to the lone dissenter with amusement. Contagious laughter spread through the group at the droll minority of 1. Of significance is the fact that the members lacked awareness that they drew their strength from the majority, and that their reactions would change radically if they faced the dissenter individually. These observations demonstrate the role of social support as a source of power and stability, in contrast to the preceding investigations which stressed the effects of social opposition. Both aspects must be explicitly considered in a unified formulation of the effects of group conditions on the formation and change of judgments.

TABLE 3: Errors of Critical Subjects with Unanimous Majorities of Different Size

SIZE OF MAJORITY	CONTROL	1	2	3	4	8	10–15
N	37	10	15	10	10	50	12
Mean number of errors	0.08	0.33	1.53	4.0	4.20	3.84	3.75
Range of errors	0–2	0–1	0–5	1–12	0–11	0–11	0–10

The Role of the Stimulus-Situation. It is obviously not possible to divorce the quality and course of the group forces which act upon the individual from the specific stimulus-conditions. Of necessity the structure of the situation molds the group forces and determines their direction as well as their strength. Indeed, this was the reason that we took pains in the investigations described above to center the issue between the individual and the group around an elementary matter of fact. And there can be no doubt that the resulting reactions were directly a function of the contradiction between the observed relations and the majority position. These general considerations are sufficient to establish the need to vary the stimulus-conditions and to observe their effect on the resulting group forces.

Accordingly we have studied the effect of increasing and decreasing the discrepancy between the correct relation and the position of the majority, going beyond the basic experiment which contained discrepancies of a relatively moderate order. Our technique permits the easy variation of this factor, since we can vary at will the deviation of the majority from the correct relation. At this point we can only summarize the trend of the results which is entirely clear. The degree of independence increases with the distance of the majority from correctness. However, even glaring discrepancies (of the order of 3–6″) did not produce independence in all. While independence increases with the magnitude of contradiction, a certain proportion of individuals continues to yield under extreme conditions.

We have also varied systematically the structural clarity of the task, employing judgments based on mental standards. In agreement with other investigators, we find that the majority effect grows stronger as the situation diminishes in clarity. Concurrently, however, the disturbance of the subjects and the conflict-quality of the situation decrease markedly. We consider it of significance that the majority achieves its most pronounced effect when it acts most painlessly.

SUMMARY

We have investigated the effects upon individuals of majority opinions when the latter were seen to be in a direction contrary to fact. By means of a simple technique we produced a radical divergence between a majority and a minority, and observed the ways in which individuals coped with the resulting difficulty. Despite the stress of the given conditions, a substantial proportion of individuals retained their independence throughout. At the same time a substantial minority yielded, modifying their judgments in accordance with the majority. Independence and yielding are a joint function of the following major factors: (1) The character of the stimulus situation. Variations in structural clarity have a decisive effect: with diminishing clarity of the stimulus-conditions the majority effect increases. (2) The character of the group forces. Individuals are highly sensitive to the structural qualities of group opposition. In particular, we demonstrated the great importance of the factor of unanimity. Also, the majority effect is a function of the size of group opposition. (3) The character of the individual. There were wide and, indeed, striking differences among individuals within the same experimental situation.

Selection 17

Thought Reform and the Psychology of Totalism

Robert J. Lifton

During the Korean War, Americans were shocked by the fact that some American prisoners-of-war had defected to the Communists and had accepted the Chinese and Soviet explanation of the war as caused by the aggressive and militaristic foreign policy of the United States. In the aftermath of discussion about the defectors, a new term, *brainwashing*, became part of our vocabulary. At the time, it was naively believed that brainwashing represented a Communist breakthrough in the manipulation of the human mind. But the following selection from Lifton's study of brainwashing in China shows that group pressures similar in essence to those operating in the Asch experiment are the key to understanding this psychological process.

A prisoner of the Chinese Communists, Dr. Vincent, who corresponds to the naive subject in the Asch situation, was led into a cell where eight other prisoners, who correspond to Asch's instructed subjects, had been given instructions: they had been told that the newcomer was an espionage agent for the West, and they were to make known to him that they knew he was a spy. Thus the first approximation to the Asch situation took place in the tiny prison cell during the "struggle" between the old prisoners and the new one. But the similarity does not end there. The prisoner was then led to a judge's chamber, where during repeated "interrogations" he was told that he was a spy and was asked to confess. The Asch-like situation was further reinforced by years of re-education sessions that lasted from ten to sixteen hours a day. It is important to note that new stages did not supersede the previous ones but were superimposed on them.

Of course, unlike the situation in Asch's laboratory, the Chinese Communists were able to use more than ridicule—although ridicule was a very effective form of punishment in the jails—to coerce Dr. Vincent into accepting the "people's" explanation of reality. Dr. Vincent was chained, was forced to eat on all fours, was not allowed to sleep during the first days of his imprisonment, and had to perform his natural functions in the most abject way.

There was another important difference between the Asch experiment and Dr. Vincent's experience as a prisoner of the Chinese Communists. The naive experimental subject who agreed that the shortest line was the same as the longest line but did not really believe it was permitted to get away with surface conformity. Not so in the Chinese jail. Dr. Vincent was not only forced to admit that he was a spy, but he also had to believe his confession. Assent just for the sake of avoiding further punishment was not enough.

Essentially, however, the conditions of Dr. Vincent's experience were the same as those in Asch's laboratory. The prisoner found himself overwhelmed by a new theory of events and history, one that was markedly different from his own. As Asch illustrated when he assigned a partner to aid the naive subject, social support is necessary if one is to maintain his own ideas. But Dr. Vincent received no support for his old ideas when he was faced with persistent and unanimous arguments to uphold the Communist version of history. This absence of support, combined with a sanctions system which severely punished those who did not accept that version resulted in Dr. Vincent's confession and his adoption of Communist views. In Dr. Vincent's words, "They built up a criminal. . . . Then your invention becomes a reality."

I first heard of Dr. Charles Vincent through a newspaper article announcing his arrival in Hong Kong by ship after three and one-half years of imprisonment and twenty previous years of medical practice in China. I was put in touch with him through another subject of mine who had known him in the past. When I telephoned him at the boarding house where he was staying, he readily agreed to talk with me; but when I began to describe to him the location of my office, he showed some hesitation and then made it clear that he wanted me to come and pick him up. I consented to this arrangement and met him in the lobby of his rooming house just five days after he crossed the border. Dr. Vincent was a short,

dark-complexioned, muscular Frenchman in his early fifties. He was not emaciated, but he did look pale; and in his eyes was that characteristic combination of fear and distance which has been aptly labeled "the thousand-mile stare."

He said little during the brief automobile ride, but in response to my inquiries about how he was getting on in Hong Kong, he described feeling frightened and nervous. Upon entering my study, he sat down hesitantly, and listened with-

Reprinted from *Thought Reform and the Psychology of Totalism* by Robert Jay Lifton, M.D., pp. 19-32. By permission of W. W. Norton and Company, Inc. Copyright © 1961 by Robert Jay Lifton.

out comment to my few sentences of explanation about my research. When I had finished, he looked at me directly for the first time and asked a quick series of questions: How old was I? How long had I been in Hong Kong doing this work? And then, with particular emphasis, "Are you standing on the 'people's side,' or on the 'imperialists' side'?" I told him I was part of the non-Communist world, but that I tried as much as possible to take no side in order to gain an understanding of the process of thought reform. He went on to explain that this was important because

"From the imperialistic side we are not criminals; from the people's side we are criminals. If we look at this from the imperialists' side, re-education is a kind of compulsion. But if we look at it from the people's side, it is to die and be born again."

Having expressed both his fear and his dilemma —and indeed, the paradox of thought reform itself—he needed no more prompting to go into the details of his ordeal. I said little during this first three-hour interview, and not much more during the remaining fifteen hours (five additional meetings) which we spent together, for Dr. Vincent had a great need to talk about what he had been through, and he did so in an unusually vivid fashion.

As one of the few remaining foreign physicians in Shanghai, he had been conducting a lucrative practice which included several Communist officials—until suddenly confronted on the street one afternoon by five men with revolvers. They produced a warrant for his arrest and took him to the "detention house" (or "re-education center") where he was to spend the next three and a half years.

INTERROGATION AND "STRUGGLE"

After a few preliminaries he was placed in a small (8′ x 12′) bare cell which already contained eight other prisoners, all of them Chinese. They were a specially selected group, each of them "advanced" in his personal "reform," each eager to apply himself enthusiastically to the reform of others as a means of gaining "merits" toward his own release. Their greeting was hardly a friendly one: the "cell chief" identified himself, and addressing Vincent in Chinese by his newly-acquired prison number, instructed him to sit in the center of the cell while the other prisoners formed a circle around him. Each in turn then shouted invectives at Vincent, denouncing him as an "imperialist" and a "spy," demanding that he "recognize" his "crimes" and "confess everything"

to the "government." Vincent protested: He was not a spy. He was a doctor. He had worked as a doctor in China for twenty years. But this only resulted in more vehement accusations: "The government has all the proof. They have arrested you and the government never makes a mistake. You have not been arrested for nothing." Then his cellmates went on to question him further about all the activities in which he engaged as a physician to "cover up" his "spy personality." This procedure in the cell was known as a "struggle," conducted for the purpose of "helping" a prisoner with his "confession," and it was an experience which Vincent had to undergo frequently, particularly during the early phases of his imprisonment.

After several hours of this disturbing treatment, Vincent was called for his first interrogation. He was taken to a small room with three people in it: the interrogator or "judge," an interpreter, and a secretary. The judge opened the session with a vague accusation and an emphatic demand: "You have committed crimes against the people, and you must now confess everything." Vincent's protestations of innocence were countered with the angry declaration: "The government never arrests an innocent man." The judge went on to ask a series of general questions concerning Vincent's activities, professional associations, organizational contacts, friends, and acquaintances during his entire twenty years in China. He answered these as accurately as he could, but was unable to satisfy his interrogator. The judge's demands always contained a tantalizing combination of hint, threat, and promise: "The government knows all about your crimes. That is why we arrested you. It is now up to you to confess everything to us, and in this way your case can be quickly solved and you will soon be released."

After a few hours of this interrogation, questions began to focus more and more upon alleged connections with people from several groups: his own embassy, American government officials, and Catholic, Japanese, and Nationalist Chinese agencies. By 6 a.m., after ten successive hours of interrogation, he had produced much information; but he still asserted his innocence, denied that he was a spy or had any subversive relationship with these organizations, and again said that he did not understand why he had been arrested. This angered the judge, who ordered handcuffs applied to Vincent's wrists, holding his arms behind his back. He dismissed the prisoner from the room, demanding that he "think over" his "crimes." But when he was returned ten minutes later, Vincent still stated that he could not recognize crimes of any kind. The judge again became incensed, ordered chains placed about Vincent's ankles, and sent him back to his cell. His return there was the occasion for continuous struggle and humiliation.

"When you get back with your chains, your cellmates receive you as an enemy. They start 'struggling' to 'help' you. The 'struggle' goes on all day to 8 p.m. that night. You are obliged to stand with chains on your ankles and holding your hands behind your back. They don't assist you because you are too reactionary. . . . You eat as a dog does, with your mouth and teeth. You arrange the cup and bowl with your nose to try to absorb broth twice a day. If you have to make water they open your trousers and you make water in a little tin in the corner. . . . In the W.C. someone opens your trousers and after you are finished they clean you. You are never out of the chains. Nobody pays any attention to your hygiene. Nobody washes you. In the room they say you are in chains only because you are a reactionary. They continuously tell you that, if you confess all, you will be treated better."

Toward the end of the second day, Vincent was concerned only with finding some relief ("You start to think, how to get rid of these chains. *You must get rid of the chains*"). That night, when called for interrogation, he made what he called a "wild confession"—a description of espionage activities which he knew to be nonexistent. As he explained it:

"We see in the judge someone who wants to press something on us. And if we show we are a big criminal, maybe we will get better treatment. . . . Everyone of us tries to cheat the government this way. We know they are angry with the Americans . . . so we become a member of an American spy ring. . . . I invented a whole organization."

But when he was pressed for details, he could not substantiate his story, and inconsistencies appeared. The confession was rejected, and he was once more summarily dismissed by the judge. The round of interrogation and struggle continued.

On the third night, he changed his tactics. Aware that the officials were greatly interested in his activities and contacts, he began to reconstruct and confess every detail of every conversation with friends and associates which he could remember from the whole of his twenty years in China. He did this because "I thought they were trying to prove I gave intelligence to friends."

Now that he was talking freely, his captors began to press home their advantage. Interroga-

tions, ever more demanding, took up the greater part of each night; these were interrupted every two or three hours for a rapid and painful promenade (in chains) which served to keep the prisoner awake, to increase his physical discomfort, and to give him a sense of movement ("in order to convince you to speed up your confession"). During the day, he was required to dictate to another prisoner everything he had confessed the night before, and anything additional he could think of. When he was not dictating the confessions or making new ones, he was being struggled. Every activity in the cell seemed to be centered around him and his confession. He soon realized that the cell chief was making daily reports to prison officials and receiving regular instructions on how to deal with him. Everything he did or said—every word, movement, or expression—was noted and written down by other prisoners, then conveyed to the prison authorities.

For eight days and nights, Vincent experienced this program of alternating struggle and interrogation, and was permitted no sleep at all. Moreover, he was constantly told by his cellmates that he was completely responsible for his own plight. ("You want the chains! You want to be shot! . . . . Otherwise, you would be more 'sincere' and the chains would not be necessary.") He found himself in a Kafka-like maze of vague and yet damning accusations: he could neither understand exactly what he was guilty of ("recognize his crimes") nor could he in any way establish his innocence. Overwhelmed by fatigue, confusion, and helplessness, he ceased all resistance.

"You are annihilated. . . . exhausted. . . . you can't control yourself, or remember what you said two minutes before. You feel that all is lost. . . . From that moment, the judge is the real master of you. You accept anything he says. When he asks how many 'intelligences' you gave to that person, you just put out a number in order to satisfy him. If he says, 'Only those?,' you say, 'No, there are more.' If he says, 'One hundred,' you say, 'One hundred'. . . . You do whatever they want. You don't pay any more attention to your life or to your handcuffed arms. You can't distinguish right from left. You just wonder when you will be shot—and begin to hope for the end of all this."

A confession began to emerge which was still "wild"—full of exaggerations, distortions, and falsehoods—but at the same time closely related to real events and people in Vincent's life. Every night Vincent would sign a written statement of his newly confessed material with a thumbprint, as his hands were not free for writing. He was so compliant by this time that he made no attempt to check upon the accuracy of what he was signing.

After three weeks, the emphasis again shifted; now he was required to report on others, to make exhaustive lists of all of the people he had known in China, and to write out their addresses, their affiliations, and anything at all which he knew about their activities. Vincent complied, again supplying a mixture of truths, half-truths, and untruths. But after two weeks of this, under the continuing pressures of his captors, these descriptions became exposés and denunciations; friends, associates became drawn into the web. Still the clamor from the judge, officials, and cellmates was the same as it had been since the moment of imprisonment: "Confess! . . . Confess all! . . . You must be frank! . . . You must show your faith in the government! . . . Come clean! . . . Be sincere! . . . Recognize your crimes! . . ."

At this point—about two months from the date of his arrest—Vincent was considered to be ready for a beginning "recognition" of his "crimes." This required that he learn to look at himself from the "people's standpoint"—to accept the prevailing Communist definition of criminal behavior, including the principle that "the people's standpoint makes no distinction between news, information, and intelligence." He described two examples of this process:

"For instance, I was the family physician and friend of an American correspondent. We talked about many things, including the political situation. . . . The judge questioned me again and again about my relationship with this man. He asked me for details about everything we had talked about. . . . I admitted that at the time of the 'liberation,' when I saw the horsedrawn artillery of the Communist army, I told this to my American friend. . . . The judge shouted that this American was a spy who was collecting espionage material for his spy organization, and that I was guilty of supplying him with military intelligence. . . . At first I did not accept this, but soon I had to add it to my confession. . . . This is adopting the people's standpoint. . . .

"I knew a man who was friendly with an American military attaché. I told him the price of shoes and that I couldn't buy gasoline for my car. I had already agreed that this was economic intelligence. So I wrote that I gave economic intelligence to this man. But they made it clear that I must say that I received an espionage mission from the American military attaché through the other person, to collect economic intelligence. . . . This was the people's standpoint."

"LENIENCY" AND "STUDY"

Just as Vincent was beginning to express himself from the "people's standpoint"—but in a dazed, compliant, and unenthusiastic manner—he was suddenly surprised by a remarkable improvement in his status: the handcuffs and chains were removed, he was permitted to be comfortably seated when talking to the judge, and he was in turn addressed in friendly tones. He was told that the government regretted that he had been having such a difficult time, that it really wanted only to help him, and that in accordance with its "lenient policy" it would certainly treat him kindly, and soon release him—if only he would make an absolutely complete confession, and then work hard to "reform" himself. And to help things along, pressures were diminished, and he was permitted more rest. This abrupt reversal in attitude had a profound effect upon Vincent: for the first time he had been treated with human consideration, the chains were gone, he could see a possible solution ahead, there was hope for the future.

Now he was offered more friendly "guidance" in rewriting (not once but many times) his entire confession, including descriptions and denunciations of other people; and his change of fortune gave him added incentive in applying himself to the task. But he soon found that this guidance was not to be taken lightly, and on three occasions when he expressed some measure of resistance, saying, "This I didn't do," the chains were re-applied for two or three days, accompanied by a return to the harsh treatment of previous weeks.

Once "leniency" had been initiated, however, Vincent was never again to experience anything as overwhelming as the assaults of his early prison period. Given the luxury of eight hours of sleep a night, of relatively calm and restrained interrogations (he was even permitted to sit on a chair), of practically no harassment in the cell, Vincent spent the next two or three weeks doing nothing but developing in even greater detail his confession material. During his sessions with the judge, he received further instructions upon the proper way to apply the "people's standpoint" to all that he was writing and saying.

Meanwhile, he was initiated into the regular cell routine: carefully regimented arrangements for sleeping and awakening, for eating and for relieving oneself. Freed of the chains, he could join the others on the two daily excursions to the toilet (everyone running head down, to an area with two open toilets, each permitted about forty-five seconds to attend to his needs with sharp criticism directed at anyone who took longer than this), and in the use of the urine bucket in the cell. He was still addressed only by prison number, and continued to receive food adequate for survival but poor in quality. And the sores and infections caused by his chains and handcuffs were given more attention, including local applications and penicillin injections.

Then, three weeks after the beginning of "leniency," he began to take part in the cell's organized "re-education" procedures. This meant active involvement in the group study program —the *hsüeh hsi*—whose sessions took up almost the entire waking existence of the prisoners, ten to sixteen hours a day. Led by the cell chief, its procedure was simple enough: one prisoner read material from a Communist newspaper, book, or pamphlet; and then each in turn was expected to express his own opinion and to criticize the views of others. Everyone was required to participate actively, and anyone who did not was severely criticized. Each had to learn to express himself from the "correct" or "people's standpoint"—applied not only to personal actions, but to political, social, and ethical issues. With each of the prisoners feeling that his freedom or even his life might be at stake, the zeal of the participants was overwhelming.

For a long time after Dr. Vincent joined the group (and probably because of his presence), discussions centered upon past Western insults to China: territorial aggrandizement, infringements upon sovereignty, special privileges demanded for Western nationals. And the message was conveyed to him personally that "under the cloak of medicine" he was nothing but a representative of "exploitation," an agent of the "imperialists," a life-long "spy," whose actions were from the beginning "harmful to the Chinese people."

Discussions starting at an intellectual level would quickly become concerned with personal analysis and criticism. When Dr. Vincent was found wanting in his adoption of the "people's standpoint" or when his views were considered "erroneous," it became necessary for him to "examine himself" and look into the causes of these "reactionary" tendencies. He had to search out the harmful "bourgeois" and "imperialistic" influences from his past for further evaluation and self-criticism. Every "question" or "problem" had to be "solved," according to the "facts," in order to get to the "truth," viewing everything, of course, from the "people's standpoint."

Special "movements" would take place, jolting the prisoners from the ordinary routine into renewed emotional efforts. Sometimes these were part of broad, all-China campaigns, sometimes

related to national prison movements, and sometimes locally initiated; but whether directed at "thought attitude," prison discipline, hygiene problems, or personal confessions, they always served to plunge each prisoner into a more thorough and compelling self-examination. Everyone was intent upon demonstrating his own "reform" and "progressive viewpoint." The atmosphere came to resemble that of a great moral crusade.

Dr. Vincent was still receiving more personal attention than anyone else in the cell. At first he simply gave lip-service to what he knew to be the "correct" point of view, but over a period of weeks and months, he began to accept these judgments inwardly, and to apply them to himself.

"In the cell, you work in order to recognize your crimes. . . . They make you understand your crimes are very heavy. You did harm to the Chinese people. You are really a spy, and all the punishment you received was your own fault. . . . In the cell, twelve hours a day, you talk and talk —you have to take part—you must discuss yourself, criticize, inspect yourself, denounce your thought. Little by little you start to admit something, and look to yourself only using the 'people's judgment.' "

At times, the prison would take on a highly academic atmosphere. Vincent and his fellow prisoners would focus their attention on applying Marxist theory to Chinese and international problems; prisoners would be referred to as "schoolmates," prison officials would be called "instructors," and all would emphasize that only "discussion" and "persuasion" should be used to teach the ignorant. As Vincent became more and more involved in the process, he began to experience its impact.

"They put in evidence, in a compulsory way, the progress of the people. The people have a future. The theories of Marx about history teach us that imperialism is condemned to be destroyed. . . . They put in evidence all the examples of repression by the imperialists in China, the missions, their charity, helping landlords, helping the KMT [Kuomintang, or Nationalist Party]—all against the people. . . . They put in evidence the development of the Soviet Union—its industries, re-education, culture, uplifting of the people, the friendly help of the Soviet to China. They told us of the victory against imperialism in the Korean war, the gradual remolding of Chinese society, the three- and five-year plans in order to arrive at a socialist society, the transformation of agriculture, the development of heavy industries, military improvement to defend the people, peace movement. . . . Living conditions of the Soviet state are very high; we see it in the movies, magazines, newspapers. We see the better condition of Chinese people in comparison with pre-liberation times—the hygiene movement in China, the cultural, the economic movement, the rights for minorities, rights between man and woman, free elections, the difference between freedom in the socialist and the imperialist worlds. . . . They solve every problem through discussion—the Korean war, the Indo-Chinese war. . . . They never use force; every question is solved through conference."

But always, the emphasis would shift back to the individual emotional experience—to the "thought problems" which prevented prisoners from making progress. Dr. Vincent learned to express "spontaneously" all of his reactions and attitudes during the discussions and especially to bring out his "wrong thoughts." And as he did so, he became ever more enmeshed in the special problem-solving techniques of this ideological world.

"You have to get rid of and denounce all your imperialist thoughts, and you must criticize all of your own thoughts, guided by the official. If not, they will have someone else solve your problem and criticize you more profoundly. . . . You have a problem—you have to denounce it—a schoolmate has to help you—his help has to have 'proper standpoint'. . . . I am quiet—they say, 'You have a problem'; I say, 'I wonder why the Chinese didn't confiscate all of the capitalist properties like the Soviets. I think it might be better to do it like the Russians—this is my problem.' They have schoolmates to solve my problem, to demonstrate I am on the wrong side because the Chinese Communists have to proceed in another way. Their way is reform rather than compulsion. He demonstrates that the Soviet revolution was different from the Chinese revolution—that the Chinese capitalist suffered through the imperialists because we imperialists never gave them the opportunity to develop their industries. Now the Chinese capitalists have to be useful to the Chinese government and undergo reform. If they follow the government they will have a bright future. . . . They have to explain the facts until I am convinced. If I am not convinced I must say I don't understand, and they bring new facts. If I am still not satisfied, I have the right to call an inspector—but I wouldn't, I would just accept, otherwise there might be a struggle. . . . You are all day under the compulsion of denouncing your thoughts and solving your problems. . . . You understand the truth of

the people—day by day, moment by moment—and you cannot escape, because from your external manifestation they say they can understand your internal situation. If you continually denounce your thoughts, you can be happy denouncing yourself. You are not resisting. But they keep a record, and after one week if you are not saying anything, they tell you you are resisting your re-education. . . . If you think out five or six problems it is a good manifestation; you are progressing because you like to discuss your imperialist thoughts. This is necessary, because if you don't get rid of these thoughts, you can't put in new ones."

When Vincent was too quiet and did not produce enough "wrong thoughts," he was criticized for not being "sincere"—for not taking an active enough part in thought reform. When his views showed the slightest deviation from Communist orthodoxy, he was told that he was "too subjective," "individualistic," or that he retained "imperialist attitudes." When it was felt that he was not wholeheartedly involved in his reform—but was merely going through the motions—he was accused of "spreading a smokescreen," "window dressing," "finding a loophole," or "failing to combine theory with practice." And after a while he followed the others' lead in seeking out these faults in himself through self-criticism, and analyzing their cause and their significance.

A portion of the study hours each day were devoted to "daily-life criticisms": general conduct, attitudes toward others, willingness to do one's share of work in the cell, eating and sleeping habits. Where Vincent was found wanting in any of these, this was attributed to "imperialist" or "bourgeois" greed and exploitation, in contrast to the "people's attitude" of sharing and co-operation. When considered lax in his work, he was criticized for lacking the "correct labor point of view"; when he dropped a plate, this was wasting the people's money; if he drank too much water, this was "draining the blood of the people"; if he took up too much room while sleeping, this was "imperialistic expansion."

Vincent would still hear talk of men who were shot because "they resisted"; and on the other hand he heard of the "bright future"—early release or happy existence in China—for those who "accepted their re-education."

ADVANCED STANDING

After more than a year of this continuous "re-education," Vincent was again subjected to a series of interrogations aimed at once more reconstructing his confession—"because after one year the government hopes you understand a little better your crimes." Now from among the great mass of material which he had already produced, the judge focused upon a few selected points, all of which had some relationship to actual events. And thus, "from a wild confession, you go to a more concrete confession." Then, eight "crimes" emerged—including membership in a right-wing French political organization, several forms of "espionage" and "intelligence" in association with American, Catholic, and other "reactionary" groups, other anti-Communist activities, and "slanderous insults to the Chinese people." But now Vincent was more deeply immersed in the "people's standpoint," and the confession had a much greater sense of reality for him than before.

"You have the feeling that you look to yourself on the people's side, and that you are a criminal. Not all of the time—but moments—you think they are right. 'I did this, I am a criminal.' If you doubt, you keep it to yourself. Because if you admit the doubt you will be 'struggled' and lose the progress you have made. . . . In this way they built up a spy mentality. . . . They built up a criminal. . . . Then your invention becomes a reality. . . . You feel guilty, because all of the time you have to look at yourself from the people's standpoint, and the more deeply you go into the people's standpoint, the more you recognize your crimes."

And at this point he began, in the "correct" manner, to relate his own sense of guilt to the Communist world view:

"They taught us what it means to be a capitalist . . . . to enslave and exploit the people so that a small group of persons can enjoy life at the expense of the masses, their capital coming from the blood of the people, not from labor . . . . that all property comes from the blood of the peasant . . . . that we helped this bad policy, that our mind is the capitalistic mind . . . . and in our profession we exploited everyone. We used our profession to exploit people, as we can see from our crimes."

Then came another fourteen months of full-time re-education. Vincent continued to concentrate upon applying Communist theory to his personal situation, demonstrating an ever-expanding "recognition" of his "crimes."

"After two years, in order to show that you are more on the people's side, you increase your crimes. . . . I said I wasn't frank before, there were really more intelligences. . . . This is a good point. It means that you are analyzing your crimes. . . . It means that you realize your crimes are very big, and that you are not afraid to denounce yourself . . . . that you trust the people, trust your re-education, and that you like to be reformed."

By this time his activities were no longer limited to his own case; he had by now become active—and skillful—in criticizing others, "helping" them to make progress in confession and reform. He had become an experienced prisoner, and was beginning to be looked upon as a true progressive. He even came to believe a great deal of what he was expressing—although not in a simple manner:

"You begin to believe all this, but it is a special kind of belief. You are not absolutely convinced, but you accept it—in order to avoid trouble—because every time you don't agree, trouble starts again."

During his third year of imprisonment, he was once more called in for a revision of his confession. The document became even more brief, concrete, "logical," and convincing. Now Vincent began to think of his sentence, estimating it from the "people's standpoint" which had become so much a part of him.

"You have the feeling that your sentence is coming and that you will be sent somewhere else. . . . and you are waiting. . . . You think, 'How long— maybe twenty, twenty-five years'. . . . You will be sent to reform through labor . . . to a factory or to a field. . . . They are very generous about this. . . . The government is very generous. The people are very generous. . . . Now you know that you cannot be shot. . . . But you are thinking that your crimes are very heavy."

Now Vincent was told that his "attitude" had greatly improved. He was transferred to a different wing of the prison—and given treasured privileges, such as an hour of outdoor exercise a day and additional recreation periods in the cell. He found himself living in harmony with his captors, and during the last few months of his imprisonment was even permitted to give French lessons to other prisoners and to conduct medical classes for students brought to the prison for this purpose. All of this was not without its effect:

"They used this as a premium in order to show me that they weren't against my work or my profession, but were only against my reactionary mind. To show that my work was well accepted, that they accepted my theories. . . . To show what it means to live among the people, if I become one of the people. . . . To put in my mind that life among the people is good."

Soon he was called in for a formal signing of his confession—both a French version in his own handwriting, and a Chinese translation. Photographers and moving-picture cameramen were on hand, and he also read it for sound recording.

With many others like it, it was widely disseminated throughout China and other parts of the world. A short time later he was called before the judge, and after three years of "solving" his case, he was read both the charges and the sentence: for "espionage" and other "crimes" against the people, three years of imprisonment—this considered to be already served. He was expelled immediately from China, and within two days, he was on a British ship heading for Hong Kong.

Selection 18

Role, Personality, and Social Structure in the Organizational Setting

Daniel J. Levinson

Berger's discussion of role theory properly emphasized the importance of that concept in sociology. Indeed, since its introduction it has become one of the most widely used concepts in sociology. Yet few sociologists have taken the time to define the term precisely, and its meaning has changed not only with different sociologists but frequently with the same sociologist as well. It is often not clear whether the word *role* refers to society's expectations about a person's behavior, to the way the person himself thought he should behave, or to the way he actually behaved. Linton suggested a distinction between *status*—society's definition—and *role*—actual behavior—but the term *status* has other meanings as well and Linton's usage is disappearing.

In order to handle the possible discrepancies between society's and the individual's definitions of both required behavior and actual role-performance, Levinson suggests a careful distinction between *role-demands* and *personal role-definition*. Role-demands refer to the way the individual is expected to behave according to the norms of the group; these norms may have been derived from the formal charter of an organization or from custom and tradition. It is difficult to know with certainty what role-demands are, since there is rarely consensus about them. The student may ask his friends and relatives to specify how husbands and wives should perform their marital roles in American society to document this lack of agreement.

Personal role-definition refers to the way an individual adapts his behavior to role-demands. There are two levels of adaptation. First, individual *role-conception* defines the way a person *thinks* his role should be performed. Although group members may not share identical role-conceptions, there must be some agreement among them for any system to operate with a reasonable degree of stability. If deans, students, professors, trustees, and parents all had different norms for the role of student, it is hard to see how the process of education could take place. The second level of adaptation is that of individual *role-performance,* which refers to the way a person *actually* performs his role. Just as role-demands and personal role-definitions may not be congruent, so an individual's behavior—his role-performance—does not always correspond to the norms he associates with a particular role—his role-conception.

The sources of the discrepancies between the way a person is expected to behave, the way he thinks he ought to behave, and the way he actually behaves are varied. For example, even when the individual and the group concur, the individual's behavior may deviate because he simultaneously fills other roles whose requirements conflict with those of the role in question. Similarly, different groups in society set different role-demands for the same role, and the actor who accepts the standards of one group may find himself at odds with those of another. Levinson discusses further sources for the lack of agreement and concludes that actual role-performance is the result of the individual's choosing a compromise from among several pressures.

Levinson worked out his analysis of the elements of role by doing research on the behavior of persons working in large-scale bureaucratic organizations, such as factories and hospitals. But his findings about the concept may be applied generally to nonorganizational settings such as the family or the neighborhood.

"SOCIAL ROLE" AS A UNITARY CONCEPT

The concept of role is related to, and must be distinguished from, the concept of social position. A position is an element of organizational anatomy, a location in social space, a category of organizational membership. A role is, so to say, an aspect of organizational physiology; it involves function, adaptation, process. It is meaningful to say that a person "occupies" a social position; but it is inappropriate to say, as many do, that one occupies a role.

There are at least three specific senses in which the term "role" has been used, explicitly or implicitly, by different writers or by the same writer on different occasions.

a. Role may be defined as the *structurally given demands* (norms, expectations, taboos, responsibilities, and the like) associated with a given social position. Role is, in this sense, something outside the given individual, a set of pressures and facilitations that channel, guide, impede, support his functioning in the organization.

b. Role may be defined as the member's *orientation* or *conception* of the part he is to play in the organization. It is, so to say, his inner definition of what someone in his social position is supposed to think and do about it. Mead (1934) is probably the main source of this view of social role as an aspect of the person, and it is commonly used in analyses of occupational roles.

c. Role is commonly defined as the *actions* of the individual members—actions seen in terms of their relevance for the social structure (that is,

seen in relation to the prevailing norms). In this sense, role refers to the ways in which members of a position act (with or without conscious intention) *in accord with or in violation of a given set of organizational norms.* Here, as in (*b*), role is defined as a characteristic of the actor rather than of his normative environment.

Many writers use a definition that embraces all of the above meanings without systematic distinction, and then shift, explicitly or implicitly, from one meaning to another. The following are but a few of many possible examples.

Each of the above three meanings of "role" is to be found in the writings of Parsons: (*a*) "From the point of view of the actor, his role is defined by the normative expectations of the members of the group as formulated in its social traditions" (Parsons, 1945). (*b*) "The role is that organized sector of an actor's orientation which constitutes and defines his participation in an interactive process" (Parsons & Shils, 1951). (*c*) "The status-role (is) the organized subsystem of acts of the actor or actors . . ." (Parsons, 1951).

More often, the term is used in a way that includes all three meanings at once. In this *unitary,* all-embracing conception of role, there is, by assumption, a close fit between behavior and disposition (attitude, value), between societal prescription and individual adaptation. This point of view has its primary source in the writings of Linton, whose formulations of culture, status, and

From the *Journal of Abnormal and Social Psychology,* Vol. 58 (1951), 172–177.

role have had enormous influence. According to Linton (1945), a role "includes the attitudes, values and behavior ascribed by the society to any and all persons occupying this status." In other words, society provides for each status or position a single mold that shapes the beliefs and actions of all its occupants.

Perhaps the most extensive formulation of this approach along sociopsychological lines is given by Newcomb (1950). Following Linton, Newcomb asserts, "Roles thus represent ways of carrying out the functions for which positions exist—ways which are generally agreed upon within (the) group." And, "Role is strictly a sociological concept; it purposely ignores individual, psychological facts." Having made this initial commitment to the "sociological" view that individual role-activity is a simple mirroring of group norms, Newcomb later attempts to find room for his "psychological" concerns with motivation, meaning, and individual differences. He does this by partially giving up the "unitary" concept of role, and introducing a distinction between "prescribed role" and "role behavior." He avers that prescribed role is a sociological concept, "referring to common factors in the behaviors required," whereas role behavior is a psychological concept that refers to the activities of a single individual. The implications of this distinction for his earlier general definition of role are left unstated.

Whatever the merits or faults of Newcomb's reformulation, it at least gives conceptual recognition to the possibility that social prescription and individual adaptation may not match. This possibility is virtually excluded in the definition of social role forwarded by Linton and used by so many social scientists. In this respect, though certainly not in all respects, Linton's view is like Weber's: both see individual behavior as predominantly determined by the collective matrix. The matrix is, in the former case, culture, and in the latter, bureaucracy.

In short, the "unitary" conception of role assumes that there is a 1:1 relationship, or at least a *high degree of congruence,* among the three role aspects noted above. In the theory of bureaucratic organization, the rationale for this assumption is somewhat as follows. The organizationally given requirements will be internalized by the members and will thus be mirrored in their role-conceptions. People will know, and will want to do, what is expected of them. The agencies of role socialization will succeed except with a deviant minority—who constitute a separate problem for study. Individual action will in turn reflect the structural norms, since the appropriate role-conceptions will have been internalized and since

the sanctions system rewards normative behavior and punishes deviant behavior. Thus, it is assumed that structural norms, individual role-conceptions and individual role-performance are three isomorphic reflections of a single entity: "the" role appropriate to a given organizational position.

It is, no doubt, reasonable to expect some degree of congruence among these aspects of a social role. Certainly, every organization contains numerous mechanisms designed to further such congruence. At the same time, it is a matter of common observation that organizations vary in the degree of their integration; structural demands are often contradictory, lines of authority may be defective, disagreements occur and reverberate at and below the surface of daily operations. To assume that what the organization requires, and what its members actually think and do, comprise a single, unified whole is severely to restrict our comprehension of organizational dynamics and change.

It is my thesis, then, that the unitary conception of social role is unrealistic and theoretically constricting. We should, I believe, eliminate the single term "role" except in the most general sense, i.e., of "role theory" as an over-all frame of analysis. Let us, rather, give independent conceptual and empirical status to the above three concepts and others. Let us investigate the relationships of each concept with the others, making no assumptions about the degree of congruence among them. Further, let us investigate their relationships with various other characteristics of the organization and of its individual members. I would suggest that the role concepts be named and defined as follows.

ORGANIZATIONALLY GIVEN ROLE-DEMANDS

The role-demands are external to the individual whose role is being examined. They are the situational pressures that confront him as the occupant of a given structural position. They have manifold sources: in the official charter and policies of the organization; in the traditions and ideology, explicit as well as implicit, that help to define the organization's purposes and modes of operation; in the views about this position which are held by members of the position (who influence any single member) and by members of the various positions impinging upon this one; and so on.

It is a common assumption that the structural requirements for any position are as a rule defined with a *high degree of explicitness, clarity, and consensus* among all the parties involved. To take the position of hospital nurse as an example: it is assumed that her role-requirements will be understood and agreed upon by the hospital administration, the nursing authorities, the physicians, etc. Yet one of the striking research findings in all manner of hospitals is the failure of consensus regarding the proper role of nurse. Similar findings have been obtained in school systems, business firms, and the like.

In attempting to characterize the role-requirements for a given position, one must therefore guard against the assumption that they are unified and logically coherent. There may be major differences and even contradictions between official norms, as defined by charter or by administrative authority, and the "informal" norms held by various groupings within the organization. Moreover, within a given-status group, such as the top administrators, there may be several conflicting viewpoints concerning long range goals, current policies, and specific role-requirements. In short, the structural demands themselves are often multiple and disunified. Few are the attempts to investigate the sources of such disunity, to acknowledge its frequency, or to take it into conceptual account in general structural theory.

It is important also to consider the specificity or *narrowness* with which the normative requirements are defined. Norms have an "ought" quality; they confer legitimacy and reward-value upon certain modes of action, thought and emotion, while condemning others. But there are degrees here. Normative evaluations cover a spectrum from "strongly required," through various degrees of qualitative kinds of "acceptable," to more or less stringently tabooed. Organizations differ in the width of the intermediate range on this spectrum. That is, they differ in the number and kinds of adaptation that are normatively acceptable. The wider this range—the less specific the norms—the greater is the area of personal choice for the individual. While the existence of such an intermediate range is generally acknowledged, structural analyses often proceed as though practically all norms were absolute prescriptions or proscriptions allowing few alternatives for individual action.

There are various other normative complexities to be reckoned with. A single set of role-norms may be internally contradictory. In the case of the mental hospital nurse, for example, the norm of maintaining an "orderly ward" often conflicts with the norm of encouraging self-expression in patients. The individual nurse then has a range of choice, which may be narrow or wide, in balancing these conflicting requirements. There are also ambiguities in norms, and discrepancies between those held explicitly and those that are less verbalized and perhaps less conscious. These normative complexities permit, and may even induce, significant variations in individual role-performance.

The degree of *coherence* among the structurally defined role-requirements, the degree of *consensus* with which they are held, and the degree of *individual choice* they allow (the range of acceptable alternatives) are among the most significant properties of any organization. In some organizations, there is very great coherence of role-requirements and a minimum of individual choice. In most cases, however, the degree of integration within roles and among sets of roles appears to be more moderate. This structural pattern is of especial interest from a sociopsychological point of view. To the extent that the requirements for a given position are ambiguous, contradictory, or otherwise "open," the individual members have greater opportunity for selection among existing norms and for creation of new norms. In this process, personality plays an important part. I shall return to this issue shortly.

While the normative requirements (assigned tasks, rules governing authority-subordinate relationships, demands for work output, and the like) are of great importance, there are other aspects of the organization that have an impact on the individual member. I shall mention two that are sometimes neglected.

Role-facilities

In addition to the demands and obligations imposed upon the individual, we must also take into account the techniques, resources, and conditions of work—the means made available to him for fulfilling his organizational functions. The introduction of tranquillizing drugs in the mental hospital, or of automation in industry, has provided tremendous leverage for change in organizational structure and role-definition. The teacher-student ratio, an ecological characteristic of every school, grossly affects the probability that a given teacher will work creatively with individual students. In other words, technological and ecological facilities are not merely "tools" by which norms are met; they are often a crucial basis for the maintenance or change of an organizational form.

Role-dilemmas or problematic issues

In describing the tasks and rules governing a given organizational position, and the facilities provided for their realization, we are, as it were, looking at that position from the viewpoint of a higher administrative authority whose chief concern is "getting the job done." Bureaucracy is often analyzed from this (usually implicit) viewpoint. What is equally necessary, though less often done, is to look at the situation of the position-members from their own point of view: the meaning it has for them, the feelings it evokes, the ways in which it is stressful or supporting. From this sociopsychological perspective, new dimensions of role analysis emerge. The concept of role-dilemma is an example. The usefulness of this concept stems from the fact that every human situation has its contradictions and its problematic features. Where such dilemmas exist, there is no "optimal" mode of adaptation; each mode has its advantages and its costs. Parsons (1951), in his discussion of "the situation of the patient," explores some of the dilemmas confronting the ill person in our society. Erikson (1957) and Pine and Levinson (1958) have written about the dilemmas of the mental hospital patient; for example, the conflicting pressures (from without and from within) toward cure through self-awareness and toward cure through repressive self-control. Role-dilemmas of the psychiatric resident have been studied by Sharaf and Levinson (1957). Various studies have described the problems of the factory foreman caught in the conflicting cross-pressures between the workers he must supervise and the managers to whom he is responsible. The foreman's situation tends to evoke feelings of social marginality, mixed identifications, and conflicting tendencies to be a good "older brother" with subordinates and an obedient son with higher authority.

Role-dilemmas have their sources both in organizational structure and in individual personality. Similarly, both structure and personality influence the varied forms of adaptation that are achieved. The point to be emphasized here is that every social structure confronts its members with adaptive dilemmas. If we are to comprehend this aspect of organizational life, we must conceive of social structure as having intrinsically *psychological* properties, as making complex psychological demands that affect, and are affected by, the personalities of its members.

PERSONAL ROLE-DEFINITION

In the foregoing we have considered the patterning of the environment for an organizational position—the kind of sociopsychological world with which members of the position must deal. Let us turn now to the individual members themselves. Confronted with a complex system of requirements, facilities, and conditions of work, the individual effects his modes of adaptation. I shall use the term "personal role-definition" to encompass the individual's adaptation within the organization. This may involve passive "adjustment," active furthering of current role-demands, apparent conformity combined with indirect "sabotage," attempts at constructive innovation (revision of own role or of broader structural arrangements), and the like. The personal role-definition may thus have varying degrees of fit with the role-requirements. It may serve in various ways to maintain or to change the social structure. It may involve a high or a low degree of self-commitment and personal involvement on the part of the individual.

For certain purposes, it is helpful to make a sharp distinction between two levels of adaptation: at a more *ideational* level, we may speak of a role-conception; at a more *behavioral* level, there is a pattern of role-performance. Each of these has an affective component. Role-conception and role-performance are independent though related variables; let us consider them in turn.

Individual (and modal) role-conceptions

The nature of a role-conception may perhaps be clarified by placing it in relation to an ideology. The boundary between the two is certainly not a sharp one. However, ideology refers most directly to an orientation regarding the entire organizational (or other) structure—its purposes, its modes of operation, the prevailing forms of individual and group relationships, and so on. A role-conception offers a definition and rationale for one position within the structure. If ideology portrays and rationalizes the organizational world, then role-conception delineates the specific functions, values, and manner of functioning appropriate to one position within it.

The degree of uniformity or variability in individual role-conceptions within a given position will presumably vary from one organization to another. When one or more types of role-conception are commonly held (consensual), we may speak of modal types. The maintenance of structural stability requires that there be at least moderate consensus and that modal role-conceptions be reasonably congruent with role-requirements. At the same time, the presence of incongruent modal role-conceptions may, under certain conditions, provide an ideational basis for major organizational change.

Starting with the primary assumption that each member "takes over" a structurally defined role, many social scientists tend to assume that there is great uniformity in role-conception among the members of a given social position. They hold, in other words, that for every position there is a *dominant, modal role-conception corresponding to the structural demands,* and that there is relatively little individual deviation from the modal pattern. Although this state of affairs may at times obtain, we know that the members of a given social position often have quite diverse conceptions of their proper roles. After all, individual role-conceptions are formed only partially within the present organizational setting. The individual's ideas about his occupational role are influenced by childhood experiences, by his values and other personality characteristics, by formal education and apprenticeship, and the like. The ideas of various potential reference groups within and outside of the organization are available through reading, informal contacts, etc. There is reason to expect, then, that the role-conceptions of individuals in a given organizational position will vary and will not always conform to official role-requirements. Both the diversities and the modal patterns must be considered in organizational analysis.

Individual (and modal) role-performance

This term refers to the overt behavioral aspect of role-definition—to the more or less characteristic ways in which the individual acts as the occupant of a social position. Because role-performance involves immediately observable behavior, its description would seem to present few systematic problems. However, the formulation of adequate variables for the analysis of role-performance is in fact a major theoretical problem and one of the great stumbling blocks in empirical research.

Everyone would agree, I suppose, that role-performance concerns only those aspects of the total stream of behavior that are structurally relevant. But which aspects of behavior are the important ones? And where shall the boundary be drawn between that which is structurally relevant and that which is incidental or idiosyncratic?

One's answer to these questions probably depends, above all, upon his conception of social structure. Those who conceive of social structure rather narrowly in terms of concrete work tasks and normative requirements, are inclined to take a similarly narrow view of role. In this view, role-performance is simply the fulfillment of formal role-norms, and anything else the person does is extraneous to role-performance as such. Its proponents acknowledge that there are variations in "style" of performance but regard these as incidental. What is essential to *role*-performance is the degree to which norms are met.

A more complex and inclusive conception of social structure requires correspondingly multi-dimensional delineation of role-performance. An organization has, from this viewpoint, "latent" as well as "manifest" structure; it has a many-faceted emotional climate; it tends to "demand" varied forms of interpersonal allegiance, friendship, deference, intimidation, ingratiation, rivalry, and the like. If characteristics such as these are considered intrinsic properties of social structure, then they must be included in the characterization of role-performance. My own preference is for the more inclusive view. I regard social structure as having psychological as well as other properties, and I regard as intrinsic to role-performance the varied meanings and feelings which the actor communicates to those about him. Ultimately, we must learn to characterize organizational behavior in a way that takes into account, and helps to illuminate, its functions for the individual, for the others with whom he interacts, and for the organization.

It is commonly assumed that there is great uniformity in role-performance among the members of a given position. Or, in other words, that there is a *dominant, modal pattern of role-performance corresponding to the structural requirements.* The rationale here parallels that given above for role-conceptions. However, where individual variations in patterns of role-performance have been investigated, several modal types rather than a single dominant pattern were found.

Nor is this variability surprising, except to those who have the most simplistic conception of social life. Role-performance, like any form of human behavior, is the resultant of many forces. Some of these forces derive from the organizational matrix; for example, from role-demands and the pressures of authority, from informal group influences, and from impending sanctions. Other determinants lie within the person, as for example his role-conceptions and role-relevant personality characteristics. Except in unusual cases where all forces operate to channel behavior in the same direction, role-performance will reflect the individual's attempts at choice and compromise among diverse external and internal forces.

The relative contributions of various forms of influence to individual or modal role-performance can be determined only if *each set of variables is defined and measured independently of the others.* That is, indeed, one of the major reasons for emphasizing and sharpening the distinctions among role-performance, role-conception, and role-demands. Where these distinctions are not sharply drawn, there is a tendency to study one element and to assume that the others are in close fit. For example, one may learn from the official charter and the administrative authorities how the organization is supposed to work—the formal requirements—and then assume that it in fact operates in this way. Or, conversely, one may observe various regularities in role-performance and then assume that these are structurally determined, without independently assessing the structural requirements. To do this is to make structural explanations purely tautologous.

More careful distinction among these aspects of social structure and role will also, I believe, permit greater use of personality theory in organizational analysis. Let us turn briefly to this question.

ROLE-DEFINITION, PERSONALITY, AND SOCIAL STRUCTURE

Just as social structure presents massive forces which influence the individual from without toward certain forms of adaptation, so does personality present massive forces from within which lead him to select, create, and synthesize certain forms of adaptation rather than others. Role-definition may be seen from one perspective as an aspect of personality. It represents the individual's attempt to structure his social reality, to define his place within it, and to guide his search for meaning and gratification. Role-definition is, in this sense, an *ego-achievement*—a reflection of the person's capacity to resolve conflicting demands, to utilize existing opportunities and create new ones, to find some balance between stability and change, conformity and autonomy, the ideal and the feasible, in a complex environment.

The formation of a role-definition is, from a dynamic psychological point of view, an "external function" of the ego. Like the other external (reality-oriented) ego functions, it is influenced by the ways in which the ego carries out its "internal functions" of coping with, and attempting to synthesize, the demands of id, superego, and ego. These internal activities—the "psychodynamics" of personality—include among other things: unconscious fantasies; unconscious moral conceptions and the wishes against which they are directed; the characteristic ways in which unconscious processes are transformed or deflected in more conscious thought, feeling, and behavioral striving; conceptions of self and ways of maintaining or changing these conceptions in the face of changing pressures from within and from the external world.

In viewing role-definition as an aspect of personality, I am suggesting that it is, *to varying degrees,* related to and imbedded within other aspects of personality. An individual's conception of his role in a particular organization is to be seen within a series of wider psychological contexts: his conception of his occupational role generally (occupational identity), his basic values, life-goals, and conception of self (ego identity), and so on. Thus, one's way of relating to authorities in the organization depends in part upon his relation to authority in general, and upon his fantasies, conscious as well as unconscious, about the "good" and the "bad" parental authority. His ways of dealing with the stressful aspects of organizational life are influenced by the impulses, anxieties, and modes of defense that these stresses activate in him.

There are variations in the degree to which personal role-definition is imbedded in, and influenced by, deeper-lying personality characteristics. The importance of individual or modal personality for role-definition is a matter for empirical study and cannot be settled by casual assumption. Traditional sociological theory can be criticized for assuming that individual role-definition is determined almost entirely by social structure. Similarly, dynamic personality theory will not take its rightful place as a crucial element of social psychology until it views the individual within his sociocultural environment. Lacking an adequate recognition and *conceptualization* of the individual's external reality—including the "reality" of social structure—personality researchers tend to assume that individual adaptation is primarily personality-determined and that reality is, for the most part, an amorphous blob structured by the individual to suit his inner needs.

Clearly, individual role-conception and role-performance do not emanate, fully formed, from the depths of personality. Nor are they simply mirror images of a mold established by social structure. Elsewhere, I have used the term "mirage" theory for the view, frequently held or implied in the psychoanalytic literature, that ideologies, role-conceptions, and behavior are mere epiphenomena or by-products of unconscious fantasies and defenses. Similarly, the term "sponge" theory characterizes the view, commonly forwarded in the sociological literature, in which man is merely a passive, mechanical absorber of the prevailing structural demands.

Our understanding of personal role-definition will remain seriously impaired as long as we fail to place it, analytically, in *both intrapersonal and structural-environmental contexts.* That is to say, we must be concerned with the meaning of role-definition both for the individual personality and for the social system. A given role-definition is influenced by, and has an influence upon, the *psyche* as well as the *socius.* If we are adequately to understand the nature, the determinants, and the consequences of role-definition, we need the double perspective of personality and social structure. The use of these two reference points is, like the use of our two eyes in seeing, necessary for the achievement of depth in our social vision.

Theory and research on organizational roles must consider relationships among at least the following sets of characteristics: structurally given role-demands and -opportunities, personal role-definition (including conceptions and performance), and personality in its role-related aspects. Many forms of relationship may exist among them. I shall mention only a few hypothetical possibilities.

In one type case, the role-requirements are so narrowly defined, and the mechanisms of social control so powerful, that only one form of role-performance can be sustained for any given position. An organization of this type may be able selectively to recruit and retain only individuals who, by virtue of personality, find this system meaningful and gratifying. If a congruent modal personality is achieved, a highly integrated and stable structure may well emerge. I would hypothesize that a structurally congruent modal personality is one condition, though by no means the only one, for the stability of a rigidly integrated system. (In modern times, of course, the rapidity of technological change prevents long-term stability in any organizational structure.)

However, an organization of this kind may acquire members who are not initially receptive to the structural order, that is, who are *incongruent* in role-conception or in personality. Here, several alternative developments are possible.

1. The "incongruent" members may change so that their role-conceptions and personalities come better to fit the structural requirements.
2. The incongruent ones may leave the organization, by choice or by expulsion. The high turnover in most of our organizations is due less to technical incompetence than to rejection of the "conditions of life" in the organization.
3. The incongruent ones may remain, but in a state of apathetic conformity. In this case, the person meets at least the minimal requirements of role-performance but his role-conceptions continue relatively unchanged, he gets little satisfaction from work, and he engages in repeated "sabotage" of organizational aims. This is an uncomfortably frequent occurrence in our society. In the Soviet Union as well, even after 40 years of enveloping social controls, there exist structurally incongruent forms of political ideology, occupational role-definition, and personality.
4. The incongruent members may gain sufficient social power to change the organizational structure. This phenomenon is well known, though not well enough understood. For example, in certain of our mental hospitals, schools and prisons over the past 20–30 years, individuals with new ideas and personal characteristics have entered in large enough numbers, and in sufficiently strategic positions, to effect major structural changes. Similar ideological and structural transitions are evident in other types of organization, such as corporate business.

The foregoing are a few of many possible developments in a relatively monolithic structure. A somewhat looser organizational pattern is perhaps more commonly found. In this setting, structural change becomes a valued aim and innovation is seen as a legitimate function of members at various levels in the organization. To the extent that diversity and innovation are valued (rather than merely given lip-service), variations in individual role-definition are tolerated or even encouraged within relatively wide limits. The role-definitions that develop will reflect various degrees of synthesis and compromise between personal preference and structural demand.

In summary, I have suggested that a primary distinction be made between the structurally given role-demands and the forms of role-definition achieved by the individual members of an organization. Personal role-definition then becomes a linking concept between personality and social structure. It can be seen as a reflection of those aspects of individual personality that are activated and sustained in a given structural-ecological environment. This view is opposed both to the "sociologizing" of individual behavior and to the "psychologizing" of organizational structure. At the same time, it is concerned with both the psychological properties of social structure and the structural properties of individual adaptation.

Finally, we should keep in mind that both personality structure and social structure inevitably have their internal contradictions. No individual is sufficiently all of a piece that he will for long find any form of adaptation, occupational or otherwise, totally satisfying. Whatever the psychic gains stemming from a particular role-definition and social structure, there will also be losses: wishes that must be renounced or made unconscious, values that must be compromised, anxieties to be handled, personal goals that will at best be incompletely met. The organization has equivalent limitations. Its multiple purposes cannot all be optimally achieved. It faces recurrent dilemmas over conflicting requirements: control and freedom; centralization and decentralization of authority; security as against the risk of failure; specialization and diffusion of work function; stability and change; collective unity and diversity. Dilemmas such as these arise anew in different forms at each new step of organizational development, without permanent solution. And perpetual changes in technology, in scientific understanding, in material resources, in the demands and capacities of its members and the surrounding community, present new issues and require continuing organizational readjustment.

In short, every individual and every sociocultural form contains within itself the seeds of its own destruction—or its own reconstruction. To grasp both the sources of stability and the seeds of change in human affairs is one of the great challenges to contemporary social science.

Selection 19

Invitation to Sociology

Peter L. Berger

If it is accurate to say that norms originating in social groups determine what we do, it is no less accurate to say that social roles—systems of norms appropriate to individual social situations—determine what we are. As Berger states in the following selection, long before any person enters the world, society prepares for him the roles he may play. New social roles may appear during a lifetime, of course, but it is safe to say that most of the roles any actor comes to fill were written before he was born.

This does not mean that every aspect of social interaction is strictly determined prior to an individual's entrance upon the scene. Role-conformity is required in varying degrees. On the one hand, some roles are rigidly defined; the priest who performs a ritual ceremony is given little opportunity for innovation—even the gestures he makes and the words he speaks are outlined for him. On the other hand, whether an outfielder pounds his hand in his glove three times, two times, or not at all before making a catch is irrelevant to his role-performance. Roles that allow the more restless members of society freedom from regimen and opportunity for novelty are available in all societies. Furthermore, as Stouffer illustrates in Selection 21, every actor plays many roles simultaneously, and role-expectations may vary with each—in fact, the requirements of one role may conflict with those of another. The model of behavior in which an actor merely unfolds the conduct that is built into his social role does not exist other than as a model.

Included in each role are not only appropriate actions but also corresponding emotions: the professor dispenses knowledge and comes to feel wise; the G.I. tapes a grenade to his jacket lapel and assumes the attitude of a fighting man. As Berger points out, once an individual has internalized the demands of a role, he becomes a professional actor—he becomes what he plays at. It is through playing a role that a person acquires his identity, what Berger calls the *essential self*. But since actors simultaneously play different roles, Berger prefers the plural "essential selves." Sometimes the various roles an individual fills have a related quality—the martinet commanding officer is also an authoritarian husband-father

—but this is not always the case. Most persons play a "kaleidoscope of roles and identities." Two people may both know a third individual well and yet have radically different views about him because they encounter him in different roles. Berger makes a strong case for the sociological view of personality as opposed to psychological theories that stress the importance of integrated personalities.

On college campuses, students are often said to be struggling to find their identities. Berger's examination of the properties of identity helps illuminate the students' problem. In the first place, identity is based on roles and is, therefore, not self-selected but socially assigned. In his earliest roles—male, son, brother, grandson—the actor has no choice. Later, in an open society, he can try out for additional roles, but these still depend on assignment by other actors since every role is a system of rights and obligations and involves two or more actors. That is, if one actor has a right, he has it because other actors are willing to meet an obligation. In the absence of such reciprocity, an actor deludes himself about his identity. The support of others is necessary to maintain an identity.

The identity problem of young Americans is a complex one for further reasons. Learning to play a male role is difficult if there is no male model in the home. Choosing an occupation is extremely crucial in a society in which one's job determines his whole style of life. Courtship and marriage are especially critical steps in a kinship system that focuses on marriage. The young person must decide not only which roles supply the identities he desires, but he must also try to "manipulate his affiliations" in order to fill them successfully. In a society where many roles are left open to competition, it is not enough to know which ones constitute an actor's "essential selves."

So far, approaching society mainly under the aspect of its control systems, we have viewed the individual and society as two entities confronting each other. Society has been conceived as an external reality that exerts pressure and coercion upon the individual. If this picture were left unmodified, one would obtain a quite erroneous impression of the actual relationship, namely, an impression of masses of men constantly straining at their leashes, surrendering to the controlling authorities with gnashing teeth, constantly driven to obedience by fear of what may happen to them otherwise. Both commonsense knowledge of society and sociological analysis proper tell us that this is not so. For most of us the yoke of society seems easy to bear. Why? Certainly not because the power of society is less than [formidable]. Why then do we not suffer more from this power? The sociological answer to this question has already been alluded to—because most of the time we ourselves desire just that which society expects of us. We *want* to obey the rules. We *want* the parts that society has assigned to us. And this in turn is possible not because the power of society is less, but because it is much more than we [ordinarily believe it to be]. Society not only determines what we do but also what we are. In other words, social location involves our being as well as our conduct. To explicate this

crucial element of sociological perspective we shall now look at three further areas of investigation and interpretation, those of role theory, the sociology of knowledge and reference-group theory.

Role theory has been almost entirely an American intellectual development. Some of its germinal insights go back to William James, while its direct parents are two other American thinkers, Charles Cooley and George Herbert Mead. It cannot be our purpose here to give a historical introduction to this quite fascinating portion of intellectual history. Rather than try this even in outline, we shall start more systematically by beginning our consideration of the import of role theory with another look at [William I.] Thomas' concept of the definition of the situation.

The reader will recall Thomas' understanding of the social situation as a sort of reality agreed upon *ad hoc* by those who participate in it, or, more exactly, those who do the defining of the situation. From the viewpoint of the individual participant this means that each situation he enters confronts him with specific expectations and demands of him specific responses to these expectations. As we have already seen, powerful pressures exist in just about any social situation to ensure that the proper responses are indeed forthcoming. Society can exist by virtue of the fact that most of the time most people's definitions of the most important situations at least coincide approximately. The motives of the publisher and the writer of these lines may be rather different, but the ways the two define the situation in which this book is being produced are sufficiently similar for the joint venture to be possible. In similar fashion there may be quite divergent interests present in a classroom of students, some of them having little connection with the educational activity that is supposedly going on, but in most cases these interests (say, that one student came to study the subject being taught, while another simply registers for every course taken by a certain redhead he is pursuing) can coexist in the situation without destroying it. In other words, there is a certain amount of leeway in the extent to which response must meet expectation for a situation to remain sociologically viable. Of course, if the definitions of the situation are too widely discrepant, some form of social conflict or disorganization will inevitably result—say, if some students interpret the classroom meeting as a party, or if an author has no intention of producing a book but is using his contract with one publisher to put pressure on another.

While an average individual meets up with very different expectations in different areas of his life in society, the situations that produce these expectations fall into certain clusters. A student may take two courses from two different professors in two different departments, with considerable variations in the expectations met with in the two situations (say, as between formality or informality in the relations between professor and students). Nevertheless, the situations will be sufficiently similar to each other and to other classroom situations previously experienced to enable the student to carry into both situations essentially the same overall response. In other words, in both cases, with but a few modifications, he will be able to *play the role* of student. A role, then, may be defined as a typified response to a typified expectation. Society has predefined the fundamental typology. To use the language of the theater, from which the concept of role is derived, we can say that society provides the script for all the *dramatis personae*. The individual actors, therefore, need but slip into the roles already assigned to them before the curtain goes up. As long as they play their roles as provided for in this script, the social play can proceed as planned.

The role provides the pattern according to which the individual is to act in the particular situation. Roles, in society as in the theater, will vary in the exactness with which they lay down instructions for the actor. Taking occupational roles for an instance, a fairly minimal pattern goes into the role of garbage collector, while physicians or clergymen or officers have to acquire all kinds of distinctive mannerisms, speech and motor habits, such as military bearing, sanctimonious diction or bedside cheer. It would, however, be missing an essential aspect of the role if one regarded it merely as a regulatory pattern for externally visible actions. One feels more ardent by kissing, more humble by kneeling and more angry by shaking one's fist. That is, the kiss not only expresses ardor but manufactures it. Roles carry with them both certain actions and the emotions and attitudes that belong to these actions. The professor putting on an act that pretends to wisdom comes to feel wise. The preacher finds himself believing what he preaches. The soldier discovers martial stirrings in his breast as he puts on his uniform. In each case, while the emotion or attitude may have been present before the role was taken on, the latter inevitably strengthens what was there before. In many instances there is every reason to suppose that nothing at all anteceded the playing of the role in the actor's consciousness. In other words, one becomes wise by being appointed a professor, believing by engaging in activities that presuppose belief, and ready for battle by marching in formation.

Let us take an example. A man recently commissioned as an officer, especially if he came up through the ranks, will at first be at least slightly embarrassed by the salutes he now receives from the enlisted men he meets on his way. Probably he will respond to them in a friendly, almost apologetic manner. The new insignia on his uniform are at that point still something that he has merely put on, almost like a disguise. Indeed, the new officer may even tell himself and others that underneath he is still the same person, that he simply has new responsibilities (among which, *en passant*, is the duty to accept the salutes of enlisted men). This attitude is not likely to last very long. In order to carry out his new role of officer, our man must maintain a certain bearing. This bearing has quite definite implications. Despite all the double-talk in this area that is customary in so-called democratic armies, such as the American one, one of the fundamental implications is that an officer is a superior somebody, entitled to obedience and respect on the basis of this superiority. Every military salute given by an inferior in rank is an act of obeisance, received as a matter of course by the one who returns it. Thus, with every salute given and accepted (along, of course, with a hundred other ceremonial acts that enhance his new status) our man is fortified in his new bearing—and in its, as it were, ontological presuppositions. He not only acts like an officer, he feels like one. Gone are the embarrassment, the apologetic attitude, the I'm-just-another-guy-really grin. If on some occasion an enlisted man should fail to salute with the appropriate amount of enthusiasm or even commit the unthinkable act of failing to salute at all, our officer is not merely going to punish a violation of military regulations. He will be driven with every fiber of his being to redress an offence against the appointed order of his cosmos.

It is important to stress in this illustration that only very rarely is such a process deliberate or based on reflection. Our man has not sat down and figured out all the things that ought to go into his new role, including the things that he ought to feel and believe. The strength of the process comes precisely from its unconscious, unreflecting character. He has become an officer almost as effortlessly as he grew into a person with blue eyes, brown hair and a height of six feet. Nor would it be correct to say that our man must be rather stupid and quite an exception among his comrades. On the contrary, the exception is the man who reflects on his roles and his role changes (a type, by the way, who would probably make a poor officer). Even very intelligent people, when faced with doubt about their roles in society, will involve themselves even more in the doubted activity rather than withdraw into reflection. The theologian who doubts his faith will pray more and increase his church attendance, the businessman beset by qualms about his rat-race activities starts going to the office on Sundays too, and the terrorist who suffers from nightmares volunteers for nocturnal executions. And, of course, they are perfectly correct in this course of action. Each role has its inner discipline, what Catholic monastics would call its "formation." The role forms, shapes, patterns both action and actor. It is very difficult to pretend in this world. Normally, one becomes what one plays at.

Every role in society has attached to it a certain identity. As we have seen, some of these identities are trivial and temporary ones, as in some occupations that demand little modification in the being of their practitioners. It is not difficult to change from garbage collector to night watchman. It is considerably more difficult to change from clergyman to officer. It is very, very difficult to change from Negro to white. And it is almost impossible to change from man to woman. These differences in the ease of role changing ought not to blind us to the fact that even identities that we consider to be our essential selves have been socially assigned. Just as there are racial roles to be acquired and identified with, so there are sexual roles. To say "I am a man" is just as much a proclamation of role as to say "I am a colonel in the U.S. Army." We are well aware of the fact that one is born a male, while not even the most humorless martinet imagines himself to have been born with a golden eagle sitting on his umbilical cord. But to be biologically male is a far cry from the specific, socially defined (and, of course, socially relative) role that goes with the statement "I am a man." A male child does not have to learn to have an erection. But he must learn to be aggressive, to have ambitions, to compete with others, and to be suspicious of too much gentleness in himself. The male role in our society, however, requires all these things that one must learn, as does a male identity. To have an erection is not enough—if it were, regiments of psychotherapists would be out of work.

This significance of role theory could be summarized by saying that, in a sociological perspective, identity is socially bestowed, socially sustained and socially transformed. The example of the man in process of becoming an officer may suffice to illustrate the way in which identities are bestowed in adult life. However, even roles that are much more fundamentally part of what psychologists would call our personality than those associated with a particular adult activity are bestowed in very similar manner through a social process. This has been demonstrated over and over again in studies of so-called socialization—the process by which a child learns to be a participant member of society.

Probably the most penetrating theoretical account of this process is the one given by Mead, in which the genesis of the self is interpreted as being one and the same event as the discovery of society. The child finds out who he is as he learns what society is. He learns to play roles properly belonging to him by learning, as Mead puts it, "to take the role of the other"—which, incidentally, is the crucial sociopsychological function of play, in which children masquerade with a variety of social roles and in doing so discover the significance of those being assigned to them. All this learning occurs, and can only occur, in interaction with other human beings, be it the parents or whoever else raises the child. The child first takes on roles *vis-à-vis* what Mead calls his "significant others," that is, those persons who deal with him intimately and whose attitudes are decisive for the formation of his conception of himself. Later, the child learns that the roles he plays are not only relevant to this intimate circle, but relate to the expectations directed toward him by society at large. This higher level of abstraction in the social response Mead calls the discovery of the "generalized other." That is, not only the child's mother expects him to be good, clean and truthful, society in general does so as well. Only when this general conception of society emerges is the child capable of forming a clear conception of himself. "Self" and "society," in the child's experience, are the two sides of the same coin.

In other words, identity is not something "given," but is bestowed in acts of social recognition. We become that as which we are addressed. The same idea is expressed in Cooley's well-known description of the self as a reflection in a looking glass. This does not mean, of course, that there are not certain characteristics an individual is born with, that are carried by his genetic heritage regardless of the social environment in which the latter will have to unfold itself. Our knowledge of man's biology does not as yet allow us a very clear picture of the extent to which this may be true. We do know, however, that the room for social formation within those genetic limits is very large indeed. Even with the biological questions left largely unsettled, we can say that to be human is to be recognized as human, just as to be a certain kind of man is to be recognized as such. The child deprived of human affection and attention becomes dehumanized. The child who is given respect comes to respect himself. A little boy considered to be a *schlemiel* becomes one, just as a grown-up treated as an awe-inspiring young god of war begins to think of himself and act as is appropriate to such a figure—and, indeed, merges his identity with the one he is presented with in these expectations.

Identities are socially bestowed. They must also be socially sustained, and fairly steadily so. One cannot be human all by oneself and, apparently, one cannot hold on to any particular identity all by oneself. The self-image of the officer as an officer can be maintained only in a social context in which others are willing to recognize him in this identity. If this recognition is suddenly withdrawn, it usually does not take very long before the self-image collapses.

Cases of radical withdrawal of recognition by society can tell us much about the social character of identity. For example, a man turned overnight from a free citizen into a convict finds himself subjected at once to a massive assault on his previous conception of himself. He may try desperately to hold on to the latter, but in the absence of others in his immediate environment confirming his old identity he will find it almost impossible to maintain it within his own consciousness. With frightening speed he will discover that he is acting as a convict is supposed to, and feeling all the things that a convict is expected to feel. It would be a misleading perspective on this process to look upon it simply as one of the disintegration of personality. A more accurate way of seeing the phenomenon is as a reintegration of personality, no different in its sociopsychological dynamics from the process in which the old identity was integrated. It used to be that our man was treated by all the important people around him as responsible, dignified, considerate and aesthetically fastidious. Consequently he was able to be all these things. Now the walls of the prison separate him from those whose recognition sustained him in the exhibition of these traits. Instead he is now surrounded by people who treat him as irresponsible, swinish in behavior, only out for his own interests and careless of his appearance unless forced to take care by constant supervision. The new expectations are typified in the convict role that responds to them just as the old ones were integrated into a different pattern of conduct. In both cases, identity comes with conduct and conduct occurs in response to a specific social situation.

Extreme cases in which an individual is radically stripped of his old identity simply illustrate more sharply processes that occur in ordinary life. We live our everyday lives within a complex web of recognitions and nonrecognitions. We work better when we are given encouragement by our superiors. We find it hard to be anything but clumsy in a gathering where we know people have an image of us as awkward. We become wits when people expect us to be funny, and interesting characters when we know that such a reputation has preceded us. Intelligence, humor, manual skills, religious devotion and even sexual potency respond with equal alacrity to the expectations of others. This makes understandable the previously mentioned process by which individuals choose their associates in such a way that the latter sustain their self-interpretations. To put this succinctly, every act of social affiliation entails a choice of identity. Conversely every identity requires specific social affiliations for its survival. Birds of the same feather flock together not as a luxury but out of necessity. The intellectual becomes a slob after he is kidnapped by the army. The theological student progressively loses his sense of humor as he approaches ordination. The worker who breaks all norms finds that he breaks even more after he has been given a medal by management. The young man with anxieties about his virility becomes hell-on-wheels in bed when he finds a girl who sees him as an avatar of Don Giovanni.

. . . [T]he individual locates himself in society within systems of social control, and every one of these contains an identity-generating apparatus. Insofar as he is able the individual will try to manipulate his affiliations (and especially his intimate ones) in such a way as to fortify the identities that have given him satisfaction in the past—marrying a girl who thinks he has something to say, choosing friends who regard him as entertaining, selecting an occupation that gives him recognition as up-and-coming. In many cases, of course, such manipulation is not possible. One must then do the best one can with the identities one is thrown.

Such sociological perspective on the character of identity gives us a deeper understanding of the human meaning of prejudice. As a result, we obtain the chilling perception that the prejudging not only concerns the victim's external fate at the hands of his oppressors, but also his consciousness as it is shaped by their expectations. The most terrible thing that prejudice can do to a human being is to make him tend to become what the prejudiced image of him says that he is. The Jew in an anti-Semitic milieu must struggle hard not to become more and more like the anti-Semitic stereotype, as must the Negro in a racist situation. Significantly, this struggle will only have a chance of success when the individual is protected from succumbing to the prejudiced program for his personality by what we could call the counterrecognition of those within his immediate community. The Gentile world might recognize him as but another despicable Jew of no consequence, and treat him accordingly, but this nonrecognition of his worth may be balanced by the counterrecognition of him within the Jewish community itself as, say, the greatest Talmudic scholar in Latvia.

In view of the sociopsychological dynamics of this deadly game of recognitions, it should not surprise us that the problem of "Jewish identity" arose only among modern Western Jews when assimilation into the surrounding Gentile society had begun to weaken the power of the Jewish community itself to bestow alternate identities on its members as against the identities assigned to them by anti-Semitism. As an individual is forced to gaze at himself in a mirror so constructed as to let him see a leering monster, he must frantically search for other men with other mirrors, unless he is to forget that he ever had another face. To put this a little differently, human dignity is a matter of social permission.

The same relationship between society and identity can be seen in cases where, for one reason or another, an individual's identity is drastically changed. The transformation of identity, just as its genesis and its maintenance, is a social process. We have already indicated the way in which any reinterpretation of the past, any "alternation" from one self-image to another, requires the presence of a group that conspires to bring about the metamorphosis. What anthropologists call a rite of passage involves the repudiation of an old identity (say, that of being a child) and the initiation into a new one (such as that of adult). Modern societies have milder rites of passage, as in the institution of the engagement, by which the individual is gently led by a general conspiracy of all concerned over the threshold between bachelor freedom and the captivity of marriage. If it were not for this institution, many more would panic at the last moment before the enormity of what they are about to undertake.

We have also seen how "alternation" operates to change identities in such highly structured situations as religious training or psychoanalysis. Again taking the latter as a timely illustration, it involves an intensive social situation in which the individual is led to repudiate his past conception of himself and to take on a new identity, the one that has been programmed for him in the psychoanalytic ideology. What psychoanalysts call "transference," the intense social relationship between analyst and analysand, is essentially the creation of an artificial social milieu within which the alchemy of transformation can occur, that is, within which this alchemy can become plausible to the individual. The longer the relationship lasts and the more intensive it becomes, the more committed does the individual become to his new identity. Finally, when he is "cured," this new identity has indeed become what he is. It will not do, therefore, to dismiss with a Marxist guffaw the psychoanalyst's claim that his treatment is more effective if the patient sees him frequently, does so over a long time and pays a considerable fee. While it is obviously in the analyst's economic interest to hold to this position, it is quite plausible sociologically that the position is factually correct. What is actually "done" in psychoanalysis is that a new identity is constructed. The individual's commitment to this new identity will obviously increase the more intensively, the longer and the more painfully he invests in its manufacture. Certainly his capacity to reject the whole business as a fake has become rather minimal after an investment of several years of his life and thousands of dollars of hard-earned cash.

The same kind of "alchemistic" environment is established in situations of "group therapy." The recent popularity of the latter in American psychiatry can again not be interpreted simply as an economic rationalization. It has its sociological basis in the perfectly correct understanding that group pressures work effectively to make the individual accept the new mirror-image that is being presented to him. Erving Goffman, a contemporary sociologist, has given us a vivid description of how these pressures work in the context of a mental hospital, with the patients finally "selling out" to the psychiatric interpretation of their existence that is the common frame of reference of the "therapeutic" group.

The same process occurs whenever an entire group of individuals is to be "broken" and made to accept a new definition of themselves. It happens in basic training for draftees in the army; much more intensively in the training of personnel for a permanent career in the army, as at military academies. It happens in the indoctrination and "formation" programs of cadres for totalitarian organizations, such as the Nazi SS or the Communist Party elite. It has happened for many centuries in monastic novitiates. It has recently been applied to the point of scientific precision in the "brainwashing" techniques employed against prisoners of totalitarian secret-police organizations. The violence of such procedures, as compared with the more routine initiations of society, is to be explained sociologically in terms of the radical degree of transformation of identity that is sought and the functional necessity in these cases that commitment to the transformed identity be foolproof against new "alternations."

Role theory, when pursued to its logical conclusions, does far more than provide us with a convenient shorthand for the description of various social activities. It gives us a sociological anthropology, that is, a view of man based on his existence in society. This view tells us that man plays dramatic parts in the grand play of society, and that, speaking sociologically, he *is* the masks that he must wear to do so. The human person also appears now in a dramatic context, true to its theatrical etymology (*persona,* the technical term given to the actors' masks in classical theater). The person is perceived as a repertoire of roles, each one properly equipped with a certain identity. The range of an individual person can be measured by the number of roles he is capable of playing. The person's biography now appears to us as an uninterrupted sequence of stage performances, played to different audiences, sometimes involving drastic changes of costume, always demanding that the actor *be* what he is playing.

Such a sociological view of personality is far more radical in its challenge to the way that we commonly think of ourselves than most psychological theories. It challenges radically one of the fondest presuppositions about the self—its continuity. Looked at sociologically, the self is no longer a solid, given entity that moves from one situation to another. It is rather a process, continuously created and re-created in each social situation that one enters, held together by the slender thread of memory. How slender this thread is. . . . Nor is it possible within this framework of understanding to take refuge in the unconscious as containing the "real" contents of the self, because the presumed unconscious self is just as subject to social production as is the so-called conscious one, as we have seen. In other words, man is not *also* a social being, but he is social in every aspect of his being that is open to empirical investigation. Still speaking sociologically, then, if one wants to ask who an individual "really" is in this kaleidoscope of roles and identities, one can answer only by enumerating the situations in which he is one thing and those in which he is another.

Now, it is clear that such transformations cannot occur *ad infinitum* and that some are easier than others. An individual becomes so habituated to certain identities that, even when his social situation changes, he has difficulty keeping up with the expectations newly directed toward him. The difficulties that healthy and previously highly active individuals have when they are forced to retire from their occupation show this very clearly. The transformability of the self depends not *only* on its social context, but also on the degree of its habituation to previous identities and perhaps also on certain genetically given traits. While these modifications in our model are necessary to avoid a radicalization of our position, they do not detract appreciably from the discontinuity of the self as revealed by sociological analysis.

If this not very edifying anthropological model is reminiscent of any other, it would be of that employed in early Buddhist psychology in India, in which the self was compared to a long row of candles, each of which lights the wick of its neighbor and is extinguished in that moment. The Buddhist psychologists used this picture to decry the Hindu notion of the transmigration of the soul, meaning to say thereby that there is no entity that passes from one candle to another. But the same picture fits our present anthropological model quite well.

One might obtain the impression from all of this that there is really no essential difference between most people and those afflicted with what psychiatry calls "multiple personality." If someone wanted to harp on the word "essential" here, the sociologist might agree with the statement. The actual difference, however, is that for "normal" people (that is, those so recognized by their society) there are strong pressures toward consistency in the various roles they play and the identities that go with these roles. These pressures are both external and internal. Externally the others with whom one must play one's social games, and on whose recognition one's own parts depend, demand that one present at least a relatively consistent picture to the world. A certain degree of role discrepancy may be permitted, but if certain tolerance limits are passed society will withdraw its recognition of the individual in question, defining him as a moral or psychological aberration. Thus society will allow an individual to be an emperor at work and a serf at home, but it will not permit him to impersonate a police officer or to wear the costume assigned to the other sex. In order to stay within the limits set to his masquerades, the individual may have to resort to complicated maneuvers to make sure that one role remains segregated from the other. The imperial role in the office is endangered by the appearance of one's wife at a directors' meeting, or one's role in one circle as an accomplished *raconteur* is threatened by the intrusion of someone from that other circle in which one has been typed as the fellow who never opens his mouth without putting his foot into it. Such role segregation is increasingly possible in our contemporary urban civilization, with its anonymity and its means of rapid transportation, although even here there is a danger that people with contradictory images of oneself may suddenly bump into each other and endanger one's whole stage management. Wife and secretary might meet for coffee, and between them reduce both home-self and office-self to a pitiable shambles. At that point, for sure, one will require a psychotherapist to put a new Humpty Dumpty together again.

There are also internal pressures toward consistency, possibly based on very profound psychological needs to perceive oneself as a totality. Even the contemporary urban masquerader, who plays mutually irreconcilable roles in different areas of his life, may feel internal tensions though he can successfully control external ones by carefully segregating his several *mises en scène* from each other. To avoid such anxieties people commonly segregate their consciousness as well as their conduct. By this we do not mean that they "repress" their discrepant identities into some "unconscious," for within our model we have every reason to be suspicious of such concepts. We rather mean that they focus their attention only on that particular identity that, so to speak, they require at the moment. Other identities are forgotten for the duration of this particular act. The way in which socially disapproved sexual acts or morally questionable acts of any kind are segregated in consciousness may serve to illustrate this process. The man who engages in, say, homosexual masochism has a carefully constructed identity set aside for just these occasions. When any given occasion is over, he checks that identity again at the gate, so to speak, and returns home as affectionate father, responsible husband, perhaps even ardent lover of his wife. In the same way, the judge who sentences a man to death segregates the identity in which he does this from the rest of his consciousness, in which he is a kindly, tolerant and sensitive human being. The Nazi concentration-camp commander who writes sentimental letters to his children is but an extreme case of something that occurs in society all the time.

It would be a complete misunderstanding of what has just been said if the reader now thought that we are presenting a picture of society in which everybody schemes, plots and deliberately puts on disguises to fool his fellow men. On the contrary, role-playing and identity-building processes are generally unreflected and unplanned, almost automatic. The psychological needs for consistency of self-image just mentioned ensure this. Deliberate deception requires a degree of psychological self-control that few people are capable of. That is why insincerity is rather a rare phenomenon. Most people are sincere, because this is the easiest course to take psychologically. That is, they believe in their own act, conveniently forget the act that preceded it, and happily go through life in the conviction of being responsible in all its demands. Sincerity is the consciousness of the man who is taken in by his own act. Or as it has been put by David Riesman, the sincere man is the one who believes in his own propaganda. In view of the sociopsychological dynamics just discussed, it is much more likely that the Nazi murderers are sincere in their self-portrayals as having been bureaucrats faced with certain unpleasant exigencies that actually were distasteful to them than to assume that they say this only in order to gain sympathy from their judges. Their humane remorse is probably just as sincere as their erstwhile cruelty. As the Austrian novelist Robert Musil has put it, in every murderer's heart there is a spot in which he is eternally innocent. The seasons of life follow one another, and one must change one's face as one changes one's clothes. At the moment we are not concerned with the psychological difficulties or the ethical import of such "lack of character." We only want to stress that it is the customary procedure.

To tie up what has just been said about role theory with what [has been said] about control systems we refer to what Hans Gerth and C. Wright Mills have called "person selection." Every social structure selects those persons that it needs for its functioning and eliminates in one way or another those that do not fit. If no persons are available to be selected, they will have to be invented—or rather, they will be produced in accordance with the required specifications. In this way, through its mechanisms of socialization and "formation," society manufactures the personnel it requires to keep going. The sociologist stands on its head the commonsense idea that certain institutions arise because there are certain persons around. On the contrary, fierce warriors appear because there are armies to be sent out, pious men because there are churches to be built, scholars because there are universities to be staffed, and murderers because there are killings to be performed. It is not correct to say that each society gets the men it deserves. Rather, each society produces the men it needs. We can derive some comfort from the fact that this production process sometimes runs into technical difficulties. . . . [I]t can also be sabotaged. . . . [H]owever, we can see that role theory and its concomitant perceptions add an important dimension to our sociological perspective on human existence.

Selection 20

Sex-Role Differentiation in an Equalitarian Society
Yonina Talmon

The following selection is illuminating not only because it deals with discrepancies between role-demands, role-conceptions, and role-performances but also because it suggests bases for the assignment of roles. The biological factor of sex is one reference point for such assignment. Until recently, at least, men and women have played distinctly different roles within a society, although, except for obvious biological functions, definitions of proper male or female behavior vary from one society to another. In Western society, the male is usually required to play the role of breadwinner; this represents his primary obligation. Men have been largely exempt from other familial obligations. At the same time, they have dominated the roles associated with political leadership. Female roles, on the other hand, have been more directly concerned with the care of children, the preparation of food, cleaning, and economic activities within the home. If women worked outside the family, their jobs were frequently related to the kinds of work done in the home—domestic chores, nursing, teaching.

What happened in a society, or rather a segment of a society—the collective settlements of Israel—in which group values opposed the traditional sex differentiation of roles is the subject of Talmon's study. The people of the collectives wanted men and women to play the same roles; that is, they wished to obliterate sex differences. In Levinson's terms, they did not differentiate between male and female activities when defining role-demands. Women were expected to work and fight alongside the men and to share political leadership in the collective councils; the limited tasks involved in the socialization of children and care of the flat were to be performed jointly by husbands and wives; and men were to participate in what used to be regarded as strictly female activities.

What was the relationship between the egalitarian ideology governing sex roles, the different conceptions individuals had about these roles, and the actual performance of the roles? Talmon found that general egalitarian values remained strong among both sexes on the collectives, but that individual conceptions governing particular activities changed and that sex-role specialties developed in both the "internal system" of the family and the "external system" of the occupational and leadership areas. Women were more likely than men to be responsible for cleaning the home and caring for clothes; they were less likely to be found in heavy agricultural work—in transportation, equipment and machinery maintenance, and the like. Individual role-conceptions developed according to the way roles were performed. Sex differentiation was less marked regarding participation in the committees that organized and planned the activities of the settlements, but it was definitely apparent in this area, too.

What was the source of these discrepancies between role-demands, role-conceptions, and role-performances? Perhaps the traditional Western ideas that many Israeli women held about the "proper" role of women contributed to the gap. Perhaps the egalitarian ideology upon which the role-demands were based had gone beyond the limits of biological possibility. For example, women were able to work and fight when they were young and unencumbered by pregnancy and lactation, but child-bearing made it necessary that they perform work which did not interfere with or jeopardize biological functions. Talmon's study implies that sex-role differences are inherently linked to biological differences and that cultures must assign roles consistent with these differences, and it also implicitly questions the possibility of constructing a society with complete equality of the sexes.

INTRODUCTION

The purpose of this paper is an analysis of the emergence of sex-role differentiation in a society originally based on a denial of sex differences. The Kibbutzim[1] in Israel have consciously cultivated a predominantly masculine image of the feminine role in their systems of training and education. The tenet of sex equality still occupies a central place in their proclaimed ideology. Yet, in spite of the systematic efforts to conduct role allocation in accordance with this ideal, a fairly clear-cut though fairly flexible sex-role differentiation has emerged in internal family activities as well as in work assignment and in nomination to committees and central offices. Most of the general theory on sex-role differentiation is based on one model. It deals with the transition from a sharply differentiated role allocation to a less differentiated one. It seems that the study of this process in reverse might further clarify the interrelations between the institutional and the ideological factors operating in this transition.

The main foci of our analysis will be: (a) analysis of the interrelation between differentiation in internal family tasks and differentiation in external activities; (b) analysis of the interrelation between differentiation in role allocation on the one hand and redefinition of sex-role models on the other; (c) analysis of the main institutionalised mechanisms evolved in order to bridge or cover up the

gap between the proclaimed ideology and reality in this sphere.

SEX-ROLE DIFFERENTIATION IN THE FAMILY

We shall start our analysis with an examination of the division of labor and sex-role models within

From "Sex-Role Differentiation in an Equalitarian Society," a paper by Yonina Talmon.

[1] The main features of collective settlements (Kvutzot or Kibbutzim) are: common ownership of property except for a few personal belongings and communal organization of production and consumption. Members' needs are provided for by communal institutions on an equalitarian basis. All income goes into the common treasury; each member gets only a very small annual allowance for personal expenses. The community is run as a single economic unit and as a single household. Husband and wife have independent jobs. Main meals are taken in the communal dining hall. In most Kibbutzim children live apart from their parents and are looked after by members assigned to this task. They spend a few hours every day with their parents and siblings, but from their birth on they sleep, eat and study in special children's houses. Each age group leads its own life and has its autonomous arrangements. The Kibbutz is governed by a general assembly, which convenes as a rule once a week, by a secretariat and by various committees. Each Kibbutz is affiliated to one of the Federations of Collectives. The Federations recruit most of their new members from youth movements which channel their members to Kibbutzim.

the family. The most important determinants of internal sex-role allocation during the initial phases of the movement were the far-reaching limitation of family functions and the equalitarian ideology. Spouses tended their small and simply-furnished rooms and looked after their children during their daily reunion, but had few other household responsibilities. Internal relations between members of the elementary family were patterned to a large extent on relations between co-members and emphasized equality and companionship. Execution of family tasks was based on a tenet of strict sex equality. Husbands were expected to participate in looking after the family living quarters and take care of the children just as much as their wives. Spouses had no right to impose their authority on each other, and there was hardly any differentiation between their spheres of special competence.

An analysis of our data on the families in the Kibbutzim in our sample reveals a gradual increase of family functions and a concomitant increase in sex-role specialisation. The family has regained some of its lost functions in the sphere of housekeeping. Most families have their afternoon tea at home with their children. In some of the Kibbutzim, families will sometimes eat their evening meal at home too. Housework has become much more time consuming. The typical dwelling unit now consists of a semi-detached flat containing one or two rooms, a kitchenette and private sanitary facilities. While the style of internal decoration has remained on the whole functional and uncluttered, the standard of equipment and the number of items of furniture supplied to each unit have increased considerably. The flat requires now more elaborate and more systematic care. Though most clothing still goes to the communal laundry, many families tend to look after their best clothes at home so that there is a little extra washing, mending and ironing now and then. An increase of the personal money allowance and a certain widening of the range of choice of consumer goods have brought about the need for planning and budgeting. Most important of all changes in this sphere is the partial reversal of functions in the sphere of child care and socialisation. Parents take a more active part in looking after their children. There is much closer cooperation between nurses, instructors, teachers and parents. Parents help in looking after their young children. They take turns in watching them at night and nurse them when they are ill. They help in the preparation of festivals arranged for the children and attend most of them. There is considerably more parental supervision of the children's behaviour, their choice of friends and

their reading habits. Some of the Kibbutzim have introduced a more radical reorganization. Children in these Kibbutzim no longer sleep in the children's houses. They stay with their age groups during the day but return home every afternoon.

An examination of our data on the families in our sample of Kibbutzim and a more systematic and rigorous observation of the division of labour in a subsample of 60 families indicate that a fairly specialised albeit flexible and fluctuating division of labour has emerged in most families. The husband will usually help his wife to clean the flat and prepare the afternoon tea. Few husbands perform these tasks regularly, but all of them do it now and then. A considerable number of the husbands take over household duties only in case of emergency when their wife is either very tired, ill or away. Clothes are exclusively the concern of the wife. The husband does not take much interest in clothes and in almost all cases does not help his wife to look after them at all. In most of the families the wife does most of the housekeeping and it is mainly her responsibility. Her husband is regarded as her assistant or as her temporary stand-in but not as co-worker on equal terms. Budgeting of personal allowances of the whole family is almost invariably the responsibility of the wife. Officially these allowances are personal and not transferable, but in practice this injunction is overruled and the allowances are pooled together and treated as a family allowance. Most men are not very interested in this small-scale budgeting and leave the planning and management of the family "finances" to their wives.

In the sphere of child care, there is considerably more cooperation and interchangeability than in housekeeping. This is clearly the effect of the system of socialisation. As parents do not carry the main responsibility for either maintenance or socialisation of their children, emphasis is put on affective ties. The main function of the parents is to minister to their children's need for security and love. Both of them interact with their children in much the same way and play a common protective role. Fathers usually take a lively interest in their children and participate actively in looking after them. They play with them, take them for walks and put them to bed about as much as the mothers. Mothers have closer contacts with babies and small children but fathers come into the picture very early. Sex of the children has no marked effect either. Fathers are only a little more concerned with boys. Mothers look after both boys and girls.

In spite of the considerable blurring of differences between the father role and the mother role, there are some signs of differentiation even in this sphere. The mother is as a rule more concerned with the bodily well-being of the children and takes care of them while they are at home. She has usually more contact with the children's institutions and the school and supervises the upbringing of her children there. There is not much routine disciplining in the family but such as there is, is more often than not the mother's responsibility. The source of this responsibility is primarily in her duties as housekeeper and part-time caretaker of her children. The child has to conform to certain standards of cleanliness and order. The living quarters of the family in the Kibbutz are small. In many cases one room serves all purposes. While standards of order are by no means very strict and exacting, there is a concern with the neatness of the flat. Even with a maximum of permissiveness the child has to be controlled and restricted to some extent. There are also the problems of personal cleanliness and health preservation. The father is less involved in these problems and the child may find in him an ally in cases of exaggerated concern with them on the part of the mother. The father's main responsibilities are outside the home—in the yard, on the farm, in dealing with communal affairs which concern the Kibbutz as a whole. Mothers have more say in routine matters and practical problems. Fathers have more say in matters of principle. In the eyes of the growing child, the father emerges gradually as the representative of the Kibbutz and its values within the family, while the mother acts primarily as the representative of the family in the Kibbutz.[2]

It should be stressed that while the emergent pattern is based on a division of spheres of competence and authority, it is not a clear-cut and uniform pattern. The family has remained basically equalitarian and does not enforce an institutionalised position of pivotal authority for either of the spouses. Division of labour is more specialised than decision-making but it is not segregated and rigid either. The pattern of role allocation differs appreciably during different phases of the life cycle in any given family and from family to family.

So far we have dealt with actual division of tasks and authority in the family. The ideological aspect of intra-familial differentiation was examined by means of four questions included in our interview schedule. The first question was a general one: "How in your opinion should internal family tasks be divided between the spouses?" This question was followed by more specific questions on the norms pertaining to child rearing, care of the flat and care of clothes.

For the classification of the answers given to these questions two cross cutting criteria were used—extent of sex-role differentiation and degree of flexibility postulated by the norms pertaining to internal division of family tasks. Four distinctive ideological patterns emerge from this classification:

(a) An "equalitarian" pattern, based on strict equality and complete interchangeability.

(b) A "joint" pattern, based on close cooperation between husband and wife. This pattern is less equalitarian and more flexible than the equalitarian pattern. It allows for some sex-role differentiation but demands joint activities and mutual help.

(c) A "differentiated" pattern in which specialised activities outnumber shared ones. Most adherents of this pattern are against any rigid general norm and hold that the division of labour within the family should be decided by the spouses. They saw it as a matter of opinion and convenience and not so much as a matter of principle. This pattern is more flexible and considerably less equalitarian than the former patterns.

(d) A "segregated" pattern, based on a clear-cut and rigid sex-role differentiation. Household work and child care are defined as women's work.

The table shows that respondents tend to be most equalitarian when dealing with the problem on a high level of ideological generalisation but become less equalitarian when dealing with more specific norms. Norms pertaining to child care are more equalitarian than norms pertaining to household duties. Norms of care of clothing are least equalitarian of all. It should be noted that the number of respondents who are undecided, reluctant or unwilling to express their explicit opinion increases progressively when we pass from the general ideological question to the questions pertaining to child care, care of flat and care of clothing. Only 7 of the respondents failed to take a definite stand on the general ideological issue whereas the number of uncommitted and undecided respondents rises to 103 when we reach the most specific issue. The decrease in equalitarianism is accompanied by an increase in ambivalence and indecision.

Comparison of the proclaimed ideology and actual practice in our sub-sample of families indicates that the ideological position is on the

---

[2] Our data disprove the hypothesis that the mother figure is always the more permissive and supportive and the father more denying and demanding as far as the administering of specific disciplines and as far as everyday relations are concerned. It reinforces the hypothesis of "positional" differentiation. The mother is the representative of the family while the father is the representative of the community at large.

whole more equalitarian than the actual practice. While the general ideological position lags far behind there is only a small gap between the more specific norms and actual behaviour. There is in fact quite a close fit between the continuum obtained when examining actual practice and the continuum obtained when considering norms— child care is least differentiated; care of the flat comes next in this respect; care of clothes is almost exclusively feminine.

ROLE ALLOCATION AND ROLE MODELS IN THE EXTERNAL SYSTEM

We turn now to the examination of the extent of sex-role differentiation in work assignments and in nomination to committees.

The original ideology postulated that women should participate equally in hard productive work, especially in agriculture. The main emphasis of the ideology pertaining to intra-familial tasks was on the participation of men in activities traditionally defined as feminine tasks. The main emphasis of the ideology pertaining to work assignment was on the participation of women in masculine tasks. Work assignment was not completely equalitarian even during the initial phases of development but crossing of the line between the masculine and feminine tasks was common. A considerable number of the women were assigned to predominantly masculine occupations and a certain percentage of the men worked in predominantly feminine tasks.

Examination of the work histories of our respondents during the last ten years indicates that there is a gradual but cumulative trend of growing sex-role specialisation in work assignment. [Table 2] shows that a fairly clear-cut division of labour has emerged in this sphere.

Men are concentrated mainly in agriculture, in production services[3] and in central public offices. Women are concentrated in services and in education. A more detailed analysis of each category indicates considerable sex-role specialisation. No woman is assigned to field crops, to fodder, to fishery or to bee keeping, and they are a very small minority in the fruit orchards. Quite a number of them work in the vegetable gardens and in the tree-nursery but even in these branches they are only a third of the workers. Women are a small minority in the dairy and flocks. They constitute about half of the workers in poultry. If we take production services we see that women are found only in accountancy. No women are found in either carpentry, electricity, maintenance of machines or construction. When we turn to the predominantly feminine categories we find indications of an even sharper differentiation. Workers in the kitchen, in the clothing-shops and stores are almost exclusively women. Workers in the shoe-repair shop and in sanitation are almost exclusively men. There is a fairly sharp differentiation in education too. Nurses and kindergarten teachers are exclusively women. Women are a majority in teaching but they are concentrated mainly in primary school teaching. Teachers in high school and instructors are predominantly male. To sum up, most occupations are segregated or almost segregated. There is a small number of occupations where a majority of one sex participates with a minority of the other sex. Women participate in predominantly masculine occupations more than men do in predominantly feminine occupations. Interchangeability is thus limited and asymmetrical.

[3] In this category we include: transportation, equipment and machinery maintenance shop, electrical shop, carpentry shop, construction.

TABLE 1:   Distribution of Ideological Patterns Pertaining to Sex-role Differentiation in Internal Family Tasks (in Percentages)

	EQUALITARIAN	JOINT	DIFFERENTIATED	SEGREGATED	TOTAL	N
General..........	29	44	22	5	100	311
Care of children ...	16	64	8	12	100	278
Care of flat	9	41	24	26	100	233
Care of clothing ...	5	15	5	70	100	215

TABLE 2:   Sex-role Differentiation in Work Assignment (in Percentages)

	AGRICULTURAL	NON-AGRICULTURAL PRODUCTION	PRODUCTION SERVICES	SERVICES	EDUCATION	CENTRAL PUBLIC OFFICES	OTHERS	TOTAL
Men	32	4	27	6	5	11	16	100
Women.....	8	2	1	38	35	2	14	100

We have examined the ideological aspects of work assignment by means of the following questions: "How in your opinion should the jobs be divided between men and women? Are you for or against sex-role differentiation in this sphere?" Classification of the answers to this question leads us again to the four ideological patterns encountered in the ideological analysis of intra-familial differentiation. We present the distribution of these patterns in [Table 3].

The main emphasis is on the "differentiated" pattern while the "joint" pattern is second in importance. The gap between ideology and reality is narrower than in the internal system but has not disappeared completely. Ideological acknowledgement of segregation still lags behind reality.

Let us now turn to an examination of *participation in committees* and *overall leadership* of the community. Examination of the membership of committees in the last 10 years indicates that in most Kibbutzim there is a gradual yet cumulative trend towards growing sex-role differen-

tiation. In the following tables we present the data on the extent of differentiation at the time of our inquiry.

Men predominate in central offices, in the secretariat which is the most important committee in most Kibbutzim, in the economic committee which is second in importance and is sometimes even more important than the secretariat. The members of the committees for planning and security are exclusively male. Though the educational committee is, as we shall soon see, predominantly female, men predominate in the committee in charge of youth activities.

We find approximately proportional representation[4] in three important committees—in the committee in charge of work assignments, in the committee in charge of social relations and personal needs of the members and in the com-

[4]Women are about 45% of the population of the Kibbutzim.

TABLE 3: Ideological Patterns—Sex-role Differentiation in Work Assignment (in Percentages)

EQUALITARIAN	JOINT	DIFFERENTIATED	SEGREGATED	TOTAL	N
10	38	48	4	100	316

TABLE 4: Predominantly Masculine Committees (in Percentages)

	CENTRAL PUBLIC OFFICES	SECRETARIAT	ECONOMIC COMMITTEE	PLANNING COMMITTEE	SECURITY COMMITTEE	YOUTH ACTIVITIES COMMITTEE
Men	97	88	95	100	100	78
Women	3	12	5	—	—	22
Total	100	100	100	100	100	100

TABLE 5: Joint Committees (in Percentages)

	WORK ASSIGNMENT	SOCIAL COMMITTEE	CULTURAL COMMITTEE	ABSORPTION COMMITTEE	HOUSING COMMITTEE	LIBRARY COMMITTEE	LANDSCAPING COMMITTEE
Men	65	60	67	55	55	55	50
Women	35	40	33	45	45	45	50
Total	100	100	100	100	100	100	100

TABLE 6: Predominantly Feminine Committees (in Percentages)

	EDUCATION COMMITTEE	HEALTH COMMITTEE	CONSUMPTION COMMITTEE	SOLDIERS COMMITTEE	PARENTS COMMITTEE
Men	38	39	33	28	—
Women	62	61	67	72	100
Total	100	100	100	100	100

mittee in charge of cultural activities. Joint participation is found also in a number of small committees which are sub-committees of either the social or cultural committees.

Women predominate in the committees in charge of education, health and consumption. They are a majority in the sub-committee in charge of members who serve in the army. Members of the sub-committee in charge of aged parents are exclusively women.

To sum up, there are more exclusively masculine committees than exclusively feminine committees. Men predominate in overall leadership and in central committees. Men predominate in overall planning, in management of economic production and security. Men and women co-operate in the management of social and cultural affairs. Women predominate in committees in charge of consumption, education, health and welfare. Differentiation in this sphere is thus considerable. It should, however, be pointed out that it is neither rigid nor clear-cut. The number of exclusively masculine or exclusively feminine committees is comparatively small. In most committees both sexes are represented. There is quite a number of committees with proportional or near proportional representation.

The ideological attitudes towards participation in committees were examined by means of the following question: "Should women participate as actively as men in communal affairs? Are you for or against sex-role differentiation in this sphere?" The classification of the answers to these questions leads us again to the four ideological patterns encountered in the examination of attitudes towards familial and occupational division of labour.

The main emphasis is on the "joint" pattern, the "differentiated" pattern coming next. A comparatively high percentage of the respondents adhere to the "equalitarian" pattern. As in the former spheres there is more equalitarianism in theory than in practice.

We conclude our examination of internal and external role differentiation by a comparison of actual and ideal division of labour in the three spheres. Differentiation is most marked in the occupational sphere. It is difficult to compare differentiation in the family to differentiation in committees but it is quite clear that there is less segregation in these spheres than in the sphere of work assignment.

Let us now compare the distribution of the ideological patterns.

Norms pertaining to the occupational system are most differentiated. Next in this respect come the norms pertaining to nomination to committees. Norms pertaining to the family are the most equalitarian.

We have already noted above that ideology lags behind reality in both the internal and external systems. This leads to the conclusion that the main pressures in the process of differentiation are institutional and that ideological reformulation follows suit. The original ideology accommodates itself to the changing reality, but lags behind it, conducting a rear-guard action against extreme differentiation. It is perhaps significant that the gap between ideology and reality is narrower in the occupational sphere than in the other spheres. The comparatively sharp occupational sex-role differentiation is sanctioned by the ideology more than the more flexible and more equalitarian sex-role differentiation in the other spheres. This seems to indicate that the pressure towards differentiation is at its strongest in the occupational sphere and that analysis of the process of differentiation in this sphere is of crucial importance.

DYNAMICS OF DIFFERENTIATION

How can we account for the considerable sex-role differentiation revealed by our analysis? Examination of our data on stages of institutional

---

TABLE 7:   Ideological Patterns—Sex-role Differentiation in Social Participation (in Percentages)

	EQUALITARIAN	JOINT	DIFFERENTIATED	SEGREGATED	TOTAL	N
Men	23	38	33	6	100	297

TABLE 8:   Ideological Patterns—Sex-role Differentiation in the Internal and External Systems (in Percentages)

	EQUALITARIAN	JOINT	DIFFERENTIATED	SEGREGATED	TOTAL	N
Family	29	44	22	5	100	312
Occupation........	10	38	48	4	100	316
Committees	23	38	34	5	100	297

differentiation and scrutiny of the assumptions and considerations which underlie the choice of each of the ideological patterns, indicate that *the sex differentiated role allocation emerges out of an interplay between changes in the internal and external systems.* We shall first examine the development of the interrelations between the family and the occupational sphere and then proceed to analyze the dynamic interplay between these institutional spheres and social participation.

There was very little pressure towards sex-role differentiation in the family at first. The Kibbutzim transferred most of the functions which loom so large in other types of family to communal institutions. All families were young and the birth rate was very low. Since the family unit was small and had very few tasks to accomplish, there was little objective need for a clear-cut division of labour or for a unified command to ensure co-ordination. Moreover, since the spouses had very few common objectives and tasks, the unity of the family depended primarily on close, affective contacts and companionship. This pattern of companionship operated against differentiation and rigidity. The process of differentiation sets in with the rise of the birth rate and with the overall increase of family functions. The family regains some of its lost functions and becomes more involved in internal activities. Our material indicates that the more task-oriented the family is the more marked is the tendency towards role differentiation within it.

How can we account for the fact that most of the reassumed family responsibilities fall on the wife? Analysis of the interviews reveals that the effects of former socialisation and the influence of differentiation in the outside world are not eliminated. The equalitarian ideology does not penetrate very deeply and certain traditional norms persist in spite of it. The attitudes towards care of clothes, to take just one example, indicate clearly the effect of a sex differentiated role prototype. We were surprised to find such a strong and emphatic opposition to interchangeability in this sphere. Many of the respondents who were equalitarian on a high level of generalisation stopped short and retracted from their equalitarian position when it came to care of clothes. It was considered as 'inappropriate, effeminate and slightly ridiculous for men to be engaged in such tasks. Quite a number of the respondents felt that it was somehow "unnatural." Covert conventional role images underlie the attitudes to many other tasks. We should take into consideration also the effects of differentiation of initial training—most wives have had more preparatory experience in performing household tasks and are more competent than their husbands in this sphere.

The initial tendency to differentiation is precipitated by the internal dynamics of family living. The advent of children accentuates the importance of familial roles. The identification with the specifically and typically feminine role of mother undermines the masculine image of the feminine role upheld by the official ideology and weakens the resistance to sex-role differentiations. We observe a gradual process of generalisation which leads from childbirth to childrearing to household duties. The various tasks involved in these responsibilities are correlated and are conceived as parts of a complex yet coherent whole.

A similar though more intense process of differentiation occurs in the sphere of work assignment. During the first phases of development the equalitarian ideology was reinforced by the demographic and economic structure of the Kibbutz. The Kibbutzim put an almost exclusive emphasis on productive labour and the standard of living was kept very low. The simple and small-scale services did not require many workers and a considerable number of the women could turn to productive labour. Most members were young and unattached. Innate biological differentiation was not very noticeable and could be ignored. The primary determinant of the shift in the division of labour is the woman's sex-linked childbearing role which accentuates biological differentiation. Communal institutions replace the mother very early but they cannot completely eliminate her special ties to her baby. Pregnancy and nursing of babies partially incapacitate the woman for hard labour in outlying orchards and fields. Pregnant women are usually transferred to lighter tasks and nursing mothers work only part time. Since they have to nurse and feed their babies every few hours it is more convenient for them to work in one of the communal service institutions which are situated near the children's houses. As long as they look after their babies during work hours they have to resign themselves to taking a leave of absence from productive labour. At first this leave of absence was kept to the bare minimum. Communal institutions took over as soon as possible and the mother, no longer hampered during working hours, returned to productive labour. With the birth of more children and with increasing age mothers usually found it increasingly difficult to return to hard physical labour and the maternity leave grew longer. The recurrent and prolonged interruptions entailed serious discontinuity. Mothers lost touch with their former job and drifted away from it.

In the course of time many of them tended to leave agriculture permanently.

The birth of children affects the economic structure of the Kibbutz in yet another way. It entails a growing need for more workers for services and children's care. The balance between productive and non-productive labour changes considerably. This process is further enhanced by the gradual rise in the standard of living. Non-productive labour now absorbs about 50 per cent of the labour force. Women are only about 45 per cent of the total population. The services, child care and education need all the female working power they can get.

The dividing line between masculine and feminine tasks is determined by the ecological setting and by the economic structure of the Kibbutz. We can discern the effect of the following factors: (a) the extent to which a given job requires considerable physical strength and strenuous exertion; (b) the extent to which it requires specialised technical skill; (c) the extent to which it requires spatial mobility; (d) the extent to which it requires continuity of effort for considerable blocks of time from the point of view of the time rhythm of the working day and from the point of view of the overall work career. Considerations of rationalisation and productivisation work against the blurring of sex job differentiation. Agriculture in the Kibbutz is becoming increasingly large scale and heavily mechanised. It seems now a waste to assign able-bodied and technically skilled men to the services. Women cannot fully replace them in productive labour because of the limitations that physical disability and childbirth impose on them. Work assigners find it increasingly difficult to allow women to work in agriculture or to draft men to work in the services. When practical considerations of efficiency gain precedence over ideological considerations, sex differentiated job allocation comes to be regarded as inevitable.

Sex differentiation is an outcome of internal pressures within each sphere as well as of an interplay between them. The occupational sphere exercises pressure on the internal division of labour in the family. Productive labour and overall administration draw the men far afield. Women's work does not take them far from their flat and from the children's houses. They find it easier to fit the care of the flat into their timetable. The children's houses are nearby and the mothers can drop in during the day. They take the children to their flat on their way home. As they are concentrated in occupations closely allied to housekeeping and child care, they find it easier to cope with these tasks at home.

Role differentiation within the family in its turn exerts pressure on the occupational sphere. The emergence of an outright feminine prototype of the woman's role precipitates the process of differentiation in work assignment. There is a growing concern with the preservation of a feminine and youthful appearance. Considerations of beauty care are not quite acceptable and are met with ridicule when admitted openly, yet they have a marked effect on work assignment. Women are not as eager as they used to be to work in agriculture and one of the main reasons for this reluctance is the fear that strenuous and exhausting physical labour and work in the open throughout the year will have an adverse effect on their figure and complexion. There is a growing concern with the maintenance of the right balance between external and internal roles. Women tend to avoid work in overall administration because jobs in this sphere are very demanding and preoccupying and do not leave them enough time and energy for their familial roles. Quite a number of members feel that as a rule women should be assigned to jobs that do not interfere with their paramount duties as wives and mothers.

We have already noted that while sex-role differentiation within the family is considerable, it is less clear-cut than in work assignment. This difference is closely related to the division of functions between the family and the occupational sphere. The dividing line between internal family activities and external activities has shifted considerably but this did not entail a radical change in the institutional division of labour. The Kibbutzim put the main emphasis on the occupational sphere and it has remained the major focus of activities for both men and women. The fact that both husband and wife work fulltime in communal institutions exerts pressure towards sharing of household chores performed after work and obviates the tendency to turn household duties and child care into the wife's exclusive task areas. It should be noted also that the internal pressure towards differentiation within the family is not very strong either. The core of specific family responsibilities has remained comparatively small and most of the tasks involved are not very specialised. These counter-pressures account for the fact that the considerable sex-role specialisation in internal family activities did not lead to rigidity and polarisation.

The attenuation of the equalitarian ideology and the loosening of communal control over the family lead to a considerable variation in familial role allocation during different stages of the life cycle of any given family, and from family to family. The family has a certain leeway to develop a pattern which suits the personally held values, the needs and interests of its members. A change in the size and in the age and sex composition of the family, a shift to a more or less arduous or time-consuming job, lead to role reallocation. Equally important is the interplay between the personalities of husband and wife and the variation in the nature and intensity of the emotional bonds between them. The tendency to sex-role differentiation is evident in all families, yet each family works out its own dynamic pattern.

How do these processes of differentiation affect the patterns of voluntary participation in the committees and how, in their turn, are they affected by them? Participation in committees serves as an important alternative direction of emancipation from sex differentiation. This outlet for activity and avenue of ascent very often compensates the women for their partial exclusion and for the limitation of their opportunities in the occupational sphere. The sphere of participation is less differentiated than the occupational sphere, but it cannot escape from the pressure towards differentiation. This pressure comes from both directions. Lines of cleavage between the sexes in committees are about the same as in the occupational sphere and in the family. Since women are gradually excluded from production and overall administration they lose touch with these aspects of community life and can contribute very little to the work of committees which deal with production, planning or overall administration. When they are elected to one of these committees they are usually very passive and often drop out after a while. They concentrate in committees in charge of organisation, of consumption, of children, of health and of personal problems. Only in these committees can they draw on the experience that they have gained in their jobs and at home and give expert advice. Only in such committees do they feel competent and in their element.

The Kibbutzim realise that joint participation is an indispensable bridge between the sexes and make special efforts to avoid under-representation and segregation. These efforts are only partly successful because most women are not very keen on nomination to committees and many of them try to avoid it as much as possible. The reluctance to accept responsibilities in committees is closely related to the limitation of the family sphere in the Kibbutzim. Participation in committees is an important outlet for housewives since it emancipates them from domesticity and isolation. Women in the Kibbutzim work outside their home all day. Work in service institutions entails intensive, constant, and very often strained contacts with many members. By the end of the day they usually crave for their children and for a quiet evening with their husbands at home. The short time spent together in the evening is the main manifestation of the unity of the family. Cutting it short by active participation in committees during off-hours encroaches on family life.

Yet another important determinant of differentiation is the persistence and resurgence of sex differentiated role stereotypes. Behind the equalitarian façade we find considerable differentiation. The conception of women as reticent, passive and placating has not disappeared. Many feel that a great deal of drive and self-assertion and a strong involvement in public affairs are unfeminine. Attempts of women to make their mark in the general assembly and in the committees are often met with condescension and excessive criticism. Women who hold important leadership positions are treated with a mixture of admiration and vague discomfort. Women tend to be self-conscious and self-deprecating when evaluating their roles in this sphere. The considerable ambivalence concerning feminine social participation reinforces their tendency to withdrawal.

To sum up, the three spheres are closely interconnected. Division of functions among them has many repercussions on internal differentiation within each of them. Concessions made to segregation in one of the spheres call for similar concessions in the others. The task-determined division of labour undermines the equalitarian ideology and reinforces sex differentiated stereotypes which persist and develop in spite of it. The redefinition of role models precipitates the tendency to sex-role differentiation.

INSTITUTIONAL MECHANISMS

The discrepancy between the proclaimed equalitarian ideology and the growing differentiation between the sexes is a source of severe strain. Since women are mainly concentrated in occupations and tasks which are closely allied to traditional housekeeping, they very often feel that they might as well perform these tasks within their own home rather than outside it. They retreat to their private sphere and press for a far-reaching redefinition of the relations between the family and communal institutions. Women are, in fact, the main agents of the familistic trend. The Kibbutzim are thus faced with a dilemma. Institutional exigencies and normative pressures lead to growing differentiation. The Kibbutzim cannot yield to segregation since marked inequality between the sexes breeds discontent and disaffection which threaten to overthrow the collective organization of consumption and child care. This dilemma has led to the emergence of ingenious "intermediate" institutional mechanisms which partly bridge and cover up the gap between ideals and reality and check differentiation. These supplementary mechanisms operate in all three systems but they are most prominent in the occupational sphere.

Rationalisation and mechanisation of service institutions

Until very recently the Kibbutzim have concentrated most of their efforts on improving efficiency in production branches and the services lagged far behind in this respect. Most service branches operated with a minimal budget and with inadequate and outdated equipment. Their organisational structure was, in addition, very loose and ill-defined. The efficiency drive leads to a certain formalisation of communication and control in the work teams and to a far-reaching mechanisation of most work processes. This reorganisation affects the service branches in many ways. It reduces the number of workers engaged in them so that a certain percentage of the women working power can be assigned to other occupations. It raises the standard of services rendered and enhances confidence in collective institutions. Work becomes easier and more manageable. There is less tension within the team and fewer complaints from "clients."

Professionalisation

The Kibbutzim are making a persistent effort to develop scientifically tested techniques in the sphere of housekeeping and child care and to turn these occupations into semi-professions. Workers in these fields are sent to get professional training in institutions outside the community. The Federations organize seminars and refresher courses in home economics, nursing and child care in which members get some theoretical grounding and practical guidance. The training is kept up and continued by means of extensive reading in semi-scientific literature and by occasional lectures. Professionalisation makes manifest the hidden potentialities of collectivistic organisation of the services. It leads to cultivation of different talents and capabilities by specialisation and systematic training. It enables workers to develop high levels of competence and encourages them to perfect their mastery of certain spheres of activity. The professional aura enhances the prestige of jobs in housekeeping and child care and establishes them as full-fledged occupational roles. The specialized training supplies the incumbents of these roles with certain objective criteria of excellence. Their position as competent experts bolsters their status vis-à-vis their "clients" and protects them from excessive criticism.

Diversification of feminine occupations

The occupational opportunities available to women in the Kibbutz are rather limited, but the range of choice open to them can be widened by branching out into new spheres of activity. A recent development in this sphere is the beginning of a training programme in social work, psychological therapy and counseling. Training in arts and crafts provides additional openings. A certain increase of suitable employment opportunities results from the development of local industries and crafts.

De-differentiation

Cultivation of spheres of joint activity. The Kibbutzim make many efforts to cut the number of exclusively feminine or exclusively masculine occupations. They often develop new branches which are suitable for men as well as for women. They try to achieve proportional or nearly proportional representation in as many committees as possible and pressure is put on the women to accept nomination. The nomination committee will often prefer a female candidate to a male one of equal or even better qualifications. This balancing mechanism serves as an antidote to the limiting effects of occupational sex-role differentiation and overcomes to some extent women's reluctance to accept office. Apprenticeship in a committee enables women to gain experience and to develop new interests and new skills. Quite a number of women who were at first very insecure in their new role have gradually become active and competent participants in the deliberations of their committee. Such an *"equilibrating" system of recruitment* helps to discover untapped energies and hidden talents and opens up new avenues of satisfying activity.

Symbolic denial of differentiation. The persistence of specifically feminine and specifically masculine roles is partly covered up and neutralized by the *temporary participation of men in specifically feminine roles and vice versa.* The Kibbutzim make a point of assigning a number of men to specifically feminine occupations on a short-term basis. The most important example is participation of men in work in the kitchen and the dining hall. They are drafted by a system of rotation in which each man serves a two- to three-month period. Most of the men serve in the dining hall where everyone can see them every day. Similar mechanisms operate in the family too, particularly in the participation of fathers in taking their children out for their daily walk and in putting them to bed in the children's houses. Their participation in what is regarded as a typically feminine task serves as a *highly visible symbolic denial of segregation*.

Participation of men in feminine tasks has a practical value, but its main significance lies in its symbolic meaning as "atonement" for differentiation. Essentially, it is a token interchangeability. Women participate in masculine tasks much more and for much longer stretches than men in feminine tasks. Girls and young women are assigned to work in masculine occupations for a number of years. When they grow older and have children they leave these occupations and settle down in services and child care. Work in productive labour is regarded as an indispensable *rite de passage* for most women.

A more durable crossing of the lines occurs in exceptional cases. The Kibbutzim encourage women who continue to work in productive labour, in overall administration and in central committees, to hold out as long as they can. These exceptions to the rule serve as living proof that there is no deliberate discrimination. The exemplary life stories of such women who have achieved equality in spite of serious difficulties travel far and wide in all Kibbutzim and have become an important part of popular lore. Some of these women have become larger-than-life heroic figures.

In some of the Kibbutzim in our sample we discern signs of the emergence of a *cycle pattern*. This pattern is based on a system of role allocation which combines continuity of career with controlled mobility. It institutionalises a sequence of changes of occupations during the life cycle coupled with patterned shifts of the centre of gravity from one institutional sphere to another. During the first phase of the cycle the main emphasis is on joint participation in the occupational system. As long as they are young and have no children, women tend to concentrate on either predominantly masculine or in joint occupations. When their children come, they settle down in services and child care and become engrossed in family affairs. When the children grow up and the mothers have more free time, they put more emphasis on social participation. The second phase is based on considerable sex differentiation but it is preceded and followed by more equalitarian stages. The cycle pattern is not rigid and allows for many combinations and variations. It does not try to erase sex differentiation completely, but neither does it yield to polarization and segregation. It takes into full consideration the developmental aspects of family life and defines the inter-relations between the external systems and the internal family system accordingly. It combines equality and differentiation in an ordered yet flexible and continually changing pattern.

Selection 21

An Analysis of Conflicting Social Norms

Samuel A. Stouffer

In the previous selection Levinson discussed the lack of congruence between role-demands—that is, between social norms governing the behavior of a person in a given social position and individual role-conception and performance. One of the reasons for such discrepancy is the fact that people fill several roles simultaneously. One is not simply a son, or a student, or a friend; he is all these things and frequently the demands of the several roles are contradictory. A father is expected to be a companion to his wife and children, for example, but as an executive he is required to spend most of his time away from them.

How are conflicting role-demands handled? Sometimes conflicting demands do not arise simultaneously. Other times the norms defining behavior allow for flexibility and variability. Students, for example, are expected to do all the required reading in a course, attend all classroom sessions, listen attentively, ask the right questions, and spend long hours studying for exams. If no flexibility were allowed in these role-demands, it would be difficult to see how they could fail to conflict with a student's other roles.

The problem of role-conflict is the subject of this selection by Stouffer, who asked each of his subjects to predict his actions as a proctor if he saw an "ordinary" student—that is, one he did not know—cheating on an examination or if he saw a roommate and close friend who he knew "desperately" needed a good grade. A proctor, of course, must report cheating, but a friend must not. In addition, the subjects were asked how they thought the authorities and the student body expected them to act.

Different categories of persons may have different expectations about the same role. Subjects in Stouffer's study agreed that the role-demands of their fellow-students and those of the authorities were similar in the case of an ordinary student caught cheating: the proctor was expected to report him. In the case of a friend, the subjects reported that the role-demands of the authorities remained unchanged; that is, authorities recognized no friendship obligations on the part of a proctor. However, subjects did not feel that other students expected a proctor to turn in a friend; they felt that friendship obligations took precedence over proctor responsibilities.

The majority of subjects said they would report an ordinary student; it made little difference to them whether or not authorities or other students were aware of their action. In the case of a friend, however, nearly two thirds of the subjects alleged that they would not report the cheating incident if they knew no one would learn of their not doing so. Although this proportion decreased somewhat if the negligence was certain to be called to the attention of the authorities, the number of subjects who said they would report a friend was still much smaller than the number who said they would report an ordinary student.

Why did some students resolve the hypothetical proctor-friend conflict by reporting the cheat, while others sought a solution that they felt would be consistent with the role-demands of both authorities and students, and while yet a third group solved the dilemma by giving primacy to the role of friend? The answer to this question requires further research into the problem of role-conflict. Stouffer's study does show how the existence of variability in role-demands makes possible three adaptations to role-conflict, how given norms are variously interpreted to allow a wide range of acceptable behavior. Complete consensus on role-demands was lacking: a few subjects felt that even the authorities would approve of the proctor's acting as though nothing had happened in the case of a cheating friend, while a few others felt that students would approve of the proctor's turning in a friend. It is such flexibility, or "social slippage," that helps alleviate problems caused by having to play many roles simultaneously.

This paper illustrates an empirical procedure for studying role obligations, with particular reference to simultaneous role obligations which conflict.

The writer became especially interested in the problem when considering the strains to which the non-commissioned officer in the Army was subjected. On the one hand, the non-com had the role of agent of the command and in case the orders from above conflicted with what his men thought were right and necessary he was expected by his superiors to carry out the orders. But he also was an enlisted man, sharing enlisted men's attitudes, often hostile attitudes, toward the commissioned ranks. Consequently, the system of informal controls was such as to reward him for siding with the men in a conflict situation and punish him if he did not. There was some evidence that unless his men had confidence that he could see their point of view, he was an ineffective leader; on the other hand, open and

From the *American Sociological Review*, Vol. 14 (1949), 707-717. Reprinted by permission of the American Sociological Association.

flagrant disobedience by him of an order from above could not be tolerated by the command.

The general theoretical viewpoint behind this paper involves several propositions:

1. In any social group there exist norms and a strain for conformity to these norms.

2. Ordinarily, if the norms are clear and unambiguous the individual has no choice but to conform or take the consequences in group resentment.

3. If a person has simultaneous roles in two or more groups such that simultaneous conformity to the norms of each of the groups is incompatible, he can take one of only a limited number of actions, for example:

(1) He can conform to one set of role expectations and take the consequences of nonconformity to other sets.

(2) He can seek a compromise position by which he attempts to conform in part, though not wholly, to one or more sets of role expectations, in the hope that the sanctions applied will be minimal.

It need hardly be pointed out that conflicts of role obligations are a common experience of all people, especially in our complex Western society. The foreman in industry, like the non-com in the Army, is an obvious example; the "marginal man," as represented by the second-generation foreign born, for example, has been much studied. But role conflicts are not limited to such situations. Every adolescent is certain to experience situations in which his family and his peer group are in conflict, such that conformity to the norms of the one is incompatible with conformity to the norms of the other. Most adults are subject to strains to conformity to norms incompatible from one group to another; although, often enough to make life tolerable, either the conflicts do not arise simultaneously or there is a broad enough range of tolerated behavior to provide some flexibility.

In any authoritarian situation, it is axiomatic that adherence to the rules prescribed by the authority depends to no small extent on the compatibility of the rules with dominant values of those who must obey them. It is likely, in most social situations, that the compatibility is not absolute but a matter of degree. There may be variability among members of the group in the extent to which a given value is held in common. The existence of such variability is a factor which should weaken the sanctions against any particular act and facilitate compromise solutions.

With respect to any social value, there are at least two classes of variability which need to be distinguished:

(1) Each individual may perceive a narrow range of behavior as permissible, but for different individuals the ranges, though small, may constitute different segments of a continuum.

(2) Each individual may perceive a rather wide range of behavior as permissible, even though there is considerable consensus as to the termini of this range.

It is the viewpoint of this paper that the *range* of approved or permissible behavior as perceived by a given individual is an important datum for the analysis of what constitutes a social norm in any group, and especially for the analysis of conflicting norms.

In order to illustrate some of these concepts and to make some preliminary attempts to define them such that statistical operations could be performed with them, an empirical study was made of conflicting role expectations in a sample of 196 Harvard and Radcliffe students, mostly undergraduates. Since the concern was wholly methodological, no effort was made to obtain a random or representative sample of the student body, and the data here reported can not necessarily be regarded as typical of how a properly drawn sample would respond. The students were all taking the same course, Social Relations 116. The data were collected on the first day of the course, without any explicit prior discussion of the theoretical problems involved.

Each student filled out a brief questionnaire, anonymously. He was told first:

"Imagine that you are proctoring an examination in a middle-group course. About half way through the exam you see a fellow student openly cheating. The student is copying his answers from previously prepared notes. When he sees that you have seen the notes as you walked down the aisle and stopped near his seat, he whispers quietly to you, 'O. K., I'm caught. That's all there is to it.'

"*You do not know the student.* What would you as proctor do:

"If you knew that, *except for your action,* there could be very little chance that either the authorities or your student friends would hear about your part in the incident, which of the following actions (*see Table A*) would you as proctor be most likely to take? Next most likely? Least likely? Next least likely?"

After he had finished checking these questions he was presented with a new complication, as follows:

"Now, assume that *except for your action,* there could be very little chance that your student friends would hear about your part in the incident. But assume that, for some reason, there is

TABLE A

	CHECK ONE IN EACH VERTICAL COLUMN			
	MY MOST LIKELY ACTION (CHECK ONE)	MY NEXT MOST LIKELY ACTION (CHECK ONE)	MY LEAST LIKELY ACTION (CHECK ONE)	MY NEXT LEAST LIKELY ACTION (CHECK ONE)
A. Take away his notes and exam book, dismiss him and report him for cheating.........	____	____	____	____
B. Take away his notes, let him finish the exam, but report him for cheating........	____	____	____	____
C. If he can be led to withdraw from the exam on some excuse, do *not* report him for cheating; otherwise report him...........	____	____	____	____
D. Take away his notes, but let him finish the exam, and *not* report him for cheating.....	____	____	____	____
E. Act as if nothing had happened and *not* report him for cheating.................	____	____	____	____

a good chance, whatever you do, of the authorities finding out about it. Which of the following actions would you as proctor be most likely to take? Next most likely? Least likely? Next least likely?"

This was followed by exactly the same check list as before.

Next the respondent was asked to fill out the following check list:

A. Suppose now that a proctor's action would be: *Take away his notes and exam book, dismiss him, and report him for cheating.*

How would the university authorities feel if they knew you as proctor did this? (check one)

_____ Would expect one to do something like this
_____ Would not necessarily expect one to do this, but would not disapprove
_____ Would disapprove
_____ Would not tolerate it

How would your friends in the student body feel if they knew you did this? (check one)

_____ Would expect one to do something like this
_____ Would not necessarily expect one to do this, but would not disapprove
_____ Would disapprove
_____ Would not tolerate it

B. Suppose that a proctor's action would be: *Take away his notes, let him finish the exam, but report him for cheating.*

C. Suppose now that a proctor's action would be: *If he can be led to withdraw from the exam on some excuse, do not report him for cheating; otherwise report him.*

D. Suppose now that a proctor's action would be: *Take away his notes, but let him finish the exam, and not report him for cheating.*

E. Suppose now that a proctor's action would be: *Act as if nothing had happened and not report him for cheating.*

(For B, C, D, and E, the same check lists were used as for A, but are here omitted to save space.)

Next the respondent was confronted with what it was hoped, for the methodological purposes of this illustrative study, would be more of a dilemma. He was told:

"Now suppose the facts in the case in which you as proctor see a fellow student are exactly the same as in the first case, except for one difference. The student you as proctor see cheating is *your own roommate and close friend.* You know that your roommate is a hard working, though not a brilliant, student and desperately needs a good grade in this course.

"If you knew that, *except for your action,* there could be very little chance that either the authorities or your student friends would know about your part in the incident, which of the following actions would you as proctor be most likely to take? Next most likely? Least likely? Next least likely?"

The check list was the same as in the ordinary case presented first. This was followed by:

"Now assume that *except for your action*, there could be very little chance that your student friends would hear about your part in the incident. But assume that, for some reason, there is a good chance, whatever you do, of the authorities finding out about it. Which of the following actions would you as proctor be most likely to take? Next most likely? Least likely? Next least likely?"

Again the check list was the same.

Finally, the identical series of questions about expectations on the part of authorities and students was repeated for this roommate-friend situation.

The five actions described were designed to constitute, from A to E, an ordered sequence along a dimension of *degree of punitiveness*. That they were so perceived generally by the respondents can be shown easily. To illustrate: If a person said that the authorities, for example, would expect or approve more than one act, it is necessary for unidimensionality that the two or more acts be contiguous (for example, A and B, or B and C, or A, B, and C, but not A and C only). Actually, as we shall see, most students reported at least two acts which would be either expected or approved by the authorities; likewise most reported at least two acts which would be either expected or approved by their friends in the student body. In all, there were 4 chances for each respondent to designate such ranges. Of the 744 responses designating ranges of two or more, the acts checked were entirely contiguous in all but 41; in other words, 95 per cent of the responses were consistent with the perception of the sequence of acts as a continuum.[1]

Attention should be called to the likelihood that the responses as to the approval or disapproval of the authorities or of one's friends in the student body to a given act have an intrinsic merit which for our purposes could be superior to the merit of the estimates of one's own probable action in a hypothetical case. In any social situation, we have some kind of awareness of the group expectations as to an act affecting the group. We can verbalize those, and these responses when tabulated are *primary data* as to the agreement among group members concerning such expectations. On the other hand, a guess as to what one would do one's self in a particular hypothetical conflict situation has a more "iffy" quality which, though possibly quite highly correlated with actual behavior, need not necessarily be so correlated. The main stress in the present paper, it will be seen, is on the reported *role expectations*. The hypothetical personal action is introduced mainly to suggest how concepts like role expectations, when adequately measured, can be applied in the study of an individual's behavior in that role. Ideally, in place of the individual's hypothetical behavior we would like to substitute actual behavior, either in a natural or experimental situation, or reported past behavior. Studies may be devised in the future with such improvements, but in any case the basic sorting variables would be the reported role expectations as perceived by different group members.

Chart I is a picture of social norms, as perceived and reported by the respondents in this study. At the left, we see (heavy line) that almost all of the respondents thought the authorities would approve acts A and B, about a fifth thought the authorities would approve act C, and almost nobody thought the authorities would approve acts D and E.[2] Also at the left we see (dotted line) that the majority of the respondents felt that their friends in the student body would approve the most punitive acts, namely, A and B. But, in addition we see that three-fourths of the respondents thought act C would be approved and a bare majority said the same for act D. Only a few felt E would meet student approval. In other words, if a proctor took action consistent with the authorities' expectations he would not be in conflict with student expectations, although the range of expectations is wider for students than for the authorities.

The left diagram in Chart I portrays the estimate of the situation where the offender was an ordinary student. By contrast, the right-hand diagram shows far less overlap in expectations imputed to authorities and students respectively. The offender in this case was one's roommate and

---

[1] To simplify the subsequent presentation the inconsistencies are here treated as checking errors, although in some cases the respondent may actually have perceived an act as not fitting into an ordered sequence (for example, when he said A and C would be approved, but B would be disapproved, he may really have viewed B in a different way from other respondents). Fortunately, the inconsistencies were so few that it is possible to edit them without appreciable effect one way or another, except to simplify the ensuing presentation materially.

[2] To simplify the presentation, "approval" is here taken to mean that the respondent checked either of the following categories:

—Would expect one to do something like this
—Would not necessarily expect one to do this, but would not disapprove

CHART I: Percentage Saying That a Specific Action As Proctor Would Be Approved by Authorities and by Fellow Students, Respectively

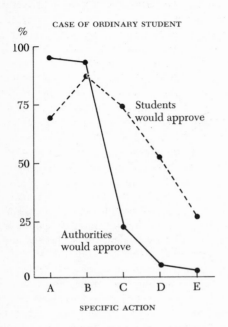

CASE OF ORDINARY STUDENT

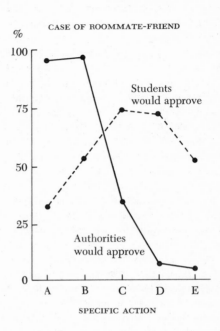

CASE OF ROOMMATE-FRIEND

TABLE 1: Percentage Who Attribute Given Role Expectations on the Part of Authorities and/or Students with Respect to Each Specific Act

| | PERCENTAGE DISTRIBUTION FOR EACH SPECIFIC ACTION | | | | | |
	A	B	C	D	E	ALL ACTIONS
CASE OF ORDINARY STUDENT Think given action would be approved by:						
Authorities only	28	12	3	—	—	9
Both authorities and students	68	81	19	4	2	35
Students only	1	6	55	48	24	27
Neither authorities nor students	3	1	23	48	74	29
	100	100	100	100	100	100
CASE OF ROOMMATE-FRIEND Think given action would be approved by:						
Authorities only	63	44	9	1	—	24
Both authorities and students	33	53	25	6	4	24
Students only	—	—	49	66	48	33
Neither authorities nor students	4	3	17	27	48	19
	100	100	100	100	100	100

N = 196

friend. Feelings that the proctor in punishing an ordinary offender was behaving consistently with the long-range interest of the students are now overshadowed by the obligations involved in codes of personal friendship: "You can't rat on a friend; you can't let a friend down."

In the case of the friend, the respondents perceived the authorities' position to be about the same as in the case of the ordinary student, except that about a third now thought the authorities might let the proctor get away with C in view of the proctor's personal dilemma. But only a third of the respondents thought the students would approve act A. The modal acts are C and D. About half believed that the least punitive of all, E, would be approved by most of the students.

In Table 1 each act (separately for the case of the ordinary student and the friend, respectively) is broken down according to the percentage who think it would be approved by (a) the authorities only, (b) both the authorities and students, (c) students only, and (d) by neither the authorities nor students.

Let us now examine the relationship between these role expectations and the respondent's own hypothetical behavior as proctor. It will be recalled that in both the case of the ordinary student and the roommate-friend, the respondent was asked what he personally would do under two hypothetical conditions: (1) if neither the authorities nor his student friends would hear about his part in the incident; and (2) if there could be very little chance that the authorities would hear about his part in the incident.

In Table 2 we have a percentage distribution of the acts which each student said he would be *most* likely to choose in the given situation. In the case of the ordinary student, as Table 2 shows, the majority of respondents say they would be most likely to employ acts A or B, the most punitive. There is not a large difference between the hypothetical behavior in private or in public (public only in the restricted sense that the authorities would hear about it in any case, though students need not). The main difference is a small increase, from a private 21 per cent to a public 30 per cent, in first choices for the most severe act A. However, the hypothetical behavior in the roommate-friend case shows a very different

pattern. As can be seen in Table 2, nearly two-thirds of the respondents elect acts D or E as their first preferences in private action, and only 16 per cent say they would employ as first choice punitive acts A or B. But if the authorities were sure to find out about it, the picture changes. Less than a third would elect D or E as first choice and 40 per cent would prefer A or B. Yet this is still only about half as large as the proportion who would prefer A or B in comparable circumstances in the case of the ordinary student.

Table 2, while of a good deal of interest in itself, is subject to the caveats entered earlier in this paper against taking reports on such hypothetical behavior too literally. But the main purpose for introducing the material in Table 2 is to enable us to see how such hypothetical behavior is related to the reported perceptions of authorities' and students' expectations, respectively, of proper behavior from a proctor. The data in Table 2 are, therefore, next broken down according to the categories used in Table 1. . . .

In such a study as this, it would be interesting first to differentiate individuals into types according to the way they perceive conflicting role expectations and then to ask how these different types of persons vary according to other social and psychological characteristics. Information of the latter type was not collected in the present study. However, the foregoing analysis has suggested how typologies could be set up and related to such outside variables. To take a simple illustration from the roommate-friend situation:

One could classify most of our respondents into three main types according as they perceived the role conflict.

Type I—Those who thought the range of ap-

TABLE 2: Percentage Distribution of Hypothetical Actions Which the Respondents Say They Would Be Most Likely to Take as Proctor

ACTION	IN CASE OF ORDINARY STUDENT		IN CASE OF ROOMMATE-FRIEND	
	PRIVATE *	PUBLIC †	PRIVATE	PUBLIC
A	21	30	4	6
B	47	48	12	34
C	16	13	18	31
D	15	7	38	18
E	1	2	28	11
	100	100	100	100
		N = 196		

* "*If you knew that,* except for your action *there could be very little chance that either the authorities or your student friends would hear about your part in the incident.*"
† "*If you knew that,* except for your action *there could be very little chance that your student friends would hear about your part in the incident, but that there is a good chance, whatever you do, of the authorities finding out about it.*"

TABLE 3:   Frequency with Which Various Ranges of Acts Are Perceived as Approved by Authorities and Students, Respectively

RANGE		CASE OF ORDINARY STUDENT ACTS APPROVED BY		CASE OF ROOMMATE-FRIEND ACTS APPROVED BY	
		AUTHORITIES	STUDENTS	AUTHORITIES	STUDENTS
1	A	13	4	4	3
	B	5	1	4	3
	C	—	—	—	2
	D	—	3	—	2
	E	—	—	—	4
		18	8	8	14
2	AB	134	37	120	12
	BC	3	10	2	10
	CD	—	7	—	14
	DE	—	5	—	26
		137	59	122	62
3	ABC	33	42	52	20
	BCD	—	14	—	18
	CDE	—	7	1	42
		33	63	53	80
4	ABCD	5	27	8	11
	BCDE	—	14	1	11
		5	41	9	22
5	ABCDE	3	25	4	18
	Total	196	196	196	196

proved acts identical from the point of view of authorities and students. (21 cases) For such respondents the problem of conformity in their own hypothetical acts could not have been difficult.

Type II—Those who thought the range of acts approved by the authorities did not overlap in any way with the range of acts approved by the students. (56 cases) For them simultaneous conformity to both was impossible. It is noteworthy, parenthetically, that 51 of the 56 said their own private act would be one conforming to student expectation, though 16 of these 51 shifted their act to a non-student position in the public situation.

Type III—Those who perceived a difference in the range of authorities' and students' expectations but who found at least one act which would be tolerated by both. (119 cases) Privately, only 36 of these individuals would take an action satisfactory to both. Publicly, however, 73 out of the 119 were able to find in an act perceived to be mutually acceptable the basis for their own hypothetical solution.

Why did these three types differ so markedly in their definition of the situation? Why, within these types did different sub-types prefer different solutions? These are the kinds of questions which subsequent research can explore. But first we must have a way of defining and classifying the role expectations relevant to our problem and the purpose of the present study is to illustrate a technique for accomplishing this first step.

From the theoretical standpoint, the most important implication of this paper may stem from its stress on variability. In essay writing in this field it is common and convenient to think of a social norm as a point or at least as a very narrow band on either side of a point. This probably is quite unrealistic as to most of our social behavior. And it may be precisely the ranges of permissible behavior which most need examination, if we are to make progress in this realm which is so central in social science. For it may be the very existence of some flexibility or social slippage—but not too much—which makes behavior in groups possible.

Recent Research

Leo P. Chall and Irene Taviss

Traditionally, research in the areas of personality and interpersonal relations has been conducted by psychologists, and research in normative behavior and in status and role by sociologists. The ambiguousness of such a division of labor among the people working in these related areas was apparent for decades, and a different field straddling all these areas has subsequently developed: social psychology. In this new field, it is not always sociologists who lead the way with new subjects for researches or with new ways of looking at socialization, development of norms, and the process whereby new roles and statuses develop—as the work by Sherif, Asch, and Lifton illustrates. Frequently, clinical psychologists and other specialists try to solve a problem in clinical practice or pursue an idea, and a new approach, new questions, and new areas for research are thereby opened. In several areas—child rearing (socialization), maternal employment, expectations of sex-role behavior, and clarification of the concept of role—recent research promises many new insights as well as an improved understanding of these aspects of behavior which affect the lives of individuals. These are not the only areas of intellectual endeavor that are continuously helping us better understand the development of the social self and the effects of family, group, and societal environments on the self, but they appear at this time to be the most significant.

Child rearing. Recent studies of the socialization process have tended to focus on the relationship between child-rearing practices and the resultant personality and character structures of children. Attempts are being made to spell out current changes in methods of child rearing. Bronfenbrenner's work (see Selection 14) is highly representative of this trend. With a theme similar to his "The Changing American Child" is the work of Miller and Swanson on *The Changing American Parent*.[1] Miller and Swanson see modern child-rearing practices as concerned with naturalness in the parent-child relationship and with the proper timing of training. Child-training methods reflect to a certain degree the state of flux of our modern, constantly changing society, but more generally the views and practices associated with child rearing appear to reflect the social position of the parents. Therefore, in their study of six hundred families in the Detroit area, Miller and Swanson distinguished between the "individuated-entrepreneurial" and the "welfare-bureaucratic" middle classes. The first group represents independent entrepreneurs, the owners of businesses and independent professionals. Children reared according to the values of this group are encouraged to be self-reliant, manipulative towards their environment, highly rational, and self-controlled. In contrast, the welfare-bureaucratic middle class is composed of those professional and white collar people who work in large bureaucratic organizations. These people employ child-rearing techniques that encourage their children to be accommodative, to allow their impulses some spontaneous expression, and to seek direction from the organizations in which they participate. It seems that the social class and the entrepreneurial-bureaucratic distinctions may provide a more meaningful and useful orientation for the study of child rearing than does a simple middle- and lower-class dichotomy, because it has been found that differences in the parents' education, in their ethnic and religious background, and in their economic position make no appreciable difference in the child-rearing practices used.

From another viewpoint, the socialization process produces conformity to societal norms "by inculcating an awareness of custom and tradition, by instilling a self-regulating conscience that incorporates social values, and by sensitizing the individual to the judgments and expectations of others."[2] Although these three elements of the process are always present, they receive differential emphases. David Riesman[3] has suggested that in mid-twentieth-century United States, some parts of the middle class have placed increasing emphasis on the development of sensitivity to the judgments and expectations of others, thus producing a prevalence of "other-directed" personalities. Such sensitivity to others, Riesman contends, is useful to the individual who must function in an increasingly bureaucratized world. He contrasts the other-directed personality, which emphasizes friendliness and ready adjustment to the demands of one's associates, with the "inner-directed" personality, which functions on the basis of a self-regulating conscience and maintains individuality and self-assertiveness. Miller and Swanson do not confirm this association between the bureaucratic middle class and other-directedness, however. A recent study by Richard Centers,[4] testing adults in Los Angeles for inner- and other-direction, also failed to find any correlation between other-direction and social class. Centers found instead that inner- and other-directed traits were normally distributed within any population studied. Nevertheless, he did find that other-directedness was most common in young people, thus supporting Riesman's contention that other-directedness is becoming more prevalent in the United States.

Maternal employment. The impact of maternal employment on the personality and development of the child is another recent area of study. In a study by Burchinal and Rossman,[5] the effects of maternal employment during various stages in the growth of the child were examined for a sample of 1,172 seventh- and eleventh-grade children. No relationship was found between maternal employment and the following personality characteristics of the children: over-sensitivity to others, excessive introspection, envy and withdrawal, propensity to disease, nervous symptoms, fatigue, anxiety, and fright. Further, no relationship was found between maternal employment and the following social relationship patterns of the children: intelligence and achievement scores, participation in school activities, and participation in community activities. The authors point out, however, that different results might have been obtained if such factors as the mother's attitude toward child rearing, her motivations in seeking employment, and the adequacy of substitute care for younger children had been considered. A great deal of additional research along these lines will be most productive.

Sex-role behavior. The entrance of females—not only mothers—into the labor force in large numbers has prompted discussions regarding changing sex roles. Interesting work is being done in this area in attempting to ascertain the conceptions that children hold with respect to what constitutes proper male and female roles. In a recent study, Hartley and Klein[6] asked 28 eight- and eleven-year-old upper-middle-class private school girls and 25 school teachers to identify various roles as "male," "female," or "not sex-linked." They found that the differences between the girls whose mothers worked and those whose mothers did not work were greater than the differences between either of these groups and the adult sample. Girls whose mothers worked tended to sex-type fewer roles than girls whose mothers did not work. In another study of children's conceptions of sex roles, Hartley[7] found that boys whose mothers worked assigned work-role activities to females more frequently than those whose mothers did not work. Girls expected to work after marriage more than boys expected their future wives to work. However, the work role of the female was seen as one of helping the family in time of need rather than as one in opposition to the accepted domestic role. It would appear, then, that while there have been changes in the concept of the female role, children do not seem to see conflict between female work roles and domestic roles. They do, however, tend to see fewer roles as distinctly masculine or feminine if their mothers work. A study of working mothers themselves indicated that they view work as an addition to the traditional domestic roles rather than as a radical change.[8] Some of the working women felt guilty about enjoying the time spent away from home. Thus, despite the minimizing of conflict gained by viewing the female work role as an addition to the traditional domestic role, there is conflict and confusion in the female role. Such confusion is further attested in a study of college students undertaken by Lovejoy.[9] The students in this survey expressed the belief that sex roles in the family today are not as well defined as they were in their own families. Both males and females felt that family decisions should be made jointly to a greater extent than had been the case in their own families, but this view was held to a greater degree among the females than among the males. Moreover, more males than females expected the wife to play the traditional domestic roles, suggesting the possibility of future conflict when these students marry and establish their own families.

Role-concepts. Studies of changing sex roles are only one example of the type of work being done in the area of studying specific roles. Studies of various occupational roles and of the processes of socialization by which people are trained in the necessary behaviors and attitudes for their roles are also proceeding.

In addition to studying specific roles and role-behaviors, an attempt is being made to clarify the concept of role itself, especially in relation to the problem of role-conflicts. An excellent example of the latter is Neal Gross' study[10] of the school superintendency role. Gross distinguished between *inter-role conflicts*—stemming from an individual's simultaneously occupying two positions, such as occupational and family roles—and *intra-role conflict*—resulting from conflicting expectations about a single position. Intra-role conflicts for the school superintendent involve the conflicting expectations of the school board, the PTA, the teachers, the students, etc. The 105 superintendents in Gross' study were asked to define the expectations of 19 different groups regarding the hiring of teachers and similar matters. Gross found three types of solutions to such intra-role conflicts: (1) moral—in which the superintendent conforms to those demands he conceives as legitimate; (2) expedient—in which he behaves on the basis of weighing the positive and negative sanctions involved in choosing an alternative; and (3) moral-expedient—in which he behaves according to the perceived "net balance" of the two dimensions. Generally, it was found that those who perceived role-conflict found less gratification in their jobs than those who did not perceive any conflict.

It is apparent that studies of child-rearing practices contribute to our understanding of the personality of children and that, in turn, studies of sex-role expectations as verbalized by children further contribute to our understanding of the formation of norms on the one hand and of the development of identification on the other. The studies presented above are but a sample of the many studies of personality and interpersonal relations which will help further unravel the complicated phenomena that constitute the fascinating area of socialization.

References

1. Daniel R. Miller and Guy E. Swanson, *The Changing American Parent* (New York: John Wiley & Sons, Inc., 1958).
2. Ely Chinoy, *Society: An Introduction to Sociology* (New York: Random House, 1961), p. 338.
3. See David Riesman *et al.*, *The Lonely Crowd: A Study of the Changing American Character* (New Haven, Conn.: Yale University Press, 1950).
4. Richard Centers, "An Examination of Riesman Social Character Typology; A Metropolitan Survey," *Sociometry*, 25 (September 1962), 231-240.
5. Lee G. Burchinal and Jack E. Rossman, "Relations Among Maternal Employment Indices and Developmental Characteristics of Children," *Marriage and Family Living*, 23 (November 1961), 334-340.
6. Ruth E. Hartley and Armin Klein, "Sex-Role Concepts Among Elementary-School-Age Girls," *Marriage and Family Living*, 21 (February 1959), 59-64.
7. Ruth E. Hartley, "Children's Concepts of Male and Female Roles," *Merrill-Palmer Quarterly*, 6 (January 1960), 83-91.
8. Ruth E. Hartley, "Some Implications of Current Changes in Sex Roles," *Merrill-Palmer Quarterly*, 6 (April 1960), 153-164.
9. Debi D. Lovejoy, "College Student Conceptions of the Roles of the Husband and Wife in Family Decision-Making," *The Family Life Coordinator*, March-June 1961, 43-46.
10. Neal Gross, Ward S. Mason, and Alexander W. M. McEachern, *Explorations in Role Analysis: Studies of the School Superintendency Role* (New York: John Wiley & Sons, Inc., 1958).

Part IV

Groups and Collective Behavior

Sociology is frequently distinguished from other social sciences because of its focus upon the *group*. This is because the group both influences the formation of the individual personality and represents a basic component of society.

Social groups should not be confused with social *aggregates* or social *categories*. Persons included in a social category have some common attribute or status, but they are not necessarily engaged in interpersonal relations. For example, all the college students in the United States constitute a social category. A social aggregate is composed of the persons in a given area who may or may not be in interaction. A music hall audience, the people on a train, and the population of Brazil are all social aggregates. A social group is any number of persons in interaction. Because the general concept of group is so broad, most sociological studies of groups are of those that are more enduring and consequently more structured, such as families or work groups.

The concept of *norm,* which is almost inseparable from that of *role,* is also closely associated with the term *social group.* As patterns of personal interaction endure through time, those persons involved in them develop symbols for communication, understandings about their interpersonal behaviors—such as what is "right" and what is "wrong" for particular persons to do or to be—and a memory of their mutual experiences. From the individual's point of view, norms dictate proper behavior in his social roles. But the matrix of the individual's norms—as was pointed out in Part III—is the social group whose members share a distinctive pattern of norms. Furthermore, adherence to the group's norms is vital to the group's survival; the obverse of the fact that the individual must have normative guidance for his action—so well documented in the Asch experiment (Selection 16)—is that a group cannot continue to exist unless its members conform to its norms.

Given the central position of the concept, it is little wonder that the attempt to classify groups has drawn the attention of many sociologists. One distinction frequently made is between groups that are *primary* and those that are *secondary.* A primary group is characterized by intimate, personal relationships that are emotionally satisfying in themselves. To such a group each person commits his entire personality, rather than only a portion of his self. The family is almost universally the first primary group encountered by all individuals. On the other hand, the individual may also be involved in many less intimate secondary groups. The satisfactions to be derived from such associations come from that group's capacity to satisfy more circumscribed needs of its members. Membership in a secondary group is often used as a means to a particular goal; for example, a lawyer may join the local chamber of commerce in order to drum up business. Kingsley Davis further defines primary groups in Selection 22.

The preponderance of primary or secondary groups in the social environment varies with the type of society. Ferdinand Tönnies, a nineteenth-century German sociologist, distinguished between *Gemeinschaft* and *Gesellschaft* societies. The *Gemeinschaft* society was a stable, rural, agricultural society with few specialized institutions; all activities necessary for the maintenance of society were carried on within the framework of the family and the religious organization. Where kinship relationships were the major cues for ordering the behavior of the members of society, virtually all of a person's time was spent in primary groups.

As industrialization and urbanization transformed this society into the *Gesellschaft* type, major changes occurred in man's social milieu. Activities primarily associated with the family were transferred to new institutions. The factory replaced the farm as the place of work for most men, and in the process the occupational role was separated from the familial role. Children, too, were away from the family for at least part of the day, since they prepared for adult life in school rather than at home. Other activities—care of the aged, treatment of the sick, recreation—were similarly absorbed by specialized institutions. Thus as kinship declined as a principle for organizing behavior in the *Gesellschaft* society, more and more of a person's social relationships took place in relatively formal groups.

It is frequently said that the decline in importance of warm primary group relationships is the major ill of industrial society. The sociologist Will Herberg feels that the current "religious revival" in the United States can be partly attributed to the fact that many Americans join a church in hopes of discovering there the primary associations that are absent elsewhere in their society.[1] The family, of course, is still an important source of primary group gratifications even in urban-industrial society, but once the individual leaves the home, he is thrown into contact with strangers, and—as noted—it is characteristic of modern society that the person spends many of his waking hours away from the family. The mother, who even in the earlier stages of *Gesellschaft* society remained at home and symbolized the warmth and intimacy of the family as a primary group, is increasingly being drawn away into the work force.

Thus in urban-industrial society the individual is often deprived of those relationships which would best support him in the face of hardships. In one of the classics of sociology, *Suicide*, Emile Durkheim demonstrated that the proclivity to suicide tended to be lowest (in the early part of the twentieth century) for persons with strong primary group ties. Durkheim did not use the term *primary group*, but he did refer to a condition of society in which individuals were no longer sure what values and norms might legitimately be pursued. To say that individuals are confused about ideal behavior is to suggest an absence of primary group ties, since it is in the primary group that the individual is indoctrinated with the major values and norms of the wider society. Further, because every social group must have a set of shared norms in order to survive,

---

[1]Will Herberg, *Protestant-Catholic-Jew* (Garden City, N.Y.: Doubleday & Co., Inc., 1955).

individuals who are confused about standards of behavior tend to be isolated. It is thus important to note that Durkheim found high rates of suicide among the single, the divorced, and the city-dweller—in short, among those who are most isolated from primary ties. Selection 23 by Edward Shils and Morris Janowitz, a remarkable study of the role of the primary group in the German army during World War II, documents some of these contentions.

It has been stated that conformity to group norms is a condition for group survival. As noted, one way to insure conformity is to reward those members whose behaviors reflect the norms and to punish those who deviate. One of the most important rewards available is high standing within the group. Status thus tends to be conferred on those whose behavior is consistent with the expectations of the group and to be withheld from those who are less able, unable, or who do not want to conform to the norms.

There is, of course, an important difference between the person whose behavior falls short of group expectations because he lacks education, experience, or competence and one who deviates because he rejects the group culture in favor of the norms of another group. In the first case the actor is loyal, but in the second case he is not. From the point of view of the group members, disloyalty challenges the beliefs that were firmly entrenched in their personalities during the process of learning their social roles, so they react harshly toward the transgressor. But where mobility from one group to another is possible, the person who deviates is no longer interested in the values of his former group, although he is very concerned with the norms of the new group, which he now uses as his standard.

This implies that the individual's attitudes, values, and behavior are not always shaped by the group in which he finds himself. It is likely, for example, that the subject who refused to go along with the incorrect response in the Asch situation was using a standard learned in and supported by some group existing outside the experimental situation. He had the choice of accepting the norm of the experimental or some other group. An ideal group that supplies one with standards for behavior and perspectives of society is called a *reference group*.[2]

Reference group behavior is useful in explaining leadership within a group and upward mobility—improvement of social status—within a society. The person who achieves success by moving from a group with low standing to one with high standing rejects the group of his origins, accepts the high-ranking group as his reference group, and adapts his personality in terms of its norms. Selections 24 and 25, by William Foote Whyte and George C. Homans respectively, support these propositions.

The norms of all groups must deal with the distribution of authority. Since every group faces problem situations and therefore must have a way of making decisions, it needs rules about which group members should bear the responsibility and authority for making them. Such authority may be concentrated entirely in one person; a fascist or communist dictator and a patriarchal father exemplify this authoritarian principle. At the other extreme, each group member may have an equal voice, with final action determined by a majority vote; the

---

[2] Sometimes a person will reject most of the norms of a particular group but will still use it as a reference group to compare with his own group—as, for example, when American Negroes contrast their economic plight with that of the white majority. See Tamotsu Shibutani, "Reference Groups as Perspectives," *American Journal of Sociology*, LX (May 1955), 562-569.

New England town meeting is a familiar example of the democratic principle. Still another possibility is a mixture of the extremes: the leaders may be chosen democratically, but they then make all decisions.

A variety of studies have been made that investigate stability and change in the relationships of group members; the selection by Whyte is an example of such a study. As behavior recurs in the same pattern again and again, it gains stability—that is, the probability that it will continue to recur increases so that it is increasingly predictable. As a group becomes increasingly stable, it may also be said to be increasingly *structured*. When a sociologist uses the term *group structure,* he is referring to recurrent patterns of behavior that reflect stable relationships among the group members.   S. H. A.

Although it has been stated that sociologists *specialize* in the study of behavior that occurs within a group context, they also study forms of human behavior that do not occur in groups as such but in aggregates and among the members of social categories. The apparent spontaneity with which structured behavior emerges in crowds, mobs, and audiences, however, belies a basic organization often derived from group interaction. The same is true in the unstructured public and in the highly structured social movement. The general term for organized behavior on the part of aggregates or categories of people is *collective behavior*. The designation of this special area indicates that sociologists are interested in developing laws, principles, and general statements about aggregates and categories of people as well as about groups.

Social movements ordinarily involve categories of people rather than aggregates, partly because they are of longer duration than other forms of collective behavior and partly because they usually appeal to persons who have some common need. Hence a social movement usually has as its host a segment of a public—people with some common interest as their identifying characteristic. Examples are the prohibition movement, the women's suffrage movement, and the civil rights movement.

A *crowd* is always an aggregate rather than a category; that is, one criterion of a crowd is that its participants are near one another. The proximity of crowd members is important because it enables people who are responding to the stimulus that caused the crowd to gather—for example, the sight of a Negro trying to enter a restaurant whose owner refuses to serve members of racial minorities—to incite one another. A *mob* is a crowd in a state of heightened suggestibility and emotional contagion.

Another form of collective behavior is *mass behavior*. The persons involved in mass behavior respond independently but in the same way to a common stimulus. In some situations there are norms governing mass behavior, as in the national mourning that followed the assassination of President Kennedy; in other situations institutionalized behavior is absent, as in the panic that accompanies fires, floods, and earthquakes. It is also possible for action that begins as mass behavior to change to crowd behavior; people who at first respond independently to the same stimulus subsequently find themselves close to one another and begin to act like a typical crowd. This transformation of mass behavior into crowd behavior is illustrated by John Houseman in Selection 28.

Although the group process does not appear at first glance to be involved in collective behavior, it is always present in the form of group-learned sentiments and behaviors brought by the persons engaging in the collective behavior. Every person's acculturation begins through group process; even the learning of a language is initiated through group interaction. The norms and values involved in collective behavior are the internalized norms and values learned in group interaction. Political, religious, and moral norms and values learned in the family group tend to carry over into later behavior, and when they are modified, they are usually modified through interaction with new groups. Social movements, particularly, depend on the group process in at least two ways: (1) group-learned norms and values usually attract individuals to social movements in the beginning, and (2) although the social movement always transcends any single group as it endures through time and attracts more people, it is invariably implemented through local support groups, cells, committees, or boards. In crowd and audience behavior, too, there is an underlying cultural organization and institutionalization of behavior, as Selection 27 by John Howard Griffin and Theodore Freedman illustrates.

The development of the mass media of communication has added a new dimension to collective behavior and has threatened to transform modern society into a gigantic mob or mass whose members are deprived of meaningful and emotionally supporting primary group relationships. These statements will be elaborated upon in Selection 29 by E. B. White, as well as in the Houseman piece.

T.E.L.

Selection 22

Primary Groups

Kingsley Davis

The importance of the group in influencing the attitudes, values, and behavior of the individual has been vividly demonstrated in the work of Asch and Lifton, which was presented in Selections 16 and 17. Their studies showed that the way a person perceives the world is largely determined by the way the members of his groups see it. The group not only makes it possible for the newborn infant to stay alive but also guides the development of his potentiality for human qualities. Since membership in social groups makes it possible for the individual to become a person, the group is as basic a unit of society as is the person. Thus it is not surprising that sociologists have spent a great deal of time and energy studying the nature of groups and classifying different types of them.

The term *social group* refers to a cluster of persons who have some kind of relationship to one another. The nature of these relationships varies from one type of group to another; for instance, the obligations and feelings parents and children have for one another are radically different from those felt by the members of a local chamber of commerce. In the latter group, the interests and involvements of the actors are limited, whereas family relationships are characterized by total emotional commitment.

The dimensions along which groups vary are discussed in this selection. Davis refines and develops the concept of primary group first suggested in the work of Charles Horton Cooley, a founding father of American sociology. Primary groups are small, durable, and intimate because of both the physical and especially the social nearness of their members. Members of primary groups share an identity of interests and regard social relationships themselves as important ends. Furthermore, interaction is spontaneous and engages every aspect of the persons involved. The term *primary* is appropriate, for the individual's primary loyalties, interests, affectional ties, and sympathies go to the members of this group. It was not, of course, just the fact that Dr. Vincent of Lifton's study had no social support for his own ideas that led him to "confess" his "crimes" against the Chinese Communist government; the more he was integrated into the primary group of his cell mates, the more he felt obliged to tell them what they wanted to hear.

Secondary groups are characterized by segmented relationships between members—that is, relationships that do not commit an individual's entire personality but are specialized and limited. Secondary groups are composed of persons whose interests and goals vary and who come together in order to satisfy a particular purpose. Secondary relationships do not have the sacred quality of primary ones, which often means that the secondary type of association is exploited in order to achieve personal ends. The individual has friends and loved ones in the primary group but "contacts" in the secondary group.

Primary and secondary groups vary with reference to the types of constraints and controls they exercise to enforce conformity to group norms. In the primary group, informal methods are utilized: ridicule, gossip, ostracism. The secondary group is more likely to set forth its norms in a formal constitution, a set of laws, or some similar body of regulations.

It is important to note, as Davis does, that the terms *primary group* and *secondary group* refer to "ideal types"—that is, abstract models. Examination reveals no real groups that resemble in every respect those dealt with in the abstract. All real groups demonstrate elements of both primary and secondary group relationships.

In the classification of human groups one of the broadest and most fundamental distinctions is that between small and intimate groups on the one hand and large and impersonal groups on the other. In its formulation of this dichotomy American sociological theory has generally followed Charles H. Cooley's distinction between primary and secondary groups, as set forth in 1909 in his book, *Social Organization*.[1] European theory has followed a somewhat similar distinction formulated in 1887 by Ferdinand Tönnies between *Gemeinschaft* (close communal relationship) and *Gesellschaft* (organized impersonal relationship). Other authors have stated the same dichotomy in one form or another, not only because it is an obvious fact but also because it is a fundamental one.

Cooley's classic definition runs as follows:

"By primary groups I mean those characterized by intimate face-to-face association and cooperation. They are primary in several senses, but chiefly in that they are fundamental in forming the social nature and ideals of the individual. The result of intimate association . . . is a certain fusion of individualities in a common whole, so that one's very self, for many purposes at least, is the common life and purpose of the group. Perhaps the simplest way of describing this wholeness is by saying that it is a 'we'; it involves the sort of sympathy and mutual identification for which 'we' is the natural expression."

Two things in this quotation are worth noting: first, that the author means to designate a class of *concrete* groups (into which he puts families, play groups, neighborhood groups, and others); second, that he uses the phrase "face-to-face association" but places the emphasis upon particular *qualities* of the relationship such as "sympathy and mutual identification." These points have led to some confusion. It is generally agreed that *all* groups tend in some degree to possess consensus

Reprinted with permission of the publisher from *Human Society* by Kingsley Davis, pp. 52-61. Copyright 1948, 1949 by The Macmillan Company.
[1] Charles Horton Cooley, *Social Organization* (New York: Charles Scribner's Sons, 1909).

—to engender a "we" feeling in their members. This was implied by Cooley himself in his subsequent discussion of the necessary extension of "primary ideals" to larger groups. Without the "we" feeling large groups cannot retain their cohesion. If primary association is thus conceived as a quality of all groups, it does not constitute a means for separating concrete groups into two types called primary and secondary. Furthermore, this particular quality cannot be said to be limited to "face-to-face" groups. There are relationships that are friendly and intimate but involve indirect contacts (such as the friendship of two distant scholars or the love affairs of soldiers and girls initiated through correspondence), and there are relationships that are formal and impersonal but involve face-to-face contacts (such as the military salute or the act of prostitution). Close scrutiny of Cooley's statement seems therefore to reveal some ambiguity.

In order to clarify the nature of primary groups our discussion will stress the following points: (1) There is a primary, or *gemeinschaftliche*, type of relationship. (2) This type of relationship is characterized by a number of interrelated qualities. (3) It, with its distinctive qualities, is found more abundantly in some concrete groups than in others. (4) The particular groups in which it is found most abundantly are those most likely to rest upon certain physical conditions. Let us begin with the last point and work backwards.

THE PHYSICAL CONDITIONS OF PRIMARY GROUPS

Cooley's idea of "face-to-face" contact expressed an important fact, but he did not sufficiently analyze this fact to see both its broader implication and its narrower limitation. He should have realized that there are not one but three essential conditions which, when present, tend to give rise to primary groups. The first of these is close (face-to-face) physical proximity of the group members; the second is smallness of the group; and the third, durability of the bond. All of these three conditions—closeness, smallness, and continuation—seem to be equally essential as well as mutually related. But note that they are *physical* conditions. They merely constitute the external setting in which a certain kind of social milieu is extremely likely to arise. It does not follow that this milieu will inevitably arise under these conditions, or that it may not arise under other conditions.

It often happens that a primary relation arises with only one or two of the conditions present. Thus "the historic friendships like that of Emerson and Carlyle did not rest on physical presence" but they did rest on the fewness of the persons involved and the long duration of the acquaintance. The essential thing is not so much the physical conditions as the values, the regard for each other, that drew these persons together in spite of physical separation. It is necessary to keep the temporal and spatial conditions of primary association analytically separate from its social nature. Why each condition is so closely related to the social characteristics will be clear only after discussion of these characteristics, but for the present a word more should be said about each condition.

Physical proximity

In order for intimacy to arise it is necessary that people have rather close contact, and nothing provides such contact better than face-to-face association. Seeing and talking with each other facilitates the subtle exchange of ideas, opinions, and sentiments. It makes possible the "conversation of gestures". . . . So true is this that close contact has come to symbolize good feeling and identity between persons. Caressing, kissing, and sexual intercourse; eating and dwelling together; playing, traveling, studying together—all tend to be regarded as external symbols of close solidarity. True, these symbols may become formalized as in the handshake of a stranger or the kiss of a French general, but even such formal usages imply a certain element of mutual regard which ultimately stems from the role of face-to-face contact in primary groups. A part of our horror of prostitution apparently derives from our customary association of sexual contact with affection, and the significance of the "kiss of Judas" would be utterly nil without a similar association of kissing with affection.

Physical proximity thus provides an opportunity for the development of primary groups, but whether or not that opportunity will be utilized depends on the situation as defined in the culture. In the first place the normative order regulates the conditions under which physical contact may take place. As between individuals of different status there are usually barriers—e.g. between members of different classes and castes, different religions and occupations, different ages and sex. These barriers prevent physical proximity from providing an opportunity for intimacy to develop; they thus keep different strata and different groups distinct. The existence of such barriers serves, in the second place, to emphasize the fact that physical intimacy in other relations is normatively prescribed. For instance the customary ban on close physical contact between the sexes serves to emphasize the necessity and importance of such contact in marriage. In these two ways— by *proscribing* and *prescribing* it according to the situation—a social system controls physical proximity in the interest of the existing social organization. In some cases where physical contact is necessary but not socially prescribed, it is treated in a tolerant but not encouraging manner. Physical nearness in a packed subway, a crowded restaurant, or a public lavatory may be much greater than the parties would in ordinary situations consider correct, but it is recognized that the circumstances make it necessary. Such tolerated physical proximity sometimes develops into a social relationship but not often. The effect of close physical proximity on the social relationship depends in the last analysis on the cultural definition of the situation.

Smallness of the group

A face-to-face group must also be a small group, for it is impossible to be in sensory contact with many people at the same time. A speaker may address an audience containing thousands of persons, but this is under special conditions; and it illustrates perfectly the necessity of smallness in addition to proximity as a condition favorable to the development of intimacy. Other factors being equal (such as the nature of the occasion— whether a show, a lecture, or a funeral), the smaller the group the more intimate it is.

Undoubtedly the character of the group tends to change with its size, and interesting attempts have been made to demonstrate the relationship between the two. As the group becomes larger each person counts less as a unique personality but more as a sheer cipher or unit; the group tends to acquire a more complex and formal organization; representative and substitute agencies arise in greater abundance; the rules of association become more explicit and the means of control more official; and the group increasingly acquires a character of its own apart from that of its specific members. With very small groups even the addition of one more member makes a difference. Thus a group of three is notoriously different from a group of two, and a group of four is different from one of three. But when the group numbers five or six the addition of one more does not necessarily change its character

although the addition of several more will do so. With very large groups, of course, it requires a great addition to change the character of the group. There is not much difference between a city of 100,000 and one of 125,000, but there is a big difference between either of these and a city of 500,000.

In a small group the members can know one another personally and can all participate directly in group decisions. Furthermore, they can develop a group character and a group intimacy rather quickly (e.g. in a small boat). If the group is larger more time is required to establish full mutual acquaintance between the members. When people live together all their lives, however, as in a peasant village, it is possible for 200 or more to know one another intimately. This brings us to the time factor as a condition of primary group association.

Duration of the relationship

Intimacy is largely a matter of the frequency and intensity of association. Other things equal, the longer the group remains together the more numerous and deeper are the contacts between its members. Social ties deepen in time through the gradual development of interlocking habits. An oft-repeated association, like any other experience, becomes part of one's way of life. Although a husband and wife may have quarreled for ten years, the very fact that they have lived together for that long makes it hard for them to do without each other. A nation is a durable entity but not a small or intimate one.

It thus becomes clear that physical proximity, small size, and long duration are the conditions most favorable to the development of intimate ties. It is possible for one of these conditions to be present without the other two, but the most favorable situation for the development of a primary group occurs when all three are present to a high degree. Let us now examine more closely the qualities of association that these conditions tend to develop.

THE CHARACTER OF PRIMARY RELATIONS

A primary relationship involves, first of all, an identity of ends as between the parties. Among the identical ends is of course the relationship itself, which is not regarded by the participants as a means to an end but as a good in its own right. This means that the relationship is non-contractual, noneconomic, nonpolitical, and nonspecialized. Instead it is personal, spontaneous, sentimental, and inclusive. A brief discussion of each of these major traits will indicate their importance.

Identity of ends

In a perfect primary relationship there is an interpenetration of ends in two different senses. First, the parties have similar desires and attitudes so that they are striving for similar things and can be together without disagreement. They look at the world through the same eyes. Two friends who are united by a common intellectual interest afford an example of this. Second, there is an interpenetration in a deeper sense: each party pursues as one of his ends the welfare of the other. He may superficially and in a given connection define the other's welfare differently from the way the other party himself views it, but in the last analysis he must accept the basic desires, the ends, of the other party as also his own ends. Thus a man who tries to dissuade his friend from a given line of conduct does so only on the ground that what the friend appears to want now is not what he will want later. He may explain to him, for example, that to throw up his job now in a pique at his boss will only cause him to regret the act later. This function—that of helping an individual interpret and understand his own welfare—is one of the great values of friendship, and it implies at bottom that the ends of one become by that very fact also the ends of the other. Another example is the behavior of a mother who injures her own health looking after that of her child. Not only is the child's welfare a supreme end for her but the joys and sorrows of the child are also her joys and sorrows, because she is in such sympathetic understanding with the child.

Seldom is the identity of ends complete. A man may distrust and resent his friend to some extent; a child may resist his parent. Seldom, moreover, is the relationship entirely mutual; it is usually a bit one-sided with one party entering much more than the other into the spirit of it. But at least we can visualize a theoretical asymptote—a complete and mutual identity of ends—which primary relations approach but do not attain.

The identification of ends is connected with a certain fusion of personalities within the group, so that what one experiences the other also tends to experience. This fusion can be observed, for example, in the case of stage-fright on the part of persons who are not actually on the stage but are close relatives of someone who is. They often experience the ordeal as vividly as if they were on the stage themselves, or even more so. There is the case of the mother of a student actress in a college play who when asked how she had enjoyed the play said she had not paid any attention to it, she was so worried when her daughter was on the stage. This fusion of personalities constitutes an important part of the "we" feeling that Cooley wrote about. It gives the relation an altruistic character, at least in one sense of the word. It does not mean that one party sacrifices his own interests for the benefit of the other, but simply that the other's interests are also his. If a mother injures her health in caring for her child, she is not going contrary to her own ends; rather she is avoiding the pain of seeing her child suffer. The child's needs become her ends.

The relationship is an end in itself

A primary relationship, ideally considered, is not regarded by the parties as simply a means to an end but rather as a value or end in itself. It is in their eyes its own excuse for being. If a friendship is formed for a purpose—say, to make a sale—we do not regard it as a genuine friendship. If a marriage is made purely with an eye to economic gain, it lacks a certain quality which we think should go into marriage.

The intrinsic value attached to the primary relationship helps explain the sense of spontaneity and freedom felt by the parties. The relationship is not compulsory, not a means to a superior end, but is intrinsically enjoyable. From an objective point of view such a relationship may look like a subtle prison for the parties concerned. We speak of a couple being so attached to each other as to be oblivious to everything else; we speak of "fascination," "infatuation," "entanglement," etc. Yet subjectively the relationship seems spontaneous because it is purely voluntary. Only when a close relationship is forced on one or is simulated for an ulterior purpose does it become burdensome; and in this case scarcely anything can be more confining. A love affair in which one no longer feels any love but which cannot be broken off is exceedingly trying.

The relationship is personal

In the primary group the interest of each is centered in the others *as persons*—i.e. as objects of value. The relationship disappears if the particular person disappears from it.

"No offense is greater in a lover than this: that he should treat his love 'impersonally.' . . ."

"The distinction between personal and impersonal relationships is a vital one in human affairs. Personal relationships, be they those of friend to friend or of husband to wife, be they motivated by love or by hatred, be they transitory or permanent, stand apart in a class by themselves. . . ."

"The most obvious and inevitable quality of a personal relationship is that it is *not transferable*. It attaches to determinate individuals who cannot be duplicated nor replaced. A new personal relationship can be established, an old one can be abandoned, perhaps the driving force that initiated the relationship may give way to another, but no substitution can be made of one individual for another in the same relationship. If Helen leaves Menelaus and flees with Paris, it is absurd to describe the new situation as a continuation of the personal attachment of Menelaus and Helen, with Paris acting as a substitute. The personal relationship between Helen and Menelaus continues, with love changed to fear and resentment. The attachment of Helen and Paris is a new entity, a new relationship."

"On the other hand, any relationship which can be transferred from one individual to another is to that extent impersonal. When citizens enter and leave the allegiance of a State, when laborers enter and leave the employ of a factory, when men supplant each other in all the diverse functions of organized society, their personality is only incidental to the political, economic, or social tie which they assume or avoid. We consider that these relationships themselves are constantly in being, whoever may be the persons bound therein."[2]

The primary relationship is a matter of persons; it exists because of the person, not despite him. Cigarettes can be bought from anybody. Our attention is focused on getting them, not on the person who sells them to us. The less the seller intrudes his personality, the better. A vending machine will do just as well except that it will not cut prices. If one man or one machine will not sell us cigarettes, another will; and it makes no great difference which one does.

The personal nature of the primary relationship has a further consequence—namely, that things trivial in other contexts may be important in this one. "As every lover who is not a bungler knows, there is no external distinction between great things and trivial things in matters of love."[3] This is because, since the relationship is personal, whatever either party chooses to regard as important necessarily becomes important. The essential thing is the attitude of each person towards the other; and anything that reveals this attitude, be it small or large, has great significance attached to it. A careless gesture, an idle remark, may be sufficient to start a quarrel. Events are not important in themselves but rather as symbols of the subjective attitudes that each is taking toward the other.

The relationship is inclusive

The person in a personal relationship is not an abstraction. He is not merely a legal entity, an economic cipher, or a technological cog. He is all of these rolled into one. He is the complete concrete person and the relationship involves him in all his completeness, extending to his whole being. His value attaches not to any particular aspect or activity of himself but to his whole self. This is why long acquaintance and close contact are so essential to a primary relationship. Each person comes to know the other in all the details of his life. In this way the primary relation differs from all other social relations, because the others do not involve complete personalities.

The relationship is spontaneous

A purely primary relationship is voluntary. In this it does not differ from a purely contractual relationship, but in a contract the conditions are laid down explicitly and the other person is held to these conditions. Furthermore, the contract exists for an ulterior purpose and is not an end in itself. As a consequence the personal relationship, which depends always on the will of either party at any point in the interaction, is voluntary in a more complete sense; and as mentioned before, it therefore implies the greatest spontaneity on the part of the participants.

[2] Robert C. Binkley and Frances W. Binkley, *What Is Right with Marriage?* (New York: Appleton-Century-Crofts, Inc., 1929), pp. 31-32.
[3] *Ibid.*, p. 34.

In actual groups, of course, the very inclusiveness and closeness of primary association means that great control over the person is exercised. Neighborhood and family control is very complete control, and the individual often wishes to escape it by getting into the anonymous and more impersonal life of a larger setting such as a big city. The truth is that such actual groups embody only imperfectly the primary relationship. They demand a great deal of loyalty and they have an element of status, of institutionalization, in them which makes them something less than spontaneous and free. Even so, the control is in general voluntarily accepted by the members of the group. One does not feel that a marriage relationship is onerous even though it imposes many limitations on one. If one does feel it to be onerous this is a sign that the relation is involuntary and therefore is not completely primary.

CONCRETE GROUPS AND
PRIMARY RELATIONSHIPS

We have now described some of the essential qualities of primary relationships—the identity of ends, the intrinsic value, the personal, inclusive, and spontaneous character which they possess. We have also given the physical conditions which favor the occurrence of such relationships. It has become increasingly clear, however, that primary relationships as we have described them do not exist in concrete form. They are merely the extreme pole, the asymptote, toward which some actual forms of interaction tend but never reach. It has also become clear, as the preceding paragraph suggests, that in actual groups of a close and intimate kind certain characteristics of a type opposite to those we have described may be found. Thus the small and durable group may be characterized by hate and conflict rather than love and harmony. Obviously then there are some theoretical problems remaining that require clarification.

The groups embodying most completely the characteristics of primary relationship are those that are freest from any connection with social organization. They imply no larger obligation, no fixed status, no involuntary element. Such, for example, is the relation of two friends who come together simply because they want to do so and who are under no obligation to continue the bond if either loses interest. Even here some rudimentary sense of obligation is inevitably incurred and there is some cultural standardization of the relationship. In primitive societies friendships are often sealed with a ceremony and are expected to continue for life. In our own society they are remarkably free. If the number of friends is increased, the element of obligation and control becomes greater; yet the boy's gang, based on similar age and similar interests, embodies primary relationships to a high degree. Like friendship, the love relationship of a man and woman apart from any marital or parental ties has a strong primary character; but here the fact of potential connection with the family system of the society places the relationship on a precarious footing.

The truth is that every society is of necessity inimical to the full expression of primary association. If it is to control individuals, it must control their relationships. Even in the most personal affairs it must define mutual obligations. It must take advantage of personal affection, of the sense of spontaneity, of the identity of ends to furnish organization for the performance of societal functions. It cannot let individuals associate simply on the basis of personal attraction or on a purely voluntary basis. Instead it must use the propulsive power inherent in these, and in using them it must inevitably destroy them in part. Thus in countless ways it limits contacts in such a way that friendship will develop along functional lines that fit into the total organization. It tries to limit or at least control the boys' gang, because it recognizes in such a group an anarchic force. Similarly it limits and controls sexual love between man and woman in the interest of reproduction, child-rearing, and the continuity of the system of stratification. It recognizes in the voluntary unregulated liaison an anarchic force.

But if organized society is inimical to the full expression of primary relationships, it is also friendly to a partial expression of them. At the bottom of human society is the fact of communicative contact between one person and another. The self cannot develop on the basis of secondary contacts; it requires close, intimate, personal contacts. It requires the security of a stable and familiar group, the sense of identity with others, the sympathetic interest and personal evaluation which others show. The intricate process of socialization, then, is handled in those concrete groups —notably the family and the play group—where an emphasis is placed on the conditions and the qualities of primary association. Such groups are institutionalized and organized, giving their members mutual rights and obligations defined in the culture, and as such they are not purely spontaneous and voluntary; yet so far as possible an attempt is made to give them an identity of ends, an intrinsic evaluation of the group as such, a sense of personal closeness, and an unawareness of the impingement of social controls.

In the last analysis the society relies heavily on the physical conditions of primary group formation—proximity, smallness, and long duration—to provide some of the qualities of primary association despite their socially organized character. In this way the family and the neighborhood (the local territorial group) provide the archetypes of what may be called organized primary groups. It happens that human beings throughout most of their history have lived chiefly in groups characterized by proximity, smallness, and durability.

But precisely because so much of their lives was passed in such groups, these groups were thoroughly organized from a social point of view. For this reason familial relations and in fact all personal relations seem more formalized in primitive groups than among ourselves. It is only in modern society that secondary contacts have come to play an important role, and consequently some of the burden of social organization has been lifted from the small primary groups which have thus gained in spontaneity and informality.

Selection 23

Cohesion and Disintegration in the Wehrmacht in World War II

Edward A. Shils and Morris Janowitz

Primary group relationships are the chief source of affection and emotional support for the individual throughout life. In a simple, preindustrial society, a person's social milieu consists almost entirely of primary group affiliations; in a more complex, industrial society, secondary relationships as embodied in factories, professional organizations, voluntary associations, and so on become more important, but most people are still bound to the larger society mainly by primary group affiliations. Even those who have many secondary associations satisfy their affectional needs in primary group relationships. One of the reasons why the institution of the family has endured in industrial society, despite the many trials to which it is subjected, is that it remains an emotional haven amidst anxiety and insecurity.

It seems strange to use such words as *affection* and *emotional security* to introduce an article concerning the German army in World War II. Yet Shils and Janowitz in their perceptive study of the Nazi military argue that it was the ability of the Wehrmacht to reproduce in the infantry company the intimacy and affection formerly furnished by the soldiers' civilian primary groups that largely explains its success. High-powered Allied propaganda delivered by means of the latest media of communication had but slight effect on Nazi soldiers.

Sociologists have not always looked favorably upon the social changes accompanying industrialization, especially the asserted disappearance of primary groups. Critics of modern society further believed that with the loss of the more traditional and conservative primary groups people found their values and their cues for behavior in the omnipotent mass media and that isolated individuals were helpless in the face of the propaganda of these media.[1] However, as we have indicated, primary relationships continued to be important

---

[1] For an excellent study of the views of the founding fathers of sociology as well as of the role of American society in criticizing these views, the student is urged to read Leon Bramson's *The Political Context of Sociology* (Princeton, N.J.: Princeton University Press, 1961).

to the German soldiers. Shils and Janowitz discovered that comparatively few soldiers were able to understand the abstract symbols of propaganda. Other studies (for example, the study of voting behavior by Lazarsfeld, Berelson, and Gaudet presented in Selection 30) have shown that propaganda tends to be mediated and interpreted by opinion leaders in the group.

Thus Allied propaganda did not bring about an early collapse of the German army. Despite defeats in North Africa, Sicily, Italy, France, Russia, and Poland which made it apparent as early as 1943 that it could not win, the German army managed to maintain its effective organization. How did the Wehrmacht manage to hold out so long? Significantly, Nazism as a political ideology did not help sustain the unity of the army to any appreciable extent; Nazism was important to but a handful of German soldiers, although the majority supported and gave their allegiance to Hitler. What did contribute to the high morale of the German fighting men despite heavy losses was the degree to which successful primary group relationships were built into the structure of combat units. To the extent that this was the case, the soldiers fought well. Of course, certain basic physical needs had to be satisfied reasonably well, but morale depended mainly on the ability of each soldier to give and receive affection and support within the primary group of his fighting unit. It is important to note that deserters tended to be those with personality difficulties—those who could neither give nor receive affection.

For its part, the German High Command did all it could to exploit primary group associations. Groups that had long fought together were maintained as a unit; replacements were given a chance to assimilate themselves into the unit and were not as a rule sent into action until they had definitely become part of the primary group. Soldiers were warned against deserting lest reprisals be taken against their comrades who remained behind.

From a practical point of view, the German experience raises serious questions about the assumption that a major motivating force for the individual soldier is knowledge, in terms of abstract philosophical principles, about why he is fighting. Fighting ability depends on training, equipment, the satisfaction of basic needs, and—perhaps most important of all—the organization of combat units into emotionally supportive groups. As soon as the primary groups within the German army disintegrated, so did its last-ditch resistance.

THE ARMY AS A SOCIAL GROUP

This study is an attempt to analyze the relative influence of primary and secondary group situations on the high degree of stability of the German Army in World War II. It also seeks to evaluate the impact of the Western Allies' propaganda on the German Army's fighting effectiveness.

Although distinctly outnumbered and in a strategic sense quantitatively inferior in equipment, the German Army, on all fronts, maintained a high degree of organizational integrity and fighting effectiveness through a series of almost unbroken retreats over a period of several years. In the final phase, the German armies were broken into unconnected segments, and the remnants were overrun as the major lines of communication and command were broken. Never-theless, resistance which was more than token resistance on the part of most divisions continued until they were overpowered or overrun in a way which, by breaking communication lines, prevented individual battalions and companies from operating in a coherent fashion. Disintegration through desertion was insignificant, while active surrender, individually or in groups, remained extremely limited throughout the entire Western campaign.

In one sense the German High Command effected as complete a defense of the "European Fortress" as its own leadership qualities and the technical means at its disposal permitted. Official military analyses, including General Eisenhower's

From *The Public Opinion Quarterly*, Vol. 12 (1948), 280-294, 314-315.

report, have shown that lack of manpower, equipment, and transportation, as well as certain strategical errors, were the limiting factors. There was neither complete collapse nor internally organized effort to terminate hostilities, such as signalized the end of the first world war.

This extraordinary tenacity of the German Army has frequently been attributed to the strong National Socialist political convictions of the German soldiers. It is the main hypothesis of this paper, however, that the unity of the German Army was in fact sustained only to a very slight extent by the National Socialist political convictions of its members, and that more important in the motivation of the determined resistance of the German soldier was the steady satisfaction of certain *primary* personality demands afforded by the social organization of the army.

This basic hypothesis may be elaborated in the following terms.

1. It appears that a soldier's ability to resist is a function of the capacity of his immediate primary group (his squad or section) to avoid social disintegration. When the individual's immediate group, and its supporting formations, met his basic organic needs, offered him affection and esteem from both officers and comrades, supplied him with a sense of power and adequately regulated his relations with authority, the element of self-concern in battle, which would lead to disruption of the effective functioning of his primary group, was minimized.

2. The capacity of the primary group to resist disintegration was dependent on the acceptance of political, ideological, and cultural symbols (all secondary symbols) only to the extent that these secondary symbols became directly associated with primary gratifications.

3. Once disruption of primary group life resulted through separation, breaks in communications, loss of leadership, depletion of personnel, or major and prolonged breaks in the supply of food and medical care, such an ascendancy of preoccupation with physical survival developed that there was very little "last-ditch" resistance.

4. Finally, as long as the primary group structure of the component units of the Wehrmacht persisted, attempts by the Allies to cause disaffection by the invocation of secondary and political symbols (e.g., about the ethical wrongfulness of the National Socialist system) were mainly unsuccessful. By contrast, where Allied propaganda dealt with primary and personal values, particularly physical survival, it was more likely to be effective.

Long before D-Day in Western France, research was undertaken in the United Kingdom and North Africa on these social psychological aspects of the enemy's forces. These studies were continued after D-Day by the Intelligence Section of the Psychological Warfare Division of SHAEF. Although of course they are subject to many scientific strictures, they provide a groundwork for the evaluation of the experiences of the German soldier and for the analysis of the social organization of the German Army. Methods of collecting data included front line interrogation of prisoners of war (Ps/W) and intensive psychological interviews in rear areas. Captured enemy documents, statements of recaptured Allied military personnel, and the reports of combat observers were also studied. A monthly opinion poll of random samples of large numbers of Ps/W was also undertaken. This paper is based on a review of all these data.

Modes of disintegration

Preliminary to the analysis of the function of the primary group in the maintenance of cohesion in the German Army, it is necessary to classify the modes of social disintegration found in any modern army:

1. Desertion (deliberately going over to the enemy lines)
  a) by individual action
    (1) after discussion with comrades
    (2) without prior discussion with others
  b) by groups acting in concert

2. Active surrender (deliberate decision to give up to the enemy as he approaches and taking steps to facilitate capture, e.g., by sending emissaries, by calling out, by signalling, etc.)
  a) by single individuals
  b) by group as a unit
    (1) by mutual agreement
    (2) by order of or with approval of NCO or officer
  c) by plurality of uncoordinated individuals

3. Passive surrender
  a) by individuals acting alone
    (1) non-resistance (allowing oneself to be taken prisoner without taking effective steps to facilitate or obstruct capture; passivity may be a means of facilitating surrender)
    (2) token resistance (allowing oneself to be taken prisoner with nominal face-saving gestures of obstruction to capture)
  b) by plurality of uncoordinated individuals

4. Routine resistance: rote or mechanical, but effective execution of orders as given from above

with discontinuance when the enemy becomes overwhelmingly powerful and aggressive.

5. "Last-ditch" resistance which ends only with the exhaustion of fighting equipment and subsequent surrender or death. (This type of soldier is greatly underrepresented in studies of samples of Ps/W. Therefore the study of Ps/W alone does not give an adequate picture of the resistive qualities of the German soldier.)

A more detailed description of each of the above classes will be useful in the following analysis:

Desertion involved positive and deliberate action by the German soldier to deliver himself to Allied soldiers for capture by crossing the lines, e.g., by planfully "losing himself" while on patrol and "blundering" into the enemy's area of control or by deliberately remaining behind during a withdrawal from a given position so that when the Allied troops came up they could take him.

In *active surrender* by the group as a unit, the positive act of moving across to enemy lines was absent but there was an element common with desertion in the deliberate attempt to withdraw from further combat. Like many cases of desertion, the decision to surrender as a group was arrived at as a result of group discussion and mutual agreement. The dividing line between active surrender and desertion brought about by lagging behind was shadowy. There were other forms of group surrender which were clearly different from desertion, e.g., the sending of an emissary to arrange terms with the enemy, the refusal to carry out aggressive orders, or to fight a way out of encirclement.

In *passive surrender,* the intention of a soldier to remove himself from the battle was often not clear even to himself. The soldier who was taken prisoner by passive surrender might have been immobilized or apathetic due to anxiety; he might have been in a state of bewildered isolation and not have thought of passive surrender until the perception of an opportunity brought it to his mind. Non-resistant passive surrender frequently occurred in the case of soldiers who lay in their foxholes or hid in the cellars or barns, sometimes self-narcotized by fear, or sometimes deliberately waiting to be overrun. In both cases, they made only the most limited external gestures of resistance when the enemy approached. In the second type of passive surrender—token resistance—the surrendering soldier desired to avoid all the stigma of desertion or surrender but nevertheless showed reluctance to undertake aggressive or defensive actions which might have interfered with his survival.

An examination of the basic social organization of the German Army, in terms of its primary group structure and the factors which strengthened and weakened its component primary groups, is first required in order to account for the stability and cohesion of resistance, and in order to evaluate the impact of Allied propaganda.

THE FUNCTION OF THE PRIMARY GROUP

"The company is the only truly existent community. This community allows neither time nor rest for a personal life. It forces us into its circle, for life is at stake. Obviously compromises must be made and claims be surrendered. . . . Therefore the idea of fighting, living, and dying for the fatherland, for the cultural possessions of the fatherland, is but a relatively distant thought. At least it does not play a great role in the practical motivations of the individual."

Thus wrote an idealistic German student in the first world war. A German sergeant, captured toward the end of the second world war, was asked by his interrogators about the political opinions of his men. In reply, he laughed and said, "When you ask such a question, I realize well that you have no idea of what makes a soldier fight. The soldiers lie in their holes and are happy if they live through the next day. If we think at all, it's about the end of the war and then home."

The fighting effectiveness of the vast majority of soldiers in combat depends only to a small extent on their preoccupation with the major political values which might be affected by the outcome of the war and which are the object of concern to statesmen and publicists. There are of course soldiers in whom such motivations are important. Volunteer armies recruited on the basis of ethical or political loyalties, such as the International Brigade in the Spanish Civil War, are affected by their degree of orientation toward major political goals. In the German Army, the "hard core" of National Socialists were similarly motivated.

But in a conscript army, the criterion of recruitment is much less specialized and the army is more representative of the total population liable to conscription. Therefore the values involved in political and social systems or ethical schemes do not have much impact on the determination of a soldier to fight to the best of his ability and to hold out as long as possible. For the ordinary German soldier the decisive fact was that he was a member of a squad or section which maintained its structural integrity and which coincided roughly with the *social* unit which satisfied some of his major primary needs. He was likely to go on fighting, provided he had the necessary weapons, as long as the group possessed leadership with which he could identify himself, and as long as he gave affection to and received affection from the other members of his squad and platoon. In other words, as long as he felt himself to be a member of his primary group and therefore bound by the expectations and demands of its other members, his soldierly achievement was likely to be good.

Modern social research has shown that the primary group is not merely the chief source of affection and accordingly the major factor in personality formation in infancy and childhood. The primary group continues to be the major source of social and psychological sustenance through adulthood. In the army, when isolated from civilian primary groups, the individual soldier comes to depend more and more on his military primary group. His spontaneous loyalties are to its immediate members whom he sees daily and with whom he develops a high degree of intimacy. For the German soldier in particular, the demands of his group, reinforced by officially prescribed rules, had the effect of an external authority. It held his aggressiveness in check; it provided discipline, protection, and freedom from autonomous decision.

Army units with a high degree of primary group integrity suffered little from desertions or from individually contrived surrenders. In the Wehrmacht, desertions and surrenders were most frequent in groups of heterogeneous ethnic composition in which Austrians, Czechs, and Poles were randomly intermixed with each other. In such groups the difficulties of linguistic communication, the large amount of individual resentment and aggressiveness about coercion into German service, the weakened support of leadership due to their inability to identify with German officers—all these factors hampered the formation of cohesive groups.

Sample interviews with Wehrmacht deserters made in North Africa in 1943 and in France and Germany in 1944 and 1945 showed an overwhelmingly disproportionate representation of elements which could not be assimilated into primary groups. A total of 443 Wehrmacht Ps/W captured toward the end of the North African campaign, consisting of 180 Germans, 200 Austrians and 63 others (Czechs, Poles, Yugoslavs, etc.), had very markedly different tendencies towards desertion: 29 per cent of the Germans were deserters or potential deserters; 55 per cent of the Austrians fell into these two classes, as did 78 per cent of the Czechs, Poles, and Yugoslavs. Of the 53

German deserters, only one declared that he had "political" motives for desertion. In the Western European campaign, the bulk of the deserters came from among the "Volksdeutsche," Austrians, Poles, and Russians who had been coerced into German military service. It was clear that in view of the apolitical character of most of the deserters, the grounds for their desertion were to be sought among those variables which prevented the formation of close primary group bonds, the chief of which were insuperable language differences, bitter resentment against their coerced condition, and the unfriendliness of the Germans in their units.

Among German deserters, who remained few until the close of the war, the failure to assimilate into the primary group life of the Wehrmacht was the most important factor, more important indeed than political dissidence. Deserters were on the whole men who had difficulty in personal adjustment, e.g., in the acceptance of affection or in the giving of affection. They were men who had shown these same difficulties in civilian life, having had difficulties with friends, work associates, and their own families, or having had criminal records. Political dissidents on the other hand, when captured, justified their failure to desert by invoking their sense of solidarity with their comrades and expressed the feeling that had they deserted when given a post of responsibility their comrades would have interpreted it as a breach of solidarity. For the political dissident, the verbal expression of political dissent was as much anti-authoritarianism as he could afford, and submission to his group was the price which he had to pay for it.

The persistent strength of primary group controls was manifested even in the last month of the war, when many deserters felt that they would not have been able to have taken the initial step in their desertion unless they had discussed the matter with their comrades and received some kind of legitimation for the action, such as a statement of approval. And, on the other hand, the same ongoing efficacy of primary group sentiment was evident in the statements of would-be deserters who declared they had never been able to cross the threshold because they had been told by their officers that the comrades who remained behind (i.e., the comrades of the men who had deserted) would be shot. Hence, one of the chief forms of disintegration which occurred in the last stages of the war took the form of group surrender in which, after ample discussion within the unit, the authorization of the leading personalities and often of the NCO's had been granted for the offering of token resistance to facilitate capture, or even for outright group surrender.

Factors strengthening primary group solidarity

The Nazi nucleus of the primary group: the "hard core." The stability and military effectiveness of the military primary group were in large measure a function of the "hard core," who approximated about ten to fifteen per cent of the total of enlisted men; the percentage was higher for non-commissioned officers and was very much higher among the junior officers. These were, on the whole, young men between 24 and 28 years of age who had had a gratifying adolescence in the most rewarding period of National Socialism. They were imbued with the ideology of *Gemeinschaft* (community solidarity), were enthusiasts for the military life, had definite homo-erotic tendencies and accordingly placed a very high value on "toughness," manly comradeliness, and group solidarity. The presence of a few such men in the group, zealous, energetic, and unsparing of themselves, provided models for weaker men, and facilitated the process of identification. For those for whom their charisma did not suffice and who were accordingly difficult to incorporate fully into the intimate primary group, frowns, harsh words, and threats served as a check on divisive tendencies. The fact that the elite SS divisions and paratroop divisions had a larger "hard core" than other divisions of the army—so large as to embrace almost the entire group membership during most of the war—accounted for their greater fighting effectiveness. And the fact that such a "hard core" was almost entirely lacking from certain *Volksgrenadier* divisions helped to a considerable extent to account for the military inferiority of these units.

One of the functions of the "hard core" was to minimize the probability of divisive political discussions. There was, of course, little inclination to discuss political matters or even strategic aspects of the war among German soldiers. For this reason widespread defeatism concerning the outcome of the war had little consequence in affecting behavior (until the spring of 1945) because of the near impossibility—objective as well as subjective —of discussing or carrying out alternative plans of action.

In contrast with the "hard core," which was a disproportionately large strengthening factor in the integrity of the military primary group, the "soft core" was a source of infection which was by no means comparable in effectiveness. Unlike the first world war experience in which anti-war attitudes were often vigorously expressed and eagerly listened to by men who were "good comrades," in the second world war the political anti-militarist or anti-Nazi who expressed his views with frequency and vigor was also in the main not a "good comrade." There was a complete absence of soldiers' committees and organized opposition, even in March and April 1945 (except for the Bavarian Freiheitsaktion which was constituted by rear-echelon troops). On isolated occasions, the Western Allies were able to exploit a man who had been a "good comrade" and who, after having been captured, expressed his defeatism and willingness to help end the war; he was thereupon sent back into the German line to talk his comrades into going over with him to the Allied lines. Here the "soft core" man exploited his comradely solidarity and it was only on that basis that he was able to remove some of the members of his group from the influence of the "hard core."

Community of experience as a cohesive force. The factors which affect group solidarity in general were on the whole carefully manipulated by the German general staff. Although during the war Germany was more permeated by foreigners than it had ever been before in its history, the army was to a great extent carefully protected from disintegrating influences of heterogeneity of ethnic and national origin, at least in crucial military situations. German officers saw that solidarity is fostered by the recollection of jointly experienced gratifications and that accordingly the groups who had gone through a victory together should not be dissolved but should be maintained as units to the greatest degree possible.

The replacement system of the Wehrmacht operated to the same end. The entire personnel of a division would be withdrawn from the front simultaneously and refitted as a unit with replacements. Since new members were added to the division while it was out of line they were thereby given the opportunity to assimilate themselves into the group; then the group as a whole was sent forward. This system continued until close to the end of the war and helped to explain the durability of the German Army in the face of the overwhelming numerical and material superiority of the Allied forces.

Deterioration of group solidarity in the Wehrmacht which began to appear toward the very end of the war was most frequently found in hastily fabricated units. These were made up of new recruits, dragooned stragglers, air force men who had been forced into the infantry (and who felt a loss of status in the change), men transferred from the navy into the infantry to meet the emergency of manpower shortage, older factory workers, concentration camp inmates, and older married men who had been kept in reserve throughout the war and who had remained with the familial primary group until the last moment.

The latter, who were the "catch" of the last "total mobilization" carried with them the resentment and bitterness which the "total mobilization" produced and which prevented the flow of affection necessary for group formation. It was clear that groups so diverse in age composition and background, and especially so mixed in their reactions to becoming infantrymen, could not very quickly become effective fighting units. They had no time to become used to one another and to develop the type of friendliness which is possible only when loyalties to outside groups have been renounced—or at least put into the background. A preview of what was to occur when units became mixed was provided by the 275th Fusilier Battalion which broke up before the First U.S. Army drive in November. Thirty-five Ps/W interrogated from this unit turned out to have been recently scraped together from fifteen different army units.

The most ineffective of all the military formations employed by the Wehrmacht during the war were the Volkssturm units. They ranged in age from boys to old men, and were not even given basic training in the weapons which they were supposed to use. Their officers were Nazi local functionaries who were already objects of hostility and who were therefore unable to release a flow of affection among equals. They had moreover not broken their family ties to the slightest extent. They still remained members of a primary group which did not fuse into the military primary group. Finally, they had no uniforms. They had only brassards to identify them and through which to identify themselves with one another. The mutual identification function of the uniform which plays so great a role in military units was thereby lost. As soon as they were left to their own devices, they disintegrated from within, deserting in large numbers to their homes, hiding, permitting themselves to be captured, etc.

Factors weakening primary group solidarity

Isolation. The disintegration of a primary group depends in part on the physical and spatial variables which isolate it from the continuous pressure of face-to-face contact. The factor of spatial proximity in the maintenance of group solidarity in military situations must not be underestimated. In February and March of 1945, isolated remnants of platoons and companies were surrendering in groups with increasing frequency. The tactical situation of defensive fighting under heavy American artillery bombardment and the deployment of rear outposts forced soldiers to take refuge in cellars, trenches, and other underground shelters in small groups of three and four. This prolonged isolation from the nucleus of the primary group for several days worked to reinforce the fear of destruction of the self, and thus had a disintegrative influence on primary group relations. A soldier who was isolated in a cellar or in a concrete bunker for several days and whose anxieties about physical survival were aggravated by the tactical hopelessness of his situation, was a much more easily separable member of his group than one who, though fearing physical destruction, was still bound by the continuous and vital ties of working, eating, sleeping, and being at leisure together with his fellow soldiers.

This proposition regarding the high significance of the spatial variable for primary group solidarity and the maintenance of the fighting effectiveness of an army is supported by the behavior of the retreating German Army in North Africa in 1943, and in France and Germany in September-October 1944 and March 1945. As long as a retreat is orderly and the structure of the component units of an army is maintained, strategic difficulties do not break up the army. An army in retreat breaks up only when the retreat is poorly organized, when command is lost over the men, so that they become separated from their units and become stragglers, or when enemy penetrations isolate larger or smaller formations from the main group.

Stragglers first became a moderately serious problem in the German Army in October 1944. On October 22, 1944, General Keitel ordered that a maximum of one to three days be allowed for stragglers to reattach themselves to their units. The previous limit had been five days. The aggravation of the straggler problem was further documented by General Blaskowitz's order of March 5, 1945, according to which the category of stragglers was declared to have ceased to exist. Soldiers who lost contact with their own units were directed to attach themselves immediately to the "first troops in the line which he can contact. . . ."

Familial ties and primary group disintegration. Prisoners of war remarked with considerable frequency that discussions about alternative paths of action by groups of soldiers who were entirely defeatist arose not from discussions about the war in its political or strategic aspects, but rather from discussions about the soldiers' families. The recollection of concrete family experiences reactivated sentiments of dependence on the family for psychological support and correspondingly weakened the hold of the military primary group. It was in such contexts that German soldiers toward the end of the war were willing to discuss group surrender.

To prevent preoccupation with family concerns, the families of German soldiers were given strict instructions to avoid references to family deprivations in letters to the front. In the winter and spring of 1945, when Allied air raids became so destructive of communal life, all telegrams to soldiers at the front had to be passed by party officials in order to insure that no distracting news reached the soldiers. On the other hand, care was taken by party and army authorities that soldiers should not be left in a state of anxiety about their families and to this end vigorous propaganda was carried on to stimulate correspondence with soldiers at the front. For those who had no families and who needed the supplementary affection which the army unit could not provide, provisions were made to obtain mail from individuals (including party officials) who would befriend unmarried or family-less soldiers, with the result that the psychic economy of the soldier was kept in equilibrium.

There was, however, a special type of situation in which the very strength of familial ties served to keep the army from further disintegration. This arose towards the end of the war, when soldiers were warned that desertion would result in severe sanctions being inflicted on the deserter's family.

Toward the end of the war, soldiers tended to break away from the army more often while they were on leave and with their families, and therefore isolated from personal contact with their primary group fellows. When soldiers returned to visit their families, then the conflict between contradictory primary group loyalties became acute. The hold of the military primary group became debilitated in the absence of face-to-face contacts. The prospect of facing, on return to the front, physical destruction or a prolonged loss of affection from the civilian primary group, especially the family, prompted an increasing number of desertions while on furlough.

All of these factors contributed to loosen the solidarity of the German Army, especially when the prospect of physical destruction began to weigh more heavily. Severe threats to the safety of the civilian primary group created anxiety which often weakened the hold of the military primary group. When the area of the soldier's home was occupied by the enemy or when the soldier himself was fighting in the area, there was strong disposition to desert homeward. One such soldier said: "Now I have nothing more for which to fight, because my home is occupied."

The strong pull of the civilian primary group became stronger as the coherence of the army group weakened. But sometimes, the former worked to keep the men fighting in their units, i.e., when they reasoned that the shortest way home was to keep the group intact and to avoid capture or desertion. Otherwise there would ensue a long period in an enemy P/W camp. On the other hand, in event of the defeat of a still intact army, there would be only a short period of waiting before demobilization.

Demand for physical survival. The individual soldier's fear of destruction ultimately pressed to weaken primary group cohesion; nevertheless it is striking to note the degree to which demands for physical survival could be exploited by Wehrmacht authority to the end of prolonging resistance. Where the social conditions were otherwise favorable, the primary bonds of group solidarity were dissolved only under the most extreme circumstances of threat to the individual organism— in situations where the tactical prospects were utterly hopeless, under devastating artillery and air bombardment, or where the basic food and medical requirements were not being met. Although aware for a long time of the high probability of German defeat in the war and of the hopelessness of the numerous individual battles, very many German soldiers continued to resist without any serious deterioration in the quality of their fighting skill. But where the most basic physiological demands of the German soldier were threatened with complete frustration, the bonds of group solidarity were broken.

Concern about food and about health always reduces the solidarity of a group. Throughout the war, and until the period just before the end, German army medical services were maintained at a high level of efficiency; the decline in their efficiency coincides with the deterioration in the morale of the men. Special care was also observed in the management of the food supply and accordingly few German soldiers felt that the food supplies were inadequate. Indeed, as late as October 1944, only 15 per cent of a sample of 92 Ps/W declared that they were at all dissatisfied with army food. By January, however, the situation changed and Ps/W reported increased preoccupation with physical survival, with food, and the shortage of clothing. Soldiers in certain units were beginning to "scrounge." The extreme cold of the winter of '44-'45 also began to tell on the men whose military self-esteem was being reduced by the raggedness of their uniforms and the failure to obtain replacements for unsatisfactory equipment.

Thus, to keep groups integral, it was necessary not only to provide positive gratifications but also to reduce to a minimum the alternative possibilities of increasing the chances for survival by leaving the unit. For this reason the Nazis sought to counteract the fear of personal physical destruction in battle by telling the men that accurate records were kept on deserters and that not only would their families and property be made to suffer in the event of their desertion, but that after the war, upon their return to Germany, they, too, would be very severely punished. They were also told by their officers that German agents were operating in American and British P/W cages in order to report on violations of security and on deserters. A Wehrmacht leaflet to German soldiers mentioned the names of two deserters of the 980th Volksgrenadiere who were alleged to have divulged information and stated that not only would their families be sent to prison and suffer the loss of their property and ration cards, but that the men themselves would also be punished after the war. In actuality, they were often punished in the P/W camps by the extreme Nazis who exercised some control in certain camps.

For the same reason, as long as the front was relatively stable, the Wehrmacht officers increased the natural hazards of war by ordering mine fields to be laid, barbed wire to be set up, and special guards to be posted to limit the freedom of movement of isolated and psychologically unattached individuals who, in situations which offered the chance of safely withdrawing from the war, would have moved over to the enemy's lines. Although the number of avowedly would-be deserters remained very small until near the end of the war, even they were frequently immobilized for fear of being killed by the devices set up to prevent their separation from the group. The danger of destruction by the Allies in event of desertion also played a part in keeping men attached to their military units. As one P/W who had thought of desertion but who never took action said, "by day our own people shoot at us, by night yours do."

Another physical narcissistic element which contributed somewhat to resistance on the Western front was fear of castration in event of the loss of the war. (This was effective only among a minority of the German soldiers.) The guilt feelings of the Nazi soldiers who had slaughtered and marauded on the Eastern front, and elsewhere in Europe, and their projection onto the enemy of their own sadistic impulses, heightened their narcissistic apprehensiveness about damage to their vital organs and to their physical organism as a whole. Rumors of castration at the hands of the Russians circulated in the German Army throughout the last three years of the war

and it is likely that they were largely the result of ruthless methods on both sides.

The Nazis perceived the function of fear of personal destruction in the event of capture as a factor in keeping a group intact after the internal bonds had been loosened. There were accordingly situations in which SS detachments deliberately committed atrocities on enemy civilians and soldiers in order to increase the anxieties of German soldiers as to what would befall them in the event of their defeat and capture. This latter policy was particularly drastically applied by the Waffen-SS in the von Rundstedt counteroffensive. It appears to have been an effort to convince German soldiers that there were no alternatives but victory or resistance to the very end and that surrender or desertion would end with slaughter of the German soldiers, as it had in the cases of the Allied soldiers. This was not effective for the mass of the German soldiers, however, who were becoming convinced that the law-abiding British and Americans would not in most situations harm them upon capture.

The dread of destruction of the self, and the demand for physical survival, while breaking up the spontaneous solidarity of the military primary group in most cases, thus served under certain conditions to coerce the soldier into adherence to his group and to the execution of the orders of his superiors.

THE ROLE OF "SOLDIERLY HONOR"

American and British soldiers tend to consider their wartime service as a disagreeable necessity, as a task which had to be performed because there were no alternatives. For the German, being a soldier was a more than acceptable status. It was indeed honorable. The King's Regulations which govern the British Army (1940) begin with the statement that the army consists of officers and men serving for various lengths of time. The German equivalent in the Defense Laws of 1935 opens with a declaration that "military service is a service of honor for the German people, the Wehrmacht is the armed barrier and the soldierly school of the German people."

Emphasis on the element of honor in the military profession has led in Germany to the promulgation of elaborate rules of conduct regulating the behavior of both officers and men in a great variety of specific military and extra-military situations. The explicit and implicit code of soldierly honor, regulating the responsibilities of officers for their men, determined behavior in battle and established conditions under which surrender was honorable. It also provided a very comprehensive body of etiquette. This elaborate ritualization of the military profession had a significantly positive influence on group solidarity and efficiency during periods of stress. "Honor" rooted in a rigid conscience (superego) served in the German Army to keep men at their tasks better than individual reflection and evaluation could have done. When the individual was left to make decisions for himself, the whole host of contradictory impulses toward authority of officers and of the group as an entity was stimulated.

Domination by higher authority was eagerly accepted by most ordinary soldiers, who feared that if they were allowed to exercise their initiative their *innere Schweinhunde*, i.e., their own narcissistic and rebellious impulses, would come to the fore. On the other hand, rigorous suppression of these impulses constituted an appeasement of the superego which allowed the group machinery to function in an orderly manner.

The belief in the efficacy and moral worth of discipline and in the inferiority of the spontaneous, primary reactions of the personality was expressed in the jettisoning of the German Army Psychiatric Selection Services in 1942. When the manpower shortage became stringent and superfluities had to be scrapped, the personnel selection system based on personality analyses was one of those activities which was thought to be dispensable. Apparently taking individual personality differences into account was thought to be too much of a concession to moral weakness which could and in any case *should* be overcome by hard, soldierly discipline.

Strength as an element in honor.   For persons who have deep-lying uncertainties over their own weaknesses, who fear situations which will reveal their weakness in controlling themselves and their lack of manliness, membership in an army will tend to reduce anxieties. Subjugation to discipline gives such persons support; it means that they do not have to depend on themselves, that someone stronger than themselves is guilding and protecting them. Among young males in middle and late adolescence, the challenges of love and vocation aggravate anxieties about weakness. At this stage fears about potency are considerable. When men who have passed through this stage are placed in the entirely male society of a military unit, freed from the control of adult civilian society and missing its gratifications, they tend to regress to the adolescent condition. The show of "toughness" and hardness which is regarded as a virtue among soldiers is a response to these reactivated adolescent anxieties about weakness.

In the German Army, all these tendencies were intensified by the military code, and they accounted for a considerable share of the cohesion and resistance up to the very last stages of the war. Among those at the extreme end of the scale —the "hard core" of Nazi last-ditch resisters—in whom the preoccupation with strength and weakness is to be found in most pronounced form— this attitude was manifested in unwillingness of some to acknowledge defeat even after capture. . . .

CONCLUSION

At the beginning of the second world war, many publicists and specialists in propaganda attributed almost supreme importance to psychological warfare operations. The legendary successes of Allied propaganda against the German Army at the end of the first world war and the tremendous expansion of the advertising and mass communications industries in the ensuing two decades had convinced many people that human behavior could be extensively manipulated by mass communications. They tended furthermore to stress that military morale was to a great extent a function of the belief in the rightness of the "larger" cause which was at issue in the war; good soldiers were therefore those who clearly understood the political and moral implications of what was at stake. They explained the striking successes of the German Army in the early phases of the war by the "ideological possession" of the German soldiers, and they accordingly thought that propaganda attacking doctrinal conceptions would be defeating this army.

Studies of the German Army's morale and fighting effectiveness made during the last three years of the war throw considerable doubt on these hypotheses. The solidarity of the German Army was discovered by these studies—which left much to be desired from the standpoint of scientific rigor—to be based only very indirectly and very partially on political convictions or broader ethical beliefs. Where conditions were such as to allow primary group life to function smoothly, and where the primary group developed a high degree of cohesion, morale was high and resistance effective or at least very determined, regardless in the main of the political attitudes of the soldiers. The conditions of primary group life were related to spatial proximity, the capacity for intimate communication, the provision of paternal protectiveness by NCO's and junior officers, and the gratification of certain personality needs, e.g., manliness, by the military organization and its activities. The larger structure of the army served to maintain morale through the provision of the framework in which potentially individuating physical threats were kept at a minimum—through the organization of supplies and through adequate strategic dispositions.

The behavior of the German Army demonstrated that the focus of attention and concern beyond one's immediate face-to-face social circles might be slight indeed and still not interfere with the achievement of a high degree of military effectiveness. It also showed that attempts to modify behavior by means of symbols referring to events or values outside the focus of attention and concern would be given an indifferent response by the vast majority of the German soldiers. This was almost equally true under conditions of primary group integrity and under conditions of extreme primary group disintegration. In the former, primary needs were met adequately through the gratifications provided by the other members of the group; in the latter, the individual had regressed to a narcissistic state in which symbols referring to the outer world were irrelevant to his first concern—"saving his own skin."

At moments of primary group disintegration, a particular kind of propaganda less hortatory or analytical, but addressing the intensified desire to survive, and describing the precise procedures by which physical survival could be achieved, was likely to facilitate further disintegration. Further-more, in some cases aspects of the environment towards which the soldier might hitherto have been emotionally indifferent were defined for him by prolonged exposure to propaganda under conditions of disintegration. Some of these wider aspects, e.g., particular strategic considerations, then tended to be taken into account in his motivation and he was more likely to implement his defeatist mood by surrender than he would have been without exposure to propaganda.

It seems necessary, therefore, to reconsider the potentialities of propaganda in the context of all the other variables which influence behavior. The erroneous views concerning the omnipotence of propaganda must be given up and their place must be taken by much more differentiated views as to the possibilities of certain kinds of propaganda under different sets of conditions.

It must be recognized that on the moral plane most men are members of the larger society by virtue of identifications which are mediated through the human beings with whom they are in personal relationships. Many are bound into the larger society only by primary group identifications. Only a small proportion possessing special training or rather particular kinds of personalities are capable of giving a preponderant share of their attention and concern to the symbols of the larger world. The conditions under which these different groups will respond to propaganda will differ, as will also the type of propaganda to which they will respond.

Selection 24

Street Corner Society
William Foote Whyte

At this point the imperiousness of the group may have the reader feeling powerless. Not only does the group insist on determining what is real (witness the work of Asch and Lifton) but the individual cannot get along without the support of the group (note Davis and Shils and Janowitz) and his standing within the group depends on the degree to which he conforms to its norms (as Homans will demonstrate in Selection 25). It is worth repeating, however, that the potentiality for personality that each infant brings into the world would not develop into actual personality without group associations. Furthermore, the group is not as constraining as it might appear, for the individual always has a choice about which norms he will follow by virtue of his ability to change affiliations. This is especially true in complex industrial societies with their proliferations of groups. Of course, an individual's initial assignment to a family and a neighborhood is ascribed—that is, determined by birth—but as he matures and develops interests, his memberships are less determined by ascriptive factors; he can decide which groups are most congenial to him and can join them.

There is, then, considerable opportunity to escape group norms that are felt to be repressive by joining more congenial groups. Before a person is accepted, of course, he must conform to group norms, at least to some extent. Thus limits are imposed on the opportunity to change associations, inasmuch as people vary in their ability to adopt the norms of a new group. If a person is uneducated, for example, it would be virtually impossible for him to learn the values, norms, and related behavior expected of members of the American Philosophical Society. However, it rarely happens that an uneducated person aspires to join such a group. People also have different kinds of exposure to the various groups in society.

Which individuals are successful in shifting their affiliations to new groups? One of the most promising concepts in sociology, that of the reference group, has begun to provide clues. During World War II it was discovered that soldiers who identified with their officers and accepted the necessity of military discipline and courtesy were more likely to be promoted than those who rejected military authority and mores and whose deepest loyalty was to the primary group that developed in the barracks. What differentiated these two groups of soldiers was their reference group. The reference group of the G.I.'s who supported the officers and army norms was not the one in which they found themselves but the one whose values they internalized or accepted as their own by studying military manuals, listening carefully to lectures, saluting smartly, and maintaining a soldierly appearance.

A reference group is the group toward which the individual is oriented—the group whose values and goals he accepts. It may or may not actually exist. Whether he aspires to membership or simply identifies with an ideal group, he will, insofar as his position allows, assume the attitudes and behavior patterns he believes to be characteristic of that group. If the individual aspires to membership in a real group, such "anticipatory socialization" makes it easier to be subsequently accepted only insofar as his attitudes and behavior correspond to the actual norms and values of the group, and then only if the group approves of emulation by "outsiders."

In his study of an Italian community, Cornerville, Whyte found a civilian counterpart of the soldier who seeks promotion. Chick Morelli, the son of Italian immigrants and the leader of the college boys, differed from the majority of Italian youths in Street Corner Society because his reference groups consisted of people who belonged to high status groups—college students, lawyers, Ivy League law students, girls from well-to-do neighborhoods, social workers who stressed the values of education and achievement, and members of the Republican party. Chick's subsequent success cannot be explained in terms of greater ability, for Doc, the leader of the Nortons, a juvenile gang, was as competent as Chick, but Doc accepted the gang as his reference group. Doc's loyalty required sacrifices to the gang which destined him to failure in terms of the standards of the larger American society.

The concept of reference group by itself, however, does not explain why individuals choose the particular groups they do. Why did some students use the experimental group as a reference group in the Asch experiment while the independent subjects rejected it? Why do some soldiers want to become officers while others are satisfied to remain privates? Why did Chick aim for high status groups while Doc rejected them? One clue may be that Chick had more exposure to alternative reference groups than Doc did. While Chick was working in a liquor store, an irate customer taunted him about his lack of ability to do college work. A prominent attorney took an interest in Chick; another lawyer pointed out the advantages of attending Ivy Law School. Significantly, Chick owned and read a book of biographies of great men. Doc might have similarly idealized other groups than his own—Chick and his club, for one—but instead he remained "loyal" to the gang and deprecated the efforts of the college boys toward achievement. In fact, the attitude of the majority of youths in Cornerville toward those who wanted to move out was expressed in the terms *stooges* or *flunkies*. These epithets are equivalents of such terms as *apple polisher*, used by some enlisted men to describe G.I.'s who identified with officers. But in spite of such clues, there is no satisfactory answer to why individuals choose the reference groups they do.

Chick Morelli told his story in this way:

"I was born in Italy. I didn't come over here until I was eight years old. . . . I was born in Avellino, near Naples. My father was quite a powerful man over there. He started a political party, and he ran for mayor and was almost elected. I guess politics runs in the family. . . . I think I get my intellectualism from my father. I realize now that the things I have done are the sort of things that he wanted to do.

"My father came to Eastern City nine or ten years before my mother and I came here. He set up a fruit and vegetable store, and he also had a small bakery. We hadn't been here long before my father died and left my mother, my older sister, and me to take care of ourselves. We got a little money selling his property, but that didn't last long.

"I started to work selling papers. From the beginning I used to make $5 a week on my paper business. I worked hard. I was anxious to get ahead. After a while, I was making $2 on Saturday with the papers and about $10 a week altogether. I always brought home every nickel to my mother, because I didn't know how to spend it. And she didn't know how to spend money in this country, so she saved it too. . . . I used to go out for wood. I provided all the fuel for the stove, except in the coldest weather, when we would buy a little coal. . . . Then I got a job after school behind an ice-cream counter. I was making $10 a week at that for a while. . . . When I was in high school, I had a job with my uncle. He was in the bootlegging business. I had to take the job; I had no choice, because I needed the money. I worked there for a while, mixing the alky, selling over the counter. Once I nearly got arrested. It was just lucky that I didn't. . . .

"When I was working in the bootlegging business, I had plenty of money. And I was a free spender at that time. I went to plenty of dances, and whenever a couple of fellows were with me, I would invite them to have coffee or a drink. I wasted a lot of money that way, but now that I look back on it, it seems to me that it was better for me to have learned my lesson early when money didn't count for so much as it does now. . . . One summer I was going different places with one particular friend. All summer we went out to dances and parties three times a week, and I always paid for him. At other times I would hand him a couple of bucks so that in case he met a girl, he wouldn't be embarrassed. I never thought the time would come when I would ask him for a dime and he wouldn't give it to me, but that time did come. It was just before I was going back to school. On this particular night I knew he had just gotten his pay check. He came up to me and asked me to go to a dance with him. I said I would gladly go, but I didn't have enough to buy the ticket. I needed ten cents more.

"He said, 'Well, I've got $30, but I need it all myself.'

"I said, 'Don't trouble yourself, I'll get it from somebody else.'

"That taught me a lesson. After that I would never go so far out of my way for anybody. I would always hold back just a little. . . . I don't know if you have found it so, but it has been my experience that I make more friends and better friendships when I act a little reserved and don't go running after the person. . . . Probably I was influenced somewhat by my mother. She always believed that you shouldn't trust a person too far, you should keep something in reserve, and she often said that to me."

I asked him if he had found it hard to adjust when he came from Italy.

"I did. I was ridiculed by my classmates be-

"Chick and His Club" by William Foote Whyte, pp. 52-65. Reprinted from *Street Corner Society* by permission of The University of Chicago Press. © 1943 by The University of Chicago Press.

cause of the way I spoke. But they didn't mean anything by it. After all, we were all Italians down here. But, still, I was always sensitive about my way of speaking. I don't think I had an accent for very long, but it wasn't until recently that someone pointed out to me that I never pronounced my *th* sounds. . . .

"I did a lot of things with the boys. I played the rubber-ball game that you play with your fist. I was a champ at that. I wasn't so good at baseball or football, perhaps because I spent so much time at the other game."

I asked him if there had been a gang of fellows with whom he associated. He said there had been. Was he the leader of it?

"I don't know. I wouldn't say just that. I know that they always used to call for me instead of me calling for them. I used to wait up at my house for them. It wasn't that I wanted them to come for me. It just got to be a habit. When we played cards, it was always up at my house. We would play there evenings, and sometimes I would say, 'Sorry, fellows, I have to go out,' and the games would break up.

"I took an academic course in high school. I don't know why I did, except that I always liked those studies. At that time I didn't think I would be able to go to college, but I don't know what I would have done if I couldn't have gone. I wanted to get out in the world. I wasn't satisfied to stay just where I was. . . . When I was working in my uncle's store, I was associating with the lowest of the low, the bums and the drunks. Sometimes I would wonder if I was going to wind up like them. . . . We did have some good customers. One was a judge. There was another man who was very well educated. Once this man came in and wanted to buy some liquor on credit. I couldn't give it to him, not because I didn't want to, but because I had orders from my uncle. We got in an argument, and he said some things that hurted me. He said, 'Chick, I like to see you in college, you'd make a jackass of yourself the way you talk and act.' . . . I was very sensitive about those things, and that hurted me. Right after that I went uptown and bought two books. One was a book on English, and the other was a book of etiquette. I don't know why I bought that book of etiquette, but when I got home, I read it through. I wanted to know everything I should do and not do.

"The summer of my Junior year in high school, when I was at a dance down at the beach, I met a girl by the name of Edith Clark. We got along all right, and she took down my telephone number. She said she would look me up when we got back to Eastern City. A few months passed, and I didn't hear anything from her. I decided to forget about it. But then one day in my Senior year a fellow came up to me in the library and told me that a girl by the name of Edith had called in my uncle's shop. I had even forgotten who she was, but I called her, and after that we got together. I was seeing her about every other night for almost two years. She lived with a woman named Mrs. Burroughs. Mrs. Burroughs took a liking to me from the beginning. She would introduce me to people before her own sons. I learned a lot of things from her and from Edith. I began mingling in with different people. Wherever I went with Edith, I would watch what she did, and I would act the same way. Sometimes I noticed that she didn't do things just right according to the book of etiquette, but, of course, I didn't say anything. I learned a lot from her. . . . Once I asked her if there was anything wrong with the way I talked, and she said that she had never noticed anything. I know now that I didn't pronounce my *th* sounds at that time, but probably she didn't want to hurt my feelings. . . . After a while, I began to notice that there were other people that didn't know as much as I did. I would be in an elevator with some fellows and girls in a hotel, and I would notice that the other fellows didn't have their hats off. Or I would be sitting at a table with another fellow when a girl came up. I would get up, and he wouldn't. I began to think I wasn't so bad off. . . .

"Bill, if there is one thing I have a talent for, if I have a talent for anything, it is a talent for imitation. When a person says something in a certain way, I can usually imitate him, not 100 per cent but pretty well. When I was in college, I used to pay attention to everything the professor said so that I could learn from the way he said things. And when I was home at night, besides my regular studies, I used to set a book of biographies of great men before me and a dictionary beside it. I would read in the biography, and any word I didn't understand I would look up in the dictionary and write down on a piece of paper. I would review them before I went to bed. Then every night I would read aloud for ten or fifteen minutes. It didn't matter what I was reading. I wanted to make my voice come out better. . . . I always had that desire for refinement. I was always seeking refinement. . . .

"When my mother told me that I was going to college, I was surprised. But she had some money saved, and I always worked summers. A couple of summers I couldn't find a job, so I set up a pushcart with Lou Danaro. Once a friend of mine asked me if I wasn't ashamed to be working on a pushcart. I told him, 'Why should I be? This is my bread and butter.'

"In grammar school we were all Italians. In high school [in Welport] the races were mixed. At St. Patrick's College there were only about a hundred Italians out of 1,400 students. About 1,200 were Irish, and the other hundred were different races. I noticed the difference when I got in college. We felt discriminated against. In the beginning I was very timid. Sometimes even when I knew the right answer I wouldn't raise my hand because I was afraid people would laugh at the way I expressed myself. But in my Sophomore year, I began coming out. I talked more in class. I remember one English class when we were discussing *Macbeth*. I said something about the play, and the professor disagreed with me; but I stuck to my point, and he gave me a lot of credit for that. He referred to 'Mr. Morelli's theory.' That gave me a lot of confidence.

"In my Junior year some Italian students came over from Italy to visit different colleges. I was appointed head of a committee of thirty at St. Patrick's to show them around. . . . At that time there was no Italian taught there. It wasn't right. To think that they should teach Spanish instead of Italian. What have the Spaniards contributed to literature to compare with the Italian contributions? . . . I organized an Italian Academy at St. Patrick's, and I was its first president. At my own expense I got up petitions for the Italian lauguage. I talked with Father Donnelly, the dean of the college. He wasn't so sympathetic. I argued with him. I asked him if he could name a greater poet than Dante. He said he couldn't. I said that, for every Irishman in any field that he could name, I could name an Italian who was a greater man. He argued that there might not be enough students to take the course. I told him that there would be at least twenty students, and if there weren't, he could drop it. . . . That fall there was an Italian course, and Professor Salerno came to the college. . . . There were thirty students taking the course. I couldn't take it myself because I was a Senior, but the Italian Academy expanded and put on plays and many other activities."

Concerning his personal contacts, Chick told me that he valued especially his friendship with Thomas L. Brown, a prominent Eastern City lawyer. He said that Brown had a strong influence on him, often correcting his mistakes and giving him advice. Once he asked Brown if he thought the Italian people were discriminated against. The lawyer answered: "Don't be an ass, Chick; it's only the jackasses that discriminate against the Italian people. No intelligent people would do that."

Chick said that this impressed him. He began to think that the Italians themselves were at fault.

"The Italian boys down here have that feeling of inferiority. I have it myself. I really mean that. When I hear that some people think I'm pretty good, I wonder what it is that I have. I can't see it. I'm not just pretending when I say that I feel inferior. That's the truth. . . . I think the only way to overcome that inferiority is to go out and mingle with other people. Until you can mingle in, you will never overcome that feeling."

I asked Chick how he happened to go to Ivy University Law School.

"I took a law course with Professor Martini at St. Patrick's. I was proud that an Italian was teaching the law course. I asked him where I should go for my law studies. He suggested St. Patrick's Law School. So I made my applications, and I was going there when I met a lawyer named Marino. He asked me why I didn't go to Ivy Law School, instead. I said: 'I know my own limitations. I couldn't get into a place like that. I'll be content to stay in my own station.'

"He told me: 'Chick, don't be a jackass. If you've got the marks, you can get into Ivy, and a degree from Ivy will mean much more to you than one from St. Patrick's.'

"I thought it over. I went home and talked with my mother. It would cost me $420 to go to Ivy, not counting books, or carfare. It would cost only $250 at St. Patrick's. I made a bargain with my mother. If she would pay my tuition, I would pay for everything else. She asked me how she could be sure that I would keep to my bargain. I told her that if I didn't, I would just drop out. So she agreed. And that's the bargain we've been keeping to ever since. . . . I was anxious to be the first Italian boy from Cornerville to go to Ivy Law School. I made my application and sent in my marks along with a letter from Mr. Brown. He boosted me to the skies. A few days later I heard that I was accepted."

Chick's entrance into Ivy University Law School constituted an important step forward in his social and professional career. There was still a hard struggle ahead of him. The next few years would be decisive in determining his position in society. Against that background we can understand what the Italian Community Club meant to Chick Morelli.

ORGANIZING THE CLUB

The roots of Chick's Italian Community Club can be traced as far back as junior high school. The ninth-grade home-room teacher had a system of seating her pupils according to her estimate of their scholastic performance. The special recognition they received led to the development of a clique among the boys of the first row and the front of the second row. They even formed a short-lived club. The ninth-grade clique included Chick Morelli, Pat Russo, Tony Cardio, Joe Gennusi, Paul DiMatia, Leo Marto, and Jerry Merluzzo, with Phil Principio upon its periphery. Eight and a half years later Chick called upon these men to form the nucleus of the Community Club. He invited five other Cornerville men, Tom Scala, Mike Ferrara, Frank and Al Perino, and Jim Filippo, to be charter members.

Pat Russo, Chick's closest friend, had begun a social work course at St. Patrick's. Tony Cardio had an office job and was going to law school at night. Joe Gennusi was selling insurance and also studying law at night school. Paul DiMatia was completing a business course at Eastern College. Leo Marto and Jerry Merluzzo were studying medicine at the recently organized Meridian Medical School.

Tom Scala was a Junior at Ivy College, where he was majoring in English literature. Mike Ferrara was in his last year at St. Patrick's. Frank Perino, a graduate of St. Patrick's, was taking a medical course at Sheldon University, which ranked next to Ivy University in this field in the Eastern City region. His younger brother, Al, was in his Junior year at St. Patrick's. Jim Filippo was a Senior at Eastern College, where he was majoring in accounting.

The club's organization meeting was held at the Norton Street Settlement House early in January, 1937. Chick Morelli was elected president; Leo Marto, vice-president; Tom Scala, secretary; and Frank Perino, treasurer.

Tom Scala gave this description of the meeting in his minutes:

"Mr. Morelli roughly outlined to the assembled group the purpose of the assembly. He stated that Italians have made a brilliant reputation in the civilization of the world; hence we should consider ourselves a vital element of the American race.

"We must create social bonds, principally with our intellectual equals, for chiefly among these can the influence of the Italian mind in the fields of Arts and Sciences be fully realized.

"Our next aim is to instruct our community as to their duty concerning amelioration of their own educational and sectional interests.

"The president [in the second meeting] presented his outline of the year's activities. The outline proposed points that were social as well as intellectual in nature.
  I. Weekly talks by the members in their respective fields preferably.
 II. Monthly articles for the _____ [local newspaper], one article a month by every individual member.
III. A monthly forum for Italian parents.
IV. Production of a play.
 V. A debate.
VI. Oratorical contests for nonmembers.

Social Program
  I. Monthly socials for the members.
 II. Smokers for intellectuals of Italian extraction.
III. Dance for benefit of Italian Orphan's Home.
IV. Bi-monthly stag parties.
 V. Fraternity pin."

The second meeting also approved a constitution that had been drawn up by Chick Morelli and Tony Cardio. Provision was made for an annual election of officers, initiation fees, dues, penalties, and the appointment of committees, but no clear statement was made upon the necessary qualifications of an applicant for membership. It was understood that the club was to be made up of a superior class of young men, but exactly what should constitute this superiority remained to be decided.

The club had a dual purpose: the social betterment of the members and the improvement of Cornerville. There seemed to be no necessary conflict between these aims when the club was organized, but it proved impossible to pursue both at the same time. Consequently, almost every issue implied a decision as to which aim was to be emphasized. When new men were admitted and when new activities were planned, the members were deciding in effect what kind of club they were to have; and, while they did not express it in these terms, they knew what was involved.

The first issue arose over the question of whether the club should admit men who had had no college or professional education. While some of the members were afraid of lowering the standing of the club, they nevertheless had friends among the noncollege men. Joe Gennusi argued that it was undemocratic to exclude them, and, after the issue had been discussed at several meetings, it was finally agreed that the membership committee should have discretion in such cases.

When the way was opened to noncollege men, Doc and Angelo Cucci were admitted to membership, and in the course of the next several months Lou Danaro, Fred Mackey, Art Testa, and Patsy Donato were voted in. Art and Patsy had both been members of the Sunset Dramatic Club. Art had an office job, and Patsy had a small contracting business.

In this same period a number of college men were added. Mike Ferrara introduced a friend, who was also a Senior at St. Patrick's. Chick brought in Vincent Pelosi, a Westland man who, like himself, was going to Ivy University Law School. Tony Cardio brought in Ernest Daddio, who had spent two years at St. Patrick's and had left to take a white-collar job.

In April, Doc invited me to a meeting of the club and asked me to join. He told me that it would be necessary to change the constitution in order to get me in, since membership was limited to Italian-Americans. Actually there was no such provision, but the written constitution was rarely referred to, and everyone believed that an amendment was necessary. Doc submitted my name to the membership committee of Tony Cardio, Tom Scala, and Phil Principio. He told me that when he entered the club most of the members were new to him, but now he looked forward with confidence to the political maneuvers necessary in my behalf. I said that I did not want to make an issue out of my application, but Doc said that he did.

At a much later time Doc reviewed for me the progress of my case. Tony Cardio had been against me, but Tom Scala and Phil Principio gave me a majority on the membership committee. However, since several others were also against me, Tony's vote was necessary to pass the amendment. He was finally persuaded to pledge his vote to me. As Doc told me:

"I had it all arranged, Bill. The vice-president of the club [Leo Marto] was against you, so if we needed the vote, I was going to have Chick stay away so he would have to take the chair. But there were only three at the meeting that told me they were against you, so I told Chick to come up. Then when we voted—by the Australian ballot—there were five votes against you. They double-crossed me, Bill. I was sore. I accused two of them of voting against you, but they swore they didn't. . . . It didn't make any difference, Bill. I was only sore because they double-crossed me. . . ."

Doc and Chick thought that Tony Cardio had broken his word by voting against me, and, although Tony denied it, Chick said after the meeting that he would never trust Tony again. In the same meeting I was elected to the newly created status of guest membership. In the next meeting Tom Scala said that it was stupid to have a special status for me and moved that I be made a regular member. This time the motion carried.

My application for membership brought about the first sharp division of opinion in the club, but it did not give rise to the college and noncollege division. The corner boys wanted to get me in, but so did some of the college boys.

SOCIAL ACTIVITIES

The program outlined by President Morelli was ambitious enough to occupy the attention of a dozen clubs. It soon became evident that only a small part of his plan could be put into effect. No action was taken upon the monthly articles, the forum for parents, the debate, the smokers for intellectuals, the benefit dance, the stag parties, or the fraternity pin. An oratorical contest for nonmembers was planned and announced, but interest in this project was insufficient to carry it through. The college men took turns in giving talks, which were held with some degree of regularity upon meeting nights. In the first season the production of a play became the center of interest.

Chick Morelli took it upon himself to select the play to be given. His choice was *Night of Horror,* which, he explained, was amusing and exciting and had the additional advantage that it could be had for a ten-dollar royalty. Doc was voted into the club after the choice had been made, but he confided to me his opinion that *Night of Horror* was a bad play which Chick liked simply because he saw a good part for himself in it.

One of the members suggested that Doc be asked to direct the play, but Chick said, "No, Doc would play favorites." Chick recommended a man by the name of Felix DiCarlo, who lived next door to him. None of the other members knew DiCarlo, but they accepted Chick's suggestion.

When the tryouts were held, Frank Perino, who had starred in amateur theatricals at St. Patrick's, sat in the back of the hall and refused to participate. He said to Doc, "What's the use of trying out? Chick will get the lead anyway." A short time later Frank resigned from the club, and his brother followed him.

Doc and Chick both tried for the leading role, and DiCarlo selected Chick. Some of the members were so outspoken in their opinion that Doc deserved the part that Chick finally suggested that Doc take his place. However, neither Doc nor DiCarlo would stand for a change.

There were four feminine roles to be filled. Doc told me that there was a great interest in dramatics in Cornerville, and he felt that giving Cornerville girls the opportunity of learning how to express themselves on the stage was in accord with the local improvement aim of the club. Chick felt that this was an opportunity for the club to make beneficial social contacts. He proposed that he get in touch with the president of the Italian Junior League, an exclusive organization of girls outside Cornerville, to see if they could provide the necessary actresses. This was agreed upon.

The results of Chick Morelli's approach to the Italian Junior League were given in the club minutes.

"President outlined events which occurred during the session with President _____ and her governing board. Final results being very favorable. They agreed to grant us their assistance in our social endeavors. We in turn are to give them our aid. This is considered by both parties as a mutual verbal agreement."

Felix DiCarlo's direction was a spectacle. As Doc commented, "He's more dramatic than any of the actors." The girls were so impressed that they asked him to direct the play to be given by the Italian Junior League. Most of the men were impressed at first, but as time went on they became tired of DiCarlo's temperament. Doc felt from the start that the director was a "phoney."

Doc and Angelo wanted to give the play in the Norton Street Settlement out of loyalty to Cornerville. Chick and Tony Cardio wanted to get a larger and more professional hall outside Cornerville. Their views prevailed.

Chick arranged to have some of the Junior League girls act as ushers. Too late it occurred to him that he should have invited girls from the Clarion Club, another exclusive Italian organization, so that his club could make contacts with both groups of girls.

The play was considered a great success by the club members. Chick, who played the hero, and Tony Cardio, who played the villain, were particularly enthusiastic. Doc and Angelo were the only ones who expressed to me privately their adverse opinions.

Whatever the merits of *Night of Horror* as drama, it opened the channels of social advancement to the Community Club. The actresses who took part in the play were working girls, but, unlike most Cornerville girls, they worked in offices instead of factories. They were attractive and well dressed, and they had social standing. There was much social activity in connection with

the rehearsals. Chick and Tony set the pace in entertaining the girls but all the members felt obligated to give them a good time.

. . . Association with the girls created a . . . serious disturbance. After the play, Chick was eager to continue the social contacts with the Italian Junior League. When the Community Club planned a social, he called the president of the Junior League and asked her to invite some of her members. It was the Cornerville custom for men and girls to go to dances separately. The Junior League girls were not used to this system, and the college men tended to break away from it, especially when going with girls from outside Cornerville. Chick's arrangements were a compromise. He asked that the girls come down by themselves, but if five girls were invited, he asked five of the members to see to it that they were entertained. Cornerville girls, especially members of clubs meeting in the settlement house, were also invited, but Chick was particularly anxious that the Junior League girls should have a good time. He and Tony Cardio made a point of dancing with each one. The other college men were shy and hung back, except when they were goaded by Chick and Tony. Paul DiMatia and Phil Principio were particularly backward. Doc divided his attentions between the two groups of girls and was popular with both of them, but he never danced. The other noncollege men confined their attentions largely to the local girls. . . .

REPUBLICAN POLITICS

. . . Forty young men from Cornerville, with representatives of other racial groups, attended "All-American Night" at the Women's Republican Club. Joe Gennusi, Paul DiMatia, Chick Morelli and Pat Russo were present.

The evening program began with a supper served by the ladies of the club. Mrs. Dillingham, who had once employed an Italian gardener, was in charge of entertaining the visitors from Cornerville. After supper she showed us around the luxurious clubrooms. "You can use this hall any time for your meetings. . . . This can be your smoking-room. . . . Just make this your home."

There was music, a speech by the chairman of the state committee, and another by the gubernatorial candidate, Percival Wickham. As the meeting broke up, Wickham shook hands with each of the Cornerville men.

The Community Club members accepted this hospitality with certain reservations. During supper Chick poured his impressions into my ear:

"I don't like this, Bill. . . . It looks like I'm

being bought off. Let them convince me by argument, not by food. After all, I have my own political ambitions to think of. . . . It's all very nice and friendly here, but how would I be received if I went to call at the home of one of these ladies? I'll tell you how. She would come to the door and tell me, 'I'm afraid you have the wrong address.' "

While Mrs. Dillingham was showing us around, Paul DiMatia pointed at a picture of a buffalo hanging on the wall, and said to me, "They should have a bull there."

As we walked home, I asked him to sum up his impressions. He smiled and said, "It was a little patronizing."

Nevertheless, the meeting served its purpose. Afterward the Cornerville group gathered on the sidewalk to decide what should be done next. Tony Cardio joined us here. John Carrideo asked Paul DiMatia to be chairman of the next meeting of the local unit. Paul agreed. He said to me, "I have nothing to lose."

"I'm convinced," said Joe Gennusi.

Tony Cardio said, "I've always been a Republican at heart."

Chick Morelli said that he was reserving his judgment, and Pat Russo followed Chick, as he always did.

Republican money flowed into Cornerville as soon as the campaign got under way. A local headquarters was opened for committee meetings and political rallies.

College men made up the nucleus of the local Republican club. There were some corner boys active at the start, but many of them dropped out later. Although a college man, Paul DiMatia was now hanging on Norton Street, and he withdrew with the other corner boys. He told me that the new organization was entirely made up of men who wanted to be leaders. They were all prepared to give orders but not to execute them. Instead of doing the spade work of canvassing the district for votes, they preferred to stay at headquarters, where they could discuss what should be done. When men prominent in the state organization appeared in Cornerville, the members of the local club tried to outjockey one another so as to gain recognition.

In the midst of the campaign Tony Cardio won the Eastern City Young Republican's Oratorical Contest with an address on "The Constitution as Guardian of Our Liberties." On the strength of this he was chosen chairman of the largest rally held in Cornerville. Tony gained prominence as a speaker, but his personal limitations were recognized in the Republican Club as well as upon the street corner. As Joe Gennusi told me:

"We were having a committee meeting to discuss getting men for certain positions. During the meeting Tony Cardio made that speech that he always likes to make. He said we must get a man with a college education. He doesn't think that a man without a college education is qualified. . . . A couple of days later, I was talking with one of the boys that was at the meeting. He had never met Tony before, but from that one time, he hated him. He said, 'Who does he think he is anyway?' . . . Now that man wouldn't even give Tony the right time.

"When we had election of officers in the Republican Club, Tony was nominated for president. John Carrideo was elected, and Tony got only two votes, his own and one other. The man who seconded the nomination didn't even vote for him. I turned in a blank ballot. I figured, they're both my friends. I knew John would get it anyway. . . . After the meeting, I told Tony that the blank ballot was mine. He began to get mad. I told him, 'Why didn't you decline the nomination?'

"He asked, 'Why should I?'

"I said, 'Because you're not well liked.' . . . That burned him up.

"He said, 'Now I know who my real friends are.' He hasn't spoken to me since that meeting. . . . It must be annoying to Tony to know that he has all the qualifications, and yet he can't be elected to anything."

Wickham was elected governor that fall, but Murphy carried Cornerville for the Democrats by almost six to one. The Republicans did poll a somewhat larger vote in Cornerville than they had in 1936, but the gain was not nearly so great as had been expected, and there was no way of telling what proportion of the gain was accounted for by the efforts of the college men. Some of the most prominent racketeers in Cornerville were also working for Percival Wickham.

CHICK MORELLI'S CAREER

One evening in the spring of 1938, as we were walking through the market district, Chick discussed his political ambitions. He said that he could already count on five hundred votes if he ran for the board of aldermen but that he wanted to build up more support before he entered such a contest. As we passed a line of fruit stands, he stopped to pick up a couple of apples, said a few words to the dealer, and walked on without offering payment. As we munched our apples, he explained that these men all rented their stands from his uncle and that if he, Chick Morelli, ran for office, they would have to work for him or else lose their stands. He added, reflectively:

"If I got a good job, maybe I wouldn't get in the fight, but politics seems to be in my blood. . . .

"Pat Russo says that charity is important. That's all right, but after all, self-preservation is the first law of man. . . . If I get in office, I'll try to help the district, but I'll advance myself first."

In the fall of 1938 Chick was not yet prepared to join in the Republican campaign. That would have meant sacrificing his ambitions in ward politics, which could only be realized through the Democratic party. Chick looked for another outlet for his political activity and found it in the campaign of Charles Madden, candidate for the Democratic nomination for district attorney. Michael Flaherty, the incumbent, had the support of all the local political organizations. If Madden proved to be a strong candidate, organizing his local campaign might give a Cornerville man who had no place in the existing organizations a favorable opportunity for the launching of his own political career.

By the time Chick decided to support Madden, a one-time member of the Sunset Dramatic Club was already in charge of the candidate's Cornerville organization. Chick set about forming an organization of his own and made himself district co-chairman. He had small boys distributing handbills, he had a group of young men and girls canvassing the district, and he made a number of political speeches.

Charles Madden was defeated, but in Cornerville he polled nearly as many votes as his opponent. Encouraged by this "moral victory," Chick formed the Alexander Hamilton Club, with fifteen young men and girls that had worked for Madden and several former members of the Community Club. Doc, Phil Principio, Paul DiMatia, and Angelo Cucci accepted Chick's invitation to join the new club. Doc explained his membership in this way:

"Last summer, when I was going to run for representative, Chick came up to me and pledged his support. . . . I told him that he should think of his own political ambitions. It wouldn't do him any good to support me when I wasn't going to win. . . . But he said, 'No, you're my friend, and I'm going to support you.' . . . It really meant something for him to do a thing like that. I felt obligated to him, so when he came around and asked me to join his club, I let him put my name down.

"I never go to the club meetings. Chick is lucky that I don't. If I was an active member of the club, I couldn't let Chick get away with the things he does. I don't know why they stand for it.

"I think Chick is doing the right thing for himself politically. He's got a bunch of young kids in that club. Those are the people he has to count on. With fellows my age, he's ruined himself already. We know him too well."

In January, 1939, Chick, Doc, Phil, Angelo, and some of the other members of the Hamilton Club attended a meeting in honor of Charles Madden. Doc had this to say about it:

"They announced a dance to be given in honor of Madden, and they asked all those in the audience who thought they could sell tickets to come up on the stage and get them. . . . Chick was on and off the stage seven times. Some others came back more than once, but—seven times—that's too much. . . . Chick just wanted to get into the limelight. All the boys noticed that."

Later, Phil told me:

"I've dropped out of the club. . . . You know, Chick invited us to come up to that meeting for Madden. When we got there, he didn't pay any attention to us. He was too busy getting in with the important people to have anything to do with his own club members. That's bad, Bill."

This was Angelo's story:

"I'm out of the club too. After the last meeting I talked to Chick out in the hall. I think he is just out for himself, and I told him that right to his face. . . . Well, he said he had to look out for himself so that when he got in a good position, he could help out all the members. . . . That's what he said, but I don't believe him. If he gets himself a good job, I don't think he'll try to help us. I really don't."

By the summer of 1939 the Alexander Hamilton Club was dead.

Chick had not yet hit upon the right combination. That fall he told me, "If I have the right fellows with me, we'll go places." Thereupon he set about reviving the Italian Community Club. This time the membership was limited to college men. Joe Gennusi and several other former members joined, but the membership was largely recruited from among those that had not previously belonged.

The main feature of the Community Club program for the 1939-40 season was to be the production of a play written by Ed Preziosa, who, I was told, was one of the outstanding members of the club.

Rehearsals began with Chick in the leading role

and Ed directing, but the play did not proceed smoothly. Doc told me that several members of the Community Club reported serious friction between Chick and Ed: "It seems they don't get along. Ed thinks Chick is trying to toss him around. Ed is a strong-minded kid himself. If anybody is going to be tossed around, he'll do the tossing."

In the early stages of rehearsals Chick had another idea. He proposed that the club sponsor a scholarship drive to send needy and deserving Italian students to college. The drive was to be launched with a banquet in the ballroom of one of Eastern City's largest hotels. The members voted to support the scholarship project, and Chick busied himself with making arrangements for it. He became so preoccupied with the scholarship drive that he decided to drop his part in the play.

The conflict between the drive and the play split the club into two parts. Those who were more interested in Ed Preziosa and the play withdrew from the Community Club and formed the Buskin Players. They filled Chick's part with one of their members and brought in Doc to substitute for one of Chick's adherents. Angelo Cucci wrote the music for a dance that was used in the play. Ed became very friendly with Doc, and after his own play had been produced he suggested that the Buskin Players merge with Doc's dramatic club. Doc was noncommittal, but the proposal showed the wide breach that separated Ed and his friends from Chick and his friends.

Chick delivered the first invitation to the banquet to Governor Percival Wickham. The governor's secretary told Chick that His Excellency was very much interested in the project but would not be able to find time to attend. Undaunted, Chick conferred with Attilio Volpe, a Cornerville banker who had been active in Republican politics and knew the governor's secretary. Volpe went in person and managed to get a pledge of the governor's personal appearance. This made it obviously a function which all prominent Italian-Americans should attend. Over five hundred

people paid two dollars each to launch the scholarship drive. . . .

Toward the end of the program, Alfred Martini, the master of ceremonies who had also been one of Chick's professors at St. Patrick's, called upon Chick Morelli. Clearly, this was the big moment in Chick's life, and he outdid himself. He spoke of the Italians who had made great contributions to civilization. He spoke of the difficulties faced by immigrant Italians in their struggle for recognition, and he proposed more education as the solution of the problems of his people. Chick received an ovation from his audience, and the following day the Italian news commentator characterized his speech as "un' orazione veramente maravigliosa."

The Italian Community Club did not inaugurate the fund-raising campaign immediately after the banquet. Summer was coming on, and the members voted to postpone it until fall.

When fall came, politics held the center of the stage. Chick worked hard for the election of Willkie for president, Wickham for governor, Bingham for attorney-general, and the other Republican candidates. Cornerville remained overwhelmingly Democratic in the state election, but the Republicans swept all the offices.

The following winter Chick revived the scholarship campaign. He enlarged the committee to include some men and women who were prominent in Italian-American society.

The second scholarship banquet was an even more impressive affair than the first. This time the mayor attended as well as the governor. It was announced that the drive had brought in something over a thousand dollars. While this fell far short of the ten-thousand-dollar goal, the drive was expected to continue from year to year so that more funds would be available.

In the midst of the fund-raising campaign, it was announced that Attorney-General Bingham had appointed Chick Morelli to his staff. It was a small position, but it was a start in politics. Chick had come a long way since he had first organized the Italian Community Club.

Selection 25

Social Ranking

George C. Homans

One of the most persistent criticisms of industrial society made by the founding fathers of sociology was that the primary group was disappearing and with it the warmth, intimacy, and support it provided. However, examination of modern society by empirically oriented American sociologists has demonstrated conclusively that primary groups have not vanished but rather that the range of social milieux that gave rise to them has broadened. Among other things, Shils and Janowitz's article on the German army showed that primary groups develop in large, impersonal, bureaucratic organizations. In fact, one of the most important sources of primary group formation in industrial society is the work group. Persons start out in a shop or office as strangers but soon develop groups that are similar in cohesion and organization to the family or friendship clique and that, ironically, frequently challenge the goals of the bureaucracy.

The classic example of this process was discovered in the Bank Wiring Observation Room of the Hawthorne Works of the Western Electric Company and is reported in part in the following excerpt from Homan's *The Human Group*. The managers of this plant, worried about low morale and poor productivity, invited industrial psychologists to study the problem after efficiency experts had failed to improve the situation. The psychologists, like their predecessors, assumed that the physical conditions of work—the quality of lighting, for example—were the most important factors influencing productivity. After controlled observations, however, it was apparent that sociological and psychological variables were the crucial factors. An important finding to the researchers—who apparently had never worked in a factory—was the existence of informal primary groups which held the loyalty of the workers and which had rules about how much work a man should do. Though the workers were paid according to the amount of work they did, the norms of the informal primary group were strong enough to enforce restriction of output.

Why did these workers hold their output down and thereby limit their take-home pay? The student who has noted carefully how important groups are to the individual knows the answer. We have suggested that the group determines what is right and what is wrong; if the group says that it is better to restrict rather than increase output, group members will tend to agree. We have also emphasized the importance of the primary group to the individual's sense of security; primary group relationships satisfy his need for affection and sympathy. But the group does not offer its support gratuitously; it does so only to individuals who conform to group norms.

By supporting people who conform and punishing those who do not, the group differentiates between those granted approval and those denied it. The differentiation of individuals within groups is one of the most important processes of group life. Repeated interaction of group members inevitably results in their being ranked or stratified according to the amount of prestige they are accorded. The basis for ranking—especially as one climbs the prestige hierarchy—seems to be a somewhat complicated relationship between the actors and the norms of the group. Those who deviate most sharply from the norms are ranked lowest. On the basis of his first approach to the data of the Bank Wiring Room, Homans concluded that the leaders at the top of the hierarchy could get "power only by conforming more closely than anyone else to the norms of the group." While Homans recognized that high status people sometimes deviated from group norms—the eccentric millionaire, for example—he clearly implied that they conformed more closely than middle-ranking persons.

In a later work, Homans revised his theory and located maximum conformity not at the top of the hierarchy but rather in the middle.[1] He emphasized

---

[1] George C. Homans, *Social Behavior: Its Elementary Forms* (New York: Harcourt, Brace & World, Inc., 1961), pp. 352-353.

much more than he did in *The Human Group* the degree to which high status people deviated. "Upper status people are better able to take [risks] than others," he wrote, "for they have less than the others to gain by doing the same old thing and less to lose by trying something different." According to this view, middle-ranking persons are most likely to conform, since they have more to lose than the lowest class by deviation and more to gain than the top stratum by conformity. Obviously, other variables are also related to hierarchical differentiation: length of time in the group, level of aspiration, access to important values, and so on. The newcomer must conform in order to be accepted; the socially mobile person must comply if he is to improve his position. Once accepted, they may—for reasons that are not yet clear—relax from rigid conformity. The explanation may, as Homans suggests, have something to do with the way the group develops new norms, or it may be that deviation from less important norms is one of the rewards of status. However, some norms are inviolable for all group members.

Although Homans' theory accounts for social differentiation within groups, it may also be applied to social stratification between groups, a topic to be dealt with in Selections 69-71.

. . . As soon as two subgroups are set apart from one another and conscious of their differences, at least one of the two is apt to feel that it is somehow better than the other. Not only are foreigners different from us, they also have no manners and filthy customs. How often we take a moral stand! How often the laws of sociology are the laws of snobbery! Sometimes the quarrel between the two subgroups ends in mutual recriminations, because there is no way of settling it, but sometimes there is a sort of way. In effect, though the process is perfectly unplanned and spontaneous, at least one of the parties demands that the norms and unconscious assumptions, accepted by the group as a whole, be used as a yardstick for evaluating its behavior more highly than that of the other party. The members of a group are more nearly alike in their norms of behavior than in their behavior itself, and a subgroup is ranked or evaluated as better or worse than another depending on how closely its behavior approaches the norms of the group as a whole. The higher the rank of the subgroup, the more closely its behavior "measures up."

. . . [I]n American society at large, assumptions are current to the effect that a job carrying higher wages, greater skill, and more seniority than another, even a job that is placed "in front of" another, is a "better" job. It is more highly valued. It may be that these assumptions are really corollaries of a still more profound one. By and large in organizations, the persons with higher wages, skill, and seniority than others are also in a posi-

tion to direct or control the activities of others. This is even true of being "in front." The teacher stands in front of his class, the captain in front of his company, and each directs his group. These things are the outward and visible signs of control, and a high value is always given to control, to authority. At any rate, the arrangements of the external system of the Bank Wiring group combined with the unconscious assumptions of American society to make the connector wiremen feel that they had better jobs than the selector wiremen.

We shall now see how the feeling of the connector wiremen that their jobs were somehow better than those of the selector wiremen was connected with other elements of the behavior of the Bank Wiring group.

SOCIAL RANKING AND ACTIVITY

A feeling on the part of an individual and of the other members of his group that he is in some way better (or worse) than another individual, that he ranks higher (or lower) than the other, is by our definition a *sentiment*. The evaluation of a man relative to the evaluation of other members of his group we shall call his *rank* rather than his *status*, because . . . rank is only one of the ele-

From *The Human Group* by George C. Homans, pp. 139-149, copyright 1950, by Harcourt, Brace & World, Inc., and reprinted with their permission.

ments of status as that word is usually defined. Evaluation is a sentiment released or stimulated by a comparison of a man's *activities* with those of other members of his group in accordance with some standard, the standard being provided by the *norms* and *assumptions* of the group. Unless there were some intellectual standard of judgment, it is hard to see how the comparison could be made. For a man to rank high in his group, it is not enough that he should evaluate himself highly; his group must also accept his evaluation, and the norms of the group provide the only possible basis for agreement. The reasoning that we have applied to an individual can also be applied to a subgroup. Thus the connector wiremen felt superior (sentiment) to the selector wiremen because their jobs (activity) were better in terms of some of the unconscious assumptions of American society.

Assuming the norms and assumptions of the group constant, let us look further at the mutual relationship between social rank and social activity. The wiremen of clique A (connector wiremen) thought that their jobs were better than those of the wiremen of clique B (selector wiremen), and they extended this feeling of superiority to all their activities. They believed their games were less boisterous and their conversations more refined. Moreover, their activities were superior not only by common American assumptions but also by the norms of the group. Thus they came much closer than the selector wiremen to meeting the standards of the group in the matter of output. The members of clique A put out close to two equipments per man per day; the members of clique B somewhat less. We can state as a hypothesis, then, that persons who set a high value on their activities in the external system will set a high value on their activities in the internal system. From this we can go on to the more fundamental hypothesis that *the higher the rank of a person within a group, the more nearly his activities conform to the norms of the group.* The hypothesis holds for subgroups as well as for individuals. The relationship is strictly mutual: the closer the person's activities come to the norm, the higher his rank will tend to be, but it is also true that, rank being taken as the independent variable, the higher the person's rank, the closer his activities will come to the norm, or, even more simply, *noblesse oblige.* To rank high in his group, a man must live up to all of its norms, and the norms in question must be the actual or sanctioned norms of the group and not just those to which the group gives lip service.

We must now consider the effect on the selector wiremen of the behavior of the connector wiremen. As far as their special jobs were concerned, the selector wiremen were not altogether ready to accept the judgment laid down by the other group. They resented the implication of inferiority, and with some reason. The differences between the two wiring jobs were slight, and the selector wiremen seem to have felt that their companions made too much of a few little things. In their relations with inspectors and supervisors, all the wiremen were on a par with one another, and in the organization of work the connector wiremen in no way directed or controlled the work of the selector wiremen. If in some ways the former could be made out as superior, in other ways all were equals.

At any rate, the selector wiremen were resentful, and as resentment, like all sentiment, seeks an outlet in activity, they expressed their feelings in activities that, in kind and in amount, they knew would be distasteful to the connector wiremen of clique A. The noisiness of their talks, games, and bickerings may have been adopted because they knew that clique A would not like this kind of behavior; their low output certainly was adopted for this reason. The activities of any one subgroup always tend to become somewhat different from those of another. Here a further factor of differentiation was the desire of one subgroup to pursue activities that would deliberately outrage the norms of the other.

If the members of clique B wished to irritate clique A, they certainly were successful. The next act in the drama found the connector wiremen hitting back—heckling clique B for its low output and damning its members as "chiselers." . . . "The interesting thing about these tactics was that they served to subordinate clique B still further and as a result to strengthen their internal solidarity still more. So, instead of increasing their output, the members of clique B kept it low, thus 'getting back' at those who were displaying their superiority."[1]

. . . "It may be concluded that the various performance records for the members of clique B were reflecting their position in the group. There was a clear-cut relation between their social standing and their output. But, it may be asked, did their low output determine their position in the group or did their position in the group determine their output? The answer is that the relation

---

[1] Fritz Jules Roethlisberger and W. Dickson, *Management and the Worker* (Cambridge, Mass.: Harvard University Press, 1939), p. 521.

worked both ways: position in the group influenced output, and output influenced position in the group. In other words, these two factors were in a relation of mutual dependence."[2] In our language, the relation in question is the mutual dependence of sentiment (social ranking) and activity (output).

The connector wiremen kept trying to bring the output of the selector wiremen closer to the standard; the latter kept trying to keep their output low just because they knew that this would anger the connectors. How far this process of attack and counterattack might have gone in other circumstances we do not know, but in the Bank Wiring Room there were forces that brought the vicious spiral to a halt and prevented the output of the selector wiremen from remaining indefinitely low. After all, both cliques were members of the same group and in a measure both accepted its norms. The output level of clique B can be looked on as the resultant of at least three forces: (a) the desire of the clique to differentiate its behavior, in the direction of irritation, from that of clique A, (b) its desire to conform to the output standard of the group as a whole, and (c) the economic interests of the selector wiremen, which must never be forgotten. If their output had gone too far down, they would have been fired. At any rate, the behavior of both clique A and clique B bears out our rule that the closer the activities of a subgroup approach the norms of the group as a whole, the higher will be its social rank. The social rank of clique B was lower than that of clique A, and the activities of its members were also further from the group norms.

According to the group norm, a wireman should not have turned out less than two equipments a day, but neither should he have turned out more. It is interesting that, while clique B was violating the norm in one way, Capek and Mueller, the social isolates among the wiremen, tended to violate it in another. The selector wiremen were too low; Capek and Mueller, particularly the latter, were apt to be too high. They were connector wiremen, and therefore unwilling to identify themselves with clique B by turning out too little work, but neither were they members of clique A, so their output, instead of lying below, or close to, the group norm, tended to lie a little above it.

In the Bank Wiring Observation Room, there were two cliques, the one higher in social rank being also the one conforming most nearly to the norms of the group as a whole. The ways of men are infinitely subtle, and some situations are not as simple as this. Occasionally we notice that the persons who stand highest in a group do not conform with undue strictness to some of the group norms, and controls are not seriously applied to them. Well-established members will suffer only a little joking when they break a rule, whereas newcomers will be severely punished with ridicule and scorn. "Here is an apparent paradox: Admittance to the group may be secured only by adherence to the established definitions of the group, while unquestioned membership carries the privilege of some deviant behavior. This is, of course, not a paradox at all; for it is characteristic of social groups to demand of the newcomer a strict conformity which will show that he accepts the authority of the group; then, as the individual approaches the center of the group and becomes an established member, they allow him a little more leeway."[3] This is probably not the whole story, but we can recognize a new factor here, which we may call the factor of social security. Up to a point, the surer a man is of his rank in a group, the less he has to worry about conforming to its norms. This new factor will under some circumstances modify our earlier generalization, just as the factor of authority modifies our generalization that frequency of interaction and sentiments of liking are positively linked. Neither factor invalidates our hypotheses but must be added to them if they are to approximate the concrete reality more and more closely.

SOCIAL RANKING AND INTERACTION

The relationship between the sentiments of social ranking and the scheme of interaction in the internal system can be seen in the matter of job trading. Job trading meant that a wireman exchanged jobs with a solderman, against the rules of the company. Most of the trades were made with Cermak, the solderman for the three selector wiremen. In 33 of the 49 observed instances of job trading, he was a participant. The reason for the great excess was that wiremen from soldering units 1 and 2 (the connector wiremen) traded with all three soldermen, but no selector wireman ever traded outside his own clique. "The connector wiremen apparently felt free to change jobs either with their own soldermen or with the solderman for the selector wiremen, but the latter did not feel free to trade outside of their own unit."[4] Now

[2] *Ibid.*, p. 520.
[3] E. C. Hughes, "The Knitting of Racial Groups in Industry," *American Sociological Review*, XI:517 (1946).
[4] Roethlisberger and Dickson, p. 504.

job trading involved interaction, and so we can suggest, as a tentative hypothesis, that *the higher a person's social rank, the wider will be the range of his interactions.* Note that we are talking about the range of interaction here, that is, the number of persons a man interacts with, and not just about the sheer frequency of interaction. Perhaps the wider contacts react to reinforce sentiments of superiority, but we have no immediate evidence for this. We must also notice . . . that the two connector wiremen who traded jobs with Cermak were Mueller and Capek and that neither of the two were fully accepted members of clique A. Through their actions they may in effect have been saying to the selector wiremen: "Though we are not full members of clique A, we are still connector wiremen and, as such, superior to you."

Something of the same sort can be seen in the origination of interaction. The originator of interaction is the person whose activity, verbal or otherwise, is followed by the activity of one or more other persons. When the output of clique B remained below the group's norm of two completed equipments per man per day, the members of clique A started originating interaction, through criticism and heckling, for the members of clique B. The latter did not originate interaction for clique A, but reacted only by keeping output down. We can suggest, then, as a further hypothesis that *a person of higher social rank than another originates interaction for the latter more often than the latter originates interaction for him.* . . . [W]hen the members of clique A originated interaction for the selector wiremen, they were trying to increase the output of the latter, that is, they were trying to control the behavior of the selector wiremen, and it may be that the attempt at control is a more fundamental phenomenon than the sheer origination of interaction. . . .

SOCIAL RANKING APART FROM CLIQUES

In discussing social ranking we have so far concentrated on the relation between cliques, or rather on the relation between connector and selector wiremen, for not all the connector wiremen were fully members of clique A. Many of the points we need to make can be made by studying clique relations alone. Yet there were other differences in social ranking besides the difference between connector and selector wiremen, and they deserve brief mention.

Between wiremen and soldermen no such conflict existed as that between connector and selector wiremen. The external system made the soldermen too clearly inferior in rank. A solderman earned substantially less than any wireman, and in the organization of work, he had to "wait on" his wiremen, to "serve" them by soldering in place the connections they had made. That is, the wireman originated the activity that was followed by the activity of the solderman. In the unconscious assumptions of American society, a man who is paid less than another and who must respond to activity that the other originates, especially when the origination implies control, is inferior to the other. On every count, then, the soldermen were judged the inferiors of the wiremen, and this judgment the soldermen, unlike the selector wiremen when judged inferior by the connectors, accepted without reservation. And note that in the internal system, as in the external, the soldermen allowed the wiremen to originate interaction: a solderman traded jobs with a wireman only when the latter asked him to do so. *A person who originates interaction for another in the external system will also tend to do so in the internal.* This submission by the soldermen was the price of their admission to the cliques. For Steinhardt and Cermak were members, though subordinate ones, of cliques A and B respectively. Matchek, with a speech defect, was not a member of any clique.

In relation to one another, the social rank of Steinhardt and Cermak was determined by the ranking of their cliques. As the solderman of clique A, Steinhardt was considered the social superior of Cermak, the solderman of clique B, and his superiority was demonstrated in his successful effort to pass on to Cermak the job of getting lunches from the company cafeteria, which was felt to be menial work. Once again, low social rank is associated with activity that is inferior according to some standard recognized by the group.

As for the relation between inspectors and wiremen, the former had in some ways the better jobs. They were paid more than the wiremen and, since they might accept or reject the work of the other men, their position was semisupervisory. In other ways the inspectors were in a weak position. Only two of them worked in the room—they were a minority group—and they were members of the separate inspecting organization—they were outsiders. Moreover, they responded, like the soldermen, to activities that the wiremen originated; that is, they inspected equipments only after the wiremen had finished making connections. As a group the wiremen were dominant in the room, and if the two inspectors wished to be accepted by the others they had to submit to the group norms, one of which required that no one should act officiously, like a supervisor. Allen made the adjustment successfully, became a member of clique A, and kept some of his superiority besides. In arguing with the supervisors, he took many more liberties than the wiremen dared to take. Mazmanian could not conform and was driven from the room.

SOCIAL RANKING AND LEADERSHIP

The same kind of analysis that has been given to the behavior of cliques may be given to the behavior of individuals in the Bank Wiring Observation Room. Let us look in particular at Taylor. He was a connector wireman—an extremely skillful and dependable one. He was a key member of the superior clique, and he was, with Krupa, one of the two men whose output conformed most closely and consistently to the accepted idea of a proper day's work. In every way, indeed, he embodied the norms the group had adopted as its own. He never broke a rate, "chiseled," "squealed," or took a superior tone. For this individual, as for a clique, conformity to the norms carried with it high social evaluation (mutual dependence of activity and sentiment). Taylor was the best-liked man in the room.

His high social rank had consequences that reacted to strengthen it. As the best-liked man, Taylor was the most helped man in the room (mutual dependence of sentiment and activity), in spite of the fact that he did not return the help, perhaps because giving help implied inferiority. Instead he offered much advice, which was often taken, to other members of the group, and got into many arguments, which he often won. That is, his high social rank allowed him to go some distance in controlling the behavior of the others. Turning now to the interaction aspect of his position, we can see that his activities in accepting help and taking control meant that much of the interaction, or, if we prefer, much of the communication, in the group focused on him (mutual dependence of activity and interaction). If other members of the group frequently originated interaction with him, he in turn frequently originated interaction with them. As we have seen, the higher the rank of a subgroup, the wider the range of interaction of its members. The same relationship holds even more strongly for a particularly high-ranking individual. At any rate, Taylor found himself at the center of a web of communications. His position in the web helped

confirm his high social rank (mutual dependence of interaction and sentiment), but we must never forget that it could do so only if his incipient control was accepted, and such acceptance depends, as we shall see, not on any one man but on the constitution of the group as a whole. Furthermore, Taylor's rank within the group no doubt depended to some extent on his influence outside it. It is significant that he alone was much more successful than Winkowski and Oberleitner together in getting a supply of wire from the department.

In short, the Bank Wiremen were, in Taylor, beginning to develop a leader of their own, different from the supervisors given them by the company. To be sure, they were only just beginning, and Taylor's position had hardly become recognized. We do not know how far this development might have gone if the experiment had lasted longer. . . .

We looked earlier at the way personality factors —and we admitted that this word *personality* covers many different things—prevented some developments from taking place in the Bank Wiring Observation Room that might otherwise have taken place. But if personality can inhibit some social developments, it can encourage others. Leadership might not have appeared in the room if Taylor had not been the kind of a man he was. It is not enough that a group tends to create its own leader; a man who is capable of being a leader must also be available. Taylor could not have behaved in any other way than he did and still have remained the most influential of the Bank Wiremen, but what enabled him to behave as he did? His score on the intelligence test was only fourth highest in the room; he must have had qualities other than sheer intelligence. Apparently he was especially well informed, and it may be significant that he was very active, keeping up a steady stream of chatter and always holding himself ready to take part in a game or conversation. But Krupa was active too, although not in quite the same way, and came about as close as Taylor to observing the group's code of output. Why did not Krupa become a leader? The only answer seems to be that, though he lived up to some of the norms, he did not live up to them all. In particular, he sought leadership, he tried to dominate, and was obvious in doing so. Krupa sought greatness; Taylor had it thrust upon him, and the latter was the only road to greatness the group would tolerate. The reasons why Taylor was able to take this course and Krupa was not must lie far back in their biological inheritance and early family history.

Selection 26
_____

Primitive Traits in Religious Revivals

Frederick M. Davenport

In Part III and in Selections 22-25 of this Part, the emphasis has been on the
formal aspects of social interaction. Socialization of personality was defined
primarily in terms of an individual's learning appropriate roles as he broadens
his social horizons through ever-widening group memberships. As Ackerknecht
demonstrated, an individual can learn to *prefer* to play the role of an Indian—
and not in the sense that American boys generally play that role. A role defines
the behavior expected of an actor in a given situation, although, as discussed,
there are often wide discrepancies between what the norms direct an actor to
do and what he does.

One area of social relationships, however, seems at first glance to challenge
the explanation of behavior as the elaboration of norms. History is full of
accounts of lawless groups that rise spontaneously on city streets and defy
social rules; since such aggregates are not always technically *groups*, they are
referred to as *mobs* or *crowds*. Sociologists classify these relatively unstructured
social gatherings under the heading *collective behavior*.

The basic elements of collective behavior were described in 1925 by Gustave
LeBon in a classic volume entitled *The Crowd*, which has been widely admired
by totalitarian dictators and respectable sociologists alike. LeBon described
crowds as assemblages of individuals closely grouped together with maximum
opportunity for communication and interstimulation, whose sentiments and ideas
have one and the same direction and whose individual personalities disappear
into a "collective mind." LeBon believed that the group mind is caused by
common sentiments found in the unconscious personalities of a given race.

One need not accept LeBon's questionable racist concepts to appreciate his
insights into crowd processes. Personality theory stresses the connection between
shared socialization practices and modal personality types in a society; that is,
individuals who are socialized in the same society tend to develop kindred
character structures. Personality, of course, includes an individual's unconscious
as well as his conscious strivings. The group mind is perhaps composed of the
unconscious strivings of many (not all, because there are many personality types
in any given society) individuals in the crowd—strivings that are similar because
they are products of similar socialization processes.

LeBon was on surer ground when he described the typical processes of a
mob. An aggregate of individuals—not yet a crowd—has its attention diverted by
some object or stimulus. As people begin to congregate, their heightened
emotional state becomes contagious. One person's excitement infects another,
and his excitement in turn inflames still others and increases the excitation of
the first person. A herd of stampeding cattle presents a somewhat parallel
situation. The norms learned during socialization weaken with the excitement,
and repressed unconscious strivings emerge. Mob norms are quickly formed,
and acts usually considered heinous crimes are approved, although in some

crowds—a revolutionary mob, for example—the new norms may be considered heroic even under normal standards.

Sociologists caution against placing too much stress on the unstructured or non-normative approach to crowd behavior. Certain groups in society internalize crowd norms at a very conscious level during the socialization process. The members of such groups refrain from implementing these norms because they fear punishment or because the behavior that elicits them—the stimulus—has been kept in check. Racists do not form mobs as long as Negroes "keep their place."

That mob behavior is actually traditional in American society is illustrated in the first and second readings in this section. One of the earliest expressions of crowd behavior in the United States is described in Davenport's account of religious revivals and camp-meetings in frontier Kentucky in 1800. The action he writes about closely resembles LeBon's model of crowd processes. It has frequently been observed that intense and prolonged meditation upon man's relation to God, the world, and a judgment to come can produce powerful emotions. Spiritual sentiment itself provided the stimulus that brought about the "season of high excitement" among churchgoing frontiersmen and transformed them into frenzied mobs. Furthermore, pioneer life with its hard work, Indian attacks, isolation, and lack of opportunity for emotional expression made the settler a willing member of the mob. Milling together at camp-meetings—it is important to note that the church was too small to hold and thus control huge gatherings—encouraged excitement, suggestibility, the weakening of controls, and the liberation of unconscious desires. One person became seized and started to shriek and shake, and before long the entire "congregation" was infected. Violent spasmodic actions, body contortions, sexual orgies, hypnotic rigidity, trances, visions—all were manifestations of crowd processes at camp-meetings.

Inasmuch as the frontier was removed from the more settled areas with their traditional restraints, social arrangements for controlling behavior were ineffective for preventing religious gatherings from turning into mobs. Davenport's account is funny, and one does not have to go beyond rock and roll or twist sessions to find modern equivalents. However, when the frontier disappeared in the West and the Southwest, one of its bequests was a tradition that encouraged mob action in other situations—especially those involving race relations.

. . . And so it happened that in the summer of 1799 two McGee brothers, William, a Presbyterian, and John, a Methodist, when crossing the pine barrens into Ohio, determined to turn aside and visit a sacramental solemnity at Red River, that they might observe for themselves the remarkable power and influence that everywhere attended the ministry of this pulpit Boanerges. What they actually happened upon that day, and furthered by their presence, was the beginning of one of the most tremendous religious revivals in modern history. In narrating the occurrences of this occasion I am following a letter written in 1820 by John McGee. I do this because, while there is no important variation in the historical accounts, there is some slight difference of detail, and the testimony of an eye-witness and participant is therefore particularly valuable. Several

preachers spoke. First John McGee, the Methodist, and never, as he says himself, did he preach with more light and liberty. Then his Presbyterian brother and the Rev. Mr. Hodge spoke with much animation and power. While the latter was discoursing, a woman in the east end of the house, unable to repress the violence of her emotions, gave vent to them with shoutings loud and long. At the close of the sermon the other ministers went out, but the two McGees and the people seemed loath to depart. "William felt such a power come over him that *he quit his seat and sat down on the floor of the pulpit, I suppose not knowing what he did.* A power which caused me

Reprinted with permission of the publisher from *Primitive Traits in Religious Revivals* by Frederick Morgan Davenport (New York: The Macmillan Company, 1905), pp. 69-84.

to tremble was upon me. There was a solemn weeping all over the house. At length I rose up and exhorted them to let the Lord God Omnipotent reign in their hearts, and submit to Him, and their souls should live. Many broke silence. The woman in the east end of the house shouted tremendously. I left the pulpit and went through the audience shouting and exhorting with all possible ecstasy and energy, and the floor was soon covered with the slain."

The little cloud no larger than a man's hand had filled the heavens with blackness, and now came the great rain. Or, to change the metaphor, the people from this Red River sacramental service were like fire in dry stubble among their neighbors. Upon the return home, "they rushed into the arms of their friends, shouting and telling what wonderful things God had done for their souls." Elder B. W. Stone, of a congregation in Bourbon County, came not long after to the scene of this remarkable religious excitement and carried the fire to the Cane Ridge country, where it blazed with a fury unequalled in any other section. From there it spread to Ohio and into Washington County, Pennsylvania, where derangement of the nervous system and loss of physical strength were common phenomena. Foote's history of North Carolina and of Virginia is full of thrilling accounts of revival fires lighted by people who returned from McGready's meetings. While in the Cumberland country itself, no opposition, no criticism, could for a long period allay the excitement in the least. From the Green River to the Cumberland, the settlements were full of religious fervor and revival zeal. From distances of forty, fifty and one hundred miles men came with their families in covered wagons, provided with food and bedding, to listen to this group of evangelists who had so stirred the congregation at the Red River sacrament. And thus originated what is known as the first camp-meeting in America at the Gasper River church in the summer of 1800. It certainly is the first known to fame, though it is possible that this extension of the pioneer Presbyterian sacramental service into several days' duration in the open air was an imitation of the quarterly circuit meeting of the early Methodists which for twenty years had been common in America, in Kentucky, Tennessee and Ohio. If not an imitation, it certainly was a growth from the same root of necessity. McGready had advertised this Gasper River meeting as widely as he could, and a great concourse assembled. The little church was far too small, and the neighboring forest was occupied as a temple. The woodsmen worshippers, with their accustomed fertility of resource, were ready for this emergency. They cleared away the

underbrush and felled the pine trees for pews. They improvised a platform for the speakers, and the wild woods, which early in the day had rung with the sound of their axes, later in the day rang with shout and song. They had not planned to remain longer than the evening. But when night came they were far from surfeited with religious zeal. The women pieced together the extra sheets and quilts which they had brought with them in the wagons, and the men cut poles over which these coverings were stretched for tents. Some brought straw from the nearest farms and others foraged for provisions. And when the darkness fell, many fires were kindled through the new-made village among the trees.

The meeting lasted from Friday until Tuesday. The preaching, praying and singing continued almost without cessation save for a few hours in the early morning. It was not until Saturday evening, however, that any special outbreak of overwrought nature manifested itself. Then two women became greatly excited, and their fervor was communicated by contagion through the whole multitude. The camp became a battleground of sobs and cries, and ministers spent nearly the whole night in passing from group to group of the "slain."

Now imitation began in earnest upon the return of these worshippers to their homes. Ten such camp-meetings were held one after another in the Green and Cumberland settlements. They became the vocation of the people. "Age snatched his crutch, Youth forgot his pastime, the laborer quitted his task," "the crops were left forgotten, the cabins were deserted, in large settlements there did not remain one soul."

The most notorious example of this intense form of the revival "crowd" is furnished by the Cane Ridge camp-meeting of August, 1801, which took place farther north in Bourbon County, Kentucky. The biography of Elder B. W. Stone makes it clear that it was an imitation from Logan County. Elder Stone lived in Bourbon County. Word had come to him of the amazing scenes of excitement and zeal in the southwest, and he made the journey in the spring of 1801 to witness what to him was "new and passing strange." The historians of the Cumberland Presbyterian Church— which by the way was an excellent product of the Logan County revival—have been sometimes wont to contend that the disorder and superemotionalism which defile the record of these early days, were the output of the Cane Ridge quarter of Kentucky and should not be charged against the settlement in the southwest. On this point the unvarnished tale of Elder Stone reflects some light. By the side of his own Cane Ridge, which he regarded as a dead community spiritually, he set the wonderful work which he saw in Logan County. It baffled description, he says. "Many, very many, fell . . . and continued for hours together in an apparently breathless and motionless state, sometimes for a few moments reviving and exhibiting symptoms of life by a deep groan or a piercing shriek or by a prayer for mercy fervently uttered. After lying there for hours . . . they would rise, shouting deliverance." Then others would fall, under the eloquence of those who rose and related their experience. In addition he saw much which he thought fanaticism, but considered to be the devil apeing the power of God. He returned with ardent spirit to his congregations at Concord and Cane Ridge. The next Sunday morning at the latter place he met a multitude who had gathered to listen to his recital of his experience of grace at Logan. There was awful solemnity, and many wept. At night he spoke in the Concord church and told the story of what he had seen in the southwest. During that meeting two little girls were struck down under the preaching *"and in every respect were exercised as others were in the south of Kentucky."* The people were greatly moved, and not long after a vast host, estimated by a revolutionary officer on the ground to be twenty thousand souls, came together at the Cane Ridge camp.

The remembrance of that fateful gathering lingers in Kentucky after the lapse of a century. Nothing was lacking to stir to its profoundest depths the imagination and emotion of this great throng of men, women and children. It was at night that the most terrible scenes were witnessed, when the camp-fires blazed in a mighty circle around the vast audience of pioneers bowed in devotion. Beyond was the blackness of the primeval forest, above the night wind and the foliage and the stars. As the darkness deepened, the exhortations of the preachers became more fervent and impassioned, their picturesque prophecies of doom more lurid and alarming, the volume of song burst all bonds of guidance and control, and broke again and again from the throats of the people, while over all, at intervals, there rang out the shout of ecstasy, the sob and the groan. When daylight came, the temper of the assembly was somewhat modified, but there was the same tendency to boisterous emotion. Men and women shouted aloud during the sermon, and shook hands all around at the close in what was termed the "singing ecstasy." There are many suggestive bits of testimony to the highly overwrought state of these susceptible people. One of the most careful observers, the Rev. Mr. Lyle, who kept a diary and journal through this whole period, and

passed calm judgment in the midst of the wild excitement, to whom we owe the best account of the extravagances and disorders, has described the crowd at Cane Ridge rushing from preacher to preacher if it were whispered that it was "more lively" at some other point, swarming enthusiastically around a "fallen" brother, laughing, leaping, sobbing, shouting, swooning. If the assembly were languid, he says, a few shrieks and one or two instances of falling would quickly arouse them, and as far in every direction as the people could see or hear, others would be caught in the contagion and would likewise fall. Children were allowed to preach, a little girl of seven being propped up on the shoulders of a man, and exhorting to the multitude "till she sank exhausted on her bearer's head."

And when we reflect that this mighty crowd did not break up on this occasion until the food gave out, but remained for days an agitated mass of humanity in the midst of such surroundings as these, contemplating the most momentous truths, ascribing every extraordinary nervous contortion to the mysterious agency of the divine, we can well understand how many, very many, would be physically and mentally overwhelmed. The whole body of persons who actually fell helpless to the earth during the progress of the meeting was computed by the Rev. James Crawford, who avers that he endeavored to keep an accurate account, to be three thousand persons, about one in every six. The number who fell in the ghost-dance on White Clay Creek was, it will be remembered, about one out of three. Measured by this test, the Kentuckian of 1800 is certainly entitled to the distinction of being twice as civilized as the savage. Those who fell were carried to the meeting-house near by. "At no time was the floor less than half covered. Some lay quiet, unable to move or speak. Some talked, but could not move. Some beat the floor with their heels. Some, shrieking in agony, bounded about like a live fish out of water. Many lay down and rolled over and over for hours at a time. Others rushed wildly over the stumps and benches and then plunged, shouting, 'Lost! Lost!' into the forest."

When the frenzy was at its height, these revival crowds were subject to a set of nervous and muscular manifestations probably as varied and terrible as ever afflicted a population in this world. There is no question of the truth of this sad chapter of pioneer history. The evidence is too overpowering and convincing. There is no question of the reality of the manifestations, though as elsewhere it is likely there was considerable humbug and deception. But there were many doubters, and the "fallen" subjects were often put to the proof. For instance, our friend the Rev. Mr. Lyle, furnished with a phial of hartshorn by a physician, "applied it to a stout young man who was lying flat on his back, and inadvertently allowed some to run into his nostrils. But he took not the slightest notice of it, so much was his attention absorbed by devotional feeling."

With respect to extravagancies and disorders, there are a large number of corroborative references in Lyle, Peter Cartwright, Lorenzo Dow and other contemporaries. Next to the "falling" exercise the most notable and characteristic Kentucky phenomenon was the "jerks." The unhappy victim shook in every joint. Sometimes the head was thrown from side to side with great rapidity. Again the feet were affected, and the subject would hop like a frog. Often the body would be thrown violently to the ground, where it would continue to bound from one place to another. Peter Cartwright declares that he had seen more than five hundred persons jerking at once in his congregation. And Lorenzo Dow, writing of a time some years later, when the epidemic again broke out in that section, remarks that on Sunday at Knoxville "the governor being present, about one hundred and fifty had the jerking exercise." It is still a phenomenon in the religious life of that country. I saw mild cases of it in the summer of 1903 among the whites in the Chilhowee Mountains. In 1800 no one was proof against it, saint or sinner, white or black, except as Lorenzo Dow naïvely remarks, "those naturalists who wished to get it to philosophize upon it, and the most godly. The wicked are more afraid of it than of smallpox or yellow fever."

It became an infectious disease. It passed the bounds of normal imitation and became a morbid contagion, and many a scoffer bit the dust in the midst of his contempt and derision. Peter Cartwright relates a serious instance of this which he vouches for as having taken place in William McGee's congregation. "There was a great work of religion and the jerks were very prevalent." A large man with a bottle of whiskey in his pocket reviled both the jerks and the religion. In a flash the contagion pursued him, caught him, and though he started to run, it was useless. "He halted among some saplings, took out his bottle of whiskey and swore he would drink the damned jerks to death. But he could not get the bottle to his mouth, though he tried hard. At this he became greatly enraged, fetched a very violent jerk, snapped his neck, fell, and soon expired, with his mouth full of cursing and bitterness."

Another phenomenon not so common was the "barking" exercise. The votaries of this dignified rite gathered in groups, on all fours, like dogs, growling and snapping the teeth at the foot of a tree as the minister preached,—a practice which they designated as "treeing the devil"!

When this stage was reached, it is evident that the tension had invaded the brain. It is only natural, then, that we have here again the trance and the vision. The affections of the ghost-dance Indians were duplicated very exactly, so perfectly indeed that it would not be inaccurate to describe the ghost-dance ceremony as a Kentucky camp-meeting run amuck. Many of these camp-meeting folk lay insensible, sometimes for hours, but when they recovered from the swoon it was to relate, in what were called "strains of heaven," experiences of interviews with departed friends and visions of glory not vouchsafed to their normally conscious and less fortunate brethren. They claimed divine inspiration and prophesied of the end of all things. The phenomena of Millerism, spiritualism and faith healing were as manifest here as among the Cherokees or the Shakers of Puget Sound.

When nervous tension had risen to the maximum, it is interesting to mark its fall towards the minimum in the changed character of the phenomena. When a year or two had elapsed, the milder hysterical forms of muscular action began to display themselves in certain quarters, until, in 1803, the "holy laugh" became a feature of the worship. While the minister was preaching, the members would burst out one after another, and then in chorus into what was regarded as a solemn laugh. The manner was devout even when the laugh was boisterous.

There were grave charges, also, such as were commonly heard in former times with respect to camp-meetings in many parts of the country, of the extraordinarily free companionship of the sexes. And these allegations were made not by the ungodly, but by prominent ministers of standing and courage who inaugurated plans for night watches "to reconnoitre the camp and the stand." While we may admit that there has been some exaggeration of this evil in the literature of revivals, we must remember that the human love passion and the spiritual love passion appear to modern psychology to be delicately interwoven, particularly in the case of young people between fourteen and twenty-five, and the kind of spiritual excitement which a super-emotional revival generates is likely to be more harmful than helpful to the self-control of the individual as exhibited in both his sexual and spiritual activities.

There appeared also in Kentucky those more moderate forms of disorder which we shall see distinguishing the Edwards and Wesley revivals. I refer to such evidences of the absence of ordinary rational deliberation as are indicated by the singing of different hymns at the same time, the vociferous praying of many at once, and the loud ejaculations of approval.

These phenomena, some of them curious and some of them dreadful, were far more common than they are often believed to have been. The Rev. James Gallagher was the editor of an early Presbyterian publication, "The Western Sketchbook." He was also a witness and a close student of these peculiar physical exercises. In referring to the grosser forms of them, he declares it to be his judgment that of the professors of religion who were in that country at the time, perhaps one-half became subjects of these bodily disorders. They ranged all the way from the normal imitation of the "holy laugh" to the morbid contagion of the "jerks" and the blackness of insanity. Even so enthusiastic an observer as Peter Cartwright, who regarded the "jerks" as the judgment of God to bring sinners to repentance, was at one time appalled by "the fearful tide of delusion that was sweeping over the country." It is not wonderful, therefore, that rational control of this mighty sympathetic movement was for a long time impossible. At the inception, there were men in the synod of Kentucky who set themselves against the wild extravagances. But their power to resist the tide was lessened by the fact that they attacked the revival preachers perhaps more vigorously for certain alleged aberrations of doctrine than for the disorderly methods and the practical vagaries. And when the movement was well under way, the very momentum of it swept all criticism before it, and any minister who put himself in the path did so at the peril of his reputation and his influence. It was not till the summer of 1803 that the abuses were opposed with any degree of success. Then Lyle preached a sermon which attracted wide attention from the text—"God is not the author of confusion but of peace." Father Rice, an old white-haired preacher of commanding intelligence and sound judgment, insisted upon better regulations and a guard around the camp, "and exhorted powerfully against noise and false exercises." The path of opposition was sometimes thorny. An editor at Lexington arose and insisted that some ladies who had fallen needed air and nothing else, but the "ladies themselves, on being asked, professed the contrary, and the editor slunk away ashamed."

This difficulty of control was accentuated by the very considerable measure of ignorance, superstition and fear that actually existed in the population. They had firm trust in signs and omens. Peter Cartwright relates an amusing illustration, showing how inbred was the belief in magic. Two fashionably dressed young women, attended by their brothers with loaded horsewhips, came to one of his meetings in 1804. Cartwright was feeling somewhat ill, and, before he preached, took a small bottle of peppermint from his pocket and sipped a little. During the sermon which followed the two young women became afflicted with the "jerks," to their great mortification. At the close of the meeting the brothers were waiting for the preacher with the horsewhips. Cartwright professed innocence of any intention to influence the sisters after this fashion, but the brothers hotly affirmed that he need not deny it, for they had seen him take the phial out of his pocket in which was the substance that had "tricked" the young women. And this same rugged pioneer preacher, who had a fine vein of sanity in him, has also told us of the thousands of people who crowded into membership in the churches from mere fright during the period of the severe earthquakes of the Mississippi Valley in the year 1812.

Selection 27

Field Reports on Desegregation in the South—
Mansfield, Texas: A Report on the Crisis Situation
Resulting from Efforts to Desegregate the School System
John Howard Griffin and Theodore Freedman

Davenport's account of camp-meetings indicates that mob action in the United States is one of the legacies of the frontier. The frenzy of the revivals provided an emotional outlet for the anxieties of the lonely frontiersman. But frontier crowd expression was not limited to religious or sexual outlets, for it became a mechanism of social control for dealing with all sorts of deviants in the wilderness—horse thieves, murderers, shady gamblers, and claim jumpers. Although crowd processes were defined earlier as spontaneous and relatively unorganized collective behavior, a tradition developed in the South and West that governed the circumstances under which lawless mobs could be used. They were most frequently exploited to control attempts of Negroes to gain the equal treatment and the dignity guaranteed them by the American Constitution. Following the Civil War, mobs lynched thousands of American Negroes and thoroughly terrorized millions more.

It is difficult to say to what extent the behavior of lynch mobs conformed to LeBon's model of the crowd. Many members of lynch mobs experienced the excitement and emotional contagion that characterize the crowd; yet others coldly and rationally used the mob in order to maintain their domination of the Negro. Violence also seemed to be correlated with an economic challenge on the part of the racial minority and with anxieties about sex. The act of rape—a frequent provocation for mob violence—was liberally defined to include any relationship between a male Negro and a white woman. Much of the crowd behavior that occurred on these grounds was contrived by organizers of violence who, in order to "keep the Negro in his place," manipulated anti-Negro prejudice and—unwittingly—the repressed desire of some whites for sexual relations with a Negro. Race relations in the United States often combine the antithetical emotions of repulsion and attraction.

Lynch mobs are infrequent now, but race riots persist, focused on the Supreme Court decision that segregation in schools, restaurants, buses, and elsewhere is a violation of the Constitution. Thus the attendance of Negro children (even of one Negro child) at previously all-white schools and the efforts of college students to encourage Negro voter-registration have replaced "rape" as the stimuli that ignite the mob. Of course, anxieties about sex and economic competition are also very much a part of the desegregation crisis, as evidenced by the following report by Griffin and Freedman on the attempt to desegregate the schools in Mansfield, Texas, in the summer of 1956. Many Southern whites—whose anxieties are common among Northerners as well—are alarmed at the recent social advances made by Negroes and fear that equal educational opportunity would mean more competition in the struggle for status. Others fear that contact between white and Negro youths in the schools will lead to intermarriage.

Mansfield had a history of racial violence that went back to the nineteenth century; utilizing a mob to keep the Negro in his place was traditional, so to speak. The mob encirclement of Mansfield High in 1956 was organized; racists must have met to plan strategy. Anti-Negro and anti-Semitic literature was distributed, for example, and word was passed to the mob not to hit anyone. Yet once the crowd gathered, it developed an existence and quality akin to LeBon's "pure" crowd; violence occurred despite orders that no one was to be beaten. As LeBon noted, the mob does not tolerate any opposition to its norms. People who inwardly reject mob norms do not as a rule openly challenge them. Thus, on this occasion, the superintendent of schools failed to appear on the first day of registration, businessmen complied with orders to close shop, and employers fired their Negro employees.

Other aspects of mob behavior can only be questioned; we cannot explain them. Why do students on one Southern campus—the University of Mississippi, for example—start bloody riots when the first Negro registers, whereas the students of another—Clemson Agricultural College—accept the order of the courts to desegregate? When and why do people return to their "normal" selves and regain control of their unconscious needs which, as LeBon pointed out, play so large a part in motivating crowd action? Who are the leaders of a crowd? At what stage in its course does a crowd disintegrate and re-form into the various groups that constitute the structure of an orderly community?

BACKGROUND

Mansfield, Texas, is located in the southeast sector of Tarrant County. The city of Fort Worth occupies the major portion of this county. Mansfield is approximately 14 miles from the downtown Fort Worth area. State Highway #287 runs through Mansfield and represents its main street. The population of this farm-surrounded community is approximately 1,500 (about 350 Negroes). A large number of the residents are employed in Fort Worth and surrounding areas.

Mansfield is the first school system (lower than college level) in Texas for which the court ordered immediate desegregation.

Mansfield residents readily state that prior to efforts at desegregation, race relations in the community were good. What is implied here is that a traditional caste system prevailed. A check into factors relating to this reveals that between 15 and 20 years ago, the Ku Klux Klan was active in the community and that at least one lynching of a Negro occurred during that time.

PRESS: There is one newspaper in the community. According to white interviewees, the editorial policies of the former editor (Mr. B.) was a contributing factor to the tension in Mansfield. The paper printed editorials and letters from White Citizens Council leaders for about a year preceding the crisis period. The majority of these letters were signed by Mr. W., a resident of a nearby community and active in the Citizens Council of that community. During the height of the crisis in Mansfield, a Citizens Council was organized and subsequently disbanded. The points made by these editorials and letters are:

a) The Supreme Court cannot "make laws." The court is communist-dominated and therefore deserves no further respect from honest Americans. The court decision usurped legal powers not granted to it.
b) For the sake of their children, parents should defy the court and fight any attempt to desegregate.
c) Biblical quotations prove that the Bible speaks against desegregation.
d) Mansfield is being made a "guinea pig" in being forced to desegregate, since other Texas communities have had desegregation postponed.
e) Separate but equal schools work no injustice on the Negro.
f) Defying "Northern" agitation will be doing both races the greatest possible good.

(While interviewees attributed the above to the newspaper under the editorship of Mr. B.—who reportedly left the community some time prior to the crisis—an examination of several of the editorials [see appendix] during the crisis reveals generally the same policy of opposition to desegregation. This was true, in spite of reports that the owner [a woman] of the paper would have stopped this "if she had known what was being printed.")

Personal animosity between a white and Negro seems to have contributed to the general ill-feeling between the races. It is difficult to pinpoint the disagreement between the men, but it is generally known that their disagreement culminated in a face-to-face argument.

Mr. F., a white cafe owner on the extreme west of town, was readily identified by white interviewees as the leader of the anti-desegregation movement. Newspaper accounts also identify him as being one of the leaders.

Mr. C., a Negro, who operates a barbeque stand across town, reportedly enjoys a highly respected standing in the community. Reportedly, most of C's trade is with white residents; however, he maintains a section for serving Negroes.

Enmity has existed between C and F for about a year. It is reported that F attempted to get the school officials to prohibit white students from going to the barbeque stand for their lunches. When school officials ignored F's demands, he is reported to have announced that any student who went to C's would not be allowed in his cafe. Interviewees noted that F's cafe is virtually the

From *Field Report on Desegregation in the South*, by John Howard Griffin and Theodore Freedman (New York: Anti-Defamation League of B'nai B'rith), pp. 3-15.

only place in Mansfield where high school students can gather, have sodas, listen to music, and engage in teenage activities after 8:00 p.m.

It should be noted that much of the hostility in this relationship appears to stem from economic competition. It seems that C sold a tract of land adjacent to his stand (for an amount estimated at between $20,000-$25,000) to a large industrial organization which has built a plant there. Now, it is reported that C has moved his place of business closer to the highway and right next to the tract of land that he sold, so that his stand will be the most convenient eating place in the area.

CHRONOLOGY

1948-49: It was learned that during this period of time, the school board of the Mansfield Independent School District appointed several Negro patrons as sub-trustees. The sub-trustees were invited to attend all meetings of the board and, according to Negro interviewees, the members of the board welcomed their suggestions relative to the needs of the Negro school. Though the role of the sub-trustees lacked official recognition, it appeared that their opinions were welcomed and, in effect, the sub-trustees had an important say in the hiring of personnel for the Negro school.

At this time, one school was serving eight grades for the Negro students. It was described by the Negroes interviewed as a one-teacher school which had no indoor toilet facilities, no running water (the teacher had to carry water in milk cans a considerable distance if there was to be drinking water in the building), no adequate teaching materials, no school lunch program, no flag or flagpole on the school grounds, and no school bus. In addition, the school was located on a heavily trucked country road. There was no fence to restrain children from darting into the road while playing. Reports indicate that the sub-trustees were constantly pressing for improvements and that a second building (described as a barracks) was later added to the grounds. The "barracks" was replaced by a new four-room school in 1954 which provided instruction through the eighth grade.

These conditions prevailed for a number of years. According to persons interviewed, the sub-trustees made repeated requests for improvements to existing facilities. It is reported that the school board advised the trustees that it would be impossible to provide all the improvements, but that they would be given a well. Repeated requests for improvements by the sub-trustees brought about the abrupt ending of this unofficial arrangement early in 1955.

A chapter of the NAACP was organized in Mansfield in 1950.

April 7, 1955: The Negro patrons of the Mansfield Independent School District, dissatisfied with the lack of action by the school board, retained a Negro Fort Worth attorney to counsel and advise them relative to a course of action. Negro interviewees stated that at this time there was no question about bringing legal action for desegregation. The list of grievances noted were:

a) No school lunch program.
b) Absence of teaching materials.
c) No flag or flagpole on school grounds.
d) School on country road, without fence to restrain children at play from running into streets.
e) Negroes of high school age attending a segregated Fort Worth high school were exposed to undesirable conditions on their way to and from school. The young people were required to take a public service bus from Mansfield which let them off in downtown Fort Worth, some twenty blocks from the school. Though school was dismissed at 3:30 p.m., the first bus back to pick up the students was at 5:30 p.m., thus returning them to Mansfield after dark in the winter months. The specific request made by the Negro patrons was for a regular school bus.

During April to July, the attorney for the Negro patrons was in correspondence and personal communication with the superintendent of schools relative to the list of grievances of the patrons.

July, 1955: Patrons filed a petition with the school board requesting admission of their children to Mansfield High School, which was then open only to white students.

August, 1955: The attorney for the Negro patrons again wrote the school board asking that the board comply with the requests of the patrons by enrollment date, September, 1955.

September, 1955: Efforts were made to enroll Negroes in the Mansfield (white) schools. Admission was denied.

October, 1955: A suit was brought by parents and relatives of three minors but in behalf of 12 Negro high school children in the Mansfield Independent School District.

November, 1955: The Mansfield suit was tried before the Federal District Court in Fort Worth, Texas, which ruled it "premature" and "precipitate." After an appeal before Fifth Circuit Court, the court remanded and reversed the decision, and directed the district judge to issue an order to the school board to admit students without regard to race.

August 22, 1956: A cross was burned at night in the heart of the Negro section of the community.

August 23, 1956: A second cross-burning occurred at night in the Negro section of the community. It was reported that the sheriff ordered police cars to patrol the area.

(None of the persons interviewed provided any details on events which might have occurred from August 24-26.)

August 27, 1956: A Mansfield Negro (president of the local NAACP and community resident for 50 years) reported receiving several telephone threats to "get out of town."

August 28, 1956: A dummy representing a Negro was hung over the main street of Mansfield. The Mansfield chief of police considered the act, "a lot more serious than pranksters." He added, "I'm kind of uneasy over it," and noted that he wouldn't be surprised by almost anything happening in Mansfield within the next few days. Signs attached to the effigy read, "THIS NEGRO TRIED TO GO TO A WHITE SCHOOL," and "WOULDN'T THIS BE A HORRIBLE WAY TO DIE." It appears that where at first there had been some articulation of resentment by white residents of Mansfield over efforts to desegregate, now the resentment began to manifest itself in more overt forms of intimidatory behavior. It was reported that there was "lynch talk" around the community. One white woman reportedly said "it was a shame that wasn't a real nigger hanging up there instead of just a dummy." One Negro woman, returning from shopping in town, observed that, "You could feel the way they looked at a Negro . . . they wanted to kill one."

At this time, it was reported, the mayor and chief of police absented themselves from the community. This was true also of several other persons who might be considered part of the power structure of the community. It is interesting to note that some of the persons interviewed readily stated they didn't want to assume any responsibility.

August 29, 1956: The attorney for the Mansfield Independent School District filed a petition for a stay of enforcement on the Federal Court order to admit Negro students. The plea was turned down. At approximately the same time, a White Citizens Council was organized and several meetings were held. One such meeting was held on an emergency basis in the local pool hall, the day prior to registration. A story was circulated in the community that Negroes would come to school to register the following morning. According to his own account, the local leader of the Citizens Council told the group that they would meet on the school grounds at 7:00 a.m. on the first day of registration, and proceed in an orderly manner as a protest. It was specified that no violence was to be used. The leader of the Citizens Council, Mr. L, is described as a "responsible person" and well regarded in Mansfield. The group was told that in the event a Negro did appear, the Citizens Council leaders would step forward, point to the crowd, and tell the Negro that he was entering the school against the will of the community and over their protests.

White interviewees expressed the belief that the NAACP recruited a large number of Negroes to press for desegregation in Mansfield, that many of the local Negroes went along with the NAACP against their wishes and that some refused to have anything to do with the organization. Specifically identified as opposing the NAACP were C, previously mentioned, and B, principal of the Negro school. White interviewees report that C made strenuous efforts to oppose "immediate" and "compulsory" desegregation and that C made an effort to get Mansfield Negroes to stop supporting what C considered the harmful representations of the NAACP. It is interesting to note that B is described by white interviewees as frightened, but acting courageously hand in hand with C. The petition circulated by B was reportedly an attempt to quash desegregation efforts.

Interviews with Negroes point up the disparity in the information received from the two sources regarding this aspect of the problem. Negro interviewees stated that at no time to their knowledge did the NAACP or any other organization urge the Negro patrons to file suit. While their attorney was a member of the NAACP, he did not suggest legal action be taken until the school board failed to consider their grievances. With reference to C, Negro interviewees state that they do not know of any action taken by him to oppose the action of the parents, though he is reported as being more conciliatory to the point of view of the white community leaders. Negro interviewees also denied knowledge of reported efforts by C to get Negroes to withdraw from the NAACP. The role of B appears to be that of the unsuccessful go-between. Indications are that his status is based on his role of principal, rather than upon one of leadership. The following information was related: in the past, the sub-trustees had some unofficial say with regard to the hiring of personnel. In the instance of the hiring of B, there were some differences of opinion. This reportedly was not based on a personal objection to B, but rather to the Board's hiring of B in the dual role of principal and janitor. Negro interviewees admit knowledge of B's having circulated a statement, but deny that it was for the purpose of opposing desegregation. B, according to Negro interviewees, indicated that he was trying to ascertain how many of the Negro parents were planning to send their children to school.

August 30, 1956: A plea for a one-year postponement of desegregation was turned down by the Federal District judge. In explaining his decision, the judge said that the Mansfield school district "is asking me now to do exactly what I did on November 27, 1955, when I ruled in favor of the school district. On June 28, 1956, on appeal by the plaintiffs, it was held that I was wrong in granting in favor of the school board and the Appeals Court reversed my judgment. On August 17, in pursuance with the Circuit Court judgment, a mandate was issued specifically and in plain terms ordering me to enter their judgment and I did enter the judgment on August 27." The judge went on to say: "It would be a direct disobedience" of the Circuit Court to grant the school district's petition for postponement of desegregation. In conclusion the judge said: "I want to say that the attitude that has been taken in this case and that is now being taken by you is one of prayerful obedience to the law and in so doing, that high school will stand as a proud monument to the patriotism and wisdom of the school board."

The Mansfield Independent School District opened for registration. On this first day, a crowd estimated by the press at more than 250 persons, gathered on the school grounds in protest of the court order to desegregate. Other observers estimated the crowd at up to 400 persons.

Three white interviewees stated they heard one of the leaders in the anti-desegregation movement say he received a shipment of knives and was offering them free to any high school youngster who would use them. Other persons indicated that the "brutal" element began to take over—the element that favored "anything" to keep the Negroes in their place, to protect the white children from "mongrelization" and to drive the NAACP out of town. This refers to five men in Mansfield

known by conservative leaders of the White Citizens Council as "the radical element." White interviewees expressed the opinion that these men were clever in not openly advocating violence in any way that could be connected with them; however, they encouraged intimidation which was suggestive of violence. A number of persons in the mob, reportedly students, carried signs— "NIGGER STAY OUT, WE DON'T WANT NIGGERS, THIS IS A WHITE SCHOOL," "A DEAD NIGGER IS THE BEST NIGGER," "COONS EARS $1.00 A DOZEN." The dummy figure of a Negro was found hanging from the school building.

The local constable went to the school and, seeing the size of the mob, stated he placed an immediate call to the county sheriff, requesting assistance. The county sheriff arrived on the scene at 11:00 a.m. and advised the milling crowd around him that he was there to preserve law and order.

The interviews with white residents reveal that F, previously mentioned, and M, a white semi-skilled worker, and others of the "radical element" made the rounds of all the stores in the community, asking merchants to cooperate with the protest movement by closing their business and putting in an appearance on the school grounds. Reports indicate that all storekeepers complied, though originally three were unwilling—until they were told that failure to do so might bring economic pressures against them. One shop-owner merely closed up for the two-hour period, going home instead of going to the school.

At this point in the series of events it was widely reported that at a cross-burning the previous week, the ground had been mined with dynamite and that if the constable made a false move, he would have been blown up. It was also said that any white men who showed opposition to the group would be subject to reprisals. (There appears to be no public record in the press, nor corroborating information from knowledgeable people as to exactly where and when these threats were made. There appears to be an absence of adequate information also as to what the constable was or was not expected to do. There is one possibility which was brought out by a Negro: that the constable has a business that is partially dependent upon Negro clientele and, therefore, he might have been hesitant to appear openly antagonistic.)

The Tarrant County district attorney, speaking for himself and for the grand jury which was recessed until September 6, issued a stern warning that the county's law enforcement agencies would not tolerate violence in Mansfield.

A telegram to the governor, from the Fort Worth Negro attorney, representing 13 Negroes in Mansfield, issued a plea to dispatch additional law enforcement officers "to assure that law and order will be maintained." A Mansfield law enforcement officer, queried by the press, indicated "if we need additional help, we can get it quickly." He also stated that he had talked with the Ranger Captain who advised that "he and other Rangers are available if needed." The Negro attorney reportedly attempted to contact the governor by phone, without success. He also telephoned the Director of Public Safety (a wire was also sent to him), who indicated that it was the policy of his department to send men only upon the request of local law enforcement officers, and that such a request had not been forthcoming.

August 31, 1956: The Mansfield Independent School District opened for the second day of registration. This was the day it was anticipated that the Negro students would attempt to register. Approximately 500 persons were on the school grounds by 9:00 a.m. (500 persons was the estimate of newspaper men; another observer suggested the size of the mob as more like the 400 of the previous day). Part of this "mob" on the second day were the newspaper, radio and TV men from the Dallas-Fort Worth area. Also present were mothers concerned with the safety of their children since they learned that white men were carrying firearms and they feared there might be shooting. Some of the white persons interviewed indicated that there were also "agitators" and "organizers" in evidence as well. (No information is available as to whom the organizers or agitators were, or which side they were on. However, the terms themselves might connote a feeling of white interviewees that these individuals were desegregationists.)

According to reports, members of the mob "voiced open threats." A dummy figure of a Negro was found hanging from the flagpole on the school grounds. It was stated that the organizers of the anti-desegregation movement had done a good job and had taken over completely. (A white person remarked that the feeling of the mob was at such a pitch that if one man had started to run forward for any reason, all would have followed.)

While there were reports that on the previous day, the sheriff's men were armed with submachine guns and tear gas, on this day only side arms were worn, because the heavier weapons aroused considerable ire on the part of the crowd.

Interviews with white persons revealed that vigilante squads were stopping all cars coming into Mansfield asking whether they were coming to town, or merely driving through. Anyone suspected of being sympathetic to the Negro cause was escorted out of town.

The superintendent of schools intended to remain away from school the first day, reportedly afraid of the mob which resented his inability or unwillingness to do anything about the situation. A white interviewee said he went to the superintendent's home and advised him that he would go to the school and explain the superintendent's position to the crowd. Newspaper reports indicate that on the second day, the superintendent was the first member of the school staff to appear and was quoted as saying: "Now you guys know I'm with you, but I've got this mandate hanging over my head."

An observer from the Tarrant County district attorney's office appeared on the scene and reportedly made some "unfortunate remarks." The crowd closed in on him and, according to an interviewee, obeyed a pro-segregation leader's command not to strike him. However, he was shaken until his nose bled. In addition, members of the mob began kicking him until he was rescued by law enforcement officers.

It should be noted that prior to and during this time, quantities of hate materials were given widespread local distribution. Some of these materials were distributed locally, others were mailed in from other parts of the state and nation. The materials claimed that the Jews were behind the NAACP and that school desegregation was a communist plot to mongrelize the white race, etc. The following is a sampling of the sources of materials, as identified by names and addresses on same:

a) Common Sense, Union, N.J.
b) The American Nationalist, Inglewood, Calif.
c) National Citizens Protective Committee, St. Louis, Mo.
d) White Citizens Councils of Mississippi and Alabama.

It appears that at this point, the leaders of the pro-segregation movement became, according to reports, "a little dictatorship." Reports indicate that they made demands that Negroes with "good" jobs be fired, with the inference that failure to cooperate would be met by economic pressure. It was further reported that demands were made that credit be denied to Negroes. Reportedly, in one instance, not only was the employer told to fire the Negro employee, but also which white man to hire in his place. It was stated that there was compliance to these demands except in two instances. The respondents pointed out that though merchants resented these tactics they did not dare oppose them for fear that such action would be misinterpreted as approval of desegregation. (Little is made of the fact that very few Mansfield Negroes work there, with the exception of domestics, and that such pressure could only have been directed at two or three Negroes.) These efforts had somewhat of a boomerang effect: reports from a Negro interviewee revealed that these difficulties came at a time when the cotton had to be picked, and, as a result of tensions in the community and sympathy for the Mansfield Negro, those from Fort Worth and elsewhere who usually came into the community to pick cotton did not do so. Failure to bring the crop in could have had serious repercussions on all levels of the community. However, it appears that migratory labor had to be used, although in many instances these laborers worked for a day or two, just to secure enough money to go on to a point closer to their destination. It was further reported in this interview that, if nothing else, the possibility of financial loss had a sobering effect on some elements in the community.

September 1-3, 1956: School was closed for the Labor Day weekend and things appeared to have quieted down. The governor dispatched two Texas rangers to the scene, and granted the school board authority to transfer out of the district any student whose presence might incite a riot. Newspaper reports of the governor's action convey the impression that his action was based on a personal decision; however, one of the white interviewees reported that the request for the rangers came from the sheriff, another that it came from the constable. There is no corroboration of the fact that such a request was made, who made it, or whether the governor was aware of same prior to his announced decision.

September 4, 1956: With final registration set for this day, a mob of over 200 persons were on the school grounds to continue the protest against efforts to enroll the three Negro students. The Tarrant County sheriff and other officers appeared on the scene at 7:00 a.m. to curb any show of violence which threatened to erupt Thursday and Friday of the previous week. A Fort Worth Episcopal minister was harassed by the mob when he appeared on the school grounds for the stated purpose of offering a Christian solution to the racial problems in the school district. White interviewees reported that some of the local "preachers" began to speak out, notably the Catholic priest and Methodist minister, who preached against lawlessness. It was stated that as a result, the Methodist minister was severely criticized, and, subsequently, the local newspaper carried references to "pin-headed preachers" who preached the brotherhood of man.

No Negro students appeared at the school to register. All of Mansfield's Negro students of high school age enrolled in Fort Worth Negro junior and senior high schools.

September 24, 1956: The Tarrant County grand jury subpoenaed some Mansfield citizens (Negro and white) to testify on the events which had taken place. Negroes interviewed expressed concern over the general procedure utilized, i.e., all the Negro students were picked up by deputies when they debarked from the bus which brought them from Fort Worth.

At a later date the grand jury was dismissed with no announced specific action relative to events in Mansfield.

PERSONAL IMPRESSIONS

The following are Mr. Griffin's personal impressions of some of the events which transpired in Mansfield as well as his answers to specific questions put to him relative to the crisis situation:

a. During this time no Negroes appeared on the scene and no word has been heard from them. They are keeping at home and quiet.

b. The people have been rendered completely confused. The small group of fanatics more or less control the town and have the backing of the majority of the people who do not approve of them, but approve of their championing of "the cause."

c. At this point a local resident, myself, begins to prepare an article on the situation. The news gets around. Both sides immediately assume that it will be against them; but the White Citizens' Council side is the most alarmed. They tell me to stay out of it. Some express anxiety over my physical safety. I announce (and Mr. C. does at the same time), that the large majority of the people are following, against their will and conscience, a sub-human species.

d. At this time I am contacted about the study of crisis community situations. I agree to do the research locally, since we do not think the local people would cooperate with any outsiders. I begin to make extensive interviews. I let it be known that the findings whether good or bad will be published nationally.

e. The steam has died down in all except the small group of fanatics. I find great resentment, and after the interviews, I attempt to explain the situation to each interviewee. The findings become obvious and there are many embarrassed and red-faced people here, some who think that what we lost is far greater than what we gained. Those who were the scapegoats—the ones who refused to fire their Negro help, are looked upon now with a certain respect. The tide is beginning to turn.

f. At the outset, it was very difficult to get interviews. But when the story got around, many people took courage and volunteered, among them some of the conservative leaders. If this were going to be published, it was a sobering thing to them—they wanted the record straight, wanted themselves cleared and written down as opposers of violence, and as regretting the whole thing.

g. The fanatics, losing none of their ardor, gradually lost prestige. It began to play out. Still, no one spoke up. The preachers had been repudiated. The feeling of triumph was still strong. Mr. F. was still distributing his pamphlets.

h. On October 15, I sent a letter to the local newspaper, a very impersonal letter, listing the background of the distributors and publishers of these hate pamphlets. Nothing more. The editor came to see me, very contrite. She said she wanted to be on the right side and that if I thought she should, she would fire the people running the paper who had written such inflammatory editorials. I refused to express myself on this. She asked for permission to publish this information, and I gave it to her. The information appeared, as coming from me, and I expected severe repercussions. To my surprise, it was highly praised. People said they hadn't realized how they were being used by hate groups. They said it would have been better to go ahead and integrate than to be led astray in this manner.

i. The local newspaper has ceased publishing editorials having anything to do with the situation, but this week they published a very long letter from the Methodist minister, who decided to speak out in public also. The fanatic opposition is temporarily quiet, and they have lost all prestige in the community; although the community is still torn with false statistics, propaganda, and residual beliefs aroused against the Negroes and Jews. Perhaps it might be more exact to say that there are a number of individual fanatics left in town—men and women who still think they acted gloriously and who think it would have been even more glorious if a Negro or two had been killed— "just to show them." But these people have no respect for the radical leaders, and not much respect for each other.

j. The subsidiary effects arising from the crisis situation were horrifying to most of the people who now view them in retrospect. These effects would appear to be:

1) The pattern of a fanatical group taking over, forming a dictatorship as oppressive to the white race as to the Negroes.

2) The pattern of working on the young and teaching them bigotry and prejudice.

3) The pattern of the destruction of reverence for values which most people consider of prime importance: namely, destruction of reverence for law, for religion, for human persons, for privacy of conscience.

k. Most people think it will take a long time to overcome the great damage done in these crisis-weeks in this community.

SUMMARY OF ANSWERS TO QUESTIONS ASKED
BY THE AUTHOR OF CITIZENS OF MANSFIELD

Q—Do you think most people in this community favor or oppose desegregation?

A—Most people still oppose it.

Q—Is this true of the Negro population?

A—Yes, at least compulsory desegregation.

Q—Do you think that most people favor the use of force, if necessary, to maintain school segregation?

A—Certainly they did at the time. It is touch and go now. Another test might prove that most still do (out of stubbornness, rather than deep conviction). It might also, if there were enough people willing to express their true feelings, show that most people do not.

Q—Do most people believe that desegregation is inevitable?

A—Most do now.

Q—Does the Negro populace favor the use of force for desegregation?

A—Not the populace of Mansfield, certainly; but that of peripheral areas would appear to.

Q—Estimate of status of race relations before and after crisis?

A—Superficially cordial before crisis. Distrust, resentment, afterward. This will linger for a very long time, in my opinion, and nothing but a reversal (unlikely) could erase it.

Q—Is there any likelihood of reprisals against members of the white race who are involved in opposing integration?

A—No, not by other members of this community; although the most rabid ones are being looked upon with general disfavor. A healthy sign is that people are disgusted with them and that their tactics have ultimately defeated them more than any open opposition could have.

Q—Is there likelihood of reprisals against Negroes who oppose desegregation?

A—Not on the local level.

Q—Are there reprisals against whites supporting desegregation?

A—At the time of the crisis, such a man would have been in great danger. Far less so now, except perhaps by a small group. Still, he would probably be ostracized generally, even at this point.

Q—Are there reprisals against Negroes actively fighting for desegregation?

A—On the local level, such a person would be in great danger. He would at least be driven out, but most probably killed.

Q—Do you think many, some or none of the local white residents would abide by the Supreme Court decision to the extent of not using force against desegregation processes?

A—Some—but this depends entirely on the groundwork. The people will follow strong leaders whether those leaders are on the wrong or right side. This has been proved. The Methodist minister in his letter to the editor pleads for respect for the Supreme Court. But for over a year, such respect has been systematically destroyed locally by editorials and letters to the editor in the local papers. It is impossible to foretell. It would depend on whom they followed.

Q—Are white children afraid of physical assault?

A—I think they are more afraid than they admit, particularly the girls. They fear insults more than physical violence. This is not true of children, obviously, but of young teenagers.

Q—Are Negro children afraid of physical assault?

A—They were very much afraid. They are still extremely cautious and nervous.

Q—How do you think the local civic officials feel about desegregation?

A—They feel just like everyone else—they are confused, vague, persecuted, filled with doubts. They oppose it but would probably make some move to leave town again if it were to boil up again in Mansfield.

Q—What is their attitude toward the use of force?

A—They oppose it loudly, but this is lip-service. There is no real opposition to anything here, except outside criticism.

Q—Have economic pressures been brought to bear against the Negroes?

A—Yes, severe ones as demonstrated above.

Q—Have economic pressures been brought to bear against any member of the white community because of this situation?

A—No, because the whites complied under threat of such economic pressures. No severe pressures were actually employed.

Q—At whose request did law enforcement agencies enter the community?

A—At the request of the local constable.

Q—How has the local press responded?

A—It responded to the pressures brought against it—it said just what the White Citizens Councils wanted it to say until recently, when policies were clarified by the owner and new personnel.

Q—Will the students at the school accept desegregation?

A—If properly presented to them, and if their parents and others allow them to, they would certainly accept it. At the present time they would not—not because of convictions about the issue, but because of pressures and prejudices.

Q—Were there outside forces involved in the organization of resistance to desegregation?

A—I can find no evidence that there were. However, they were in evidence almost immediately afterward, and certainly were involved in the latter part of the crisis period.

Q—Were there outside forces involved in the Negroes' attempts to desegregate?

A—Unquestionably, yes. It is significant that the NAACP lost all of its local supporters within the month. Even the local leader, Mr. M., quit in disillusionment and went and apologized to Mr. C. for his part in the NAACP intervention here. It is significant, too, however, that the Negroes behaved with perfect dignity and did nothing in any way untoward during the entire period on the local level. They made themselves invisible, gave no answer, displayed no intention to use force to gain entry to the school, and behaved with perfect tact. This was significant, particularly in view of the accusations against them by the whites, which would have led most people to believe that the Negroes were virtually storming the gates. All of the bad behavior locally was that of the whites. The Negroes advanced their cause considerably by refusing to lower themselves to the indignities practiced by the whites. They showed up far better than those who demonstrated against them.

Q—Do most youngsters of high school age really fear that they, as individuals, will be involved in social mingling with the Negro if he is accepted into the school?

A—I have asked this of many high school students of both sexes, and they all think it is too ridiculous. They fear it for others, yes, but for themselves—they have not the slightest fear they will be involved in social mingling or in any form of mongrelization. Each feels that it would be bad for others, but each feels thoroughly insulated against the danger himself.

Q—What was the group identification of those who participated?

A—Virtually all groups had members there, though

not as representatives of the groups. There were no Jews, but there were Catholics, Protestants, and many White Citizens Council men (who were the only official group represented).

Q—What is your description of the crowd process?

A—This has been described above, but it might be added that they were instructed not to "hit" anyone. Their technique when they wished to oppose anyone was to fix their eyes on him and shuffle forward as a crowd, stirring up much dust and glaring silently at him. They tightened around him. One man was rescued by the rangers from this cordon, thoroughly shocked and shaken emotionally; another was physically shaken and then kicked. All agreed that had these men not been taken out by the police, they might have been trampled to death or seriously injured.

Q—Were leaders actually identified?

A—Yes, both the conservative respected ones and the radicals who assumed the real leadership very quickly.

Q—Did law enforcement officers single them out or were they allowed to remain anonymous with a feeling of security within the crowd?

A—Both—The fanatics were singled out, but sociably. Officers stayed close to them, laughed, joked with them, pretended to join in with them, but were there so that they could prevent any display of violence. However, they did little to prevent anything until the last moment in both instances, and then instead of repudiating the leaders for this violence, they merely escorted the victims to safety.

SOLUTIONS OFFERED

List of solutions suggested by various people during the course of interviews:

1. Texas should secede from the Union.

2. A law should be passed whereby all Negroes not willing to remain in the status quo of segregation, not willing to "keep on just like they are and like we want them" should be allowed to sell out and keep their money, be provided with passage to Africa, given a thousand dollar bonus, and forced to go live with their own kind. It was further suggested that they would lift the level of the savage Africans and thereby do a good service.

3. The radical element in Mansfield should have been arrested the first day of the mob action and put into jail. Anyone defying the law should have been immediately arrested. They should not have been allowed to interfere by threats of force with what is clearly the law. It is felt by this man that such an action at the outset would have solved the problem quickly and effectively and at least have averted the precedent establishing success of the Mansfield efforts. This success, he pointed out, has resulted in stickers and mottos being widely distributed, which read: REMEMBER MANSFIELD.

4. At the age of fourteen, any Negro boy who chooses would be sent, all expenses paid, to the "North"; any Negro refusing this would be subjected to painless and proper sterilization, if not by law, then by groups of responsible citizens.

5. Schools should be segregated according to sex rather than race, having all-boys schools and all-girl schools, through high school; then integrated colleges.

6. One Negro suggested that if they segregated schools according to intelligence rather than race, it might prove of interest.

7. The Congress should impeach the entire Supreme Court and begin again.

8. All Jews should be sent to Israel, all Catholics should be shipped to Rome, all Communists should be shipped to Russia, all Negroes should be shipped to Africa and leave America to the Americans. It was further suggested that each of these groups be dumped half-way across and allowed to swim the rest of the way.

All of these opinions except No. 6, were offered with complete seriousness by those proposing them.

TRACEABLE SUBSIDIARY EFFECTS

1. *Anti-Semitism,* strong since propaganda has blamed Jews for activities of NAACP.

2. *Anti-Semitism* implied, since some publicity has referred to Hitler's eradication of the Jews as a model we should follow in eradicating the threat of Negro racial "pollution."

3. *Anti-Christianity,* very pronounced in editorials denouncing "pinhead preachers" who advocate the brotherhood of man.

A) *Anti-Catholicism,* slight.

B) *Anti-Methodism,* strong in some quarters due to recent official stand taken by Methodists on desegregation issue.

C) *Anti-Episcopalianism,* pronounced due to the attempts of Rev. Clark to intervene in the mob action.

4. *Anti-Community Chest & United Fund,* due to propaganda put out by National Citizens Protective Assn., St. Louis, Mo., alleging that local United Fund supports "the anti-white conspiracies of the Urban League."

5. *Anti-Juridic,* since this has convinced many that the Supreme Court's decision was wrong and ineffectual and that thereby it need not be re-

spected. Indeed, this feeling is powerful here and it has resulted in complete loss of respect for the Supreme Courts of state and nation.

Editorial from the Mansfield News, *Sept. 20, 1956*

PRECIOUS AMERICAN HERITAGE AT STAKE

We, the American people are right back where our forefathers were when they left England to escape oppression. They wanted religious freedom and were willing to endure untold hardships to gain that freedom.

Today we are facing oppression of a different kind. Our personal freedom is at stake, our racial freedom is being violated. It is a time for all true Americans to open their eyes and their ears. None is so blind as he who WILL not see, says an old quotation. Hatreds are being promoted between races which have gotten along together for lo, these many years. Why can't the whites of this land, as well as the Negroes, see that they are both being used as pawns in a Communistic game to disrupt our nation? Some advocates of integration have been brain-washed by pin-headed, religious fanatical preachers who get up in pulpits all over the land and shout, "The Negro is your brother, the Bible says so, you must have him in your home, in your church and in your school." And, he might add, in your family. The Bible does not say anything about accepting the Negro as an equal.

The two races are as different in customs, ways of thinking and in ideals as they are in color. "East is East, West is West and never the twain shall meet," is just as true as the day it was written. In fact a seer of no mean ability must have written it.

Appendix I

ABOUT MANSFIELD

The picture of the former generations in Mansfield is clear: a town quite individualized; respect for religion, but perhaps little display of reverence for it. It was a good and necessary thing for the women. Men often used the meetings, revivals, etc. as a place to pick up girls. There was a type of delicious humor in their blasphemies and attitudes (delicious to them) that, however, left little room for doubt that when an issue of importance or honor was at stake, the men would behave according to ultimate principles. Brought up with reverence for womenfolks.

People in those days had a strange education. The schooling comprised classical studies, years of Latin, etc. The literary diet was chiefly that of Dickens, Browning, Mark Twain, etc. Families that had no conveniences, with children who worked the fields from morning till night, considered it basically necessary to have good books for the family to read during the winter or at bedtime. The humor was rough and robust, men accepted their animality almost casually insofar as modesty about their physical functions was concerned. They used a very blunt and straightforward language in connection with all of this in preference to more covered words, which they well knew how to use. It was a sort of honesty. with them and not a mark of ignorance, for most of the old timers can speak and write with a great flair for rhetorical language.

And yet the reading matter was the classics, and in letters, these men express themselves in great richness and proper choice of words.

They looked on nature with complete acceptance; they handled crimes with relative casualness —or at least they speak of it that way now. "I was riding home from a date, it was real late and I was on horseback and had to pass this cottonwood thicket where we'd hanged a man for horse stealing a couple of days earlier. They'd just cut him down and tossed his body in the creek bed, and I'm riding through there in the dark, and I began to think about that and really gave that horse the spur. I'se glad to get out of there."

Murder was considered commonplace. It has been stated that the people who today are the largest property-owners are that way because their forefathers did the most killing. On at least one occasion, straws were drawn to see who would kill the local constable. The one who drew the straw showed up in town with his shotgun, sat on a box in front of one of the stores, and talked with other men until the constable walked down the street. Then he said: "You all better get on inside. I'm going to kill Emmett." And he shot him with the calmness of doing any necessary job.

On the other hand, we see a community more than counterbalanced in the opposite direction. No farmer could get into a jam without his neighbors giving unstintingly of their help. There is a feeling of great underlying decency among the people. A superficial view might indicate that in a crisis condition such as we are now facing, the qualities of generosity, justice, kindness, rationality, etc., have faded into the background and only the tradition of violence shows through in the mob we have seen here in Mansfield. The countering qualities have become momentarily obscured.

Selection *28*

The Men from Mars

John Houseman

Davenport's account of camp-meetings and Griffin and Freedman's report of the desegregation crisis in Mansfield, Texas, were examples of crowds whose members were able to communicate and to stimulate one another. In his book LeBon dealt only with crowds whose members were close together, but he included in his typology of crowds one whose members—curiously enough—were physically separated.

What happens when widely dispersed people are all struck by the same observation or emotion at the same time? LeBon did not say, nor did he foresee the revolution in communications that would make such a situation possible. The telegraph, telephone, transatlantic cable, radio, television, and now the communications satellite, however, have made it possible for the attention of the whole world to be fixed on a single event. One of the earliest examples of crowd action stimulated by the mass media of communication was touched off by a radio broadcast on October 30, 1938. On that evening the Mercury Theater, a dramatic radio series produced and directed by the celebrated actor Orson Welles, presented an adaptation of H. G. Wells' *The War of the Worlds*. The play told of the invasion of New Jersey and New York City by Martians armed with terrifying weapons.

There is no way of knowing how many Americans panicked as a result of the program; the following account of the incident by John Houseman, co-founder of the Mercury Theater, probably exaggerates it somewhat, but a crowd response on a national scale did occur. The effect was especially marked in New Jersey where the "invaders" first appeared.

What characterized the crowd processes of the widely separated listeners? At first, emotional contagion was limited to small groups of people—families, friends, fraternities, and the like—and within these groups more rational heads may have succeeded in preventing panic. But to the extent that the radio program managed to drive small groups into the streets where they could merge with others, LeBon's typical crowd processes were operative. Indeed, in many parts of the United States people rushed outside, milled about, or tried to flee from the Martians. (This behavior also illustrates the tenet of modern sociology which holds that people react to their own definitions of reality.)

Why were so many Americans susceptible to this fantastic and logically untenable tale (the invaders marched across most of New Jersey into New York City between the start of the program and the station break)? In Davenport's account of camp-meetings, lack of opportunity for emotional expression was proposed as one factor in the evolution of mobs. Although the harshness of frontier life had disappeared by 1938, new sources of frustration had been produced by industrialization. Millions of Americans were left jobless by the Great Depression. Manager-worker conflicts erupted in sit-down strikes in the factories. The rise of Nazism and Fascism in Europe was another source of apprehension. Much of the popularity of the new media of communication—this was the heyday of the movies and soap operas—was that they afforded a temporary release from everyday troubles. People accepted the rapid course of events in the Martian invasion tale because they had become accustomed to—as Houseman calls it—"dramatic" rather than "real" time. Thus both the anxieties of the thirties and the constant exposure to the content of the new media combined to make many Americans vulnerable to the excitement and release of the Martian invasion.

What individuals were most likely to be taken in by the broadcast? The student is invited to formulate some hypotheses concerning their distribution. Was it primarily those who suffered most from the effects of the depression—the poor, the jobless, the uneducated, the oppressed minority groups, those whose lives were emotionally and materially impoverished?[1]

The revolution in mass communications has thus added a new dimension to collective behavior. Millions of people who are widely dispersed can see the same object at the same time and react like mobs, first in small groups, then in larger ones. It is even possible now for crowd behavior in one part of the world to ignite mob action in another, as when groups of anti-American students in tandem, so to speak, attack American embassies. Another such incident, the "swastika epidemic," started in West Germany in December, 1959, and spread to the United States and other countries. Over six hundred incidents occurred in the United States in which swastikas were smeared on buildings and automobiles in predominantly Jewish neighborhoods. With the instantaneous worldwide publicity given each occurrence, the emotional contagion spread from one group of anti-Semitic youths to another. This particular episode also illustrates, as did the Griffin and Freedman study, that crowd behavior is often linked to racial and ethnic hatred.

The show came off. There is no doubt about that. It set out to dramatize, in terms of popular apprehension, an attempted invasion of our world by hostile forces from the planet Mars. It succeeded. Of the several million American citizens who, on the evening of October 30, 1938, milled about the streets, clung sobbing to one another or drove wildly in all directions to avoid asphyxiation and flaming death, approximately one-half were in terror of Martians—not of Germans, Japanese, or unknown enemies—but, specifically, of Martians. Later, when the excitement was over and the shadow of the gallows had lifted, some of us were inclined to take credit for more deliberate and premeditated villainy than we deserved. The truth is that at the time, nobody was more surprised than we were. In fact, one of the most remarkable things about the broadcast was the quite haphazard nature of its birth.

In October 1938, the Mercury Theater, of which Orson Welles and I were the founding partners, had been in existence for less than a year. Our first Broadway season had been shatteringly successful—"Julius Caesar," "The Cradle Will Rock," "Shoemaker's Holiday," and "Heartbreak

House" in the order of their appearance. In April, Orson, in a straggly white beard, made the cover of *Time* Magazine. In June, the Columbia Broadcasting System offered him a radio show—"The Mercury Theater on the Air," a series of classic dramatizations in the first person singular with Orson as master of ceremonies, star, narrator, writer, director, and producer. He accepted. So, now, in addition to an empty theater, a movie in progress, two plays in rehearsal, and all seven of the chronicle plays of William Shakespeare in preparation, we had a radio show.

We opened on July 11. Among our first thirteen shows were "Treasure Island," "39 Steps," "Abraham Lincoln," "Three Short Stories" (by Saki, Sherwood Anderson, and Carl Ewald), "Jane Eyre," "Julius Caesar" (with running commentary by Kaltenborn out of Plutarch), and "The Man Who Was Thursday." Our second series, in the fall, began with Booth Tarkington's "Seventeen," "Around the World in Eighty Days," and "Oliver

From *Harper's Magazine*, December 1948, pp. 74-82.
[1] The student may check his hypotheses against the data in Hadley Cantril's *The Invasion from Mars*. (Princeton, N.J.: Princeton University Press, 1940).

Twist." Our fifth show was to be "Life with Father." Our fourth was "The War of the Worlds."

No one, as I remember, was very enthusiastic about it. But it seemed good programming, between the terrors of Dickens' London slums, and the charm of Clarence Day's New York in the nineties, to throw in something of a contrasting and pseudo-scientific nature. We thought of Shiel's *Purple Cloud,* Conan Doyle's *Lost World,* and several others before we settled on H. G. Wells' twenty-year-old novel, which neither of us, as it turned out later, remembered at all clearly. It is just possible that neither of us had ever read it.

II

Those were our golden days of unsponsored radio. We had no advertising agency to harass us, no client to cut our withers. Partly because we were perpetually overworked and partly because that was the way we did things at the Mercury, we never seemed to get more than a single jump ahead of ourselves. Shows were created week after week under conditions of soul- and health-destroying pressure. On the whole they were good shows. And we *did* develop a system—of sorts.

It worked as follows: I was editor of the series. With Welles, I chose the shows and then laid them out. The writing, most of it, was done by Howard Koch—earnest, spindly, six-foot-two—a Westchester lawyer turned playwright. To write the first draft of an hour's radio script took him about five days, working about fifteen hours a day. Our associate producer was Paul Stewart, a Broadway actor turned director. His function was to put the broadcast through its first paces and preliminary rehearsals. Every Thursday, musicless and with rudimentary sound effects, a wax record of the show was cut. From this record, played back later that night, Orson would give us his reactions and revisions. In the next thirty-six hours the script would be reshaped and rewritten, sometimes drastically. Saturday afternoon there was another rehearsal, with sound—with or without Welles. It was not until the last day that Orson really took over.

Sundays, at eight, we went on the air. Beginning in the early afternoon—when Bernard Herrmann arrived with his orchestra of twenty-seven high-grade symphony players—two simultaneous dramas were regularly unfolded in the stale, tense air of Studio Number One: the minor drama of the current show and the major drama of Orson's gargantuan struggle to get it on. Sweating, howling, disheveled, and single-handed he wrestled with Chaos and Time—always conveying an effect of being alone, traduced by his collaborators, surrounded by treachery, ignorance, sloth, indifference, incompetence and—more often than not—downright sabotage! Every Sunday it was touch and go. As the hands of the clock moved relentlessly toward air time the crisis grew more extreme, the peril more desperate. Often violence broke out. Scripts flew through the air, doors were slammed, batons smashed. Scheduled for six—but usually nearer seven—there was a dress rehearsal, a thing of wild improvisations and irrevocable disaster. (One show was found to be twenty-one minutes overlength, another fourteen and one-half minutes short.)

After that, with only a few minutes to go, there was a final frenzy of correction and reparation, of utter confusion and absolute horror, aggravated by the gobbling of sandwiches and the bolting of oversized milkshakes. By now it was less than a minute to air time. . . .

At that instant, quite regularly week after week—with not one second to spare . . . the titanic buffoonery stopped. Suddenly out of chaos, the show emerged—delicately poised, meticulously executed, precise as clockwork, and smooth as satin. And above us all, like a rainbow over storm clouds, stood Orson on his podium, sonorous and heroic, a leader of men surrounded by his band of loyal followers; a giant in action, serene and radiant with the joy of a hard battle bravely fought—a great victory snatched from the jaws of disaster.

In later years, when the Men from Mars had passed into history, there was some bickering among members of the Mercury as to who, exactly, had contributed precisely what, to that particular evening's entertainment. The truth is that a number of us made a number of essential and incalculable contributions to the broadcast. (Who can accurately assess, for instance, the part played by Johnny Dietz's perfect engineering, in keeping unbroken the shifting illusion of imperfect reality? How much did the original old H. G. Wells, who noisily repudiated us, have to do with it? Or the second assistant sound man? Or individual actors? Or Dr. Goebbels? Or Charlie McCarthy?) Orson Welles had virtually nothing to do with the writing of the script and less than usual to do with its preliminary rehearsals. Yet first and last it was his creation. If there had been a lynching that night, it is Welles the outraged populace would have strung up—and rightly so. Orson was the Mercury. "The War of the Worlds," like everything we did, was his show.

Actually, it was a narrow squeak. Those Men from Mars barely escaped being still-born. Tuesday afternoon—five days before the show—Howard

Koch telephoned. He was in deep distress. After three days of slaving on H. G. Wells' scientific fantasy he was ready to give up. Under no circumstances, he declared, could it be made interesting or in any way credible to modern American ears. Koch was not given to habitual alarmism. To confirm his fears, Annie, our secretary, came to the phone. She was an acid and emphatic girl from Smith College with fine blond hair, who smelled of fading spring flowers. "You can't do it!" she whined. "Those old Martians are just a lot of nonsense. It's all too silly! We're going to make fools of ourselves! Absolute fools!"

For some reason which I do not clearly remember our only possible alternative for that week was a dreary one—"Lorna Doone." I tried to reach Welles. He was at the theater and wouldn't come to the phone.

The reason he wouldn't come to the phone was that he was in his thirty-sixth successive hour of dress-rehearsing "Danton's Death," a beautiful, fragmentary play by Georg Buechner out of which Max Reinhardt, in an augmented form, had made a successful mass-spectacle in the twenties. Not to be outdone, Orson had glued seventeen hundred masks on to the back wall of the Mercury Theater, and ripped out the entire stage. Day after day actors fell headlong into the rat-ridden basement, leaped on and off erratically moving elevators, and chanted the "Carmagnole" in chorus under the supervision of Marc Blitzstein.

Unable to reach Welles, I called Koch back. I was severe. I taxed him with defeatism. I gave him false comfort. I promised to come up and help. When I finally got there—around two the next morning—things were better. He was beginning to have fun laying waste the State of New Jersey. Annie had stopped grinding her teeth. We worked all night and through the next day. Wednesday at sunset the script was finished.

Thursday, as usual, Paul Stewart rehearsed the show, then made a record. We listened to it rather gloomily, long after midnight in Orson's room at the St. Regis, sitting on the floor because all the chairs were covered with coils of unrolled and unedited film. We agreed it was a dull show. We all felt its only chance of coming off lay in emphasizing its newscast style—its simultaneous, eyewitness quality.

All night we sat up, spicing the script with circumstantial allusions and authentic detail. Friday afternoon it went over to CBS to be passed by the network censor. Certain name alterations were requested. Under protest and with a deep sense of grievance we changed the Hotel Biltmore to a non-existent Park Plaza, Trans-America to Intercontinent, the Columbia Broadcasting Build-ing to Broadcasting Building. Then the script went over to mimeograph and we went to bed. We had done our best and, after all, a show is just a show. . . .

Saturday afternoon Paul Stewart rehearsed with sound effects but without Welles. He worked for a long time on the crowd scenes, the roar of cannon echoing in the Watchung Hills and the sound of New York Harbor as the ships with the last remaining survivors put out to sea.

Around six we left the studio. Orson, phoning from the theater a few minutes later to find out how things were going, was told by one of the CBS sound men, who had stayed behind to pack up his equipment, that it was not one of our better shows. Confidentially, the man opined, it just didn't come off. Twenty-seven hours later, quite a few of his employers would have found themselves a good deal happier if he had turned out to be right.

III

On Sunday, October 30, at 8:00 P.M., E.S.T., in a studio littered with coffee cartons and sandwich paper, Orson swallowed a second container of pineapple juice, put on his earphones, raised his long white fingers and threw the cue for the Mercury theme—the Tchaikovsky Piano Concerto in B Flat Minor #1. After the music dipped, there were routine introductions—then the announcement that a dramatization of H. G. Wells' famous novel, *The War of the Worlds*, was about to be performed. Around 8:01 Orson began to speak, as follows:

Welles

"We know now that in the early years of the twentieth century this world was being watched closely by intelligences greater than man's and yet as mortal as his own. We know now that as human beings busied themselves about their various concerns they were scrutinized and studied, perhaps almost as narrowly as a man with a microscope might scrutinize the transient creatures that swarm and multiply in a drop of water. With infinite complacence people went to and fro over the earth about their little affairs, serene in the assurance of their dominion over this small spinning fragment of solar driftwood which by chance or design man has inherited out of the dark mystery of Time and Space. Yet across an immense ethereal gulf minds that are to our minds as ours are to the beasts in the jungle, intellects vast, cool, and unsympathetic regarded this earth with envious eyes and slowly and surely drew their plans against us. In the thirty-ninth year of the twentieth century came the great disillusionment.

"It was near the end of October. Business was better. The war scare was over. More men were back at work. Sales were picking up. On this particular evening, October 30, the Crossley service estimated that thirty-two million people were listening in on their radios. . . ."

Neatly, without perceptible transition, he was followed on the air by an anonymous announcer caught in a routine bulletin:

Announcer

". . . for the next twenty-four hours not much change in temperature. A slight atmospheric disturbance of undetermined origin is reported over Nova Scotia, causing a low pressure area to move down rather rapidly over the northeastern states, bringing a forecast of rain, accompanied by winds of light gale force. Maximum temperature 66; minimum 48. This weather report comes to you from the Government Weather Bureau. . . . We now take you to the Meridian Room in the Hotel Park Plaza in downtown New York, where you will be entertained by the music of Ramon Raquello and his orchestra."

At which cue, Bernard Herrmann led the massed men of the CBS house orchestra in a thunderous rendition of "La Cumparsita." The entire hoax might well have exploded there and then—but for the fact that hardly anyone was listening. They were being entertained by Charlie McCarthy—then at the height of his success.

The Crossley census, taken about a week before the broadcast, had given us 3.6 per cent of the listening audience to Edgar Bergen's 34.7 per cent. What the Crossley Institute (that hireling of the advertising agencies) deliberately ignored, was the healthy American habit of dial-twisting. On that particular evening, Edgar Bergen in the person of Charlie McCarthy temporarily left the air about 8:12 P.M., E.S.T., yielding place to a new and not very popular singer. At that point, and during the following minutes, a large number of listeners started twisting their dials in search of other entertainment. Many of them turned to us—and when they did, they stayed put! For by this time the mysterious meteorite had fallen at Grovers Mill in New Jersey, the Martians had begun to show their foul leathery heads above the ground, and the New Jersey State Police were racing to the spot. Within a few minutes people all over the United States were praying, crying, fleeing frantically to escape death from the Martians. Some remembered to rescue loved ones, others telephoned farewells or warnings, hurried to inform neighbors, sought information from newspapers or radio stations, summoned ambulances and police cars.

The reaction was strongest at points nearest the tragedy—in Newark, New Jersey, in a single block, more than twenty families rushed out of their houses with wet handkerchiefs and towels over their faces. Some began moving household furniture. Police switchboards were flooded with calls inquiring, "Shall I close my windows?" "Have the police any extra gas masks?" Police found one family waiting in the yard with wet cloths on faces contorted with hysteria. As one woman reported later:

"I was terribly frightened. I wanted to pack and take my child in my arms, gather up my friends and get in the car and just go north as far as we could. But what I did was just sit by one window, praying, listening, and scared stiff, and my husband by the other sniffling and looking out to see if people were running. . . ."

In New York hundreds of people on Riverside Drive left their homes ready for flight. Bus terminals were crowded. A woman calling up the Dixie Bus Terminal for information said impatiently, "Hurry please, the world is coming to an end and I have a lot to do."

In the parlor churches of Harlem evening service became "end of the world" prayer meetings. Many turned to God in that moment:

"I held a crucifix in my hand and prayed while looking out of my open window for falling meteors. . . . When the monsters were wading across the Hudson River and coming into New York, I wanted to run up on my roof to see what they looked like, but I couldn't leave my radio while it was telling me of their whereabouts."

"Aunt Grace began to pray with Uncle Henry. Lily got sick to her stomach. I don't know what I did exactly but I know I prayed harder and more earnestly than ever before. Just as soon as we were convinced that this thing was real, how petty all things on this earth seemed; how soon we put our trust in God!"

The panic moved upstate. One man called up the Mt. Vernon Police Headquarters to find out "where the forty policemen were killed." Another took time out to philosophize:

"I thought the whole human race was going to be wiped out—that seemed more important than the fact that we were going to die. It seemed awful that everything that had been worked on for years was going to be lost forever."

In Rhode Island weeping and hysterical women swamped the switchboard of the Providence *Journal* for details of the massacre, and officials of the electric light company received a score of calls urging them to turn off all lights so that the city would be safe from the enemy. The Boston *Globe* received a call from one woman "who could see the fire." A man in Pittsburgh hurried home in the midst of the broadcast and found his wife in the bathroom, a bottle of poison in her hand, screaming, "I'd rather die this way than that." In Minneapolis a woman ran into church screaming, "New York destroyed this is the end of the world. You might as well go home to die I just heard it on the radio."

The Kansas City Bureau of the AP received inquiries about the "meteors" from Los Angeles; Salt Lake City; Beaumont, Texas; and St. Joseph, Missouri. In San Francisco the general impression of listeners seemed to be that an overwhelming force had invaded the United States from the air—was in process of destroying New York and threatening to move westward. "My God," roared an inquirer into a telephone, "where can I volunteer my services, we've got to stop this awful thing!"

As far south as Birmingham, Alabama, people gathered in churches and prayed. On the campus of a Southeastern college—

"The girls in the sorority houses and dormitories huddled around their radios trembling and weeping in each other's arms. They separated themselves from their friends only to take their turn at the telephones to make long distance calls to their parents, saying goodbye for what they thought might be the last time. . . ."

There are hundreds of such bits of testimony, gathered from coast to coast.

IV

At least one book and quite a pile of sociological literature has appeared on the subject of "The Invasion from Mars." Many theories have been put forward to explain the "tidal wave" of panic that swept the nation. I know of two factors that largely contributed to the broadcast's extraordinarily violent effect. First, its historical timing. It came within thirty-five days of the Munich crisis. For weeks, the American people had been hanging on their radios, getting most of their news no longer from the press, but over the air. A new technique of "on-the-spot" reporting had been developed and eagerly accepted by an anxious and news-hungry world. The Mercury Theater on the Air by faithfully copying every detail of the new technique—including its imperfections—found an already enervated audience ready to accept its wildest fantasies. The second factor was the show's sheer technical brilliance. To this day it is impossible to sit in a room and hear the scratched, worn, off-the-air recording of the broadcast, without feeling in the back of your neck some slight draft left over from the great wind of terror that swept the nation. Even with the element of credibility totally removed it remains a surprisingly frightening show.

Radio drama was taken seriously in the thirties—before the Quiz and the Giveaway became the lords of the air. In the work of such directors as Reis, Corwin, Fickett, Welles, Robson, Spier, and Oboler there was an eager, excited drive to get the most out of this new, all too rapidly freezing medium. But what happened that Sunday, up on the twentieth floor of the CBS building was something quite special. Beginning around two, when the show started to take shape under Orson's hands, a strange fever seemed to invade the studio—part childish mischief, part professional zeal.

First to feel it were the actors. I remember Frank Readick (who played the part of Carl Phillips, the network's special reporter) going down to the record library and digging up the Morrison recording of the explosion of the Hindenburg at Lakehurst. This is a classic reportage—one of those wonderful, unpredictable accidents of eyewitness description. The broadcaster is casually describing a routine landing of the giant gasbag. Suddenly he sees something. A flash of flame! An instant later the whole thing explodes. It takes him time—a full second—to react at all. Then seconds more of sputtering ejaculations before he can make the adjustment between brain and tongue. He starts to describe the terrible things he sees—the writhing human figures twisting and squirming as they fall from the white burning wreckage. He stops, fumbles, vomits, then quickly continues. Readick played the record to himself, over and over. Then, recreating the emotion in his own terms, he described the Martian meteorite as he saw it lying inert and harmless in a field at Grovers Mill, lit up by the headlights of a hundred cars—the coppery cylinder suddenly opening, revealing the leathery tentacles and the terrible pale-eyed faces of the Martians within. As they begin to emerge he freezes, unable to translate his vision into words; he fumbles, retches —and then after a second continues.

A few moments later Carl Phillips lay dead, tumbling over the microphone in his fall—one of the first victims of the Martian Ray. There followed a moment of absolute silence—an eternity of waiting. Then, without warning, the network's emergency fill-in was heard—somewhere in a quiet studio, a piano, close on mike, playing "Clair de Lune," soft and sweet as honey, for many seconds, while the fate of the universe hung in the balance. Finally it was interrupted by the manly reassuring voice of Brigadier General Montgomery Smith, Commander of the New Jersey State Militia, speaking from Trenton, and placing "the counties of Mercer and Middlesex as far west as Princeton and east to Jamesburg" under Martial Law! Tension—release—then renewed tension. For soon after that came an eyewitness account of the fatal battle of the Watchung Hills; and then, once again, that lone piano was heard—now a symbol of terror, shattering the dead air with its ominous tinkle. As it played, on and on, its effect became increasingly sinister—a thin band of suspense stretched almost beyond endurance.

That piano was the neatest trick of the show— a fine specimen of the theatrical "retard," boldly conceived and exploited to the full. It was one of the many devices with which Welles succeeded in compelling, not merely the attention, but also the belief of his invisible audience. "The War of the Worlds" was a magic act, one of the world's greatest, and Orson was just the man to bring it off.

For Welles is at heart a magician whose particular talent lies not so much in his creative imagination (which is considerable) as in his proven ability to stretch the familiar elements of theatrical effect far beyond their normal point of tension. For this reason his productions require more elaborate preparation and more perfect execution than most. At that—like all complicated magic tricks—they remain, till the last moment, in a state of precarious balance. When they come off, they give—by virtue of their unusually high intensity—an impression of great brilliance and power; when they fail—when something in their balance goes wrong or the original structure proves to have been unsound—they provoke, among their audience, a particularly violent reaction of unease and revulsion. Welles' flops are louder than other men's. The Mars broadcast was one of his unqualified successes.

Among the columnists and public figures who discussed the affair during the next few days (some praising us for the public service we had rendered, some condemning us as sinister scoundrels) the most general reaction was one of amazement at the "incredible stupidity" and "gullibility" of the American public, who had accepted as real, in this single broadcast, incidents which in actual fact would have taken days or even weeks to occur. "Nothing about the broadcast," wrote Dorothy Thompson with her usual aplomb, "was in the least credible." She was wrong. The first few minutes of our broadcast were, in point of fact, strictly realistic in time and perfectly credible, though somewhat boring, in content. Herein lay the great tensile strength of the show; it was the structural device that made the whole illusion possible. And it could have been carried off in no other medium than radio.

Our actual broadcasting time, from the first mention of the meteorites to the fall of New York City, was less than forty minutes. During that time men traveled long distances, large bodies of troops were mobilized, cabinet meetings were held, savage battles fought on land and in the air. And millions of people accepted it—emotionally if not logically.

There is nothing so very strange about that. Most of us do the same thing, to some degree, most days of our lives—every time we look at a movie or listen to a broadcast. Not even the realistic theater observes the literal unities; motion pictures and, particularly, radio (where neither place nor time exists save in the imagination of the listener) have no difficulty in getting their audiences to accept the telescoped reality of dramatic time. Our special hazard lay in the fact that we purported to be, not a play, but reality. In order to take advantage of the accepted convention, we had to slide swiftly and imperceptibly out of the "real" time of a news report into the "dramatic" time of a fictional broadcast. Once that was achieved—without losing the audience's attention or arousing their skepticism, if they could be sufficiently absorbed and bewitched not to notice the transition—then, we felt, there was no extreme of fantasy through which they would not follow us. We were keenly aware of our problem; we found what we believed was the key to its solution. And if, that night, the American public proved "gullible," it was because enormous pains and a great deal of thought had been spent to make it so.

In the script, "The War of the Worlds" started extremely slowly—dull meteorological and astronomical bulletins alternating with musical interludes. These were followed by a colorless scientific interview and still another stretch of dance music. These first few minutes of routine broadcasting "within the existing standards of judgment of the listener" were intended to lull (or maybe bore) the audience into a false security and to furnish a solid base of realistic time from which to accelerate later. Orson, in making over the show, extended this slow movement far beyond our original conception. "La Cumparsita," rendered by "Ramon Raquello, from the Meridian Room of the Hotel Park Plaza in downtown New York," had been thought of as running only a few seconds; "Bobby Millette playing 'Stardust' from the Hotel Martinet in Brooklyn," even less. At rehearsal Orson stretched both these numbers to what seemed to us, in the control room, an almost unbearable length. We objected. The interview in the Princeton Observatory—the clockwork ticking monotonously overhead, the woolly-minded professor mumbling vague replies to the reporters' uninformed questions—this, too, he dragged out to a point of tedium. Over our protests, lines were restored that had been cut at earlier rehearsals. We cried there would not be a listener left. Welles stretched them out even longer.

He was right. His sense of tempo, that night, was infallible. When the flashed news of the cylinder's landing finally came—almost fifteen minutes after the beginning of a fairly dull show—he was able suddenly to spiral his action to a speed as wild and reckless as its base was solid. The appearance of the Martians; their first treacherous act; the death of Carl Phillips; the arrival of the militia; the battle of the Watchung Hills; the destruction of New Jersey—all of these were telescoped into a space of twelve minutes without overstretching the listeners' emotional credulity. The broadcast, by then, had its own reality, the reality of emotionally felt time and space.

v

At the height of the crisis, around 8:31, the Secretary of the Interior came on the air with an exhortation to the American people. His words, as you read them now, ten years later, have a Voltairean ring. (They were admirably spoken—in a voice just faintly reminiscent of the President's—by a young man named Kenneth Delmar, who has since grown rich and famous as Senator Claghorn.)

The Secretary

"Citizens of the nation: I shall not try to conceal the gravity of the situation that confronts the country, nor the concern of your Government in protecting the lives and property of its people. However, I wish to impress upon you—private citizens and public officials, all of you—the urgent need of calm and resourceful action. Fortunately, this formidable enemy is still confined to a comparatively small area, and we may place our faith in the military forces to keep them there. In the meantime placing our trust in God, we must continue the performance of our duties, each and every one of us, so that we may confront this destructive adversary with a nation united, courageous, and consecrated to the preservation of human supremacy on this earth. I thank you."

Toward the end of this speech (*circa* 8:32 E.S.T.), Davidson Taylor, supervisor of the broadcast for the Columbia Broadcasting System, received a phone call in the control room, creased his lips, and hurriedly left the studio. By the time he returned, a few moments later—pale as death—clouds of heavy smoke were rising from Newark, New Jersey, and the Martians, tall as skyscrapers, were astride the Pulaski Highway preparatory to wading the Hudson River. To us in the studio the show seemed to be progressing splendidly—how splendidly Davidson Taylor had just learned outside. For several minutes now, a kind of madness had seemed to be sweeping the continent—somehow connected with our show. The CBS switchboards had been swamped into uselessness but from outside sources vague rumors were coming in of deaths and suicides and panic injuries.

Taylor had requests to interrupt the show immediately with an explanatory station-announcement. By now the Martians were across the Hudson and gas was blanketing the city. The end was near. We were less than a minute from the Station Break. The organ was allowed to swirl out under the slackening fingers of its failing organist and Ray Collins, superb as the "last announcer," choked heroically to death on the roof of Broadcasting Building. The boats were all whistling for a while as the last of the refugees perished in New York Harbor. Finally, as they died away, an amateur shortwave operator was heard, from heaven knows where, weakly reaching out for human companionship across the empty world:

"2X2L Calling CQ
2X2L Calling CQ
2X2L Calling CQ
Isn't there anyone on the air?
Isn't there anyone?"

Five seconds of absolute silence. Then, shattering

the reality of World's End—the Announcer's voice was heard, suave and bright:

Announcer

"You are listening to the CBS presentation of Orson Welles and the Mercury Theater on the Air in an original dramatization of *The War of the Worlds*, by H. G. Wells. The performance will continue after a brief intermission."

The second part of the show was extremely well written and most sensitively played—but nobody heard it. It recounted the adventures of a lone survivor, with interesting observations on the nature of human society; it described the eventual death of the Martian Invaders, slain— "after all man's defenses had failed by the humblest thing that God in his wisdom had put upon this earth"—by bacteriological action; it told of the rebuilding of a brave new world. After a stirring musical finale, Welles, in his own person, delivered a charming informal little speech about Halloween, which it happened to be.

I remember, during the playing of the final theme, the phone starting to ring in the control room and a shrill voice through the receiver announcing itself as belonging to the mayor of some Midwestern city, one of the big ones. He is screaming for Welles. Choking with fury, he reports mobs in the streets of his city, women and children huddled in the churches, violence and looting. If, as he now learns, the whole thing is nothing but a crummy joke—then he, personally, is coming up to New York to punch the author of it on the nose! Orson hangs up quickly. For we are off the air now and the studio door bursts open. The following hours are a nightmare. The building is suddenly full of people and dark blue uniforms. We are hurried out of the studio, downstairs, into a back office. Here we sit incommunicado while network employees are busily collecting, destroying, or locking up scripts and records of the broadcast. Then the press is let loose upon us, ravening for horror. How many deaths have *we* heard of? (Implying they know of thousands.) What do *we* know of the fatal stampede in a Jersey hall? (Implying it is one of many.) What traffic deaths? (The ditches must be choked with corpses.) The suicides? (Haven't you heard about the one on Riverside Drive?) It is all quite vague in my memory and quite terrible.

Hours later, instead of arresting us, they let us out a back way. We scurry down to the theater like hunted animals to their hole. It is surprising to see life going on as usual in the midnight streets, cars stopping for traffic, people walking. At the Mercury the company is still stoically rehearsing—falling downstairs and singing the "Carmagnole." Welles goes up on stage, where photographers, lying in wait, catch him with his eyes raised up to heaven, his arms outstretched in an attitude of crucifixion. Thus he appeared in a tabloid that morning over the caption, "I Didn't Know What I Was Doing!" The *New York Times* quoted him as saying, "I don't think we will choose anything like this again."

We were on the front page for two days. Having had to bow to radio as a news source during the Munich crisis, the press was now only too eager to expose the perilous irresponsibilities of the new medium. Orson was their whipping boy. They quizzed and badgered him. Condemnatory editorials were delivered by our press-clipping bureau in bushel baskets. There was talk, for a while, of criminal action.

Then gradually, after about two weeks, the excitement subsided. By then it had been discovered that the casualties were not as numerous or as serious as had at first been supposed. One young woman had fallen and broken her arm running downstairs. Later the Federal Communications Commission held some hearings and passed some regulations. The Columbia Broadcasting System made a public apology. With that the official aspects of the incident were closed.

As to the Mercury—our new play, "Danton's Death," finally opened after five postponements. Not even our fantastic publicity was able to offset its generally unfavorable notices. On the other hand, that same week the Mercury Theater on the Air was signed up by Campbell Soups at a most lavish figure.

Of the suits that were brought against us— amounting to over three quarters of a million dollars for damages, injuries, miscarriages, and distresses of various kinds—none was substantiated or legally proved. We did settle one claim however, against the advice of our lawyers. It was the particularly affecting case of a man in Massachusetts, who wrote:

"I thought the best thing to do was to go away. So I took three dollars twenty-five cents out of my savings and bought a ticket. After I had gone sixty miles I knew it was a play. Now I don't have money left for the shoes I was saving up for. Will you please have someone send me a pair of black shoes size 9B!"

We did.

Selection 29
_____

Preposterous Parables: The Decline of Sport

E. B. White

E. B. White's classic, fantastic, and funny short story "The Decline of Sport" suggests that modern industrial society resembles a giant mob. The trend that White travesties is also illustrated by the popularity of the terms introduced by sociologists—the *lonely crowd* and *mass society*. Welles' Martian "invasion" forcefully demonstrated the power of the radio to produce crowd behavior. As noted, the revolution in mass media has continued, thus making the situation White describes not entirely "preposterous."

White's story carries the American passion for spectator sports to an extreme but logical conclusion: a three-day work week to permit people to keep up with the world of sports; the multi-game spectator who simultaneously watches a football game in a stadium, views a horse race on a giant-screen television set provided by thoughtful stadium officials, and listens to the World Series on a portable radio. Indeed, the modern football game itself has become mob-like, with substitutions of players made so often that the main actors have come to have the anonymity typical of crowds. Games are attended by millions of people who drive to stadiums in millions of automobiles on jammed highways—until White's mob-that-ended-all-mobs brings about the inevitable climax. The tale is utterly ridiculous, but so was the very real "invasion" by the Martians—and, after all, people *do* bring transistor radios to sporting events.

Although White deals with the problem only implicitly, the student should consider the forces responsible for mass society. There have been frequent references in this text to the social consequences of industrialization and urbanization. What is the modern city like? It is large, crowded, impersonal; the city-dweller is anonymous. The reader has only to review the accounts of the camp-meeting in Kentucky and the Mansfield race riot to see that the anonymity an individual enjoys in a crowd makes it difficult for traditional controls to restrain his actions. Thus the modern city with its faceless individuals presents optimum conditions for the expression of mob behavior.

The American city was once a collection of many small local communities, each of which had its own organization that influenced the actions of most of its members. But with the introduction of mammoth housing developments, old neighborhoods have been torn down, and informal community organizations—gatherings on the front stoop, fiestas, sodalities, political clubs, and the like—have been lost amid the rubble. Adults who in earlier days were almost totally involved in the community find their activities segmented; they leave the community for work, for recreation—as White shows so well—and for visits with friends. The tightly knit neighborhood organization that used to draw parents together has gone with the slum buildings, with the result that neighbors do not know one another, no longer exchange views with other parents, and hence are unable to develop accepted standards of behavior to impose on their children. The formation of juvenile gangs, which often act like LeBon's typical mob, is greatly facilitated by the loss of both family and community controls. Thus hordes of people in modern society are unorganized and undifferentiated and play no role in community decisions.[1]

White does not deal with all the dimensions of mass society, but he does, implicitly at least, appreciate the contributions to its development made by the passion for sports, modern means of transportation, and the mass media. Not only do sporting events provide the stimulus for people to gather together and act like mobs—there are, after all, riots at games—but they also distract the individual from community participation.

In the third decade of the supersonic age, sport gripped the nation in an ever-tightening grip. The horse tracks, the ballparks, the fight rings, the gridirons, all drew crowds in steadily increasing numbers. Every time a game was played, an attendance record was broken. Usually some other sort of record was broken, too—such as the record for the number of consecutive doubles hit by left-handed batters in a Series game, or some such thing as that. Records fell like ripe apples on a windy day. Customs and manners changed, and the five-day business week was reduced to four days, then to three, to give everyone a better chance to memorize the scores.

Not only did sport proliferate but the demands it made on the spectator became greater. Nobody was content to take in one event at a time, and thanks to the magic of radio and television nobody had to. A Yale alumnus, class of 1962, returning to the Bowl with 197,000 others to see the Yale-Cornell football game would take along his pocket radio and pick up the Yankee Stadium, so that while his eye might be following a fumble on the Cornell twenty-two-yard line, his ear would be following a man going down to second in the top of the fifth, seventy miles away. High in the blue sky above the Bowl, skywriters would be at work writing the scores of other major and minor sporting contests, weaving an interminable record of victory and defeat, and using the new high-visibility pink news-smoke perfected by Pepsi-Cola engineers. And in the frames of the giant video sets, just behind the goalposts, this same alumnus could watch Dejected win the Futurity before a record-breaking crowd of 349,872 at Belmont, each of whom was tuned to the Yale Bowl and following the World Series game in the video and searching the sky for further news of events either under way or just completed. The effect of this vast cyclorama of sport was to divide the spectator's attention, over-subtilize his appreciation, and deaden his passion. As the fourth supersonic decade was ushered in, the picture changed and sport began to wane.

A good many factors contributed to the decline

of sport. Substitutions in football had increased to such an extent that there were very few fans in the United States capable of holding the players in mind during play. Each play that was called saw two entirely new elevens lined up, and the players whose names and faces you had familiarized yourself with in the first period were seldom seen or heard of again. The spectacle became as diffuse as the main concourse in Grand Central at the commuting hour.

Express motor highways leading to the parks and stadia had become so wide, so unobstructed, so devoid of all life except automobiles and trees that sport fans had got into the habit of travelling enormous distances to attend events. The normal driving speed had been stepped up to ninety-five miles an hour, and the distance between cars had been decreased to fifteen feet. This put an extraordinary strain on the sport lover's nervous system, and he arrived home from a Saturday game, after a road trip of three hundred and fifty miles, glassy-eyed, dazed, and spent. He hadn't really had any relaxation and he had failed to see Czlika (who had gone in for Trusky) take the pass from Bkeeo (who had gone in for Bjallo) in the third period, because at that moment a youngster named Lavagetto had been put in to pinch-hit for Art Gurlack in the bottom of the ninth with the tying run on second, and the skywriter who was attempting to write "Princeton 0—Lafayette 43" had banked the wrong way, muffed the "3," and distracted everyone's attention from the fact that Lavagetto had been whiffed.

Cheering, of course, lost its stimulating effect on players, because cheers were no longer asso-

"The Decline of Sport" from *The Second Tree from the Corner* by E. B. White, pp. 41-45. Copyright 1948 by E. B. White. Originally appeared in *The New Yorker*, and reprinted with the permission of Harper & Row, Publishers, Incorporated.
[1] For an excellent discussion of the changing American community, the student is referred to James S. Coleman's "Community Disorganization," in Robert K. Merton and Robert A. Nisbet, eds., *Contemporary Social Problems* (New York: Harcourt, Brace & World, Inc., 1961), pp. 553-604.

ciated necessarily with the immediate scene but might as easily apply to something that was happening somewhere else. This was enough to infuriate even the steadiest performer. A football star, hearing the stands break into a roar before the ball was snapped, would realize that their minds were not on him, and would become dispirited and grumpy. Two or three of the big coaches worried so about this that they considered equipping all players with tiny ear sets, so that they, too, could keep abreast of other sporting events while playing, but the idea was abandoned as impractical, and the coaches put it aside in tickler files, to bring up again later.

I think the event that marked the turning point in sport and started it downhill was the Midwest's classic Dust Bowl game of 1975, when Eastern Reserve's great right end, Ed Pistachio, was shot by a spectator. This man, the one who did the shooting, was seated well down in the stands near the forty-yard line on a bleak October afternoon and was so saturated with sport and with the disappointments of sport that he had clearly become deranged. With a minute and fifteen seconds to play and the score tied, the Eastern Reserve quarterback had whipped a long pass over Army's heads into Pistachio's waiting arms. There was no other player anywhere near him, and all Pistachio had to do was catch the ball and run it across the line. He dropped it. At exactly this moment, the spectator—a man named Homer T. Parkinson, of 35 Edgemere Drive, Toledo, O.—suffered at least three other major disappointments in the realm of sport. His horse, Hiccough, on which he had a five-hundred-dollar bet, fell while getting away from the starting gate at Pimlico and broke its leg (clearly visible in the video); his favorite shortstop, Lucky Frimstitch, struck out and let three men die on base in the final game of the Series (to which Parkinson was tuned); and the Governor Dummer soccer team, on which Parkinson's youngest son played goalie, lost to Kent, 4–3, as recorded in the sky overhead. Before anyone could stop him, he drew a gun

and drilled Pistachio, before 954,000 persons, the largest crowd that had ever attended a football game and the *second*-largest crowd that had ever assembled for any sporting event in any month except July.

This tragedy, by itself, wouldn't have caused sport to decline, I suppose, but it set in motion a chain of other tragedies, the cumulative effect of which was terrific. Almost as soon as the shot was fired, the news flash was picked up by one of the skywriters directly above the field. He glanced down to see whether he could spot the trouble below, and in doing so failed to see another skywriter approaching. The two planes collided and fell, wings locked, leaving a confusing trail of smoke, which some observers tried to interpret as a late sports score. The planes struck in the middle of the nearby eastbound coast-to-coast Sunlight Parkway, and a motorist driving a convertible coupé stopped so short, to avoid hitting them, that he was bumped from behind. The pileup of cars that ensued involved 1,482 vehicles, a record for eastbound parkways. A total of more than three thousand persons lost their lives in the highway accident, including the two pilots, and when panic broke out in the stadium, it cost another 872 in dead and injured. News of the disaster spread quickly to other sports arenas, and started other panics among the crowds trying to get to the exits, where they could buy a paper and study a list of the dead. All in all, the afternoon of sport cost 20,003 lives, a record. And nobody had much to show for it except one small Midwestern boy who hung around the smoking wrecks of the planes, captured some aero newssmoke in a milk bottle, and took it home as a souvenir.

From that day on, sport waned. Through long, noncompetitive Saturday afternoons, the stadia slumbered. Even the parkways fell into disuse as motorists rediscovered the charms of old, twisty roads that led through main streets and past barnyards, with their mild congestions and pleasant smells.

Recent Research

Leo P. Chall and Irene Taviss

Small group behavior

The growth of research in the nature of groups has been so pronounced in the last few decades that some commentators have referred to it as "the rediscovery of the primary group." Of all the areas of research, the small group field has become most firmly institutionalized for a variety of reasons. Military needs have encouraged the study of bomber crews as small groups, industrial sociologists look into work groups, and psychologists are interested in task groups. The availability of students as experimental subjects and the rapid development of exactness and specificity in research techniques and experimental designs have also contributed to the development of this area of study.

A review of *Sociological Abstracts* indicates that particular emphasis has been placed on the study of group cohesiveness, social influence, leadership, and group structure.

Group cohesiveness. Studies of group cohesiveness have attempted to determine what factors make for greater or lesser cohesiveness and to examine the correlates of such cohesiveness. In addition, the bases of attraction to the group are also studied, including such questions as: Why are certain individuals attracted to specific types of groups, and what types of people are accorded social acceptance in certain types of groups?

Three recent studies reported on different aspects of group cohesion and attraction. Aronson and Mills[1] studied the relationship between different kinds of initiations and attraction to the group. The subjects, all college students, were divided into three groups: one group read embarrassing material to another group as a condition of entrance to a discussion group; a second group read only mildly embarrassing material; and a third group was not required to read any material. All subjects listened to what was supposedly a taped recording of a previous meeting of the discussion group and then were asked for their reactions to the discussion—that is, they were asked whether or not they found it interesting. The results confirmed Aronson and Mills' hypothesis that people who undergo an unpleasant initiation to become members of a group (those who read embarrassing material) find the group more attractive than those who become members without undergoing severe initiation (groups two and three). Such studies are useful to organization leaders and all those concerned with the problem of attracting potential members to their groups. Various devices akin to severe initiation, such as rigorous selection procedures, can be employed to increase the desire for participation and the attractiveness of groups to non-members.

Lott and Lott[2] used natural groups of friends in a laboratory to study the relationship between group cohesiveness, conformity, and communication between members. Measures of each of these variables confirmed the prediction that there would be a greater degree of conformity to the group and more communication between members in groups having a high degree of cohesiveness. Many other studies have also noted that conformity to group norms varies directly with group cohesiveness.

Goslin[3] used nineteen groups of adolescent boys and girls to study the relationship between group members' self-perceptions and their acceptance in the group. He found that those who saw themselves differently from the way others in the group saw them, and/or those who were unable to predict how the others saw them, were isolated from the group—unable to interact with the others. Sociological theory has long noted the importance of the perceptions of others about one's self in the formation of a self-concept.

Social influence. An interesting study of social influence was that of Hunt and Synnerdahl,[4] who performed an Asch experiment with young children.

They found that children showed very little tendency to go along with group judgments. The children seemed almost totally unaware of "social pressure," though they were cooperative and interested in the experiment. If these findings can be duplicated with other children, they raise some interesting questions regarding sensitivity to social pressures: At what point in the life cycle do people become aware of such pressures, and under the influence of what forces or agents of socialization?

Another interesting study by Hollander[5] followed the lead of Homans regarding influence processes in small groups and tried to determine the relationship between influence and competence. Hollander found that group members who showed the greatest competence in group tasks also had the greatest influence within the group. In addition, he examined the effect of conformity or nonconformity on influence, finding that the influence of those who showed nonconformity in early group meetings was reduced, whereas those who exhibited nonconformity later did not suffer a reduction in their influence.

Leadership.   Fox[6] found that positive leadership produced a more permissive, friendlier group atmosphere than negative leadership. Greater group satisfaction with leadership and greater acceptance of group solutions were also found in groups where leaders employed a positive style.

Yet another study indicated that a leader must not be too psychologically close to his group if the group is to accomplish its tasks effectively. Fiedler[7] found that "psychologically distant leaders are more effective in promoting the productivity of task groups than are leaders with psychologically closer interpersonal relations. . . ." But leadership traits can operate in influencing group productivity only when the leader has considerable power in the group. Thus it is not only the manner of leadership which is important but also the extent to which the leader has power in the group. Power, of course, may in turn be influenced by the qualities of the leader.

A further example of the work that is being done in the area of group structure is the work of Turk and Turk,[8] who examined the nature of group interaction in a three-person group, a triad. They found that triads were free of coalitions if the power of one member was greater than that of the other two combined. The flow of communication and emotional support between pairs went from the member with greater power to the member with less power. The element of power is thus important in determining not only the success of a leader but also the nature of the interaction between group members.

Beyond the experimentally created groups in which leadership has been studied, a number of descriptive studies have been made of leadership processes in community development, in protest movements such as CORE and the NAACP, and in other political and social movements.

Collective behavior

There has been a tendency in recent studies of collective behavior to look for primary groups within larger aggregations. Research in mass communications has indicated that the primary group is often the mediating influence between the mass media and the individual-in-the-mass.

Much work has also been done to distinguish various types of collective behavior—the acting crowd, the expressive crowd, the public, the audience, etc. Among the most recent attempts to formulate a general theory of collective behavior is that of Neil Smelser.[9] In his *Theory of Collective Behavior*, Smelser suggests the following as determinants of collective behavior: (1) Structural conduciveness—the social structure in a particular social situation permits or encourages definite types of responses. Thus, for example, economic panic cannot occur in a system in which property is closely linked to the kinship structure and can be transferred only to the first-born son at the death of the father. (2) Structural strain—e.g., conflicts and other kinds of deprivations. (3) Growth and spread of a generalized belief—which identifies the source of strain and specifies certain responses as appropriate. (4) Precipitating factors—events which set collective behavior in motion as opposed to the first three factors which act as predisposing elements. A precipitating factor might be a Negro family's moving into a white neighborhood. But a fistfight will not lead to a race riot unless it occurs in the light of a general situation established by conduciveness, strain, and a generalized belief. (5) Mobilization of participants for action—i.e., something must bring the affected group into action. Here leadership plays a very important role. (6) The operation of social control—the counter-determinants that prevent or inhibit stages 1-5. These are of two types: those which minimize conduciveness and strain, and those which operate after an episode has begun to minimize. The nature and effectiveness of social controls affect the form which collective behavior may take, or indeed whether it occurs at all.

Also of interest are the major studies of "unstructured situations" sponsored by the Disaster Research Group of the National Academy of Sciences. A variety of natural and accidental disasters have been described and analyzed, such as a coal mine disaster, a panic, a fireworks explosion in Texas, a tornado in Worcester, the Rio Grande flood, and an unexpected air raid warning. An interesting project of this kind was undertaken by Quarantelli,[10] who reviewed over fifty studies of community disasters in the last decade. He found, among other things, that, contrary to all discussions of the weakness of extended family ties in industrialized, urbanized societies, the extended family is a major source of help for disaster victims. On the basis of this finding, Quarantelli suggests that the physical dispersion of the kinship group in modern societies may actually be functional in preventing crises from simultaneously incapacitating all members of an extended family.

In another interesting study, Winick[11] interviewed 1,392 New Yorkers at the time that they experienced a generalized threat from the "Mad Bomber." Interestingly enough, almost 66 per cent of the respondents were able, when asked, to identify the race and religion of the unknown bomber. Winick suggested that this fact reflects the hostility of the respondents towards various racial or religious groups, which was given expression by the "unstructured situation."

New studies of collective behavior will soon be reported in various journals. It is suggested that the student carefully peruse *Sociological Abstracts* and *Psychological Abstracts* as well as *The Public Opinion Quarterly, Sociometry, Studies in Communication, Journalism Quarterly*, and other academic and lay periodicals.

References

1. Elliot Aronson and Judson Mills, "The Effect of Severity of Initiation on Liking for a Group," *Journal of Abnormal and Social Psychology*, 59 (1959), 177-181.

2. Albert J. Lott and Bernice Eisman Lott, "Group Cohesiveness, Communication Level, and Conformity," *Journal of Abnormal and Social Psychology,* 62 (March 1961), 408-412.

3. David A. Goslin, "Accuracy of Self-Perception and Social Acceptance," *Sociometry,* 25 (September 1962), 283-296.

4. Raymond G. Hunt and Vonda Synnerdahl, "Social Influence Among Kindergarten Children," *Sociology and Social Research,* 43 (January-February 1959), 171-174.

5. E. P. Hollander, "Competence and Conformity in the Acceptance of Influence," *Journal of Abnormal and Social Psychology,* 61 (November 1960), 365-370.

6. William M. Fox, "Group Reaction to Two Types of Conference Leadership," *Human Relations,* 10 (1957), 279-289.

7. Fred E. Fiedler, "The Leader's Psychological Distance and Group Effectiveness," in Dorwin Cartwright and Alvin Zander, eds., *Group Dynamics: Research and Theory* (Evanston, Illinois: Row, Peterson & Company, 1960), pp. 586-606.

8. Theresa and Herman Turk, "Group Interaction in a Formal Setting: Case of the Triad," *Sociometry,* 25 (March 1962), 48-55.

9. Neil J. Smelser, *Theory of Collective Behavior* (New York: The Free Press of Glencoe, 1963), pp. 15-18.

10. Enrico L. Quarantelli, "A Note on the Protective Function of the Family in Disasters," *Marriage and Family Living,* 22 (1960), 263-264.

11. Charles Winick, "How People Perceived 'The Mad Bomber,'" *The Public Opinion Quarterly,* 25 (1961), 25-38.

Part V

SOCIAL PROCESSES

Interaction constitutes the basic process of human social life, and hence its conceptualization is one of the most fundamental sociological elements and tools for sociological study. The special kind of interaction with which sociology deals is symbolic and is concerned largely with norms, statuses, values, and reciprocal relationships.

Sociologists believe and teach that human behavior can be understood only by realizing that the social behavior of individuals is oriented toward other human beings and by conceptualizing behavior as interplay between the self and the expected or actual behavior of others. Thus, while the basic unit of study in psychology is the individual, in sociology the basic unit is the group—two or more persons influencing each other's behavior.

Erving Goffman's article, Selection 32, illustrates the point that even behavior which at first appears highly individualistic and idiosyncratic may actually be a very subtle and functional pattern of communication. Social interaction is never truly random or chaotic; rather, it tends to manifest itself in patterns or streams of interaction that persist over time to establish social relationships and, eventually, social structures.

These patterns of interaction do not develop in a social vacuum. Selection 30 by Paul Lazarsfeld, Bernard Berelson, and Hazel Gaudet illustrates how patterns of interpersonal communication are shaped by social forces, and Selection 31 by Warren A. Peterson and Noel P. Gist demonstrates that even rumor, which takes place upon a somewhat ambiguous stage of human interaction, may be regarded as reciprocal social interaction.

The consistent patterns of interaction that can be identified in a society have traditionally been referred to as *social processes*. The term as used here is not meant to suggest an entirely new idea; rather, *process* should be seen as a stage upon which transitions from one social condition to another are accomplished—as a basic and repetitive way in which humans interact.

Georg Simmel, sometimes referred to as the founder of the "formal school" of sociology, was one of the first to point out the importance of interactive processes. Simmel felt that one could abstract from concrete social situations a number of relatively stable patterns of interaction, the most important of them being conflict, cooperation, and competition. Since his abstractions or generalizations were based upon concrete social situations, Simmel, by using this method, countered the claims of those who said that no social science was possible because each individual and each situation was unique and nonrepetitive.

Simmel's work deeply influenced American sociology, especially at the University of Chicago where Robert E. Park and Ernest W. Burgess refined and further developed the concept of social processes. For those following their teachings, social processes came to be viewed in terms of four major types of interaction, each of which has several subtypes: (1) competition, (2) conflict, (3) accommodation, and (4) assimilation. Later students have sometimes used slightly different lists.

It is generally agreed that there are two basic forms of interaction—*associative processes,* which make for group consensus, and *dissociative processes,* which tend toward disunity. The difference between these two forms of interaction can be demonstrated by the difference between competition and cooperation. As a social process, *competition* is mutually opposed effort to secure the same scarce resources or objectives, while *cooperation* implies mutual aid and complementary and supplementary behavior. Peter M. Blau in Selection 36 and Melville Dalton in Selection 37 illustrate the ways in which cooperation and competition are related to such vital concepts as group cohesion and productivity.

Although competitors may utilize different means, they share a desire for like ends. All of us actively participate in many competitive relationships every day—for example, students compete for grades and scholarships, organizations attempt to recruit the same people, nations attempt to secure the same scarce resources, and retail businessmen attempt to influence the public to spend money for the goods and services they provide. Two particular aspects of competition should be noted: (1) it does not necessarily occur on a conscious or personal level, and (2) it does not always involve direct interaction.

Do the ways in which groups relate to one another have latent consequences for group structure and character? Arnold M. Rose tests this very interesting question in Selection 38 and points out that certain internal patterns of behavior which develop within competing or conflicting groups are not associated with other types of groups. It is interesting to note that many of these latent consequences are of a positive nature—for example, increased participation and loyalty—thus emphasizing that competition and conflict are not necessarily harmful.

Rivalry, as opposed to competition, obtains when individuals or groups not only seek the same scarce objective but do so in a conscious, emotionally toned manner. For example, two males seek the affection of the same girl, two colleges engage in an athletic contest, or two politicians run for the same public office. *Conflict* refers to situations in which the clash of interests is so keen and the emotion engendered so intense that opposing groups do not merely compete for scarce resources and objectives but seek to destroy or displace one another.

One seldom finds individuals or groups attempting to pursue either competition or cooperation to their extremes. Instead, a readjustment of power or status occurs—they accommodate themselves to one another. "*Accommodation,* then, may be defined as a social process in which conflict or alienation is brought to an end through adjustment of the conflicting individuals or groups to one another. So defined it may be considered one sequel of conflict, competition, or rivalry. On the other hand, it may be akin to the social process making for unity since it limits conflict. Obviously, it is a common condition, holding elements of both conflict and cooperation."[1]

An excellent example of accommodation is the way in which industrial conflict is usually resolved. Labor unions do not pursue goals that could destroy industry, and management seldom exerts all-out efforts to subjugate workers completely. Instead, both parties, while still trying to maximize their relative portions of the fruits of production, realize that it would be to their disadvantage to eliminate the other completely. On another level, the teen-age culture or clique may represent an accommodation of parent-child conflict.

There are numerous forms of accommodation, some of which lead to such a degree of similarity between opposed parties that *assimilation* can be said to have occurred. The classic definition says assimilation is "a process of interpenetration and fusion in which persons and groups acquire the memories, sentiments, and attitudes of the other persons or groups, and, by sharing their experience and history, are incorporated with them in a common cultural life."[2] For example, adopted children are assimilated into their new homes and give up old ways for new, and newly married couples give up their separate identities and establish families.

Closely related to assimilation is *acculturation,* which is commonly defined as the borrowing or acceptance of cultural items or patterns. Acculturation may lead to full assimilation; both acculturation and assimilation are much more one-way than two-way processes. Selection 33 by Howard Woolston points out that if assimilation is to be complete it must take place within a cooperative and reciprocal setting. The study by Erich Rosenthal, Selection 34, emphasizes that assimilation should be viewed as a complex social-psychological process that does not necessarily follow acculturation. S. N. Eisenstadt, in Selection 35, provides an excellent analysis of the factors that make for successful, complete assimilation. To a large degree, culture determines the exact form in which each social process occurs.

As is apparent, social processes encompass persistent patterns of interaction that occur between all types of social units—individuals, groups, and even whole societies. Furthermore, each process is relative: cooperation often exists within groups that are in conflict with one another. Within a single society such as the United States, political factions may be in open conflict with one another for the spoils of office; economic groups and institutions may be in competition; labor unions and corporations may be in the process of working out certain accommodative compromises; and immigrant Poles, Italians, and Scandinavians may be merging their common cultural values in the reciprocal process of assimilation. Indeed the basic social processes can be clearly viewed *only* in relation to one another, for they function simultaneously and reciprocally in dynamic organizations.

The reader should consider three general questions when analyzing the selections in Part V. First, how are the origins and nature of social processes found? Second, how do social relationships or social structures develop and mature? And third, what are the reciprocal relations among individuals, groups, and social processes?

[1] G. Sellen, P. H. Furfey, and W. T. Gaughan, *An Introduction to Sociology* (New York: Harper & Brothers, 1958), p. 323.

[2] Robert E. Park and Ernest W. Burgess, *Introduction to the Science of Sociology,* 2nd ed. (Chicago: University of Chicago Press, 1924), pp. 735-736.

Selection *30*
_____

The Nature of Personal Influence
Paul F. Lazarsfeld, Bernard Berelson, and Hazel Gaudet

When social interaction is regarded as two-way communication and response, it is implied that actor B not only receives some communication from actor A but also evaluates and responds to that stimulus. If A has influence over B, A may be able to affect the behavior of B toward certain goals or in certain directions. A proper area of sociological study therefore is "What determines whether or not A's communication behavior will influence B?" How an individual reacts to communication is often related to the relative status of the person doing the communicating—that is, an individual tends to respond most favorably to communication received from those members of his own groups who have high status or prestige.

In some communities a few individuals are especially able to influence the attitudes or behavior of their associates; hence they may be called opinion leaders. Because their opinions and points of view are valued, opinion leaders are looked to by their friends and neighbors for advice and counsel. Although opinion leaders are active in practically all spheres of community life, their importance was illustrated by Lazarsfeld, Berelson, and Gaudet in *The Peoples' Choice* (1944), which was the first attempt to analyze the role of informal personal influence on the formation of political opinions and public policy. In this study, a sample population (a panel) of Erie County, Ohio, was interviewed once each month throughout the presidential election campaign of 1940. This unique method allowed the researchers to trace the development of, and analyze as a process, the voting decision. The concept of opinion leaders developed out of the discovery that certain people exerted significant influence on the political opinions of others.

Since opinion leaders exist at all social and economic levels and since the authors hypothesize that the effect of informal communication with an opinion leader may be more pronounced than that of any formal communication, one can see the significance of this study to both the social scientist and the student of political behavior, and therefore he should not be surprised at the wealth of additional research to which it has led. This selection is a classic in the fields of sociology, public opinion, and political science and is widely known and used in all three disciplines.

The political homogeneity of social groups is promoted by personal relationships among the same kinds of people. But for a detailed and systematic study of the influence of such relationships—the political role of personal influence—a systematic inventory would be needed of the various personal contacts and political discussions that people had over a sample number of days. . . . Such complete data are not available in the present study, but enough information has been collected to indicate the importance of personal relationships so far as their direct political influence is concerned. Our findings and impressions will be summarized without much formal statistical data. The significance of this area of political behavior was highlighted by the study but further investigation is necessary to establish it more firmly.

In comparison with the formal media of communication, personal relationships are potentially

From *The People's Choice* by Paul F. Lazarsfeld, Bernard Berelson, and Hazel Gaudet (New York: Columbia University Press, 1948), pp. 150-158.

more influential for two reasons: their coverage is greater and they have certain psychological advantages over the formal media.

PERSONAL CONTACTS REACH THE UNDECIDED

Whenever the respondents were asked to report on their recent exposure to campaign communications of all kinds, political discussions were mentioned more frequently than exposure to radio or print. On any average day, at least 10% more people participated in discussions about the election—either actively or passively—than listened to a major speech or read about campaign items in a newspaper. And this coverage "bonus" came from just those people who had not yet made a final decision as to how they would vote. Political conversations, then, were more likely to reach those people who were still open to influence.

For example, people who made up their minds later in the campaign were more likely to mention personal influences in explaining how they formed their final vote decision. Similarly, we found that the less interested people relied more on conversations and less on the formal media as sources of information. Three-fourths of the respondents who at one time had not expected to vote but were then finally "dragged in" mentioned personal influence. After the election, the voters were given a check list of "sources from which they got most of the information or impressions that caused them to form their judgment on how to vote." Those who had made some change during the campaign mentioned friends or members of their family relatively more frequently than did the respondents who kept a constant vote intention all through the campaign.

THE TWO-STEP FLOW OF COMMUNICATIONS

A special role in the network of personal relationships is played by the "opinion leaders." . . . [T]hey engaged in political discussion much more than the rest of the respondents. But they reported that the formal media were more effective as sources of influence than personal relationships. This suggests that ideas often flow *from* radio and print *to* the opinion leaders and *from* them to the less active sections of the population.

Occasionally, the more articulate people even pass on an article or point out the importance of a radio speech. Repeatedly, changers referred to reading or listening done under some personal influence. Take the case of a retired school teacher who decided for the Republicans: "The country is ripe for a change . . . Willkie is a religious man. *A friend read and highly recommended* Dr. Poling's article in the October issue of the *Christian Herald* called 'The Religion of Wendell Willkie'."

So much for the "coverage of personal contacts." The person-to-person influence reaches the ones who are more susceptible to change, and serves as a bridge over which formal media of communications extend their influence. But in addition, personal relationships have certain psychological advantages which make them especially effective in the exercise of the "molecular pressures" finally leading to the political homogeneity of social groups. We turn now to a discussion of five such characteristics.

NON-PURPOSIVENESS OF PERSONAL CONTACTS

The weight of personal contacts upon opinion lies, paradoxically, in their greater casualness and non-purposiveness in political matters. If we read or tune in a speech, we usually do so purposefully, and in doing so we have a definite mental set which tinges our receptiveness. Such purposive behavior is part of the broad area of our political experiences, to which we bring our convictions with a desire to test them and strengthen them by what is said. This mental set is armor against influence. The extent to which people, and particularly those with strong partisan views, listen to speakers and read articles with which they agree in advance is evidence on this point.

On the other hand, people we meet for reasons other than political discussion are more likely to catch us unprepared, so to speak, if they make politics the topic. One can avoid newspaper stories and radio speeches simply by making a slight effort, but as the campaign mounts and discussion intensifies, it is hard to avoid some talk of politics. Personal influence is more pervasive and less self-selective than the formal media. In short, politics gets through, especially to the indifferent, much more easily through personal contacts than in any other way, simply because it comes up unexpectedly as a sideline or marginal topic in a casual conversation. For example, there was the restaurant waitress who decided that Willkie would make a poor president after first thinking he would be good. Said she: "I had done a little newspaper reading against Willkie, but the real reason I changed my mind was from *hearsay*. So many people don't like Willkie. Many customers in the restaurant said Willkie would be no good." Notice that she was in a position to overhear bits of conversation that were not intended for her. There are many such instances. Talk that is "forbidden fruit" is particularly effective because one need not be suspicious as to the persuasive intentions of the speakers; as a result one's defenses are down. Furthermore, one may feel that he is getting the viewpoint of "people generally," that he is learning how "different people" think about the election.

Such passive participation in conversation is paralleled in the case of the formal media by accidental exposure, e.g., when a political speech is heard because it follows a favorite program. In both conversation and the formal media, such chance communication is particularly effective. And the testimony to such influence is much more frequent in the case of personal contacts. The respondents mentioned it time and again: "I've heard fellows talk at the plant . . . I hear men talk at the shop . . . My husband heard that talked about at work. . . ."

FLEXIBILITY WHEN COUNTERING RESISTANCE

But suppose we do meet people who want to influence us and suppose they arouse our resistance. Then personal contact still has one great advantage compared with other media: the face-to-face contact can counter and dislodge such resistance, for it is much more flexible. The clever campaign worker, professional or amateur, can make use of a large number of cues to achieve his end. He can choose the occasion at which to speak to the other fellow. He can adapt his story to what he presumes to be the other's interests and his ability to understand. If he notices the other is bored, he can change the subject. If he sees that he has aroused resistance, he can retreat, giving the other the satisfaction of a victory, and come back to his point later. If in the course of the discussion he discovers some pet convictions, he can try to tie up his argument with them. He can spot the moments when the other is yielding, and so time his best punches.

Neither radio nor the printed page can do anything of the kind. They must aim their propaganda shots at the whole target instead of just at the center, which represents any particular individual. In propaganda as much as in other things, one man's meat is another man's poison. This may lead to boomerang effects, when arguments aimed at "average" audiences with "average" reactions fail with Mr. X. The formal media produced several boomerangs upon people who resented what they read or heard and moved in the opposite direction from that intended. But among 58 respondents who mentioned personal contacts as concretely influential, there was only one boomerang. The flexibility of the face-to-face situation undoubtedly accounted for their absence.

REWARDS OF COMPLIANCE

When someone yields to a personal influence in making a vote decision, the reward is immediate and personal. This is not the case in yielding to an argument via print or radio. If a pamphlet argues that voting for the opposite party would be un-American or will jeopardize the future, its warning may sound too remote or improbable. But if a neighbor says the same things, he can "punish" one immediately for being unimpressed or unyielding: he can look angry or sad, he can leave the room and make his fellow feel isolated. The pamphlet can only intimate or describe future deprivations; the living person can create them at once.

Of course all this makes personal contacts a powerful influence only for people who do not like to be out of line. There are certainly some people who gain pleasure from being nonconformists, but under normal circumstances they are probably very much in the minority. Whenever propaganda by another person is experienced as an expression of the prevailing group tendencies, it has greater chances of being successful than the formal media because of social rewards. For example, here is a woman who was for Roosevelt until the middle of the campaign: "I have always been a Democrat and I think Roosevelt has been all right. But my family are all for Willkie. They think he would make the best president and they have been putting the pressure on me." She finally voted for Willkie. This aspect of personal contacts was especially important for women.

The rewards of compliance to other people are learned in early childhood. The easiest way for most children to avoid discomfort is to do what others tell them to do. Someone who holds no strong opinions on politics and hence makes up his mind late in the campaign may very well be susceptible to personal influences because he has learned as a child to take them as useful guides in unknown territory. The young man who was going to vote for Roosevelt because "my grandfather will skin me if I don't" is a case in point.

TRUST IN AN INTIMATE SOURCE

More people put reliance upon their personal contacts to help them pick out the arguments which are relevant for their own good in political affairs than they do in the more remote and impersonal newspaper and radio. The doubtful voter may feel that the evaluations he reads or hears in a broadcast are plausible, for the expert writer can probably spell out the consequences of voting more clearly than the average citizen. But the voter still wonders whether these are the issues which are really going to affect *his own* future welfare. Perhaps these sources see the problem from a viewpoint entirely different from his own. But he can trust the judgment and evaluation of the respected people among his associates. Most of them are people with the same status and interests as himself. Their attitudes are more relevant for him than the judgments of an unknown editorial writer. In a formal communication the content can be at its best; but in a face to face contact the transference is most readily achieved. For example, here is the case of a young laborer who professed little or no interest in the campaign and who did not even expect to vote until late October: "I've been discussing the election with *the fellows at the shop* and I believe I'll vote, but I haven't decided yet who for." His constant exposure to the views of his fellow-workers not only brought him to the ballot booth but also brought out his final Democratic vote in line with his colleagues.

A middle-aged woman who showed great interest in the campaign was undecided until late October and then voted for Willkie: "*I was talking politics just this morning with a friend, a businessman.* He says business will improve if Willkie is elected and that Willkie promises to keep us out of the war. FDR is getting too much power. He shouldn't have a third term." Her friend had apparently run out for her what amounted to a small catalogue of Republican arguments and he was impressive enough to clinch her vote, which had been in the balance throughout the campaign. Her trust in his judgment settled her mind.

Trust in another person's point of view may be due to his prestige as well as to the plausibility of what he has to say or its relevancy to one's interests. It is obvious that in all influences prestige plays a considerable role. The degree of conformity is greater the higher the prestige of the person in our group who seeks to influence us. The plausibility of the consequences he presents will seem greater if he is important. (Of course, the formal media are also important in this respect.) The heightening of trust through the prestige of certain personal contacts was clear in the case of the driver of a bread truck who changed to Willkie because the prominent president of a business firm had done him the honor

of persuading him in that direction. Then, too, there is the case of a middle-aged housewife with little education who was for Willkie from May through September, became undecided in October, and finally voted for Roosevelt. She left Willkie because of the statements of people whom she considered authorities: "I talked with *a college student* from Case, in Cleveland, and students are for Roosevelt because he has helped recreation. I talked, too, with a *man from Chicago who is very interested in politics,* and he doesn't seem to think that Willkie is a big enough man to handle international affairs."

PERSUASION WITHOUT CONVICTION

Finally, personal contacts can get a voter to the polls without affecting at all his comprehension of the issues of the election—something the formal media can rarely do. The newspaper or magazine or radio must first be effective in changing attitudes related to the action. There were several clear cases of votes cast not on the issues or even the personalities of the candidates. In fact, they were not really cast for the candidates at all. They were cast, so to speak, for the voters' friends.

"*I was taken to the polls* by a worker who insisted that I go."

"*The lady where I work wanted me to vote.* She took me to the polls and *they all voted Republican so I did too.*"

In short, personal influence, with all its overtones of personal affection and loyalty, can bring to the polls votes that would otherwise not be cast or would be cast for the opposing party just as readily if some other friend had insisted. They differ from the formal media by persuading uninterested people to vote in a certain way without giving them a substantive reason for their vote. Fully 25% of those who mentioned a personal contact in connection with change of mind failed to give a real issue of the campaign as a reason for the change, but only 5% of those who mentioned the formal media omitted such a reason. When personal influence is paramount in this way, the voter is voting mainly for the personal friend, not the candidate.

PRACTICAL IMPLICATIONS

In a way the outcome of the election in Erie County is the best evidence for the success of face-to-face contacts. It so happened that for some time the Republican machine in that area worked much more vigorously than its Democratic opponent. When asked whether they knew people who had good ideas about politics, our respondents mentioned considerably more Republican than Democratic local politicians. A few people who did not expect to vote but finally went to the polls mentioned Republican canvassers as the main influence, but we could not trace a similar success for the Democratic machine.

However, one should not identify the personal contacts discussed in this [selection] with the efforts of the *professional* political machines. These personal contacts are what one might call *amateur machines* which spring up during elections—individuals who become quite enthusiastic or special groups that try to activate people within their reach. One might almost say that the most successful form of propaganda—especially last-minute propaganda—is to "surround" the people whose vote decision is still dubious so that the only path left to them is the way to the polling booth. We do not know how the budget of the political parties is distributed among different channels of propaganda but we suspect that the largest part of any propaganda budget is spent on pamphlets, radio time, etc. But our findings suggest the task of finding the best ratio between money spent on formal media and money spent on organizing the face-to-face influences, the local "molecular pressures" which vitalize the formal media by more personal interpretation and the full richness of personal relationships into the promotion of the causes which are decided upon in the course of an election.

In the last analysis, more than anything else people can move other people. From an ethical point of view this is a hopeful aspect in the serious social problem of propaganda. The side which has the more enthusiastic supporters and which can mobilize grass-root support in an expert way has great chances of success.

Selection 31

Rumor and Public Opinion
Warren A. Peterson and Noel P. Gist

One of the most common but least understood modes of interaction is that of *rumor.* Although the social functions of rumor are not completely understood, rumor most often occurs during "anomic," or normless, conditions. This means that rumors—unverified accounts or explanations of events—serve to define and explain situations of importance that appear ambiguous.

Rumors are unlike the other types of communication and interaction described later in this part. Embarrassment, for example, may be properly viewed as functionally useful to the group, whereas rumor is commonly viewed as dysfunctional and harmful to group relations. The preceding selection concerned itself with a fairly well-structured situation in which leadership roles were apparent and well-developed systems of status and prestige existed. Rumor, on the other hand, is usually associated with conditions of an ambiguous, unstructured, or fluid nature.

Recently, social scientists have tried to offer systematic explanations of how rumors develop. Such knowledge could conceivably contribute to a better understanding if not to the elimination, of rumors. Remembering that interaction is two-way communication should remove the likelihood of mistakenly viewing rumors as unilateral verbal behavior. Peterson and Gist feel that rumors should be considered a form of public opinion, with public opinion seen as a complex collective process. By *collective process* is meant the temporary and fluctuating behavior or attitudes that arise from group efforts to interpret and adjust to a novel situation. *Collective* implies a reciprocal give-and-take between social units. Rumors are seldom started by one person and then passively transmitted by others. Rather, the development and transmission of rumors involve interpretation, discussion, speculation, and even creative imagination. If this view of rumor is valid, then psychological descriptions of rumor in terms of distortions of memory or perception should be supplemented by an explanation of the changes in meaning and motivation that occur in the give and take of informal discussion.

What is important about the approach suggested by Peterson and Gist is that rumor is treated as a process. Only in this way can a systematic analysis be made of a normal process which at first appears on the surface to be abnormal or pathological.

I

"Rumor," in general usage, refers to an unverified account or explanation of events, circulating from person to person and pertaining to an object, event, or issue of public concern. Whether, beginning with such a definition, rumors can be treated as a single and separate generic class is problematic. There are significant differences among rumors of various types: retrospective rumors focused upon the implications of past events, in contrast with prospective or predictive rumors anticipating the future; rumors planted and systematically transmitted to serve the ends of special groups, as compared with those which arise, apparently spontaneously, under conditions of social unrest; rumors which represent extreme flights of imaginative fantasy, as opposed to those which carry a rational, newslike quality. Because of this wide variation, attention must be given to the definition and classification of rumors and to their position in the field of collective behavior. In particular, the objective analysis of rumor is contingent upon the systematic treatment of various public opinion processes.

Our present concern is with rumors which appear to arise spontaneously after a public has been formed through common interest in an issue or event. Rumors of this type can be considered the product of collective efforts to interpret a problematic situation, when the public views the situation affectively and when authoritative information is lacking.

"Public opinion," in contrast to more static concepts like "culture," designates temporary and fluctuating attitudes and beliefs resulting from collective efforts to interpret constantly emerging new situations. A group of people develops an interest in an event or issue, reciprocally communicates attitudes and beliefs pertaining to it, and interprets these in terms of the existing cultural context and their specialized frames of reference. This occurs within a social organization and is dependent upon the leadership, group affiliations, and channels of communication within the society.

Because of the constant flow of new events and issues, institutionalized channels have developed in our society for the communication of new attitudes and beliefs. Communications of broad social significance are usually transmitted, at least in part, by mass media. Communications significant to a specific group or organization are commonly transmitted in the form of official statements or are passed down, more informally, with the explicit understanding that there is some kind of authoritative sanction. Public opinion is always more than an automatic response to authoritative opinion. Even when no conflicting authoritative opinion is presented, issues are discussed informally and are related to the specialized attitudes and beliefs of particular groups.

Rumor "opinion" differs significantly from other forms of public opinion, in that it is not verified through customary channels. The common-sense assumption that rumor is abnormal or pathological reflects the fact that the persons involved are normally expected or accustomed to rely upon authority or upon a different kind of authority. A social setting conducive to rumor occurs when a public is interested and concerned about a past or anticipated event, when authoritative information and explanation are lacking, and when social controls relevant to the situation are external to most members of the public.

Under these conditions there is greater recourse to informal discussion, in the course of which the interest of individuals tends to be intensified. The public may be extended to include persons who originally were neither interested in, nor informed about, the situation. As persons move from one discussion group to another, speculation tends to be passed as rumor; and rumor comes

"Rumor and Public Opinion" by Warren A. Peterson and Noel P. Gist. Reprinted from *The American Journal of Sociology*, Vol. LVII (1951), 159-167, by permission of The University of Chicago Press.

to be represented as fact, often supported by citing supposedly authoritative sources.

Typically, the rumor public is more emotional than other publics. At times it borders incipiently on crowd behavior. Rumor objects tend to be affectively evocative—fascinating, weird, bizarre. Recurrently, in American society at least, issues which involve arson, murder, and sex deviation serve as rumor topics. To the extent that a public reacts affectively to an issue, rational controls are released, and speculation and imagination are evoked. . . . Rumor seems more likely to occur when public interest focuses on a person, although groups tagged with affect-laden stereotypes seem to serve nearly as well.

In the early stages of the process, members of a rumor public vary greatly in attitudes toward the object, issue, or event, according to the intensity and the kind of interest, concern, or anxiety. This variation is probably greater than in most other publics. The communication of rumor tends to reduce the divergence in attitudes and to produce a common definition of the situation and a common feeling or mood. Rumor is one means by which a collectivity, albeit a temporary and unstable collectivity, emerges from an aggregate.

II

The work of Allport and Postman represents one of the most comprehensive attempts to examine rumor objectively.[1] Taking methodological cues from psychological experiments on memory and recall, these investigators designed a series of carefully controlled experiments, using chains of six or seven selected subjects. A visual stimulus, in the form of a picture of a suggestive social scene, was presented to the first subject, who passed on his impressions of it to the second, who subsequently passed on his impressions of the first subject's report to the third, and so on. Conclusions about the nature of rumor were derived by comparing the "terminal report" with the initial stimulus.

Allport and Postman summarize their conclusions under the concepts *leveling, sharpening,* and *assimilation.* "Leveling" refers to the tendency of a rumor, as it travels, to "grow shorter, more concise, more easily grasped and told. In successive versions fewer words are used and fewer details are mentioned." "Sharpening" is defined as "the selective perception, retention, and reporting of a limited number of details from larger context." And "assimilation" "has to do with the powerful attractive force exerted upon rumor by the intellectual and emotional context existing in the listener's mind." . . .

The Allport-Postman approach is different from that which deals with rumor as a form of public opinion and with public opinion as a complex collective process. They assume that the social context in which rumors occur can be reduced to a single chain of subjects; that, by implication, the wide circulation of rumor is nothing more than the adding-together of such chains; and that rumor can be explained, at least in part, by reference to uniform and pervasive psychological mechanisms like "the economizing process of memory."

Moreover, and perhaps more important, Allport and Postman proceed on the assumption that rumor basically results from distortion in perception and in *unilateral* verbal communication. Thus in the course of their experiments they completely rule out changes in meaning and in motivation which occur in the give and take of informal discussion. They also overlook the possibility that the same individual, transmitting rumor to a succession of persons, may communicate a different version in each instance, not just because of faulty memory, but because of differences in his relationship with them.

It is superficially evident that persons who develop and transmit rumors are not passively reacting to a stimulus, as Allport and Postman imply, but are acting in a situation that is problematic and affectively evocative to them. Public expectations, fears, anxieties, hostilities, and aspirations are often clearly manifest in rumors. Their development and transmission involve interpretation, discussion, speculation, and creative imagination.

Similarly, simple observation discloses that communication is a complicated time-space network, relating persons who are receiving, discussing, interpreting, forgetting, and transmitting attitudes and beliefs in a variety of social situations. The rapidity and complex nature of the process make rumor a difficult subject for objective examination. It is very unlikely that the methodological problems can be solved by applying the orthodox procedures of simplification and control employed in experimental psychology. . . .

. . . A set of rumors investigated by the writers is presented here as an empirical test of the Allport-Postman approach and as a general case study of rumor.

III

Rumors were circulated in a small midwestern city during a period of public concern about an

---

[1] Gordon W. Allport and Leo Postman, *The Psychology of Rumor* (New York: Henry Holt & Co., 1947).

unsolved crime—the rape and murder of a fifteen-year-old girl. The rumors, or set of rumors, had many variations, but a common theme: that the householder who had employed the victim as a babysitter for the evening had returned home without his wife and murdered the girl. Although there was no authoritative verification at the time or subsequently, the rumors circulated throughout the community, resulting in considerable excitement. Two weeks intervened between the occurrence of the crime and the circulation of these rumors. During the first two days, press and radio devoted themselves to reporting all possible details of the murder and to reviewing similar incidents in the preceding few years in the same residential neighborhood.

Later, a number of events served to stimulate interest in the case and speculation about the identity of the murderer. The police appealed, through press and radio, for any type of information that might be relevant. Citizens were requested to report to the police any male who had scratches or cuts on his face or hands. A campaign was conducted to raise a reward for information leading to the apprehension of the murderer. The National Guard was called out to screen the area for possible clues. In a neighborhood near the place of the murder the police chased and exchanged shots with a prowler, but failed to apprehend him. Police cars constantly patrolled all streets in the vicinity.

Various activities expressed the special concern of particular groups and, being noted by others, served to intensify general public interest. Large numbers of residents drove past the scene of the crime. Others devoted themselves to gathering information about the family of the girl and the family which had employed her as a babysitter. Measures were taken to safeguard homes against intruders. Girls and young women were warned against being alone after dark. The rape-murder case became a common topic of conversation wherever persons gathered and associated.

Almost immediately after the crime, rumors began to circulate about the identity of the murderer. These rumors (or speculations) were widely varied, scattered, and of short duration. It was suggested or speculated that the murderer was a Negro; a high-school student; a cab driver; and a feeble-minded boy.

There were also rumors about the inefficiency and corruptness of the police. The issue of police competence persisted as a general topic of public discussion during and after the period when the babysitter's employer was rumored to be the murderer. The latter, whom we shall refer to as "Mr. X," was alleged to have left a party which

he and his wife were attending, returned to their home, entered the house, raped and murdered the girl, and subsequently returned to the party after changing his clothes. In general, this was the common element in the rumors which circulated for three or four days.

The numerous variations which developed from this central theme indicate interpretation, speculation, and creative imagination on the part of members of the public in the direction of coordinating the story with previous conceptions of the murder, of attributing stereotyped sex-criminal characteristics to Mr. X, of constructing a basis for sympathizing with his wife, of supplying authentic verification, and of generally molding a sensational account.

The writers, both residents of the community, observed as carefully as possible the communication of this particular set of rumors and assembled all possible information on the preceding events. About one hundred university students, residing in various parts of the community, were asked to set down in writing any rumor or any information heard during the previous week concerning the rape-murder case.[2] The assortment of rumors collected by this procedure presents a configuration having a basic theme but a wide variety of detailed interpretations, some of which are contradictory in ideational content.

Mr. X's absence from the party

"Mr. X left the party for two hours, from 9:30 to 11:30."

Variously reported as ½ hour, 1½ hours, from 11:00 to 12:30, and from 11:00 to 12:00.

"When Mr. X returned to the party he had completely changed clothes, had scratches on his face."

Variously reported as scratches on his back and on his chest.

"It is said that X left the party for about two hours. He said he was going out for more liquor, but instead returned home and completely surprised the young girl."

Also reported that he said he had been filling out an income tax form during his absence.

"When Mr. X came back to the party, he had blood and mud on his shoes."

"Mr. X had left the party, taken a bus, done the killing, and returned to the party."

---

[2] This does not, of course, represent a sampling of rumors that were current at that time; not all rumors that were circulating in the community are necessarily represented. Virtual duplicates of those given here are not included.

The detection and arrest of Mr. X

"Mr. X was picked up and questioned all day."

"Mr. X is being held in Jackson City" (30 miles distant).

"Blood hounds followed the trail three times to where Mr. X was playing cards, but because of political reasons no arrests were made on this clue."

"Mr. X has confessed to the crime in Jackson City."

"When questioned by the police, X gave several stories as to where he was during his absence."

"X has been held in the local jail for questioning. He has been there two days. He can't account for the two hours he was absent from the party."

"X has signed a confession. He moved immediately to California and then his conscience got the better of him and he sent the signed confession to the local police."

"The police and the FBI have been trailing him since the day of the funeral."

"I've heard that he is now being held for questioning and that the police are trying to beat it [confession] out of him."

"Mr. X is in the penitentiary."

"The police picked him up last night and rushed him off to Jackson City. They are afraid to keep him here."

"Mr. X is being held in Jackson City for questioning and various tests, i.e., the lie detector."

"Mr. X is not being held; in fact, they believe he may be in California."

"Mr. X is hiding out with his family in Utah."

"X is being held for the murder; he was taken into custody in Minnesota."

"The police questioned him several times and he gave no satisfactory answer as to where he had been" [during his absence from the party].

Evidence concerning the attack

"He . . . entered the front door; that's why the porch light was on, because Miss B had recognized him and let him enter. He put the sawhorse by the window and broke the window to make it look as if the murderer had entered that way."

"In the house there were no fingerprints except those of the X family."

"The cord that was around Miss B's neck had been in a very dark part of a closet and wouldn't have been found if he [the attacker] hadn't already known where it was. Later I heard the window had been broken from the inside."

"Mud tracks led into the living room showing the front door had been used."

"The latch on the window he was supposed to have entered was broken from the inside."

"He went into the front door of his home, then staged the window scene."

"There were no scratches on the piano in front of the window, so he came in the front door."

"When he and his wife arrived home that evening, he would not let his wife go into the house but insisted on going in himself and then came out and told what he had seen."

"The window was too small for a man to crawl through."

"When his little boy was asked if he had been scared that night, he had said, 'No, my daddy was here.' "

"When the X child was questioned as to what he saw or heard the night of the murder, he said, 'I saw a man who looked like daddy.' "

"The police have found the blood-soaked clothes he wore when he killed her."

"The clothes he had been wearing were found in the basement."

"The clothes he had been wearing were found in the car."

"He has blonde hair like that found at the scene of the crime."

"He undressed in the bathroom, so his wife could not see the scratches on his body."

"He entered the front door, and the window was smashed in the struggle. His footprints match those found."

Evidence supplied by individuals

"The information about the absence of Mr. X was supplied by a couple who were at the party on the night of the murder."

"Mr. X, who hired the babysitter, was turned in by his wife because he left the party one and one half hours at the time the murder was committed."

"Mr. X was turned in by his wife. She missed him for an hour at the time of the crime. She found some blood-soaked clothes of his in the basement."

"Mrs. X furnished the lead which led to his arrest; she has declared her intention 'never to live with him again' as a result of previous marital disagreements."

"Mrs. X spied on him while he was undressing in the bathroom and observed scratches upon his body. This she reported to the police."

"His wife has left him; she knew the truth all along."

"Either his wife or his father-in-law has reported him."

"His mother turned him in to the police, saying that he was an habitual sexual pervert, and that he had 'finally gone too far.' "

"Some one at the party sent a letter to the police reporting Mr. X's absence."

Reactions of Mrs. X

"His wife is covering up for him, but has gone to California to have her second child."

"The day of the funeral he took his wife to her home in Minnesota. From there she called her priest in Canton and asked him to help her. It is doubtful whether Mrs. X or the priest turned in X to the police. As a result of the shock of finding the murdered girl, Mrs. X lost a child."

"Mr. X had his wife leave town until it all blows over."

"Mrs. X has gone to her home in North Dakota."
Also reported as Wisconsin, Texas, and Illinois.

"His wife is having a nervous breakdown."

"Mrs. X is four months pregnant and has lost her child."[3]

"Mrs. X has gone insane."

"Mrs. X is in California, where she had a baby which was born dead, due to the effects of this case on her physiological well-being."

"His wife and child went to her mother's home in Wisconsin. It supposedly caused her to have a miscarriage."

"It was said that Mrs. X was pregnant, and that she lost consciousness when her husband was arrested. She is reported to be in a hospital, having been in a coma for ten days or so."

Images of Mr. X

"I have heard that he was a known sex pervert from youth."

"He is an exceptionally intelligent man, a C.P.A., and talented in music."

"Miss K, aunt of the slain girl, went to school with Mr. X and she said that he was a queer-acting fellow."

"His wife reported that he had become 'woman crazy' during the past six months."

"Mr. X had at one time been in an insane asylum."

"Mr. X and his wife had not been getting along lately."

"Mr. X was said to be a no-good drunkard and carouser about town."

"Mr. X had been shell-shocked during the war, and insanity spells were not uncommon for him."

"The marriage of Mr. and Mrs. X has been 'on the rocks' for a year. She has filed suit now."

"Mr. X has been under suspicion for the Ferguson case five years ago."

"They [Mr. and Mrs. X] are sexually incompatible."

"There is a connection between him and the Ferguson murder a few years ago."

"He often left parties and returned later, so no one thought his behavior strange."

"He was drunk and unable to account for himself for these hours."

IV

It is probable that the central theme—that Mr. X had raped and murdered the girl during his absence from a party—developed in the course of speculations about the identity of the attacker. Since this theme appeared first, it is almost certain that the rumor did not emerge in full form. Among the elaborations, versions which tended to co-ordinate the story with previous conceptions of the murder seem to have followed the central theme almost immediately.

It was not, however, a simple case of one wave of elaboration spreading throughout the community, to be followed by another wave. Many persons did not hear the original version until it had been elaborated considerably. There is no reason to believe that each specialized version originated independently and ran its course in isolation from the others.[4] There must have been additions to the rumor as it was passed from person to person, discussed in a variety of social situations, and interpreted by individuals with special interests or preconceptions.

Whether this rumor "snowballed" in the process of transmission depends upon the perspective used in interpretation. "Snowballing" suggests increasing enlargement and implies that details are retained as new ideas are superimposed. Viewing the entire phenomenon as a *Gestalt* of interrelated rumors, probably derived from a common origin and differentiated into a profusion of details, the phenomenon does appear to have grown like a snowball. Certainly, there was an accumulation of details; whether any were completely lost in the course of transmission and elaboration is not known.

[3] The information that Mrs. X was pregnant was correct. However, she was duly delivered several months later.

[4] It also seems improbable that the central theme could have originated with the perceptual experience of an event, because of the time lapse between the murder and the rumors. Allport and Postman's position is that "most rumors start as a report of an actual episode—that is to say, with someone's perceptual experience of an event. . . ." (*op. cit.*, p. 226).

If one views each of the particular rumors as having an independent origin and a separate "career," then the case for leveling as opposed to snowballing can be supported very effectively, largely because it is logically impossible for independent, particularistic rumor to snowball. In our opinion, such a frame of reference limits the possibility of securing information that would shed light on the nature of rumor—if rumor is fundamentally an aspect of public opinion and · if communication in a public follows multilateral associational channels.

Apparently, something similar to what Allport and Postman call "assimilation" does occur. The stereotyping of Mr. X as the type of man who could commit such a crime; the portrayal of Mrs. X as reacting as a woman faced with such a situation might be expected to react; the alleged behavior of the police in apprehending and questioning Mr. X—all might be considered expressions of cultural preconceptions assimilated into the central theme, making the entire configuration more impressive and sensational but not necessarily more "coherent, plausible, and well-rounded."

Assimilation is not simply "the powerful attractive force exerted upon rumor by the intellectual and emotional context in the listener's mind." The listener-interpreter-communicator is motivated in a social situation. From the latent residue of attitudes and beliefs in his memory, he consciously or unconsciously selects those which are appropriate in the situation as he defines it. The variety of such situations which occur in a public almost necessitates changes in meaning and emphasis.

The setting in which the rumors used in this report occurred was very different from an artificially constructed experimental situation. The rape and murder were real, not fictitious events. The public was composed of girls and women concerned about their personal safety; of sympathetic friends, relatives, and neighbors; of young men who had searched for clues with the National Guard; and a great mass of persons who took a vicarious interest in the whole range of activities.[5] Where a public is composed of people with a variety of interests—and nearly every public is—any event or situation is likely to be diversely defined and interpreted.

There is no evidence in the present study of a general "economizing process of memory." It seems more likely that persons with very little interest forget details, while those who are keenly interested remember details, at least details which they consider crucial.

Allport and Postman generalize that proper names and titles tend to be omitted in the transmission of rumor. "In virtually all experiments names of places and persons either dropped out or were distorted beyond recognition." There is no evidence of wholesale omissions of proper names and titles in the rumors examined for this report. In fact, nearly all respondents stated specifically the names of the alleged attacker and the victim, and in a great many cases mentioned the place where Mr. and Mrs. X were spending the evening.

There may be a tendency to omit names and titles in certain types of rumors in which the basic content is not affected; in others, the effectiveness of the rumor seems to depend on their retention. If persons are intensely interested and emotionally aroused, they recall certain items with clarity and accuracy; they may even take items from other experiences and, with varying degrees of accuracy, apply them to the one at hand. There was, for instance, a tendency among some persons to incorporate into the rumor information taken from the original press and radio version of the murder.

A portion of the distortion may be explained by the fact that a person, in the role of transmitter, is likely to have more personal interest in a rumor than he had in the role of receiver. Inside information bearing on an issue of public concern places a person temporarily in a position of prestige; and the prestige-position of the transmitter is more secure if the story can be made to sound authentic. The transmitter is sufficiently motivated to forget details that make the story dubious, to emphasize details that make it plausible, and to introduce new corroborating details.

The major limitation in the experimental study of rumor and of other forms of collective behavior lies in the failure to produce, or even to simulate, affectively toned motivational states comparable to those which occur in real life. This is true both of the small discussion group and of the public.

The study of rumor in uncontrolled situations manifestly presents serious methodological difficulties. Rumor appears as an ephemeral, elusive phenomenon which cannot be fruitfully approached in historical perspective. To wait until interest has waned is to lose a large part of the basic information and to run the risk of ex post facto rationalization.

The essential characteristics of rumor are such as to require, at this stage at least, careful on-the-spot observation, preferably by a team of investigators. Although the ideational content of

---

[5] The police department's call to citizens to report any male with scratches or cuts on his face or hands made all men and older boys potential suspects and tended to intensify anxiety, especially after reports were circulated that innocent persons had been arrested and subjected to questioning.

rumor is the easiest information to obtain and is superficially the most objective, it is not necessarily the most sociologically relevant. In the systematic investigation of rumor, attention should be given to such problems as the composition of the public, the establishment of cultural beliefs and attitudes through rumor communication, role behavior in groups where rumor is discussed, and personality characteristics of persons who specialize in rumor transmission.

It is particularly important that the emergence and communication of rumor be treated as a process. Consideration should be given to the question of whether there is a typical rumor cycle involving, perhaps, the formation of a public through common interest in an issue or event; relatively unfocused discussion gradually defining objects of interest; growing concern and increased discussion; the emergence of rumor; the growth of a rumor public and the proliferation of rumor; the dissolution of the rumor public; and the reorganization of public attitudes and beliefs.

Selection 32

Embarrassment and Social Organization
Erving Goffman

One of the most significant differences between man and other animals is that man alone achieves *selfhood*. In other words, by reflecting and internalizing the ways that "significant others" react to him, man acquires a mental image of his *self*. The possession of an adequate or emotionally satisfying self-concept is an important aspect of mental health.

The judgments that others make of one's self are based upon the extent to which he fulfills certain behavioral expectations and possesses attributes and capacities valued by others in the groups to which he belongs. Goffman describes what he calls *social encounters*, which consist of effectively projected claims to an acceptable self and the confirmation of like claims made by others. The results of these encounters often are related to the relative amount of social status or prestige an individual possesses.

But an individual does not always satisfy the expectations of others. What happens then? Possibly an "unsatisfactory" social encounter can be restructured so as to compensate for the individual's failure to conform to group expectations.

Goffman states that a certain process, usually learned early through basic socialization, teaches us a way of conveying to others (sometimes unintentionally) our concern over our inabilities to present a fully acceptable self (plus related behaviors). This process, embarrassment, communicates (1) our recognition that such inability is undesirable and (2) our desire for future conformity. In other words, if a person cannot meet expected standards of behavior, the social function of embarrassment is to demonstrate to others that he is disturbed by the self he is presenting and that he wishes to prove himself worthy of the group's acceptance at a later time.

The full significance of this process can be seen better in cases where the group feels a person should be embarrassed but that person is not. That is, embarrassment is the social expectation in such a situation, and social conformity demands that it either actually occur or be seriously feigned. To the extent that this explanation is correct, a person who fails to present a proper self but acts embarrassed is considered a conforming member of the group, albeit he probably loses some status in the process. Conversely, a person who fails to present a proper self but does not feel and demonstrate embarrassment at his failure is considered nonconforming, and he appears as one who either does not belong to the group or is fast on his way out. Embarrassment, thus viewed, is one of the basic types of communication associated with human interaction. It is caused not only by "self" consciousness but also by "group" consciousness and as such may even be useful as a measure of the integration of an individual into a group or of the degree of acculturation of a person or group into a new culture. Certainly this viewpoint gives feelings of shame, spontaneous "flustering," and blushing new meanings, which are primarily social rather than individual in nature.

An individual may recognize extreme embarrassment in others and even in himself by the objective signs of emotional disturbance: blushing, fumbling, stuttering, an unusually low- or high-pitched voice, quavering speech or breaking of the voice, sweating, blanching, blinking, tremor of the hand, hesitating or vacillating movement, absent-mindedness, and malapropisms. . . . There are also symptoms of a subjective kind: constriction of the diaphragm, a feeling of wobbliness, consciousness of strained and unnatural gestures, a dazed sensation, dryness of the mouth, and tenseness of the muscles. In cases of mild discomfiture these visible and invisible flusterings occur but in less perceptible form.

In the popular view it is only natural to be at ease during interaction, embarrassment being a regrettable deviation from the normal state. The individual, in fact, might say he felt "natural" or "unnatural" in the situation, meaning that he felt comfortable in the interaction or embarrassed in it. He who frequently becomes embarrassed in the presence of others is regarded as suffering from a foolish unjustified sense of inferiority and in need of therapy.

To utilize the flustering syndrome in analyzing embarrassment, the two kinds of circumstance in which it occurs must first be distinguished. First, the individual may become flustered while engaged in a task of no particular value to him in itself, except that his long-range interests require him to perform it with safety, competence, or dispatch, and he fears he is inadequate to the task. Discomfort will be felt *in* the situation but in a sense not *for* it; in fact, often the individual will not be able to cope with it just because he is so anxiously taken up with the eventualities lying beyond it. Significantly, the individual may become "rattled" although no others are present.

This paper will not be concerned with these occasions of instrumental chagrin but rather with the kind that occurs in clear-cut relation to the real or imagined presence of others. Whatever else, embarrassment has to do with the figure the

individual cuts before others felt to be there at the time. The crucial concern is the impression one makes on others in the present—whatever the long-range or unconscious basis of this concern may be. This fluctuating configuration of those present is a most important reference group.

VOCABULARY OF EMBARRASSMENT

A social encounter is an occasion of face-to-face interaction, beginning when individuals recognize that they have moved into one another's immediate presence and ending by an appreciated withdrawal from mutual participation. Encounters differ markedly from one another in purpose, social function, kind and number of personnel, setting, etc., and, while only conversational encounters will be considered here, obviously there are those in which no word is spoken. And yet, in our Anglo-American society at least, there seems to be no social encounter which cannot become embarrassing to one or more of its participants, giving rise to what is sometimes called an incident or false note. By listening for this dissonance, the sociologist can generalize about the ways in which interaction can go awry and, by implication, the conditions necessary for interaction to be right. At the same time he is given good evidence that all encounters are members of a single natural class, amenable to a single framework of analysis.

By whom is the embarrassing incident caused? *To* whom is it embarrassing? *For* whom is this embarrassment felt? It is not always an individual for whose plight participants feel embarrassment; it may be for pairs of participants who are together having difficulties and even for an encounter as a whole. Further, if the individual for whom embarrassment is felt happens to be

"Embarrassment and Social Organization" by Erving Goffman. Reprinted from *The American Journal of Sociology*, Vol. LXII (1956), 264-271, by permission of The University of Chicago Press.

254   *Part 5: Interaction and Communication*

perceived as a responsible representative of some faction or subgroup (as is very often the case in three-or-more-person interaction), then the members of this faction are likely to feel embarrassed and to feel it for themselves. But, while a *gaffe* or *faux pas* can mean that a single individual is at one and the same time the cause of an incident, the one who feels embarrassed by it, and the one for whom he feels embarrassment, this is not, perhaps, the typical case, for in these matters ego boundaries seem especially weak. When an individual finds himself in a situation which ought to make him blush, others present usually will blush with and for him, though he may not have sufficient sense of shame or appreciation of the circumstances to blush on his own account.

The words "embarrassment," "discomfiture," and "uneasiness" are used here in a continuum of meanings. Some occasions of embarrassment seem to have an abrupt orgasmic character; a sudden introduction of the disturbing event is followed by an immediate peak in the experience of embarrassment and then by a slow return to the preceding ease, all phases being encompassed in the same encounter. A bad moment thus mars an otherwise euphoric situation.

At the other extreme we find that some occasions of embarrassment are sustained at the same level throughout the encounter, beginning when the interaction begins and lasting until the encounter is terminated. The participants speak of an uncomfortable or uneasy situation, not of an embarrassing incident. In such case, of course, the whole encounter becomes for one or more of the parties an incident that causes embarrassment. Abrupt embarrassment may often be intense, while sustained uneasiness is more commonly mild, involving barely apparent flusterings. An encounter which seems likely to occasion abrupt embarrassment may, because of this, cast a shadow of sustained uneasiness upon the participants, transforming the entire encounter into an incident itself.

In forming a picture of the embarrassed individual, one relies on imagery from mechanics; equilibrium or self-control can be lost, balance can be overthrown. No doubt the physical character of flustering in part evokes this imagery. In any case, a completely flustered individual is one who cannot for the time being mobilize his muscular and intellectual resources for the task at hand, although he would like to; he cannot volunteer a response to those around him that will allow them to sustain the conversation smoothly. He and his flustered actions block the line of activity the others have been pursuing. He is

present with them, but he is not "in play." The others may be forced to stop and turn their attention to the impediment; the topic of conversation is neglected, and energies are directed to the task of re-establishing the flustered individual, of studiously ignoring him, or of withdrawing from his presence.

To conduct one's self comfortably in interaction and to be flustered are directly opposed. The more of one, the less, on the whole, of the other; hence through contrast each mode of behavior can throw light upon the characteristics of the other. Face-to-face interaction in *any* culture seems to require just those capacities that flustering seems guaranteed to destroy. Therefore, events which lead to embarrassment and the methods for avoiding and dispelling it may provide a cross-cultural framework of sociological analysis.

The pleasure or displeasure a social encounter affords an individual, and the affection or hostility he feels for the participants, can have more than one relation to his composure or lack of it. Compliments, acclaim, and sudden reward may throw the recipient into a state of joyful confusion, while a heated quarrel can be provoked and sustained, although throughout the individual feels composed and in full command of himself. More important, there is a kind of comfort which seems a formal property of the situation and which has to do with the coherence and decisiveness with which the individual assumes a well-integrated role and pursues momentary objectives having nothing to do with the content of the actions themselves. A feeling of discomfiture per se seems always to be unpleasant, but the circumstances that arouse it may have immediate pleasant consequences for the one who is discomfited.

In spite of this variable relation between displeasure and discomfiture, to appear flustered, in our society at least, is considered evidence of weakness, inferiority, low status, moral guilt, defeat, and other unenviable attributes. And, as previously suggested, flustering threatens the encounter itself by disrupting the smooth transmission and reception by which encounters are sustained. When discomfiture arises from any of these sources, understandably the flustered individual will make some effort to conceal his state from the others present. The fixed smile, the nervous hollow laugh, the busy hands, the downward glance that conceals the expression of the eyes, have become famous as signs of attempting to conceal embarrassment. . . . These gestures provide the individual with screens to hide behind while he tries to bring his feelings back into tempo and himself back into play.

Given the individual's desire to conceal his

embarrassment, given the setting and his skill at handling himself, he may seem poised according to some obvious signs yet prove to be embarrassed according to less apparent ones. Thus, while making a public speech, he may succeed in controlling his voice and give an impression of ease, yet those who sit beside him on the platform may see that his hands are shaking or that facial tics are giving the lie to his composed front.

Since the individual dislikes to feel or appear embarrassed, tactful persons will avoid placing him in this position. In addition, they will often pretend not to know that he has lost composure or has grounds for losing it. They may try to suppress signs of having recognized his state or hide them behind the same kind of covering gesture that he might employ. Thus they protect his face and his feelings and presumably make it easier for him to regain composure or at least hold on to what he still has. However, just as the flustered individual may fail to conceal his embarrassment, those who perceive his discomfort may fail in their attempt to hide their knowledge, whereupon they all will realize that his embarrassment has been seen and that the seeing of it was something to conceal. When this point is reached, ordinary involvement in the interaction may meet a painful end. In all this dance between the concealer and the concealed-from, embarrassment presents the same problem and is handled in the same ways as any other offense against propriety.

There seems to be a critical point at which the flustered individual gives up trying to conceal or play down his uneasiness: he collapses into tears or paroxysms of laughter, has a temper tantrum, flies into a blind rage, faints, dashes to the nearest exit, or becomes rigidly immobile as when in panic. After that it is very difficult for him to recover composure. He answers to a new set of rhythms, characteristic of deep emotional experience, and can hardly give even a faint impression that he is at one with the others in interaction. In short, he abdicates his role as someone who sustains encounters. The moment of crisis is of course socially determined: the individual's breaking point is that of the group to whose affective standards he adheres. On rare occasions all the participants in an encounter may pass this point and together fail to maintain even a semblance of ordinary interaction. The little social system they created in interaction collapses; they draw apart or hurriedly try to assume a new set of roles.

The terms "poise," "*sang-froid*," and "aplomb," referring to the capacity to maintain one's own composure, are to be distinguished from what is called "graciousness," "tact," or "social skill,"

namely, the capacity to avoid causing one's self or others embarrassment. Poise plays an important role in communication, for it guarantees that those present will not fail to play their parts in interaction but will continue as long as they are in one another's presence to receive and transmit disciplined communications. It is no wonder that trial by taunting is a test that every young person passes through until he develops a capacity to maintain composure. Nor should it come as a surprise that many of our games and sports commemorate the themes of composure and embarrassment: in poker, a dubious claim may win money for the player who can present it calmly; in judo, the maintenance and loss of composure are specifically fought over; in cricket, self-command or "style" is supposed to be kept up under tension.

The individual is likely to know that certain special situations always make him uncomfortable and that he has certain "faulty" relationships which always cause him uneasiness. His daily round of social encounters is largely determined, no doubt, by his major social obligations, but he goes a little out of his way to find situations that will not be embarrassing and to by-pass those that will. An individual who firmly believes that he has little poise, perhaps even exaggerating his failing, is shy and bashful; dreading all encounters, he seeks always to shorten them or avoid them altogether. The stutterer is a painful instance of this, showing us the price the individual may be willing to pay for his social life.

CAUSES OF EMBARRASSMENT

Embarrassment has to do with unfulfilled expectations but not of a statistical kind. Given their social identities and the setting, the participants will sense what sort of conduct *ought* to be maintained as the appropriate thing, however much they may despair of its actually occurring. An individual may firmly expect that certain others will make him ill at ease, and yet this knowledge may increase his discomfiture instead of lessening it. An entirely unexpected flash of social engineering may save a situation, all the more effectively for being unanticipated.

The expectations relevant to embarrassment are moral, then, but embarrassment does not arise from the breach of *any* moral expectation, for some infractions give rise to resolute moral indignation and no uneasiness at all. Rather we should look to those moral obligations which surround the individual in only one of his capacities, that of someone who carries on social encounters.

The individual, of course, is obliged to remain composed, but this tells us that things are going well, not why. And things go well or badly because of what is perceived about the social identities of those present.

During interaction the individual is expected to possess certain attributes, capacities, and information which, taken together, fit together into a self that is at once coherently unified and appropriate for the occasion. Through the expressive implications of his stream of conduct, through mere participation itself, the individual effectively projects this acceptable self into the interaction, although he may not be aware of it, and the others may not be aware of having so interpreted his conduct. At the same time he must accept and honor the selves projected by the other participants. The elements of a social encounter, then, consist of effectively projected claims to an acceptable self and the confirmation of like claims on the part of the others. The contributions of all are oriented to these and built up on the basis of them.

When an event throws doubt upon or discredits these claims, then the encounter finds itself lodged in assumptions which no longer hold. The responses the parties have made ready are now out of place and must be choked back, and the interaction must be reconstructed. At such times the individual whose self has been threatened (the individual *for* whom embarrassment is felt) and the individual who threatened him may both feel ashamed of what together they have brought about, sharing this sentiment just when they have reason to feel apart. And this joint responsibility is only right. By the standards of the wider society, perhaps only the discredited individual ought to feel ashamed; but, by the standards of the little social system maintained through the interaction, the discreditor is just as guilty as the person he discredits—sometimes more so, for, if he has been posing as a tactful man, in destroying another's image he destroys his own.

But of course the trouble does not stop with the guilty pair or those who have identified themselves sympathetically with them. Having no settled and legitimate object to which to play out their own unity, the others find themselves unfixed and discomfited. This is why embarrassment seems to be contagious, spreading, once started, in ever widening circles of discomfiture.

There are many classic circumstances under which the self projected by an individual may be discredited, causing him shame and embarrassment over what he has or appears to have done to himself and to the interaction. To experience a sudden change in status, as by marriage or promotion, is to acquire a self that other individuals will not fully admit because of their lingering attachment to the old self. To ask for a job, a loan of money, or a hand in marriage is to project an image of self as worthy, under conditions where the one who can discredit the assumption may have good reason to do so. To affect the style of one's occupational or social betters is to make claims that may well be discredited by one's lack of familiarity with the role.

The physical structure of an encounter itself is usually accorded certain symbolic implications, sometimes leading a participant against his will to project claims about himself that are false and embarrassing. Physical closeness easily implies social closeness, as anyone knows who has happened upon an intimate gathering not meant for him or who has found it necessary to carry on fraternal "small talk" with someone too high or low or strange to ever be a brother. Similarly, if there is to be talk, someone must initiate it, feed it, and terminate it; and these acts may awkwardly suggest rankings and power which are out of line with the facts.

Various kinds of recurrent encounters in a given society may share the assumption that participants have attained certain moral, mental, and physiognomic standards. The person who falls short may everywhere find himself inadvertently trapped into making implicit identity claims which he cannot fulfil. Compromised in every encounter which he enters, he truly wears the leper's bell. The individual who most isolates himself from social contacts may then be the least insulated from the demands of society. And, if he only imagines that he possesses a disqualifying attribute, his judgment of himself may be in error, but in the light of it his withdrawal from contact is reasonable. In any case, in deciding whether an individual's grounds for shyness are real or imaginary, one should seek not for "justifiable" disqualifications but for the much larger range of characteristics which actually embarrass encounters.

In all these settings the same fundamental thing occurs: the expressive facts at hand threaten or discredit the assumptions a participant finds he has projected about his identity. Thereafter those present find they can neither do without the assumptions nor base their own responses upon them. The inhabitable reality shrinks until everyone feels "small" or out of place.

A complication must be added. Often important everyday occasions of embarrassment arise when the self projected is somehow confronted with another self which, though valid in other contexts, cannot be here sustained in harmony with the first. Embarrassment, then, leads us to the matter of "role segregation." Each individual has more than one role, but he is saved from role dilemma by "audience segregation," for, ordinarily, those before whom he plays out one of his roles will not be the individuals before whom he plays out another, allowing him to be a different person in each role without discrediting either.

In every social system, however, there are times and places where audience segregation regularly breaks down and where individuals confront one another with selves incompatible with the ones they extend to each other on other occasions. At such times, embarrassment, especially the mild kind, clearly shows itself to be located not in the individual but in the social system wherein he has his several selves.

DOMAIN OF EMBARRASSMENT

Having started with psychological considerations, we have come by stages to a structural sociological point of view. Precedent comes from social anthropologists and their analyses of joking and avoidance. One assumes that embarrassment is a normal part of normal social life, the individual becoming uneasy not because he is personally maladjusted but rather because he is not; presumably anyone with his combination of statuses would do likewise. In an empirical study of a particular social system, the first object would be to learn what categories of persons become embarrassed in what recurrent situations. And the second object would be to discover what would happen to the social system and the framework of obligations if embarrassment had not come to be systematically built into it.

An illustration may be taken from the social life of large socal establishments—office buildings, schools, hospitals, etc. Here, in elevators, halls, and cafeterias, at newsstands, vending machines, snack counters, and entrances, all members are often formally on an equal if distant footing. . . . Cutting across these relationships of equality and distance is another set of relationships, arising in work teams whose members are ranked by such things as prestige and authority and yet drawn together by joint enterprise and personal knowledge of one another.

In many large establishments, staggered work hours, segregated cafeterias, and the like help to insure that those who are ranked and close in one set of relations will not have to find themselves in physically intimate situations where they are expected to maintain equality and distance. The democratic orientation of some of our newer establishments, however, tends to throw differently placed members of the same work team together at places such as the cafeteria, causing them uneasiness. There is no way for them to act that does not disturb one of the two basic sets of relations in which they stand to each other. These difficulties are especially likely to occur in elevators, for there individuals who are not quite on chatting terms must remain for a time too close together to ignore the opportunity for informal talk—a problem solved, of course, for some, by special executive elevators. Embarrassment, then, is built into the establishment ecologically.

Because of possessing multiple selves the individual may find he is required both to be present and to not be present on certain occasions. Embarrassment ensues: the individual finds himself being torn apart, however gently. Corresponding to the oscillation of his conduct is the oscillation of his self.

SOCIAL FUNCTION OF EMBARRASSMENT

When an individual's projected self is threatened during interaction, he may with poise suppress all signs of shame and embarrassment. No flusterings, or efforts to conceal having seen them, obtrude upon the smooth flow of the encounter; participants can proceed as if no incident has occurred.

When situations are saved, however, something important may be lost. By showing embarrassment when he can be neither of two people, the individual leaves open the possibility that in the future he may effectively be either. His role in the current interaction may be sacrificed, and even the encounter itself, but he demonstrates that, while he cannot present a sustainable and coherent self on this occasion, he is at least disturbed by the fact and may prove worthy at another time. To this extent, embarrassment is not an irrational impulse breaking through socially prescribed behavior but part of this orderly behavior itself. Flusterings are an extreme example of that important class of acts which are usually quite spontaneous and yet no less required and obligatory than ones self-consciously performed.

Behind a conflict in identity lies a more fundamental conflict, one of organizational principle, since the self, for many purposes, consists merely of the application of legitimate organizational principles to one's self. One builds one's identity out of claims which, if denied, give one the right to feel righteously indignant. Behind the apprentice's claims for a full share in the use of certain plant facilities there is the organizational principle: all members of the establishment are equal in certain ways qua members. Behind the specialist's demand for suitable financial recognition there is the principle that the type of work, not mere work, determines status. The fumblings of the apprentice and the specialist when they reach the Coca-Cola machine at the same time express an incompatibility of organizational principles.

The principles of organization of any social system are likely to come in conflict at certain points. Instead of permitting the conflict to be expressed in an encounter, the individual places himself between the opposing principles. He sacrifices his identity for a moment, and sometimes the encounter, but the principles are preserved. He may be ground between opposing assumptions, thereby preventing direct friction between them, or he may be almost pulled apart, so that principles with little relation to one another may operate together. Social structure gains elasticity; the individual merely loses composure.

Selection 33

The Process of Assimilation
Howard Woolston

The most simple theoretical model of a nation would be one that contained only one racial and cultural element. Such an "ideal" never seems to exist, however. Although nations vary widely in their racial and cultural composition, most of them have some diversity of ethnic and cultural groups. For a long time, sociologists have tended to assume that unity in a nation was to be preferred over diversity. Nations like the United States that have had to deal with a wide range of racial and cultural groups have encountered many difficulties in attempting to assimilate these groups into the central culture stream. This selection discusses assimilation in general as a process. Rosenthal, in Selection 34, addresses himself to the question of whether a group can take on most of the culture traits of the host nation and still not be assimilated fully, using the Jewish community in Chicago as his case study. In Selection 35, Eisenstadt, an Israeli sociologist, describes the assimilation problems of his new nation and seeks to isolate some of the variables that make assimilation either easier or more difficult for new immigrants to Israel.

Assimilation is only one of the possible ways in which a society can relate racial and cultural minorities to the dominant social order. This approach assumes that the groups involved are reasonably equal and that the differences which exist are primarily superficial and can be overcome by joint effort. The assumption of eventual "alikeness" is essential to choosing the approach of assimilation. But sometimes the majority group (or at least the most powerful group) does not see the minority group in question as potentially equal or desirable or as eventually becoming indistinguishable from the majority group; under these conditions, the most likely reaction is one of segregation and social avoidance. This results in the isolation of the minority so that few if any of its members have the opportunity for either the security or challenges of complete citizenship. Not only the United States South but also many areas of Latin America, Africa, and Asia show examples of this subordinate-superordinate attitude syndrome.

Woolston feels that assimilation programs in the United States often were less successful than they could have been because assimilation was viewed as mere conformity ("Americanization") and those in charge of the programs often sought only external conformity—even imposed conformity—without realizing that true assimilation is more essentially a matter of attitudes and values than of externals such as food, knowledge, language fluency, customs, and etiquette. Furthermore, all too frequently those in charge of assimilation programs sought a wholly one-way transfer, tacitly assuming that the immigrant's culture had nothing useful to offer—was, in fact, inferior—and hence that all ties with the old culture should be severed, the sooner the better. With this type of Americanization approach prevailing, it is no wonder that the Chinese in America at first resisted assimilation almost to a man, sometimes feeling that the attempts of "white barbarians" to push aside the ancient Chinese culture in favor of the new, crude, materialistic American culture were somewhat like a child trying to get an adult to trade good money for counterfeit. Assimilation is a noncoercive process in which each party profits from and learns from the other, however unequally.

Woolston feels that tension or conflict between nations is of the same order as that occurring between diverse racial and cultural groups within a nation. Hence, our failure to establish a means of alleviating international discord reflects our failure to devise an assimilation model that can work within a democratic framework. Somewhere between segregation and Americanization, Woolston believes, lies another possible course of action which he calls *cooperative culture*. More recently a related term, *cultural pluralism*, has been used to indicate that attitudinal approach to the close living together of diverse groups which holds, in brief, that a society or nation is strongest when it represents a "unity of diversity" rather than a sort of mechanical alikeness. Division of labor, it is said, makes for a stronger, more diverse, more dynamic, more efficient institution, program, or nation than does imposed mechanical uniformity. Similarly, what is "best" in the long run is more likely to come from the "best" of a number of cultures combined than from the "best" of any single culture.

The student reading this selection should bear in mind that the principles discussed in it are applicable not only to cultural groups, ethnic groups, races, and nations but probably also to the smaller social groups in which he participates in everyday life.

In the first scene of Goethe's Faust, the old scholar appears, seated at his desk. His opening soliloquy expresses frustration. Long years of study have not disclosed the meaning of life. Faust invokes the aid of magic; but shrinks before its frightful consequences. Then, glancing around his library, he exclaims, "These works I have inherited. Now I must make them mine." So ultimately, with the help of the Devil, he does discover the redemptive power of love and of human sacrifice.

When the ancient Greeks sent out a colony to found a settlement in some distant place, they gave the emigrants a brand from the civic altar. This sacred fire was guarded and used to kindle a flame in the central shrine of the new city. From it the founders lit their family hearths. In this way, the extension of spiritual power was sym-

bolized. A cold altar was the sign of an abandoned home and of a dying state.

We, too, have received from our fathers gifts material and spiritual. Some of these we have scarcely earned. We merely use them or extol their virtues. But we do not really possess them until we understand their meaning and rekindle their inspiration in our own lives. This constant renewal of thought and social life is the subject of our discussion.

Many people assume that *assimilation* means simply making individuals alike in appearance or manners. Such external resemblance does not imply uniformity in all respects. A son may be like

From *Social Forces*, Vol. 23 (1944-1945), 416-424. Published by the University of North Carolina Press.

his mother in complexion or speech, and yet show marked differences in behavior and associates. Evidently superficial likeness does not always indicate fundamental agreement in character. Social counterfeits are not uncommon. Make-up is cheap, and books on etiquette can be borrowed. . . .

Students of biology and human behavior use the term *assimilation* to designate internal change. Physiologists mean by it the absorption of food prepared through digestion. Psychologists refer to the process by which different experiences are fused into a new unit of perception. Teachers hope their students will "get the idea" illustrated by an example or "grasp the principle" underlying a test case. The ability to discern what is essential in a situation, to convert the experience into clews for further action, and to apply such measures effectively under appropriate circumstances, demonstrates that an individual knows his business.

Now individuals live in families, communities and nations. So they must play a part in several institutions. If they miss their cues, the show is spoiled and they are disgraced. Training actors for our civic pageant is also called *assimilation*. Students of society use the term to indicate the process by which individuals are conditioned and accepted into the life of a community. This implies the learning of roles by candidates and, ultimately, their incorporation into the company. Only when the players are competent and are willingly received by their associates can the troupe be said to have assimilated its personnel. Thus Leviathan (the State) lives on the energy of its citizens, while they are sustained by its massive organization.

What do the people assimilate? Not merely bread and thrills, but also ideas about agriculture and the Air Force—hunches, notions, prejudices, if you will. Yet this inner arrangement of significant marks furnishes a background for social action. These patterns of behavior are not peculiar to each person, but are fashioned from group experience and are followed by most of its members. Such common ways of thinking, judging, and believing become norms of conduct for a people. The rules are accepted and approved as furnishing a fit design for living by folks who understand their value. Indeed, recognition and response depend largely upon awareness of the meaning of standard signals for concerted action.

These related and loosely integrated codes we call collectively *culture*. The term includes language and literature, art and industry, custom, morals and law, religion and philosophy, science. We distinguish the inner meaning of such systems from their outward manifestations in material objects, such as books, tools, prisons, churches and school houses, on the one hand; and also from groups of people who use the codes in institutional arrangements, such as families, business corporations, states, congregations, academies and clubs, on the other. We prefer to label the mass of physical things as *wealth* and to designate the organization of people as *civilization*.

For example, a university has grounds, buildings, and technical equipment. It is manned by Regents, Faculty and students, working together in meetings, classes, and assemblies. The central purpose of all these arrangements is to transmit and develop the great traditions of letters, art, science, technology and human relations. It is these latter subjects that we have in mind when we speak of *culture*.

Let me remind you of certain characteristics of the American brand of culture. We have been told that all its ingredients were not found first by us. Many parts were imported and borrowed from various sources. So our culture is not entirely original. Some of its traits have been developed more notably than others. For example, interest in economics and politics has expanded more rapidly among us than has concern for aesthetics and theology. This trend may signify an unbalanced and inconsistent scheme of life, as judged from the standpoint of older and more stable cultures. Nevertheless, the kind of tradition we have evolved to meet conditions in this country seems to be satisfactory to most Americans. At least we are unwilling to alter it radically now. Still, our national history shows that we have been obliged repeatedly to depart from precedent in order to master changing circumstances. Perhaps we have not yet arrived at a final formula. We are accustomed to certain ways of thinking and acting, which we believe are best for us. We may be convinced that all the strange views and practices of other people are inferior to our own procedures. Such an attitude would indicate a limited outlook, and might result in attempts to proselyte humanity under the standard of provincial ideals.

Who assimilate the American tradition? All of us. That is, everybody who really belongs within our varied associations. Of course, everyone does not absorb our culture to the same extent, because there are marked differences of individual capacity and of social opportunity. However, some knowledge of a common language and local customs is necessary for all persons who share in the life of any community.

Those individuals who do not understand and adopt the ways of their neighbors and fellow citizens are soon regarded as outsiders. This is true of "queer" natives as well as of "outlandish" foreigners. The stranger shows differences in speech, dress or manners, in politics, religion or attitudes toward recognized authority. Such divergence seems to challenge and threaten accepted codes. So the peculiar person becomes an object of suspicion, and often the butt of ridicule or the victim of hostility. We don't like people who differ markedly from us, unless we can subject them to our purposes. Otherwise, we prefer to segregate or to exclude them. They don't seem to fit into our scheme of life. The color line, foreign districts, anti-Semitism and Red baiting are not unknown in this Land of the Free.

Such discrimination against minorities often drives them closer together for mutual support. They become sensitive to criticism and rally defiantly about their impugned standards. They may even exaggerate differences that separate them from the majority of people about them. In that case, assimilation becomes difficult, because overtures from outside are regarded as decoys, and yielding to them is considered disloyal.

How are people assimilated? Ordinarily, contact and communication will establish some common tradition among them. But the extent of acculturation varies greatly with the means employed to produce it. Perhaps the crudest method is *conquest and subjugation*. The vanquished people are forced to relinquish some of their customary privileges and to observe the decrees of their masters. This they may do sullenly, with a determination to throw off the oppressor as soon as they are able. Such people are not assimilated: they are merely saddled and ridden, as the Slavs under Hitler, for instance.

Another way of bringing about a new order of thought and action is through *trade and exploitation*. Such methods characterized the penetration of the West Indies by white men. Natives were offered a wider market for their products and skill. They were paid with impressive baubles and were given wages that seemed princely—for servants. Soon the country was overrun with exacting bosses; its natural resources were drained into company stores; the people had work which they dared not leave; stern authorities insisted that contracts be fulfilled, under penalty. Presently, the blessings of forced labor and subsidized debauchery begin to pall upon primitive field hands and jaded factory workers. They still obey orders and spend their wages for unaccustomed luxuries. But little sympathy and cooperation exist between masters and men. Each gets what he can out of hard bargaining. Some people

say this type of economy persists, even among us, today.

A third way of extending the benefits of culture into backward regions is through *colonization*. People are sent from the home country to reclaim land, to control the natives and to strengthen national frontiers. They develop natural resources, promote trade and elevate morality in benighted provinces. Some authority to manage local affairs is conceded to them; but they remain dependent upon the grand policy of the capital. Not infrequently the colonists are more concerned about meeting immediate issues than in following the tradition of remote statesmen. The frontier affects their attitudes. They do not always dress for dinner. Thus colonial standards gradually change from those maintained in the mother country. In such a case, differentiation rather than similarity is the result. For example, consider the English in Australia.

To influence men's minds and to bring their conduct into harmony with what some people consider best for everybody, a questionable process, called *propaganda or proselyting*, is often used. The former consists in presenting selected facts and opinions so as to sway unstable judgment into agreement. The latter frequently employs threats and promises to detach men from their traditional allegiance and to add them to the ranks of another sect or party. Such missionary effort may have noble ends in view and may follow them sincerely. The dubious aspect of the diversion is the sudden break with previous reasoning required, and the consequent uncertain foundation of the new faith. Nobody can deny the efficacy of basic reorientation and conversion. The difficulty is to produce lasting effects by the superficial methods frequently employed. Strong emotional appeal does not always carry deep conviction and concurrence. Assimilation requires time.

One more short-sighted method recommended for securing agreement among people is *amalgamation*. This is simply cross-breeding different biological stocks so as to modify marked peculiarities of each. It has little to do with culture traits. Language and morals are not transmitted through the genes. Actually, much assimilation of common ways of thought and action is necessary before successful mixed marriages are possible. Doubtless mutual accommodation occurs subsequently. However, mere interbreeding does not automatically produce unified culture in parents or offspring. Unfortunately, it often results in a human variety that is rejected with contempt by both lines of kindred. The mongrel lives in a half-world, unsure of full participation on either side. The marginal status of Eurasians in India exemplifies such unhappy lot.

Now let us consider more effective means for unifying human purposes. Perhaps the most thorough process is through the *education of children*. Babies are plastic, and soon acquire the habits of diet, speech and personal relationship followed in the home. Then comes a period of systematic instruction in fundamental lines of thought and action through school, playground and church. Since this stage is discussed by experts we may merely note other agencies at work in the formation of youthful character.

Children live in communities, where certain patterns of behavior are strikingly exemplified in the conduct of neighbors, friends and public officers. The gang on the corner show how "regular guys" are supposed to act, more convincingly than do tales of Robin Hood or Knights of the Round Table. Policemen and the Mayor represent practical standards of civic virtue more vividly than do speeches about Cato and George Washington. The "funnies," the movies and the radio translate ancient codes of morals and manners into the vernacular. Thus current expression modifies classic tradition. School teachers may be comforted by realizing that they are not solely responsible for ordering the lives of other people's children.

An outstanding problem in this country, especially during the past fifty years, has been how to *assimilate immigrants*. About 38 million foreigners landed on our shores within a century. They and their descendants constitute nearly half our present population. At first they came mostly from the lands of northwestern Europe, where traditional ways of life were not unlike those of the colonial stock that preceded them. After 1890 the main current flowed from central and southern Europe, wherein marked differences of language, economic standards and morality were evident. Some of the uprooted individuals sought refuge here from persecution because of their religious or political views and practices. Most of them came to gain more comforts than they could secure at home. A few expected to return with small fortunes earned here. The great majority stayed and sent for relatives and friends to join them.

By 1890, cheap land, the peasant's ideal property, was no longer available. The natural frontier was closed. So most of the newcomers settled in cities near the Eastern seaboard. Some Orientals dropped into West Coast towns. There aliens formed groups to sustain one another in the midst of our strange civilization. Often they continued to use their native language and customs, which were the only ones they understood. Some of them were slow to become naturalized, possibly because they could not readily accomplish the necessary steps to do so. Being without strong legal representatives, they were not infrequently exploited by unscrupulous landlords and employers. Thus some foreigners gained a reputation for stupidity, stubbornness and disloyalty, which was imputed to all of their kind. In this way, new cultural barriers were set up in our midst.

The children of these outsiders went to school, learned our language and customs, entered business and professions, and were often accepted as native Americans. Discrimination due to skin color usually made such transition impossible. Some children were confused by the difference between the standards of conduct observed by their foreign-born parents and those enforced by the rest of the community. In the slums of our cities, not a few of the second generation fell into evil ways, because divided authority left them free to follow their unguided impulses. Such failures lowered the reputation of parents and relatives, so the flow of immigration was checked by law. Some Americans even ventured to assert that no foreign stock (except, perhaps, that of their own forbears) can be successfully assimilated, because bad manners are born in the blood. Heredity alone determines ability, they affirm. So inbreeding must replace education and social reform. That sounds like Nazi Aryanism. If the theory holds—which is more than doubtful—we have been wasting time in discussing assimilation. This process involves transforming different dispositions instead of merely multiplying those that are already alike.

The intolerant attitude of older immigrants toward those who arrived later prompts another question: How thoroughly are traditional Americans assimilated into the body of our growing society? An answer is difficult, because we may not agree as to what is essential in so-called *Americanism*. Certainly legal criteria of parentage, birthplace, and residence do not guarantee participation. The Juke family (mostly paupers, thieves and prostitutes) were old Dutch-American stock. Neither do wealth, schooling and social responsibility insure fidelity. Recently a leader in American finance, the scion of an outstanding family, spent time in Sing Sing for embezzlement. Nor does prominence in artistic and literary circles prove that Hollywood actors and metropolitan columnists grasp the basic meaning of American life.

Students and critics of our traditions are apt to present a list of desirable and undesirable culture traits that all of us are believed to share. Americans are supposed to love personal freedom, and also to favor restrictive legislation; they demand equal opportunity, and also enjoy fierce competition; they are friendly and resent interference. Americans are said to be lofty idealists, as well as gross materialists; they are efficient and wasteful; they radiate optimism while planning frantically against disaster. Such platitudes fail to indicate where and when these diverse traits prevail. They do not tell us how far and among whom the qualities are dominant. We are flattered by some descriptions and grow indignant at unfair aspersions. These characterizations do not help us to understand the strength and weakness of our way of life. They merely say that we are *human*. They do not always disclose the standpoint or the competence of the person who pronounces Olympian judgment.

It seems to me that nobody can evaluate any phenomenon without comparing it with similar manifestations. If behavior is viewed only from the standpoint of habits familiar to the observer, all deviations from custom appear strange, wrong, bad. Unless a common base can be found from which to estimate both old models and novel types of action, selection between them depends merely upon personal preference. . . .

. . . We cannot appreciate the worth of our own institutions until we view them in the perspective of history. Then many temporary and local expedients assume their just proportions. Some ancient tribal rites may appear childish, some parochial boundaries seem to cramp expanding life. Laws against witchcraft and heresy have to be revised in the light of modern science. Caste and party lines disappear beneath the stress of industry and war. We may discover that men on the other side of the earth are driving toward goals like those we have set up, by roads that, until yesterday, we thought impassable.

At this time, when the United States is emerging from continental retirement to assume a leading part in world affairs, it would be disappointing if our representatives spoke only hackneyed words in a provincial dialect. Perhaps it is fear of such poor performance that is expressed in the phrase "winning the war and losing the peace." Have we any comprehensive plan to unite the nations and to blend their cultures? We should have mastered its rudiments in composing the differences among the various peoples in our own country. If we have failed to do so, the fault may lie in the belief that assimilation is a one-way process. Certainly we have gained much from the traditions of other nations. Can we now return

their contributions enlarged and enriched through our experience?

The need of assimilation is obvious. Men cannot communicate without some means of expression and recognition. Language, including gesture and symbolic marks, furnishes a basis for mutual understanding. But nations speak not only different tongues; they use words with various shades of meaning. Terms that are roughly equivalent do not refer to qualities of objects or actions that are exactly alike. So literal translation often conveys a wrong impression. Some acquaintance with the background of a speaker or writer is necessary in order to appreciate the force of his words. . . .

Behind the score is the composer's theme. What do the notes suggest? An interpretation of nature, an appeal to human sentiment is conveyed. Men's emotions and activities are thus arranged in some intelligible scheme. The clash of individual wills is gradually resolved in a plan that allows to each a field of self-expression and also preserves order within the group. A system of human relations is established. This is the basis of social harmony. . . .

How is assimilation promoted? Different policies have been followed in the United States. The first to gain wide approval was based upon the so-called *melting pot theory*. The general idea is that if all kinds of people are thrown together and left to stew in their own juice, the good qualities of each will permeate the others and a superior blend will emerge. Presumably, dregs will sink and scum will be automatically removed in the process. The rationale of this scheme agrees with the theory of natural selection and laissez faire economy popular at one time.

The results obtained by this process were disappointing. The pot was not big enough for immigrants to circulate freely. They settled in lumps at the bottom and stuck there. Children raised in the slum absorbed its sodden flavor. Natives refused to mix with a lower economic stratum. The mess began to separate like curds and whey. An upper level formed a crust containing rich fats extracted from the mass below. The kettle boiled furiously, but no cook was at hand to stir and season the broth. Judges pronounced the dish unpalatable. The experiment was termed a failure.

Belief in social Darwinism has suffered a setback during the past fifty years. Uncontrolled natural forces are often destructive. Those forms of life that survive are not always the best from a human standpoint. All individuals do not rise or fall by virtue of innate capacity alone. Training and opportunity also affect success. Men cannot go far without materials and assistance supplied by their fellows. The depression and the war have worked a remarkable change in our views regarding rugged individualism. Social planning is now the fashion.

In marked contrast with the free and easy temper of our people at the turn of the century, is the disposition manifested during the last twenty-five years. *Americanization* became the slogan. Immigration was checked and naturalization was encouraged. Schools for foreigners were opened and social workers invaded Hobohemia. Children were taught to salute the flag and teachers were sworn to uphold the Constitution. Textbooks were revised under the scrutiny of one-hundred-percent patriots. Commissions investigated subversive (*i.e.* "un-American") activities and bureaus were set up to check them. Laws were passed to regulate predatory business. Labor organization was favored. Social security went into effect. Literary expatriates returned and native artists decorated our walls with local color.

Some of these reforms were long overdue; others seem to be drastic corrections of time-honored folkways. America has outgrown its non-age, and is now prepared to take its place as a world power. However it would be an irony of history if this recent arrival in the family of great nations should maintain a stiff-necked pharisaic attitude toward its older relatives. Some ridiculous manifestations of national conceit may be noted in passing.

Self-made business men volunteer to direct foreign trade and diplomacy. Local politicians advocate home-grown simples for national ills. Self-taught pundits arise to tell the world how it should be saved. Schoolmen and clergy exalt their particular brands of dogma and insist upon indoctrinating their followers with its peculiar theories. Amateur critics tell poets and playwrights what is wrong with their productions. The man on the street is ready to say just how America can win the war. Polls of uninformed public opinion serve as directives for hesitant leaders.

A reasonable amount of ethnocentrism is to be expected among any people. The ways they and their fathers have pursued must seem good to them. Habit, authority and rationalization establish certain lines of conduct. Ignorance of other forms of behavior, fear of attempting a dangerous transition and pure laziness inhibit rapid change. But when beaten trails of custom are replaced by iron rails of law, some alteration of grade and direction is necessary. Intolerance of suggestions from outside the group, suppression of variants within it and a domineering attitude toward lesser nations are not becoming in a democracy.

The spirit of nationalism (*i.e.*, "my country above all others") readily induces a people to adopt strong measures to check interference with its favored policy. Regimentation may be necessary in war time. But army discipline does not furnish a model for the conduct of art and industry. Any attempt to dam the flow of original thought or to cut off its connections with outside sources results in stagnation and desiccation. The springs that fed the reservoir may lie on distant mountain sides. Pipes and channels are required to bring them in. Such devices cannot regulate the amount of snow that falls on the peaks.

The principal weakness of imposed conformity lies in its external approach. A man may obey the law perforce, although he thoroughly disapproves of it. Such compliance often leads to clever evasion. A student may repeat a required formula without understanding its derivation or application. Such defective knowledge results in what has been called "the higher illiteracy," that is, ability to read words without meaning. A woman may perform the rites of hospitality prescribed by fashion, with bitterness in her heart. Her conduct might be considered hypocritical. In ways like these, people are induced to wear uniforms with slight attachment to the cause they represent. Such compliance does not deserve the name of assimilation. It is a lifeless show that carries no conviction.

Is there any other way of leading men to share vitally in the great tradition of our common life? Certainly! The two contrasting policies just mentioned by no means fill the wide logical interval that lies between them. Like many other questions, this one cannot be answered by choosing one horn of an imaginary dilemma. The real problem is to find how far to one side or the other we must go to locate a reasonably safe course. This cannot be plotted in detail, because the factors involved are many and variable. Still we can indicate an angle of approach. Let us call the objective *cooperative culture* and illustrate the means for attaining it in terms of foreign immigration. . . .

The first step is *selection*. The term here means intelligent choice of the number and kind of persons wanted to fill places in our national economy. The numbers will vary with changing conditions. The qualities desired have reference to the functions to be performed. Accidents of birthplace, residence, and racial origin are obviously less significant than are personal traits of health, intelligence and moral integrity. Arbitrary distinctions based upon wealth, politics and religion do not seem so important. Picking the right people is not a matter for legislators, but for administrative experts.

The second step is *registration*. This means identifying every alien who enters the country and recording his movements while here. Such measures have been used in many foreign countries for a long time. . . . The purpose is to avoid losing track of an individual and his performance. Anonymity is a dangerous gift, and mistaken identity may have serious consequences. This plan keeps a man and his record in line. Its use in wartime is obvious.

A third requirement is *distribution*. This implies rapid movement by new-comers to places where they are wanted, instead of settling in pools or drifting without ties. Where a man finds a home, a job and friends, there he is apt to stay as a useful and contented member of the community. . . .

The last point is the one we have been discussing in this paper—*assimilation*. It connotes agreement in the ways of life and participation in all their vital phases. When we have selected our guests and have placed them properly, we take them into our confidence, unless they misbehave. Their reception into churches, offices, clubs, and homes, is a sign that now the strangers belong among us. They recognize it too, and usually return the hospitality. Thus our circle of friends is enlarged and new bonds are formed among them.

The same process may be observed in any association. Suitable persons are selected for membership. Their experience is noted and their conduct is scrutinized. Soon they are assigned to appropriate positions. They learn the rules and presently show willingness to conduct themselves accordingly. Then, we say, "they have gotten the idea," "they enter into the spirit of the group." They are assimilated.

The new members also contribute enthusiasm and practical suggestions to the association. We do not expect them to renounce all former connections and to derive every idea from a single source. Discussion, correction, and improvement are believed to result from fresh contacts. This is what we mean by *cooperative culture*.

If people are free to seek association with others who have similar interests, they soon find their places in a new social order. Old lines of race and nationality tend to disappear in functional arrangements to promote art or industry. The most effective methods from any source tend to prevail. Good technique replaces ardent custom. Styles are modified and combined along broader lines. So cities and nations grow. . . .

The process of assimilation may now be summarized in three steps:

1. When men begin to live together they learn to communicate with one another by words and other symbols. These signs convey to each some knowledge of the other's experience and intention. As acquaintance grows, sympathy or dislike develops. Thus lines of unification and division are set up between individuals.

2. Persons of like mind cooperate to promote their common interests. They participate in essential phases of group activity and adopt codes of behavior that require obedience. Thus communities are organized according to institutional patterns.

3. Those members who comprehend the purpose of social arrangements strive to carry on a creative tradition. Compliance with conventional authority is not enough for them. They seek to establish the spirit of law that lives in them. Through communion with such men of good will a deep sense of unity pervades a people.

In conclusion, let us consider a graphic illustration of these stages. Suppose we represent three persons in communication with one another by a triangle of equal sides. Then join the corners to a point above them in the form of a pyramid. That indicates their union in some occupation or agency. When their corresponding faces are similar, twenty such pyramids can be packed into a regular solid by pointing their summits toward one center. If these units are duplicated and superimposed with their tips directed outward, the body expands into a starlike crystal having symmetrical connections between the exterior points and the core, as in the figure below. So elementary forms of human relations (institutions) developed into stable bodies (communities), which are combined in a design of many dimensions (civilization). An individual who enters into these relations absorbs social meaning from them and transmits its significance to others. *That is assimilation.*

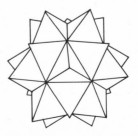

Selection *34*

Acculturation Without Assimilation?
The Jewish Community of Chicago, Illinois
Erich Rosenthal

Few people would doubt that the relatively successful manner in which so many millions of immigrants have been integrated into American society constitutes one of the world's major social experiments. One cannot accept without reservation the "melting pot" theory of Americanization, because what actually happened may have been that the country developed a system of synthesizing diverse and often antagonistic ethnic elements into its own social framework; yet one can say that assimilation usually followed a fairly predictable pattern. This pattern, often referred to as the *race relations cycle,* involved a distinct sequence of behavior. Although many ethnic groups originally tended to concentrate their settlement in certain urban neighborhoods near the center of the city, a movement away from older neighborhoods occurred as people moved to newer, more desirable residential areas. Alienation of immigrants from fellow ethnic members was seen by the American majority as a social-psychological process symbolic of *acculturation,* with acculturation defined as taking the beliefs, values, and customs of the American culture. Then it was thought that acculturation, facilitated by such factors as economic integration, political freedom, educational opportunities, and intermarriage, would lead to a relatively complete *assimilation* of the ethnic minority into the mainstream of American society, so that the immigrants would become more or less indistinguishable from the majority.

The intriguing question asked by Rosenthal is this: Is it possible for acculturation to occur without assimilation? Put another way, the problem is: Does mere conformity with dominant norms and codes of behavior assure complete integration into the community? Basically, the answer to these questions hinges on one's definitions of acculturation and assimilation. Most properly, *acculturation* should be reserved for the acquiring of knowledge, skill, behavior patterns, language, and the like, in a degree presumably comparable to that of persons who have learned that culture from birth. (Incidentally, acculturation, like socialization, is always partial and to some extent unique, in that no one partakes fully of all aspects of a culture.) The term *assimilation* should be reserved for a process in which the person (or group) develops a set of sentiments, social relationships, loyalties, and particularly a feeling of identification with the society involved. When an adult learns about the American Revolution, he takes one step toward acculturation; but when a Japanese-American child reports at home, with shining eyes, that he learned in school that "We won the American Revolution!" then he has passed from the area of acculturation into the area of assimilation.

Rosenthal interprets the settlement pattern of the Jewish population of Chicago, Illinois, in terms of the successive stages of the race relations cycle from acculturation to assimilation. The resistance to assimilation on the part of the Jewish community of Chicago, which brings the universality of the race relations cycle into question, may be explained by three special circumstances: (1) the Jewish education of the community, (2) the wish of the Jews themselves to remain segregated from the rest of the Chicagoans, and (3) the social and psychological accompaniments of living in a high-status area.

In Selection 35, Eisenstadt uses the absorption of new immigrants into Israel to describe large-scale successful integration and to demonstrate how the successful assimilation of diverse ethnic elements into a community or nation is to a considerable extent a function of those individuals' past experiences and psychological predispositions.

For over forty years American sociologists under the leadership of the Department of Sociology of the University of Chicago have paid close attention to the distribution of population within our northern industrial cities, of which Chicago may well be taken as the prototype. They have found that at a given time racial, ethnic, and religious groups are not randomly scattered but are concentrated in neighborhoods and that the movement of an ethnic or religious group from one neighborhood to another follows a pattern. Usually the movement is directed away from older neighborhoods near the center of the city toward newer and more desirable residential areas, at or near the periphery, where both the physical condition of housing and social conditions are better than those in the area left behind.

. . . In *The Ghetto*—first published in 1928 and reissued in 1956—the late Louis Wirth gave a detailed description of the area of first settlement around the turn of the century, its eventual liquidation, and the movement of the Jewish population to areas of second and third settlement.[1] However, he was not satisfied with describing the movements from area to area but looked upon the sequence of moves as symbols of cultural, social, and social-psychological processes. Such movement is the expression of a further step toward Americanization and acculturation. Whenever a family moves to a "better" location, it does so in the hope of improving its social status. . . . Finally, according to this theory, the move from a Jewish neighborhood is motivated by the desire to flee, to alienate oneself from one's fellow Jews, to live in a neighborhood that has lost all traces of ethnicity. Assimilation and integration are the terminal phases of these processes.

It is the purpose of this paper to pick up the thread and describe the flow of Jewish communal life since the late twenties and to examine whether and to what extent the cultural, social, and psychological forces that were projected have made an impact upon the community.[2]

In the late twenties a newcomer to Chicago learned rather quickly that the Jewish population of the city was dispersed over all parts of the city, not evenly, of course, but in well-defined local communities. Each community offered its residents a specific type of housing, a particular set of Jewish and public institutions, and a differential level of status.

In 1930 the Jewish population of the city was estimated at 270,000, of which just about half lived in local communities on the West Side. Of these, North Lawndale, with its 75,000 Jewish residents, constituting about 67 per cent of the total population of the area, was the most distinctive Jewish community of the city. As the successor to the old "ghetto," the area of first settlement, it had become the center of Jewish life. An additional one-fourth of the Jewish population—about 69,000—lived on the Northwest Side, with the community of Albany Park containing the largest Jewish settlement, about 23,000 persons. On the North and South Sides the Jewish population amounted to about 12 per cent each.

"Acculturation Without Assimilation? The Jewish Community of Chicago, Illinois" by Erich Rosenthal. Reprinted from *The American Journal of Sociology*, Vol. LXVI (1960), 275-288, by permission of The University of Chicago Press.

[1] Louis Wirth, *The Ghetto*, "Phoenix Books," No. 7 (Chicago: University of Chicago Press, 1956).

[2] This study is based on a combination of sociological methods. The writer spent most of his time in local communities, where he studied the signs of physical change, collected local newspapers, and studied the history of the neighborhood. The directors of social agencies, schools, libraries, and religious organizations were interviewed to determine the nature of the change in the neighborhood, the impact of the change upon local institutions, and their adaptation to it. Since many institutions are trying to meet the threat to their survival by a systematic study of the changes in their constituency, the personnel made excellent informants who were anxious to exchange ideas with a specialist who had made the effort to come all the way from New York. The research staffs of city-wide public and private planning agencies furnished the writer with the most recent demographic and economic analyses.

Rogers Park on the North Side and South Shore on the South Side contained the largest Jewish settlements, with about 11,000 persons each. Within the city a residence in a South Side neighborhood conferred the highest status, followed by the North, Northwest, and West Sides, in that order. Outside the city, residence in a North Shore suburb bestowed the highest status, surpassing any area within the city limits.

This pattern of spatial distribution was well correlated with the pattern of acculturation: the West Side, with the largest number and proportion of foreign-born, was the seat of orthodoxy and of secular Jewish movements. Albany Park to the northwest was a transitional community characterized by one reform and a few orthodox synagogues, while the North and South Side communities were dominated by reform temples. At the same time, the pattern of internal migration functioned in accordance with the sociological scheme: the West Side was losing population in a small but steady stream which was directed to the other neighborhoods in a predictable manner.

A study of the shifts in the distribution of the Jewish population between 1930, the onset of the depression, and 1946, the end of World War II and the height of the housing shortage, corroborated the sociological expectations: the older communities with the largest numbers and highest concentrations experienced the greatest losses, while the neighborhoods near the edges of the city showed the greatest gains. The fact that the North Side communities showed a considerably greater gain than the older South Side communities was interpreted as a continuation of the existing trend toward a more even distribution of the Jewish population over all parts of the city and toward a continued process of acculturation and rise in status.

Today we know that the spectacular growth of the Jewish population on the North Side between 1930 and 1946 was the initial step toward high concentration. Since the end of the war, the nearly even distribution of the Jewish population over all parts of the city, together with the orderly streams of internal migration from one status area to another, has given way to a high concentration in the northern neighborhoods and suburbs. Today, of the total Jewish population of the Chicago area—estimated at 282,000—nearly 60 per cent have settled into one area, stretching from Albany Park in the southwest within the city to Highland Park, the northernmost suburb on Lake Michigan. While the overall proportion of Jewish to non-Jewish residents in this area appears to be about 40 per cent in the city and 30 per cent in suburban towns, each contains neighborhoods where the density is as high as 90 per cent or more. The next step, then, is to discover the cause for this reversal of a long-time trend and to examine whether these facts require a revision of long-cherished social theories.

The settlement pattern of the Jewish group—or, for that matter, of any group—is determined by the "push," the pressure that other ethnic and racial groups exert, as well as by the "pull" that draws a group to a new neighborhood. It is well to remember that "pull," as well as "push," is involved in shortening the period of occupancy of an area by a given group and in shortening the life span of the unique set of institutions designed to serve the group during its tenure. The current settlement pattern of the Jewish population of Chicago has been greatly influenced by the "push," the pressure exercised by the influx of southern in-migrants, white as well as Negro; of the two, Negro in-migrants have been by far the stronger force in the relocation of the Jewish population and its communal institutions. . . . The absorption of this large wave of in-migrants was aided to a considerable extent by the removal of the Jewish population from West Side communities, particularly from North Lawndale, which between 1915 and 1945 had the highest concentration of Jewish population and which, through its array of institutions, was the most distinguishable Jewish community of the city. Although in 1946 North Lawndale had been all white, by 1954 the area had become an all-Negro community. In eight years about 100,000 whites, of whom an estimated 64,000 were Jewish, had evacuated the neighborhood and were replaced by an estimated 120,000 Negroes. A considerably smaller number of Jewish persons was displaced from the lakefront communities on the South Side as the so-called Black Belt began to expand eastward into Kenwood, Woodlawn, and parts of Hyde Park at about the time that the Supreme Court issued its ruling against the enforcement of race-restrictive covenants.

While the Negro in-migrants have made their homes on the West and South Sides of the city, the southern white in-migrant, the so-called hillbilly, has found his new habitat on the North Side, mainly in the Uptown community. It is estimated that this group displaced about 25,000 Jewish persons.

Although the settlement of southern in-migrants is undoubtedly the largest force in the relocation of Jewish neighborhoods, there are other, comparably smaller forces at work in uprooting Jewish neighborhoods. According to one informant—whom I shall call Rabbi Brightman—the Jewish residents of the North Side community of Logan

Square, which is far removed from the scenes and problems of racial succession, have left the area because of a change in the rules governing admission to public high schools. It appears that, until recently, the students of this area had a choice of attending the local high school or one outside the district in a large Jewish community to the north. The Jewish families had made intensive use of this option and sent their high-school youth to the school outside the area. When the Chicago Board of Education issued a new ruling under which the students would have to attend the local high school, the Jewish parents who had disapproved of the standards of the local school all along left the neighborhood for the far North Side as soon as possible.

The rapid evacuation of Jewish neighborhoods and the concomitant lack of resistance to the possession of these areas can be attributed to three attributes of the Jewish population of the city, namely, relatively low home ownership, relatively high income, and demand for residence in high-status areas. The surrender of an area to another group is probably greatly facilitated if the majority of the residents do not own their own homes, as was the case with the Jewish population. In 1940, five years before the population exchange began, only 13.5 per cent of foreign-born Jewish persons were home-owners, compared with an average of 36.9 per cent of foreign-born persons from "old" countries and 39.2 per cent from "new" countries. The difference between native-born Jews of foreign or mixed parentage and the averages for such persons from "old" and "new" countries is of the same magnitude. Although income data for the total Jewish population are not available, returns of the 1950 census indicate that foreign-born Jewish persons had higher incomes in 1949 than did foreign-born persons from other ethnic groups. Therefore, some segments of the Jewish population did not have to resist the newcomers for economic reasons but were able and, as will be shown below, rather eager to move to newer and better housing in higher-status areas eight miles or more from the old neighborhood.

It has been demonstrated that the demand for high-status areas by the Jewish population precedes the surrender of older neighborhoods to the non-white population. A detailed study into the causes of the liquidation of North Lawndale, the most "ghetto-like" Jewish community of Chicago, revealed that the young adults had left the area for other neighborhoods in the city. The loss of 10,000 people between 1930 and 1940 was confined to persons under forty-five years of age, while the population aged over sixty-five

years increased by 50 per cent. The same pattern was repeated for the next decade. This vacuum was filled by the Negro population, which needed housing desperately. Since cities up to now have not succeeded in developing and maintaining racially mixed neighborhoods, even those people who would be better off by staying in the old area are compelled to swell the stream of migrants. This is particularly true of old persons and households with marginal status.

Since the displacement of the Jewish groups is in large measure due to the settlement of a large body of non-white in-migrants, the question arises whether the resettlement pattern of the Jewish population, namely, the heavy concentration on the North Side, has also been influenced by the arrival of about one-quarter million Negroes in the last decade. To the extent that a combination of the growth of the non-white population together with continued and increased segregation . . . begets increased white segregation, the answer must be affirmative. But the major reason for the concentration of the Jewish population to the north of the city must be sought elsewhere, namely, in the fact that the Jewish population directs its housing demand toward—and perhaps even limits it to—the area of highest status. . . .

Although the North Side had steadily gained social ascendancy over the South Side since the end of the first World's Fair in 1893, within the Jewish community a residence in a lakeside community on the South Side conferred very high status at least until the end of World War I. The preference for the North Side and North Shore, however, was evident as early as 1925, fully twenty-five years before Jews arrived there in any large numbers, and was commented upon in a Jewish newspaper: "It is unfortunate that the Jewish population has the moving spirit and neighborhoods change practically overnight. First it was Douglas and Independence Boulevards, then the North Shore district, then Rogers Park: now it is Wilmette, Winnetka, Glencoe, etc." It appears that at the same time young people were consciously oriented toward the North Shore suburbs. The director of the Jewish People's Institute, which in 1925 was still located in the area of first settlement, recorded in his annual report that the students in the JPI evening school had, under the guidance of their teachers, organized summer outings to the North Shore, namely, to Highland Park and to Ravinia Park, the site of the outdoor music festival.

It therefore comes as no surprise when one informant says that his strong desire to leave the North Lawndale area for Wilmette had been formed when, as a youngster, he gained the impression from the local newspapers that all the good things in life could be found in the North Shore suburbs. . . . The attraction to this area is buttressed by the fact that it is predominantly, if not exclusively, white. It therefore relieves its residents from psychological anxiety about status and economic anxiety about problems of tenancy and home ownership in a neighborhood threatened by racial succession. . . .

Before an attempt is made to relate this recent spatial consolidation to the sociological scheme of acculturation and assimilation, status gain, and alienation, the most salient features of the new community of the North Side will be described. First of all, the recent consolidation of the Jewish community has not done away with income, housing, or status differentials. As a matter of fact, the resettlement in the new area proceeded in such a manner as to maintain these differentials. The swift relocation of the Jewish population was accomplished in a two-step move. Those Jewish families who at the end of the war had been residents of the North Side within the city limits made space for the newcomers by moving into the north suburbs. A study of the recent migration of Jewish families to these suburbs shows not only that each town attracts a specific income and occupational level but also that the newcomers typically come from one area rather than another. For example, a former resident of Albany Park is more likely to settle in Skokie, while a family from West Rogers Park will probably move to Glencoe or Highland Park. For the local communities within the city similar regularities of migration streams can be observed between sites of departure and arrival. This differential income and status pattern is reflected by the distribution of religious institutions: There is a predominance of orthodox synagogues in the communities within the city limits, of conservative congregations in Skokie, and of reform temples on the North Shore.

The second most salient attribute of this new community is the fact that the center of strictest orthodoxy is no longer far removed from the relatively well-acculturated areas. Rather, it forms the southernmost tier of the new area of Jewish settlement and is within walking distance from the adjacent Jewish neighborhoods. It fell to Albany Park to become the center of strictest orthodoxy and the seat of the most "foreign" expression of Jewish life. Apparently, at one time Albany Park had played a crucial role in the process of acculturation and status gain for the Jewish population. Unfortunately, a detailed social history of this area is not available. However, there are some indications that in the early twenties, when Albany Park had its heyday, this community was the launching platform for families with the greatest impetus for rapid economic advancement, rapid secularization, and Americanization. By the end of the thirties, however, this neighborhood had taken on the characteristics of older neighborhoods to the south, such as a growing number of orthodox synagogues, a community center, and a boys' club. It appears that the local leadership had not realized the slow aging and downward drift of the area and reacted with severe shock after the war when they were confronted with the fact that this area was in the process of becoming the most "ghetto-like" community of the city. Today, Albany Park has become the residential area for those households which would have preferred to stay in the old neighborhoods—particularly in North Lawndale—but were swept into the stream of migration by the onrush of the Negro population. These newcomers to Albany Park have the following characteristics: They are, according to the local merchants, less affluent than the previous residents. The new families probably comprise the weakest economic stratum of the Jewish community of Chicago. Among the new residents are a great number of aged people. . . .

We can now examine the question as to whether and to what extent this spatial consolidation of the Jewish community has affected the processes of acculturation, accretion in status, and alienation. According to the theory known as the "race-relations cycle," increased segregation of an ethnic group should signify the stoppage, if not the reversal, of these cultural, social, and psychological processes. According to this scheme, which calls for progressively smaller clusters, as well as progressively lower densities of Jewish residents, the process of alienation has been reversed. Apparently, the Jewish population was willing to pay this price for residence in a high-status area. While the process of Americanization has probably been only minimally affected, another aspect of acculturation, namely, secularization, appears to have been reversed. Witness the growth in the new area of religious institutions, temple and synagogue membership, religious-school attendance, and the revival of selected ceremonials, Bar Mitzvahs in particular. Finally, the very fact that an ethnic group occupies a new area in such large numbers may tend to lower the status of the area in its own eyes and in those of the community at large. To sum it up, the race-relations cycle which ran its course up to the end of World War II seems to have been brought to a standstill and experienced a serious setback. It should be of some interest that the American Council for Judaism has drawn exactly this conclusion and defined the current situation as one of "self-segregation, secular withdrawal and self-ghettoization" resulting from Zionist activity and propaganda. . . .

However, the relocation of the Jewish population can be interpreted in a different—and, in my opinion, a more correct—manner by putting the race-relations cycle into historical perspective as well as by reexamining the causes for the spatial mobility of the Jewish population. To start with the latter, I question the validity of investing the spatial movement of the Jewish population with such a high degree of cultural, social, and psychological significance. It might be more correct to give the housing market a greater weight as a determinant in the location of the Jewish population. Such factors as changing land use, changing land values, racial segregation of non-white populations, a marked shortage of adequate housing, and attempts to restrict this short supply to selected groups combine to define the location of a social group at a given time within an urban area. As was shown above, the surrender of the West and South Sides to the non-white population, the availability of residential vacant land on the North Side, the desire and economic ability to get housing that meets today's standards, all contributed to the relocation of the Jewish population in a specific area. Similarly, the encroachment of industry and railroads, street widening, and the influx of Negroes were important factors in the destruction of the original "ghetto" on the Near West Side of Chicago as was the desire for more healthful housing in a better neighborhood. It appears that the liquidation of the area of first settlement was more in the nature of upward *economic* mobility than of "social mobility altering occupation and status." I propose to put the race-relations cycle into historical perspective with the aid of the following considerations, namely, the difference between the process of acculturation in the United States and the process of assimilation in Europe and the difference in the rate of speed of acculturation between the Jewish group and other ethnic groups. In central and western Europe assimilation was the price demanded from the Jews for their legal and social emancipation. It was the individual person or nuclear family which, in expectation of economic and social rewards, severed its tie with the relatively small Jewish community. However, for the Jews in the United States there were internal as well as external reasons for becoming acculturated in a collective rather than an individual manner. Based on the much more pronounced attributes of peoplehood, such as language, autonomous community life, and size and settlement pattern of the population, for the descendants of Jews from eastern Europe, cohesion and group survival rather than assimilation are supreme values. Therefore, the group must do everything in its power to prevent assimilation. Concrete experience with the economic, social, and political organization in the United States has helped to sustain the value of group cohesion at least until very recently. . . .

The available evidence indicates that the Jewish population has gone through the process of acculturation at a faster rate than have other ethnic groups that arrived in the United States at about the same time. Since acculturation and social mobility are interrelated, it appears that the Jewish population has achieved a high economic, education, and occupational status. . . .

The collective approach to, as well as the rapid rate of, social mobility has an important bearing on the process of alienation, the need to flee one's fellow Jews. It appears, first of all, that the extent of alienation cannot have been as great as it would have been if acculturation and social mobility had proceeded exclusively by individual efforts. In recent years a definite case of alienation occurred in the local community of Albany Park, the most "ghetto-like" neighborhood in Chicago in the last decade. There, acculturated Jews resented the influx of a Hasidic sect whose members not only have a "foreign" appearance but also reject acculturation in principle. This instance leads me to believe that alienation was most pronounced in the first stage of acculturation and was directed particularly sharply against those persons and groups who insisted on their foreign ways and that the intensity of alienation was progressively reduced with increased Americanization and rapid upward mobility. There can be no doubt that the cessation of Jewish mass immigration, over three decades ago, has contributed significantly to the decline of alienation as well as to rapid social mobility.

The decline of this centrifugal force, then, contributes its share to the consolidation of the Jewish community. Are there any other factors that are responsible for the current voluntary segregation? When I asked Rabbi Brightman—as I asked all my informants—what his explanation is for the recent aggregation of the Jewish community on the North Side of Chicago, his reply was that the one thing that parents fear more than anything else and fear more than at any other time in history is amalgamation, the marriage of their children to "outsiders." While at one time Jewish identity was no problem for the individual who lived a distinctively Jewish life in his home, his synagogue, and the community, today there is little that marks the Jew as a Jew except Jewish self-consciousness and association with fellow Jews. If one were to depend on the religiocultural rather than on the associational tie, large-scale amalgamation would be the order of the day. To forestall this, the parents favor residence in a neighborhood that has such a high density of Jewish families that the probability of their children marrying a Jewish person approaches certainty. . . .

The one factor which currently operates against assimilation, the final step in the race-relation cycle, is Jewish self-consciousness, or identification with the Jewish group. The decline in cultural differences has not been accompanied by a decline in Jewish self-consciousness; on the contrary, it appears that the latter has increased. Many persons have what amounts to a "false consciousness," where the behavior pattern and value system cannot be reconciled with the practices and religious beliefs of Judaism. To a considerable extent this heightened self-consciousness is a result of the growth of anti-Semitism in the thirties and of the Nazi definition of Jews along "racial" and ancestral lines. . . . The second major event in the recent history of the Jewish people, the creation of the state of Israel, is commonly held to have contributed to a heightened Jewish self-consciousness of a more positive nature. However, this assumption seems not to have been subjected to any empirical tests.

Jewish educators and rabbis are keenly aware of the rift between the decline in the practice of Judaism and the height of Jewish self-consciousness. To the question whether there can be Jewishness without Judaism, they answer that "Jewish survival requires both." Jewish educators are eager to use this high consciousness as a motivating force to give this formal commitment a substantial base through Jewish education. It appears that this attempt has been eminently successful: The enrolment in Jewish schools increased by 131 per cent between 1948 and 1958. But a closer examination of the performance of the Jewish schools reveals that, compared to the twenties and thirties their standards have been lowered considerably. A generation ago the average afternoon school provided each student with eight to ten hours of instruction per week, forty-eight weeks per year, as compared with current average of four to five hours per week, thirty-eight weeks a year. While the professional educators want to achieve a maximum of commitment, a thorough knowledge of Hebrew, and a continuity of study through high school, the average afternoon falls far short of this goal and provides only a minimum program of education that prepares

for and ends at the Bar Mitzvah ceremony at the age of thirteen years. The result is that "hundreds of thousands of Jews enter the threshold of adult Jewish life with little understanding and less knowledge of their Jewish heritage." The resistance to a more intensive Jewish education stems from the parents. . . . [T]he historian Ismar Elbogen, in recording the occurrence of such resistance one hundred years ago, attributes it to parental concern "lest too much Jewish knowledge should serve to isolate their children, burden them with a heavy load, render them unfit for the struggle of life; and so they [the parents] hindered rather than promoted intensive Jewish education for their children."[3] It appears, then, that the basic function of Jewish education is to implant Jewish self-consciousness rather than Judaism, to "inoculate" the next generation with that minimum of religious practice and belief that is considered necessary to keep alive a level of Jewish self-consciousness that will hold the line against assimilation.

A modicum of Jewish education and voluntary segregation are two parts of a three-part device designed to forestall large-scale assimilation. The third is residence in a high-status area. We are now in a position to understand more fully the quest of the Jewish population for residence in such an area. Settlement there removes the stigma that is usually attributed to a separate ethnic community which, according to the scheme of the race-relations cycle, is reserved for unacculturated immigrants. Residence in a high-status area indicates the voluntary nature of the settlement of Jews as well as non-Jews and lifts the burden of alienation from the younger generation in particular. . . .

The question thus arises whether the survival formula—voluntary segregation in a high-status area plus a modicum of Jewish education—is successful in preventing the final step of assimilation. . . . If one is satisfied with taking intermarriage as a simple and convenient index of assimilation, the picture is as follows: Private communal surveys undertaken in the thirties revealed that about 6 per cent of Jewish families were intermarried. The first government survey of the religious composition of the American people revealed that in 1957, 7.2 per cent of all Jewish families had a non-Jewish marriage partner. A recent survey of the Jewish population of Washington, D.C., found that 11.5 per cent of all households were intermarried. An analysis of marriage licenses in

---

[3] Ismar Elbogen, *A Century of Jewish Life* (Philadelphia: Jewish Publication Society, 1953), p. 100.

the state of Iowa for 1953 showed 31 per cent of Jewish marriages to be mixed. A recent survey of the Jewish population of the San Francisco area indicated that the proportion of mixed marriages was 17.2 per cent in San Francisco, 20 per cent on the peninsula, and 37 per cent in Marin County. In Canada, where government statistics on intermarriage are available, the rate of Jewish intermarriage has steadily increased from 4.9 per cent in 1926-30 to 11.7 per cent for 1951-55.

. . . If we accept the findings of the 1957 survey of the United States Bureau of the Census of a national intermarriage rate of 7.2 per cent, and if, at the same time, we assume that the statistics for Iowa and the San Francisco area are merely regional variations of the over-all rate, we can probably be justified in defending the current survival formula as adequate for the preservation of the Jewish group. If we assume, however, that the findings for Iowa and San Francisco are the first indications of the future over-all rate of intermarriage, then the efficacy of the survival formula must be seriously doubted. There can, however, be no doubt that the likelihood of intermarriage increases with increased acculturation. The recent Washington survey was detailed enough to show that persons born in the United States with an educational achievement beyond high school and with high professional status are most likely to enter into intermarriage.

Selection 35

The Process of Absorption of New Immigrants in Israel
S. N. Eisenstadt

The rebirth of the state of Israel is one of the most remarkable events of history. A people oppressed and humiliated for 2000 years sought to build anew in a desolate land. Today the world is aware of the technological, agricultural, and political successes of this new state.

The new nation has had a full measure of economic, military, political, and even religious problems; yet some of the citizens of Israel would argue that one of the most difficult problems which faced the new nation was the integration of all its new immigrants into a single society. The range of variability of languages, types of Judaism, socio-cultural backgrounds, experiences, and personality syndromes seemed to approach the infinite. As a result, large numbers of immigrants experienced difficulty in adjusting to the new country. In fact, some of the problems were so great that one might almost say the new country had trouble adjusting to immigrants.

Eisenstadt set out to analyze those conditions, predispositions, and past experiences that contributed to an immigrant's successful adaptation to his new state. First, his investigation revealed that the successful immigrants as a group could be characterized as possessing an adequate predisposition to change. Eisenstadt next sought the social-psychological sources of this predisposition. Which sectors of which populations seemed most likely to be characterized by this quality? Does family membership promote or undermine the attitudes and orientations of the new immigrant? How does a predisposition to change manifest itself in terms of an individual's aspiration level and identification with the Jewish state?

The student should not regard Eisenstadt's findings as relevant only to the state of Israel. Successful migration in the United States is probably amenable to the same kind of analysis, and it would not be surprising to find similar forces influencing migrant adjustment.

The field work on which this material is based has been carried on in ten centres of new immigrants' settlements—three urban quarters, three semiurban quarters, and four cooperative agricultural settlements. The field work was carried out from October 1949 to November 1950, and dealt mainly with "new" immigrants—those who arrived after the establishment of the State of Israel. The average length of stay of the immigrant in Israel was, at the end of the field work, about 19 months. The field work was executed in the following way: In each location a field worker, or—in the urban centres—a group of two-three field workers, established themselves as students of the problems of new immigrants. They worked in three directions: 1. Continuous, systematic observation of the behaviour of the new immigrants in various typical social situations—work, school, public life, religious life, relief agencies, and, to some degree, also in their homes. 2. Intensive "free," "open-ended" interviewing of a selected sample in each location—usually a random sample within each main "ethnic" group—according to prearranged schedules, which were not, however, shown during the interviews. These interviews took place either in the immigrants' homes or in informal walks and like situations, and usually included the adult and adolescent members of the family. The schedule dealt with a variety of topics, namely, their general background, motives for immigration, general interest, levels of aspiration in different spheres, social participation and identification, and so on. This sample served also as a panel for repeated interviewing on different problems of attitudes and behaviour, such as identification with the new country and participation in the new social setting, in regard to which changes may have taken place during the year. The interviews were undertaken only after the field workers established themselves in the locations. They were extended in time, and on many topics repeated three or four times, according to changing conditions and situations. 3. More extensive and freer conversations and interviews with a larger sample of immigrants, usually with a great part of the inhabitants of a given quarter. These were used for obtaining more general background information and for investigation of various points raised during the interviews. All

these interviews varied in the degree of their intensity. . . .

The general problem of the research

The most general problem with which this research was concerned was the conditions under which successful adaptation of immigrants took place. Adaptation was broadly defined as the immigrants' effective capacity to perform successfully those basic roles inherent in the main institutional spheres (family, economic, political, etc.) of the social structure of the absorbing country. This effective capacity can be subdivided into three main spheres: 1. The actual learning of new social roles and their performance in different spheres; 2. the extent of stable social participation with old inhabitants, either in existing or in new types of groups; and 3. the evolution and maintenance of positive identification with the new social structure and its values, and the minimization of aggressive behaviour oriented against it. It is, of course, obvious that the achievement of maximal adaptation is a slow, gradual, and uneven process which can be attained, if at all, only under specific conditions. Broadly speaking, two main sets of such conditions can be distinguished: (a) those relating to the immigrants' own motivations and predispositions to action in the new social field, and (b) those relating to the conditions existing within the new social field, which define the opportunities available to the new immigrants and the attitudes existing towards them. In this paper we shall concentrate mainly on some aspects of the first set of conditions.

Some social characteristics of immigration and adaptation

The process of immigration is a process of physical transition from one society to another. Through it the immigrant is taken out of a more or less stable social system and transplanted into another.

This process of transplantation involves considerable frustrations and gives rise to many social problems among the immigrants. The initial immigration is usually motivated by some feelings of inadequacy and insecurity within the old social system, and by the hope to resolve this insecurity

From *Human Relations*, Vol. 5 (1952), 223-246.

in the new one. In the first stages of transplantation, the immigrant encounters, however, an additional element of insecurity, caused by two interdependent factors: First, the mere necessity to act in a new, relatively strange social field may increase the feeling of insecurity; and second, the process of immigration and transplantation involves a considerable shrinking of the immigrants' social life and participation. Immigration usually takes place in groups which do not encompass all the social spheres of the people, and for some time at least the immigrant is confined to such smaller groups as his mainstay of social participation and identification. Thus throughout this period the immigrant can perform adequately only some of his roles, as only in these smaller groups are his role-expectations more or less institutionalized. In other, wider spheres the immigrant lives in an unstable, unstructured field, with only minimal institutionalization of role-expectations.

The immigrants' integration within the new country may, then, be visualized as a process of extension of the immigrants' field of social participation through mutual adaptation of their role-expectations and the institutionalized norms of the absorbing society. Through this process the immigrants may find solutions to the double social and psychological insecurity in which they are involved. . . .

The nature and manifestations of predisposition to change

Our first task is to set out a set of indices (or attributes) of these (positive) predispositions. The mere undertaking or performance of new roles could not constitute such an index, as almost every immigrant has to perform some of the roles, especially in the occupational field. It is the immigrant's definition of, and attitude toward, this change that is of interest to us and which should be indicated by these indices.

The most general attribute of a positive predisposition to change is a *high level of frustration-toleration*. Such factors as the exigencies of the absorbing situation and the necessity for reorientation constitute definite frustrations, and an attitude which accepts these conditions as inescapable necessarily entails a high level of frustration-toleration. The main concrete manifestations of this attribute are the following:

1. *Ego-integrity* in face of frustrations imposed by the new situation, which can be seen in (a) a low degree of personal apathy and/or aggression as a reaction to these frustrations; (b) the maintenance of personal initiative within the new

situation—a high degree of selective activity in the exploration of the new environment, in utilization of different opportunities, etc.; and (c) a general "experimental" attitude towards the new environment, which is closely related to (b), and which also manifests itself in a low incidence of complaining and bitterness and in a preparedness to "try out" the new roles and to perform them faithfully.

2. *Flexibility of levels of aspirations*, which manifests itself in (a) the readiness to change aspirations if found to be unrealizable in the existing situation, and to adjust them to present possibilities, and (b) "open-mindedness" with regard to aspirations oriented to the future and preparedness to "experiment" with alternative future possibilities.

Both ego-integrity and flexibility of levels of aspirations were also manifested in a strong positive future-perspective, i.e., the evaluation of the present as a preparatory stage for the future, making possible the endurance of present hardships, as opposed to "fixation" on the present and evaluation of the future in terms of present difficulties only. . . .

[The] difference between ego-strength and ego-weakness [which is related to frustration-tolerance] may be related to a psychological characteristic recently investigated by Fraenkel-Brunswick and Rokeach—namely, the "tolerance of ambiguity."[1] The initial absorbing situation is, we think, highly ambiguous for the immigrants, both because of its novelty and because of the almost always present discrepancy between their hopes and the existing reality. It seems that those with a positive predisposition to change have a high level of ambiguity-toleration and can resolve this ambiguity (and give some positive meaning to their situation) through their own self-integrative principles; while those with a negative predisposition to change lack these principles and this strength and consequently cannot resolve and tolerate the existing ambiguity.

Ego-strength and evaluation of status-symbols

In our sample, this characteristic can best be seen in the different ways of self-evaluation of

---

[1] W. Fraenkel-Brunswick, "Intolerance of Ambiguity as an Emotional and Perceptual Personality Variable," *Journal of Personality*, 18 (1949), 108-143; M. Rokeach, "Generalized Mental Rigidity as a Factor in Ethnocentrism," *Journal of Abnormal and Social Psychology*, 43 (1948), 259-278.

status and occupational standing. The necessity for change of roles is, as we have seen, most pressing in this sphere, and it may involve forgoing many of the amenities, patterns of behaviour, and expressive symbols, such as standard of living, style of dress, dwelling, occupational choice, etc., that are. either closely interwoven with social status or constitute its main symbols. The attitude towards this necessity differs markedly as between those with positive and those with negative predisposition to change. Those with positive predisposition to change are quite prepared to forgo some of these symbols and the expressive gratifications inherent in them, as long as they feel they can achieve *through* their present activities—even if only in a future time—some basic economic and social security. They do not renounce any aspirations of achieving some high social status in the future—but their image of this status is not bound to any of the "symbolic" patterns of behaviour, and they are quite prepared to experiment with many different possibilities and avenues of achievement, and to vary them according to the necessities and demands of the situation. Throughout this process of "experimentation" and change their self-evaluation does not suffer to any great extent because of the necessary changes, and is not dependent on their clinging to these various amenities and symbols. In the present stage their evaluation of all these symbols and amenities is essentially an "instrumental" one, e.g., as a means to social and economic security.

The interpretation of status is entirely different among those with a negative predisposition. Here we find a definitely "ritualistic" attitude which makes their self-esteem dependent on the acquisition and holding of these different symbols and amenities, which become, as it were, ends in themselves, and necessary symbols of self. . . .

These different evaluations of self and own status were also found to be very highly correlated with different types of identification with the Jewish nation (or the State of Israel). We have seen earlier that the type of orientation that the immigrant has toward his new country is of great importance for the process of adaptation, and here we could find a definite correlation between this orientation and those attributes which make for differential-tempo and direction of adaptation, viz., the predisposition to change. Among those with positive predisposition, it was found that belonging to the Jewish community and coming to Israel were defined, in themselves, as sources of security, strength and "feeling of belongingness." It was non-conditional identification, evaluated mainly in terms of "living together"; "among own people"; "without disturbances"; "being at home." Among those with a negative predisposition this identification was mainly conditional on the possibility of their maintaining—or, usually, acquiring—within this community symbols of status which had for them the above-mentioned ritual quality. Belonging to the Jewish community as such does not constitute for them a source of security. . . .

We may, then, sum up by saying that the immigrant with a positive predisposition to change is usually one with considerable ego-strength, which enables him not to cling "ritually" to various status characteristics as prerequisites for self-esteem and social acceptance, and whose ego-strength is, at least to some degree, connected with his positive, non-conditional identification with the Jewish community as a source of security and belongingness.

It is this "ego-strength" and self-assurance which enable those with positive predisposition to change to participate actively in the structuring and "rebuilding" of the social field in which they are placed through the process of immigration, and to contribute to their own social reintegration. The flexibility of their role-expectations enables them to adapt them to the institutional norms of the absorbing society, and to achieve full institutionalization of their role-expectations. On those with negative predisposition the forces of the social field impinge sharply without their being able to reinterpret and reintegrate them actively in their social field. For them the social field remains unstructured, and their situation mainly "anomic."

Conditions of predisposition to change: sources of ego-strength

Our next step was the analysis of the social conditions under which positive and negative predisposition to change develop among different types of immigrants.

First, we tried to see whether any significant correlations existed between the predisposition to change and some "usual" objective, socio-economic variables—such as country of origin, occupation, economic status, education level, and age at time of marriage.

Among these it was found that the positive predisposition is relatively higher among unmarried people within the age-groups of 15-22 than in other comparable groups, and that no significant correlations exist with the other variables. It was found, however, that the distribution of these two types is not the same among immigrants of different countries of origin [see Table 1]. . . .

This focus is in line with the general exposition of our problem as outlined above. If the existence of a positive predisposition to change can be more or less equated with "ego-strength," then in looking into conditions giving rise to it we should look into possible sources of such strength (or weakness) within the immigrants' social groups and settings. Although ego-strength has been defined as relative independence from "external" evaluation, it is obvious that (a) ego-strength is acquired through distinct types of social interaction, in which psychological security is assured, and that (b) for its maintenance it is dependent on the continuity of some such relations. The problem, then, could be restated in terms of which groups, relations, and identifications provide the immigrant with enough emotional support to enable him not to be dependent on the expressive symbols of status and to withstand the ambiguity and lack of structuring of the absorbing situation.

Family solidarity

It was assumed that the greatest importance should be attributed here to those basic groups which continued to exist throughout the process of immigration and which constituted the immigrants' mainstay and the centre of their most continuous and effective social relations. Among

these, the family stood out clearly as of greatest importance, and we have focused our analysis on some aspects of family structure related to our problem.

Two main types of families could be distinguished in their ways of facing the difficulties inherent in immigration: the solidary and the non-solidary types. The main distinction between the two types of families is based on the extent of their internal cohesion and collectivity-orientation. The solidary family is a cohesive group, the existence of which is perceived by its members as an end in itself. Their activities and relations are oriented towards the maintenance and perpetuation of the collectivity, with its common goals and norms; and the mutual relations of its members are to a very large extent evaluated accordingly. Every member of the group is highly valued as such because of his belonging to the group. The non-solidary family, on the other hand, does not evince any high degree of cohesion, of sharing goals and ends, and its existence is mainly perceived as a means for attaining the discreet goals of its members. The same holds true, of course, of the mutual relations of its members. . . .

A very high correlation has been found between positive predisposition to change and membership in a solidary family, and negative predisposition and unsolidary types. . . .

It should be emphasized that these two types of families to a large extent cut through cultural and structural differences, although they are un-

TABLE 1: The Distribution of Positive and Negative Predisposition to Change Among Immigrants of Different Countries of Origin

COUNTRIES OF ORIGIN	HEADS OF FAMILIES WITH POSITIVE PREDISPOSITION TO CHANGE		HEADS OF FAMILIES WITH NEGATIVE PREDISPOSITION TO CHANGE	
	NUMBER	PER CENT	NUMBER	PER CENT
Yemen	86	85	16	15
Turkey	55	65	36	35
North Africa:				
Tunisia	24	40	34	60
Morocco	41	33	82	67
Algiers	20	35	38	65
Tripoli	32	40	46	60
Bulgaria	100	80	25	20
Yugoslavia	62	65	33	35
Central and Eastern Europe:				
Poland	18	25	54	75
Czechoslovakia	11	25	32	75
Hungary	12	27	33	73
Rumania	13	20	51	80
Total:	474		480	

equally distributed among the different countries of origin. Both types can be found, however, within the traditional patriarchal, extended family of the Balkan Jews, and within the conjugal, individualistic, small, "modern" family of Central and Eastern European Jews. Our typology refers not to the formal structure and distribution of power within the family, but to the internal processes of the family as a functioning unit. It seems that these processes may sometimes even run counter to the formal structure, or are at least to some extent independent of it. What the exact limits of this independence are, and to what extent structural and cultural differences facilitate the existence of these types, has . . . not been investigated by us at this stage, as it was considered of relatively little concern for our immediate purposes. From our point of view the most important fact is that membership in each of these types of families affects the immigrant's behaviour (predisposition to change) in the same way, irrespective of such conditions as his country of origin or cultural tradition. . . .

Jewish identification

The importance of family solidarity to the predisposition to change is not, however, in itself sufficient to account for all the sources of security and ego-strength of the immigrants. Although the family constituted the main stable social unit throughout the process of immigration, this very process, its motivation and course, are interwoven within wider social settings. It is the insecurity felt within the society of origin which gives rise to migration, and it is within the entire social fabric of the new country that the immigrant hopes to resolve this insecurity. Therefore it is important to investigate what security and strength the immigrant can derive from this wider orientation, and under what conditions this orientation hampers the achievement of this security. In our sample, the importance of this problem was accentuated by the specific Jewish element. Most of the immigrants came to Israel because they felt insecure as Jews in their countries of origin, and because they hoped to be able to overcome this insecurity in Israel—as a new, independent, Jewish society. From the outset it was some sort of Jewish identification that motivated them to immigrate to Israel. The exact nature of this Jewish insecurity and identification varies, however, from country to country; and we have already seen that positive and negative predisposition to change is closely connected with different types of Jewish identification. Thus our problem here is to investi-

gate to what extent specific types of Jewish social structure serve as bases of personal security or insecurity for the immigrant. We therefore classified and analysed the different Jewish communities according to those elements and aspects of their social structure most closely related to our problem.

The most important characteristic of Jewish social structure in the Diaspora, from this point of view, is the ambivalence of the Jews with regard to the wider, Gentile society. The Jewish community in the more or less traditional countries of the Diaspora lives within the cological and political orbit of the general society, in a situation of (formal or informal) discrimination, segregation, and social inferiority, at the same time maintaining its own tradition, regarded by its members as of higher value than that of the surrounding society. This inferiority-superiority role necessarily gives rise to a feeling of insecurity on the one hand, and of ambivalence (based on tension between actual inferiority and evaluative cultural superiority) towards the Gentile society, on the other. This ambivalence is usually centred around problems of acceptance within the Gentile society. The structuring and resolution of this ambivalence vary from one Jewish community to another according to the possibilities of (a) segregating the relative spheres of superiority and inferiority; (b) limiting the bestowal of status effective within the community to those spheres in which cultural superiority can be maintained; (c) orienting the aggressive tendencies accruing from ambivalence towards the out-group, while at the same time maintaining a high degree of in-group cohesion and solidarity.

These characteristics can be maintained only under specific conditions, among which the extent of social autonomy, self-regulation and "autarchy" of the different Jewish communities is most important.

The main types of Jewish communities

From this point of view we have been able to distinguish in our sample the following main types of Jewish communities:

1. The traditional sector, which comprises the Yemenite Jews and some sectors of North African Jewry. This sector is characterized by a relatively wide extent of social autonomy and orientation towards particularistic Jewish values and traditions (although the degree of intensity of this orientation and of the activities of specifically Jewish *élites* varies greatly from place to place). Cultural orientation towards the out-group is

mainly negative, and the Jewish community succeeds in maintaining independent, autonomous status criteria not directly related to or dependent on the parallel criteria of the Gentile society. This community therefore evinces a very high degree of· solidarity and cohesion in relation to the out-group, and insecurity within the surrounding Gentile society is resolved, or overcome, through this in-group solidarity. Segregation of the relative spheres of superiority-inferiority is achieved, and serves to enhance the solidarity.

2. The "insecure" transitional sector, which comprises great parts (especially urban) of the North African Jewish communities, and most of the Central and Eastern European communities which remained intact after the war. Its main characteristics are the following: (a) A very small extent of social autonomy; (b) relatively strong aspirations towards entrance into the Gentile society and identification with it; (c) social and occupational mobility towards the Gentile society; and (d) a feeling that belongingness to a Jewish community usually constitutes an impediment for the achievement of status and successful mobility towards the Gentile society. . . .

. . . These sectors live in a constant state of tension, status-anxiety, and insecurity, which does not find any permanent solution in the structure of their societies.

3. The secure, transitional sector, which comprises Jewish communities settled within Gentile society and approved by it. This group, in our sample, is confined mainly to Serbian and Bulgarian Jewries, which constituted, it seems, a unique type of Jewish society. Their most important characteristics are the following: (a) Small degree of social autonomy, mainly confined to family traditions and religious worship; (b) strong primary identification with the general community and secondary, associational identification with the Jewish community; (c) acceptance of their Jewishness by the Gentile community as a sub-system within the general social structure, and, consequently, their Jewishness usually fostering, or emphasizing, their social status. It is very important and characteristic that only in these countries was the social crisis which prompted them to immigrate to Israel not a specifically Jewish one, i.e., they were not deported, etc., because of being Jews but mainly because of general social and political upheavals, and, for them, belonging to the Jewish community proved to be a source of a specifically strong feeling of security.

4. The sector of ex-inmates of D.P. camps, survivors of the destroyed Jewish communities in Eastern Europe, for whom the experience of destruction and camp-life overshadowed any other social traditions and feeling in their self-consciousness as Jews. (In our further analysis we shall subsume the fourth sector under the second, and the third sector will be called the "insecure transitional sector.")

The different types of predisposition to change (both positive and negative) were unquestionably connected with these characteristics of Jewish communities and their crises. Positive predisposition took place mostly among those coming from countries where belongingness to the Jewish community constituted an approval of social status and/or a source of group cohesion against the outside world, namely, in the first and third sectors. Negative predisposition took place mostly among those for whom belongingness to the Jewish nation was a factor of insecurity and status-anxiety—the second and fourth sectors. . . .

The importance of the different types of Jewish life stands out clearly also in the social organization of the immigration movement itself. We have already emphasized the importance of the "small," basic group which remains intact throughout the process of immigration. The attitudes and identifications evolved in these groups influence to a very great extent the immigrants' perception and role-expectations. It is in these groups that the immigrants' orientation towards the new country is moulded and articulated. . . .

Family solidarity and Jewish identification

Our next problem was to see whether any relation exists between the two main conditions of predisposition to change—family structure and the type of crisis of Jewish societies, i.e., whether the degree of family solidarity is related to these broader structures of Jewish social life. [Table 2] shows us the extent of overlapping of the two factors.

From this table we see that although there exists no full overlapping between these two factors, it still exists to a very large extent, especially within the first three sectors. Our material bears out the fact that this relation is not accidental. While it would be futile to assert that all the personality characteristics associated with family solidarity can be accounted for by "structural" or cultural factors, there still exists a strong relation between these two. . . .

From this analysis and discussion of the conditions under which different types of predispositions to change develop, some general conclusions relating to the process of adaptation can be stated.

The type of the immigrant's predisposition to

change is important with respect to the extension of his social field from the small group in which immigration takes place to the new social setting, i.e., the bridging over by him of the "unstructured" parts of this field. The higher the positive predisposition, the quicker the achievement of stable relations within this field and, consequently, the tempo of adaptation as well. This predisposition is dependent mainly on the extent of basic psychological security provided by (a) the primary family unit in which immigration usually takes place; and (b) the immigrant's orientation to the new country and his identification with it. In so far as this security is provided both by the small group and by the *general* social framework towards which the immigrant is oriented, the bridging over of the unstructured field which exists between the two is relatively easy. In so far as this security is not provided, the predisposition to change is usually negative, and the "bridging over" is hampered, delayed, and sometimes not achieved at all.

"Open flexibility"

In our former discussion we have not differentiated between various degrees of predisposition

and have dealt with "negative" and "positive" types only. The nature of our material and methods of investigation would make any such differentiation at this stage very artificial. It is only with respect to one element that some differentiation could be made, a differentiation which was also connected—even if in a tentative way only—with some important social factors. This element is the flexibility of the levels of aspiration. Here a differentiation can be made between those whose flexibility was limited to the present only, i.e., those who were prepared to accept any situation in the present as a preparatory stage for the future, but had very fixed aspirations for the future—usually connected with their former occupational status. On the other hand, there were those whose flexibility extended to the future also, and who maintained throughout the "instrumental" approach to social status. We shall refer to the latter as those with "open" flexibility.

It was found that women in the traditional and transitional (Oriental) sector have a more "open" flexibility than men; adolescents and unmarried young adults more than married adults, and that, within the traditional sector, members of the Jewish *élite* have more "closed" flexibility than other non-*élites*. There was no difference between women and men in non-traditional sectors, and

---

TABLE 2:   The Disposition of Predisposition to Change and Family Solidarity Among the Different Sectors of the Jewish Community

	POSITIVE PREDISPOSITION TO CHANGE		NEGATIVE PREDISPOSITION TO CHANGE	
	SOLIDARY FAMILIES	NON-SOLIDARY FAMILIES	SOLIDARY FAMILIES	NON-SOLIDARY FAMILIES
North Africa:				
1. Traditional Sector	87	10	10	15
2. Transitional Sector with Status-anxiety	—	5	15	155
3. Secure Transitional Sector	15	—	—	—
Central and Eastern Europe:				
1. Traditional Sector	18	2	23	12
2. Transitional Sector with Status-anxiety	5	2	10	52
2a. Ex-D.P. Camp Inmates	—	2	45	28
3. Secure Transitional Sector	25	—	—	—
Turkey:				
1. Traditional Sector	40	5	6	2
2. Transitional Sector with Status-anxiety	5	5	10	18
Bulgaria and Yugoslavia:				
1. Transitional Sector with Status-anxiety	5	6	8	38
2. Secure Transitional Sector	144	7	5	7
Yemen:				
1. Traditional Sector	70	16	5	11
Total	414	60	137	338

between members of different occupational and social "strata" outside the traditional sectors. . . .

The data at our disposal do not allow any definite explanation, but a tentative one may be suggested at this stage. It seems that within the scope of solidary families and positive, unconditional community-identification, it is those who have least "vested interest" in high social positions and roles who can show the greatest "openness" and flexibility in their levels of aspiration, as change cannot affect their privileged positions. They enjoy, as it were, the benefits of social and psychological security inherent in these groups without being tied to any special positions within

them. While this explanation accounts for our data, it does not show why the difference between *élites* and non-*élites* existed only within the traditional sector. The tentative explanation of this may be that the difference holds only in those groups which have maintained themselves and their cultural identifications intact through the process of immigration, and who could have hoped to maintain their old patterns of life in the new social setting. This holds true only for the more active parts of the traditional sector, while in all other sectors the process of immigration has involved a thorough reshuffling of social groups emergence of new *élites*.

Selection 36

Co-operation and Competition in a Bureaucracy

Peter M. Blau

The following selections deal with three of the basic social processes by which men interact—cooperation, competition, and conflict. By way of review, the chief difference between the latter two is that while both involve a striving for scarce goods or goals, competition is relatively impersonal and universal, but in conflict the aim is to hinder, harm, or destroy the opposing person or group. The personalized aspect of competition, rivalry, stands between competition and conflict. In addition to dealing with the basic social processes, these three selections give special insight into bureaucracy, industrial organization, and voluntary associations, respectively.

Two of the most significant findings of industrial sociology have been (1) that within formal organizations, personal contacts and interaction patterns (informal organizations) develop that seem to be necessary not only for the operation of formal organizations themselves but also for the preservation of individual integrity through cohesive relationships; and (2) that competition *per se* may not be related to increased productivity in a simple one-to-one ratio. For example, informal work norms develop that may or may not support official work rules but must be considered a very real part of the industrial social organization. Also, management today rarely resorts only to economic incentives to spur competition and hence production.

As is usually the case, many related questions developed as logical extensions of this successful research. For example, what factors encourage and promote individual and group productivity? Are individual and group productivity always positively related to one another? Does competition sometimes have latent dysfunctional consequences? What advantages and disadvantages result when competition between individuals and groups is encouraged?

Unfortunately, few sociological hypotheses can be stated in the simple form in which variable A is said to be a definite and limited function of variable B. Usually other variables have to be controlled or at least taken into account.

Blau's hypothesis, that competition is positively related to individual productivity but negatively related to group productivity, should be carefully evaluated. If the hypothesis is valid, the cultural emphasis currently placed upon the desirability of competition in our society may actually be dysfunctional in some situations, in which case other forms of social organization and other patterns of interaction perhaps ought to be encouraged. For example, the existence over an extended period of time of the kind of competition between different sectors of management that Dalton treats in Selection 37 constitutes a very real hindrance to our type of industrial organization.

This paper discusses performance and variations in competitiveness among twelve interviewers in two small sections of a public employment agency. The duties of the interviewers in both sections were essentially alike. They received requests for workers over the phone. The order forms on which job openings were described were filed in a common pool in each section. Most of the official's time was spent interviewing applicants for jobs. After ascertaining the client's qualifications, the interviewer searched the sectional files for suitable vacancies. If an acceptable job was found, he referred the client to it and later phoned the employer to determine whether the client had been hired.

"The statistics which show how many interviews and how many placements each person in the section did are passed around to all interviewers. Of course, you look at them and see how you compare with others. This creates a competitive spirit," said one of the interviewers, voicing the sentiments of most of his fellows. In a period of job shortages, competition took the form of trying to utilize job openings before anybody else did. Interviewers were so anxious to make placements that they even resorted to illicit methods. Said one:

"When you take an order, instead of putting it in the box, you leave it on your desk. There was so much hiding of orders under the blotter that we used to ask, 'Do you have anything under your rug?' when we looked for an order. You might leave an order you took on the desk, or you might leave it on the desk after you made no referral. . . . Or, you might take an order only partially; you write the firm's name, and a few things; the others you remember. And you leave it on the pad [of order blanks]. You keep on doing this, and all these orders are not in the box.

"You can do some wrong filling out. For instance, for a rather low-salary job, you fill out 'experience required.' Nobody can make a placement on that except you, because you, alone, know that experience isn't required. Or, if there are several openings [on one order], you put the order into 'referrals' [file category for *filled* job

openings] after you make one placement. You're supposed to put it into 'referrals' but stand it up, so that the others can see it. If you don't, you have a better chance of making the next placement than somebody else. And time and again you see four, five openings on one order filled by the same person." [In one case on file eight out of nine openings on one order had been filled by the same interviewer.]

The major opportunity for competitive monopolization of job openings occurred when they were received from employers. Since illicit practices were concealed from the observer, the extent of competition could not be determined through questioning or direct observation[1] but was betrayed by the record of official transactions. The extent to which an interviewer filled the vacancies he had received over the phone with his own clients in excess of chance expectations furnishes an index of competitiveness. (Col. 4 in Table 1 shows this index; Cols. 1-3 present the data on which it is based.)

STRUCTURAL CONDITIONS AND COMPETITIVENESS

The members of Section A were more competitive than those of Section B. The last two columns in Table 1 also show that the interviewer's competitiveness was related to his productivity in Section A (Pearsonian $r = +.92$), but this was not the case in Section B ($r = -.20$). In other words, hoarding of jobs was an effective way to

"Co-operation and Competition in a Bureaucracy" by Peter M. Blau. Reprinted from *The American Journal of Sociology*, Vol. LIX (1954), 530-535, by permission of The University of Chicago Press.

[1] This is clearly indicated by the comment of one of a group of special interviewers, who were expected to use the job openings of the regular interviewers but usually had great difficulty in doing so: "Oh, they hide everything from us. We got more orders when you [the observer] sat in the middle of that section than ever before. We laughed about it. Interviewers would hand us orders asking whether we could use them—when you were looking. That had never happened before."

TABLE 1: Competitiveness and Productivity in Section A and in Section B

	OPENINGS RECEIVED * (1)	REFERRALS MADE BY RECIPIENT (2)	RATIO OF REFERRALS TO OPENINGS (3)	COMPETI-TIVENESS † (4)	PRODUC-TIVITY ‡ (5)	NUMBER OF PLACEMENTS (6)
Section A:						
Adams.......	34	19	0.56	3.9	0.70	100
Ahman	62	27	.44	3.1	.49	70
Ajax.........	40	28	.70	4.9	.97	139
Akers........	71	32	.45	3.2	.71	101
Ambros	69	18	.26	1.8	.45	65
Atzenberg....	106	43	.41	2.9	.61	87
Auble	10	3	.30	2.1	.39	56§
Section B:						
Babcock	16	7	.44	2.2	.53	46
Beers........	58	19	.33	1.6	.71	62
Bing	51	15	.29	1.5	.75	65
Borden	17	7	.41	2.1	.55	48§
Bush	43	19	0.42	2.1	0.97	84
Section A ..	392	170	0.43	3.0	0.59	590
Section B ..	185	67	0.36	1.8	0.67	289

* *The great differences between interviewers in this column show that some were much more successful than others in inducing employers, or telephone operators, to channel requests for workers to them personally. This form of rivalry does not involve competitive interaction.*

† *Competitiveness index (col. 4): The proportion of job openings received to which the recipient made a referral (col. 3) times the number of members of the section. (This represents the observed divided by the expected frequency of referrals made by the recipient of a job opening.) Base period: First half of April, 1949.*

‡ *Productivity index (col. 5): The number of placements made (col. 6) divided by the number of job openings available, that is, the number of openings in the section per interviewer. Base period: April, 1949.*

§ *The number of placements was adjusted for the two interviewers absent for more than five days during April. Since the sectional numbers of placements were not revised, the values in col. 6 add up to more than the two totals shown.*

improve an interviewer's placement record only in one of these two groups.

The members of Section B were more cooperative: they discouraged competitive practices by making them ineffective. When they learned about interesting vacancies, they often told one another, but an interviewer who manifested competitive tendencies was excluded from the network of reciprocal information and lost the respect of his co-workers. Any advantage of hoarding jobs was, at least, neutralized by such lack of cooperation, as is indicated by the absence of a relation between competitiveness and productivity in this group. Since competitive practices made an interviewer unpopular and failed to raise his productivity, they were infrequent.

These officials themselves attributed the greater competitiveness in Section A to the ambitiousness of several members: "There is usually one individual who starts it, who becomes a pace-setter. Once it has started, it is too late." The others, so interviewers claimed, have to follow suit. How-

ever, the most competitive member of Section A in recounting her reactions when production records were first introduced made it clear that this explanation of competition on the basis of personality characteristics is inadequate:

"When they introduced statistics, I realized how fast I worked. I even wanted to drop lower. I didn't mind working fast as long as it didn't show, but when it showed up like that on the record, I wanted to work less. But you know what happened? Some of the others started to compete with each other and produced more than I did. Then I thought to myself, 'Since I can do it, it's silly to let them get ahead of me.' I'm only human. So I worked as fast as before."

When statistical records made the superior performance of this interviewer public knowledge, she decided to work less, possibly in response to pressures the others had brought to bear upon her. While complaining about her unfair standards, however, the other members of the section also improved their own performance. Consequently, this interviewer, just like the others, felt constrained by colleagues to compete for an outstanding record. One or two members of Section B, on the other hand, were also accused of competitive tendencies, but their colleagues successfully discouraged their expression in monopolistic practices. It is in this sense that the competitive practices of one group and the co-operative practices of the other were social factors, calling for explanation in sociological rather than psychological terms. . . .

Differential conditions affected the development of these two groups. First, the supervisor in Section A relied heavily on performance records in evaluating interviewers: "And here, in the production figures, is the answer to the question: How good are you? Here you see exactly how good the work you did was." Interviewers often mentioned the pressure thus exerted: "[Especially] around rating time, you get this competition. You don't care whether the best person gets the job, but you try to make the placement yourself." In contrast, the new supervisor in Section B surprised his subordinates by rating them more leniently than they had expected, and not primarily on the basis of production records. Consequently, as one interviewer reported, "we became less anxious about statistics; another experience like that, and we might forget all about placement credit."

Second, a common professional orientation existed only in Section B. While the members of Section A had been assigned, and had received their training, at different times, the majority of those in Section B received their training together after World War II, at a time when intensive counseling had been stressed, since many returning veterans needed occupational advice. One official said of this period:

"When I first came here, in May, 1946, we had a very nice bunch. It was like an all-day consultation; we discussed placements with each other all day long. At that time, the veterans came back, and there was a lot of emphasis on counseling. Nobody asked you how many placements you made, then. The emphasis was on quality, and we consulted with each other all day."

In this situation, the group developed a common professional code, which discouraged speedy placement as constituting defective employment service. In effect, this orientation transformed competitive practices from illegitimate means for desirable ends into illegitimate means for worthless ends. If such practices did occur, they were vigorously opposed on moral grounds as violating the interest of clients. Nevertheless, as will be shown presently, competition could not have been effectively curbed if the supervisor's evaluation practice had engendered acute anxiety over productivity. However, the existence of this code would have made it difficult for the supervisor to judge performance mainly by productivity, since doing so would have stamped him as ignorant of the essentials of good employment service.

No opportunity for the development of a *common* professional code had existed in Section A. Since competitiveness prevailed in this group, the individual whose personal professional standards made him reluctant to compete either became the deviant whose productivity suffered or modified his standards and entered the race with the others.

Third, most members of Section A had been appointed to temporary civil service positions during World War II. They were on probation pending permanent appointments when production records were originally introduced and even afterward remained subject to layoffs due to reductions in staff. Their insecurity led them to strive to impress superiors with outstanding performance. In contrast, all but one of the members of Section B were veterans, whose employment could not be terminated except for cause. As one envious colleague put it, "They felt that nothing could happen to them, because they were veterans, and had super-seniority."

Differences in these three conditions—security of employment, opportunity for the development of a common professional orientation, and the evaluation practice of the supervisor—gave rise to two dissimilar social structures. Productivity was highly valued in Section A and became associated with the individual's standing in the group, while striving for sheer productivity was disparaged in Section B. Thus, whereas the most productive and most competitive member of Section A was considered the best interviewer by her co-workers and was most popular with them,[2] the most productive member of Section B was least respected and least popular. As a result of these structural differences, co-operative norms prevailed only in Section B.

The interviewers in *both* sections disliked working in a competitive atmosphere. A member of Section A said: "If I see that an interviewer keeps orders on her desk, I take them and put them in the box. . . . Of course, you don't make friends that way." Since the majority in this section, including its most popular members, were

_____
[2] She was most often mentioned by members of her own section in answer to the questions, respectively, "Who are the best interviewers?" and "Who are your friends in the office?"

highly competitive, to antagonize them was to threaten one's own standing in the group. This deterred interviewers from discouraging competitive practices. Antagonizing a deviant, however, does not endanger one's status. Consequently, since a striver was unpopular in Section B, its members could use sanctions freely to combat competitive practices and enforce co-operative norms.

SOCIAL COHESION AND PRODUCTIVITY

Table 1 shows that the group most concerned with productivity was less productive than the other group. Fifty-nine per cent of the job openings received in Section A were filled, in contrast to 67 per cent in Section B. (The 8 per cent difference is significant on the .01 level.) Another implicit paradox is that competitiveness and productivity were directly related for individuals in Section A but inversely related for the two groups.

Anxious concern with productivity induced interviewers in Section A to concentrate blindly upon it at the expense of other considerations. In their eagerness to make many placements they often ignored their relationships with others as well as official rules. Competitiveness in this group weakened social cohesion, while co-operativeness in Section B strengthened it. This difference is further shown by the fact that usually none of the members of Section A spent their rest periods together, whereas all but one of those of Section B, a newcomer when this study was being made, did. Social cohesion enhanced operating efficiency by facilitating co-operation and by reducing status anxiety.

Although the members of both groups had occasion to assist one another, greater effort was required to elicit such co-operation in Section A. The social interaction that occurred in the office during the twenty-four busiest hours of one week was recorded and classified as official and private contacts, that is, those directly concerned with a specific job or client, and all others. The frequency of an interviewer's official contacts with colleagues was related to his productivity in Section A (rank correlation $= +.98$) but not in Section B (rank correlation $= +.08$). This suggests that only interviewers who kept, as one put it, "hopping around all the time" to retrieve job orders that others kept on their desks were able to make many placements in the competitive section. In the cohesive group, on the other hand, the co-operation needed for making placements occurred as a matter of course, and not only in response to special requests. This effort was not required for high productivity.

To maximize his placements, the interviewer in Section A hoarded jobs and simultaneously tried to prevent others from doing so, thereby antagonizing his co-workers, whose co-operation he needed if he was to do well. The members of this section therefore attempted to conciliate colleagues whom their competitive practices had alienated. Often, shortly after having interfered with her operations, an interviewer paid another a compliment about her work or her apparel. The most competitive interviewer was in the habit of taking time out to joke with her co-workers and was proud of making more placements than anybody else, "nevertheless." Actually, this compensating friendliness, which made her popular despite her competitiveness, helped her to be productive.

In Section A, interviewers had to make special efforts at conciliation in order to make placements, but this was not necessary in Section B. At least, this impression is corroborated by the finding that frequency of private contacts with others was also related to productivity in Section A (rank correlation $= +.84$) but not in Section B (rank correlation $= +.13$). The members of the cohesive group, whose operating practices did not put colleagues at a disadvantage, did not have to devote time and energy to solicit and encourage co-operation, since it was not extended reluctantly. Their spontaneous co-operation improved operating efficiency.

Social cohesion also lessened the status anxiety generated by the evaluation system. Such anxiety is most acute in the individual who does not feel integrated in his work group and therefore seeks to derive social recognition from excelling at his task and from approval of superiors. Friendly relations with co-workers made the standing of the individual in the cohesive group independent of his productivity, particularly since fast work was disparaged as a sign of superficial service. The consequent reduction of anxiety in the antiproductivity-oriented group actually raised its productivity.

Fluctuations in productivity illustrate the dysfunction of status anxiety. Section B had not always operated more efficiently than Section A. Its productivity had been lower during the two months preceding the last rating but had abruptly increased then, while that of Section A had declined. . . .

The two groups found themselves in different situations before and after they were rated. The members of Section A were familiar with the rating standards of their supervisor, for she had rated them in previous years. Their anxiety led them to work especially hard immediately before the annual rating. The members of Section B, on the other hand, had never before been rated by their new supervisor. They were also concerned about their record but could not calm their anxiety by concentrating upon certain tasks, because they did not know what the supervisor would stress; the explanation he gave to his subordinates was too vague and adhered too strictly to official procedures to help them to foresee his actual practices. This unfocused anxiety was particularly detrimental to efficient performance. Later, when the interviewers found out that they were not rated primarily on the basis of statistical records, their anxiety largely subsided and their productivity increased. In contrast, the experience of the members of Section A, whose rating was strongly influenced by their production records, intensified their status anxiety, but, when the rating was over, anxiety was no longer channeled into exceptionally hard work, with the result that their productivity declined below that of Section B.

Social cohesion is no guaranty against anxiety in a bureaucracy. Civil service status is too important to officials for them to remain immune to the threat of losing it. But when no such threat is felt, social cohesion reduces anxiety by divesting productivity of its significance as a symbol of status in the work group. Diminished anxiety as well as smoother co-operation then enable those in the cohesive group to perform their tasks more efficiently than the others.

In the absence of social cohesion, competitive striving for an outstanding performance record became a substitute means for relieving status anxiety in Section A. This psychological function of competition is illustrated by the following incident: The interviewers in this section became very irritable, and one of them even became physically ill, when a temporary supervisor, who tried to prevent competitive practices, interfered with their method of allaying anxiety. Status anxiety reduced operating efficiency. Even in the cohesive group, productivity was low when the unknown rating standards of a new supervisor produced acute and diffuse anxiety. Otherwise, however, the cohesive group was more productive, because social cohesion relieved status anxiety by making the individual's standing in the group independent of his productivity. The very competitive striving that undermined the group's cohesiveness also served to lessen the individual's status anxiety in a non-cohesive situation. The hypothesis that the cohesiveness of the group and the competitiveness of the individual in the less cohesive group both reduce status anxiety explains the paradox that the *less competitive group* as well as the *more competitive individual* in the competitive group each was particularly productive.

Selection 37

Conflicts Between Staff and Line Managerial Officers
Melville Dalton

The most common early focus of study in industrial sociology for both economists and sociologists was union-management relations and its economic, social, and organizational effects. As the area of industrial sociology has grown, sub-areas of study have become popular, particularly those that investigate social processes. One such sub-area is explored by the following selection—namely, the interaction (and its consequences) between the two major vertical groupings of industrial management, the *staff* and the *line*. The line hierarchy has authority over production procedures; the staff hierarchy is made up of functionaries in management, research, personnel, and advisory capacities whose tasks have to do with efficiency, progress, coordination, and other specialties. Theoretically, these two groups should work together in harmony; in practice, cooperation may be most conspicuous by being supplanted by competition or even conflict. Although staff-line competition is not structured or planned as was that of the interviewers in the preceding selection, its harmful consequences are much the same. This replacement of cooperation by negative modes of interaction means that manifest (readily recognizable) changes in organizational structure and process have latent (concealed) consequences that not only are unanticipated by the plant leadership but are often contradictory to, and destructive of, the organization's formal aims.

What are the sources of staff-line conflict? How does staff-line conflict relate itself to the general conflict system of a modern industrial plant? These are some of the vital issues with which Dalton deals in his penetrating analysis of a modern, highly technical form of social organization. Dalton's work is important not only because of the systematic analysis of conflict he presents, however, but also because of the thought-provoking, remedial measures he suggests. These remedial measures have consequences for the industrial world and for many other segments of our society as well.

The present paper is the result of an attempt to study processes among industrial managers. It is specifically a report on the functioning interaction between the two major vertical groupings of industrial management: (1) the *staff* organization, the functions of which are research and advisory; and (2) the *line* organization, which has exclusive authority over production processes.

Industrial staff organizations are relatively new. Their appearance is a response to many complex interrelated forces, such as economic competition, scientific advance, industrial expansion, growth of the labor movement, and so on. During the last four or five decades these rapid changes and resulting unstable conditions have caused top industrial officials more and more to call in "specialists" to aid them toward the goal of greater production and efficiency. These specialists are of many kinds including chemists, statisticians, public and industrial relations officers, personnel officers, accountants, and a great variety of engineers, such as mechanical, draughting, electrical, chemical, fuel, lubricating, and industrial engineers. In industry these individuals are usually known as "staff people." Their functions, again, for the most part are to increase and apply their specialized knowledge in problem areas, and to advise those officers who make up the "line" organization and have authority over production processes.

This theoretically satisfying industrial structure of specialized experts advising busy administrators has in a number of significant cases failed to function as expected. The assumptions that (a) the staff specialists would be reasonably content to function without a measure of formal authority over production, and that (b) their suggestions regarding improvement of processes and techniques for control over personnel and production would be welcomed by line officers and be applied, require closer examination. In practice there is often much conflict between industrial staff and line organizations and in varying degrees the members of these organizations oppose each other.

The aim of this paper is, therefore, to present and analyze data dealing with staff-line tensions.

Data were drawn from three industrial plants in which the writer had been either a participating member of one or both of the groups or was intimate with reliable informants among the officers who were.

Approached sociologically, relations among members of management in the plants could be viewed as a general conflict system caused and perpetuated chiefly by (1) power struggles in the organization stemming in the main from competition among departments to maintain low operating costs; (2) drives by numerous members to increase their status in the hierarchy; (3) conflict between union and management; and (4) the staff-line friction which is the subject of this paper.[1] This milieu of tensions was not only unaccounted for by the blue-print organizations of the plants, but was often contradictory to, and even destructive of, the organizations' formal aims. All members of management, especially in the middle and lower ranks, were caught up in this conflict system. Even though they might wish to escape, the obligation of at least appearing to carry out formal functions compelled individuals to take sides in order to protect themselves against the aggressions of others. And the intensity of the conflict was aggravated by the fact that it was formally unacceptable and had to be hidden.

For analytical convenience, staff-line friction may be examined apart from the reciprocal effects of the general conflict system. Regarded in this way, the data indicated that three conditions were basic to staff-line struggles: (1) the conspicuous ambition and "individualistic" behavior among

From the *American Sociological Review*, Vol. 15 (1950), 342-351. Reprinted by permission of the American Sociological Association.
[1] Because these conflict areas were interrelated and continually shifting and reorganizing, discussion of any one of them separately—as in the case of staff-line relations—will, of course, be unrealistic to some extent.

staff officers; (2) the complication arising from staff efforts to justify its existence and get acceptance of its contributions; and, related to point two, (3) the fact that incumbency of the higher staff offices was dependent on line approval. The significance of these conditions will be discussed in order.

MOBILE BEHAVIOR OF STAFF PERSONNEL

As a group, staff personnel in the three plants were markedly ambitious, restless, and individualistic. There was much concern to win rapid promotion, to make the "right impressions," and to receive individual recognition. Data showed that the desire among staff members for personal distinctions often over-rode their sentiments of group consciousness and caused intra-staff tensions.

The relatively high turnover of staff personnel quite possibly reflected the dissatisfactions and frustrations of members over inability to achieve the distinction and status they hoped for. Several factors appeared to be of importance in this restlessness of staff personnel. Among these were age and social differences between line and staff officers, structural differences in the hierarchy of the two groups, and the staff group's lack of authority over production.

With respect to age, the staff officers were significantly younger than line officers. This would account to some extent for their restlessness. Being presumably less well-established in life in terms of material accumulations, occupational status, and security, while having greater expectations (see below), and more energy, as well as more life ahead in which to make new starts elsewhere if necessary, the staff groups were understandably more dynamic and driving.

Age-conflict was also significant in staff-line antagonisms. . . . The older line officers disliked receiving what they regarded as instruction from men so much younger than themselves, and staff personnel clearly were conscious of this attitude among line officers. In staff-line meetings staff officers frequently had their ideas slighted or even treated with amusement by line incumbents. Whether such treatment was warranted or not, the effects were disillusioning to the younger, less experienced staff officers. Often selected by the organization because of their outstanding academic records, they had entered industry with the belief that they had much to contribute, and that their efforts would win early recognition and rapid advancement. Certainly they had no thought that their contributions would be in any degree unwelcome. This naiveté was apparently due to lack of earlier first-hand experience in industry

(or acquaintance with those who had such experience), and to omission of realistic instruction in the social sciences from their academic training. The unsophisticated staff officer's initial contacts with the shifting, covert, expedient arrangements between members of staff and line usually gave him a severe shock. He had entered industry prepared to engage in logical, well-formulated relations with members of the managerial hierarchy, and to carry out precise, methodical functions for which his training had equipped him. Now he learned that (1) his freedom to function was snared in a web of informal commitments; (2) his academic specialty (on which he leaned for support in his new position) was often not relevant for carrying out his formal assignments; and that (3) the important thing to do was to learn who the informally powerful line officers were and what ideas they would welcome which at the same time would be acceptable to his superiors.

Usually the staff officer's reaction to these conditions is to look elsewhere for a job or make an accommodation in the direction of protecting himself and finding a niche where he can make his existence in the plant tolerable and safe. If he chooses the latter course, he is likely to be less concerned with creative effort for his employer than with attempts to develop reliable social relations that will aid his personal advancement. The staff officer's recourse to this behavior and his use of other status-increasing devices will be discussed below in another connection.

The formal structure, or hierarchy of statuses, of the two larger plants from which data were drawn, offered a frustration to the ambitious staff officer. That is, in these plants the strata, or levels of authority, in the staff organizations ranged from three to five as against from five to ten in the line organization. Consequently there were fewer possible positions for exercise of authority into which staff personnel could move. This condition may have been an irritant to expansion among the staff groups. Unable to move vertically to the degree possible in the line organization, the ambitious staff officer could enlarge his area of authority in a given position only by lateral expansion—by increasing his personnel. Whether or not aspiring staff incumbents revolted against the relatively low hierarchy through which they could move, the fact remains that (1) they appeared eager to increase the number of personnel under their authority, (2) the personnel of staff groups *did* increase disproportionately to those of the line, and (3) there was a trend of personnel movement from staff to line, rather than the reverse, presumably (reflecting the drive and ambition of staff members) because there were more positions of authority, as well as more authority to be exercised, more prestige, and usually more income in the line.

Behavior in the plants indicated that line and staff personnel belonged to different social status groups and that line and staff antipathies were at least in part related to these social distinctions. For example, with respect to the item of formal education, the staff group stood on a higher level than members of the line. In the plant from which the age data were taken, the 36 staff officers had a mean of 14.6 years of schooling as compared with 13.1 years for 35 line superintendents, 11.2 years for 60 general foremen, and 10.5 years for 93 first-line foremen. The difference between the mean education of the staff group and that of the highest line group (14.6-13.1) was statistically significant at better than the one per cent level. The 270 non-supervisory staff personnel had a mean of 13.1 years—the same as that of the line superintendents. Consciousness of this difference probably contributed to a feeling of superiority among staff members, while the sentiment of line officers toward staff personnel was reflected in . . . name-calling. . . .

Staff members were also much concerned about their dress, a daily shave, and a weekly hair-cut. On the other hand line officers, especially below the level of departmental superintendent, were relatively indifferent to such matters. Usually they were in such intimate contact with production processes that dirt and grime prevented the concern with meticulous dress shown by staff members. The latter also used better English in speaking and in writing reports, and were more suave and poised in social intercourse. These factors, and the recreational preferences of staff officers for night clubs and "hot parties," assisted in raising a barrier between them and most line officers.

The social antipathies of the two groups and the status concern of staff officers were indicated by the behavior of each toward the established practice of dining together in the cafeterias reserved for management in the two larger plants. Theoretically, all managerial officers upward from the level of general foremen in the line, and general supervisors in the staff, were eligible to eat in these cafeterias. However, in practice the mere taking of one of these offices did not automatically assure the incumbent the privilege of eating in the cafeteria. One had first to be invited to "join the association." Staff officers were very eager to "get in" and did considerable fantasying on the impressions, with respect to dress and behavior, that were believed essential for an invitation. One such staff officer, a cost supervisor, dropped the following remarks:

"There seems to be a committee that passes on you. I've had my application in for three years, but no soap. Harry [his superior] had his in for over three years before he made it. You have to have something, because if a man who's in moves up to another position the man who replaces him doesn't get it because of the position—and he might not get it at all. I think I'm about due."

Many line officers who were officially members of the association avoided the cafeteria, however, and had to be *ordered* by the assistant plant manager to attend. One of these officers made the following statement, which expressed more pointedly the many similar spontaneous utterances of resentment and dislike made by other line officers:

"There's a lot of good discussion in the cafeteria. I'd like to get in on more of it but I don't like to go there—sometimes I have to go. Most of the white collar people [staff officers] that eat there are stuck-up. I've been introduced three times to Svendsen [engineer], yet when I meet him he pretends to not even know me. When he meets me on the street he always manages to be looking someplace else. G—d— such people as that! They don't go in the cafeteria to eat and relax while they talk over their problems. They go in there to look around and see how somebody is dressed or to talk over the hot party they had last night. Well, that kind of damn stuff don't go with me. I haven't any time to put on airs and make out I'm something that I'm not."

COMPLICATIONS OF STAFF NEED TO PROVE ITS WORTH

To the thinking of many line officers, the staff functioned as an agent on trial rather than as a managerial division that might be of equal importance with the line organization in achieving production goals. Staff members were very conscious of this sentiment toward them and of their need to prove themselves. They strained to develop new techniques and to get them accepted by the line. But in doing this they frequently became impatient, and gave already suspicious line officers the impression of reaching for authority over production.

Since the line officer regards his authority over production as something sacred, and resents the implication that after many years in the line he needs the guidance of a newcomer who lacks such experience, an obstacle to staff-line cooperation develops the moment this sore spot is touched.

On the other hand, the staff officer's ideology of his function leads him to precipitate a power struggle with the line organization. By and large he considers himself as an agent of top management. He feels bound to contribute something significant in the form of research or ideas helpful to management. By virtue of his greater education and intimacy with the latest theories of production, he regards himself as a managerial consultant and an expert, and feels that he must be, or appear to be, almost infallible once he has committed himself to top management on some point. With this orientation, he is usually disposed to approach middle and lower line with an attitude of condescension that often reveals itself in the heat of discussion. Consequently, many staff officers involve themselves in trouble and report their failures as due to "ignorance" and "bull-headedness" among these line officers.

On this point, relations between staff and line in all three of the plants were further irritated by a rift inside the line organization. First-line foremen were inclined to feel that top management had brought in the production planning, industrial relations, and industrial engineering staffs as clubs with which to control the lower line. Hence they frequently regarded the projects of staff personnel as manipulative devices, and reacted by cooperating with production workers and/or general foremen (whichever course was the more expedient) in order to defeat insistent and uncompromising members of the staff. Also, on occasion (see below), the lower line could cooperate evasively with lower staff personnel who were in trouble with staff superiors.

EFFECT OF LINE AUTHORITY OVER STAFF PROMOTION

The fact that entry to the higher staff offices in the three plants was dependent on approval of top line officers had a profound effect on the behavior of staff personnel. Every member of the staff knew that if he aspired to higher office he must make a record for himself, a good part of which would be a reputation among upper line officers of ability to "understand" their informal problems without being told. This knowledge worked in varying degrees to pervert the theory of staff-line relations. Ideally the two organizations cooperate to improve existing methods of output, to introduce new methods, to plan the work, and to solve problems of production and the scheduling of orders that might arise. But when the line offers resistance to the findings and recommendations of the staff, the latter is reduced to evasive practices of getting some degree of acceptance of its programs, and at the same time of convincing top management that "good relations" exist with officers down the line. This necessity becomes even more acute when the staff officer aspires (for some of the reasons given above) to move over to the line organization, for then he must convince powerful line officers that he is worthy. In building a convincing record, however, he may compromise with line demands and bring charges from his staff colleagues that he is "selling out," so that after moving into the line organization he will then have to live with enemies he made in the staff. In any case, the need among staff incumbents of pleasing line officers in order to perfect their careers called for accommodation in three major areas: (1) the observance of staff rules, (2) the introduction of new techniques, and (3) the use of appropriations for staff research and experiment.

With respect to point one, staff personnel, particularly in the middle and lower levels, carried on expedient relations with the line that daily evaded formal rules. Even those officers most devoted to rules found that, in order not to arouse enmity in the line on a scale sufficient to be communicated *up* the line, compromising devices were frequently helpful and sometimes almost unavoidable both for organizational and career aims. The usual practice was to tolerate minor breaking of staff rules by line personnel, or even to cooperate with the line in evading rules, and in exchange lay a claim on the line for cooperation on critical issues. In some cases line aid was enlisted to conceal lower staff blunders from the upper staff and the upper line.

Concerning point two, while the staff organizations gave much time to developing new techniques, they were simultaneously thinking about how their plans would be received by the line. They knew from experience that middle and lower line officers could always give a "black eye" to staff contributions by deliberate mal-practices. Repeatedly top management had approved, and incorporated, staff proposals that had been verbally accepted down the line. Often the latter officers had privately opposed the changes, but had feared that saying so would incur the resentment of powerful superiors who could informally hurt them. Later they would seek to discredit the change by deliberate mal-practice and hope to bring a return to the former arrangement. For this reason there was a tendency for staff members to withhold improved production schemes or other plans when they knew that an attempt to introduce them might fail or even bring personal disrepute.

Line officers fear staff innovations for a number

of reasons. In view of their longer experience, presumably intimate knowledge of the work, and their greater remuneration, they fear being "shown up" before their line superiors for not having thought of the processual refinements themselves. They fear that changes in methods may bring personnel changes which will threaten the break-up of cliques and existing informal arrangements and quite possibly reduce their area of authority. Finally, changes in techniques may expose forbidden practices and departmental inefficiency. In some cases these fears have stimulated line officers to compromise staff men to the point where the latter will agree to postpone the initiation of new practices for specific periods.

In one such case an assistant staff head agreed with a line superintendent to delay the application of a bonus plan for nearly three months so that the superintendent could live up to the expedient agreement he had made earlier with his grievance committeeman to avoid a "wildcat" strike by a group of production workmen. The lower engineers who had devised the plan were suspicious of the formal reasons given to them for withholding it, so the assistant staff head prevented them (by means of "busy work") from attending staff-line meetings lest they inadvertently reveal to top management that the plan was ready.

The third area of staff-line accommodations growing out of authority relations revolved around staff use of funds granted it by top management. Middle and lower line charged that staff research and experimentation was little more than "money wasted on blunders," and that various departments of the line could have "accomplished much more with less money." According to staff officers, those of their plans that failed usually did so because line personnel "sabotaged" them and refused to "cooperate." Specific costs of "crackpot experimentation" in certain staff groups were pointed to by line officers. Whatever the truth of the charges and counter-charges, evidence indicated (confidants in both groups supported this) that pressures from the line organization (below the top level) forced some of the staff groups to "kick over" parts of the funds appropriated for staff use by top management. These compromises were of course hidden from top management, but the relations described were carried on to such an extent that by means of them—and line pressures for manipulation of accounts in the presumably impersonal auditing departments—certain line officers were able to show impressively low operating costs and thus win favor with top management that would relieve pressures and be useful in personal advancement. In their turn the staff officers involved would receive more "co-operation" from the line and/or recommendation for transfer to the line. The data indicated that in a few such cases men from accounting and auditing staffs were given general foremanships (without previous line experience) as a reward for their understanding behavior.

SUMMARY

Research in three industrial plants showed conflict between the managerial staff and line groups that hindered the attainment of organizational goals. Privately expressed attitudes among some of the higher line executives revealed their hope that greater control of staff groups could be achieved, or that the groups might be eliminated and their functions taken over in great part by carefully selected and highly remunerated lower-line officers. On their side, staff members wanted more recognition and a greater voice in control of the plants.

All of the various functioning groups of the plants were caught up in a general conflict system; but apart from the effects of involvement in this complex, the struggles between line and staff organizations were attributable mainly to (1) functional differences between the two groups; (2) differentials in the ages, formal education, potential occupational ceilings, and status group affiliations of members of the two groups (the staff officers being younger, having more education but lower occupational potential, and forming a prestige-oriented group with distinctive dress and recreational tastes); (3) need of the staff groups to justify their existence; (4) fear in the line that staff bodies by their expansion, and well-financed research activities, would undermine line authority; and (5) the fact that aspirants to higher staff offices could gain promotion only through approval of influential line executives.

If further research should prove that staff-line behavior of the character presented here is widespread in industry, and *if* top management should realize how such behavior affects its cost and production goals—and be concerned to improve the condition—then remedial measures could be considered. For example, a corrective approach might move in the direction of (1) creating a separate body whose sole function would be the coordination of staff and line efforts; (2) increasing the gradations of awards and promotions in staff organizations (without increase of staff personnel); (3) granting of more nearly equal pay to staff officers, but with increased responsibility (without authority over line processes or personnel) for the practical working of their projects; (4) requiring that staff personnel have a minimum supervisory experience and have shared repeatedly in successful collaborative staff-line projects before transferring to the line; (5) steps by top management to remove the fear of veiled personal reprisal felt by officers in most levels of both staff and line hierarchies (This fear—rising from a disbelief in the possibility of bureaucratic impersonality—is probably the greatest obstacle to communication inside the ranks of management); (6) more emphasis in colleges and universities on realistic instruction in the social sciences for students preparing for industrial careers.

Selection 38

Voluntary Associations Under Conditions of Competition and Conflict

Arnold M. Rose

Although sociologists generally have been concerned with the structure and function of groups, they often have restricted their study to nonvoluntary or informal groups. However, voluntary associations or formal organizations, as opposed to temporary informal groups, develop stable patterns of interaction over longer periods of time that can be observed and related to other organizational or societal factors. For this reason, Rose felt that it was vital to analyze the ways formal associations relate to one another and the consequences of such interaction in terms of its effect upon group structure. Specifically, Rose's study "attempts to test a series of related hypotheses concerning voluntary associations that have competing or opposing associations in the same community and those that do not."

Inter-group competition usually means that two or more groups are desirous of obtaining scarce community resources—for instance, membership, wealth, material, or prestige. In terms of an ends-means schema, inter-group competition is quite different from inter-group conflict. While competing groups seek to obtain the same ends, conflicting organizations may seek quite dissimilar ends in society and not hesitate to apply negative sanctions to one another.

Rose's central hypothesis, which is confirmed in this study, is that certain internal patterns of behavior and social structures develop within either competing or conflicting groups that are not characteristic of groups which neither compete with nor manifest conflict toward other community associations.

Since some of the latent consequences of group competition and conflict include such important matters as rate of participation, identification with the association, organizational flexibility with regard to goal-setting, etc., Rose's work is of importance not only to the social scientist but also to students who may become community leaders and development workers.

. . . There has been a gap in the research literature, at least until recently, on formally organized voluntary associations. Yet many of the hypotheses about groups advanced by sociologists can best be tested on voluntary associations and we have the word of our most distinguished foreign observers that voluntary associations are a distinctively important type of social structure in American society. This paper attempts to test a series of related hypotheses concerning voluntary associations that have competing or opposing associations in the same community and those that do not.

The data were collected by means of structured

From *Social Forces*, Vol. 34 (1955-1956), 159-163. Published by the University of North Carolina Press.

interviews with the chief executive officers of 91 organizations constituting a rough cross-section of voluntary associations of all types in Minneapolis and St. Paul. . . . Among many other matters, inquiry was made concerning the existence of organizations opposed to and/or competing with the organization under study. A classification of the groups was made according to their major purposes, and there were practically no differences in the distribution of groups by major purpose between those having opposers, those having competitors but no opposers, and those having neither competitors nor opposers. There were also no differences among these three categories relative to the age of the group. Thus any differences discovered in this study among the three categories cannot be attributed to the general nature of their major purposes or the age of the groups studied.

We shall now present our findings in connection with our series of related hypotheses about conflict and competition among organized groups. We define group conflict or opposition operationally as the existence within the same community of at least two groups whose primary functions are opposed to each other and the recognition by the leaders of at least one of these groups that this opposition exists. We define group competition operationally as the existence within the same community of at least two independent groups whose primary functions are the same and the recognition by the leaders of at least one of these groups that their goals are the same as those of the other group. Thus the distinction between conflict and competition, as used here, is that the former involves a difference in ends whereas the latter involves a difference in means but not ends. Phrasing it in this manner suggests that it is of little concern that most (20 out of 24) of the conflicting groups in our sample also have competitors, but we have not included in our category of "competing groups" any of those competing groups which also have opposers.

1. *Groups faced with opposition are more active in pursuit of group goals than are groups faced only with competition, and the latter are more active than groups that are faced with neither opposition nor competition.* Table 1 presents the relevant evidence, which supports our hypothesis: The activity reported for both primary and secondary functions, especially the latter, decreases as we move from conflicting group to competing groups to non-competing, non-conflicting groups. The last-named are less likely to have secondary functions, but when they have them they are at least as likely to have several.

2. *Groups faced with opposition are more likely*

TABLE 1: Degree of Activity Among Groups

	PERCENTAGE DISTRIBUTION OF		
	ASSOCIATIONS WITH OPPOSERS	ASSOCIATIONS WITH COMPETITORS BUT NOT OPPOSERS	ASSOCIATIONS WITH NEITHER OPPOSERS NOR COMPETITORS
Degree of activity reported for primary function			
Very inactive	0.0	2.1	0.0
Fairly inactive	0.0	0.0	5.3
Moderately active	16.7	10.4	21.1
Fairly active	12.5	27.1	15.8
Very active	70.8	60.4	57.8
Number of secondary functions reported			
None	12.5	20.8	31.6
One	62.5	47.9	36.8
Two	25.0	31.3	31.6
Average degree of activity reported for secondary functions			
Very to fairly inactive	8.3	33.4	42.1
Moderately to fairly active	41.7	25.0	31.6
Very active	50.0	41.6	26.3
(Number of cases)	(24)	(48)	(19)

TABLE 2:   Degree of Structure Among Groups

	PERCENTAGE DISTRIBUTION OF		
	ASSOCIATIONS WITH OPPOSERS	ASSOCIATIONS WITH COMPETITORS BUT NOT OPPOSERS	ASSOCIATIONS WITH NEITHER OPPOSERS NOR COMPETITORS
Number of paid staff members			
None	37.5	47.9	68.4
One	12.5	18.7	15.8
Two to five	41.7	20.9	5.3
Six or more	8.3	12.5	10.5
Number of unpaid staff members			
None	79.1	85.4	78.8
One	0.0	6.2	5.3
Two to five	8.4	4.2	5.3
Six or more	12.5	4.2	10.6
Possession of filing system			
Yes	66.7	45.8	21.0
No	33.3	54.2	79.0
Keep minutes of meetings			
Yes	91.6	89.6	84.2
No	8.4	10.4	15.8
Frequency of following Robert's *Rules of Order*			
All the time	54.1	35.4	47.3
Most of the time	25.0	45.8	21.1
Some of the time	4.2	8.3	0.0
Once in a while	4.2	4.2	10.5
Never	12.5	6.3	21.1
(Number of cases)	(24)	(48)	(19)

to develop a complex structure than are groups faced only with competition, and the latter have more structure than groups that are faced with neither opposition nor competition. Table 2 shows that groups with neither opposition nor competition are more likely to get along without paid staff members, and that competing groups are likely to have fewer paid staff members than are conflicting groups. Yet when it comes to unpaid staff members, there are no significant differences among our three categories of groups. The conflicting groups are most likely to keep a systematic file, to keep minutes of meetings, and to follow Robert's *Rules of Order,* and the competing groups are also more likely to do these things than groups which have neither competitors nor opposers. This second conclusion is related to the first one: Groups that are most active in pursuit of their goals are also most likely to develop the structure which they believe will aid them in attaining these goals.

3. *Groups that are faced with opposition are*

more likely to meet frequently than are groups faced only with competition, and the latter are more likely to meet frequently than are groups which are faced with neither opposition nor competition. This hypothesis is also intimately related to the first; groups which have more activity are more likely to meet together to plan and consummate this activity. It is interesting that the greatest differences are in the number of executive meetings, which are planning meetings, rather than in membership or other meetings, which are more likely to be meetings that carry on or consummate the group activity (Table 3).

4. *Groups that are faced with opposition are more likely to be flexible in activities and techniques than are groups faced only with competition, and the latter are more likely to be flexible than are groups which are faced with neither opposition nor competition.* At first glance, this hypothesis might appear to be opposed to the second hypothesis concerning the degree of structure among groups, since it might be supposed

TABLE 3: The Number of Group Meetings

	PERCENTAGE DISTRIBUTION OF		
	ASSOCIATIONS WITH OPPOSERS	ASSOCIATIONS WITH COMPETITORS BUT NOT OPPOSERS	ASSOCIATIONS WITH NEITHER OPPOSERS NOR COMPETITORS
Number of executive meetings per year			
None	37.5	50.1	68.4
One to three	8.3	8.3	21.1
Four to eleven	33.4	25.0	10.5
Twelve or more	16.7	8.3	0.0
Indefinite or no answer	4.1	8.3	0.0
Number of membership meetings per year			
None	20.8	8.3	15.8
One to three	41.7	45.9	36.8
Four to eleven	12.5	27.1	21.1
Twelve or more	20.9	16.6	26.3
Indefinite or no answer	4.1	2.1	0.0
Number of other meetings per year			
None	54.2	58.3	84.2
One to three	8.3	12.5	10.5
Four to eleven	12.5	14.5	0.0
Twelve or more	16.6	8.4	5.3
Indefinite or no answer	8.4	6.3	0.0
(Number of cases)	(24)	(48)	(19)

TABLE 4: Flexibility Among Groups

	PERCENTAGE DISTRIBUTION OF		
	ASSOCIATIONS WITH OPPOSERS	ASSOCIATIONS WITH COMPETITORS BUT NOT OPPOSERS	ASSOCIATIONS WITH NEITHER OPPOSERS NOR COMPETITORS
Change in number of activities since organization began			
Increased considerably	66.7	43.7	31.6
Increased a little	12.5	20.8	21.1
Remained the same	8.3	18.7	36.8
Decreased a little	4.2	6.2	5.3
Decreased considerably	0.0	8.3	5.3
No answer	8.3	2.1	0.0
Change in functions during lifetime of organization			
Added functions	12.5	12.5	5.3
Eliminated functions	0.0	4.2	5.3
Change in emphasis	12.5	0.0	0.0
No change	75.0	83.3	89.4
Change in techniques of working toward group goals			
Change very frequently	8.3	4.2	0.0
Change rather frequently	16.7	4.2	5.3
Change occasionally	41.7	43.7	21.1
Change very seldom	12.5	27.1	26.3
Never change	20.8	20.8	47.3
(Number of cases)	(24)	(48)	(19)

that a large amount of structure inhibits flexibility. While it is probably true that a huge amount of structure can prevent flexibility, apparently few voluntary associations get a very large functioning membership or allow structure to get out of hand. Actually this fourth hypothesis clarifies the second one in the light of the first: Opposition and, to a lesser extent, competition require special efforts on the part of the group; this may be expressed both in amount of structure and in flexibility. This suggests that when groups with opposition develop a heavy structure they can also change or get rid of this structure. The concern which some

sociologists and other critics express concerning the overstructuring of some voluntary associations should, if this hypothesis is correct, be directed only at those groups which face neither opposition nor competition. Table 4 presents the evidence for the hypothesis: The conflicting groups are by far the most likely to have considerably increased their activities since the inauguration of the organization, and they are to a lesser extent the most likely to have changed the functions of the organization. It is in respect to change of techniques in working toward group goals that the conflicting groups are most different from the

TABLE 5:   Internal Solidarity Among Groups

	PERCENTAGE DISTRIBUTION OF		
	ASSOCIATIONS WITH OPPOSERS	ASSOCIATIONS WITH COMPETITORS BUT NOT OPPOSERS	ASSOCIATIONS WITH NEITHER OPPOSERS NOR COMPETITORS
Percentage of "loyal" members *			
Less than 15%	8.4	10.4	21.0
15% to 34%	20.8	22.9	15.8
35% to 75%	20.8	29.2	10.5
75% and over	25.0	22.9	31.6
No answer	25.0	14.6	21.1
Direct personal benefits to members from work of organizations			
Benefit a good deal	45.8	35.4	36.8
Benefit to a limited extent ., ...	25.0	35.4	21.1
Benefit only a little	4.2	12.5	5.3
Benefit practically not at all	12.3	12.5	26.3
No answer	12.3	8.3	10.5
"Do you [executive officer] like members to also be members of other organizations?"			
Yes.............................	58.3	77.1	47.4
Indifferent.......................	33.3	20.8	36.8
No	4.2	0.0	5.3
No answer	4.2	2.1	10.5
Influence of leaders on members			
Very influential	37.5	43.8	21.1
Fairly influential	41.7	20.8	21.1
Moderately influential	0.0	14.6	26.3
Not very influential	8.3	10.4	10.5
Not influential at all	0.0	4.2	10.5
No answer	12.5	6.2	10.5
(Number of cases)	(24)	(48)	(19)

* *The percentage of "loyal" members was arrived at in the following way: The following question was asked, "How much can the membership be relied on to contribute time and money to the organization?" and interviewers were instructed to get the percentage of the membership allocated to each of the following categories: (1) "A great deal, they are a most loyal and self-sacrificing membership"; (2) "A good deal, they give what they can"; (3) "A moderate amount of time and money, what is spare or extra"; (4) "Not very much, only when we put the pressure on"; (5) "Very little, they hardly help at all." The percentages indicated for the first two categories were combined for reporting in this table.*

competing groups, and the competing groups from the groups facing neither opposition nor competition.

5. *Groups that are faced with opposition have a more cohesive relationship among their members than do groups faced only with competition, and the latter are more cohesive than groups that face neither opposition nor competition.* This is, of course, only a restatement of an old sociological hypothesis that opposition increases group solidarity. It also fits in with our preceding hypotheses that opposition makes for increased activity and increased frequency of meetings. The data only partially support the hypothesis, however, suggesting that other factors in group solidarity may work against the influence of conflict and competition. The direct-measure of loyalty of the members (at the top of Table 5) indicates that a low percentage of loyal members is most characteristic of groups with neither opposers nor competitors—which is what our hypothesis predicts—but that a high percentage of loyal members is also most characteristic of other groups of this type—which is contrary to our hypothesis. The direct personal benefits to the members of the work of the organization are distributed, as we expected, in descending order from conflicting groups to competing groups to groups which face neither opposition nor competition, although the differences are not sharp.

When the question was asked of the executive officers, "Do you like members of your organization to also be members of other organizations?" the most favorable responses came from the officers of the competing organizations. Again we are faced with a conflicting finding: We expected indifference to be greatest in the groups facing neither opposition nor conflict, which actually turned out to be the fact, but we also expected opposition to be greatest in the conflicting groups, which was not found to be the fact. Our general hypothesis is confirmed, however, by the question concerning the estimated influence of group leaders on rank-and-file members. The influence of the leaders, which is an index of group cohesiveness, is greatest in the conflicting groups and next greatest in the competing groups. Insofar as charismatic leaders are to be found in voluntary associations, they probably most frequently gravitate to, or are created in, conflicting groups. The leadership in groups that face neither opposition nor competition probably comes closer to Max Weber's conception of bureaucratic leadership.

We have examined the relationships between and the supporting evidence for five hypotheses concerning conflicting and competing voluntary associations. The study confirms our expectation that a study of this type of functioning group would prove to be as fruitful as the more frequent studies of nonvoluntary groups or *ad hoc* groups.

Recent Research
Charles L. Mulford

An analysis of such leading journals as the *American Sociological Review, American Journal of Sociology, Sociology and Social Research, Phylon, Sociometry, Social Forces, Journal of Social Issues, Journal of Human Relations,* and *Sociological Abstracts,* as well as a sampling of books published in recent years, reveals that sociologists have needed to consider at least three kinds of problems in order to make contributions to a sociology of "interaction and process."

First, sociologists have been concerned with a general theoretical development and reformulation of hypotheses. Second, attempts have been made to refine, or construct where none existed, the tools used to measure or operationalize* the many facets of interaction and process. And finally, sociologists have

---

* *operationalize:* To make a term or concept operational is to define it in such a way that it can be observed directly. Terms such as *pain, fear,* or *hunger* may never be satisfactorily operationalized since they can only be inferred, not observed. To make a concept such as *competition* operational is no small task, since one must define it in terms of that which can be directly observed; no vestige of inference on the part of the observer is permitted.

sought ways of extending to real-life situations the applications and generalizations that their research allows them to make.

In terms of theory development, it has been recognized for some time that the structural-functional, or equilibrium, school of sociological theory has tended to focus upon more-or-less static structural relations at a given moment of time, while ignoring the dynamic, or process, elements of behavior. With regard to this criticism, Charles P. Loomis'[1] recent work may represent a step in the right direction. Loomis has attempted to develop a model that stresses "processes over time"—that is, a dynamic model of social systems.

In general, one will find that most researchers now differentiate between interaction and process that occurs within the *internal system* of a group[2] and that which occurs in the *external system*. The internal system has to do with interaction centered around sentiment and social-emotional needs of group members, while the external system has to do with patterns of interaction which display the group's adjustment to its environment and pursuit of goals.

The internal-external approach has suggested a number of interesting research problems now being analyzed: (1) Do changes in external system interaction cause changes in internal system interaction? (2) What type of interaction predominates in each system? (3) What type of leadership is needed in each system, and do the same individuals usually play leadership roles in both systems?

It has become increasingly clear that small-group experiments often lead to findings that can be generalized to communities or even to whole societies. For this reason, one finds a wealth of studies that mainly relate patterns of interaction to such variables as (1) size of group, (2) type of task, (3) type of reward, (4) time allotted for interaction, (5) spatial considerations, (6) personality structure, and (7) perception.

It is interesting to note that social theorists are seeking not only the sources of conflict and answers to other traditional questions, but also are showing interest in the positive aspects of social conflict. Lewis A. Coser[3] feels that sociology should be at least as concerned with the functions as with the dysfunctions of social conflict. For example, conflict often leads to increased morale, results in new alliances, and forces people to cooperate against a common foe; international as well as national and local interaction systems are actually conducted on a conflict basis, rather than on the basis of some equilibrium or even cooperative model.

Measurement in this area of sociology has required and still does require a wide variety of approaches. Social distance testing continues to occupy a prominent position in the area of inter-group relations, with the Bogardus technique still the most popular tool. This instrument is being administered to many different social and ethnic groups, and scores on it are being related to many socio-economic-psychological variables. Now, also, attitude and personality dimensions of behavior are seen as playing major roles in determining how people and groups interact with one another.[4, 5]

Often the historical approach is used as a means of unraveling patterns of inter-group cooperation and tensions. The Records' *Little Rock U.S.A.*,[6] a chronologically constructed case study of school desegregation, is an excellent example of the application of this method.

Large samples of respondents are needed if one wishes to measure public opinion, determine dominant attitudes toward ethnic groups, etc. One institution carrying out empirical research on a nation-wide scale is the National Opinion Research Center at the University of Chicago.

The most concise and well-integrated theories, as well as precisely conducted research, may be of only limited value if applications or generalizations cannot be made that will be useful in predicting or describing real-life behavior. In this sense, the social processes have been fruitful indeed. For example, a major project since the Supreme Court decision in 1954 has been to analyze the process of desegregation in the border states. The results of these studies are being used to predict, and perhaps avoid, trouble spots in desegregation of the Deep South.

Findings from desegregation studies have indicated the need for further research of several types: (1) both white and Negro communities, since desegregation is now seen as interaction between these communities, and (2) the new, rising, Negro middle class (represented by Reverend Martin Luther King) which is assuming an active, aggressive (as opposed to the traditionally accommodative) approach to civil rights. The Ford Foundation through its Fund for the Advancement of Education underwrote and sponsored a series of studies relating especially to desegregation and school integration.

As a result of recent research, the following general statements about the assimilation of ethnic, racial, or regional migrant groups can now be made: assimilation (1) is not an inevitable process that will "naturally" occur if given enough time, (2) should be seen as a two-way process, (3) may be at best a slow process, and (4) always involves both conscious and unconscious processes.

Large firms, whose bureaucratic organization consists of several divisions or branch plants engaged in similar productive efforts, have found that it is profitable to encourage consciously those competitive patterns that are so dominant in our society. These same organizations, however, have come to recognize the benefits of cooperation within divisions and have learned to encourage loyalty, esprit de corps, and group solidarity in them.

Several experimental housing and recreational projects have been or are now being conducted with members of various racial and ethnic groups. Each program has been a direct product of well-documented research carried on by social scientists.

It is very significant to note that several scholarly journals exist solely for the purpose of disseminating research findings directly related to inter-group relations. For example, the *Journal of Conflict Resolution,* published at the University of Michigan, contains theoretical as well as empirical statements related to world peace and the reduction of inter-group tension. UNESCO, and other United Nations affiliates, not only has organized programs for the scientific study of groups, with special emphasis on tension reduction, but also publishes the UNESCO *Courier,* a monthly bulletin that contains a regular account of its highly diversified activities in addition to a list of the publications it sponsors.

References

1. Charles P. Loomis, *Social Systems: Essays on Their Persistence and Change* (Princeton, N.J.: D. Von Nostrand Company, Inc., 1960).
2. George C. Homans, *The Human Group* (New York: Harcourt, Brace & Co.; 1950), especially chapters 4-6.
3. Lewis A. Coser, *The Functions of Social Conflict* (Glencoe, Ill.: The Free Press of Glencoe, 1956).
4. Theodor W. Adorno, *The Authoritarian Personality* (New York: Harper & Brothers, 1950).

5. Gordon W. Allport, *The Nature of Prejudice* (Reading, Mass.: Addison-Wesley Publishing Company, Inc., 1954).
6. Wilson Record and Jane Cassels Record, eds., *Little Rock, U.S.A.* (San Francisco: Chandler Publishing Company, 1960).

Part VI

THE HUMAN AGGREGATE

The aggregation of living human beings in a defined physical space is called a *population*. When special categories of persons are considered, the term may be given a modifier, as in "the female population," "the school-age population," or "the indigent population."

Population cannot be conceptualized without reference to *space*. A statement such as "There are 13,151 persons" does not convey meaning. Given a spatial referent, such as "There are 13,151 persons per square mile in the District of Columbia," or "There are 13,151 persons in the city of Fairbanks, Alaska," or "There are 13,151 American Indians in Minnesota," the statement becomes meaningful.

Nor can population have significance without reference to *time*. A population that would be considered sparse in one period of time might be considered burdensome in another. In the ancient world, the perishability of food, limited water supplies, crude sanitation practices, and other factors fixed the absolute limit for an urban population aggregate at one million persons. Today, sixty-four cities of the world exceed that figure, and Tokyo has more than nine million inhabitants. (Tokyo's 1960 population was roughly equal to the population of the United States during John Quincy Adams' presidency, or to the population of the entire world in the Stone Age!)

The study of population categories, their size and composition, is called *demography*—a term whose Greek roots might be freely translated as "a description of the people."

It is essential that modern states take accurate inventories of their populations. The Constitution of the United States made the machinery of government dependent on such inventories when it stipulated that the apportionment of taxes and congressional representation be based on a national census conducted every ten years. Today, a census provides population statistics that serve many other purposes as well. It furnishes a basis for long-range planning in every department of the government and in many private enterprises. By supplying information about the distribution of population and about age categories within the population, censuses make possible estimates of future educational needs; social security expenditures; persons eligible for induction into the armed services; and suitable locations for interstate highways, hydroelectric dams, and other facilities. Population statistics are also used in "basic research"—the construction and verification of ·sociological studies of social class, social change, social movements, and similar phenomena that lead to general understanding of society and social dynamics.

Demography involves the study of regional and urban aggregates as well as national and continental aggregates. In the first reading in Part VI (Selection 39), Frank W. Notestein shows how population changes result from and are reflected in population growth and shifts in distribution—both of which are related to migration and natural increase. *Migration* includes immigration (movement into an area) and emigration (movement out of an area). *Natural increase* refers to the excess of births over deaths or vice versa; it is the general term for changes caused by fluctuations of the birth and death rates, even when the result is a net decrease in population. (An excess of deaths over births would yield a negative rate of natural increase.) As Notestein points out, immigration and a positive rate of natural increase have been the order of the day for the United States ever since its founding.

A great deal of information of interest to sociologists is revealed by vital statistics that are secondary to birth and death rates. Fecundity rates, marriage rates, divorce rates, longevity rates, and morbidity rates permit the analysis and prediction of changes in birth and death rates as well as changes in the composition of the population.

A *fecundity rate* is an index of a population's capacity to reproduce. The number of women in a given population is a better index of the size of its next generation than is the number of men. Consider a logging camp composed of 100 men and 3 women versus an oriental harem with 102 women and 1 man. The total populations are the same—103—but the contrast in reproductive potential is clear. Of course, not all women have the capacity to reproduce; it is common demographic practice to consider girls under the age of fifteen and women past the age of forty-four incapable of conceiving children. In a preliterate tribe where the average female dies before the age of thirty, a woman has the capacity to reproduce during only half her lifetime. If the same tribe has an equal number of males, none of whom—by definition—can give birth, it is statistically impossible for more than one fourth of the population to be pregnant at any given instant. On the other hand, in a population where the average woman lives to the age of forty-five, the same statistical treatment and logic would place the maximum fraction of the population that could possibly be pregnant at any instant at one third instead of one fourth. But when the life span of women goes beyond forty-five years, the reproductive potential begins to decline again; in an imaginary society where everyone lived to be ninety years of age, the maximum fraction of the population that could be pregnant would be one sixth of the total. In "The Case of the G. E. Babies," Selection 41, the reader will see what happens when general vital statistics are applied to particular cases that do not constitute a representative sample of the population.

The recent "population explosion" in the United States makes Donald O. Cowgill's article on population growth cycles especially timely. Changes in life expectancy—the average number of years people live—affect the number of people living at any given time. Some of the alarmism about the population explosion might be reduced if people paused to consider that we have been postponing deaths, not preventing them. The first cohorts of persons in the United States whose lives have been extended are rapidly approaching the limits of their postponements. For example, the average person born in 1895 was expected at birth to live until approximately 1940, but by 1940 the invention of wonder drugs, better working conditions, better nutrition, and improved medical care had given him a "stay of execution." In fact, there are "even odds" that he is still living at the age of seventy years, although his expectation of life at the time he was born was only forty-five years.

Maximum longevity has not increased much, if any, in the past three or four thousand years. In the fifteenth century B.C., Moses said, "The days of our age are threescore years and ten; and though men be so strong that they come to fourscore years: yet is their strength then but labour and sorrow; so soon passeth it away, and we are gone." The difference in expectation of life between 1500 B.C. and the present lies not in the span of human life but in the number of people who live out their life spans.

Demography is one phase of the broader area of *human ecology*, a field of study which investigates and theorizes about the processes, patterns, and social products of human beings in dynamic aggregate as they compete for survival and for the achievement of their values in their natural environments. In its broadest sense, human ecology is an approach to the science of society.

Sociological curiosity leads us to ask questions about the ways in which individual organisms relate to each other and to their collective habitats. Bees swarm together, build a common hive, reproduce, rear their young, allocate functions to their members, and fend off enemies. What bees might do if they were not organized is a hypothetical question: "social organization" is an inherent part of being a bee. Since their lives are biologically ordered, bees have no problems of sharing values, no questions about norms or sanctions, no truths or fallacies. When humans "swarm," however, the kind of housing they will build is not universally predictable; birth control and child-rearing practices become public and private issues; morals affect employability; occupational specialization is to some extent the result of rational decisions; and enemies are not always recognized and may not even be mutual.

The coming together of a large number of people appears to be a very complex and hazardous (if not potentially disastrous) thing. Certainly it would be difficult to predict how a "swarm" of humans would become organized—or would even survive—if each person somehow had been reared without communication with other humans. It is fortunate that human beings are seldom deprived of other human association, for from human interactions emerge social organization and freedom from dependence upon instinct for the perpetuation of society and consequently of the species. The problems of human ecology differ to some extent from the problems of the ecologies of plants and of other animals. Amos H. Hawley's article, Selection 45, deals with basic issues relating to the ecology of human beings.

The most obvious point at which to begin the study of human ecology is the human community. Human communities may have many kinds of significance and may be studied from many perspectives, several of which are apparent in the following selections. Identification of a writer's perspective is important, since failure to recognize it may result in a misinterpretation of his work.

First, a community may be considered a *sociocultural environment*. The community is the medium for the transmission of culture. It is in the community that ways of doing things become common; it is there that the members of a society congregate to create, learn, and transmit those ways. Whether he is Bantu, Eskimo, or New Yorker, the small child discovers the "natural" and "right" way to do things in a locality rather than in a nation in macrocosm. If the family is the cradle of human nature, the community is its school.

Those anthropologists who emphasize the impact of the community on the basic personality characteristics of societies represent the maximum development of this first perspective. They believe that the community stamps an indelible mark on the personality of each of its constituents in the form of basic, often unconscious, attitudes toward life. The oriental calm, the German concern for orderliness, the French preoccupation with love, the Southerner's concern for the comfort of his guests are all cited as examples by those who believe in a basic societal personality structure. This perspective is clearly present in Selection 48 by Louis Wirth and in Selection 44 by Arthur J. Vidich and Joseph Bensman.

Second, the community may be viewed as an *economic device*. Since before the days of the social contract theorists, many scholars have viewed the community as a contrivance through which men can obtain their individual goals more easily or can obtain more of them than they might in isolation. Community life allows more people to subsist and more of them to achieve a better level of living. In the community market place, nonmaterial goods as well as material goods are exchanged. Survival, protection, education, religious experiences, and entertainment are quite as much involved in the economy of the community as are food, shelter, and clothing. This perspective of the community is indispensable to the economist as well as to the sociologist; it will be illustrated in Gideon Sjoberg's article, Selection 49.

Third, the community can be viewed as a unit of *social organization*. From such a perspective, a community is a population of mutually significant persons, mutually understood symbols, and shared definitions of situations. John Smith, for example, is able to define a situation, to "know what he is doing," at least in part because he is able to relate himself to other persons, events, places, and ideas. He relates himself to the meter-reader who knocks at his door by permitting him to enter the basement and read his water meter, even though he may not relate strongly to him in any other way. John Smith's image of his wife is much more complex: even though he has been married to her for ten years, some aspects of his relationship to her stem from the fact that she is Mr. William Jones' daughter; he relates to her in other ways because she is the mother of his children. His relationship to her is generally stable because he knows what kind of behavior to expect from each relationship in literally thousands of situations—and his expectations are usually borne out.

It would be an endless task even to list the relationships that constitute John Smith's personal perspective of social organization; not only are they myriad, but they keep changing as long as he is in interaction with other people. The same can be said of Mrs. Smith, Mr. Jones, and the meter-reader, who are all significant to one another. The sight, sound, or even idea of one of them in a situation elicits expectations, feelings, and behavioral responses in the person who perceives it. Each of these persons "makes sense" out of the interactions of a population of many significant persons, who are in turn related to other persons, events, places, and ideas. In Selection 42, Robert Redfield describes an ideal community with the most stable social organization occurring among humans.

Fourth, community can be viewed as the *product* of the human aggregate, an *effect* achieved by interacting persons rather than by the population itself. In this sense, community is an *artifact of society*. This usage is predominantly ecological; it will be discussed in more detail in Selections 46 and 47 by Walter Firey and H. Laurence Ross and in the introductions to these articles.

Fifth, community can be considered a *collective representation.* In this usage, the community is a symbol that becomes meaningful to local residents in somewhat the same way that a college or university becomes meaningful to its students. It is more than a way of life; it is an object of strong sentiment. Its residents identify with it so that it becomes a symbol of solidarity toward which they react emotionally, giving them a sense of unity and mutually understood status. "My L. A." becomes a popular newspaper column while promoting a collective representation; "Chi-ca-go" means more than just another song to many residents of that city; a Navy signalman who hails from Minneapolis says, "You can get your kicks just by walkin' down Hennepin Avenue." The community becomes a social-psychological symbol, a personal sentiment that plays a part in the attitudes, motivations, and behaviors of the individual. Anselm Strauss in Selection 50 as well as Wirth and Ross deal with this aspect of community in their articles.

One cannot discuss population and community in the contemporary world without making some reference to the city. Certainly the social organization of the city is the most complex order of social aggregate in existence today. In no other form of social life is there so much interdependence among so many people. Most Americans live in such aggregates, and the lives of even those who are not city dwellers are profoundly influenced by those who are, as is documented in the story of Springdale told by Vidich and Bensman.

In a society with a rural heritage—especially one that attributes many virtues to rural living—a certain amount of disorganization and discontent may be expected if pressures to live in urban areas become great. In the United States, such pressures are increasing. The mechanization and commercialization of agriculture creates increasing unemployment in rural areas; the relatively high wages paid industrial labor and the cultural advantages believed to exist in the city beckon to those in the hinterlands; the urban orientation of mass media tacitly or openly presses for the general adoption of urban norms; the economic advantages of centralized industry pull factories toward other factories, and factories pull more and more employees into ever-growing megalopolises. On the other hand, success in America means space for living, clean air, quiet nights, trees, birds, dogs, community churches and schools, golf courses and bridle paths. People want to have the good life that urban living can give them plus the good life that rural living can give them. One solution—or partial solution—that some people have found is to have the wage-earner employed in the city but the remainder of the family living in the country. The suburb and the exurb make such a double life possible when the wage-earner is willing to commute between home and place of employment to gain an optimum in both.

What kind of community is a commuter town—a place of homes but no industry? Will any of the concepts of community that we have discussed above apply to such a population aggregate? Questions like these are the special concern of Alvin H. Scaff in Selection 43 and of Anselm Strauss in Selection 50. Budding sociologists will be particularly interested in the ways in which Scaff went about finding answers to these and other questions—answers in which he could place the kind of confidence that a research scholar demands.

The civilization and the population characteristics of the United States seem to demand the growth of modern cities. Sociologists would be remiss if they did not study the adaptation of people to urban living as it now exists and the ongoing social processes by which the cities of tomorrow and a thousand years from now are being shaped by human acts in the present.   *T.E.L.*

Selection 39

Population

Frank W. Notestein

This report, by one of America's most eminent demographers, concerns the state of the population of the world and of the United States at mid-twentieth century. Notestein has gathered pertinent statistics relating to the distribution and composition of the population of the United States and other selected areas; then, by a careful analysis of vital statistics, he has forecast trends and problems that loom ahead. Not only is this report complete and well-written—an example of demography at its best—but since it was prepared on the basis of the United States Census of 1950, the reader can compare Notestein's predictions and forecasts with the actual occurrences since that date.

Changes in the number of members in a family result from the processes of birth, death, marriage, adoption, and migration of members; and the processes of population growth or decline on a national or even a world scale are fundamentally quite as simple. The three factors of birth, death, and migration determine the size of the population in any area.

As Notestein observes, the factor of migration is an extremely complex one. It may involve political philosophies, climate, economic changes, cultural values, and sometimes even sex ratios. Some of the aspects of migration will be brought out in the readings on human ecology (Selections 45-47). Here, selections have been limited to those dealing with birth and death, or, in the terminology of the demographer, with fertility and mortality. Notestein presents the empirical case of the United States in 1950. Cowgill summarizes the theories of population growth cycles which should explain the reasoning that underlies the prediction of population changes. Finally, "The Case of the G. E. Babies" shows how careful one must be to account for all the variables involved in predicting future births for a specific population.

The tense international situation . . . seems to have fostered many misconceptions about the power position of the U.S. We hear talk of our being hopelessly outnumbered in a struggle for survival with the rapidly increasing peoples of the Far East. This pessimistic account runs to the effect that our population is small, whereas the Far Eastern population is huge; that our numbers are not increasing, while unlimited reproduction is multiplying those in Asia; that our nation is no longer rich in young men, whereas China's population is heavily loaded with youths. From these notions many draw the inference that our power is waning while that of the Far East is rising rapidly. Actually there are several errors in this picture.

It is true that the U.S. has a very small part of the world's two and a third billion people: in 1950 only six out of every 100 of the world's people lived within our continental boundaries. But our proportion of the world's population has been increasing, not falling. A hundred years ago the U.S. accounted for only two per cent of the world population, and 50 years ago only five per cent. Our population has increased more rapidly than that of the world in general or of the Far East in particular. It is increasing more rapidly now, and may well continue to do so for some time to come. Moreover, a larger proportion of our population is in the age groups from which the labor force is drawn, and we probably have even

From the *Scientific Monthly*, September 1951, pp. 28-35. Reprinted by permission of the American Association for the Advancement of Science.

a larger proportion in the ages between 20 and 40 than China has.

Most important, we are much the healthiest and wealthiest of the world's great powers. Our influence and that of our friends in the Western world has never depended mainly on numbers; we always have been, and shall remain, a rather small minority of the world's people. The prosperity, prestige and power of the U.S. have been based largely on the rich natural resources at our command, our excellent health, our high skills and our effective political and economic organization. Taken together, these spell large per capita production. In agriculture we make more efficient use of our manpower than most other countries. Whereas in Asia three or four out of every five workers work on the land and produce only a meager per capita supply of food and fiber, in the U.S. our people are fed and clothed much better with only about one worker in every eight working on farms. This leaves the other seven of the eight available for nonagricultural pursuits. That circumstance, coupled with our high industrial efficiency, accounts for the fact that the U.S., with only about six per cent of the world's population, produces almost one half of the world's industrial goods.

The huge population of Asia (well over a billion) and its very high birth rates are not the threat to our leadership that they may seem. With the mass of the population living close to the margin of subsistence, the death rates in the Far East are tragically high, so the rate of population increase is in general rather low in spite of the high birth rates. Any substantial reduction of the death rates through improvement of the food supply would bring a rapid population increase, but the new mouths to feed would absorb most of the increased production; hence it will be extremely difficult to achieve sustained improvements in living conditions. For some decades to come the situation in Asia spells poverty and not power— except power to absorb suffering and punishment. The fact is that the Far East probably would be more prosperous and more powerful if it had half as many people as it has now.

It is not in the Far East but in Eastern Europe and the U.S.S.R. that the most significant new developments are occurring. This quarter of the world has a large population which until recently has been technologically backward. But these peoples are now rapidly acquiring the skills needed to turn their fairly abundant resources into economic products. Barring major catastrophes or the grossest sort of mismanagement, they should achieve rapid increases in per capita production and in population during the next few decades.

In industrialization they should advance rapidly because they are moving along a path already well charted by the Western world. Their populations should grow swiftly because they are getting the knowledge and the production with which to reduce their high death rates. This segment of the human race is the one that would seem to have the best chance, among the hitherto backward peoples, of becoming a major new focus of political power in the world and of maintaining its position.

All this suggests two major guides to policy for the U.S.: (1) as a small minority people it will be well for us to gain and keep as many likeminded friends as possible; (2) as the more numerous peoples modernize themselves technologically, we shall be able to maintain our leadership in peace and war only by rapidly increasing our own efficiency. In other words, our leadership in the future, as in the past, must be based on quality of performance, not on the number of people. The task is not a simple one, for it requires ever-advancing innovation.

Let us look at our recent population trends to see in what directions they seem to be taking us. During the past 100 years the population of the U.S. increased more than sixfold, while the world's population only doubled; our average annual rate of increase was almost two per cent, in contrast with about three quarters of one per cent for the world as a whole. This increase was due only in relatively small part to immigration; most of the growth was accounted for by the native-born white population. But our rate of growth has been falling decade by decade. It dropped from three per cent a year between 1850 and 1860 to .7 per cent a year in the depression decade 1930-1940. In the 1940s there was a spectacular resurgence of growth; we added 19 million to our population and the average annual rate of increase was twice that in the 1930s. . . .

Between 1900 and 1950, when the total population almost doubled, the rural population increased by only a little more than one-third. By 1950 the people living in rural areas, including unincorporated villages and towns, amounted to only 41 per cent of the total population. Those actually living on farms, not all of whom gained their livelihood from agriculture, constituted 16 per cent of the total. Thus in 1950 a farm population some millions smaller than that of 1900 was producing a more ample food supply for nearly twice as many people. The shrinkage of the farm population does not mean that it produced less than its share of the nation's natural increase. With its high birth rates and favorable death rates, it contributed more than its share to the

Age and sex distribution of the population notably shows the effects of the economic depression of the 1930s. The pyramids on these two pages show the number of men and women in each age group in 1900, 1920, 1940, 1950, and 1960. The pyramids at the top are broadest at the base; the pyramids at the bottom are notched by the declining birth rate of the 1930s. In 1960, however, the base of the pyramid broadened again.

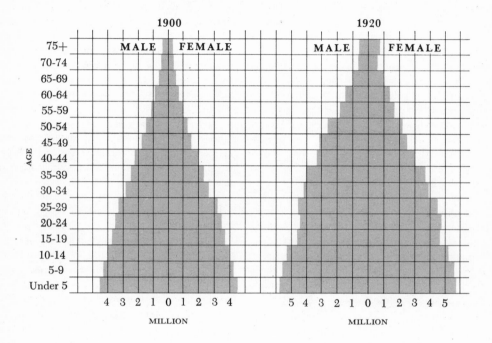

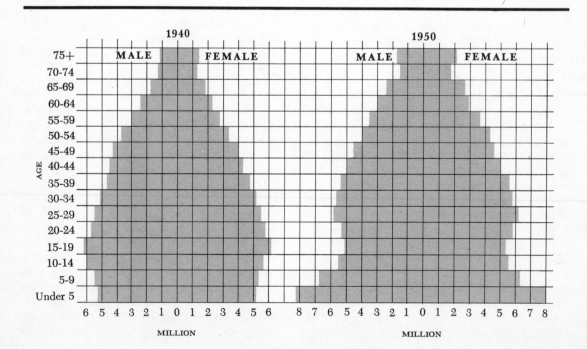

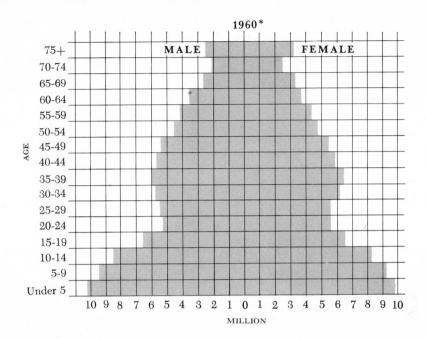

1960*

| | MALE | FEMALE |

AGE

75+
70-74
65-69
60-64
55-59
50-54
45-49
40-44
35-39
30-34
25-29
20-24
15-19
10-14
5-9
Under 5

10 9 8 7 6 5 4 3 2 1 0 1 2 3 4 5 6 7 8 9 10

MILLION

*Source: Department of Commerce, Bureau of the Census, *United States Census of Population: 1960,* Vol. I, in United States Bureau of the Census, *Statistical Abstract of the United States: 1963* (Washington, D.C.: Government Printing Office, 1963), p. 26.

growth of the population, but as job opportunities on the farm shrank, there was a huge and continuous movement of farm sons and daughters toward the cities. Farm families have done extraordinarily well in supplying the nation both with food and with the people to eat it.

During the past 50 years great changes also have occurred in the regional distribution of the population. The sections that have shown the most marked growth are the South, which had the largest absolute increase in numbers, and the West, which had the largest proportionate increase. The two regions achieved their increases in diametrically opposite fashions. The South has grown mainly because of a very high birth rate, which has more than offset the fact that more people have migrated away from the region than to it. The West, on the other hand, has had a comparatively low rate of natural increase, but it has grown prodigiously by attracting migrants from other regions. In general the highest natural increases have come in areas of low economic opportunity. The freedom of internal migration in the U.S. has been one of the sources of our great economic strength, for it has permitted the flexible adjustment of discrepancies between the rate of natural increase and economic opportunity in a region. People have been able to move easily to

areas where economic expansion is taking place. Without such migration, the regional differences in the levels of living and per capita productivity would be very much greater than they are.

Another great element of strength in our demographic situation is the age composition of the population. In our population only a little more than one-fourth are children under age 15, whereas in Asia, for example, about four persons of each ten are in that generally unproductive group. The rearing of children of course is the soundest investment that a nation can make, and in our case the investment is a particularly good one, for at current rates of survival more than 95 per cent of those born will live at least to age 15 and more than 60 per cent will live to age 65. But in the Far East the investment is much more precarious; a conservative estimate is that a smaller proportion of those born live to age 15 there than live to age 65 in the U.S. Probably more than 40 per cent of the children in the Far East never reach the productive years of life.

A hundred years ago our own age distribution was much like that of the Far East today. The median age of our population was only 18.8. Fifty years ago it had risen to 22.9. Since 1900 the picture has changed radically. At the turn of the century the age structure was represented by a pyramid that was broadest at the base (representing the number in the youngest age group) and narrowed in rather regular steps for each five-year age group from youth to old age (*see page* 308). This structure reflected the fact that both the birth rates and the death rates before 1900 had been high: each year's crop of babies was larger than that of the year before, and the older birth classes, besides being smaller to begin with, had tended to die at a relatively early age.

Now the way to produce an older population is to cut both the risks of death and the rate of expansion of the birth crops. Since 1900 the U.S. has done both, with the result that the median age of the population has risen to 30.1. By 1940 the base of the pyramid had been sharply narrowed, because of the decline in the number of births. At that time many demographers, including the writer, suggested that the U.S. might reach its maximum population in a few decades. But events in the 1940s upset these predictions. Death rates declined with unexpected speed, and birth rates rose spectacularly. The base of the age pyramid broadened again. The pyramid for 1950 in the illustration on page 309 clearly shows the extent of our error, and should warn the reader that current predictions also may be invalidated by future events.

We had a dip in the number of births during the depression and a sharp rise during the 1940s. As a result there will be considerable swings in the next few years in the size of classes coming of age for school, military service, work and marriage. We have already felt the complications of these changes. . . . The fluctuations in the size of the birth classes will, of course, be felt for many years, as wave following trough breaks on the schools, the labor market, the hospitals, the pension funds and the insurance systems.

Thus far, however, the recent swings in births have not changed the total picture much. In 1950, as in 1940, about 58 per cent of the population was of working age, as against 45 per cent in 1850. In the past 100 years the proportion of old dependents in the population has risen considerably, but the proportion of young dependents has declined sharply, the proportion of young workers has increased somewhat and the proportion of old workers has more than doubled. In short, from the point of view of economic productivity the age distribution of our population has been improving. If we make effective use of our older workers, in all probability that improvement will continue.

This brings us to the consideration of what the future trends in our population are likely to be.

Predictions are risky, as we have seen, but we have some facts to go on and can examine the possibilities. We shall leave out of the discussion the uncertain factor of immigration, which has played an important, though not predominant, part in our population growth in the past. We might increase our numbers greatly by opening the doors again, for it is clear that so long as the U.S. remains free and wealthy in a poverty-stricken world, we can have as many newcomers as we care to accept. But this seems an unlikely event, and in any case immigration policy is a large subject of its own that is beyond the scope of this article.

The two major factors that shape population change in a nation are mortality and fertility. Let us consider mortality first. It can be said at once that the growth of our population would not be affected much by any further reductions in mortality rates, unless we lengthened life by reducing the mortality among oldsters (*i.e.*, over 60). A statistical example will illustrate why this is so.

We shall consider a group of 1,000 live-born white girls. In 1901 the risks of death were such that barely more than half of the 1,000 could expect to live to the age of 60. In 1948 more than half would live to the age of 75, assuming that the death risks remained at the 1948 level. To put it another way, at the 1901 survival rate for white females 1,000 births a year would maintain a total population of 51,000 persons, while at the 1948 rate the same number of births would maintain a population of 71,000, with an average life-expectancy of 71 years. (In India, according to the most recent official life tables— for 1921-1931—the death risks were so high that 1,000 female births a year would maintain a population of no more than 27,000.)

Now most of the gain in average life-expectancy in the U.S. between 1901 and 1948 was due to a spectacular reduction in the mortality of people under 45. There is relatively little further room for improvement in mortality rates below that age. Even if there were no deaths at all before the age of 45 among white females in the U.S., 1,000 births a year would support a population only six per cent larger than the 71,000 figure given above, assuming that the death rates of people above 45 were not reduced. This hypothetical maximum gain of six per cent is much less than the 30 per cent gain that was actually achieved by the reduction of mortality under 45 between 1901 and 1948. By eliminating or greatly reducing deaths before 45 among Negroes, whose mortality rates are still far higher than those of whites in spite of great improvement since 1901, we could add somewhat more to our population

Fertility of the white population steadily decreased from the 1800s to the end of the 1930s. The diagram at the right shows in greater detail the area indicated by the gray rectangle on the diagram at the left.

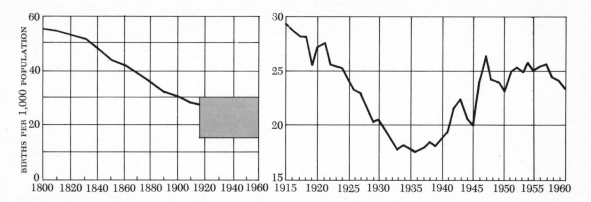

Source of data for 1951-1960: United States Department of Health, Education, and Welfare, *Health, Education, and Welfare Trends,* 1960 Edition (annual).

potential. But it remains true that the maximum mortality reduction we could achieve for people under 45, or even up to 60, would not greatly increase our population growth. There is, of course, no theoretical limit to the population increases that we might obtain by cutting mortality rates among people over 60; if no one ever died, a population recruited even by only one birth a year would grow indefinitely. Perhaps future advances in the control of the degenerative diseases of old age will have great effects on the size and character of our population, but such speculation seems futile at present. It seems safe to say that the growth of the U.S. population under 60 will not be influenced to any important extent by changes in mortality.

Consequently the major determinant of our growth probably will be fertility, that is, the trend in the birth rate. The events of the past decade have made this very difficult to forecast. Until the early 1940s the direction of the trend seemed perfectly clear. There had been an almost unbroken decline in the birth rate since 1800. All available evidence seemed to point toward a continuation of that decline. The nation was rapidly adopting the small-family system, apparently in all strata of the population. There was ample evidence that the reductions in births were coming about mainly through the growing prevalence and increasing effectiveness of contraceptive practices. It seemed that the people, poor and well-to-do alike, wanted fewer children and were rapidly finding the means of fulfilling that want.

Further declines in the birth rate could confidently be predicted.

So went the reasoning; the events took another course, as the charts on page 309 demonstrate. From a depression low of 2.3 million in 1933 the annual number of births rose to 3.9 million in 1947 and stayed at about 3.7 million through 1950. But it is far from certain that the birth boom of the 1940s foreshadows a continuation of high birth rates in the future. There are indications to the contrary in some of the characteristics of the boom.

For example, the increase in births has been most marked in those sectors of the population where fertility has been under the most effective control and is normally low—among city families, those living in the Northeast and those with college education. The groups that are usually the most fertile—farm families, those living in the South, those with the least education—had the smallest increases.

Moreover, the indications are that the huge increase in births during the 1940s was due mainly to the fact that more families were having children or adding a second or third child, rather than to any abandonment of the small-family system. First, second and third children accounted for most of the increases in births. It is true that there were also considerable increases in the numbers of families that had a fourth or fifth child, but this appears to be attributable to the fact that more women were exposed to that risk, because of the sharp rise in marriage rates in

1940 and 1941. The actual proportion of mothers who bore fourth and fifth children, of the total number of married women in a position to do so, probably declined throughout the baby boom. . . .

The increase in first and second children almost certainly has been due in part to the growing social disapproval of childless and one-child families. If this attitude continues, it will tend to produce a permanent increase in births. However, the increase seems to have been due in even larger part to the fact that people have been marrying at progressively younger ages, which has resulted in a very large increase in the number of marriages. This process cannot go on indefinitely. When the trend toward earlier and earlier marriage ages stops, the marriage rate will fall sharply, and if the marriage age should then rise, the drop in the number of marriages would be precipitous. That in turn, of course, would result in a sharp drop in the number of births.

. . . [T]he fact that couples marry younger means that the wife is exposed to the possibility of having children for a larger part of the child-bearing period of her life, and the parents therefore have more chances of exceeding the number of children they want or more time to change their minds about wanting additional children. On the other hand there is every indication that the major part of the increase has come from those sectors of the population that have their fertility under the most effective control, and the increase from this group may be canceled to a considerable extent by the continued decline of the truly large families—a decline that has gone on throughout the baby boom.

. . . It is unlikely . . . that we shall return to the low birth rates of the depression years in the foreseeable future, provided the marriage age stays young and the proportion of those who never marry does not increase. No one knows whether these conditions will continue. We have learned a good deal about the manner in which the resurgence in births developed, but we still know rather little about the motivating forces. Evidently the revival of the economy after the great depression released a backlog of postponed marriages and births. . . . The expansion of social security, increases in tax exemptions for dependents, [and] the current period of full employment . . . probably have had something to do with the increases in births. The present military service act, which defers the induction of fathers, adds a new stimulus to procreation.

Yet we do not really know what were the most important factors behind the baby boom; it is possible that less tangible causes, on which no systematic evidence is available, have been more influential than any we have mentioned. Apparently the wartime experience taught young America that it was fun to marry young and rear a small family. . . . If this is so, and if new economic difficulties do not arise, we may expect the stream of births to be sustained well above that of the depression years, though below the current level.

Our population should therefore continue to grow, at a rate somewhat lower than that of the 1940s. But we are not in a position to make any precise estimates of our future size; there are too many unknown variables at work. . . .

It is by no means certain that it would be to the advantage of the nation to have a continuation of the recent high rate of population increase. Growth of the population reduces the amount of natural resources available per person, which means that the nation must turn to the use of inferior or substitute resources, and such uses generally entail higher costs. Technological advances may well cancel such added cost, but income used in canceling higher costs is not available for other uses. From the standpoint of the economic welfare of the population as a whole, the only economic advantage that comes from a large population as such lies in the economies it makes possible through specialization in production. It is not at all certain, however, that larger numbers would greatly increase such economies in the U.S.

Rapid growth undoubtedly supplies a kind of stimulus to the economy, making it more dynamic and flexible, but growth is only one of the ways of achieving this, and if the costs of the growth are high, it may not be the most efficient way. Precipitous changes in the rate of growth are troublesome. As we have seen, such changes introduce waves and troughs into the age distribution, and these require the nation to maintain more facilities to care for its population than it would if the same numbers were distributed more smoothly over the life span. School buildings are one striking example; they must be built to take care of peaks of population. The ebb and flow of births is, in the long run, a costly affair.

From the military point of view the matter of population size may have a somewhat different aspect. Even from this point of view, however, it is questionable whether the desirability of a larger population is as great as is commonly supposed. Since our population will in any case remain a relatively small one in world-wide terms, our main asset lies in our power to produce more material than we require to maintain ourselves. This asset can be retained only if we are able to invest heavily in the health and training of our youth, which involves retaining a high level of living. These considerations suggest that it is wise to avoid growth that presses on our resources, even when the object is to maximize national power. On the whole it seems to the writer that the nation is fortunate to have come through its period of rapid growth without generating a population that seriously strains our resources.

From the point of view of power and economic welfare the characteristics of the population may be more important than its size. One of our most important assets will continue to be the favorable distribution of the population between the working and the dependent ages. The value of this asset will depend to a considerable extent on the effectiveness with which we employ the older worker. The number of young workers will continue to grow, but the older workers will increase even more rapidly. The aged will increase most rapidly of all. The "problems of the aged" are difficult human and social problems, but these are minor liabilities of one of our most magnificent assets—the fact that relatively little of the life created in the U.S. is lost before it reaches the age when it can contribute to the social product.

If the strength of the nation lies less in numbers than in per capita productivity, then we need to place great and growing emphasis on the quality of the population. Here we have some disturbing problems. . . . [I]t is unfortunate that the states whose high birth rates produce the heaviest educational burdens are also the ones least able to carry the loads. If the leadership of the U.S. is to be maintained, in our increasingly complex world, it is essential that we develop the skills of all our people to the maximum of their inborn potential. This we have not done, and shall not do until the ability of the child replaces the income of the parents as the major criterion for educational opportunity.

If the population problems facing us in the future seem difficult, it may be pointed out that under peacetime conditions the problems ahead will be small compared with those already solved. Western civilization for the first time in man's long history has learned to substitute the control of fertility for death as a means of checking unlimited increase. Our reduction of peacetime mortality since 1900 has saved many more lives than have been lost in the wars of this century. With all our tragic failings we have become relatively efficient producers of life, and given peace and moderate wisdom we should continue to increase that efficiency.

Selection 40

The Theory of Population Growth Cycles
Donald O. Cowgill

At the beginning of the nineteenth century, an English scholar named Thomas Robert Malthus observed that the human population has the capacity to increase at a much more rapid rate than does the available supply of food. In fact, he deduced that population would increase at an exponential rate if it was not checked, while the food supply could not be expected to increase at more than a straight-line rate. In other words, for each generation the food supply would *increase by a fixed amount*, while the population would be *multiplied by a fraction of itself*. Although Malthus' mathematical model has fallen into some disrepute among scholars, few are willing to deny that in recent years population has increased more rapidly than the food supply, at least in underdeveloped countries.

If Malthus' proposition is correct, how can we account for the fact that the population of the earth has not already stripped it of its food supply? Malthus pointed out that when the natural increase exceeds the food supply, the population is *checked* by starvation. There are, he said, two broad classes of population checks: (1) positive and (2) preventive. Preventive checks are those factors that reduce the number of *births*, such as late marriage, celibacy, sterilization, and birth control. Positive checks, on the other hand, are those factors that increase the number of *deaths,* such as war, disease, disaster, accident, murder, suicide, and ultimately (if the positive and preventive checks combined do not limit the population to a size commensurate with its available food supply) famine and starvation.

Since the appearance of Malthus' writings, several scholars have attempted to trace the patterns of natural increase. In the article presented here, Cowgill reviews some of the chief theories that have been set forth. Since the initial publication of Cowgill's article, here somewhat abridged, events have occurred which suggest that Cycle IV, rather than Cycle III (as they are labeled in the article), is likely to be the future cycle. In the preceding article by Notestein, it was shown that the birth rate in the United States reached a nadir in the period 1933-1939, increased until 1947, and began another decline which continued until 1950. Demographers attributed the increase to factors associated with U.S. participation in World War II (1941-1945) and the homecoming from it and believed that the decline evident in 1948 would continue, possibly to a rate as low or lower than that of 1936.

But, as we shall see in "The Case of the G. E. Babies," there are many more variables operating than are apparent on the surface, and a logical prediction must take all of them into account. It now appears that the abnormal condition that affected both fertility and mortality rates was not so much World War II as the Great Depression of the mid-1930's. The birth rate did not continue to decline much after 1950 but stabilized at about the level of the mid-1920's. In the meantime, the death rate dropped as a result of many factors, including the invention of antibiotics, and helped produce the "population explosion" by *deferring* a tremendous number of deaths. We are presently at the threshold of an era of increasing death rates unless man's life span is lengthened. In other words, we appear to be at approximately the point shown by the arrow in the diagram below.

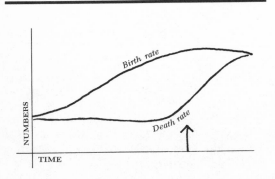

The systematic study of population began with the broad, supposedly universal principles enunciated by Malthus. Much of the development of later population theory has been a reaction to these Malthusian principles, largely by way of pointing out specific exception to the general principle arising in the last century and a half and attempting to adjust the theory to meet these new facts. This emphasis on events of recent times plus the dearth of population facts for other periods has tended to foster the impression that principles adequate to explain modern phenomena are adequate for all time. One specific area in which this seems to be the case is in the theory relating to population cycles.

The chief cycle theories have been based exclusively upon modern human populations or laboratory experiments with subhuman species. One of the best known is that of Raymond Pearl:

"Growth occurs in cycles. Within one and the same cycle, and in a spatially limited area or universe, growth in the first half of the cycle starts slowly but the absolute increment per unit of time *increases* steadily until the midpoint of the cycle is reached. After that point the increment per unit of time becomes *smaller* until the end of the cycle."

"The Theory of Population Growth Cycles" by Donald Olen Cowgill. Reprinted from *The American Journal of Sociology,* Vol. LV (1949), 163-170, by permission of The University of Chicago Press.

This theory, based first on experiments with the *Drosophila melanogaster* [fruit fly] in the limited environment of a milk bottle, was stated as a mathematical law, using a formula for the logistic curve to describe the curve of population growth. This type of curve is illustrated in Figure I. Pearl found that the same curve could be fitted to the growth pattern of yeast and of chickens, again under the ideal conditions of a spatially limited universe. . . .

. . . [I]n the unsuccessful effort to secure an unsophisticated human population that would most closely resemble fruit flies in a bottle, Pearl studied the people of Algeria after their subjugation by the French in the middle of the nineteenth century. The analogy was not that the French "bottled them up" in this period but that the pacific condition of the Algerians in subsequent decades permitted expansion of population as the fruit flies expanded in the bottle. Here a reasonably close fit to the logistic curve was obtained, in part due to neglect of the gross inaccuracy of early population data for Algeria.

From this Pearl generalized that "growth occurs in cycles." . . .

A somewhat similar cycle theory, though less precise, is that of the Italian, Gini, who . . . adduced . . . that a human population has a life-cycle similar to that of the individual, characterized by an early period of rapid growth, a period of maturity and stability, followed by senescence and decline. . . .

takes place. . . . [W]e shall disregard the effects of migration and treat only of natural increase. It is in regard to the mechanics of the cycle that . . . theorists come into sharp disagreement. Malthus inferred that any growth cycle would ultimately be curtailed and brought to a close by an increase in the death rate. Gini [and] Pearl . . . see the close of the cycle effected by a falling birth rate. . . . It might be assumed that, as they explain the cessation of growth by a decline in the birth rate, they would ascribe its origin to an increase in the birth rate. However, this is not specifically stated, and the general implication seems to be that they assume the normal situation to be a much higher birth rate than death rate. The highly artificial environmental situation in which Pearl conducted his biological experiments were amenable to this interpretation. In these experiments he was much more concerned with what stopped the cycle than how it started, and it is perhaps not surprising that he carried this emphasis over into the study of human populations. . . . [B]irth and death ratios would produce Pearl's logistic curve of growth only under the ideal conditions of transplantation of a few individuals into an ideal environment—conditions approximated to a degree in the New World since the discovery of America if we disregard the indigenous American population. . . . By contrast, the implication of Malthus appears clear cut; any technological improvement, any new resources, any new territory for exploitation will tend to increase the population by temporarily depressing the death rate. . . .

FIGURE 1: A population growth cycle

Assuming, then, that growth cycles may be observed in many and varied populations, and assuming that, in general, such cycles do result in an S-curve of growth, the object of this paper is to examine the mechanics by which such growth

Theoretically, a cycle of growth through natural increase could be inaugurated by either an increased birth rate or a decreased death rate and terminated by either a decreased birth rate or an increased death rate. But there is a dynamic relationship between these two variables that requires consideration of the whole cycle.

Four simple theoretical patterns of relationship emerge as possible combinations.

This does not exhaust the possibilities; there are numerous other combinations and permutations that might be remarked. But these will serve as the most obvious and simple pure forms of the cycle. Each of these in the regular form presented above will result in an S-curve of population growth.

Now let us see when and where these different forms of the cycle have occurred.

FIGURE 2:   The mechanics of Cycle I (the primitive cycle).

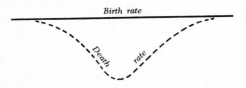

Cycle I. While the birth rate remains stationary, the death rate falls, then rises again to terminate the cycle (see Figure 2).

FIGURE 3:   The mechanics of Cycle II (the modern cycle).

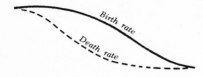

Cycle II. This cycle is characterized by both falling birth rates and falling death rates; but in the initial stages the death rate drops more rapidly than the birth rate, only to be overtaken by a more rapidly falling birth rate in the later stages of the cycle (see Figure 3).

FIGURE 4:   The mechanics of Cycle III (the future cycle).

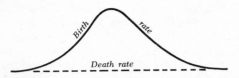

Cycle III. This cycle is initiated by a rising birth rate and brought to a close by a recession of the birth rate, while the death rate remains stable (see Figure 4).

Prior to the recent decline in the birth rate in countries affected by the Industrial Revolution and concomitant developments, there is no reliable evidence of growth cycles produced by rising birth rates. Bowen admits of a possible increase in the birth rate during the Middle Ages.[1] However, there is no proof of this development, and the safer generalization is that in the main the birth rate in pre-industrial times was relatively high and reasonably stable. Of this situation Thompson has the following to say:

"Before the development of the more efficient methods of machine production in Western countries and before the accompanying agricultural revolution got under way, steady and rapid population growth was the exception rather than the rule. There was a severe struggle for mere subsistence. When for some reasons conditions were favorable, when there was a series of good crop years, when favorable 'runs' of fish appeared, or when disease was less prevalent than usual, there was an increase in population, its rate depending on how favorable these conditions were at the time. But, when dearth and disease came, the death rate rose and population did not grow or even declined."[2]

The inference from this quotation is that the fluctuating variable in these circumstances is the death rate, not the birth rate. A little later Thompson says:

"These facts, coupled with the observations of population growth in the nonindustrialized nations of today, lead us to believe that in pre-Industrial Revolution days all death rates were high and averaged very little lower than the birth rates. . . . A violently fluctuating death rate with a very slow increase of population over long periods probably characterized most peoples before the advent of the Industrial Revolution."[3]

Thus we arrive at the hypothesis that cycles of growth in primitive or pre-industrial societies

---

[1] "It is quite probable that birth rates may have had some slight age-long decline. There is, however, the strong possibility of a perceptible upward trend during the Middle Ages" (Ezra Bowen, *An Hypothesis of Population Growth*, New York: Columbia University Press, 1931, p. 169).

[2] Warren S. Thompson, *Population and Peace in the Pacific* (Chicago: University of Chicago Press, 1946), p. 22.

[3] *Ibid.*, p. 23.

follow the pattern of Cycle I above, i.e., the initial growth is accounted for by a falling death rate, and the cycle closes with a return of the death rate to its previous high level.

There are a number of authenticated cases where this has happened. In Finland between 1810 and 1870 this pattern of growth is evident. In 1810 the death rate stood above the birth rate but, by 1820, was ten points lower than the birth rate. Approximately the same margin was maintained until about 1856, when the death rate rose again to about the same level as the birth rate. Subsequently, of course, Finland has gone into the typical growth cycle which has accompanied industrialization, a cycle which differs in mechanics, as we shall see in a moment.

Recurring famines in many lands induce an appearance of such cycles. India, up to about 1910, gave evidence of alternating patterns of growth and stability or decline, correlated with alternating good crop years and bad. During the limited period for which statistics are available, it appears that the birth rate fluctuated little up to 1910, while the death rate fluctuated widely in the manner described by Thompson.

Again, this is the pattern in China according to Ta Chen:

". . . the data seem to show that Chinese population changes in the past have been cyclical rather than linear and that the cyclical trends may be roughly explained as follows: At the beginning of a new dynasty, when peace and order were maintained, population normally increased by the excess of births over deaths, and cultural development advanced apace through the division of labor. As time went on, the increased density, coupled with the lack of inventions and improvements in farming technology, gradually intensified the struggle for existence by the masses. Nevertheless, population continued to increase until it reached a saturation point, the apex of the cycle. Then came pestilence and famine, symptoms of overpopulation, until life became increasingly more intolerable and revolution or war broke out. This temporarily relieved the pressure of population and brought a new dynasty into being. Population continued to decrease until it reached the lowest possible level, the bottom of the cycle. Then another cycle began, and the cyclical trends were thus repeated, each lasting several hundred years, the length of time being largely determined by the severity of the population pressure prior to the downfall of the reigning dynasty."[4]

The estimates cited by this author indicate little

FIGURE 5:   The mechanics of Cycle IV

Cycle IV. This cycle is also initiated by a rising birth rate but is terminated by a subsequent rise in the death rate (see Figure 5).

increase in the Chinese population from the year 2 A.D. to the year 1620. Instead, he postulates periods of growth counterbalanced by periods of loss. While, of course, there are no adequate birth or death statistics for this period, it is significant that Ta Chen cites famine, pestilence, and war as the factors which bring a growth cycle to an end. These are mortality-inducing factors, and the presumption is that a rising death rate closes the cycle. Here again, then, we get the picture of a fluctuating death rate without much change in the birth rate.

The historical and descriptive material dealing with famine and pestilence, all too prevalent in primitive societies, uniformly supports the conclusion that this was the general condition in primitive societies.

The cycle of population increase in primitive society then conforms more closely to Malthus' explanation than it does to the explanation of Pearl, Gini, . . . and others who have believed that the close of the cycle was marked by declining fertility. . . .

THE MODERN CYCLE

It is common knowledge today that population tends to increase with the influences of industrialization, the widening of commercial trade areas, the development of mechanized agriculture, improved medical science, and mass education. Pearl's logistic curve does approximate the growth cycle of most areas subjected to these influences.

The mechanics of this modern population cycle are too well known to require extended treatment. This is the pattern of Cycle II above, with a declining death rate and a declining birth rate but

[4] Ta Chen, *Population in Modern China*, Suppl. to the *American Journal of Sociology*, LII (July 1946).

with the birth rate lagging several decades behind the death rate. This cycle is described by Thompson as follows:

"The data for Sweden show the pattern of a growing natural increase for several decades after the birth rate began to decline. . . . Here the natural increase—birth rate minus death rate—was greater every decade from 1851 to 1911 than in the corresponding decade a century earlier, although there can be no doubt that Sweden's birth rate had begun to decline as early as 1830. . . .

"This period of an increasing margin between birth rate and death rate, or of a rather large but steady margin, as in Finland, is in time succeeded by a period generally shorter but varying considerably in length from country to country, in which the rate of natural increase begins to decline because the birth rate is falling faster than the death rate but during which natural increase still remains quite high.

"Thus the modern cycle of population growth in industrialized lands is completed and the population again approaches the stationary or has too few births to maintain itself, as it was in preindustrial days—although it no longer fluctuates largely between excess and deficit as in earlier days. The failure of population to grow today is not because of the high and fluctuating death rate, as was usually the case in the past, but because of the low birth rate."[5]

Here we have the same pattern of initial reduction in the death rate that characterized the primitive cycle; but, from there on, the pattern is radically different. Instead of a subsequent return to its former height, the death rate remains low—or so it has thus far. Thus the cycle can be concluded only by a reduction in the birth rate, or, more accurately, it is possible to maintain a low death rate indefinitely only if the birth rate is brought under control and reduced commensurately. In any event, the modern cycle shows not only the new feature of a low death rate remaining low but, probably for the first time in history, a . . . decline in the birth rate. Both may then tend to become stabilized at a new and lower level. . . .

FUTURE CYCLES

. . . [Low] birth rates are more amenable to increase than are high birth rates. A corollary proposition is that it is an easier matter to lower a death rate of 40 than it is to lower one of 10. In other words, there appears to be a ceiling over birth rates and a floor under death rates. On the

latter point Bowen says: ". . . there is an apparent, and presumably inescapable, lower limit which the death rate may approach but never pass, . . . *there is no real lower limit* to the birth rate—or rather, *it is zero.*"

From these propositions we may derive the hypothesis that in Western industrialized areas that have completed the modern population cycle eventuating in both low birth rates and low death rates, any growth cycle in the future will require an increase in the birth rate. Thus we have a reversal of the primitive conditions in which birth rates were high and relatively stable and in which the death rates showed the greatest fluctuation, accounting for any cycles of growth or decline. In the postindustrial phase of population phenomena, it appears that the birth rate must assume the role of greatest freedom and fluctuation, while the death rate becomes relatively stable.

This obviously leads to the further hypothesis that in the postindustrial phase of population, any growth cycle in the future will be of the general pattern of Cycle III and that, as we have labeled Cycle I the "primitive cycle" and Cycle II the "modern cycle," so might we appropriately call Cycle III the "future cycle."

It will be noted, however, that this subsumes a continued control of the death rate which would prevent this cycle from assuming the form of Cycle IV. . . .

CONCLUSION

In conclusion, then, it may be remarked that, while there have been many cycles of growth that may have approximated the regular and ideal pattern hypotheticated by Pearl, there is no theoretical or historical justification for the conclusion that the mechanics of all population growth cycles are the same. Instead, it appears that in primitive societies cycles of growth are produced by a falling death rate, which subsequently returns to the original high level, while the birth rate remains relatively constant. This general pattern we may call the "primitive cycle." Populations significantly affected by the Industrial Revolution and concomitant factors shows a decidedly divergent pattern characterized by both falling birth rates and falling death rates, but with the birth rate lagging behind the death rate in its descent in the first phase, followed by a second phase of a more rapid drop in the birth rate, with the lines ultimately meeting at a low level for both rates.

---

[5] Thompson, pp. 25-26.

This we have called the "modern cycle." A third pattern is that produced by a rising birth rate which subsequently falls again to a balance with the death rate, which meanwhile remains constant. Some semblance of this pattern has been apparent in many Western countries during the last fifteen years, but otherwise it was virtually unknown in the history of past population growth cycles. However, it is probable that any growth cycles of the future of those populations which have already passed through the modern cycle will manifest this general pattern. For this reason we have referred to it as the "future cycle."

Each of these growth patterns, if regular and symmetrical, would produce a growth curve of the S-form. The mechanics of each obviously differ from one another, and, consequently, so do the conditions producing them. . . .

Selection *41*

The Case of the G.E. Babies

Statistics—particularly demographic statistics—can easily be misused. The student who has read the earlier article by Notestein will be able in the present selection to account for some of the factors which the General Electric Company failed to take into consideration and which the editors of *Fortune* did not report, even with the advantage of hindsight.

Vital statistics gathered from a national sample cannot be applied to a special subsample. During World War II, for instance, members of the U.S. armed services were offered National Service Life Insurance, which was designed to provide life insurance to servicemen at actual cost while remaining actuarially sound. NSLI has been paying annual dividends that occasionally run to as much as 80 per cent of the premiums, even though the premiums are far below those of commercial insurance companies. The high dividend rate must be due to NSLI's computing premium rates on the basis of national statistics, despite the fact that the members of the armed services are not a cross section of the population either mentally or physically. The insured servicemen were first carefully screened mentally and physically by examinations at induction, then further screened during the performance of their duties.

Similarly, General Electric employees do not constitute a representative sample of the United States population. As the article points out, there are neither children nor old people employed at General Electric, no persons with tuberculosis, and no seriously mentally deficient or mentally deranged individuals—but all of these non-child-bearing categories are included in the population on which the national birth rate is computed.

The factor of incentive probably played a smaller role in the production of G.E. babies than the editors of *Fortune* suggest. Not only did the company fail to take into account their nonrepresentative population sample, but they also failed to consider that the population of which their current employees were a sample was establishing the highest United States birth rate for three decades. If we can infer from our discussion of population growth cycles that the low birth rates of the Great Depression were due to unemployment, it seems safe to assert that this factor should not depress the G.E. birth rate, since G.E. employs no unemployed employees!

The perils and complexities of birth forecasting were encountered last year, in rather extraordinary circumstances, by General Electric. Last January 14, G.E. announced that it would award five shares of its common stock to any employee who had a baby on October 15—the latter date being the company's seventy-fifth anniversary. Originally the company said it expected about thirteen winners. It arrived at this figure by applying a daily U.S. birth rate to its own 226,000 employees. This computation actually yielded a prediction of fifteen births; but a G.E. public-relations man thought it might be nice to trim the figure to thirteen, since the latter was the number of original G.E. investors. The mathematics suffered from more than public relations, however. G.E. employees, since they include no children and no one over sixty-five, are obviously a much more fertile group than the population as a whole. When this fact sank in, a company statistician made a new assault on the problem. He estimated that the size of an average G.E. family was 4.2. This meant that the total number of people in

the G.E. families was close to a million. Applying the crude annual birth rate to *this* group, and dividing by 365, he came up with a new prediction of seventy-two births on the big day.

As it turned out, there were not thirteen, fifteen, or seventy-two babies born to G.E. employees on October 15. There were 189.

Subtracting the company's highest expectation of seventy-two from 189 gives 117 "extra" babies. Where did G.E. go wrong? Well, among other things, the company made no allowance for the incentive provided by its own stock. This oversight, remarkable in a company that has had a lot to say about capitalist incentives, was apparently rectified by the employees. The latter not only enjoy having children but, it appears, they rather enjoy the idea of becoming capitalists. And they seem to have known a good thing. In a generally declining stock market, G.E. common rose, during the pregnant months, from 69% to 78%.

From *Fortune*, January 1954, p. 95. Reprinted courtesy of Fortune Magazine.

Selection 42

The Folk Society
Robert Redfield

The role of taxonomy in research and theory construction was discussed in Part I of this book. Stated simply, a taxonomy is the set of classes into which a thing might be classified, an all-inclusive system of mutually exclusive categories. The twelve phyla of biology constitute a taxonomy, and so do the elements in chemistry. However, even some of the oldest and most widely accepted taxonomies are occasionally presented with cases which defy categorization by the established criteria. The *Obelia* is such a case in biological taxonomy, and so is slime mold. The taxonomist must establish "cutting points" between categories to serve as boundaries for each class.

Even though borderline cases attract the most attention in taxonomy, the taxonomist must begin with a general idea of the objects in each class. This general mental image of a whole class may be given artificial concreteness in the form of a model that portrays all of the requisite characteristics of any specimen in the class and ignores other and deviant characteristics. The model, in other words, is a "pure" specimen of the class. Since it is not likely to exist in fact, it is called an *ideal type*.

Ideal types are syntheses of the essential characteristics of a category of objects. They are, of course, abstractions. Pertinent characteristics are selected from real cases and combined to describe a "perfect" example. All empirically observable cases have irrelevant, inconsistent, and imperfect characteristics that constitute variations or deviations from the ideal, either major or minor.

No actual case is expected to correspond exactly to the ideal case. Empirical cases are classified according to their relative similarity or dissimilarity to the ideal types. Sometimes the description of an empirical case will refer to several ideal types, pointing out the relevant characteristics of each.

Logically, a set of ideal types can be conceptualized as a taxonomy turned upside down, as a muffin pan viewed from the bottom instead of from the top. Where taxonomies emphasize boundaries for categorizing cases (like fences for dividing fields), ideal types are models of the perfect cases in each category (like claim stakes or flags identifying the field at its center). Taxonomies show where the muffin must go; ideal types reveal the positive shape of the muffin.

In the article at hand—considered a classic by both anthropologists and sociologists—Redfield essays to construct an ideal type, a prototype to which communities may be compared. He suggests at least one other type—the modern city—toward the construction of a comprehensive typology but limits his work to the folk society.

In the two subsequent selections, two more ideal types are added to the growing typology of communities—the bedroom town and the small town. In Selection 49, Sjoberg describes another ideal type—the preindustrial city. The student will be able to furnish additional categories for the taxonomy from his own direct or vicarious experiences—the metropolis, the regional city, the satellite city, the county seat, the farming community, and the college town, to name a few possibilities.

I

Understanding of society in general and of our own modern urbanized society in particular can be gained through consideration of the societies least like our own: the primitive, or folk, societies. All societies are alike in some respects, and each differs from others in other respects; the further assumption made here is that folk societies have certain features in common which enable us to think of them as a type—a type which contrasts with the society of the modern city.

This type is ideal, a mental construction. No known society precisely corresponds with it, but the societies which have been the chief interest of the anthropologist most closely approximate it. The construction of the type depends, indeed, upon special knowledge of tribal and peasant groups. The ideal folk society could be defined through assembling, in the imagination, the characters which are logically opposite those which are to be found in the modern city, only if we had first some knowledge of nonurban peoples to permit us to determine what, indeed, are the characteristic features of modern city living. The complete procedure requires us to gain acquaintance with many folk societies in many parts of the world and to set down in words general enough to describe most of them those characteristics which they have in common with each other and which the modern city does not have.

In short, we move from folk society to folk society, asking ourselves what it is about them that makes them like each other and different from the modern city. So we assemble the elements of the ideal type. The more elements we add, the less will any one real society correspond to it. As the type is constructed, real societies may be arranged in an order of degree of resemblance to it. . . .

II

"The conception of a 'primitive society' which we ought to form," wrote Sumner, "is that of small groups scattered over a territory." The folk society is a small society. There are no more people in it than can come to know each other well, and they remain in long association with each other. Among the Western Shoshone the individual parental family was the group which went about, apart from other families, collecting food; a group of families would assemble and so remain for a few weeks, from time to time, to hunt together; during the winter months such a group of families would form a single camp. Such a temporary village included perhaps a hundred people. . . . A Southwestern Pueblo contained no more than a few thousand persons.

"The Folk Society" by Robert Redfield. Reprinted from *The American Journal of Sociology*, Vol. LII (1947), 293-306, by permission of The University of Chicago Press.

The folk society is an isolated society. Probably there is no real society whose members are in complete ignorance of the existence of people other than themselves; the Andamanese, although their islands were avoided by navigators for centuries, knew of outsiders and occasionally came in contact with Malay or Chinese visitors. Nevertheless, the folk societies we know are made up of people who have little communication with outsiders, and we may conceive of the ideal folk society as composed of persons having communication with no outsider.

This isolation is one half of a whole of which the other half is intimate communication among the members of the society. A group of recent castaways is a small and isolated society, but it is not a folk society; and if the castaways have come from different ships and different societies, there will have been no previous intimate communication among them, and the society will not be composed of people who are much alike.

May the isolation of the folk society be identified with the physical immobility of its members? In building this ideal type, we may conceive of the members of the society as remaining always within the small territory they occupy. There are some primitive peoples who have dwelt from time immemorial in the same small valley, and who rarely leave it. Certain of the pueblos of the American Southwest have been occupied by the same people or their descendants for many generations. On the other hand, some of the food-collecting peoples, such as the Shoshone Indians and certain aborigines of Australia, move about within a territory of very considerable extent; and there are Asiatic folk groups that make regular seasonal migrations hundreds of miles in extent.

It is possible to conceive of the members of such a society as moving about physically without communicating with members of other groups than their own. Each of the Indian villages of the midwest highlands of Guatemala is a folk society distinguishable by its customs and even by the physical type of its members from neighboring villages, yet the people are great travelers, and in the case of one of the most distinct communities, Chichicastenango, most of the men travel far and spend much of their time away from home. This does not result, however, in much intimate communication between those traveling villagers and other peoples. The gipsies have moved about among the various peoples of the earth for generations, and yet they retain many of the characteristics of a folk society.

Through books the civilized people communicate with the minds of other people and other times, and an aspect of the isolation of the folk society is the absence of books. The folk communicate only by word of mouth; therefore the communication upon which understanding is built is only that which takes place among neighbors, within the little society itself. The folk has no access to the thought and experience of the past, whether of other peoples or of their own ancestors, such as books provide. Therefore, oral tradition has no check or competitor. Knowledge of what has gone before reaches no further back than memory and speech between old and young can make it go; behind "the time of our grandfathers" all is legendary and vague. With no form of belief established by written record, there can be no historical sense, such as civilized people have, no theology, and no basis for science in recorded experiment. The only form of accumulation of experience, except the tools and other enduring articles of manufacture, is the increase of wisdom which comes as the individual lives longer; therefore the old, knowing more than the young can know until they too have lived that long, have prestige and authority.

The people who make up a folk society are much alike. Having lived in long intimacy with one another, and with no others, they have come to form a single biological type. The somatic homogeneity of local, inbred populations has been noted and studied. Since the people communicate with one another and with no others, one man's learned ways of doing and thinking are the same as another's. Another way of putting this is to say that in the ideal folk society, what one man knows and believes is the same as what all men know and believe. Habits are the same as customs. In real fact, of course, the differences among individuals in a primitive group and the different chances of experience prevent this ideal state of things from coming about. Nevertheless, it is near enough to the truth for the student of a real folk society to report it fairly well by learning what goes on in the minds of a few of its members, and a primitive group has been presented, although sketchily, as learned about from a single member. The similarity among the members is found also as one generation is compared with its successor. Old people find young people doing, as they grow up, what the old people did at the same age, and what they have come to think right and proper. This is another way of saying that in such a society there is little change.

The members of the folk society have a strong sense of belonging together. The group which an outsider might recognize as composed of similar persons different from members of other groups is also the group of people who see their own resemblances and feel correspondingly united.

Communicating intimately with each other, each has a strong claim on the sympathies of the others. Moreover, against such knowledge as they have of societies other than their own, they emphasize their own mutual likeness and value themselves as compared with others. They say of themselves "we" as against all others, who are "they."

Thus we may characterize the folk society as small, isolated, nonliterate, and homogeneous, with a strong sense of group solidarity. Are we not soon to acknowledge the simplicity of the technology of the ideal folk society? Something should certainly be said about the tools and tool-making of this generalized primitive group, but it is not easy to assign a meaning to "simple," in connection with technology, which will do justice to the facts as known from the real folk societies. The preciseness with which each tool, in a large number of such tools, meets its needs in the case of the Eskimo, for example, makes one hesitate to use the word "simple." Some negative statements appear to be safe: secondary and tertiary tools—tools to make tools—are relatively few as compared with primary tools; there is no making of artifacts by multiple, rapid, machine manufacture; there is little or no use of natural power.

There is not much division of labor in the folk society: what one person does is what another does. In the ideal folk society all the tools and ways of production are shared by everybody. The "everybody" must mean "every adult man" or "every adult woman," for the obvious exception to the homogeneity of the folk society lies in the differences between what men do and know and what women do and know. These differences are clear and unexceptional (as compared with our modern urban society where they are less so). "Within the local group there is no such thing as a division of labor save as between the sexes," writes Radcliffe-Brown about the Andaman Islanders. ". . . . Every man is expected to be able to hunt pig, to harpoon turtle and to catch fish, and also to cut a canoe, to make bows and arrows and all the other objects that are made by men." So all men share the same interests and have, in general, the same experience of life.

We may conceive, also, of the ideal folk society as a group economically independent of all others: the people produce what they consume and consume what they produce. Few, if any, real societies are completely in this situation; some Eskimo groups perhaps most closely approach it. Although each little Andamanese band could get along without getting anything from any other, exchange of goods occurred between bands by a sort of periodic gift-giving.

The foregoing characterizations amount, rough-ly, to saying that the folk society is a little world off by itself, a world in which the recurrent problems of life are met by all its members in much the same way. This statement, while correct enough, fails to emphasize an important, perhaps the important, aspect of the folk society. The ways in which the members of the society meet the recurrent problems of life are conventionalized ways; they are the results of long intercommunication within the group in the face of these problems; and these conventionalized ways have become interrelated within one another so that they constitute a coherent and self-consistent system. Such a system is what we mean in saying that the folk society is characterized by "a culture." A culture is an organization or integration of conventional understandings. It is, as well, the acts and the objects, in so far as they represent the type characteristic of that society, which express and maintain these understandings. In the folk society this integrated whole, this system, provides for all the recurrent needs of the individual from birth to death and of the society through the seasons and the years. The society is to be described, and distinguished from others, largely by presenting this sytem.

This is not the same as saying, as was said early in this paper, that in the folk society what one man does is the same as what another man does. What one man does in a mob is the same as what another man does, but a mob is not a folk society. It is, so far as culture is concerned, its very antithesis. The members of a mob (which is a kind of "mass") each do the same thing, it is true, but it is a very immediate and particular thing, and it is done without much reference to tradition. It does not depend upon and express a great many conventional understandings related to one another. A mob has no culture. The folk society exhibits culture to the greatest conceivable degree. A mob is an aggregation of people doing the same simple thing simultaneously. A folk society is an organization of people doing many different things successively as well as simultaneously. The members of a mob act with reference to the same object of attention. The members of a folk society are guided in acting by previously established comprehensive and interdependent conventional understandings; at any one time they do many different things, which are complexly related to one another to express collective sentiments and conceptions. When the turn comes for the boy to do what a man does, he does what a man does; thus, though in the end the experiences of all individuals of the same sex are alike, the activities of the society, seen at a moment of time, are diverse, while interdependent and consistent.

The Papago Indians, a few hundred of them, constituted a folk society in southern Arizona. Among these Indians a war party was not so simple a thing as a number of men going out together to kill the enemy. It was a complex activity involving everybody in the society both before, during, and after the expedition and dramatizing the religious and moral ideas fundamental to Papago life. Preparation for the expedition involved many practical or ritual acts on the part of the immediate participants, their wives and children, previously successful warriors, and many others. While the party was away, the various relatives of the warriors had many things to do or not to do—prayer, fasting, preparation of ritual paraphernalia, etc. These were specialized activities, each appropriate to just that kind of relative or other category of person. So the war was waged by everybody. These activities, different and special as they were, interlocked, so to speak, with each other to make a large whole, the society-during-a-war-expedition. And all these specialized activities obeyed fundamental principles, understood by all and expressed and reaffirmed in the very forms of the acts—the gestures of the rituals, the words of songs, the implied or expressed explanations and admonitions of the elders to the younger people. All understood that the end in view was the acquisition by the group of the supernatural power of the slain enemy. This power, potentially of great positive value, was dangerous, and the practices and rituals had as their purposes first the success of the war party and then the draining-off of the supernatural power acquired by the slaying into a safe and "usable" form.

We may say, then, that in the folk society conventional behavior is strongly patterned: it tends to conform to a type or a norm. These patterns are interrelated in thought and in action with one another, so that one tends to evoke others and to be consistent with the others. Every customary act among the Papago when the successful warriors return is consistent with and is a special form of the general conceptions held as to supernatural power. We may still further say that the patterns of what people think should be done are closely consistent with what they believe is done, and that there is one way, or a very few conventional ways, in which everybody has some understanding and some share, of meeting each need that arises. The culture of a folk society is, therefore, one of those wholes which is greater than its parts. Gaining a livelihood takes support from religion, and the relations of men to men are justified in the conceptions held of the supernatural world or in some other aspect of the

culture. Life, for the member of the folk society, is not one activity and then another and different one; it is one large activity out of which one part may not be separated without affecting the rest.

A related characteristic of the folk society was implied when it was declared that the specialized activities incident to the Papago war party obeyed fundamental principles understood by all. These "principles" had to do with the ends of living, as conceived by the Papago. A near-ultimate good for the Papago was the acquisition of supernatural power. This end was not questioned; it was a sort of axiom in terms of which many lesser activities were understood. This suggests that we may say of the folk society that its ends are taken as given. The activities incident to the war party may be regarded as merely complementarily useful acts, aspects of the division of labor. They may also, and more significantly, be seen as expressions of unquestioned common ends. The folk society exists not so much in the exchange of useful functions as in common understandings as to the ends given. The ends are not stated as matters of doctrine, but are implied by the many acts which make up the living that goes on in the society. Therefore, the morale of a folk society —its power to act consistently over periods of time and to meet crises effectively—is not dependent upon discipline exerted by force or upon devotion to some single principle of action but to the concurrence and consistency of many or all of the actions and conceptions which make up the whole round of life. In the trite phrase, the folk society is a "design for living."

What is done in the ideal folk society is done not because somebody or some people decided, at once, that it should be done, but because it seems "necessarily" to flow from the very nature of things. There is, moreover, no disposition to reflect upon traditional acts and consider them objectively and critically. In short, behavior in the folk society is traditional, spontaneous, and uncritical. In any real folk society, of course, many things are done as a result of decision as to that particular action, but as to that class of actions tradition is the sufficient authority. The Indians decide now to go on a hunt; but it is not a matter of debate whether or not one should, from time to time, hunt.

The folkways are the ways that grow up out of long and intimate association of men with each other; in the society of our conception all the ways are folkways. Men act with reference to each other by understandings which are tacit and traditional. There are no formal contracts or other agreements. The rights and obligations of the individual come about not by special arrangement; they are, chiefly, aspects of the position of the individual as a person of one sex or the other, one age-group or another, one occupational group or another, and as one occupying just that position in a system of relationships which are traditional in the society. The individual's status is thus in large part fixed at birth; it changes as he lives, but it changes in ways which were "foreordained" by the nature of his particular society. The institutions of the folk society are of the sort which has been called "crescive"; they are not of the sort that is created deliberately for special purposes, as was the juvenile court. So, too, law is made up of the traditional conceptions of rights and obligations and the customary procedures whereby these rights and obligations are assured; legislation has no part in it.

If legislation has no part in the law of the ideal folk society, neither has codification, still less jurisprudence. Radin has collected material suggesting the limited extent to which real primitive people do question custom and do systematize their knowledge. In the known folk societies they do these things only to a limited extent. In the ideal folk society there is no objectivity and no systematization of knowledge as guided by what seems to be its "internal" order. The member of this mentally constructed society does not stand off from his customary conduct and subject it to scrutiny apart from its meaning for him as that meaning is defined in culture. Nor is there any habitual exercise of classification, experiment, and abstraction for its own sake, least of all for the sake of intellectual ends. There is common practical knowledge, but there is no science.

Behavior in the folk society is highly conventional, custom fixes the rights and duties of individuals, and knowledge is not critically examined or objectively and systematically formulated; but it must not be supposed that primitive man is a sort of automaton in which custom is the mainspring. It would be as mistaken to think of primitive man as strongly aware that he is constrained by custom. Within the limits set by custom there is invitation to excel in performance. There is lively competition, a sense of opportunity, and a feeling that what the culture moves one to do is well worth doing. . . . The interrelations and high degree of consistency among the elements of custom which are presented to the individual declare to him the importance of making his endeavors in the directions indicated by tradition. The culture sets goals which stimulate action by giving great meaning to it.

It has been said that the folk society is small and that its members have lived in long and intimate association with one another. It has also been said that in such societies there is little critical or abstract thinking. These characteristics are related to yet another characteristic of the folk society: behavior is personal, not impersonal. A "person" may be defined as that social object which I feel to respond to situations as I do, with all the sentiments and interests which I feel to be my own; a person is myself in another form, his qualities and values are inherent within him, and his significance for me is not merely one of utility. A "thing," on the other hand, is a social object which has no claim upon my sympathies, which responds to me, as I conceive it, mechanically; its value for me exists in so far as it serves my end. In the folk society all human beings admitted to the society are treated as persons; one does not deal impersonally ("thing-fashion") with any other participant in the little world of that society. Moreover, in the folk society much besides human beings is treated personally. The pattern of behavior which is first suggested by the inner experience of the individual—his wishes, fears, sensitivenesses, and interests of all sorts—is projected into all objects with which he comes into contact. Thus nature, too, is treated personally: the elements, the features of the landscape, the animals, and especially anything in the environment which by its appearance or behavior suggests that it has the attributes of mankind—to all these are attributed qualities of the human person.

In short, the personal and intimate life of the child in the family is extended, in the folk society, into the social world of the adult and even into inanimate objects. It is not merely that relations in such a society are personal; it is also that they are familial. The first contacts made as the infant becomes a person are with other persons; moreover, each of these first persons, he comes to learn, has a particular kind of relation to him which is associated with that one's genealogical position. The individual finds himself fixed within a constellation of familial relationships. The kinship connections provide a pattern in terms of which, in the ideal folk society, all personal relations are conventionalized and categorized. All relations are personal. But relations are not, in content of specific behavior, the same for everyone. As a mother is different from a father, and a grandson from a nephew, so are these classes of personal relationship, originating in genealogical connection, extended outward into all relationships whatever. In this sense, the folk society is a familial society. . . . [T]he primitive society is organized in terms of kinship rather than territory. It is true that the fact that men are neighbors contributes to their sense of belonging together. But the point to be emphasized in understanding the folk society is that whether mere contiguity or relationship as brother or as son is the circumstance uniting men into the society, the result is a group of people among whom prevail the personal and categorized relationships that characterize families as we know them, and in which the patterns of kinship tend to be extended outward from the group of genealogically connected individuals into the whole society. The kin are the type persons for all experience.

This general conception may be resolved into component or related conceptions. In the folk society family relationships are clearly distinguished from one another. Very special sorts of behavior may be expected by a mother's brother of his sister's son, and this behavior will be different from that expected by a father's brother of his brother's son. Among certain Australian tribes animals killed by a hunter must be divided so that nine or ten certain parts must be given to nine or ten corresponding relatives of the successful hunter—the right ribs to the father's brother, a piece of the flank to the mother's brother, and so on. The tendency to extend kinship outward takes many special forms. In many primitive societies kinship terms and kinship behavior (in reduced degree) are extended to persons not known to be genealogically related at all, but who are nevertheless regarded as kin. . . . In the folk society groupings which do not arise out of genealogical connection are few, and those that do exist tend to take on the attributes of kinship. Ritual kinship is common in primitive and peasant societies in the forms of blood brotherhood, godparental relationships, and other ceremonial sponsorships. These multiply kinship connections; in these cases the particular individuals to be united depend upon choice. Furthermore, there is frequently a recognizedly fictitious or metaphorical use of kinship terms to designate more casual relationships, as between host and guest or between worshipper and deity.

The real primitive and peasant societies differ very greatly as to the forms assumed by kinship. Nevertheless, it is possible to recognize two main types. In one of these the connection between husband and wife is emphasized, while neither one of the lineages, matrilineal or patrilineal, is singled out as contrasted with the other. In such a folk society the individual parental family is the social unit, and connections with relatives outside this family are of secondary importance. Such family organization is common where the population is small, the means of livelihood are by precarious collection of wild food, and larger units cannot permanently remain together because the natural resources will not allow it. But where a somewhat larger population remains together, either in a village or in a migratory band, there often, although by no means always, is found an emphasis upon one line of consanguine connection rather than the other with subordination of the conjugal connection. There results a segmentation of the society into equivalent kinship units. These may take the form of extended domestic groups or joint families (as in China) or may include many households of persons related in part through recognized genealogical connection and in part through the sharing of the same name or other symbolic designation, in the latter case we speak of the groups as clans. Even in societies where the individual parental family is an independent economic unit, as in the case of the eastern Eskimo, husband and wife never become a new social and economic unit with the completeness that is characteristic of our own society. When a marriage in primitive society comes to an end, the kinsmen of the dead spouse assert upon his property a claim they have never given up. On the whole, we may think of the family among folk peoples as made up of persons consanguinely connected. Marriage is, in comparison with what we in our society directly experience, an incident in the life of the individual who is born, brought up, and dies with his blood kinsmen. In such a society romantic love can hardly be elevated to a major principle.

In so far as the consanguine lines are well defined (and in some cases both lines may be of importance to the individual) the folk society may be thought of as composed of families rather than of individuals. It is the familial groups that act and are acted upon. There is strong solidarity within the kinship group, and the individual is responsible to all his kin as they are responsible to him. . . . Thus, in folk societies wherein the tendency to maintain consanguine connection has resulted in joint families or clans, it is usual to find that injuries done by an individual are regarded as injuries against his kinship group, and the group takes the steps to right the wrong. The step may be revenge regulated by custom or a property settlement. A considerable part of primitive law exists in the regulation of claims by one body of kin against another. The fact that the folk society is an organization of families rather than an aggregation of individuals is further expressed in many of those forms of marriage in which a certain kind of relative is the approved spouse. The customs by which in many primitive societies a man is expected to marry his deceased brother's widow or a woman to marry her deceased sister's husband express the view of marriage as an undertaking between kinship groups. One of the spouses having failed by death, the undertaking is to be carried on by some other representative of the family group. Indeed, in the arrangements for marriage—the selection of spouses by their relatives, in bride-price, dowry, and in many forms of familial negotiations leading to a marriage—the nature of marriage as a connubial form of social relations between kindreds finds expression.

It has been said in foregoing paragraphs that behavior in the folk society is traditional, spontaneous, and uncritical, that what one man does is much the same as what another man does, and that the patterns of conduct are clear and remain constant throughout the generations. It has also been suggested that the congruence of all parts of conventional behavior and social institutions with each other contributes to the sense of rightness which the member of the folk society feels to inhere in his traditional ways of action. In the well-known language of Sumner, the ways of life are folkways; furthermore, the folkways tend to be also mores—ways of doing or thinking to which attach notions of moral worth. The value of every traditional act or object or institution is, thus, something which the members of the society are not disposed to call into question; and should the value be called into question, the doing so is resented. This characteristic of the folk society may be briefly referred to by saying that it is a sacred society. In the folk society one may not, without calling into effect negative social sanctions, challenge as valueless what has come to be traditional in that society.

Presumably, the sacredness of social objects has its source, in part, at least, in the mere fact of habituation; probably the individual organism becomes early adjusted to certain habits, motor and mental, and to certain associations between one activity and another or between certain sense experiences and certain activities, and it is almost physiologically uncomfortable to change or even to entertain the idea of change. . . . Probably the sacredness of social objects in the folk society is related also to the fact that in such well-organized cultures acts and objects suggest the traditions, beliefs, and conceptions which all share. There is reason to suppose that when what is traditionally done becomes less meaningful because people no longer know what the acts stand for, life becomes more secular. In the repetitive character of conventional action (aside from technical action) we have ritual; in its expressive character we have ceremony; in the folk society ritual tends also to be ceremonious, and ritual-ceremony tends to be sacred, not secular.

The sacredness of social objects is apparent in the ways in which, in the folk society, such an object is hedged around with restraints and protections that keep it away from the commonplace and the matter-of-fact. In the sacred there is alternatively, or in combination, holiness and dangerousness. When the Papago Indian returned from a successful war expedition, bringing the scalp of a slain Apache, the head-hairs of the enemy were treated as loaded with a tremendous "charge" of supernatural power; only old men, already successful warriors and purified through religious ritual, could touch the object and make it safe for incorporation into the home of the slayer. Made into the doll-like form of an Apache Indian, it was, at last, after much ceremonial preparation, held for an instant by the members of the slayer's family, addressed in respect and awe by kinship terms, and placed in the house, there to give off protective power. The Indians of San Pedro de la Laguna, Guatemala, recognize an officer, serving for life, whose function it is to keep custody of ten or a dozen Latin breviaries printed in the eighteenth century and to read prayers from one or another of these books on certain occasions. No one but this custodian may handle the books, save his assistants on ceremonial occasions, with his permission. Should anyone else touch a book he would go mad or be stricken with blindness. Incense and candles are burnt before the chest containing the books, yet the books are not gods—they are objects of sacredness.

In the folk society this disposition to regard objects as sacred extends, characteristically, even into the subsistence activities and into the foodstuffs of the people. Often the foodstuffs are personified as well as sacred. " 'My granduncle used to say to me,' explained a Navajo Indian, ' "if you are walking along a trail and see a kernel of corn, pick it up. It is like a child lost and starving." According to the legends corn is just the same as a human being, only it is holier. . . . When a man goes into a cornfield he feels that he is in a holy place, that he is walking among Holy People. . . . Agriculture is a holy occupation. Even before you plant you sing songs. You continue this during the whole time your crops are growing. You cannot help but feel that you are in a holy place when you go through your fields and they are doing well.' "[1] In the folk society, ideally conceived, nothing is solely a means to an immediate practical end. All activities, even the means of production, are ends in themselves, activities expressive of the ultimate values of the society. . . .

[1] W. W. Hill, *The Agricultural and Hunting Methods of the Navaho Indians,*" Yale University Publications in Anthropology, No. 18 (New Haven: Yale University Press, 1938), p. 53.

III

... The conception sketched here takes on meaning if the folk society is seen in contrast to the modern city. The vast, complicated, and rapidly changing world in which the urbanite and even the urbanized country-dweller live today is enormously different from the small, inward-facing folk society, with its well-integrated and little-changing moral and religious conceptions. At one time all men lived in these little folk societies. For many thousands of years men must have lived so; urbanized life began only very recently, as the long history of man on earth is considered, and the extreme development of a secularized and swift-changing world society is only a few generations old.

Selection *43*

The Effect of Commuting on Participation in Community Organizations
Alvin H. Scaff

Although the following article has been included here in Part VI because it deals with a particular type of community—a type markedly different from the folk society described by Redfield in the preceding article—it is also illustrative of several research methods in sociology. First of all, it is a case study—a thorough study of one "specimen" of a "species" viewed from a particular perspective. While one cannot reach general conclusions on the basis of a single case, a single documentation can serve as the starting point for the inductive development of theory, principles, and general statements. The author properly begins by calling attention to the ways in which his specimen is known to differ from other specimens. Scaff's questions do not purport to be hypothetical facts or principles; they are simple, direct inquiries, asking for factual answers that appear to be well within the scope of the research design.

Scaff's study also provides an example of area sampling—a technique highly respected by sociologists, botanists, and other field researchers because it can be used to obtain a representative sample of items distributed in space. Briefly, the underlying principle of area sampling is that if a large enough sample is dispersed regularly, the various qualities to be found in the population will occur in proportion to their occurrence in the whole community.

The author reports his findings in an orderly fashion and sets down the inferences that he has drawn from those findings. This kind of presentation is customary in reports of empirical research—so much so that it could be called a sociological folkway. Accordingly, the readers of sociological journals have come to expect it (in other words, it is normative). Reports that differ greatly in form are likely to be considered disorganized and to evoke negative sentiments from sociologists. Thus we observe that sociologists can be as ethnocentric as anyone else!

The findings of Scaff's research are of special interest because the commuter is a product of cultural change whose significance for social change needs to be studied. The rapidly growing number of commuters in the United States gives emphasis to this need. Other processes of social and cultural change at work in still another ideal type of community will be described by Bensman and Vidich in Selection 44.

The suburban communities, sometimes referred to as bedroom towns, are the fastest growing communities in the nation. One of the clearest demonstrations of this community development is to be seen in the Los Angeles Metropolitan area. Between 1940 and 1950 Los Angeles City increased its population by 31 per cent; during the same period of time the Metropolitan area increased its population by 50 per cent. Out of 40 incorporated cities in Los Angeles County other than Los Angeles itself only eight had rates of growth equal to or less than that of the central city. The seven cities in Pomona Valley at the eastern edge of the county showed a rate of growth of 65 per cent between 1940 and 1950. One of these communities, West Covina, had increased by 320 per cent; the city of Pomona showed a 49 per cent gain. Claremont, a town of 6,212 in the Pomona Valley with an increased population of 103 per cent since 1940, was selected for the present study. Approximately half the gain for Claremont is attributed to the fact that in 1950 for the first time the Census enumerated students present in Claremont rather than reporting them as living in their home communities. If this student group (those living on campus in college dormitories) is omitted, as is actually done in the present study, the population gain for Claremont is approximately the same as the average for all the outlying communities in the Metropolitan District.

Although Claremont is typical of the Los Angeles Metropolitan area in terms of rate of population increase and perhaps in terms of its commuting pattern, it probably is not typical in many other regards. Claremont has four colleges, maintains three retirement centers, enjoys a "cultural" atmosphere, and prides itself upon its New England heritage. Using this community as the area of investigation, an attempt was made to measure the effects of commuting on participation in organized groups.

The research problem may be stated in the form of four questions:

1. To what extent is Claremont becoming a commuter town?

2. What are some of the differences between the commuter and the non-commuter groups?

3. Is participation in community organizations affected by commuting?

4. What is the effect of factors other than commuting upon community participation?

SOURCE OF DATA AND NATURE OF SAMPLE

The data were gathered in personal interviews and recorded by the interviewer on schedules, from which tabulations were made. The data represent a sampling of the Claremont community according to an adaptation of the Bureau of Census area sampling procedure. The sampling, which might be described as stratified area sampling, involved locating every household in the natural community on a map, then outlining blocks or combinations of blocks throughout the area of the community so that each block-unit contained approximately the same number of households. The block-units were then consecutively numbered from 1 to 105, listing those of similar ethnic composition, rental value, age of inhabitants, and distance from the center of the community—thus maximizing the probability of including in the sample proportionate representatives of all strata and areas within the community. One block out of every five was then chosen at random and the schedule administered to every other household in the sample blocks. The sample is therefore approximately ten per cent of the total population. This was a larger sample than necessary to obtain a reliable percentage of commuters in the working force; but with the larger sample we were able to secure reliable data on such subjects as education, length of residence, and occupational status in relation to commuter and non-commuter groups.

DEFINITIONS AND PROCEDURE

The unit of investigation was the small family group composed of the income receiver and his dependents, if any, living with him. Thus, husband, wife, and dependent children under 21 years of age were included on one schedule. Other adults, even if they lived in the same dwelling place, were listed on a separate schedule. Limiting the information on each schedule to the small family unit was necessary in securing a clear picture of the influence of commuting on the participation of families where the chief breadwinner was a commuter.

Organized groups included any group with regular meetings and some regular membership whether official or informal; such as, church services, parent-faculty associations, or bridge clubs. One credit toward a participation score was given for membership in each group. A person holding an elected or appointed office that carried with it special responsibilities was given two units credit toward his participation score.

In the course of each interview, the informant

From the *American Sociological Review*, Vol. 17 (1952), 215-220. Reprinted by permission of the American Sociological Association.

was asked to name the groups to which each member of the family belonged, indicating any in which an appointive or elective office was held. He was then supplied with a master list of all the organized groups in the community to be sure that he had not overlooked some affiliations. With this information each individual could be assigned a participation score simply by adding his organizations and any offices that he held. In comparing individuals this score was sufficient, but in comparing families the total family scores had to be corrected for family size.

The corrected family participation score was obtained by dividing the total score on each schedule by the total number of adults plus four-tenths for each child between the ages of three and nineteen. The value of four-tenths was arrived at by calculating the average participation score for each age in the entire sample. It was discovered that children under three had no participation in organized groups; therefore they were omitted from consideration. Children between three and nineteen participated in only four-tenths as many organized groups as did the average adult over age nineteen.

FINDINGS

The schedules were classified into four groups according to the employment status of the chief breadwinner. The commuter group was composed of families whose chief breadwinner held a job outside of the community. The retired group included all persons who had completed their period of gainful employment and did not expect to enter the labor force again. A third group was made up of families whose chief breadwinner was

employed in Claremont. Finally, the unemployed were those temporarily out of work but who expected to return to work when a suitable job was found. The retired group, those employed in Claremont, and the unemployed, together composed the non-commuter population. See summary comparison in Table 1.

Forty-six per cent of the working force in Claremont travel to jobs outside of the community. The families in this group, the commuter families, compose 30 per cent of all the families in Claremont. The largest single group of families, 35 per cent of the total, were those where the chief breadwinner was retired. Families with employment in Claremont total 32 per cent of the total family population. Only 3.5 per cent of the family heads were unemployed.

The highest participation in organized groups in Claremont was achieved by the retired group with a corrected average family participation score of 2.4. The lowest participation score (1.7) was made by the commuter families. Families whose chief breadwinner was employed in Claremont made an average score of 2.2, which means that they participated in community activities 29 per cent more than did the members of commuter families. If the comparison is made between the breadwinners employed in Claremont and those employed outside of the community, the participation score for those working within the community was 1.9 compared with a score of 1.2 for the commuting breadwinners. Therefore, whether the comparison is between individuals employed or between the families of commuter and non-commuter groups, commuting is associated with low participation in organized groups.

Approximately 27 per cent of all the families in the community belonged to no organized

---

TABLE 1:   Comparison Between Commuter and Non-Commuter Families, Claremont, California, 1951

	PER CENT OF ALL FAMILIES	AVERAGE LENGTH OF RESIDENCE IN YEARS	AVERAGE FAMILY SIZE	AVERAGE AGE OF BREAD-WINNER	AVERAGE NUMBER SCHOOL YEARS COMPLETED	PER CENT FAMILIES WITH PARTICIPATION SCORE OF 0	PARTICIPATION SCORE OF BREADWINNER	PARTICIPATION SCORE FOR FAMILIES CORRECTED FOR FAMILY SIZE
Commuters......	29.7	7.6	3.4	38.4	14.0	31.3	1.2	1.7
Non-Commuters..	70.3	13.0	1.9	55.5	13.7	19.3	2.1	2.3
Non-Commuters in Working Force.........	31.6	12.8	2.8	44.4	12.8	26.8	1.9	2.2
Non-Commuters Retired	35.1	13.1	1.5	72.1	13.8	12.7	2.4	2.4

groups. Among the non-commuters 19 per cent had zero participation scores, while 31 per cent of the commuting families failed to register a single affiliation with an organized group.

An analysis of the figures on length of residence indicates that Claremont is increasingly becoming a commuter town. While the percentage of commuter families in the whole community is 30, the percentage of commuter families among those who have lived in Claremont fewer than five years is 42.7, and the corresponding figure for families living in the community fewer than three years is 43.4 per cent. An increasing percentage of the newcomers consists of commuters. The average length of residence for the commuters is 7.6 years and for the non-commuters 13.0 years. The average commuter family has resided in Claremont only slightly more than half as long as the average non-commuter family. Length of residence has an important bearing on community participation. The average participation score for those who had lived in the community less than three years was .9; for those who had lived in the community three years but less than five years the score was 1.4; and for the group with 20 years or more residence in the community the participation score was 2.9. This means that the long-time resident participated in more than twice as many community organizations as did the newcomer.

The participation of the commuter is affected by the distance he must travel to his place of employment. Those traveling a distance of fewer than 17 miles from Claremont had an average participation score of 1.3; but beyond that distance the community participation was insignificant, the average score being .5. Place of work outside of Claremont for the commuting group varied from nearby Pomona, to Los Angeles 40 miles away, and to some distant points 60 miles or more from Claremont.

A map showing the direction and the size of this flow of traffic indicated wide diversity in the place of employment of the commuter, and graphically demonstrated that the commuter is not principally attracted from the suburban town to the central city of the metropolitan area.

The commuting population adds young families and comparatively larger families to this community. The average age of the adult commuter is 38 years; of the adult non-commuter, 55 years. The average size of commuter families is 3.4; of non-commuter families, 1.9. Omitting the retired group from the non-commuters, the average family size is still only 2.6. Without question the presence of the commuter group in the community introduces younger adults and children and helps to balance an age distribution that is otherwise heavily weighted by elderly people.

Educational status was measured by the average number of school years completed by husband and wife. The average score of the commuter group was slightly higher (14.0) than that of the non-commuter adults (13.7). The difference is greater if the comparison is limited to those gainfully employed in Claremont. For this group, the educational score was 12.8. The addition of retired persons with high educational achievement raised the average for the non-commuter population.

An analysis of the relationship between education and community participation proved interesting. Persons who had not completed high school participated least in community organizations; those with college education made the highest scores. Participation increased without exception for each year of schooling completed from the eighth grade through the second year of graduate work beyond college. An analysis of the figures in Table 2 indicates a relatively good participation score for those with less than eighth grade education. The explanation for this variation lies in the participation of Mexican-American families in the Catholic Church and in their own ethnic organizations. At the upper end of the educational scale those with a third year of graduate schooling made a lower participation score than those with one or two years of graduate work; however, the high participation score for those with more

TABLE 2: Educational Achievement and Community Participation, Claremont, California, 1951

AVERAGE NUMBER OF SCHOOL YEARS COMPLETED FOR HUSBAND AND WIFE	AVERAGE FAMILY PARTICIPATION SCORE CORRECTED FOR FAMILY SIZE
0–7*	1.38
8	.71
9	.82
10	1.00
11	1.25
12	1.53
13	1.96
14	2.04
15	2.82
16	2.92
17	2.94
18	3.67
19	2.84
20–25*	3.77

* *Grouping necessary in order to avoid the danger of distortion in a small number of cases.*

TABLE 3:   Community Participation and Family Size, Claremont, California, 1951

FAMILY SIZE	AVERAGE PARTICIPATION SCORE CORRECTED FOR FAMILY SIZE
1	2.30
2	1.46
3	1.85
4	2.35
5 and over	2.2

than three years of graduate schooling would suggest that additional schooling beyond college is related to increased participation in community organizations.

There was no consistent increase or decrease in community participation according to family size. Families of single individuals had a higher participation than families of two and three individuals. Families of four individuals had the highest participation score of any size family, and

families of five or more persons participated more than the families of two and three persons but not as much as families of one individual.

On the assumption that participation in organized groups in the community might be affected by the age distribution of children in the family, or the presence or absence of children, all families in the sample were classified and ranked according to dependency. This classification and the corresponding average family participation scores are presented in Table 4. Unfortunately the number of families in many of the categories was too small to yield statistically reliable averages; therefore the lack of correlation between dependency and community participation may be more apparent than real.

A division of the working force of Claremont into occupational groups indicated some significant differences in the occupational composition of the commuter and non-commuter groups. The largest proportion of the non-commuters was found in professional service (31.4 per cent) and in agriculture (23.9 per cent). Commuters were employed largely in industry (36.9 per cent) and in professional service (30.8 per cent). The most significant comparison between the two groups was the

TABLE 4:   Family Composition and Community Participation, Claremont, California, 1951

FAMILIES CLASSIFIED BY AGE DISTRIBUTION OF CHILDREN AND RANKED ACCORDING TO DEPENDENCY	NUMBER IN SAMPLE	AVERAGE PARTICIPATION SCORE CORRECTED FOR FAMILY SIZE
1. Single parent with any dependent children under ten years of age	3	1.98
2. Single parent with all dependent children ten years and over	5	2.51
3. a*	10	1.00
4. a, b	6	.28
5. a, b, c	2	2.10
6. a, c	3	2.16
7. b, c	8	2.11
8. a, b, d	0	—
9. a, c, d	0	—
10. a, b, c, d	1	.75
11. b	5	.82
12. c	8	.94
13. a, d	3	4.37
14. b, c, d	0	—
15. b, d	1	4.28
16. c, d	9	1.65
17. d	27	3.32
18. Husband and wife only	62	1.46
19. Single individual	71	2.28

* *Key to classifications 3-17: Husband and wife and*
   a. Children under 3 years.
   b. Children 3-4 years.
   c. Children 5-9 years.
   d. Children 10-20 years.

TABLE 5: Occupational Status and Community Participation, Claremont, California, 1951

OCCUPATION	PER CENT	AVERAGE PARTICIPATION SCORE EMPLOYED INDIVIDUALS
All Occupations	100.0	1.6
Agriculture	14.3	1.7
Industry and Construction	24.8	.9
Commerce...........	13.6	1.0
Clerical Service	8.4	1.5
Professional Service ...	25.3	2.8
Public Service	3.9	4.5*
Domestic Aid Personal Service	9.7	.5

* *The number of cases in terms of which this average was made is too small for the statistic to be interpreted as more than an indication of a high degree of community participation for this occupational group.*

different proportion of each employed in industry: 36.9 per cent of the commuters were employed in industry as compared with 13.4 per cent of non-commuters. As Claremont grows, the proportion of its population in the commuter group will increase, the size of the industrial group will therefore increase, and the occupational composition of the community as a whole will be altered by this increase in industrial employees.

Significant variations in participation were observed for different occupational groups. The lowest score (.9) was made by employees in industry and the highest score by those in professional service (2.8) and in public service (4.5).

If the future commuter population of Claremont becomes increasingly industrial, as is likely, the participation of the commuter group, already low, will probably become still lower.

1. The suburban town is a community with an increasing commuter population. A significant proportion of the young adult male population commutes to outside jobs. The commuters do not work exclusively in the central city but scatter to their places of employment in many directions within the metropolitan area. Only four per cent of the commuters from Claremont, for example, work in Los Angeles.

2. Whatever community interest the commuter expresses is likely to be divided between his place of residence and his place of work. This often complicates the task of the Community Chest and other agencies dependent upon private, volunteer, local support.

3. Usually the commuter participates very little in community affairs. Thus, the organizations of the community are largely left in the hands of elderly retired people or women.

4. The presence of a large group of commuters does help to balance the age groups in the population, but with the additional child population the tax burden for providing adequate schooling and the pressure for park space are increased.

5. Without any conscious effort to be exclusive, the organizations in the community are highly selective of the educated and professional groups. Education and membership in a profession become a badge of acceptance. High participation scores are thus made by these groups; the lowest participation scores, by the poorer educated and the employees in industry. If the community wishes to achieve a wider participation in its organized activities, the organizations must become more diversified and must appeal to all the different occupational groups. The commuting process has in fact given Claremont a cosmopolitan population without developing at the same time a cosmopolitan pattern of community organization.

Selection 44

Springdale and the Mass Society

Arthur J. Vidich and Joseph Bensman

The ideas, beliefs, and behaviors of the members of a community are profoundly influenced by face-to-face interpersonal communications and actions.

This is true in the industrial city as well as in the folk community. Such influences, coming directly from persons with whom interaction has occurred, is occurring, or may occur, are called *group influences.*

Through the group process, people acquire ideas, memories, and beliefs which may be held in common by all the members of a society, whether it be a village or a nation. When this is the case, the responses of an individual to a specific stimulus may be remarkably like those of others, even though he is alone or does not take other group members into consideration when the stimulus is received. (It is not difficult to predict how a normal American would react to cannibalism, regardless of his company!) Such a response is called a *mass response.*

Mass responses are made without immediate reference to other persons, but because of common acculturation they are nevertheless quite uniform. *Mass communication* is possible because the symbols transmitted are received by most people with a relatively high degree of understanding. Generally, the more homogeneous a society, the greater the number of stimuli to which a mass response might be expected and hence the more successful the attempts at mass communication.

Common sources of information (books, newspapers, public education, motion pictures, radio, television, and magazines) advance the formation of mass beliefs, ideas, and behaviors on a grand scale. A common cultural heritage; the relatively large amount of residential mobility and migration; channels of communication through travel, correspondence, and telephone; compulsory military service; compulsory education; and even neolocal marriage (the practice of couples establishing a distinct new household at marriage)—all work toward the maintenance of a mass society in the United States.

Occasionally a community, neighborhood, family, or individual becomes distressed over the idea of "conforming" to the mass and resists by striving to emphasize its (or his) individuality. Unless the collectivity or person is truly innovative, however, the result is likely to be a more rigorous conformity to a slightly different mass culture: thus the norms for nonconformity are often well established. A jazz musician, for example, is not only restricted in performance to what the group will accept, but often the norms are so subtle that they can be expressed only in music; a beatnik who is so "far out" that he wears a gray flannel suit is rejected by other beatniks.

The following selection describes how Springdale (a real town of about a thousand persons in upstate New York, though the name is fictitious) is affected by the mass society of which it seems inescapably a part. In this respect, Springdale as the potential ideal type is exactly the opposite of the folk society described by Redfield.

THE AMBIVALENT ATTITUDE TO MASS SOCIETY

Springdalers have a decided respect for the great institutions that characterize American society. The efficiency, organizational ability and farflung activities of giant government and business enterprise inspire them with awe. The military might of the nation and the productive capacity of industry lend a Springdaler a sense of pride and security, and the continuous development and successful application of science assure him that he is a participant in the most forward-looking and progressive country in the world.

Reprinted from *Small Town in Mass Society: Class, Power, and Religion in a Rural Community* by Arthur J. Vidich and Joseph Bensman, pp. 79-105, by permission of Princeton University Press. Copyright © 1958 by Princeton University Press.

Anyone who would attack the great institutions of America would have no audience in Springdale: "Everybody knows this country wouldn't be what it is if it weren't for free enterprise and the democratic form of government." . . .

The Springdaler also sees that the urban and metropolitan society is technically and culturally superior to his own community. He sees this in his everyday life when he confronts the fact that his community cannot provide him with everything he needs: almost everyone goes to the city for shopping or entertainment; large numbers of people are dependent on the radio and television; and everyone realizes that rural life would be drastically altered without cars and refrigerators. Springdalers clearly realize how much of local life is based on the modern techniques, equipment and products which originate in distant places.

The community is constantly dependent on cultural and material imports and welcomes these as a way of "keeping up with the times." However, they believe that the very technical and cultural factors that make for the superiority of the "outside" also account for the problems of living that cities exhibit. The "city masses," while they have easier access to progress, are also the ready-made victims of the negative aspects of progress. In contrast, rural life, because it is geographically distant, can enjoy progress and avoid the worst features of the industrial mass society; Springdalers can believe that they are in a position to choose and utilize only the best of two worlds, that the importations, if properly chosen, need not affect the inner life of the community.

Because it is possible to choose only the best, the Springdaler can believe, that in spite of some disadvantages, his is the better of two worlds. This belief in the autonomy or, at worst, the self-selective dependency of rural life makes it possible for the community member publicly to voice the following conceptions concerning the relationships between his town and mass society:

1. That the basic traditions of American society —"grass-roots democracy," free and open expression, individualism—are most firmly located in rural society. The American heritage is better preserved in the small town because it can resist bad city influences and thereby preserve the best of the past.

2. That the future hope of American society lies in rural life because it has resisted all "isms" and constitutes the only major bulwark against them.

3. That much of the progress of society is the result of rural talent which has migrated to the cities. In this way rural society has a positive

influence on urban life; rural migrants account for the virtues of city life. "Everyone knows that most of the outstanding men in the country were raised in small towns" and Springdalers proudly point to several local names that have made good on the outside.

4. That "when you live in a small town you can take or leave the big cities—go there when you want to and always come back without having to live as they do." There is the belief that "if more people lived in small towns, you wouldn't have all those problems."

These summarize the types of beliefs that are frequently stated in public situations. The observer who is willing to go beyond the public statements discovers that Springdale has a great variety of direct and intimate connections with a wide range of institutions of the mass society. Moreover, these institutions affect many phases of the community, have consequences for its internal local functioning and in some ways control the direction of social change within it.

Springdale is connected with the mass society in a variety of different forms. The cumulative effect of these various connections makes possible the continuous transmission of outside policies, programs and trends into the community, even though the effects of the transmission and the transmitting agents themselves are not always seen. . . .

The external agents of cultural diffusion range from specific observable individuals placed in the local community by outside institutions to the impact of mass media of communications and successive ways of migration. The consequence of these modes of diffusion lies in the effect which they have on local styles of living.

Formal importing organizations

The adult extension program of the [nearby] land grant college is mediated at the local level by the county agent and the home demonstration agent who respectively are concerned with farming methods and production, and patterns of home-making and family life. These agents carry out their program through the Farm and Home Bureau organizations. . . . As a type of executive secretary to the local Farm Bureau whose officers are local farmers, the agent acts as an advisor in planning the organization's program, which includes such items as production and marketing problems, parity price problems and taxation problems.

The organizational structure of the Home Bureau parallels the Farm Bureau. From skills and techniques and personnel available at the extension center, local programs consist, for example, of furniture refinishing or aluminum working as well as discussions on such topics as child-rearing, nutrition, penal institutions and interior design. The Home Bureau extension specialist trains a local woman in information and techniques which are reported back to the local club. This program, geared as it is to modern home-making, child-rearing and the feminine role, has the effect of introducing new styles and standards of taste and consumption for the membership.

Other institutional connectors similar to the above in organizational structure account for the introduction of still other social values and social definitions. The 4-H Club, the Future Farmers of America and the Boy and Girl Scouts, as well as the Masons, Odd Fellows, American Legion, Grange and other local branches of national organizations and their auxiliaries, relate the Springdaler to the larger society through the social meanings and styles of activity defined in the programs, procedures and rituals of the national headquarters. State and national conventions . . . of these as well as church organizations directly link individuals to the outside. . . .

New cultural standards are also imported by agents who are not permanent residents of the town or who have only a transient relationship with it. These include the teachers at the central school, many of whom view their jobs as a temporary interlude in a progression of experience which will lead to a position in a city system. The other agents of contact are a wide variety of salesmen and "experts" who have a regular or irregular contact with business, government and private organizations. From the surrounding urban centers and the regional sales offices of farm implement and automobile manufacturers and nationally branded products, modern methods of merchandizing and business practice are introduced. Experts in civil defense, evangelism, fire-fighting, gardening, charity drives, traffic control and youth recreation introduce new techniques and programs to the local community. This great variety and diversity of semi-permanent and changing contacts in their cumulative effect act as a perpetual blood transfusion to local society. The net effect that these agents have as transmitters of life styles depends in a measure on their position and prestige in the community. The differential effect of these cultural contacts is treated below.

The ubiquity of mass media

Social diffusion through the symbols and pictorial images of the mass media of communications has permeated the community, reducing the local paper to reporting of social items and local news already known by everyone. Few individuals read only the local weekly paper; the majority subscribe to dailies published in surrounding cities and in the large metropolitan areas. This press, itself part of larger newspaper combines, presents an image of the passing scene in its news and nationally syndicated features to which the population of an entire region is exposed.

The mass culture and mass advertising of television and radio reach Springdale in all their variety. Television, particularly, is significant in its impact because for the first time the higher art forms such as ballet, opera and plays are visible to a broad rural audience. National events such as party conventions, inaugurations and investigative hearings are visible now to an audience which was previously far removed from the national centers of action and drama. Because of the relative geographic isolation of Springdale, television has made available entirely new areas of entertainment, information and education. It has created new leisure-time interests, has introduced new modes of leisure-time consumption and has led to the acceptance of standardized entertainment models. . . . Equally available and pervasive among the classes and individuals to whom they appeal are pocket books, comic books, and horror and sex stories. . . . The intrusion of the mass media is so overwhelming that little scope is left for the expression of local cultural and artistic forms.

However, the diffusion of the printed word is not limited to the mass media; it is present also in the realm of education, both religious and secular. The state department of education syllabus defines minimum standards and content for subject matter instruction. Courses of Sunday School instruction are available for all age levels, and each faith secures its material from its own national religious press. In each of these major institutional areas the standards and *content* of instruction are defined in sources available only in standardized form.

The immigrant as cultural carrier

Specific individuals are carriers of cultural diffusion, and the volume and extent of migration in and out of the community suggests the degree and intimacy of its contact with the mass society. . . .

Each decade and each generation introduces a new layer of immigrants to the community. The agricultural and business prosperity of the 1940's and early 1950's has brought city dwellers to farms and to businesses on main street. . . . Each new wave of migrants, bringing with it the fashions and thought styles of other places, influences the cultural development of the community.

The cumulative consequences of these channels of diffusion and the quantity and quality of the "material" diffused denies the existence of a culture indigenous to the small town. In almost all aspects of culture, even to speech forms, and including technology, literature, fashions and fads, as well as patterns of consumption, to mention a few, the small town tends to reflect the contemporary mass society.

Basically, an historically indigenous local culture does not seem to exist. The cultural imports of each decade and generation and the successive waves of migration associated with each combine to produce a local culture consisting of layers or segments of the mass culture of successive historical eras. In the small town the remaining elements of the gay-ninety culture are juxtaposed against the modern central school. The newer cultural importations frequently come in conflict with the older importations of other eras. The conflict between "spurious" and "genuine" culture appears to be a conflict between two different ages of "spurious" culture.

THE ECONOMIC NEXUS: OCCUPATIONAL GATEKEEPERS TO THE MASS SOCIETY

Simply because individuals pursue given occupations, their interconnections with mass society follow given patterns. They may be direct employees of specific organizations of the mass society; they may be the objects and targets of the programs of mass organizations; they may be trained by and in great institutions or their skills may be utilized only in urban areas. Because of these occupational characteristics they are specially qualified, accessible and available as transmitters of specific organizational and cultural contacts and contents.

Because these individuals in their occupational roles as gatekeepers are treated as specialists by both the community and mass society, occupation even more than life style becomes a crucial dimension of community life. The content, quality and amount of cultural importation accounted for by an individual is a function of the specific occupational nexus which he has to both the community and mass society.

The professionals

A number of institutional representatives who are residents of the town receive their position in the community by virtue of their connections with outside agencies. Their position in the community is secured in part by the institution to which they are connected and by the evaluation of the role they are imputed to have in the agency which they locally represent.

The group of individuals who possess a borrowed prestige based on their external affiliations fall largely in the professional category. They are individuals who uniformly possess a college education. Among their ranks are included lawyers, ministers, doctors, teachers, engineers, and a variety of field representatives of state and federal agencies who settle in the community for occupational purposes. All of these individuals, except one or two, have migrated to the community as adults. In addition to the prestige which they are accorded by virtue of being "educated," their overwhelming characteristic as a group lies in the influence which they have in mediating between the town and the larger society. They possess the knowledge and techniques necessary for connecting the small town to the intricate organization of the mass bureaucratic society. They possess "contacts" with outside agencies and their role requires an ability to understand "official" documents and forms, and to write appropriate letters to appropriate bureaus. Thus, for example, the lawyer is counsel to political bodies as well as to free associations and other local organizations, in which capacities he gains an extensive and intimate knowledge of affairs of the town and thereby acquires a position of influence. In like manner the technical knowledge of state educational regulations and policies possessed by the high-school principal is indispensable to the locally constituted school board.

In addition to the prestige and influence which segments of this group possess by virtue of their education and institutional role, they are accorded a respect and, in some cases, awe because of the power which they are imputed to have in manipulating the outside world; they can accomplish things for the community which no one else can.

Moreover, this professional group as a whole, including the relatively transient teaching staff, are felt to have access to styles of taste and consumption which are considered different from those available to the rest of the community. As a result these institutional connectors are considered outside the ordinary realm of prestige assignments and social stratification. That is, their social position in the community is not guaranteed by conforming to standards which are indigenous to the community but, rather, by imputed conformance to "alien" or "exotic" standards of urban life.

As a result of this dual position, individuals in this group, especially those who have come from or have resided for some time outside the community, are able to influence styles of consumption and thought in the community. They do this in three main areas of activity: in organizational activities, community projects and social fashions. They have been prime movers in setting up a formal program of youth recreation and in vigorously participating in and supporting local cultural activities such as plays, recitals and educational talks. In the P.T.A. they constitute the block favoring those modern methods and programs which bring the outside world to the small town— talks by foreign university students, race relations discussions and socio-dramas in dating and parent-child relationships. Ideas for the development of a community center and adult education programs emanate from and are supported by them. In terms of dress styles and personal adornment as well as home furnishings and styles of party giving, this group is in the forefront of innovation.

This innovating group of middle-class newcomers is supported by a group of college-educated locals who act as a bridge between the new standards and local society. In supporting these new standards, the local group absorbs some of the resentment which is directed at the innovating group by both the farmers and merchants.

It must be noted that the professionals' psychological orientation to accentuate the "elite" cultural values of mass society is more than merely a product of their residence, education or background in the mass society. The limitations on economic success and the limited professional opportunities in the community means that the drive toward success through work and investment is not fully available to them. The possession of alien cultural standards makes it possible for the professionals to reject the success drive by accepting meaningful standards alternative to those available to the rest of the community; they distinguish themselves in the community by their identification with external values.

Businessmen

For storekeepers, filling station operators, appliance dealers, automobile and farm equipment dealers and feed mill operators, the external world is a source of supply for the goods and commodities which they sell on the local market. Their position in relation to their source of supply and the overall condition of the national economy determines the level of their business activity, ceilings on their potential income, and hence indirectly their style of life. To analyze this group we must consider separately the position of the independent shopkeeper, the businessman who operates on a franchise and the feed mill and farm implement dealer.

The shopkeepers who make up the bulk of the business community have experienced a slow and gradual decline in their class position relative to other groups in the community. This is mainly due to the breakdown of their monopolistic position with respect to the local market, but it is also related to the rise of other groups. The development of the automobile, the appearance of the chain stores in surrounding areas and the expansion of mail order sales have placed them in a competitively disadvantageous position. Moreover, the nationally branded and advertised product, with its fixed profit margin determined by the producer, has tended in a general way to determine his volume/profit ratio in a way increasingly disadvantageous to him. His decrease in profits in relation to volume has driven him to a greater competition with other local shopkeepers —a competition which takes place in the form of despecialization, greater reliance on credit trade and keeping his shop open for long hours. The first two of these responses to his dilemma have further depressed his profit/volume ratio: in the one case by reducing his return on his investment and in the other case by increased losses due to bad debts. He keeps his business open in an effort to improve his investment/profit ratio and this he can do only by staying in the store himself.

The economic position of the small shopkeeper prevents him from reinvesting earnings in his own business. He sees little to be gained by modernizing and expanding his store in an effort to increase profits. Hence, the very basis on which the business group could achieve a class ascendancy are not open to it. Moreover, the long hours which he keeps in his store prevent him from holding a secondary occupation and limit his activities in community affairs. As a result he lives in an atmosphere of social and economic scarcity relative to his position thirty years ago and relative to other segments of the community. This accounts for the dominant psychology of scarcity-mindedness which is characteristic of this most numerous segment of the business class.

The position of the businessman who operates on a *franchise* is more obviously linked to the mass society. Usually he not only has a single source of supply, but also his source of supply (a petroleum company, for example) specifies the business practices and standards which must be maintained in order to retain the franchise. If the retail outlet is owned by the supplier (as with some filling stations) rents may be charged on a sliding scale according to volume of business—less volume, less rent—with the consequence that the profit margin of the local operator is not fixed.

More important, however, are the combined effects of the distribution policies of the petroleum products companies and appliance producers. Most of the big producers of these products maintain a local outlet; in some cases a single product may be retailed in two or three small-scale local outlets. In at least one line, household appliances, price cutting has become a standard form of competition. The effect of this proliferation of outlets is to depress the business chances of any single operator retailing a given branded product.

This group responds to its economic situation by increasing business hours, by carrying secondary lines and by intensive competition for "service" trade. Business is conducted at almost any hour of the day or night. Since these are one-man businesses, other members of the family are soon incorporated in the work process; children are helpers, wives act as secretaries and clerks. In the extreme case, the family life of the filling station operator orients itself almost completely to "keeping the business open"; the husband and wife are on duty together or the husband is absent from home except to sleep. This group is known to the community primarily through its occupational circumstances and its relationships are based upon being entrepreneurs and having a clientele. As individuals they are relatively unimportant to the community since there is a high rate of turnover of franchises.

There are three individuals in the business class who are exceptions. These are the feed mill operators and the farm implement dealers who in Springdale consist of one feed mill operator located on the periphery of the township, one implement dealer located in the village, and one large-scale combined feed mill, housing supply and farm implement partnership. Because they service an agricultural industry which since the early Forties has been prosperous, they are favorably situated in the local economy.

In terms of their customer relationships they are most intimately tied to the farmers, especially to the prosperous farmers who do most of the buying. Because of their market position their economic fate is intimately related to that of the farmers. In the period of farm ascendancy at the time of the study, they too were prosperous. . . . In addition, however, because they are business-

men and the most successful businessmen, they have achieved the respect, admiration and enmity of the business community as well as of the town at large.

They are the most heavily capitalized group of individuals in the community and play an important credit function in the local agricultural economy. Because of the farmer's economic dependence on them and the interlocking character of their mutual fate, the feed mill and implement dealers identify themselves with the farmer's interests. In local politics they are in a position to provide the leadership in organizing the farmer's interests and frequently act as spokesmen for the farm community. This is particularly true of the feed mill and implement partnership since it is the community's dominant enterprise. . . .

Thus two sub-groups of the business community, shopkeepers and franchise operators, experience a social and economic decline relative to a third, the feed and implement dealers.

These shifts in relative success are linked to accessibility to economic opportunity which is largely defined by external forces. . . .

Farmers

. . . Although the status of all farmers is equally linked to decisions and policies of . . . larger institutional structures (the price structure and federal agricultural legislation), all farmers do not equally orient their operations to legislation and regulations oriented to them. At this point the rate of status ascendancy of the individual farmer is probably directly related to the extent to which he accepts the preferential treatment accorded him in these larger policy decisions. Those who have been most swift and efficient in adjusting to the changing conditions of the agricultural economy over the past twenty years constitute the most rapidly ascending segment of farmers. . . .

This analysis does not exhaust the class groups. Other groups are occupationally less directly connected with the mass society and its markets. The aristocrats are oriented to the market only by fixed interest rates established in previous economic periods; their income from annuities, insurance payments and fixed inheritances declines in an inflationary period. The shack people, with the exception of their consumption function, are separated from the market by their unwillingness to direct their attention to it for any sustained period of time, even though their consumption standards are inflated at those times when they do address themselves to the market. The marginal middle-class groups economically are not in a position to be directly and importantly related to the market except through the general price level. Their relationship to the market is mediated through their imitation of more prestigeful and successful groups which are located in the community. . . .

THE POLITICAL SURRENDER TO MASS SOCIETY

. . . The village board . . . is dependent on its own taxable resources (taxes account for almost half its revenues) and best illustrates the major dimensions of local political action. The village board in Springdale accepts few of the powers given to it. Instead, it orients its action to the facilities and subsidies controlled and dispensed by other agencies and, by virtue of this, forfeits its own political power. Solutions to the problem of fire protection are found in agreements with regionally organized fire districts. In matters pertaining to road signs and street signs action typically takes the form of petitioning state agencies to fulfill desired goals "without cost to the taxpayer." On roads built and maintained by the state there is no recourse but to accept the state traffic bureau's standards of safety. A problem such as snow removal is solved by dealing directly with the foreman of the state highway maintenance crew through personal contacts: "If you treat him right, you can get him to come in and clear the village roads." In other areas of power where there are no parallel state agencies, such as for garbage collection or parks, the village board abdicates its responsibility.

As a consequence of this pattern of dependence, many important decisions are made for Springdale by outside agencies. Decisions which are made locally tend to consist of approving the requirements of administrative or state laws. In short the program and policies of local political bodies are determined largely by acceptance of grants-in-aid offered them—i.e., in order to get the subsidy specific types of decisions must be made—and by facilities and services made available to them by outside sources.

Psychologically this dependence leads to an habituation to outside control to the point where the town and village governments find it hard to act even where they have the power. Legal jurisdictions have been supplanted by psychological jurisdictions to such an extent that local political action is almost exclusively oriented to and predicated on seeking favors, subsidies and special treatment from outside agencies. The narrowing of legal jurisdictions by psychologically imposed limits leads to an inability to cope with local problems if outside resources are not available.

Power in local political affairs, then, tends to be based on accessibility to sources of decision in larger institutions. Frequently this accessibility consists merely of the knowledge of the source, or it may mean a personal contact, or an ability to correspond to get necessary information. Under these circumstances, power in the political arena is delegated to those with contacts in and knowledge of the outer world and to those who are experts in formal communication with impersonal bureaucratic offices. . . .

THE SOCIAL PSYCHOLOGICAL CONSEQUENCES OF THE RURAL SURRENDER

A central fact of rural life then, is its dependence on the institutions and dynamics of urban and mass society. The recognition of this dependence and the powerlessness associated with it give to the agents and institutions of the great society a degree of respect and admiration which, however, does not always connote approval. Rather, there is a high degree of ambivalence with respect to these agents and institutions. They have respect because of their power and wealth, and because their norms have the legitimacy of acceptance in wide areas of the society at large. On the other hand, the very dominance of the mass institutions causes resentments, since, in the light of this dominance, rural life in its immediacy is devalued. Hence, for example, although the standards of the land grant college are accepted, the institution and its agents may be resented for the role they play in innovation.

The phenomenon of psychological ambivalence to the mass society is particularly reinforced by the fact that slight changes in the policies and dynamics of the mass institutions can have profound effects on the rural way of life and on its major social and economic classes—i.e., parity policies, industrial relocations, new state roads and state subsidization formulas. In response to these conditions, the members of the rural community and their political spokesman resent their dependency and powerlessness and channelize it into anti-urban politics and policies. In relation to the outer world, there exist two types of political victory; when rural rather than urban areas get a disproportionately large share of the benefits of the state budget and when the city can be made the object of investigation on grounds of corruption or vice by politicians surrounded by a halo of rural images. At the same time a personal identification with important urban political officials lends an individual prestige in the rural community.

But this continuous transvaluation of the attitudes toward urban life and its representatives are never so simple as the dependence-resentment mechanism would suggest. For such political and psychological currents are supported by intricately articulated images of the mass society and rural self images . . . which for the purposes of this discussion can be termed counterimages.

These images, themselves, are a product of complex institutional developments and reflect the process of urban penetration. For it is uniquely ironical that the self-image of the rural community and its image of urban life are in part the products of the penetration of urban mass media. Through these media the people of Springdale see urban life dominated by crime, dirt, filth, immorality, vice, corruption and anti-Americanism. The urban center is seen as a jungle of man's inhumanity to man; the large political center as a "dog-eat-dog" world of investigations and counterinvestigations with few clearly defined heroes. It sees the urban middle classes confronted by apparently hopeless personal problems and moving from crisis to crisis without end. It is because of the mechanism of resentment that the Springdaler can see wide class differences in urban society and be unaware of class in his own environment.

Contrariwise, the mass media frequently present rural life in idyllic terms. . . . The weekly press carries syndicated columnists who extol the virtues of ruralism. Political as well as feature speakers who come to town invariably reinforce the town's image of itself: "The false life of cities." "If America were made up of small towns like Springdale, this would be a better country." "The goodness of America lies in the small town where life and nature meet to make for genuine living." The urban man of knowledge and the university scientist verbalize their own image of rural life and in doing so shape the self-image of the rural audience.

Separate urban images exist for the various segments which epitomize the rural community. The farmer is strong, self-reliant and capable. He is warm, affectionate and devoted but these characteristics are frequently hidden under a crusty, gruff exterior. He is a good businessman and a sharp trader capable in the final analysis of outwitting others, especially the city slicker. Outside of a few old gossips, community life is richly warm and filled with a wide variety of social interchange, gatherings and genuinely spontaneous self-expression. The rural dweller is religious, moral and upright, though capable of "cutting-up" in a way which is both amusing and tolerable. The villains, the sharp-dealers, the frauds, when not urban types, exist in order to provide the

protagonist and the community with an effective demonstration of its values in action.

The above picture, of course, is only a profile of the images presented to the rural consumer of mass media. Numerous exceptions exist, as, for example, the image of rural corruption often present in the violent type of pocket novel. Another notable exception is the absence in the mass media of an image of the rural, commuting, industrial worker. His place in rural society is difficult to stereotype, particularly since it stands in sharp contrast to the image of the self-reliance and independence of the rural community as personified by the farmer. Thus the lack of definition of the rural industrial worker in the mass media corresponds to the lack of a definition of industrial workers held by the residents of Springdale, including the lack of a self-definition by the industrial workers themselves.

The mass media then provide the raw materials out of which the rural resident can and does form personal images which enable him to approach the psychological demands of his situation. The rural target of the mass media thus can select those elements of the total output which enable him to meet those psychological needs, ignoring both the materials and the implications which are not congruent with the manner in which he wishes to structure his perception and images.

From the standpoint of the producer of mass media, to complete the picture, the image presented of rural life and life in general reflects not only his estimate of his audience (since not all of the mass media are specifically aimed at the rural market) but also the psychological climate of the urban centers where images of rural life are produced. The romanticization of rural life in press and radio reflects the need of the urban dweller to conceive of rural life as simpler and freer from the complexities, tensions and anxieties which he faces in his own world. Rural life is thus conceived as a counterimage which highlights his own situation. However, when presented to the rural resident, it serves as an image which enables the rural dweller to form symbolic and ideological resistance to urban society. It is thus through the mass media that the negative reactions to mass society of both the rural and urban dweller are linked; and it is as sets of similar responses to the negative aspects of urbanism that both urban and rural dwellers find a common symbolic meeting ground.

In addition to images which may be the peculiar product of the mass media, Springdalers hold negative images of the major urban institutions. Washington is populated by corrupt politicians, influence peddlers and communists. Cities are hotbeds of radicalism and atheism. Industrial workers led by racketeers are lazy, highly paid and incapable of performing the complex managerial practices necessary to success in farm and small business management. Big universities and city churches are seats of secularism and the city influence is held responsible for local immorality and corruption. These images in their complex articulation enable the rural resident to take pride in his situation, to meet the psychological threat of his powerlessness in a mass society and to organize political action which expresses both his economic interest and his psychological needs.

It must be remembered, however, that the central fact of rural life is ambivalence: the negative image of urban life goes hand in hand with respect for the power, the wealth and the legitimacy of acceptance of urban values. The most contrary values are thus held in complex, psychologically balanced constellations. As a result, the response of rural residents to urban institutions is not stable through time. Slight shifts in their situations can cause the most varied responses. Their political loyalties are subject to sudden shifts in phase with shifts in farm income, price levels and the policies of state and federal govern-ments. Anti-urban elements are held in check or can develop relatively easily. Furthermore, the balance of power and influence within the community can and does vary with relatively slight shifts in the external situation affecting these groups.

Hence, those factors which appear to be decisive in determining the action of the rural community are factors which originate in areas outside the rural community. Thus, even when the rural community attacks the urban mass society, the nature of the attack, its intensity and the situations which bring it forth are, in large part, the products of urban mass society. Rural life, then, can be seen as one area in which the dynamics of modern urban mass society are worked out.

There is always the danger of considering all aspects of mass society as responding only to the dynamics of mass society, so that when one completes one's analysis mass society dissolves into a reponse to itself. It must be remembered that there is a reciprocal relationship between Springdale and mass society in which Springdale, taken as one of thousands of similar communities, exerts itself upon and shapes the mass society. . . .

Selection *45*

Ecology and Human Ecology
Amos H. Hawley

Human ecology, like ecology generally, has to do with the relationships between organisms and their environments. Out of such relationships emerge a balance, an organization, a tenuous and ever-changing stability. If this were not so, life on earth would long since have perished. The study of ecology is essentially the study of the survival of life.

For life to continue, the disruption wrought by invention, invasion, the exhaustion of natural resources, cultural change, the excessive reproduction of a species, the failure of a species to reproduce, and the vagaries of climate—to name only a few of the factors involved—must be resolved. Sometimes the resolution is a change in size in the respective populations of various species that can be accommodated in a given space; sometimes the resolution is brought about by the survival of a mutant of a species and the disappearance of the original strain; sometimes the resolution involves the total extinction of a species. Occasionally no adjustment is possible (as in the case of a volcanic eruption), and all life disappears.

There are some important differences between human beings and other forms of life in adjusting to a natural setting. The ability to reason abstractly, the capacity to communicate in symbols and hence to transmit the cultural heritage which he has acquired from his predecessors, and the *existence* of that cultural heritage enable man to alter his environment more extensively and in more complex ways than is possible for other animals. Memory, the ability to classify phenomena, and (if it differs from these two) the ability to *think* enable man to forecast events that have not yet occurred and to alter his environment on a rational, rather than on an instinctive, basis before they do occur. (This does not necessarily imply that rational behavior always produces results that are superior to those of instinctive behavior, but it does permit a greater variety of behaviors.) There are, therefore, valid grounds for distinguishing between ecology generally and human ecology.

From 1915 to 1945, human ecologists devoted most of their energies to studying the spatial patterns of the human community and to exploring the effects of the process of competition. Hawley's challenge to ecologists to expand the scope of ecological theory stimulated much serious thought, with the result that contemporary ecologists direct more attention toward the integration of empirical research findings into a broader theory. Hawley is concerned with an ecological explanation of the development and perpetuation of human communities generally, as well as of particular types of communities, such as those described in previous articles—the folk community, the bedroom town, and the small town—and those to be described in subsequent articles—the urban community, the preindustrial city, and the modern suburb.

Human ecology, from its inception to a comparatively recent date, is reminiscent of Alice's curious experience in the rabbit hole when she, after consuming the pretty little cake, opened out "like the largest telescope that ever was." . . .

Perhaps it is to be expected that the sudden ascent to popularity of an innovation in scientific thought should be accompanied by a certain amount of confusion as to its specific connotation. . . . One finds it variously argued that the study deals essentially with "sub-social" phenomena, with the effects of competition, with spatial distributions, with the influence of geographic factors, and with still other more or less intelligibly delineated aspects of human behavior. There are some writers who would have human ecology encompass the whole field of social science, and there are others who prefer to relegate it to the status of a mere sociological research technique. Between these wide extremes the subject can be found identified in turn with biology, economics, human geography, sociology, and, as if not to overlook a possibility, it is sometimes described as marginal to all other life sciences. . . .

Probably most of the difficulties which beset human ecology may be traced to the isolation of the subject from the mainstream of ecological thought. Although it seems almost too elementary to mention, the only conceivable justification for

a human ecology must derive from the intrinsic utility of ecological theory as such. . . .

. . . That ecology is basically a social science has long been clear to most serious students of the subject. It is apparent, moreover, in almost every aspect of the discipline: in the root of the term ecology; in the historical details of the subject's development; in the large place given to sociological concepts such as community, society, niche, commensalism, symbiosis, dominance, succession, etc.; and in the manner in which problems for investigation are stated. . . .

Briefly stated, ecology is concerned with the elemental problem of how growing, multiplying beings maintain themselves in a constantly changing but ever restricted environment. It is based on the fundamental assumption that life is a continuous struggle for adjustment of organism to environment. However, the manifest interrelatedness of living forms, which heads students to speak of the "web of life," suggests that adjustment, far from being the action of independent organisms, is a mutual or collective phenomenon. Drawing together the relevant facts, it seems that the inevitable crowding of living forms upon limited resources produces a complex action and

From *Social Forces*, Vol. 22 (1944), 398-405. Published by the University of North Carolina Press.

344   Part 6: Human Ecology

reaction of organism with environment and organism with organism in the course of which individuals become related to one another in ways conducive to a more effective utilization of the habitat. As the division of labor which thus develops approaches equilibrium, such that the number of organisms engaged in each of the several activities is sufficient to provide all the needs that are represented, the aggregate of associated individuals assumes the aspect of a compact viable entity, a superorganism, in fact. The (biotic) community, as such a functionally or symbiotically[1] integrated population may properly be called, is in effect a collective response to the habitat; it constitutes the adjustment in the fullest sense of the term, of organism to environment.

The subject of ecological inquiry then is the community, the form and development of which are studied with particular reference to the limiting and supporting factors of the environment. Ecology, in other words, is a study of the morphology of collective life in both its static and its dynamic aspects. It attempts to determine the nature of community structure in general, the types of communities that appear in different habitats, and the specific sequence of change in community development.

Two elements, one implicit and the other explicit, in the conception as outlined here merit special emphasis. Not immediately evident perhaps, though nevertheless of basic importance, is the fact that the units of observation, i.e., the data, are neither physiological processes nor anatomical structures but are rather the activities of organisms. Taxonomic characteristics are relevant only so far as they serve as indexes of behavior traits. . . .

Secondly, as already indicated, life viewed ecologically is an aggregate rather than an individual phenomenon. The individual enters into ecological theory as a postulate and into ecological investigation as a unit of measurement; but as an object of special study he belongs to other disciplines, e.g., physiology, genetics, psychology, etc. The focus of attention in ecology is upon the population which is either organized or in process of becoming organized. This cannot be too strongly emphasized, for it places ecology squarely in the category of social science.

Human ecology, like plant and animal ecology, represents a special application of the general viewpoint to a particular class of living things. It involves both a recognition of the fundamental unity of animate nature and an awareness that there is differentiation within that unity. Man is an organism and as such he is dependent on the same resources, confronted with the same ele-

mentary problems, and displays in essential outline the same mode of response to life conditions as is observed in other forms of life. Thus the extension of patterns of thought and techniques of investigation developed in the study of the collective life of lower organisms to the study of man is a logical consummation of the ecological point of view. One important qualification is necessary, however; the extraordinary degree of flexibility of human behavior makes for a complexity and a dynamics in the human community without counterpart elsewhere in the organic world. It is this that sets man apart as an object of special inquiry and gives rise to a human as distinct from a general ecology.

While to reason from "pismires to parliaments" would do violence to the facts, it is nevertheless necessary to keep the phenomenon of culture in proper perspective. When man by virtue of his culture-producing capacity is regarded as an entirely unique type of organism the distortion is no less acute than if this quality were completely ignored. Human behavior, in all its complexity and variability, is but further evidence of the tremendous potential for adjustment inherent in life. Culture is nothing more than a way of referring to the prevailing techniques by which a population maintains itself in its habitat. The component parts of human culture are therefore identical in principle with the appetency of the bee for honey, the nest-building activities of birds, and the hunting habits of carnivora. To argue that the latter are instinctive while the former are not is to beg the question. Ecology is concerned less now with how habits are acquired, than with the functions they serve and the relationships they involve.

Thus despite the great difference between the behavior of men and that of lower forms of life—a difference which appears to be of degree rather than of kind, the approach described as general ecology may be applied to the study of man without radical alteration. In simplest terms, human ecology is the descriptive study of the adjustment of human populations to the conditions of their respective physical environments. The necessity that life be lived in a specific place and time, operating upon man as it does upon other organisms, produces an inescapable compulsion to adjustment which increases as population increases or as the opportunities for life decrease. And out of the adaptive strivings of aggregated individuals there develops, consciously or unconsciously, an organization of interdependencies which consti-

---

[1] Symbiosis may be defined as the mutually beneficial living together of unlike forms.

tutes the population a coherent functional entity. The human community, in other words, is basically an adaptive mechanism; it is the means whereby a population utilizes and maintains itself in its habitat. Human ecology, then, may be defined more fully as the study of the development and the form of communal structure as it occurs in varying environmental contexts.

The human community, of course, is more than just an organization of symbiotic relationships and to that extent there are limitations to the scope of human ecology. Man's collective life involves, in greater or less degree, a psychological and a moral as well as a symbiotic integration. But these, so far as they are distinguishable, should be regarded as complementing aspects of the same thing rather than as separate phases or segments of the community. Sustenance activities and interrelations are inextricably interwoven with sentiments, value systems, and other ideational constructs. Human ecology is restricted in scope then not by any real or assumed qualitative differences in behavior but simply by the manner in which its problem is stated. The question of how men relate themselves to one another in order to live in their habitat yields a description of communal structure in terms of its overt and visible features. It does not, however, provide explanations of all the many ramifications of human interrelationships. The external and descriptive approach of ecology is ill-suited to the direct study of the psychological counterpart of symbiosis, although it may serve as a fruitful source of hypotheses concerning that aspect of the community.

It may be helpful to call attention to the fact that the problems of human ecology, and ecology in general, are basically population problems. The broad question, as previously indicated, concerns the adjustment of population to the resources and other physical conditions of the habitat. This resolves itself into a number of related problems, such as: (1) the succession of changes by which an aggregate passes from a mere polyp-like formation into a community of interdependences; (2) the ways in which the developing community is affected by the size, composition, and rate of growth or decline of the population; (3) the significance of migration for both the development of the community and the maintenance of community stability; and (4) the relative numbers in the various functions composing the communal structure, together with the factors which make for change in the existing equilibrium and the ways in which such change occurs.

Clearly, human ecology has much in common with every other social science. The problem with which it deals underlies that of each of the several specialized studies of human social life. Its data are drawn from the same sources and it employs many of the same techniques of investigation. The points of convergence are, in fact, too numerous to detail in this paper. There is no basis therefore to conclude from what has been said that human ecology is an autonomous social science: it is quite unlikely that there is any autonomy in science. The distinctive feature of the study lies in the conception of the adjustment of man to habitat as a process of community development. Whereas this may be an implicit assumption in most social science disciplines, it is for human ecology the principal working hypothesis. Thus human ecology might well be regarded as the basic social science.

Selection *46*

Sentiment and Symbolism as Ecological Variables
Walter Firey

The preoccupation of ecologists with competition and with spatial patterns of the community leads directly to a consideration of the operational definitions used in the empirical study of actual communities. It follows that one of the basic tools of the ecologist should be a map of the community that he is studying. It follows further that two kinds of information should be among the first to appear on the map: (1) the use of specific parcels of land and (2) the rent or cost of each parcel.

A good Marxist would be expected to predict that the cost and use of land would be inextricably related and that temporary dislocations would ultimately be forced to give way to economic determinism. And a good functionalist might be expected to predict that the law of supply and demand, the values of the society involved, and the integrity of the community would both determine and reflect land usage and land costs.

In the article that follows, Firey does not directly refute either the economic determinists or the functionalists, but he does introduce several considerations that merit the attention of both groups. Basing his report on the investigation of three areas in Boston, he points out that there are more important factors than market value in determining the use of land. Beacon Hill, the Boston Common, and the North End all have special significance to particular persons. The symbolic nature of these areas and the sentiments about them held by the population appear to be more important than either money or efficiency in determining their use. To the fact that human beings are rationally capable of achieving economic values, Firey adds that sentimental attachments as well as logical decisions are reflected by the actual economic organization of a community.

. . . In common with many of the older American cities Boston has inherited from the past certain spatial patterns and landmarks which have had a remarkable persistence and even recuperative power despite challenges from other more economic land uses. The persistence of these spatial patterns can only be understood in terms of the group values that they have come to symbolize. We shall describe three types of such patterns: first, an in-town upper class residential neighborhood known as Beacon Hill; second, certain "sacred sites," notably the Boston Common and the colonial burying-grounds; and third, a lower class Italian neighborhood known as the North End. In each of these land uses we shall find certain locational processes which seem to defy a strictly economic analysis.

The first of the areas, Beacon Hill, is located some five minutes' walking distance from the retail center of Boston. This neighborhood has for fully a century and a half maintained its character as a preferred upper class residential district, despite its contiguity to a low rent tenement area, the West End. During its long history Beacon Hill has become the symbol for a number of sentimental associations which constitute a genuine attractive force to certain old families of Boston. Some idea of the nature of these sentiments may be had from statements in the innumerable pamphlets and articles written by residents of the Hill. References to "this sacred eminence," "stately old-time appearance," and "age-old quaintness and charm," give an insight into the attitudes attaching to the area. One resident reveals rather clearly the spatial referability of these sentiments when she writes of the Hill:

"It has a tradition all its own, that begins in the hospitality of a book-lover, and has never lost that flavor. Yes, our streets are inconvenient, steep, and slippery. The corners are abrupt, the contours perverse. . . . It may well be that the gibes of our envious neighbors have a foundation and that these dear crooked lanes of ours were indeed traced in ancestral mud by absent-minded kine."[1]

Behind such expressions of sentiment are a number of historical associations connected with the area. Literary traditions are among the strongest of these; indeed, the whole literary legend of Boston has its focus at Beacon Hill. Many of America's most distinguished literati have occupied homes on the Hill. Present day occupants of these houses derive a genuine satisfaction from the individual histories of their dwellings. One lady whose home had had a distinguished pedigree remarked:

"I like living here for I like to think that a great deal of historic interest has happened here in this room."

Not a few families are able to trace a continuity of residence on the Hill for several generations, some as far back as 1800 when the Hill was first developed as an upper class neighborhood. It is a point of pride to a Beacon Hill resident if he

From the *American Sociological Review*, Vol. 10 (1945), 140-148. Reprinted by permission of the American Sociological Association.
[1]Abbie Farwell Brown, *The Lights of Beacon Hill* (Boston: 1922), p. 4.

can say that he was born on the Hill or was at least raised there; a second best boast is to point out that his forebears once lived on the Hill.

Thus a wide range of sentiments—aesthetic, historical, and familial—have acquired a spatial articulation in Beacon Hill. The bearing of these sentiments upon locational processes is a tangible one and assumes three forms: retentive, attractive, and resistive. Let us consider each of these in order. To measure the retentive influence that spatially-referred sentiments may exert upon locational activities we have tabulated by place of residence all the families listed in the Boston *Social Register* for the years 1894, 1905, 1914, 1929, and 1943. This should afford a reasonably accurate picture of the distribution of upper class families by neighborhoods within Boston and in suburban towns. In Table I we have presented the tabulations for the three in-town concentrations of upper class families (Beacon Hill, Back Bay, and Jamaica Plain) and for the five main suburban concentrations (Brookline, Newton, Cambridge, Milton, and Dedham)... The most apparent feature of these data is, of course, the consistent increase of upper class families in the suburban towns and the marked decrease (since 1905) in two of the in-town upper class areas, Back Bay and Jamaica Plain. Although both of these neighborhoods remain fashionable residential districts their prestige is waning rapidly. Back Bay in particular, though still surpassing in numbers any other single neighborhood, has under-

gone a steady invasion of apartment buildings, rooming houses, and business establishments which are destroying its prestige value. The trend of Beacon Hill has been different. Today it has a larger number of upper class families than it had in 1894. Where it ranked second among fashionable neighborhoods in 1894 it ranks third today, being but slightly outranked in numbers by the suburban city of Brookline and by the Back Bay. Beacon Hill is the only in-town district that has consistently retained its preferred character and has held to itself a considerable proportion of Boston's old families.

There is, however, another aspect to the spatial dynamics of Beacon Hill, one that pertains to the "attractive" locational role of spatially referred sentiments. From 1894 to 1905 the district underwent a slight drop, subsequently experiencing a steady rise for 24 years, and most recently undergoing another slight decline. These variations are significant, and they bring out rather clearly the dynamic ecological role of spatial symbolism. The initial drop is attributable to the development of the then new Back Bay. Hundreds of acres there had been reclaimed from marshland and had been built up with palatial dwellings. Fashion now pointed to this as the select area of the city and in response to its dictates a number of families abandoned Beacon Hill to take up more pretentious Back Bay quarters. Property values on the Hill began to depreciate, old dwellings became rooming houses, and businesses began to invade some of the streets. But many of the old families remained on the Hill and a few of them made efforts to halt the gradual deterioration of the district. Under the aegis of a realtor, an architect, and a few close friends there was launched a program of purchasing old houses, modernizing the interiors and leaving the colonial exteriors intact, and then selling the dwellings to individual families for occupancy. Frequently adjoining neighbors would collaborate in planning their improvements so as to achieve an architectural consonance. The results of this program may be seen in the drift of upper class families back to the Hill. From 1905 to 1929 the number of *Social Register* families in the district increased by 120. Assessed valuations showed a corresponding increase: from 1919 to 1924 there was a rise of 24 percent; from 1924 to 1929 the rise was 25 percent. The nature of the Hill's appeal, and the kind of persons attracted, may be gathered from the following popular write-up:

TABLE I: Number of Upper Class Families in Boston, by Districts of Concentration, and in Main Suburban Towns, for Certain Years

	1894	1905	1914	1929	1943
Within Boston					
Beacon Hill	280	242	279	362	335
Back Bay	867	1166	1102	880	556
Jamaica Plain ..	56	66	64	36	30
Other districts ..	316	161	114	86	41
Suburban Towns					
Brookline	137	300	348	355	372
Newton	38	89	90	164	247
Cambridge.....	77	142	147	223	257
Milton.........	37	71	106	131	202
Dedham	8	29	48	69	99
Other towns	106	176	310	403	816
Total in Boston ...	1519	1635	1559	1364	962
Total in Suburbs ..	403	807	1049	1345	1993
Totals	1922	2442	2608	2709	2955

Tabulated from: Social Register, Boston

"To salvage the quaint charm of Colonial Architecture on Beacon Hill, Boston, is the object of a well-defined movement among writers and professional folk that promises the most delightful opportunities for the home seeker of moderate means and conservative tastes. Because men of discernment were able to visualize the possibilities presented by these architectural landmarks, and have undertaken the gracious task of restoring them to their former glory, this historic quarter of old Boston, once the centre of literary culture, is coming into its own."[2]

The independent variable in this "attractive" locational process seems to have been the symbolic quality of the Hill, by which it constituted a referent for certain strong sentiments of upper class Bostonians.

While this revival was progressing there remained a constant menace to the character of Beacon Hill, in the form of business encroachments and apartment-hotel developments. Recurrent threats from this source finally prompted residents of the Hill to organize themselves into the Beacon Hill Association. Formed in 1922, the declared object of this organization was "to keep undesirable business and living conditions from affecting the hill district." At the time the city was engaged in preparing a comprehensive zoning program and the occasion was propitious to secure for Beacon Hill suitable protective measures. A systematic set of recommendations was drawn up by the Association regarding a uniform 65-foot height limit for the entire Hill, the exclusion of business from all but two streets, and the restriction of apartment house bulk. It succeeded in gaining only a partial recognition of this program in the 1924 zoning ordinance. But the Association continued its fight against inimical land uses year after year. In 1927 it successfully fought a petition brought before the Board of Zoning Adjustment to alter the height limits in one area so as to permit the construction of a four million dollar apartment-hotel 155 feet high. Residents of the Hill went to the hearing en masse. In spite of the prospect of an additional twenty million dollars worth of exclusive apartment hotels that were promised if the zoning restrictions were withheld the petition was rejected, having been opposed by 214 of the 220 persons present at the hearing. In 1930 the Association gained an actual reduction in height limits on most of Beacon street and certain adjoining streets, though its leader was denounced by opponents as "a rank sentimentalist who desired to keep Boston a village." One year later the Association defeated a petition to rezone Beacon street for business purposes. In other campaigns the Association successfully pressed for the rezoning of a business street back to purely residential purposes, for the lowering of height limits on the remainder of Beacon street, and for several lesser matters of local interest. Since 1929, owing partly to excess assessed valuations of Boston real estate and partly to the effects of the depression upon families living on securities, Beacon Hill has lost some of its older families, though its decline is nowhere near so precipitous as that of the Back Bay.

Thus for a span of one and a half centuries there have existed on Beacon Hill certain locational processes that largely escape economic analysis. It is the symbolic quality of the Hill, not its impeditive or cost-imposing character, that most tangibly correlates with the retentive, attractive, and resistive trends that we have observed. And it is the dynamic force of spatially referred sentiments, rather than considerations of rent, which explains why certain families have chosen to live on Beacon Hill in preference to other in-town districts having equally accessible location and even superior housing conditions. There is thus a non-economic aspect to land use on Beacon Hill, one which is in some respects actually diseconomic in its consequences. Certainly the large apartment-hotels and specialty shops that have sought in vain to locate on the Hill would have represented a fuller capitalization on potential property values than do residences. In all likelihood the attending increase in real estate prices would not only have benefited individual property holders but would have so enhanced the value of adjoining properties as to compensate for whatever depreciation other portions of the Hill might have experienced.

If we turn to another type of land use pattern in Boston, that comprised by the Boston Common and the old burying grounds, we encounter another instance of spatial symbolism which has exerted a marked influence upon the ecological organization of the rest of the city. The Boston Common is a survival from colonial days when every New England town allotted a portion of its land to common use as a cow pasture and militia field. Over the course of three centuries Boston has grown entirely around the Common so that today we find a 48-acre tract of land wedged directly into the heart of the business district. On three of its five sides are women's apparel shops, department stores, theaters and other high-rent locational activities. On the fourth side is Beacon street, extending alongside Beacon Hill. Only the activities of Hill residents have prevented business from invading this side. The fifth side is occupied by the Public Garden. A land value map portrays

---

[2] Harriet Sisson Gillespie, "Reclaiming Colonial Landmarks," *The House Beautiful*, 58 (September, 1925), 239-241.

a strip of highest values pressing upon two sides of the Common, on Tremont and Boylston streets, taking the form of a long, narrow band.

Before considering the ecological consequences of this configuration let us see what attitudes have come to be associated with the Common. There is an extensive local literature about the Common and in it we find interesting sentiments expressed. One citizen speaks of:

". . . the great principle exemplified in the preservation of the Common. Thank Heaven, the tide of money making must break and go around that."[3]

Elsewhere we read:

"Here, in short, are all our accumulated memories, intimate, public, private."[4]

"Boston Common was, is, and ever will be a source of tradition and inspiration from which the New Englanders may renew their faith, recover their moral force, and strengthen their ability to grow and achieve."[5]

The Common has thus become a "sacred" object, articulating and symbolizing genuine historical sentiments of a certain portion of the community. Like all such objects its sacredness derives, not from any intrinsic spatial attributes, but rather from its representation in peoples' minds as a symbol for collective sentiments.

Such has been the force of these sentiments that the Common has become buttressed up by a number of legal guarantees. The city charter forbids Boston in perpetuity to dispose of the Common or any portion of it. The city is further prohibited by state legislation from building upon the Common, except within rigid limits, or from laying out roads or tracks across it. By accepting the bequest of one George F. Parkman, in 1908, amounting to over five million dollars, the city is further bound to maintain the Common, and certain other parks, "for the benefit and enjoyment of its citizens."

What all this has meant for the spatial development of Boston's retail center is clear from the present character of that district. Few cities of comparable size have so small a retail district in point of area. Unlike the spacious department stores of most cities, those in Boston are frequently compressed within narrow confines and have had to extend in devious patterns through rear and adjoining buildings. Traffic in downtown Boston has literally reached the saturation point, owing partly to the narrow one-way streets but mainly to the lack of adequate arterials leading into and out of the Hub. The American Road Builders Association has estimated that there is a loss of $81,000 per day in Boston as a result of

traffic delay. Trucking in Boston is extremely expensive. These losses ramify out to merchants, manufacturers, commuters, and many other interests. Many proposals have been made to extend a through arterial across the Common, thus relieving the extreme congestion on Tremont and Beacon streets, the two arterials bordering the park. Earlier suggestions, prior to the construction of the subway, called for street car tracks across the Common. But "the controlling sentiment of the citizens of Boston, and of large numbers throughout the State, is distinctly opposed to allowing any such use of the Common."[6] Boston has long suffered from land shortage and unusually high real estate values as a result both of the narrow confines of the peninsula comprising the city center and as a result of the exclusion from income-yielding uses of so large a tract as the Common. A further difficulty has arisen from the rapid southwesterly extension of the business district in the past two decades. With the Common lying directly in the path of this extension the business district has had to stretch around it in an elongated fashion, with obvious inconvenience to shoppers and consequent loss to businesses.

The Common is not the only obstacle to the city's business expansion. No less than three colonial burying-grounds, two of them adjoined by ancient church buildings, occupy downtown Boston. The contrast that is presented by 9-story office buildings reared up beside quiet cemeteries affords visible evidence of the conflict between "sacred" and "profane" that operates in Boston's ecological pattern. The dis-economic consequences of commercially valuable land being thus devoted to non-utilitarian purposes goes even further than the removal from business uses of a given amount of space. For it is a standard principle of real estate that business property derives added value if adjoining properties are occupied by other businesses. Just as a single vacancy will depreciate the value of a whole block of business frontage, so a break in the continuity of stores by a cemetery damages the commercial value of surrounding properties. But, even more than the Common, the colonial burying-grounds of Boston have become invested with a moral significance which renders them almost inviolable. Not only

---

[3] William Everett, speech quoted in *The Boston Transcript*, March 7, 1903.
[4] T. R. Sullivan, *Boston New and Old* (Boston: 1912), pp. 45-46.
[5] Joshua H. Jones, Jr., "Happenings on Boston Common," *Our Boston*, 2 (January, 1927), 9-15.
[6] *First Annual Report of the Boston Transit Commission* (Boston: 1895), p. 9.

is there the usual sanctity which attaches to all cemeteries, but in those of Boston there is an added sacredness growing out of the age of the grounds and the fact that the forebears of many of New England's most distinguished families as well as a number of colonial and Revolutionary leaders lie buried in these cemeteries. There is thus a manifold symbolism to these old burying-grounds, pertaining to family lineage, early nation-hood, civic origins, and the like, all of which have strong sentimental associations. What has been said of the old burying-grounds applies with equal force to a number of other venerable landmarks in central Boston. Such buildings as the Old South Meeting-House, the Park Street Church, King's Chapel, and the Old State House—all foci of historical associations—occupy commercially valu-able land and interrupt the continuity of business frontage on their streets. Nearly all of these land-marks have been challenged at various times by real estate and commercial interests which sought to have them replaced by more profitable uses. In every case community sentiments have resisted such threats.

In all these examples we find a symbol-sentiment relationship which has exerted a significant influ-ence upon land use. Nor should it be thought that such phenomena are mere ecological "sports." Many other older American cities present similar locational characteristics. Delancey street in Phila-delphia represents a striking parallel to Beacon Hill, and certain in-town districts of Chicago, New York, and Detroit, recently revived as fashionable apartment areas, bear resemblances to the Beacon Hill revival. The role of traditionalism in rigidifying the ecological patterns of New Orleans has been demonstrated in a recent study. Further studies of this sort should clarify even further the true scope of sentiment and symbolism in urban spatial structure and dynamics.

As a third line of evidence for our hypothesis we have chosen a rather different type of area from those so far considered. It is a well known fact that immigrant ghettoes, along with other slum districts, have become areas of declining population in most American cities. A point not so well established is that this decline tends to be selective in its incidence upon residents and that this selectivity may manifest varying degrees of identification with immigrant values. For resi-dence within a ghetto is more than a matter of spatial placement; it generally signifies acceptance of immigrant values and participation in immi-grant institutions. Some light on this process is afforded by data from the North End of Boston. This neighborhood, almost wholly Italian in popu-lation, has long been known as "Boston's classic land of poverty." Eighteen percent of the dwell-ings are eighty or more years old, and sixty percent are forty or more years old. Indicative of the dilapidated character of many buildings is the recent sale of a 20-room apartment building for only $500. It is not surprising then to learn that the area has declined in population from 21,111 in 1930 to 17,598 in 1940. To look for spatially referable sentiments here would seem futile. And yet, examination of certain emigration differentials in the North End reveals a congruence between Italian social structure and locational processes. To get at these differentials recourse was had to the estimation of emigration, by age groups and by nativity, through the use of life tables. The procedure consists of comparing the actual 1940 population with the residue of the 1930 popula-tion which probably survived to 1940 according to survival rates for Massachusetts. Whatever deficit the actual 1940 population may show from the estimated 1940 population is a measure of "effective emigration." It is not a measure of the actual volume of emigration, since no calculation is made of immigration *into* the district between 1930 and 1940. Effective emigration simply indi-cates the extent of population decline which is attributable to emigration rather than to death. Computations thus made for emigration differen-tials by nativity show the following: (Table II.)

TABLE II: Effective Emigration from the North End, Boston, 1930 to 1940, by Nativity

NATIVITY	1930 POPULATION	PER CENT OF 1930 POPULATION IN EACH NATIVITY GROUP	EFFECTIVE EMIGRATION 1930-1940	PER CENT OF EMIGRATION ACCOUNTED FOR BY EACH NATIVITY GROUP
American-born (second generation)..	12553	59.46	3399	76.42
Italian-born (first generation)	8557	40.54	1049	23.58
Totals	21110	100.00	4448	100.00

Calculated from: census tract data and survival rates

Thus the second generation, comprising but 59.46 percent of the 1930 population, contributed 76.42 percent of the effective emigration from the North End, whereas the first generation accounted for much less than its "due" share of the emigration. Another calculation shows that where the effective emigration of second generation Italians represents 27.08 percent of their number in 1930, that of the first generation represents only 12.26 percent of their number in 1930.

Equally clear differentials appear in effective emigration by age groups. If we compare the difference between the percentage which each age group as of 1930 contributes to the effective emigration, and the percentage which each age group comprised of the 1930 population, we find that the age groups 15-24 account for much more than their share of effective emigration; the age groups 35-64 account for much less than their share. . . . In brief, the North End is losing its young people to a much greater extent than its older people.

These differentials are in no way startling; what is interesting, however, is their congruence with basic Italian values, which find their fullest institutionalized expression in the North End. Emigration from the district may be viewed as both a cause and a symbol of alienation from these values. At the core of the Italian value system are those sentiments which pertain to the family and the *paesani*. Both of these put a high premium upon maintenance of residence in the North End.

Paesani, or people from the same village of origin, show considerable tendency to live near one another, sometimes occupying much of a single street or court. Such proximity, or at least common residence in the North End, greatly facilitates participation in the *paesani* functions which are so important to the first generation Italian. Moreover, it is in the North End that the *festas*, anniversaries, and other old world occasions are held, and such is their frequency that residence in the district is almost indispensable to regular participation. The social relationships comprised by these groupings, as well as the benefit orders, secret societies, and religious organizations, are thus strongly localistic in character. One second generation Italian, when asked if his immigrant parents ever contemplated leaving their North End tenement replied:

"No, because all their friends are there, their relatives. They know everyone around there."

It is for this reason that the first generation Italian is so much less inclined to leave the North End than the American born Italian.

Equally significant is the localistic character of the Italian family. So great is its solidarity that it is not uncommon to find a tenement entirely occupied by a single extended family: grandparents, matured children with their mates, and grandchildren. There are instances where such a family has overflowed one tenement and has expanded into an adjoining one, breaking out the partitions for doorways. These are ecological expressions, in part, of the expected concern which an Italian mother has for the welfare of her newly married daughter. The ideal pattern is for the daughter to continue living in her mother's house, with she and her husband being assigned certain rooms which they are supposed to furnish themselves. Over the course of time the young couple is expected to accumulate savings and buy their own home, preferably not far away. Preferential renting, by which an Italian who owns a tenement will let apartments to his relatives at a lower rental, is another manifestation of the localizing effects of Italian kinship values.

Departure from the North End generally signifies some degree of repudiation of the community's values. One Italian writes of an emigrant from the North End:

"I still remember with regret the vain smile of superiority that appeared on his face when I told him that I lived at the North End of Boston. 'Io non vado fra quella plebarlia.' (I do not go among those plebeians.)"[7]

As a rule the older Italian is unwilling to make this break, if indeed he could. It is the younger adults, American-born and educated, who are capable of making the transition to another value system with radically different values and goals.

Residence in the North End seems therefore to be a spatial corollary to integration with Italian values. Likewise emigration from the district signifies assimilation into American values, and is so construed by the people themselves. Thus, while the area is not the conscious object of sentimental attachment, as are Beacon Hill and the Common, it has nonetheless become a symbol for Italian ethnic solidarity. By virtue of this symbolic quality the area has a certain retentive power over those residents who most fully share the values which prevail there. . . .

[7] Enrico C. Sartorio, *Social and Religious Life of Italians in America* (Boston: Christopher Publishing House, 1918), pp. 43-44.

Selection *47*

The Local Community

H. Laurence Ross

The importance of maps in the study of ecology was mentioned in the introduction to Firey's article. A map can show much more about an area than can an aerial photograph; a series of maps can show changes through time that are abstract and symbolic as well as structural. It is not surprising to discover that the ecologist must be an amateur cartographer, if not a professional one.

It is easy to make maps of rivers and lakes, canyons and mountain ranges. It is also easy to show political boundaries on maps. But Firey implied that sentiments have a bearing on the significance of land areas. Can such significant areas be bounded on a map? If one wished to try to bound such an area, how would he proceed? To what extent do the people who live in or near a sentimentally significant area agree on the boundaries of the area and on the name of the area? To what extent does living in a named area cause characteristics to be imputed to its residents generally (or, as Ross says, cause statuses to be ascribed)? In the following article, Ross addresses himself to these and similar questions.

Several years ago a professor of sociology at the University of Southern California assigned one of his classes the task of finding the boundaries of Hollywood—which was politically an unbounded section of Los Angeles at that time—by asking people on the street whether or not they were in Hollywood. Consensual and precise boundaries appeared from the very first. Even though people did not seem to be aware of all the boundaries of Hollywood as such, everyone had a very definite idea about whether he was or was not in Hollywood at a given instant.

Ross explores the knowledge that residents of the central part of Boston have of its natural areas or, to use a term that suggests social and cultural differentiation a little more strongly, local communities.

The model of the local community was proposed by Robert E. Park and Ernest W. Burgess as a framework for the description of social structure in American cities. The original model underlies several more recent investigations of urban life. Among the distinctive features of this model are the divisibility of the city into "natural" areas delimited by "natural" boundaries, the recognition of the areas as communities by their inhabitants, and the organization of social life within the areas around distinctive local facilities. This paper reports on a study using survey methods to investigate these aspects of the local community model.

A further concern of the study was the status-ascriptive function suggested for named areas in the work of W. Lloyd Warner.

The research attempted, first, to determine whether named and bounded areas are recognized by a sample of urban residents who were asked to name and bound their own area of residence and to identify other named areas within the city. Second, the status-ascriptive functions were investigated through analysis of free responses to

From the *American Sociological Review*, Vol. 27 (1962), 75-84. Reprinted by permission of the American Sociological Association.

the stimuli of selected area names. Third, the residents were questioned concerning the location of various common activities that appeared to be relevant to the local community model. The results of this paper both amplify and qualify portions of the original model.

THE LOCAL COMMUNITY MODEL

In the industrial metropolis, depicted . . . as a collection of overstimulated, blasé, and reserved individualists, Robert E. Park and his colleagues noted many regions where social life was intense, informal, and intimate. Prototypical of such regions was the immigrant ghetto, integrated by the institutions of a quasi-folk society and isolated from other parts of the metropolis by language barriers and prejudice. The limits of the immigrant colonies were often marked by physical barriers to travel, such as elevated railway walls and watercourses. Impressed by the fact that the entire urban landscape was divided into small areas by the network of transportation and industry, these early ecologists put forward a model in which the interstices of this network, termed "natural areas," contained the units of urban social structure, which they called "local communities." Starting with a map of Chicago containing the expected natural boundaries, they began a search for "the correspondence, if any, between this physical formation of the city . . . and the currents of the economic and social life of the city." The latter were determined by the following tests:

(1) Well-recognized historical names and boundaries of local communities and the changes which these have undergone.
(2) Dividing lines that are at present recognized by the residents, as when on one side of the street persons state that they live in one community and persons on the other side of the street state that they live in another community.
(3) Boundaries of areas claimed by local organizations as businessmen's associations, by local newspapers, and by improvement associations, and in caes of dispute checking claims by plotting memberships of these groups.
(4) Plotting membership or attendance or patronage of local community institutions or enterprises and noting the effect of barriers like parks and railroad lines.
(5) Plotting the distributions and the movements of cultural groups like immigrant colonies and noting the effect of these barriers.[1]

According to Burgess, the model was appropriate to Chicago. On the other hand, simultaneously with this effort to demonstrate that the metropolis is made up of community areas segregated by natural boundaries, students following Park's research suggestions were noting certain limitations of the model, especially in some central city areas. Among these was Zorbaugh, who, after studying the Near North Side "community" in Chicago, stated:

". . . the older organization of the community, based on family ties and local associations, is being replaced by an organization based upon vocational interests and attitudes. This vocational organization cuts across local areas; defines itself spatially as city-wide; and takes much of a person's life out of the local community."[2]

In American cities of the fifties and sixties, many of the cultural differences that once distinguished among, and isolated, the local communities appear to have diminished. The large immigrant ghettoes of the early twentieth century have declined in size and have been reduced in variety and number, and the association "based on vocational interests and attitudes" appears increasingly prevalent. The question arises: can one identify today entities analogous to the local community as described by Park and his colleagues? Furthermore, if such entities are found, what functions do they serve in modern urban life? . . .

RECOGNITION OF NAMED AREAS

With rare exceptions, surveys concerned with the identification of a local community, in terms of respondents' naming and bounding an area in which their residences are located, have been unsuccessful. . . .

The present study was initiated on the assumption that these negative findings were in large part the result of methodological weaknesses, including the use of the ambiguous term "neighborhood" and the placement of questions concerning the name and boundary of the area at the end of questionnaires concerning "your block" or "the area within five blocks from home." Therefore, the first question asked of respondents in this study was, "What is the name of this part of [the city]?" There followed a request to state the boundaries of the area so named. The hypothesis

[1] Ernest W. Burgess, "Basic Social Data," in T. V. Smith and Leonard D. White, eds., *Chicago: An Experiment in Social Science Research* (Chicago: University of Chicago Press, 1929), pp. 47-66; see particularly p. 58.
[2] Harvey Zorbaugh, *The Gold Coast and the Slum* (Chicago: University of Chicago Press, 1929), p. 241.

to be tested was that residents agree on the name and boundaries of the area in which they live, and it was arbitrarily decided in advance that the criterion of "agreement" would be a simple majority.

A census tract in central Boston was chosen for study. The choice was made in order to depart as much as possible from the ghetto prototype of the local community. The tract in question was an apartment house area. It contained population of mixed class and ethnic background. Because of a large proportion of young, unmarried people, the area had a very high mobility rate. Two hundred fifty respondents, representing 87 per cent of a random sample of households, participated in the study.

Tables 1 and 2, presenting the distributions of names and boundaries given in answer to the above questions, show that there was a great deal more agreement in this study than in previous . . . studies that the respondents lived in a certain named and bounded area of the city. Majority agreement was found on a name for the area and on three of four boundaries. Moreover, the boundaries were those predicted in advance from natural area considerations. To the north, the boundary was a heavily traveled street, and to the south and west the boundaries were parks, major streets, and a river.

The presence of a second name for the area, on which a minority agreed, was not expected. It was noted that the boundaries given by respondents terming the area "the West End" tended to include territory lying farther north than the region defined by respondents using the name "Beacon Hill," and the hypothesis was advanced that the respondents might be living in a border region between two more clearly defined areas. In order to test this hypothesis, two small samples of people in tracts adjacent to the study area were asked the same questions. To the north, 24 respondents agreed unanimously that they lived in the West End. To the south, 22 of 23 agreed

that they lived in Beacon Hill. Thus, the border region nature of the study area appears to explain the bi-modal distribution of names among the original sample. . . .

In summary, it can be said that residents of the area studied regard themselves as living in a named area of the city, and agree on the boundaries of their area in all but one direction. The criterion of majority agreement was satisfied despite the fact that the study happened to be conducted in a border region formed by the intersection of two clearly defined named areas. Furthermore, residents of this region can correctly identify several other named areas within the city. These results were achieved in spite of the fact that many residents were new to the city, and that the census tract studied was highly urbanized, being central to the city and heterogeneous in population.

FUNCTIONS OF THE NAMED AREA IN ASCRIBING STATUS

Some sociologists, not primarily concerned with the study of local communities, have found the concept of named urban areas to be useful in other respects. One important use that has been made of area names is in ascertaining the social class of an individual. Warner's instructions for scoring the Index of Status Characteristics are illustrative:

"By previous knowledge or interview, establish the major social areas and their relative ranking . . . make a map of the areas and indicate the value of each area by putting its rating after its name on the map. Sub-areas of higher and lower ranking should be delineated and ranked. People living in the area know the differences."[3]

While these instructions, quoted in their entirety, are not very precise, Warner seems to be proposing the interview as a method for determining the named areas and finding out the degree of prestige associated with each area name. This technique would presumably be increasingly useful in large cities, where ratings that depend on intimate knowledge of individuals (for instance, Evaluated Participation) are less feasible.

Others have suggested that what is useful to the sociologist is also useful to the average man. Shevky and Williams write:

"In urban-industrial society, the unfailing indicators of the social position of others readily accessible to everyone are houses and areas of

TABLE 1:   Distribution of Names Ascribed to the "Part of Town" by Respondents in the Study Area

NAME	PER CENT USING NAME
Beacon Hill	68%
Modified form of Beacon Hill[a]	6
West End	23
Other name	2
D. K.	1
Total	100% (250)

[a] e.g., *"the Back Side of Beacon Hill," "Bohemian Hill,"* etc.

[3] W. Lloyd Warner *et al.*, *Social Class in America* (Chicago: Science Research Associates, 1949), p. 238.

TABLE 2: Distribution of Boundaries Ascribed to the "Part of Town" by Respondents in the Study Area

NORTHERN BOUNDARY		SOUTHERN BOUNDARY		EASTERN BOUNDARY		WESTERN BOUNDARY	
STREET	PER CENT	STREET	PER CENT	STREET	PER CENT	STREET	PER CENT
Cambridge	80%	Beacon[a] or Boston Common	81%	Joy	12%	Charles St., Charles River and Embankment[c]	87%
		Myrtle or Pinckney	5	State House and streets bordering Scollay and Tremont[b]	43		
					21		
Other	9	Other	3	Other	9	Other	5
D.K., vague	11	D.K., vague	11	D.K., vague	15	D.K., vague	8
Total	100% (250)	Total	100% (250)	Total	100% (250)	Total	100% (250)

[a] Combined because Beacon Street forms the near border of the Boston Common.
[b] Combined because Tremont Street begins at and forms an extension of Scollay Square.
[c] Combined because the Embankment is a park that follows the Charles River, and Charles Street parallels and borders the Embankment in the immediate vicinity of the census tract studied.

TABLE 3: Indices for 1950 of Class and Ethnicity for Five Named Areas in Boston

INDEX	NORTH END[a]	BACK BAY[b]	SOUTH END[c]	BEACON HILL[d]	WEST END[e]
Percentage professionals, proprietors, managers, and officials in the labor force	8.0%	39.0%	9.7%	34.0%	13.8%
Percentage laborers and operatives in the labor force	46.2	3.7	27.5	6.4	31.3
Percentage of population foreign born	18.9	14.0	11.6	15.5	26.3
Percentage of population non-white	0.0	0.6	22.2	0.9	1.1

[a] Tracts F-2, F-4, and F-5.
[b] Tracts K-3 and K-5.
[c] Tracts I-1, I-2, I-3, I-4, L-1, L-4, and L-5.
[d] Tracts K-1 and K-2.
[e] Tract H-1.
Source: United States Census of Population: 1950. Vol. III, Census Tract Statistics. *Chapter 6.*

TABLE 4: How Respondents Characterize Three Named Areas in Terms of Status

COMMUNITY	WHITE COLLAR	BLUE COLLAR	BOTH	TOTAL	NO MENTION	GRAND TOTAL	N
North End	1%	14%	1%	16%	84%	100%	166
Back Bay	33	4	3	40	60	100	199
South End	1	45	1	47	53	100	142

residence. As every occupation is evaluated and generally accorded honor and esteem on a scale of prestige in society, so every residential section has a status value which is readily recognized by everyone in the city."[4]

Consideration of such names as Chinatown, Little Italy, Kilgubbin and Harlem suggests that

[4] Eshref Shevky and Marilyn Williams, *The Social Areas of Los Angeles* (Berkeley, Calif.: University of California Press, 1949), pp. 61-62.

TABLE 5:   How Respondents Characterize Three Named Areas in Terms of Ethnicity

	PERCENTAGE OF THOSE DEMONSTRATING KNOWLEDGE OF THE AREA WHO MENTION ETHNICITY						
COMMUNITY	NEGROES	ITALIANS	OTHER ETHNIC	TOTAL	NO MENTION	GRAND TOTAL	N
North End	a	67%	1%	68%	32%	100%	166
Back Bay	a	a	4	4	96	100	199
South End	37%	a	7	44	56	100	142

a *Not coded separately.*

ethnic connotations as well as status connotations are conveyed by the names of areas. A possible conclusion from these considerations is that area names play an important role in identifying the status and ethnicity of individuals, in a manner resembling that of occupational title for social class and family name for ethnicity. If area names are to perform this function in large cities, the names must be well-known, and the connotations they bear concerning class and ethnicity must be appropriate to the population of the areas. The diffusion of knowledge of area names in different parts of the metropolis was suggested in the previous section of this paper. Evidence concerning the appropriateness or accuracy of the connotations evoked by names of urban areas will be presented in the following paragraphs.

. . . Indices of social class and ethnic composition for the areas are presented in Table 3. Residents of the studied tract were asked to give a description of the three distant areas. Respondents denying knowledge of an area or citing a street not within the wider boundaries . . . were not counted in the following tabulations. The descriptions, coded for mentions of class and ethnicity, were compared with the demographic indices for each area. Among the three areas, it was expected that the Back Bay would be described as white-collar, in contrast to the other areas; that the South End would be seen as Negro; and that the North End would be seen as Italian, since 96 per cent of its foreign-born were from Italy. Tables 4 and 5 support these expectations. Given the very open nature of the question, the absolute number of class and ethnic symbols mentioned is evidence that these associations are among the first to be made to the stimulus of an area name.

A similar pattern appears in Table 6, in which respondents thinking of themselves as living in Beacon Hill are compared with those thinking of themselves as living in the West End. In this tabulation, direct questions were asked of the respondents about the class and national origin of the people in the area named, so the propor-

tions mentioning class and ethnic composition cannot be taken as an index of the salience of these characteristics. The respondents speaking of Beacon Hill thought of it as an upper- and middle-class area of North European Protestant stock. Those speaking of the West End thought of it as a working- and lower-class area of ethnic stock. These characterizations are supported, for the cores of these areas, by the census statistics presented in Table 3.

The preceding paragraphs have shown that accurate characterizations of class and ethnicity of the residents are among the salient connotations of area names. It follows that these names are available for use in social interaction between non-intimates in defining their respective statuses. . . . This study is not able to supply proof that these names are actually used for this purpose, but one of the tabulations made suggests that people act as if this were so. The study took place in a border region between two named areas with different status connotations, and residents

TABLE 6:   Differences in Characteristics Attributed to the Area Among Respondents Identifying with Beacon Hill and West End

CLASS DESIGNA-TION OF AREA	RESPONDENTS SPEAKING OF BEACON HILL	RESPONDENTS SPEAKING OF WEST END
Upper or middle	70%	31%
Working or lower	27	66
Both, or D.K.	3	3
Total	100% (169)	100% (58)
ETHNIC DESIGNA-TION OF AREA		
North European Protestant a	54%	7%
Ethnic b	24	81
Both, or D.K.	22	12
Total	100% (169)	100% (58)

a *Old Yankee, English, Scottish, German, Dutch, Scandinavian origin.*
b *All other countries of origin.*

of the region had a choice between the names of Beacon Hill and the West End. If people are socially typed by the name of their area of residence, those with a choice may be expected to choose the name with status connotations corresponding most closely to their own self-conceptions. Thus, in the present case, people conceiving of themselves as upper- and middle-class should tend to choose Beacon Hill as the name of their residence area, whereas people conceiving of themselves as working- and lower-class should choose the West End, allowing a margin of error for working-class people who would like to "rise" to Beacon Hill and for middle-class people who do not accept the stereotype of the West End as working-class.

The results of the survey support the predictions. Among the respondents describing themselves as upper- and middle-class, 81 per cent "chose" Beacon Hill as their area of residence, compared with 58 per cent of the respondents thinking of themselves as working- and lower-class. A similar situation exists with respect to national origin. Among the North European Protestants, 76 per cent "chose" Beacon Hill, as against 65 per cent of the ethnics. Proximity to the cores of the respective areas was found to be associated with this decision, but cartographic analysis revealed that proximity operated independently, and that at any distance from the cores of the communities, working- and lower-class individuals were more likely to "choose" the working- and lower-class West End label for their area of residence.

THE NAMED AREA AS A COMMUNITY

. . . [T]he proposal that the local community is organized around distinctive facilities must be strongly qualified. The nature of the qualification can be illustrated by considering the kinds of facilities that are locally used. While only food shopping and church attendance are modally local in these studies, the distribution of retail outlets in the city suggests that drugs, some kinds of banking, purchasing at variety stores, and other similar activities, are also typically local. This type of activity can be characterized as convenience shopping, involving goods which are used in small quantities and purchased fairly often, in which price differentials are not very important, and which are relatively highly standardized. It is, in other words, precisely in those lines in which goods are *not* strongly differentiated that local shopping is done. Goods and corresponding outlets that are distinctive appear to require a larger market than that supplied by a typical named area.

These data indicate that the local facilities usage of the modal urbanite, in the areas studied in this project and in Foley's previous work, tends to be confined to convenience goods. However, it should be kept in mind that local facilities usage in almost all categories appears greater than a chance model would predict, especially considering the absence of opportunities in the area. . . .

The research reported here supports the proposition, contained in the local community model of the metropolis, that the city is perceived by its residents as containing named areas, bounded by such barriers to travel as parks, rivers, and large streets. On the background of many studies yielding negative evidence, this study succeeded, using a new method that avoided the ambiguity of the term "neighborhood" and presented definitional questions at the beginning of the questionnaire.

The names of areas apart from the one of residence were found to be well-diffused in this study. Furthermore, these names were shown to have class and ethnic connotations that were in harmony with indices derived from the census. This evidence can be interpreted as support for the proposition that one function of named areas is the attribution of class and ethnic positions in the secondary social relations typical of the city.

An investigation of the proposition that residents of a named area use distinctive local facilities yielded generally negative results. Little use was made of local facilities except in items commonly termed convenience items, which are similar from area to area.

These results, based on a sample of households in one census tract in Boston, are statistically generalizable only to the census tract sampled. However, there is evidence to indicate that the results are not entirely due to peculiar local conditions in Boston and in the study area. In pre-tests of the questionnaire used in this study, residents of three Chicago "local communities" as defined by the Chicago Community Inventory— South Shore, Near North Side, and New City— were asked to name and bound their part of Chicago. Agreement on name and boundaries in these areas compared favorably with that found in the Boston case, although residents of New City uniformly used the more pungent name of Back-of-the-Yards in referring to their area of residence. Similar results were found in a secondary analysis by the author of data gathered in outlying areas of Boston by Morton Rubin of Northeastern University. Consciousness of living in a named and bounded area thus does not appear to be confined to residents of high-status and historic areas of an old city. With respect to the other findings in this paper, Warner's use of the Index of Status Characteristics in various cities supports the characterization of named areas as a source of status ascription, and the previously noted similarity between areas in Boston and St. Louis and Rochester supports the generalizability of the results reported for use of facilities.

This study supports the local community conception of the city by demonstrating that named units with "natural" boundaries are recognized by residents of an urban area. It further suggests that named areas have a status-ascriptive function not stressed in the original model. The research qualifies as aspect of the model concerning the usage of local facilities. Other features of the local community model, such as the presence of participation in local organizations and a network of local friendships, were not specifically tested in this study, and await further research.

Selection *48*

Urbanism as a Way of Life

Louis Wirth

For the Census of the United States, urban territory has been defined as: (1) places of 2,500 or more inhabitants incorporated as cities, boroughs, and villages; (2) the densely settled urban fringe, incorporated or unincorporated, around cities of 50,000 or more; (3) unincorporated places of 2,500 or more inhabitants outside of any urban fringe; or (4) incorporated towns of 2,500 or more except in those states in which a "town" is simply a division of a county. By the time one has finished reading such a definition, even in the abbreviated form in which it appears here, he will probably have entertained, at least briefly, two additional ideas: (1) that the line between urban and rural communities is probably not so clearly drawn by him as it is by the census; and (2) that, by his standards, it is probably drawn in the wrong place. He will probably question the inclusion in a directory of urban places such aggregations as the following:

Bad Axe, Michigan (2,998)
Hominy, Oklahoma (2,866)
Painted Post, New York (2,570)
Sedro-Woolley, Washington (3,705)
Truth or Consequences, New Mexico (4,269)
(The compiler of this directory regrets that Helper, Utah, listed in the 1950 Census at 2,850, can no longer be included as its population has declined to 2,459!)

In this article Wirth reviews the usual indexes for distinguishing urban from rural populations: size, density of population, and heterogeneity of population. After relating the findings of sociology to these three indexes, he goes on to develop three more criteria for distinguishing the urban way of life—namely, the physical structure of the city, the attitudinal and behavioral characteristics of its constituents, and its social organization.

This classic article is a bench mark in the study of urban sociology, because Wirth departs from a strictly demographic concept of urbanism and introduces cultural and sentimental aspects of city life as an important part of the definition of urbanism. He develops the concept of the city as an ideal type in a fashion that resembles Redfield's development of the ideal type of the folk society.

THE CITY AND CONTEMPORARY CIVILIZATION

Just as the beginning of Western civilization is marked by the permanent settlement of formerly

"Urbanism as a Way of Life" by Louis Wirth. Reprinted from *The American Journal of Sociology*, Vol. XLIX (1938), 46-63, by permission of The University of Chicago Press.

nomadic peoples in the Mediterranean basin, so the beginning of what is distinctively modern in our civilization is best signalized by the growth of great cities. Nowhere has mankind been farther removed from organic nature than under the conditions of life characteristic of great cities. The contemporary world no longer presents a picture of small isolated groups of human beings scattered over a vast territory. . . . The distinctive feature of the mode of living of man in the modern age is his concentration into gigantic aggregations around which cluster lesser centers and from which radiate the ideas and practices that we call civilization.

The degree to which the contemporary world may be said to be "urban" is not fully or accurately measured by the proportion of the total population living in cities. The influences which cities exert upon the social life of man are greater than the ratio of the urban population would indicate, for the city is not only in ever larger degrees the dwelling-place and the workshop of modern man, but it is the initiating and controlling center of economic, political, and cultural life that has drawn the most remote parts of the world into its orbit and woven diverse areas, peoples, and activities into a cosmos. . . .

[The] shift from a rural to a predominantly urban society, which has taken place within the span of a single generation in such industrialized areas as the United States and Japan, has been accompanied by profound changes in virtually every phase of social life. It is these changes and their ramifications that invite the attention of the sociologist to the study of the differences between the rural and the urban mode of living. The pursuit of this interest is an indispensable prerequisite for the comprehension and possible mastery of some of the most crucial contemporary problems of social life since it is likely to furnish one of the most revealing perspectives for the understanding of the ongoing changes in human nature and the social order.

Since the city is the product of growth rather than of instantaneous creation, it is to be expected that the influences which it exerts upon the modes of life should not be able to wipe out completely the previously dominant modes of human association. To a greater or lesser degree, therefore, our social life bears the imprint of an earlier folk society, the characteristic modes of settlement of which were the farm, the manor, and the village. This historic influence is reinforced by the circumstance that the population of the city itself is in large measure recruited from the countryside, where a mode of life reminiscent of this earlier form of existence persists. Hence we should not

expect to find abrupt and discontinuous variation between urban and rural types of personality. The city and the country may be regarded as two poles in reference to one or the other of which all human settlements tend to arrange themselves. In viewing urban-industrial and rural-folk society as ideal types of communities, we may obtain a perspective for the analysis of the basic models of human association as they appear in contemporary civilization.

A SOCIOLOGICAL DEFINITION OF THE CITY

Despite the preponderant significance of the city in our civilization, however, our knowledge of the nature of urbanism and the process of urbanization is meager. Many attempts have indeed been made to isolate the distinguishing characteristics of urban life. Geographers, historians, economists, and political scientists have incorporated the points of view of their respective disciplines into diverse definitions of the city. While in no sense intended to supersede these, the formulation of a sociological approach to the city may incidentally serve to call attention to the interrelations between them by emphasizing the peculiar characteristics of the city as a particular form of human association. A sociologically significant definition of the city seeks to select those elements of urbanism which mark it as a distinctive mode of human group life.

The characterization of a community as urban on the basis of size alone is obviously arbitrary. It is difficult to defend the present census definition which designates a community of 2,500 and above as urban and all others as rural. The situation would be the same if the criterion were 4,000, 8,000, 10,000, 25,000, or 100,000 population, for although in the latter case we might feel that we were more nearly dealing with an urban aggregate than would be the case in communities of lesser size, no definition of urbanism can hope to be completely satisfying as long as numbers are regarded as the sole criterion. Moreover, it is not difficult to demonstrate that communities of less than the arbitrarily set number of inhabitants lying with the range of influence of metropolitan centers have greater claim to recognition as urban communities than do larger ones leading a more isolated existence in a predominantly rural area. Finally, it should be recognized that census definitions are unduly influenced by the fact that the city, statistically speaking, is always an administrative concept in that the corporate limits play a decisive role in delineating the urban area. Nowhere is this more clearly apparent than in the concentrations of population on the peripheries of great metropolitan centers which cross arbitrary administrative boundaries of city, county, state, and nation.

As long as we identify urbanism with the physical entity of the city, viewing it merely as rigidly delimited in space, and proceed as if urban attributes abruptly ceased to be manifested beyond an arbitrary boundary line, we are not likely to arrive at any adequate conception of urbanism as a mode of life. The technological developments in transportation and communication which virtually mark a new epoch in human history have accentuated the role of cities as dominant elements in our civilization and have enormously extended the urban mode of living beyond the confines of the city itself. The dominance of the city, especially of the great city, may be regarded as a consequence of the concentration in cities of industrial and commercial, financial and administrative facilities and activities, transportation and communication lines, and cultural and recreational equipment such as the press, radio stations, theaters, libraries, museums, concert halls, operas, hospitals, higher educational institutions, research and publishing centers, professional organizations, and religious and welfare institutions. Were it not for the attraction and suggestions that the city exerts through these instrumentalities upon the rural population, the differences between the rural and the urban modes of life would be even greater than they are. Urbanization no longer denotes merely the process by which persons are attracted to a place called the city and incorporated into its system of life. It refers also to that cumulative accentuation of the characteristics distinctive of the mode of life which is associated with the growth of cities, and finally to the changes in the direction of modes of life recognized as urban which are apparent among people, wherever they may be, who have come under the spell of the influences which the city exerts by virtue of the power of its institutions and personalities operating through the means of communication and transportation.

The shortcomings which attach to number of inhabitants as a criterion of urbanism apply for the most part to density of population as well. . . . [I]t is clear that unless density is correlated with significant social characteristics it can furnish only an arbitrary basis for differentiating urban from rural communities. Since our census enumerates the night rather than the day population of an area, the locale of the most intensive urban life—the city center—generally has low population density, and the industrial and commercial areas of the city, which contain the most characteristic

economic activities underlying urban society, would scarcely anywhere be truly urban if density were literally interpreted as a mark of urbanism. Nevertheless, the fact that the urban community is distinguished by a large aggregation and relatively dense concentration of population can scarcely be left out of account in a definition of the city. But these criteria must be seen as relative to the general cultural context in which cities arise and exist and are sociologically relevant only in so far as they operate as conditioning factors in social life.

The same criticisms apply to such criteria as the occupation of the inhabitants, the existence of certain physical facilities, institutions, and forms of political organization. The question is not whether cities in our civilization or in others do exhibit these distinctive traits, but how potent they are in molding the character of social life into its specifically urban form. Nor in formulating a fertile definition can we afford to overlook the great variations between cities. By means of a typology of cities based upon size, location, age, and function, . . . we have found it feasible to array and classify urban communities ranging from struggling small towns to thriving world-metropolitan centers; from isolated trading centers in the midst of agricultural regions to thriving world ports and commercial and industrial conurbations. Such differences as these appear crucial because the social characteristics and influences of these different "cities" vary widely.

A serviceable definition of urbanism should not only denote the essential characteristics which all cities—at least those in our culture—have in common, but should lend itself to the discovery of their variations. An industrial city will differ significantly in social respects from a commercial, mining, fishing, resort, university, and capital city. A one-industry city will present different sets of social characteristics from a multi-industry city, as will an industrially balanced from an imbalanced city, a suburb from a satellite, a residential suburb from an industrial suburb, a city within a metropolitan region from one lying outside, an old city from a new one, a southern city from a New England, a middle-western from a Pacific Coast city, a growing from a stable and from a dying city.

A sociological definition must obviously be inclusive enough to comprise whatever essential characteristics these different types of cities have in common as social entities, but it obviously cannot be so detailed as to take account of all the variations implicit in the manifold classes sketched above. Presumably some of the characteristics of cities are more significant in conditioning the nature of urban life than others, and we may expect the outstanding features of the urban-social scene to vary in accordance with size, density, and differences in the functional type of cities. Moreover, we may infer that rural life will bear the imprint of urbanism in the measure that through contact and communication it comes under the influence of cities. It may contribute to the clarity of the statements that follow to repeat that while the locus of urbanism as a mode of life is, of course, to be found characteristically in places which fulfill the requirements we shall set up as a definition of the city, urbanism is not confined to such localities but is manifest in varying degrees wherever the influences of the city reach.

While urbanism, or that complex of traits which makes up the characteristic mode of life in cities, and urbanization, which denotes the development and extensions of these factors, are thus not exclusively found in settlements which are cities in the physical and demographic sense, they do, nevertheless, find their most pronounced expression in such areas, especially in metropolitan cities. In formulating a definition of the city it is necessary to exercise caution in order to avoid identifying urbanism as a way of life with any specific locally or historically conditioned cultural influences which, while they may significantly affect the specific character of the community, are not the essential determinants of its character as a city.

It is particularly important to call attention to the danger of confusing urbanism with industrialism and modern capitalism. The rise of cities in the modern world is undoubtedly not independent of the emergence of modern power-driven machine technology, mass production, and capitalistic enterprise. But different as the cities of earlier epochs may have been by virtue of their development in a preindustrial and precapitalistic order from the great cities of today, they were, nevertheless, cities.

For sociological purposes a city may be defined as a relatively large, dense, and permanent settlement of socially heterogeneous individuals. On the basis of the postulates which this minimal definition suggests, a theory of urbanism may be formulated in the light of existing knowledge concerning social groups.

A THEORY OF URBANISM

In the rich literature on the city we look in vain for a theory of urbanism presenting in a systematic fashion the available knowledge concerning the city as a social entity. We do indeed have excellent formulations of theories on such special problems as the growth of the city viewed as a historical trend and as a recurrent process, and we have a wealth of literature presenting insights of sociological relevance and empirical studies offering detailed information on a variety of particular aspects of urban life. But despite the multiplication of research and textbooks on the city, we do not as yet have a comprehensive body of compendent hypotheses which may be derived from a set of postulates implicitly contained in a sociological definition of the city, and from our general sociological knowledge which may be substantiated through empirical research. . . .

In the pages that follow we shall seek to set forth a limited number of identifying characteristics of the city. Given these characteristics we shall then indicate what consequences or further characteristics follow from them in the light of general sociological theory and empirical research. We hope in this manner to arrive at the essential propositions comprising a theory of urbanism. Some of these propositions can be supported by a considerable body of already available research materials; others may be accepted as hypotheses for which a certain amount of presumptive evidence exists, but for which more ample and exact verification would be required. At least such a procedure will, it is hoped, show what in the way of systematic knowledge of the city we now have and what are the crucial and fruitful hypotheses for future research.

The central problem of the sociologist of the city is to discover the forms of social action and organization that typically emerge in relatively permanent, compact settlements of large numbers of heterogeneous individuals. We must also infer that urbanism will assume its most characteristic and extreme form in the measure in which the conditions with which it is congruent are present. Thus the larger, the more densely populated, and the more heterogeneous a community, the more accentuated the characteristics associated with urbanism will be. It should be recognized, however, that in the social world institutions and practices may be accepted and continued for reasons other than those that originally brought them into existence, and that accordingly the urban mode of life may be perpetuated under conditions quite foreign to those necessary for its origin.

Some justification may be in order for the choice of the principal terms comprising our definition of the city. The attempt has been made to make it as inclusive and at the same time as denotative as possible without loading it with unnecessary assumptions. To say that large numbers are necessary to constitute a city means, of course, large numbers in relation to a restricted area or high density of settlement. There are, nevertheless, good reasons for treating large numbers and density as separate factors, since each may be connected with significantly different social consequences. Similarly the need for adding heterogeneity to numbers of population as a necessary and distinct criterion of urbanism might be questioned, since we should expect the range of differences to increase with numbers. In defense it may be said that the city shows a kind and degree of heterogeneity of population which cannot be wholly accounted for by the law of large numbers or adequately represented by means of a normal distribution curve. Since the population of the city does not reproduce itself, it must recruit its migrants from other cities, the countryside, and—in this country until recently—from other countries. The city has thus historically been the melting-pot of races, peoples, and cultures, and a most favorable breeding-ground of new biological and cultural hybrids. It has not only tolerated but rewarded individual differences. It has brought together people from the ends of the earth *because* they are different and thus useful to one another, rather than because they are homogeneous and like-minded.

There are a number of sociological propositions concerning the relationship between (a) numbers of population, (b) density of settlement, (c) heterogeneity of inhabitants and group life, which can be formulated on the basis of observation and research.

Size of the population aggregate

Ever since Aristotle's *Politics*, it has been recognized that increasing the number of inhabitants in a settlement beyond a certain limit will affect the relationships between them and the character of the city. Large numbers involve, as has been pointed out, a greater range of individual variation. Furthermore, the greater the number of individuals participating in a process of interaction, the greater is the *potential* differentiation between them. The personal traits, the occupations, the cultural life, and the ideas of the members of an urban community may, therefore, be expected to range between more widely separated poles than those of rural inhabitants.

That such variations should give rise to the spatial segregation of individuals according to color, ethnic heritage, economic and social status, tastes and preferences, may readily be inferred. The bonds of kinship, of neighborliness, and the sentiments arising out of living together for generations under a common folk tradition are likely to be absent or, at best, relatively weak in an aggregate the members of which have such diverse origins and backgrounds. Under such circumstances competition and formal control mechanisms furnish the substitutes for the bonds of solidarity that are relied upon to hold a folk society together.

Increase in the number of inhabitants of a community beyond a few hundred is bound to limit the possibility of each member of the community knowing all the others personally. . . . The multiplication of persons in a state of interaction under conditions which make their contact as full personalities impossible produces that segmentalization of human relationships which has sometimes been seized upon by students of the mental life of the cities as an explanation for the "schizoid" character of urban personality. This is not to say that the urban inhabitants have fewer acquaintances than rural inhabitants, for the reverse may actually be true; it means rather that in relation to the number of people whom they see and with whom they rub elbows in the course of daily life, they know a smaller proportion, and of these they have less intensive knowledge.

Characteristically, urbanites meet one another in highly segmental roles. They are, to be sure, dependent upon more people for the satisfactions of their life-needs than are rural people and thus are associated with a greater number of organized groups, but they are less dependent upon particular persons, and their dependence upon others is confined to a highly fractionalized aspect of the other's round of activity. This is essentially what is meant by saying that the city is characterized by secondary rather than primary contacts. The contacts of the city may indeed be face to face, but they are nevertheless impersonal, superficial, transitory, and segmental. The reserve, the indifference, and the blasé outlook which urbanites manifest in their relationships may thus be regarded as devices for immunizing themselves against the personal claims and expectations of others.

The superficiality, the anonymity, and the transitory character of urban-social relations make intelligible, also, the sophistication and the rationality generally ascribed to city-dwellers. Our acquaintances tend to stand in a relationship of utility to us in the sense that the role which each one plays in our life is overwhelmingly regarded as a means for the achievement of our own ends. Whereas, therefore, the individual gains, on the one hand, a certain degree of emancipation or freedom from the personal and emotional controls of intimate groups, he loses, on the other hand, the spontaneous self-expression, the morale, and the sense of participation that comes with living in an integrated society. This constitutes essentially the state of *anomie* or the social void to which Durkheim alludes in attempting to account for the various forms of social disorganization in technological society.

The segmental character and utilitarian accent of interpersonal relations in the city find their institutional expression in the proliferation of specialized tasks which we see in their most developed form in the professions. The operations of the pecuniary nexus lead to predatory relationships, which tend to obstruct the efficient functioning of the social order unless checked by professional codes and occupational etiquette. The premium put upon utility and efficiency suggests the adaptability of the corporate device for the organization of enterprises in which individuals can engage only in groups. The advantage that the corporation has over the individual entrepreneur and the partnership in the urban-industrial world derives not only from the possibility it affords of centralizing the resources of thousands of individuals or from the legal privilege of limited liability and perpetual succession, but from the fact that the corporation has no soul.

The specialization of individuals, particularly in their occupations, can proceed only, as Adam Smith pointed out, upon the basis of an enlarged market, which in turn accentuates the division of labor. This enlarged market is only in part supplied by the city's hinterland; in large measure it is found among the large numbers that the city itself contains. The dominance of the city over the surrounding hinterland becomes explicable in terms of the division of labor which urban life occasions and promotes. The extreme degree of interdependence and the unstable equilibrium of urban life are closely associated with the division of labor and the specialization of occupations. This interdependence and instability is increased by the tendency of each city to specialize in those functions in which it has the greatest advantage.

In a community composed of a larger number of individuals than can know one another intimately and can be assembled in one spot, it becomes necessary to communicate through indirect media and to articulate individual interests by a process of delegation. Typically in the city, interests are made effective through representation. The individual counts for little, but the voice of the representative is heard with a deference roughly proportional to the numbers for whom he speaks.

While this characterization of urbanism, in so far as it derives from large numbers, does not by any means exhaust the sociological inferences that might be drawn from our knowledge of the relationship of the size of a group to the characteristic behavior of the members, for the sake of brevity the assertions made may serve to exemplify the sort of propositions that might be developed.

Density

As in the case of numbers, so in the case of concentration in limited space, certain consequences of relevance in sociological analysis of the city emerge. Of these only a few can be indicated.

As Darwin pointed out for flora and fauna and as Durkheim noted in the case of human societies, an increase in numbers when area is held constant (i.e., an increase in density) tends to produce differentiation and specialization, since only in this way can the area support increased numbers. Density thus reinforces the effect of numbers in diversifying men and their activities and in increasing the complexity of the social structure.

On the subjective side, . . . the close physical contact of numerous individuals necessarily produces a shift in the mediums through which we orient ourselves to the urban milieu, especially to our fellow-men. Typically, our physical contacts are close but our social contacts are distant. The urban world puts a premium on visual recognition. We see the uniform which denotes the role of the functionaries and are oblivious to the personal eccentricities that are hidden behind the uniform. We tend to acquire and develop a sensitivity to a world of artifacts and become progressively farther removed from the world of nature.

We are exposed to glaring contrasts between splendor and squalor, between riches and poverty, intelligence and ignorance, order and chaos. The competition for space is great, so that each area generally tends to be put to the use which yields the greatest economic return. Place of work tends to become dissociated from place of residence, for the proximity of industrial and commercial establishments makes an area both economically and socially undesirable for residential purposes.

Density, land values, rentals, accessibility, healthfulness, prestige, aesthetic consideration, absence of nuisances such as noise, smoke, and dirt determine the desirability of various areas of the city as places of settlement for different sections of the population. Place and nature of work, income, racial and ethnic characteristics, social status, custom, habit, taste, preference, and prejudice are among the significant factors in accordance with which the urban population is selected and distributed into more or less distinct settlements. Diverse population elements inhabiting a compact settlement thus tend to become segregated from one another in the degree in which their requirements and modes of life are incompatible with one another and in the measure in which they are antagonistic to one another. Similarly, persons of homogeneous status and needs unwittingly drift into, consciously select, or are forced by circumstances into, the same area. The different parts of the city thus acquire specialized functions. The city consequently tends to resemble a mosaic of social worlds in which the transition from one to the other is abrupt. The juxtaposition of divergent personalities and modes of life tends to produce a relativistic perspective and a sense of toleration of difference which may be regarded as prerequisites for rationality and which lead toward the secularization of life.

The close living together and working together of individuals who have no sentimental and emotional ties foster a spirit of competition, aggrandizement, and mutual exploitation. To counteract irresponsibility and potential disorder, formal controls tend to be resorted to. Without rigid adherence to predictable routines a large compact society would scarcely be able to maintain itself. The clock and the traffic signal are symbolic of the basis of our social order in the urban world. Frequent close physical contact, coupled with great social distance, accentuates the reserve of unattached individuals toward one another and, unless compensated for by other opportunities for response, gives rise to loneliness. The necessary frequent movement of great numbers of individuals in a congested habitat gives occasion to friction and irritation. Nervous tensions which derive from such personal frustrations are accentuated by the rapid tempo and the complicated technology under which life in dense areas must be lived.

Heterogeneity

The social interaction among such a variety of personality types in the urban milieu tends to break down the rigidity of caste lines and to complicate the class structure, and thus induces a more ramified and differentiated framework of social stratification than is found in more integrated societies. The heightened mobility of the individual, which brings him within the range of stimulation by a great number of diverse individuals and subjects him to fluctuating status in the differentiated social groups that compose the social structure of the city, tends toward the acceptance of instability and insecurity in the world at large as a norm. This fact helps to account, too, for the sophistication and cosmopolitanism of the urbanite. No single group has the undivided allegiance of the individual. The groups with which he is affiliated do not lend themselves readily to a simple hierarchical arrangement. By virtue of his different interests arising out of different aspects of social life, the individual acquires membership in widely divergent groups, each of which functions only with reference to a single segment of his personality. Nor do these groups easily permit of a concentric arrangement so that the narrower ones fall within the circumference of the more inclusive ones, as is more likely to be the case in the rural community or in primitive societies. Rather the groups with which the person typically is affiliated are tangential to each other or intersect in highly variable fashion.

Partly as a result of the physical footlooseness of the population and partly as a result of their social mobility, the turnover in group membership generally is rapid. Place of residence, place and character of employment, income and interests fluctuate, and the task of holding organizations together and maintaining and promoting intimate and lasting acquaintanceship between the members is difficult. This applies strikingly to the local areas within the city into which persons become segregated more by virtue of differences in race, language, income, and social status, than through choice or positive attraction to people like themselves. Overwhelmingly the city-dweller is not a home-owner, and since a transitory habitat does not generate binding traditions and sentiments, only rarely is he truly a neighbor. There is little opportunity for the individual to obtain a conception of the city as a whole or to survey his place in the total scheme. Consequently he finds it difficult to determine what is to his own "best interests" and to decide between the issues and leaders presented to him by the agencies of mass suggestion. Individuals who are thus detached from the organized bodies which integrate society comprise the fluid masses that make collective behavior in the urban community so unpredictable and hence so problematical.

Although the city, through the recruitment of variant types to perform its diverse tasks and the accentuation of their uniqueness through competition and the premium upon eccentricity, novelty, efficient performance, and inventiveness, produces a highly differentiated population, it also exercises a leveling influence. Wherever large numbers of differently constituted individuals congregate, the process of depersonalization also enters. This leveling tendency inheres in part in the economic basis of the city. The development of large cities, at least in the modern age, was largely dependent upon the concentrative force of steam. The rise of the factory made possible mass production for an impersonal market. The fullest exploitation of the possibilities of the division of labor and mass production, however, is possible only with standardization of processes and products. A money economy goes hand in hand with such a system of production. Progressively as cities have developed upon a background of this system of production, the pecuniary nexus which implies the purchasability of services and things has displaced personal relations as the basis of association. Individuality under these circumstances must be replaced by categories. When large numbers have to make common use of facilities and institutions, an arrangement must be made to adjust the facilities and institutions to the needs of the average person rather than to those of particular individuals. The services of the public utilities, of the recreational, educational, and cultural institutions must be adjusted to mass requirements. Similarly, the cultural institutions, such as the schools, the movies, the radio, and the newspapers, by virtue of their mass clientele, must necessarily operate as leveling influences. The political process as it appears in urban life could not be understood without taking account of the mass appeals made through modern propaganda techniques. If the individual would participate at all in the social, political, and economic life of the city, he must subordinate some of his individuality to the demands of the larger community and in that measure immerse himself in mass movements.

THE RELATION BETWEEN A THEORY OF URBANISM AND SOCIOLOGICAL RESEARCH

By means of a body of theory such as that illustratively sketched above, the complicated and many-sided phenomena of urbanism may be analyzed in terms of a limited number of basic categories. The sociological approach to the city thus acquires an essential unity and coherence enabling the empirical investigator not merely to focus more distinctly upon the problems and processes that properly fall in his province but also to treat his subject matter in a more integrated and systematic fashion. A few typical findings of empirical research in the field of urbanism, with special reference to the United States, may be indicated to substantiate the theoretical proposition set forth in the preceding pages, and some of the crucial problems for further study may be outlined.

On the basis of the three variables, number, density of settlement, and degree of heterogeneity, of the urban population, it appears possible to explain the characteristics of urban life and to account for the differences between cities of various sizes and types.

Urbanism as a characteristic mode of life may be approached empirically from three interrelated perspectives: (1) as a physical structure comprising a population base, a technology, and an ecological order; (2) as a system of social organization involving a characteristic social structure, a series of social institutions, and a typical pattern of social relationships; and (3) as a set of attitudes and ideas, and a constellation of personalities engaging in typical forms of collective behavior and subject to characteristic mechanisms of social control.

Urbanism in ecological perspective

Since in the case of physical structure and ecological processes we are able to operate with fairly objective indices, it becomes possible to arrive at quite precise and generally quantitative results. The dominance of the city over its hinterland becomes explicable through the functional characteristics of the city which derive in large measure from the effect of numbers and density. Many of the technical facilities and the skills and organizations to which urban life gives rise can grow and prosper only in cities where the demand is sufficiently great. The nature and scope of the services rendered by these organizations and institutions and the advantage which they enjoy over the less developed facilities of smaller towns enhances the dominance of the city and the dependence of ever wider regions upon the central metropolis.

The urban-population composition shows the operation of selective and differentiating factors. Cities contain a larger proportion of persons in the prime of life than rural areas which contain more old and very young people. In this, as in so many other respects, the larger the city the more this specific characteristic of urbanism is apparent. With the exception of the largest cities, which have attracted the bulk of the foreign-born males, and a few other special types of cities, women predominate numerically over men. The heterogeneity of the urban population is further indicated along racial and ethnic lines. The foreign born and their children constitute nearly two-thirds of all the inhabitants of cities of one million and over. Their proportion in the urban population declines as the size of the city decreases, until in the rural areas they comprise only about one-sixth of the total population. The larger cities similarly have attracted more Negroes and other racial groups than have the smaller communities. Considering that age, sex, race, and ethnic origin are associated with other factors such as occupation and interest, it becomes clear that one major characteristic of the urban-dweller is his dissimilarity from his fellows. Never before have such large masses of people of diverse traits as we find in our cities been thrown together into such close physical contact as in the great cities of America. Cities generally, and American cities in particular, comprise a motley of peoples and cultures, of highly differentiated modes of life between which there often is only the faintest communication, the greatest indifference and the broadest tolerance, occasionally bitter strife, but always the sharpest contrast.

The failure of the urban population to reproduce itself appears to be a biological consequence of a combination of factors in the complex of urban life, and the decline in the birth-rate generally may be regarded as one of the most significant signs of the urbanization of the Western world. While the proportion of deaths in cities is slightly greater than in the country, the outstanding difference between the failure of present-day cities to maintain their population and that of cities of the past is that in former times it was due to the exceedingly high death-rates in cities, whereas today, since cities have become more livable from a health standpoint, it is due to low birth-rates. These biological characteristics of the urban population are significant sociologically, not merely because they reflect the urban mode of existence but also because they condition the growth and future dominance of cities and their basic social organization. Since cities are the consumers rather than the producers of men, the value of human life and the social estimation of the personality will not be unaffected by the balance between births and deaths. The pattern of land use, of land values, rentals, and ownership, the nature and functioning of the physical structures, of housing, of transportation and communication facilities, of public utilities—these and many other phases of the physical mechanism of the city are not isolated phenomena unrelated to the city as a social entity, but are affected by and affect the urban mode of life.

Urbanism as a form of social organization

The distinctive features of the urban mode of life have often been described sociologically as consisting of the substitution of secondary for primary contacts, the weakening of bonds of kinship, and the declining social significance of the family, the disappearance of the neighborhood, and the undermining of the traditional basis of social solidarity. All these phenomena can be substantially verified through objective indices. Thus, for instance, the low and declining urban-reproduction rates suggest that the city is not conducive to the traditional type of family life, including the rearing of children and the maintenance of the home as the locus of a whole round of vital activities. The transfer of industrial, educational, and recreational activities to specialized institutions outside the home has deprived the family of some of its most characteristic historical functions. In cities mothers are more likely to be employed, lodgers are more frequently part of the household, marriage tends to be postponed, and the proportion of single and unattached people is greater. Families are smaller and more frequently without children than in the country. The family as a unit of social life is emancipated from the larger kinship group characteristic of the country, and the individual members pursue their own diverging interests in their vocational, educational, religious, recreational, and political life.

Such functions as the maintenance of health, the methods of alleviating the hardships associated with personal and social insecurity, the provisions for education, recreation, and cultural advancement have given rise to highly specialized institutions on a community-wide, state-wide, or even national basis. The same factors which have brought about greater personal insecurity also underlie the wider contrasts between individuals to be found in the urban world. While the city has broken down the rigid caste lines of pre-industrial society, it has sharpened and differentiated income and status groups. Generally, a larger proportion of the adult-urban population is gainfully employed than is the case with the adult-rural population. The white-collar class comprising those employed in trade, in clerical, and in professional work, are proportionately more numerous in large cities and in metropolitan centers and in smaller towns than in the country.

On the whole, the city discourages an economic life in which the individual in time of crisis has a basis of subsistence to fall back upon, and it discourages self-employment. While incomes of city people are on the average higher than those of country people, the cost of living seems to be higher in the larger cities. Home ownership involves greater burdens and is rarer. Rents are higher and absorb a larger proportion of the income. Although the urban-dweller has the benefit of many communal services, he spends a large proportion of his income for such items as recreation and advancement and a smaller proportion for food. What the communal services do not furnish the urbanite must purchase, and there is virtually no human need which has remained unexploited by commercialism. Catering to thrills and furnishing means of escape from drudgery, monotony, and routine thus become one of the major functions of urban recreation, which at its best furnishes means for creative self-expression and spontaneous group association, but which more typically in the urban world results in passive spectatorism on the one hand, or sensational record-smashing feats on the other.

Being reduced to a stage of virtual impotence as an individual, the urbanite is bound to exert himself by joining with others of similar interest into organized groups to obtain his ends. This results in the enormous multiplication of voluntary organizations directed toward as great a variety of objectives as there are human needs and interests. While on the one hand the traditional ties of human association are weakened, urban existence involves a much greater degree of interdependence between man and man and a more complicated, fragile, and volatile form of mutual interrelations over many phases of which the individual as such can exert scarcely any control. Frequently there is only the most tenuous relationship between the economic position of other basic factors that determine the individual's existence in the urban world and the voluntary groups with which he is affiliated. While in a primitive and in a rural society it is generally possible to predict on the basis of a few known factors who will belong to what and who will associate with which in almost every relationship of life, in the city we can only project the general pattern of group formation and affiliation, and this pattern will display many incongruities and contradictions.

Urban personality and collective behavior

It is largely through the activities of the voluntary groups, be their objectives economic, political, educational, religious, recreational, or cultural, that the urbanite expresses and develops his personality, acquires status, and is able to carry on the round of activities that constitute his life-career. It may easily be inferred, however, that the organizational framework which these highly differentiated functions call into being does not of itself insure the consistency and integrity of the personalities whose interests it enlists. Personal disorganization, mental breakdown, suicide, delinquency, crime, corruption, and disorder might be expected under these circumstances to be more prevalent in the urban than in the rural community. This has been confirmed in so far as comparable indices are available; but the mechanisms underlying these phenomena require further analysis.

Since for most group purposes it is impossible in the city to appeal individually to the large number of discrete and differentiated individuals, and since it is only through the organizations to which men belong that their interests and resources can be enlisted for a collective cause, it may be inferred that social control in the city should typically proceed through formally organized groups. It follows, too, that the masses of men in the city are subject to manipulation by symbols and stereotypes managed by individuals working from afar or operating invisibly behind the scenes through their control of the instruments of communication. Self-government either in the economic, the political, or the cultural realm is under these circumstances reduced to a mere figure of speech, or, at best, is subject to the unstable equilibrium of pressure groups. In view of the ineffectiveness of actual kinship ties we create fictional kinship groups. In the face of the disappearance of the territorial unit as a basis of social solidarity we create interest units. Meanwhile the city as a community resolves itself into a series of tenuous segmental relationships superimposed upon a territorial base with a definite center but without a definite periphery and upon a division of labor which far transcends the immediate locality and is worldwide in scope. The larger the number of persons in a state of interaction with one another the lower is the level of communication and the greater is the tendency for communication to proceed on an elementary level, i.e., on the basis of those things which are assumed to be common or to be of interest to all.

It is obviously, therefore, to the emerging trends in the communication system and to the production and distribution technology that has come into existence with modern civilization that we must look for the symptoms which will indicate the probable future development of urbanism as a mode of social life. The direction of the ongoing changes in urbanism will for good or ill transform not only the city but the world. Some of the more basic of these factors and processes and the possibilities of their direction and control invite further detailed study.

It is only in so far as the sociologist has a clear conception of the city as a social entity and a workable theory of urbanism that he can hope to develop a unified body of reliable knowledge, which what passes as "urban sociology" is certainly not at the present time. By taking this point of departure from a theory of urbanism such as that sketched in the foregoing pages to be elaborated, tested, and revised in the light of further analysis and empirical research, it is to be hoped that the criteria of relevance and validity of factual data can be determined. The miscellaneous assortment of disconnected information which has hitherto found its way into sociological treatises on the city may thus be sifted and incorporated into a coherent body of knowledge. Incidentally, only by means of some such theory will the sociologist escape the futile practice of voicing in the name of sociological science a variety of often unsupportable judgments concerning such problems as poverty, housing, city-planning, sanitation, municipal administration, policing, marketing, transportation, and other technical issues. While the sociologist cannot solve any of these practical problems—at least not by himself—he may, if he discovers his proper function, have an important contribution to make to their comprehension and solution. The prospects for doing this are brightest through a general, theoretical, rather than through an *ad hoc* approach.

Selection 49

The Preindustrial City

Gideon Sjoberg

The concept of *ideal types* was discussed in the introduction to Redfield's article, "The Folk Society." It refers to the construction of a word-model describing the epitome of some class or kind of phenomenon. Actual cases often vary from the ideal type, and in fact no perfect example may ever be found. If the reader is not familiar with ideal types, he should read pages 320-321 in order to assure an understanding of Sjoberg's purpose in the following article, which describes the preindustrial city as an ideal type.

In the preceding selection, Wirth suggested a continuum of community types, with the pole at one end being the rural-folk ideal type and the pole at the other end being the urban-industrial type. In "The Preindustrial City" Sjoberg defines as a distinct type a city that does not fit into either of Wirth's polar categories. Some cities can be placed in each of the three categories at some point in their histories, although so placing them usually involves the assumption that a folk village preceded the preindustrial city. For example, the preindustrial city of Rome was probably created when The Etruscans captured a few folk hamlets on the Palatine Hill and subjected them to a uniform political rule. (The exact nature of the occurrence is not known; probably no record of it was made at the time.) Today, Rome is patently an industrial city. Not every city has such a history; many cities in the New World were never preindustrial, let alone folk-rural.

Many characteristics of the preindustrial city are unique; they do not appear in either the folk society or the industrial city. It is possible that the preindustrial city does not belong on the continuum suggested by Wirth but is a distinct polar type in itself.

Although folk elements may exist in neighborhoods of both preindustrial and industrial cities, both of the latter are too large and too heterogeneous to have either the uniformity of values and mores or the personal involvement in community activities to which Redfield referred. Also, the feudal city that developed from the growth of permanent settlements prior to the industrial revolution can hardly be classed with the modern metropolis—such as New York, Los Angeles, or Chicago—as an ideal type. Although preindustrial cities are decreasing in number, many of them can be found today in underdeveloped countries. The way of life and the sentiments of the people in such cities appear to have much more in common with the cities of medieval Europe than with the industrial metropolises of the present day. Hence *preindustrial* refers to a type rather than to a period in history.

In the past few decades social scientists have been conducting field studies in a number of relatively non-Westernized cities. Their recently acquired knowledge of North Africa and various parts of Asia, combined with what was already learned, clearly indicates that these cities are not like typical cities of the United States and other highly industrialized areas but are much more like those of medieval Europe. Such communities are termed herein "preindustrial," for they have arisen without stimulus from that form of production which we associate with the European industrial revolution. . . .

ECOLOGICAL ORGANIZATION

Preindustrial cities depend for their existence upon food and raw materials obtained from without; for this reason they are marketing centers. And they serve as centers for handicraft manufacturing. In addition, they fulfil important political, religious, and educational functions. Some cities have become specialized; for example, Benares in India and Karbala in Iraq are best known as religious communities, and Peiping in China as a locus for political and educational activities.

The proportion of urbanites relative to the peasant population is small, in some societies about 10 per cent, even though a few preindustrial cities have attained populations of 100,000 or more. Growth has been by slow accretion. These characteristics are due to the nonindustrial nature of the total social order. The amount of surplus food available to support an urban population has been limited by the unmechanized agriculture, transportation facilities utilizing primarily human or animal power, and inefficient methods of food preservation and storage.

The internal arrangement of the preindustrial city, in the nature of the case, is closely related to the city's economic and social structure. Most streets are mere passageways for people and for animals used in transport. Buildings are low and crowded together. The congested conditions, combined with limited scientific knowledge, have fostered serious sanitation problems.

More significant is the rigid social segregation which typically has led to the formation of "quarters" or "wards." In some cities (e.g., Fez, Morocco, and Aleppo, Syria) these were sealed off from each other by walls, whose gates were locked at night. The quarters reflect the sharp local social divisions. Thus ethnic groups live in special sections. And the occupational groupings, some being at the same time ethnic in character, typically reside apart from one another. Often a special street or sector of the city is occupied almost exclusively by members of a particular trade; cities in such divergent cultures as medieval Europe and modern Afghanistan contain streets with names like "street of the goldsmiths." Lower-class and especially "outcaste" groups live on the city's periphery, at a distance from the primary centers of activity. Social segregation, the limited transportation facilities, the modicum of residential mobility, and the cramped living quarters have encouraged the development of well-defined neighborhoods which are almost primary groups.

Despite rigid segregation the evidence suggests no real specialization of land use such as is functionally necessary in industrial-urban communities. In medieval Europe and in other areas city dwellings often serve as workshops, and religious structures are used as schools or marketing centers.

Finally, the "business district" does not hold the position of dominance that it enjoys in the industrial-urban community. Thus, in the Middle East the principal mosque, or in medieval Europe the cathedral, is usually the focal point of com-

"The Preindustrial City" by Gideon Sjoberg. Reprinted from *The American Journal of Sociology*, Vol. LX (1955), 438-445, by permission of The University of Chicago Press.

munity life. The center of Peiping is the Forbidden City.

ECONOMIC ORGANIZATION

The economy of the preindustrial city diverges sharply from that of the modern industrial center. The prime difference is the absence in the former of industrialism which may be defined as that system of production in which *inanimate* sources of power are used to multiply human effort. Preindustrial cities depend for the production of goods and services upon *animate* (human or animal) sources of energy—applied either directly or indirectly through such mechanical devices as hammers, pulleys, and wheels. The industrial-urban community, on the other hand, employs inanimate generators of power such as electricity and steam which greatly enhance the productive capacity of urbanites. This basically new form of energy production, one which requires for its development and survival a special kind of institutional complex, effects striking changes in the ecological, economic, and social organization of cities in which it has become dominant.

Other facets of the economy of the preindustrial city are associated with its particular system of production. There is little fragmentation or specialization of work. The handicraftsman participates in nearly every phase of the manufacture of an article, often carrying out the work in his own home or in a small shop near by and, within the limits of certain guild and community regulations, maintaining direct control over conditions of work and methods of production.

In industrial cities, on the other hand, the complex division of labor requires a specialized managerial group, often extra-community in character, whose primary function is to direct and control others. And for the supervision and co-ordination of the activities of workers, a "factory system" has been developed, something typically lacking in preindustrial cities. (Occasionally centralized production is found in preindustrial cities —e.g., where the state organized slaves for large-scale construction projects.) Most commercial activities, also, are conducted in preindustrial cities by individuals without a highly formalized organization; for example, the craftsman has frequently been responsible for the marketing of his own products. With a few exceptions, the preindustrial community cannot support a large group of middlemen.

The various occupations are organized into what have been termed "guilds." These strive to encompass all, except the elite, who are gainfully employed in some economic activity. Guilds have existed for merchants and handicraft workers (e.g., goldsmiths and weavers) as well as for servants, entertainers, and even beggars and thieves. Typically the guilds operate only within the local community, and there are no large-scale economic organizations such as those in industrial cities which link their members to their fellows in other communities.

Guild membership and apprenticeship are prerequisites to the practice of almost any occupation, a circumstance obviously leading to monopolization. To a degree these organizations regulate the work of their members and the price of their products and services. And the guilds recruit workers into specific occupations, typically selecting them according to such particularistic criteria as kinship rather than universalistic standards.

The guilds are integrated with still other elements of the city's social structure. They perform certain religious functions; for example, in medieval European, Chinese, and Middle Eastern cities each guild had its "patron saint" and held periodic festivals in his honor. And, by assisting members in time of trouble, the guilds serve as social security agencies.

The economic structure of the preindustrial city functions with little rationality, judged by industrial-urban standards. This is shown in the general nonstandardization of manufacturing methods as well as in the products and is even more evident in marketing. In preindustrial cities throughout the world a fixed price is rare; buyer and seller settle their bargain by haggling. (Of course, there are limits above which customers will not buy and below which merchants will not sell.) Often business is conducted in a leisurely manner, money not being the only desired end.

Furthermore, the sorting of goods according to size, weight, and quality is not common. Typical is the adulteration and spoilage of produce. And weights and measures are not standardized: variations exist not only between one city and the next but also within communities, for often different guilds employ their own systems. Within a single city there may be different kinds of currency, which, with the poorly developed accounting and credit systems, signalize a modicum of rationality in the whole of economic action in preindustrial cities.

SOCIAL ORGANIZATION

The economic system of the preindustrial city, based as it has been upon animate sources of power, articulates with a characteristic class structure and family, religious, educational, and governmental systems.

Of the class structure, the most striking component is a literate elite controlling and depending for its existence upon the mass of the populace, even in the traditional cities of India with their caste system. The elite is composed of individuals holding positions in the governmental, religious, and/or educational institutions of the larger society, although at times groups such as large absentee landlords have belonged to it. At the opposite pole are the masses, comprising such groups as handicraft workers whose goods and services are produced primarily for the elite's benefit. Between the elite and the lower class is a rather sharp schism, but in both groups there are gradations in rank. The members of the elite belong to the "correct" families and enjoy power, property, and certain highly valued personal attributes. Their position, moreover, is legitimized by sacred writings.

Social mobility in this city is minimal; the only real threat to the elite comes from the outside—not from the city's lower classes. And a middle class—so typical of industrial-urban communities, where it can be considered the "dominant" class—is not known in the preindustrial city. The system of production in the larger society provides goods, including food, and services in sufficient amounts to support only a small group of leisured individuals; under these conditions an urban middle class, a semileisured group, cannot arise. Nor are a middle class and extensive social mobility essential to the maintenance of the economic system.

Significant is the role of the marginal or "outcaste" groups (e.g., the Eta of Japan), which are not an integral part of the dominant social system. Typically they rank lower than the urban lower class, performing tasks considered especially degrading, such as burying the dead. Slaves, beggars, and the like are outcastes in most preindustrial cities. Even such groups as professional entertainers and itinerant merchants are often viewed as outcastes, for their rovings expose them to "foreign" ideas from which the dominant social group seeks to isolate itself. Actually many outcaste groups, including some of those mentioned above, are ethnic groups, a fact which further intensifies their isolation. (A few, like the Jews in the predominantly Muslim cities of North Africa, have their own small literate religious elite which, however, enjoys no significant political power in the city as a whole.)

An assumption of many urban sociologists is that a small, unstable kinship group, notably the conjugal unit, is a necessary correlate of city life.

But this premise does not hold for preindustrial cities. At times sociologists and anthropologists, when generalizing about various traditional societies, have imputed to peasants typically urban kinship patterns. Actually, in these societies the ideal forms of kinship and family life are most closely approximated by members of the urban literate elite, who are best able to fulfil the exacting requirements of the sacred writings. Kinship and the ability to perpetuate one's lineage are accorded marked prestige in preindustrial cities. Children, especially sons, are highly valued, and polygamy or concubinage or adoption help to assure the attainment of large families. The preeminence of kinship is apparent even in those preindustrial cities where divorce is permitted. Thus, among the urban Muslims or urban Chinese divorce is not an index of disorganization; here, conjugal ties are loose and distinctly subordinate to the bonds of kinship, and each member of a dissolved conjugal unit typically is absorbed by his kin group. Marriage, a prerequisite to adult status in the preindustrial city, is entered upon at an early age and is arranged between families rather than romantically, by individuals.

The kinship and familial organization displays some rigid patterns of sex and age differentiation whose universality in preindustrial cities has generally been overlooked. A woman, especially of the upper class, ideally performs few significant functions outside the home. She is clearly subordinate to males, especially her father or husband. Recent evidence indicates that this is true even for such a city as Lhasa, Tibet, where women supposedly have had high status. The isolation of women from public life has in some cases been extreme. In nineteenth-century Seoul, Korea, "respectable" women appeared on the streets only during certain hours of the night when men were supposed to stay at home. Those women in preindustrial cities who evade some of the stricter requirements are members of certain marginal groups (e.g., entertainers) or of the lower class. The role of the urban lower-class woman typically resembles that of the peasant rather than the urban upper-class woman. Industrialization, by creating demands and opportunities for their employment outside the home, is causing significant changes in the status of women as well as in the whole of the kinship system in urban areas.

A formalized system of age grading is an effective mechanism of social control in preindustrial cities. Among siblings the eldest son is privileged. And children and youth are subordinate to parents and other adults. This, combined with early marriage, inhibits the development of a "youth culture." On the other hand, older persons hold considerable power and prestige, a fact contributing to the slow pace of change.

As noted above, kinship is functionally integrated with social class. It also reinforces and is reinforced by the economic organization: the occupations, through the guilds, select their members primarily on the basis of kinship, and much of the work is carried on in the home or immediate vicinity. Such conditions are not functional to the requirements of a highly industrialized society.

The kinship system in the preindustrial city also articulates with a special kind of religious system, whose formal organization reaches fullest development among members of the literate elite. The city is the seat of the key religious functionaries whose actions set standards for the rest of society. The urban lower class, like the peasantry, does not possess the education or the means to maintain all the exacting norms prescribed by the sacred writings. Yet the religious system influences the city's entire social structure. (Typically, within the preindustrial city one religion is dominant; however, certain minority groups adhere to their own beliefs.) Unlike the situation in industrial cities, religious activity is not separate from other social action but permeates family, economic, governmental, and other activities. Daily life is pervaded with religious significance. Especially important are periodic public festivals and ceremonies like Ramadan in Muslim cities. Even distinctly ethnic outcaste groups can through their own religious festivals maintain solidarity.

Magic, too, is interwoven with economic, familial, and other social activities. Divination is commonly employed for determining the "correct" action on critical occasions; for example, in traditional Japanese and Chinese cities, the selection of marriage partners. And nonscientific procedures are widely employed to treat illness among all elements of the population of the preindustrial city.

Formal education typically is restricted to the male elite, its purpose being to train individuals for positions in the governmental, educational, or religious hierarchies. The economy of preindustrial cities does not require mass literacy, nor, in fact, does the system of production provide the leisure so necessary for the acquisition of formal education. Considerable time is needed merely to learn the written language, which often is quite different from that spoken. The teacher occupies a position of honor, primarily because of the prestige of all learning and especially of knowledge of the sacred literature, and learning is traditional and characteristically based upon sacred writings. Students are expected to memorize rather than evaluate and initiate, even in institutions of higher learning.

Since preindustrial cities have no agencies of mass communication, they are relatively isolated from one another. Moreover, the masses within a city are isolated from the elite. The former must rely upon verbal communication, which is formalized in special groups such as storytellers or their counterparts. Through verse and song these transmit upper-class tradition to nonliterate individuals.

The formal government of the preindustrial city is the province of the elite and is closely integrated with the educational and religious systems. It performs two principal functions: exacting tribute from the city's masses to support the activities of the elite and maintaining law and order through a "police force" (at times a branch of the army) and a court system. The police force exists primarily for the control of "outsiders," and the courts support custom and the rule of the sacred literature, a code of enacted legislation typically being absent.

In actual practice little reliance is placed upon formal machinery for regulating social life. Much more significant are the informal controls exerted by the kinship, guild, and religious systems, and here, of course, personal standing is decisive. Status distinctions are visibly correlated with personal attributes, chiefly speech, dress, and personal mannerisms which proclaim ethnic group, occupation, age, sex, and social class. In nineteenth-century Seoul, not only did the upper-class mode of dress differ considerably from that of the masses, but speech varied according to social class, the verb forms and pronouns depending upon whether the speaker ranked higher or lower or was the equal of the person being addressed. Obviously, then, escape from one's role is difficult, even in the street crowds. The individual is ever conscious of his specific rights and duties. All these things conserve the social order in the preindustrial city despite its heterogeneity.

CONCLUSIONS

Throughout this paper there is the assumption that certain structural elements are universal for all urban centers. This study's hypothesis is that their form in the preindustrial city is fundamentally distinct from that in the industrial-urban community. A considerable body of data not only from medieval Europe, which is somewhat atypical, but from a variety of cultures supports this point of view. Emphasis has been upon the static features of preindustrial city life. But even those preindustrial cities which have undergone considerable change approach the ideal type. For one thing, social change is of such a nature that it is not usually perceived by the general populace.

Most cities of the preindustrial type have been located in Europe or Asia. Even though Athens and Rome and the large commercial centers of Europe prior to the industrial revolution displayed certain unique features, they fit the preindustrial type quite well. And many traditional Latin-American cities are quite like it, although deviations exist, for, excluding pre-Columbian cities, these were affected to some degree by the industrial revolution soon after their establishment.

It is postulated that industrialization is a key variable accounting for the distinctions between preindustrial and industrial cities. The type of social structure required to develop and maintain a form of production utilizing inanimate sources of power is quite unlike that in the preindustrial city. At the very least, extensive industrialization requires a rational, centralized, extra-community economic organization in which recruitment is based more upon universalism than on particularism, a class system which stresses achievement rather than ascription, a small and flexible kinship system, a system of mass education which emphasizes universalistic rather than particularistic criteria, and mass communication. Modification in any one of these elements affects the others and induces changes in other systems such as those of religion and social control as well. Industrialization, moreover, not only requires a special kind of social structure within the urban community but provides the means necessary for its establishment.

Anthropologists and sociologists will in the future devote increased attention to the study of cities throughout the world. They must therefore recognize that the particular kind of social structure found in cities in the United States is not typical of all societies.

Selection 50

The Changing Imagery of American City and Suburb
Anselm L. Strauss

Two predominant themes run through Part VI. One of them is concerned with describing categories of things that are alike—categories of population, types of city structures, kinds of attitudes toward communities that characterize collectivities of people. The other theme deals with the eternal ferment of humanity—changing population qualities, changing material traits which reflect changing economies, changing political relationships, and changing attitudes toward home and work and "the good life" and God. These stabilities and instabilities reflect and are reflected in the relationships between people and places.

In this article by Strauss, the reader may pause to ponder the effects on living habits of the lengthening of life expectancy. One of the changes that seems in retrospect to have been inevitable, considering all the factors, is that people expect to live in many different houses during a lifetime. This was not the case in 1900. What has changed? (1) People live longer—in 1900 the expectation of life at birth was forty-five years; today it is roughly seventy years. (2) People marry earlier—the age at marriage has declined two years since 1900. (3) Children are born into the family earlier—the average mother bears her last child when she is twenty-eight years old. (4) Families are neolocal —few people plan to live in the homes their parents occupied (in part because the parents are still living). (5) Fewer people live on farms—their source of income is away from their residence. (6) Children leave home while the parents are relatively young—few parents of fifty still have children at home. Hence, housing needs change drastically during the life cycle. Most young people today plan to: (1) take an apartment or small house apart from their parents when they marry; (2) move to a house in a good school district when they have children; (3) move to a bigger house in a better residential area when their children reach adolescence and when their earning power and social needs are at a maximum; (4) move into a smaller house or an apartment when the last child has married and left home; and (5) move into a small community in a good climate when they retire. Viewed in this way, it is not strange that Strauss finds perspectives of the city and suburb changing from what they were earlier in the century. City and suburb mean different things with respect to housing; one may expect to live in both of them during a lifetime.

One of the images of the city which Strauss describes is that it is the core, or nucleus, of a concentration of population. He refers to a concept similar to Wirth's *urbanism* rather than to a strictly man-land ratio; it is the *attitudes* of the people rather than the numbers of people that are important. In this image, dwellers in city, suburb, and exurb alike assume that the center of the city contains the major and most enduring objects of value—cultural, economic, religious, and others—but that certain minor or temporary values are to be gained by living near the city rather than in it. The emphasis in this attitude is on the accessibility of city values from the suburb, not on the accessibility of suburban values from the city.

The reader may infer from Strauss' article that he—like Sjoberg—envisions the highest expression of a society's cultural values to be those expressed in its cities. This perspective is diametrically opposed to the stated opinions of the small-town dwellers described in the article by Vidich and Bensman. The citizens of Springdale felt that cities destroyed the "American heritage" of independence and democracy.

In Part VI we have studied man and the biological, cultural, and social factors involved in his adaptation to the earth. We have studied the patterns of people living in aggregate and the material implementation of these patterns and the cultural residuum after the society has changed. We have studied, too, the psychological orientation of men to these patterns and processes and its constantly emerging effects on them. Strauss ends Part VI on an urban note, perhaps subtly hinting that if human life is to continue, it will *have to* have an urban orientation. In view of the reports of Notestein and Cowgill, it seems unlikely that we can look forward to any peaceful decline in population in the foreseeable future.

As the United States progressed from an agricultural nation to markedly urbanized status, largely during the last half of the nineteenth century, each step of the way was paralleled by Americans' attempts to make sense of what was happening. Making sense of what was happening merged easily with complaints over the way things were going and with predictions and suggestions for the way things ought to go. The United States has had a very rich history of such ideological accompaniments to the objective facts of its urbanization. (Some of these accompaniments were actually quite potent, too, in affecting that urbanization. Almost ninety years ago, for instance, Frederick Olmstead, the urban landscape planner argued that American cities were to outweigh the countryside in the nation's scale, and introduced influential concepts of getting air and light and other rural qualities into the crowded cities by way of planned parks. Olmstead had already built Central Park in New York and was soon to become one of America's most influential city planners.) American urbanization today is still rich in ideological accompaniments which serve as interpretations and criticisms of the most recent urbanization phenomena and which quite possibly may affect future urbanization in the States.

Today's urban imagery is no longer concerned with the imagined polarity of countryside and city which for so long preoccupied Americans. This polarity was succeeded some decades ago by a presumed polarity of city and suburb—a polarity which followed in the wake of a vastly increased suburbanization of American cities, and the flight of great numbers of city dwellers to the suburbs in search of fresh air, safe and quiet streets,

From *The Sociological Quarterly*, Vol. 1 (1960), 15-24.

genuine communal life, better standards of domestic living, and—as American sociologists have so often stressed—more prestigeful locales in which to live. But the imagined polarity of suburb and city is already breaking down, and new imagery is beginning to take its place. In this paper, I shall briefly consider some of this newer imagery, which imagery should suggest some of the kinds of questions that Americans are raising about the destinies of their metropolitan areas. These are questions which planners are raising too—as well as questions which planners are going to have to take into account.

The first question is: What is going to be the fate of American cities? The broadest range of envisioned alternatives is the continued dominance of cities versus the actual disappearance of cities. The *New York Times,* perhaps only for purposes of provocation, recently raised the alternatives in this way:

"One hundred million Americans are now living in metropolitan areas, including their central cities.

"Will the new pattern of settlement result in the eventual dwindling of great cities like New York, Chicago and San Francisco? Will they be just islands of national business headquarters, financial clearing houses and other specialized functions within great flat seas in which the other activities of our national life will mingle?

"Or will our historic cities sparkle brighter by contrast with the sprawling urbanized regions which they will serve as centers of culture as well as commerce?"[1]

Far from dominating the American scene today, the big cities are on the defensive, at least in some ways. Our magazines are full of stories about cities fighting to make a "comeback," and cities are combating "the threat of strangulation by the suburbs." One emerging concept of the fate, and function, of the metropolis is that it can serve as the core of the entire metropolitan area. By "the core," urban planners and civic propagandists may mean either business or cultural functions, or both. For instance, the mayor of Detroit like many other civic leaders, advocates strengthening downtown districts so that they can serve as a strong magnet to attract people from distant suburbs, either for daily visits or for permanent residence in a resurrected city. Hence he advocated building expressways to bring suburbanite shoppers into the downtown area: "If we don't make it possible for them to come back, they will build large shopping areas in the outlying communities and we will lose that business." To some

other metropolitan champions, "the new metropolis" connotes somewhat less hard-headed emphasis upon business and more upon the cultural and political leadership of cities.

New concepts are also emerging of who shall —or should—live in the central city. Here, for instance, is the view of William Zeckendorf, probably the most influential of American urban redevelopers:

"There is a swing back to the cities of the highest-grade type of tenant. He is generally aged 45 and upward. He has raised his children; he has reached the peak of his earning power; his house is now superfluous in size; he is tired of commuting.

"That man, if you provide him with appropriate living conditions in the central areas of the cities, can be reattracted on a scale never dreamed of before to a way of life that is impossible to obtain in the suburbs."

He adds, and here we may see what a new concept is involved, that "For each 10 people that the city loses to the suburbs, it can get 10 times their collective buying power in people who return."[2] In the hands of people like Zeckendorf, the concept of "redevelopment" has now come to mean a combination of things: partly the replacement of slums with upper-income housing; partly the renovation of "downtown U.S.A." But other planners and influential citizens urge—on moral as well as on economic grounds—that the city ought not to be given over only to the wealthier residents; and in fact, others meanwhile keep pointing to the steady abandonment of the large cities to Negroes, who are thus effectively segregated within the greater urban area.

While cities are "fighting back" against suburbia, the transformation of suburban areas is accompanied by a reinterpretation of life as it is lived there. In place of a relatively undifferentiated "suburb"—a symbolic area contrasting with an equally symbolic city—a differentiated set of popular concepts is appearing. As those suburbs located near the city's actual boundaries become increasingly crowded, becoming virtually part of the city, the "better class" of residents who live further out refer disdainfully to those older suburbs. They make subtle distinctions about the relative qualities of various communities—knowl-

---

[1] "Expansion of Cities Alters Patterns of Living in U.S.," *New York Times,* January 17, 1957.
[2] William Zeckendorf, "Can the Big Cities Come Back?" *U.S. News and World Report,* July 19, 1957, p. 73.

edge essential when unwanted ethnic groups or Negroes may tomorrow set up residence in certain of those locales. Especially with the enormous extension of the suburban rings clear out into the next states, it was inevitable that someone would make a distinction between suburbs and suburbs-beyond-the-suburbs—and Spectorsky's "exurbia" and "suburbia" have met this need for drawing such boundaries.[3] . . .

In past decades, a momentous aspect of the suburban dream was the wish to reinstitute, or establish, the emotionally satisfying bonds of community and neighborhood. For more civic-minded souls, a suburban community also represented a reasonably good way to enter into the political process, something that was much more difficult to effect within the crowded city wards. Both aspirations have attracted a good deal of acid comment in recent decades. The imagery of a truer political democracy has not always been easy to put into practice, especially as the suburbs have grown larger, or have become the locus of clashes between uncompromising social classes. As for the bonds of community and neighborhood, two kinds of criticism have been directed against these. One kind is uttered by suburbanites who have expected the friendliness and democracy of an ideal small town only to be bitterly disappointed by the realities of suburban living. They accuse the suburb of false friendliness, of mock neighborliness; it has not a democratic atmosphere at all; it is ridden with caste and snobbery. Another kind of criticism is leveled, by suburbanites and outsiders alike, against the achievement of too much "community." It is said that there is no real privacy in most suburbs; and that so deadening is the round of sociability that little time can remain for genuine leisure. While most critics are willing to admit that friendship and communal ties are to be valued, they deride the standardization of suburban communities and their all too visible styles of life (the barbecue suppers, the PTA's, the suburban clothing, the commuting). Since World War II, criticism has continued to mount about suburbia as a way of life. The new kinds of suburbs are so homogeneous in population, so child-dominated, so domestic-oriented, so little concerned with intellectual or cultural pursuits—or thus it would seem to the critics.

When conceived in such terms suburbanization seems to represent to inveterate lovers of the city a genuine threat to urban values—a threat even to the nation. In place of an earlier derision of the suburb as an uncomfortable or inconvenient place to live, and added to the fear of the suburb as a threat to true democracy (because it enhances class distinctions), we have now an increasing concern over the continued exodus to suburbs. If it is true that suburban life is inimical to much that has made the city exciting, freeing, and innovative, then—it is felt—there is cause for alarm. Despite the counterargument that the suburbs now have theaters and concerts, the city as the great central locale for the arts and for civilized institutions generally still remains convincing as an image to many city residents. Even intellectuals living in the suburbs betray some uneasiness about their abandonment of former habitats and pursuits; and a growing literature of the suburban novel portrays the city as a creative foil to the dull, if necessary, domesticity of suburbia.

The intellectuals are not the only city people disposed to bemoan the strength of the suburban movement; they are joined by urban politicians and by urban businessmen. "Satellite towns, which are the product of decentralization, are parasites" —I quote Zeckendorf again—"jeopardizing the entire fiscal and political future of our great municipalities."[4] He, like others, argues how detrimental it is to the whole metropolitan community, and thus ultimately to the nation, that suburban cities should refuse to be incorporated into the near-by dominant metropolis. . . .

Thus a new imagery about the city and its suburbs is appearing. The city as an invading malignant force which threatens the beauty of the suburban village has been a fearful imagery of suburbanites for many years—an imagery which has aroused antagonism against new kinds of neighbors, in complaints about loss of rural atmosphere, and in the continual flight further outward. But a reverse aspect of the city is supplementing the other imagery—namely, that the former idyllic suburban landscape is, or is becoming, a thing of the past. The services which the central city can offer the near-by communities are inestimable, or at least better than can be locally supplied, for the suburbs are no longer relatively isolated, autonomous, proud towns. They have been swamped with populations, if old; and if new, erected too quickly and without adequate services or without an eye to future growth of population.

Although most suburbanites still undoubtedly imagine the central city to be different from the suburbs, already some prophets are beginning to visualize very little true difference between the two locales. They take delight in pointing out, if they are themselves city dwellers, that the suburbs are fully as noisy as the city; that traffic

---

[3] A. C. Spectorsky, *The Exurbanites* (New York: J. B. Lippincott Co., 1955).
[4] William Zeckendorf, "Cities versus Suburbs," *Atlantic*, 190 (July, 1952), 24.

is getting to be as onerous in the towns as it is downtown; that city people are wearing the same kinds of informal attire. The suburbanite is beginning to notice these things himself.

The flattening out of differences between suburb and city—by the increasing suburban densities and the possibility of planning cities for good living—seems destined to bring about further changes in the imagery of Americans. Very recently several new images have appeared. Thus one sociologist, Nathan Glazer, who loves cosmopolitan city life and who is afraid that it cannot flourish in suburbia, has argued that suburbia itself is in danger of invading, in its turn, the big city.[5] This is a new twist, is it not? Glazer's argument is that because redevelopers have combined certain features of the garden city (superblocks, curving paths) and Corbusier's skyscraper in the park, they have in a large measure destroyed "the Central values of the city—as meeting place, as mixing place, as creator and consumer of culture at all levels." If poorer classes are better off now than they were in our older great cities, the rich and the middle class are worse off, while artists, poets, intellectuals, and professors have less propitious circumstances in which to flourish. The city core itself,

"the part that people visit, that eager migrants want to live in, that produces what is unique, both good and bad, in the city, as against the town and the suburb. What has happened to that? Strangely enough, it loses the vitality that gave it its attraction."

Glazer asserts that the very density of nineteenth-century cities forced city planners to build towns at the rim of existing cities rather than to plan for better cities. We have now, he argues, to plan for the metropolis without losing that essential cosmopolitanism which makes it great. A rich and varied urban texture must be created, "and this . . . cannot be accomplished by reducing density." Whatever it is that has gone wrong with our cities, he concludes, "one thing is sure: nothing will be cured by bringing the suburb, even in its best forms, into the city." This is a radically different kind of argument—and imagery—from that of the city boy who merely refuses to take up residence in the suburb because he believes life there is intellectually stultifying.

In either case, though, the critic of suburbia takes the city as his measuring rod: he assumes the city as the locus for a frame of mind, a style of life. The proponent of suburbia reverses the procedure and measures the city against a healthier, saner, more sociable, or some other reputed

suburban counterpart. There is, of course another, and transcending, position whereby one may avoid taking sides, saying that both city and suburb have their respective advantages—and people who own homes in both locales doubtless subscribe to that particular imagery.

Yet another transcending imagery is possible:

"We are going to have to learn a wholly new concept of a city—a great sprawling community covering hundreds of square miles, in which farms and pastures mingle with intense residential developments, factories and shopping centers, with the entire area run purposefully for the common good. . . . These wonderful new cities [the writers promise] aren't as far in the future as they may sound."[6]

Notice their wording. We have to learn a "wholly new concept of a city" and "these wonderful new cities" that are just around the corner. What these terms signify is that the dichotomy of city *versus* suburb is no longer defensible in the eyes of some Americans. In its turn, this dichotomy is in some danger of dissolution like its predecessor, the country-city polarity. When Americans can maintain no longer that the two locales differ then we can expect new imageries to arise—interpretations of the latest phases of urbanization.

One can almost see them being born. Not many months ago, *Fortune Magazine* published a series of articles on the "exploding metropolis," closing with William H. Whyte's "Urban Sprawl."[7] Whyte begins his report on the state of American metropolitan areas by warning that their fate will be settled during the next three or four years. "Already huge patches of once green countryside have been turned into vast, smog-filled deserts that are neither city, suburb, nor country." Note that last phrase: it forebodes the invention in the near future of a less neutral, more descriptive, term than the sociologists' colorless "metropolitan area." Whyte himself coins no new term, but his attitude toward the region eaten into by urban sprawl reflects something new. He reports a conference of planners, architects, and other experts that was convened by *Fortune Magazine* and by *Architectural Forum* to tackle the problem of remedying the worst features of urban sprawl. This group made recommendations, based upon the assumption that large amounts of suburban

---

[5] Nathan Glazer, "The Great City and the City Planners" (unpublished paper).
[6] T. H. Reed and D. D. Reed, "Does Your City Suffer from Suburbanitis?" *Collier's Magazine*, 130 (October 11, 1952), 20.
[7] William H. Whyte, "Urban Sprawl," *Fortune Magazine*, 57 (January 1958), 103.

land need to be rescued before they get completely built upon in distressingly unplanned ways. As Whyte says, "it is not too late to reserve open space while there is still some left—land for parks, for landscaped industrial districts, and for just plain scenery and breathing space."[8] The language—and the outlines of these recommendations —are consciously very like that of earlier generations of city planners who were concerned with the problems of urban density; although the current situations, as everyone recognizes, involve a more complex interlocking of city, suburb, county, and state.

Americans are now being told in their mass media that soon they will "be living in fifteen great, sprawling, nameless communities—which are rapidly changing the human geography of the entire country."[9] They are beginning to have spread before them maps of these vast urban conglomerations which are not cities but are nevertheless thoroughly urban: "super-cities" and "strip cities." They are being warned that America's urban regions are already entering upon a new stage of development, "even before most people are aware that urban regions exist at all." And already before the recently coined concept of "exurbia" is more than a few years old they are being confronted with "interurbia," which is simply all the land not actually within the denser urban strips of land but which lies within the urban regions; an area within which few people live on farms but where almost everybody commutes to work—not necessarily to cities "but to factories and offices located in small towns."[10] As the polar concepts of city and suburb thus dissolve, Americans are being invited to think of urbanization in newer, more up-to-date terms. The new terms, however technically they may be sometimes used, refer no less than did the older vocabulary to symbolic locales and associated sentiments.

---

[8] *Ibid.*, p. 104.
[9] C. Tunnard, "America's Super-cities," *Harpers*, 217 (August 1958), 59-65.
[10] *Ibid.*, pp. 61-62.

Recent Research

H. Laurence Ross*

POPULATION

One of the chief sources of sociological interest in the study of population remains the Malthusian problem of the relationship of population to resources. In 1798 the English clergyman Thomas Malthus noted that if population can increase at a geometric rate (e.g., 2, 4, 8, 16, 32 . . .) while food resources can increase only at an arithmetic rate (e.g., 2, 4, 6, 8, 10 . . .), eventually there will not be enough food to go around. In the absence of voluntary birth control, the human race can look forward only to vice and misery, caused by the pressure of population on food resources.

Malthus had the ill fortune to write his essay just prior to the arrival in Europe of bumper crops of grain from the American prairies, and his thesis soon appeared to look rather far into the future. Moreover, for reasons still not completely understood, European birth rates declined precipitously with maturing industrialization. Far from increasing geometrically, the population of nations like France and Sweden actually declined for several years.

A revival of interest in the Malthusian problem has occurred since World War II, when overpopulation was noticed in various parts of the world such as

---

* I am indebted to Irwin Sanders and Herbert Gans for advice and criticism in writing this chapter.

Southeast Asia and Central America. Population pressure is now seen to interfere with economic development[1] as well as with political stability.[2]

A second development that increased interest in the Malthusian problems is the totally unexpected resurgence of population growth in the industrialized countries of Europe and North America. It had been assumed that population stability could be achieved through a "demographic transition," whereby voluntary birth control would lower the birth rates to equal the reduced death rates achieved by the "death control" of modern medicine and public health technology. The classic Indianapolis Study had indicated that widespread acceptance of contraception was the cause of the decline in births among American families in the Depression and World War II years.[3] However, the rise in births since World War II has taken place against a background of continued acceptance of contraception, and recent research has found little to explain the increased birth rate.[4] For families using effective contraceptives, births are largely a result of a deliberate decision to have children, but the sociological causes of decisions in favor of additional children are still obscure. This fact creates considerable difficulties in planning programs to cope with present and projected cases of overpopulation.

A further recent development connected with the study of population is the extension of Malthusian thinking to other resources, both natural and cultural. Natural resources other than food have been regarded in a Malthusian perspective by conservationists for many years, as evidenced by our country's national parks and legislation for the protection of wildlife. Air, water, and raw materials for industry as economic resources were the subject of a strongly Malthusian book written by Fairfield Osborn in 1948, and similar concern, modified by guarded optimism, is apparent in more recent reports.[5] Quite analogous to the conservation of food in the Malthusian formula is the conservation of adequate transportation resources in contemporary urban planning. Congestion of streets and parking areas, which chokes off the flow of people into the center of the city, is figuratively choking off the city's "food supply."[6]

Implicit in all sociological discussion of population is the conception that both births and deaths, as well as the provision of resources, are influenced by social factors. The study of population is progressing in the direction of decreasing interest in sheer description and forecasting, and increasing interest in the factors that lie behind the presence of different kinds of populations (for instance, those with unusual sex ratios or age distributions), as well as in the social effects that different population situations yield.[7]

COMMUNITIES

The term *community* is a vague and ambiguous concept in sociology, since it may refer to nearly any group larger than a primary group and smaller than a society. It generally refers to the sociologist's heuristic preconception that there exists a level of social integration intermediate between the small group and the large society. It is usually considered to have a territorial base, although such concepts as "community of scholars" or "American financial community" lack this presumption. Most studies of communities deal with either small towns or neighborhoods within cities.

Recent discussion of communities takes place against a background of assertions that the community is declining and that it is being superseded by the mass society, in which there are no intermediate levels of organization between the primary group and the state.[8] Most researchers are inclined to disagree with such assertions. Continuing studies of social participation in urban areas find considerable evidence of social integration in city and suburban neighborhoods.[9] On the other hand, the functions performed by the communities described in these recent studies appear definitely secondary to those performed at lower and higher levels. Janowitz' conception of the "community of limited liability" seems valid as a description of the entity found in these studies.[10] Residents identify with the community, and it is a locus of much social participation and of a good deal of facilities usage, but most of the activity is parochial and without consequence for the larger society.[11] A similar picture is drawn for the rural community in recent studies like *Small Town in Mass Society.*[12]

A continuing aspect of interest in the community is the study of power structure, launched by a 1953 book by Floyd Hunter.[13] The community referred to in the power-structure literature is usually an entire city or metropolitan area. Using the technique of interviewing influential people in the city, Hunter identified the perceived sources of power in a Southern city. His model of power structure, which has been generally supported by students using the same technique, is that of a rather closed circle of power wielders, somewhat divided internally into "crowds" representing different economic interests. A correlation between economic and political power, with a dominance of the economic, occurs in nearly all studies of American cities in this tradition. A contrasting point of view, exemplified by the work of Robert Dahl, sees community power structure as more fluid, varying with the issue at hand and involving different people with different interests on varying occasions.[14] The discussion of community-power studies is very heated because, although the issues mainly concern research methods, the implications of the Hunter model are at odds with the body of American ideology.[15]

HUMAN ECOLOGY

Human ecology in its classical phase (1915-1935) was more a research tool than a systematic theory. Its flower was a set of models of urban structure, the Burgess and Hoyt structural hypotheses.[16] Numerous studies were undertaken to demonstrate a linkage between distance and direction from the center of a city on the one hand and such variables as crime, mental illness, quality of housing, and proportions of Negroes and foreign-born on the other. The interest that these fascinating models generated has been maintained to this day, and the consensus of recent research is that a model combining the features of both the Burgess and the Hoyt hypotheses is valid in the North American context. However, investigations in other societies suggest that the validity of this model may be confined to industrial societies in which land is considered a commodity that can be freely sold to maximize its economic potential. Where this assumption is unrealistic, other structural patterns prevail, some of them entirely reversing the pattern contained in the Burgess model.[17]

Recent work in human ecology is more theoretical and of broader scope. It attempts to explain social organization in general as a product of the adjustment by a population to an environment, in contrast to the more traditional sociological approach which traces social organization to cultural sources. The contrast is nicely brought out in a recent article by Duncan and Schnore.[18]

Urban sociology, and the conception of urbanism prevalent in sociology, was traditionally based entirely on American data. In fact, until 1935 the socio-logical study of the city was almost uniquely the study of Chicago, where a vigorous academic department of sociology at the University of Chicago centered its efforts on the problems of this growing metropolis. A significant recent development has been the enlargement of urban sociology to a world scope. To the comparative study of American cities, based largely on the United States Census, has been added consideration of cities abroad and in other historical periods. The best summation of much of this work appears in Gideon Sjoberg's *The Pre-Industrial City*.[19] This research has considerably qualified the Simmel-Park-Wirth model of urbanism (contained in the reading by Wirth presented in this book). In the social contexts of other times and places, size, density, and heterogeneity do not necessarily produce the isolation and loneliness, nor the cosmopolitanism and freedom, which infuse this model derived from modern American and European investigations. Moreover, careful observational studies of neighborhoods in highly industrialized societies underscore the exaggerated nature of the model; the title of Gans' recent book, *The Urban Villagers*, suggests the intimate and parochial social life evident in these studies.[20]

A phenomenon that has excited a great deal of comment and stimulated much research is increasing urbanization. Throughout the world cities are growing in size and are coming to include increasingly larger proportions of the total population. Especially in industrial societies, urban populations are over-flowing the political limits of cities, creating suburbs, metropolitan areas, and Melgalopolises."[21] One of the centers of sociological interest in this phenomenon is the suburb and its hypothesized way of life.

The preponderance of ideology concerning the suburb has been negative. The suburb is said to be the home of white-collar drudges who spend their lives in an attempt to conform to the norms of a depressing and uninspiring mass culture.[22] Although some aspects of the ideology have been supported by research, the studies that yield this support—such as Whyte's study of Park Forest, Illinois[23]—are based on middle-class suburbs and may presumably reflect the facts of life in the middle classes rather than in suburbs *per se*. An increasing body of literature suggests that suburban areas in general differ little from corre-sponding areas in central cities,[24] and studies of working-class suburbs show little difference from what is known of working-class areas in the central city.[25]

Even a brief review of recent developments in the sociology of the city must acknowledge the role of city planning in stimulating theory and research. The advent of planning, vastly stimulated by the participation of the federal govern-ment through the Housing Acts of 1949 and 1954, has focused attention on urban problems and the values with which cities are imbued. Two recent polemical works state extreme cases. Lewis Mumford is negative about most developments in urban societies since the Middle Ages.[26] He decries the spread of the city across the landscape in the form of low-density suburbs, as well as the mixture of functions that has accompanied urban growth, the prevailing standards of sanitation and other urban services, etc. He supports plans that have as their goal the reorganization of the metropolis in the form of associated but distinct smaller agglomerations. Jane Jacobs, in contrast, takes the side of the *status quo*, rejecting nearly all current theories of planning.[27] The random mixture of land uses that appears in areas marginal between two or more prevailing uses is her ideal, and what to Mumford is overcrowding and congestion is intensity and life to Jacobs. Although the intrusion into sociology of a value controversy with political implications has led to instances of overstatement and intemperance, it has resulted also in increased interest and a new liveliness in the sociological study of the city.

References

1. W. F. Ogburn, "Population, Private Ownership, Technology and the Standard of Living," *American Journal of Sociology,* 56 (1951), 314-319.
2. Philip M. Hauser, "Demographic Dimensions of World Politics," *Science,* 131 (1960), 1641-1647. See also recent issues of *Population Bulletin.*
3. P. K. Whelpton and Clyde V. Kiser, eds., *Social and Psychological Factors Affecting Fertility* (New York: Milbank Memorial Fund, 1946-1958).
4. Charles F. Westoff, Robert G. Potter, Philip C. Sagi, and Elliot G. Mishler, *Family Growth in Metropolitan America* (Princeton, N.J.: Princeton University Press, 1961).
5. Fairfield Osborn, *Our Plundered Planet* (Boston: Little, Brown & Co., 1948).
6. The Editors of *Fortune, The Exploding Metropolis* (New York: Doubleday & Company, Inc., 1958).
7. Kingsley Davis, "The Sociology of Demographic Behavior," in Robert K. Merton, Leonard Brown, and Leonard S. Cottrell, Jr., eds., *Sociology Today* (New York: Basic Books, Inc., 1959).
8. Maurice R. Stein, *The Eclipse of Community* (Princeton, N.J.: Princeton University Press, 1960).
9. Scott Greer, "Urbanism Reconsidered: A Comprehensive Study of Local Areas in a Metropolis," *American Sociological Review,* 21 (1956) 19-25. See also Sylvia Fleis Fava, "Contrasts in Neighboring: New York and a Suburban County," in William M. Dobriner, ed., *The Suburban Community* (New York: G. P. Putnam's Sons, 1958).
10. Morris Janowitz, *The Community Press in an Urban Setting* (New York: The Free Press of Glencoe, 1952).
11. Peter H. Rossi and Robert A. Dentler, *The Politics of Urban Renewal* (New York: The Free Press of Glencoe, 1961). See also Herbert Gans, *The Urban Villagers* (New York: The Free Press of Glencoe, 1962).
12. Arthur J. Vidich and Joseph Bensman, *Small Town in Mass Society* (Princeton, N.J.: Princeton University Press, 1958).
13. Floyd Hunter, *Community Power Structure* (Chapel Hill, N.C.: University of North Carolina Press, 1953).
14. Robert Dahl, *Who Governs?* (New Haven: Yale University Press, 1961).
15. See the debate between Nelson W. Polsby, Raymond E. Wolfinger, and others in *American Sociological Review,* 27 (1962), 838-854.
16. Theodore R. Anderson and Janice A. Egeland, "Spatial Aspects of Social Area Analysis," *American Sociological Review,* 26 (1961), 392-398.
17. George A. Theodorson, *Human Ecology* (Evanston: Row, Peterson & Co., 1961).
18. Otis Dudley Duncan and Leo Schnore, "Cultural, Behaviorial, and Ecological Perspectives in the Study of Social Organization," *American Journal of Sociology,* 65 (1959), 132-146.
19. Gideon Sjoberg, *The Pre-Industrial City* (New York: The Free Press of Glencoe, 1960).
20. Gans, *The Urban Villagers, op. cit.*
21. Jean Gottmann, *Megalopolis* (New York: Twentieth Century Fund, 1961).
22. David Riesman, "The Suburban Sadness," in Dobriner, *The Suburban Community, op. cit.*
23. William H. Whyte, *The Organization Man* (New York: Simon & Schuster, Inc., 1956).
24. Herbert Gans, "Urbanism and Suburbanism as Ways of Life: A Re-evaluation

of Definitions," in Arnold M. Rose, ed., *Human Behavior and Social Processes* (Boston: Houghton Mifflin Co., 1961).

25. Bennett Berger, *Working-Class Suburb* (Berkeley: University of California Press, 1960).
26. Lewis Mumford, *The City in History* (New York: Harcourt, Brace & World, 1961).
27. Jane Jacobs, *The Death and Life of Great American Cities* (New York: Random House, 1961).

Part VII

SOCIAL INSTITUTIONS

Throughout history, students of mankind have noted that some forms of behavior seemed to be repetitive, organized, standardized, and, within homogeneous societies, somewhat predictable. Sociologists not only have noted these common forms of behavior but have considered them major objects for study. Commonly these uniformities are called *institutions,* and although they are variously defined, there is considerable agreement among professional behavioral scientists —but not always among laymen—about what they are.

One of the most inclusive and descriptive definitions is that of Joyce O. Hertzler[1] who says, "Social institutions are purposive, regulatory, and consequently primary cultural configurations, formed, unconsciously and/or deliberately, to satisfy individual wants and social needs bound up with the efficient operation of any plurality of persons. They consist of codes, rules, and ideologies . . . and essential symbolic organizational and material implementations. They evidence themselves socially in standardized and uniform practices and observances, and individually in attitudes and habitual behavior." Probably the briefest good definition is that of Martindale,[2] who states simply that institutions are standardized solutions to collective problems.

The generic term *institution* is an abstraction, not a perceivable reality. One may perceive, visually and otherwise, *a* family, but one cannot observe *the* family as a social institution. Institutions are essentially systems of social relationships which embody the ultimate values men hold in common. Because these values are widely shared, they become foci around which life in the society revolves. There may be some value differences from culture to culture; an example of this is Selection 52, by Harold T. Christensen and George R. Carpenter, which describes differences of values and behavior regarding premarital coitus in Sweden and among American Mormons. Institutions are accepted not only by their own participants and functionaries, but also by

---

[1] Joyce O. Hertzler, *Social Institutions* (Lincoln, Neb.: University of Nebraska Press, 1946), pp. 4-5.
[2] Don Martindale, *American Society* (Princeton, N.J.: D. Van Nostrand Company, 1960), p. 260.

the great majority of people in the society that they serve. Thus institutions are social patterns directing the ordered behavior of human beings in basic activities. They have two important characteristics, formality and continuity. Every society organizes its institutional behavior more formally and rigidly than it does behavior that it thinks is less important. Out of this formality and rigidity comes a large degree of continuity, for as behavior becomes patterned and repetitive it becomes more ingrained and is thus more likely to survive in the minds and personalities of subsequent generations. This is why particular participants may die and be replaced, outward manifestations may be destroyed and reconstructed, rules and rituals and procedures may change, but an entity survives: the system of social relationships, the complex behavior systems and culture traits, that collectively are an institution.

Confusion sometimes arises between the use of the concept *institution* and of the term *association*. An association is an organized group with some structure and continuity; such an organization might express an institution or be patterned by institutionalized factors, but an association is no more an institution than anatomy is physiology. In spite of the loose use of the term by the man on the street, neither a church, a university, a mental hospital, nor a penitentiary is an institution. In the final analysis, an association is essentially composed of people; an institution is essentially composed of patterns of interaction and interrelationships. The difference is the same as that between twenty-two chosen men on a football field and the game of football. Thus Selection 55 by David O. Moberg, which describes the life cycle of a church, is not concerned with the generality of religion itself nor with the history of a specific association, such as the Centerville First Methodist Church, but rather with the rise and growth of sects and denominations.

The institutionalized family may meet many more needs in a primitive society than it does in a complex society. In a considerably differentiated society, one might find institutionalization of recreation, health, science, aesthetics, communication, transportation, and labor, as well as the more universal institutions of religion, education, family, economics, and government to which the following selections are devoted.

Nothing could be more incorrect than to infer that every institution is separate from every other institution. The interrelationships are numerous, varied, and deep. First, each participant in one institutionalized system is also a participant in other institutionalized systems. For the sake of personal integrity, each institutional role that an individual plays must be brought into reasonable conformity with all other roles he plays in other systems. In a highly institutionalized society, personal attitudes, values, and behavior patterns which conflict with institutional norms may result in the expulsion, isolation, or punishment of deviant persons. Second, institutions often have common functions and goals. For example, the family, religion, and education are all directly and vitally concerned with the transmission of the social heritage. Selection 59 by Robert Gordis shows some of the relationships between religion and the schools, and Selection 65 by Seymour Martin Lipset investigates some relationships between economics and politics. Selection 61, "Homunculus," by Mary Garraway, goes even further and speculates on some effects of technology—specifically, computers—on economic and other institutions.

Institutions perform two general types of functions. One is specific and often relates more to one particular institution than to others; e.g., the chief function of religion is to relate man to the supernatural. Other tasks may be jointly shared, as socialization may be shared by the family, education, and possibly other institutions as well. Such an interrelationship helps explain why changes in one institution may lead to significant, if unintentional, changes in another institution. The second institutional function is general and is shared by all institutions; since all institutions are normative—and thus social control agencies—all of them conserve and transmit the social heritage and all are builders and influencers of personality. When we speak of an institution as consisting of a *concept* and a *structure,* we mean that it consists of an idea of what the institution should do (the concept) and the patterns of techniques and relationships necessary to enact that idea (the structure). The idea may be either a general value that cannot be fully achieved at one time—such as being a "good father"—or a concrete, achievable goal—such as disposing of dead persons. Very briefly, we will list some of the major institutions in our own society and outline some of their chief functions.

The family once performed, more or less effectively, all major institutional functions. This contention is supported by studies of primitive groups and of earlier civilizations such as the early Hebrew and traditional Chinese societies. Certainly during historic times the family has been the most multifunctional of our institutions. Today, both the family and the church perform fewer functions. The public school and the commercial laundry have become institutionalized patterns for carrying out functions that were formerly relegated to the family, just as service clubs, welfare agencies, and psychotherapists perform many functions that were formerly provided by the church. This does not represent a societal "weakness" or "failure" in any real sense, for institutions are simply cultural patterns that have no life or power or volition of their own. The transfer indicates, rather, the belief that other institutions can and should perform these functions as well as or better than the family can. Even though it now shares some of its functions, however, the family is still the socially sanctioned institution for the reproduction of children and for the satisfaction of sexual needs of the marital partners, and it retains the responsibility for the care of young children and for providing much socialization and considerable education. It still is a major consuming unit; a chief source of affection, companionship, and security; and a likely provider of needs in the areas of recreation, physical and mental health, and sometimes religion and welfare. Society as a whole is organized on the premise of the unity and continuous functioning of each individual family. Selection 51 by Ernest W. Burgess indicates some of the factors closely associated with family stability.

Religion, once used to meet economic, political, and artistic ends, still serves as the chief institution for relating man to the supernatural, for seeking peace of mind, for explaining the meaning of life and meeting its crises, and for providing moral guidance and control. In various ways religion still may aid in attaining the goals of security, education, welfare, recreation, and a sense of belonging. Selection 56 by Albert J. Mayer and Harry Sharp reports some of the relationships of religious preference and worldly success. James S. Coleman's article, Selection 54, reports on some ways in which religious conflicts may be related to social cleavage and vice versa.

As the family and religion are less used to achieve certain goals, government, education, and economic organizations have begun to take them over and have become more multifunctional than they were in the past. Government now performs a large number of economic, educational, and recreational functions. It conserves natural resources, subsidizes transportation and communication, and engages in a wide variety of research projects, besides performing a multitude of other functions.

Education, once found chiefly in the family, has as its basic function the transmission of special aspects of the cultural heritage needed for full socialization. During relatively recent years it has acquired such additional functions as the imparting of attitudes and values, recreation, communication, research, and the extension of knowledge, and it even has assumed something of a status-giving function. An institution may become conscious of its "self" and seek to study itself. It even may be studied by the functionaries of other institutions or by members of associations within the institution. As a case in point, in Selection 57 Professor Neal Gross, a functionary of a university, studies the institution of education from the specialized viewpoint of the discipline of sociology.

The institutionalized aspects of the economy are organized primarily around satisfying physical needs, production, distribution, consumption, and the general area of subsistence; secondary functions include services, transportation, research, and welfare. The direct, personal relationship of the economy to the individual is exemplified in Selection 62, by William A. Faunce, Einar Hardin, and Eugene H. Jacobson, on automation and the employee. Valentin Chu's article on Red China, Selection 64, shows how political ideology unintentionally may bring about extremely important negative economic results.

Each institutional complex contains a great deal of behavior that is *functional*—i.e., that meets the needs or goals toward which the institution is oriented. Normally the complex also contains behavior that no longer serves its original purpose or at best is very peripheral. In addition, it may include behavioral patterns that are actually *dysfunctional* in that they contravene or make more difficult the attainment of the stated goals of the institution. For example, at one time marriage was supervised by the family and the church and involved fairly rigorous courtship mores. Under those conditions, it was desirable that legal permission to wed be secured easily. Today, the family and the church exercise much less control, and courtship patterns vary widely. Yet the ease of legal marriage remains the same, with numerous states requiring no waiting period. Since hurried marriages lead to a disproportionate share of marital failures, the permission of hasty marriages is *dysfunctional* in meeting many of the previously stated functions of the family. Selection 58, Coleman's study of a high school subculture, shows that this culture values athletic prowess more than academic achievement, which logically should be its highest goal. Robert K. Merton's article on the old-time political machine (Selection 63) shows how it may perform latent functions—unintended and not fully observed —for which the "reform" machine must provide if it wishes to continue in power.

Of the general societal functions of institutions, none is more important and observable than that of social control. One of the most commonly quoted statements on this subject is that of Parsons, who says institutions "are *normative* patterns which define what are felt to be, in the given society, proper, legitimate, or expected modes of action or of social relationship."[3] Institutions exert much of their control by defining situations and then indoctrinating these definitions into the impressionable young. The individual rather unconsciously internalizes

---

[3] Talcott Parsons, *Essays in Sociological Theory, Pure and Applied* (Glencoe, Ill.: The Free Press, 1949), p. 203.

these definitions as values and thereafter "polices" himself in accordance with them. Informal controls may be exercised by members over other members, and formal controls are exerted by organizations, associations, or functionaries.

Another generalized function that all institutions perform is the formation of personality. Personality consists chiefly of biological, social, cultural, and experimental factors, with the latter three particularly important. In every group, organization, association, or institution in which the individual is involved, he has a certain *status,* the dynamic behavioral aspects of which we call *role.* Roles form a considerable portion of the person's social experience, are related to his attitudes and values, and hence affect his personality strongly. Each role has certain expected characteristics, which have a tendency to become a part of the total personality of the individual. The acquisition of an important new role means changes in behavior; in one sense this is the significance of the findings of Kingsley Davis in his study of the trend in our society toward an early assumption of the status and role of a married person (Selection 53). William Foote Whyte's report on the social structure of the restaurant, Selection 60, points up clearly both the easily recognized roles in larger restaurants and the significance for the smooth functioning of the restaurant of the interaction of the personalities playing those roles.

Institutions characteristically tend to be permanent and to resist change. Institutions exist because they have been reasonably successful in meeting needs. They have solidified around the "best" ways of meeting the needs involved, and their members and functionaries tend to view new ways as dangerous. To illustrate, if a man has a deep well in which a pumping system operates reasonably satisfactorily, he may be quite reluctant to exchange his old pump for a new one that promises to work better—for it just might not work as well. Or, to continue the analogy, suppose a man has a good job running the old pump and the new pump will be fully automatic. This man has a *vested interest* in the pump (institution) as it now exists, for he will lose something very important to him as a functionary if the new pumping system (institutional change) is installed, even though it produces more water and thus even better meets the need for which the system originally was designed. Because they are repetitive, patterned forms of behavior based on the past, institutions and their functionaries consciously resist change and, possibly unconsciously, contribute to stagnation and cultural lag. Certainly every institution retains some traditions and practices that have outlived their usefulness.

Those institutions that are felt to meet the most important needs resist change the most. Also, those that have a sacred orientation tend to resist change more than secular ones. Nevertheless, institutional changes do occur. Aspects of the world, the culture, or the society related to the institutions change, and the more these aspects change, the greater the pressure, tension, and strain placed on the institution. Moreover, the persons who enact an institution also change, and opportunity for change arises when new personnel are drawn into the network of relationships. Institutional personnel tend to be ambivalent toward institutional change. They may recognize rationally that change is needed but reject it emotionally, or they may support change in one aspect of an institution while violently opposing it in another. If we agree with the institutional change proposed by a leader, he is a statesman; if we oppose his change, he is an irresponsible crackpot. Thus institutions are the greatest preservers of our traditions, of the past, and of the status quo; at the same time, they can change, and do so slowly but inexorably.   *J. H. B.*

Selection *51*

Predictive Methods and Family Stability

Ernest W. Burgess

Despite the increasing significance of secondary groups, mass culture, and mass media of communication, primary groups still fulfill the major portion of man's universal needs and wishes. Only primary groups make such an impact on the personality and character of the person, and of these groups none is as important as the family. The old axiom that the family is the cornerstone of society is still unequivocally true. Yet it is a shaky cornerstone and a far from perfect method of meeting basic needs. Widespread social problems, maladjustments, and personal disorganization prove that the family is not fulfilling its appointed tasks with full effectiveness.

Not all of the reasons for the failure of the family to function effectively are found within the family itself, but one undeniable factor is its failure to stay together. The previous sentence is not a polemic against divorce—far from it. Divorce, properly viewed and used, is simply the legal and official burial of a marriage already dead. If a polemic is needed, it should be against the deficiencies of marriages, against a society and culture that make easy so much unwise mate selection by couples who are not properly prepared for marriage, and against the shortage of adequate premarital and postmarital counseling.

Sociologists who are concerned less with "grand theory" than with theories of the middle range consider successful prediction of human behavior the proof of the success of their theory building. But, as in all fields, sociological prediction is in terms of probability, likelihood, generality, uniformity, or odds, not in terms of absolutes. Valid predictions consist of such statements as "the great majority . . . ," "in eight out of every ten cases . . . ," "the odds are over 90 out of a hundred that . . . ," or "the higher the marital prediction score, the higher the chances of marital happiness." Prediction is mathematical only in a probabilistic way, but within limits it can be accurate.

The selection by Burgess describing prediction of marital stability is particularly useful to the beginning student because it shows the difference between the intuitive, off-the-cuff predictions of the man on the street and the carefully prepared, scientifically organized and administered predictive techniques applied by the professional behavioral scientist. Selection 52 by Christensen and Carpenter and Selection 53 by Davis are quite different in content; they deal with the specific topics of premarital sex and of early marriage. The former also demonstrates the combination of theory and research. The latter combines the descriptive and scientific approaches, a method that is well suited to a number of practical areas in today's social life, including marriage.

In the following selection, Burgess reviews what we know about the prediction of marital success by testing and the possibility of applying these tests or their findings to actual engagements and marriages. He concludes that predictive studies are useful in five areas—(1) general preparation for marriage,

(2) mate selection, (3) screening for premarital counseling, (4) premarital counseling, and (5) early postmarital counseling—and that when properly used they can contribute significantly to marital stability.

The purpose of this paper is an attempt to answer the questions: Can methods of predicting success and failure in marriage help in stabilizing the American family? If so, under what conditions and to what extent?

The instability of the American family derives from many conditions. . . . This article . . . will assume that the change from a rural to an urban society has undermined the traditional basis of the American family. It will assume without restating evidence that many young people today do not have knowledge adequate either to select a mate or to make successful adjustments in marriage.

One-fourth of all marriages terminate in divorce. Probably another fourth constitute unhappy and unstable unions. Perhaps an additional fourth have unresolved difficulties and problems which could either have been prevented or remedied by early treatment.

When the increasing divorce rate first excited alarm two generations ago, pillars of society and the general public believed that the solution lay in strengthening the laws against divorce. The proposal for a uniform national divorce law was widely accepted as a promising way of decreasing the divorce rate.

In recent years students of marriage and the family are in the main agreed that the concern with divorce is essentially dealing with effects rather than causes. They are convinced by their studies of happy and unhappy unions that the factors making for failure in marriage are unwise mate selection and lack of preparation for marriage. They regard the majority of divorces followed by remarriages as a process of trial and error on the part of couples. They are convinced that research findings of the psychological and social sciences are now offering a basis for programs of preparation for marriage and for premarital and early postmarital counseling. These programs, while promising, are not yet commensurate with the magnitude of the problem. As they expand and reach larger groups of young people before and after marriage, they should have a very real effect in contributing to family stability.

HISTORY AND NATURE
OF PREDICTIVE METHODS

The first attempt to discover factors predictive of success or failure in marriage was made by Katharine B. Davis in 1926. In the intervening two decades a large number of studies have been made correlating factors assumed to be predictive of success in marriage with some criterion of success such as "happiness," "permanence of the union," "satisfaction," and "adjustment." The findings of many of these studies and a detailed analysis of them have been prepared by Clifford Kirkpatrick and published under the title *What Science Says About Happiness in Marriage*.

While in a sense all these studies could be termed predictive, they fall into two broad groups. The first are those which consider only single items and indicate their individual relation to the selective criterion of success in marriage. The second group are those which deal with several items combined into an expectancy table of the probabilities of marital success. The principal studies of the latter type have been those made by Terman[1] and his associates, by Burgess and Cottrell,[2] and by Burgess and Wallin.[3]

Our main emphasis in this paper will be upon studies dealing with a combination of factors as related to an index of success and failure in marriage. . . .

STEPS IN PREDICTION

What are the steps in prediction? They involve the following:

1. *The selection of a criterion of success in marriage.* In the studies by Terman, by Burgess and Cottrell, and by Burgess and Wallin, the criterion is an index of success composed of answers of husband and wife to a large number of questions dealing with self-reports on happiness, satisfaction, agreements and disagreements, and common interests. By giving a numerical value to answers to these questions, a total score representing the degree of success of the union is obtained.

From *The Annals of the American Academy of Political and Social Science*, Vol. 272 (1950), 47-52.
[1] Lewis M. Terman, *Psychological Factors in Marital Happiness* (New York: McGraw-Hill Book Co., 1938).
[2] Ernest W. Burgess and Leonard S. Cottrell, *Predicting Success or Failure in Marriage* (New York: Prentice-Hall, Inc., 1939).
[3] Unpublished study of 1,000 engaged and 700 married couples.

2. *The choice of items assumed to be predictive.* These may be taken from the literature on human behavior, from previous research in the field of marital relations, and from the theories and hunches of the investigator. Appropriate questions are devised to be answered by the members of the engaged or married couples.

3. *The correlation of these items assumed to be predictive with the success score.* Certain items are found not to be correlated, and only those which show correlations are retained.

4. *The construction of an expectancy or experience table of the probabilities of marital success.* This is accomplished by getting a total prediction score for each couple on a basis of the answers which they give to the items that are found to be associated with success in marriage. This total prediction score for each person is then correlated with his corresponding success score. It is then possible to relate groups of prediction scores to the percentage of those who will succeed or fail in marriage. Such an expectancy table was prepared by Burgess and Cottrell[4] for a group of 519 couples, and is reproduced here in adapted form.

TABLE 1: Relation Between Prediction Scores and Marriage-Success Scores (Percentage Distribution)

PREMARITAL PREDICTION SCORE	MARRIAGE-SUCCESS SCORE			NO. OF CASES
	VERY LOW	LOW	HIGH & VERY HIGH	
700 to 779	0.0	10.0	90.0	10
620 to 699	1.5	12.1	86.4	66
540 to 619	5.8	21.9	72.3	137
460 to 539	27.6	29.4	43.0	170
380 to 459	39.8	31.1	29.1	93
300 to 379	57.2	25.7	17.1	35
220 to 299	75.0	25.0	0.0	8
Total				519

It will be noted in the study that husbands and wives with the highest premarital prediction score (700 to 779) have no cases with a very low marriage-success score, while those with a very low prediction score (220 to 229) have no cases with high or very high marriage-success scores.

5. *Application of the expectancy table to a new group of cases.* This was done by Burgess and Cottrell for a new sample of 155 couples with the same general socioeconomic level of the first group. The test of its validity was a correlation of .48 between the correlations of premarital predic-

tion scores and success scores as compared with a correlation of .51 in the original sample. . . .

QUESTIONS OF APPLICATION

Certain questions have been raised about the practical application of prediction tests. These may be taken up in the following order:

1. *Are the findings of these predictive studies representative of the general public?* It is true that the studies by Terman and Burgess and Cottrell had a higher proportion of couples at the college and high school level than that in the general population. On the other hand, they did include persons of only grade school training, and a larger number who had not completed high school. Other studies have been made where the sample included predominantly those who had not completed the grades or had not completed high school. Clarence Schroeder made a study of divorced and nondivorced couples, in a midwest city of 100,000, who were predominantly of low economic, low educational, and low social status. Locke compared background factors of divorced and nondivorced couples in the county in which was located a city of 400,000. They were also predominantly of low economic, low educational, and low social status. Both Schroeder and Locke found, however, that the same chief background factors were correlated with divorce and non-divorce as Terman and Burgess and Cottrell found associated with success or failure in marriage.

An unpublished study in a small city indicates that the majority of background factors operate in the same way with southern Negroes as with white couples previously studied. Differences in predictive factors are perhaps not so great by social class and by region of the country as had been expected. . . .

2. *Are background and personality information secured after marriage truly predictive?* The answer to this question is flatly, No. They can only be tentatively held as predictive until they are corroborated by studies of these items in the engagement period. Even then, they should be tested on a new sample to determine whether they are efficient predictors.

This point applies particularly to personality traits. Burgess and Wallin find that personality characteristics as measured by self-reports are subject to some change after marriage. For example, a person with a relatively high neurotic score in the engagement period may have a low score three years after marriage. The reverse is

---

[4] Burgess and Cottrell, p. 284.

also the case. Research in the future should be directed to securing, if possible, personality characteristics that are not subject to change and are also predictive of marital success.

3. *Are not statistical methods of prediction in terms of probabilities of success for a group of cases rather than for the individual?* It is evident from Table 1 that the prediction is by risk groups. For example, a premarital prediction score of 700 to 779 may be interpreted to mean that 90 per cent of engaged persons will have a high or very high marriage-success score. But it is not possible to state from the premarital prediction score above whether a given person will fall in the 10 per cent with a low marriage-success score or in the 90 per cent with a high marriage-success score. The prediction is in terms of probabilities and not of certainties.

4. *Can a statistical prediction score take account of the particular configuration of factors operating in every engagement relation?* It cannot at the present stage of development of statistical prediction. It should be possible over a long period of research to convert more and more case-study findings into quantitative expression. For the time being, however, a predictive factor indicates the way it operates in the majority of cases. In particular cases, under certain conditions, a factor may have the reverse influence.

These different objections need to be kept in mind in any attempts at the practical application to the solution of family problems of predictive factors or expectancy tables.

APPLICATION OF PREDICTIVE STUDIES

Predictive studies have been undertaken for the purpose of securing scientific knowledge about factors making for or against success in marriage. The question inevitably arises, can this knowledge and the predictive methods employed in research also be used to improve mate selection and in this and other ways increase the stability of marriage? The answer to this question will be taken up under the following heads: (1) general preparation for marriage, (2) function in mate selection, (3) screening for premarital counseling, (4) premarital counseling, and (5) early postmarital counseling.

General preparation for marriage

The knowledge of factors associated with marital success is now being disseminated in high school and college texts and courses on prepara-

tion for marriage. Since World War II a rapid growth has occurred in the number of college and university marriage courses and in the enrollment in them.

The crucial question, of course, is whether or not this knowledge is effective upon conduct. No proof of this through research findings is yet available. In the opinion of the writer, the chief value of these courses may lie not so much in the absorption of this new knowledge but in the changes in attitude of the students. Young people exposed to these courses inevitably adopt the attitude of adaptability. They perceive that love is not enough for success in marriage. They come to realize that marriage requires adjustment of personalities, preparation for it by future husbands as well as wives, and the acquirement of certain skills.

Function in mate selection

What place, if any, have prediction schedules in mate selection? Their most effective use is before young people fall in love. Findings of studies indicate that marriages are likely to be happier when young people are of similar rather than dissimilar family backgrounds, have had the advantages of a harmonious and happy home life, are comparable in personality, possess common interests, and cherish the same life values. They show that adjustments in marriage are easier to make if the two spouses have the same or similar cultural backgrounds, belong to the same social class, hold the same religious faith, and espouse the same degree of interest in religion or in a cause to which they hold allegiance. They reveal the factors which make for difficulty and conflict. They indicate that couples with divergent backgrounds and interests must work harder than others to make a success of marriage.

Screening for premarital counseling

The personality prediction schedules are particularly valuable in the selection of those in need of special preparation for marriage, including premarital counseling. The schedules may be used to identify those persons and couples with low prediction scores for marital success. Individuals falling somewhere in the lower half of the prediction scores may be regarded as those who should receive the best available preparation for marriage. Those with scores in the lowest quartile of the prediction should be specially encouraged.

They are also the group who will benefit most by premarital counseling on an individualized basis.

Premarital counseling

A brief discussion of the different sections of the prediction schedule will indicate their value for premarital counseling. These sections are (*a*) background factors, (*b*) personality items, (*c*) engagement history, (*d*) engagement adjustment, and (*e*) anticipations of marriage behavior.

The first two sections, on backgrounds and personality, are concerned with the independent characteristics of each member of the engaged couple. The last three sections deal with the engagement relation between the two. Persons cannot change their background and personality traits, but they can modify their engagement adjustment and their anticipations of marriage behavior.

Those couples with low scores predictive of marital success need not feel that their union is doomed to failure. The majority of them can achieve domestic happiness, but they must work harder than others to obtain it. Difficulties of adjustment during the engagement period have been found to be predictive of a low score for adjustment in marriage. The counselor may suggest that the engaged couple postpone marriage until these problems are solved. The study by Judson T. Landis[5] indicates how long a time it may take to make various adjustments after marriage where the couple has not solved these problems before marriage.

In particular cases, the marriage counselor will be able to forecast probable sources of difficulty in the marriage. These "danger zones" can be discussed with the couple. To the extent that young people are forewarned about these, they may be forearmed to meet them successfully. This preventive aspect of premarital counseling should promote the stability of marriage.

Early postmarital counseling

The marriage-success score may be used to help husbands and wives who have problems of adjustment. These may be either major or minor difficulties. Certain components of the success score—areas of agreement and disagreement, presence or absence of complaints about marriage and the spouse, and so forth—indicate points of conflict and tension. Other components show the over-all attitudes of the members of the couple, such as their report of happiness or unhappiness, general satisfaction or dissatisfaction with their marital relation, and the strength or weakness of their love for each other.

. . . Lewis M. Terman[6] presents evidence of the value of postmarital tests in showing which marriages would be broken and which would be unbroken eight years after the tests were given. Three tests were given to over 600 married couples. . . . The marital aptitude test contained 150 items on personality, childhood, family background, education, occupational history, and opinions about the ideal marriage. The marital happiness test contained 15 items, including self-reports, on happiness, activities enjoyed with and without spouse, and satisfaction with the spouse and with marriage. The sex adjustment score was obtained for the husband and wife separately through their replies to questions about sexual aspects of the marriage. Terman found that scores on all three tests were predictive for both husbands and wives, but more predictive for wives than for husbands. He also discovered that for both husbands and wives the happiness score was the most predictive, and that the scores for the other two tests added only slightly to the efficiency of prediction when happiness scores were used alone.

The findings of Terman's study indicate the value of marital happiness scores and of other criteria of success in marriage for screening couples for postmarital counseling. This study also underscores the finding of his original study and of the Burgess and Wallin unpublished report that in a large proportion of marriages there is considerable difference between husband and wife in happiness and in sexual adjustment.

It is evident that there exists an unexplored field for the use of tests of marital happiness, aptitude for marriage, and sex adjustment. These tests, if given early in the marriage as a basis of selection of cases for marriage counseling, might avert many separations and divorces. At present, couples wait until one member wishes a divorce before calling upon the services of a marriage counselor. By that time, it is generally too late to save the marriage.

CONCLUSION

The prediction of marital adjustment is still in the pioneer stage of research. At best, present use in practical application is in providing data

[5] Judson T. Landis, "Adjustments After Marriage," *Marriage and Family Living*, 9 (1947), 32.
[6] Lewis M. Terman, "Predicting Marriage Failure from Test Scores," *Marriage and Family Living*, 12 (May 1950), 52-54.

(1) for courses on preparation for marriage and (2) for screening cases in premarital and postmarital counseling. This screening should be accomplished by selecting those cases with low predictive scores in the fields of personality traits, social background, engagement history, engagement adjustment, and anticipations and plans for the marriage period.

Marriage counseling centers are already beginning to use prediction schedules for research purposes. Undoubtedly individual counselors are using them cautiously in addition to clinical methods for analyzing the problem areas of cases which they are studying. . . .

Indispensable to any program for strengthening the stability of the American family are research findings in human behavior. The disciplines of biology, cultural anthropology, psychology, psychiatry, social psychology, and sociology are making increasing contributions to our knowledge. Studies in the prediction of success and failure in marriage utilizing the basic findings of these sciences of human behavior are concentrating upon the study of marriage. The results of this research, even in its pioneer stage, have already made contributions and will continue to make contributions that can be utilized in the field of education for marriage and for marriage counseling.

Selection 52

Value-Behavior Discrepancies Regarding Premarital Coitus

Harold T. Christensen and George R. Carpenter

The following selection by Christensen and Carpenter combines theory with research and adds previously unreported data to the total store of the social sciences. Methodologically, the authors combine the techniques of cross-cultural comparison, statistics, and attitude measurement.

There is a long history of studies that attempt to measure premarital sexual behavior and to find and state the causes for the observed variations in such behavior. Some students of the subject have sought the reasons for variations in the individual psyche and ego-orientation; others, in the psychological needs and desires of the individual's conscious or subconscious. Still others have postulated imitation and the control of the peer group (which does seem significant in the relatively infrequent "sex gangs"), home and family experiences and examples, or the amount and kind of sex education and the age at which it was received.

The following article in essence concerns itself with none of these but instead hypothesizes about variations between groups rather than between individuals. That is, the study does not concern itself with why persons number 121 and 122 in sample A differ from each other in premarital behavior but with why the average of sample A differs from the average of sample B. The student should note that this difference in approach—dealing with groups rather than with individuals—illustrates one of the differences between clinical psychology and sociology. Each approach is valid and useful and each is related to the other, but their aims and results are not coequal.

The geographic areas of the United States from which the samples come are not necessarily representative of any total cultural pattern. Students from the Far West, Southwest, Deep South, New England, or Middle Atlantic areas may wish to compare the findings of the study with their estimate of the geographic area with which they themselves are most familiar. Speculation on the amount of under-reporting of tabooed behavior in relation to the findings of this study is also entirely proper, even though the authors do not report data on this area. Other studies have indicated a very general, almost universal, tendency to somewhat under-report societally disfavored behavior and to somewhat over-report societally approved behavior.

In an earlier article, it was shown that premarital pregnancy and its consequences are in certain respects related to the general culture of the society involved. A . . . comparison of samples from three modern Western societies—the sexually restrictive Mormon culture of Utah, the more typical United States culture as found in Indiana, and the sexually permissive Scandinavian culture of Denmark—revealed that the last named had not only the highest incidence of premarital pregnancy, but also the least negative effects therefrom. In Denmark there was found to be less pressure than in the American samples to either hasten into marriage or to dissolve the marriage as a consequence of premarital pregnancy.

This report has been prepared as a companion piece to the work just cited. Whereas the first publication was based upon official registration data and was restricted to the phenomenon of premarital pregnancy, the present analysis was built from questionnaire responses of university students and it deals with: (1) attitudes respecting premarital sexual intimacy, (2) actual rates of premarital coitus, and (3) comparisons between the two. Nevertheless, both articles are concerned with the same three general cultures and both focus upon the problem of cultural relativism applied to premarital sex norms. By the use of complementary data, this second article attempts to retest and to further complete the theory suggested in the first.

SAMPLES AND PROCEDURES

Though university populations cannot be considered as cross-sections of the societies in which they are located, students are perhaps the most accessible and cooperative of all possible subjects for research purposes. For this reason, and since cross-cultural research involves some unusual difficulties at best, it was decided to use college students and thereby minimize the problem of achieving uniformity in the data gathering procedures. In line with this decision, our samples were drawn from a Danish university, from a university in Midwestern United States, and from a university of the Intermountain region of the United States having a high proportion of Mormons in its student body.

A questionnaire was constructed, translated into Danish, pretested on both sides of the Atlantic, and exposed to criticism and revised several different times. . . .

The questionnaires were administered in university classes during regular class hours . . . . Brief verbal instructions were generally given stressing the importance of the research and the voluntary and anonymous nature of participation. Response was almost one hundred per cent.

. . . The resulting samples consisted of 149 males and 86 females (total 235) from the Danish university, 213 males and 142 females (total 355) from the Midwestern university, and 94 males and 74 females (total 168) from the Intermountain university.

As a first step in analysis, it was desired to test the original assumption of intercultural variability regarding sexual permissiveness-restrictiveness. A Guttman type scale was constructed for this purpose, thereby permitting us to represent each respondent's attitude concerning premarital intimacy with a single numerical symbol.

We started with twenty-one different items, but tests for unidimensionality reduced this number to ten. These are: agreeing with the statement, "I would prefer marrying a non-virgin;" disagreeing with the statement, "I would prefer marrying a virgin;" approving of petting any time before marriage for oneself; approving of petting any time before marriage for the daughter; approving of coitus any time before marriage for the daughter; approving of coitus on random or casual dates; approving of coitus when a couple is in love and going steady; approving of coitus when a couple is in love and formally engaged to be married; agreeing that premarital pregnancy is nothing to be ashamed of or to hide providing the couple is in love and later gets married; and agreeing that it is best not to try to prohibit erotic and obscene literature and pictures by law, but rather to leave people free to follow their judgments and tastes in such matters.

All ten items were stated in terms of permissiveness, and, therefore, the higher the resulting scale value the greater the permissiveness of the respondent being considered. The range of possible scores was from zero through ten. . . .

From the *American Sociological Review*, Vol. 27 (1962), 66-74. Reprinted by permission of the American Sociological Association.

INTIMACY PERMISSIVENESS

In Table 1 are presented mean intimacy permissiveness scores for males and females, and then for the total, in all three cultures. (1) The most striking thing to be observed is the very great and consistent decreases in scores as one moves from left to right. Danish scores are almost twice as large as the Midwestern, and Midwestern scores are almost twice as large as the Intermountain—which is practically a geometric decline. Furthermore, the comparison holds for males and females considered separately, as well as for the total, and in all cases the differences are statistically significant. (2) A second observation is that the Midwestern scores are closer to the Intermountain than to the Danish. These two findings give further support to the hypothesis . . . that Danish culture is sexually permissive, Intermountain Mormon culture sexually restrictive, and Midwestern culture somewhere in between but closer to the restrictive norms. (3) Thirdly, males are shown to have higher scores than females in all three cultures, indicating that they are more permissive regarding sexual matters. However, these differences were found to be statistically significant in the Midwestern sample only.

The sequence of Danish-Midwestern-Intermountain on the permissive-restrictive continuum is clear for every type of attitude test that has been run. Statistically significant differences in this direction were found, not only for totals and when sex as a variable was controlled, as shown in Table 1, but when two factors were controlled simultaneously (sex combined one at a time with each of the following factors: age, educational level, religious participation, social class, happiness of parents' marriage, and courtship-marriage status), and even when three factors were controlled simultaneously (sex, age, and religious participation; and sex, age, and social class). It was the most consistent and significant relationship revealed in the entire study.

TABLE 1:   Mean Intimacy Permissiveness Scores by Sex and Culture

SEX	DANISH	MIDWESTERN	INTER-MOUNTAIN
Males.....	8.4	4.8	2.7
Females...	8.2	3.4	2.0
Total	8.3	4.1	2.4

TABLE 2:   Percentage Having Experienced Premarital Coitus, by Sex and Culture

SEX	DANISH (N-228)	MIDWESTERN (N-351)	INTER-MOUNTAIN (N-168)
Males.....	63.7	50.7	39.4
Females...	59.8	20.7	9.5
Total	62.3	38.8	26.2

PATTERNS OF PREMARITAL COITUS

Responses to our query on most advanced stages of intimacy revealed varying percentages who had experienced premarital coitus, as shown in Table 2. The points to be observed, as might have been expected, are similar to those of Table 1 for Intimacy Permissiveness scores: (1) Danish respondents show the highest percentages, with Midwestern intermediate and Intermountain lowest.[1] This is true for males and females alike (especially the latter) and for totals. All three sets of differences were found to be statistically significant. (2) For the females at least, Midwestern percentages are closer to the Intermountain than to the Danish. Male percentages, however, show approximately equal intercultural gaps. (3) In all three cultures, significantly higher percentages of males than females had experienced premarital coitus. It can be observed, however, that in the Danish sample the rates are within four percentage points of each other whereas in both the Midwestern and Intermountain samples the rates are approximately thirty points apart. Furthermore, all six tests wherein other factors (age, educational level, courtship-marriage status, religious participation, social class, and happiness of parents' marriage) were controlled, one at a time, revealed nonsignificant male-female differences for the Danish sample but significant differences for the Midwestern and Intermountain samples.

When the cross-cultural analysis is refined by controlling other factors, two and three at a time, the picture remains essentially the same as above described—for females *but not for males.* . . . The major intervening variable for males was age. The fact that advanced age is related to higher rates of premarital coitus, together with the fact that

[1] A separate analysis of percentages who stopped their premarital intimacy with petting showed the reverse order; that is, Intermountain high and Danish low. This opposite cross-cultural relationship for petting would suggest that in the United States, as compared with Denmark, the tendency is to preserve the chastity norm by substituting petting for coitus.

the Danish sample has disproportionately more older males, suggest that for males part of the higher coital rate in Denmark is due to the different age distribution there.

Additional aspects of premarital coitus, for those who had experienced it, are presented in Table 3. Following are some relevant observations. (1) The Danish males and females had their first coital experience about a year and a half later in life than did the Midwestern and Intermountain males and females. The former were about nineteen and one-half years of age whereas the latter were approximately eighteen. These cross-cultural differences were found to be statistically significant. In the Danish and Midwestern samples, females at first coitus were slightly older than males at first coitus, whereas Intermountain males and females were the same age. (2) Not only did males tend to start coitus earlier but they tended to be more promiscuous; that is, more of them had had more than one sexual partner. This was true in all three cultures, but especially in the Midwestern and Intermountain. Here is another example of males and females being more similar in behavior in Denmark than in the United States . . . . (3) Still another example of the point just made is demonstrated by the percentage having first coital experience with either a "steady" or a fiance(e). Here, also, are the Danish males and females rather close together in their responses while the males and females of the other two samples are extremely far apart. By this measure, the Danish males were less promiscuous and the Danish females more promiscuous than the respective males and females of the other two samples. In all three cultures, however, more females than males had their first coital experience under conditions of relative stability and commit-

ment; that is, with a steady or a fiance(e). . . . (4) In the majority of cases, first coitus was claimed to have been voluntary because of desire; and the percentages claiming this were highest for the Danish sample, next highest for the Midwestern sample, and lowest for the Intermountain sample. . . . [M]ore males than females in every culture gave "desire" as their reason for first coitus.[2] . . . (5) Finally, a majority of the Danish respondents but only minorities of the Midwestern and Intermountain respondents had "pleasant" reactions on the day after first coitus. As might be expected, pleasant reaction percentages were lowest in the Intermountain sample. Also as might be expected, pleasant reaction percentages were lower for females than males—except for the Danish sample where the familiar pattern of greater male-female similarity held. . . .

ATTITUDE-BEHAVIOR COMPARISONS

The two points just made are suggestive of an important cross-cultural relationship. If coitus *by desire*, and also *pleasant feelings* the day after first coitus, both decrease in relative magnitude from Denmark to the Midwest to the Intermountain, as has been shown, there must be a reason. Perhaps the reason is that in sexually permissive societies there is less guilt and hence more desire

---

[2] In all three samples, many more females than males indicated that the first coital experience was either forced upon them or was voluntary on their part because of a felt obligation.

TABLE 3: Selected Responses by Persons Having Had Premarital Coital Experience, by Sex and Culture

ITEMS	MALES			FEMALES		
	DANISH	MID-WESTERN	INTER-MOUNTAIN	DANISH	MID-WESTERN	INTER-MOUNTAIN
Number of persons having had premarital coitus	93	107	37	49	29	7
Median age at first coital experience	19.5	17.9	17.8	19.9	18.6	17.8
Percentage having had only one coital partner	40.9	33.7	35.1	42.9	65.5	57.1
Percentage where first coitus was with a "steady" or fiance(e)	64.5	42.1	46.0	71.4	75.9	100.0
Percentage where first coitus was voluntary because of desire	95.6	90.7	86.5	64.4	62.1	57.1
Percentage having "pleasant" feelings on day after first coitus . . .	71.4	44.8	33.3	72.9	34.5	14.3

and pleasure, while in sexually restrictive societies there is more guilt and hence less desire and pleasure.[3] . . .

It already has been observed that the variations of Table 1 and Table 2 are substantially the same. Thus, premarital coital experience was found to be more likely in those categories showing the highest Intimacy Permissiveness scores; attitudes and behavior tended to line up.

Another approach was to compare *individual* score values on the Intimacy Permissiveness scale with the presence or absence of premarital coital experience. When this was done a positive relationship was found. In other words, the higher the permissiveness score, the larger the per cent having had premarital coitus. The relationship held in all three cultures and differences were found to be statistically significant.

By considering for each sex and culture the percentage who approved of coitus before marriage, and then superimposing upon this the percentage who had actually experienced premarital coitus, we were able to study the several patterns of discrepancy between attitude and behavior in this regard. Comparisons are given in two ways: first, by showing numerical ratios of approval to experience; and second, by picturing graphically for each subdivision both the per cent approving and the per cent experiencing the phenomenon. (See Figure 1.) The following points stand out: (1) First and most important, both males and females in the Danish sample gave greater approval than actual experience whereas those of the other two samples indicated more experience than approval. Apparently, in the Danish sample, there were a number of both sexes who had not experienced premarital coitus but thought they would do so later on. Obviously, where there has been premarital coitus by more people than approve, some of these will be harboring guilt feelings about their behavior. Both Midwestern and Intermountain students (especially the latter) fell into this category. In the Intermountain—where guilt over premarital sex may be presumed to be the greatest—a larger percentage of total males than total females experienced coitus without approving it, but of the sexually experienced the situation was the reverse of this (compare graph bars with approval-experience ratios). (2) As with previous comparisons, females showed up more conservative than males. This may be observed in all three cultures and for both approved behavior and actual coital experience. Furthermore, each of the female approval-experience ratios were lower than the corresponding ones for males. Thus, of the sexually experienced, proportionately more females

than males apparently had compromised their standards. . . .

THE MEASUREMENT OF EFFECTS

From the beginning, it has been our contention that premarital sexual behavior is related to the general culture in which it occurs: first, in respect to the attitudes or values which people hold; second, in respect to the actual overt behavior which takes place; but third, *in respect to the consequences or effects of this behavior.* Specifically on this last point, it has been hypothesized that the most permissive culture would have the least negative effects from premarital sexual intimacy, because behavior there would be in line with accepted values, while the most restrictive culture would show the greatest negative effects, since in that situation behavior would tend to be in violation of the values held. Therefore, in considering the three cultures dealt with in this study, we have expected the Danish sample to show the least and the Intermountain sample the greatest negative effects from premarital coitus.

One important measure of effects was provided by the senior author's earlier analysis of these three cultures. . . . It was shown that premarital pregnancy in Denmark does not cause either the hurried up marriage or the same pressure for divorce later on as it tends to do in America.

Another clear indication of effects was suggested above by three different but complementary findings: first, that the percentages of respondents who said their first premarital coitus was "voluntary because of desire" were highest for Denmark and lowest for Intermountain (Table 3); second, that the percentages of respondents who had "pleasant" reactions the day after first premarital coitus were highest for Denmark and lowest for Intermountain (Table 3); and third, that the Danish respondents indicated greater approval of premarital coitus than they had actually experienced, whereas both the Midwestern and Intermountain respondents indicated the reverse of this (Figure 1). Thus, the Danish respondents had a margin of tolerance in which they could feel relatively comfortable, whereas many Midwestern and Intermountain respondents (especially the latter) had over-stepped the moral

---

[3] Actually, responses concerning feelings the day after first coitus showed only 2.2 per cent of the combined male and female sample from Denmark feeling guilt, as compared with 12.7 per cent from Midwestern, and 25.6 per cent from Intermountain. This, of course, supports our hypothesis.

bounds of their groups and so must have been experiencing some guilt. Actually, the guilt expressed for the day after first coitus was greatest for the Intermountain sample and least for the Danish sample, which bears out the claim just made. The probable explanation for these cross-cultural differences in sexual desire at first coitus, and pleasant feelings the day following first coitus, seems to be the relative lack of inner conflict over sexual matters in the permissive culture as against the presumed inner conflict in the more restrictive cultures due to the value-behavior discrepancies existing there.

SUMMARY AND CONCLUSIONS

This paper is the complement of an earlier one dealing with the cultural relativism of premarital sexual intimacy. Three cultures have been analyzed by means of both governmental record data and university questionnaire data. The cultures involved are Denmark with its rather permissive sex norms; Midwestern United States with its somewhat typically American sex norms, and the Mormon culture of the Intermountain West with its rather restrictive sex norms. No claim is made for precise representativeness of the samples or for exact comparability of the data. Yet, it is believed that the data are reasonably qualified in these respects. Furthermore, the fact that both sets of data present the same general cross-cultural pattern, tends to increase one's confidence in the results.

The general pattern revealed is as follows: (1) Denmark has the most permissive and Intermountain the most restrictive *attitudes* regarding premarital sexual intimacy. This was shown through citations from the literature and by means of an Intimacy Permissiveness Scale. (2) Likewise, Denmark has the most permissive and Intermountain the most restrictive *behavior patterns* in the area of premarital sexual intimacy. This was shown by means of indices for premarital coitus and premarital pregnancy. (3) But when it comes to *negative effects* resulting from premarital intimacy, Denmark has the least and Intermountain the most. The effects analyzed in this regard were lack of sexual desire at first coitus, unpleasant feelings on the day following first coitus, . . . tendency to hurry the marriage after discovery of pregnancy, and tendency to terminate the marriage by divorce. (4) In most of the above comparisons, Midwestern United States is intermediate, though closer to the Intermountain Mormon culture than to the Danish culture. The largest gap, in other words, was found to be between the Danish and the United States cultures.

It must be remembered that, for males, the higher coital rate in Denmark may be accounted for in part by the larger percentage of older males in the Danish sample.

Also to be kept in mind are the facts that larger percentages of Danish men had only one sexual partner and had their first coitus with a steady or fiance, which means that they are *less promiscuous,* and that Danish men and women had their first sexual experience at a later age than was true in the United States. In other words, sexual intimacy in Denmark is more a part of the marriage process; the culture there is actually less permissive of intimacy for its own sake; in this sense, the Danish pattern is the more conservative. This closer association of sexual intimacy with the marriage process in Denmark may help account for the greater likelihood of pleasant feelings accompanying first coital experience there.

There is some evidence that sexual restrictiveness tends to converge male and female *attitudes,* perhaps by idealizing the male; while sexual permissiveness tends to converge male and female *behavior,* perhaps by liberalizing the female. Apparently, a possibly stronger male sex drive causes males more than females in the restrictive cultures to "break over the traces;" so that—in

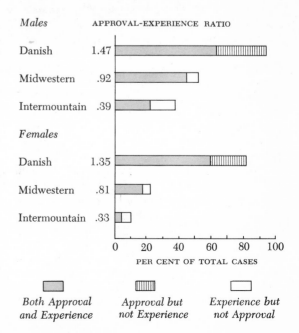

FIGURE 1: Comparisons of Approval with Experience in Premarital Coitus

Males   APPROVAL-EXPERIENCE RATIO

Danish	1.47
Midwestern	.92
Intermountain	.39

Females

Danish	1.35
Midwestern	.81
Intermountain	.33

PER CENT OF TOTAL CASES

Both Approval and Experience   *Approval but not Experience*   *Experience but not Approval*

regards to behavior but not in regards to attitude—cross-cultural differentials are less for males than for females.

But, though the male in the restrictive culture seems to have the greater discrepancy between what he believes and how he behaves sexually, both sexes within such cultures experience some discrepancy in this direction. And it seems prob-able that it is this discrepancy that causes the guilt feelings, the dulled sexual experiences, . . . the higher rate of divorce, and possibly other negative effects which seem to be highest in restrictive cultures. In other words, it may be the *value-behavior discrepancy*, as much or even more than the behavior itself, that is causing the difficulty.

Selection 53

The Early Marriage Trend

Kingsley Davis

Davis, in the following selection, presents conclusive evidence that the average age at marriage is decreasing and has decreased for a number of decades. In the past, urban, well-educated people married latest, but today we as a nation are more urban and better educated than ever before and are marrying earlier. Davis sees the "why" of earlier marriage not as a capricious whim but as the result of basic changes in society that make marriage less of a "fateful commitment" than it was once; these changes do not directly "cause" earlier marriage, but they do "lower the threshold" for this kind of behavior. Chief among the significant factors, in Davis' opinion, are the pressure of sex, the elimination of serious financial handicaps when both partners work, control over the timing of children through contraception, and the increasing use of divorce to relieve mistakes.

Several of the serious implications of early marriage are that: (1) families have more children, earlier, and over a shorter time span; (2) there is little emphasis on a career for the wife—if employed, she works at a dead-end, non-challenging job that may be a serious waste of talent and education; (3) it "catapults" youth into adulthood and "accelerates all phases of the family cycle except the final one"; (4) the younger the marital partners, the higher the divorce rate.

Davis' personal evaluation of the trend toward earlier marriage is negative: "The emphasis . . . is upon group conformity rather than individual initiative, on security rather than achievement, on slackness rather than self-discipline." Today's youth "adopt a conformist mode of life; circumstances have made marriage easy for them, and they have embraced it."

Not all sociologists and certainly not all students will agree with Davis. Despite greater knowledge of contraception, our illegitimacy rate is not drop-ping rapidly, and in some areas it seems to be increasing. Whether even earlier marriage would improve this condition cannot be said, but it seems logical that later marriage would not inevitably be beneficial. Certainly social norms and expectations are more important factors in the problem of illegitimacy than age alone.

In our society, marriage tends to signify adulthood. For example, in some states a girl of seventeen may not be served beer because she is a minor; but if she marries, she is no longer a minor and so legally may be served. If she gets a divorce, still at seventeen, is she again a minor, or once having been an adult is she always thereafter an adult? The answer to this question is not yet legally clear. Particularly important is the assumption that any man is ready to support a wife when he has finished his education, training, apprenticeship, or what have you. This is true in theory more often than fact, however. Parents as well as young couples are faced with the alternatives of stopping formal education or continuing it under handicaps. All too frequently the parental generation sees the latter choice as an unfair desire to "have your cake and eat it, too" on the part of the young couple.

For many lower-middle- and upper-lower-class young couples, whether or not they continue formal education, early marriage means that both work full time, that they live in a small apartment or "rooms," that they maintain close family ties, and that they hope there will be no children for a while. If the wife does become pregnant, she tries every way short of illegal abortion to prevent the birth. When children do come, they are very quickly placed with the grandparents—usually hers—throughout the day and often for the night as well, since the young couple frequently are loath to give up their earlier entertainment habits. This pattern is broken only if the children become too numerous, if the grandmother's health begins to give way, or, rarely, if the husband's financial situation improves markedly. More commonly the pattern runs full cycle: the young couple's children grow up and have children of their own, and the new grandmother gives up her job and stays home to play the role her own mother played seventeen to twenty years before.

As for the future of the early marriage trend, any trend is simply a directional movement observable in the past and present and is useful for predicting the future only to the extent that conditions do not change—which they often do in our dynamic, modern world.

Recently the question of age at marriage was highlighted by the visit of a Tennessee rock-'n'-roll singer to Britain. The singer, aged 22, was accompanied by his *third* wife, aged 13! The British expressed strong disapproval, evidently not realizing that the singer is as up-to-date in his matrimonial life as he is in his music, that he and his wife merely represent the extreme expression of the modern trend toward early marriage found in all industrial societies, particularly in the United States.

Several features of this trend are worth noting:

—First, the age at marriage has tended to drop in all the advanced countries, especially in recent years; but in the United States, which had a low age at marriage already, the decline evidently began earlier and has lasted longer than elsewhere. The only thing that interrupted the decline was the great depression, when apparently the age at marriage rose slightly; after that the downward trend was so sharp as to make up for the depression-born interruption.

—Second, the decline has been greater for men, the median age falling by more than three years for the men and by barely two years for women. As a result, the age gap between husband and wife has been reduced.

—Third, the magnitude of the decline can be appreciated when we realize the relatively narrow age range within which most people in this country get married for the first time. Among the women who entered their first marriage during 1950-53, half got married within the age band of 18 to 21; for half the men, it was 20 to 24.

These features make it clear that the trend is a persistent and a sizable one. A further fact suggests that it may be revolutionary as well. Not only has the trend reversed what was probably a lengthy tendency to *postpone* marriage (doubtless characterizing much of the nineteenth century), but it has occurred during a period when many of the changes in America have been such as to lead to an extension rather than a reduction in the age at marriage. We know that city folk generally marry later than country folk; since the United States has rapidly urbanized during the last century, the age at marriage should have risen. We know that well-educated persons normally marry later than poorly educated ones; since the amount of schooling has greatly increased in America, the marrying age should have gone up. That the marriage trend

From *What's New*, No. 207 (1958), 2-6.

has been in the opposite direction suggests that other forces of a powerful character have been affecting the lives of young people.

WHY ARE THEY MARRYING YOUNGER?

A glance at the figures shows that marital age fluctuates with business conditions. The depression definitely interrupted the rush toward youthful marriage. Doubtless the long-term rise in real income has played a role in the long-term drop in the age of marriage—both movements cutting through minor variations. Business changes, however, explain shorter fluctuations in marriage better than they explain long-range changes. To understand the protracted decline in the marital age, we have to call upon some additional factors.

The basic principle explaining the trend is this: anything that makes marriage less of a fateful decision, less of an economic and social commitment, less of an irreversible step, will tend to lower the age at marriage. This is particularly true when, as in our country, there continues to be a prejudice against premarital intercourse despite great freedom of association between boys and girls. The postponement of marriage in the past was due to the serious prerequisites and subsequent obligations tied to wedlock by social expectation. Yet young people are naturally impelled to get together to have sex relations, and they will do so in the easiest way they can find. If circumstances favor the socially accepted avenue of marriage, they will take this path. The fundamental reason why marriage is occurring earlier, then, is that there are fewer obstacles and countervalues to getting married than there used to be.

One of the traditional obstacles to marriage for the man was that he had to have enough income to support a family. In the old days of agrarian Europe or early America, this meant that he had to have enough land of his own; for with this land he could put both himself and his wife to work. As industrialism came along, the principle was altered to mean that he had to have a steady job; but owing to the separation of home and workplace, it was *his* job, and his alone, that was meant, for the wife was expected, at least in respectable circles, to remain at home. For seventy years in this country, however, the proportion of married women in the labor force has been rising. In 1890, of the wives who were under age 35 and living with their husbands, only about 5.5 percent were in the labor force. Half a century later, by 1940, the proportion (18.4 percent) was more than three times as high. By 1957 it was up to 27.7 percent.

The rise since 1940 in job-holding by married women living with their husbands is remarkable, because it has occurred simultaneously with the baby boom. This does not mean that mothers of young children are flocking into the labor force, but simply that young wives now tend to work *until* they have children and to work *again* as soon as the last child reaches school age. In other words, marriage itself does not keep them out of the labor force, but solely the presence of young children. This explains why there are more married women (spouse present) in the labor force at ages 35 to 54 than there are at younger ages. Even at young ages, however, an amazing number of married women are helping their husbands bring home the bacon. In 1957, for instance, 28 percent of the wives aged 18-19 were working, and 30 percent of those aged 20-24. This willingness of young women to work after marrying enables many a youth to decide that he can "afford" to get married.

Since the coming of children has the double effect of removing the wife from the labor force and increasing the financial burdens of the couple, another important factor lessening the automatic costs of marriage is birth control. Although the knowledge and use of contraception had started by 1890, it had not diffused through all social classes. In the 1930's, however, virtually all couples had access to it, and under the adverse conditions of the depression the birth rate fell so low that, if it had continued, it would eventually have led to population decline. With the return of prosperity, couples have had more children, but this reversal has been due to deliberate planning rather than to ignorance of birth control—as shown by the fact that the upper classes (those previously with the lowest fertility) have shown the steepest rise in childbearing.

The significance of contraception as an encouragement to early marriage does not lie, therefore, in a reduction of the number of children, but rather in *control* over the number. Whereas formerly marriage automatically led to children in the normal case, it needn't do so now if the couple's economic circumstances are adverse. Accordingly, a young man contemplating marriage does not have to be in a position to "support a family." If conditions turn out to be good after the wedding, he and his wife will usually have children, and they have been doing so abundantly during the last two decades; but if conditions are bad, the young couple will postpone this phase of marriage.

Another factor reducing the commitment implied by matrimony is the increased rate of divorce and the growing tendency to remarry after divorce. The divorce rate rose steadily until after World War II. The number of divorced persons in ratio to the married was more than five times greater in 1948 than it was in 1890. The peak year for marital dissolutions was 1946; since then the rate has been cut nearly in half, though it has remained higher than the pre-war rate. It looks as though we have reached a high plateau in marital dissolution, with something like a fifth to a fourth of marriages ending in divorce or annulment.

The willingness of young people to get married early is thus enhanced by their implicit knowledge that the act is not irrevocable. They see around them many persons who have gone into wedlock and safely emerged again. They know that second and third marriages are common and often happy. They feel that if they themselves are making a mistake in their first marriage, it is not a fatal mistake. The girls especially realize that the earlier an unsatisfactory marriage occurs, the better their chances of getting into an advantageous second marriage.

Still other factors have encouraged youthful marriages, such as the wartime support of soldiers' dependents, postwar G.I. educational and housing benefits, and the federal subsidy of home ownership. In sum, however, the effect of all these elements is to make marriage less of a fateful commitment. The employment of wives and the control of contraception both protect the man from the automatic responsibilities that wedlock formerly entailed. No longer does marriage necessarily endanger his career; instead, it may help him. The wife's working may cushion even the financial burden of children, for she may hold a job specifically for the purpose of saving money in order to have children. These changes explain why it is the man's age at marriage that has fallen faster. A young man today is simply deciding to get married; he is not deciding to support a wife or to have a long chain of progeny, at least not immediately. Furthermore, he and his bride half-consciously realize that if their early marriage does not work out, they can readily get a divorce or an annulment and try again.

SOCIAL CLASS AND AGE AT MARRIAGE

The reduction in the age at marriage has not characterized all groups equally. In general it still remains true that the higher the person's status, the later he marries; but this is less true now than formerly, because the high-status groups have shown the most pronounced decline in the marital age. Between 1940 and 1950, for instance, the proportion of persons aged 20-24 who were married rose by 11 percent among those with only

four years or less of elementary education, but by 102 percent among those with a college education.

As Paul C. Glick, one of our outstanding authorities on family statistics, has pointed out, the waiting period between quitting school and getting married tends to diminish as the amount of schooling increases. Today, with the lowering of the age at marriage among those receiving advanced education, the waiting period is tending to disappear altogether. In 1957, for instance,

Median Age at First Marriage

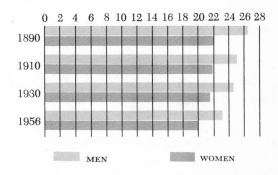

Source: *Bureau of the Census, Current Population Reports, Series P-20, No. 72 (Dec. 21, 1956), p. 3.*

Percentage of Ever-Married in Each Age Group*

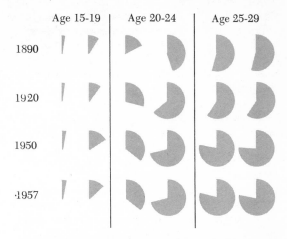

Sources: *U.S. Census, 1940, Vol. IV, Part 1, p. 16. U.S. Census, 1950, Special Reports, P.E. No. 20, pp. 2D-16 to 2D-18. Current Population Report, Series P-20, No. 81 (Mar. 19, 1958), p. 8.*

The "ever-married" include those who are currently married, widowed, divorced or separated. In other words, each percentage is the reciprocal of the percentage single.

28.8 percent of male college students were married and living with their wives. This is a much higher proportion than the 9.7 percent of female college students who are married and living with their husbands. The difference suggests that the working-wife-and-studying-husband pattern is very widespread. At older ages among the college students, the proportion married is greater. Since the medical student is often still going to school in his middle twenties, and since his education is expensive, we can expect that young working wives are now subsidizing a substantial share of medical education in this country. Such wives are trading their present hardships for their future status as wives of medical doctors. That the high divorce rate will bilk some of them out of the reward is intimated by "Not as a Stranger."

IMPLICATIONS OF YOUTHFUL MARRIAGE

Just as the lessening age at marriage derives from basic changes in our society, so it tends in its own right to create additional, mostly unanticipated changes.

One effect is to increase the number of children that each woman has. Earlier marriage means that the woman spends a greater proportion of her reproductive span within wedlock. The two-year reduction in age at marriage gives the American woman, for example, a 7-percent increase in the sheer time of exposure to the risk of pregnancy. Since the two years are added at the lower and more fecund end of the reproductive span, the increased exposure to legal conception amounts to much *more* than 7 percent. Furthermore, the younger the couple, the more flexible they feel about the hardships of having children. Mothers of 17 to 21 can fall asleep most any time, can stand noise and trouble and distraction more readily than a woman of 28 to 33. It is not strange, then, that with the lowering of the age at marriage, women are tending to begin childbearing at an earlier and more fecund age than formerly, and that there are far fewer childless and one-child couples than there used to be. It is not strange, either, that women are *completing* their reproduction when they are much younger. As Glick has shown, the average wife today has her last child at about 26, already having had from two to four.

The question of whether or not girls of 17 to 22 make *good* mothers is another matter. In the absence of firm knowledge in the field of infant training, the best bet is probably a young and healthy mother who is flexible and not too burdened with a sense of responsibility.

One thing is clear, however. Women now have even less ambition than they had formerly. They seem entirely satisfied to enter marriage and start childbearing at the earliest opportunity. Such distractions impede the man trying to place himself favorably in the occupational scale; for the woman, they utterly rule out occupational aspirations. It is startling to find that the increase of women in the labor force has not been accompanied by an improvement in the occupational *level* they attain. They have become increasingly concentrated in the dead-end jobs of the middle white-collar range. Their participation in the labor market is therefore not a bold stroke for feminine independence; it is rather a mark of the subordination of their occupational role to their family role. This fact may seem satisfactory, depending on the observer's values, but one must realize the price paid for it by the nation. The exclusion of women from the learned and practicing professions is the greatest waste of talent that occurs in our society. In Russia, for example, most of the M.D.'s and many of the scientists and engineers are women. Our low age at marriage and high rate of reproduction are part of a general return to primitivism at a time when we can ill afford to waste talent.

A further consequence of early marriage leads in the same direction. Somehow, if the last years of youth are to be maximized from the standpoint of training and effort, some kind of discipline has to be maintained. Marriage has traditionally been the badge of adulthood, of freedom from parental authority. For this reason many young people, especially girls, get married for the purpose of "getting away from home." The result of early marriage, then, is to catapult young people into adulthood before they have acquired adult capacities in a society whose future depends on technology and science.

Not only does early marriage push adolescents into premature adulthood, but it accelerates all phases of the family cycle except the final one. Having married early, a couple complete their childbearing much earlier than formerly, and they are much younger than they used to be when their last child marries (at an early age) and leaves home. At the same time, the length of life has been greatly extended, and therefore the couple now have a much longer period remaining after their last child has gone. In 1890 most couples were separated by death before the last child married and left home; today both partners are still living some 15 years after the last child has departed, and the average woman lives more than 30 years afterwards. The result is that parents devote more attention than formerly to preparing for a long period of life when they will be alone.

The woman in particular is now able to re-enter the labor force at a younger age and to spend the third of her life that precedes senility in a greater spirit of independence. Unfortunately, her premature preoccupation with marriage and children has usually robbed her of the chance for any distinctive contribution in this sphere, regardless of whether or not she originally had talent.

As we have seen, the willingness of youth to risk an early marriage is predicated on the ease of divorce or annulment if the relation does not work out. Evidently many youthful marriages do not work out; for the younger the parties are, the less stable is the marriage. The statistics on remarriage in relation to age at first marriage suggest that a union in which the bride is below age 20 is roughly three times as likely to end in a divorce as one in which the bride is aged 22 to 24. Somewhat similar conclusions are reached by the data on the "separated." Since this category is applied by the Census Bureau only to *estranged* couples living apart, it is a fair index of marital instability. In 1950 the percentage of married persons in each age group who were separated from their spouses was:

	Males	*Females*
14-17	10.9	5.9
18-19	4.1	4.0
20-24	3.0	3.4

By increasing the rate and the youthfulness of divorce, the lower age at marriage tends to step up the amount of remarriage. In 1955 about 31 percent of the marriages in the United States represented a remarriage for at least one of the partners.

A more youthful age at marriage also tends to reduce the death rate slightly: first, the married have a lesser age-specific death rate than the unmarried; second, a lowered average age of women when they bear children reduces the incidence of maternal and perinatal mortality.

WILL THE MATRIMONIAL AGE FALL FURTHER?

There is no doubt that the age at marriage in the United States has fallen to an amazingly low point for an industrial country. The question of whether it will continue to fall or begin to reverse itself depends upon the interpretation we give to the facts. Broadly stated, the reduced age at marriage seems part of the widespread movement toward anti-intellectualism and anti-effort in our society. The emphasis, as Remmers, Radler, Riesman, Hollingshead and other sociologists and psychologists have shown, is upon group conformity rather than individual initiative, on security rather than achievement, on slackness rather than self-discipline. If our young people marry early, they are hardly expressing any spirit of rebellion or innovation. They are conforming to the ancient public sentiment that marriage is a good thing.

Presumably the youth of today could enjoy their sexual freedom without entanglement in marriage. In this way they could focus on preparation for adult life in a society that depends for its existence on highly trained manpower. Instead, they dawdle through years of superficial schooling, start "going steady" in the grades or in junior high, and get married when they are still wet behind the ears. They thus adopt a conformist mode of life; circumstances have made marriage easy for them, and they have embraced it.

It seems unlikely, however, that the marriage age will drop further. It has not changed much between 1950 and 1956. Our country's slackness may so weaken its competitive position that the value of rigorous training and individual achievement will once again be emphasized. Theoretically, early marriage would be no bar to such values, but copious reproduction certainly would be, especially for women. Conceivably our youth might adopt a pattern of very early marriage but postponement of children. If reproduction is postponed, however, the question arises, why get married? The coming generation may answer that question negatively.

Selection 54

Social Cleavage and Religious Conflict
James S. Coleman

It is in the nature of any society that each of its major institutions interweaves in both obvious and covert ways throughout the whole of the societal structure.

Selections 54-56 show some of the less obvious societal relationships—between religion and social conflict, between religion and bias, and between religion and social classes.

In any society there are at least three basic social processes always at work: cooperation, competition, and conflict. Students socialized into the Judeo-Christian culture may be somewhat more likely to think of religion in connection with cooperation and competition than with conflict, but in point of fact religion is fully immersed in all three processes, and in turn each of the three processes can easily be exemplified in religion.

The selection by Coleman has the dual merit of re-emphasizing process theory discussed in previous selections and of giving insight into religion as a locus of value and attachment in American society. The author points out that men may enter into conflict over anything which they feel is important and over which they disagree; religion is thus a likely area of cleavage and contention because certain of its characteristics make it particularly susceptible to "opposition" behavior.

Generally, when lines of cleavage exist and conflict results, the more equally matched are the groups involved, and the greater and longer will be the conflict. If the groups are quite unequal, either the conflict will be short, or it will result in the establishment of a subordinate-superordinate relationship with a minimum of actual conflict occurring. In the case of religion, the conflicting parties are sometimes quite equal and other times quite disparate in strength toward conflict; hence conflict related to religion covers a wide range of types and degrees. Religious conflict may be interreligious, intra-religious, or between church and state, but in each case religion has certain peculiarities which make it particularly susceptible to conflict. These include: the private nature of religious experience; the social power of religion as a social institution and of its leaders; the varying values to be found among religious groups and the possibility of conflict between these values and those of secular groups or of other religious groups; the likelihood that persons of the same religious group will associate with each other but not with persons of other religious groups; and the generation-to-generation transmission of religious values in early youth.

Religious conflict can mean many things, and it is important at the outset to be clear just which of these meanings is under discussion. For one, there is conflict *between established religious groups,* such as may exist in a community controversy centered around two local churches. There is conflict *within* a religious group, which sometimes leads to the breaking off of a new sect from the main body. The number of Christian sects all stemming from a single source attests to the frequency of such conflict. And there is conflict *between religious groups and secular society.*

Keeping in mind that because of these and other variations religious conflict is no simple and unitary social phenomenon, it is the purpose of this paper to point out (a) some of the sources of social conflict which seem inherent in the organization of society; and (b) some of the sources peculiar to religious conflict which seem inherent in the nature of religion.

SOURCES OF SOCIAL CONFLICT

Consensus and cleavage in society

First of all, it is important to recognize that cleavage between groups is in many respects only the obverse of consensus within groups. When people feel strong identification with a particular group, whether it is national, religious, ethnic, or another, they are necessarily setting themselves

From *The Journal of Social Issues,* Vol. 12 (1956), 44-56.

off from persons not in the group. The double-edged meaning of the verb "to discriminate" illustrates this well: to discriminate is to select and to judge, to choose between the good and bad; but to discriminate is also to exclude, to keep out, to set up barriers.

Given that men do identify themselves with groups, given that there is high consensus within such groups, then cleavage is simply the other side of the coin. The analysis of social controversy, then, is not so much an analysis of *why* there is *cleavage* between groups, but a study of *which* groups are the foci of consensus and cleavage. It is like the problem of locating walls in a house: it is not a question of whether there will be walls to delineate rooms, but rather a question of how the walls will be located, and what consequences a particular location will have for living convenience.

Thus the interesting question becomes this one: What are the different consequences of the lines of cleavage in society running one way rather than another? What are the consequences, for example, of having the primary psychological attachments being to national groups rather than religious groups? Or to local communities rather than a national community? Or to race rather than social class? The possibilities are numerous, and each configuration has, just like each floor plan for a house, its own set of consequences.

In some simple cases these differing consequences are obvious. If the waves of immigrants to this country in the 19th century had not come with an initial and remarkably strong identification as "Americans," they could hardly have been assimilated. They would have held to their old world culture as some Southerners hold to their Southern accent, and that "melting pot" would never have melted them. Much has been made of the evils of the melting pot concept of assimilation because of the debilitation of culture; and third-generation Americans often look with nostalgia at the cultural values their first- and second-generation parents have so eagerly shed. Yet if their parents had not shed these values, and had failed to make being "American" a major group identification, this country might have been little more than a battleground for different ethnic groups. The Irish immigration is a case in point, for as histories of the period from 1830-1860 in this country show, Eastern cities became a battleground for the immigrant Irish Catholics and the native Protestants. It is fortunate that not all of America's immigrants were so strongly identified with the old country and with a religion different from the prevailing Protestantism of this country. A second example makes even clearer the effect

of configurations of attachment. Suppose that social class overrode race as a boundary between groups in the United States, as it does in some European countries. Then since class carries no ineradicable distinguishing marks as does race, a man could move from stratum to stratum in an anonymous society like ours. It would be impossible to classify a man irrevocably, as a Negro is classified by his skin color, and thus impossible to deny him the potentiality of society's highest rewards.

More generally, the consequences stem from this one question: When a crucial choice exists, when the issues are clear, then how are men going to line up: Which attachments are going to come to the fore and delineate the lines of cleavage? A man has many roles, and the crucial question is which of them dominates in a situation where they lead to different paths of action. The one underlying reason why interreligious conflict has been so important through the ages is that religious attachments have been among the most powerful men can feel. Only insofar as religion comes to play a lesser role in men's lives can the potential for religious conflict become weaker. This does not mean, of course, that the level of conflict between religious groups is fixed and invariant whenever the importance of religion in men's lives is fixed. Many other factors play a part; but insofar as religion is important to men, it constitutes the *potential* battle lines along which men may divide when conditions are right.

Lines of cleavage and levels of conflict

Perhaps the most important variable having to do with the location of lines of social cleavage is the level at which these lines crosscut society. By this I mean that major lines of cleavage may come *within* individuals or *between* individuals. If the lines of cleavage come within the individual, this is tantamount to saying that numerous roles are important to him, and that he will feel cross-pressures when faced with an issue—such as, for example, the issue of released time from public schools for religious instruction. The cross-pressured man is the man whose attachments lead him in both directions at once: to side with his religious beliefs, and to side with his attachments to secular public education.

The question is, what makes for or against cross-pressures? What brings the lines of cleavage within individuals or keeps them between individuals? The answer is simple: cross-pressures are absent when the major meaningful kinds of classification in society coincide. When such important lines of potential cleavage as ethnicity and religion and social status coincide, then there are few cross-pressures. That is, when Catholics are mostly Irish or Italian and mostly working-class, while Protestants are mostly n-th generation Americans of English and middle European backgrounds, and are white-collar workers or farmers, then the potential lines of cleavage in society coincide, and reduce the possibility of cross-pressures within individuals.

One of the reasons that Jews have been a major focal point of conflict is that there have seldom been cross-cutting lines of cleavage which tied various segments of them to other persons in society. Partly out of choice, partly out of necessity created by persecution, they have constituted not only a religious group, but a cultural group, an ethnic group, a particular economic stratum of society, and a group closely knit by associational bonds. Thus in countries like Poland and Germany, there have been few ties between them and Gentiles which would create cross-pressures in either group when issues of potential conflict arose.

Group conflicts are at their strongest, are most likely to develop and least easily dissipated, when no conflict is felt within the person. This is one reason that conflicts between religious groups, as conflicts between national groups, have often been of considerable intensity. Members of a religious group feel little cross-pressure when faced with a conflict between their religious group and another. In contrast, conflicts between a religious group and the secular society comprised primarily of the same persons have been less strong. And least intense, in terms of the actual tactics of combat, has been the conflict within a religious group like the Catholic Church, resulting in the splitting off of fragmentary groups. It is only after a splinter group has irrevocably cut the bonds, so that such internal cross-pressures no longer exist, that these conflicts reach the intensity of interreligious conflicts. Martin Luther, for example, until his unequivocal break with the Church used tactics completely different from and much milder than those used when the conflict is between discrete religious groups.

When men are cross-pressured, they characteristically take one of several alternatives: they withdraw from the controversy, they delay taking sides, they attempt to keep others to whom they are attached out of the conflict, they maintain a low intensity of feeling toward either side. But one response is to take one side or the other. When this occurs, as it does initially when the conflict is between men who feel no cross-pressures, then a whole new set of responses occur. Men attempt to influence others who are uncommitted, they break off attachments which are inconsistent with their position, they change from mere disagreement with the other side to direct antagonism toward it, they invent new and diverse issues with which to gain new adherents and reinforce their position. This set of responses closely corresponds to the well-known "runaway" or "explosive" nature of conflict. When such responses exist among large numbers of people, that is, when large numbers of people are not at all cross-pressured, then the conflict takes on this explosive character, and can no longer be contained.

From this point of view, then, it is of extreme importance whether an issue lodges itself within people or between them, whether it creates cross-pressures in people or only mobilizes them for action. For in the first case, it brings into play a whole set of responses which dampen the conflict; while in the second, it brings in responses which amplify it.

When one looks at the potential for cross-pressures in our society between religious attachments and others, interesting changes are evident. The economic, ethnic, and other groups which have paralleled religious groupings in the past are coming to cross-cut them now: Catholics have diffused upwards in the economic structure, and outward geographically to the suburbs; Jews similarly are less concentrated in particular economic roles and geographic locations than before; Protestants who grew up in one sect in a community are dispersed and recongregated in communities where sects must combine to survive. In sum, economic and geographic mobility is imposing new conditions of association and group identification on persons of different religious groups. These conditions will not break down religious cleavages; to the contrary, they may sometimes thrust together in a single community a combination of religious groups which makes for conflict; yet this dispersion has its effect in many ways; certainly by increasing the possibilities of cross-pressure; perhaps by bringing religious conflict more often to the community level, less often to the national or state level; perhaps by reducing the intergroup suspicion and hostility which feed on dissociation; perhaps by initial disputes followed by gradual reduction of tensions. . . .

Lines of cleavage and the size of minority groups

One area about which little is known is the effect of the *size* of a minority group on intergroup conflict. Yet there are certain regularities which await research. In the South today, one of the few generalizations arising from segregation controversies is the relation between proportion of Negroes and resistance to desegregation. The more Negroes, the more resistance by whites. And in the history of political differences in the South, one of the primary cleavages has been between high-Negro areas and low-Negro areas, with a two-party system among the whites sometimes evolving in low-Negro areas, but never in high-Negro areas.

The history of religious restrictions in civil law in this country is also suggestive concerning the effects of minority size. When the colonies were religiously homogeneous without any organized minority in the earliest days, religious restrictions in civil laws were great, and religious conflict took the form of persecution. Yet from the early 19th century until the early 20th century, as religious diversity increased with immigration and mobility within the country, these restrictions were broken down. For example, laws requiring Bible reading in school were prevalent at the end of the 18th century. Yet few were added after that time, and from then until about 1913 there was a continual reduction in such laws. It appears that organized minority groups, Catholics, Jews, and different Protestant sects, in areas which had once been religiously homogeneous, easily broke down such laws through court action. Without such an organized opposition a religiously homogeneous community could maintain laws restricting religious liberty in violation of the constitution; but once organized minorities *did* exist, then restrictions were easily overcome.

However since 1913, and despite some Supreme Court decisions, there has been a growth of local and state laws compelling Bible reading in the classroom, released time for religious instruction, and similar measures re-affiliating religious and secular education.* The reason for this is obscure, but one possibility is this: minority religions, particularly the Catholic Church, which once opposed an affiliation of religion and education because this threatened their existence, have now become well-established and powerful enough so that, rather than being threatened by such an affiliation, they are aided by it. Thus the very minority religious groups which once opposed such measures now support them, merely as a consequence of a shift in size and security. Whether this explanation is a correct one or not is uncertain; yet it indicates the gains that would accrue in our knowledge of religious conflict if we knew more about the general relations between the size of a minority and the development of controversy.

Other examples of the effect of minority size on the group's response are abundant. Jews in the Bronx, surrounded by a majority of Jews, behave differently from Jews in the Midwest, surrounded by a majority of Protestants. And Protestants in the South, with few Catholics around them, behave differently in voting than do Protestants in the North, where Catholics are politically important. Southern Protestants shifted their votes in record numbers to defeat Alfred E. Smith for president; yet Protestants in the North who were Democratic, with Catholics dispersed among them not only geographically but socially as well, and in their party organizations, failed to turn against Al Smith to the same extent as did their colleagues in the South.** Yet such a reaction might not have occurred; the existence of a deviant minority within a group often makes the group *more* cohesive than it would otherwise be, while this example suggests the opposite.

Little is known systematically about the effect of the size of minorities on the behavior of the minority group and the majority group members. This is one point at which research could be extremely enlightening—and enlightening on a point which has important implications for the future of religious conflict, as religious groups diffuse more and more throughout the different economic and geographic segments of society.

INTRINSIC SOURCES OF RELIGIOUS CONFLICT

The paragraphs above have discussed some of the propositions which arise from a general study of social conflict. But there are certain peculiarities of religion which make it particularly susceptible to conflict, whether it be interreligious, intrareligious, or between a religious group and the state. The remainder of this paper will examine some of these attributes of religion, some of these sources of conflict intrinsic to religion.

The private nature of religious experience

Much has been made by social scientists of the organized, institutional character of religion. But religious experience is also a mystical, private thing, a relation between a man and his God. Sometimes, as in Protestantism, this individual, private nature of religion is carried to the extreme. Yet Catholicism and Judaism, even with all their

---

* Note that this article was written before the now famous case in which the Supreme Court ruled against prayers and Bible reading in public schools.—*Ed.*
** Note that this trend continued and increased with the election of President Kennedy, his popularity before his assassination, and the virtual national adulation immediately after it.—*Ed.*

institutional aspects, have nearly as important a private meditative character as well. One consequence of this "communication with God" is that every man who so indulges is in communication with a different "person outside society," a person he has in part shaped with his own thoughts. That is, whenever a mystic or a monk or a devout believer engages in meditation and interpretation of the scripture, he can create a new creed. This possibility poses a constant threat of cleavage within a religious group. In an organized doctrinal religion, like Catholicism, this threat comes mainly from individual *interpretation* of the doctrine; in sects, it comes mainly from individual *communication* with the deity. But in both cases, the threat to religious unity arises from religion's private and personal character.

Examples are abundant. Think of the Mormons' beginning: Joseph Smith takes himself to a hill, has a private revelation, and by this very revelation establishes a creed which sets off a myriad of social controversies. Jehovah's Witnesses provide an equally good example. Pastor Russell in Pittsburgh meditates on the scriptures, interprets them anew, and with his small flock founds Jehovah's Witnesses, and with them a set of tenets which has never ceased to arouse religious conflict. The examples multiply endlessly, particularly within Protestantism, with its emphasis on religion as an affair between a man and his God. But even in Catholicism, whenever such meditation, mysticism, and individual interpretation occur, as they do among monks, diversity and cleavage arise. It may be that millions of followers accept the interpretations of a Joseph Smith, a Pastor Russell, a Martin Luther, or a Pope; nevertheless, the very nature of religion itself as a mystical experience offers the constant potential for a new revelation, and with it a new set of beliefs. The path is always open for a revelation from God, establishing a new sect at odds with those around it. Nothing more may be required than a man who is ambitious or who seeks to "discover God for himself," and who has the necessary leadership qualities.

The divisive potential of such a situation is reflected by the Catholic Church's strict ban on freethinking, its insistence on the Pope as mediator between man and his God, in order to interpret the scriptures aright to him. In fact, the institution of confessionals in the Church could hardly be better designed to undermine the potential for cleavage. The priest (a member of the hierarchy and thus himself subject to discipline for possible deviation) is the mediator who insures that the "word of God" which a supplicant hears is always the same word, and can be depended upon not to lead a follower into deviant paths. Yet even with such stringent restrictions built into the religious creed, deviations within the Church continue to arise from the personal inner-experience character of religion. The tradition of miracles and sainthood constitutes one of the Church's means of coping with mystics; but saints have always been a problem for the Church, arising as they do outside the hierarchy of established religious authority.

The power and status functions of religious leadership

Another source of cleavage within religious groups arises from the other half of religion's double nature as a private experience and a social institution. As a recognized organization in society, a religious group provides status and power for its leaders. Men feel the "call" to become a preacher, priest, or rabbi for a multitude of reasons; not the least of them is the status this leadership confers. For an ambitious man, the possibility of swaying the multitudes, of leading one's flock, of having an impact upon the lives of men can be almost irresistible when combined with the rationale of fulfillment of a moral and religious duty. Such ambitions are often appeased by leadership within an existing sect or church; but how much greater are the possibilities of immortality if one leads his flock in a new direction, pointed by a direct revelation from God.

Here as elsewhere is apparent the curious combination of private and public, individual and social, which constitutes organized religion: it is much more appealing to an ambitious leader to strike out on his own, gathering his flock around him to nurture a new belief; yet a religious belief depends for survival on social acceptance and respect, which a new sect may never win. A religion ridiculed by everyone is no religion at all; and unless a group of followers reaches a "critical size" so that its members can effectively reassure one another in the face of ridicule, the infant sect cannot survive. The emphasis in religious creeds on adhering to the one true belief, and the sanctions applied to those who break away from the organization which purports to uphold this belief, are a strong deterrent to religious deviation. But even with such deterrents built into all religious creeds, there remains the attractiveness for an ambitious leader of leading his people in really new directions. The zeal of many religious leaders for foreign missions and for evangelistic preaching have been two manifestations of this ambition; another is the multiplication of religious creeds and sects, with the potential for conflict which they create.

Religion as a source of alternative values

A further basis for religious conflict—this time conflict between religious and secular society, or between different religions—is perhaps even more fundamental, for it derives from the function which religion has always performed for poor, oppressed, or unhappy people. It was Karl Marx who pointed out that religion acted as an opiate of the masses to divert them from pure class consciousness and from their struggle for a classless society. This is simply another way of saying that religion serves a peculiar and important function for the oppressed and the poor in society: it provides them with a hope and belief that sometime, somewhere, there will be a different set of values by which status is derived, a set of values which will make them the "chosen people" or those who "inherit the earth." As one writer put it recently:

If a small boy one day comes upon the fact that he is a member of the poorest family in his block, and that his block is in a slum, he should have at least the comfort of another identity, in another world, where he is rich rather than poor and where he is not only the equal of everyone, but his superior, being the beloved of God.[1]

It is easy to see the necessity for some such belief if a depressed person is to maintain his self-esteem, if in fact he is to maintain his personal equilibrium and continue to function in society. It is equally easy to see that the comfort provided by such beliefs may act as the "opiate" of which Marx spoke, for this very comfort lessens tensions which could otherwise be channeled into activity against economic oppression. But what is not so evident is the fact that this fundamental function of religion sets the stage for religious cleavage which may carry over into more general social conflict. Perhaps the best example in present-day society is to be found in Africa. Much of Africa has been converted to Christianity from tribal religions, and it is an established fact that those tribes and areas where the conversion has been greatest have showed the greatest nationalism. In particular, Jehovah's Witnesses, who have played the most important part in these African conversions, have been widely accused of fomenting nationalism among the natives. But also the Anglican Church and even the Catholic Church seem to have been the source of nationalism in places like Ugandi, where both religious groups are powerful. The rebellions which occur are the unintended consequences of creeds which provide an alternative set of values for the natives, values which subvert any possibility that the natives will accept fully the values imposed by the whites in civil authority.

When religion tells the oppressed and burdened that *they* are the chosen people, or that *they* are among the select few who will pass through the gates of heaven, religion thereby gives them a release from the values of a society which locates them so low in the eyes of themselves and others. Though their religious creed seldom dictates that they actively rebel against others (an exception is the Hebrew religion which brought the Jews out of Egypt), it provides the potentialities for such rebellion simply by telling each religious group that they are superior. To be sure, it may comfort them so that they are pacified, and need not revolt or work to gain prestige in the eyes of the rest of society; but without such an alternative set of values which religion provides (or which, it may be noted, a socialist ideology also provides), they would not even have the psychological *basis* for rebellion or other activity. A belief in religion thus acts just as does a deviant political ideology in freeing men from the value constraints imposed by society. If they were forced to hold these accepted social values and no others, a psychological equilibrium would hardly be possible for the poor and oppressed. Religious values, in helping maintain such an equilibrium, also provide the possibility of cleavage, division, and ultimately conflict.

Examples are abundant of religious belief serving as the basis for conflict stemming from a rejection of socially accepted values. Probably the most striking is that of African natives discussed above. The escape of the Jews from Egypt, the Crusades, and Gandhi's non-violent resistance movement, predicated on religion, are three other important cases; though in all of these cases other factors such as nationalism and ethnicity added fuel to the flames started by religion. In the South today, under the impact of industrialization, the strong Protestantism among poorly paid workers has in some cases provided the basis for rebellion. Also in the South, the religious values of Catholicism have generated conflict by treating the Negro as a person with equal rights, again providing an alternative set of values to those held by persons having power in secular society.

---

[1] Thomas Sugrue, *A Catholic Speaks His Mind on America's Religious Conflict* (New York: Harper & Brothers, 1951), p. 17.

One of the most important derivatives of religion's "alternative-value" function is the establishment of strong in-group feelings. Particularly if the group is small, such feelings are necessary if the group members are to maintain their alternative values in a hostile or indifferent environment; but in turn such feelings are further generated by these values, which emphasize the goodness of one's fellow-members. Each religious sect is, in a sense, a mutual admiration society.

Feelings of group identity of course help set the stage for conflict, as discussed earlier, for they establish a "we" and "they," and bring about an investment of the ego in the group. This ego-investment, in turn, means that all the defenses and needs of the ego are expanded to encompass the whole group. Whether a man is a Jehovah's Witness, a Jew, a Catholic, or a Presbyterian, a slight or insult to his religious group is a personal one, to be reacted to as a personal insult. It is obvious, then, that such group identification, derived in part from the alternative values which religion provides, creates a basis for conflict between religions or between a religious group and secular society.

The genesis of cleavage by association and dissociation

One fundamental social process which plays an important role in conflict between religious groups is the genesis of disagreement through dissociation. Catholics associate with Catholics, Jews with Jews, and Protestants with Protestants. Now given that this is true (and numerous empirical studies have shown that religion is as important a basis of association in our society as any other except race), numerous consequences follow. The process through which dissociation leads to disagreement is one of the most important. Socio-psychological mechanisms come into play to create suspicion, hostility, and fear within each group that is socially isolated from another. An account of a community conflict in the twenties between Presbyterians and Methodists in the same community illustrates these processes well:

"In a small farming community of the Northeast, there had been intense rivalry between the churches. The Presbyterians of the early days are said to have been of an unusually 'Blue' variety. They called the Methodists 'howling Methodists.' The school was near the Methodist Church, and some of the parents would warn their children not to pass this church in going to school, lest they be contaminated by the Methodist ideas."[2]

Similarly, a Catholic writes of his childhood as a Catholic among Protestants:

"I began to hear what came to be familiar phrases: 'those people,' 'the Prods,' 'our own kind,' 'they don't want us.' I became aware that we did not live in a community of friendly neighbors, but that as Catholics we were camped instead in the middle of warlike Protestants."[3]

These accounts of dissociation coupled with feelings of religious group identity illustrate how strongly reinforcing these two elements are: *feeling* together and *associating* together, or alternatively feeling apart from others and associating apart from them. Religion has been so fully tied to numerous other social institutions (ethnic groups, nationality groups, economic groups, communities, and such ancillary religious institutions as welfare organizations, schools, youth groups, informal associations, and so on) that it has been a major means by which boundaries of association have been defined in society. As a consequence, religious groups have constituted closed "pockets" within which opinions can resonate and values can evolve in isolation from others.

Generational transmission

Another source of religious conflict, obvious though it may be, is nevertheless distinct from those that have gone before. It is due to the fact that religion is usually a family matter, transmitted from generation to generation as part of a general cultural heritage. Thus religious differences are built into children at an early age, either as direct transmission of values, or indirectly through their effect on child-rearing practices. Such differences have a double effect in creating diversity paralleling religion: they provide different sets of *values* from a very early age; but even more fundamentally, they create different *personalities*. A Baptist mother, a Catholic mother, and a Jewish mother bring up their children quite differently. It could almost be predicted that these children would fail to understand each other as adults, when their personality structures as well as their values differ.

Parochial schools of course reinforce these potentialities for cleavage, for they maintain an environment for the child which shapes his whole perception of the world. An excellent indication of how these differences arise is provided by

[2] The Inquiry, *Community Conflict* (New York: The Inquiry, 1929), p. 119.
[3] Sugrue, p. 47.

passages from three textbooks used in a small Dutch community in a Catholic school, a Calvinist school, and a Dutch Reform school:[4]

CATHOLIC

Philip II was a religious sovereign. To him the Catholic cause was beyond anything else. In those days, apostasy was generally considered as a crime and had to be punished. Very many sovereigns did not bother about it too much. But Philip did. He was not too popular in the Netherlands. He was a proud Spaniard, and did not feel quite at home in the Netherlands.

The tensions and agitations in the country increased. Everywhere hedge-sermons were held; the preachers often used inflammatory words to incite rebellion.

CALVINIST

Philip did not like the Dutchmen and the Dutchmen did not like him. He was a typical Spaniard: proud, ambitious, unfriendly, and a merciless persecutor of heretics. People understood quite well why the Spanish soldiers received orders to stay here. It was to wipe out heresy from the country, to rob the Dutchmen of their freedom, in the long run.

These calm people who came to sing here in the fields and pray and listen to the old man who speaks to them from the Bible? These women and children? Oh no, this all seems to be so calm and weak. From these people there comes obviously no force, no redemption for the poor, suppressed country.

DUTCH REFORM

Philip II was by far not such a clever sovereign as his father. He was a typical Spaniard, and had nothing in common with the Dutchmen. He could not even understand their language. The purpose of his rule was as follows: the extirpation of the reformed religion in the Netherlands. Everybody had to become a Catholic!

Suddenly, a grave incident took place. In Flanders, the Calvinists revolted. They broke into the Catholic churches and smashed the statues and paintings to pieces, destroyed the altars and windows and stole what they could. There was naturally much scum among these bands. This riot, known as "iconoclasm" spread to Holland and Zeeland. There was a great tumult throughout the country.

These passages treat the same historical events; yet they perceive these events in three quite different ways. With such differences "built into" children from the very beginning, the seeds of religious cleavage are well sown. It is no wonder that such cleavages regenerate themselves with each new generation.

SUMMARY

The major argument of the present paper has been this: the potential for social conflict exists by the very way in which people identify themselves with groups, forming lines of consensus and cleavage in society; but beyond this, the potential for religious conflict exists by virtue of the very functions which religion performs for people. For both these reasons, insofar as religion fulfills the same functions for people as it has in the past, it will be attended by intergroup diversity, conflict, and cleavage.

The sources of general social conflict examined were:

(a) Cleavage between groups exists in society as the simple obverse of consensus within groups. This means that the question for analysis is not *why* is there cleavage, but *what* are the lines of potential cleavage in society, and what are the consequences of one configuration rather than another.

(b) One important variation in patterns of consensus and cleavage is the degree to which lines of potential conflict are lodged *within* individuals rather than *between* individuals. If they are within, this creates internal cross-pressures, and as a consequence a set of responses which dampen and dissipate controversy. If they are between individuals, this creates a set of responses which amplify controversy and provide an explosive potential.

(c) The size of minority groups has an important effect on the potentialities for controversy in a number of ways. Both majority- and minority-group members act differently when the minority is not permanent, and a small one; but perhaps more important, an organization acts differently when it is secure and potentially dominant than when it is in a rigid and one-sided majority.

These factors affecting social conflict are supplemented by some attributes peculiar to religion, which create a potential for religious conflict:

(a) A major source of cleavage within religious groups is the private, personal nature of religion. Since any man can communicate with his own God or interpret the scriptures anew, a diverse array of beliefs can spring up, inhibited only by the fact that religious belief needs the company of at least a few if it is to survive.

(b) A second source of cleavage within religious groups, closely tied to the first, is the status and power rewards available to a leader by successfully establishing a new cult or sect. Given the private revelations which constitute the basis of religion, an ambitious leader has the possibility of breaking away and has much to gain from a successful break with the parent church (though, to be sure, much to lose if he fails).

(c) Religion's function of providing an *alternative set of values* creates a potential for conflict between religion and secular society. These values

---

[4] I. Gadourek, *A Dutch Community* (Leiden, Neth.: Stenfert Kroese, 1956), pp. 545-547.

elevate in one's own eyes his religious group above its social position. Thus like a political ideology they provide the ferment for conflict by releasing members from the dominant values in society and providing an alternative set of values, and a group identity to go with them.

(d) Closely related to feelings of group identity is a pattern of *association*. Both induced by feelings of identity, and acting in turn to reinforce these feelings, the in-group associations of religion determine lines of social interaction to a degree

surpassed only by a few other groupings, such as race. Lack of association with other groups generateš the familiar feelings of distrust, fear, and hostility between groups, and these are the stepping-stones to social conflict.

(e) A final source of religious diversity, cleavage, and conflict is the generational transmission of religious values and of personality derivative from these values. Thus the cultural heritage which is so much a part of us from early childhood has a high religious component.

Selection 55

The Life Cycle of the Church

David O. Moberg

The following selection is the concluding portion of the chapter entitled "The Rise and Growth of Churches" in Moberg's recent book, *The Church as a Social Institution: The Sociology of American Religion.* In the earlier portions of the chapter, Moberg reiterates the traditional statement of the life cycle of religious bodies—from cult to sect to denomination to church. To oversimplify, the *cult* is small, loosely structured, self-centered, and "different"; the *sect* is still small, claims to "have the only answer," is anti-status quo, differentiates itself from the rest of the religious world, and often suffers persecution; the *denomination* is larger, is more liberalized and institutionalized, and tolerates and is tolerated; the *church* is even larger, conservative, bureaucratic, broad in its approach, and extremely influential in society. Christianity, an especially good illustration of the traditional life cycle, originated as a despised Jewish cult, grew into a persecuted sect, evolved into a tolerated and tolerating denomination, and eventually became a state church. According to Moberg, the Methodists, the Baptists, and the Salvation Army followed this general pattern closely, but the Mormons and the Christian Scientists did not. Moberg goes on to describe a series of social sources from which cults and sects arise: migration and transplantation, social disorganization, social change, conflict, socioeconomic differentiation, racial attitudes, or charismatic personal leadership.

In the following analysis, Moberg synthesizes and organizes existing theories of the general life cycle of institutions and applies it to churches, describing in some detail a theoretical five-stage institutional cycle. There yet remains to be either explained or described the life cycle of a particular church as an institution.

As an institution develops, it creates an informal and a formal structure; a set of traditions, values, goals, and objectives; policies and rules; a division of labor; expectations and hopes; collective feelings (*esprit de corps*) and morale among members. All these are progressively modified in the institution's evolution by processes operating within it. If it survives, it tends increasingly to impose

formal rules upon members, in time producing a conformity that is no longer a product of primarily

Reprinted from *The Church as a Social Institution* by David O. Moberg (Englewood Cliffs, N.J.: Prentice-Hall, Inc., 1962), pp. 118-125. Adapted from *Social Institutions* by J. O. Hertzler (Lincoln, Neb.: University of Nebraska Press, 1946). Reprinted by permission of the University of Nebraska Press.

voluntary interaction. This bureaucratic growth tends to increase efficiency. Ultimately, however, a vicious circle of increasing formalization may impair effectiveness; the institution may collapse, unless renewal occurs through relaxation of formal rules, increased stress upon informal relations, or other changes. Informal, unofficial relationships, practices, and organization are of as great importance as the formal and official in an institution's life.

The process by which an institution develops may be called its natural history. Study of many churches reveals a typical pattern through which they pass as they emerge, grow, decline, and ultimately die. Each recurrent growth cycle of stability, experimentation, and integration may be described as involving five stages. Out of the last may come reorganization or repetition of a similar cycle either within the same church or in another that arises out of its ruins.

1. The stage of *incipient organization* is usually one of unrest and dissatisfaction with existing churches. The uneasiness may be generally diffused, or it may be limited to one segment of the population, often the lower classes who complain about the "corruption" of privileged groups and the churches' complacency with their departure from traditional folkways and mores. The social unrest may arise out of a crisis which the church has failed to meet satisfactorily. It may be a reaction against ritualism that replaces personal spontaneity and devotion, against the church's involvement with "secular" affairs, or against the clergy's lack of certain spiritual or moral qualifications. When leadership arises, a new cult or sect emerges, typically as a reform movement within the parental body.

Many emerging sects have a high degree of collective excitement. Unplanned and uncontrolled emotions in crowd situations may lead to a sense of bodily possession by the Holy Spirit or by Satan that produces intense joy or fear. Physical reactions that identified such groups as the Quakers, Shakers, and "Holy Rollers" are a common result. New beliefs that deviate from those previously held may appear to upset the balance of members' personalities and subject them to the suspicion of insanity. The charismatic, authoritarian, prophetic leader is characteristic of this stage. Yet in sects that emerge as a result of gradually changing mores or rational planning, leadership is apt to be so diffused that historians have a difficult time designating a "founder."

2. A period of *formal organization* closely follows the rise of leadership. An attempt is made to develop a sense of union and of common interests. Followers are asked to commit themselves by formally joining the new group, which now separates itself completely from the parental church. Goals are formulated and publicized to attract additional members, who may either object to the established society and its churches or seek to bring about the perfection of society, religion, or individuals. A creed is developed to preserve and propagate orthodoxy. Great emphasis is placed upon symbolic expressions of the difference between the new sect and worldly nonmembers. The symbols may seem trivial or foolish to the outsider, but to the sect member they are of utmost importance. Some center upon slogans that reflect the group's theological orientation ("saved by the blood," "baptized in the Holy Ghost," "Jesus only," etc.); others emphasize behavior that deviates from society's folkways. The use of automobiles, neckties, tobacco, instrumental music, cosmetics, or wedding rings may be considered sinful; card playing, movie attendance, dancing, or military service may be tabooed. Thus codes of behavior are developed and enforced; these distinguish members from others and often draw persecution or ridicule that increases in-group feelings and strength. Agitational forms of leadership gradually diminish as the next stage is approached.

3. In the stage of *maximum efficiency* leadership has a much less emotional emphasis and is dominated by statesmen. Effectively voicing group convictions, they lead to an increasingly rational organization that replaces charismatic leadership. Historians and apologists emerge. Propaganda is prominent; the mass media are used to publicize activities and aims of the sect. Programs of action are formulated by rational consideration of relevant facts; intellectuals repelled by the previous display of emotion may give their approval or even transfer allegiance to it. It has moved psychologically from the position of a despised sect to one of near-equality with previously recognized denominations. Hostility toward others diminishes; with it the fanatical resolution to maintain sharply different ways relaxes, for the first generation of converts usually has died by this time.

The group's formal structure rapidly develops as new committees, boards, and executives are appointed to meet the needs of the growing organization. Official leaders perform their duties enthusiastically and efficiently; the rituals and procedures in worship and in administration are still viewed as means rather than as ends in themselves. The institution is at its stage of maximum vitality or "youthful vigor"; its growth may be very rapid. . . . This growth is likely to be uneven, each period of rapid growth being followed by one in which new members are integrated. If such integration is not successfully accomplished, diverse purposes, interpretations of doctrines and creeds, and social interests may lead to internal dissension; new splinter groups may arise, or the sect may even disintegrate. The Assemblies of God appear to be at this stage. The gradual acceptance of Seventh-day Adventists into fundamentalist circles illustrates movement into denominational status in this period.

4. During the *institutional* stage, formalism saps the group's vitality. Its leadership is dominated by an established bureaucracy more concerned with perpetuating its own interests than with maintaining the distinctives that helped bring the group into existence. Administration centers in boards and committees that tend to become self-perpetuating. . . . Mechanisms of the group's structure have largely become an end in themselves. The church has become a bureaucracy. Creeds become little more than venerated relics from the past. Organized worship gradually develops into a ritual which by this stage is a nearly or wholly empty formality to most "worshipers." Religious symbolism encroaches and persists beyond its usefulness because it is capable of repetition without fresh thought and always at command, in striking contrast to internal, personal devotion. The institution has become the master of its members instead of their servant, making many demands upon them, suppressing personalities, and directing energies into serving the "organization church."

By this stage conflict with the outside world has been replaced completely by toleration. Conformity to societal folkways and mores is typical even on issues clearly in conflict with implications of the church's official dogma. Ulterior motives of "respectability" are often involved in joining; membership standards are relaxed as the church tries to gain all socially respectable people. Increased membership is correlated with increased heterogeneity of sentiments, interests, and dedication. Feelings of intimacy in the group decline. Membership becomes passive and remote from leadership. Interests and activities once considered secular become major attractions as the church attempts to become a center of community activity through sponsoring cultural events, scout troops, athletic organizations, counseling bureaus, and camping programs. Sermons become topical lectures dealing with social issues, rather than fervent discourses on sin, salvation, and church dogma. Many major denominations are in at least the beginning phases of this stage; many of their local churches are far into it.

5. With overinstitutionalism *disintegration* sets in. "Diseases" of formalism, indifferentism, obsolescence, absolutism, red tape, patronage, and corruption are common symptoms of disintegration. Lack of responsiveness by the institutional machine to the personal and social needs of constituents causes loss of their confidence. Many withdraw into new sects or drift without any formal church connections. Those who nominally continue to embrace the church ignore it in practice, or they conform to its teachings only half-heartedly, supporting it because they feel it is not consistent or logical to change their attitudes even after losing all belief in their value. Leadership with a vested interest in the institution, and followers who are emotionally attached to it, attempt to preserve it. As a result, an internal reform movement may restore the church to a position of vitality and usefulness. However, the church's strength may be gradually sapped by waning membership or by the growth of new sects until complete collapse occurs.

Frequently the death of a Protestant church involves three stages. First, as a result of diminishing financial support, it is vacated by the pastor. Second, finding it difficult to secure a full-time successor, the church secures a part-time pastor either by yoking itself with another church, by hiring a lay minister who has a source of independent income, or by securing a retired or student pastor. The program of the church is attenuated. As a result, membership dwindles, some seeking a more active church. When the relatively inactive church has become so small that attempts to continue seem futile, the third stage is reached: the church "dies" by complete abandonment or by merger into another group.

Of 62 closed rural Pa. churches, 28 per cent had closed for a lack of available membership, although 38 per cent of the latter were in areas of increasing population. At the time of closing they had an average of 28 members and 21 persons attending services. Shifts of population which brought persons of other faiths into the community led to the closing of 22 per cent of the churches. Overchurching, with its accompanying competition for status and survival, was the chief factor in the closing of 13 per cent of them. Congregational disputes, arising most often out of personality clashes, caused 13 per cent to close, and 11 per cent were closed because of unsatisfactory professional leadership. Financial difficulties were the chief cause in 8 per cent, changes in transportation in 3 per cent, and destruction of the church building by fire was the precipitating factor in one church. When the churches were closed by administrative action of denominational agencies, the after-feelings of people in the community were more often harmonious than when the churches closed "on their own." . . .

The stage of disintegration is apparent in many churches. Abandoned church buildings are a witness to its past operation. Part-time pastors with meager salaries, poorly attended churches maintained largely by endowment funds, and churches with declining memberships, though located in areas of increasing population, often reflect the process of disintegration.

The five stages in the church's life cycle overlap. Not all religious institutions pass through all five, but a cult tends to arise in the first stage and develop into a sect in the second, a denomination in the third, and a church in the fourth. Reaction sets in at the fifth stage, and reorganization or death of the religious body is the usual result. Many are arrested at one stage or another. Some skip certain stages in a sequence of rapid development. The entire process may be completed in little more than a generation, or it may take hundreds of years for the sect to enter the denominational stage. The process may be reversed; it is not inevitable. It grows out of natural patterns of cause and effect relationships that as yet have been explored only superficially.

As institutions come under increased rational control, the result may be continuous adjusting and adapting rather than progression into the stage of disintegration with its pathological effects. When churches change with the changing conditions of their environments, they may remain in a stage of constant reorganization instead of degenerating pathologically. Social institutions of the past, however, seem to have followed distinct patterns of growth and decline. U.S. religious census data for three periods of time indicate that, from 1890 to 1906, 13.8 per cent of denominations that were listed became defunct compared to 8.8 per cent in 1906-1916, and 15.3 per cent in 1916-1926. These dissolutions and other data suggest . . . that the broad rivers of the great religions flow for a long time, the rivulets of denominations and sects for a short time, and small organizations within a given church appear and disappear even more quickly. Variables apparently related to churches' longevity include the rapidity of the organization's creation and development, its optimum size, the balance of homogeneity and heterogeneity in its membership, its rigidity and elasticity, its willingness to accept new members, the degree to which members' talents are used, and the environmental forces in operation.

Occasionally entire religious systems die. Of sixteen historical religions which had millions of adherents, only ten survive, and two of these are no longer located in the land of their origin. Some died as a result of violence from outside sources, others as a result of internal decadence. Some that died appear to have been succeeded by religions which bear a new name in a changed social order. . . .

Certain self-corrective processes that lead to recuperation in time of disintegration operate in social institutions. Even without the benefit of specific planning, there is a natural, often unconscious, tendency of disintegrating churches to move toward an equilibrium of adjustment. The adjustment may rejuvenate the institution, or it may involve emergence of a new organization out of the ruins of the old. . . .

The factors contributing to the life cycle of emergence, growth, and decline of religious bodies are all interrelated. They can be treated as separate items only in the abstract work of the scholar or scientist. In "real life" they combine with one another to form a complex network of interacting circumstances which operate together to produce new cults and sects. Thus it was not only Father Divine, a charismatic leader, who produced his Kingdom, but Father Divine plus a host of interrelated social forces which made emergence of his cult almost inevitable. Social disorganization, social change, conflict with and within society, race and class distinctions, and migration were all involved in the rise of his cult. Similar social factors are reciprocally involved in the life cycle of every sect and denomination.

Selection 56

Religious Preference and Worldly Success
Albert J. Mayer and Harry Sharp

In 1906 Max Weber, a German professor of economics and sociology, wrote *The Protestant Ethic and the Spirit of Capitalism*. Weber was much concerned with explaining why capitalism arose rapidly and with great strength in Western Europe and in the United States, for example, but failed to make comparable strides in other locales in which the economic and industrial potential appeared equally great. He concluded that Protestantism contained certain values and precepts—he called them the "Protestant ethic"—which were particularly sympathetic and conducive to the type of capitalism that arose in Western Europe and the United States. Throughout his work he emphasized the importance of human values as they affect an economic system. His theory was purposely in contrast to that of Marx, who held that religion was determined by the economic system and that Protestantism arose more or less as a by-product of capitalism. The traditional Catholic attitude was nonmaterialistic; it put matters of the soul far above matters of economic success and frequently intimated that too much concern with economic success might be good evidence of poor Christianity. According to Weber, Protestantism held a different value, the idea that making money (honestly, of course) was good and desirable and indeed might be visible proof of God's favor for those who followed His will. This attitude (here oversimplified considerably), along with an emphasis on thrift, is what Weber termed the "spirit of capitalism." The correlation between the spirit of capitalism and the Protestant ethic led Weber to hypothesize that the rise of the latter was one major source of modern capitalism. His studies of Confucianism in China, Hinduism in India, and their related economic consequences confirmed his belief that religious values were significantly related to economic success in a world of industrial capitalism.

Mayer and Sharp are fully aware of the various Marxian and Weberian hypotheses concerning the relationship between religion and economic success. In order to test the relationship empirically, they compared the religious preferences and economic success of a large sample of adults from the Detroit area. The results of their study offer some support for a contemporary interpretation of Weber's thesis, while presenting some modifications.

To what extent does the theory of the Protestant ethic apply to the population of a modern American metropolitan community? Previous research has pointed out some of the significant social and economic differences that exist among the major religious groupings in the United States. In this paper we are concerned primarily with the specific relationship between religious preference and worldly success. Dependence on the writings of Weber, Sombart, and Tawney is obvious. . . . [T]he "Weberian controversy" . . . is an important concern of many social scientists who basically are interested in understanding contemporary western society.

An inquiry into the meaning of religion to different denomination groups and the strength of religious expression, valuable as this would be, is beyond the scope of the present paper. Rather, we are here accepting only the denominational label with which an individual associates himself, and investigating the hypothesis that differing religious preferences are associated with varying degrees of worldly success.

This hypothesis is founded on the assumption of a basic distinction in the life orientations which are held by Catholics as compared with Protestants. The powerfully reinforced and traditional Roman Catholic Church tends to orient its members toward the hereafter; successful performance in the market place and the acquisition of the symbols of economic achievement are of relatively little importance as an indication of the Catholic's status after death. On the other hand, adherents of Protestantism are assumed to be highly concerned with worldly success and the attainment of material possession, status, and the prestige that is associated with upward social mobility. These things often are viewed as indications that salvation is assured, or at least is more probable.

From the *American Sociological Review*, Vol. 27 (1962), 218-227. Reprinted by permission of the American Sociological Association.

To the degree that religious orientations toward life are reflected in behavior, this theory would lead us to expect Protestants to excel Catholics in the race for worldly success. Protestantism in contemporary America, however, is hardly a homogeneous religious faith. We expect variations among the major Protestant denominations both with respect to adherence to the Protestant ethic and to economic achievement. Thus, this research does not group all Protestants under a common rubric, but considers the major denominations separately.

Members of the Jewish faith and adherents of the Eastern Orthodox Church do not fit into the theory as summarized above. According to Sombart, the Jews played a prominent supportive role in the rise of capitalism. On this basis, we would hypothesize that the Jewish group should bear a greater resemblance to Protestants rather than to Catholics, were all religious groups measured by a scale of economic achievement. The comparative standing on an achievement scale of the adherents of Eastern Orthodoxy was not predicted at the start of the research.

Religion does not exist as an independent attribute of the individual, but is closely bound to important cultural variables such as urbanism, ethnicity, nativity, and experience in a specific community. Thus, in an investigation of the type proposed here, the question must be answered: Is it the religion itself, operating through a network of values stemming from one's religious faith, that produces varying degrees of economic success? Or are other factors, correlated with but not "caused by" a given religious preference, instrumental in the degree of success achieved by a given religious group?

THE DATA

The data employed in this research were collected by The University of Michigan's Detroit Area Study. Each year since 1952 the Detroit Area Study has conducted a survey of the metropolitan Detroit community. . . . The objectives of these surveys required a sample of the adult population of greater Detroit that would be representative, within known confidence limits, of all non-institutionalized adults in the community.

For this research, strict probability samples were constructed which allowed the assignment of specific addresses at which interviews were to be obtained. No substitutions of any kind were permitted. Certain information was obtained about every adult who lived in the sampled dwelling units. . . . By doing so, we are able to work with a maximum N of over 9,000 adults.

Adults in the sample were classified by religious preference on the basis of their answers to these questions:

"Do you have a religious preference?"
(If Yes) "Are you Protestant, Catholic, Jewish, or something else?"
(If Protestant) "What specific denomination is that?"

For purposes of analysis, the total sample was grouped into twelve denominational categories: Catholic, Jewish, Eastern Orthodox, Episcopalian, Lutheran, Calvinist,[1] Methodist, Baptist, Small Neo-Fundamentalist Protestant Sects,[2] Non-Denominational Protestant, Semi-Christian Churches,[3] and No Religious Preference.

ANALYSIS PROCEDURE

From one perspective, life in a modern community may be viewed as a hotly contested foot race in which families vie with one another in the hope of material reward. The rewards are rather well defined in western society; they include such achievements as economic success, collection of worldly assets, and the status to be derived from the attainment of these culturally approved goals.

Through the use of a number of indices, all of which repeatedly have been shown to be highly interconnected, we have measured the relative success of the major religious denominations in this race. At the same time, we have attempted to account for the fact that not all denominations are equally favored with background factors that are helpful in the winning of economic success in a metropolitan community.

Each of the variables measured by the indices used here can be categorized as *achieved* or *ascribed*, following the conceptualization developed by Linton. The relative position of a given religious group on an *achieved* variable index may be regarded as the result of the efforts of the individuals comprising that group. Correspondingly, the position of a given group on the *ascribed* variable index is here regarded as an

---

[1] Included in this classification are Presbyterians, Congregationalists, Evangelical and Reformed, and Dutch Reformed.
[2] E.g., Jehovah's Witnesses, United Missionary, Pentecostal Churches.
[3] This category includes such groups as the Latter Day Saints, the Christian Scientists, and the Spiritualists. The classification, of course, represents more of a residual grouping than a meaningful distinction.

"accident of birth;" ascribed status is given to the individual when he is born or while he is still a dependent minor.

Continuing with the analogy to a foot race, a system of "handicapping" has been devised which at least partially removes the effect of ascribed factors on worldly success. The handicapping consists of weighting the ascribed variables in such a way that no group has an unfair advantage at the start of the contest. Thus, the relationship of religion to achievement can be more clearly seen.

ASCRIBED FACTORS

Ascribed background factors were analyzed through the use of three continua: rural-urban background, foreign-native background, and extent of experience in metropolitan Detroit. Each major religious group in the Detroit area was ranked with respect to these factors. In this ranking, one polar extreme would be a religious group all of whose members had no rural experience, were born in this country of fathers who

were also native-born, and had spent their entire adult lives in greater Detroit. The advantages for this hypothetical group are maximal since its members would have had the greatest opportunity to acquire property, education, and maximum familiarity with the cultural setting in which they now live. The opposite extreme would consist of a group all of whose members had a rural background, are of foreign birth, and have had a relatively short residence in greater Detroit. For this hypothetical denomination, familiarity with the ways and customs of a modern metropolis, and hence opportunities for success, would be at a minimum; their ascribed advantage would therefore be minimal.

Each of these ascribed background factors was further redefined. Rural-urban experience was measured in three ways: (1) percentage of each group having no farm experience (the higher the proportion without farm experience, the greater the presumed familiarity with an urban way of life); (2) percentage of each group born in cities of 50,000 or more persons; and (3) percentage of each group born outside the rural South. An additional handicap was given for rural southern

TABLE 1:   Ascribed Factors, by Religious Group and Race

RELIGIOUS GROUP AND RACE	RURAL BACKGROUND			FOREIGN BACKGROUND			SPECIFIC DETROIT BACKGROUND		NUMBER OF CASES [*]
	% WITH NO FARM BACK-GROUND	% BORN IN CITIES OF 50,000+	% NOT BORN IN RURAL SOUTH	% WITH NATIVE BORN FATHERS	% WITH FATHERS OF N-W EUROPEAN STOCK	% BORN IN U.S. OR CANADA	% BORN IN DETROIT AREA	% IN DETROIT BEFORE AGE 15	
White									
Catholic	77	54	99	36	46	81	45	68	3,307
Episcopalian.....	84	44	100	46	95	82	32	42	289
Lutheran	74	53	99	52	84	90	42	55	778
Calvinist	75	46	98	59	90	90	33	46	723
Methodist	64	34	92	69	92	95	24	36	750
Baptist	44	24	72	80	96	97	17	29	727
Small sects	49	26	85	68	87	93	21	33	232
No denomination .	60	35	70	68	91	92	12	42	194
Semi-Christian ...	64	50	92	63	89	96	26	39	96
Jewish..........	90	63	100	4	10	70	42	58	234
Eastern Orthodox.	61	33	99	3	8	42	19	33	169
No preference ...	74	44	94	49	64	85	39	54	239
Negro									
Catholic	76	50	89	—	—	—	23	41	75
Methodist	62	39	73	—	—	—	12	26	316
Baptist	43	23	68	—	—	—	7	20	938
Other	60	36	72	—	—	—	18	32	164

[*] *The N's given here are applicable to all following tables.*

United States birth under the assumption that cultural differences between the North and the South constitute a substantial disadvantage for those residents of metropolitan Detroit who were born in the southern United States.

Three indices, each with a somewhat different connotation, were used in measuring the effect of foreign background: (1) percentage of each group whose fathers were born in the United States; (2) percentage of each group whose fathers were of Northwestern European derivation (this measure attempts to "correct" for ethnically based differences in social status by assigning a higher handicap to persons of non-Northwest European stock); and (3) percentage of the members of each group who themselves are native-born Americans or were born in Canada.

It was also assumed that adults who have spent all or a major share of their lives in greater Detroit have an economic advantage over more recent arrivals in the community. Two indices were built for this ascribed factor: (1) the proportion of a given group's adherents who are native Detroiters; and (2) the percentage of each group's members

who came to the Detroit area before the age of fifteen. Together, these indices measure specific experience in this particular cultural environment.

Table 1 presents the data for the ascribed factors. White and Negro Detroiters are considered separately in this table; given the social significance of race in American society, it would be completely unrealistic to do otherwise.

Although the figures in Table 1 reveal some striking relationships, full comprehension of these data is difficult without further summarizing. Therefore, in Table 2 each index of the three ascribed factors was analyzed in terms of quartiles. Of the twelve religious preferences in the white population, the three ranking highest on each ascribed characteristic were given the weight of four, the next three highest were given the weight of three, and so forth. The four religious categories in the Negro population were handled in a comparable manner on the relevant variables, with the obvious exception that only one preference was in each quartile of the index.

For whites, the foreign and rural background categories each consisted of three indices. The

TABLE 2:   Quartile Ranking and Total Weights of Ascribed Factors, by Religious Group and Race

RELIGIOUS GROUP AND RACE	\% WITH NO FARM BACK-GROUND	\% BORN IN CITIES OF 50,000+	\% NOT BORN IN RURAL SOUTH	\% WITH NATIVE BORN FATHERS	\% WITH FATHERS OF N-W EUROPEAN STOCK	\% BORN IN U.S. OR CANADA	\% BORN IN DETROIT AREA	\% IN DETROIT BEFORE AGE 15	GRAND TOTAL ALL ASCRIBED FACTORS
	RURAL BACKGROUND			FOREIGN BACKGROUND			SPECIFIC DETROIT BACKGROUND *		
White									
Catholic	4	4	3.3	1	1	1	6	6	26.3
Episcopalian.....	4	2.5	4	4	2	2	4.5	3.8	26.7
Lutheran	3	4	3.3	2	2	2.5	6	6	28.8
Calvinist	3	3	3	3	3	2.5	4.5	4.5	26.5
Methodist	2	2	2	4	4	4	3	3	24.0
Baptist	1	1	1	4	4	4	1.5	1.5	18.0
Small sects	1	1	1	2	3.5	3	3	1.5	16.0
No denomination .	1	2	1	3	3.5	3	1.5	3.7	18.7
Semi-Christian ...	2	3	2	3	3	4	3	3	23.0
Jewish..........	4	4	4	1	1	1	6	6	27.0
Eastern Orthodox.	2	1	3.3	1	1	1	1.5	1.5	12.3
No preference ...	3	2.5	2	2	2	2	4.5	4.5	22.5
Negro									
Catholic	4	4	4	—	—	—	6	6	24.0
Methodist	3	3	3	—	—	—	3	3	15.0
Baptist	1	1	1	—	—	—	1.5	1.5	6.0
Other	2	2	2	—	—	—	4.5	4.5	15.0

QUARTILE RANKING ON ASCRIBED FACTORS

* *Quartile weights for Specific Detroit Background inflated by 50 per cent to equalize weights between background factors.*

third factor (Specific Detroit Background) consisted of two indices. Specific Detroit Background was given a weight equivalent to each of the first two factors by increasing it 50 per cent. As a result, each of the three ascribed variables had a possible maximum weight of twelve (4 x 3, or 6 x 2). The grand total maximum weight for the ascribed factors in the white population would therefore be 12 x 3, or thirty-six.

For Negro Detroiters, quartile rankings on Specific Detroit Background were also increased by 50 per cent. Since foreign background was not a variable for Negroes, the grand total weight for this population group was 12 x 2, or twenty-four.

In the white population, Lutherans (with a value of 28.8) are in the most advantageous position with respect to the ascribed factors, followed by a cluster of three groups: Jews (27.0), Episcopalians (26.7), and Calvinists (26.5). Detroiters of the Eastern Orthodox faith possess the least advantage (12.3) with the members of the small sects (16.0) and the Baptists (18.0) also at a comparative disadvantage.

The rankings on the ascribed variables are generally in accord with preconception. Detroit area Lutherans, Jews, Episcopalians, and Calvinists are highly urban, and, as a group, have a very large proportion of native-born Detroiters. The Jewish advantage is tempered, however, by the greater proportion of foreign-born among Jews as compared to other religious preferences. The Eastern Orthodox are economically handicapped, not only because a majority of these persons are foreign-born, but also because of their limited urban background before coming to Detroit and the comparatively late age at which they arrived in this community. The Baptists, although largely of native birth, are among the lowest of the religious groups in urban background and specific Detroit experience.

Among Negro Detroiters, the Baptist faith is by far the most common denomination. Negro Baptists also are in the least advantageous position with respect to the possession of those ascribed characteristics which, we have assumed, lead most readily to economic achievement. Negro Catholics (a minority within a minority, to be sure) are a comparatively urban group and therefore rank at the top of each of the indices of ascribed factors.

In following the above procedure, we obviously have assumed that one unit of urban experience, one unit of specific Detroit experience, and one unit of foreign birth can be considered as equiva-

TABLE 3:   Achieved Factors, by Religious Group and Race

RELIGIOUS GROUP AND RACE	ACHIEVED FACTORS				
	% $2,000 AND ABOVE MEDIAN INCOME	% SELF-EMPLOYED	% IN HIGH STATUS OCCUPATIONS	MEDIAN SCHOOL YEAR COMPLETED	% IN THREE OR MORE FORMAL GROUPS
White					
Catholic	27	7	19	10.0	14
Episcopalian	35	9	42	12.5	42
Lutheran	30	6	28	12.2	17
Calvinist	35	11	37	12.5	21
Methodist	32	8	27	12.3	23
Baptist	21	6	15	9.8	8
Small sects	16	11	17	9.5	9
No denomination	29	11	26	12.0	17
Semi-Christian	24	15	39	12.4	19
Jewish	42	41	62	12.5	45
Eastern Orthodox	35	15	13	9.3	8
No preference	23	9	28	10.0	7
Negro					
Catholic	6	4	7	10.0	8
Methodist	7	5	6	9.8	12
Baptist	8	3	3	9.1	7
Other	12	10	15	9.8	10

lent. This assumption was necessary as a result of summing these different measures to produce a unique index value. Given the present level of knowledge, the degree to which this assumption is in error cannot be evaluated. We offer this procedure as an admittedly rough approximation to "reality," and hope that further research in this area will result in progressively more accurate refinements.

ACHIEVED FACTORS

Five indices were used in measuring the social and economic achievements of the major religious groups in greater Detroit: (1) relative ranking on family income, given as the percentage of each group earning $2,000 or more *above* the median Detroit area family income for a given year; (2) percentage of self-employed in each group; (3) percentage of the members of each group who are in high status white-collar occupations (professionals, managers, proprietors, or officials); (4) median school year completed; and (5) percentage of persons of each religious preference who are members of three or more formal social

groups. These five indices, then, attempt to measure worldly success. They are shown in Table 3.

The quartile grouping described above for the ascribed factors was applied in a comparable manner to the achieved factors. For both whites and Negroes, the total maximum weight that any religious group might have on the achieved factors would be twenty (4 x 5). The results of these operations may be seen in Table 4.

With respect to the white population, Jews (with a rating of 20.0) show the greatest achievement as we have measured it. They are followed by Episcopalians (17.7), Calvinists (16.7) and the Semi-Christian group (16.0). The other end of the scale represents low achievement. Here are found Baptists (5.0), and Catholics and small Protestant sects (both with a rating of 8.0).

Among Negroes, the greatest achievement is shown by adults who are categorized as "Other" in Table 4. They score 17.5 on our measure. Negro Methodists rank second on achievement (13.5), and are followed closely by Negro Catholics (12.0). Negro Baptists are a rather distant fourth with a rating of 7.0.

In general, the achievement rankings shown here are consistent with the findings of previous research, both on a national basis and for indi-

TABLE 4: Quartile Ranking and Total Weights of Achieved Factors, by Religious Group and Race

	QUARTILE RANKING ON ACHIEVED FACTORS					
RELIGIOUS GROUP AND RACE	% $2,000 AND ABOVE MEDIAN INCOME	% SELF-EMPLOYED	% IN HIGH STATUS OCCUPATIONS	MEDIAN SCHOOL YEAR COMPLETED	% IN THREE OR MORE FORMAL GROUPS	GRAND TOTAL ALL ACHIEVED FACTORS
White						
Catholic	2	1	1	2	2	8.0
Episcopalian..............	3.7	2	4	4	4	17.7
Lutheran.................	3	1	3	3	2.5	12.5
Calvinist	3.7	3	3	4	3	16.7
Methodist	3	2	2	3	4	14.0
Baptist	1	1	1	1	1	5.0
Small sects	1	3	1	1	2	8.0
No denomination	2	3	2	2	2.5	11.5
Semi-Christian	2	4	4	3	3	16.0
Jewish...................	4	4	4	4	4	20.0
Eastern Orthodox	3.7	4	2	1	1	11.7
No preference	1	2	3	2	1	9.0
Negro						
Catholic	1	2	3	4	2	12.0
Methodist	2	3	2	2.5	4	13.5
Baptist	3	1	1	1	1	7.0
Other....................	4	4	4	2.5	3	17.5

vidual communities. Episcopalians, Calvinists, and Unitarians are usually ranked high on economic status. Also, Jews generally are a relatively high economic status group in metropolitan centers other than New York City. Moreover, the very low status of Baptists and small Protestant sects is not surprising, although the relatively low ranking of Detroit area Catholics is not consistently reported by other studies.

RELATIONSHIP OF ASCRIBED TO
ACHIEVED FACTORS

To evaluate the contribution of ascribed background factors to variations in socio-economic status, the ascription handicap was subtracted from a *weighted* achievement rating for each religious group. Weighting of the achievement measure was necessary to convert this variable to the same scale as the ascribed rating. The total achievement rating for each white denomination was weighted by nine-fifths; for Negro religious groups, the weight was six-fifths. It should be noted that this process in no way changes the relative weights, but simply facilitates comparison between achieved and ascribed factors. The results of this procedure are shown in Table 5.

Returning once more to the analogy of a foot race, we are now in a position to judge the results of this contest. To review, in investigating the relationships between religious preference and worldly success in metropolitan Detroit, we endeavored to place all denominations on an "equal footing" with respect to those background factors which are conducive to high economic achievement in an urban environment. Actual achievement was then measured against the potential for this performance. The final ranking of the religious groups, taking the starting handicaps into consideration, is as follows:

White: Jewish
   Eastern Orthodox
   Semi-Christian
   Episcopalian
   Calvinist
   Protestant, no denomination
   Methodist
   Small sects
   No preference, Lutheran (tie)
   Baptist
   Catholic
Negro: Other than the below
   Baptist
   Methodist
   Catholic

TABLE 5: Total Inflated Weights of Achieved Factors Less Total Weights of Ascribed Factors, by Religious Group and Race

RELIGIOUS GROUP AND RACE	TOTAL OF FACTORS		
	ACHIEVED FACTORS*	ASCRIBED FACTORS	ACHIEVED LESS ASCRIBED
White			
Catholic	14.4	26.3	−11.9
Episcopalian	31.9	26.7	+ 5.2
Lutheran	22.5	28.8	− 6.3
Calvinist	30.0	26.5	+ 3.5
Methodist	25.2	24.0	+ 1.2
Baptist	9.0	18.0	− 9.0
Small sects	14.4	16.0	− 1.6
No denomination ..	20.7	18.7	+ 2.0
Semi-Christian	28.8	23.0	+ 5.8
Jewish	36.0	27.0	+ 9.0
Eastern Orthodox ..	21.0	12.3	+ 8.7
No preference	16.2	22.5	− 6.3
Negro			
Catholic	14.4	24.0	− 9.6
Methodist	16.2	15.0	+ 1.2
Baptist	8.4	6.0	+ 2.4
Other	21.0	15.0	+ 6.0

* Totals inflated by 1.8 for whites and by 1.2 for Negroes to equalize weights between ascribed and achieved factors.

For many religious groups, the handicapping produced a final ranking which was comparable to that based on achievement alone. However, several interesting exceptions may be seen. The most significant change in rank occurred in the Eastern Orthodox group which, when its handicap was applied, jumped high on the scale. The Baptists also rose one notch on the scale, thereby surpassing Catholics among both whites and Negroes.

A striking picture emerges from these data. Members of the Jewish, Greek Orthodox, and Semi-Christian faiths appear to have made the greatest achievements, given the system followed here. Behind these three groups are the several major Protestant denominations, with Baptists ranking below those white Detroiters who have no religious preference. For both whites and Negroes, the Catholics have had the least economic success as measured by our index.

Although these indices are crude and the resultant quantification somewhat specious, the major findings are not easily dismissed. We believe that no amount of statistical manipulation, even if more precise or elegant than that employed here, would appreciably change the broad outline of these rankings. To summarize our findings as they apply to white residents of greater Detroit: (1) Jews, followed closely by Episcopalians and Calvinists, have achieved the greatest worldly success. In the middle range are the remaining Protestant groups, with Baptists falling toward the end of the economic scale. Catholics have achieved the least. (2) If an ascription "handicap" is considered, the Eastern Orthodox group, closely followed by adherents of the Semi-Christian faiths, join the Jewish group at the top of the scale. An additional conclusion is that Catholicism is related to economic achievement among Negroes much as it is among whites.

INTERPRETATION

Previous research, in general, has failed to reach agreement as to the nature of the relationship between religious preference and economic achievement. Several investigations have discovered a comparative absence of Catholics among the economic and social élite of America. Low Catholic achievement motivation has also been pointed out. On the other hand, a number of researchers have found little evidence for the proposition that the Protestant ethic hypothesis is descriptive of the relationship between religious preference and worldly success in contemporary urban society.

The results of the present study may be interpreted as supporting the Weberian approach in part, while presenting some important modifications. Religious preferences appear to have meaningful consequences for economic success, quite apart from other background factors associated with religion. It would seem, therefore, that religion continues to play an essential role in controlling, limiting, and guiding economic behavior. As Weber proposed, most Protestant denominations far exceed the Catholics in economic standing. The various Protestant denominations are ranked

in a general order which further supports the Weberian thesis. As Sombart proposed, moreover, the Jews seem to be the most successful and worldly oriented. Thus, where it has been hypothesized that a general ordering would appear, it has appeared.

Not all religious preferences, however, fall into a neat, predictable rank order. This finding leads to a further interpretation in which religion per se is of lesser importance in guiding economic achievement in contemporary society than are other cultural factors associated with the religion. As part of their cultural heritage, members of particular religious groups may have certain occupational roles. The Eastern Orthodox in Detroit, for example, are primarily Syrians, Lebanese, and Greeks—traditionally traders, shopkeepers, merchants, and entrepreneurs. Granting that originally their religion strengthened, abetted, and possibly even forced them into these pursuits, their total cultural environment presently is consistent with entry into these occupations.

Much the same case can be made for Jews. Although three or four generations ago the Jewish religious link to worldly success was probably direct, the contemporary teachings of this religion may not be nearly as crucial as are other cultural characteristics which foster success and achievement patterns. Thus, the presence of intervening variables may alter the original linkage between religion and worldly success.

Future phases of this study will turn to an investigation of intervening variables such as residential segregation, family solidarity, and specific occupational inheritances. It is also planned further to refine our measurement of religious affiliation by introducing such factors as church attendance and church membership. The significance of the present study will be greatly enhanced if it is found, for example, that active Catholics are less successful than inactive Catholics; and conversely, that active Calvinists are more successful than inactive Calvinists.

Selection *57*

Some Contributions of Sociology to the Field of Education

Neal Gross

In regard to two of the major social institutions of our time, the family and education, the student frequently is unable to recognize a forest because he personally is surrounded by so many trees. His very closeness to these institutions—in terms of both habituation and personal involvement—makes it difficult for him to analyze them objectively. Yet in modern America there are no more important, influential, and pervasive institutions than these for him to study.

Because of its readily observable significance, education has been subjected to scrutiny, research, contributions, and theorizing by many major disciplines. In the following selection, the particular discipline involved is sociology; Gross examines some of the major theories, techniques, and insights that accrue to education by applying sociological theory and techniques to the social situation of the school and the classroom.

The social system has long been an area of sociological study, and much data has been gathered, analyzed, and formed into various theories of social systems. These theories have been applied to a wide variety of systems—prisons, armed forces units, neighborhoods, camps, business firms, and others. In the following selection Gross first examines the entire school as a social system, the kind of social system we call a formal organization; then he considers each separate classroom as a small social system; and finally he repeats the sound hypothesis that no institution, organization, discipline, or movement is isolated from the forces impinging on it from the wider society and demonstrates how the school is strongly influenced by its social milieu.

Specifically, the student will learn some of the major organizational barriers to the effective functioning of the school as a large formal organization and some of the sources of the strain and tension felt by the professional personnel of the school. The student should consider his own high school or college as he reads the analysis of how the social class structure and the power structure of the community affect the school as a formal organization and of the need for a school to change as the community and the society change. The student should also, in terms of functionaries he himself knows, attempt to gain greater insight into the conflicts that educational personnel face because of the different and sometimes incompatible roles they must play in the school and in the community.

Gross ends his essay on an unusually candid note. He repeats that sociologists have developed investigative techniques and theories that may offer real insight and assistance in understanding the school; but he warns that not all of the information and suggestions that some sociologists offer can be accepted indiscriminately and that theories and research findings should be evaluated carefully in terms of each particular situation before they are put to use.

The purpose of this paper is to delineate for the educational practitioner some specific contributions of sociological analysis to the field of education. We propose to focus on a limited set of substantive sociological contributions that teachers, supervisory personnel, school principals, or school superintendents may find of value in dealing with their work environment in a more realistic and effective manner.

Of the many approaches possible in describing some "practical contributions" of sociology to the field of education, the following procedure has been adopted. Specific contributions will be discussed under three headings that constitute sociological perspectives in the examination of school systems as functioning social systems. The first is that educational relationships occur in the context of a formal organizational setting. Students, teachers, supervisors, principals, and school superintendents interact as incumbents of positions in a social system which has an organizational goal, the education of children. To accomplish this task the work that goes on in a school must be assigned, coordinated, and integrated. Educational practice involves a number of people in a complicated division of labor; this necessitates networks of role relationships within

From the *Harvard Educational Review*, Vol. 29 (1959), 257-287.

an organizational environment. The second perspective derives from the fact that the basic work of the school, the educational transaction, takes place primarily in a relatively small social system, the classroom. The third perspective emerges from an observation that the sociologist would make about the school as a social system: Like all organizations, it is influenced by forces external to it. The impact of these external factors on the functioning of the school therefore comes under his scrutiny as a focal point of inquiry. It is from these three limited perspectives—the school system as a formal organization, the classroom as a social system, and the external environment of the schools—that we propose to delineate some contributions of sociology to practitioners in the field of education.

THE SCHOOL SYSTEM AS A FORMAL ORGANIZATION

A school system from a sociological point of view shares many common characteristics with other kinds of large-scale organizations. Two of these are of special relevance for our purpose. The first is that a school system, like business firms and hospitals, has an organizational objective. It is a goal-directed social system. Second, it contains a network of interrelated positions (for example, teachers, supervisors, and administrators) that are directly linked to the accomplishment of the organizational goal.

According to the "organizational model" for public schools, the business of the school is to impart knowledge and skills to students and therefore teachers are employed for this purpose. The function of supervisors is to help teachers to do a more effective job, and the formal duties of school administrators are to coordinate and integrate the diverse activities of the school. The incumbents of these positions have certain rights and obligations in their relationships with incumbents of other positions with whom they interact. Implicit in discussions of these aspects of the organizational structure of the school are two assumptions that deserve empirical examination. The first is that there is basic agreement on the organizational objective of the schools. The second is that there is agreement on the rights and obligations associated with the various positions in education. Sociological analysis suggests that both assumptions may in fact be tenuous in many school systems, and that lack of agreement on educational objectives and role definition may constitute major dysfunctional elements in the

functioning of the school and may affect the gratification educators derive from their jobs.

The formal organizational goal of public school systems is vague and is characterized by ambiguity. This observation emerges from a comparison of school systems with other types of organizations, for example, a business firm. The formal organizational goal of a business firm is unambiguous: to produce products or services for a profit. Labor unions may fight with management over the distribution of profits but typically there is no quarrel over the organizational goal itself. The situation is quite different, however, when an effort is made to specify the organizational objective of a school system. "To educate children" is a largely meaningless statement unless the purposes of the education are specified. And here lies the difficulty.

The specification of educational purposes invokes value issues such as the respective responsibilities of the home and the school or the meaning of a "good education." Whether the schools should give greater primacy to the intellectual, social, or emotional development of the child; whether or not they have the responsibility to impart moral values; whether the schools have different obligations to the "typical" and "atypical" child; whether they should encourage or discourage the questioning of the status quo; whether driver education, physical education, and courses in home economics and family living are legitimate or illegitimate functions of the school—each of these is a value question on which there may be contradictory points of view within and outside of school systems. An unpublished Harvard study involving personnel at different levels in eight New England school systems revealed dramatic differences in the beliefs teachers hold about educational goals and revealed that principals and teachers frequently do not share common views about educational objectives. Striking disagreements between superintendents and school boards have also been uncovered in regard to certain educational objectives. Research evidence further indicates that one of the major sources of pressures to which school administrators are exposed consists in conflicting viewpoints in their communities about school objectives and programs. Educational practitioners need to recognize that a fundamental source of controversy within the schools may be related to basic and unrecognized value conflicts over its organizational objectives. These differences in beliefs are infrequently brought to the surface for frank and open discussion. They may constitute basic blocks to effective group action and harmonious social relationships. The second "organizational assumption," that there is agreement on the role definition for educational positions, also appears to be suspect. Although textbooks in education glibly speak about the role of the teacher and of the school administrator as if everybody agreed on what they are, and many educational practitioners make this assumption, the organizational fact in many school systems may be that those people who work together frequently do not share similar views about the rights and obligations associated with their positions.

Should teachers be expected to attend PTA meetings regularly? Does the teacher's job include the counseling function? What are the teacher's obligations to the especially bright or especially dull child? Or the problem child? What are the teacher's obligations in handling discipline problems? Should teachers be expected to participate in in-service training programs? Does the teacher have the right to expect that the administrator will always support him when parents complain about his behavior? On these and many other phases of a teacher's job there may be considerable disagreement between principals and teachers as well as among teachers.

The findings of a study concerned with the role definition of approximately 50 per cent of the superintendents and school board members in Massachusetts revealed a basic lack of agreement over the division of labor between them. On the issue of hiring new teachers, seven out of ten superintendents interviewed reported that the arrangement they desired was this: when a new teacher was to be hired, the school board should act *solely* on the nominations of the superintendent. But only one out of five of the school board members agreed with them. How about the selection of textbooks? Nearly nine out of ten superintendents felt that the school board should always accept the recommendation of the superintendent in choosing a textbook. But less than one-half of the school board members agreed. What about teacher grievances? Nearly 90 per cent of the superintendents believed that teachers should always bring their grievances to the superintendent before they went to the school board. Only 56 per cent of the school board members agreed. What should the procedure be when a community group wishes to use school property? Nine out of ten school superintendents thought that this decision should be the superintendent's responsibility. Nearly one-half of the school board members, however, felt that these decisions should be made by the school board. What about recommendations for salary increases for school system employees? Over two-thirds of the superintend-

ents felt that the superintendent should make all such recommendations. Only one-third of the school board members agreed with them. These findings imply that in many school systems disagreements over the rights and obligations associated with educational positions may constitute basic sources of stress in the school system. They also suggest that intra-role conflicts appear to be "built into" many educational positions.

By an intra-role conflict we mean conflicting expectations to which an individual is exposed as a consequence of his occupancy of a *single* position. Teachers are frequently exposed to conflicting expectations from their principal and supervisors, from guidance personnel and their principal, from parents and administrators, and even from students in their classrooms. School principals are exposed to conflicting expectations from their superintendent and their staff over such matters as the supervision of classroom instruction and the handling of discipline problems. School administrators are confronted with conflicting expectations among their school staff. For example, some teachers expect their principal to make all important decisions affecting their welfare, but other teachers expect to participate in such decisions. In addition, parents and teachers frequently hold contradictory expectations for the principal's behavior in regard to student promotion and discipline practices. It is the school superintendent, however, who probably is exposed most frequently to intra-role conflict. A major source of these conflicting expectations arises from the differential views held by his school board and his staff for his behavior. Whose views should he support when the school board and the staff hold conflicting expectations for his behavior on such issues as the size of the school budget or promotion policies? Superintendents, like school principals, must also frequently deal with differential expectations among the teaching staff. And their most difficult problems may emerge from conflicting expectations held by their school board members for their performance.

To sum up: Viewing school systems as organizations from a sociological perspective suggests major organizational barriers to their effective functioning. We have emphasized two of these blocks: lack of agreement on organizational goals and lack of consensus on the role definitions associated with educational positions.

THE CLASSROOM AS A SOCIAL SYSTEM

. . . At this stage of sociological and sociopsychological inquiry on the classroom as a social system, the major empirical contributions of the sociologist have undoubtedly been to draw attention to the sociometric structure of the classroom and to isolate basic sources of strain and tension to which teachers are exposed in the classroom. Sociometric studies reveal that classrooms typically contain "stars" and "isolates," and they have uncovered factors that affect student interpersonal relations in the school class. Of especial importance to educators is the finding that teachers appear to misperceive frequently the interpersonal relationships among students in their classrooms. They do not show high sensitivity to the way children actually react to each other and they frequently allow their own biases toward students to hinder a correct assessment of the "sociometric facts of life."

A second sociological contribution to the understanding of classroom behavior stems from the isolation of some potential sources of strain for the classroom teacher. One source of stress is the collision between the authority structure of the school and the professional status of the teaching staff. A school system must provide for the coordination and integration of the work of its members. Someone has to assign responsibilities, see that tasks are accomplished, and have the power to sanction teachers of students for deviant behavior. The elementary school principal, for example, as the formal leader of his school has to make room assignments and final decisions about the disposition and discipline problems. He must also see that the educational experiences of the child in the first grade are integrated with those he receives in the second and third grades. This requires some type of control over the work content and work output of teachers at each of these levels. Their classroom behavior is part of his concern. The authority structure, however, conflicts with another characteristic of school organization—the school is staffed with professional personnel. A professional worker is supposed to have autonomy over his own activities. . . . It is this built-in source of strain that in part accounts for the "social distance" that frequently exists between school principals and their teachers and for the charge—by teachers—that administrators upset "their" classes. The clash between the authority structure and the professional status of teachers is also undoubtedly reflected in the latent and overt opposition of teachers to the introduction of new educational practices.

A second source of strain derives from the differential norms held by teachers and students for the student's behavior. Gordon's analysis of a high school suggests the differential frames of reference that may be operating in many classrooms. His analysis indicates that teachers expected students to perform in a manner that approximated their knowledge and ability potential. But students' expectations were in part based on the informal social structure and values of the students. He indicates that student stereotypes had an important influence on the "roles" students assigned each other and played themselves, and that these stereotypes therefore affected their role performance. When student-defined and teacher-defined roles and values were incompatible, the net result was strain for the teacher in his transactions with students.

Another contribution of a sociological perspective on classroom behavior is demonstrated by the current work of Lippitt and his associates at the University of Michigan on the "socially unaccepted" child in the classroom. In addition to showing the need for a typology of such children, their studies suggest the powerful group forces operating on the unaccepted child. The major barriers to changing his behavior may be in the classroom, rather than or in addition to forces within the child. This finding has important implications for teachers and also for school guidance practices which are usually based on the assumption that individual counseling is the only way to change a student's behavior. The observation that the attributes and stereotypes of classmates as well as the teacher are barriers to behavior changes is one demanding rigorous exploration.

In addition, sociological analysis strongly suggests that the attitudes and behavior of the individual are strongly linked to those groups to which he belongs or aspires. These reference groups constitute "anchoring points" which have to be considered in inducing changed behavior. For the classroom teacher, the important consequence of this observation is that to deal effectively with a child may require isolating group forces that are constraining his behavior and inducing changes in clique norms and values.

THE EXTERNAL ENVIRONMENT OF THE SCHOOL

A school system does not exist in a vacuum. Its existence and functioning depend in part on its outside world, its external environment. This sociological point of view has many implications for the analysis of school systems.

One implication is that changes in the larger social system of the community materially affect the composition of the student body in a school system, and therefore may require modifications in the curriculum. The heavy migration of the rural population in the South to metropolitan centers implies that many large city school systems need to undertake a critical review of the ability of their school program to meet the needs of the school's changed clientele. The empty school buildings in the center of many cities and the needed new school buildings in suburban areas, associated with the recent "flight to the suburbs," suggest the need for a metropolitan approach to school planning, a concept infrequently considered in educational circles. In short, the educational implications of demographic studies require considerably greater attention by educators.

A second aspect of the external environment of public school systems to which sociologists have given considerable attention is the social class structure of communities. Studies in this area reveal that most aspects of school functioning are influenced by social class phenomena. Research on social class strongly supports the notion that teacher grading practices and the criteria which teachers apply to children are related to the social class placement of the child and the teacher. The mobility aspirations of children, the drop-out rate, participation in extra-curricular activities, dating behavior, and friendship patterns are in part accounted for by the socio-economic characteristics of the child's family.

A third "external environment" factor that has important implications for the public schools is the power structure or structures of the community. School systems absorb a large portion of the local tax dollar and the influence of informal and formal power agents in the community on educational budgetary decisions is without doubt a basic influence on the quality of the staff and the program of a school system. It is not surprising that national meetings of educational administrators usually have sessions devoted to "techniques for studying community power structure" and that sociologists are invited to participate in them.

A fourth contribution of sociology to the understanding of the external environment of the schools is the analysis of the basic link between the community and the schools—the school board. Charters has questioned the assumption, frequently found in the educational literature, that the disproportionate incidence of school board members from upper socio-economic strata results in "a conservative bias" in public education. Sociological research has demonstrated the impact of the behavior of school board members and of their

motivation for seeking election to this position on the superintendent's job satisfaction and his job performance. The effect of such factors as religion, occupation, and income on the school board member's behavior as well as the pressures to which school administrators are exposed by their school boards have also been examined. These findings lead to the general conclusion that a crucial, but frequently neglected, variable influencing the operation of the school is the behavior of the small group of laymen who are its official policy-makers. This conclusion has had many important ramifications, one of which is the National School Board Association's current effort to improve the "quality" of school board members.

A fifth sociological contribution emerges from the analysis of inter-role conflicts to which educational personnel are exposed as a consequence of their occupancy of positions in schools and in other social systems. Getzels and Guba found that many of the expectations linked to the teacher's position conflict with other positions he occupies, and that some of these conflicts are a function of local school and community conditions.

The school superintendent's position is especially exposed to inter-role conflict. His job and the way he carries it out influence in some way virtually all members of the community. In dealing with him, members of his church, his personal friends, members of other organizations to which he may belong, and, of course, his wife and family, are inclined to identify him not only as a fellow church member, for example, but as a fellow church member who is at the same time the superintendent of schools.

Some unpublished findings of the School Executive Studies shed light on the kinds of inter-role conflicts to which school superintendents are exposed. Twenty per cent of the superintendents reported that they faced incompatible expectations deriving from their simultaneous occupancy of positions in the *educational and religious systems.* The formal leaders and certain members of their church expected them to act in one way regarding certain issues, while other individuals and groups expected contrary behavior. One Catholic superintendent said that he faced situations like this all the time:

"Sometimes, the situation gets pretty touchy. I want to keep good relations with the Church. Don't forget—most of my school committee members and the local politicians belong to my church. Take this for example: one of the Catholic groups wanted to let the kids out early from school.

They were having some special meetings, and they wanted the kids to be there. I knew that wouldn't be right. It wasn't fair to the other kids. So what did I do? I refused to give an official o.k. to the request, but at the time I simply winked at it [letting them out early]. I would have offended them if I'd stopped the kids from going, and I just couldn't afford to do that. It really left me bothered. Should I have stopped it? Legally, I could and I would have been right. But I know I would have had hell to pay."

Another superintendent, a Protestant, told the interviewer:

"[My] minister wants all kinds of special favors because I am a member of his church. He expected me to turn over our gym to the church basketball team. He wanted me to support his idea of giving out a Bible to each public school child. He told me that he thought I ought to see that more of 'our people' get jobs in the school. None of these are fair requests. I'm supposed to represent all the people, and I want to use the criterion of 'what's best for the schools,' not 'what's best for my church.' I might give him the gym, but it would be worth my job to give in on the Bibles in this community. I try not to play favorites, but sometimes it's hard to know what is the right thing to do."

Of perhaps as great personal and emotional significance to superintendents are the role conflicts arising from the expectations of their *personal friends* which are incompatible with those held by other individuals and groups in the community. Thirty-five percent of the superintendents reported conflicts of this kind.

Although some superintendents said that their "personal friends" expected special consideration in the areas of personnel decisions and the allocation of school contracts, more often the superintendents said that their friends expected special consideration for their children. These included requests that teachers be reprimanded for treating their children unfairly, that their children be transferred to a school in another district, that transportation be provided for children who are not entitled to it, that their children be promoted against the best judgment of the teacher and principal involved, and so on. Each of these "special consideration" expectations is incompatible with procedures and principles which the superintendent is expected to follow and which are set by the school board, by the teachers, and by PTA groups. Undoubtedly there are many requests of this kind which superintendents automatically ignore or refuse and which they did not mention in the interview; it is when these requests come from personal friends and when these friends expect the superintendent to make particular concessions, that the superintendents describe them as "role conflict" situations.

One superintendent said:

"[One of the] nastiest aspects of my job is bus transportation. Good friends of mine have the nerve to telephone me, the superintendent of schools, and ask that a bus pick up their children, when they know, and I know, and the bus driver knows, that they live within the one-mile limit. I tell them I don't drive the bus. I'm just superintendent of schools. Talk to the bus driver. They think I'm saying okay, and I guess I am if you come right down to it. Someday I guess I'll get into trouble when someone who doesn't have the gall to come to me goes to the committee and says 'so and so, the superintendent's friend, has his kids picked up. Why can't I have mine?' It's all in the game and sometimes the game is rough."

A third role conflict situation frequently mentioned involved the *superintendency and the father positions.* Forty-eight per cent of the superintendents described conflicts of this type.

The superintendents reported a wide variety of situations in which their children expected one thing and others expected something quite different. One superintendent who was greatly troubled by problems in this area described his situation in this way:

"You know one of the worst things about this job that you never think of before you get into it is its effect on your children. You don't have time for your children. You have to be out every night and it just isn't fair to them. They don't like it; they resent it. And then the kids have a cross to bear. Either they get especially soft or especially rough treatment by the teachers. And the teachers are just waiting for you to throw your weight around.
"For example, my boy has told me certain things about one of his teachers—the way she behaves in the classroom. He's an honest youngster so I have no reason to doubt him, and if I were not the superintendent you can be darn sure I'd raise a lot of cain. But as the superintendent I'm not supposed to invade a teacher's classroom. So I try to support the teacher even though I know she is in the wrong. I feel pretty mean

about this, but what else can I do? I hope my boy will understand the situation better later on."

Eighteen percent of the superintendents mentioned inter-role conflicts stemming from incompatible expectations held for their behavior as a *member of a local community association and as the superintendent*. For example, in many communities certain local organizations to which the superintendent belonged expected him to allow them to use the time of students and staff to achieve their own organizational objectives, whereas the professional school staff expected him to protect the schools from this type of "invasion." School superintendents are exposed to requests for school children to be active in fund raising activities, for the school band to play in parades, and for the schools to participate in youth activities. Local community groups expect the superintendent to facilitate their use of these school resources. On the other hand, many superintendents know that one of the major complaints of their faculty is that this type of activity frequently disrupts classroom activities and planned school programs. This constitutes a difficult area of decision making, especially when the organization in question has a powerful voice in community affairs.

These findings support the proposition that inter-role conflicts stemming from occupancy of positions in the school system and in the environment external to it constitute a basic source of potential stress for the educator.

There are dangers to be avoided as well as benefits to be derived from the closer alignment between the fields of sociology and education. One of these dangers is to overgeneralize sociological research findings that apply to a single case or a small population to American education or American society when there is no logical basis for such induction. Sociologists as well as educators have erred in this respect. A second pitfall is the uncritical acceptance of unverified pronouncements of sociologists as verified propositions. There are many statements to be found in textbooks of educational sociology that are speculative in nature and which are not based on rigorous research evidence. Hunches and speculations need to be distinguished from verified propositions. A third danger is the acceptance of sociological research findings without critical examination of their assumptions, the adequacy of their research methods, and their conclusions. The literature on the influence of social class structure in American education is permeated with each of these, as well as other, pitfalls in the sociology-

education mating process. The educational practitioner needs to be aware of these difficulties in his utilization of sociological analyses of educational problems.

These precautionary observations lead to the consideration of the major contribution of the sociologist to educational practitioners. The teacher or school administrator must constantly bear in mind that he is working in a complex environment in which many variables are at play. The forces are multidimensional and his environment, although it shares common features with the situation confronting other educational practitioners, has many unique features. The sociologist, however, usually defines his problem so that he is working with one or a few independent variables (for example, social class or leadership structure) and one dependent variable (for example, academic achievement or sociometric choice), and he attempts to control other variables that may be influencing the relationships he is investigating. Of necessity he must simplify his problem so he can deal with it. He usually assumes multiple causation but his methodological tools allow him to deal with only a very limited number of the forces that may account for the phenomena he is trying to explain. He never deals with *all* the variables that the practitioner probably needs to take into account in his decision making. Further, the research findings of the sociologist may not be applicable to the particular set of conditions confronting the practitioner. Research findings based on a sample of suburban school systems may not hold for city school systems. These considerations lead to the following point of view about the sociologist's major contribution to the educational practitioner. What the sociologist has to offer is basically a series of sensitizing and analytic concepts and ideas based on theoretical and empirical analysis that will allow the practitioner to examine in a more realistic and more incisive way the multiple forces operating in his social environment. The sociologist cannot make the educational practitioner's decisions for him, nor can the sociologist's research findings based on one population be applied to any educational population indiscriminately. The practitioner's task is to assess the various forces that have a bearing on the achievement of his objectives, assign them relative weights, and make a decision based on these calculations. The basic sociological contribution is to add to the educator's kit of intellectual tools a set of sociological insights and concepts that will allow him to take account in his decision-making organizational, cultural, and interpersonal factors at work in his environment.

Selection 58

The Adolescent Subculture and Academic Achievement
James S. Coleman

In modern-day America, high school youths spend a great many of their waking hours either in school or with groups of their schoolmates. From one standard of reference theory, each high school consists of a social system made up primarily of adolescents. Commonly, a definite enough subsystem exists that the adolescent can be said to be living in a "world of his own" for the greater part of his waking hours. All too frequently, schools, parents, and programs oriented toward adolescents fail to comprehend the reality, solidity, and strength of the high school subsystem and its influence on its members. Intelligent direction of this subculture by the larger parent culture is possible and would seem to be useful and desirable.

Studies devoted to documenting the existence of these subsystems and describing them (the essential primary step in cultural research) have been successful for a number of years. In fact, much evidence acquired from interviews, autobiographies, records, etc., indicates that the phenomenon of an adolescent subculture, only recently studied sociologically, actually existed during the era of the Charleston, bell-bottomed trousers, enameled shoes, long necklaces, and hip flasks, when the parents and grandparents of those adolescents presently being studied were themselves adolescents. How much further back in history this type of subculture goes we cannot say, but evidence indicates the probability that adolescent subsystems existed in English private schools a century ago.

Available evidence on modern adolescent (high school) subcultures suggests that these subsystems hold much in common but that observable differences do exist. These differences are "variations on a theme," however, rather than distinct and unrelated subcultures. For example, each subsystem has a value system that includes academic achievement, athletic prowess, popularity, extracurricular achievement, etc.; the variations are in the importance given to each of these sometimes competing values. The following selection reports not on the existence of adolescent subsystems, which it accepts as proved, but on the variations between high school subsystems in regard to one particular value—academic achievement.

Industrial society has spawned a peculiar phenomenon, most evident in America but emerging also in other Western societies: adolescent subcultures, with values and activities quite distinct from those of the adult society—subcultures whose members have most of their important associations within and few with adult society. Industrialization, and the rapidity of change itself, has taken out of the hands of the parent the task of training his child, made the parent's skills obsolescent, and put him out of touch with the times—unable to

"The Adolescent Subculture and Academic Achievement" by James S. Coleman. Reprinted from *The American Journal of Sociology*, Vol. LXV (1960), 337-347, by permission of The University of Chicago Press.

understand, much less inculcate, the standards of a social order which has changed since he was young.

By extending the period of training necessary for a child and by encompassing nearly the whole population, industrial society has made of high school a social system of adolescents. It includes, in the United States, almost all adolescents and more and more of the activities of the adolescent himself. A typical example is provided by an excerpt from a high-school newspaper in an upper-middle-class suburban school:

SOPHOMORE DANCING FEATURES CHA CHA

SOPHOMORES, this is your chance to learn how to dance! The first day of sophomore dancing is Nov. 14 and it will begin at 8:30 A.M. in the Boys' Gym. . . .

No ONE IS required to take dancing but it is highly recommended for both boys and girls. . . .

If you don't attend at this time except in case of absence from school, you may not attend at any other time. Absence excuses should be shown to Miss _____ or Mr. _____.

In effect, then, what our society has done is to set apart, in an institution of their own, adolescents for whom home is little more than a dormitory and whose world is made up of activities peculiar to their fellows. They have been given as well many of the instruments which can make them a functioning community: cars, freedom in dating, continual contact with the opposite sex, money, and entertainment, like popular music and movies, designed especially for them. The international spread of "rock-and-roll" and of so-called American patterns of adolescent behavior is a consequence, I would suggest, of these economic changes which have set adolescents off in a world of their own.

Yet the fact that such a subsystem has sprung up in society has not been systematically recognized in the organization of secondary education. The theory and practice of education remains focused on *individuals;* teachers exhort individuals to concentrate their energies in scholarly directions, while the community of adolescents diverts these energies into other channels. The premise of the present research is that, if educational goals are to be realized in modern society, a fundamentally different approach to secondary education is necessary. Adults are in control of the institutions they have established for secondary education; traditionally, these institutions have been used to mold children as individuals toward ends which adults dictate. The fundamental

change which must occur is to shift the focus: to mold social communities as communities, so that the norms of the communities themselves reinforce educational goals rather than inhibit them, as is at present the case.

The research being reported is an attempt to examine the status systems of the adolescent communities in ten high schools and to see the effects of these status systems upon the individuals within them. The ten high schools are all in the Midwest. They include five schools in small towns (labeled *0-4* in the figures which follow), one in a working-class suburb (*6*), one in a well-to-do suburb (*9*), and three schools in cities of varying sizes (*5, 7,* and *8*). All but No. 5, a Catholic boys' school, are coeducational, and all but it are public schools.

The intention was to study schools which had quite different status systems, but the similarities were far more striking than the differences. In a questionnaire all boys were asked: "How would you most like to be remembered in school: as an athletic star, a brilliant student, or most popular?" The results of the responses for each school are shown in Figure 1, where the left corner of the triangle represents 100 per cent saying "star athlete"; the top corner represents 100 per cent saying "brilliant student"; and the right corner represents 100 per cent saying "most popular." Each school is represented by a point whose location relative to the three corners shows the proportion giving each response.

The schools are remarkably grouped somewhat off-center, showing a greater tendency to say "star athlete" than either of the other choices. From each school's point is a broken arrow connecting the school as a whole with its members who were named by their fellows as being "members of the leading crowd." In almost every case, the leading crowd tends in the direction of the athlete —in all cases *away* from the ideal of the brilliant student. Again, for the leading crowds as well as for the students as a whole, the uniformity is remarkably great; not so great in the absolute positions of the leading crowds but in the direction they deviate from the student bodies.

This trend toward the ideal of the athletic star on the part of the leading crowds is due in part to the fact that the leading crowds include a great number of athletes. Boys were asked in a questionnaire to name the best athlete in their grade, the best student, and the boy most popular with girls. In every school, without exception, the boys named as best athletes were named more often—on the average over twice as often—as members of the leading crowd than were those named as best students. Similarly, the boy most popular with girls was named as belonging to the leading crowd more often than the best student, though in all schools but the well-to-do suburb and the smallest rural town (schools 9 and 0 on Fig. 1) less often than the best athlete.

These and other data indicate the importance of athletic achievement as an avenue for gaining status in the schools. Indeed, in the predominantly middle-class schools, it is by far the most effective achievement for gaining a working-class boy entrée into the leading crowd.

Similarly, each girl was asked how she would like to be remembered: as a brilliant student, a leader in extracurricular activities, or most popular. The various schools are located on Figure 2, together with arrows connecting them to their leading crowd. The girls tend slightly less, on the average, than the boys to want to be remembered as brilliant students. Although the alternatives are different, and thus cannot be directly compared, a great deal of other evidence indicates that the girls—although better students in every school— do not want to be considered "brilliant students." They have good reason not to, for the girl in each grade in each of the schools who was most often named as best student has fewer friends and is less often in the leading crowd than is the boy most often named as best student.

There is, however, diversity among the schools in the attractiveness of the images of "activities leader" and "popular girl" (Fig. 2). In five (9, 0,

3, 8, and 1), the leader in activities is more often chosen as an ideal than is the popular girl; in four (7, 6, 2, and 4) the most popular girl is the more attractive of the two. These differences correspond somewhat to class background differences among the schools: 2, 4, 6, and 7, where the activities leader is least attractive, have the highest proportion of students with working-class backgrounds. School 9 is by far the most upper-middle-class one and by far the most activities-oriented.

The differences among the schools correspond as well to differences among the leading crowds: in schools 2, 4, and 6, where the girls as a whole are most oriented to being popular, the leading crowds are even more so; in the school where the girls are most oriented to the ideal of the activities leader, No. 9, the leading crowd goes even further in that direction. In other words, it is as if a pull is exerted by the leading crowd, bringing the rest of the students toward one or the other of the polar extremes. In all cases, the leading crowd pulls away from the brilliant-student ideal.

Although these schools vary far less than one might wish when examining the effects of status systems, there are differences. All students were asked in a questionnaire: "What does it take to get into the leading crowd?" On the basis of the answers, the relative importance of various activities can be determined. Consider only a single activity, academic achievement. Its importance for

---

FIGURE 1: Positions of schools and leading crowds in boys' relative choice of brilliant student, athletic star, and most popular.

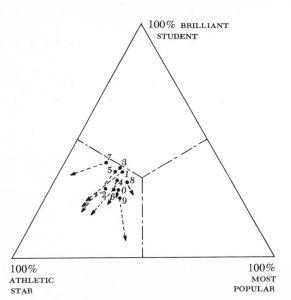

FIGURE 2: Titles as in Figure 6, but without last parentheses.

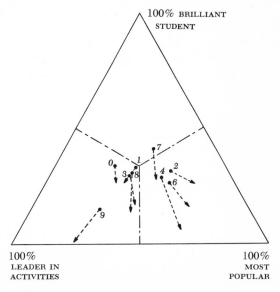

status among the adolescents in each school can be measured simply by the proportion of responses which specify "good grades," or "brains" as adolescents often put it, as a means of entrée into the leading crowd. In all the schools, academic achievement was of less importance than other matters, such as being an athletic star among the boys, being a cheerleader or being good-looking among the girls, or other attributes. Other measures which were obtained of the importance of academic achievement in the adolescent status system correlate highly with this one.

If, then, it is true that the status system of adolescents *does* affect educational goals, those schools which differ in the importance of academic achievement in the adolescent status system should differ in numerous other ways which are directly related to educational goals. Only one of those, which illustrates well the differing pressures upon students in the various schools, will be reported here.

In every social context certain activities are highly rewarded, while others are not. Those activities which are rewarded are the activities for which there is strong competition—activities in which everyone with some ability will compete. In such activities the persons who achieve most should be those with most potential ability. In contrast, in unrewarded activities, those who have most ability may not be motivated to compete; consequently, the persons who achieve most will be persons of lesser ability. Thus in a high school where basketball is important, nearly every boy who might be a good basketball player will go out for the sport, and, as a result, basketball stars are likely to be the boys with the most ability. If in the same school volleyball does not bring the same status, few boys will go out for it, and those who end up as members of the team will not be the boys with most potential ability.

Similarly, with academic achievement: in a school where such achievement brings few social rewards, those who "go out" for scholarly achievement will be few. The high performers, those who receive good grades, will not be the boys whose ability is greatest but a more mediocre few. Thus the "intellectuals" of such a society, those defined by themselves and others as the best students, will not in fact be those with most intellectual ability. The latter, knowing where the social rewards lie, will be off cultivating other fields which bring social rewards.

To examine the effect of varying social pressures in the schools, academic achievement, as measured by grades in school, was related to I.Q. Since the I.Q. tests differ from school to school, and since each school had its own mean I.Q. and

its own variation around it, the ability of high performers (boys who made A or A— average) was measured by the number of standard deviations of their average I.Q.'s above the mean. In this way, it is possible to see where the high performers' ability lay, relative to the distribution of abilities in their school.

The variations were great: in a small-town school, No. *1*, the boys who made an A or A— average had I.Q.'s 1.53 standard deviations above the school average; in another small-town school, No. *0*, their I.Q.'s were only about a third this distance above the mean, .59. Given this variation, the question can be asked: Do these variations in ability of the high performers correspond to variations in the social rewards for, or constraints against, being a good student?

Figure 3 shows the relation for the boys between the social rewards for academic excellence (i.e., the frequency with which "good grades" was mentioned as a means for getting into the leading crowd) and the ability of the high performers, measured by the number of standard deviations their average I.Q.'s exceed that of the rest of the boys in the school. The relation is extremely strong. Only one school, a parochial boys' school in the city's slums, deviates. This is a school in which many boys had their most important associations outside the school rather than in it, so that its student body constituted far less of a social system, less able to dispense social rewards and punishments, than was true of the other schools.

Similarly, Figure 4 shows for the girls the I.Q.'s of the high performers. Unfortunately, most of the schools are closely bunched in the degree to which good grades are important among the girls, so that there is too little variation among them to examine this effect as fully as would be desirable. School 2 is the one school whose girls deviate from the general relationship.

The effect of these values systems on the freedom for academic ability to express itself in high achievement is evident among the girls as it is among the boys. This is not merely due to the school facilities, social composition of the school, or other variables: the two schools highest in the importance of scholastic achievement for both boys and girls are *1* and *8*, the first a small-town school of 350 students and the second a city school of 2,000 students. In both there are fewer students with white-collar backgrounds than in schools 9 or 3, which are somewhere in the middle as to value placed on academic achievement, but are more white-collar than in schools 7 or 4, which are also somewhere in the middle. The highest expenditure per student was $695 per year in school 9, and the lowest was little more than half that, in school 4. These schools are close together on the graphs of Figures 3 and 4.

It should be mentioned in passing that an extensive unpublished study throughout Connecticut, using standard tests of achievement and ability, yielded consistent results. The study found no correlation between per pupil expenditure in a school and the achievement of its students relative to their ability. The effects shown in Figures 3 and 4 suggest why: that students with ability are led to achieve only when there are social rewards, primarily from their peers, for doing so—and these social rewards seem little correlated with per pupil expenditure.

So much for the effects as shown by the variation among schools. As mentioned earlier, the variation among schools was not nearly so striking in this research as the fact that, in all of them, academic achievement did not count for as much as other activities. In every school the boy named as best athlete and the boy named as most popular with girls was far more often mentioned as a member of the leading crowd, and as someone to "be like," than was the boy named as the best student. And the girl named as best dressed, and the one named as most popular with boys, was in every school far more often mentioned as being in the leading crowd and as someone "to be like," than was the girl named as the best student.

The relative unimportance of academic achievement, together with the effect shown earlier, suggests that these adolescent subcultures are generally deterrents to academic achievement. In other words, in these societies of adolescents those who come to be seen as the "intellectuals" and who come to think so of themselves are not really those of highest intelligence but are only the ones who are willing to work hard at a relatively unrewarded activity.

The implications for American society as a whole are clear. Because high schools allow the adolescent subcultures to divert energies into athletics, social activities, and the like, they recruit into adult intellectual activities people with a rather mediocre level of ability. In fact, the high school seems to do more than allow these subcultures to discourage academic achievement; it aids them in doing so. To indicate how it does and to indicate how it might do differently is another story, to be examined below.

Figures 1 and 2, which show the way boys and girls would like to be remembered in their high school, demonstrate a curious difference between the boys and the girls. Despite great variation in social background, in size of school (from 180 to

---

FIGURE 3: I.Q.'s of high achieving boys by importance of good grades among other boys.

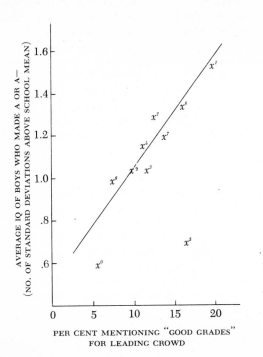

FIGURE 4: I.Q.'s of high achieving girls by importance of good grades among other girls.

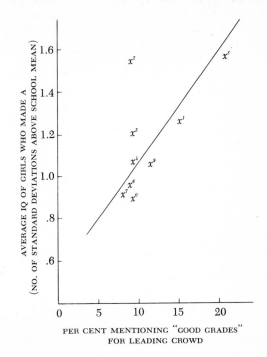

2,000), in size of town (from less than a thousand to over a million), and in style of life of their parents, the proportion of boys choosing each of the three images by which he wants to be remembered is very nearly the same in all schools. And in every school the leading crowd "pulls" in similar directions: at least partly toward the ideal of the star athlete. Yet the ideals of the girls in these schools are far more dispersed, and the leading crowds "pull" in varying directions, far less uniformly than among the boys. Why such a diversity in the same schools?

The question can best be answered by indirection. In two schools apart from those in the research, the questionnaire was administered primarily to answer a puzzling question: Why was academic achievement of so little importance among the adolescents in school 9? Their parents were professionals and business executives, about 80 per cent were going to college (over twice as high a proportion as in any of the other schools), and yet academic excellence counted for little among them. In the two additional schools parental background was largely held constant, for they were private, coeducational day schools whose students had upper-middle-class backgrounds quite similar to those of school 9. One (No. 10) was in the city; the other (No. 11), in a suburban setting almost identical to that of No. 9. Although the two schools were added to the study to answer

the question about school 9, they will be used to help answer the puzzle set earlier: that of the clustering of schools for the boys and their greater spread for the girls. When we look at the responses of adolescents in these two schools to the question as to how they would like to be remembered, the picture becomes even more puzzling (Figs. 5 and 6). For the boys, they are extremely far from the cluster of the other schools; for the girls, they are intermingled with the other schools. Thus, though it was for the boys that the other schools clustered so closely, these two deviate sharply from the cluster; and for the girls, where the schools already varied, these two are not distinguishable. Furthermore, the leading crowds of boys in these schools do not pull the ideal toward the star-athlete ideal as do those in almost all the other schools. To be sure, they pull away from the ideal of the brilliant student, but the pull is primarily toward a social image, the most popular. Among the girls, the leading crowds pull in different directions and are nearly indistinguishable from the other schools.

The answer to both puzzles, that is, first, the great cluster of the boys and now, in these two additional schools, the greater deviation, seems to lie in one fact: the boys' interscholastic athletics. The nine public schools are all engaged in interscholastic leagues which themselves are knit together in state tournaments. The other school of

---

FIGURE 5: Title as in Figure 1, but with added: (two private schools [*10, 11*] included).

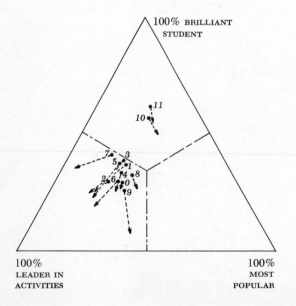

FIGURE 6: Positions of schools and leading crowds in girls' relative choice of brilliant student, activities leader, and most popular (two private schools [*10, 11*] included).

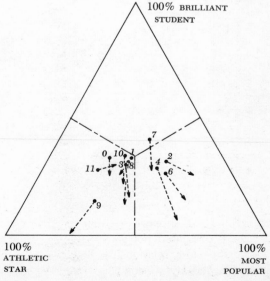

the first ten, the Catholic school, is in a parochial league, where games are just as hotly contested as in the public leagues and is also knit together with them in tournaments.

Schools *10* and *11* are athletically in a world apart from this. Although boys in both schools may go in for sports, and both schools have interscholastic games, the opponents are scattered private schools, constituting a league in name only. They take no part in state or city tournaments and have almost no publicity.

There is nothing for the girls comparable to the boys' interscholastic athletics. There are school activities of one sort or another, in which most girls take part, but no interscholastic games involving them. Their absence and the lack of leagues which knit all schools together in systematic competition means that the status system can "wander" freely, depending on local conditions in the school. In athletics, however, a school, and the community surrounding it, cannot hold its head up if it continues to lose games. It *must* devote roughly the same attention to athletics as do the schools surrounding it, for athletic games are the only games in which it engages other schools, and by representation, other communities.

These games are almost the only means a school has of generating internal cohesion and identification, for they constitute the only activity in which the school participates *as* a school. (This is well indicated by the fact that a number of students in school *10*, the private school which engages in no interscholastic games, has been concerned by a "lack of school spirit.") It is as a consequence of this that the athlete gains so much status: he is doing something for the school and the community, not only for himself, in leading his team to victory, for it is a school victory.

The outstanding student, in contrast, has little or no way to bring glory to his school. His victories are always purely personal, often at the expense of his classmates, who are forced to work harder to keep up with him. It is no wonder that his accomplishments gain little reward and are often met by ridiculing remarks, such as "curve-raiser" or "grind," terms of disapproval which have no analogues in athletics.

These results are particularly intriguing, for they suggest ways in which rather straightforward social theory could be used in organizing the activities of high schools in such a way that their adolescent subcultures would encourage, rather than discourage, the channeling of energies into directions of learning. One might speculate on the possible effects of city-wide or state-wide "scholastic fairs" composed of academic games and tournaments between schools and school exhibits to be judged. It could be that the mere institution of such games would, just as do the state basketball tournaments in the midwestern United States, have a profound effect upon the educational climate in the participating schools. In fact, by an extension of this analysis, one would predict that an international fair of this sort, a "Scholastic Olympics," would generate interscholastic games and tournaments within the participating countries.

Selection 59

Education for a Nation of Nations
Robert Gordis

The two previous selections have described specialized aspects of education studied by sociologists. The present selection upholds the status quo as being more desirable than certain proposed educational changes. This selection also differs from the two preceding ones in that it is little concerned with methods and research findings, but instead it emphasizes the underlying philosophy, the societal goals, and the role of religion in education.

The following article definitely has a "point of view" to express, one that the reader will support or condemn in terms of his own value orientation. The article is presented not so much because of its point of view but because it shows the close relationship between religious belief, value orientation, and governmental law. Secondarily—and this is always useful—it shows that social issues are rarely if ever strictly black or white but may be of all shades of gray or striped or spotted.

On the issue of public and parochial schools, the author states and defends the position that parents' sending their children to a parochial school does not relieve the parents of the responsibility of supporting the institution (public schools) that Gordis believes to be "the basic agency for building mutuality of relationship among the citizens of various faiths and backgrounds." He also holds that a parochial school does not just give its students a secular education to which religious studies have been added, but is rather a school in which "religion permeates every course . . . so that no aspect of culture would be exempt from its influence."

Yet an education that ignores religion can be a partial one at best and a seriously distorted one at worst. The older the student, the more satisfactory and the less controversial is the inclusion of religious material in the curriculum. Certainly the present state of religious illiteracy of much of our population is to be deplored.

Those who favor church-affiliated education say that persons who pay taxes have an inherent right to receive a just return for them. The argument goes that we have passed compulsory school attendance laws; we have agreed that these laws can be fully satisfied by parochial school attendance; *ergo*, parochial schools should receive an equitable share of tax assistance—free textbooks, free transportation, free surplus food commodities, financial grants, etc. Thus, the argument concludes, it is unfair to require Catholics to pay for both their own schools, which conscientious Catholics are bound to support, and for public schools which their children do not attend.

The above argument is in many ways cogent, yet not even the most democratic community can permit individual citizens to pay taxes only for the specific purposes which they at a particular time want to support. Every citizen supports a greater or lesser degree of government activity of which he does not approve, but, except for expressing oneself through the polls, no democratic remedy for this situation in education or in other areas seems to exist.

SEPARATION OF CHURCH AND STATE:
THE AMERICAN EXPERIMENT

In 1783, when the American Constitution was adopted, these United States embarked upon a new experiment in government. In the intervening period, the American goal of a democratic society has been widely espoused by other nations, but the specific forms in which the ideal has been concretized in America have never been duplicated.

As is well-known, the American system is that of a self-limiting government, which has voluntarily surrendered any claim to the total control or supervision of the life of its citizens. This limitation on the power of the state finds its legal formulation in the Bill of Rights. But this is not all. It has been built into the very structure of government, through the separation of the executive, the legislative, and the judicial branches. This emphasis upon the division of powers, which some may regard as an obsession, . . . undoubtedly creates serious problems with regard to the liaison among the various branches of government and between the federal government and the states, but it has proved a far more effective safeguard of the liberties of the citizenry than a merely abstract formulation in a written document. . . .

The most striking instance of a specific American method for achieving a democratic ideal lies in the area of freedom of religion. Here again the principle has been accepted universally as basic to a free society, but the American policy of the separation of church and state has rarely, if ever, been followed elsewhere. After the century and three-quarters that have elapsed since the ratification of the Constitution, the unique American experiment still remains largely unique.

It is because of this determination to safeguard

From *Religion and the Schools* (The Fund for the Republic, 1959), pp. 5-33.

the rights and liberties of the citizen that religion was made one of the subjects of the First Amendment in the Bill of Rights: "Congress shall make no law respecting an establishment of religion, or prohibiting the free exercise thereof . . ."

Prodigious efforts have been expended in seeking to establish the original intent of the Founding Fathers in drafting the First Amendment. Some students have suggested that its sole purpose was to prevent the federal government from establishing a national church . . . .

Another school of thought has argued with great vigor that the Founding Fathers were far too friendly to religion to have wished to create "a wall of separation," in Jefferson's phrase, between church and state. . . .

On the other hand, some scholars have assembled evidence . . . to buttress the view that the creation of such a wall was precisely the intent of the First Amendment. Thus the frequently quoted words of Justice Black in the *Everson* case: "The 'establishment of religion' clause of the First Amendment means at least this: Neither a state nor the Federal Government can set up a church. Neither can pass laws which aid one religion, aid all religions, or prefer one religion over another."

Equally well-known is the utterance of Justice Douglas in the *Zorach* case which, in the opinion of many, modifies this standpoint substantially, if it does not contravene it directly: ". . . The First Amendment within the scope of its coverage permits no exception; the prohibition is absolute. The First Amendment, however, does not say that in every and all respects there shall be a separation of church and state. Rather, it studiously defines the manner, the specific ways, in which there shall be no concert or union or dependency one on the other. That is the common sense of the matter. Otherwise the state and religion would be aliens to each other—hostile, suspicious, and even unfriendly."

. . . Had it been the intention of the Founding Fathers to permit non-preferential aid to all religions and to prohibit only preferential aid to one religious sect, they would have worded the First Amendment so as to forbid "the establishment of a church" or "of a religion," not "the establishment of religion."

Be this as it may, . . . [t]he real issue that must be met is: Which interpretation of the classical American doctrine of the separation of church and state is most likely to advance the interests of a free society in the twentieth century? Which position shall we adopt—the more restricted interpretation of the First Amendment, which sees in it only the prohibition of preferential aid to one religion, or the broader one which sees in it the impermissibility of direct aid to religion even on a non-preferential basis?

Several preliminary observations are in order. It is clear that the separation of church and state was adopted principally to safeguard the stability of the state against the divisiveness of sectarian strife. This direct purpose has been achieved to a very high degree—America has largely been spared the ravages of a *Kulturkampf* between the religious and non-religious elements in society. As a result we have been free both from the clerical political parties common on the European continent and from the violent anticlerical movements which flowered into the Nazi, Fascist, and Communist dictatorships. Moreover, the differences among the various sects, Protestant, Catholic, and Jewish, have rarely been exacerbated to the point of violent conflict in America.

At least as important as the direct purpose of the First Amendment have been its indirect results. Religious diversity is encountered everywhere in the modern world. But while it is treated elsewhere as a disagreeable fact, to be minimized, if not suppressed, it is characteristic of the American way to regard religious diversity as a good, worthy of being accorded full freedom.

The Amendment, moreover, has not only safeguarded the stability of the state; it has contributed to the vitality of religion as a whole. As a completely voluntary agency in American life, organized religion has attained a position of influence and prestige, outstripping by far its status in lands where the alliance of church and state is the norm. In the steadily rising percentage of the total population which is affiliated with a church, in the level of development and prestige which religious education has reached, in the range and extent of other religious activities, and, by no means least, in the attitude of respect, or at least of non-hostility, on the part of the non-affiliated that religion enjoys in the United States, it has attained to a position without parallel anywhere else in the world.

Observers of the current American scene frequently criticize, and with substantial justice, the superficiality of the current wave of religiosity, which has been described as a faith in faith, rather than as a faith in God and submission to His will. . . . The protagonists of a vital religion may find far too little of what they are seeking in America, and that is the challenge confronting them. But a little is infinitely more than nothing. It is phenomena such as these in American life which led to Justice Douglas' now famous dictum: "We are a religious people whose institutions presuppose a Supreme Being."

Out of both sections of the First Amendment—

the prohibition of the establishment of religion and the guarantee of "the free exercise thereof"— have emerged the two elements of the basic American attitude: The state is friendly to religion and respects it as a beneficial activity, hence it must do nothing to injure it; but the state is precluded from giving religion direct support even on a non-preferential basis.

Today, there is evident a growing demand for a revision of this position about direct aid to religion by the state. On the legal issue involved, it is contended that while the Supreme Court has generally sought to maintain the wall of separation between church and state, this has by no means been the universal pattern. In permitting fringe benefits like free text-books and bus transportation for parochial-school pupils, the Court has in effect recognized the emergent pattern in the church-state relationship of the future. Moreover, it is argued, this is by no means a radical break with the past, for there are many other instances of "breaches" in the alleged "wall of separation" which have persisted for decades and have never been ruled unconstitutional.

Now it is undeniable that American practice with regard to church-state relationship, both in law and in life, has not been thoroughly consistent. In seeking to fashion the shape of things to come, we may therefore adopt one of two alternatives:

A) We may hold the doctrine of "separation" to be the vestigial remains of an older order, which is to be allowed to wither away, either through the process of an increasingly restricted interpretation of the First Amendment or by its nullification in practice, as the state gives an ever greater measure of support to organized religion and to sectarian education.

B) On the other hand, we may feel that the principle of the separation of church and state, and not the exceptions to the doctrine, should remain normative in American life. This conviction would be based not merely on a view of the original intent of the First Amendment, but on the evidence that both the stability of the American commonwealth and the vitality and progress of religion owe not a little to the doctrine of the separation of church and state as historically understood. . . .

I believe that the second alternative is infinitely preferable. If the principle of separation of church and state is at least as valid today as ever in the past, how are we to understand the various deviations from this norm? I believe that they fall into several categories. Some may have a measure of justification, while others must be adjudged as indefensible violations of the basic principle, even if no remedy is presently in sight:

1) Such practices as the opening of Congress with prayer, the swearing in of government officials on the Bible or its use in court oaths, and references to the Deity in Thanksgiving Proclamations are sufficiently general in character as to offend neither the rights nor the sensibilities of the overwhelming majority of Americans. Moreover, they are so slight in scope as not to constitute a major infraction of the principle of separation— *de minimis non curat lex.*

2) The establishment and support of chaplaincies in the armed forces and in government prisons flow out of the recognition that men who are in service or behind bars have been forcibly removed from their usual environment by the state. The government therefore may be legitimately called upon to replace such facilities as they enjoyed while at liberty in civilian society. These include various kinds of entertainment, access to books and music, exercise, and sport. Obviously a very high priority among these facilities is occupied by the ministrations of religion.

3) Tax-exemption for houses of worship and religious schools presupposes a recognition of the beneficial character of religion in the life of the citizenry and is parallel to the tax-exemption granted other institutions like museums, hospitals, universities, and other specialized schools. To be sure, each of them serves only a fraction of the population, but their functioning is regarded as beneficial to the body politic as a whole.

The three categories we have noted above are justifiable, or at least are reconcilable with the traditional American doctrine of separation of church and state. This is the obverse of the coin, the reverse of which is the maintenance of a relationship of respect and cooperation between religion and society.

The following category, on the other hand, would seem to be completely at variance with this point of view:

4) In many public schools throughout the country, various forms of religious activity are widespread, such as Bible reading, Christmas celebrations, and the recitation of the Lord's Prayer. It is obvious that these practices are not likely to be modified in the foreseeable future. In fact, new features of sectarian belief and practice are

being introduced, like the erection of crèches on public-school grounds and the recitation of the Ten Commandments in a "non-denominational" version, which, with apologies to George Orwell, can only be described as more "non-denominational" for some than for others.

Efforts to oppose this trend are arousing such violent reactions that the month of December, traditionally the season of good-will, is fast becoming the most tension-laden in the American school year. In this climate of clashing opinion and charged emotion, minority groups may well feel it prudent to desist from all-out opposition to the dominant pattern and seek to safeguard, on a local basis, and as well as they can, the rights and sensibilities of their own children. Nonetheless, it is difficult to see how these sectarian practices, however widespread and well-intentioned, can be regarded as anything other than a violation of a fundamental principle of the American way of life. . . .

Many of those who urge government support of religion in the area of education are well aware of these potential perils to freedom of religion and the cohesion of American society. They are nevertheless impelled to adopt their position from a deep-seated conviction that religion is a basic enterprise in the life of the human spirit which cannot be eliminated from the educational process. The corollary is then added that the American public-school system, as constituted at present, from which religious teaching is excluded, does not adequately fulfill the task of fashioning human personality.

How is the problem to be met? Here there is a divergence of opinion among the protagonists of religion in the school system. There are those who believe that the public school, by its very nature as a non-sectarian or even multi-sectarian institution, suffers from incurable ills and that only a religiously permeated, church-controlled school system can be regarded as ideal. Others are convinced that the situation can be remedied by the introduction of the teaching of religion in the public-school curriculum. . . .

GOVERNMENT AID TO PAROCHIAL SCHOOLS

. . . The ethical argument for government support of parochial schools has particular force. Parents who send their children to these schools are bearing the onus of double taxation, both for the public schools, enforced by the state, and for the parochial schools, enjoined by their sense of religious duty. This works especially great hardship upon millions of American Catholics, who represent every economic level in society, though Lutherans, Jews, and other groups also conduct day schools under religious auspices.

Two theoretical considerations are advanced to buttress this contention. It is maintained (a) that no one but the parent has a natural right regarding the education of his children and that this right is prior to all other claims in this area, and (b) the state in the field of education is merely acting as surrogate for the parent, making it possible for him to exercise his right through state collection of taxes from all residents into a general education fund.

In some quarters, the secular public school has been described as an agency for such parents as are not concerned or competent to establish an educational system by themselves, while those concerned and competent would establish schools administered by themselves or by appointed trustees. A less invidious and juster distinction would define the public school as the instrumentality created for such parents as do not wish any religious instruction for their children within the rubric of secular education, and the parochial school as the instrument of those parents for whom education implies a religious orientation organically related to the entire curriculum. In any event, the argument runs, both groups of parents and both types of schools are equally entitled to governmental support or, more concretely, to their proportionate share from the public-education fund to which all have contributed. In sum, the secular school and the religious school are equally "public" and thus equally deserving of tax support.

With regard to the social utility of the proposal, proponents claim that the vast system of parochial education cannot permanently survive through the voluntary self-taxation of the Catholic community, so that public support is a necessity as well as a right. As for the charges of "segregation" and "Un-Americanism" leveled in some quarters against the parochial school, these are refuted by the statement that such a school actually accords with the highest American ideals. Ours is a pluralistic culture, which necessarily implies the free expression and intensive cultivation of the varying religious traditions in America. Attention is also called to the strong emphasis placed upon morality and patriotism in the parochial schools as proof of their devotion to the welfare and unity of the American people.

As evidence that the democratic spirit is compatible with government support of parochial schools, the example of Holland is frequently invoked. Here government support is provided for the secular public schools, as well as for Catholic parochial schools and other private schools.

Now, one cannot fail to be profoundly impressed by the magnificent devotion to their faith exhibited by American Catholics in the creation of their far-flung system of education or to be moved by the burdens that they have voluntarily assumed in maintaining it. Yet with all genuine sympathy for their problem, the theoretic contentions which are advanced must be subjected to careful analysis, and other aspects must be taken into consideration.

The conception of the state as merely the administrator of a public-education fund to which each individual contributes and from which he is free to withdraw his "share" is an over-simplification and a totally unrealistic picture of the functions of government.

It will be generally agreed, and freely granted, that "the very purpose of a Bill of Rights was to withdraw certain subjects from the vicissitudes of political controversy, to place them beyond the reach of majorities and officials, and to establish them as legal principles to be applied by the courts. One's right to life, liberty, and property, to free speech, a free press, freedom of worship and assembly, and other fundamental rights may not be submitted to vote; they depend on the outcome of no elections." It is, however, a *non-sequitur* to infer that the activity of the government in the safeguarding of "life, liberty, and property" is merely that of an agency collecting the funds required to carry out these purposes, and that the individual or a group is therefore free to secede from the collective enterprise at will.

Conscientious objectors must pay their taxes to the federal government, most of which are allocated today to military purposes. A group of citizens may feel that the sanitation system in their community . . . is inadequate or even hazardous to health. They cannot withhold their share of municipal taxes, in order to create their own system of garbage removal. There is nothing to prevent them from arranging for a private carting service to remedy the delays of the public Sanitation Department. A business concern or an individual may feel the need for more protection of property and life than the police department affords. He would not be permitted, however, to retain part of his taxes in order to pay for a burglar-alarm system, a private police force, or a bodyguard. In the field of education, the role of the state is far more central and inclusive than serving as the repository of a public-education pool.

Moreover, it may well be denied that the school is merely a surrogate for the parent, for its functions are both more and less extensive than the parental obligation. They are less, because important elements of the child's education, such as religious doctrine and practice, ethical standards of behavior, etiquette, and other aspects of personal conduct, are not entrusted to the school but are, and should be, the functions of the home and the church. They are more, because the school is concerned with the transmission of group values which society regards as essential for its survival and unity and which are not the primary concern of the parent.

Moreover, the assumption of a primal and prior right to the parents in regard to education seems highly questionable on two grounds: the order of the alleged priorities and, consequently, the nature of the relationships involved. It is obvious that man is not merely a biological creature but a social being, and it is this second characteristic which sets him apart from the lower animals. *Hence a child possesses concurrent and parallel relationships both to his parents and to society, and both are equally rooted in his nature.* Moreover, on grounds of religion and of logic one may argue that the nature of these relationships is to be subsumed under the category of *duty* rather than of *right,* since the newborn child finds himself born into a family and a society not of his own choosing. . . .

In sum, both the parents and the state have *concurrent obligations* to prepare the young for life in the environment in which they find themselves, by training them to be useful, respected, and self-fulfilling members of society and by transmitting to them the necessary tools for making a living and for being at home in the world.

Not the least of these obligations, both of the parents and of society, is to recognize the child as an independent personality. Though procreated by his parents and nurtured by society, the child is not a creature of either, nor is he required to be a facsimile of the one or a robot in the other. Safeguarding the child's individuality and affording him the opportunity for free self-development constitute ethical imperatives of the highest order, of which a free society must always be aware. That awareness is frequently charged with pain and peril, as both parents and society can testify out of their experience, but it is an inevitable feature of the human situation.

To be sure, this parallel duty of the parents and of the state gives rise to corresponding rights. Parents have the right to inculcate in the young the ideals by which the family lives and maintains its character. Society has the right to transmit the values needed for the civic good. It is not reasonable to expect that either the parents or the social order should be burdened with obligations toward the younger generation and at the same time be denied the power to help assure their own preservation.

Hence, the public school teaches not merely spelling and arithmetic, as well as vocational arts and skills, but the English language, American literature, and American history, in order to imbue the coming generation with a sense of communal unity and national loyalty. Similarly, parents have a right to transmit the religious and ethical values they regard as precious and lifegiving. For some parents, supplemental religious instruction after public-school hours may appear adequate, whether in Sunday Schools or in afternoon schools. For others, religion is too important to be relegated to a subordinate position and religious culture too extensive to be adequately taught in the interstices of a child's leisure hours. Such parents will necessarily seek to satisfy their needs through a parochial school, in which religion and secular studies are integrated. Parents have a right to establish such schools, but they have no right to claim the help of the state in maintaining them.

Moreover, the proponents of governmental support for parochial schools seem to have committed the error of the undivided middle. Since parochial schools are not conducted for private gain, it is insisted that they are "public schools." Actually, communal institutions fall into three—not two—principal categories:

1) *Public institutions*, which are tax-supported, being directed, controlled, and staffed by the government—like the public schools, municipal and state hospitals, and local, state, and national museums and parks. It is not merely a theoretical procedure that dictates that these activities supported by public funds be under the supervision of the government. A government agency is the instrumentality created by the citizens for achieving those socially desirable ends they all share in common.

2) *Private institutions*, conducted for profit, such as privately owned hospitals, commercial museums, private business and vocational schools.

3) *Non-public, voluntary institutions* created by free associations of individuals who alone are responsible for their program and functioning. The role of the state here is essentially negative and regulatory, to make sure that minimal standards of competence, safety, and sanitation are maintained. Within this category fall the voluntary community hospitals, homes for the aged and infirm, child-shelter and family guidance agencies, specialized museums like the Museum of Modern Art, and musical organizations like the New York Philharmonic. That institutions in this third category should be exempted from the burden of taxation is fair and just, in recognition of the values they contribute to society, but, being free from governmental control, they cannot expect maintenance from public funds.

The economist may argue that exemption from taxation is no less a subvention than a direct grant. This is undoubtedly true in theory, but life has a logic of its own and recognizes a distinction between the two procedures. The existence of institutions in this third, intermediate category is paralleled by the presence of a third, intermediate position with regard to public funds—no direct allocation, but no tax obligation.

By far the most compelling argument for public support for parochial schools is the issue of "double taxation" and the genuine burdens it imposes. But here the Catholic (or Lutheran or Jewish) parent would do well to recall that he has a double obligation, to the American people, of which he is a part, as well as to his own religious community. The nature of this obligation is often overlooked.

The past one hundred years, which coincide with the history of the American public school, have witnessed the emergence of the American nation as a living entity. It was during this time that the overwhelmingly white, Protestant, Anglo-Saxon complexion of the American nation underwent its most far-reaching and potentially critical transformation. The small island of Anglo-Saxon Americans was inundated by successive waves of immigration, consisting of untold ethnic groups, notably the Irish, Scandinavian, German, Slavic, and Italian and including substantial numbers of Catholics and Jews. Their impact subjected the American body politic to substantial strains, which are far from spent even today. Yet, by and large, the nation fulfilled its originally projected goal of *E Pluribus Unum,* and an overwhelming sense of unity, beyond the prevalent ethnic and religious diversity, was engendered among the old and the new Americans. The three major wars America fought in the twentieth century underlined this unity in blood, but it had come into being long before the outbreak of hostilities.

Social cleavages, economic conflicts, political differences, and religious divergences were very much in evidence. But it was the public school that created the basis for American unity and loyalty, for here children of all backgrounds and levels in society met as equals, played and studied together, learning to live not merely as neighbors but as fellow-citizens of the Republic.

The home and the church taught the beliefs and the practices that were to serve as the firm foundations of the child's personality. The public school completed the ethical training of the youth by inculcating a respect for the right of others to differ with him as well as a feeling of friendship and camaraderie with those of other races and creeds. Martin Buber has eloquently reminded our age that it is the personal confrontation of human beings that is decisive in building their relationships, not the forensic or written word however elevated in sentiment.

The diversity of the student body in the public school was matched by the variety of background and outlook among the teachers with whom the children came into contact. The pupil developed a recognition of the truth that intelligent and well-meaning men and women might well differ among themselves on many issues, cherishing their specific viewpoints, yet finding it entirely possible to live and function in cooperation, harmony, and mutual respect with one another. One need not exaggerate the merits of the public school to see in it a unique laboratory for the democratic process.

Nor does this task belong only to the past. Unlike the racially more homogeneous nations of Western Europe, America is, in Walt Whitman's words, "a nation of nations, a people of peoples." This cultural and ethnic diversity may not remain a feature of the American landscape forever, but its disappearance is still a long way off. Besides, religious pluralism is recognized by nearly all Americans as a good, worthy of permanent preservation. If there is to be a maximum degree of freedom in American society, it must be counterbalanced by an equally powerful instrument for building unity and mutual fellowship. . . . There is no other institution in American life that can rival the public school in fulfilling this indispensable function for the present and the future.

The living tension between these two poles of unity and diversity is the measure of the vitality of the democratic way of life. If either principle is submerged, true freedom is imperiled. Hence, when the Supreme Court in the *Pierce* case affirmed the legitimacy of parochial schools, and, more recently, when California voters rejected the attempt to void tax-exemptions for parochial schools, Americans were defending one of the two indispensable elements of a free society. At the same time, it should be recognized that the destruction of the public-school system or even its attenuation would seriously affect the moral and social values of national unity. The weakening of the social fabric would ultimately undermine the religious and cultural diversity of the American way.

The example of Holland, often advanced as an instance of a democratic government which supports all types of schools, is not altogether reassuring in this respect. In 1948 the so-called "public-school system" numbered only about 27 per cent of the school population (328,000), while the Catholic parochial schools contained 43 per cent (525,000) and "other private schools" 29 per cent (349,000). This stratification has apparently become permanent. In 1955, according to the Ministry of Education of the Netherlands, of the 1,413,402 children of elementary-school age, 28 per cent attended the "public schools" (407,034), 27 per cent were pupils of Protestant schools (387,318), 41 per cent were enrolled in the Catholic schools (592,356), and 1 per cent attended "other schools" (26,694). A school system which includes only one child out of four can be called "public" only by courtesy. One may anticipate that the absence of a fund of shared experience and common living for Dutch youth is bound to affect the sense of unity in the Dutch people as time goes on. Be this as it may, the Dutch, like most other West European nations, are ethnically homogeneous. The task of creating a nation out of disparate elements no longer confronts the Netherlands as it does America.

One can scarcely expect American society to help underwrite the cost of parochial education, the merits of which may be freely granted, but one of the results of which may well be the destruction of the public-school system. This is not merely a matter of group strategy. What is being suggested here is that parents whose loyalty to their church leads them to send their children to parochial schools are not on that account freed from the obligation to support the public schools as the basic agency for building mutuality of relationship among the citizens of various faiths and backgrounds. Nor is this duty obviated by attacks upon the "godlessness" of the public schools, which have always been friendly to religion and which have contributed to the character-building of at least four generations of Americans with gratifying success.

Throughout this discussion thus far, a theory with regard to the nature of the parochial-school program has been implicitly taken for granted. The implication has been that a parochial school gives its pupils what is essentially a secular education, to which religious studies have been added. On this basis, it has been argued that the public educational fund amassed by the state through taxation should be dipped into to support the secular elements of the parochial-school program.

The truth is, however, that no religious educator, Catholic, Lutheran, or Jewish, would be willing to define his educational philosophy in such terms. For him, religion should permeate every course in the curriculum, in greater or lesser degree, so that no aspect of culture would be exempt from its influence. Many religious educators would go further and wish to have the children's entire lives spent in an atmosphere created and informed by their specific tradition and way of life. Often it is the desire to create this pervasive religious spirit rather than the wish to impart specific religious knowledge to the children that is the driving force behind the creation of parochial schools.

From this underlying philosophy of education, however, flow constitutional consequences which cannot fairly be evaded. Since all parochial education is religious in character and intent, it follows that governmental support of schools would represent aid to religion, direct, concrete, and substantial, and thus run counter to the "nonestablishment" clause of the First Amendment.

American Catholics possess a deep dedication to their faith and a zeal for their children's education that cannot be too highly praised. They should recognize that the American Catholic school system, which is unequaled elsewhere, is one more sign of the strength of religion in a free society, relying upon its own inner resources rather than upon the compulsive power of the state. The record of history, both past and present, demonstrates that wherever the state buttresses the church, the results are often an external, soulless conformity at best and a violent antagonism at worst. Rarely do men give the free allegiance of their spirit to God, which is the essence of true religion.

Moreover, protagonists of the parochial or day school of all faiths should recognize the duty they share with all other Americans, including those who may send their children to private schools, or who have no children at all, to maintain the public school as the basic instrumentality for the education of American children, while maintaining their right to create parochial schools for the intensive cultivation of the religious spirit for as many children as are willing or able to be accommodated within them.

As a non-Catholic who possesses a deep sympathy with the widespread desire of Catholic parents to give their children a Catholic education, I would urge the need of recognizing the legitimacy of the two ideals here in tension, the resolution of which can come only through a painful and partial process of accommodation between them. The same problem, on a lesser scale, confronts the Jewish community in America. The difficulties of transmitting the rich and complex content of Jewish culture and inculcating the values and practices of the Jewish religion are tremendous, particularly in an open society in which Judaism is the heritage of a minority group.

To fulfill this task, American Jews have created a vast array of supplementary schools, some meeting on Sunday mornings, others on weekday afternoons after public-school hours. Because of limitations in the child's time and energy after a full schoolday, these supplementary schools cannot satisfy those parents and educators who are committed to an intensive Jewish religious education. As a result, Jewish day schools have been rapidly increasing in number, though they include only a small minority of the Jewish school population in America.

It is safe to say that even the Jewish leaders who are most devoted to the day-school idea do not look forward to having all, or even most, Jewish children enrolled in these private schools. Their goal is the creation of a corps of Jewish men and women in the coming generation who, possessing a more extensive knowledge of Judaism and a correspondingly deeper sense of personal commitment, will supply the professional and lay leadership for the Jewish community and its spiritual life. This objective does not preclude recognizing the value of the American public school as "the potter's house where the soul of the nation is fashioned." Most American Jews believe that it is in the public school that most Jewish children should continue to receive their general education, supplemented by the training supplied by the religious school.

Undoubtedly the problem is more intense for Catholics, but the difference is one of degree, not of kind—the reconciliation of the basic needs of the American people as a whole with the equally legitimate requirements of religious education. It is far better that both goals be met, albeit imperfectly, than that either be totally ignored.

The extraordinary success achieved by Catholics in America in establishing their educational system suggests the need of a special self-restraint that cannot perhaps be logically justified but is a very real necessity nonetheless. It is a truism in the social-economic order that large aggregations of power, be they corporations or labor unions, because of their very size, create special problems such as monopoly, price-fixing, and the exercise of pressure on government which do not arise for similar groups of smaller compass and lesser influence. In the face of phenomena such as these, society must impose effective safeguards of its over-all interests.

Conversely, where the unit is smaller, society can afford the luxury of greater latitude. American law thus offers considerable freedom to conscientious objectors to war, even in the case of aliens applying for citizenship. Were the day to arrive when most Americans, for whatever reason, become conscientious objectors, it is highly doubtful whether the state could afford to leave itself defenseless before a potential enemy. The need for the preservation of the state would limit, if not totally abrogate, the freedom of conscience of the citizen which is involved in the refusal to bear arms.

Were the Catholic school system small in extent, it would pose no challenge to the public-school system. By the same token, American Catholics would not be confronted by the problem of reconciling two goals, both of which deserve their allegiance.

The vast economic problem confronting American Catholics in maintaining the far-flung parochial-school system deserves the sympathy of all their fellow-citizens, as surely as their achievement should command universal admiration. Yet, in spite of the hardships and tensions involved, we believe that both ideals—concern for national unity and zeal for religious commitment—receive their optimum fulfillment under the present arrangement, which grants tax-exemption to parochial schools without giving them tax support. The "middle way" is the best for America as a whole and for the various religious faiths which undergird its way of life.

RELIGION IN THE PUBLIC SCHOOLS

The parochial school represents one effort to counter the "secularism" of the public school, by establishing an alternative religious school system. The other approach seeks to remedy the condition by introducing religion into the public school itself by the practice of certain religious observances or through the teaching of religion or both.

As we have seen, religious observances in the public schools are no innovation. In their origin, they are survivals from an earlier era, when the schools were, in fact if not in law, Protestant institutions. Bible readings, generally from the King James' Version, are all but universal, and scarcely less so is the inclusion of some hymns into the assembly and music programs. The Lord's Prayer is also widely used, its constitutionality having been upheld by some courts, as in New Jersey.*

The most widespread aspect of religious observance has revolved around Christmas, through decorations in the classroom, art work, plays, and celebrations participated in by the pupils. The degree of specific sectarian content in these cele-

brations has naturally varied with the community and the school administration through the years. In the last decade, religious leaders have made thoroughly justifiable attempts to oppose the secularization and commercialism of Christmas. The call to "put Christ back into Christmas" has had a marked effect on the schools. Probably on the assumption that since Christmas celebrations are already in the school system they might as well be really "Christian," pressures have been growing for giving them a more markedly sectarian character. Determined efforts have been made to have Nativity scenes enacted by the children and to have crèches erected on public-school grounds. That these practices, growing in extent and intensity, have confronted the Jewish community, among others, with grave problems has already been noted.

For a period, some well-meaning educators and parents, both Christian and Jewish, thought that joint Christmas-Hanukkah celebrations in the public schools might be the solution. It is true that the Maccabean struggle for religious freedom, which is commemorated by the Jewish Hanukkah holiday, poses no basic theological difficulties for Christians as does Christmas for Jews. Quite the contrary, had the Maccabean victory not taken place, Christianity may not have come into the world. This the church recognized by including the *Books of the Maccabees* in the canon of Scripture (in the Catholic Church) and in the Apocrypha (in Protestantism)—a status of sanctity, incidentally, which these books do not occupy in Judaism. For several centuries, the church observed a special feast called "the Birth of the Maccabees" on the first of August.

Nevertheless, signs are multiplying that Catholic and other religious leaders are objecting to the participation by Christian children in Hanukkah plays and pageants. Most Jewish religious leaders have been opposed all along to these joint celebrations, holding that bi-sectarianism is also a form of sectarianism that has no place in the public school. The Jewish laity, originally more favorable to the project, is now increasingly conscious of its inadequacy. Such instances as the statement by the chairman of the public-school board in New Hyde Park, New York, that Hanukkah should not be mentioned "where it interferes with the Christmas season" has helped speed the sense of disenchantment with the idea.

Far less charged with emotion and prejudice than the issue of religious observances and celebrations and therefore conducted on a far more

---

* Note that the Supreme Court now has ruled against prayers and Bible reading in public schools.—*Ed.*

rational level are the various proposals for introducing the teaching of religion into the public-school system. Such responsible agencies as the American Council on Education, the Religious Education Association, and various educational and religious bodies have explored possible avenues of solution and shed considerable light on the issue.

That the widespread "religious illiteracy" of our day poses a problem for contemporary education is universally conceded. Religion has been one of the most potent factors in human history, and its influence is written large in literature, music, and art, as well as in politics and morals. It follows that some knowledge of the scriptures, beliefs, rites, history, and heroes of the great religious traditions of the world is indispensable to a truly educated person.

Thus far the problem. With regard to the solution, too, there is a substantial measure of agreement. It is generally agreed that whatever difficulties inhere in the teaching of religion they are minimal on the college level. Here the relative maturity of the students and the atmosphere of free intellectual inquiry offer assurance that not indoctrination but education will be the guiding principle, both in the discussion of the religious factor in history and in special courses in religion offered in the curriculum. Hence, colleges and universities, and in some instances even state universities, have witnessed the expansion of courses in religion. Nearly always they are offered on an elective basis and generally they have elicited considerable interest from students. While the major religious traditions generally receive adequate treatment in the curricula of Departments of Religion, it should be noted that this is not always true of the minority faiths. Though overt prejudice is rarely the cause, the lesser sects do run the risk of having their viewpoint overlooked or minimized or distorted by inexpert or unsympathetic instructors. These liabilities are, however, inherent in the pluralistic pattern of American religious life. By and large, good-will prevails in this area, and the position of religion as an integral element in the college curriculum seems assured.

A lesser, but still substantial, measure of agreement exists with regard to the teaching of religion on the elementary-school level. It is generally recognized that there are many pitfalls and few advantages in undertaking the teaching of religion in the elementary school, particularly the lower grades. The young and impressionable age of the children, their inability to react critically to material presented to them, and the fact that their own specific loyalties are still in process of formation—factors such as these have persuaded most

Americans that religion does not belong in the curriculum of the elementary school.

The problem is most acute with regard to the secondary school. It is not difficult to make out a convincing case for objective teaching about religion, its institutions, tenets, and practices, as a branch of civics in the high-school curriculum. Churches constitute an important part of the social scene, no less than the institutions of government, culture, education, and recreation. To ignore the religious life of the community means to create a vast lacuna in the children's understanding of the society in which they live and function.

The truth of this position is incontrovertible, but the major difficulties involved in implementing such a plan cannot be glossed over. The history of recent years gives ground for feeling that the danger of the "camel's head in the tent" is not imaginary. It cannot be denied that there are those who would regard "teaching *about* religion" merely as the entering wedge for the "teaching *of* religion" along denominational lines within the public-school curriculum, or at least with the authority and prestige of the state behind it. The good faith of most advocates of the introduction of the teaching *about* religion in the school system is not in question. But they are not representative of those who want to see outright religious instruction in the schools.

Where such bona-fide programs in "teaching about religion" have been experimented with, important practical problems have come to light. The study materials thus far produced in this area leave much to be desired from the standpoint of objectivity and content and raise the serious question whether adequate material can be prepared to meet this need. The growing shortage of personnel in the teaching profession as a whole would be aggravated by this new and delicate assignment, which would necessitate special training in the untried art of teaching about religion. It is also difficult to see how the introduction of such an arrangement could be prevented from leading to a "religious test" for teachers to the school system, in fact if not in law, particularly in view of the mounting pressures by church groups for "positive" religious values in the schools. Besides, it is highly doubtful whether most Catholics, Protestants, or Jews would be willing to have their tenets and rites presented by those outside their respective traditions.

Difficulties such as these have led to another approach to the problem. It has been suggested that the teaching about religion be given by the priests, ministers, and rabbis in the community, whose houses of worship would be visited by the classes as part of the course in civics, similar to trips taken to other institutions. To be sure, this procedure would relieve the present school staffs of most of the burdens mentioned above, but it would create new problems of major proportions. It is doubtful whether most ministers of religion, who are trained to be devoted advocates of their respective faiths, would be willing or able to give objective instruction on religion, overcoming their natural and legitimate impulse to "win souls" for the convictions they hold sacred.

Moreover, the multiplicity of denominations in Protestantism, as well as the variety of viewpoints in Judaism, would necessarily mean the elimination of most sects and the favored treatment of a few. It would hardly be practical for high-school students to visit five or more Protestant churches, three Jewish synagogues, in addition to the Catholic Church, in order to cover the major traditions. There would still remain such groups as Unitarianism, Ethical Culture, Christian Science, Jehovah's Witnesses, and Theosophy, which would presumably be ignored. In addition, it is certain that many denominations would not sanction their children's visiting other houses of worship and studying alien doctrines from their ministers. Whether such convictions are justifiable or not is irrelevant; they need to be reckoned with. Given these circumstances, however, it seems clear that the comprehensiveness and impartiality of the program would be gravely compromised.

Besides, if the "teaching about religion" were successfully introduced into the public high schools and all these problems were overcome, it might prove a Pyrrhic victory for the cause of religion. If this type of teaching became widespread, many parents might regard it as an adequate substitute for religious education in church schools, which requires the expenditure of additional time, energy, and substance. Thus the fabric of the traditional religious school would be weakened still further and the difficult struggle to give religious education greater breadth and depth might well receive the kiss of death.

Finally, the objective presentation of religious beliefs and practices, with a scrupulous avoidance of any effort to secure the pupil's commitment to the faith under discussion, would seem to many, if not to most, religiously minded people to be highly objectionable. Such teaching of religion would be playing Hamlet without the Prince of Denmark, or, if we may heap Pelion on Ossa, keeping the bath while throwing the baby out. There would be the very real danger that the objectivity of the teacher would be translated by the pupil into indifference to all genuine religious commitment.

In sum, the problem is genuine, but so are the drawbacks confronting the various proposals advanced for the teaching of religion in the public schools. What would therefore seem to be indicated is the need for further concentrated study of the question, to be followed by experimentation in selected areas, through adequate teacher-training, the preparation of proper curriculum material, and the careful orientation of the community in question to the program. Perhaps many of the difficulties envisaged in advance might be dissipated in the bright sunlight of reality; conversely, new and unanticipated problems might well arise.

Until such programs for "teaching about religion" in the public-school system are tried and found thoroughly feasible, we would do well to recall some basic truths about religion and life. In spite of the inbred American propensity for panaceas, the truth remains that the total education of the child as a human being, as a citizen, and as a child of God cannot be entrusted to any single agency. The home, the public school, the religious school, the church, and, by no means least, "the street" all play their part in molding the personality of the child and the youth. Never in American history, even before the emergence of the secular public school, was the school expected to assume the full burden of educating a generation that would be loyal to religious and ethical values. The home and the church never abdicated their roles in this complex undertaking.

Much of the impetus for introducing religion into the curriculum and the extra-curriculum program of the public school in our day stems from a sense of frustration felt by many teachers of religion. Even in this day of "religious revival," they see the weakening of religion in the home and the consequent ineffectiveness of the church and the church school. Religious leaders and institutions, their energies already taxed to the full, would be less than human if they were not tempted to seek the help of the state to achieve their purpose.

Yet there is no escaping the law that water cannot rise higher than its source; it is an illusion to imagine that America can be made "religious" in spite of itself. If the public-school system were to be saddled with the tasks that should be borne by the church, the religious school, and the home, we might well develop a religion-by-rote which would spell decay for religious vitality. Who, more than the teacher of religion, should know that there is no short-cut to the New Jerusalem?

There are vast dimensions to the problem of religion and education in a free society. Yet we may cling to the conviction that basically America has been on the right path during the past century and three-quarters of its history and should persevere on it in the future. Will the tensions and conflicts that are mounting in this area be resolved on grounds of reason and moral principle? One has doubts, but also hopes. In any event, we may continue to believe that as the issues are clarified, the various protagonists will understand better their own presuppositions, as well as those they find unacceptable. If the discussion is conducted on a rational level, we may hope that the solutions finally achieved will be both moderate and just.

Selection *60*
***

The Social Structure of the Restaurant
William Foote Whyte

In the following selection, Whyte discusses the social structure, organization, and interaction found in fairly large restaurants. This study is an example of the sociological contributions to the fields of industrial relations, human relations, industrial sociology, and, to some degree, to the sociology of occupations. In approved sociological style, Whyte relates theory to facts and facts to theory, to the mutual advantage of each.

A business organization is, among other things, an interrelated and interdependent social system, consisting of the members of that organization and their relations to each other. How people relate to each other is, of course, the major element in this social structure. However, since people may participate in this social system in an almost infinite number of ways, it seems neither necessary nor desirable to attempt to account for all their behavior. Hence, research usually ignores behavior not directly related to the social structure or organization and instead emphasizes the purposeful, repeated interaction or the interaction at points of stress in the structure. Narrowing research to significant, repetitive behavior makes theory building, hypothesis testing, and model construction much more possible and the gathering of data much more fruitful. Long ago, sociologists proved how significant the influence of the social environment was on human behavior; studies such as the one presented in Selection 61 demonstrate this significance. Other structural-functional studies of industries or occupations that are recommended to the student include Hughes' study of the "grid of informal relationships" that exist within production units in an industry,[1] Caplow and McGee's studies of the academic profession,[2] Habenstein and Lamers' study of morticians,[3] and Habenstein and Christ's studies of interaction among nurses.[4]

The last two paragraphs of Whyte's article may mislead the beginning student of sociology, for, despite their significance, they state all too briefly one of the exciting methodological problems that modern sociologists are seeking to solve—namely, how to combine the necessary empirical, statistical handling of the characteristics of a "universe" and yet retain the dynamic, interactional, nonstatistical, personal aspects which, although less verifiable and replicable, bring to life the data under study.

[1] Everett C. Hughes, *Men and Their Work* (Glencoe, Ill.: The Free Press, 1958).
[2] Theodore Caplow and Reece J. McGee, *The Academic Marketplace* (New York: Basic Books Inc., 1958).
[3] Robert W. Habenstein and William M. Lamers, *History of American Funeral Directing* (Milwaukee: National Funeral Directors Association of the United States, 1955).
[4] Robert W. Habenstein and Edwin A. Christ, *Nurses at Work* (Columbia, Mo.: University of Missouri Press, 1955).

While research has provided a large and rapidly growing fund of knowledge concerning the social organization of a factory, studies of other industrial and business structures are only beginning. Sociologists who are concerned with working out the comparative structures of economic organizations must therefore look beyond as well as into the factory. This paper represents one effort in that direction. It grows out of a fourteen-month study of restaurants.[1] We do not claim to have studied a representative sample of restaurants. In an industry having so many types of operations and sizes of units, such a task would have taken years. We did aim to find out, at least in a general way, what sort of structure a restaurant is and what human problems are found within it. . . .

CHARACTERISTICS OF THE RESTAURANT

The restaurant is a combination production and service unit. It differs from the factory, which is solely a production unit, and also from the retail store, which is solely a service unit.

The restaurant operator produces a perishable product for immediate sale. Success requires a delicate adjustment of supply to demand and skillful co-ordination of production with service. The production and service tie-up not only makes for difficult human problems of co-ordinating action but adds a new dimension to the structure of the organization: the customer-employee relationship.

The contrast between factory and restaurant can be illustrated by this simple diagram, representing the direction of orders in the two structures:[2]

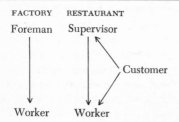

FACTORY   RESTAURANT
Foreman   Supervisor

Worker   Worker
                    Customer

The problems of co-ordination and customer relations are relatively simple in the small restaurant, but they become much more difficult as the organization grows. This may be illustrated structurally in terms of five stages of growth.

In the first stage, we have a small restaurant where the owner and several other employees dispense short orders over the counter. There is little division of labor. The owner and employees serve together as cooks, countermen, and dishwashers.

STAGE 1   STAGE 2

M   M

C   C

W   D ← K ← S

M — Manager   S — Service employees
C — Customers   K — Kitchen employees
W — Workers   D — Dishwashers

In the second stage, the business is still characterized by the informality and flexibility of its relationships. The boss knows most customers and all his employees on a personal basis. There is no need for formal controls and elaborate paper work. Still, the organization has grown in complexity as it has grown in size. The volume of business is such that it becomes necessary to divide the work, and we have dishwashers and kitchen employees, as well as those who wait on the customers. Now the problems of co-ordination begin to grow also, but the organization is still small enough so that the owner-manager can observe directly a large part of its activities and step in to straighten out friction or inefficiency.

As the business continues to expand, it requires a still more complex organization as well as larger quarters. No longer able to supervise all activities directly, the owner-manager hires a service supervisor, a food production supervisor, and places one

"The Social Structure of the Restaurant" by William Foote Whyte. Reprinted from *The American Journal of Sociology*, Vol. LIV (1949), 302-310, by permission of The University of Chicago Press.
[1] The research was financed by the National Restaurant Association. The field work was done by Margaret Chandler, Edith Lentz, John Schaefer, and William Whyte. We made interview or participant-observation studies of twelve restaurants in Chicago and did some brief interviewing outside Chicago. From one to four months was spent upon each Chicago restaurant. In *Human Relations in the Restaurant Industry* (New York: McGraw-Hill Book Co., 1948), I report the study in detail. Since the book is primarily addressed to restaurant operators and supervisors, the sociological frame of reference given here does not duplicate the more detailed publication.
[2] This is, of course, an oversimplified picture, for many factory workers interact also with inspectors, engineers, time-study men, etc., but the frequency of such interaction does not compare with that which we observe between customers and waiters or waitresses in a restaurant.

of his employees in charge of the dishroom as a working supervisor. He also employs a checker to total checks for his waitresses and see that the food is served in correct portions and style.

STAGE 3

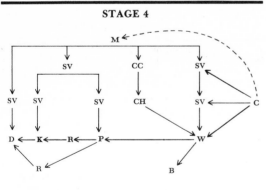

M — Manager
SV — Supervisor
CH — Checker
C — Customer

W — Waitress
K — Kitchen worker
D — Dishwasher

In time, the owner-manager finds that he can accommodate a larger number of customers if he takes one more step in the division of labor. Up to now the cooks have been serving the food to the waitresses. When these functions are divided, both cooking and serving can proceed more efficiently. Therefore, he sets up a service pantry

---

STAGE 4

M — Manager
SV — Supervisor
CH — Checker
CC — Cost control
    supervisor
C — Customer

W— Waitress
B — Bartender
P — Pantry worker
K — Kitchen worker
R — Runner
D — Dishwasher

apart from the kitchen. The cooks now concentrate on cooking, the runners carry food from kitchen to pantry and carry orders from pantry to kitchen, and the pantry girls serve the waitresses over the counter. This adds two more groups (pantry girls and runners) to be supervised, and, to cope with this and the larger scale of operation,

the owner adds another level of supervision, so that there are two supervisors between himself and the workers. Somewhere along the line of development, perhaps he begins serving drinks and adds bartenders to his organization.

Stage 5 need not be diagrammed here, for it does not necessarily involve any structural changes in the individual unit. Here several units are tied together into a chain, and one or more levels of authority are set up in a main office above the individual unit structures.

This expansion process magnifies old problems and gives rise to new ones. They may be considered under three headings: administration, the customer relationship, and the flow of work. Whenever we lengthen the hierarchy, adding new levels of authority to separate top executive from workers, the problem of administration becomes more complex. However, this is true for any organization, and therefore these problems of hierarchy need not be given special attention in an article on restaurants.

The particular problem of the large restaurant is to tie together its line of authority with the relations that arise along the flow of work. In the first instance, this involves the customer relationship, for here is where the flow of work begins. The handling of the customer relationship is crucial for the adjustment of the restaurant personnel, and a large part of that problem can be stated in strictly quantitative interaction terms: Who originates action for whom and how often? In a large and busy restaurant a waitress may take orders from fifty to one hundred customers a day (and perhaps several times for each meal) in addition to the orders (much less frequent) she receives from her supervisor. When we add to this the problem of adjusting to service pantry workers, bartenders, and perhaps checkers, we can readily see the possibilities of emotional tension —and, in our study, we did see a number of girls break down and cry under the strain.

Our findings suggested that emotional tension could be related directly to this quantitative interaction picture. The skilful waitress, who maintained her emotional equilibrium, did not simply respond to the initiative of customers. In various obvious and subtle ways she took the play away from customers, got them responding to her, and fitted them into the pattern of her work. She was also more aggressive than the emotionally insecure in originating action for other waitresses, service pantry people, and supervisor.

While in the rush hour the waitress works under a good deal of tension at best, the supervisor can either add to or relieve it. Here again we can speak in quantitative terms. In one restaurant we observed a change in dining-room management when a supervisor who was skilful in originating action for customers (thus taking pressure off waitresses) and who responded frequently to the initiation of waitresses was replaced by a supervisor who had less skill in controlling customers and who originated for the girls much more frequently and seldom responded to them. (Of the new supervisor, the waitresses would say, "She's always finding something to criticize"; "She's never around when we need her"; "She's always telling you; she doesn't care what you have to say"; etc.) This change was followed by evidences of increased nervous tension, especially among the less experienced waitresses, and finally by a series of waitress resignations.

Here we see that the customer-waitress, waitress-supervisor, waitress–service-pantry-worker relationships are interdependent parts of a social system. Changes in one part of the system will necessarily lead to changes in other parts. Furthermore, if the people involved in the system are to maintain their emotional balance, there must be some sort of compensatory activity to meet large interactional changes. For example, when waitresses are subject to a large increase in the originations of customers (at the peak of rush hours), the supervisor allows them to originate action for her with increasing frequency and diminishes the frequency with which she gives them orders. This is, in fact, the sort of behavior we have observed among supervisors who enjoy the closest co-operation with waitresses, as reported by the waitresses.

The customer relationship is, of course, only one point along the flow of work which brings orders from dining-room to kitchen and food from kitchen to dining-room. In a large restaurant operating on several floors, this is a long chain which may break down at any point, thus leading to emotional explosions in all quarters. The orders may go from waitress to pantry girl and then, as the pantry girl runs low in supplies, from pantry girl to pantry supplyman, from pantry supplyman to kitchen supplyman, and from kitchen supplyman to cook. And the food comes back along the same route in the opposite direction. Where drinks are served, the bar must be tied in with this flow of work, but there the chain is short and the problem less complex.

We have here a social system whose parts are interdependent in a highly sensitive manner. Thus the emotional tension experienced by waitresses is readily transmitted, link by link, all the way to the kitchen.

I have already noted how a skilful dining-room supervisor may help to relieve the tension on the entire system at its point of origin. Here we may consider other factors which affect the relations among employees along the flow of work: status, sex relations, and layout and equipment.

I would propose the hypothesis that relations among individuals along the flow of work will run more smoothly when those of higher status are in a position to originate for those of lower status in the organization and, conversely, that frictions will be observed more often when lower-status individuals seek to originate for those of higher status. (This is, of course, by no means a complete explanation of the friction or adjustment we observe.)

While more data are needed on this point, we made certain observations which tend to bear out the hypothesis. For example, in one kitchen we observed supplymen seeking to originate action (in getting food supplies) for cooks who were older, of greater seniority, more highly skilled, and much higher paid. This relationship was one of the sore points of the organization. Still, we discovered that there had been one supplyman who got along well with the cooks. When we got his story, we found that he had related himself to the cooks quite differently from the other supplymen. He sought to avoid calling orders to the cooks and instead just asked them to call him when a certain item was ready. In this way, he allowed them to increase the frequency of their origination for him, and, according to all accounts, he got better co-operation and service from the cooks than any other supplyman.

Much the same point is involved in the relations between the sexes. In our society most men grow up to be comfortable in a relationship in which they originate for women and to be uneasy, if not more seriously disturbed, when the originations go in the other direction. It is therefore a matter of some consequence how the sexes are distributed along the flow of work. On this question we gave particular attention to the dining-room–service pantry and dining-room–bar relationships.

In the dining-room–pantry situation there are four possible types of relationship by sex: waiter-counterman, waiter–pantry girl, waitress–pantry girl, and waitress-counterman. We were not able to give much attention to the first two types, but we did make intensive studies of two restaurants illustrating the third and fourth types. Ideally, for scientific purposes, we would want to hold everything else constant except for these sex differences. We had no such laboratory, but the two restaurants were nevertheless closely comparable. They were both large, busy establishments, operating on several floors, and serving the same price range of food in the same section of the city.

Perhaps the chief differences were found in the dining-room–pantry relationship itself. In restaurant A, waitresses gave their orders orally to the pantry girls. On the main serving floor of restaurant B, waitresses wrote out slips which they placed on spindles on top of a warming compartment separating them from the countermen. The men picked off the order slips, filled them, and put the plates in the compartment where the waitresses picked them up. In most cases there was no direct face-to-face interaction between waitresses and countermen, and, indeed, the warming compartment was so high that only the taller waitresses could see over its top.

These differences were not unrelated to the problems of sex in the flow of work. One of the countermen in restaurant B told us that, in all his years' experience, he had never before worked in such a wonderful place. Most workers who express such sentiments talk about their relations with their superiors or with fellow-employees on the same job or perhaps about wages, but this man had nothing to say about any of those subjects. He would discuss only the barrier that protected him from the waitresses. He described earlier experiences in other restaurants where there had been no such barrier and let us know that to be left out in the open where all the girls could call their orders in was an ordeal to which no man should be subjected. In such places, he said, there was constant wrangling.

This seems to check with experience in the industry. While we observed frictions arising between waitresses and pantry girls, such a relationship can at least be maintained with relative stability. On the other hand, it is difficult to prevent blowups between countermen and waitresses when the girls call their orders in. Most restaurants consciously or unconsciously interpose certain barriers to cut down waitress origination of action for countermen. It may be a warming compartment as in this case, or, as we observed in another restaurant, there was a man pantry supervisor who collected the order slips from the waitresses as they came in and passed them out to the countermen. There are a variety of ways of meeting the problem, but they all seem to involve this principle of social insulation.

The rule that all orders must be written also serves to cut down on interaction between waitresses and countermen, but this in itself is not always enough to eliminate friction. Where there is no physical barrier, there can be trouble unless the men who are on the receiving end of the orders work out their own system of getting out

from under. Such systems we observed at one bar and at one of the serving counters in restaurant B. The counter in this case was only waist high. While the girls wrote out their orders, they were also able to try to spur the men on orally, and there was much pulling and hauling on this point both at the bar and at the pantry counter.

The men who did not get along in this relationship played a waiting game. That is, when the girls seemed to be putting on special pressure for speed, they would very obviously slow down or else even turn away from the bar or counter and not go back to work until the offending waitresses just left their order slips and stepped away themselves. Thus they originated action for the waitresses. While this defensive maneuver provided the men with some emotional satisfaction, it slowed down the service, increased the frustrations of the waitresses, and thus built up tensions, to be released in larger explosions later.

One bartender and one counterman not only enjoyed their work but were considered by waitresses to be highly efficient and pleasant to deal with. Both of them had independently worked out the same system of handling the job when the rush hour got under way. Instead of handling each order slip in turn as it was handed to them (thus responding to each individual waitress), they would collect several slips that came in at about the same time, lay them out on the counter before them, and fill the orders in whatever order seemed most efficient. For example, the bartender would go through the slips to see how many "Martinis," "Old Fashions," and so on were required. Then he would make up all the "Martinis" at once before he went on to the next drink.

When the work was done this way, the girl first in was not necessarily first out with her tray, but the system was so efficient that it speeded up the work on the average, and the girls were content to profit this way in the long run. The men described the system to us simply in terms of efficiency; but note that, in organizing their jobs, they had changed quantitatively the relations they had with the waitresses. Instead of responding to each waitress, they were originating action for the girls (filling their orders as the men saw fit and sending them out when the men were ready).

Along with our consideration of layout and equipment in the flow of work, we should give attention to the communication system. Where the restaurant operates on one floor, the relations at each step in the flow can be worked out on a face-to-face basis. There may be friction, but there is also the possibility of working out many problems on a friendly, informal basis.

When a restaurant operates on two or more

floors, as many large ones do, face-to-face inter-action must be supplemented by mechanical means of communication. We saw three such mechanical means substituted for direct inter-action, and each one had its difficulties.

People can try to co-ordinate their activities through the house telephone. Without facial ex-pressions and gestures, there is a real loss of understanding, for we do not generally respond solely to people's voices. Still, this might serve reasonably well, if the connection between kitchen and pantry could be kept constantly open. At least in the one restaurant where we gave this subject special attention, that solution was out of the question, as one call from kitchen to pantry tied up the whole house phone system and nobody could call the manager, the cashier, or anybody else on this system as long as another call was being made. Consequently, the telephone could be used only to supplement other mechanical aids (in this case, the teleautograph).

The public address system has the advantage over the telephone that it can be used all the time, but it has the great disadvantage of being a very noisy instrument. Busy kitchens and service pan-tries are noisy places at best, so that the addition of a public address system might be most un-welcome. We do not yet know enough of the effect of noise upon the human nervous system to evaluate the instrument from this point of view, but we should recognize the obvious fact that surrounding noise affects the ability of people to communicate with each other and becomes there-fore a problem in human relations.

The teleautograph makes no noise and can be used at all times, yet it has its own disadvantages. Here we have an instrument in the service pantry and one in the kitchen. As the pantry supplyman writes his order, it appears simultaneously on the kitchen teleautograph. The kitchen's replies are transmitted upstairs in the same way. The ma-chine records faithfully, but it does not solve the problem of meaning in interaction. We may pass over the problem of illegibility of handwriting, although we have seen that cause serious diffi-culties. The more interesting problem is this: How urgent is an order?

When the rush hour comes along, with custom-ers pushing waitresses, waitresses pushing pan-try girls, and pantry girls pushing supplymen, the supplyman is on the end of the line so far as face-to-face interaction is concerned, and he is likely to get nervous and excited. He may then put in a larger order than he will actually use or write "Rush" above many of his orders. If he overorders, the leftovers come back to the kitchen at the end of the meal, and the kitchen supplymen

and cooks learn thus that the pantry supplyman did not really know how much he needed. They take this into account in interpreting his future orders. And, when everything is marked "Rush," the kitchen supplymen cannot tell the difference between the urgent and not so urgent ones. Thus the word becomes meaningless, and communica-tion deteriorates. Stuck in this impasse, the pantry supplyman may abandon his machine and dash down to the kitchen to try to snatch the order himself. The kitchen people will block this move whenever they can, so, more often, the pantry supplyman appeals to his supervisor. In the heat of the rush hour, we have seen pantry supervisors running up and down stairs, trying to get orders, trying to find out what is holding up things in the kitchen. Since they have supervisor status, the kitchen workers do not resist them openly, but the invasion of an upstairs supervisor tends to disrupt relations in the kitchen. It adds to the pressures there, for it comes as an emergency that lets everybody know that the organization is not functioning smoothly.

It is not the function of this article to work out possible solutions to this problem of communica-tion. I am concerned here with pointing out a significant new area for sociological investigation: the effects on human relations of various mechani-cal systems of communication. It is difficult enough to co-ordinate an organization in which the key people in the supervisory hierarchy are in direct face-to-face relations. It is a much more difficult problem (and one as yet little understood) when the co-ordination must be achieved in large meas-ure through mechanical communication systems.

IMPLICATIONS FOR THEORY AND METHODOLOGY

In presenting our observations on the restaurant industry, I have discussed formal structure, quan-titative measures of interaction, symbols in rela-tions to interaction, attitudes and interaction, and layout and equipment (including mechanical sys-tems of communication). Data of these categories must be fitted together. The uses of each type of data may be summarized here.

1. *Formal structure.*—We have ample data to show that the formal structure (the official alloca-tion of positions) does not *determine* the pattern of human relations in an organization. Neverthe-less, it does set certain limits upon the shape of that pattern. Thus, to analyze the human problems of a restaurant, it is necessary to outline its struc-ture in terms of length of hierarchy, divisions into departments, and flow of work (as done in the five stages above).

2. *Quantitative measures of interaction.*—Within the limits set by the formal structure, the relations among members of the organization may fall into a variety of patterns, each of which is subject to change.

The pattern we observe we call the *social system*. A social system is made up of *interdependent* parts. The parts are the *relations* of individuals in their various positions to each other. This is simply a first description of a social system, but there are important theoretical and practical conclusions which flow from it.

The relations of individuals to one another are subject to *measurement*, sufficient to allow them to be compared and classified. We can, for example, count the number of times that a waitress originates action for her customers compared with the number of times they originate it for her in a given period and observe how often she originates action for her supervisor and how often the supervisor does so for her, and so on, through the other relations in the system. So far, mathematically precise measurements of interaction have only been made in laboratory situations involving interviewer and interviewee. Nevertheless, in the present state of our knowledge, we can get, through interviewing and observation, quantitative data which, though only approximate, are sufficiently accurate to allow us to predict the course of developments or explain how certain problems have arisen and point the way to their possible solution.

As the terms are used here, *interaction, origination,* and *response* are abstractions without content. That is, they are indices which have no reference to either the symbols used or the subjective reactions felt by the interacting individuals. Such measures do not, of course, tell us all it is useful to know of human relations. Indeed, many students will think it absurd to believe that any useful data can come from abstractions which leave out the "content" of human relations. To them I can only say that science is, in part, a process of abstraction, which always seems to take us away from the "real world." The value of such abstractions can be determined only by testing them in research to see whether they enable us better to control and predict social events.

Since the social system is made up of *interdependent relations*, it follows that a change in one part of the system necessarily has repercussions in other parts of the system. For example, a change in origin-response ratio between waitresses and supervisor necessarily affects the waitress-customer and waitress–service-pantry-girl relations, and changes in those parts lead to other changes in the system. Therefore, in order to study

the social system or to deal with it effectively, it is necessary to discover the *pattern* of relations existing at a given time and to observe changes within that pattern. The nature of the interdependence of the parts of the system can be discovered only through observing how a change in Part A is followed by change in Part B, is followed by change in Part C, etc. Therefore, social systems must be studied *through time*. A static picture of the social structure of an organization is of little value. Science requires that we develop methods of study and tools of analysis to deal with constantly changing relations.

3. *Symbols in relation to interaction.*—We cannot be content simply with quantitative descriptions of interaction. We need to know why A responds to B in one situation and not in another or why A responds to B and not to C. In part, this is a matter of habituation, for we respond to the people we are accustomed to responding to and in the sorts of situations to which we are accustomed. But we must go beyond that to explain the development of new patterns and changes in old patterns of interaction.

We observe that individuals respond to certain symbols in interaction. I have discussed here status and sex as symbols affecting interaction (the problems of the originating from below of action for high status individual or by woman for man).

I have noted some problems in language symbols in the discussion of mechanical means of communication. That leaves the whole field of symbols in face-to-face interaction untouched, so that it represents only the barest beginning of an attempted formulation of the relations between symbols of communication and interaction. . . .

As we analyze social systems, symbols should always be seen in terms of their effects upon interaction. They are *incentives* or *inhibitors* to interaction with specific people in certain social situations. Thus, to put it in practical terms, the manager of an organization will find it useful to know both the pattern of interaction which will bring about harmonious relations and also how to use symbols so as to achieve that pattern.

4. *Attitudes and interaction.*—Changes in relations of individuals to one another are accompanied by changes in their *attitudes* toward one another and toward their organizations. In recent years we have developed excellent methods for attitude measurement, but the measurement in itself never tells us how the attitudes came about. The whole experience of our research program leads us to believe that the dynamics of attitude formation and change can best be worked out as we correlate attitudes with human relations in the organizations we study.

5. *Layout and equipment.*—Here the sociologist is not directly concerned with the problems of the mechanical or industrial engineer. He does not undertake to say which machine or which arrangement of work space and machines will be most productively efficient. However, he cannot help but observe that, for example, the height of the barrier between waitresses and countermen or the nature of the mechanical communication system have important effects upon human relations. Only as these effects are observed do the physical conditions come in for sociological analysis. (Of course, human relations have a bearing upon efficiency, but the sociologist, if he tackles the problem of efficiency, uses types of data and schemes of analysis quite different from those used by the engineer.)

A few years ago there was a great debate raging: statistics versus the case study. That debate is no longer waged publicly, but it still troubles many of us. On the one hand, we see that an individual case study, skilfully analyzed, yields interesting insights—but not scientific knowledge. On the other hand, we find that nearly all statistical work in sociology has dealt with the characteristics of aggregates: How much of a given phenomenon is to be found in a given population? Such an approach does not tell us anything about the relations among the individuals making up that population. And yet, if we are to believe the textbooks, the relations among individuals, the *group* life they lead, are the very heart of sociology.

So let us have more individual case studies, but let us also place the individual in the social systems in which he participates and note how his attitudes and goals change with changes in the relations he experiences. And let us have more quantitative work, but let us at last bring it to bear upon the heart of sociology, measuring the relations among individuals in their organizations.

Selection 61

Homunculus
Mary Garraway

The following selection has very special interest and merit in that from it the student learns something of basic social theory and at the same time something of the uses of computers for basic social research in industry. The article describes elementary social behavior between individuals in terms of sound social hypotheses and then attempts to determine whether the results obtained in the abstract setting of computer simulation are applicable to an organization operating in the real world. The simulation results, obtained under conditions of complete control (computer), as specified by theory, enable researchers to interpret their findings in real life with greater certainty.

More or less incidentally, the imaginative student can visualize the workings of a humanized robot or a roboticized human in the attempt to reduce reaction and behavior to simple, repetitive operations. He may even support a flight of fancy concerning the extent to which computors can "behave" intelligently, while at the same time considering the extent, if any, to which free will enters into man's routine social life.

The "Homunculus" project is the effort of John and Jeanne Gullahorn, working at the System Development Corporation—a nonprofit research organization—to make an analogy between social phenomena that have been generated largely by historical processes in real life and a model that has been created in the laboratory by rational processes. As the analogy becomes more apt, it may enable more rational procedures to be introduced intentionally into institutional change. Thus the project has both practical and scientific potential.

Picture a pigeon wandering around and pecking away in his cage in a laboratory. When the pigeon hits a round red target, an automatic machine feeds him grain. The hungrier the pigeon is, the more often he will emit an activity that has been reinforced with food. The more nearly satiated the pigeon is, the less often he will emit an activity reinforced with food. The more often an activity is punished by drenching the pigeon with water, the less often the animal emits the activity.

If the pigeon has been regularly fed when he pecked the target and then the feeding is abruptly stopped, he will probably show frustration and anger by turning away from the target, flapping his wings, and cooing excitedly. It is soon evident that the withdrawal of a positive reinforcer releases aggression. In contrast, a positive reinforcer may release, besides the reinforced activity, some degree of positive emotional behavior.

HOMANS' SOCIOLOGICAL TREATISE

In his book *Social Behavior: Its Elementary Forms*, George C. Homans combines certain of these psychological hypotheses about animal behavior, along with some principles from classical economics. He states that if an activity is often reinforced, it is often emitted, but that frequent reinforcement may also satiate the animal and so decrease the frequency of emission. Or, if an activity is often reinforced, it is often emitted, but the very emission precludes other activities, and this inescapable cost may in time decrease the frequency of emission.

While the response repertoires of pigeon and man may greatly differ, Homans suggests that the behavior of the two organisms may be similar in that they follow certain basic principles which he has formalized into five propositions. In trying to explain elementary social behavior, Homans views human behavior as a function of its payoff, and individual response as dependent on the amount and quality of reward and punishment his actions elicit.

BLAU'S INTERACTION SEQUENCE

In an application of these propositions, Homans uses an interaction sequence described in Peter M. Blau's book, *The Dynamics of Bureaucracy, A Study of Interpersonal Relations in Two Government Agencies*. Sixteen agents holding the same title, but varying in competence, are employed in a federal office. The more skilled receive more requests for assistance from their coworkers. Although the agent requesting help usually is rewarded by being able to do a better job, he pays the cost of implicitly admitting his inferiority to a colleague who by title is supposedly his equal. While the consultant gains prestige, he incurs the cost of time taken from his own work. Social justice is realized in this situation if the rewards of both participants are proportional to their costs. Both workers will net a social profit if their rewards from the interaction exceed their personal costs.

HOMUNCULUS MODEL

SDC [System Development Corporation] consultants John and Jeanne Gullahorn use this relatively simple interaction sequence between two hypothetical agents in a project called HOMUNCULUS. They have worked on the project since the summer of 1961 under the aegis of the artificial intelligence research area, Research Directorate. HOMUNCULUS attempts to actualize, in a computer program, the dynamic implications of Homans' propositions. The translation of these propositions into computer routines is expected ultimately to contribute to the goal of naturalistic prediction of behavior in small groups.

In the HOMUNCULUS model, a person is conceived as an information processing organism. He is programmed to receive, recognize, and store stimuli in memory, and to compare and contrast stimuli; to emit activities, to differentiate between reward and punishment, and to associate a stimulus-situation with a response and a response with a reinforcement; on the basis of past experience, to predict the probability of reward resulting from each response contemplated; and in social situations, to differentiate among other members of a group, to evaluate a social stimulus in terms of the specific person emitting it, and to select his response accordingly for the purpose of eliciting a positive reaction in turn.

The social being, just described, is programmed into the computer by means of IPL-V (Information Processing Language, Version V). This list-processing language represents a person as a hierarchy of lists and description lists. These lists specify an individual's identity, abilities, relative and absolute positions in various social groups, image lists of his reference groups and of other group members, as well as lists containing elements of his past history and his resulting values and needs.

From the *Systems Development Corporation Magazine*, Vol. 6 (1963), 1-5.

HOMANS' PROPOSITIONS	DESCRIPTION OF DECISION MAKING IN INTERPERSONAL BEHAVIOR
Proposition 1: "If in the recent past the occurrence of a particular stimulus-situation has been the occasion on which a man's activity has been rewarded, then the more similar the present stimulus-situation is to the past one, the more likely he is to emit the activity, or some similar activity, now."	The interaction sequence begins with an agent, Ted, requesting help from his colleague, George, in completing a job assignment. After determining that the stimulus-situation has been a rewarding occasion in the past and that Ted has been an agent of reinforcement, George considers response alternatives. If he has interacted in similar situations with Ted and has emitted several different activities that Ted has rewarded, George must choose among these possible reactions to Ted's request.
Proposition 2: "The more often within a given period of time a man's activity rewards the activity of another, the more often the other will emit the activity."	George estimates the frequency with which Ted has rewarded each of the activities he is considering in response to Ted's current request for help.
Proposition 3: "The more valuable to a man a unit of the activity another gives him, the more often he will emit activity rewarded by the activity of the other."	George considers more carefully the particular reward he expects Ted to give to each of the three responses so that he may determine the inherent worth to him of each anticipated reward.
Proposition 4: "The more often a man has in the recent past received a rewarding activity from another, the less valuable any further unit of that activity becomes to him."	George now considers how much of each reward—for example, approval—he has received from Ted in the recent past and determines how much he is currently in need of such reinforcement.
(Subsumed under Propositions 3 and 4) "The cost . . . of a unit of a given activity is the value of the reward obtainable through a unit of an alternative activity, foregone in emitting the given one."	At this point, George ranks his contemplated responses in terms of their expected payoff. He is tentatively planning to give Ted direct assistance on his problem, because in the past Ted has praised him for this activity, and social approval is a reinforcement George values highly and one for which he feels relative deprivation at present. But George has an important assignment to complete. Taking time from it might detract from the quality of his work and lessen the approval he anticipates from his boss for a good job. In this case George would incur a loss rather than a profit in helping Ted directly. Therefore George continues to determine whether one of the other activities contemplated might yield a profit. George will probably decide that referring Ted to another source will net him a profit, since he expects some approval for this activity, and he will incur a very small cost in terms of time taken from his own work.
Proposition 5: "The more to a man's disadvantage the rule of distributive justice fails of realization, the more likely he is to display the emotional behavior called anger." (The full implications of the proposition deal with whether a participant receives from interaction rewards commensurate with his cost and social profit proportional to his investments of energy, skill, education, etc. Thus the man who receives a greater reward than called for experiences feelings of guilt, whereas one who receives a smaller reward than expected becomes angry.)	Through repetition of interaction situations within a group, certain behavior patterns become stabilized so that expectations develop regarding what constitutes justice in the distribution of rewards and costs between persons. It is an accepted office norm that a worker who asks for help should do it openly in a manner acknowledging the superiority of his consultant. In one interaction sequence, Ted seeks aid in a devious manner. George decides Ted is violating the norms of fair exchange by evading the cost of thanking him for his assistance and conceding his superiority. Ted persists in presenting George with problems without acknowledging his own need for assistance, causing George to respond with anger or to store up aggression to be expressed against someone else. Before actively punishing Ted, George first assesses the consequence of such behavior. In one interaction sequence, George finds that Ted is in favor with George's boss; therefore he suppresses his aggression at the moment and releases it the next time he interacts with a subordinate.

INFORMATION PROCESSING IN THE COMPUTER MODEL

In executing the process of George's decision on what action he will emit in response to Ted's request, one routine representing a retrieval function of the programmed agent (George) searches a memory list of reinforced stimulus-situations to determine whether the present input is among them.

To check on past interactions with Ted, one routine locates George's image list, finds the sublist that describes George's previous interactions with Ted, determines whether George has received the present stimulus from Ted before, and if so, whether Ted has rewarded the responses.

In the program, George selects up to three activities from a memory list of responses Ted has rewarded and then processes further information on these contemplated activities.

A five-point ordinal scale for reward frequency is used, ranging from an estimate that a response is "nearly always rewarded," through a judgment that it is "rewarded about half the time," to an assessment that it is "almost never rewarded."

The routines retrieve the responses Ted has previously made to each of George's past activities to help determine which one Ted is likely to emit now, and search description lists for finding the subjective value of the reward for George.

The routines search the description lists of each of the anticipated rewards to determine the degree of George's current deprivation or satiation in connection with them. A deprivation-satiation score based on a simple ordinal scale is stored as the value of a special attribute on the description list of each activity.

In order to determine the relative value of working on his assigned task, George follows a procedure analogous to that described above, processing information concerned with the frequency of past reinforcement and the value of the anticipated reward ensuing from this activity, as well as his relative satiation with the reward. Further routines enable George to compare the over-all expected reward from his contemplated response to Ted with the anticipated reward from continuing with his own work, allowing him finally to compute what Homans terms the psychic profit—the reward of an activity less its cost.

The list structures of the agents are programmed to have "consciences," including a repertoire of appropriate guilt and anger responses.

George is programmed to treat time spent solving a problem of another worker as help to that person for which recognition and social approval are due. When his colleague evades this cost, George finds this input inappropriate in terms of his expectations regarding distributive justice. Routines then change George's image list of Ted so that the next time he expects more recognition and thanks to atone for the present evasion. After several repetitions of this interaction sequence, the discrepancy between Ted's behavior and George's expectations will be so great that when George evaluates Ted's responses he will plant a signal, in his image list of Ted, indicating that interaction with Ted is not rewarding because he violates group norms.

The routines processing the negative branch of Proposition 5 not only modify image lists, but also use some of the routines from the other propositions to evaluate the probable consequences of direct anger responses.

As Homans' propositions apply generally to all humans regardless of their cultural backgrounds and institutional relationships, the information processing involved in the routines is common for all simulated subjects. However, each list structure describing a group participant is highly specific. Consequently, individual idiosyncrasies and recent past histories determine whether certain subroutines will be executed and what their outputs will be in specific interaction sequences. The computer programs embodying the model have been successfully run on the IBM 7090, as well as on the Philco 2000.

To better understand how HOMUNCULUS works, the preceding chart shows the relationship between Homans' propositions, an interpretation of Blau's description of interpersonal behavior in a bureaucracy, and the translation of verbal statements into computer routines by the Gullahorns.

COMPUTER SIMULATIONS

The Gullahorns have chosen to simulate elementary social behavior on a computer for several reasons. First, the systematization allows comparisons between sets of generalizations, comparisons that are not possible with verbal theory. The very process of translation forces preciseness about variables and their relationships and identifies ambiguities in expression and implicit assumptions in the verbal model.

Another reason for the computer simulation is that the complexity of a model is not a serious obstacle because of the computer's step-by-step mode of operation. The steps in the program can be complicated without effect from constraints in mathematical expression.

Furthermore, computer simulation not only tests and verifies theory, but also develops theory. When the computer program begins to operate, each logical manipulation advances it one step beyond where it was before. Routines are executed in a successive manner, each operating on the output of its predecessor. With this technique, the consequences of hooking up hypothetical processes into complex sequences can be directly observed.

More than a thousand operations are required for a person to determine his response to a social stimulus. When programs run with groups of five and six persons and include more sophisticated routines, four to ten thousand operations will be required to determine each interaction unit or activity emitted. Even at present, after a sequence consisting of fifty activities is exchanged between two individuals, at least 50,000 logical operations

intervene between pushing the "GO" button and terminating the interaction.

ADDITIONS TO HOMUNCULUS

Additional routines are now being written to introduce refinements into the basic HOMUNCULUS model. The most important of these is the coding of the present detailed activities into a system of categories described in R. F. Bales' book *Interaction Process Analysis*. The range of activities a person can emit is broadened by the use of these categories, which depict six dimensions of group interaction. These dimensions include communication problems where an individual either gives orientation (information, repetition, clarification, and confirmation) or asks for orientation; evaluation problems where an individual either offers an opinion (evaluation, analysis, and expression of feeling) or asks for an opinion; control problems where an individual either presents a suggestion (direction and possible ways of action) or asks for suggestions; decision problems where an individual either agrees (shows passive acceptance, understands, concurs, and complies) or disagrees; tension reduction problems where an individual either releases tension (jokes, laughs, and is satisfied) or displays tension; and reintegration problems where an individual either shows solidarity (by raising the other's status and by giving help and receiving reward) or shows antagonism.

These problem areas in group interaction are compatible with the HOMUNCULUS model, and the categorization will enable various experiments to be run without introducing a new set of actions for each one.

SMALL-GROUP EXPERIMENTS

Interaction in a triad is now being programmed. In a group of three unacquainted persons, sooner or later one of them initiates interaction with another. Each time their interactions prove rewarding, information is stored in their image lists that will lessen the cost of finding rewarding acts to emit to each other. Thus the rate of interaction between them increases, the repertoire of rewarded activities increases, and the likelihood of the bond being disrupted is lessened. The third man does not have the opportunity to let the other two know how rewarding he might be and remains an enigma. In other words, the interaction leads to a dyad and an isolate.

But assume that the first interaction is punishing to one or both of the two involved. The probability then becomes higher that interaction will be initiated with the third person. Assuming his values and norms make rewarding interaction likely, then whichever one captures him first will, no doubt, form a dyad with him and leave the other as the isolate.

With a group of three persons in which each pair is already well-acquainted, the same principles lead to different expectations. Each already has established a repertoire of activities that he knows he can emit to the other two and that will be rewarded. Therefore, when there is slight satiation with the rewards one of them can provide, attention is temporarily transferred to the other.

Or perhaps the interrupt mechanism programmed for group participants will lead the one, temporarily not paired, to join into the conversation. Since the others know interaction with him will be rewarding, he will not be rebuffed, but will be taken into the group.

EXPERIMENTS IN ORGANIZATION DESIGN

In reaching beyond the simulation of small-group laboratory experiments, the Gullahorns plan to use HOMUNCULUS for testing theories of organization design. Their first project in this area of research will be to examine the relative effectiveness of the traditional authoritarian hierarchy *vs.* the overlapping-group design advocated by Rensis Likert (see Fig. 1).

In the traditional structure, communication occurs between adjacent men up and down the line, with information transmitted up, decisions made at the top, and instructions flowing down the line. Theoretically, lateral communication does not occur. In the overlapping-group organization, each member within a group is in regular communication with every other member; decisions are reached by the group rather than the superordinate; and the members are responsible for passing on the information to other groups of which they are members.

Computer simulation of decision-making activities by both types of organization is expected to produce information showing the relative efficiency of the two designs. Such factors are considered as the amount of information available to those making decisions; the effect of the decision-making process on the motivation of the workers to perform; and the impact of each type structure on the satisfaction of individual workers, on their sentiments toward each other, and on their sentiments toward the organization.

This study is only now moving into the flow-chart stage. The program built for the project will then be used for research on stability and flexibility of leadership (suggested in discussions with Sydney and Beatrice Rome, SDC Research Directorate).

Two experimental groups will be programmed within the computer. In group A, the persons in authority positions will be composed of three men who possess qualities considered essential for leadership, e.g., a large repertoire of skills, decisiveness, knowledge of human motivation, plus past experience of successful leadership. Other members will possess few of these attributes. In group B, the persons in authority positions will possess few of the attributes described. Those who are in positions of followers will be high in both sets of attributes.

Two other dimensions will be varied: the environment and the group structure. One environment will be structured to facilitate accomplishment of the task and continued existence of the group. The second environment will be designed so that accomplishing the task will be extremely difficult and costly, and the group will be threatened with destruction. In addition, three types of group structure will be introduced, ranging from complete authoritarianism with despotic leadership through mild authoritarianism with paternalistic leadership to a Likert-type of group leadership.

While adequate results must await actual simu-

FIGURE 1

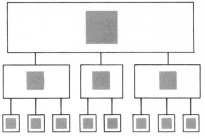

TRADITIONAL STRUCTURE

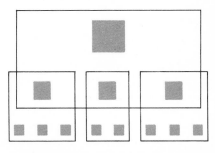

OVERLAPPING-GROUP STRUCTURE

lation runs, the Gullahorns predict, on the basis of the HOMUNCULUS model, that when the highly skilled and experienced leaders are in positions of authority they will remain there throughout the experimental changes. With the less competent leaders, however, the other experimental factors are expected to influence the outcomes. As long as the environment remains benign the organization will continue to function relatively smoothly, its members will remain satisfied, and the authority of the leaders will not be challenged. But when the organization confronts a threatening environment, trouble is likely to result.

In the absolute dictatorship, the members will be dissatisfied, but the high cost of deviance and the slight possibility of success will prevent rebellion to overthrow the incompetent leaders.

Under a paternalistic leadership, with decisions being made by superiors but subordinates being permitted to voice their opinions, it is predicted that under stress conditions the highest rate of rebellion will occur. Communication nets will have been established among subordinates; the organization will probably fail under continued in-

competent leadership; and there will be a chance of saving it if the skilled men take over.

Within the overlapping-group structure, the rate of rebellion will again decline. With an established pattern of group contribution to decision-making, the suggestions of subordinates are already being considered. A revolt by the skilled men would disrupt established relationships and increase the probability of organization failure, even if they established their authority.

ABSTRACT SETTING VS. REAL WORLD

Laboratory experiments, a test in a pilot plant, and a trial run in a full-scale organization are required before the results obtained in the abstract setting of computer simulation are proved applicable to an organization operating in the real world. Nevertheless, the simulation results obtained under conditions of complete control, as specified by theory, enable researchers like John and Jeanne Gullahorn to interpret the findings in real life with greater certainty.

Selection 62

Automation and the Employee

William A. Faunce, Einar Hardin, and Eugene H. Jacobson

At one time, the fields of economics and sociology in the United States were closely allied, especially in their mutual interest in poverty and dependency, class structure, immigration, and the then-emergent field of labor relations. The vastly increased specialization in the two fields then became a divisive factor, but recently there have arisen certain aspects of specialization that can be studied best by drawing from both sociology and economics—e.g., the sociology of occupations, industrial sociology, and the social effects of technology. It is with the last area that the following selection is particularly concerned.

The actuality of automation and the major importance of its present and future economic and social effects are accepted by laymen and professionals alike; but acceptance and understanding are not synonymous, and there has been no agreement about the effects of automation. To help fill this void, the *Annals of the American Academy of Political and Social Science* devoted an entire issue to the topic of automation. Charles C. Killingsworth, in his introduction to the *Annals* symposium, reminds us that mechanization has been increasing for centuries and that some machines which perform mental tasks have been in use for many decades. However, recent years have been marked by the growth of the electronic computer, the awesome machine that has been called the most significant postwar development in technology. Today, says

Killingsworth, we can link together "measuring instruments, computers, and control devices to provide integrated, self-regulating systems which are capable of performing extremely complicated operations with little or no human assistance." These developments lead him to define automation as "the mechanization of sensory, thought, and control processes." He continues, ". . . the basic techniques of automation are applicable to an extremely broad range of activities, including as examples petroleum refining, chemical processing, steel rolling, preparation of payrolls, accounting, language translation, airplane navigation, medical diagnosis and many others. . . . Many decisions which . . . were thought to require human judgment can be reduced to clearcut rules which the computer can apply more accurately and far more rapidly than humans. It seems justifiable to suggest . . . [that] we have again reached a point in technological development where fundamental changes in the relationship between men and machines are taking place."

In the following selection on the reported effects of automation on employees and on their reaction to it, the authors show that office employees rarely reject mechanization as such but that their feelings about their specific jobs (if affected by automation) are likely to be ambivalent. Sources of satisfaction and dissatisfaction seem to vary with the type of job and the attitude of the employee toward change in general. Negatively, any change tends to be disruptive, and automation is more likely to eliminate jobs than to produce them. On the other hand, machines are doing more of the less desirable kinds of labor, and the consequent reduction of work hours continues the present trend toward a more leisure-oriented society.

Field research suggests that the impact of office automation upon job satisfaction varies depending on whether affected job aspects are intrinsic or contextual, whether the employees are in electronic data-processing departments which gain work tasks or in other affected departments that lose tasks, whether the computer is of large or medium size, and on several other circumstances. Office employees think the broad impact of office automation is to eliminate jobs and regard the methods changes as temporarily disruptive, but they often welcome change and rarely reject mechanization as such. Attitudes toward change appear to depend on the ability of the individual to deal effectively with change and on the skill with which the organization manages the change. Studies of factory automation suggest that automated plants are preferred as work places to less advanced plants, although they provide important sources of dissatisfaction. The sources of satisfaction and dissatisfaction vary over the course of adjustment to automation. Automation may affect the significance of work in our society by changing job content, redistributing employment opportunities, or decreasing working hours. Its effect will probably be a decrease in the importance of work and a continuation of the trend toward a leisure-oriented society.

Three aspects of the relationship between auto-

mation and the employee are discussed in this article. First, how does automation affect the job satisfaction and material welfare of employees? Second, what are the attitudes of employees toward automation and toward the very process of change? Third, how does automation affect the role of work in the lives of the employees? Although automation has occurred in many thousands of factories and offices, there have been few field studies pertinent to these questions. Furthermore, the relevant studies differ considerably in focus and method, so that meaningful generalizations are hazardous to make. Our aim is to illustrate the diversity of effects rather than to make a broad, over-all assessment.

EFFECTS OF OFFICE AUTOMATION

In one study dealing with automation and job satisfaction, attitude surveys were conducted before and after the installation of a small to medium-size computer (IBM 650) in an insurance company having about 400 employees. Satisfaction with variety in work, accuracy requirements, importance of the job to the company, skill

From *The Annals* of the American Academy of Political and Social Science, Vol. 340 (1962), 60-68.

requirements, responsibility involved, and several other intrinsic characteristics of the work increased for most employees. At the same time, there was no clear trend of change in satisfaction with such contextual aspects of the job as pay, promotion chances, the way the company handled changes in organization and procedures, and the nature of the company's information program.

The changes in job satisfaction varied depending upon the extent to which the computer affected the work methods and work load. The computer-area employees, who were initially in the key-punching and tabulating jobs, showed more increases than decreases in satisfaction with intrinsic jobs aspects, while the reverse was true for contextual aspects. The employees in the underwriting departments, who lost tasks to the computer area and had to adjust their work methods to its requirements, showed a mixed pattern, with about the same number of increases as decreases in satisfaction for both intrinsic and contextual aspects. The employees in the rest of the company, accounting for more than two-thirds of total employment, had essentially unchanged work methods and work load. They became less satisfied with the company's way of handling changes and with the lack of accuracy and promptness of company information, and became more satisfied with virtually all other aspects of their jobs. The differences among the three department groups were frequently small enough, however, to be random fluctuations.

The employees were also asked, in the survey after the installation, how much the computer had changed fourteen aspects of their jobs, most of which were intrinsic. The computer-area employees felt the computer exerted a large and favorable impact on the variety, work load, and skill requirements of their jobs but influenced only slightly their job security, promotion chances, and pay. The employees of the underwriting departments felt the computer brought a great deal of change in variety, work load, and accuracy requirements; lowered their job security and promotion chances more often than it raised them; and made for less variety in work, less work load, and lowered work interest in a number of instances. Employees of unaffected departments were not aware of much impact upon themselves.

While the preceding differences illustrate the employee perceptions of the role of the computer, the actual effect of the computer upon various aspects of the job is better reflected by a different set of findings. The employees were asked in the second survey what changes, regardless of cause, there had been in the job aspects. The computer-area employees continued to report more change than the other employees, but the differences between the two groups were usually smaller. The underwriting departments and the unaffected departments perceived much the same frequency of change, although changes were more often in the undesirable direction in the former group. Neither the computer nor other factors had materially altered the work methods and work load of the unaffected departments. This suggests that the effect of automation upon the fourteen job aspects, though real, was quite moderate, except in the computer area itself. The indication that the computer had only moderate effects on work environment and job satisfaction was corroborated in a study of another insurance company that had also installed an IBM 650 computer.

Somewhat different findings were indicated in a preliminary report on a larger but less common computer. Mann and Williams found that the installation of an IBM 705 computer in a large public utility brought changes in organization, procedures, control, and job structure. They described the impact on the individuals by saying [that] "for many individuals this was a period of growth; for others a period of failure and disillusionment. The change severely tested marginal employees and supervisors, while at the same time giving the more experienced and able ones the opportunity to develop and to demonstrate their work potential. The dislocation and the loss of duties and jobs was a serious problem for some employees."

A Bureau of Labor Statistics study of office automation in twenty large business firms showed that, one year after automation, there had been increases in salary grade for more than four-fifths of the computer-area employees, as compared with one third of the employees of other affected departments. Virtually none were lowered in grade or lost their jobs. That office automation may well lead to different long-run results, however, is suggested in preliminary reports by Ida Hoos on another study of about twenty organizations. Centralization of functions from branch offices to main offices occurring after a few years of automation reduced branch-office employment enough to necessitate layoffs or transfers with lower pay or poorer advancement opportunities and, hence, affected many employees adversely. Deterioration was not only found in the surviving routine, nonsupervisory jobs, which appeared less interesting and more machine-paced than before automation, but also in the middle-management jobs outside the electronic data-processing area, which became fewer and, thus, reduced the training and advancement opportunities of supervisors seeking to rise in the organization. The highly skilled elite of programmers and systems analysts, who, according to other studies, tends to consist of young and well-educated men, was strongly prone toward empire building and likely to become involved in conflict with other departments because of its own autonomy, key position, stress on efficiency, and lack of social sensitivity.

EFFECTS OF FACTORY AUTOMATION

Several studies of factory automation have also been made. One of these dealt with the attitudes of workers transferred to an automated automobile-engine plant. Three-fourths of the workers preferred the new automated jobs to their old nonautomated jobs, and the strongest preferences for the new jobs were expressed by those whose jobs were the most automated. The substantial reduction in materials handling which accompanied automation was the major reason for preferring the new jobs. Physical working conditions seemed to vary considerably from one department to the next and were, on balance, no better in the automated plant than in the nonautomated plant. Changes in earnings, except those associated with general contract changes, appeared to be few.

The new technology, however, increased the distance between work stations, the amount of machine noise, the amount of attention required by the job, and the extent to which the workers were paced by the machines. In consequence, the workers were less able to talk with each other during the work, tended to confine their communications to work-related matters, thought they made fewer friends at work, and felt socially isolated. Because they were required to pay closer attention to their work, were supervised more frequently by the foremen, and felt a constant pressure to avoid machine breakdowns, they experienced greater mental fatigue and work tension. In fact, where it existed, preference for the old jobs could most often be attributed to the social isolation of the worker and the increase in work tensions.

Mann and Hoffman studied the attitudes of workers in two power plants at different levels of automation. The operators in the advanced plant liked their current jobs more than did those in the standard plant, when everything was considered. They felt they had more responsibility on their jobs, required more training, had to spend less time doing dirty jobs, learned more on the job, could move around in the plant, and had more contacts with the other workers than two years earlier, before the more advanced plant was completed and staffed. They felt more nervous and tense, however, which may have been caused by a feeling of greater dependence on others combined with the belief that they were inadequately trained and prepared for the automated technology. Because the two plants differed from each other in many respects in addition to level of technology, it is difficult to determine the exact role of the changing technology in the attitude differences of the two groups of workers. In particular, the careful selection of the work force and the use of job rotation, job enlargement, and a changed pattern of shift work in the advanced plant may account for much of the higher satisfaction of its workers. In so far as this interpretation is true, it underlines the importance of management practices to facilitate adjustment to automation.

A study by Charles R. Walker of an automated steel mill showed that job satisfaction may vary during the process of adjustment to the new technology. Automation increased the amount of attention and responsibility required, lessened the physical demands of the job, limited possibilities for promotion, and affected patterns of social interaction on the job. Response to these changes varied during the four-year period of the study. Walker summarizes this finding . . . [by saying that] "the majority of crew members, though not all, were able to move from semi-manual jobs to semi-automatic ones and derive personal satisfaction from the immediate job content of those positions. They did not derive this satisfaction at first but after a period of acclimatization and experience. The same job characteristics, all stemming from the automatic or semi-automatic operations of the mill which had at first been feared and hated, *were later the source of satisfaction.*"

RESPONSE TO CHANGE

In addition to knowing how employees respond to work situations at different levels of technological development, it is important to understand employee response to the fact and prospect of change in the work situation. From the point of view of the employee, the work situation probably involves continuous change, more apparent and dramatic when new technologies are introduced rapidly, but always present in complex organizations. The normal pattern of change, like many constant influences, may not receive regular attention. But when one of the aspects of change is accelerated, as in the introduction of new technologies into relatively stable, well-established work procedures, change becomes the focus of attention. As an example, when even relatively small electronic data-processing devices are installed in established business offices, the consequences become a matter of concern to a large part of the work force, even though many employees may not be affected by the change. Employee response to innovation and change of this sort, as determined through questionnaire and interview studies conducted by the authors and their colleagues, will be examined in the following paragraphs.

Prominent among the initial effects of the installation of a computer is concern with the possibility that the new equipment will throw some people out of work. The employees we questioned were very much aware of the potential of the computer for replacing workers. About three-quarters of them reported that machines were replacing workers in insurance companies. But, when questioned about their own job prospects, about four-fifths felt that it was very unlikely that they, themselves, would be replaced by machines. This reflected the actual work situation, in which no employees had lost jobs because of the computer installation.

More than half of the employees felt that their jobs had changed because of the new equipment. They saw themselves as having been promoted or transferred or as having the content of their jobs altered. The company officials and the research team, on the other hand, estimated that less than one third of the work force was affected in any significant way by the change. Apparently employees were associating many aspects of their own jobs with this very visible new influence in their lives. Changes that would have occurred if the computer had not been installed could be interpreted as related to it. Changes of a small magnitude or of a kind not noted by management might loom large in the eyes of the employee.

An additional facet of technological change to which the employee responds is the readjustment that occurs no matter how effectively the change-over may be managed. While two-thirds of the employees we questioned felt that the change-over significantly interrupted their normal work procedures, most of them thought they had adjusted to the change relatively quickly, within a few weeks. About one quarter of the employees felt that developments in machines and methods for doing work in industry as a whole were taking place more rapidly than is desirable, and only a small proportion felt they were taking place too slowly. But, when asked about the kind of job that they themselves liked, 70 per cent expressed a preference for a situation in which the work process changed from time to time. Apparently,

with too little change, the job would be routine and monotonous, and with too much change, change itself would be threatening.

The major characteristic of the office automation we studied was the shift from human to machine processing of data. The employees anticipated that this shift would continue and would directly affect the jobs they were doing. Most of them liked to work with office machinery, would like to make more use of office machinery, and would be pleased to attend a training school to learn how to work with the new equipment, if job changes required this.

In general, then, employees perceived that the broad industry impact of automation and technological change was to eliminate some jobs. And many felt that these changes, at the industry and society level, were occurring too rapidly. But they distinguished these effects from the consequences of a particular adjustment in their own work situation which they judged on the basis of actual experience. When an abrupt introduction of a new technology was experienced, a larger proportion of the employees would see themselves as affected than might be anticipated by management on an objective basis. Usually, they saw the methods changes as being temporarily disruptive but quickly integrated into the system. They often welcomed change in their own work situations and expressed a preference for having some part of their work mechanized. We found no rejection of mechanization as such.

VARIABLES AFFECTING RESPONSE TO CHANGE

These generalizations about employee attitudes toward change should be understood in terms of some factors that are related to them and that are likely to vary considerably from organization to organization and within large organizations. These include the differences among employees in readiness for change and the history of the management of change in a given organization.

In Trumbo's analysis of readiness for change, employees that had better education, obtained better scores on personnel tests, were freer from job anxieties, and had benefited from past changes were more likely to indicate a readiness for change. These variations in individual attitudes toward change seemed to reflect differences in ability to deal effectively with the demands of a changing situation and beliefs that the stress involved in change would be compensated by the opportunities that change offered.

It appeared that where change in the job implied change in the work group, those who attached higher value to social satisfactions in work had less favorable attitudes toward change. Another element of the social context, the supervisor-employee relations, also appeared to have a bearing upon attitudes toward change. The attitudes of the members of work groups were similar to those of their supervisors. Supervisors who were relatively authoritarian were less often in charge of employees who favored change. Perhaps authoritarian supervisors were usually put in charge of persons least likely to benefit from change.

The way in which the change is managed by the organization is a central concern of the employee. Mann and Williams used a case study of the introduction of a computer into an accounting division of a public utility to show that management skill in handling change has an important influence on employee response to the change. If the organization has a record of concern for the employee and manages change so that the employee is protected, and, if possible, his situation is enhanced, employees are more likely to welcome change.

It is interesting to find, however, that employees who were better informed about the anticipated impact of technological change, as reported by Nangle, were not more favorable toward the change. A more important factor was the employee's attitudes toward the company and its policies.

Office employees with relatively high social status, from urban rather than rural backgrounds, and in high status positions in the organization, were found more likely to welcome change. This suggests, among other things, that a positive attitude toward change is likely to be associated with greater possibility of being involved in decision-making about the change.

AUTOMATION AND THE MEANING OF JOB SATISFACTION

Another important variable affecting both job satisfaction and attitudes toward job change is the significance of work to the individual. Satisfaction with an activity which is of major importance clearly differs in meaning and in behavioral consequences from satisfaction with an activity which is of little concern. Attitudes toward change in any activity can also be expected to be conditioned by the significance of the activity to the individual.

There is considerable evidence of variation in the function and meaning of work. Morse and Weiss found that a sense of accomplishment on the job, interest in a particular task area, and, in general, the assigning of importance to a specific work role were more characteristic of professional and managerial than of clerical and blue-collar workers. Dubin found that work and the work place were not "central life interests" for almost three-fourths of the industrial workers he studied, and Orzack, in a replication of the Dubin study, found that four-fifths of a group of professional nurses did regard work and the work place as "central life interests." In a study conducted by the authors, it was found that the importance of work to the individual varied considerably with the job level.

This evidence suggests that the level of responsibility and skill required by the job has an important bearing upon the degree of significance of work to the individual. To the extent that automation changes these aspects of job content, it may affect the meaning of job satisfaction and job change.

Automation does appear to increase the proportion of the total operation for which the worker is responsible. The integration of separate operations into a continuous-flow production process means that a single worker observing lights or gauges on an automatic control panel may have responsibility for a large number and wide variety of production processes. The clerical worker who feeds stacks of cards into an electronic computer is also likely to be responsible for a larger share of information processing in the office. There is evidence that some workers regard their jobs as more important as a result of increased responsibility in this sense.

It is obvious, however, that technological integration of separate operations is not the same thing as job enlargement. Many jobs in automated plants and offices involve less personal responsibility in the sense that neither quality of product nor work pace are controlled by the worker. Automatic inspection, control, and information-processing systems are designed to supplant human judgment in the production process. The elimination of direct participation in the work process can be expected to have an effect upon the function and meaning of work. The following quotation from interviews with workers in an automated plant seems to illustrate the feeling of estrangement from work:

"[I don't like] the lack of feeling responsible for your work. The feeling that you're turning out more work but know it's *not yours really* and not as good as you could make it if you had control of the machine like before."

Irrespective of its effect upon the content of jobs, automation might result in an increase in the significance of work in our society if it increased the proportion of the labor force employed in more skilled, responsible, and prestigeful jobs. Studies of effects of automation suggest that there is a higher proportion of skilled workers in plants where automated equipment is used. This does not result from the creation of many new skilled jobs, however, but from a reduction in the employment of semiskilled and unskilled workers. Such changes mean that the work force in the automatic factory may be composed primarily of skilled workers for whom work is intrinsically important and to whom job satisfaction means pride in workmanship, but this work force may be small. Automation may contribute somewhat to the increased demand in certain professional and technical fields. These fields, however, in spite of their current rate of growth, still employ a relatively small proportion of the total labor force. The primary effect of automation upon occupational distribution will undoubtedly be to decrease the proportion of semiskilled and unskilled factory operatives. A majority of new workers who·might otherwise have been employed as operatives will probably be absorbed into expanding clerical, sales, and service occupations.

There is little empirical evidence regarding the function and meaning of work for people in these occupations. The existing evidence, however, along with an assessment of the nature of the tasks and social structural conditions of work in lower level white-collar occupations, would lead us to expect that work would not be regarded as a central life interest by people in these occupations. C. Wright Mills, in *White Collar*, concludes that for the "white collar masses," as for wage workers generally, the job is not intrinsically meaningful, and success, in the sense of technical craftsmanship, is not regarded as an end in itself. The substitution of what Daniel Bell has called the new "salariat" for the proletariat as comprising the bulk of the labor force in industrial societies could not be expected to reverse the apparent tendency in these societies toward de-emphasis of work and an increasing leisure orientation.

In the long run, a reduction of working hours made possible by automation may have a greater impact upon the importance of work than will any of the other factors we have considered. Productivity increases in the past have always resulted in a decrease in the average number of hours worked per week. There is little reason to suppose that increases in productivity attributable to automation will not sooner or later have the same effect. Where work requires a diminishing proportion of time and energy, activities unrelated to work will probably assume increasing importance. So long as professional, technical, and upper-level managerial positions employ less than a majority of our labor force, most people can be expected to use their increased leisure to seek meaningful activities which provide some relief from the functionally specialized nature of their work. The net effect of automation would appear to be a continuation of the already existing trend toward a leisure-oriented society in which work is viewed as an exclusively economic activity and in which activities other than work serve to provide meaningful experiences for the individual and to relate him to his community.

Selection 63

Some Functions of the Political Machine
Robert K. Merton

The following analysis of the functions performed by the urban political machine is taken from a chapter entitled "Manifest and Latent Functions," which is primarily concerned with the explanation and clarification of certain aspects of social theory. Earlier in the chapter Merton says that an appropriate way to view or analyze a social phenomenon is through its functions (and its dysfunctions, if any). The functions of a social phenomenon include not just those that are obvious, direct, external, and *manifest* but also those that are *latent*; although these latent functions are below the threshold of superficial observation, they are so important that they may outweigh the manifest functions. For example,

Thorstein Veblen's *conspicuous consumption* concept explains that the manifest function of using consumer goods is to satisfy the need for which they are designed, whereas the latent function of using conspicuously expensive consumer goods is to heighten social status. That is, neither the behavior of the man who lights a cigar with a ten dollar bill nor that of the woman who lights her cigarette with a thousand dollar lighter can be understood solely in terms of the manifest function—that of putting fire to tobacco. In studying social phenomena, the sociologist must search for and take into account their latent as well as their manifest functions.

Selections 63-65, which all deal with political institutions, are widely different, thus indicating the great range of the topic. Merton's discussion is both narrow and general—narrow in that it touches on only a few of the numerous aspects of urban political machines, general in that it can be applied to political machines as a group as well as to a single one and also in that the concept of latent function is applicable far more broadly than just to political machines. Chu's article on Communist China is a nonempirical, nontheoretical report of political conditions in China, particularly as they affect China's economic life. Although Chu does not use the term *latent function*, this concept and the concept of dysfunction are seen in the unintended effects of political and economic action in China. Lipset's article, although quite unrelated to the other two, nevertheless shows by empirical observation both manifest and latent functional relationships between economic development and democracy. Merton's area of study is a very small portion of a nation, Chu's area is an entire nation, and Lipset's is a considerable number of nations.

Merton's selection is recommended to the student as a particularly fortuitous combination of understandable social theory, penetrating analysis, and verifiable, clear, and competent description of a socio-political phenomenon.

. . . Veblen's analysis of latent functions departs from the common-sense notion that the end-product of consumption is "of course, the direct satisfaction which it provides": "People eat caviar because they're hungry; buy Cadillacs because they want the best car they can get; have dinner by candlelight because they like the peaceful atmosphere." The common-sense interpretation in terms of selected manifest motives gives way, in Veblen's analysis, to the collateral latent functions which are also, and perhaps more significantly, fulfilled by these practices. To be sure, the Veblenian analysis has, in the last decades, entered so fully into popular thought, that these latent functions are now widely recognized. [This raises the interesting problem of the changes occurring in a prevailing pattern of behavior when its *latent* functions become generally recognized (and are thus no longer latent). . . .]

The discovery of latent functions does not merely render conceptions of the functions served by certain social patterns more precise (as is the case also with studies of manifest functions), but introduces a *qualitatively different increment in the previous state of knowledge*.

Since moral evaluations in a society tend to be largely in terms of the manifest consequences of a practice or code, we should be prepared to find that analysis in terms of latent functions at times runs counter to prevailing moral evaluations. For it does not follow that the latent functions will operate in the same fashion as the manifest consequences which are ordinarily the basis of these judgments. Thus, in large sectors of the American population, the political machine or the "political racket" are judged as unequivocally "bad" and "undesirable." The grounds for such moral judgment vary somewhat, but they consist substantially in pointing out that political machines violate moral codes: political patronage violates the code of selecting personnel on the basis of impersonal qualifications rather than on grounds of party loyalty or contributions to the party war-chest; bossism violates the code that votes should be based on individual appraisal of the qualifications of candidates and of political issues, and not on abiding loyalty to a feudal leader; bribery, and "honest graft" obviously offend the proprieties of property; "protection" for crime clearly violates the law and the mores; and so on.

In view of the manifold respects in which political machines, in varying degrees, run counter to the mores and at times to the law, it becomes pertinent to inquire how they manage to continue in operation. The familiar "explanations" for the continuance of the political machine are not here in point. To be sure, it may well be that if "respectable citizenry" would live up to their political obligations, if the electorate were to be alert and enlightened; if the number of elective officers were substantially reduced from the dozens, even hundreds, which the average voter is now expected to appraise in the course of town, county, state and national elections; if the electorate were activated by the "wealthy and educated classes without whose participation," as the not-always democratically oriented Bryce put it, "the best-framed government must speedily degenerate";— if these and a plethora of similar changes in political structure were introduced, perhaps the "evils" of the political machine would indeed be exorcized. But it should be noted that these changes are often not introduced, that political machines have had the phoenix-like quality of arising strong and unspoiled from their ashes, that, in short, this structure has exhibited a notable vitality in many areas of American political life.

Proceeding from the functional view, therefore, that we should *ordinarily* (not invariably) expect persistent social patterns and social structures to perform positive functions *which are at the time not adequately fulfilled by other existing patterns and structures,* the thought occurs that perhaps this publicly maligned organization is, *under present conditions,* satisfying basic latent functions.[1] A brief examination of current analyses of this type of structure may also serve to illustrate additional problems of functional analysis.

SOME FUNCTIONS OF THE POLITICAL MACHINE

Without presuming to enter into the variations of detail marking different political machines—a Tweed, Vare, Crump, Flynn, Hague are by no means identical types of bosses—we can briefly examine the functions more or less common to the political machine, as a generic type of social organization. We neither attempt to itemize all the diverse functions of the political machine nor imply that all these functions are similarly fulfilled by each and every machine.

The key structural function of the Boss is to organize, centralize and maintain in good working condition "the scattered fragments of power" which are at present dispersed through our political organization. By this centralized organization of political power, the boss and his apparatus can satisfy the needs of diverse subgroups in the larger community which are not adequately satisfied by legally devised and culturally approved social structures.

To understand the role of bossism and the machine, therefore, we must look at two types of sociological variables: (1) the *structural context* which makes it difficult, if not impossible, for morally approved structures to fulfill essential social functions, thus leaving the door open for political machines (or their structural equivalents) to fulfill these functions and (2) the subgroups whose distinctive needs are left unsatisfied, except for the latent functions which the machine in fact fulfills.

Structural context

The constitutional framework of American political organization specifically precludes the legal possibility of highly centralized power and, it has been noted, thus "discourages the growth of effective and responsible leadership. The framers of the Constitution, as Woodrow Wilson observed, set up the check and balance system 'to keep government at a sort of mechanical equipoise by means of a standing amicable contest among its several organic parts.' They distrusted power as dangerous to liberty: and therefore they spread it thin and erected barriers against its concentration." This dispersion of power is found not only at the national level but in local areas as well. "As a consequence," Sait goes on to observe, "when *the people or particular groups* among them demanded

---

[1] I trust it is superfluous to add that this hypothesis is not "in support of the political machine." The question whether the dysfunctions of the machine outweigh its functions, the question whether alternative structures are not available which may fulfill its functions without necessarily entailing its social dysfunctions, still remain to be considered at an appropriate point. We are here concerned with documenting the statement that moral judgments based *entirely* on an appraisal of manifest functions of a social structure are "unrealistic" in the strict sense, *i.e.,* they do not take into account other actual consequences of that structure, consequences which may provide basic social support for the structure. As will be indicated later, "social reforms" or "social engineering" which ignore latent functions do so on pain of suffering acute disappointments and boomerang effects.

positive action, no one had adequate authority to act. The machine provided an antidote."[2]

The constitutional dispersion of power not only makes for difficulty of effective decision and action but when action does occur it is defined and hemmed in by legalistic considerations. In consequence, there developed "a much *more human system* of partisan government, whose chief object soon became the circumvention of government by law. . . . The lawlessness of the extra-official democracy was merely the counterpoise of the legalism of the official democracy. The lawyer having been permitted to subordinate democracy to the Law, the Boss had to be called in to extricate the victim, which he did after a fashion and for a consideration."[3]

Officially, political power is dispersed. Various well-known expedients were devised for this manifest objective. Not only was there the familiar separation of powers among the several branches of the government but, in some measure, tenure in each office was limited, rotation in office approved. And the scope of power inherent in each office was severely circumscribed. Yet, observes Sait in rigorously functional terms, "Leadership is necessary; and *since* it does not develop readily within the constitutional framework, the Boss provides it in a crude and irresponsible form from the outside."

Put in more generalized terms, *the functional deficiencies of the official structure generate an alternative (unofficial) structure to fulfill existing needs somewhat more effectively.* Whatever its specific historical origins, the political machine persists as an apparatus for satisfying otherwise unfulfilled needs of diverse groups in the population. By turning to a few of these subgroups and their characteristic needs, we shall be led at once to a range of latent functions of the political machine.

Functions of the political machine for diverse subgroups

It is well known that one source of strength of the political machine derives from its roots in the local community and the neighborhood. The political machine does not regard the electorate as an amorphous, undifferentiated mass of voters. With a keen sociological intuition, the machine recognizes that the voter is a person living in a specific neighborhood, with specific personal problems and personal wants. Public issues are abstract and remote; private problems are extremely concrete and immediate. It is not through the generalized appeal to large public concerns that the machine operates, but through the direct, quasi-feudal relationships between local representatives of the machine and voters in their neighborhood. Elections are won in the precinct.

The machine welds its link with ordinary men and women by elaborate networks of personal relations. Politics is transformed into personal ties. The precinct captain "must be a friend to every man, assuming if he does not feel sympathy with the unfortunate, and utilizing in his good works the resources which the boss puts at his disposal."[4] The precinct captain is forever a friend in need. In our prevailingly impersonal society, the machine, through its local agents, fulfills the important social *function of humanizing and personalizing all manner of assistance* to those in need. Food-baskets and jobs, legal and extra-legal advice, setting to rights minor scrapes with the law, helping the bright poor boy to a political scholarship in a local college, looking after the bereaved—the whole range of crises when a feller needs a friend, and, above all, a friend who knows the score and who can do something about it,—all these find the ever-helpful precinct captain available in the pinch.

To assess this function of the political machine adequately, it is important to note not only that aid *is* provided but *the manner in which it is provided.* After all, other agencies do exist for dispensing such assistance. Welfare agencies, settlement houses, legal aid clinics, medical aid in free hospitals, public relief departments, immigration authorities—these and a multitude of other organizations are available to provide the most varied types of assistance. But in contrast to the professional techniques of the welfare worker which may typically represent in the mind of the recipient the cold, bureaucratic dispensation of limited aid following upon detailed investigation of *legal* claims to aid of the "client" are the unprofessional techniques of the precinct captain who asks no questions, exacts no compliance with legal rules of eligibility and does not "snoop" into private affairs.

For many, the loss of "self-respect" is too high a price for legalized assistance. In contrast to the gulf between the settlement house workers who so often come from a different social class, educational background and ethnic group, the precinct worker is "just one of us," who understands what

[2] Edward M. Sait, "Machine, Political," in Edwin R. A. Seligman, ed.-in-chief, *Encyclopedia of the Social Sciences*, 15 Vols. (New York: The Macmillan Co., 1937), IX, 658 b [italics supplied]; *cf.* A. F. Bentley, *The Process of Government* (Chicago: University of Chicago Press, 1908), Chapter 2.
[3] Herbert Croly, *Progressive Democracy* (New York: The Macmillan Co., 1914), p. 254, cited by Sait, 658 b.
[4] *Ibid.*, 659 a.

it's all about. The condescending lady bountiful can hardly compete with the understanding friend in need. In *this struggle between alternative structures for fulfilling the nominally same function* of providing aid and support to those who need it, it is clearly the machine politician who is better integrated with the groups which he serves than the impersonal, professionalized, socially distant and legally constrained welfare worker. And since the politician can at times influence and manipulate the official organizations for the dispensation of assistance, whereas the welfare worker has practically no influence on the political machine, this only adds to his greater effectiveness. More colloquially and also, perhaps, more incisively, it was the Boston ward-leader, Martin Lomasny, who described this essential function to the curious Lincoln Steffens: "I think," said Lomasny, "that there's got to be in every ward somebody that any bloke can come to—no matter what he's done—and get help. *Help, you understand; none of your law and justice, but help.*"[5]

The "deprived classes," then, constitute one subgroup for whom the political machine satisfies wants not adequately satisfied in the same fashion by the legitimate social structure.

For a second subgroup, that of business (primarily "big" business but also "small"), the political boss serves the function of providing those political privileges which entail immediate economic gains. Business corporations, among which the public utilities (railroads, local transportation and electric light companies, communications corporations) are simply the most conspicuous in this regard, seek special political dispensations which will enable them to stabilize their situation and to near their objective of maximizing profits. Interestingly enough, corporations want to avoid a chaos of uncontrolled competition. They want the greater security of an economic czar who controls, regulates and organizes competition, providing that this czar is not a public official with his decisions subject to public scrutiny and public control. (The latter would be "government control," and hence taboo.) The political boss fulfills these requirements admirably.

Examined for a moment apart from any moral considerations, the political apparatus operated by the Boss is effectively designed to perform these functions with a minimum of inefficiency. Holding the strings of diverse governmental divisions, bureaus and agencies in his competent hands, the Boss rationalizes the relations between public and private business. He serves as the business community's ambassador in the otherwise alien (and sometimes unfriendly) realm of government. And, in strict business-like terms, he is well-paid for his economic services to his respectable business clients. In an article entitled, "An Apology to Graft," Lincoln Steffens suggested that "Our economic system, which held up riches, power and acclaim as prizes to men bold enough and able enough to buy corruptly timber, mines, oil fields and franchises and 'get away with it,' was at fault." And, in a conference with a hundred or so of Los Angeles business leaders, he described a fact well known to all of them: the Boss and his machine were an *integral part* of the organization of the economy. "You cannot build or operate a railroad, or a street railway, gas, water, or power company, develop and operate a mine, or get forests and cut timber on a large scale, or run any privileged business, without corrupting or joining in the corruption of the government. You tell me privately that you must, and here I am telling you semi-publicly that you must. And that is so all over the country. And that means that we have an organization of society in which, *for some reason*, you and your kind, the ablest, most intelligent, most imaginative, daring, and resourceful leaders of society, are and must be against society and its laws and its all-around growth."

Since the demand for the services of special privileges are built into the structure of the society, the Boss fulfills diverse functions for this second subgroup of business-seeking-privilege. These "needs" of business, as presently constituted, are not adequately provided for by conventional and culturally approved social structures; consequently, the extra-legal but more-or-less efficient organization of the political machine comes to provide these services. To adopt an *exclusively* moral attitude toward the "corrupt political machine" is to lose sight of the very structural conditions which generate the "evil" that is so bitterly attacked. To adopt a functional outlook is to provide not an apologia for the political machine but a more solid basis for modifying or eliminating the machine, *providing* specific structural arrangements are introduced either for eliminating these effective demands of the business community or, if that is the objective, of satisfying these demands through alternative means.

A third set of distinctive functions fulfilled by the political machine for a special subgroup is that of providing alternative channels of social mobility for those otherwise excluded from the more conventional avenues for personal "advancement." Both the sources of this special "need" (for social mobility) and the respect in which the political machine comes to help satisfy this need

---

[5] *The Autobiography of Lincoln Steffens* (Chautauqua, New York: Chautauqua Press, 1931), p. 618.

can be understood by examining the structure of the larger culture and society. As is well known, the American culture lays enormous emphasis on money and power as a "success" goal legitimate for all members of the society. By no means alone in our inventory of cultural goals, it still remains among the most heavily endowed with positive affect and value. However, certain sub-groups and certain ecological areas are notable for the relative absence of opportunity for achiev-ing these (monetary and power) types of success. They constitute, in short, sub-populations where "the cultural emphasis upon pecuniary success has been absorbed, but where there is *little access to conventional and legitimate* means for attaining such success. The conventional occupational op-portunities of persons in (such areas) are almost completely limited to manual labor. Given our cultural stigmatization of manual labor, and its correlate, the prestige of white-collar work, it is clear that the result is a tendency to achieve these culturally approved objectives *through whatever means are possible.*" These people are on the one hand, "asked to orient their conduct toward the prospect of accumulating wealth [and power] and, on the other, they are largely denied effective opportunities to do so institutionally."

It is within this context of social structure that the political machine fulfills the basic function of providing avenues of social mobility for the otherwise disadvantaged. Within this context, even the corrupt political machine and the racket "represent the triumph of amoral intelligence over morally prescribed 'failure' when the channels of vertical mobility are closed or narrowed *in a society which places a high premium on economic affluence, [power] and social ascent for all its members.*"[6] As one sociologist has noted on the basis of several years of close observation in a slum area:

"The sociologist who dismisses racket and po-litical organizations as deviations from desirable standards thereby neglects some of the major elements of slum life. . . . *He does not discover the functions they perform for the members* [of the groupings in the slum]. The Irish and later immigrant people have had the greatest difficulty in finding places for themselves in our urban social and economic structure. Does anyone believe that the immigrants and their children could have achieved their present degree of social mobility without gaining control of the political organiza-tion of some of our largest cities? The same is true of the racket organization. *Politics and the rackets have furnished an important means of social mo-bility for individuals, who, because of ethnic background and low class position,* are blocked from advancement in the 'respectable' channels."[7]

This, then, represents a third type of function performed for a distinctive subgroup. This func-tion, it may be noted in passing, is fulfilled by the *sheer* existence and operation of the political machine, for it is in the machine itself that these individuals and subgroups find their culturally induced needs more or less satisfied. It refers to the services which the political apparatus provides for its own personnel. But seen in the wider social context we have set forth, it no longer appears as *merely* a means of self-aggrandizement for profit-hungry and power-hungry *individuals,* but as an organized provision for *subgroups* otherwise excluded from or handicapped in the race for "getting ahead."

Just as the political machine performs services for "legitimate" business, so it operates to perform not dissimilar services for "illegitimate" business: vice, crime and rackets. Once again, the basic sociological role of the machine in this respect can be more fully appreciated only if one tempo-rarily abandons attitudes of moral indignation, to examine in all moral innocence the actual work-ings of the organization. In this light, it at once appears that the subgroup of the professional criminal, racketeer or gambler has basic similari-ties of organization, demands and operation to the subgroup of the industrialist, man of business or speculator. If there is a Lumber King or an Oil King, there is also a Vice King or a Racket King. If expansive legitimate business organizes administrative and financial syndicates to "ration-alize" and to "integrate" diverse areas of produc-tion and business enterprise, so expansive rackets and crime organize syndicates to bring order to the otherwise chaotic areas of production of illicit goods and services. If legitimate business regards the proliferation of small business enterprises as wasteful and inefficient, substituting, for example, the giant chain stores for hundreds of corner groceries, so illegitimate business adopts the same businesslike attitude and syndicates crime and vice.

Finally, and in many respects, most important, is the basic similarity, if not near-identity, of the economic role of "legitimate" business and of "illegitimate" business. *Both are in some degree concerned with the provision of goods and services*

---

[6] Robert K. Merton, "Social Structure and Anomie," *Social Theory and Social Structure* (Glencoe, Ill.: The Free Press of Glencoe, 1957), Chapter IV.

[7] William F. Whyte, "Social Organization in the Slums," *American Sociological Review*, 8 (February 1943), 34-39 [italics supplied].

for which there is an economic demand. Morals aside, they are both business, industrial and professional enterprises, dispensing goods and services which some people want, for which there is a market in which goods and services are transformed into commodities. And, in a prevalently market society, we should expect appropriate enterprises to arise whenever there is a market demand for certain goods or services.

As is well known, vice, crime and the rackets *are* "big business." Consider only that there have been estimated to be about 500,000 professional prostitutes in the United States of 1950, and compare this with the approximately 200,000 physicians and 350,000 professional registered nurses. It is difficult to estimate which have the larger clientele: the professional men and women of medicine or the professional men and women of vice. It is, of course, difficult to estimate the economic assets, income, profits and dividends of illicit gambling in this country and to compare it with the economic assets, income, profits and dividends of, say, the shoe industry, but it is altogether possible that the two industries are about on a par. No precise figures exist on the annual expenditures on illicit narcotics, and it is probable that these are less than the expenditures on candy, but it is also probable that they are larger than the expenditure on books.

It takes but a moment's thought to recognize that, *in strictly economic terms,* there is no relevant difference between the provision of licit and of illicit goods and services. The liquor traffic illustrates this perfectly. It would be peculiar to argue that prior to 1920 (when the 18th amendment became effective), the provision of liquor constituted an economic service, that from 1920 to 1933, its production and sale no longer constituted an economic service dispensed in a market, and that from 1934 to the present, it once again took on a serviceable aspect. . . . Examples of this sort can of course be multiplied many times over. Can it be held that in European countries, with registered and legalized prostitution, the prostitute contributes an economic service, whereas in this country, lacking legal sanction, the prostitute provides no such service? Or that the professional abortionist is in the economic market where he has approved legal status and that he is out of the economic market where he is legally taboo? Or that gambling satisfies a specific demand for entertainment in Nevada, where it constitutes the largest business enterprise of the larger cities in the state, but that it differs essentially in this respect from motion pictures in the neighboring state of California?

The failure to recognize that these businesses

are only *morally* and not *economically* distinguishable from "legitimate" businesses has led to badly scrambled analysis. Once the economic identity of the two is recognized, we may anticipate that if the political machine performs functions for "legitimate big business" it will be all the more likely to perform not dissimilar functions for "illegitimate big business." And, of course, such is often the case.

The distinctive function of the political machine for their criminal, vice and racket clientele is to enable them to operate in satisfying the economic demands of a large market without due interference from the government. Just as big business may contribute funds to the political party warchest to ensure a minimum of governmental interference, so with big rackets and big crime. In both instances, the political machine can, in varying degrees, provide "protection." In both instances, many features of the structural context are identical: (1) market demands for goods and services; (2) the operators' concern with maximizing gains from their enterprises; (3) the need for partial control of government which might otherwise interfere with these activities of businessmen; (4) the need for an efficient, powerful and centralized agency to provide an effective liaison of "business" with government.

Without assuming that the foregoing pages exhaust either the range of functions or the range of subgroups served by the political machine, we can at least see that *it presently fulfills some functions for these diverse subgroups which are not adequately fulfilled by culturally approved or more conventional structures.*

Several additional implications of the functional analysis of the political machine can be mentioned here only in passing, although they obviously require to be developed at length. First, the foregoing analysis has direct implications for *social engineering.* It helps explain why the periodic efforts at "political reform," "turning the rascals out" and "cleaning political house" are typically (though not necessarily) short-lived and ineffectual. It exemplifies a basic theorem: *any attempt to eliminate an existing social structure without providing adequate alternative structures for fulfilling the functions previously fulfilled by the abolished organization is doomed to failure.* (Needless to say, this theorem has much wider bearing than the one instance of the political machine.) When "political reform" confines itself to the manifest task of "turning the rascals out," it is engaging in little more than sociological magic. The reform may for a time bring new figures into the political limelight; it may serve the casual social function of re-assuring the electorate that the moral virtues remain intact and will ultimately triumph; it may actually effect a turnover in the personnel of the political machine; it may even, for a time, so curb the activities of the machine as to leave unsatisfied the many needs it has previously fulfilled. But, inevitably, unless the reform also involves a "re-forming" of the social and political structure such that the existing needs are satisfied by alternative structures or unless it involves a change which eliminates these needs altogether, the political machine will return to its integral place in the social scheme of things. *To seek social change, without due recognition of the manifest and latent functions performed by the social organization undergoing change, is to indulge in social ritual rather than social engineering.* The concepts of manifest and latent functions (or their equivalents) are indispensable elements in the theoretic reper-toire of the social engineer. In this crucial sense, these concepts are not "merely" theoretical (in the abusive sense of the term), but are eminently practical. In the deliberate enactment of social change, they can be ignored only at the price of considerably heightening the risk of failure.

A second implication of this analysis of the political machine also has a bearing upon areas wider than the one we have considered. The paradox has often been noted that the supporters of the political machine include both the "respect-able" business class elements who are, of course, opposed to the criminal or racketeer and the distinctly "unrespectable" elements of the under-world. And, at first appearance, this is cited as an instance of very strange bedfellows. The learned judge is not infrequently called upon to sentence the very racketeer beside whom he sat the night before at an informal dinner of the political big-wigs. The district attorney jostles the exonerated convict on his way to the back room where the Boss has called a meeting. The big business man may complain almost as bitterly as the big racket-eer about the "extortionate" contributions to the party fund demanded by the Boss. Social op-posites meet—in the smoke-filled room of the successful politician.

In the light of a functional analysis all this of course no longer seems paradoxical. Since the machine serves both the businessman and the criminal man, the two seemingly antipodal groups intersect. This points to a more general theorem: *the social functions of an organization help deter-mine the structure (including the recruitment of personnel involved in the structure), just as the structure helps determine the effectiveness with which the functions are fulfilled.* In terms of social status, the business group and the criminal group are indeed poles apart. But status does not fully determine behavior and the inter-relations be-tween groups. Functions modify these relations. Given their distinctive needs, the several sub-groups in the large society are "integrated," what-ever their personal desires or intentions, by the centralizing structure which serves these several needs. In a phrase with many implications which require further study, *structure affects function and function affects structure.*

Selection *64*

The Famine Makers
Valentin Chu

According to classic institutional theory, institutions arise (or are enacted) to meet one or more basic, recurring human needs. In actual practice, major insti-tutions (economics, politics, religion, education, etc.) meet needs conjointly, with variations in time and place determining which institutional patterns actually meet particular needs or goals.

Contrary to the belief that the government which governs least governs best, communism as a political entity attempts to undertake or control almost all the needs (goals) which were previously allocated to economics, education, the family, etc. Theoretically, such central control should make for greater efficiency in meeting these needs.

Pre-Communist China, without particularly attempting to hide anything, was a considerable enigma to the Western world. Communist China, with its extensive propaganda, distortion, and secrecy, is a much greater enigma. The following article gives the student some factual knowledge of Communist China's activities and of life in China today. It also demonstrates that the mere will of the functionaries of one institution (political) to take over and improve the activities of another (economic) may not result in increased efficiency of the usurped functions but may even result in decreased efficiency in meeting basic human needs, thereby causing an increase in human misery. Chu, who is of course by no means unbiased in this matter, points out numerous major failures of the Communist political regime in China to meet the economic needs of the people.

Chu's approach is quite different from that of Lipset (Selection 65), who shows the definite possibility that kinds of government grow out of economic situations. Carried to an extreme, this would mean that the economic order determines the political order. Chu's article, on the other hand, shows how a political order is attempting, with doubtful success, to determine an economic order. The student may decide for himself which interpretation is the more nearly correct. The student also should judge for himself the latent functions or dysfunctions connected with China's fertilizer drivers, new large-scale communal living, deforestation, new plows, crop changes, water conservation, the canal network, "calamity fighters," sparrow killing, and the like.

Thirty years ago, totalitarian governments such as those in Italy and Germany were praised for their efficiency at the same time that they were being damned for their lack of democracy. If Chu's report is at all correct, Communist China is equally if not more totalitarian, equally or more lacking in democracy, and at the same time not only far more inefficient than Hitlerite Germany but even more inefficient in food production than previous, inefficient Chinese regimes. All of this can be understood better through the application of the social concepts of function, dysfunction, and latent function.

In the third century B.C. the ruler of a Chinese kingdom suffering from a severe famine sought advice from the sage Mencius. The King had been energetically shifting his people and his resources about the country in an all-out effort to alleviate the starvation and to govern effectively. Yet the nation failed to prosper. He wondered why.

Mencius told the King: "If the seasons of cultivation are not interfered with, the grain will be more than you can eat. If close-knit nets are not cast in the pools and ponds, the fish and turtles will be more than you can eat. If axes enter the hills and forests only at the proper time, the wood will be more than you can use. But your dogs and swine eat the food of men, and you curb them not. People are starving by the wayside, and you open not your granaries. When people die, you say: 'I am not responsible; it is the year.' What difference is this from stabbing a man to death and saying: 'I am not responsible; it is the weapon'?"

Twenty-two centuries later Mao Tse-tung, the ruler of another Chinese empire suffering from famine, is energetically moving his people and his resources all over the country in a similar effort to govern effectively. He, too, must wonder why

hunger remains the plague of his people. And it is something to wonder about. For during the decade 1949-59 Communist China's food increase was seven times its population increase. Even under the severest natural conditions, there should have been enough reserve to forestall a famine. The answer to this riddle can only be understood after a long look at both China's traditional agricultural economy and the program of the present regime since its take-over in 1949.

The land of China, slightly larger in area than the United States, is hardly ideal for agriculture. China is more mountainous than the U.S., the USSR or India. Almost 70 per cent of its land is over 3,000 feet above sea level, and only 15 per cent is under 1,600 feet. Its climate varies from sub-tropic summer to Siberian winter. Arable land on the mainland amounts to 264 million acres, or only one-tenth the total area. Of this, 30 per cent is good soil, 40 per cent medium quality and the rest inferior. To maintain a subsistence level four-fifths of China's population has to toil on one-tenth of its land. In Soviet Russia, half of the population works on one-eleventh of

From *The New Leader,* June 11, 1962, pp. 13-21.

the land to provide a meager standard of living. In the United States, one-eighth of the population farms one-fifth of the land to create a national overweight problem and pile up great surpluses.

The trouble with the Chinese is that the fecundity of their soil can never match the fecundity of their loins; in their land it is easier to breed than to feed. But too little arable land and too large a population are not the only problems. In China a year without natural calamities is indeed a year for thanksgiving. The country's peasants have always been at the mercy of their eroded mountains and capricious rivers.

China's history records 1,397 serious droughts since Christ was born. Floods have also been disastrous. The Huai River, draining an area six times the size of the Netherlands but without a mouth of its own, flooded its valley 979 times in 2,200 years. The mighty Yangtze River, the world's third longest, in whose valley nearly half the population lives, had 242 floods and droughts in 265 years. From mythical times there have been attempts to tame the Yellow River, known as "China's Sorrow." This 2,900-mile river, with a basin equal in area to Italy, Switzerland and Norway combined, devastated its plain 1,500 times in 3,000 years, and made nine major changes of its course, swinging its mouth in wild arcs up to 500 miles long.

Add to all this frequent dust storms in the arid northwest, typhoons along the coast, insect pests everywhere, rare but severe earthquakes, and it can be seen that the lot of the Chinese peasant has been tied to natural calamities. Because the peasants obtain three-quarters of their food directly from their own land, when famine strikes it always means hunger and often means starvation. One million people were killed in the 1887 flood alone. Some 800,000 lost their lives in the great earthquake of 1556, and another 246,000 perished in a similar disaster in 1920.

Moreover, after many centuries of exploitation by a vast farming population, China has very little natural vegetation left. Forests make up only one-tenth of its total area (about 80th down the list among the world's countries on a percentage area basis). The water-holding capacity of the soil is therefore extremely poor, and excessive run-off is a major cause of floods. Another major cause is the breaching of dykes. The Yellow River, the world's siltiest, deposits enough sediment on its delta to fill up one-and-a-half Empire State Buildings daily. For hundreds of miles it flows between dykes on a river bed high *above* the surrounding countryside, with the silt raising the bottom continuously. A single breach can empty the entire river on to the flat, densely populated Yellow Plain for as far as the eye can see, sometimes inundating the region for as long as a year. Many other rivers in North China have similar skyway river beds between precarious dykes, and floods in this area are the most destructive. When too much water goes to one place, there is bound to be too little elsewhere. And in China drought occurs oftener than floods, is even more destructive and more extensive in area, and lasts longer.

Since historically China is a land of catastrophes, it is tempting to conclude that the current famine is just one of those things. This is not so. True, Peking has publicized the natural causes and played down other factors. But the present famine is due not so much to sudden dramatic blows from nature as to the grave errors of a bureaucracy highly efficient in control but childishly lacking in common sense. A sizeable portion of the floods and droughts which China has suffered during the past few years have been aggravated, and at times directly caused, by a decade of pseudo-scientific methods in farming, irrigation and soil treatment. Each year since the Communists came to power in 1949, the total area of farmland affected by natural calamities has risen steadily: It was only 13 million acres in 1950; 29 million in '54; 38 million in '56; 78 million in '58; 107 million in '59; and 148 million in '60. It is safe to assume that the 1961 total, although never officially announced, was probably at least as large as 1960's.

What China is now facing is no common natural disturbance, affecting a few provinces for a short time. It is a nation-wide exhaustion of the land and the people, the cumulative result of 12 years of abusing nature and human nature. Peking's search for a breakthrough in agriculture has resulted in a breakdown.

In the beginning, the Chinese Communists attempted to implement a titanic program of farm mechanization on the Russian or American scale. But unlike either the Soviet Union or the United States, both of which have vast plains that are thinly settled, China's huge population is extremely dense wherever the land is arable. Most of the farmland consists of cut up wet paddies or terraced hillside plots where modern tractors are of no use. The U.S. has 5 million tractors, the USSR 1.7 million. China has fewer than 33,500 tractors, with some 6,700 in disrepair, but despite their limited usefulness this is less than 4 per cent of the number required as estimated by the regime. In October 1957 the *People's Daily*, Peking's official organ, finally had to admit: "It is too early to talk about general mechanization. We have no oil, too few animals. Steel is expensive. The cost of machinery is prohibitive."

Attention was then turned to "semi-mechanization," which meant improved animal-powered farming implements. The glamour star of "semi-mechanization" was the Double-Wheel Double-Share Plow, an ordinary all-metal plow pulled by animals. With great fanfare, Peking turned out 3.5 million Double Plows in 1956 and 6 million in '57. But they were a flop. Not only were they too heavy for China's wet paddies and terraced fields; they were also badly manufactured, with many brand-new plows missing parts. Soon peasants all over the country refused to use what they called the "Sleeping Plow." Peking accused the peasants of "hostility toward innovations" and "backward conservatism." But six months later the production of a new, lighter model was announced.

Lately, the regime has been encouraging the use of small, handmade instruments. The quality of the newly made small implements, however, leaves much to be desired. A recent *People's Daily* editorial recalled wistfully the days of the pre-Communist peasant, when "a hoe would last three generations . . . the property of the man who used it, repaired it and cared for it." Today a hoe often does not last one season, especially when it is made of the "steel" from the backyard furnaces. Nor does the peasant own it, repair it or care for it. Instead, the small implements are "lost, wasted or destroyed . . . left scattered in the open air in the fields where rains and winds ruined them."

Mechanization having failed as a panacea, Peking has been trying its luck with fertilizer. Each winter since 1957 tens of millions of peasants and city residents have been taking part in fertilizer marches. With gongs clanging, drums beating and red pennants fluttering in the scented breezes, these brigades, singing and moving in military formation, transport their precious commodity to the fields. In wooden buckets, bamboo baskets, tin cans and earthen pots slung from bamboo poles, or in makeshift carts pulled by children, the brigades carry the excrement of China's 700 million human beings and 265 million farm animals, plus sewage silt, garbage, river mud, peat, green meal, fumigated earth, chimney ashes, brackish water and industrial waste.

For all its bizarreness, the fertilizer drive is intended to make up for a real agricultural deficiency. Communist China produces less than 3 million tons of chemical fertilizer a year; it needs at least 10 times that amount. Peking cannot afford to build enough modern fertilizer plants or to import fertilizer from abroad, and China must still depend largely on compost. The population daily returns to the earth, in the form of manure, more than 700 tons of phosphorus, 1,200 tons of

potassium and a large amount of nitrogen. Yet human and animal excrement, green compost and river mud have been used by Chinese farmers for 40 centuries. Thus, the fertilizer drive has not really increased fertilizing strength, even though mixing compost with adulterating ingredients has increased the total tonnage.

In the summer of 1958, after it took over direct control of agriculture, the Party ordered nearly half of the crop land deep-plowed and close-sown. But such practices demand discretion and careful coordination with fertilization. The regime acted indiscriminately, with the result that many plants either weakened or died, and much soil was debilitated. By the fall of 1959 Peking conceded: "What we gained was not up to what we lost."

Further damage was caused by the so-called Battle of Crops. In its early stages, this involved an ambitious simultaneous assault on agriculture, fishing, animal husbandry and forestry. The result was a reduction in the food crop. The regime then reversed its policy: Concentrate on food crops; ignore subsidiary activities. So the Party *kanpu* (cadre) had hundreds of thousands of acres of cotton, hemp, tea, mulberry, peaches, oranges, lychees and bamboo razed and turned into unstable, unfit, ill-conditioned fields for wet rice, wheat and potatoes.

In agricultural China each valley and plain has its own special combination of soil, climate and economic requirements. Over the centuries, the peasants have learned which crops are the best and the most profitable. In a silk-producing area near Canton, for example, the peasants engage in fish culture as a sideline. They use the waste from the silkworms to feed the fish, then dig up the fertile mud from the fish ponds to fertilize mulberry trees, the leaves of which are fed to the silkworms. Everything is used, nothing wasted. When the mulberry trees in a village near Canton were razed by zealous Party robots to plant rice, the entire cycle of agricultural economy was upset. Similar disruption was caused by plowing too deeply, sowing too closely, planting too early, using the wrong crops or wrong seeds, employing too much or too little or inadequate fertilizer, and not fallowing fields that should have been fallowed. All these mistakes dealt the harvests a severe blow.

The 1959 locust disaster is another enlightening example of the Party bureaucrats' knack for worsening natural calamities. In early April of that year, peasants in Honan discovered some young locusts and reported their find to the commune's *kanpu*. But the *kanpu* scolded the peasants: "The corn and soybean have just sprouted and the wheat will ripen soon. We don't even have enough people for weeding and fertilizing. How can we divert labor for insect pests? We must take care of urgent business first." The peasants then appealed to the county Party commissar. They were again pushed aside: "Little ghost and big fright! You saw an insect and you bring us a heap of blind words. We shall have an insect-destroying campaign some day anyway. Why make the fuss now?"

Two months later the crops in two counties were eaten up by locusts in one night. Immediately the provincial Party secretary pushed the panic button and issued a set of "Regulations Pertaining to the Swift Extermination of Locusts." During three days in mid-June, 1.3 million peasants were hurled into a sea of locusts for an epic extermination battle. By then, however, it was too late. Crops, grass and tree leaves on a million acres in 48 counties in Honan were stripped clean. The locusts next invaded the neighboring provinces of Anhwei, Kiangsu and Shantung, damaging nearly five million acres of farmland in 179 counties. Peasants from 6-80 were pressed into the fight. Airplanes were used to spray insecticide. But the spraying, done with frenzy and inexperience, killed 100,000 farm animals. By Peking's own estimate, insect pests damage 10 per cent of the country's grain, 20 per cent of the cotton and 40 per cent of the fruits every year.

Given China's limited means, water conservation seems the only practical means of improving the country's agriculture. In sheer quantity, China has plenty of water, but its distribution is lopsided. Every year 668 cubic miles of water flow over the mainland's 3.6 million square miles of land, averaging 12 tons of water for each person daily. Three-quarters of this water, however, is in the Yangtze valley and south of it. North China has less than 5 per cent.

The regime claims that during the first 10 years of its rule the nation's irrigated area increased from 40 million to 180 million acres. Official figures speak of 40 billion man-days used to dig 105 billion cubic yards of earth (equivalent to 450 Panama Canals, or a wall 3.3 feet high and wide girdling the earth 2,000 times). The work, according to Peking, consisted of building or repairing some 60 large reservoirs, 1,000 medium ones, 4 million small reservoirs and canals, 74,600 miles of dykes, 15 million farm weirs and 10 million wells.

The official statistics are impressive. One imagines millions of Chinese peasants, ant-like and faceless, digging and hauling all over the land, disciplining the savage rivers and salving the fields with gentle moisture. With this image in mind, it is even possible to rationalize that the misery of millions forced to labor today might bring some good to additional millions who will inherit the land tomorrow. But the fact is that China's water conservation efforts have done more harm than good. Indeed, they are an important factor in the current famine.

Until 1957, Peking concentrated its energies on big, hydroelectrically oriented dams. Many of these expensive projects were either ill-planned or badly executed. The largest and most important project was a TVA-like system to regulate the Yellow River and its tributaries; by the time the river passed the vicinity of Kaifeng and reached the flat Yellow Plain, its flow was to be controlled. When the project was initiated Peking proudly announced that the Yellow River, perhaps the world's most unmanageable body of water, would not only be tamed forever but that by 1961 its lower reaches would be "crystal clear."

The key to the Yellow River system was to be the mammoth Sanmen Gorge Dam, at a point just before the river leaves the mountains. To protect it, 59 high dams were to be constructed in the upper river. By 1956 half of the high dams were completed. The same year, floods destroyed or silted up almost all of them. Despite a Chinese specialist's warning to re-examine the whole plan, the Sanmen Gorge Dam, with a one-million kilowatt power plant, was started in 1957. The dam was planned, model-tested and supervised by Russian technicians. Because of structural defects, its design and construction had to be altered time and again. In 1958 there was another flood, and this time 70 per cent of the swollen water came from *below* the Sanmen Gorge. An official technical journal, *Water Conservation and Power*, then admitted this proved that even after the completion of the project, major floods could not be prevented.

Another big pride of Communist China's hydraulic engineering is the much-ballyhooed Futseling Reservoir and Power Plant in Anhwei. This project was completed with Russian aid in 1954. Soon after the Huai River overflowed its banks and inundated the entire plain the reservoir was supposed to protect. Five years later the reservoir was still not functioning: The sluice gates had turned out to be heavier than designed, and it was feared that they would not open when the reservoir was filled with water. A similar fate befell the Yungting Reservoir Tunnel near Peking, which was also opened with a loud blast of propaganda. After the hosannas came the flood, inundating 7 million acres and washing away 2.6 million houses. Then there is the incident of the Tahuofang Dam, the country's second biggest reservoir, near Fushun in Manchuria. After a year's work on it, construction had to be halted in 1954 because it was discovered that the structure "had the consistency of rubber."

Some of the mistakes are almost unbelievable. During the dry season, fields in many areas could not get a single drop of water even though the reservoirs were full. It was discovered that no one had been ordered to build water conveyance systems for the reservoirs—no sluice gates, no canals, no ditches. In June 1959, the *People's Daily* summed up the results of many of the large-scale projects: "There are reservoirs without water, reservoirs with water but without aqueducts. . . . A great number of flood-prevention works which have to be renewed yearly were not renewed, or, if they were started, were not finished." And *Water Conservation and Power* reported that a number of hydroelectric dams were leaking badly, that many reservoirs "look all right as long as water is not let in," and that on some projects equipment was installed but no power could be produced. Medium and small works, by Peking's own admission, have fared even worse.

Water conservation is a complicated science. It requires detailed study, careful surveys and co-ordinated planning. The planners must have intimate knowledge of river flow, flood history, silt content, topography, soil characteristics, water tables, weather patterns and the needs of surrounding areas. But Peking has never had any overall water conservation plan. Technical direction often has not matched actual working conditions. Quality has always been less important than quantity and speed. For large projects, there has never been enough steel and cement available. For smaller ones, only earth and stone have been used because of shortages. Everywhere substitute materials and short cuts in construction have been favored—and praised as "technical innovations." Is it any wonder that China has registered such spectacular water conservation failures?

The dam fiascoes touched off an orgy of canal-digging in 1958-59. Peking finally realized that the much-vaunted huge projects, which had so impressed foreign visitors, often turned out to be mere monuments to stupidity. In 1958, the year of the Great Leap Forward, it turned its attention from big dams to regional irrigation projects of medium and small dams, wells and, especially, canals.

In August of that year, the Party Central Committee announced a stupendous project: a network of canals which would criss-cross the entire area of the China Plains and link the three great rivers —the Yellow, the Yangtze and the Huai. The canals were to be of five sizes, ranging from small irrigation ditches to large ones accommodating 3,000-ton ships. They would serve as inland waterways, as a gigantic reservoir, and as a water-regulating system to bring water from South to North China. When the plan was announced, millions of peasants had already been digging for months. By early 1960 half of the canals in some provinces were completed.

But after months of confused experience, the small canals proved inadequate. They were too numerous, creating problems for future farm mechanization. They were also too small, providing little protection in times of flood or drought. To further complicate matters, the village *kanpu* in charge of digging were unclear about the various canal measurements, and they varied greatly. In the winter of 1958 the plan was revised: Small canals already dug were abandoned or filled up; medium and large canals were dug at relocated sites.

The frenzied canal digging created problems undreamed of in the Communist philosophy: The canals took away much valuable farmland. They leaked badly (in many cases 60 per cent of the water escaped). In some areas where the water table was near the surface, excessively deep canals drained the land, creating an artificial drought where none had existed. In other areas, mainly in dry North China, where the water table was low and the soil unleached, water leaking from the canals raised the water table, thus accentuating capillary action through the lime-rich earth. This brought up harmful salts and alkali from the subsoil and formed a crust on the surface after evaporation, spoiling formerly dry but good farmland. By 1959, the *People's Daily* sensed something was wrong: "During the past one or two years, the alkalization of much soil in many irrigated areas in the North has spread." But the canal digging went on. In 1960, the same paper again reported that saltpeter, which normally appears only in serious drought, had affected millions of acres of farmland. And in April 1961 the *Kuang Ming Daily* noted that "arable land is continuously shrinking and alkalized soil spreading."

In a country like China, where the water balance has already been upset by centuries of intensive cultivation and population weight, the best place to store water is not behind big dams or in sloppy canals, but underground near where it falls. Not surprisingly, Peking has also had insanely grandiose forestation plans. The original Great Vision Program—no longer mentioned today —consisted of a number of bold forestation projects, which included two "Green Great Walls." One was to be a 1,000-mile protective windbreaker, starting from the Chinese-Korean border, winding along the China Coast, and ending at the mouth of the Yangtze. The other, equally long, was to be a forest shield against the sand from Outer Mongolia. It was to start from the vicinity of the Old Silk Road in Kansu, cut across the sand dunes of the Alashan Desert and the Ordos Desert in Inner Mongolia, and end at the great bend of the Yellow River.

In early 1956, a campaign to "green up China in 12 years" was begun. The job would be easy: "If every one of the country's 500 million peasants plants two trees each year, we shall have one billion trees in a single year." Peking believed that in 12 years it could change China's arid land, barren hills and deserts into 160 million acres of sylvan delight. So millions of school children were ordered to plant trees all over the country. In most cases the entire program consisted of digging holes, inserting cuttings or saplings, and watering them for a few days. Then the human sea surged in other directions, for other campaigns, and the trees were left to die of thirst.

While forestation surged up and died off, deforestation seemed to progress systematically. Forest fires and the incidence of tree diseases have increased. Artificial deforestation has also been on the increase, especially since 1958. Farm cooperatives and communes have set their cattle to graze on saplings, and have chopped down roadside trees and whole forests for timber or to "open virgin land." During the 1958 steel-making campaign many mountains were stripped bare for fuel. A commune in Kwangtung close-shaved 13 forest-covered hills in one swoop. Timber industries in forest areas, led by quota-conscious *kanpu*, competed with each other in cutting down big and small trees without replanting. Even saplings were not left to protect the soil, which soon became barren. Since the 1958 Great Leap, the Chinese have been too busy making steel, digging canals and fighting calamities to worry about reforestation. But deforestation is continuing at an even faster pace, reducing the already poor moisture-capturing capacity of the soil, extending the erosion area, heightening excessive run-off of rain water, and insuring severer damage from floods and droughts for generations to come.

The foolish squandering of resources and manpower on big, haphazard projects before 1958, and the wanton canal digging since then, has deteriorated the water and soil in China's richest farming regions. It is no coincidence that the worst droughts of the past four years have taken place in the very provinces where millions dug canals from 1957-59. The entire hydrologic cycle in China is now upset by faulty water conservation and deforestation. Communist China has unwittingly changed nature.

While food coming out of the earth is decreasing, crops already harvested are increasingly spoiled or wasted. For centuries wasting food was considered a sin in China. Under the Communists a good deal of food is unnecessarily spoiled. Many granaries are haphazardly built; others are created from decrepit temples or ancestral shrines; still others are without doors and windows—though all have fences or walls to prevent theft. One year an investigation revealed serious conditions in grain storage in seven provinces. In Kwangsi, for example, of the 740,000 tons of grain inspected, 83 per cent was spoiled by worms. One granary reported 10 per cent of its grain mildewed. Another, in Shensi, had 30 per cent mildewed and 40 per cent sprouting. The Party *kanpu* in charge of food supply in the communes are nicknamed by the peasants: "The Five Don't Knows": They don't know how much grain is harvested; don't know how much is eaten; don't know how much is in the commune kitchen; don't know how much is stored in the granaries; and don't know how long the store will last. When famine became acute late in 1960, a *People's Daily* editorial revealed that the total amount of grain stored in Communist China was unknown. It launched a national campaign to weigh the stored grain, explaining: "We shall only know the real situation if we weigh and clearly account for the food grain collected." Since 1961, Peking has imported grain. The real situation, apparently, is now known.

The efficiency of China's farm labor, low in the old days because of inadequate equipment, has been lowered even further by Peking's administrative epilepsy. The peasants always worked hard; each knew what to do and how to do it with the limited means available. Today, they are told how to plow, when to sow and what to plant. They are pressed into a robot army and maneuvered with human-sea strategy and commando tactics.

In the winter of 1955, many millions were "volunteered" into constructing dams and dykes. The following summer, when it was found that subsidiary farm work had slumped to half its normal amount, they were shunted back to the fields. In some provinces the Party ordered up to 40 per cent of the peasants to stick to subsidiary farm work, although drought was spreading. Left unharvested, much rice and sweet potatoes were damaged by the drought. When this was discovered, the peasants were hurried back to plant more food crops. Meanwhile, the half-finished dams and dykes they had left were damaged by floods.

In 1958 some 60 million people, most of them

peasants, were told to make village steel, creating a labor shortage on the farms. In many areas fertilizer was not put into the fields and rice was not harvested in time. Forty per cent of the land in Hopei province that needed sowing was left untended. In North China cotton and potato picking were not done on time. Elsewhere 650,000 tons of tobacco leaves were plucked but unsorted, and the damp leaves began to spoil. For three consecutive winters, up to 70 million peasants were commandeered to dig canals. More recently, the peasants have been recruited to fight flood and drought. The number of calamity-fighters now exceeds 10 million in each seriously affected province. When the fertilizer drive was on, 80 million had to forage for manure. When there was a coal shortage, 20 million were sent to the hills to dig for dubious fuel.

The madcap use of farm labor is responsible for at least one unnatural disaster, the "weed calamity." This term was coined by the Communists to denote fields left unplanted or unattended which subsequently were found covered with weeds. The weed calamity first came to light in 1959. By the fall of 1960 weeds were reported in at least 13 provinces, from northern Manchuria to Kiangsu, and covered 20 per cent of China's farmland. In many areas the weeds were taller than the crops. In Shantung one-third of the farmland was covered by weeds, which at places grew so thick that a "man was unable to walk into the fields." Soon the Ministry of Agriculture sounded another alarm, this time to fight weeds. Peasants, city people, students, civil servants and even soldiers were ordered to forsake whatever they were doing and hand-pluck weeds from the fields. In Hopei, 6 million were mobilized; in Shantung, more than 7 million. In Liaoning, two-thirds of the students and civil servants from the cities were diverted to the countryside. In Shansi, half of the total farm labor was used.

The more the peasants work under the Party's blundering policy, of course, the less they produce. And the less they produce, the more they have to work. The end result is debilitating famine.

At present, an ordinary resident in show cities like Peking and Shanghai receives a small ration of inferior rice or flour, plus a monthly allotment of about half a pound of pork, three ounces of sugar and three ounces of edible oil. For a small quantity of vegetables, he has to line up as early as 3 A.M. Eggs, poultry and fish have virtually disappeared. The peasant in the commune receives much less—usually two bowls of semi-liquid gruel or paste, made from bad cereals, gritty flour or sweet potatoes, for each meal.

Since 1959, Communist China has officially ordered the eating of rice husks, bean waste, potato leaves, pumpkin flowers, wild plants and algae. During the past two winters, each province sent from a half a million to 3 million peasants and city dwellers to forage for wild plants in the hills. Newspapers praised the high nutritive value of wild plants and recommended recipes for these and other novel foods. Rice straw, soaked in lime solution, dried, ground into powder and mixed with flour, is made into cakes and served in restaurants upon surrender of ration coupons.

China's streets and villages, formerly cluttered with friendly dogs and cats, are now empty of domestic animals. Common birds such as sparrows, pigeons, crows and cuckoos are also gone. Some 2.2 billion sparrows were systematically exterminated as predatory birds in a nation-wide campaign. The campaign ended when a sizeable increase in predatory insects was noted.

The appearance of a wild rabbit or a crow in China today is an occasion for a mass hunt for extra food. Sweet potatoes, turnips and other vegetables grown in city suburbs must be guarded throughout the night, or they will be stolen by city people who raid the fields and sometimes eat the loot on the spot. Beggars openly wait by restaurant tables for leftover food, often grabbing food from the patrons. Policemen merely shrug at such petty crimes. The blackmarket is growing, supplied by corrupt Communists controlling food supply centers. Blackmarket rings sometimes have their own sampans and armed escorts.

Until late 1960, Communist China limited food parcels from Hong Kong and Macao. Immediately after the restrictions were lifted, the tiny Hong Kong post office was buried under a daily avalanche of 50,000 food parcels from frantic relatives; at present, more than 200,000 parcels are sent daily. The little British colony now has more than 1,000 firms specializing in sending food parcels to China. Not long ago, Hong Kong Communist newspapers eagerly quoted a Japanese visitor to China who said, "I did not see any hunger in Peking." On the same pages where this story appeared were advertisements of firms offering to deliver food parcels to China, with such screaming titles as "Fast, Fast, Fast!" and "Rocket Speed!"

A normal man in the Far East, according to the United Nations' Food and Agriculture Organization, requires a minimum of 2,300 calories of food daily. In food-short India, according to a United Nations survey, the daily average intake is 2,000 calories. In prewar China it was 2,234 calories. At present, a great number of Chinese peasants, who must put in 14-18 hours of hard labor a day, receive less than 1,000 calories.

Like most Asian countries, China has always had major public health problems. Modern doctors number only one to every 10,000 people. Except for those in the big cities, people have to depend on the traditional herb doctors, who are good at common ailments but have little knowledge of contagious diseases and surgery. In certain rural areas diseases like schistosomiasis (a chronic intestinal malady involving enlargement of the liver and spleen), hookworm and beriberi have always been common. But the bulk of the population has fared well, perhaps because of strong immunities and wise eating habits. Except for fresh fruits, the Chinese have never eaten uncooked food or unboiled water. And most Chinese food is eaten piping hot.

During the first few years of Communist rule, a real attempt was made to improve health. Notable were the campaigns of fly-swatting, rat-exterminating and street-sweeping, all amply reported by foreign visitors. But since the mid-1950s, and particularly since the Great Leap, conditions have changed drastically. Drinking water in the communes is no longer boiled because of fuel shortage, although in many villages water is often taken from polluted creeks and ponds. Manure, green compost and garbage are handled with bare hands during the fertilizer drives. (Newspapers often praise fertilizer heroes who, after handling manure, refuse to wash their hands as a patriotic gesture.) And collective working and living without adequate sanitary precautions has resulted in widespread food poisoning and epidemics.

According to recent refugee information, one out of three or four peasants has dropsy. It is not uncommon for laborers working in the fields to collapse and drop dead suddenly. A former Government technician from Nanchang has reported that in his bureau 20 per cent of the civil servants had liver inflammation or infectious hepatitis. A nurse from Peking said 10 per cent of her colleagues were hospitalized. Hospitals in all cities are full of patients suffering from hepatitis and other diseases, but only serious cases are admitted. Tuberculosis is also spreading widely, but sufferers are not even treated because TB is less alarming than other prevalent diseases. Many babies are born dead. Families of people who die have to make reservations at the busy crematoriums; those who supply firewood get priority.

These grisly first-hand accounts are supported by the official press in its guarded but still revealing stories. In July 1959 the *Honan Peasant's Daily,* a provincial paper not even allowed outside Honan, divulged that many peasants were dying from malnutrition and overwork. During two summer weeks in 1959, 367,000 peasants collapsed and 29,000 died in the fields of Honan. In the same summer 60,000 peasants collapsed after six days and nights of flood-fighting with little sleep or rest. Other press reports reveal that during similar periods 7,000 peasants died in the fields in Kiangsi, 8,000 in Kiangsu and 13,000 in Chekiang.

Epidemics have been developing in China for four years, though their full extent is not known. At first the press was able to cover up the situation, but during the past two years there have been partial admissions and reports of "seasonal contagious diseases." Moreover, the Minister of Health, Li Te-ch'uan, recently admitted that in 1959 a total of 70 million cases of schistosomiasis, filariasis (parasitic worms in the blood), hookworm and malaria were treated. She has also admitted that influenza, measles, diphtheria and spinal meningitis are spreading at water conservation sites, in commune nurseries and primary schools. In April 1960, too, the People's Congress revealed that *kala-azar* (infection of the liver, spleen and bone marrow, especially prevalent among children) was spreading; that *ke-shan* (a disease caused by infected water) had erupted in Inner Mongolia; and that there was large-scale chemical poisoning in industrial cities. Six months later, an emergency public health committee warned that careless handling of manure, garbage and dirty water had spread "all kinds of diseases: schistosomiasis, tapeworm, hookworm, diphtheria, typhus, liver inflammation and animal diseases."

Actual epidemic conditions have never been publicly reported. They can only be gathered from press reports about large numbers of public health teams rushing madly from cities to unnamed rural areas at short notice. In the Spring of 1960, some 500,000 city people from eight provinces were sent to the countryside to enforce emergency public health measures. In the summer of that year, 110,000 were sent to villages in Szechwan, 60,000 to Hunan, and 2,000 to Fukien. According to refugees, cholera killed 30,000-50,000 in Kwangtung last year alone. After the plague spread to Hong Kong, Macao, Indonesia and North Borneo, Peking finally admitted the outbreak of cholera to the Geneva Red Cross.

The regime is worried not so much about the people's suffering, however, as it is about the loss of manpower. The basic rule was sternly laid down by the *People's Daily* in late 1959: "The point of departure is production. It must be our unwavering determination in fighting pests and extinguishing diseases that this work shall be subservient to production. Public health as a purpose in itself—a bourgeois way of thinking—should not be permitted."

When a government fails to fill its people's stomachs, it finds it even harder to wash their brains. Escapees report that food riots occurred throughout South China in 1960 and '61, with many killed. Tens of thousands of peasants have deserted famine-stricken northern Kiangsu and converged on once-prosperous Shanghai, searching for food. Other groups are moving from Chekiang into Fukien. Of course, only last month 70,000 from Kwangtung sought refuge across the border in Hong Kong.

In December 1960, workers at the Anshan steel mills and the Fushun coal mines, China's biggest steel and coal centers, staged a strike demanding food and cotton as wages. Later, in Sian, students of 38 colleges and high schools turned a memorial meeting into an "anti-hunger demonstration." Similar demonstrations broke out in Szechwan cities. In Hunan, soldiers sent to pursue granary robbers deliberately let the thieving peasants escape. In an Army barrack in Kiangsu, soldiers refused to get out of their beds for morning drills, protesting against short rations, which have now affected all the armed forces. And a strong, well-organized underground movement is making its presence felt repeatedly in Shanghai, where most of modern China's revolutions have begun.

All this could be a mere straw in the wind. Impulsive demonstrations and spontaneous food riots are no match against a monolithic regime with a powerful secret police and armed forces. But if overt resistance is not effective at the moment, the conditions breeding it are likely to persist and will probably get worse. Thus the monolithic picture could be deceptive. No one realizes this more than the Chinese Communists

themselves. Peking recently resuscitated the regional political bureaus to tighten its control over the provinces. It has replaced militiamen in strategic areas with regular troops, and steadily moved stored grain from the communes to bigger granaries near cities, which are easier to guard.

Communist China is estimated to have 2.5 million regular troops and 20 million militiamen. The militia is no longer trusted because it is part of the local peasantry. Nearly 90 per cent of the regular troops are recruited from the peasantry. Their families, who formerly received special privileges, are now living the same hard life as other peasants. The morale of the regular troops will become an increasingly significant factor if peasant livelihood is not improved. Furthermore, among the peasants and water conservation workers there are 10 million demobilized soldiers. These veterans are the bitterest and the most articulate complainers. Since 1958, a vast number of low-level *kanpu*, who have been sent to the countryside to live, work and eat with the peasants, have been "infected." They have been repeatedly blamed by Peking for being "afraid of the peasants" and for their "misguided sentimentality."

It would be highly unrealistic to ignore the significant realignment of forces which has taken place in China during the past few years. Many Westerners tend to appraise the Communist regime by simply gawking at its production statistics, or weighing its military equipment, or guessing what is up its diplomatic sleeves. They seldom try to probe into the cross-currents of China's complex economy, or the subtle psychological undertow of its silent millions. This is food for thought for the free world.

Selection 65

Some Social Requisites of Democracy:
Economic Development and Political Legitimacy
Seymour Martin Lipset

The particular form of political institutions has varied widely through time and from place to place. The majority of Americans are vitally concerned about the growth of democracy and the growth of communism in the world today. The following selection analyzes certain factors that seem to be related to the growth of democracy.

Using the comparative method, Lipset analyzed the relationship between economic development and democracy in a large number of countries. He found that the average wealth, the degree of industrialization and urbanization, and the level of education were much higher for the more democratic countries—enough higher that these three factors can be considered as one common factor that carries with it the political correlate of democracy. Evidence suggests that while these factors are causally related to democracy, democracy is equally causally related to these factors. It may also be argued that the factors making for democracy have also produced capitalism and that factors which help maintain one also help maintain the other, but not invariably.

Lipset's article essentially contains two theses: that democracy is related to economic development, and that it is related to political legitimacy. The second thesis is not included in the following excerpt, but the deleted section describes legitimacy as the degree to which institutions are valued for themselves and are considered right and proper. This degree is shown to be related to the effectiveness of the system, which is primarily a function of economic development, and to the kinds and degrees of cleavage and conflict found in a society. To accept the data on which Lipset bases his conclusions, one must agree with him on the interrelationship of economic, political, community, and educational institutions and on the close relationship between certain aspects of these institutions and the growth and maintenance of democracy during modern times.

Any viable and dynamic institution in a society exists because it is an established, organized, commonly accepted means of meeting recurrent basic human needs. No major institution (religion, economics, politics, family, education, etc.) meets only one need; each meets several or many needs. No institution exists in a vacuum; any major aspect of society does and must interact with all other major aspects of society. In previous selections we have seen how education, politics, religion, and economics all interact and mutually affect each other. Another approach is to say that a society is made up of people who collectively evolve institutions to meet their needs; it would be surprising if these institutions did not overlap and were not closely related, for each is originally a tool of the people. Moreover, it is only to be expected that people with certain attitudes and values will devise ways of meeting their needs which differ from the ways used by people with other attitudes and values.

Following this line of reasoning, Lipset demonstrates that people who live under certain sets of conditions tend to have both democratic political institutions and a relatively high and complex economic development, and that a nation which does not have *both* of these characteristics is unlikely to have either one. That Lipset finds higher wealth, greater industrialization, more urbanization, and a higher level of education to be positively related to democracy and capitalism is not illogical. Certainly, if the United States is a fair example, each factor represents a positive value, with no one of them negating or hindering any other. That these factors represent a pattern of characteristics—a "social syndrome" so to speak—is, for the average American, gratifying rather than shocking and certainly is not contradicted by Chu's description of Communist China.

The conditions associated with the existence and stability of democratic society have been a leading concern of political philosophy. In this paper the problem is attacked from a sociological and behavioral standpoint, by presenting a number of hypotheses concerning some social requisites for democracy, and by discussing some of the data available to test these hypotheses. In its concern with conditions—values, social institutions, historical events—external to the political system itself which sustain different general types of political systems, the paper moves outside the generally recognized province of political sociology. . . .

From *The American Political Science Review*, Vol. LIII (1959), 69-103.

INTRODUCTION

A sociological analysis of any pattern of behavior, whether referring to a small or a large social system, must result in specific hypotheses, empirically testable statements. Thus, in dealing with democracy, one must be able to point to a set of conditions that have actually existed in a number of countries, and say: democracy has emerged out of these conditions, and has become stabilized because of certain supporting institutions and values, as well as because of its own internal self-maintaining processes. The conditions listed must be ones which differentiate most democratic states from most others. . . .

The advantage of an attempt such as is presented here, which seeks to dissect the conditions of democracy into several interrelated variables, is that deviant cases fall into proper perspective. The statistical preponderance of evidence supporting the relationship of a variable such as education to democracy indicates that the existence of deviant cases (such as Germany, which succumbed to dictatorship in spite of an advanced educational system) cannot be the sole basis for rejecting the hypothesis. A deviant case, considered within a context which marshals the evidence on all relevant cases, often may actually strengthen the basic hypothesis if an intensive study of it reveals the special conditions which prevented the usual relationship from appearing. Thus, electoral research indicates that a large proportion of the more economically well-to-do leftists are underprivileged along other dimensions of social status, such as ethnic or religious position.

Controversy in this area stems not only from variations in methodology, but also from use of different definitions. Clearly in order to discuss democracy, or any other phenomenon, it is first necessary to define it. For the purposes of this paper, democracy (in a complex society) is defined as a political system which supplies regular constitutional opportunities for changing the governing officials. It is a social mechanism for the resolution of the problem of societal decision-making among conflicting interest groups which permits the largest possible part of the population to influence these decisions through their ability to choose among alternative contenders for political office. In large measure abstracted from the work of Joseph Schumpeter and Max Weber,[1] this definition implies a number of specific conditions: (a) a "political formula," a system of beliefs, legitimizing the democratic system and specifying the institutions—parties, a free press, and so forth—which are legitimized, *i.e.*, accepted as proper by

all; (b) one set of political leaders in office; and (c) one or more sets of leaders, out of office, who act as a legitimate opposition attempting to gain office.

The need for these conditions is clear. *First*, if a political system is not characterized by a value system allowing the peaceful "play" of power—the adherence by the "outs" to decisions made by "ins" and the recognition by "ins" of the rights of the "outs"—there can be no stable democracy. This has been the problem faced by many Latin American states. *Second*, if the outcome of the political game is not the periodic awarding of effective authority to one group, a party or stable coalition, then unstable and irresponsible government rather than democracy will result. This state of affairs existed in pre-Fascist Italy, and for much, though not all of the history of the Third and Fourth French Republics, which were characterized by weak coalition governments, often formed among parties which had major interest and value conflicts with each other. *Third*, if the conditions facilitating the perpetuation of an effective opposition do not exist, then the authority of officials will be maximized, and popular influence on policy will be at a minimum. This is the situation in all one-party states; and by general agreement, at least in the West, these are dictatorships. . . .

No detailed examination of the political history of individual countries will be undertaken in accordance with the generic definition, since the relative degree or social content of democracy in different countries is not the real problem of this paper. Certain problems of method in the handling of relationships between complex characteristics of total societies do merit brief discussion, however.

An extremely high correlation between aspects of social structure, such as income, education, religion, on the one hand, and democracy, on the other, is not to be anticipated even on theoretical grounds, because to the extent that the political sub-system of the society operates autonomously, a particular political form may persist under conditions normally adverse to the *emergence* of that form. Or, a political form may develop because of a syndrome of fairly unique historical factors, even though major social characteristics favor another form. Germany is an example of a nation in which the structural changes—growing industrialization, urbanization, wealth, and education—

[1] Joseph Schumpeter, *Capitalism, Socialism and Democracy* (New York: Harper and Bros., 1947), pp. 232-302, esp. 269; Max Weber, *Essays in Sociology* (New York: Oxford University Press, 1946), p. 226.

all favored the establishment of a democratic system, but in which a series of adverse historical events prevented democracy from securing legitimacy in the eyes of many important segments of society, and thus weakened German democracy's ability to withstand crisis.

The high correlations which appear in the data to be presented between democracy and other institutional characteristics of societies must not be overly stressed, since unique events may account for *either* the persistence *or* the failure of democracy in any particular society. Max Weber argued strongly that differences in national patterns often reflect key historical events which set one process in motion in one country, and a second process in another. To illustrate his point, he used the analogy of a dice game in which each time the dice came up with a certain number they were increasingly loaded in the direction of coming up with that number again. To Weber, an event predisposing a country toward democracy sets a process in motion which increases the likelihood that at the next critical point in the country's history democracy will win out again. This process can only have meaning if we assume that once established, a democratic political system gathers some momentum, and creates some social supports (institutions) to ensure its continued existence. Thus a "premature" democracy which survives will do so by (among other things) facilitating the growth of other conditions conducive to democracy, such as universal literacy, or autonomous private associations. This paper is primarily concerned with explicating the social conditions which serve to *support* a democratic political system, such as education or legitimacy; it will not deal in detail with the kinds of internal mechanisms which serve to *maintain* democratic systems such as the specific rules of the political game.

Comparative generalizations dealing with complex social systems must necessarily deal rather summarily with particular historical features of any one society within the scope of the investigation. In order to test these generalizations bearing on the differences between countries which rank high or low in possession of the attributes associated with democracy, it is necessary to establish some empirical measures of the type of political system. Individual deviations from a particular aspect of democracy are not too important, as long as the definitions unambiguously cover the great majority of nations which are located as democratic or undemocratic. The precise dividing line between "more democratic" and "less democratic" is also not a basic problem, since presumably democracy is *not* a quality of a social system which either does or does not exist, but is rather a complex of characteristics which may be ranked in many different ways. For this reason it was decided to divide the countries under consideration into two groups, rather than to attempt to rank them from highest to lowest. Ranking *individual* countries from the most to the least democratic is much more difficult than splitting the countries into two classes, "more" or "less" democratic, although even here borderline cases such as Mexico pose problems.

Efforts to classify all countries raise a number of problems. Most countries which lack an enduring tradition of political democracy lie in the traditionally underdeveloped sections of the world. It is possible that Max Weber was right when he suggested that modern democracy in its clearest forms can only occur under the unique conditions of capitalist industrialization. Some of the complications introduced by the sharp variations in political practices in different parts of the earth can be reduced by dealing with differences among countries within political culture areas. The two best areas for such internal comparison are Latin America as one, and Europe and the English-speaking countries as the other. More limited comparisons may be made among the Asian states, and among the Arab countries.

The main criteria used in this paper to locate European democracies are the uninterrupted continuation of political democracy since World War I, *and* the absence over the past 25 years of a major political movement opposed to the democratic "rules of the game."[2] The somewhat less stringent criterion employed for Latin America is whether a given country has had a history of more or less free elections for most of the post-World War I period. Where in Europe we look for stable democracies, in South America we look for countries which have not had fairly constant dictatorial rule (See Table I). No detailed analysis of the political history of either Europe or Latin America has been made with an eye toward more specific criteria of differentiation; at this point in the examination of the requisites of democracy, election results are sufficient to locate the European countries, and the judgments of experts and impressionistic assessments based on fairly well-known facts of political history will suffice for Latin America.

---

[2] The latter requirement means that no totalitarian movement, either Fascist or Communist, received 20 per cent of the vote during this time. Actually all the European nations falling on the democratic side of the continuum had totalitarian movements which secured less than seven per cent of the vote.

TABLE 1:   Classification of European, English-speaking and Latin American Nations by Degree of Stable Democracy

| EUROPEAN AND ENGLISH-SPEAKING NATIONS | | LATIN AMERICAN NATIONS | |
STABLE DEMOCRACIES	UNSTABLE DEMOCRACIES AND DICTATORSHIPS	DEMOCRACIES AND UNSTABLE DICTATORSHIPS	STABLE DICTATORSHIPS
Australia	Austria	Argentina	Bolivia
Belgium	Bulgaria	Brazil	Cuba
Canada	Czechoslovakia	Chile	Dominican Republic
Denmark	Finland	Colombia	Ecuador
Ireland	France	Costa Rica	El Salvador
Luxemburg	Germany (West)	Mexico	Guatemala
Netherlands	Greece	Uruguay	Haiti
New Zealand	Hungary		Honduras
Norway	Iceland		Nicaragua
Sweden	Italy		Panama
Switzerland	Poland		Paraguay
United Kingdom	Portugal		Peru
United States	Rumania		Venezuela
	Spain		
	Yugoslavia		

ECONOMIC DEVELOPMENT AND DEMOCRACY

Perhaps the most widespread generalization linking political systems to other aspects of society has been that democracy is related to the state of economic development. Concretely, this means that the more well-to-do a nation, the greater the chances that it will sustain democracy. From Aristotle down to the present, men have argued that only in a wealthy society in which relatively few citizens lived in real poverty could a situation exist in which the mass of the population could intelligently participate in politics and could develop the self-restraint necessary to avoid succumbing to the appeals of irresponsible demagogues. A society divided between a large impoverished mass and a small favored elite would result either in oligarchy (dictatorial rule of the small upper stratum) or in tyranny (popularly based dictatorship). And these two political forms can be given modern labels: tyranny's modern face is Communism or Peronism; oligarchy appears today in the form of traditionalist dictatorships such as we find in parts of Latin America, Thailand, Spain or Portugal.

As a means of concretely testing this hypothesis, various indices of economic development—wealth, industrialization, urbanization and education—have been defined, and averages (means) have been computed for the countries which have been classified as more or less democratic in the Anglo-Saxon world and Europe and Latin America.

In each case, the average wealth, degree of industrialization and urbanization, and level of education is much higher for the more democratic countries . . . . If we had combined Latin America and Europe in one table, the differences would have been greater.

The main indices of *wealth* used here are per capita income, number of persons per motor vehicle and per physician, and the number of radios, telephones, and newspapers per thousand persons. The differences are striking on every score . . . . In the more democratic European countries, there are 17 persons per motor vehicle compared to 143 for the less democratic countries. In the less dictatorial Latin American countries there are 99 persons per motor vehicle, as against 274 for the more dictatorial ones. Income differences for the groups are also sharp, dropping from an average per capita income of $695 for the more democratic countries of Europe to $308 for the less democratic ones; the corresponding difference for Latin America is from $171 to $119. The ranges are equally consistent, with the lowest per capita income in each group falling in the "less democratic" category, and the highest in the "more democratic" one.

Industrialization—indices of wealth are clearly related to this, of course—is measured by the percentage of employed males in agriculture, and the per capita commercially produced "energy" being used in the country, measured in terms of tons of coal per person per year. Both of these indices show equally consistent results. The average percentage of employed males working in agriculture and related occupations was 21 in the "more democratic" European countries, and 41 in the "less democratic," 52 in the "less dictatorial" Latin American countries, and 67 in the "more dictatorial." The differences in per capita energy employed in the country are equally large.

The degree of *urbanization* is also related to the existence of democracy. Three different indices of urbanization are available from data compiled by International Urban Research (Berkeley, California), the percentage of the population in places of 20,000 and over, the percentage in communities of 100,000 and over, and also the percentage residing in standard metropolitan areas. On all three of these indices of urbanization, the more democratic countries score higher than the less democratic, for both of the political culture areas under investigation.

Many have suggested that the better educated the population of a country, the better the chances for democracy, and the comparative data available support this proposition. The "more democratic" countries of Europe are almost entirely literate: the lowest has a rate of 96 per cent, while the "less democratic" nations have an average literacy rate of 85 per cent. In Latin America, the difference is between an average rate of 74 per cent for the "less dictatorial" countries and 46 per cent for the "more dictatorial." The educational enrollment per thousand total population at three different levels, primary, post-primary, and higher educational, is equally consistently related to the degree of democracy. The tremendous disparity is shown by the extreme cases of Haiti and the United States. Haiti has fewer children (11 per thousand) attending school in the primary grades than the United States has attending colleges (almost 18 per thousand).

The relationship between education and democracy is worth more extensive treatment since an entire philosophy of democratic government has seen in increased education the spread of the basic requirement of democracy. . . . Education presumably broadens men's outlooks, enables them to understand the need for norms of tolerance, restrains them from adhering to extremist and monistic doctrines, and increases their capacity to make rational electoral choices.

The evidence bearing on the contribution of education to democracy is even more direct and strong in connection with individual behavior *within* countries, than it is in cross-national correlations. Data gathered by public opinion research agencies which have questioned people in different countries with regard to their belief in various democratic norms of tolerance for opposition, to their attitudes toward ethnic or racial minorities, and with regard to their belief in multi-party as against one-party systems have found that *the most important single factor differentiating those giving democratic responses from others has been education.* The higher one's education, the more likely one is to believe in democratic values and support democratic practices. All the relevant studies indicate that education is far more significant than income or occupation.

These findings should lead us to anticipate a far higher correlation between national levels of education and political practice than in fact we do find. Germany and France have been among the best educated nations of Europe, but this by itself clearly did not stabilize their democracies. It may be, however, that education has served to inhibit other anti-democratic forces. Post-Nazi data from Germany indicate clearly that higher education is linked to rejection of strong-man and one-party government.

If we cannot say that a "high" level of education is a sufficient condition for democracy, the available evidence does suggest that it comes close to being a necessary condition in the modern world. Thus if we turn to Latin America, where widespread illiteracy still exists in many countries, we find that of all the nations in which more than half the population is illiterate, only one, Brazil, can be included in the "more democratic" group.

There is some evidence from other economically impoverished culture areas that literacy is related to democracy. The one member of the Arab League which has maintained democratic institutions since World War II, Lebanon, is by far the best educated (over 80 per cent literacy) of the Arab countries. In the rest of Asia east of the Arab world, only two states, the Philippines and Japan, have maintained democratic regimes without the presence of large anti-democratic parties since 1945. And these two countries, although lower than any European state in per capita income, are among the world's leaders in educational attainment. The Philippines actually ranks second to the United States in its proportion of people attending high school and university, while Japan has a higher level of educational attainment than any European state.

Although the various indices have been presented separately, it seems clear that the factors of industrialization, urbanization, wealth, and education, are so closely interrelated as to form one common factor. And the factors subsumed under economic development carry with it the political correlate of democracy.

Before moving to a discussion of the inner connections between the development complex and democracy, mention may be made of a study of the Middle East, which, in its essential conclusions, substantiates these empirical relationships for another culture area. A survey of six Middle Eastern countries (Turkey, Lebanon, Egypt, Syria, Jordan, and Iran), conducted by the Columbia University Bureau of Applied Social Research in 1950-51, found high associations between urbanization, literacy, voting rates, media consumption and production, and education. Simple and multiple correlations between the four basic variables were computed for all countries for which United Nations statistics were available, in this case 54. The multiple correlations, regarding each as the dependent variable in turn, are as follows:

Dependent Variable	Multiple Correlation Coefficient
Urbanization	.61
Literacy	.91
Media Participation	.84
Political Participation	.82

In the Middle East, Turkey and Lebanon score higher on most of these indices than do the other four countries analyzed, and Lerner points out that the "great post-war events in Egypt, Syria, Jordan and Iran have been the violent struggles for the control of power—struggles notably absent in Turkey and Lebanon, where the control of power has been decided by elections."[3]. . .

Lerner introduces one important theoretical addition, the suggestion that these key variables in the modernization process may be viewed as historical phases, with democracy a part of later developments, the "crowning institution of the participant society," one of his terms for a modern industrial society. His view on the relations between these variables, seen as stages, is worth quoting at some length:

"The secular evolution of a participant society appears to involve a regular sequence of three phases. Urbanization comes first, for cities alone have developed the complex of skills and resources which characterize the modern industrial economy. Within this urban matrix develop both of the attributes which distinguish the next two phases—literacy and media growth. There is a close reciprocal relationship between these, for the literate develop the media which in turn spread literacy. But, literacy performs the key function in the second phase. The capacity to read, at first acquired by relatively few people, equips them to perform the varied tasks required in the modernizing society. Not until the third phase, when the elaborate technology of industrial development is fairly well advanced, does a society begin to produce newspapers, radio networks, and motion pictures on a massive scale. This in turn, accelerates the spread of literacy. Out of this interaction develop those institutions of participation (*e.g.*, voting) which we find in all advanced modern societies."[4]

. . . A number of processes underlie these correlations, observed in many areas of the world, in addition to the effect, already discussed, of a high level of education and literacy in creating or sustaining belief in democratic norms. Perhaps most important is the relationship between modernization and the form of the "class struggle." For the lower strata, economic development, which means increased income, greater economic security, and higher education, permit those in this status to develop longer time perspectives and more complex and gradualist views of politics. . . . Increased wealth and education also serve democracy by increasing the extent to which the

---

[3] The study is reported in Daniel Lerner, *The Passing of Traditional Society* (Glencoe, Ill.: The Free Press of Glencoe, 1958).

[4] *Ibid.*, p. 60. Lerner also focuses upon certain personality requirements of a "modern" society which may also be related to the personality requirements of democracy. According to him, the physical and social mobility of modern society requires a mobile personality, capable of adaptation to rapid change. Development of a "mobile sensibility so adaptive to change that rearrangement of the self-system is its distinctive mode" has been the work of the 20th century. Its main feature is *empathy*, denoting the "general capacity to see oneself in the other fellow's situation, whether favorably or unfavorably." (p. 49 ff.) Whether this psychological characteristic results in a predisposition toward democracy (implying a willingness to accept the viewpoint of others) or is rather associated with the anti-democratic tendencies of a "mass society" type of personality (implying the lack of any solid personal values rooted in rewarding participation) is an open question. Possibly empathy, a more or less "cosmopolitan" outlook, is a general personality characteristic of modern societies, with other special conditions determining whether or not it has the social consequence of tolerance and democratic attitudes, or rootlessness and anomie.

lower strata are exposed to cross pressures which will reduce the intensity of their commitment to given ideologies and make them less receptive to supporting extremist ones. . . . [T]his process . . . essentially . . . functions through enlarging their involvement in an integrated national culture as distinct from an isolated lower class one, and hence increasing their exposure to middle-class values. Marx argued that the proletariat were a revolutionary force because they have nothing to lose but their chains and can win the whole world. But Tocqueville in analyzing the reasons why the lower strata in America supported the system paraphrased and transposed Marx before Marx ever made this analysis, by pointing out that "only those who have nothing to lose ever revolt."[5]

Increased wealth is not only related causally to the development of democracy by changing the social conditions of the workers, but it also affects the political role of the middle class through changing the shape of the stratification structure so that it shifts from an elongated pyramid, with a large lower-class base, to a diamond with a growing middle-class. A large middle class plays a mitigating role in moderating conflict since it is able to reward moderate and democratic parties and penalize extremist groups.

National income is also related to the political values and style of the upper class. The poorer a country, and the lower the absolute standard of living of the lower classes, the greater the pressure on the upper strata to treat the lower classes as beyond the pale of human society, as vulgar, as innately inferior, as a lower caste. The sharp difference in the style of living between those at the top and those at the bottom makes this psychologically necessary. Consequently, the upper strata also tend to regard political rights for the lower strata, particularly the right to share in power, as essentially absurd and immoral. The upper strata not only resist democracy themselves, but their often arrogant political behavior serves to intensify extremist reactions on the part of the lower classes.

The general income level of a nation will also affect its receptivity to democratic political toler-ance norms. The values which imply that it does not matter greatly which side rules, that error can be tolerated even in the governing party can best develop where (a) the government has little power to affect the crucial life chances of most powerful groups, or (b) there is enough wealth in the country so that it actually does not make too much difference if some redistribution does take place. If loss of office is seen as meaning serious loss for major power groups, then they will be readier to resort to more drastic measures in seeking to retain or secure office. The wealth level will also affect the extent to which given countries can develop "universalistic" norms among its civil servants and politicians (selection based on competence; performance without favoritism). The poorer the country, the greater the emphasis which is placed on nepotism, *i.e.*, support of kin and friends. The weakness of the universalistic norms reduces the opportunity to develop efficient bureaucracy, a condition for a modern democratic state.

Less directly linked but seemingly still associated with greater wealth is the presence of intermediary organizations and institutions which can act as sources of countervailing power, and recruiters of participants in the political process in the manner discussed by Tocqueville and other exponents of what has come to be known as the theory of the "mass society." They have argued that a society without a multitude of organizations relatively independent of the central state power has a high dictatorial as well as a revolutionary potential. Such organizations serve a number of functions necessary to democracy: they are a source of countervailing power, inhibiting the state or any single major source of private power from dominating all political resources; they are a source of new opinions; they can be the means of communicating ideas, particularly opposition ideas, to a large section of the citizenry; they serve to train men in the skills of politics; and they help increase the level of interest and participation in politics. Although there are no reliable data which bear on the relationship between national patterns of voluntary organizations and national political systems, evidence from studies of individual behavior within a number of different countries demonstrates that, independently of other factors, men who belong to associations are more likely to hold democratic opinions on questions concerning tolerance and party systems, and are more likely to participate in the political process—to be active or to vote. Since we also know that, within countries, the more well-to-do and the better educated one is, the more likely he is to belong to voluntary organizations, it seems likely that the propensity to form such groups is a function of level of income and opportunities for leisure within given nations.

It is obvious that democracy and the conditions related to stable democracy discussed here are essentially located in the countries of northwest

---

[5] Alexis de Tocqueville, *Democracy in America*, Vol. I (New York: Alfred A. Knopf, Vintage edition, 1945), p. 258.

Europe and their English-speaking offspring in America and Australasia. It has been argued by Max Weber among others that the factors making for democracy in this area are a historically unique concatenation of elements, part of the complex which also produced capitalism in this area. The basic argument runs that capitalist economic development (facilitated and most developed in Protestant areas) created the burgher class whose existence was both a catalyst and a necessary condition for democracy. The emphasis within Protestantism on individual responsibility furthered the emergence of democratic values. The greater initial strength of the middle classes in these countries resulted in an alignment between burghers and throne, an alignment which preserved the monarchy, and thus facilitated the legitimation of democracy among the conservative strata. Thus we have an interrelated cluster of economic development, Protestantism, monarchy, gradual political change, legitimacy and democracy. Men may argue as to whether any aspect of this cluster is primary, but the cluster of factors and forces hangs together. . . .

PROBLEMS OF CONTEMPORARY DEMOCRACY

The characteristic pattern of the stable western democracies in the mid-20th century is that of a "post-politics" phase—there is relatively little difference between the democratic left and right, the socialists are moderates, and the conservatives accept the welfare state. In large measure this reflects the fact that in these countries the workers have won their fight for citizenship and for political access, *i.e.*, the right to take part in all decisions of the body politic on an equal level with others.

The struggle for citizenship had two aspects, political (access to power through the suffrage) and economic (institutionalization of trade union rights to share in the decisions affecting work rewards and conditions). The representatives of the lower strata are now part of the governing classes, members of the club. Political controversy has declined in the wealthier stable democracies because the basic political issue of the industrial revolution, the incorporation of the workers into the legitimate body politic, has been settled. The only key domestic issue today is collective bargaining over differences in the division of the total product within the framework of a Keynesian welfare state; and such issues do not require or precipitate extremism on either side.

In most of Latin and Eastern Europe, the struggle for working-class integration into the body politic was not settled before the Commu-

nists appeared on the scene to take over leadership of the workers. This fact drastically changed the political game, since inherently the Communists could not be absorbed within the system in the way that the Socialists have been. Communist workers, their parties and trade unions, cannot possibly be accorded the right of access by a democratic society. The Communists' self-image and more particularly their ties to the Soviet Union lead them to accept a self-confirming hypothesis. Their self-definition prevents them from being allowed access and this in turn reinforces the sense of alienation from the system (of not being accepted by the other strata) which workers in nations with large Communist parties have. And the more conservative strata are reinforced in their belief that giving increased rights to the workers or their representatives threatens all that is good in life. Thus, the presence of Communists precludes an easy prediction that economic development will stabilize democracy in these European countries.

In the newly independent nations of Asia, the situation is somewhat different. In Europe at the beginning of modern politics, the workers were faced with the problem of winning citizenship, the right to take part in the political game, from the dominant aristocratic and business strata who controlled politics. In Asia the long-term presence of colonial rulers has identified conservatism as an ideology and the more well-to-do classes with subservience to colonialism; while leftist ideologies, usually of a Marxist variety, have been dominant, being identified with nationalism. The trade unions and the workers' parties of Asia have been part of the political process from the beginning of the democratic system. Conceivably such a situation could mean a stable democracy, except for the fact that these lower-strata rights pre-date the development of a stable economy with a large middle class and an industrial society.

The whole system stands on its head. The left in the European stable democracies grew gradually in a fight for more democracy, and gave expression to the discontents involved in early industrialization, while the right retained the support of traditionalist elements in the society, until eventually the system came into an easy balance between a modified left and right. In Asia, the left is in power during the period of population explosion and early industrialization, and must accept responsibility for all the consequent miseries. As in the poorer areas of Europe, the Communists exist to capitalize on all these discontents in completely irresponsible fashion, and currently are a major party, usually the second largest in most Asian states.

Given the existence of poverty-stricken masses, low levels of education, an elongated pyramid class structure, and the "premature" triumph of the democratic left, the prognosis for the perpetuation of political democracy in Asia and Africa is bleak. The nations which have the best prospects, Israel, Japan, Lebanon, the Philippines and Turkey, tend to resemble Europe in one or more major factors, high educational level (all except Turkey), substantial and growing middle class, and the retention of political legitimacy by non-leftist groups. The other emerging national states in Asia and Africa are committed more deeply to a certain tempo and pattern of economic development and to national independence, under whatever political form, than they are to the pattern of party politics and free elections which exemplify our model of democracy. It seems likely that in countries which avoid Communist or military dictatorship political developments will follow the pattern developing in countries such as Ghana, Tunisia or Mexico, where an educated minority uses a mass movement expressing leftist slogans to exercise effective control, and holds elections as a gesture toward ultimate democratic objectives, and as a means of estimating public opinion, not as effective instruments for legitimate turnover in office of governing parties. Given the pressure for rapid industrialization and for the immediate solution of chronic problems of poverty and famine through political agencies, it is unlikely that many of the new governments of Asia and Africa will be characterized by an open party system representing basically different class positions and values.

Latin America, underdeveloped economically like Asia, is, however, politically more like Europe in the early 19th century than like Asia today. Most Latin American countries became independent states before the rise of industrialism and Marxist ideologies, and contain strongholds of traditional conservatism. The countryside is often apolitical or traditional, and the leftist movements secure support primarily from the industrial proletariat. Latin American communists, for example, have chosen the European Marxist path of organizing urban workers, rather than the "Yenan way" of Mao, seeking a peasant base. If Latin America is allowed to develop on its own, and is able to increase its productivity and middle classes, there is a good chance that many Latin American countries will follow in the European direction. Recent developments, including the overthrowal of a number of dictatorships, in large measure reflect the effects of an increased middle class, growing wealth, and increased education. There is, however, also the possibility that these countries may yet follow in the French and Italian direction rather than that of northern Europe, that the communists will seize the leadership of the workers, and that the middle class will be alienated from democracy.

The analysis of the social requisites for democracy contained in this paper has sought to identify some, though obviously far from all, of the structural conditions which are linked to this political system. It has been possible in a very limited fashion to attempt some tests of the hypotheses suggested. These preliminary efforts to apply the method of science to comparative political systems can still be considered only as illustrative since we can say so little about actual variations in national social structures. Considerably more research must be done specifying the boundaries of various societies along many dimensions before reliable comparative analysis of the sort attempted here can be carried out. . . .

The data available are, however, of a sufficiently consistent character to support strongly the conclusion that a more systematic and up-to-date version of Aristotle's hypothesis concerning the relationship of political forms to social structure is valid. Unfortunately, as has been indicated above, this conclusion does not justify the optimistic liberal's hope that an increase in wealth, in the size of the middle class, in education, and other related factors will necessarily mean the spread of democracy or the stabilizing of democracy. As Max Weber, in discussing the chances for democracy in Russia in the early 20th century pointed out: "The spread of Western cultural and capitalist economy did not, *ipso facto*, guarantee that Russia would also acquire the liberties which had accompanied their emergence in European history. . . . European liberty had been born in unique, perhaps unrepeatable, circumstances at a time when the intellectual and material conditions for it were exceptionally propitious."

These suggestions that the peculiar concatenation of factors which gave rise to western democracy in the nineteenth century may be unique are not meant to be unduly pessimistic. Political democracy exists and has existed in a variety of circumstances, even if it is most commonly sustained by a limited cluster of conditions. To understand more fully the various conditions under which it has existed may make possible the development of democracy elsewhere. Democracy is not achieved by acts of will alone; but men's wills, through action, can shape institutions and events in directions that reduce or increase the chance for the development and survival of democracy. . . .

Recent Research
Don Martindale

Institutions are collective human arrangements arising in the course of the survival of human pluralities through time, as they wrest the things needed for life from nature and create them by their own efforts. In short, institutions are solutions to collective problems.[1]

The study of institutions has three natural divisions: (1) the examination of the internal structure of institutions as a response to the empirical problems of social life (for example, the distribution of activities in various component roles of group members or the study of the psychological components—Oedipal relations, authoritarian demands, etc.—of various role occupants); (2) the exploration of the influence of institutions arising in one area of social life on those in another (for instance, the influence of religious ethic on economic behavior, illustrated by Max Weber's famous studies)[2]; and (3) the study of changes in the internal structure of institutions as a product of the external social *milieu* (as when women follow domestic industry from the home into the factory, thereby securing a more nearly equal economic status with men, and return to the home as democratic equals). Any one (or all three) of the divisions of institutional study may be considered within a theoretical or a practical context.

The theoretical study of institutions is undertaken to extend scientific knowledge. It normally takes the form of research into one or more of the problems of a variety of institutions from the standpoint of hypotheses derived from some general theory of social life. In the inter-war period, for example, much research was carried on in a variety of institutions (families, religious groups, political parties, etc.) in an attempt to ascertain the extent to which their internal structures were a product of the types of psychological configurations (such as the Oedipus complex) described by Freudian psychology. A second group of studies of institutions was conducted during the same period to verify hypotheses derived from the role-theory of George Herbert Mead.

The practical study of institutions, on the other hand, is undertaken to resolve current issues and not primarily to extend the growing body of scientific knowledge—though this may occur incidentally. As the changes in on-going society bring the institutions of one sphere into conflict with those of another, trends may appear which, if they persist, threaten to transform the traditional values of the institutional area. Consequences of the dynamics of social change are experienced as tensions, strains, and crises for which solutions are sought: depressions may destroy the economic foundations of families and threaten their members with a temporary or permanent decline in socioeconomic status; wars uproot families and tear them from the contexts of local, normative controls that once held them firmly in place, leading to increased numbers of mixed social and ethnic marriages; periods of prosperity may lead to baby booms which eventually place new tensions on educational systems; technological displacements send new masses into universities and other institutions of higher learning and not only strain their facilities to the breaking point but open long-range possibilities for the formation of a new white-collar proletariat.

In the long run, the significance of institutional research for laymen and professionals alike can be assessed only when the theoretical or practical (or joint) context within which the research appears is established. A conventional kind of ceremonial obeisance is given to the need to anchor a given piece of research to its relevant context by the practice of "reviewing the literature." Unfortunately, however, the "review of the literature" which prefaces written accounts of most sociological research is seriously deficient in definitely establishing the theoretical or practical context of the research findings. It usually consists of little more than the citation of a few items more or less in accord with the task at hand or, preferably, against which an argument is to be made. Furthermore, the literature reviewed often is more in need of contextual assessment than the research itself. As a result, sociological research in the field of institutions superficially resembles a kaleidoscopic collection of fragments.

THEORETICAL CONTEXTS OF POST-WAR INSTITUTIONAL RESEARCH

Most scientifically significant research arises in response to theoretical problems derived from sets of basic hypotheses about the nature and composition of social life. All sociologists agree that, in detail, human social life consists of specific interhuman acts and that these interhuman acts are formed into groups and communities. However, quite different implications for social life flow from assuming one or another of these phenomena to be basic. Moreover, different implications flow from the manner in which a given supposedly fundamental social phenomenon is analyzed into subcomponents.

In the brief space available here, only the broadest characterization of the types of theory is possible.[3] Nevertheless, no distortion is involved in visualizing the range of sociological theories as falling into two very broad basic types: atomistic (conceiving the primary social reality to be social acts or some other type of interhuman behavior which serve as basic building blocks to all other social phenomena) and holistic (conceiving the primary social reality to be some form of the collective within which individuals and their behaviors are working parts). Atomistic and holistic social theories are further differentiated in terms of the peculiar "atom" or "collective" considered primary. The major sociological theories are charted in the following table.

Basic Suppositions of the Major Types of Sociological Theories

	TYPES OF THEORIES	PRIMARY SOCIAL REALITY CONSISTS OF:
Atomistic	1. Social Behaviorism	meaningful social acts
	2. Phenomenological Sociology	psychic states
	3. Neo-Kantian Formalism	forms of interhuman processes
	4. Conflict Sociology	encounters of conflict processes
Holistic	1. Functionalism	the total social system conceived as an organic whole
	2. Marxian Sociology	economic class
	3. Neo-Thomistic Sociology	the religious collective or church

If researchers into institutions and their interrelations progressed in a self-conscious manner from all of these theoretical perspectives, the spectacle would be wondrous to behold, but few of the atomistic theories have ever had major followings in the United States. Phenomenological sociology, however, is sponsored in Europe at present by such giants as Georges Gurvitch and Karl Jaspers. Neo-Kantian formalism had largely run its course by the mid-1930's without significantly influencing research; recently some of the small-group theorists have worked with a few of its formulations (particularly those of Georg Simmel, but in an unsystematic manner. Since the great days of Albion Small, the individualistic forms of conflict theory have had few sponsors in the United States (except for notable individuals such as George B. Vold).[4]

Among the holistic theories, neither Marxism nor neo-Thomism has had any major influence on institutional research in the United States. Neo-Thomistic orientations have gradually been introduced in several Roman Catholic colleges and universities, but too recently to have yet made a major impact on institutional research. Marxian sociology has been even less influential. In a notable study, H. D. Lasswell and Dorothy Blumenstock[5] demonstrated that even during the 1930's, when Marxist perspectives had their greatest opportunity for success, they exercised little influence even on practical social action in this country, to say nothing of research. During and since the war, the United States has been distinctly hostile to Marxism.

Only two major theoretical perspectives have had discernible influence upon institutional research in the United States—social behaviorism and functionalism—and only functionalism has become fully established. Social behavioristic views have occasionally appeared either as common-sense orientations or in hypotheses drawn from outstanding social behaviorists, but not in relation to the broader theory of which they were a part.

The influence of social behaviorism on institutional research in the postwar period in the United States derives from two sources. Many of America's greatest social theorists were research-oriented social behaviorists. They included such persons as Robert MacIver, William I. Thomas, Charles Cooley, George Herbert Mead, William Ogburn, and F. Stuart Chapin, and their research activities were continued in the postwar period either by themselves or by their students. Added to this research impulse was the introduction of Max Weber's ideas, first by the translation of many of his key essays by Hans Gerth and C. Wright Mills and then by the translation of Henderson and Parsons.[6] Suggestions from this pool of social behavioristic ideas, particularly those of Weber, have been taken particularly for the study of political and religious institutions and, to some extent for the study of educational and business-industrial institutions. Hypotheses drawn from Weber's theories concerning such phenomena as "bureaucratization," "class," "status," "party," "legitimate order," "the rationalization of social structure," "charismatic," "traditional," "legalistic authority," and "the influence of religious ethic on economic conduct" have been central to many of the studies. Unfortunately, most of these researches have not systematically related the hypotheses drawn from Weber or other social behaviorists back to the original body of theory. Hence the social behavioristic impulse in recent institutional research has been desultory and chaotic and has led to such ironic consequences as the failure of research students to follow up with concrete research the brilliant theoretical integration (from a social behavioristic point of view) of political sociology by H. D. Lasswell and Abraham Kaplan.[7]

In contrast to the unself-conscious manner in which social behaviorist perspectives have guided institutional research, functionalistically oriented research has constituted a well organized program. It is a tribute to the influence of the prestigeful private colleges and to the position of the sociological leaders of this movement (particularly Robert Merton,[8] Talcott Parsons,[9] and George Caspar Homans[10]) that for a time in the postwar period functionalistic perspectives were clamped down so firmly on American sociology as to cause many persons to believe that functionalism and social theory are virtually identical terms. Self-conscious functionalistic perspectives have been most prominent in the institutional spheres of the family, medicine, education, and, above all, industry. By contrast, social behaviorist perspectives have been strongest in the spheres of political and administrative structures and religion.

There is some evidence, however, that many contemporary sociologists have grown somewhat restive under the functionalist regime; the functionalistic analysis of institutions may well have reached a temporary saturation point. The turning point in the extension of functionalistic perspectives may be marked by Sherman Krupp's critical review of the consequences of institutional research on the business firm in terms of functionalistic suppositions.[11] He observes that "the functionalistic approach characteristically assumes the unity or purpose of the whole and views the parts as they contribute to this unity. Like arms, or legs, or the brain, the parts work in harmony to serve or fulfill the good of the whole." However, Krupp continues, the danger of the functionalist approach is its tendency to conceal "harmony-laden teleologies. Thus, an interpretation of the business firm through the language of 'group cooperation' may be analogous to a description of a jungle using a theory of a farm."

Although criticisms equivalent to those of Krupp of the functionalistic analyses of the family, medical institutions, and educational institutions remain to be investigated, there is some evidence that in these areas, also, distortions have occurred that are similar to those that Krupp demonstrated in the functionalistic studies of the business firm. The effect on institutional research of the growing dissatisfaction with functionalism will probably be two-fold: to raise to new self-consciousness the social behavioristic research perspectives and to create new interest in other theoretical perspectives, such as conflict theory or perhaps even phenomenological sociology.

PRACTICAL CONTEXTS OF POSTWAR INSTITUTIONAL RESEARCH

Ideally, research in a science should proceed out of its theories. However, in a field such as sociology, characterized by fragmented theoretical perspectives on the one hand and by the slight differentiation of its problems from those of common sense on the other, a mutually disadvantageous separation of theorists and researchers has developed. As a result, much institutional research is undertaken merely because the researcher has a talent for securing research funds and is guided by a feeling that certain problems are in some unspecified sense important.

The hypothesis is tentatively offered that when common theoretical-practical grounds are sought to guide institutional research, it will be found that changes in the structure of social life have begun to place pressure on traditional values and practices. If this hypothesis is correct, it would help account (in connection with the prevailing functionalism of the postwar period) for the fragmentation of perspectives in research situations. Functionalism operates on the assumption that there is an essential organism-like harmony in the social system, but many researchers take up their problems not because they represent harmonies in the social system but because the problems seem to be tendencies destructive of traditional features of the way of life. Research workers in concrete situations, thus, have often found functionalistic theory an obstacle rather than an aid and have then dismissed it (and all theory) as unrealistic, if not false.

Some attempt was made in *American Social Structure*[12] and in *American Society*[13] to document the hypothesis that the dynamism of American society has been supplied by the destruction of forms of the local community and by the formation and consolidation of the national community. In the course of this transformation, an extensive liquidation of traditional values takes place, with consequences for all institutions and all major formations of traditional culture. As a product of these changes, the old division of institutions as economic, political, religious, etc. has become obsolete, and a reorganization of institutions into those concerned with *socialization, the mastery of nature, and social control* has been proposed. It is hoped that such a reorganization will bring the theoretical and practical contexts of institutional research into closer accord.

References

1. Don Martindale, *Social Life and Cultural Change* (Princeton, N.J.: D. Van Nostrand Co., Inc., 1962), p. 39. For alternative definitions of institutions, see the footnote on pp. 39-40.
2. Max Weber, *The Protestant Ethic and the Spirit of Capitalism*, 2nd ed., trans. Talcott Parsons (New York: Charles Scribner's Sons, 1958).
3. For a fuller examination, see Don Martindale, *The Nature and Types of Sociological Theory* (Boston: Houghton Mifflin Co., 1960).
4. Don Martindale, *The Nature and Types of Sociological Theory* (Boston: Houghton Mifflin Company, 1960), Ch. 8.
5. H. D. Lasswell and Dorothy Blumenstock, *World Revolutionary Propaganda* (Alfred A. Knopf, Inc., 1939).
6. Hans H. Gerth and C. Wright Mills, trans. and eds., *From Max Weber: Essays in Sociology* (New York: Oxford Press, 1958). A. M. Henderson and Talcott Parsons, *The Theory of Social and Economic Organizations* (New York: Oxford University Press, 1947).
7. H. D. Lasswell and Abraham Kaplan, *Power and Society* (New Haven, Conn.: Yale University Press, 1950).
8. Robert Merton, *Social Theory and Social Structure* (Glencoe, Ill.: The Free Press, 1957).
9. Talcott Parsons, *The Structure of Social Action* (Glencoe, Ill.: The Free Press, 1949).
10. George Homans, *The Human Group* (New York: Harcourt, Brace & World, Inc., 1950).
11. Sherman Krupp, *Pattern in Organization Analysis* (Philadelphia: Chilton Company, 1961).
12. Don Martindale, *American Social Structure* (New York: Appleton-Century-Crofts, 1960).
13. Don Martindale, *American Society* (Princeton: D. Van Nostrand Co., Inc., 1960).

Part VIII

THE SOCIAL RANKS

It may be good politics to say that all men are created equal, but it is a fairly obvious social fact that while this might be true at the ballot box it is not true in *all* respects in the United States. Moving forward from the inequalities of birth, the observers will note an increasing number of inequalities in the objective characteristics of men. Further, these inequalities may be multiplied by the perspectives of the persons to whom the subject men are significant. As a matter of fact, our society would be both confused and confusing if men were equal in all respects in the eyes of all. American society is not presently organized in terms of general equality. In fact, the most significant features of the persons with whom we interact are usually the ones that are *different* from those of other persons.

In our society, age makes a difference in the way we interact with others. (It even makes a difference at the ballot box mentioned above.) Sex makes a difference in the way we interact with others, too. Differences in occupation, education, income, race, family background, nearness of kin, religious belief, and many other factors clearly play a part in the way people behave toward one another in different situations. In each of these factors there are inequalities, at least in the minds of some perceivers. The division of a population into discrete categories of occupations, extent of education, or some other factor such as those mentioned above is called *social differentiation* in sociological research literature.

When Herbert Spencer first used the term *social differentiation* he referred to social "organs" comprised of persons who developed specialized functions in the structure of society as the society evolved. Spencer modeled his theory of society upon a biological analogy; his use of the term *differentiation* was borrowed directly from embryology. Since Spencer's day, a somewhat different concept of social differentiation has come into vogue. As many sociologists now use it, the term is virtually synonymous with social categorization. It refers to the division of a social aggregate into categories according to some referent such as sex, age, income, race, and so forth, or an index combining several such referents. The persons in each category have in common a range of the referent, in kind or degree, and are distinguished from persons in other categories who share different ranges. Each category is called a *status* in structure-functional explanations of society.

As developed in Selections 66-68 by Richard T. LaPiere, Ray Gold, and Thomas E. Lasswell, the concept of social status implies the comparison of a person (or persons) with other persons or categories of persons. Because an individual has many qualities, because there are many perspectives from which he may be perceived, and because he may be perceived or imagined in many different social contexts or situations, it is impossible to assign any summary or general status to an individual. Thus *the* status of a person is not very meaningful unless it has an implicit or explicit referent. Every person has many statuses.

Let us review a few of the statuses of Oliver Wendell Holmes, Senior, some of whose several statuses are widely known. For example, his family name, Holmes, indicates a kind of status; it identifies him as a member of one of the Holmes families—an item of special significance to such persons as genealogists, geneticists, students of Americana, socially minded Bostonians, and many lawyers and physicians. Holmes not only assumed the status of a poet for himself, but he was also assigned this status both by other poets and by readers. If we take the status of poet in its usual sense, it implies the status of being literate. It implies for many that Holmes must have had average or better-than-average intelligence, a status that is supported by his status as a physician.

Holmes' first name, Oliver, reveals that he had the status of a male. He also had the status of husband and the status of father (the father of a United States Supreme Court Justice, at that). He was a graduate of Harvard University. He was a Bostonian. Furthermore, we might compute his status within many of the categories mentioned. His status as a poet may be debated, but probably he can be assigned to a range of statuses upon which almost everyone would agree— most persons, for example, would certainly agree that he was a lesser poet than William Shakespeare and a greater poet than Edgar A. Guest.

Can there be an expression of Holmes' *general* status? Is it possible to place him in a master category that will express *all* of his statuses or his standing relative to the *total* community? We are inclined to think not, although some scholars have used *social class* to designate the "sum" of all a person's statuses.

The term *social class* is part of the normal vocabulary of all Americans; even those relatively few who deny the existence of social classes in this country impute some meaning to the phrase when it is used. Investigation of its uses by Americans reveals not merely that different persons use the term with different meanings, but even that the same person often uses *social class* to refer to several rather distinct concepts. Sometimes he uses the term to denote an associational phenomenon, referring to clubs, parties, schools, families, cliques, and friendship circles. Defined in this way, a social class is composed of real, whole people whose belonging together is the essence of their class membership.

A second use of *social class* refers not to associations but to culture as revealed by a person's speech patterns, his ways of thinking, his manners, his taste in clothes, furniture, art, and music, and the way he rears his children. While people do not need to be in interaction to constitute a social class according to this definition, they are still real, whole people whose social class is judged as an integral category by those with whom they are in interaction. An upper-class person from Charleston, South Carolina, has, in this sense of social class, ways of thinking, feeling, believing, and behaving that are quite similar to those of an upper-class person from Seattle, Washington—or that would at least be recognized as upper class should these two persons meet. In many ways, the thoughts, feelings, beliefs, and behaviors of the two would be more alike than those of either are like those of lower-class persons in their own home towns. In this usage, a social class is a category of persons who have a common culture within the context of a great culture—a special variant of the national culture that is distinguishable from other such variants. This concept of social class underlies Clifton Fadiman's article (Selection 72).

A third way in which *social class* is used is to refer to influence or power categories in a society. Although the members of a social class defined in this sense may be in interaction and may indeed share a common culture, these qualities are peripheral. The central quality of social class is the extent to which categories of people are able to influence or to control behaviors and beliefs, lives and fortunes of others either informally or through the formal agencies of government, the church, education, and so forth. Once again, people in the various influence classes are whole people, integrated organisms that are inseparable from the influence they exert, just as persons in the classes previously defined are inseparable from their associational selves or their cultural selves.

A fourth and more recent usage of the term *social class* differs conceptually from the first three to a marked degree. It deals largely with abstract qualities of persons rather than with integral personalities. It is concerned with the division of society into horizontal strata having characteristic ranges of income, years of education, occupational statuses, types of housing, or socioeconomic scores derived by arranging several such factors along a common scale. Since the categories of social class are determined from abstract demographic data, it is not necessary for research personnel to observe people in interaction or to hear their judgments of one another to determine their social class assignments according to this concept, which is essentially that of John F. Cuber and William F. Kenkel in Selection 69. Because the underlying assumptions of this definition of social class are so different from the basic assumptions of the three preceding definitions, some scholars feel that it should not properly be called social class. Such is the conviction of Arnold Rose, who presents this position in Selection 73.

The concept of social class presented in the paragraph above is widely used in current sociological research under the name *social stratification,* which is defined as the division of a large social entity into unequal categories. Sometimes the unequal categories are called social classes; sometimes they are called *social strata.* Since there are many bases for the division of a society into unequal categories, it seems logical to use *social stratification* as a general term and *social class* as a more specific term. Social classes, in other words, constitute *one kind* of social strata. Thus we might speak of income stratification, racial stratification, socioeconomic stratification, or social class stratification, all under the general heading of social stratification.

Factors of social organization may be lacking in demographic studies of stratification. Such factors are not included because they are often nonquantifiable, nonrational, or local in applicability. On the other hand, these same factors are frequently essential to assessment of social class when it is defined according to the associational, cultural, or influence concepts. No demographic device has yet been used which can measure the impact of family history and reputation or of close friendships on social class as it is traditionally defined. Demographic data are not available in large-scale quantities on voice melody, the choice of phrases in conversation (of which Fadiman speaks), or the use of cloth napkins for breakfast. The social classes identified by means of demographic indexes are therefore at best only approximations of the social classes observed in interaction.

One cannot predict the taste or the social influence of Miss Minnie Masterson of Moss Point, Mississippi, on the basis of demographic data alone; one needs to know the social history of Moss Point, the loves, hates, feuds, and friendships not only of this generation but of generations past, and the uncontemplated conjunctures of events that shaped the beliefs and behaviors of a thousand people. Even Miss Minnie incorporates the products of her social heritage into her own beliefs and behaviors largely through feelings and sentiments rather than through a rational process. The relationship between social classes and demographic social strata must be expressed in terms of probability.

The final three selections in this part deal with changes in status. Movement from one occupation to another, from one income bracket to another, from one social class to another, or from one way of life to another is as important as is movement from one dwelling to another. Such movement is called *social mobility*. The original definitive article on social mobility is Selection 74 by Pitirim A. Sorokin. Social mobility seems to be accomplished more easily in some societies than in others. A society in which one might expect to die as a constituent of a different social class from the one into which he was born—or of a different income, educational, or occupational level—is called an *open* society. At the other extreme is the *caste* society, in which social class, occupation, educational achievement, and income level are determined at birth. In a caste society, marriage across caste boundaries is unthinkable.

Social stratification involves the perception of people as different and the fixing of significance to the differences that are perceived. It may well be that our distant ancestors would consider our society homogenized if they could see it in action; surely we have moved far in the direction of becoming outwardly very much alike. Nevertheless, most of us would be greatly distressed if we had to live in a society where everyone was exactly like everyone else and where we did not have the opportunity to be superior (or, if we chose, inferior) to other people in ways that we value.   *T. E. L.*

Selection *66*

The Dimensions of Social Status
Richard T. LaPiere

Although *status* is one of the most frequently used terms in sociological literature and, according to a recent survey, is rated by American sociologists as one of the most indispensable concepts, it varies in usage from a quite specific denotation to a rather indefinite generality. Pronounced "stay'-tus" by professional sociologists interested in this particular area of sociology, it deals in its most specific sense with the comparison of a person (or persons) to others or with the nature of the relationship between a person (or persons) and others.

In its comparative usage, status designates a category into which a person falls in contrast to the categories into which other people fall. The status of being "rich" indicates which of the categories concerned with the possession of material wealth is applicable to a particular person. "Rich" implies that other people are "poor" or "of modest means" or "comfortable" with regard to the same value-referent (wealth), even though these other categories are not specifically designated. The designation of a person as "a professional man" refers usually to the occupational category into which he falls and thus implicitly compares his occupational status to that of others.

The status of "mother" indicates the relationship between one person and another or others. Although it is true that the term *mother* may also be used as a category of persons, it generally indicates a specific relationship between specific persons. Whether or not a person is your mother depends very particularly upon who you are! Being rich or being a professional person may not designate a particular relationship to a particular person, but being a mother does. In Selection 67, Gold studies the categorical and particular relationships between janitors and tenants.

Apart from the specific denotations of status described in the two paragraphs above is a usage that refers to a person's general standing in society. Sometimes there is a high degree of consensus in a community about the general standing of specific persons, but in most communities the variety of perspectives precludes the ordering of their members into categories of "general status" except by means of indexes developed from particular statuses.

In the present reading, LaPiere undertakes an analysis of how status assignments affect persons. The student will recognize that it is impossible to comprehend all the statuses of any person, since many of them relate to specific other people and cannot have an objective meaning in the usual sense of that term.

Given the socially granted right to live, a right that is always subject to withdrawal, the level of life that any individual enjoys is mainly dependent upon his social status. Social status is commonly thought of as the position which an individual has in his society. It is not, however, a position comparable to the position that a building occupies relative to other structures in a city. In the first place, the individual has not only one but many positions in society; he may be king to his subjects, but he is also husband to his wife and father to his children. In the second place, the social status or position of an individual is not a static condition, as is the location of a building. It is, rather, the product of a dynamic process of interaction, a process that is somewhat analogous to the vast complex of molecular behaviors which determine the position of a given molecule relative to all the other molecules which make up a fluid at a given moment.

Like his right to live, the status that an individual enjoys in his society is socially granted. The individual has no social status in subsocial nature. The fictional castaway Robinson Crusoe was devoid of social status until he discovered his man Friday and was wholly dependent upon his own efforts; for nature—the fishes in the sea, the plants and animals of the land, etc.—never bows to man's will, never caters to his needs, responds to his pleas, or even concedes him the right to survival. Man can and often does domesticate lower animals; and in so doing he gains a kind of status with them. Thus the farmer's cows may come at his call, and the master's dog will probably welcome him home with wagging tail and other indications of affection. But the status

that can be accorded the individual by his cows or his dog is a trifling thing compared with the social status that may be and usually is granted him by his parents in infancy, his siblings in childhood, and his wife and children and neighbors in maturity. Man's truest friend may possibly be his dog; but his best friends are his fellow men. Without fellow men to grant him social status, and unless they do grant him status, he is somewhat less than human.

Many factors determine the particular kinds of social status that a given individual will be granted, and some of these factors will be considered shortly. The provision of any particular status is accomplished through the relevant personality attributes—the sentiments, values, etc.—of those human beings who are involved in social interactions with him. The elements of such interaction are symbols (such as a welcoming smile) which reflect esteem in which the individual is held; services (including gifts and other tangible contributions to his welfare) which are evidence of the responsibilities that are felt toward him; and demands (such as the share of the crop that a landlord may take from his tenant) which are evidence of the responsibilities that he is felt to have toward others.

The evidences of social status are for the most part manifest in social situations, *i.e.*, through the conduct toward the individual of persons with whom he is for the moment situationally involved. But whereas social situations are always transitory, the social status of an individual always has considerable and often great stability through time. The maintenance of a given order of social status through many transitory social situations is accomplished in one of two ways: either through the fact that the varying personnel of successive situations accord, for whatever reason, the individual the same status position—as men may everywhere and upon all occasions recognize as and treat a woman as a lady; or through the fact that successive situations are composed of the same persons. Both these conditions presuppose the existence of organized social life, the former of such large forms of organization as those of class, and the latter of such smaller forms of organization as family, community, club, and the like. Social status may therefore be defined as the position granted an individual in the organized activities of his fellow men.

Status and self-definition

The social status that a given individual enjoys —or, more properly speaking, the various status positions that he is granted—tends to determine in large measure the definition that he makes of himself. This fact has long been recognized; and various terms—*e.g.*, "the looking-glass self," "the reflected self," "ego involvements," etc.—have been used to describe the resulting phenomenon. It is evident that, other things being equal, the status accorded a child by those who are mainly responsible for his socialization determines the personality attributes that the child will acquire. Thus a parentally idolized child will most certainly acquire, among other attributes, a much higher concept of his own value than will one who is unwanted and is so treated. Such long-run consequences of status are, however, of less interest to the student of social control than are the comparatively short-run effects on an individual's self-definition of a change—for better or worse—in any status to which he has become accustomed. Any considerable change in an individual's status, such as that which occurs when the fortunes of war or intercollegiate football result in an inconspicuous lad's being acclaimed a hero or that which occurs when a respected man is caught in a scandalous activity, is likely to lead the individual to redefine himself (a process which the psychologists sometimes describe as "restructuring" the personality). . . .

THE STATUS ROLE

The individual who is granted status of any sort . . . is expected to act in certain specified ways, even as he can expect others to act toward him in certain specified ways. He is in a sense expected to play a role, specifically the role that is prescribed for and associated with the particular status position that he has been granted. The role may range all the way from that of slave to that of king, from that of indentured servant to that of pampered daughter of the family, from that of hunted criminal to that of wealthy and respected banker. Whatever the role, he is expected to live up to its requirements, to behave in terms of it. If he is granted the status of king, he is expected to behave as king, to play the role of king, not that of slave or something else. In the analysis that follows, the term "status role" will be used whenever attention is focused, not on the status itself, but on the behavior of the individual in the particular status position that he has been accorded.

Status rights

Each status role involves a variety of more or less clearly defined and rigidly maintained rights. The tribal elder may have, among other things, the right to food—and perhaps the choicest bits of food at that—although he himself no longer hunts or works in the fields. . . .

. . . The status of professor usually has a number of obvious rights that distinguish the professor from students and from all others who do not share that status . . . .

He has the right to question the authority of tradition and to disagree on intellectual grounds with his economic and political superiors. Functionally related to this right is that of tenure in his academic position, a right which means that he cannot be punished economically for failure to agree with his superiors on intellectual matters. Even more subtle, but quite significant, is the right to say "I do not know" or, as it is usually put, "The facts are not yet evident." This right, the right to withhold judgment, is peculiarly academic; most occupational roles—*e.g.*, that of politician, priest, physician, or businessman—do not grant it.

The aforementioned and all the other obvious and subtle professorial rights are, of course, subject to considerable variation. Some institutions demand comparative subservience of the individual faculty man; thus in a religious college an agnostic either holds his tongue or loses his position. A young instructor—an apprentice professor—has somewhat fewer rights and holds even these in lesser degree than does a mature and established man. All of which is another way of getting at the fact that a given status role—professor, housewife, or priest—is actually a status category within which a variety of specific roles exist, each with something of its own special rights. Thus a professor of biology has greater right to speak freely (even to the point of contradicting one of his noted colleagues) on biological matters than does a professor of psychology, who as an authority on psychology is granted greater right to speak his mind on this subject.

What has been said of the rights, obvious and subtle, of the professorial role in our society applies in principle to all of the more clearly defined status rolls. The good neighbor may, for example, have the right to address his fellow neighbors by nickname, joke with their wives, borrow their garden tools, mow his lawn on Sunday, and give a big and noisy party for his business acquaintances once in a while; the store clerk who is liked by his fellows may have such rights as his choice of women customers (where an informal rotation system operates and he is, perhaps, exceptionally successful with women) and the right to borrow a few dollars from his co-workers when he is running short of money; the member in good standing of an informal club may have the right to play bad golf and joke about it or perhaps even the right to break a few rules in order to keep his score down, the right to assert his opinions in conversation with fellow members, and the right to a warm welcome whenever he turns up.

Individually the various rights of a status role may appear trivial, and to value them may seem a matter of petty personal pride. *In toto,* however, the rights of a status role may actually constitute the individual's most prized "possession," the direct source of most of the psychological satisfactions that he secures in life, and in many instances an essential part of his basic right to live at all.

Status symbols

One of the rights of every clearly defined status role is the use of some particular status symbol or symbols. The military, for example, wear uniforms distinctive to their particular service, thereby distinguishing themselves from brother services and from civilians. Within any particular service the clothing of officers is, moreover, sufficiently different from that of the ranks so that officers and men are distinguishable at a glance; still further differentiating both officers and men are the symbols of rank—the bars and oak leaves, the

stripes and chevrons, etc. Status symbols of nonmilitary groups are somewhat less obvious but are usually meaningful to the initiate. Clothing, in its design, color, or quality, is a common status symbol. For example, no one could possibly, even at first glance, mistake a bobby-soxer for a fashionable woman; and among fashionable women there are all sorts of meaningful symbols indicating their rank relative to one another. The businessman's uniform—currently the double-breasted wool suit—is on the one hand easily distinguished from the workingman's denims and, on the other, from the garb of the priest. Among businessmen certain vague but still important rank differences are reflected in the quality and cut of the business suit; the junior executive may buy his clothes ready-made, his superior may have his made by an expensive tailor, and the superior's superior may secure his from an "exclusive" tailor.

Badges, tags, and a great variety of more elaborate devices either worn on the person or displayed—such as a chauffeur-driven limousine—are used to indicate status position. Even verbal mannerisms and gestures often have status significance; thus Oxford University bestows on its graduates—along with other if less evident things—a distinctive mode of speech. Class status invariably carries its verbal and gestural indicators; as a consequence, the lowborn origin of an individual who has gained wealth and position can often be detected in spite of fine clothing and grand manner. Regional status, likewise, is often symbolized in speech and gesture. In some instances deliberate efforts are made to indicate region of origin, as when a Texan visiting in New York City wears the wide-brimmed hat of his homeland. The clothing and other symbols of the sex roles are so evident that they need not be described here.

Status symbols serve various functions. Within formally organized groups they are commonly used as token rewards for good behavior, thus constituting a simple social-control device that will be discussed in another connection later. Somewhat more complex in function is the use within groups of symbols of differential rank or office. In formal groups, such as military organizations, these symbols assure that the individual will receive—or, if he does not, can effectively demand—the rights of his role: that the officer will be saluted by the men, that the orders he gives will be obeyed by anyone who is his subordinate, that anyone with whom he deals will know his place in the military hierarchy and accord him the respect and prerogatives of his special office. At the same time, symbols of rank or office help to keep the individual within the confines of his role; *i.e.*, he is in effect labeled "not a general" when he is labeled "Captain."

Visible status symbols of rank or office are perhaps most commonly associated with large, relatively impersonal, regimentally organized groups, such as the military, police forces, firemen, marine services, etc., which operate under conditions of crisis and in which there is, for functional reasons, a rigid structuring of personnel into various ranks and a strong emphasis upon discipline and uncritical obedience to orders. The members of small, intimate groups do not need visible status symbols to enable them to identify a fellow member or the rank or office which he occupies; they identify the person and through him his particular role, a sequence which is reversed in military and other similar organizations. Nor is there much need for or use of visible symbols of rank or office in large, impersonal organizations, such as corporate businesses and civil government agencies, that do not operate under crisis conditions. In such organizations orders flow from the top downward in a relatively channeled and impersonal way. The subordinate does not need to identify at sight the president, vice-president, or whatnot; for governmental bureau chiefs and corporation executives do not mingle "in the heat of battle" with common workers, as may generals, police and fire chiefs, and even captains of ships at sea. Rather, when there is occasion in such organizations for a subordinate to meet one of the "big bosses," he usually goes to that person's office; if anything is needed to make identification complete, the name and title on the office door will serve.

The emphasis that is placed upon symbols of rank and office, however, is not always proportionate to the function that they serve. Many nonmilitary organizations with no functional need to do so nonetheless stress and mark out rank within the membership, as does, for example, the Masonic order; on the other hand, some organizations in which rank differences are functionally significant do not stress ranks as such. Within the academic world, for example, a professor is a professor whether he is in fact an assistant or an associate or a full professor; and the use of the title "Professor" is usually limited to formal occasions and relations with nonacademic people. Thus whereas a captain and a general are clearly distinguishable by the obviously indicated difference in rank, and neither would ever refer to the other without putting him in his special role by using his military title, the members of a university faculty are most clearly distinguishable in terms of age, which does not correlate closely with rank; and they usually address one another, in-

cluding their president, as "Mr." if they are not intimately acquainted and by first name if they are. An odd form of status indicator has developed within the past twenty years in business and, most especially, governmental bureaucracy. Referring to and in some instances addressing a superior by the initials of his given names (*e.g.*, "L.M.") is taken to indicate a sort of respectful intimacy on the part of the subordinate. . . .

Status obligations

. . . Although it would be an oversimplification to say that the clearly defined status positions of a society can be scaled in terms of their desirability to the members of the society, it is true that women have rarely competed for masculine roles, that the majority of the members of even our own laboring class make no effort to climb into the middle classes, and that only an exceedingly small proportion of America's young women go to Hollywood in hope of achieving stardom. Actually, the values that a given individual places on the various status positions of his society depend in the main upon his subcultural training; for each of the many subcultures there is, perhaps, a special system for evaluating the various status positions. In a dynamic society such as our own, most persons who are not wealthy may vaguely wish that they were; but only a few strive to become so. Most are, if not content, at least more or less reconciled to gaining promotion within their class, occupation, and other subcultural status categories.

One reason for this limited competition is that the particular values of an individual make only a few of the many status roles of his society operationally attractive to him. To the middle-class youth, the rights accruing to a Mason may be attractive; to the lower-class youth, being a Mason may seem far less desirable than being a member of some local baseball club. Moreover, ethnic, class, sex, and other limitations on eligibility to a given status role will either preclude or at least discourage efforts on the part of many individuals to gain admission to it.

But perhaps the major reason for the very limited competition for higher status roles is the fact, central to social control, that status rights tend to entail compensatory obligations. Ascribed status roles, such as that of prince and rich man's son, are only partial exceptions to this general rule. They are partial in that both a prince and a rich man's son do have at least the obligation of living up to the social standards set for them. To the outsider such social parasites may seem to get much and give nothing in return; but under most circumstances they must dress up and play up to their roles, whether they personally wish to do so or not.

Status rights and obligations are not, of course, nicely balanced in terms of some abstract principle of social justice. A generation of economists attempted to prove that a man's financial income is a fair index of his economic contribution to society, but without notable success. Even ignoring such facts as that thieves often wax rich while honest and industrious men stay poor, that fortunes are often made through such sheer inadvertence as happening to be the owner of land on which oil is discovered, and that some of the most important contributions to social welfare have no economic implication or reward, it is still difficult to demonstrate a consistent relation between economic income and economic productivity. For the fact is that economic values are everywhere intermingled with noneconomic values and are often canceled out by them. A scientist may gain renown but no wealth, whereas high economic reward may be given for the most intangible and uneconomic of services—witness, for example, the high incomes of successful professional gamblers who offer their patrons nothing but an illusory hope of quick and easy wealth.

In the long run, however, the obligations of any status role (obligations which will subsequently be discussed from the control point of view as group norms) are, from the point of view of those who strive to enter or to remain in that role, nearly but not quite the value equivalents of the rights. Status obligations cannot for long exceed status rights, for the role will disappear for lack of competitors for it; the obligations cannot for long be far less than the rights, for excessive competition for the role will lead to its being accepted at a cut price, *i.e.*, the status obligations will be accepted for less than the going status rights. An understanding of the balance of status rights and obligations depends upon realization of the fact that the value placed upon any right and the disutility placed on any obligation is a matter of social definition; the balance of rights and obligations therefore varies between different societies, between different subcultural groups within the same society, and between different individuals within such groups; and it is, moreover, subject to change through time. There is no inherent reason why as many men as do should aspire to become President of the United States; and there is no inherent reason why so comparatively few should set themselves up as professional gamblers. The income of a successful gambler is far greater than that of a successful politician,

whereas the chances of sudden death are probably not much greater, the demands upon one's time are certainly less, and each in his own circle has high prestige. But currently to be Senator, Governor, or President is respectable, whereas to be a wealthy gambler is not; just as currently to be a general, and perhaps direct the slaughter of tens of thousands, is respectable, whereas to be a gangster and kill only a few is not.

Reciprocal rights and obligations

The balance of status-role rights and obligations is perhaps most evident when the obligations of one status role satisfy the rights of another, and vice versa. To the extent that the members of a group occupy equivalent status positions (*e.g.*, housewives in a community, workers occupying the same jobs) status-role obligations are simply the obverse of status rights. The individual member of a group who has, for example, the role right to take a hand at the bridge table whenever a place is open must, as one of three who need a fourth for bridge, extend the same right to all others of the group; the stock boy who has the role right to slip out for a smoke now and then must in return protect any fellow worker who is out for a smoke (*i.e.*, cover up for him when the boss comes around); the stenographer who has the right to take a day off for shopping occasionally on the grounds that she is ill must validate a fellow worker's excuse for a similar absence when the occasion arises. Support of the rights of individual members of a group usually involves rather devious actions and, often, the exercise of considerable ingenuity. The stock boy who just says vaguely, "Oh, Joe's somewhere around" when his employer or the departmental manager inquires will probably not be living up to his role obligation in this matter; his obligation is to save Joe from being caught or even suspected by his superiors: it is Joe's "right" to protection while off the job, and it is the obligation of his fellow workers to provide him with the best possible protection under the circumstances. Likewise, the stenographer who is taking her turn at being ill expects full protection. The minimum obligation of her coworkers is to support the idea that she is ill; really adequate performance would be the more or less subtle proffering to the office manager of some "evidence" confirming her illness—*e.g.*, a slightly embarrassed reference to the phase of the moon.

The reciprocal type of status-role rights and obligations is very common. One thing required of a physician, for example, is that he defend his

fellow practitioners against any charge of mal-
practice; *e.g.,* his personal opinion of diagnosis or
treatment by another physician should never be
revealed to any layman. Similarly, the college
teacher is expected by his colleagues to divert
student criticism of any colleague and never to
reveal to students any adverse views that he may
hold of the teaching ability or scholarly pro-
ficiency of a colleague. Likewise, if it is his right
to expect the blackboard in a classroom to be
clean when he takes over that room, then it will
be obligatory for him to erase the marks he has
put on the board before leaving at the end of
the hour.

Where, as is often the case, the membership of
a group is differentiated into ranks, the obligations of each rank may differ somewhat, and they
are sometimes but not always the obverse of
the rights. Thus a superior may have the right
to be addressed as "Sir" by his inferiors; obligatory to their roles is, then, addressing the superior
as "Sir." The same is true of all the special rights
of a superior; his rights are satisfied only to the
extent that his inferiors live up to their obligations vis-à-vis him. But he too will have obligations, different in kind yet essential to the
satisfaction of at least some of the rights of his
inferiors. The newcomer in a work group may be
assigned the dullest and dirtiest work tasks; but in
return for doing these tasks, his seniors will
ordinarily aid him in a variety of ways—perhaps
by inducting him into their skills. A young physician, just starting practice, is often given—"has
referred to him" is the polite phrase—the unwanted patients of established practitioners—those
who are just tiresome neurotics, the less important
seniles, and perhaps even some nonpaying incur-
ables. He must, moreover, show respect for the
age and wisdom of his seniors and in a variety
of ways cultivate their good will. But if he does,
he will usually receive in return a variety of
services—expert help when his skills prove inadequate, protection from outside criticism, suggestions on how to build up a profitable practice, etc.
Similarly, a young instructor in a college or university is often given tasks which the older men
on the staff may feel beneath their dignity or
which they have outgrown. To some extent it is
the basic obligation of the young instructor to
relieve his elders of irksome responsibilities. But
in return those elders usually are obligated to
show consideration for his youth; perhaps in such
ways as assisting him in working up course materials, showing him how to handle student problems, and even covering up for him when he
makes a mistake.

Whether the role obligations of a superior to
his inferior or inferiors are the equivalent of their
obligations to him is perhaps in every instance
debatable. In general, it would seem that the
obligations of a superior are more difficult to fulfill, if not so numerous and so demanding of time
and energy; *i.e.,* they require greater skill and
longer experience than do those of the subordinate.
Where the role obligations of the superior are
more or less the equivalent, in terms of the scale
of values of the members and in their demands
on the individual, to the obligations of the subordinate, the superiority of status consists in the
greater rights that accrue to that role. It is to
be observed that in many instances administrative
officers in business, in clubs and other organizations, and even in colleges and universities spend
far more time on the job and work at a higher
level of intensity than do their subordinates, and
that the most respected members of the local
medical fraternity are likely to be the hardest
worked as well as the best paid.

Personal status

. . . There is always a distinction between the
status rights of a role that an individual occupies
and the rights that are actually accorded him as
a person in that role. Even in the relatively
mechanized relationships of military life, where
status rights and obligations are rigidly specified,
the treatment accorded two men of the same rank
may be quite different. Thus while each of two
company commanders may be obeyed without
overt question by his subordinates and given all
the obvious rights of his position, one may have
high personal status with his company and the
other low personal status with his. In lay terms,
the one is *as a person* respected and admired,
while the other is *as a person* held in disdain and
contempt. Differential personal status of this sort
will be reflected in a multitude of ways, all external to the rights accorded the status role itself.
For example, the officer who has high personal
status may be obeyed with some zest and with
some tendency on the part of his subordinates to
protect him from the consequences of errors of
judgment or misadventure. The rights of his status
role will often be fulfilled beyond the letter of
the law; perhaps his staff car is kept in exceptionally good condition, or perhaps in officers' mess
he is served the thickest and tenderest steak. The
officer whose personal status is low, on the other
hand, may be obeyed in a somewhat apathetic
manner; when occasion arises he may be shown
up in the worst possible light; and although his
car may be maintained in the prescribed military
manner, it will probably not receive the con-

scientious attention that makes for trouble-free operation.

Every human act can be played in a wide variety of manners. An act that is supposed to signify respect, such as the military salute, the bow of a head waiter, the "Yes, Sir" of a servant, and the "May I help you?" of the store clerk, can in actuality be made to convey anything from honest admiration to outright contempt. A service act, such as that of filling an order for a dozen eggs, fitting a suit, painting a house, or mowing the lawn, can be performed more or less promptly and more or less well. A friendly greeting can be a welcome or a rebuff; a companionable silence can be anything from warm to cold; an honor accorded a notable can be empty or sincere; a laugh accorded a joke can be perfunctory or hearty; the protest "Oh, it's early. Don't go yet" can be an invitation to stay on or a strong hint to get along.

The individual who occupies a defined status role is generally given his rights in accordance with the letter of the law; but the satisfaction that he secures from those rights ordinarily depends mainly upon his personal status as an occupier of that role. Unless he is as an individual abnormally crass and unfeeling, the way in which his rights are fulfilled considerably affects their value to him. And the way in which the rights of his role are fulfilled—whether willingly or reluctantly, as it were—is dependent upon his personal status. This, in turn, is determined in the long run by the way in which he fulfills the obligations of his role.

For example, all the regular patrons of a given restaurant may pay the proper amount for their food and, if such is the local custom, give the proper tip to the waiter. Such payment is the basic obligation of the patron. But some patrons may endear themselves to the management and staff (acquire high personal status as patrons) by the way in which they conduct themselves, while others may not. A patron who has more than fulfilled his obligations—at, perhaps, no financial cost, but rather through kindness and consideration in manner—may be accorded, in addition to the rights of his role as patron, such humanly gratifying signs of respect as the best available table, prompt service, helpful suggestions in ordering, and a sincere "Thank you" or "Good night" upon leaving. Conversely, a patron who has earned low personal status may be told off in a variety of more or less subtle ways; he may be placed in a crowded corner, served in a slightly delinquent manner, thanked in a toneless voice, etc.

In the relations of peers—*i.e.,* persons who occupy equal status roles—personal status is of major importance. An individual who belongs to the best club and plays as good a game of golf as any member but has low personal status with his fellow members may gain some satisfaction from his status as a club member by boasting of it to nonmembers; but he will gain little satisfaction from the membership itself. Although he will presumably have all the rights of a club member, he will find little pleasurable companionship within the club, he will be excluded from many of the more intimate and informal member activities, and he will be the victim of more or less covert disparagement. Conversely, the member who has exceptionally high personal status can figuratively —and upon occasion literally—"get away with murder." He will be included in all club activities, and his company will be sought rather than avoided.

The individual's personal popularity or unpopularity, to use common terms, with his peers is mainly determined by the way in which he fulfills the obligations of his role. Manner and other attributes of personal charm may even offset failure on the part of the individual to live up to some of the less important of those obligations. Even as a waiter will often take in good grace a substandard tip from a favored patron, peers will often forgive minor delinquencies on the part of the one who has through ease and affability of manner endeared himself to them. On the other hand, the one who is unpopular with them is normally held to strict accounting and given no more than the "law" requires.

Personal charm and consideration for the personal feelings of others does not always, however, determine the extent to which the status rights of a role are fulfilled. In some instances an individual with high personal status may be less effective in his role than is one with low personal status: a hated employer may secure more work from his employees than a beloved one; a disliked officer may have more power over his troops than a well-liked one; an inconsiderate and despised gangster boss may rule with fear where he could not rule if he were admired but unfeared. In some instances, moreover, high personal status is the consequence of proved efficiency in a role rather than personal charm—*i.e.,* what the individual has accomplished, rather than how he has gone about doing it. Although they may not like him as a person, the crew of a ship may admire their captain as a leader and grant him high personal status because he has brought them safely through a perilous voyage; and although a scientist may be brusque and inconsiderate, his assistants and advanced students may be loyal to him and grant him high personal status because they respect his intellectual ability and his integrity. What particular personal qualities will earn high personal status for the occupant of a given role depend upon the nature of that role, which is to say, upon the values and other criteria by which the occupant of the given role is evaluated. Personal charm is, perhaps, always an asset; but most roles require more than a pleasing manner and consideration for the feelings of others.

STATUS ASPIRATION AND CONFORMING BEHAVIOR

. . . Status aspirations vary widely both in degree and in kind. An individual may, for example, simply wish to obtain higher personal status within the status role that he occupies or to secure a higher rank or office within a group to which he belongs; or he may wish to gain entry into another group, *i.e.*, to secure status of a different kind from that which he possesses. In the latter case the individual is what is generally termed an "ambitious" man or, less kindly, a "social climber."

Status aspiration may be rather generalized. An individual may, for example, seek to rise up the class hierarchy in all dimensions—financial, residential, local prestige, etc. More often, however, status aspiration is quite specific; the individual seeks to secure promotion in his occupation, to gain recognition in his profession, to secure membership in a certain country club, to win acclaim in some hobby or artistic circle, or to become a member in good standing of the local café-society set.

In many instances in primitive and premodern societies promotion from role to higher role has been largely a matter of seniority. In the patriarchal family, for example, the first-born son took precedence over his younger brothers in all matters and ascended to the role of patriarch upon his father's death. In this family system it was also often the right of the first-born daughter to be the first daughter of the family to enter marriage; and until she was married, her younger sisters could not be. In most societies, the senior of a number of individuals has been granted precedence in many matters, both large and small —such, for example, as the right to first choice from the serving bowl or platter at meals, the right to precede his juniors through doorways and down narrow streets, the right to dominate discussions with his opinions and prejudices, and the right to many other concessions "due his age." Ordinarily, seniority rights have adhered to age per se (or, more specifically, superior age) and have not carried with them offsetting obligations.

In modern society there is a marked tendency toward a similar granting of special status rights on a seniority basis. Seniority in our society is, however, less often a matter of age, even relative age, than it is of length of time as a member in good standing within a given organization. In governmental, business, academic, and even military organizations the individual usually accumulates rights as the years pass; *i.e.*, he gains higher status as a function of time alone. The change in status may be gradual and almost imperceptible, as it is in the case of a university professor who acquires the patina of authority along with his gray hairs and in that of the old-timer in a craft who is respected not so much for what he is as for the history that he represents. The change in status may, on the other hand, be rigidly structured, as it is in most governmental bureaus, in long-established businesses, and in military forces. Here the individual gradually moves up a hierarchy of ranks (and, perhaps, offices), each of which has its specific rewards "for service," its special rights, and, often, its special symbols, such as the service stars of the railroad conductor or the rating of the civil service employee.

Status rights granted on the basis of seniority are sometimes segmental and may be limited to preferential employment (*i.e.*, the oldest worker in point of service is last to be laid off and first to be reemployed), to preferential job assignment (*i.e.*, the senior worker has his first choice of the available work tasks), or to tenure, the acquired right to retain status irrespective of performance. Some organizations, *e.g.*, scientific societies, grant life memberships on the basis of long and satisfactory prior service. In most universities, in many public-school systems, and in many governmental bureaus, the individual secures tenure upon the completion of a specified period of service; thereafter he cannot be dislodged from his position without cause, if, indeed, he can be dislodged at all.

Seniority versus merit

No doubt the granting of status rights on the basis of seniority often has a functional basis. Under some circumstances the eldest of a group will generally be best qualified to provide leadership, counsel, or other valuable service to the group. The rights granted to a soldier upon each successive reenlistment have their evident organizational function; they encourage men to make a career of military service; moreover, they probably pay for themselves in that the additional pay, etc., given an old serviceman upon his reenlistment is more than offset by the fact that he does not have to be trained as does the "rookie." In government and industry, the granting of rights on the basis of seniority may somewhat lower labor turnover, which is always costly to an organization; but that it everywhere and always, or even generally, increases the operational efficiency of groups does not follow. On the contrary, the granting of status rights on the basis of seniority is most often a means by which some group members profit at the expense of the remainder, with the consequence that the organization is less efficient than it otherwise would be. Moreover, it also imposes various restrictions on the effectiveness of leaders and in general makes the entire organization less adaptable to changing circumstances.

The individual who, because of the nature of the organization of which he is a member, can in time acquire seniority rights is as a rule encouraged by that prospect to stay on in the organization, even though he has an alternative that is currently more attractive but that lacks the promise of future seniority rights. Thus he is in effect induced to make current sacrifices in the prospect of gaining future benefits and is to this extent subject to control pressures. By making current sacrifices he is to some degree fulfilling the seniority rights of his elders in the organization, who in a sense constitute an elite that is being rewarded for past rather than current performance. Since, however, his promotion within the group is a function of time rather than merit, the individual is free from the need to strive for personal status beyond that which is just necessary to assure continued membership in the group.

By contrast, wherever the progression of an individual up a hierarchy of ranks or offices is determined by the consent of his peers or superiors rather than by simple seniority, the individual who wants to advance in rank or office must strive for higher personal status; for it is his personal status that largely determines his rate of progress. If he wants only to maintain his achieved status, he is relatively free from control pressure; for he need only conform minimally to his status obligations—*i.e.*, live up to the letter of his responsibilities and avoid doing anything which will jeopardize his personal status with his peers and superiors. If, however, he wishes to gain a higher status—*e.g.*, to secure promotion to a better-paying job, to be elected to a higher office, to be invited into a more exclusive club than the one to which he already belongs, or even to marry into one of the "best" local families—he will be highly susceptible to control pressures; and these pressures are often conflicting.

On the one hand, he must conform to the obligations of the status role that he occupies; on the other hand, he must at the same time acquire a higher than normal personal status within the role. The latter requirement may mean that he must conform, or somehow seem to conform, to two somewhat different sets of standards. Thus if he is a bookkeeper aspiring to the office of head bookkeeper, a position that may eventually become open as a consequence of the promotion of the present occupant to a higher office, he must maintain the personal status appropriate to a bookkeeper with both his peers and his superiors: for if he should gain the reputation of being "bossy" or excessively efficient he might disqualify himself for promotion in the eyes of his peers, with the consequence that his superiors may then doubt his ability to get along with his fellow workers. Yet he must at the same time prove to those superiors that he has the personal qualities which are essential to effective operation as head bookkeeper—that he is, in fact, superior to his fellow workers in energy, diligence, skill, loyalty, and personality. Almost anything that he might do to demonstrate the latter will certainly lower his status with his peers; for it is difficult, if not impossible, to be at once a "good fellow" and a superior one. In a like way the man who seeks an invitation to join a better club must somehow make himself known to and agreeable to members of that club without, however, hurting the feelings of the members of his own club or otherwise jeopardizing his personal status with them. He must maintain the latter, since he may not secure the desired invitation, in which case he will need his membership in the old club, and since the desired invitation may be contingent in part upon what members of the better club learn about his reputation among members of the other one. A man who wants to marry above his station in life usually faces a similar predicament; to the extent that he conforms to the standard of the higher class and thus demonstrates his eligibility, he may lose personal status with his own class, in whose terms he may be putting on airs or behaving snobbishly. And, as is the case with others who aspire to higher status positions, his acceptability in the higher class may depend in part upon his personal status in his own class.

TRANSFERABILITY OF STATUS

Whereas the prophet is without honor in his own country and his own house, the individual is without status except in his own country and his own house—*i.e.*, where he is known either in person, by role, or both. For in the main, status is specific, as regards both the kind of status and the social area in which that status exists. . . .

Selection *67*

Janitors Versus Tenants: A Status-Income Dilemma
Ray Gold

In the introduction to the selection by LaPiere it was noted that sometimes statuses are categorical, as in the case of occupational statuses, and that sometimes they express a relationship between persons. In the article reproduced here, the reader will have the opportunity to observe some reactions to incongruous categorical statuses: the relatively high income statuses and relatively low occupational statuses of janitors. The product of this perceived conflict was a disturbance in the interpersonal relationships between janitors and tenants.

In Gold's sample of janitors, there is little doubt that the janitor's increasing income had resulted in a re-evaluation of his self-image as well as in a disturbance of the definition of his general status on the part of the tenants in the building where he worked. Thus Gold's work points out the difficulty of assessing general status. Differences in perspective result in differences in status assignments. Persistent stereotypes may be more powerful than objective criteria in determining general status (if such exists) for some categories of people. Feelings toward people are seen to outweigh some status indexes in producing interpersonal behavior.

Selection 68, which deals with the perception of social status, is concerned not only with the meaning of statuses that are perceived but also with the implications of differential status perceptions for social organization.

There is some kind of status relationship between the worker and the person served in almost any occupation where the two meet and interact. For example, when the salesperson and the customer meet, each brings to bear on the other valuations by which the other's status category can be tentatively ascertained. This tentative status designation enables each to make a rough judgment as to how to act toward the other person and as to how he thinks the other person will act toward him. If their association is resumed, their initial judgments strongly influence the character of their subsequent interactions. If they are separated by wide barriers of social distance, they may carry on an almost formal salesperson-customer relationship for years. Or their respective status judgments may be such that the status barriers are gradually penetrated. In any case, the status relationship between them is always present, unless it is resolved into an absolute equalitarian relationship. Likewise, in the case of the physician and his patients, the plumber and his customers,

the minister and his parishioners, and in others, there is a status relationship of which both parties are more or less aware and which influences the pattern of their interactions. Such being the case, the nature and form of these status relationships can and should be studied wherever they occur.

The present example, which concerns the apartment-building janitor and his tenants, is a case study in such status relationships. The form these relationships have taken is that of a marked dilemma of status and income.

STATUS AND INCOME

The status-income dilemma may be expected to occur in two situations. One is that in which an individual earns too little to pay for the goods

"Janitors Versus Tenants: A Status-Income Dilemma" by Ray Gold. Reprinted from *The American Journal of Sociology*, Vol. LVII (1952), 486-493, by permission of The University of Chicago Press.

and services generally associated with his other social characteristics. The other is that in which he earns enough to pay for goods and services generally associated not with *his* other social characteristics but with those of members of higher social classes. When an individual in the first dilemma meets and interacts almost daily on a rather personal level with one in the second as, respectively, in the case of the tenant and the apartment-building janitor, they develop an association whose form and content are of sociological interest.

The data in this article are based entirely upon interviews with janitors. What results is a penetrating view of the janitor's conceptions of tenants and of his interpretations of their conceptions of him. Thus, we obtain an intimate understanding of the janitor's view of how he and tenants spar to resolve their respective dilemmas. Although many of the tenants may not be so sensitive as the janitor to this contest, it is safe to assume that, through his untiring efforts to play the game with his rules, the tenants are aware that he is agitating to change their traditional patterns of interaction.

In the early part of this century, before janitors in Chicago were unionized, they catered to virtually every whim of their employers and tenants in order to establish job security. Since they have become unionized, their duties have been greatly delimited, their wages increased, and their privileges extended to include a rent-free basement apartment in one of the larger buildings which they service. At present, they are required to fire the furnace to provide heat and hot water for the tenants, to remove the tenants' garbage regularly, to make minor emergency repairs, and to keep the building and grounds clean.

Having a history, the janitor also has a reputation. The tenant-public seems to look upon him as an ignorant, lazy, and dirty occupational misfit. There has developed a general belief that, if a man cannot do anything else successfully, he can always become a janitor. This stereotype has been perpetuated by the public because of a number of beliefs, principally the following: (1) many janitors are foreign-born and therefore strange and suspicious; (2) the janitor is always seen wearing dirty clothes, so the tenants seem to feel that he habitually disregards cleanliness; (3) the janitor lives in the basement, which symbolizes his low status; and (4) the janitor removes the tenants' garbage, a duty which subserves him to them. It is because the public has singled out these features in their view of the janitor that his ascribed status has been lowly. In the public's view it seems that the janitor merely is a very low-class person doing menial work for the tenants.

It is true that the performance of janitorial duties requires neither lengthy training nor a high order of mechanical or technical skills. However, the nature of the janitor's situation has led him to play roles and incorporate self-conceptions which frequently overshadow those which others expect of a combination caretaker and handy man. Because he does not work under direct supervision and can plan his work to suit himself, he feels that he is his own boss: he, alone, is in charge of the building and responsible for the safety of the tenants. After becoming proficient at making repairs for tenants, he magnifies his handy-man role into that of a master mechanic. Combining these two roles, he then sees himself as an entrepreneur who runs a cash business of attending to the tenants' service needs.

These roles, together with others which stem from the work situation, contradict the public's stereotyped view of the janitor. Being sensitive to these social conceptions, the janitor strives to gain the tenants' acceptance as a person who has risen above the disreputable fellow these conceptions describe. Toward this end he not only plays the role of a respectable, dignified human being but of one who has a very substantial income . . . . In this setting it is evident that the janitor's social relationships with the tenants are of crucial importance to him. These relationships are pervaded by his persistent disowning of his unhappy occupational heritage and the justification of his claim to middle-class status.

So important are social relationships with the tenants that the janitor defines success in terms of them. As many janitors have pointed out:

"The most important thing about a janitor's work is that you have to know how to deal with people. Then, when you show the tenants that you have a clean character and are respectable, you can train them to be good tenants, that's what's really important in being a success."

Because the janitor attempts to realize his self when interacting with his tenants, his efforts to train them are actually channeled toward the establishment of relationships which support, rather than oppose, his self-conceptions. The "good" tenants support his self-conceptions; the "bad" tenants oppose them.

It will be well now to examine the nature of these social relationships to determine how they give rise to the personal and social dilemmas which comprise the central theme of this discussion.

The janitor believes that, in general, tenants hold him in low esteem. Even the most friendly tenants maintain some social distance between the janitor and themselves. Tenants, generally, over-look his qualifications as an individual and see him only as a member of a low-status group. In their view he is merely an occupational type. The most militant proponents of this view are the "bad" tenants.

There are two characteristics of a special group of "bad" tenants which are apposite to this presentation. These characteristics, jealousy and resentment, are descriptive of only those tenants who are embittered by the janitor's economic prowess. They are people whose incomes are usually below, but sometimes slightly above, the janitor's income. The janitor often refers to these tenants as "fourflushers." They live on the brink of bankruptcy, and he knows it. Status symbols are very important to them. Unlike the janitor, they apparently strain their budgets to improve the appearance of their persons and their apartments. When they see the janitor's new car or television aerial, their idea of high-status symbols, it is almost more than they can bear. It violates their sense of social justice. In consequence of his high income, the janitor can acquire things which these tenants may interpret as a threat to the established social order.

The janitor's new car, parked conspicuously in front of the building, serves constantly to remind tenants of his pecuniary power. It draws the most criticism from the jealous tenants. Commenting on the tensions thereby engendered, Janitor No. 35 remarked:

"There is a certain amount of jealousy when janitors try to better themselves. A whole lot are jealous because the janitor makes more than they do. But they don't consider the time a janitor puts in. When I got my Dodge two years ago somebody said, 'Huh, look at that fellow. He must be making the money or he wouldn't be buying a new car.' I know one party, they think a janitor should be in working clothes all the time. Just because a janitor likes to go out in an auto and they don't have any, there is that feeling between janitor and the tenant, that's for sure."

Some of these fourflushers do own an automobile. But if the janitor's car is bigger and newer than theirs, they are extremely mortified. Janitor No. 33 experienced the wrath of such people:

"About a third of the tenants are very pleasant about it when they see my car, but the rest say, 'Holy cripe, the janitor got a new car!' The same majority is the ones you are in trouble with all the time. They say, 'How is the "nigger" with

the big car?' meaning I am a 'nigger' because I got a Buick and my car is bigger than theirs."

The janitor finds that the jealous tenants are impossible to accommodate. They do not want to be accommodated by him. "No matter what you do," protested Janitor No. 14, "they squawk." Their animosity seems to know no bounds. They deliberately attempt to create trouble for the janitor by complaining about him to his employer.

Besides complaining about him, these tenants reveal their resentment of the janitor's mobility efforts by making nasty remarks to him. This was shown very clearly in a conversation with Janitor No. 12 and his wife:

JANITOR: When we got our 10 per cent raise a short time ago, the tenants didn't like it. You see how nice this [first-floor] apartment looks. Well, there ain't another apartment in the building that's decorated as nice as this. I had all those cabinets in the kitchen tore out and got new ones put in. That brick glass and ventilator in the transom opening—I had it done. Tenants didn't like to see me do all that. They resent it.

INTERVIEWER: How do they show their resentment?

WIFE: Mostly by making snotty remarks. One woman told us that we shouldn't live in such a nice apartment on the first floor, that we should live in a hole [basement apartment] like other janitors. Then they are sarcastic in a lot of other ways. They just don't like to see us have a nice apartment and a new car. I guess they'd rather see us live like rats.

The basement apartment is symbolic of the janitor's subservient status. If he can arrange with his employer to obtain a first-floor apartment, there is nothing that the jealous tenants can do to stop him. They can only try to make life miserable for him.

Jealous tenants disdainfully address him as "Janitor," rather than using his given name. It is bad enough, from his standpoint, that all other tenants address him by his given name, thereby indicating his historically servile status. But these resentful tenants go further. They call him by his occupational name. Symbolically, their use of this "dirty" name means that they want their relationships with him to be as impersonal as possible. They want the janitor to be aware of the great social distance which he would dare to bridge. Janitor No. 14 commented on this form of address:

JANITOR: The bad ones squawk as long as they live. No matter what you do they squawk. They're the ones that don't call you by your name. They're a lower class of people, but they try to make you feel even lower than them.

INTERVIEWER: Why do they call you "Janitor"?

JANITOR: It's either out of stupidity or to make you think you are a slave to them—an underdog. . . .

These fourflushers who address him as "Janitor" are unalterably opposed to his efforts to better himself. The longer they live in the building, the worse their relationships with him become. This point was brought out by Janitor No. 4:

"Boy, I'll tell you about one thing that happened to me last Christmas morning. This woman rings my bell when I'm out and gives an envelope to my wife to give to me. I passed by the back windows here a little while later and looked in like I always do to wave at the kid, and my wife called me in because she thought there must be a present in the envelope. So I went in and opened it up and there was a note inside that said, "I'll be home today so please keep the heat up." . . . That's how the tenants get when they been living here too long. Most of them think they own the building, and you should do just what they want."

As Janitor No. 4 insisted, the fourflushers' unthinking demands for personal service, their utter disregard for the janitor's integrity and authority, and their possessiveness toward the building increase with their length of residence. The building becomes more and more like "home" to them, the longer they live there. "They can't afford to have a home and servants of their own," observed Janitor No. 18, "so they try to treat the janitor as their servant." They like to think of him as a mobile part of the building, always at their beck and call. Still, the deep-seated animosities between these tenants and the janitor preclude any mutually satisfactory adjustment of their respective roles. Through the years they continue to be jealous and resentful of him. Meanwhile, he continues to resent their unco-operativeness and disrespect. The building becomes as much "home" to him as it does to them. But there is something about "home" that can never be remedied. From the standpoint of these fourflushers, that something is the janitor. From the janitor's point of view, that something is the fourflushers.

Turning now from janitors whose tenants have incomes that are marginal to theirs to janitors whose tenants are plainly well-to-do, it is evident that there is a remarkable contrast in janitor-tenant relationships. The following conversation with Janitor No. 26 will serve as an introduction to this contrast:

INTERVIEWER: Some fellows have told me that many of their tenants resent their getting a new car or a television set. Have you ever come up against that?

JANITOR: That class of people don't live here, of course. The class of people you're talking about are making two hundred a month, don't have a car, and are lucky they're living. Yeah, I've met up with them. . . . People here aren't jealous if you got a new car. People here feel you have to have a car, like bread and butter.

Tenants whose incomes are clearly higher than the janitor's have no cause to be jealous of him. They do not compete with him for symbols of pecuniary power. There is more prestige attached to having an engineer in the building than to having a janitor, so they call him "the engineer." These people obviously do not have the status-income problems of the fourflushers who contemptuously address him as "Janitor." Clearly, then, tenants who are well-to-do have no need to make demands. As Janitor No. 17, many of whose tenants have incomes marginal to his, so penetratingly observed:

"The people that don't have anything put up the biggest front and squawk a lot. The people who got it don't need any attention. I'd rather work for rich tenants. The ones we got here are middle ones. Those tenants that sing don't have a right to. . . . Some few tenants just got here from the Negro district. They were stuck there until they could find a place to move to. Man, they're real glad to be here. They don't give me no trouble at all."

Demonstrating remarkable insight, Janitor No. 17 pointed out that the "rich" tenants do not feel that they need attention from the janitor; that the "refugee" (like the poor) tenants feel that they are in no position to make demands; and that the fourflushers or "middle" (probably lower-middle) tenants are the most troublesome.

When a janitor works for many years in a building occupied by well-to-do tenants, it is not unusual that a genuinely warm relationship develops between him and these tenants. They probably come to see him as an old family employee, while he believes that he has been accepted for himself. As Janitor No. 26 asserted, "They feel they're no better than me—I'm no better than them, and they always invite me in for coffee or something like that." There is no problem in sharing identification of "home." The building is undisputedly "home" to both the janitor and the "rich" tenants, because they most probably view their relationship with him as a status accommodation, which he interprets as an equalitarian relationship.

In the next section the status-income dilemma is illustrated in terms of the janitor's professional behavior and outlook, which are in marked contrast with the tenants' lack of respect for him.

PROFESSIONAL BEHAVIOR AND PROFESSIONAL ATTITUDES

It is likely that in every low-status occupation, where the worker associates with the customer, the workers meet with certain customer-oriented situations in which they typically behave in accordance with standards that people have traditionally called "professional." These low-status workers certainly do not label themselves "professionals," nor do others so label them. Yet, there is ample evidence that some of their behavior is ethically comparable to the behavior exhibited by members of the so-called "professions." . . .

While it is true that the janitor's self-conceptions are instrumental in forming the superstructure of his professional behavior, the foundation of such conduct is formed primarily out of situational requisites. This being the case, his status-income dilemma is intensified, because he is frequently called upon to act in a professional manner toward the disrespectful tenants. Thus, whether mainly out of choice (expression of self-conceptions) or out of necessity (fulfilment of situational requisites), the relationship between janitor and tenant sometimes assumes the character of that between professional and client.

The nature of the janitor's work leads him to find out a great deal about the personal lives of his tenants. He meets with many situations which force him to decide how much and to whom he should tell what he knows about them. Generally, he exercises scrupulous care in the handling of this intimate knowledge, as he considers himself to be intrusted with it in confidence.

The janitor gets some of his information from sources other than the tenants themselves. When he acts as an informant (e.g., for insurance checkers), he finds out a great deal about their personal affairs. One tenant tells him about another. The garbage reveals much about them. From these sources he acquires information of a very confidential nature.

The janitor also gets information directly from the tenants. They confide in him not only about illnesses but also about personal problems. As Janitor No. 20 remarked, "Some of them stop you and think they have to tell you if they got a toothache."

How the janitor dispenses his intimate knowledge about tenants was related by Janitor No. 32:

"If tenants want to know what's going on, they come to me about it. You hear and see a lot of things in your time. There are even times when you are requested to keep quiet. And there are times when you have to answer—for FBI and insurance inspectors. You can't tell them everything, either, you know. See and not see; hear and not hear—that's the best policy."

Like the bartender and the barber, whose ascribed occupational status beclouds the fact that they frequently share their customers' personal secrets, the janitor is placed in problematical situations requiring some kind of ethical rules. When it is understood that occupational problems which accrue from the same kinds of situations are basically the same without respect to status, then the similar receipt of confidences by the janitor, the lawyer, or the bartender becomes clear. These workers are, in this instance, in the kind of situation which requires them to protect the customer's personal secrets. Whether the disposition of these secrets involves as little as remaining silent or as much as stretching the truth, the workers protect their relationship with the customer by protecting his confidences. Likewise, in other given kinds of work situations which require the solution of ethical problems, the worker-customer relationship becomes overly complicated unless the worker makes and observes appropriate rules. Such ethical rules are not simply a matter of honorable self-conceptions or formalized professional codes. They are fundamentally a matter of situational requirements, irrespective of personal and occupational status.

Another area in which professional behavior is found concerns the janitor's relationships with overamorous tenants. Janitor No. 12 described what he considers to be the proper procedure for easing gracefully out of such a delicate predicament:

"Another thing about janitors—lots of women try to get you up in apartment just 'to talk' or for some phony excuse. When you walk in they are on couch, ask you to sit down, and that means only one thing. When that happens to me and I begin to sweat, I know I better leave. Thing is not to refuse them so they get embarrassed, so I act dumb. I excuse myself and say

I forgot about water running some place which I must shut off right away. It's hard to do, but it's best."

One can easily imagine hearing the bishop advise the young minister or the elderly doctor in a similar vein. The minister and the doctor must be prepared to meet such situations in a like fashion. The janitor instructs tenants to call him for repairs only during daylight hours, except for what he considers to be genuine emergencies. In the same way, the physician teaches his patients to call him only during office hours, except for a bona fide emergency. Some janitors recognize the similarity to doctors' problems. As Janitor No. 19 observed:

"Did you ever stop to think that we have a lot in common with doctors? I used to meet them in the halls at all hours of the night. We'd kid each other about making emergency calls at all hours of the night and never getting through with work."

Not only the janitor and the physician but others who deal routinely with customers' emergencies have problems of the same kind.

Yet another cluster of work situations wherein the janitor exhibits professional behavior concerns those occasions when he is called upon to do mechanical work for the tenants. The most clearcut evidence of professional behavior in this area was submitted by Janitor No. 11.

"Some of the repair work the tenant is responsible for and I'm supposed to charge for it. Well, if I replace some glass that costs me three and a half dollars, I may charge the tenant a half dollar or two dollars more for my labor, depending on how much she can afford. If it's a little thing and the tenant isn't well off, I won't charge her anything for it if she's supposed to pay."

The janitor's practice of charging for repairs on the basis of the customer's ability to pay is a high standard of service—quite in the tradition of the medical profession—and he knows it.

THE DILEMMA

The janitor's professional behavior, together with his substantial income, contradicts what he believes are his tenants' conceptions of him. His struggle to gain their respect is a struggle for status. His high standards of conduct constitute a way of favorably influencing their estimation of his worth. Still, he finds that tenants regard him as hardly more than a *janitor*. He strongly resents their failure properly to recognize him, particularly in the case of the fourflushers. As Janitor No. 18 bitterly remarked:

"They're the kind that are very important. They think you're a fireman—should drop everything and run to them. They adopt a superior attitude: 'I'm the tenant and you're the janitor.' Like the East and the West in that saying. Confidentially, a lot of us janitors could buy out most tenants. They put on airs and try to be bossy."

The janitor has a higher income than many of the tenants; yet, the latter "adopt a superior attitude." So he does considerable soul-searching to seek a satisfactory explanation of his relatively low status. The conversation which we had with Janitor No. 28 is in point:

INTERVIEWER: What things are janitors touchy about?

JANITOR: A lot of tenants figure he's just . . . a servant. Here [with "rich" tenants] it's not so bad. You say something to them and they [the "bad" tenants] say, "Hell, you're nothing but a janitor." Or when you're talking to even a working man and you tell him you're a janitor, he smiles—you know, people think there's nothing lower than a janitor. You get that feeling that they're looking down on you, because you're working for them. I know I feel that way sometimes. During the depression I was making better than most, so what the hell. It's good earned money.

INTERVIEWER: Well, why do you say you get that feeling that they are looking down on you? Why do you feel so sensitive?

JANITOR: In different places you hear people talk janitor this and janitor that, and they say they'd never be a . . . janitor. So you think people here must say and think the same, but not to you. It makes you feel funny sometimes.

It is noteworthy that Janitor No. 28 does not reject his idea of the tenants' definition of a janitor. For that matter, virtually no other janitor does so either. To explain this, it is necessary to understand how the janitor relates himself to other janitors in terms of the occupational title.

The individual janitor strongly identifies himself with the name "janitor," despite his belief that tenants look down on janitors. Their view does not annoy him very much because he, too, looks down on *other* janitors. He feels that he is different from and better than other janitors. So, when tenants (nonjanitors) speak disparagingly of janitors, he does not resent it because of the group solidarity in the occupation, for, in reality, there is little such solidarity. Rather he resents it because his self-conceptions are so involved in the name "janitor" and because the tenants fail to recognize his individual worth. Thus, when a janitor (No. 8) proudly states, "Tenants never treated *me* like a janitor," there is no doubt that he agrees with their definition of janitor but that he, by virtue of being singularly superior to other janitors, has been treated in accordance with his conception of himself.

This attitude of "different and better" may be characteristic of the members of any occupation (or other group) whose public reputation is one of censorious stereotypes. This attitude implies that the individual member agrees that most of his colleagues do have the characteristics attributed to them by the public. The interesting question is: Why does the member agree with the public? The study of janitors suggests that the answer is likely to be in terms of (1) the nature of the member's association with his colleagues (he probably knows only a few of the "better" ones) and (2) the status relationship between the member and the portion of the public he associates with in his work.

Although the individual janitor capably defends himself from the public's conceptions of janitors, he still must perform tasks which preclude advance to a higher occupational, hence social, status. The janitorial reputation refers to the members' personal characteristics and work habits. Closely related to, but distinguishable from, these alleged personal traits, are readily verified features of janitoring which involve dirty work (e.g., shoveling coal and removing garbage). Work is dirty when society defines it as such, that is, when society defines it as being necessary but undesirable or even repugnant. Middle-class people seem consciously to avoid such tasks. They apparently realize that the kind of work one does is often more important than one's income when it comes to getting established as a member of the middle class. Yet, in a materialistic society certain costly things, like a new automobile and a television set, become symbolic of high status, even to them. This accounts for the dilemma of the fourflushers.

But what about members of occupations which require the performance of dirty tasks? It seems that, like members of the janitorial occupation, they have the financial but lack the occupational qualifications for acceptance by the middle class. Speaking on this dilemma, Janitor No. 35 argued:

"A lot think they're better than the janitor because he has to take down their trash. Still the janitor makes more money. I believe the janitor *should* be making a lot more money than white-collar workers. After all, a janitor has a whole lot of responsibility and long hours."

Janitor No. 35, in summarizing the status-income dilemma, is painfully aware that tenants look down on the janitor. Their trash, the garbage, is undoubtedly the biggest single element in the janitor's continued low status. The removal of garbage is dirty work, incompatible with middle-class status. It causes the janitor to subserve the tenants, all of his individual attributes notwithstanding. The garbage symbolizes the dilemmas of the janitor-tenant relationship.

CONCLUSION

This account of the status-income dilemma suggests that, since high-prestige and high-income occupations are frequently distinguishable from one another, the *kind* of work a person does is a crucially qualifying factor in so far as his status possibilities are concerned. Viewed another way, the trend toward professionalization of occupations becomes an effort either to bring status recognition into line with high income or to bring income into line with high-status recognition. The janitor-tenant relationship has been graphically presented to call attention to a dilemma which is so prevalent that it is apt to be overlooked.

Selection 68

The Perception of Social Status

Thomas E. Lasswell

"Handsome is as handsome does" suggests that the objective observation of a person at any given instant is subject to interpretation based on previous experience with the person. To many an off-campus reader, it is difficult to understand how the "beauty queens" pictured in the college paper were selected. The smaller the student body—and hence the more intimately the students know one another, as a rule—the more likely the discrepancy between the perceptions of "objective" judges and close friends. To a great extent, as another old adage says, "Beauty is in the eye of the beholder."

In this selection, it is noted that "The locus of perception is at the perceiver, not at the perceived." In other words, the assignment of an object to a conceptual category takes place in the mind of the person who perceives the object, not at the object. So it is with the assignment of status, including the assignment of status to oneself. Hence the assignment or acquisition of status is a *social* function. A completely isolated person (a rather impossible idea, since humans are neither hatched from eggs nor self-sufficient at birth) would not only have no conception of the statuses of others but would also have no conception of his own statuses.

It is further noted in the following articles that some statuses separate persons into categories that imply inferiority or superiority while others do not. The former, called *ordered* statuses, are found in such abstractions as rich, intelligent, healthy, upper class, educated, poor, stupid, ill, lower class, and ignorant. Such statuses involve the distinguishing of categories and their *evaluation.* On the other hand, *nominal* statuses such as brother, sister, aunt, blood type A, brunette, and the like usually imply nothing about the superiority or inferiority of the subject. Often statuses that seem ordered to one person seem nominal to another. For example, a racist may perceive racial statuses to fall into a definite hierarchy, while the physical anthropologist may perceive that there are different racial categories but may be quite unconcerned about the superiority or inferiority of each category.

It is through an individual's perception of social statuses that other people become significant to him. As he perceives *who they are,* he relates himself to them and understands their relationships to the other persons in his world. In this way he comes to understand the organization of society. This is why tenants and janitors alike are disturbed when statuses are perceived as incongruous, as reported in the preceding selection. Failure to understand one's relationship with others confuses one's own position in society.

. . . The conceptualization of social status presupposes a perceptive person with some kinds of value orientations in some kind of social contact with a variety of other persons. Hence the elements of the human organism, culture, and the group are all implicit in any study of status or status perception. The status-fixing process itself is a mental device by means of which persons organize and/or rationalize social relationships. It functions through abstracting qualities of persons and relating or comparing them to similar qualities of other real or ideal persons. It involves both cognition and perception. The status-fixing process is in the legitimate area of inquiry of the social psychologist because it is involved in all human interaction and is essential to the conceptualization of social organization in the mind of the person.

The mechanism by which status is perceived consists of a cognitive response to a sensory stimulus. Wallach said, "I have the impression that I perceive . . . meanings in the object even while I realize that they do not come to me through my eyes at the moment of perceiving them but must be furnished by a memory function, for they were given by previous experience with the object." [1] . . . Social status is perceived as memory responds to sensory stimuli. Prescribed and anticipatory roles are memories. "Knowing" a person is remembering a person.

Memories are known to vary in accuracy. While some memories may be quite precise and verifiable, others may be distorted by affective components, or they may be based on inaccurate

From *Sociology and Social Research,* Vol. 45 (1961), 170-174.
[1] Hans Wallach, "Some Considerations Concerning the Relation Between Perception and Cognition," *Journal of Personality,* 18 (September 1949), 6.

perceptions or mistaken sensations. . . . Certain memories may be accentuated or repressed because of strong affective accompaniments. In such circumstances they may overshadow other elements . . . or they may be obscured. Sometimes a person rejects particular perceptions because they cannot be rationalized with existing configurations. For these reasons and others, it is not likely that "objective" statuses of persons can be depended upon for a full understanding of most social situations.

Social statuses cannot be sensed directly. Since they are abstract qualities of persons, they must be perceived through the sensing of symbols. . . . In other words, they are memories that respond to the sensing of particular symbols. One *sees* a wedding ring on the appropriate finger of another person rather than seeing that person's marital status. One *hears* a foreign accent rather than hearing a national status. The sensation received must be related to existing cognitions before status is perceived. . . .

The locus of perception is at the perceiver, not at the perceived. "An individual carries his social position around in his head, so to speak, and puts it into action when the appropriate occasion arises."[2] Not only does he carry his own social position around in his head, but he also carries positions or potential positions for every person that is significant to him.

Perceived statuses rather than "real" statuses are involved in the interaction process. When two persons are engaged in interaction, each is behaving according to his understanding of the other's status(es) if his responses are at the conscious level. If his responses are subliminal, he is still responding to stimuli as *his* nervous system senses and interprets them, not necessarily as a panel of qualified judges might perceive them. In a recent homicide case, a woman claimed that she had believed her husband to be a burglar when he was walking about in their house at night, and had shot him. As a result, he was quite as dead as if he had been a "real" burglar.

It is expedient to distinguish between *nominal* statuses and *ordered* statuses, although these two are by no means mutually exclusive. Nominal statuses are elements of organizational configurations, indicating how persons are related to one another in a social entity. They are ungraded and have no vertical implications. Mother, father, brother, sister, son, daughter are nominal statuses when they are not conceptualized with a vertical dimension. When nominal statuses are being considered, there is no implication of superiority or inferiority. When used in their normal status sense, daughter and sister designate *different* statuses, but carry no suggestion that one is better

or worse, higher or lower, with respect to any system of values.

Ordered statuses are conceptualized along continua from low to high, negative to positive, inferior to superior, or the reverse of these. In other words, ordered statuses have a vertical connotation. One cannot construct such a continuum without reference to some particular value; persons cannot be superior or inferior except with regard to some standard or index. Ordered statuses imply a cognitive scale of a higher order than a nominal scale.

Some status continua are *partially ordered* in the mind of the perceiver. In industry, a line organization suggests an ordered scale, a staff organization suggests a nominal scale, and a line-and-staff organization suggests a partially ordered scale. Occupational scales are frequently partially ordered. A perceiver may have definite vertical statuses in mind for several occupations but indefinite ones for others, even though he understands their nominal differentiation. An unskilled laborer may use no vertical component in conceptualizing the difference between a nurse and a laboratory technician, even though he comprehends the difference in their activities and in their nominal statuses. Nor does this necessarily suggest occupational farness; college professors may hesitate before assigning vertical components to the statuses of business managers, superintendents of buildings and grounds, university press editors, student deans, librarians, and others, even though they can conceptualize a vertical *range* for these occupational statuses. In the partially ordered status scale there are bench marks, but the intermediate categories are not graded individually.

Under certain conditions, the sociologist may wish to use metric scales in evaluating social status. A metric scale is a directional continuum with some sort of systematic calibration so that scaled items can be compared in independent observations by means of a cardinal index. Although any kind of systematic calibration is permissible, equal-interval calibration is so commonly used that it is assumed in the absence of contrary notation.

In interpersonal relationships metric scales may be conceptualized, but ordinarily the information available to persons in interaction is not of an appropriate variety for metric scaling. Other symbols may take precedence in the establishment of relative statuses even if metrically scaled information is available. Even though exact intelligence

---

[2] Kingsley Davis, *Human Society* (New York: The Macmillan Company, 1949), p. 87.

quotients of students are known, a teacher is quite likely to conceptualize their relative intelligence statuses along a more simply ordered or partially ordered continuum.

The perception of ordered statuses involves a cognitive configuration of a series of categories which respond to the stimuli of ordered categories of symbols. These cognitive configurations are often identified as stereotypes. Research on the nature of social class stereotypes now in process by the author and his associates suggests that cognitive configurations may be stimulated by any of an indefinite number of sensed status symbols, but that often a single symbol elicits the entire stereotype, so that all of the configuration is implicit unless special exceptions are noted. To some persons spatially distant from the southern region of the United States, for instance, the symbolic significance of a "southern accent," even though the speaker is unseen, elicits a full stereotype about his expected behaviors in various situations, his values, his intelligence, his morals, his education, his standard of living, his prejudices, and many of his other characteristics. The same stereotype might be elicited by other symbols—a white linen suit, a panama hat, a string tie—depending on the previous direct or vicarious perceptions of the stereotyper. Occasionally, neither

the symbols nor the stereotype elicited appears to have any objective validity.

It has been pointed out that when an individual is confronted by a stranger, he immediately begins to search for symbols by means of which he can assign status to the stranger. This has been called "cue searching." Status-fixing is the sequent of cue searching. The perceiver must be able to fit the perceived into a cognitive framework in order to give meaning to his own behavior toward him; otherwise, the situation is undefined and normless —a degree of anomie exists from his perceptual vantage point.

The man-in-interaction searches consciously or unconsciously for symbolic cues by means of which he can perceive the statuses of others in every social situation. He perceives these cues and compares them with his cognitive images of persons and configurations of statuses, including his image of himself and his statuses. Such images and configurations are compounded from memories and affect. Through this process he relates himself to others. Status perception is imperative for defining a social situation. Both social organization and social adjustment are inconceivable without some form of status perception, as, for that matter, are social disorganization and social maladjustment.

Selection 69

Problems in the Study of Social Stratification

John F. Cuber and William F. Kenkel

Social stratification refers to the division of a large social entity into unequal categories. As was the case with social status, such a division may be (1) an artifice of the student of society or (2) a product of the interaction of the social aggregate. The former approach to the study of social stratification is increasing in recent literature. Since it is usually based upon census information, school records, or other such readily gathered data—without direct observation of the interaction patterns of the population involved—it can be done relatively quickly and inexpensively. The latter approach involves a study of the patterns of association, power hierarchies, and cultural ways of believing and behaving which separate the population into enclaves that are differentially valued by the individual persons in the population. It therefore necessitates a great deal of expensive and time-consuming field work, as well as a broad background in the understanding of human behavior. Probably each of these methods of study has its advantages, but sociologists tend to take strong stands favoring one approach or the other.

In the following selection Cuber and Kenkel have undertaken the task of summarizing three other issues (in addition to the one discussed in the preceding paragraph) that have arisen from the efforts of sociologists to describe the stratification of societies and communities and to understand how and why social stratification occurs in human populations.

Perhaps a prefatory word should be said about the terms *multidimensional* and *unidimensional,* which are used in this article. In its simplest sense, *unidimensional* means that the phenomenon in question has only one necessary and sufficient dimension; that is, only one dimension is *necessary* to describe the phenomenon, and the same dimension is *sufficient* to describe the phenomenon. Multidimensional, on the other hand, means that one measurement is *not* sufficient to describe the phenomenon—that several measurements are necessary. Most social events, processes, and conditions seem to be multidimensional; that is, they cannot be accurately described by any single dimension.

It will be helpful to the student to interpret the positions of Landecker in Selection 70 and of Hollingshead and Redlich in Selection 71 with respect to the issues that Cuber and Kenkel treat.

One of the persistent, but *often implicit,* theoretical difficulties which obfuscate efforts to analyze social stratification concerns whether stratification . . . is unidimensional or multidimensional. Writers with a strong statistical bent sometimes approach their task with either a tacit or expressed assumption that stratification "is" a hierarchical arrangement of persons measured or manifested by *a* difference—attitudes, style of life, differential power, prestige, economic role, or what not. In contrast stand a few sociologists, but growing in number, who apparently have been influenced, whether they know it or not, by the late Max Weber.[1] Weber distinguished among at least three stratifications in a society: (1) the *economic order* ("classes"), that is, the relation of persons to the production and distribution of goods and services; (2) the *prestigial or honorific order* ("social order"); and (3) the *power structure* ("legal order"). A given person (or family) at any given time has at least these three, not one, relative positions in a society. The three positions may not correlate with one another—and often striking contrasts are manifest. Moreover, the interrelations among these three stratifications are not fixed, but rather are constantly changing.

Our own position on this issue is very well stated by Kurt Mayer.[2] (His use of the word *class* instead of *stratification* represents no inconsistency with our usage.)

"Only a class theory which recognizes these three [or more] vertical dimensions as analytically distinct and which intends to trace their interrelationship can provide a realistic understanding of the class structure of complex, industrial socie-

ties. [It must also take cognizance of the fact that the interrelationships of the three dimensions are] in constant flux."

This is a larger order than might at first appear. To apprehend and measure the three (and there may be more) dimensions is a baffling and complex problem; to analyze their interrelationship is an even more subtle and exacting task. But the objective seems to us rightly stated by Mayer, and while we must be satisfied with less than full accomplishment for the present, we should also recognize that the goal is not truly reached when we fashion a quick "solution" by unidimensional analyses.

Categorical (or discrete classes) theories claim, in effect, that in American society the patterns of prestige, power, and other privileges and disprivileges result in the creation of more or less distinct groupings of persons. Such expressions as "the working class is marked off from" some other class, imply that there is a line of demarcation which sets off the designated group of ranked people from some other group. One of these writers says, "A social class, then, is any portion of a community *marked off from* the rest by social

From *Social Stratification in the United States* by John F. Cuber and William F. Kenkel (New York: Appleton-Century-Crofts, Inc., 1954), pp. 22-30.
[1] See H. H. Gerth and C. W. Mills, *From Max Weber: Essays in Sociology* (New York: Oxford University Press, 1946), pp. 180-195, and A. M. Henderson and T. Parsons, *Max Weber: The Theory of Social and Economic Organization* (New York: Oxford University Press, 1947), pp. 424-429.
[2] Kurt Mayer, "The Theory of Social Classes," *Harvard Educational Review,* Summer, 1953, p. 165.

status."[3] In other words, it is postulated by some writers that there is in a community (or society) a collectivity of people of sufficiently similar privilege and disprivilege that they are "marked off from" other persons with different privilege-disprivilege configurations. This concept of stratification is further implied in such phrases as "class lines" and "class conflicts."

Some writers, conscious of the difficulty of defining precisely these alleged lines, point out that it is sometimes impossible to determine "just where" the line should be drawn, but that there is, "somehow," "more or less," some "sort of line" that everyone knows is there! Many persons are familiar, for example, with the upper-, middle-, and lower-class trichotomy, with the Lynds' "business class"-"working class" dichotomy,[4] and with the Warner group's sixfold class system.[5] When one attempts to place a *random* selection of individuals in their "proper" class categories, difficulties arise,[6] because the individuals in question have some attributes, say, of "lower-upper" and some attributes of "lower-middle." Where, then, do they "belong"? Proponents of these categorical systems often allege that these unclassifiable cases are really only "few," are "exceptions to the rule," or are "individuals in transition" from one status category to another. Although there is undoubtedly some truth to each of these rationalizations, we shall subsequently demonstrate that such cases are *not* few, much less "exceptional," or "persons in transition."

It should be pointed out that not all persons who use the *nomenclature* of the categorical-class analyst necessarily subscribe to the above rigidity. Sometimes expressions like "middle class" or "upper-upper" are used in a loose way to designate an approximate range in a hierarchical system for comparative purposes. They do not imply lines of demarcation any more than a person who speaks of "middle age" or "old people" necessarily implies that the categories are clear cut. Considerable caution, therefore, should be observed in analyzing a writer's theoretical position, lest we confuse nomenclature with *conceptualization*.

By implication we have already defined the *continuum theory of stratification*, namely, the idea that there are several privilege, power, and status ranges, more or less continuous from top to bottom, with no clear lines of demarcation. For statistical purposes, of course, it is entirely legitimate to set up *statistical* classes in a continuous series of data, breaking the series at any point or points which suit the purposes of the investigation. Thus, for example, if we are dealing with age, we could, logically, define "old age" as beginning at 65, because then the person is eligible for social

security payments; or at 70, because then he has outlived the average life expectancy at birth; or at 55 or thereabouts, because that seems a reasonable point at which to terminate the range called "middle age." Any of these lines of demarcation can be considered logical, so long as one does not assume that this statistical device gives him any particular grasp on reality and so long as he also realizes that any individual at a given age may fall into a number of different categories, depending on the purpose of the classifier.

Protagonists of the continuum theory of stratification in American society make a strong case for their theory.

1. First, they point out one criticism of the categorical theories, which is now more or less widely known: that there are almost as many systems as there are observers—three classes, six classes, two classes, and four classes!

2. No matter what the criteria may be, significant numbers of persons cannot be readily categorized; this being the case, what shall we do with these numerous "fringe" people?

3. Moreover, the bases of ranking change from time to time, the privileges and disprivileges of persons change with the passing and repealing of laws and the obsolescence of occupations, and in many other ways the system is in perennial flux.[7]

4. A very important line of justification for the continuum theory devolves from the nature of the data. As everyone knows, students of differential rank have "discovered" that the possession of wealth and income, family background, education, ownership of status-giving goods, and prestige give a person or family a relative ranking in the local community or even in the nation. However, when we *measure* each of these attributes, a *continuous series of data emerges*. Income and wealth form a continuous series from the multimillionaire to the person on relief. Occupational prestige has been measured and the findings form

---

[3] Robert MacIver and Charles Page, *Society: An Introductory Analysis* (New York: Rinehart and Co., 1949), pp. 348-349. Italics not in original.
[4] Robert and Helen Lynd, *Middletown* (New York: Harcourt, Brace and Co., 1929), and their *Middletown in Transition* (1937).
[5] W. L. Warner, Marchia Meeker, and Kenneth Eells, *Social Class in America* (Chicago: Science Research Associates, Inc., 1949).
[6] See, e.g., Gerhard E. Lenski, "American Social Classes: Statistical Strata or Social Groups?" *American Journal of Sociology*, 58 (September, 1952), 139-145.
[7] An excellent treatment of this point is to be found in Gideon Sjoberg, "Are Social Classes in America Becoming More Rigid?" *American Sociological Review*, 16 (December, 1951), 775-783. See also M. E. Deeg and D. G. Peterson, "Changes in Social Status of Occupations," *Occupations*, 25 (January, 1947), 205-208.

a series of scores from 96 (out of a possible 100 points) down to 33. . . . Wealth follows a pattern similar to that of income; and prestige goods and services, since they are largely dependent upon income, also follow the same pattern. Education, to be sure, does show some "natural" breaks in the series, due only, however, to the convention of terminating education at the completion of the eighth grade or of high school or of college or of a professional or other post-graduate school.

5. What is an even more important justification of the continuum theory derives from the fact that the alleged bases or criteria for ranking (whether prestige or power or privilege is focused upon) mostly do not show significant *correlations* with one another. A hypothetical case may be constructed to *illustrate* (not offered as "proof" of) this point.

"John Doe is a Jewish owner-proprietor of the largest mercantile establishment in a New England city of 100,000. Being the son of an immigrant, in a family which did not highly value education, he left high school at the end of his second year. Upon his father's death, he inherited a half-million dollar estate, including his father's old, but well-built, home in the 'zone of transition' of the city. A Jew, he cannot belong to either of the two high-prestige country clubs or to any of the high-status Protestant churches of the city, and there is not a large enough Jewish population to support a Jewish Synagogue. One of his sons married the daughter of a highly respected professor in the local university. The other son remained in the military service after the end of the war."

Now what "class" does this man belong to? In terms of lineage, it is obvious that he belongs to a group long disvalued in the Western European culture. In terms of prestige goods—home, automobile, clothes, and jewels—his rating would be approximately average. His institutional affiliations (country club, church, lodge, etc.) would do little, if anything, to attach special prestige or power to him. His educational achievements are certainly below average; those of his children only slightly better. The details in this case are admittedly somewhat extreme, but cases of this *type* are not unusual. It is well known that some of our most highly educated persons (teachers, clergymen, scientists) are on the average relatively lowly paid, and some of our most highly paid persons and groups have little formal education. Many of the "old families" are no longer well off financially and the *nouveaux riches* are found in every community. The correlations among the various criteria of rank are mostly tautological ones: wealth and/or income and the possession of goods that require wealth or income in order to possess them. This is hardly a startling discovery.

It seems for these and other reasons that we are on more sound theoretical ground as social scientists if we proceed on the assumption that the American ranking system is more accurately conceived of as a continuum than as a set of discrete categories. . . .

A third theoretical issue concerns the *raison d'être* of a stratification system. What is its rationale? Two main views on this question can be found in present sociological literature.

The *functional* point of view, stated in simple terms, holds that the existing differential distribution of privilege and disprivilege derives from the efforts of a society to fulfill its necessary goals.[8] For example, a society needs leaders in government, religion, and education. These leaders require substantial periods of training and they must defer gratification of many of their personal wants and must submit to considerable discipline in order to secure their training. After the period of training is completed, they are required to assume positions of considerable responsibility, resulting often in more self-denial. As a reward for these disprivileges, and for the value of the service performed, these persons, it is claimed, receive the privilege of higher income, higher prestige, deference, and various kinds of other perquisites.[9]

Furthermore, talent is relatively scarce. Not everyone has the necessary intelligence, physical stamina, and emotional attributes, for example, to complete the conventional training for an M.D. degree and to practice medicine thereafter. Similarly for other professions and undertakings that require special skill. Therefore, it is further argued by functionalists, unequal privilege is also the result of unequal possession of talent.[10]

A conflicting view[11] stresses that, for American society at least, there are contradictions to the functional theory. The positions of highest societal

---

[8] For a clear and forceful statement of a functionalist position, see especially Kingsley Davis and W. E. Moore, "Some Principles of Stratification," *American Sociological Review*, 10 (April, 1945), 242-249.

[9] *Ibid.*

[10] *Ibid.*

[11] For a vigorous critique of Davis and Moore's position on functionalism and stratification, see Melvin Tumin, "Some Principles of Stratification: A Critical Analysis," *American Sociological Review*, 18 (August, 1953), 387-394. A defense of their position by Davis and Moore follows Tumin's critique. The issue is reopened by Tumin again in a "Letter to the Editor," *American Sociological Review*, 18 (December, 1953), 672.

responsibility—government, religion, the judiciary, and education—are financially not highly rewarded in the American system. Are we to conclude that liquor dispensers, entertainers (including athletes), and speculators have a higher "function" in American society? They, along with racketeers, certainly receive higher incomes and are further supported in the eyes of many by high prestige. Furthermore, what is particularly functional about the accent on lineage? Moreover, cases are legion in which persons of considerable talent are summarily denied the right to exercise their talents in socially responsible positions simply because they are Negroes, or because they are Jewish, or because otherwise they have not chosen their parents wisely.

An acceptable functionalist position would seem to need, then, to take account of several conditions: (1) "Rewards" to persons, which presumably motivate the able to defer gratification and otherwise translate their aspirations into actions in the public interest, should be understood to include psychic and prestigial income as well as financial returns. The low incomes of teachers and clergymen may be counterbalanced by such factors as high prestige, pleasant working conditions, long vacations, and other non-pecuniary advantages. (2) Alternative ways of handling recruitment and reward should be recognized as being comparably, if not equally, functional in meeting the needs of the society. In other words, the functionalist should so state his position that it could not be used by the supporters of the status quo in such a way that all new ways of recruitment and reward come to be labeled "disfunctional." Change can improve as well as impede the chances for a better society. (3) Goals (values) of those who judge functionality should be recognized as affecting judgments of what is and is not functional. For example, mass education is probably not "functional" to one with pro-fascist views. (4) What is "functional" will vary from time to time because societal arrangements are not functional per se, but rather are so in part *because of* the conditions imposed on the society from the outside. For example, a large military force is functional only so long as there is a real and present danger from the outside; otherwise it is a parasite on the economy. Examined in the light of these and probably other qualifications, a stratification system can probably be objectively evaluated, either in toto or in its various parts, as to its functionality.

Selection 70

The Crystallization of Social Strata

Werner S. Landecker

At various times and places social strata have been so clearly defined and generally agreed upon that the superiority or inferiority of a given category of persons has been known to and understood by the entire population. In some countries, such as the Union of South Africa, social categories are or have been literally determined by law. At other times and in other places, the distinctions between social categories have been so subtle that one would have to live in the community for many years before he could sense their existence, and even then there may be widespread disagreement as to which people constitute each of the categories. The Mesquakie Indians have such a society, and such is the ideal of Communist countries.

Following the development of the concept of status crystallization by Gerhard Lenski, Landecker observes in the article at hand that there are degrees of rigidity (and perhaps reality) in the lines which separate social strata in different communities and that it is possible to devise an index which will reflect the pervasiveness and persistence of these lines. He then proceeds to prepare such an index, to show the results of its application, and to describe the theoretical implications of the basic concept.

Landecker uses the term *social class* in much the same way that others use the term *social stratification*. It may seem to the student, as it does to many eminent scholars, that a distinction between these terms is not necessary since they denote quite similar social phenomena. Other scholars argue that social class is only *one kind* of social stratification—that power stratification, ethnic stratification, religious stratification, and many other kinds of stratification may be found in social aggregates. As a rule, persons who equate social class and social stratification are logically forced to support the concept of general status, which was discussed earlier. This concept, in turn, suggests a unidimensional perspective of social class, as discussed in the preceding article by Cuber and Kenkel.

In this book, we distinguish social stratifications from social class and use the former as the more general term. Students whose texts or other readings equate the two terms may choose to ignore the distinction between the subject matter of Selections 69-71 and that of Selections 72-73.

Although quantitative analysis has been applied to many aspects of class, the "class" character of given strata has not been treated in quantitative terms. "Being a class" has not been described as a property that may be present in varying degrees. This is not to say that the concept has always been used with the intent of asserting the full-blown existence of a class. The point is rather that, as yet, attention has not been directed to such questions as "To what *extent* is a given system of stratification a class system?" or "How do different segments of that system compare in the *degree* to which they are classes?" The chief purpose of this paper is to develop an approach that would make it possible, both conceptually and operationally, to pursue such questions.

THE "CLASS CRYSTALLIZATION" CONTINUUM

To treat class stratification as a matter of degree should be useful in the analysis of American class systems in particular. There are several studies whose findings suggest that in American society the formation of social classes has occurred only to a limited extent. For example, while it has been widely observed that opinions on social-economic issues differ by social status, the differences obtained are ordinarily so gradual in character that the existence of underlying class differences has been questioned. Furthermore, in several community studies it has been found that the local population is in considerable disagreement as to the number of social classes in the community. It would be difficult to assume that what appears to its local participants in images of such diversity is a highly structured class system. A similar problem is posed by the results of a study concerned with the respondent's awareness of his own class status. It was found that whether a person identified himself with one or another social class

depended to a large extent on the particular technique used in phrasing the interview question. Again, such instability in self-classifications would be unlikely to occur in a clearly class-structured population.

While these findings do not imply an absence of class stratification, they pose the problem of its magnitude. A major obstacle in recognizing this problem seems to have been of a conceptual sort. What is needed is a concept of "class" which points to different degrees of "classness."

One may attempt to build this kind of concept on foundations laid in Max Weber's analysis of social classes. Weber develops his concept of "class" within the framework of a more general pattern of definitions couched in terms of "probability." Since probability is a matter of degree, objects defined in this manner are readily conceived as existing to a greater or lesser extent. Such quantitative thinking is facilitated when Weber defines "class" as a "typical probability" that a given level of opportunities in life or "life chances" will accompany a given position in the economic order. Thus class stratification exists to a higher or lower degree, depending on the greater or smaller probability that different economic positions will give access to different levels of opportunity.

Implied in Weber's treatment of "class" is a distinction between two types of social inequality. One of these is a relatively *specific* kind of inequality, as among property levels or among occupational levels; the other is an inequality in more *general* respects, designated as inequality in life chances or opportunities. For Weber, inequality in specific respects is basic to class stratification but not identical with it. Class stratification exists only to the degree to which specific inequalities give rise to a generalized inequality. This abstract

From *Social Research*, Vol. 27 (1960), 308-320.

formulation provides the framework within which a research-oriented definition can be developed.

For this purpose, inequality in "specific" respects may be represented by any status hierarchy in which a population is distributed in terms of a single characteristic. Occupation is illustrative of such a characteristic, as is education. In the present analysis any hierarchy that consists entirely of status gradations of a single characteristic will be called a "rank system."

In order to ascertain the extent to which class stratification has taken place in a social system, one may determine the degree to which the status differences specific to particular rank systems have given rise to generalized inequalities. Inequalities are generalized in so far as the specific inequalities of one rank system are consistent with those of other rank systems.

Thus if it is common for persons who face one another as superior and subordinate in one rank system to be so related in other rank systems as well, a generalized pattern of inequality is present. Under such conditions, where class stratification is highly developed, strata located on approximately the same levels of different rank systems tend to coincide in their memberships. In reverse, a merely rudimentary class system, characterized by inequalities that are situationally specific rather than generalized, will manifest itself in rank systems that are relatively independent of one another in their population distributions. If rank status is but a minor factor in the patterning of social relations, a person's status in one rank system will have little effect on his opportunities in other rank systems. Under these conditions it will frequently happen that persons who occupy the same level in one rank system will be considerably scattered in others.

In these two patterns of relationship among rank systems a highly developed class structure is contrasted with a virtual absence of classes. These patterns are opposite poles on a scale that will here be designated as the "class crystallization" continuum. It measures the extent to which equivalent strata of different rank systems converge in their composition, and thus form one class.

TOOLS FOR MEASURING CLASS CRYSTALLIZATION

The preceding considerations have served as the basis for an attempt to measure class crystallization in the metropolitan area of Detroit, as of 1952. The information required for this task was obtained through the facilities of the Detroit Area Study, by means of interviews with subjects selected by area sampling.

The first methodological problem encountered in measuring class crystallization is to decide what the major rank systems of a given population are. In the selection of such rank systems the following criteria seem generally applicable.

First, the major rank systems of a given population are only those in which virtually every member of that population can be placed. A person's placement in such a rank system may be possible either because of his own position in it, or because his status is derived from a position held by the head of his family. Thus an occupational rank system would qualify by this criterion, because one may assume that persons who lack an occupational role of their own, especially wives, will share to some extent the occupational status held by the head of their family. Differences in athletic prowess, on the other hand, are perhaps a common rank system among adolescents and young adults, but in urbanized societies they do not yield rank differences among adults in general.

Second, to serve as a potential basis of class stratification, a major rank system must be one in which it is possible for all members of a family to hold identical status (though of course this situation does not necessarily obtain). Otherwise its use would make it difficult or impossible to treat the family as a homogeneous unit of a class system. This criterion eliminates age and sex rank systems, because in both of these any single family is necessarily scattered over different strata.

Finally, in relation to any major rank system already selected, another major rank system must have a reasonable degree of conceptual and logical independence. However, the mere fact of a high correlation between two rank systems at a particular time and locality does not necessarily argue against their simultaneous use; indeed, one way of observing a high degree of class crystallization would be through a high intercorrelation among rank systems. An empirical justification for rejecting one rank system as a mere duplication of another would hinge on evidence of a relationship between them which remains uniformly close under the most diverse conditions, representing the greatest possible variety of communities. Lacking evidence of this kind, the researcher must substitute a plausible assumption. Thus in the present study it is assumed that a rank system based on the financial value of possessions would correlate with an income rank system so highly and so consistently under manifold conditions that only one of them should be accepted.

Within the limits set by these criteria, as well as by the researcher's perception of the rating scales that prevail in a population, the selection of particular rank systems will depend on the variety of available data. In the case of a large American city like Detroit, highly diversified in cultural background and ancestry as well as in economic pursuits, it seemed appropriate to rank all respondents in terms of the following four characteristics: occupation, income, education, and ethnic-racial descent.

It was, then, among four rank systems based respectively on these characteristics that crystallization, or the convergence of equivalent status levels, was to be measured. For this purpose it seemed necessary to employ a standard measure of status, in terms of which the various ranks of all rank systems could be compared. Such a measure was devised for the population of Detroit by first computing the cumulative percentage distribution of the total sample in each rank system separately, and then assigning consecutive ranges of status percentiles to the ranks found in a given rank system. Table 1 presents these status ranges in equalized intervals, thus permitting comparisons that indicate which ranks of the various rank systems in the Detroit population are approximately equivalent in status. Inasmuch as the table bypasses the fact that equivalent ranks do not completely coincide in their membership, it serves also as a theoretical construct of a fully crystallized class system.

The next step in measuring class crystallization was to determine the degree of equivalence among the ranks held by a given person in each of the four rank systems. For this purpose every rank of each individual was represented by the midpoint of its percentile range; this midpoint was designated as "status score." By inverting a measure of dispersion among his four status scores, a "crystallization score" was computed for each person. The actually obtained scores range from a minimum of 10 for the most amorphous to a maximum of 98 for the most crystallized status. When used in the aggregate, individual scores provide a basis for measuring crystallization as a property of an entire class system, or of particular levels within it. This mode of analysis is pursued in the following examination.

THE HYPOTHESIS OF
"CRYSTALLIZATION PATTERN"

It is probably unusual for a class system to be equally crystallized from top to bottom. Perhaps in a rigidly crystallized and stationary system, like the Hindu caste system in earlier centuries, one might find the extent of crystallization to be nearly uniform on all status levels. Conversely, in a rapidly changing frontier society, amorphous status combinations may be equally dominant throughout. In those systems, however, where neither the strain for consistency nor the momentum of fluid-

---

TABLE 1: Approximately Equivalent Rank Levels in Four Rank Systems[a]

STATUS PERCENTILES	OCCUPATIONAL RANK SYSTEM[b]	INCOME RANK SYSTEM (ANNUAL)	EDUCATIONAL RANK SYSTEM (IN YEARS COMPLETED)	ETHNIC-RACIAL RANK SYSTEM[c]
91–100	A	$8,000 & over	15 & over	English
81–90	B	6,000–7,999	13–14	{ Scandinavian { French
71–80	B	5,000–5,999	12 (diploma)	{ Scottish { Finnish
61–70	C	4,000–4,999	12 (others)	German
51–60	C	4,000–4,999	11	Irish
41–50	C	3,000–3,999	10	{ Greek { Italian
31–40	D	3,000–3,999	9	Polish
21–30	D	3,000–3,999	8	{ Hungarian { Russian
11–20	D	2,000–2,999	7	Negro
1–10	E	1,999 & less	6 & less	{ Mexican { Hillbilly

[a] *Upper and lower percentile limits of each rank are rounded to the nearest tenth percentile.*
[b] *Major occupations illustrative of each level are the following: A) banker, engineer, industrialist, physician, school principal; B) building contractor, electrician, newspaper reporter, registered nurse, toolmaker; C) auto mechanic, bricklayer, policeman, secretary, real estate agent; D) barber, machine operative, salesclerk, truckdriver, typist; E) dockworker, gas-station attendant, janitor, maid, waiter.*
[c] *The ethnic-racial categories listed constitute major examples. Each status decile is represented by its largest component if the latter fills more than half of that decile; otherwise it is represented by its two largest components.*

ity determines the relationship among rank systems, differences in the crystallization potential of different status levels are likely to find expression.

One would expect the potential for crystallization to be strongest at the two extremes of a class system. In so far as the elite level of any major rank system is concerned, the very fact that this level stands out in prestige and influence would seem to favor its control over objects of high esteem. High status positions in other rank systems are among these objects. It is likely, therefore, that persons who rate highest in one rank system have the most power to monopolize equivalent strata in other rank systems. On an intermediate rank level there seems to be not only less power to monopolize corresponding rank levels but also less interest in doing so, at least in mobile systems; here the goal of up-mobility will reduce the effort to solidify one's present position. On the other hand, to be near the bottom of one rank system is a handicap of such magnitude that access to higher levels in other rank systems is made particularly difficult.

It is assumed then that very high status and very low status have similar structural consequences, but each for a different reason. In the one case, equivalent rank levels tend to converge because the power to exclude competitors for status is at its maximum; in the other case, because the power to compete for higher status is at its minimum.

This hypothesized pattern is consonant with various empirical findings scattered in studies of diverse scope. Among these findings the following four are relevant: first, when judging the relative prestige of different families in a community, local raters show more agreement with respect to families at each extreme than for those on intermediate levels of the prestige range; second, prestige ratings of different occupations show the highest degree of consensus regarding occupations at each extreme of the prestige scale; third, correlations between income and education are highest for persons at each extreme of occupational status, and correlations between educational and occupational status are highest for persons at each extreme of the income distribution; and finally, residential segregation is most pronounced among persons of either extremely high or extremely low occupational status. All of these findings acquire added meaning and mutual consistency if the hypothesis of "crystallization pattern" can be established. The Detroit data have provided an opportunity for determining whether variations in class crystallization on different status levels conform indeed to the expected pattern.

In order to make possible such comparison among status levels, an arithmetic mean of crystallization scores was calculated separately for each rank in each rank system. All means were standardized for differences in the lowest crystallization scores theoretically possible for different rank levels.[1] The resulting measures were designated as "adjusted crystallization means," and series of these measures for each of the four rank systems are presented in Table 2. Within a rank system, the adjusted mean shown for a given status percentile represents the rank whose status range happens to include that percentile.

Of particular relevance for the hypothesis of

---

[1] If "a" represents the mean crystallization score for a given rank level and "b" the lowest possible crystallization score for that level, the procedure can be summarized as follows: $x = 100(a-b)/100-b$.

TABLE 2: Adjusted Crystallization Means and Class Crystallization Index for Every Tenth Status Percentile

STATUS PERCENTILES	ADJUSTED CRYSTALLIZATION MEANS				CLASS CRYSTALLIZATION INDEX
	OCCUPATIONAL RANK SYSTEM	INCOME RANK SYSTEM	EDUCATIONAL RANK SYSTEM	ETHNIC-RACIAL RANK SYSTEM	
95	70.8	60.8	60.0	62.6	63.6
85	55.7	58.2	54.0	57.4	56.3
75	55.7	60.0	59.2	55.3	57.6
65	56.4	59.4	55.7	58.9	57.6
55	56.4	59.4	57.6	57.6	57.8
45	56.4	60.3	60.4	61.4	59.6
35	59.1	60.3	58.1	62.8	60.1
25	59.1	60.3	60.0	55.4	58.7
15	59.1	60.3	59.0	60.1	59.6
5	58.7	55.1	62.1	55.2	57.8

"crystallization pattern" is the last column of this table. Since the adjusted crystallization means in the earlier columns are relative to specific rank systems, a more comprehensive measure seemed needed, capable of assessing class crystallization as a property of status levels that cut across all rank systems. The index of class crystallization, contained in the last column, is intended to provide such an overall measure. Each index value is the mean of the adjusted crystallization means shown for that status percentile.

The distribution of these index values conforms only in part to the "crystallization pattern" hypothesis in its initial formulation. The assumption that class crystallization will be particularly strong on the highest level is supported by the fact that the index of class crystallization shows a higher score for the top status level, represented by status percentile 95, than for any other level. It was additionally assumed, however, that the class crystallization of the lowest status level would also be comparatively strong, and this part of the hypothesis is not borne out by the data. Besides the top status level there are four others, status percentiles 45-15, that have higher index scores than does the lowest level. Thus the findings support the view that high status exerts a relatively strong influence on one's "life chances," to return to Weber's phrase; but they also indicate that the handicap of low status is less severe than had been anticipated.

CONCLUSIONS

The fact that the pattern of class crystallization in Detroit conforms to the hypothesis in one respect and deviates in another is not by itself a test of the hypothesis. Detroit is but one case; as long as comparable data for other communities are not available, it is impossible to decide whether the discrepancy between the observed and the expected pattern requires a general revision of the initial hypothesis or reflects the special influence of uncontrolled factors. Thus one may wonder whether some aspects of large-scale employment in mass industry have exerted a leveling effect among Detroit workers and thereby counteracted the strong crystallization potential of the lowest strata. For instance, the growth of industrial unionism in Detroit may have aided in a reduction of the linkage between the lowest ethnic-racial levels and the lowest occupational and income levels.

Within the context of this paper, however, the main function of the Detroit data has been to provide the necessary working material as well as a demonstration case for a revised approach to class stratification. In the main, an effort has been made to treat class stratification as a phenomenon that may be present in larger or smaller amounts. The concept of "class crystallization" has been introduced to indicate explicitly that the structuring of a collectivity into social classes is a matter of degree.

Even for purely descriptive purposes this shift has a manifest advantage. Familiar but oversimplified questions as to the *existence* of social classes in the United States or elsewhere give way to questions as to the *extent* of their formation. For Detroit the findings suggest a twofold answer. In the first place, the community as a whole seems to constitute a class system to a rather limited degree, as judged by the fact that the values of the crystallization index are considerably lower than the maximum crystallization scores obtained by individuals. Second, the highest status level constitutes a class to a greater extent than does any other status level in the community.

But the chief implications of the "class crystallization" variable lie in the promise it holds for the development of theoretically relevant research. It is possible to distinguish three research areas in which the use of this variable would seem to be of benefit.

One set of problems is concerned with the conditions under which different degrees of class crystallization occur. Research in this direction would include analyses of differences in class crystallization among the several strata of a given status system, as illustrated by the present study. It would also be concerned with the problem of how to account for differences in the class crystallization of entire status systems, a problem that has its roots in the familiar search for "causes of class stratification" encountered in the older literature. In its revised formulation, this problem becomes more readily amenable to investigation, since one can select a number of collectivities, such as various communities, that represent different points on the class-crystallization continuum, and compare them with respect to the presence of factors that may be thought to promote or impede class crystallization.

A second group of research problems involves the use of class crystallization as an independent variable, the goal of such investigations being to discover its social consequences. Professor Lenski has examined the Detroit data from this point of view. His findings suggest that weak class crystallization engenders emotional stress and interpersonal strain, thereby contributing to social change and to social interaction of the purposive . . . type. . . .

In a third area of research, class crystallization

occupies the role of a qualifying variable—one that affects the relationship between two other variables. Research in this area would attempt to determine whether differences in class crystallization tend to modify the social and social-psychological consequences of other stratification variables. Considerable attention could be focused on the broad hypothesis that the influence of status differences on other aspects of group life is strengthened by a high degree of class crystallization. As the crystallization of a class system increases, one would expect that status differences will function as more severe barriers to personal association and communication; that behavior patterns and attitudes will vary more closely with status; and that status will be reflected more accurately in class consciousness.

These hypotheses rest on a premise that can be expressed in substantive as well as in methodological terms. In substantive respects the basic assumption is that the weaker the crystallization of a class system, the more nearly are the consequences of one rank system canceled out by those of another; and that in a highly crystallized class system the causal influence of status differences is strengthened by their mutual reinforcement. In methodological respects the premise implies a criterion for the selection of research sites. If one wishes to determine the effects of class differences on other social phenomena, be they political ideologies or child-rearing practices, it will be advisable to collect one's data in class systems characterized by strong crystallization. Otherwise the findings may be inconclusive, because the strata were too limited in class quality to yield significant class differences.

Selection 71

Social Stratification and Psychiatric Disorders
August B. Hollingshead and Frederick C. Redlich

There are times when it is desirable to have some indicator to help locate a phenomenon in order to study it or something related to it. The "finder" is called an *index*. In the following article, Hollingshead presents an *Index of Social Position*, based on the residential area in which a family lives, the occupation of the head of the family, and the education of the head of the family. It should be stressed that an index is not a summation of the factors involved in a phenomenon but rather a guide to the absence, presence, extent, degree, or categories of the phenomenon. Hence the I.S.P. (the commonly used abbreviation for the *Index of Social Position*) is not a composite of all the factors involved in assigning general status nor of the determinants of social class.

In addition to being a "finder," the I.S.P. serves as a gauge, a measuring device, by means of which the *probable* social class of an individual or a family may be discovered. From many perspectives the population is divided into unequal categories which appear to be definitely superior or inferior to one another; the I.S.P. draws the boundary lines between five such categories. Hollingshead and Redlich maintain that the five categories into which the I.S.P. separates the population of New Haven, Connecticut, comprise respectively the five social classes found in that city.

In the description of these classes, phrases such as "often inherited," "almost all," "many are engaged," "predominantly high school graduates," and "only a small minority" demonstrate that the I.S.P. categories do not correspond *exactly* to the social classes of New Haven but that the correspondence is close enough to make possible the collection of significant data. Similar findings have been reported in other studies, notably those done by W. Lloyd Warner and his associates. The Warner studies utilize the *Index of Status Characteristics* (or I.S.C.), which is based on source of income, occupation, house type, and residential area. The implication of these findings for the issue of the continuum described by Cuber and Kenkel is that one might find discrete classes in the social organization of a community and yet find a continuum of demographic categories in the same community.

In the study that follows, Hollingshead and Redlich used the I.S.P. to identify the social class status of persons in the New Haven area. Then samples of members of different social classes were identified and studied to determine whether there were differences between the social classes in the nature and extent of mental illness patterns among their members. In similar fashion, the I.S.P. has been used by other researchers to determine whether there are class differences in speech patterns, eating habits, and many other cultural and behavioral items.

The research reported here grew out of the work of a number of men, who, during the last half century, have demonstrated that the social environment in which individuals live is connected in some way, as yet not fully explained, to the development of mental illness. Medical men have approached this problem largely from the viewpoint of epidemiology. Sociologists, on the other hand, have analyzed the question in terms of ecology, and of social disorganization. Neither psychiatrists nor sociologists have carried on extensive research into the specific question we are concerned with, namely, interrelations between the class structure and the development of mental illness. However, a few sociologists and psychiatrists have written speculative and research papers in this area.

The present research, therefore, was designed to discover whether a relationship does or does not exist between the class system of our society and mental illnesses. Five general hypotheses were formulated in our research plan to test some dimension of an assumed relationship between the two. These hypotheses were stated positively; they could just as easily have been expressed either negatively or conditionally. They were phrased as follows:

I. The *expectancy* of a psychiatric disorder is related significantly to an individual's position in the class structure of his society.

II. The *types* of psychiatric disorders are connected significantly to the class structure.

III. The type of *psychiatric treatment* administered is associated with patient's positions in the class structure.

IV. The *psycho-dynamics* of psychiatric disorders are correlative to an individual's position in the class structure.

V. *Mobility* in the class structure is neurotogenic [neurosis-producing].

Each hypothesis is linked to the others, and all are subsumed under the theoretical assumption of a functional relationship between stratification in society and the prevalence of particular types of mental disorders among given social classes or strata in a specified population. Although our research was planned around these hypotheses, we have been forced by the nature of the problem of mental illness to study *diagnosed* prevalence of psychiatric disorders, rather than *true* or *total* prevalence.

METHODOLOGICAL PROCEDURE

The research is being done by a team of four psychiatrists, two sociologists, and a clinical psychologist. The data are being assembled in the New Haven urban community, which consists of the city of New Haven and surrounding towns of East Haven, North Haven, West Haven, and Hamden. This community had a population of some 250,000 persons in 1950. The New Haven community was selected because the community's structure has been studied intensively by sociologists over a long period. In addition, it is served by a private psychiatric hospital, three psychiatric clinics, and 27 practicing psychiatrists, as well as the state and Veterans Administration facilities.

Four basic technical operations had to be completed before the hypotheses could be tested. These were: the delineation of the class structure of the community, selection of a cross-sectional control of the community's population, the determination of who was receiving psychiatric care, and the stratification of both the control sample and the psychiatric patients. . . .

From the *American Sociological Review*, Vol. 18 (1953), 163–169. Reprinted by permission of the American Sociological Association.

The community's social structure is differentiated *vertically* along racial, ethnic, and religious lines; each of these vertical cleavages, in turn, is differentiated *horizontally* by a series of strata or classes. Around the socio-biological axis of race two social worlds have evolved: A Negro world and a white world. The white world is divided by ethnic origin and religion into Catholic, Protestant, and Jewish contingents. Within these divisions there are numerous ethnic groups. The Irish hold aloof from the Italians, and the Italians move in different circles from the Poles. The Jews maintain a religious and social life separate from the gentiles. The *horizontal* strata that transect each of these vertical divisions are based upon the social values that are attached to occupation, education, place of residence in the community, and associations.

The vertically differentiating factors of race, religion and ethnic origin, when combined with the horizontally differentiating ones of occupation, education, place of residence and so on, produce a social structure that is highly compartmentalized. The integrating factors in this complex are twofold. First, each stratum of each vertical division is similar in its cultural characteristics to the corresponding stratum in the other divisions. Second, the cultural pattern for each stratum or class was set by the "Old Yankee" core group. This core group provided the master cultural mold that has shaped the status system of each sub-group in the community. In short, the social structure of the New Haven community is a parallel class structure within the limits of race, ethnic origin, and religion.

This fact enabled us to stratify the community, for our purposes, with an *Index of Social Position*. This *Index* utilizes three scaled factors to determine an individual's class position within the community's stratificational system: ecological area of residence, occupation, and education. Ecological area of residence is measured by a six point scale; occupation and education are each measured by a seven point scale. To obtain a social class score on an individual we must therefore know his address, his occupation, and the number of years of school he has completed. Each of these factors is given a scale score, and the scale score is multiplied by a factor weight determined by a standard regression equation. The factor weights are as follows: Ecological area of residence, 5; occupation, 8; and education, 6. The three factor scores are summed, and the resultant score is taken as an index of this individual's position in the community's social class system.

This *Index* enabled us to delineate five main social class strata within the horizontal dimension of the social structure. These principal strata or classes may be characterized as follows:

Class I. This stratum is composed of wealthy families whose wealth is often inherited and whose heads are leaders in the community's business and professional pursuits. Its members live in those areas of the community generally regarded as "the best;" the adults are college graduates, usually from famous private institutions, and almost all gentile families are listed in the New Haven *Social Directory*, but few Jewish families are listed. In brief, these people occupy positions of high social prestige.

Class II. Adults in this stratum are almost all college graduates; the males occupy high managerial positions, many are engaged in the lesser ranking professions. These families are well-to-do, but there is no substantial inherited or acquired wealth. Its members live in the "better" residential areas; about one-half of these families belong to lesser ranking private clubs, but only 5 per cent of Class II families are listed in the New Haven *Social Directory*.

Class III. This stratum includes the vast majority of small proprietors, white-collar office and sales workers, and a considerable number of skilled manual workers. Adults are predominately high school graduates, but a considerable percentage have attended business schools and small colleges for a year or two. They live in "good" residential areas; less than 5 per cent belong to private clubs, but they are not included in the *Social Directory*. Their social life tends to be concentrated in the family, the church, and the lodge.

Class IV. This stratum consists predominately of semi-skilled factory workers. Its adult members have finished the elementary grades, but the older people have not completed high school. However, adults under thirty-five have generally graduated from high school. Its members comprise almost one-half of the community; and their residences are scattered over wide areas. Social life is centered in the family, the neighborhood, the labor union, and public places.

Class V. Occupationally, Class V adults are overwhelmingly semi-skilled factory hands and unskilled laborers. Educationally most adults have not completed the elementary grades. The families are concentrated in the "tenement" and "cold-water flat" areas of New Haven. Only a small minority belong to organized community institutions. Their social life takes place in the family flat, on the street, or in neighborhood social agencies.

The second major technical operation in this research was the enumeration of psychiatric patients. A Psychiatric Census was taken to discover the number and kinds of psychiatric patients in the community. Enumeration was limited to residents of the community who were patients of a psychiatrist or a psychiatric clinic, or were in a psychiatric institution on December 1, 1950. To make reasonably certain that all patients were included in the enumeration, the research team gathered data from all public and private psychiatric institutions and clinics in Connecticut and nearby states, and all private practitioners in Connecticut and the metropolitan New York area. It received the cooperation of all clinics and institutions, and of all practitioners except a small number in New York City. It can be reasonably assumed that we have data comprising at least 98 per cent of all individuals who were receiving psychiatric care on December 1, 1950.

Forty-four pertinent items of information were gathered on each patient and placed on a schedule. The psychiatrists gathered material regarding symptomatology and diagnosis, onset of illness and duration, referral to the practitioner and the institution, and the nature and intensity of treatment. The sociologists obtained information on age, sex, occupation, education, religion, race and ethnicity, family history, marital experiences, and so on.

The third technical research operation was the selection of a control sample from the normal population of the community. The sociologists drew a 5 per cent random sample of households in the community from the 1951, New Haven *City Directory*. This directory covers the entire communal area. The names and addresses in it were compiled in October and November, 1950—a period very close to the date of the Psychiatric Census. Therefore there was comparability of residence and date of registry between the two population groups. Each household drawn in the sample was interviewed, and data on the age, sex, occupation, education, religion, and income of family members, as well as other items necessary for our purposes were placed on a schedule. This sample is our Control Population.

Our fourth basic operation was the stratification of the psychiatric patients and of the control population with the *Index of Social Position*. As soon as these tasks were completed, the schedules from the Psychiatric Census and the 5 per cent Control Sample were edited and coded, and their data were placed on Hollerith cards. The analysis of these data is in process.

SELECTED FINDINGS

Before we discuss our findings relative to Hypothesis I, we want to reemphasize that our study is concerned with *diagnosed* or *treated* prevalence rather than *true* or *total* prevalence. Our Psychiatric Census included only psychiatric cases under treatment, diagnostic study, or care. It did not include individuals with psychiatric disorders who were not being treated on December 1, 1950, by a psychiatrist. There are undoubtedly many individuals in the community with psychiatric problems who escaped our net. If we had *true* prevalence figures, many findings from our present study would be more meaningful, perhaps some of our interpretations would be changed, but at present we must limit ourselves to the data we have.

Hypothesis I, as revised by the nature of the problem, stated: *The diagnosed prevalence of psychiatric disorders is related significantly to an individual's position in the class structure.* A test of this hypothesis involves a comparison of the normal population with the psychiatric population. If no significant difference between the distribution of the normal population and the psychiatric patient population by social class is found, Hypothesis I may be abandoned as unproved. However, if a significant difference is found between the two populations by class, Hypothesis I should be entertained until more conclusive data are assembled. Pertinent data for a limited test of Hypothesis I are presented in Table 1. The data

TABLE 1: **Distribution of Normal and Psychiatric Population by Social Class**

SOCIAL CLASS	NORMAL POPULATION*		PSYCHIATRIC POPULATION	
	NUMBER	PER CENT	NUMBER	PER CENT
I	358	3.1	19	1.0
II	926	8.1	131	6.7
III	2,500	22.0	260	13.2
IV	5,256	46.0	758	38.6
V	2,037	17.8	723	36.8
Unknown**	345	3.0	72	3.7
Total	11,422	100.0	1,963	100.0

Chi square $= 408.16$, *P less than .001.*
These figures are preliminary. They do not include Yale students, transients, institutionalized persons, and refusals.
**The unknown cases were not used in the calculation of chi square. They are individuals drawn in the sample, and psychiatric cases whose class level could not be determined because of paucity of data.*

included show the number of individuals in the normal population and the psychiatric population, by class level. What we are concerned with in this test is how these two populations are distributed by class.

When we tested the reliability of these population distributions by the use of the chi square method, we found a *very significant* relation between social class and treated prevalence of psychiatric disorders in the New Haven community. A comparison of the percentage distribution of each population by class readily indicates the direction of the class concentration of psychiatric cases. For example, Class I contains 3.1 per cent of the community's population but only 1.0 per cent of the psychiatric cases. Class V, on the other hand, includes 17.8 per cent of the community's population, but contributed 36.8 per cent of the psychiatric patients. On the basis of our data Hypothesis I clearly should be accepted as tenable.

Hypothesis II postulated a significant connection between the *type* of psychiatric disorder and social class. This hypothesis involves a test of the idea that there may be a functional relationship between an individual's position in the class system and the type of psychiatric disorder that he may present. This hypothesis depends, in part, on the question of diagnosis. Our psychiatrists based their diagnoses on the classificatory system developed by the Veterans Administration. For the purposes of this paper, all cases are grouped into two categories: the neuroses and the psychoses. The results of this grouping by social class are given in Table 2.

A study of Table 2 will show that the neuroses are concentrated at the higher levels and the psychoses at the lower end of the class structure. Our team advanced a number of theories to explain the sharp differences between the neuroses and psychoses by social class. One suggestion was that the low percentage of neurotics in the lower classes was a direct reaction to the cost of psychiatric treatment. But as we accumulated a series of case studies, for tests of Hypotheses IV and V, we became skeptical of this simple interpretation. Our detailed case records indicate that the social distance between psychiatrist and patient may be more potent than economic considerations in determining the character of psychiatric intervention. This question therefore requires further research.

The high concentration of psychotics in the lower strata is probably the product of a very unequal distribution of psychotics in the total population. To test this idea, Hollingshead selected schizophrenics for special study. Because of the severity of this disease it is probable that very few schizophrenics fail to receive some kind of psychiatric care. This diagnostic group comprises 44.2 per cent of all patients, and 58.7 per cent of the psychotics, in our study. Ninety-seven and six-tenths per cent of these schizophrenic patients had been hospitalized at one time or another, and 94 per cent were hospitalized at the time of our census. When we classify these patients by social class we find that there is a very significant inverse relationship between social class and schizophrenia.

Hollingshead decided to determine, on the basis of these data, what the probability of the prevalence of schizophrenia by social class might be in the general population. To do this he used a proportional index to learn whether or not there were differentials in the distribution of the general population, as represented in our control sample, and the distribution of schizophrenics by social class. If a social class exhibits the same proportion of schizophrenia as it comprises of the general population, the index for that class is 100. If schizophrenia is disproportionately prevalent in a social class the index is above 100; if schizophrenia is disproportionately low in a social class the index is below 100. The index for each social class appears in the last column of Table 3.

The fact that the Index of Prevalence in Class I is only one-fifth as great as it would be if schizophrenia were proportionately distributed in this class, and that it is two and one-half times as high in Class V as we might expect on the basis of proportional distribution, gives further support to Hypothesis II. The fact that the Index of Prevalence is 11.2 times as great in Class V as in Class I is particularly impressive.

Hypothesis III stipulated that the type of psychiatric treatment a patient receives is associated with his position in the class structure. A test of this hypothesis involves a comparison of the different types of therapy being used by psychiatrists

TABLE 2: Distribution of Neuroses and Psychoses by Social Class

SOCIAL CLASS	NEUROSES		PSYCHOSES	
	NUMBER	PER CENT	NUMBER	PER CENT
I	10	52.6	9	47.4
II	88	67.2	43	32.8
III	115	44.2	145	55.8
IV	175	23.1	583	76.9
V	61	8.4	662	91.6
Total	449		1,442	

Chi square = 296.45, P less than .001.

on patients in the different social classes. We encountered many forms of therapy but they may be grouped under three main types; psychotherapy, organic therapy, and custodial care. The patient population, from the viewpoint of the principal type of therapy received, was divided roughly into three categories: 32.0 per cent received some type of psychotherapy; 31.7 per cent received organic treatments of one kind or another; and 36.3 per cent received custodial care without treatment. The percentage of persons who received no treatment care was greatest in the lower classes. The same finding applies to organic treatment. Psychotherapy, on the other hand, was concentrated in the higher classes. Within the psychotherapy category there were sharp differences between the types of psychotherapy administered to the several classes. For example, psychoanalysis was limited to Classes I and II. Patients in Class V who received any psychotherapy were treated by group methods in the state hospitals. The number and percentage of patients who received each type of therapy is given in Table 4. The data clearly support Hypothesis III. . . .

CONCLUSIONS AND INTERPRETATIONS

This study was designed to throw new light upon the question of how mental illness is related to social environment. It approached this problem from the perspective of social class to determine if an individual's position in the social system was associated significantly with the development of psychiatric disorders. It proceeded on the theoretical assumption that if mental illnesses were distributed randomly in the population, the hypotheses designed to test the idea that psychiatric disorders are connected in some functional way to the class system would not be found to be statistically significant.

The data we have assembled demonstrate conclusively that mental illness, as measured by diagnosed prevalence, is not distributed randomly in the population of the New Haven community. On the contrary, psychiatric difficulties of so serious a nature that they reach the attention of a psychiatrist are unequally distributed among the five social classes. In addition, types of psychiatric disorders, and the ways patients are treated, are strongly associated with social class position.

The statistical tests of our hypotheses' indicate that there are definite connections between particular types of social environments in which people live, as measured by the social class concept, and the emergence of particular kinds of psychiatric disorders, as measured by psychiatric diagnosis. They do not tell us what these connections are, nor how they are functionally related

TABLE 3:   Comparison of the Distribution of the Normal Population with Schizophrenics by Class, with Index of Probable Prevalence

SOCIAL CLASS	NORMAL POPULATION		SCHIZOPHRENICS		INDEX OF PREVALENCE
	NUMBER	PER CENT	NUMBER	PER CENT	
I	358	3.2	6	.7	22
II	926	8.4	23	2.7	33
III	2,500	22.6	83	9.8	43
IV	5,256	47.4	352	41.6	88
V	2,037	18.4	383	45.2	246
Total	11,077	100.0	847	100.0	

TABLE 4:   Distribution of the Principal Types of Therapy by Social Class

SOCIAL CLASS	PSYCHOTHERAPY		ORGANIC THERAPY		NO TREATMENT	
	NUMBER	PER CENT	NUMBER	PER CENT	NUMBER	PER CENT
I	14	73.7	2	10.5	3	15.8
II	107	81.7	15	11.4	9	6.9
III	136	52.7	74	28.7	48	18.6
IV	237	31.1	288	37.1	242	31.8
V	115	16.1	234	32.7	367	51.2

Chi square = 336.58, P less than .001.

to a particular type of mental illness in a given individual. The next step, we believe, is to turn from the strictly statistical approach to an intensive study of the social environments associated with particular social classes, on the one hand, and of individuals in these environments who do or do not develop mental illnesses, on the other hand. . . .

Selection 72

Is There an Upper-Class American Language?
Clifton Fadiman

Prior to the beginning of the twentieth century, it was very simple to distinguish upper-class people from lower-class people in almost any civilized country in the world. They wore different kinds of clothes, ate different kinds of foods, played different kinds of games, had different attitudes toward love and marriage, and were perceivably different in many, many ways. The increased dignity and income of laboring people have obliterated some of the highly visible cues of the past, and so have mass education and mass production of consumer goods. A common man today can own at least one suit of clothes that might easily be mistaken for that of a captain of industry, can afford his own sailboat and has the leisure to sail it, can have a good enough diet and sufficient medical and dental care to maintain an upper-class state of physical health, and through the mass media can be as well informed on public affairs and cultural events as his upper-class counterpart—at least in the United States. Nevertheless, Fadiman reminds us, there are still class differences that are important to many people.

Stephen Birmingham once observed that the upper class seemed to be on FM and the rest of the population on AM, that there were barriers to communication between the classes which seemed impenetrable. A similar thought seems to underlie Fadiman's article. Differences in speech habits between the classes seem to be manifestations of more basic differences in values and in the understandings of social organization. Speech patterns may be an *index* to social class just as occupation, education, and residential area may be indexes to general status or to social stratification. The decreasing validity of other indexes of social class does not necessarily mean that social class lines are becoming blurred or rigid. It simply means that one must look elsewhere for valid criteria for distinguishing among classes.

Recent research has shown that there is a high degree of consensus among Americans in ten different regions of the United States on the social class status of speakers whose tape-recorded voices were heard reciting "Twinkle, twinkle, little star. . . ."[1] In virtually every instance, the assigned class of the speaker was identical or adjacent to the category computed from the speaker's I.S.P. score, as described by Hollingshead and Redlich. Such findings, coupled with a number of others, indicate that there are culturally distinct social classes perceived by Americans and that one kind of cue to these cultural distinctions is transmitted by speech patterns.

[1] Charles C. Crider, "Regional Variations in the Estimation of Social Class from Auditory Stimuli," unpublished doctoral dissertation, The University of Southern California, June 1962.

Last July an American edition[1] of a book called *Noblesse Oblige* appeared and received a certain amount of gentle kidding by our reviewers. For some reason or other we tend to think the British interest in class distinctions rather funny, though actually it is just as serious and important as, let us say, our own absorption in presidential conventions.

The subject of the book is the language, more especially the vocabulary, used by the English aristocracy. When first published, the little volume kicked up an enormous fuss; and the dust is not yet laid. The fuss started in Finland. Prof. Alan Ross of Birmingham University published in Helsinki for Finnish philologists (I am not making this up) a paper called *U and Non-U: An Essay in Sociological Linguistics*. It was an attempt to define the language used by upper-class (U) Englishmen, language that sets them apart from non-U speakers. Miss Mitford, herself rather aggressively U and therefore just a shade non-U, wrote a witty and delightful commentary called *The English Aristocracy*. Uproar followed.

Why? Because (a) Miss Mitford and Professor Ross let the cat of U-vocabulary out of the closed bag of U-society; (b) according to her peers, Miss Mitford shouldn't have done it, because it is a private cat; (c) England is trying very hard to convince itself and the rest of the world that its class system is on the way out; (d) anybody who thinks that one way of speaking is better than another is a snob, isn't he, and snobs are bad people, aren't they?

I doubt that a similar tempest in a teapot will arise among us. For one thing, we are less interested in class distinctions. For another, we are less interested in language. For those few, however, who *may* be interested in language, I should like to set down a few comments on American U-sage and non-U-sage; and I hope that they will be challenged and corrected by better observers and scholars.

But before so doing I had better come clean and state that I believe there *is* an American aristocracy.

The American upper class is the lunatic aunt in our national attic. Both the family and the neighbors know she's there, but neither will own up to it. Indeed we have had an upper class ever since the founding of the Republic, an achievement made possible in large part by aristocrats and even, though one hates to admit it, by snobs, who are merely aristocrats who have lost self-confidence. We would all be a little less touchy on the subject if this simple fact could be taught to children in their first history class.

The present writer is by birth and training drastically non-upper class. That is what permits him to write about our upper class. Upper-class self-contemplation is a bit *infra dig*, not quite cricket.

Our upper class is not to be confused with our most publicized, our richest, or our most powerful citizens, though it is represented in all three groups. Its numbers are not large; its unit is the family, not the individual; it is "old"; generally of English or Scotch-English stock; respected by the community; Ivy League, West Point or Annapolis-educated; not necessarily intellectual, but respectful of the intellect; with *some* money somewhere in the family; often uncommitted to competition; and, most important, attached to a dying code of behavior, ultimately derived from eighteenth- or even seventeenth-century England.

This code, I believe, is marked by certain linguistic habits and traditions, though not so sharply as in England. I will go further. I believe our uppers speak and often write a certain *kind* of English better than the rest of us do; and, as a lover of our magnificent tongue, that interests me. I am aware that sufficient usage can eventually make the ugly, the repulsive, the unclear, the evasive, the discordant perfectly correct; and I am not in the least impressed by this fact, which seems so greatly to please our professors of linguistics. I am not urging anyone to imitate, let us say, the speech of Adlai Stevenson. It would be foolish and vain to try. I merely say that it is more admirable than certain other kinds of speech, because more efficient, clean and memorable; and for these reasons it is worthy of detached study, study quite unrelated to "snobbery."

I have not known many U-speakers. In one of my trades—entertainment—they are virtually non-existent, though there are a few English actors resident among us who are genuinely U and several more who are excellent U-mimics, which they should be, as that is part of their business. Writers are usually non-U in their speech and most of the most popular and successful ones are non-U in their writing. (An exception is Mr. John Marquand.) My observations are drawn therefore from limited experience. But this experience is more fruitful than would have been the case had I been U myself, with wider access to U families. Such families generally are not self-perceptive. The fish does not notice the water.

Reprinted by special permission from *Holiday*, October 1956, pp. 8-10, 14-15. Copyright 1956, by The Curtis Publishing Company.
[1] Nancy Mitford, ed., with an introduction by Russell Lynes, *Noblesse Oblige: An Enquiry into the Identifiable Characteristics of the English Aristocracy* (New York: Harper & Brothers, 1956).

In general, I would say that American U-sage is (always roughly) marked by:

1. Avoidance (unconscious if upper-U, conscious if garden-variety U) of the smart or topical phrase, and of trade jargon and slang. Qualify this last: there is a special U slang, derived largely from certain U sports, particularly the hunt. There is also a special U slang learned in certain Ivy League colleges or gentlemen's preparatory schools.

2. Avoidance of language-fidgets. The U-speaker economizes, often to the point of sparseness. He does not preface his sentences with "Well . . . ." A U-speaker will as a general rule use about twenty per cent fewer words than will a non-U.

3. Preference for the direct and simple, even the common, or what the non-U speaker would call the vulgar.

4. Often an inability to use *rich* or *striking* language; the wonderful inventiveness of our vernacular (when it *is* wonderful) is entirely non-U. The English of Ring Lardner is, in its coinages, its humor and its vividness, non-U. However, in its economy and directness it is U. Lardner himself came of a near-U family, though most of his later interests and associations were non-U.

5. Certain peculiarities of pronunciation, though not many, as most of our pronunciation differences are matters of region, not of class.

6. Certain minor peculiarities of syllabic accent.

7. Freedom of vocabulary. Longshoremen and U-speakers use Anglo-Saxon monosyllables casually. (So do young American novelists, but for different reasons.) My class, the middle, is relatively circumspect in its speech.

8. Neatness of enunciation, not to the point of the Oxford or Noel Coward "clipped" accent, but in general an avoidance of drawling and slurring. There is one difficulty here which I cannot resolve: Southern U-families seem to me to speak badly; but that may be because my ears are Northern.

9. A special pitch and tonality, varying of course with the region, but essentially distinct from that region's non-U. This is a rather difficult point to illustrate without the use of linguistic technicalities. I shall not illustrate it.

Suppose we begin with a few illustrations as to which there can be little debate. *Black tie* (or often *dress*) is U, which does not mean that it is not also the preferred form of many non-U speakers; whereas *tux* is not only non-U, but perhaps even sub-non-U. *Long dress*, I am told, is more or less U; *formal* is non-U, or perhaps non-U undergraduate jargon: our great Midwestern and Western colleges are mints of non-U-sage. The simple *how do you do?* is proper and has

descended to the rest of us (probably) from U speakers; *pleased to meet you* and similar unhappy phrases are non-U. U introductions are usually terse and consist of the names of the two principals; *meet the missus, the wife*, we need hardly discuss. Jocular introductions (*meet the ball-and-chain*) are sub-non-U. In England, Miss Mitford tells us, *mirror* is non-U as opposed to U *looking glass;* but this usage applies here only among certain conservative New England families. *Pardon me* is vaguely non-U, as is *I beg your pardon;* but I am not sure that *excuse me* or *sorry* are at all decisively U.

Non-U speakers are given to various euphemisms (or perhaps we should say non-euphemisms) for *bathroom* or *toilet* (this latter word, itself a euphemism, seems hardly to be used at all). In this connection we might note that *all* advertising copy is non-U, particularly when it is supposed to be exceedingly U. *Rumpus room* and *den* are non-U. Abbreviations tend to the non-U: no U speaker would call a *fraternity* a *frat*, of course. *Children* is U as opposed to non-U *kids*. In Hollywood, where only the purest undefiled non-U is current, a *cook* is generally a *housekeeper*. There is something non-U about *passed away* for *died*. A non-U speaker will often speak of an article in a newspaper or magazine as a *write-up* or sometimes a *piece;* U speakers will be more concrete and knowledgeable.

The most ordinary phrases are often the most crucial. *Have you got?* and *Do you have?* are both correct, but the first (I think) is non-U. The word *weekend* is interesting: U speakers often prefer *Friday to Monday* and many who do use *weekend* will accent the second syllable as against non-U *week'end* (either stress is correct). The tendency to accent the first syllable of certain words, by the way, is often a non-U identifier: *cig'arette, mag'azine* are non-U. So are *ice' cream* for *ice cream'* and *Moth'er Goose* for *Mother Goose'*. On the other hand *ar'istocrat* seems to be preferred by U speakers, as against non-U *aris'-tocrat*, though either is acceptable.

The scholar-critic Basil Davenport tells me that he feels *commence* is generally non-U as opposed to *begin;* but I think this a bit subtle. I am not sure of the U for *to date* (a girl) but there is no doubt the phrase itself is decisively non-U. *To keep company* used to be non-U, but today one rarely hears it except among elderly non-U's. *To go steady* is perhaps sub-non-U.

The U speaker avoids like the plague all modish "elegant" phrases, such as *I couldn't care less, I couldn't agree more, educated guess, calculated risk, I needed that one* (after a drink). This is Madison Avenue jargon; the world of advertising and popular journalism is rife with such phrases, even though many men in these trades are U by birth and education. (It is interesting that the Luce periodicals are managed in large part by U men, who do their utmost to employ and develop a writing style that will conceal their impeccable origins.) Please do not accuse me of political bias when I say that the leaders of our present Administration are prolific users of non-U English. Probably it is part of the homey, cosy, honest-American middle-of-the-roadness which is the presumed hallmark of the Republican Party as at present constituted. The late Senator Taft, on the other hand, spoke (for a politician, I mean) relatively U-English.

Vase is interesting. The nearer you are to the correct French pronunciation the more likely you are to be non-U; most U-speakers rhyme the word with *face*. On the other hand the U pronunciation of *lingerie* is apt to stick fairly close to the French; non-U is something like *lonjeray*. But probably U-speakers say *underwear*.

I am on debatable ground here, but I think U folk will say *May I have coffee?* whereas non-U will often preface the last word with *my*. A man who orders *a coffee* in a restaurant has probably spent some years in France; but the usage is gaining.

To *name* one's country house, particularly jocularly, is a trifle non-U, unless, like Alexander Woollcott's *Wit's End*, the joke is really witty. But a traditional and unexpressive name for a large estate (Mr. Baruch's *Hobcaw*) is England county-family U.

To call the *maître d'hôtel* the *maître D* is blatantly non-U. It is, once again, pure Madison Avenue in origin: all such knowing phrases have a non-U coloration.

To refer to *my wife* is more or less U; Mrs. Smith is non-U; Mrs. S. sub-non-U.

Professor Ross has an interesting footnote on the phrases used in casual toasting. English U-speakers used to say nothing, which does seem the best form. (In general, when there is no need to say anything, U-speakers say nothing.) *Cheers, down the hatch, bottoms-up* and similar locutions are all perfectly pleasant, perfectly acceptable, and perfectly non-U.

The use of first names among people who have just met each other is increasing among us: it is non-U, and probably derives from the entertainment industry.

A U-man will say *view* rather than *viewpoint, good-by* rather than *'bye now*. Jocularities such as *see you in church* or *don't do anything I wouldn't do* are pathetically non-U.

Conference (in business) used to be elegant;

then it became non-U and gave way to *meeting*. Unless a businessman is really attending a meeting, *he's busy* would appear the honest U-phrase to be used by the receptionist.

U-talk is often brutal as compared with non-U talk: *poor* is U-sage, *underprivileged* non-U-sage. The jargon of sociology and editorial journalism is responsible for a good deal of this kind of circumlocution.

A non-U will often refer to a *relative* or *relation;* a U may prefer *connection* or even, in old-fashioned U families, as well as among rural folk, *kin*, which seems to me the best word of all.

Non-U's, particularly the ladies, often love the exaggerated phrase: I cannot conceive of a U saying "I *despise* garlic!" *Tasty*, as applied to food, I find non-U; also the phrase *to go to theater*, perhaps a Yiddishism, as are *this I've got to hear, I told him off but good,* and similar vogue locutions.

Our professional students of language have quite properly called upon us to admire the venison richness of our vernacular, the coinages of a Winchell, the inventions of the hard-working journalists of *Time*, the close-to-the-people vocabulary of Ring Lardner. Well and good. But the quiet, steadying, braking influence of U-speech tends to attract small notice. Concision, understatement, exactness, even conventionality of expression (if the convention is a noble one) are not to be sniffed at. Why not give the underprivileged gentleman a fair shake?

I recollect the exact moment when this became clear to me, the moment that I decided that, despite the New Grammarians, correct usage had its value.

As a young man—I was nineteen—I got my first teaching job in a private school. The principal— Herbert W. Smith is now seventy, and I should like to record his name here—was interviewing me in his office. He asked my permission to make a necessary telephone call to one of the teachers. To the switchboard operator he said, "May I speak with Miss Jones?" Something about the question struck me as odd. I realized what it was: I would have said "May I speak *to* Miss Jones?" The difference is not unimportant. It is not only a matter of exact meaning, though it is that also. It is a matter of courtesy, even morality. The clearest English is often *good* English, in both senses of the term. It respects the communicatee just as it shows that the communicator respects himself.

My view may seem stiff-necked but here it is: no matter how many people say *to, with* is better. And it will remain better even though every English speaker on the face of the earth should reject *with* and embrace *to*.

Selection 73

The Concept of Class and American Sociology
Arnold M. Rose

In the introductions to the preceding articles, it was suggested that the manifestations of social class differences may be more or less subtle at different times or in different places but that this subtlety does not necessarily reflect the rigidity of class boundaries. The subtlety of class differences and the ease with which class boundaries may be "crossed" introduce some problems of procedure for the sociologist who undertakes the study of social classes, not the least of which is the defining of social class in terms that can be used in sociological research.

European sociologists have typically assumed that social classes comprise *discrete categories of people* who, if the occasion were sufficiently urgent, could be called together to discuss class problems. American sociologists, on the other hand, have shown a preference for the study of social classes as statistical categories comprising *clusters of abstract population qualities* related by the probability that they will occur together. Many American students of social class are no more concerned about interaction patterns of class members than they are about interaction patterns of cancer victims, insofar as social organization is concerned.

Rose questions whether statistical categories can properly be called social classes, and we are inclined to share his doubt. We are quite willing to agree, however, that statistical categories do represent population *strata* (categories of population which are distinguishable and are differentially evaluated on some continuum). When an American suggests that Barry Goldwater and Henry Cabot Lodge belong to different social classes, no one assumes that he is referring to their incomes, their occupations, their power, their years of education, or their homes. He is referring to a unique sociocultural division of the population that constitutes *one kind* of social stratification.

If the assumption that social classes are synthetic aggregates of demographic qualities is not the product of machine data-handling in American sociology, it has certainly been furthered by it. Such factors as family history, attitudes of the community, and the interaction of persons, not to mention the thousands of speech variations—accents, choice of words, speech melodies— and other cultural nuances require tremendously more effort and skill to translate onto tapes and punch cards than do categories of income, education, and house type.

Once again, the study of statistical population strata is useful and valuable in American sociology. Whether it should be called the study of social class is at best doubtful.

The comparative study of nonliterate societies has made anthropologists and sociologists aware of the great variation in institutional forms from one society to another. Few comparative studies have been made, however, of the so-called "advanced" societies, and as a result there is a

From *Social Research*, Vol. 25 (1958), 53-69.

tendency to conceive of Western societies as fairly uniform in regard to basic institutions. It is true, of course, that Western societies have a common heritage in Judaeo-Christian, Graeco-Roman civilization, and have since been molded by common technological, economic, and even political influences. But these do not exhaust the influences that mold the various cultures within the great Western complex. When a sociologist familiarizes himself with the meanings, values, and institutions of an advanced society other than that in which he has been raised he becomes aware of great cultural differences, as well as of the considerable variation within each society. And these differences are present in spite of the facile translations on a verbal level.

For example, the French *syndicat* has been considered by even well informed social scientists as equivalent to the American "trade union." Aside from the fact that the *syndicat* can be an association of employers or farmers as well as of industrial workers, there are some basic distinctions in structure and function between the *syndicat du travail* and the trade union. First, the *syndicat* is a purely voluntary association of workers; they can join or leave at any time, regardless of whether their firm is "organized" or not; and within a single firm, workers performing the same tasks may be members of three or four mutually opposed *syndicats*. Second, the *syndicats* are differentiated by their affiliation with different political parties and different philosophies of desirable industrial organization; thus some are closer to the employers in their party affiliation and philosophy than they are to other *syndicats*. Third, the *syndicats* do not engage in collective bargaining with the employers (except for one brief period, 1936-38, when the government forced them to); their activities are primarily political and associational rather than economic. And fourth, the *syndicats* do not engage in strikes in the American sense (that is, they very rarely continue a strike against a single employer until he is forced to compromise); the French strike is either a one-day protest (which usually does little damage to the employer) or a general or an industrywide strike in which all industry or a whole sector of industry is shut down (as in the case of the transportation strike in the summer of 1953), but in any case it is the government that is "damaged" and makes the concessions, if any are made. By general consensus, not by law (except in the case of minimum wages), the government has for some time set the wages and working conditions for all workers in France. In a country of great natural resources and high worker skill the government keeps the level low, and consequently the profit level high (relative to American wages and profits).

If we assume that the above statements are true (it would take us too far afield to present here the evidence for them) can we justifiably speak of the *syndicat* as equivalent to the trade union, or even of French capitalism as equivalent to American capitalism? It seems to me that the differences mentioned are so fundamental that it would be scientifically desirable not to translate the French word *syndicat* as "union."

I have chosen this example as one that is easily substantiated and that is not of great concern to the sociologist. The purpose of this paper, however, is to suggest that the French word *classe* cannot be considered equivalent to the American "class." This is more difficult to substantiate but is of considerable importance to the sociologist. My personal experience and study are fairly limited to France and Italy, but casual observation and general reading suggest that the meaning of class in France is fairly typical of Western Europe (with the partial exception of Scandinavia), and that therefore the contrast of France with the United States can be somewhat generalized.

If further study should prove this to be true, it would be questionable whether the analysis and thought applied to class in Europe can be appropriately transferred to the United States. American sociologists could then be regarded as engaged in a reverse kind of ethnocentrism, in which they inappropriately apply theory developed for a European institution to data from the American scene. But before considering the implications of this it is first necessary to substantiate empirically the statement that *classe* in France and class in the United States refer to phenomena sufficiently different to render invalid any effort by sociologists to transfer theory from one to the other.

I

The concept of class among European intellectuals grew out of their observations of and political interest in the change in the mediaeval "estates," which had more of the characteristics of what anthropologists call "caste" than of modern "class." Among the changes that caused Europeans to recognize in their countries the phenomenon of class, as distinguished from estate, were the rise in status and power of the merchants and owners of the developing industry; the decline in status and power of the mediaeval nobility and higher clergy; the great development of "free" industrial workers; and the rise of cities and modern "conveniences," which considerably expanded the number of shops and specialized services. "Class" referred to the new categories of occupations, which were closely associated with wealth and power.

But while these changes were going on, certain other important matters in the society remained roughly the same: the divisions among the categories (now called classes) remained fairly sharp in regard to status and social prerogatives; the differential behavior patterns of the classes remained, even when some of their specific content changed; higher education and "higher culture" generally remained a prerogative of the upper class, even in democratic countries and even when university tuition fees were reduced to nominal rates; and it continued to be almost impossible to change one's class during one's own lifetime or even the lifetime of one's son. Not only did it remain almost inconceivable that one could greatly improve one's education or economic status, but even if one did, this would not mean that one had moved into a higher class.

Thus the important thing about class in Europe, for our purposes, is that it was assimilated to the pre-existing system of status-differentiated estates. Several of the countries formalized this principle by granting titles of nobility to the new holders of power, the *haute bourgeoisie*. This class simply took over the privileges, duties, and sometimes even the symbols of the mediaeval nobility. Peasants and workers became free, but they did not expect to obtain power or "privileges" except by revolutionizing the social system.

Marx integrated the above and other facts about class into a philosophy of history and a political creed that are so widely accepted in Europe—even by many who think of themselves as anticommunists and non-Marxists—that "Marxism" itself has become a fact affecting the European class system. Class dominance, class aspects of interpersonal behavior, and the association of wealth and power are almost generally accepted in Europe as inevitable, and this uncritical acceptance helps to make the Marxist interpretation more permanently accurate than it might otherwise have been.

Class in Europe is now in various partial degrees of disintegration, especially in Scandinavia since 1930 and in Britain since 1945. But it is still a basic fact of everyday social life. The lower classes still engage in little ceremonies of obeisance to the upper classes, as they did in the year 1200. They still do not imagine that they can attend a university or a concert, even though these institutions are legally open to all who can pay a small fee and pass certain tests. In most of continental Europe the very language of direct address distinguishes between the upper and lower classes. Class is an all-pervading psychological as well as an economic and political fact; its core includes class *consciousness* (that is, a sense of class superiority or inferiority), which affects nearly every aspect of social behavior. People engage in specific class behaviors every hour of their waking lives, not only in their eating, clothing, working, and other habits, but—more importantly—in their interpersonal relations.

This kind of class behavior is so basic a part of European culture that it apparently does not change under communist revolution, contrary to Marx's expectations. In communist Poland "the intellectuals earn easily seven or eight times more than the average worker. One sees among them signs of wellbeing if not of luxury. They have maids, buy expensive and powerful radios, take taxis, eat in the better restaurants, and their frequent trips are paid for by the government. . . . A trade-union leader earns 40,000 zlotys and lives in a villa that costs his union more than 100,000 zlotys a month. A chauffeur, on the other hand, must work 14 hours a day to earn 1400 zlotys a month. . . . The average level of living is significantly lower than that of northern or central Italy."[1] In Western as well as in Eastern Europe the wives of communist leaders have full-time maids. . . . On December 2, 1956, according to an American newspaperman in Moscow, the Soviet leader Khrushchev "delivered a veiled warning to university students that unless they show loyalty to communism they will lose their places and will be sent to earn a living as factory workers."[2] The significance of these facts is not merely that a new bureaucratic and intellectual class has taken power from an old "capitalist" or "feudal" class; it is just as important to observe that class patterns of behavior and interpersonal relations have remained much the same since before the communist revolution.

In a democratic country like France the strength of the class system also explains, in part, why the workers seek to obtain social change through revolution rather than through the ballot box. They believe, whether rightly or wrongly, that their lot cannot be significantly improved unless the upper class is physically destroyed. In the United States, on the contrary, the great majority of workers conceive of the possibility of modifying the social position of the upper economic strata through political means, even though our political structure (because of the disproportionate electoral

---

[1] Article by Domenico Bartoli in *Corriere della Sera*, November 28, 1956, p. 3 (my translation from the Italian).

[2] I. J. Cutler, USIS, Daily Wireless File, U.S. Embassy Rome, Nos. 288-289, December 3, 1956, p. 15.

weight accorded to the South, to rural areas, and to small states) is formally less democratic than that of France.

In the United States there are, of course, great differences of wealth and status. But here there was never a mediaeval nobility or upper clergy whose privileges and duties the modern leaders of society could take over. . . . And there has generally been less class consciousness, and less acceptance of the Marxist interpretation of class. These are fundamental differences, which ought to preclude an analysis of the American class system in terms that are appropriate to the European class system. They are fundamental because they have influenced the whole attitudinal and behavioral complex associated with social differentiation. This will now be given empirical support.

II

In the United States it is possible for qualified persons of low status to obtain a higher education. For example, there are many more colored people attending college in the United States than there are British subjects attending college in all British universities—160,000 as compared to 105,461, though the respective population bases are 16 and 45 million. On the basis of comparable cutting points according to occupation of father, about 40 percent of American college students may be said to have lower status as compared to less than 3 percent of French college students, 6 percent of Swiss college students, and 11.3 percent from a prosperous northern Italian city (Turin).

It is of course true that the English and some other European universities operate on a higher educational level than do the majority of American colleges, but this is beside the point. The important fact is that in the United States children from lower-status and lower-income families can attend what they *regard* as institutions of the highest learning, while in Europe they do not think they can do so. This attitude difference is embedded in the legal structure of the two educational systems: in the United States there is a single educational ladder, from which a student may drop out or continue upward at any point, whereas in most European countries there are two or more educational ladders, from one of which (that predominantly for the lower class) there is no possibility of moving upward after the age of twelve or fourteen. This difference has importance beyond the matter of attitudes and school structure. American business draws its junior executives —the new men of top status and power—from the ranks of the well educated, and many of these young men have fathers who are farmers or indus-

trial workers; in most of Europe a business is much more likely to be a family-run affair, but in any case the rising young businessmen are almost exclusively from the upper or upper-middle class families.

In the United States education is associated with liberal attitudes toward political, economic, and social issues. Of the thousands of public-opinion polls taken in this country since 1935, nearly every one shows that the well educated are more "progressive" in their attitudes than are the poorly educated. In Europe the opposite is true: though the university students are often "temporary Marxists," the adult "progressives," of various categories, are predominantly in the lower classes. Conservatism is the mark of the educated man in most of Europe, except for a few of the radical leaders (who often regard their followers with as much contempt as do the conservative leaders).

In the United States higher education is associated with "secularism." Educated people may attend church, but the strictly "religious" are largely to be found among those who have not gone beyond secondary schools. In Europe there is a positive association between education and religious observance. The workers' communities in France, outside of Normandy, are filled with atheists, and the Catholic church classifies many of them not as parishes but as "mission areas." In Britain and Scandinavia there are two distinct categories of church attenders: the "established church" members, who are largely from the upper classes in the continental pattern, and the members of the "new" evangelical sects, who are often workers.

Vertical mobility is somewhat different in Europe and the United States. In the first place, there has been practically no downward mobility in Europe since the remnants of the mediaeval nobility were either killed off (as in the French Revolution) or assimilated by the *haute bourgeoisie* (as in England and Germany): the impoverished upper-class person in Europe remains upper-class —in manners, family, associations, and often attitudes—even when he has to take a job as salesman or bank clerk in order to live. There is considerably less downward mobility than upward mobility in the United States, but this is a function of economic expansion and the economic structure, not of the theoretical impossibility of falling in class affiliation, with the attendant changes in manners, associations, and attitudes.

Secondly, a case can be made that an upward change of status is rarer in at least continental Europe than in the United States. There have been studies of vertical mobility in several European countries and in the United States, and while their techniques of research have differed somewhat, they are partially comparable. These studies tend to show little difference in upward mobility between the United States and several European countries, as measured by change of occupation between fathers and sons. While this occupational measure has many advantages, it mixes two distinct variables, both of which are socially significant. One is the rate of expansion of the economy: in an expanding economy there is always a movement from agricultural to manufacturing to service occupations. The other variable is the possibility of changes in the prestige levels and behaviors associated with class. Since several European countries are industrializing at almost the same rate as the United States, it is natural to expect that they will have about as many occupational changes.

In this paper, however, I am concentrating on the degree of flexibility in the system of stratification, and unfortunately there are no comparable systematic studies of this factor. Even in the sphere of occupational mobility, but outside the gross measures of change from agriculture to manufacturing to service occupations, there are no data to contradict the observation that the American class structure is more open or flexible than that of continental Europe. For example, the movement into management and the professions, the possibility of becoming an individual achiever or intellectual, occurs to a much greater extent in the United States than in Europe. This situation is a function of certain aspects of social structure that are more likely to be found in the United States (and also in Canada, Australia, and New Zealand, but our comparison is with Europe): foremost, the openness and unidimensionality of the American educational ladder, already discussed; second, the "push" of a large number of European immigrants, Negroes, and Mexicans coming in at the bottom of the status scale (which prevented the formation of a permanent, indigenous white lower class); third, the relatively rapid increase of productivity, made possible by technological innovation, rich natural resources, and domination of the value of efficiency; and fourth, expansion-minded businessmen.

Another kind of upward mobility that is almost uniquely American is the upward movement among the immigrants, for whom assimilation alone was mobility, and among their offspring, some of whom achieve high-status positions in the general society. It is also possible to speak of an upper and a middle class among the Negroes, although these are not integrated into the class system of the whites. We must be cautious not to say that a social structure with possibilities of upward mobility is always good, but we must also recognize that upward mobility is factually more possible in the United States than it is in the countries of Europe.

There is still a tradition of a leisure class in Europe—originally kept prepared for war. While the strict expectation that the nobility should never work has broken down, a certain proportion of the upper-class European males do not engage in remunerative work, and this remains as an ideal among some of the others. In the United States the great majority of ablebodied men of all social categories engage in remunerative occupations, and the few who do not pretend to do so. A "gentleman of leisure" is a man to be scorned in the United States.

Closely associated is the fact that the United States has no "upper-class families" as such. While certain families have heritages of wealth and fame, they also have their "poor relations," whose status and power have fallen away. Each male individual must make his own way to a considerable extent. Compared to other societies, primitive and modern, the United States does not accord a high value to lineage. Similarly, while property is inherited in the United States, it is not so much a matter of family inheritance as in Europe. A fact seldom·recognized in this context is that a considerable proportion of the wealth of the United States is owned by groups (corporations and associations), rather than by individuals or families. This is coming to be true in Great Britain and Scandinavia, and perhaps in other European countries, but it is a relatively new fact for them.

A systematic study would probably reveal more important differences between "class" in Europe and "class" in the United States. The major exception to the present analysis is the position of the Negro in the United States, though it is an exception that supports the analysis for the white American population. The present position, and even the history of enslavement, of the American Negro is more like that of the European lower class than it is like that of the white American lower class, at least in the northern and western states. For this reason it is justifiable to speak of Negroes as the *only* American lower class (using the term in the European sense), or to use a more precise anthropological term—"caste"—to designate them. I prefer the latter approach, especially as it permits the recognition of significant status and other differences within the Negro group. In any case, the Negro is such a special and complex problem for the analysis of social differentiation in the United States, and a problem that is currently changing so rapidly, that I ask the reader's forbearance if I neglect the Negro in the remainder of this paper.

III

Turning from the comparison of similarities and differences between Europe and the United States, let us consider how the social scientist might best deal with social differentiation in this country. I have no objection to using the term "class" to speak of arbitrary divisions in the United States, on any continuum—occupation, education, status or prestige, power, or one of the many other bases of significant social differentiation—provided it is recognized that class is a different phenomenon in Europe. But I suspect it is too difficult to keep this distinction clear. Nor would finding a new word improve matters greatly, because social differentiation in the United States does not lend itself to realistic treatment in terms of arbitrary and blanket concepts.

What I propose is a reversion to the scheme of analysis frequently used before a number of empirical studies, in the late 1930s, popularized for a second time the concept of class as an aspect of American social structure. In their empirical researches before the late 1930s American social scientists were aware of what they called "social differentiation," and they described and measured education, wealth, income, occupation, prestige, and, to a lesser extent, family background and power. These traits were correlated with social behavior of one sort or another, and interesting associations were reported. . . . In these studies education was found to be a most important variable, often highly correlated with the attitudes and behaviors that were the primary object of study. Education is referred to probably more frequently than any other background variable in the published and unpublished writings of this research group.

Our interest here, however, is not in the fact that education was found to be more important than other variables—income of parents, for example—but in the fact that education and income were thought of as variables in their own right, not as indices of class. As far as I know (as a member of the group), there was never any inclination to substitute the variable "class" for the variable "education." Similar examples can be drawn from other studies in which education, occupation, and wealth were among the principal independent variables investigated.

Contrast the situation among sociological researchers in the 1950s. "Class" is now considered to be a most important object of study, and a cause (or independent variable) of many other social phenomena. . . .

It is legitimate under the canons of science to combine such variables as wealth, family background, education, and regard the combination as a new variable or concept, such as class, *provided:* first, the constituent elements and the manner of combination are made explicit; second, there is consistency in the manner of using the new concept; and third, some reasonable way is devised for handling deviations from the correlation among the variables—to decide, for example, in what class a person shall be counted if he has high education but low income. Individual researchers who use the concept of class frequently do all three of these things, but they certainly do not do them in the same way. Specifications as to the ingredients and procedures used in formulating a measure of class are almost as numerous as the researchers who use the concept. The result is that nearly anything can be shown to be related or not related to class in the United States. But the fact remains that the class measure is not so accurate a predictor of other behaviors as are such much more specific variables as power, education, or income.

Implicit in the formulation of any such combination concept as class is the belief that something is added by the combination which is not present in the constituent elements. Presumably the gain more than compensates for the loss involved in the reduction of variation caused by the combination. The loss is readily seen in such a statistical operation as multiple correlation. The correlation of some dependent variable with education, income, or occupation will inevitably be higher than the correlation of the same dependent variable with a combined index of class based on the same three independent variables. (The only condition that will produce the same degree of correlation with the dependent variable is a perfect correlation among all three of the independent variables.) Yet there has been little discussion in the American literature concerning what is added by the concept of class that is not already present in knowledge about education, income, power, family background, and whatever else is considered to be a constituent of class.

European writers have dealt with the concept of class consciousness and with power differences, which they believe or find to be related to a variety of concrete behaviors in their own countries. In fact, for them class is identified with class consciousness and differential power, while income, education, prestige, family background are considered simply as indices to measure conveniently what cannot be measured ideally. Since so much of the thinking about class has been borrowed from the European writers, some American sociologists have implicitly introduced class consciousness when they substitute class for education, income, or occupation, without considering the special independent effects of class consciousness. Other American sociologists have avoided assuming anything about class consciousness but use "class" merely as a shorthand term for a certain level of status, education, income, and the like, and therefore are speaking inaccurately for the sake of brevity and following the current fashion. Still other American sociologists, like Parsons, have used the concept of class in a special way, and to this I have no objection except that probably their readers attribute a more general definition of class to their discussions.

Certainly not all American sociologists have substituted the concept of class for its constituent variables. Many have preferred to work with the simpler, more explicit measures. Nevertheless, it is probably true that an article on "The Relation of Class to Drinking Habits" can capture more attention among sociologists than an article on "The Relation of Education and Income to Drinking Habits," even though the two are based on the same data. There has been no effort to determine which of the two procedures—keeping the independent variables separate or combining them into a measure of class—produces a better explanation of the variation in the dependent variable.

In sum, while there are legitimate reasons for using "class" as a combination concept, these reasons have not yet been made sufficiently explicit to have empirical support from those who use the concept in reference to American data. There is a great deal of evidence that the concept of class as used by European intellectuals has a different empirical reference from that in the class concept as used by American sociologists. The Europeans follow the legitimate procedure of consistently using the concept of class to refer to a power group with a certain group consciousness and characteristic "life chances"; this definition is realistic because it reflects the heritage from the mediaeval estates. There is little empirical evidence that class differences have increased over the past generation in the United States, or have affected basic behaviors that they did not previously affect. Yet there has been a sharp increase in the use of the class concept by American sociologists, as a substitute for such simpler concepts as education, occupation, and income.

These facts suggest that the use of the concept of class is a function of conditions prevailing among American sociologists as a social group rather than of conditions characteristic of the society, or of science, and that from a strictly scientific point of view we ought to revert to the simpler concepts. American sociology needs more theory to deal with the important facts of social differentiation, but the concept of class has perhaps caused as much confusion about these facts as it has clarified them.

Selection 74

Social Mobility

Pitirim A. Sorokin

A synonym for "mobility" is *movement*. Movement is inextricably related to time. To demonstrate that movement has occurred, one must show that the dimensions or qualities or locations of an item or items are different at two or more different times. All movement must thus take place with respect to points of reference—that is, one can understand at one moment that the sun moves with respect to his bedroom window and at another can imagine the sun to be quite stationary while the earth revolves about it, rotating on its axis. Reference points are quite as necessary in studying social change as they are in studying geophysical change.

The relationship between time and motion is worth noting. Actually, time is an artifice for describing change. For existentialists (and many others, too) there is no *real* time except the present. Past time is no longer time at all. Memories and records have no use in the present except as reference points, and often (since their meanings frequently change) their utility as such is severely limited. Hence the comparison of past, present, and future (or any two of them) in studies of social mobility must take into consideration the changing significance of reference points.

Movement and change are the chief symptoms of life whether one looks for them in an organism or in a society. Even stagnation produces changes, however, so not all change is good. The behavioral scientist has a tremendous challenge in the interpretation of case histories and longitudinal studies of small groups, for he must take into consideration not only reference points in the whole society but also reference points in the biological, psychological, and social lives of each person involved.

The article reproduced here appeared shortly before the publication of Sorokin's book *Social Mobility*, which was the first comprehensive treatise on the subject. Social mobility may refer, as he describes, either to movement from one status to another in terms of the same reference points or to a shift in reference points. Lipset and Bendix have chosen the former meaning for their treatment of mobility (Selection 75).

CONCEPTION OF SOCIAL MOBILITY AND ITS FORMS

By social mobility I understand any transition of an individual or social object of value—anything that has been created or modified by human activity—from one social position to another. There are two principal types of social mobility, *horizontal and vertical*. By horizontal social mobility or shifting, I mean the transition of an individual or social object from one social group to another situated on the same level. Transitions of individuals, as from the Baptist to the Methodist religious group, from one citizenship to another, from one family (as a husband or wife) to another by divorce and remarriage, from one factory to another in the same occupational status, are all instances of social mobility. So too are transitions of social objects, the radio, automobile, fashion, communism, Darwin's theory, within the same social stratum, as from Iowa to California, or from any one place to another. In all these cases, "shifting" may take place without any noticeable change of the social position of an individual or social object in the vertical direction. By the *vertical* social mobility I mean the relations involved in a transition of an individual (or a social object) from one social stratum to another. According to the direction of the transition there are two types of vertical social mobility: *ascending and descending, or social climbing and social sinking*. According to the nature of the stratification, there are ascending and descending currents of economic, political and occupational mobility, not to mention other less important types. The ascending current exists in two principal forms: an *infiltration* of the individuals of a lower stratum into an existing higher one; and as *a creation of*

a new group by such individuals, and the insertion of such a group into a higher stratum instead of, or side by side with the existing groups of this stratum. Correspondingly, the descending current has also two principal forms: the first consists in a dropping of the individuals from a higher social position into an existing lower one, without a degradation or disintegration of the higher group to which they belonged; the second is manifested in *a degradation of a social group as a whole, in an abasement of its rank among other groups, or in its disintegration as a social unit*. The first case of "sinking" reminds one of an individual falling from a ship; the second of the sinking of the ship itself with all on board, or of the ship as a wreck breaking itself to pieces.

The cases of individual infiltration into an existing higher stratum or of individuals dropping from a higher social layer into a lower one are relatively common and comprehensible. They need no explanation. We must dwell a little more, however, on the second form of social ascending and descending, the rise and fall of groups.

The following historical examples may serve to illustrate. The historians of India's caste-society tell us that the caste of the Brahmins did not always have the position of indisputable superiority which it has held during the last two thousand years. In the remote past, the caste of the warriors, and rulers, or the caste of the Kshatriyas, seems to have been not inferior to the caste of the Brahmins; and it appears that only after a long

From *The Journal of Applied Sociology*, Vol. 11 (1926), 21-32. A full development and proofs of the propositions in this article can be found in Sorokin's *Social and Cultural Mobility* (Glencoe, Ill.: The Free Press, 1959).

struggle did the latter become the highest caste. If this hypothesis be true, then this elevation of the rank of the Brahmin caste as a whole through the ranks of other castes is an example of the second type of social ascent. The group as a whole being elevated, all its members, *in corpore*, through this very fact, are elevated also. Before the recognition of the Christian religion by Constantine the Great, the position of a Christian Bishop, or the Christian clergy, was not a high one among other social ranks of the Roman society. In the next few centuries the Christian Church, as a whole, experienced an enormous elevation of social position and rank. Through this wholesale elevation of the Christian Church, the members of the clergy, and especially the high Church dignitaries, were elevated to the highest ranks of medieval society. And, contrariwise, a decrease in the authority of the Christian church during the last two centuries has led to a relative abasement of the social ranks of the high church dignitaries within the ranks of the present society. The position of the Pope or a cardinal is still high, but undoubtedly it is lower than it was in the Middle Ages. The group of the legists in France is another example. In the 12th century, this group appeared in France, as a group, and began to grow rapidly in significance and rank. Very soon, in the form of the judicial aristocracy, it asserted itself into the place of the previously existing nobility. In this way, its members were raised to a much higher social position. During the 17th, and especially the 18th centuries, the group, as a whole, began to "sink," and finally disappeared in the conflagration of the Revolution. A similar process took place in the elevation of the Communal *Bourgeoisie* in the Middle Ages, in the privileged *Six Corps* or the *Guilda Mercatoria,* and in the aristocracy of many royal courts.

To have a high position at the court of the Romanoffs, Hapsburgs, or Hohenzollerns before the Revolutions meant to have one of the highest social ranks in the corresponding countries. The "sinking" of the dynasties led to a "social sinking" of all ranks connected with them. The group of the Communists in Russia, before the Revolution, did not have any high rank socially recognized. During the Revolution the group climbed an enormous social distance and occupied the highest strata in Russian society. As a result, all its members have been elevated *en masse* to the place occupied by the Czarist aristocracy. Similar cases are given in a purely economic stratification. Before the "oil" and "automobile" era, to be a prominent manufacturer in this field did not mean to be a captain of industry and finance. A great expansion of these industries has transformed them into some of the most important kinds of industry. Correspondingly, to be a leading manufacturer in these fields now means to be one of the most important leaders of industry and finance. These examples illustrate the second—collective—form of ascending and descending currents of social mobility.

The situation is summed up in the table at the bottom of the page.

INTENSIVENESS OR VELOCITY AND
GENERALITY OF VERTICAL SOCIAL MOBILITY

From the quantitative point of view, we must further distinguish the intensiveness and the generality of the vertical mobility. By its *intensiveness* I mean the vertical social distance, or the number of strata—economic, or occupational, or political—crossed by the individual in his upward or downward movement in a definite period of time. If, for instance, one individual in one year climbed from the position of a man with a yearly income of $500 to a position with an income of $50,000, while another man in the same period succeeded in increasing his income only from $500 to $1000, in the first case the intensiveness of the economic climbing would be fifty times greater than in the second case.

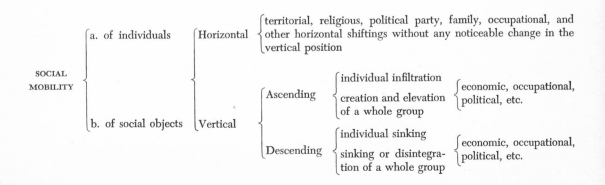

For a corresponding change, the intensiveness of the vertical mobility may be measured in the same way in the field of the political and occupational stratifications. By *the generality of the vertical mobility*, I mean the number of individuals who have changed their social position in the vertical direction in a definite period of time. The absolute number of such individuals gives the *absolute generality* of the vertical mobility in a given population; the proportion of such individuals to the total number of a given population gives *the relative generality of the vertical mobility*.

Finally, combining the data of intensiveness and relative generality of the vertical mobility in a definite field, (e.g., in the economic), we may obtain *the aggregate index of the vertical economic mobility of a given society*. In this way we may compare one society with another, or the same society at different periods, to find in which of them, or at what period, the aggregate mobility is greater. The same may be said about the aggregate index of the political and occupational vertical mobility.

IMMOBILE AND MOBILE TYPES
OF STRATIFIED SOCIETIES

On the basis of the above it is easy to see that a social stratification of the same height and profile may have a different inner structure caused by the difference in the intensiveness and generality of the (horizontal and) vertical social mobility. Theoretically, there may be a stratified society in which the vertical social mobility is nil. This means that within it there is no ascending or descending, no circulation of its members; that every individual is forever attached to the social stratum in which he was born; that the membranes or hymens which separate one stratum from another are absolutely impenetrable, and do not have any "holes" through which, or any stairs and elevators with which, the dwellers of the different strata may pass from one floor to another. *Such a type of stratification may be styled as absolutely closed, rigid, impenetrable, or immobile.* The opposite theoretical type of the inner structure of the stratification of the same height and profile is that in which the vertical mobility is very intensive and general; here the membranes between the strata are very thin and have the largest holes to pass from one floor to another. Therefore, though the social building is as stratified as the immobile one, nevertheless, the dwellers of its different strata are permanently changing; they do not stay a very long time in the same "social story," and with the help of the largest staircases and elevators are *en masse* moving "up and down." *Such a type of social stratification may be styled open, plastic, penetrable, or mobile.* Between these two extreme types there may be many middle or intermediary types of stratification.

SOME RESULTS OF A STUDY
OF THE VERTICAL MOBILITY

I have undertaken a study of the vertical mobility from the standpoint of its factors, its forms, its fluctuation in time and space, the channels through which it goes on and the social mechanism which controls it; from the standpoint of the characteristics of the people who are placed at the upper and the lower social strata, and, finally, from that of the effects of social mobility. . . .

Propositions concerning the fluctuation of the velocity and generality of the vertical mobility in space and time

1. There has scarcely been any society whose strata were absolutely closed, or in which vertical mobility in its economic, political, occupational, and other forms was not present.

2. There has never existed a society in which its vertical mobility has been absolutely free and in which the transition from one social stratum to another has had no resistance.

3. The intensiveness and generality of the vertical mobility varies from society to society (fluctuation in space) and within the same society from time to time.

4. In the fluctuation of the vertical mobility in time there seems to be no definite perpetual trend toward either an increase or a decrease of the intensiveness and generality of the mobility. All trends seem to have been only temporary, being superseded by the opposite ones in a longer period of time. This is proposed as valid for the history of a country, for that of a large social body, and, finally, for the history of mankind.

5. The nineteenth and the twentieth centuries in the history of the Western societies have been the periods of highest mobility in its occupational, economic, and political forms. However, in the past there have been periods of an equal and, perhaps, even that of a greater mobility.

6. The occupational vertical mobility of the present Western societies has the following characteristics: First, per cent of transmission of occupational status from the father to the sons fluctuates from 90 to 3 per cent according to occupation and country. The most common or typical index of the transmission varies from 20 to 50 per cent. Second, within the last three or four generations

in many occupations there seems to have been a tendency toward a decrease of the transmission of occupation from the father to the sons. In some other occupations, however, the tendency seems to have been reversed. Third, the number of inter- and intra-occupational vertical shiftings within the life of the last generation seems to be somewhat greater than within the life of the preceding generation. Fourth, within the same occupation the more qualified and better paid strata shift less intensively than the less qualified and more poorly paid strata. Members of an occupation which disappears shift more intensively than the members of an occupation which develops and prospers. Fifth, the sons of the fathers who belong to the same occupation are dispersed throughout different occupations, and the members of the same occupation are recruited from different social groups and strata. However, the closer affinities are the occupations, the more intensive among them is mutual interchange of their members; and vice versa, the greater is the difference between occupations the less is the number of individuals who shift from one group to another. Sixth, under normal conditions, these "ups" and "downs" go on gradually and orderly and are selective, being controlled by the machinery of social selection. In time of revolution they are sudden and non-selective. Seventh, different individuals move in the vertical (occupational) direction at different velocities. The greater is the number of the occupational strata to be crossed, the less is the number of the "jumpers."

7. Shifting on the economic ladder within the present Western societies is characterized by somewhat similar traits. It increases in the period of social upheavals (war, revolution, industrial transformation, and so on). Like the occupational strata, among the richest people of a country there are climbers who were born in a poor family, and among the poor population there are the people who were born in a rich family. However, in difference from the occupational mobility, there seems not to have existed the tendency toward a decrease of the transmission of economic status from the father to the sons during the last few generations. Many characteristics of the present occupational and economic mobility are applied to the present political mobility.

Propositions concerning the channels and the machinery which controls the vertical mobility of individuals

1. The most common channels through which vertical shifting of individuals goes on are the series of social institutions like: army, church, school, political parties, and different occupational institutions. They play the rôle of "elevators" through which people go "up" and "down."

2. With the exception of the periods of anarchy the vertical mobility of individuals and their placement at different social strata is controlled by a complex machinery of social testing, selection and distribution of individuals within the society. This machinery is composed out of social institutions of family, church and school which test general intelligence and character of individuals, and out of different occupational institutions which re-test the results of the family, church and school testing, and especially test the specific ability of individuals necessary for a successful performance of a definite occupational function. This "testing and selective" rôle of these institutions is no less important than their "educational and training" rôle. From this it follows that the population of different social strata is selective.

Propositions concerning the characteristics of the population of different social strata of a society

Being selective in a considerable degree the population of different social strata exhibits several bodily, mental, and moral differences. Part of them is the result of selection and heredity, another part is that of environmental differences. As a general rule, the population of the upper strata has a taller stature, a greater weight, a greater cranial capacity or greater size of head, better proportions of body and is more handsome than the population of the lower strata. The contention that the upper classes of the same society are more dolichocephalic and more blond than the lower classes is not warranted by the facts.

Concerning the vitality and health the upper strata have a greater duration of life, lower mortality, and are healthier than the population of the lower strata. Birth-rate of the upper classes at the present moment and in many periods in the past has been lower than that of the lower classes. However, the rule cannot be applied to all times and countries.

Population of the upper strata has a higher intelligence and is richer with the ambitious, bold and adventurous characters, with inventive minds, with harsh and non-sentimental natures, and with the cynical persons, than the population of the lower classes. The above means that social stratification and distribution of individuals according to physical and mental qualities are positively correlated. The correlation is, however, not perfect, and it is not constant. There are overlappings. The correlation decreases in the period of degeneration of the upper classes or of a whole society and may even disappear.

Propositions concerning the effects of mobility

1. In the field of racial composition of a society. Under the condition of lower procreation of the upper strata an intensive vertical mobility leads to wasting of the best population of society. It is probable that in the long period of time this wasting may lead to a racial depletion of the population. This is the price paid by a mobile society for its rapid progress.

2. In the field of human behavior and psychology. An intensive vertical mobility facilitates an increase of the plasticity and versatility of behavior, openmindedness, mental strain, intellectual progress, and progress of discoveries and inventions. On the other hand, it facilitates an increase of mental diseases, superficiality, insensitiveness of nervous system, scepticism, cynicism, and "idiosyncrasies"; it also diminishes intimacy in interrelations of individuals, increases their social isolation and loneliness, favors an increase of

suicide, hunting for sensual pleasure and restlessness; finally, mobility facilitates disintegration of morals.

3. In the field of social processes and organization. Mobility, under some conditions, facilitates a better and more adequate social distribution of individuals among different social strata, economic prosperity and social progress. The effects of mobility on social stability are very complex, partly positive, partly negative; all in all, rather negative. Its influence upon longevity and continuity of culture-complex is negative also. It facilitates atomisation and diffusion of solidarity and antagonisms, increase of individualism followed by a vague cosmopolitanism and collectivism.

Diagnosis concerning the future trend of the mobility

At the present moment there are several symptoms of a decrease of the vertical mobility within the present Western societies. They are, however, opposed by the symptoms of the opposite character. Therefore, it is difficult to say certainly, whether these societies continue to drift towards a greater mobility, or toward an immobility.

Selection 75

Social Mobility and Occupational Career Patterns
Seymour M. Lipset and Reinhard Bendix

The empirical study reported here illustrates many of the conceptual points set down by Sorokin in the preceding selection. Probably more empirical studies of social mobility have been focused on changes in occupation than on changes in any other single objective characteristic of the population. This is due in part to the existence of a number of scales for rating or ranking occupations and in part to the fact that many field studies have shown a high correlation between assigned social class and occupational status. Also involved are the relative ease of determining a person's occupation and the assumption of a good deal of stability in occupational categories—that is, being a physician a generation ago signified about the same thing socially as it does today and as it may be expected to signify a generation from now. In other words, the occupational scale furnishes a series of reference points for the study of social mobility. Certainly these reference points are not perfectly stable themselves, but they are probably more stable than many of the other objective status categories available or in current use (such as income, years of schooling, type of housing, residential area) and in most instances can probably be ascertained more accurately for the past and predicted more accurately for the not-too-distant future. People's occupational aspirations are generally more realistic than their income aspirations, for example.

Most studies of occupational mobility seem to be intergenerational—that is, they compare the occupations of fathers with the occupations of sons in order to show the amount or extent of change from one generation to the next. The study reproduced here, however, is concerned with changes in the occupations of particular persons during their own working lives.

UPWARD AND DOWNWARD MOBILITY

The interchange between manual and nonmanual occupations from the point of view of social mobility can most easily be shown by contrasting the proportion of time which those who work with their hands have spent in the nonmanual occupations with the proportion of time which nonmanual workers have spent as manual laborers.

Though little confidence can be placed in the over-all contrast between 11.1 and 20.2 per cent, it is of interest that the range of variation in the two groups differs markedly. Those who hold manual jobs at present have worked for from only 9 to 13 per cent of their careers in nonmanual occupations. But those now in nonmanual occupations have spent from 5 to 29 per cent of their

life-careers as manual workers. In a society in which the majority of individuals do *not* pass from the one category to the other, the instances where the crossing is made may be called cases of upward or downward mobility. These terms shall be used in the conventional sense, designating as upward mobile any individual who moves from manual to nonmanual jobs during a significant period of his work career.

Although the use of this terminology is justified on the whole, the data reveal an important aspect of social mobility, in American society, which is essentially obscured by the terms. There is perhaps less doubt about upward than about downward mobility. If a person from a worker's family obtains jobs in the nonmanual occupations, then he is likely to have risen in the hierarchy of prestige even though, economically, he may have advanced little, or not at all. Our data indicate that relatively little of this upward mobility is of a permanent character. On the other hand, it does not follow that those who are now in nonmanual occupations have been downward mobile because they have spent a portion of their careers as manual laborers. The test of a rise or fall in the socioeconomic hierarchy is clearly the permanence of the change. As already indicated, there is relatively little permanent crossing between the manual and nonmanual occupations among the respondents.

Table 2 indicates, however, that a temporary change from one to the other category occurs with considerable frequency. Significantly, the temporary crossings occur more frequently downward than upward. Workers in American society may well feel that their chances of a rise in socioeconomic status are slight. Yet those in the middle and upper brackets of the occupational hierarchy may continue to insist that ready opportunities for social and economic advancement exist, because from 40 to 80 per cent of their

TABLE 1: Percentage of Time Spent in Occupational Divisions Other than Present, by Present Occupational Group and Division

PRESENT OCCUPATIONAL GROUP AND DIVISION	NUM-BER	PERCENTAGE OF TIME SPENT	
		IN MANUAL OCCUPATIONS	IN NON-MANUAL OCCUPATIONS
Professional......	23	5.7	——
Semiprofessional..	19	13.4	——
Own business	105	26.0	——
Upper-white-collar	72	10.4	——
Lower-white-collar	67	29.5	——
Sales	42	21.2	——
All nonmanual ...	343*	20.2	——
Skilled..........	169	——	9.3
Semiskilled	98	——	13.5
Unskilled........	44	——	12.8
All manual	314*	——	11.1

* *These figures include 15 business executives and 3 manual (odd jobs) workers not shown separately. (All of the tables in this article reporting proportions of lifetime career patterns are based on males, aged thirty-one years or older. The younger workers in our sample are not considered in such tables.)*

"Social Mobility and Occupational Career Patterns" by Seymour M. Lipset and Reinhard Bendix. Reprinted from *The American Journal of Sociology*, Vol. LVII (1952), 494-504, by permission of The University of Chicago Press.

TABLE 2: Percentage Who Ever Worked in Occupational Division Other than Present, by Occupational Group and Division*

		RESPONDENTS EVER SPENDING TIME	
PRESENT OCCUPATIONAL GROUP AND DIVISION	NUM-BER	IN MANUAL OCCUPATIONS	IN NON-MANUAL OCCUPATIONS
Professional......	23	39.1	——
Semiprofessional..	19	52.6	——
Own business	105	68.5	——
Upper-white-collar	72	45.8	——
Lower-white-collar	67	82.1	——
Sales	42	64.3	——
All nonmanual ...	343†	62.4	——
Skilled..........	169	——	46.7
Semiskilled	98	——	49.0
Unskilled........	44	——	40.9
All manual	314†	——	46.8

* *These figures include 15 business executives and 3 manual (odd jobs) workers not shown separately.*
† *The jobs included in the data do not include jobs held before completing school or university.*

numbers have at one time or another worked in the manual occupations. While this is not the place to explore the subjective aspects of social mobility, we want to emphasize the importance of considering the impact of casual job experiences on the subjective appraisals of opportunities and on the presence or absence of subjective class identifications.

In using the conventional interpretations of the occupational hierarchy, two reservations must be

made. Recent studies have shown that the occupation of an individual correlates highly with his "social placement" by members of the same community. On the other hand, people's ideas about who belongs to the middle class or the working class are sufficiently vague and ideological to allow even some corporation vice-presidents to rank themselves as members of the working class. Such findings demonstrate the difficulty of using an occupational classification as a basis for assessing upward or downward mobility. Differences in earnings can be objectively ascertained, but the social evaluation of a particular job or occupation is inevitably subjective. When an individual's work career is judged by his occupational rise or fall, it is so judged because occupational classification combines to some extent the economic with the prestige aspect of social class. But, in using data such as those in this study, whose subjective judgment of social mobility should be employed? Not the individual's, since he was not asked to evaluate his own mobility, or his associates', since that was not available. Hence we fall back on the general understanding of the differences between high- and low-status jobs, which is presumed to be accepted in the country as a whole. Such an understanding, in so far as it exists, is vague indeed, and in assessing the social mobility of the respondents only crude distinctions can be made. A second reservation must be made. We speak of a lack of social mobility if an individual has remained within the same occupational group throughout his career. But this conflicts with the general understanding, however vague, which was referred to above. A man who owns his own business and who transforms it from a small store to a chain of stores in twenty years

TABLE 3: Occupational Group of Present Job by Occupational Division of Previous Job

OCCUPATIONAL DIVISION OF PREVIOUS JOB	PRESENT JOB							
	PROFESSIONAL AND SEMIPROFESSIONAL		OWN BUSINESS		UPPER-WHITE-COLLAR		LOWER-WHITE-COLLAR	
	NUMBER	PER CENT	NUMBER	PER CENT	NUMBER	PER CENT	NUMBER	PER CENT
Nonmanual.....	193	89.8	207	55.5	91	89.2	534	74.5
Farm	——	——	12	3.2	1	1.0	10	1.4
Manual	22	10.2	154	41.3	10	9.8	173	24.1
Total	215	100.0	373	100.0	102	100.0	717	100.0
	SALES		SKILLED		SEMISKILLED		UNSKILLED	
	NUMBER	PER CENT	NUMBER	PER CENT	NUMBER	PER CENT	NUMBER	PER CENT
Nonmanual.....	243	70.2	135	13.6	167	16.7	73	17.3
Farm	7	2.0	21	2.1	47	4.7	32	7.6
Manual	96	27.7	839	84.3	786	78.6	316	75.1
Total	346	99.9	995	100.0	1,000	100.0	421	100.0

will be regarded as highly mobile, both economically and socially. Yet he would not be so described if the stability of an occupational career is the only criterion of mobility. At the same time it is impossible to consider each career in detail as long as the interest is in an analysis of general career patterns. This aspect of the problem subsequently will be taken into account by linking occupational career with income data and with the degree of mobility between jobs, areas, and industries.

SPECIFIC AVENUES OF MOBILITY

Though 935 job histories provide a mass of information, this number is quickly reduced to insignificance when more than two or three breakdowns are attempted. It is, nevertheless, possible to analyze the upward and downward mobility of respondents in greater detail. "Areas" of high and of low mobility may first be distinguished on the basis of the previous tabulations of 4,530 job changes. Here again (Table 3) the pattern is similar to that evidenced in the total job-history data above. The self-employed reveal the greatest mobility from manual to nonmanual positions. Shifts from farm jobs are largely to manual labor, especially the unskilled and semiskilled positions. The lower-white-collar and sales positions are the main positions in which manual workers have an opportunity to secure other than self-employment, and these positions do not usually reflect immediate upward mobility. The professional, semiprofessional, business executive, and upper-white-collar positions are filled largely by persons who previously were in nonmanual positions. As one would expect, skilled positions are the most difficult manual jobs for nonmanual workers to secure.

It is difficult to estimate from the data how much genuine social mobility is reflected in these tables, since persons changing from manual work to lower-white-collar and sales jobs or to small business may not actually be changing their status and income level by a great deal. The fact remains, however, that a considerable amount of such shifting does occur.

"Bureaucratic" Versus "Free-Enterprise" Mobility

Table 3 suggests that the greatest social mobility occurs in the form of shifts into "own business" and that shifts into the white-collar occupation and sales rank next. These are the occupations of most of those who manage to pass from manual to nonmanual work. There is, however, a significant difference in the mobility patterns if "own business" is compared with the white-collar occupations. That is to say, the majority of persons in white-collar jobs have always been employed in such jobs, though 20 per cent of those employed in lower-white-collar occupations have previously worked with their hands. On the other hand, more than a third of the persons who own their business are "recruited" from the manual occupations.

It cannot be concluded that a person's work career is mobile if he has stayed throughout in the same occupational classification. He may be a white-collar worker at the end as well as at the beginning of his career, though he began as a salesclerk and ended as an executive vice-president. However, the study does not deal with this type of mobility here but rather with the two types of social mobility which are represented by the people who own their business and by those in the white-collar occupations, which may be called an "old" and a "new" type of mobility. To run a business of one's own is still a much-cherished ideal. But with the growth of large-scale organizations in all parts of American society

---

TABLE 4: Selected Occupational Groups* of Present Job by Major Occupational Group and Division of Previous Job

MAJOR OCCUPATIONAL GROUP AND DIVISION OF PREVIOUS JOB	PRESENT JOB					
	OWN BUSINESS		UPPER-WHITE-COLLAR		LOWER-WHITE-COLLAR	
	NUMBER	PER CENT	NUMBER	PER CENT	NUMBER	PER CENT
Professional and semiprofessional	9	2.1	4	3.3	31	3.6
Own business	92	21.6	8	6.6	16	1.9
White-collar and sales	106	24.8	79	65.8	487	57.0
All manual	154	36.2	10	8.4	273	20.2

* For simplicity, a number of miscellaneous occupational groups have been included. The percentage figures are calculated for the whole group, but, since some occupational groups have been excluded, they do not add to 100 per cent.

it has lost some of its meaning, though its ideological appeal has not necessarily been weakened thereby. Many still cherish it, though their own careers show little evidence that "private enterprise" has had much significance for them personally. Mobile persons in the white-collar occupations are mobile in the bureaucratic manner; the qualities which lead to the promotion of the salaried employee are radically different from those which would make him a successful, independent businessman. The data reveal some significant differences between the idolized "free-enterprise" career and the bureaucratic career of the white-collar worker.

Until now these occupations have been considered in terms of "all previous" jobs, meaning the occupational background of any person who owned his business or did white-collar work, if only for three months. However, the degree of mobility which characterizes these career patterns can be more accurately assessed. Other data in this study reveal that the first job is an excellent predictor of the subsequent career. Degree of social mobility may be described in terms of the "occupational distance" between the first and the present job.

The "occupational distance" between first and present job is clearly greatest for business owners and executives, almost as great for the lower-white-collar workers, and least significant for persons in the upper-white-collar brackets. A number of other variables are associated with these differences. Business owners and executives are an older group than are the white-collar workers, 7 per cent of the first but 22 per cent of the second group being thirty years or under, while 53.9 per cent of the business owners and 43.3 per cent of the white-collar-workers are forty-six years of age or older. The older age of the business owners, together with the fact that many of them have been in the manual occupations at various times, suggests that opportunities for the

manual workers to turn businessmen open up in the middle and later years. In all other respects there is little difference between the mobility patterns of business owners or white-collar workers and those of the sample as a whole: mobility among jobs, occupations, and areas is greatest in the younger age groups and decreases with age.

The mobility of these three occupational groups, considered as a whole, is, however, quite striking. That is to say, between 40 and 50 per cent of business owners and white-collar workers have had four or more different occupations as well as six or more different jobs. Although this mobility is partly reflected in the answers to a number of questions posed in the study, it may be suggested that a further investigation of the contrast between proprietorship and bureaucratic careers would be worth while. Respondents were asked whether they had known of other available positions since they began their present jobs. Answers to this question presumably reveal something of a person's potential mobility in the recent past, since mobility depends in good part on his contacts. Presumably persons who knew of other available jobs are more mobile than those who knew of no job alternative since starting in their present positions.

More than half of the semiskilled and unskilled workers and of the business owners state that they have not known of other jobs since starting on the present one. All respondents in the nonmanual and skilled occupations have known of other jobs more often than business owners. It is true of course that "available job" means different things to the different occupations and that business owners in particular are not at all concerned with other jobs but rather with how to make profitable their present, presumably small-scale investment. Thus, while business ownership is a goal of the socially mobile, especially for persons from the manual occupations, it is not in the same sense a step to other jobs. The significant difference

---

TABLE 5: Selected Occupational Groups of Present Job by Major Occupational Group and Division of First Job

MAJOR OCCUPATIONAL GROUP AND DIVISION OF FIRST JOB	PRESENT JOB					
	OWN BUSINESS		BUSINESS EXECUTIVE AND UPPER-WHITE-COLLAR		LOWER-WHITE-COLLAR AND SALES	
	NUMBER	PER CENT	NUMBER	PER CENT	NUMBER	PER CENT
Professional, semiprofessional, business owners, and executives	10	9.0	10	10.3	2	1.3
All white-collar and sales	38	34.2	61	62.9	75	48.7
All manual (including farm)	63	56.8	26	26.8	77	50.0
Total	111	100.0	97	100.0	154	100.0

between business ownership versus bureaucratic position as a goal for the socially mobile lies in the fact that in modern society the first is the final step in a person's work career, while the second is at least potentially a means to a better-paying job in the same or another large-scale organization.

Changing implications of proprietorship

That there is a certain finality in proprietorship does not mean that persons in this group never move into other occupations. But, since a good proportion of them come from the manual occupations, it is probable that their only opportunity is to choose between manual labor or proprietorship. The self-employed businessman, in so far as the data of this study represent him adequately, is today a very different person, both socially and economically, from what he was two generations ago. Then he could hope and work for real economic success which would consist in the building-up of a large enterprise out of very small beginnings. That hope and work were meaningful, regardless of the individual's particular fate, because the social and economic distance between the small business at the beginning and the large enterprise at the end of a career was very great. Today, this distance has largely disappeared. Success in proprietorship today consists in most instances in the stabilization of an enterprise at a given social and economic level, because the opportunities for building large enterprises out of very small ones are dramatically diminished, though they have certainly not disappeared. It is in part a by-product of the predominance of large-

scale organizations that those who head them have usually had a bureaucratic career. The "industrial bureaucrat" and not the small independent businessman is likely to advance most, both socially and economically. For these reasons the data on self-employed businessmen are of special interest.

The 105 individuals who were self-employed at the time of the interview have been so employed for less than half of their average working careers. Sixty-eight per cent of the group had at some time been employed in manual work (Table 2), while 59 per cent had had jobs as lower-white-collar workers or salesmen. If one considers semi-skilled, unskilled, manual (odd jobs), and farm workers, as well as lower-white-collar workers and salesmen, as the lower-status occupations in American society, then 88.6 per cent of the self-employed business owners have spent some part of their work careers in these lower-status occupations. If their work careers are considered collectively (rather than what proportion of the group has been in the lower-status occupations at some time), then the group is shown to have spent, on the average, 36.3 per cent of its work careers in these low-status jobs, which is only slightly less than the average time spent in self-employment (41.5 per cent).

Census data corroborate our finding that self-employment continues to be important as a career goal at the same time that it proves to be unattainable on a permanent basis for the overwhelming majority of Americans. Only 8 per cent of the population are presently self-employed, but many more persons have been in business for themselves at some time in their history. Every socioeconomic category contains a large group

TABLE 6: **Selected Occupational Groups by Number of Occupations and Number of Jobs**

NUMBER OF OCCUPATIONS AND NUMBER OF JOBS	PRESENT JOB					
	OWN BUSINESS		BUSINESS EXECUTIVE AND UPPER-WHITE-COLLAR		LOWER-WHITE-COLLAR AND SALES	
	NUMBER	PER CENT	NUMBER	PER CENT	NUMBER	PER CENT
Number of occupations:						
1	15	12.6	15	14.0	30	18.5
2–3	53	44.5	42	39.3	59	36.4
4 or more	51	42.9	50	46.7	73	45.1
Total	119	100.0	107	100.0	162	100.0
Number of jobs:						
1–5	56	47.1	63	58.3	97	59.9
6–10	44	37.0	39	36.1	50	30.9
11–15	13	10.9	3	2.8	10	6.2
16 or more	6	5.0	3	2.8	5	3.0
Total	119	100.0	108	100.0	162	100.0

TABLE 7: Knowledge of Other Jobs by Present Occupational Group

PRESENT OCCUPATIONAL GROUP	KNOWLEDGE OF OTHER JOBS*			
	YES		NO	
	NUM-BER	PER CENT	NUM-BER	PER CENT
Professional and semiprofessional..	31	63.3	18	36.7
Own business......	40	42.1	55	57.9
Upper-white-collar and business executive	60	65.2	32	34.8
Lower-white-collar .	47	54.0	40	46.0
Sales	33	60.0	22	40.0
Skilled	104	56.2	81	43.8
Semiskilled........	48	44.9	59	55.1
Unskilled	19	41.3	27	58.7
All groups.......	382	53.4	334	46.6

Based on replies to question: "Since you began this job, have you known about any other jobs which you might have been able to get?"

who have once been self-employed. It is especially noteworthy that over one-fifth of those persons now employed in manual work were at some time employed in their own businesses. The proportion of the previously self-employed rises to 24.3 per cent for the skilled workers and to 38.1 per cent for salesmen.

Department of Commerce statistics on turnover among business firms from 1944 to 1948 confirm the implications of our data. Table 8 presents the figures of the department.

Even during the postwar boom of 1945-48 almost 30 per cent of the businesses in the United States were discontinued, while in the same period every year with the exception of 1948 witnessed the opening of new businesses equal to about twice the number of businesses which closed. In California, where the data of the present study were collected, the entrance and discontinuance rate was much higher, as is to be expected in an area of expanding population.

The absolute figures present an even clearer picture. Over four-fifths of all the businesses which opened or closed were small firms employing three or fewer workers. A total of 1,917,000 firms opened and 1,094,400 discontinued. Assuming that these openings and closings involved different people, which is obviously not always the case, and ignoring the question of number of partners in these firms, between 1944 and 1948 about three million Americans were involved in either starting or getting out of business, a figure equal to 6 per cent of the urban work force of the entire population. Unfortunately, similar data do not exist for previous years, and it is difficult to extrapolate the postwar data backward to the war years and to the prewar depression period. Judging by the war year of 1944, however, the rate of business turnover was even greater during the war than in the following period. Thus it is safe to conclude that the Oakland labor market is not atypical. That is, somewhere between 20 and 30 per cent of the urban work force has been self-employed at some time, and self-employment in small business still constitutes an attainable goal, if a temporary one, for a large part of the population.

The majority of every occupational category in the sample admits to having had the goal of "going into business" at some time. This aspiration

TABLE 8:* Entrance and Discontinuance Rates: Number of New and Discontinued Firms per 1,000 Firms in Operation, by Area and Size of Firm, March 31, 1944-48

AREA AND SIZE	ENTRANCE RATES					DISCONTINUANCE RATES				
	1944	1945	1946	1947	1948	1944	1945	1946	1947	1948
Specified area:										
Total United States....	117	134	176	123	99	66	63	64	76	94
Far West............	207	210	243	194	131	100	81	83	94	128
California	217	205	244	205	131	102	84	81	91	124
Size of firm:										
All firms	—	134	176	123	99	—	63	64	76	94
0–3 employees	—	155	206	143	115	—	72	76	88	111
4–7 employees	—	86	124	83	75	—	34	35	48	53
8–19 employees	—	55	74	51	41	—	35	32	41	46
20 or more employees..	—	33	38	26	22	—	26	24	29	29

Source: U.S. Department of Commerce, State Estimates of Business Population (Washington, 1949), p. 5, and U.S. Department of Commerce, Survey of Current Business, May, 1950, p. 17.

TABLE 9: Business Aspirations of Males Age Thirty-one and Over by Present Occupational Group

PRESENT OCCUPATIONAL GROUP	BUSINESS ASPIRATIONS*			
	YES		NO	
	NUM-BER	PER CENT	NUM-BER	PER CENT
White-collar.......	77	55.8	61	44.2
Sales	31	73.8	11	26.2
Skilled	106	63.1	62	36.9
Semiskilled........	69	71.1	28	28.9
Unskilled	30	68.2	14	31.8
All manual	208	66.7	104	33.3

Based on replies to question: "Have you ever thought about going into business for yourself?"

It is our guess that the creed of the "individual enterpriser" has become by and large a working-class preoccupation. Though it may have animated both working class and middle class in the past, it is no longer a middle-class ideal today. Instead, people in the middle class aspire to become professionals and, as a second choice, upper-white-collar workers. But persons in the nonmanual occupations frequently work with their hands—though only for short periods of time. The belief in the social mobility of American society apparently continues its hold on people's imagination, partly because individual enterprise is frequently a goal of manual workers and partly because members of the middle class can point to their experience with manual jobs as evidence of such mobility.

has been even greater among the manual (Table 9) than among the white-collar group, though salesmen as a class seem to desire and obtain self-employment more than any other group.

Responses to the question, "Have you ever tried to own your own business?" are similar. The proportions of persons who report that they actually tried to become self-employed is lower than those who have thought of it as a goal, but here again the manual workers report more such effort than the white-collar group, the salesmen again leading.

This analysis of mobility between manual and nonmanual occupations reveals hidden and changing aspects of the belief in social mobility which is still widespread among the American people.

CONCLUSIONS

This research report is a preliminary introduction to the Oakland labor-market studies, limited to a survey of the data, especially classified by lifetime careers for males, thirty-one years of age and older. Certain conclusions may be drawn upon in future research in occupational stratification.

1. The use of present job as an index of the social experiences and pressures correlated with occupational status ignores the fact that the individuals in any given sample have a variety of work experiences. If the sample were analyzed at some point five or ten years before the interviewing, many individuals would fall into a different socioeconomic category.

TABLE 10: Percentage of Males Age Thirty-one and Over Who Attempted to Own Business, by Present Occupational Group

PRESENT OCCUPATIONAL GROUP	ATTEMPTS TO OWN BUSINESS*										HAVE BEEN IN BUSINESS†	
	TRIED		DID NOT TRY		TOTAL REPLIES		NO REPLY		TOTAL			
	NUM-BER	PER CENT	NUM-BER	PER CENT	NUM-BER	PER CENT	NUM-BER	PER CENT	NUM-BER	PER CENT	NUM-BER	PER CENT
White-collar	40	35.1	74	64.9	114	82.0	25	18.0	139	100.0	20	14.4
Sales	27	67.5	13	32.5	40	95.2	2	4.8	42	100.0	16	38.1
Skilled.........	61	44.2	77	55.8	138	81.6	31	18.3	169	100.0	41	24.3
Semiskilled	30	37.0	51	63.0	81	83.5	16	16.5	97	100.0	23	23.7
Unskilled	16	42.1	22	57.9	38	86.3	6	13.6	44	100.0	6	13.6
All manual	108	41.5	152	58.5	260	83.0	53	16.9	313	100.0	71	22.7

Based on replies to question: "Have you ever tried to own your own business?"
†Data on business ownership are from actual job histories and are shown here to provide ready comparison. Although 107 respondents have owned a business, 282 indicate that they have made attempts in this direction.

2. That the split between manual and non-manual work is basic in American society is a conclusion reinforced by this sample, taken from one of the most mobile areas in the United States. On the other hand, the majority of males over thirty-one years of age have at some time been in occupations in either category. It is important to see that both conditions exist simultaneously.

3. Those who cross from one category to the other, nevertheless, are largely persons in the nonmanual occupations who work with their hands from time to time and persons in the manual occupations who for some period become self-employed small businessmen or lower-white-collar workers. Persons in the nonmanual occupations frequently work with their hands, whether their careers are considered in terms of the over-all time they spend in the manual occupations and in terms of the proportion of nonmanual persons who have ever done so. The reverse movement of manual workers into the nonmanual occupations occurs less frequently.

4. The opportunity and the desire to enter small business may still be a major goal of American wage-earners. Statistics on the comparatively small number of self-employed at any given time conceal the fact that many more than the number now self-employed have been self-employed in the past or will try to be self-employed in the future. That people do not mention self-employment as a desired future occupation does not mean that it is not a realistic goal to them. Self-employment is one of the few positions of higher status attainable to manual workers. That most of those who try it apparently fail does not change the fact that they do try.

5. Various sociologists hold that the socially mobile have significantly different attitudes from those of the immobile, especially in respect to racial prejudice. This study indicates that Americans are still a very mobile people, regardless of long-run trends, and that it is possible within rough limits to differentiate careers which reflect a great deal of mobility from those which do not.

6. There seems to be more homogeneity at the top of the social structure than at the bottom. However, the study tells little about the very top or bottom because of the limitations of the sample. The study does suggest that generalizations about trends in social mobility made on the basis of studies of small communities may greatly distort the national picture.

Certain limiting factors prompt us to regard this inquiry as a pilot study in social mobility.

a) The study was undertaken in connection with an investigation of labor-market behavior. From the standpoint it was convenient to omit census tracts containing some 17 per cent of the Oakland population, which had the effect of excluding from consideration the areas of the highest and of the lowest socioeconomic classes. This is clearly a limitation, in a study of social mobility. Likewise, since only working heads of families were interviewed, the older age groups are overrepresented.

b) The sample was drawn from a probability random sample of segments of blocks. The sample requirements were not completed. In all, close to 18 per cent of the population drawn were not interviewed, for a variety of reasons. This was in part a result of the fact that the interviewing was done on a very small budget.

c) There were a number of biases in the data on job histories. The reliability of the interviewees is probably low. The older a worker and the more jobs he has had, the less likely is he to report his job changes accurately or to give information which permits reliable classification of the status of the job. Certain types of jobs, especially those which are considered of high status, are probably more likely to be reported than the low. Highly educated persons are more likely to give accurate information than those of lesser education. The very meaning of the job may be different in peacetime from what it is in wartime and in a small community from what it is in a metropolis.

Certain variables specific to Oakland and California may make it impossible to generalize from these results to the rest of the country. The city of Oakland has grown greatly in the last twenty years, and most especially in the last ten years. Only 24.4 per cent of the sample are native to the San Francisco Bay Area, and only 30.6 per cent have always lived in California: 69.4 per cent have resided in more than one community, and a large proportion of this group has held jobs before coming to California. An analysis of the relation between the community of origin of the interviewees and their occupational status suggests a relationship between the expansion of a city and the social mobility of its residents. This analysis will be presented elsewhere, but the limitations should be mentioned as a caveat to those who may extrapolate these data to other more static areas. On the other hand, studies conducted in other metropolitan areas will probably reveal also a great deal of heterogeneity of the occupational backgrounds of the population, although there is little doubt that the degree will vary with the size, age, and economic stability of the given community.

Selection 76

Personality and Social Mobility
Allison Davis

Occupational success is one of the yardsticks by which Americans are evaluated by their fellows. It is "too bad" when a young man aspires to an occupation beneath that of his father (or his father-in-law) on the occupational scale. On the other hand, if the son of a skilled worker aspires to become a professional man, he is praised and given encouragement and many forms of psychological rewards.

In the following article, Davis undertakes an analysis of the effects of pressures for upward mobility on the personalities of those pressured. Perhaps it should be pointed out in conjunction with this article, and as an extension of the preceding article by Lipset and Bendix, that there has been a shift in the number of persons engaged in the various occupational categories in the United States and that the general direction of this shift is upward. This in effect alters the reference points for gauging the social significance of the various occupational statuses, so that to "keep up" with the world occupationally, one must achieve some degree of upward occupational mobility. Recognition of this may be a factor in producing the pressures of which Davis writes. However, his concern is not with the objective situation in regard to the changing occupational structure but with the personal significance of status aspirations and conceptions of self.

The readings in Part VIII, in retrospect, have been concerned with the way in which the people in society distinguish between and stereotype social categories to which they assign different values. Selections 66-68 documented the social fact of differential statuses; in readings 69-71 attention was given to the nature of social strata; and Selections 72 and 73 were devoted to the development of the concept of social class and its meaning in the social world. Finally, articles 74-76 have been concerned with the dynamic nature of social strata and with the effects of the perception of differential social worth on personality development.

There is a growing feeling in America that the competition for professional status is becoming more severe and that our status system generally is tightening. Perhaps this belief contributes to the pressure for acceleration by our schools. Middle-class parents, moreover, are increasingly fearful that their children will not qualify for admission to a good college. These parents, as well as many teachers and administrators, exert strong pressure upon the child from the time he is in elementary school. The tension builds up until the months preceding the announcement by colleges of their decisions upon applications; at that time even the best students often are in a nearly frenetic condition.

This whole process is a function of our social-class system. Educators are realizing that the social-class system is a stubborn reality, which influences every aspect of the school, from the values and attitudes of teachers and pupils to the curriculum itself. The social-class system in America is becoming sharply defined. Techniques

"Personality and Social Mobility" by Allison Davis. Reprinted from The School Review, Summer 1957, pp. 134-143, by permission of The University of Chicago Press.

exist, it is true, for climbing the ladder of social status. This process of changing one's status is called "social mobility." Education is the most readily available means of rising in the world. Even with education, however, an individual's upward mobility is slow; to climb one subclass in his lifetime, such as from lower-middle class to upper-middle class, constitutes an unusually rapid rate of social mobility for an individual.

Failure attends the efforts of the majority of those individuals who wish to rise to a higher status and actually attempt to do so. A major cause of these failures lies in the personalities of the individuals. In the following pages an effort will be made to define some of the personality factors related to success or failure in upward social movement. . . . Here the purpose is to examine the functions of *aggression* and of a sense of *identity* in facilitating the processes of upward status movement.

These processes usually begin in the early family life of the individual. Many parents seek to train their children toward upward mobility. Perhaps the prototype of such a parent is the immigrant who insists that all his children become physicians, lawyers, or teachers. The son of such a father commented recently that everyone in his family had taken books seriously because his father considered the reading of English the most important factor in "getting up" in the American social system. In such a family, books have a kind of pragmatic value in addition to whatever value they may have as intellectual and imaginative stimuli. Books and school marks become "instruments" of social mobility. Although the ethnic cases may afford the more dramatic instances of the pushing and training of a child to rise above the status of his parents, it is of course true that many established American middle-class families train their children for extremely high goals, superior to those of the parents' occupational and educational standings.

Such parents really teach the child that he must be superior to his parents. To accomplish the Herculean task of becoming smarter and more successful than his own father or mother, the driven child apparently often learns to feel that he must actually be "perfect" in school and in work. Since he can never be perfect, he can never be satisfied with his success, no matter how great it may seem to others. Thus to him the game seems not worth the candle. For he can never extinguish his early learned need to be perfect, and therefore he must continue the pursuit of the ever retreating goal of perfection by driving himself toward increasingly greater attainment.

What of the parents who push their children hard and early for the attainment of the culture of a higher social level? Often such parents feel that they themselves have failed in the world. Their own hopes may have been blocked by lack of money or by undue economic responsibility for their own parents. The mother may feel that, as a woman, she has been prevented from achievement in business, law, medicine, or some other field dominated by men—an achievement which she deeply wanted. Such parents set the highest standards for their children, for they project their own ambitions upon the child. They feel that the child needs, more than anything else in life, the prestige and position in the world which the parents themselves always have desired.

Such a child may fail at upward mobility because he has been weakened, by parental guidance and pressure, in just those ego functions which are essential for upward mobility. As a child, he learned from his parents that he could not direct his own life, stand on his own feet, make his own decisions both in the present and in the future. Although such children perform well in the academic world (a relatively simple world, where books are far more important than relationships with people), they often have trouble when they begin their careers. Their difficulty apparently results from their long-repressed hostility toward the parents, which is displaced to other authority figures. It is likely that the child who believes he has not been allowed to make his own decisions will feel that he has been used and exploited, and the resultant hostility often will be transferred to his relationships with later authority figures. Such a child may also turn his (now guilty) resentment against himself and become self-punishing. In either case, whether by turning his resentment toward later parental figures, such as his boss, or by turning it inward against himself, he succeeds in being avenged upon the ambitious parent by failing in the world. These children often are harried by feelings of unworthiness, of having betrayed their parents. Their guilt really may be due not to their failure but to their own resentment against their parents.

Another area in which the driven child may have difficulty as he grows up is that of relationships with the opposite sex. Where the mother has been the driver, the son may have difficulty, not only with objective authority figures, but also with women generally, including his wife, because he views women as authority figures like his mother.

Many parents who push their children toward social mobility are members of mixed-class marriages. The most common type of mixed-class marriage is that between a woman from the lower-middle class and a man from the top part of the working class. A lower-middle-class woman who marries a man from the top part of the working class usually begins to try to recoup her original social-class status either by reforming and elevating her husband's behavior to meet lower-middle-class standards or by seeking to train and propel her children toward the status which she once had or toward an even higher status, thus compensating for her "error." A similar situation may arise with a man who has been downward mobile, due either to economic mishap or to his having married into a lower class. He may wish to help his children to avoid the kind of error which he feels he has made or the kind of deprivation which he has had to undergo.

The child of such a mixed-class marriage faces many of the conflicts typical of any marriage between individuals from different cultures. He will be caught between the lower-middle-class parent, who will have the ideas of child-rearing, the ambitions with respect to education, and the concepts of sexual renunciation which are typical of the lower-middle-class culture, and the other parent from the working class, who may have quite different views with respect to education, discipline, child-training goals, recreation, and sexual exploration and behavior. Thus the conflict will be in the basic areas of life. Such a conflict is most readily seen, however, in the area of education. The working-class father in such a mixed-class marriage often feels that the girl or the boy should go to work after she or he has finished high school, but his wife from the lower-middle-class almost always feels that the child should go on to college to train for a profession. This conflict is often bitter; it is also pivotal, since education is one of the most available means for upward mobility.

Until now this discussion has dealt with children who have been "trained" for mobility but trained, perhaps, in the wrong way. The best training for upward mobility probably is training to be independent, to make one's own decisions, to seek one's own goals, and to have a proper degree and level of aggression. It is possible here to discuss only aggression. The handling of aggression—the control, direction, and transformation of his own aggression—is especially important for the successfully upward-mobile individual. Basic means of controlling and redirecting aggression are learned in childhood and adolescence. The young child seeks, first of all, to satisfy his own impulses and reduce his tensions. When his parents or siblings block his pursuit of food, activity, and love, he feels angry. He soon learns that his physical weakness prevents his attacking the

parents. As he grows older, he also is deterred from aggression toward the parents by his learned feelings of guilt and anxiety as well as by his desire for approval. But the fact that the parents must deny him many things he wants, together with the basic status structure of privileges inherent in the social structure of the parent-child relationship, still chronically arouses the hostility of the child toward the parent.

. . . Until the child has worked out, through his culturally permitted roles, socially effective forms of initiative and aggression, he has one of two choices. He may either displace his rage from the all-powerful father or mother to a sibling, or he may turn his hostility inward and attack and depreciate himself (as he feels his parents would do if they were aware of his resentment toward them). Thus the healthy child expresses his hostility toward his parents by displacing it to his brother or sister. In this way he seeks to preserve his self-regard by counterattacking but, at the same time, saves himself the destructive guilt and anxiety which would be aroused by direct and conscious hostility toward the parents. The other recourses, that is, to repress his hostility, or to attack the parents themselves, or to turn his rage against himself, usually lead to destructive levels of guilt and anxiety.

The method by which the upward-mobile individual handles his aggression is extremely complex. It varies, moreover, from one type of personality to another. Boys may repress their hostility toward the parents, usually the father, and, owing to the repressed hate, become the victims of a great deal of vague anxiety and guilt. Other upward-mobile individuals may experience their hostility toward the father at a more nearly conscious level and therefore may suffer less guilt and less anxiety than those of the first group. This second group would presumably include many of the leaders of industry, studied by Warner and Abegglen, who depreciate their fathers in their memories and who insist that they, themselves, became successful without the help and example of their fathers. Really this is only another way of saying, "I am better than, stronger than, smarter than, my father was." Still another type of child may develop a great deal of fear and insecurity in his early relationships with the parents. Throughout the remainder of his life, he may be seeking to gain forever increasing power, applause, and prestige in an effort to satisfy his insatiable desire to be reassured.

Similarly, one may distinguish several levels of aggression which are developed in the individual's early relationships with his siblings. The normal adaptation, as has been said, is to be jealous of the sibling; every child apparently wants all of his mother's and father's love or certainly the best part of it. To be jealous of, and to be competitive with, the siblings are therefore almost universal experiences. This rivalry, however, has certain normal limits. It becomes abnormal when the child is obsessed with the feeling that the brother or sister has all the best of it; that he, himself, is rejected by the mother and father. Such a child devotes his life, so to speak, to the self-pity and the feeling of rejection which results from his belief that his sibling has been strongly preferred. Or the reaction may be one of chronic and inextinguishable rage and resentment. The third type of relationship to the sibling is that of overidentification with the sibling. In this case the child apparently feels that the effort to compete with the sibling is hopeless, owing either to the belief that the mother or father has given all his love to the sibling or to the belief that the sibling, himself, is far more able and effective. The overidentified individual then feels, apparently, "The best recourse I have is to be just like the sibling, to become another one such as he or she." This process by which a sibling loses his identity and initiative in order to escape the resentment of the parent is a destructive process to the ego. It is similar to overidentification with a parent and to identification with the aggressor.

In the social realm, realistic aggression is one of the child's basic ego functions. Aggression, in this sense, includes the ability to stand up for one's self, to fight for one's own stake in the love of the parent, to gain physical pleasure as well as prestige in the areas both of social relations and occupational competence. These ego functions are all subsumed under the general terms "aggression" or "initiative" or "autonomy," and they are strengthened or weakened in the early relationship to the parent and to the sibling. Upward-mobile individuals may come out of their early family life either highly competitive and highly hostile or skilful and realistic in their aggression. But they certainly do not come out of the early family life either as highly self-punishing individuals or as individuals overidentified with their siblings.

The individual who has been *socially,* as distinguished from occupationally, upward-mobile must be one who has especially firm control of his hostility. The socially mobile individual has learned from childhood and adolescence not to fly in the face of authority. He has somehow learned how to placate and win over the authority figures. He has not weighed himself down with fruitless and guilt-laden hostility or resentment toward the parent. With his parents, as later with his social-class superiors, he is a diplomat in aggression. He learns how far he may go, presses for his just due, but he also expects to knuckle under when necessary and is able to do so without losing his self-regard and without feeling undue humiliation and resentment.

As child and adult, such an individual has learned how to redirect and transform aggression into the socially approved virtues of competition and initiative. He has learned to walk nimbly the tightrope of his superiors' approval by skilful aggression (initiative), while avoiding defiance, on the one hand, and self-depreciation and guilt, on the other. This is his distinguishing characteristic, perhaps—this fine tempering of his aggression. He faces the constant, objective necessity to impress, and to win acceptance from, persons who have more power and more status than he has. These superiors must not, in spite of his efforts to enter their group, come to regard him as a "pusher" or as an *arriviste.* His must be an effective, but congenial and disarming, aggression.

The most difficult task faced by the upward-mobile child and adolescent is that of becoming identified with some group and of achieving a sense of personal identity. . . . To develop his identity, he must have a group, know what it is, and feel that he is intimately a part of it.

But the upward-mobile adolescent is *leaving* his family and group and therefore is losing his old identity. Moreover, his parents, if they are "ambitious for him," are urging and guiding the adolescent toward a culture and a social place which they themselves do not possess. Thus the adolescent in an upward-striving family is being directed toward an identity which neither he nor his parents can conceive in terms of those specific behaviors, goals, and values which the higher social status, or social class, demands; for the parents can define the identity goals of only that culture and that social class in which they have been participating. Thus the child or adolescent whose parents are consciously, or more often unconsciously, directing him toward a social class higher than their own cannot learn from his parents how to obtain recognition from this higher social class nor how to conceive of himself as a prospective member of the higher class. He is attempting to learn an identity without having the necessary targets for identification and without having a group which can give him, through mutual association and "recognition," the necessary help in conceiving or integrating his new ego identity.

Thus, in upward-striving families, the adolescent is faced with two life-plans: that of his family's own culture and place and that of the more privileged culture and group which he is attempting to integrate into his life. The result is to intensify in these adolescents what Erikson calls "ego-diffusion" and to drive many of them, no doubt, toward a negative identity.

Faced by two conflicting demands—to follow the demands and assume the identity of the parents or to abandon much of the parents' culture and learn a culture to which neither they nor he has social access—the adolescent finds himself confronted by more social tasks, roles, and emotional problems than he can learn to handle. In this social situation and also, no doubt . . . as a result of his deep-seated disappointment in the parents in earlier stages of his relationship to them, the adolescent may retreat to an identity which is the opposite of his parents'. Specifically he may move *downward* in his social-class participation, choosing radical groups, identifying with out-groups, marrying "out," or giving up the effort to form any identity at all.

On the other hand, those adolescents who have satisfactorily come through the earlier stages of development are capable of learning the identity of a higher social class and of eventually moving up into that class. But, in all probability, these successfully upward-moving individuals are precisely those who have *not* been dominated or overprotected or had their life-plans mapped out by their parents.

Recent Research

William F. Kenkel

During the last two decades, sociologists have produced a tremendous amount of research in the area of social stratification. Hundreds of research articles have been published, and at least a dozen books with social stratification as their only or central theme have appeared. The field, moreover, has been "discovered" by journalists and popular writers who toss about terms like *status symbol, upper-middle class,* and *status seeking,* confident that they are both communicating with and impressing their fellow citizens.

Forming the base for the current research efforts in social stratification are the various community class studies of the 1930's and 1940's. The work of the Lynds,[1] Warner,[2] Hollingshead,[3] Dollard,[4] West,[5] and others focused primarily on the status system of a particular place at a particular time. But in the course of conducting the studies, these researchers collectively touched upon almost every aspect of social stratification. Through their development of field procedures and measuring devices, their use and refinement of existing concepts, and their attention to the effects of social status on the individual, these studies have provided a rich legacy of sociological insight. They also furnished a body of "facts" against which the results of subsequent studies could be compared. But the community class study era seems to be over. Communities are still studied, of course, but they are currently viewed as laboratories where human behavior can be observed and analyzed and as a result, hopefully, general principles of social stratification can be discovered.

In not too artificial a manner, the bulk of current social stratification research can be separated into two types. One type can be thought of as theoretical or conceptual research, for it deals with the principles and concepts in the field—testing and retesting existing theories, clarifying time-honored concepts, and, at times, inventing new concepts. Included in this type of research are those efforts devoted to the measurement of social stratification variables, such as the development of a scale that allows us to measure more precisely or more purely social mobility, status aspirations, or occupational prestige.

In the second type of research, social stratification concepts are used as independent or explanatory variables. In a sense, this type of research asks the question, "How much human behavior can be explained by knowing the social class of the behaving people?" Thus the focus of such studies is on understanding and predicting various aspects of human behavior and human society. Although the studies are not designed to contribute directly to the field of social stratification, they do, of course, indicate the importance of social stratification variables and they sometimes expose gaps of uncomfortable proportions in stratification theory.

CONCEPTUAL-THEORETICAL RESEARCH

Probably the simplest way to organize the body of research that has dealt largely with stratification theory is to isolate those key concepts that seem to have attracted the most research attention. While in no case can the discussion of each concept be exhaustive, we will try to indicate what kind of studies have been made and where the field now stands with respect to the particular concept.

The nature of social class

As various readings in this book have indicated, a key concept in social stratification has been that of *social class*. Until the 1950's it was agreed that social classes were real entities, consisting of groupings of people of roughly similar social ranks who were clearly set apart from other status groupings within the community. While not all agreed on how many social classes there were in American society, there was a basic acceptance of the idea that within each community there was a fixed number of classes which were observable units to the outsider and meaningful groupings to the community members.

A major breakthrough in social stratification theory and research came when the foregoing concept of social class was challenged. At first, issue was taken chiefly with the research methods used in studies that purported to discover social classes in specific communities. Then, the reality of social classes was questioned. Finally, the field research of such people as Hetzler,[6] Cuber and Kenkel,[7] and Lenski,[8] in a county seat village, a Midwestern city, and a New England mill town, respectively, showed that social classes in the sense of real and discrete entities were simply not to be found. In a surprisingly short time, the concept of social class underwent a transformation, and it now is used chiefly to mean a logically created category or statistical grouping rather than a social grouping that constitutes a subdivision of the community.

Vertical social mobility

As indicated in the introduction to Selection 74, the first comprehensive work on vertical social mobility was written by Sorokin in 1927.[9] In this work the basic concepts necessary to study movement up and down the social ladder and to distinguish it from other types of movements were defined and explained. It is amazing that this early work did not excite more scholars to delve into the topic. Possibly the depression years evoked so much concern for the absolute plight of the masses that improvements or losses in relative ranks within society seemed less important. After World War II, however, when it became apparent that our society was "on the go" again, it seemed important to find out more about who was going, in which direction, and how far.

Much concern has rested on the topic of how much mobility is occurring and particularly whether there is more or less vertical movement than there was, for example, at the turn of the century. For a time, research seemed to show less mobility—that is, that it was becoming more difficult to climb or descend the social ladder, at least very many rungs. Studies such as Warner's *Who Shall Be Educated?*[10] and Hollingshead's *Elmtown's Youth*[3] supplied some of the explanations for this trend; the acquisition of education, an increasingly demanded requisite for filling the higher positions of society, was found to be considerably easier for children whose parents were better educated.

More recently, the notion that class lines are hardening and movement up and down is becoming more difficult has been severely challenged by Sjoberg.[11] The research of Adams[12] led him to the conclusion that probably a certain rigidity, and consequent difficulty of movement, set in during the depression but that such a situation no longer prevails. Most, but not all, subsequent research indicates that at least from generation to generation there is a great deal of vertical mobility, probably as much as there ever has been.[13] Equally important, recent research has exposed and sometimes corrected weaknesses in the concept of social mobility. One example of needed clarification is the distinction between intergenerational mobility (usually measured as the difference between a man's social rank and his father's) and intragenerational mobility (the change in position that an individual accomplishes during his adult life).[14]

Status consistency

One of the most provocative social stratification concepts that only recently has come to the fore is that of *status consistency*, sometimes called *status congruency* or *status crystallization*. Starting with a multidimensional view of stratification, interest was aroused over how consistent the various ranks of an individual were with one another. It is logical to expect, for example, that a person who ranks high in occupational prestige and very high in education but who is just barely in the upper half in terms of income will in other ways differ from the person who ranks equally high on all three scales. Lenski's studies have shown that a sample of people differ rather remarkably with respect to the consistency of their statuses[15] and that the degree of status consistency, in turn, is related to such phenomena as political behavior and social participation.[16] Jackson,[17] writing in 1962, found in a national sample that people characterized by a high degree of status inconsistency had more psychological disturbances than did those whose statuses were more consistent. Different types of inconsistencies—for example, ethnic rank higher than occupational, as opposed to occupational rank higher than ethnic—were associated with different kinds of psychological problems. Thus, the concept continues to be refined and developed through current research. Largely untapped, however, is the study of how aware people are of their status inconsistencies and what effect this awareness, as opposed to the objective differences in their several ranks, has on their feelings and behavior.

Status perception

It must be kept firmly in mind that there is an important difference between a person's social rank and his awareness or perception of that rank. In the first instance we are talking about where a person "really is," or perhaps where others judge him to be, while in the second we are referring to how he sees himself. Though a person's objective rank and his perception of that rank are related, they are not the same phenomenon. Similar distinctions can and should be made with regard to the criteria that are used to judge the status of other people and with regard to other features of the status system.

Starting from the assumption that most people are aware of their own social rank, the notion became prevalent that most people also identify themselves with others of approximately the same status and consider themselves and these others as somehow constituting a group set apart from other groups in society. It was thus held that people are conscious of belonging to a segment of society that differs from other segments by virtue of the typical social ranks of the people in each.

Belief in the existence of class consciousness seemed to be justified by the polls of *Fortune* magazine and studies of similar design which consisted of presenting people with a list of social classes (e.g., upper, middle, lower; upper, middle, working, lower) and asking them to which class on the list they felt they belonged. Alas, the conclusions inhere in the method. The existence of two, three, or four social classes can be substantiated if the method of questioning provides for only that number of responses. More recent studies that do not assume either that there is some fixed number of social classes or that people do identify with a class do not seem to find this type of class consciousness at all.[18] This does not deny, of course, that people are more or less aware of where they stand with respect to their fellows. Consciousness of one's approximate social rank is not the same as identification with a social class.

Important contributions of West's *Plainville, U.S.A.,*[5] written in 1945, were that the criteria used to judge social rank, the designation and number of strata in the community, and many other important features of the status system were found to be differentially perceived by various community members. The differential perception, moreover, was systematic in the sense that people of similar rank, as judged by certain criteria, seemed to have common views on the nature of the status system. This finding raises the question of whose views are correct and whose are distorted. It further suggests that we explore more fully why some people, or perhaps entire groups, employ different standards for ranking themselves and their fellows than do other persons or groups in the same community. Interestingly, the phenomenon of differential perception of status criteria has not attracted much research attention. There are few definitive answers that can be given to the perplexing problems in this area.

SOCIAL STATUS AS AN EXPLANATORY VARIABLE

It is reasonable to expect that unequal distribution of rewards, privileges, power, and prestige will in various ways affect the members of society. In the last couple of decades, there has accumulated a substantial body of knowledge regarding the ways in which people of varying statuses differ from one another.

It is impossible to summarize, or even properly categorize, the hundreds of research findings in this area. The following short list of the kinds of behavior found to be related to social status has been arranged, for convenience, according to the life cycle of an individual. Relationships are phrased only in terms of the lower class. It should be emphasized that these are only a few of the many, many relationships that have been discovered.

As compared with higher status groups, low status groups in America are characterized by:

Higher infant mortality rate
Greater use of physical punishment in child rearing
Less school success, despite intelligence
Higher rate of school dropouts
Higher rate of premarital sex experience
Earlier age at marriage
More children
Higher divorce rate
More political and economic "radicalism"
Higher rate of mental illness
Lower rate of church membership
Lower rate of formal group membership
More chronic illness
Less likelihood of owning health insurance
Younger age at death

Thus, beginning with one's likelihood of surviving his first year of life, various of "life's chances" are tied up with one's parents' social status or his own social status. None of the phenomena listed above is found only among lower-class people; rather, various phenomena are more or less prevalent when people in the lower class are compared with those in another.

Undoubtedly, the years immediately ahead will see retests of earlier studies and new studies discovering other characteristics, other ways of thinking and feeling, and other modes of behavior that differ according to social status. There should, however, be more research specifically designed to explain why and how the discovered relationships operate. *Why* is it, for example, that the divorce rate is higher at the lower levels of society? *Why* is it that lower status people are not as likely to belong to formal groups as are higher status members of a community? Answers to such questions would not only contribute to our knowledge of behavior affected by social status—in this case divorce and group participation—but would also add to our knowledge about the nature and impact of differential social status.

Finally, the store of knowledge about behavior and characteristics related to social status could be processed in such a way that it would make a major contribution in the mainstream of social stratification theory. If all of the findings concerning differences by social status were brought together and ordered, it would be possible to ascertain whether the differences were so many and were of such a nature and degree that we ought to think of each social stratum as having a more or less distinct "way of life." If such were true, it would be legitimate to consider each stratum as a social class, in the older sense of the term. Although present research does not suggest that we now have distinct subcultures, existing data could be analyzed in order to determine if true subcultures are emerging. In this way, the many studies that have used social stratification variables to study other social facts could be brought to bear on some central and persistent problems in social stratification theory.

References

1. Robert S. Lynd and Helen Merrell Lynd, *Middletown: A Study in Contemporary American Culture* (New York: Harcourt, Brace & Co., 1929); and *Middletown in Transition: A Study in Cultural Conflicts* (New York: Harcourt, Brace & Co., 1937).
2. W. Lloyd Warner *et al.*, *Democracy in Jonesville* (New York: Harper & Brothers, 1949).
3. August B. Hollingshead, *Elmtown's Youth: The Impact of Social Classes on Adolescents* (New York: John Wiley & Sons, Inc., 1949).
4. John Dollard, *Caste and Class in a Southern Town* (New York: Harper & Brothers, 1949).
5. James West, *Plainville, U.S.A.* (New York: Columbia University Press, 1945).
6. Stanley Hetzler, "An Investigation of the Distinctiveness of Social Classes," *American Sociological Review*, 18 (October 1953), 493-497.
7. John F. Cuber and William F. Kenkel, *Social Stratification in the United States* (New York: Appleton-Century-Crofts, Inc., 1954), pp. 132-156.
8. Gerhard Lenski, "American Social Classes: Statistical Strata or Social Groups," *American Journal of Sociology*, LVIII (September 1952), 139-144.
9. Pitirim A. Sorokin, *Social and Cultural Mobility* (Glencoe, Ill.: The Free Press, 1959).
10. W. Lloyd Warner, Robert J. Havighurst, and Martin B. Loeb, *Who Shall Be Educated?* (New York: Harper & Brothers, 1944).
11. Gideon Sjoberg, "Are Social Classes in America Becoming More Rigid?" *American Sociological Review*, 16 (December 1951), 775-783.
12. Stuart Adams, "Trends in Occupational Origins of Business Leaders," *American Sociological Review*, 19 (October 1954), 541-548.
13. See, for example, Elton F. Jackson and Harry J. Crockett, Jr., "Occupational Mobility in the United States: A Point Estimate and Trend Comparison," *American Sociological Review*, 29 (February 1964), 5-15.
14. Saburo Yasuda, "A Methodological Inquiry into Social Mobility," *American Sociological Review*, 29 (February 1964), 16-25.
15. Gerhard E. Lenski, "Status Crystallization: A Non-Vertical Dimension of Social Status," *American Sociological Review*, 19 (August 1954), 405-413.
16. Gerhard E. Lenski, "Social Participation and Status Crystallization," *American Sociological Review*, 21 (August 1956), 458-464.
17. Elton F. Jackson, "Status Consistency and Symptoms of Stress," *American Sociological Review*, 27 (August 1962), 469-480.
18. Thomas Ely Lasswell, "Social Class and Stereotyping," *Sociology and Social Research*, 42 (March-April 1958), 256-262.

Part IX

SOCIAL PROBLEMS

From its earliest history in America, sociology has been interested not only in function but in malfunction, in disorganization as well as in organization, in areas of societal weakness as well as in areas of societal strength. Although these elements are no longer the primary concern of modern sociology, they represent areas of legitimate and abiding interest.

When a crabbed old woman calls the police to "come keep these juvenile delinquents from walking on my lawn," she is expressing her own *personal* problem. Unless many people in many places object to many children walking on lawns, however, this is not a *social* problem. By definition, social problems are widespread, are recognized as undesirable, are not caused by only one or a few persons, and cannot be ameliorated or cured by only one or a few persons. Cuber, Harper, and Kenkel[1] in their text followed the definition used by Richard Fuller that "social problems . . . represent a social condition which is regarded by a considerable number of individuals as undesirable, and hence these persons believe that something 'ought to be done' about the situation." Horton and Leslie[2] agree, saying "a social problem is a condition affecting a significant number of people in ways considered undesirable, about which it is felt something can be done through collective social action." Raab and Selznick[3] differ substantially but not irreconcilably when they say "social problems are primarily problems in relationships among people. . . . A social problem exists (1) where prevailing relationships among people frustrate the important personal goals of a substantial number of people; or (2) where organized society appears to be seriously threatened by an inability to order relationships among people." Our nation had over two million serious crimes in 1964; certainly crime and delinquency may properly be considered "social" problems.

The differences between the concepts *social problem* and *social disorganization* may not seem important for introductory students. According to Francis E. Merrill,[4] both are complementary in that the former introduces the problem and describes and measures it, while the second attempts to find out how and why it arose. For example, John H. Burma's study of intermarriage in Los

---

[1] John F. Cuber, Robert A. Harper, and William F. Kenkel, *Problems of American Society* (New York: Henry Holt & Co., 1956), p. xiv.

[2] Paul B. Horton and Gerald R. Leslie, *The Sociology of Social Problems* (New York: Appleton-Century-Crofts, 1960), p. 4.

[3] Earl Raab and Gertrude J. Selznick, *Major Social Problems* (Evanston, Ill.: Row, Peterson and Company, 1959), pp. 3-4.

[4] Francis E. Merrill, "The Study of Social Problems," *American Sociological Review*, 13:3 (June 1948), 251-259.

Angeles (Selection 85) describes and measures intermarriage—who married whom, and to what extent—but presents no concrete data on *why* these people intermarried. On the other hand, Selection 79 by Walter C. Reckless is specifically concerned with "why." "The problems approach alone produces a fragmentary consideration of a number of isolated situations existing more or less independently. The social disorganization approach alone tends to lose sight of the trees for the forest, and the individual problems often fail to come alive." Horton and Leslie[5] explain the concept somewhat differently: "The term *social organization* refers to all the organized and customary ways of doing things in a society, and is characterized by order, stability, and the predictability of behavior. *Social disorganization*, a product of social change, occurs when the customary ways of doing things break down or are no longer adequate. The resulting confusion and disorder are major elements to be considered in analyzing social problems."

Clearly, the definition of social problems—and of social disorganization—is closely related to *values* held by individuals and groups. What is a social problem in one society may not be so viewed in another; the same is true for subgroups within a society. For example, representatives of management and labor might have considerable difficulty attempting to delineate a "social problem" in the labor-management area; the man in the street, however, might call anything in this area that interfered with his income, consumption, or convenience a social problem. At one time industrial child labor was not considered a social problem; then it became a great problem and was severely attacked; today it no longer is a social problem in America, not because of a change in values but because it has so nearly disappeared. Most social problems are clearly recognized as such by most persons. LaMar T. Empey and Jerome Rabow in Selection 78 do not devote any space to proving that delinquency is a social problem; our society more or less by acclamation says it is. Their report concerns, rather, a new and unique method of attempting to deal with the problem and to return society to an equilibrium. On the other hand, the Negro youths reported by Harold Finestone in Selection 82 did not recognize, at least outwardly, that their use of narcotics and their goal of pimping for prostitutes represented "social problems."

The difficulty of definition and choice is illustrated by a half-dozen recent college texts dealing with social problems. Full chapter treatment was given to only six problems: crime, family problems, juvenile delinquency, racial and ethnic problems, educational problems, and a rather general mélange of personal disorganization and pathology. Three other problems were chosen by three of the books: population problems, problems of income and dependency, and rural-urban community problems. On the other hand, twenty different problems were given chapter treatment by only one or two of these six texts; they were problems relating to religion, health, civil liberties, war, mass communication, government and politics, mental health, old age, adolescence, leisure and recreation, industrial relations, class, immigration, social reform and planning, housing, gambling, suicide, prostitution, alcoholism, and drug addiction. No matter how empirically a certain behavior is studied, the selection of this behavior as a "social problem" is subjective as well as objective and hence will vary from time to time and from place to place. The student should not be concerned about this textual confusion, for it is more apparent than real and arises primarily from value judgments concerning which of the problems are the most serious

---

[5] Horton and Leslie, p. 39.

and from the editorial decision of whether to use a considerable number and treat each briefly or to use a small number and pursue each in depth. In this book it is possible only to include a very few problems and to pursue none of them in depth.

One matter is abundantly evident: our society is far from perfect. It has area after area of strain, weakness, tension, danger, unhappiness, disequilibrium, injustice, and discord. No responsible citizen can look upon all these problem areas and shrug them off with a "so what?" Not all persons can or should take an active part in seeking to alleviate these problems, but no one can consider himself educated without having more than a merely superficial knowledge of a considerable number of them. Certainly Selections 80 and 81 by Karen Horney and Robert E. L. Faris do not reach much beyond a superficial knowledge of mental disorder, but they are at least a good beginning. No society that hopes to improve as it changes can ignore its weaknesses, lags, and faults.

It is fruitless to look forward to a time when our society will be free of social disorganization. No such period will occur, because we have such a dynamic society and culture. Change—with its resultant disorganization (and our attempts at reorganization)—is unceasing. Historically most of this change has been unplanned and often relatively unforeseen; hence no forearming against the resulting social problems was undertaken. Today planned change, although comparatively infrequent, does occur, for we are beginning to recognize that although elements of social disorganization are inevitable, their undesirable effects can be minimized. Cultural change was discussed earlier in Part II. A change in a technological aspect of a culture often occurs prior to a change in the related nonmaterial culture. To this condition we apply the concept of *cultural lag;* the breakdown in relationships that then occurs is an aspect of social disorganization. For example, we had big, fast, heavy, dangerous automobiles for a number of decades before we made any attempt to restrict who could drive these engines of potential destruction. Even today many states have no compulsory automobile insurance as a financial protection for the victims of accidents. Social problems that arise as the result of sociocultural change are truly "social" in the sense that no one or a few persons can cause them and no one or a few persons can cure them. Raab and Selznick[6] suggest that the major social changes in America have been industrialization, urbanization, mobility, heterogeneity, and the increasing awareness of seeking for, and acceptance of, social change itself. One would today be tempted to add changes in race relations to this list. Selection 83 by Otto Klineberg and Selection 84 by Donald Pierson, on race differences and race prejudice, are intended to give the student some broad background for a better understanding of racial problems.

Other social problems, however, are not so clearly related to change and society. Some social problems are "social" only in the sense that they occur to many people and affect many people. For example, alcoholism is in one sense a personal problem; if we could devise "personal" cures, it could be controlled in much the same way that we have controlled smallpox. Mental disorder, drug addiction, and some types of delinquency and crime are illustrations of this personal type of social problem that are presented in sections in this part.

Another method of analyzing social disorganization is the value-conflict approach. As has been said, a social problem must be recognized as such by many people; that is, it must in some way contravene their values. Polyandry and prostitution are social problems only if there are widely held *values* in

---

[6] Raab and Selznick, pp. 10-14.

opposition to them. This is not as simple as it sounds, for our society has no single set of values. For example, whether racial discrimination is a social problem depends on one's value system, and it is abundantly clear that in America there is no uniform attitude toward discrimination. Certain conditions viewed as seriously detrimental to one segment of the population may be advantageous and desired by another. Selection 84 by Donald Pierson on the relationships between racial situations and racial prejudice is a good illustration. Selection 85 by John H. Burma reports that the number of interethnic marriages in Los Angeles in the late 1950's was triple what it was in the late 1940's. For people with one set of values, this shows an increasing social problem; for others, this is evidence of progress toward the goal of equality for all people. Rarely, if ever, does *everyone* in our society agree that any given condition is a serious problem and should be eliminated.

The chief function of social norms is the social control of behavior, but the controlling function of social norms is not equally effective at all times for all men. The French sociologist Emile Durkheim popularized the concept of *anomie* as one explanation of this. *Anomie,* as applied to individuals, is essentially a condition of normlessness. Under ordinary conditions any society sets up, or permits to grow, series of sanctioned behaviors, of ranges of permissibility, that are called *norms.* The typical individual uses these norms successfully to meet all of the typical (normal) social situations in which he finds himself. These norms and their attendant behavior are learned through the process of *socialization* and, in a relatively stable situation, last the individual all his life. But this describes a somewhat ideal situation. If social change is slow, most people are able to change their norms to the new ones required by the new situations. But if social change is rapid, some people are unable or unwilling to accept the new norms, function in a disorganized manner, and are said to suffer *anomie.* Wars, depressions, and revolutions are great breeders of *anomie.* Sometimes the change is a sociocultural one in the sense that a person who has learned and has been successfully applying a set of norms finds himself in a very different situation. His old norms no longer fit because the situation has changed, but he has no way of readily securing new norms. Thus, the well-adjusted, Southern, rural "folk" Negro who suddenly migrates to the slum-ghetto of a large, Northern, industrialized city may suffer from what is colloquially called "slum-shock" but what is actually a clear case of *anomie.* When a person suffers from *anomie,* whatever the cause, his behavior is likely to be confused, disorganized, unpredictable, and deviant. He loses a sense of attachment to society, becomes essentially egocentric, lives for the present, is seriously insecure, bitter, frustrated, and possibly destructive and criminal. Social disorganization may bring about *anomie,* and anomic individuals, collectively, represent a source of social disorganization.

Societies cannot accept with equanimity the existence of social problems and social disorganization. The members of a society are able to function together smoothly only because each person's behavior is, within limits, predictable. Society sets norms, and most persons conform to these norms most of the time. No matter how broad and flexible the norms, society cannot tolerate much deviation from them if it is to carry out common goals and functions. Social controls are operative in every society in order to prevent deviance; many social problems result in large part from the failures of the social control system of the society. Thus at least part of the society may censure the person participating in (or the recipient of) the social problem—the prostitute, the illiterate, the welfare case, the criminal, the divorcee, etc. A special problem exists when the individual is adjusted to the norms of value and behavior in his own small group but when those norms differ from those of the larger society. Some delinquents, for example, acquire their norms in the usual fashion, from those around them, but are surrounded by a deviant subculture and thus are socialized to and internalize delinquent patterns. Selection 77 by Albert K. Cohen and James F. Short, Jr., explains this type of delinquency.

In the case of either social or personal problems, treatment and cause may not successfully be separated. Unless a proper diagnosis of causal difficulties is made, treatment must be guesswork or trial and error. Social problems are usually the result of complex causes, and therefore only complex treatments can hope to succeed. Our treatment of some social problems has failed; other problems have ceased to be serious, either because of or in spite of treatment. Causation and treatment may be considered on three levels: societal, personal, and "middle range."

On the societal level, the theory is that disorders involving individuals result largely from our having a "sick society." According to Lawrence K. Frank,[7] the oustanding exponent of this theory, American culture is the result of a confused mixture of unrelated people, societies, and cultures, which are not in unity and never were. "Our culture has no unanimity of individual or social aims, . . . no common patterns of ideas or conduct." Consequently, we are suffering from cultural disintegration. Frank says we believe we have a normal, balanced, healthy, society that is being attacked by criminals, psychopaths, families in conflict, recalcitrant juveniles, hatemongers, and deviants of all kinds who, as rebels, threaten this stable society. We look upon political, economic, family, and religious problems as resulting from attacks by persons who are basically "wrong" upon that which is basically "right." This assumption of only personal perversity or depravity gives us the false notion that our society is in fine condition; only some of its members are evil or ill. This, says Frank, is not true. *Society* is sick.* Social problems arise because of the efforts of people of limited abilities to survive in a society that is conflicting, confused, and neurotic. Treatment is badly needed; to treat only individuals merely alleviates symptoms. The entire society is sick; hence only "societal" treatment can cure social problems.

The personal approach to the causation and treatment of social problems has been proposed primarily by psychologists and in its extreme form has been proposed by only a relatively small number of psychoanalysts. Oversimplified, their assumption is that all behavior is the result of individual psychic drives, and that since all behavior arises from within the psyche, the individual psyche itself must be treated if successful change is to occur. Society is seen as a passive phenomenon, made up of congeries of autonomous individuals who are not basically influenced by it. Groups and environment are considered important, but they are viewed as being essentially the products of individuals. With these causal assumptions, treatment of social problems obviously must begin with the individual. For example, if each individual drug addict could be cured by treatment, presently there would be no more addicts and no social problem. This approach is more difficult to accept for such problems as the malfunctioning of the school system, the dependency of the aged, or slum clearance. Karen Horney in Selection 80 shows that cultural elements definitely have a bearing on type and seriousness of neurosis.

---

[7] Lawrence K. Frank, "Society as the Patient," *American Journal of Sociology*, 42 (1936-1937), 335-344, as abridged and adapted in Raab and Selznick, pp. 566-568.
* Note that Frank proposed this theory in the midst of the Great Depression, a period which undoubtedly influenced the theory itself as well as its relatively wide and immediate acclaim.

The "middle range" approach, named after Robert K. Merton's "theories of the middle range," suggests that causal and treatment factors are most manageably conceived in a range somewhere between the extremes of societal and personal. Causal factors of major social phenomena are multiple in origin and action; truly monistic causes of social problems do not exist. For example, some, but not all, crime is the result of *anomie,* of psychogenic factors, of differential association, of differential response and neutralization, of self-concept and differential identification, of criminal subcultures, of failure of the family to perform its functions successfully, or of failures in social control. Each of these factors, in combination with any or all of the other factors, may be found to be the major cause of *some* crime. Successful treatment of any one of these factors will reduce crime, but only treatment of each and every one—and even of other factors—could be expected to eliminate crime as a social problem. A special "group pressure" approach to this problem is described in Selection 78 on the Provo experiment in the rehabilitation of delinquents.

Once reasonable agreement is reached as to the major causal factors involved in a social problem, serious hurdles to the elimination of the problem still exist. A decision must be made—and dispute is common—as to whether action will be an all-out curative attempt or will consist primarily of amelioration. For example, with regard to the problem of caring for children of divorced parents, the *ameliorative* approach would be to use child guidance experts to recommend to the court the best possible placement of the children; the *curative* approach would be to prevent the husband-wife estrangement that caused the divorce. Or, with regard to the problem of delinquent gangs, the ameliorative approach would be to send group workers to the gangs to decrease their fighting, crime, and predatory actions; the curative approach would be to remove those factors that cause the adolescents to feel strong needs for the delinquent gang. It can be said that cure is better than palliation, but on the other hand, cure may involve knowledge, power, skill, insight, popular financial support, or legal machinery not now available. Amelioration may be the only present possibility. In any event, society usually must use both measures, emphasizing the ameliorative until the curative has been perfected.

A second typical issue in the treatment of social problems is coercion versus persuasion. Coercion is usually the first thought, but coercion typically involves the law, and even if the proper laws exist, the cost of full enforcement may seem excessive or the infringement on personal freedom may be too great. Also, we lack sufficient knowledge of some problems to treat them by coercion; war is a good illustration. The denial of the franchise to Southern Negroes is an example in the field of racial relations where the existence of a law did not secure the end desired by the law, because influential people on the scene desired the opposite. The combined might of our armed forces could force immediate desegregation of every school in the South, but the social costs of this coercion would be greater than we are willing to pay in order to achieve the end. Therefore, persuasive approaches are used; they are nonviolent, less open to opposition and resistance, cheaper in certain costs, and at times successful. They are also slower, less sure, and less predictable. For most problems, a mixture of coercive and persuasive methods used simultaneously may be considerably better than the use of either method alone.

A great diversity of opinion is to be found concerning most social problems. One reason for this diversity is ignorance—ignorance both of the problem and its etiology and of the effectiveness and availability of various solutions. To complicate this ignorance, on some social problems large quantities of purposive misinformation and propaganda have been disseminated by *vested interests*, who have a preferred position in the status quo and wish to maintain it. Add to these factors the differences in personal experiences, personality, and individual outlook, then a lack of full agreement concerning a given problem appears a normal and expected, but by no means hopeless, condition.

Sociologists are not the only ones who study social problems, and they are no more concerned about or affected by these problems than any other citizens, except as specialized knowledge may lead to specialized concern. In studying and reporting on social problems, sociologists have an advantage chiefly if not solely in their dedication to an unbiased, scientific, empirical point of view and presentation.

So broad is the field of social problems that Part IX with its three sections on social disorganization, personality deviations, and minorities cannot hope to do more than present a sample. The section on social disorganization, for example, includes one selection on delinquency, one on rehabilitation, and one on a combination of delinquency and crime. Yet any university may offer separate undergraduate courses in delinquency, in criminology, and in penology (the study of the treatment of criminals), plus at least one graduate course in each of these areas. Thus the purpose here is solely to give the student a foretaste and a sample.   *J. H. B.*

Selection 77
_____

Research in Delinquent Subcultures

Albert K. Cohen and James F. Short, Jr.

The Introduction to Part IX dealt with the broad theory of social problems; the following article is specifically concerned with the causes of delinquency. It presents both sides of the theory that much delinquency can be explained by the gradual socialization of certain working-class boys into the delinquent *subculture* that exists in the locality in which they grow up.

All normal persons become acculturated through the process of socialization, but in any society there are more culture traits than any one person utilizes. Nearly everyone learns most aspects of the *mass culture* (a term used to mean a sort of lowest common denominator of the culture shared by most normal people). Beyond this "mass" level there are *specialties* and *subcultures*. "Specialty" cultural items may be comparatively few in number and may relate only to one aspect of behavior, such as one's occupation; a subculture, however, includes a range of cultural elements sufficiently broad to constitute a whole characteristic way of life. These concepts may be thought of as on a continuum, with the dividing line between them arbitrary. A few older sociologists disapprove of the concept of subculture, but most sociologists and anthropologists make considerable use of it. Whether or not Cohen and Short stretch the concept somewhat to accommodate all of their types of delinquent subcultures is not a serious problem, since the aim of the authors is to understand delinquency, not contribute to concepts or theories relating to subcultures. In any event, the essence of the theory they present is that boys (or girls) who are "successfully" exposed to any delinquent subsociety come to take over its attitudes, values, and behavior patterns and become subject to its controls and may in turn exert an influence on it.

The authors describe (1) the parent male subculture which is most common and is "non-utilitarian, malicious, negativistic, versatile, and characterized by short-run hedonism and group autonomy"; (2) the conflict-oriented subculture, whose most prominent host is the fighting gang; (3) the drug addict subculture; (4) the semiprofessional theft subculture, of which theft for gain rather than for "kicks" is the most prominent characteristic; and (5) the middle-class delinquent subculture, which differs from but is functionally equivalent to the parent delinquency subculture. A little is reported about female delinquent subcultures, primarily oriented around sex and often closely related to various male subcultures. Unfortunately, nothing is said about the *pachuco* delinquent subsociety, which reaches from Los Angeles to San Antonio and is made up almost entirely of Spanish-speaking youth. It hosts one of the best examples of delinquent subcultures available, possessing as it does patterns of behavior, special values, almost a whole language of special words, emphasis on self-tattooing (especially the *pachuco cross*), a set of values reminiscent in part of the *machismo* of Mexico, and feelings both of unity and of separateness from other groups.

Sizable numbers of the American population think of delinquents as being genetically deficient or psychologically ill or as persons with full control over their behavior and attitudes who are "just plain mean." Cohen and Short refute this common misconception by eloquently pointing out the essentially social nature of the great majority of delinquent and criminal acts.

This paper is a backward look upon the book *Delinquent Boys: The Culture of the Gang*[1] and a look ahead to the kinds of theoretical and research work which it is hoped and anticipated will soon make this book obsolete.

Without trying to summarize the argument of this book, let us indicate what it tried to do. It proceeded from the premise that much delinquency—probably the vast bulk of it—represents participation in a delinquent subculture. Much of the sociological literature on juvenile delinquency has been concerned with demonstrating that this is so, and with formulating the processes whereby this subculture is taken over by the individual. *Delinquent Boys* posed the problem: Why is the delinquent subculture there in the boys' milieu to be taken over? More specifically, why is there a subculture with this specific content, and distributed in this particular way within the social system? Secondly, it set forth a general theory of subcultures, on the methodological premise that the explanation of any phenomenon consists of a demonstration that it conforms to a general theory applicable to all phenomena of the same class. Thirdly, it formulated an explanation of the delinquent subculture. In brief, it explained the delinquent subculture as a system of beliefs and values generated in a process of communicative interaction among children similarly circumstanced

by virtue of their positions in the social structure, and as constituting a solution to problems of adjustment to which the established culture provided no satisfactory solutions. These problems are largely problems of status and self-respect arising among working-class children as a result of socially structured inability to meet the standards of the established culture; the delinquent subculture, with its characteristics of non-utilitarianism, malice, and negativism, provides an alternative status system and justifies, for those who participate in it, hostility and aggression against the sources of their status frustration.

The nature of the theoretical issues raised by this book will be clearer if we pause to consider a thoughtful critique by Gresham Sykes and David Matza. These authors dispute the proposition, central to the argument of *Delinquent Boys*, that delinquency is based on a set of norms antithetical to those of the dominant culture and, indeed, deriving their content by a process of hostile and negativistic reaction against the dominant culture. They offer, in turn, what they describe as "a possible alternative or modified explanation for a large portion of juvenile delinquency." They

From *The Journal of Social Issues*, Vol. 14 (1958), 20-37.
[1] Albert K. Cohen, *Delinquent Boys: The Culture of the Gang* (Glencoe, Ill.: The Free Press, 1955).

present impressive evidence that the delinquent is by no means immune or indifferent to the expectations of respectable society, that he has internalized the respectable value system, and that in many ways he appears to recognize its moral validity. They go on to say that "the theoretical viewpoint that sees juvenile delinquency as a form of behavior based on the values and norms of a deviant sub-culture in precisely the same way as law-abiding behavior is based on the values and norms of the larger society is open to serious doubt. Instead, the juvenile delinquent would appear to be at least partially committed to the dominant social order in that he frequently exhibits guilt or shame when he violates its proscriptions. . . ." They then proceed to argue that much delinquency is based on a set of justifications for deviance that are seen as valid by the delinquent but not by the legal system or society at large; that is, on a set of techniques for neutralizing the internal and external demands for conformity, deriving from values whose legitimacy is at least on some level recognized. These techniques of neutralization are then set forth in considerable and convincing detail.

With all of this we have no quarrel. The analysis of the techniques of neutralization, in fact, we would regard as an important elaboration of the argument of *Delinquent Boys*. It is not clear, however, that this analysis provides an *alternative* explanation of delinquent behavior. The notion that the delinquent boy has internalized the respectable value system, is therefore profoundly ambivalent about his own delinquent behavior, and must contend continuously with the claims of the respectable value system is one of the central propositions of *Delinquent Boys*. Although *Delinquent Boys* does not mention the techniques of neutralization enumerated by Sykes and Matza (and the failure to do so constitutes a significant omission), it strongly emphasizes the part played by the mechanism of reaction-formation, one of the most elementary techniques of neutralization. Reaction-formation is stressed because it is not only a way of coming to terms with one's delinquent impulses; it helps to account for the nature of the delinquent behavior itself. To quote *Delinquent Boys*: ". . . we would expect the delinquent boy who, after all, has been socialized in a society dominated by middle-class morality and who can never quite escape the blandishments of middle-class society, to seek to maintain his safeguards against seduction. Reaction-formation, in his case, should take the form of an 'irrational,' 'malicious,' 'unaccountable' hostility to the enemy within the gates as well as without: the norms of respectable middle-class

society." As a final commentary on the paper by Sykes and Matza, we would add this: The formation of a subculture is itself probably the most universal and powerful of techniques of neutralization, for nothing is so effective in allaying doubts and providing moral reassurance against a gnawing superego as the repeated, emphatic, and articulate support and approval of other persons.

Wilensky and Lebeaux are concerned with other limitations of *Delinquent Boys*. The most obvious of these limitations is the fact that there is not *one* delinquent subculture but a *variety* of delinquent subcultures. This is suggested in the book but not developed there. Although there does not as yet exist a real comparative sociology of juvenile delinquency, evidence from other countries suggests that some of the features of delinquent behavior which in this country are so pervasive that we have come to take them for granted as inherent in the very idea of delinquency may be absent elsewhere. It is probable that delinquent subcultures have distinct emphases in different societies and that these can be related to differences in the respective social systems of which they are the products. Comparative research in the sociology of delinquent subcultures is to be most strongly encouraged, for it is bound to highlight aspects of delinquent behavior in the American scene which we are prone to overlook, and to make them the object of theoretical concern. Furthermore, the comparative study of delinquency in different national settings will undoubtedly focus attention on hitherto neglected aspects of the relationship of delinquency to the overall structure of society and may clarify some of the present confusion regarding *individual* and *socially structured* motivations for delinquency. These questions tend to become clouded by a sort of "cultural blindness" when we restrict our observations to our own society. . . .

In the following discussion, we present a list of the principal varieties of delinquent subcultures which can be tentatively differentiated at the present time, some descriptive notes, etiological speculations, and some problems for theory and research suggested by this discussion. . . .

DELINQUENT SUBCULTURES: MALE

The parent male subculture

This is what the book, *Delinquent Boys*, calls "the" delinquent subculture. It has been described as non-utilitarian, malicious, negativistic, versatile, and characterized by short-run hedonism and group autonomy. We refer to it as the parent subculture because it is probably the most common variety in this country—indeed, it might be called the "garden variety" of delinquent subculture—and because the characteristics listed above seem to constitute a common core shared by other important variants. However, in addition, these variants possess distinctive attributes or emphases which are not fully accounted for by the argument of *Delinquent Boys*. We believe the parent subculture is a working-class subculture. This position, however, is open to question and we shall consider the matter further in our discussion of the middle-class subculture.

The conflict-oriented subculture

This is the subculture most prominent in the news today and is probably regarded by many laymen as the typical form which delinquency takes. In its highly developed forms it has the following characteristics. It is a culture of large gangs, whose membership numbers ordinarily in the scores and may run into the hundreds; in this respect contrasting to the parent subculture, whose members consist of small gangs or cliques. These gangs have a relatively elaborate organization, including such differentiated roles as president, vice-president, war-chief, and armorer. The gang may be subdivided into sub-gangs on an age or territorial basis and may have alliances with other gangs. These gangs have names, a strong sense of corporate identity, a public personality or "rep" in the gang world. The gang is identified with a territory or "turf" which it tries to defend or to extend. The status of the gang is largely determined by its toughness, that is, its readiness to engage in physical conflict with other gangs and its prowess in intergang "rumbles." Although fighting occupies but a small portion of the gang's time, "heart" or courage in fighting is the most highly prized virtue and the most important determinant of the position of gang members within the gang as well as that of the gang among other gangs. Fighting within the gang is regulated by a code of fairness; gang members, however, are relatively unconstrained by any concepts of chivalry or fairness in warfare with other gangs. To demonstrate "heart" it is not necessary to give the other fellow a decent chance or to show forbearance toward an outnumbered or defeated enemy. There is evident ambivalence about fighting; it is not a simple outpouring of accumulated aggression. Members are afraid of rumbles, and are frequently relieved when police intervention prevents a scheduled rumble, but the ethic of the gang requires the suppression of squeamishness, an outward demeanor of toughness, and a readiness to defend turf and rep with

violence and even brutality. In their other activities, these gangs exhibit the general characteristics of the delinquent subculture. Drinking, sex, gambling, stealing, and vandalism are prominent. Such gangs include a wide age range. They are concentrated in sections of the city that are highly mobile, working-class, impoverished, and characterized by a wide variety of indices of disorganization.

This is the full-blown conflict gang. Although large conflict gangs may be found in many cities, it is doubtful that the degree of organization, including the officers and functionaries, found in the New York gangs is to be found elsewhere. Probably more common than the type of gang described here is a form intermediate between the conflict gang and the parent subculture: a loosely organized and amorphous coalition of cliques with only a vague sense of corporate identity, coalescing sporadically and frequently for displays of open violence. But the reality of gangs in New York and in other cities, similar to those we have described, cannot be doubted.

The drug addict subculture

What we know of this subculture is derived primarily from two large-scale research projects conducted in New York and Chicago respectively. Although these studies do not agree in all respects, especially with reference to etiological questions, it is clear that the subculture which centers around the use of narcotic drugs provides a markedly distinct way of life. Both studies are agreed that drug addiction and criminality go hand-in-hand, that addiction arises in communities where delinquency is already endemic, that most juvenile addicts—although not all—were delinquent prior to their addiction. They are agreed that the addict eschews the more violent forms of delinquency—rape, assault, gang warfare, "general hell-raising"—and prefers income-producing forms of delinquency, which are essential to the support of a drug habit in a society in which drugs are obtainable only in an illegal market and at great cost. The addict subculture, therefore, in contrast to the parent and the conflict gang cultures, has a marked utilitarian quality, but this utilitarianism is in support of and a precondition of the addict way of life.

The kinship of the addict and other delinquent subcultures is brought out in the finding of the New York study that addicts are usually members of organized gangs and share the general philosophy of those gangs. After the onset of addiction, however, their participation in the more violent and disorderly activities of the gangs is reduced and they tend to cluster in cliques on the periphery of the gangs. There is little moral disapproval of drug use on the part of gang members, but it is usually discouraged and the status of the addict within the larger gang is lowered on the practical grounds that addiction lowers the value of the addict to the group. The reports of the Chicago investigators, however, suggest that they were studying a more "mature" addict subculture, one that is not peripheral to more "conventional" subcultures and in a merely tolerated status, but one that has achieved a higher degree of autonomy, with a loose and informal but independent organization, enjoying a relatively high status in the communities within which it flourishes. The Chicago addict, as described, is not a hanger-on of a conflict gang but moves proudly in the world of the "cats." The characteristics of the cat culture are suggested in the reports of the New York study, but are elaborately and richly described in the Chicago reports. Central to the cat culture is the "kick," defined by Finestone as "any act tabooed by 'squares' that heightens and intensifies the present moment of experience and differentiates it as much as possible from the humdrum routine of daily life," and the "hustle," defined as "any non-violent means of making some bread (money) which does not require work." Heroin is "the greatest kick of them all"; pimping, conning, pickpocketing, and such are approved and respectable hustles. Both the kick and the hustle, notes Finestone, are in direct antithesis to the central values of the dominant culture. The cat cultivates an image of himself as "cool," self-possessed, assured, and quietly competent, places great value upon the esthetic amenities of clothes and music, and possesses a discriminating and critical taste.

Both studies locate the addict subculture in those areas of the city which are most deprived, of the lowest socio-economic status, most lacking in effective adult controls—characterized by extensive family disorganization, high mobility, and recently arrived populations. Addiction characteristically occurs after the age of sixteen and is most heavily concentrated among the most-discriminated-against minority groups, especially Negroes.

Semi-professional theft

The word "professional" is not intended to connote the "professional thief" of Sutherland's description. The latter represents the elite of the criminal underworld, skilled, sophisticated, non-violent, specialized. It is intended to suggest, rather, a stage in a life history which has been described by Sutherland and Cressey as proceed-

ing "from trivial to serious, from occasional to frequent, from sport to business, and from crimes committed by isolated individuals or by very loosely organized groups to crime committed by rather tightly organized groups." This sequence appears to characterize especially "persons who in young adult life become robbers and burglars." The earlier stage of this sequence describes what we have called the parent subculture. Most participants in this subculture appear to drop out or to taper off after the age of sixteen or seventeen. A minority, however, begin to differentiate themselves from their fellows, at about this age, and to move in the direction of more utilitarian, systematic, and pecuniary crime—what we are calling "semi-professional theft."

Systematic research on this pattern, as a differentiated variant or offspring of the parent subculture, is scanty. . . . Preliminary analysis strongly suggests that the following characteristics, all presumptive evidence of a strong utilitarian emphasis, tend to go together with the later stages of a long history of frequent stealing which began at an early age:

a. the use of strong-arm methods (robbery) of obtaining money.
b. the *sale* of stolen articles, *versus* using for oneself, giving or throwing away, or returning stolen articles.
c. stating, as a reason for continued stealing, "want things" or "need money" *versus* stealing for excitement, because others do it, because they like to, or for spite.

In the areas studied, this semi-professional stealing appears to be more of a differentiation of emphasis within a more diversified climate of delinquency than an autonomous subculture independently organized. Boys who show the characteristics listed above commonly participate in non-utilitarian delinquency as well; *e.g.,* giving or throwing away stolen articles or indicating that they steal for excitement, because they like to, or for spite. Furthermore, they belong to gangs the majority of whose members may engage in predominantly non-utilitarian delinquency. It seems probable, although it has not been demonstrated, that the semi-professional thieves constitute cliques within the larger gangs and that they are differentiated from other delinquents in the same gangs with respect to other characteristics than patterns of stealing alone. We would surmise that, to the degree to which stealing becomes rational, systematic, deliberate, planned, and pursued as a primary source of income, it becomes incompatible with anarchic, impulsive, mischievous, and malicious characteristics of non-utilitarian delinquent subcultures and that its practitioners tend to segregate themselves into more professionally oriented and "serious-minded" groups. This, however, is speculation and is a subject for further research.

The middle-class delinquent subculture

Thus far we have distinguished subcultures primarily on empirical grounds; that is, investigators have observed the differences we have described. Middle-class delinquency commonly takes a subcultural form as well, but there is as yet no firm basis in research for ascribing to it a different content from that of the parent male subculture. We distinguish it rather on theoretical grounds; since none of the problems of adjustment to which the working-class subcultures seem to constitute plausible and intelligible responses appear to be linked with sufficient frequency to middle-class status, we assume that middle-class subcultures arise in response to problems of adjustment which are characteristic products of middle-class socialization and middle-class life situations. The notion that different patterns of behavior may be "functionally equivalent" solutions to the same or similar problems is familiar. We are suggesting that the same or similar patterns of behavior may be "functionally versatile" solutions to different problems of adjustment. However, we are persuaded that further research will reveal subtle but important differences between working-class and middle-class patterns of delinquency. It seems probable that the qualities of malice, bellicosity, and violence will be underplayed in the middle-class subcultures and that these subcultures will emphasize more the deliberate courting of danger (suggested by the epithet "chicken") and a sophisticated, irresponsible, "playboy" approach to activities symbolic, in our culture, of adult roles and centering largely around sex, liquor, and automobiles.

DETERMINANTS OF THE MALE SUBCULTURES

A fully satisfactory theory of delinquent subcultures must specify the different problems of adjustment to which each of these subcultures is a response, and the ways in which the social structure generates these problems of adjustment and determines the forms which the solutions take.

Definitive theory can grow only out of research specifically concerned with differences among these subcultures. Such research is in its infancy. For example, it is not possible to determine from the published literature what are the characteristics of the cities in which the conflict gang appears and of those in which it does not; the specific characteristics which differentiate urban areas in which delinquency assumes this form and those in which it does not; or the specific characteristics of the children who become involved in this sort of delinquency and of those who do not. There is a literature, most of it growing out of the work of the New York City Youth Board, which is valuable and suggestive. Little of this literature, however, employs a systematic comparative perspective designed to throw light on the *differential* characteristics of this subculture and its social setting. With respect to the conditions which favor the emergence of a semi-professional subculture, the literature is practically silent. On the matter of middle-class delinquency, there is an enormous emotional to-do and vocal alarm, but little more. There is a great need of case studies of middle-class delinquent groups, including detailed descriptions of the specific quality of their delinquencies and the behavioral context and community settings of these delinquencies. It is interesting that some of our most adequate and illuminating research concerns the drug addict subculture, which is numerically perhaps the least significant delinquent subculture and is restricted to a few sections of our larger cities, although where it appears it is a grave social problem and is most ominous for the young people who are caught up in it.

To us, the subculture of the conflict gang is the most baffling. Several years ago Solomon Kobrin suggested, on the basis of his intimate knowledge of delinquency in Chicago, the differential characteristics of areas in which delinquency assumes the semi-professional form, and of those in which it assumes a violent, "hoodlum," conflict form. These differences he described as differences in the degree of integration between the conventional and criminal value systems. In areas in which adults are engaged in consistently profitable and highly organized illegal enterprises and also participate in such conventional institutions as churches, fraternal and mutual benefit societies, and political parties, criminal adult role models have an interest in helping to contain excesses of violence and destructiveness; in these areas youngsters may perceive delinquency as a means to the acquisition of skills which are useful to the achievement of conventional values and which may, as a matter of fact, lead to a career in the rackets, and to prestige in the community. Here delinquency tends to assume a relatively orderly, systematic, rational form. We suspect that this type of area is relatively rare and that the pattern of semi-professional theft is correspondingly rare, as compared with the occurrence of the parent and hoodlum-type patterns. In a contrasting type of area adults may violate the law, but this violation is not systematic and organized, and the criminal and conventional value systems do not mesh through the participation of criminals in the conventional institutions. "As a consequence, the delinquency in areas of this type tends to be unrestrained by controls originating *at any point* in the adult social structure." Delinquency takes on a wild, untrammeled, violent character. "Here groups of delinquents may be seen as excluded, isolated conflict groups dedicated to an unending battle against all forms of restraint."

This is the kind of provocative formulation of which we stand much in need. However, Kobrin's formulations have not, to our knowledge, led to research to test their validity. Furthermore, although this formulation specifies the kind of breakdown of controls under which a conflict subculture can flourish, it does not account for the positive motivation to large-scale organized gangs, the warlike relationships between gangs, and the idealization of toughness, relatively unregulated by an intergang code of chivalry and fairness. It is a defect of many of our theories of delinquency that they try to account for delinquency by demonstrating the absence of effective restraints. Delinquency, however, and certainly this particular form of delinquency, cannot be assumed to be a potentiality of human nature which automatically erupts when the lid is off. Nor do we believe that the emphasis on conflict can be explained as a way of expressing and channelizing aggression accumulated through a variety of frustrations. We do not deny either the frustrations or the aggression of many of the youngsters in this subculture. But it is apparent from the reports of workers that the violence we see is as much a matter of conformity, sometimes in the face of great fear and reluctance, to a highly compulsive group-enforced ideal of toughness as it is a simple outburst of pent-up hostility. We will not at this point add our own speculations to those of others. It is our purpose here merely to indicate the nature of the problem.

It is a matter for further research to determine the extent to which the patterns we have described, and other patterns, are *variants* of a common subculture or subcultures, with qualitatively distinct etiologies, or *quantitative extremes* of the common subculture with the same variables accounting for their existence and their extremity. In this paper we have chosen to describe these patterns as variants. The description of these variants, and their accounting, in etiological research and theory, is the major task of the larger project of which this paper is a partial report.

With respect to the drug addict subculture, the New York and Chicago investigators present different interpretations, and it is an interesting challenge to theory to account for these differences or to reconcile them. The New York investigators state unequivocally that "All juvenile drug addicts are severely disturbed individuals," and that "adolescents who become addicts have deep-rooted, major personality disorders." Specifically, they suffer from a weak ego, an inadequately functioning superego, and inadequate masculine identification. These defects, in turn, can be traced to family experiences. Up to the age of sixteen or so these boys do not behave very differently from the ordinary gang delinquent. At about this age the emotionally healthy youngsters develop a new conception of themselves consistent with age-graded role definitions and expectations in our culture. The gang activities become kid stuff, the gang begins to break up, the boy begins to organize his life around a job, his girl, his future. "It is at this stage that those members or hangers-on who are too disturbed emotionally to face the future as adults find themselves seemingly abandoned by their old cronies and begin to feel increasingly anxious." They take to the use of drugs because drugs help to reduce anxieties resulting from personal incapacity and because they make it easy to deny and to avoid facing deep-seated personal problems.

The Chicago investigators, on the contrary, question the concept of the addict as a "sick person," whose addiction is a symptom of personality defects. They emphasize, on the one hand, the breakdown of controls which occurs in areas which "are characterized by a high density of a recently arrived and largely unsettled population," and whose residents cannot mobilize effectively to secure law enforcement against even that behavior which offends their own standards. They emphasize, on the other hand, the problems of adjustment which are a function of the social position of the populations within those areas, the problems, that is, of the most depressed sectors of the most disadvantaged minority groups, who are increasingly sensitized to the value, goals, and conceptions of success of the dominant social order but who are categorically excluded from the opportunity for legitimately achieving them. Since they are denied participation, except in a servile and unrewarding capacity, in those activities which are defined by the dominant institutional order as the legitimate, "serious," and really important activities, these groups turn their back on this order and the sober virtues which it enjoins, and make a virtue and an ideal of "play," of irresponsible, autonomous, hedonically oriented activity which seeks its consummation and reward in the extraction of the maximum "kick" from the present moment. The problems of adjustment to which the cat culture is a response are not a function of a pathological character structure; they are socially structured strains endemic in the lower-class urban Negro and other minority group populations.

How are we to account for the contrast between the two interpretations? It is possible that one or the other represents faulty speculation which is not in keeping with the data and which is a product of a sociologistic or psychologistic bias. However, both grow out of responsible, systematic research and neither can be lightly dismissed as an autistic distortion of the plain facts. It is possible that the two populations studied cannot be equated, that we are dealing with two different addict subcultures. It is possible, also, that the cat culture described by the Chicago researchers is a logical extreme of the gradual isolation from the more conventional gangs which is documented by the New York studies. This still does not explain the differences noted in the two studies, however. It is further possible that the two sets of conclusions are not mutually exclusive. With respect to the Chicago study we may make two observations: (1) it is always a minority of young people in any given area who become addicts, and therefore there must be selective processes at work in addition to those stressed by the Chicago investigators; (2) the methods of the Chicago study were not designed to reveal the kinds of data concerning personality structure to which the New York investigators attach such importance. It may well be that, without regard to individual peculiarities and abnormalities, the social setting described in the Chicago reports is one in which the addict subculture is attractive and possible, but that, within this general setting, the attractiveness of this response is further enhanced for those with the character structure described in the New York reports. Furthermore, it is possible that this kind of character structure occurs with exceptionally high frequency in lower-class Negro areas. A family constellation of floating, irresponsible males centering around a hardworking, overburdened mother is common in this segment of the Negro population, and it is the sort of constellation that might be expected to produce the weak ego, inadequately functioning superego, and inadequate masculine identification that are ascribed to the addict's personality. In short, it is possible, although it is still speculative,

that the methods of the two studies illuminate different aspects of the same reality.

In *Delinquent Boys*, it was suggested that the middle-class delinquent subculture is a response to ambivalence and anxiety in the area of sex-role identification, aggravated by the prolonged dependence of the boy upon his family, and the indefinite postponement of adult self-sufficiency and self-determination. This interpretation has been questioned by Wilensky and Lebeaux who argue that anxiety about male identity is greater in the *lower class*. The working-class delinquent subculture, therefore, is determined by both status anxiety and sex-role anxiety; the middle-class subculture is determined by anxiety about becoming a man, an adult. Wilensky and Lebeaux conclude that this theory would predict even sharper contrasts between working-class and middle-class delinquency than the official statistics would show.

A recent study based on self-reported behavior of western and mid-western high school students does not support this prediction or suggest that there is any significant difference in middle-class and working-class delinquency rates in the several communities studied. The same findings might not obtain in large urban areas or non-caucasian populations, which were not studied, but at least in this one respect the findings are not consistent with inference from the Wilensky and Lebeaux hypothesis. This argument does not lack plausibility, however, and research is obviously necessary to decide between what are, at this point, rival speculations.

In an effort to account for the apparent increase in middle-class delinquency, Cohen suggested that, as a result of changes in the structure of our economy, labor market, and school system, the traditional deferred gratification pattern of the middle-class boy is breaking down. In an economy of scarcity this pattern of deferred gratification did, as a matter of fact, "pay off." It was a prerequisite to movement through the schools and to the economic opportunities to which the schools were an avenue. Furthermore, middle-class parents could point to the obviously greater economic affluence of themselves in contrast to the unskilled and generally unprotected mass of working class people. Thus, with support from parents, the economy, and the school, the "college boy" way of life, to use Whyte's felicitous phrase, was inculcated in middle-class children and in working-class children who aspired to "better themselves." This pattern was incompatible with commitment to a delinquent way of life. . . .

Sociologists have pointed out that our society provides no well-defined role for adolescence, a period in the child's life when the problem of establishing his personal identity becomes especially crucial. With the weakening of the deferred gratification pattern, the choice among alternatives as the boy seeks to fill this status void is more likely to become a delinquent choice. When he tries to establish his identity as an adult, or as a man, he finds the "conventional," the "respectable," the "responsible" criteria of adult status denied him. Hence, he tends to symbolize his adulthood by irresponsible, hedonically oriented behavior involving the courting of danger, liquor, sex, cars, etc.

Still other changes in society and in child rearing patterns, especially among middle class parents, may have contributed to an increase in delinquency in this class of youngsters. These changes have to do with the relatively greater independence from each other of family members as a result of the economic changes we have talked about, the democratization of family relations, vacillation in child rearing philosophy as a result of increasing concern with what the "experts" in the field have to say (together with vacillation on the part of the latter), and the "cult of youth" which holds that all pain, especially psychic pain, is injurious to children and that it is the responsibility of parents to minimize pain and frustration for their children. All of these things require documentation in the form of carefully conducted research. All, however, appear to weaken the deferred gratification pattern of socialization and the authority of parental figures, to retard the internalization of authority, to reduce the ability to tolerate frustration, and to contribute to an increase in delinquency among middle-class children.

This is, perhaps, more than enough speculation on the conditions which might facilitate the formation of middle-class delinquent subcultures. The saddest commentary, however, is that we are faced with a poverty of speculation, without which there can be no meaningful research, without which, in turn, there can be no conclusions that are more than speculation.

DELINQUENT SUBCULTURES: FEMALE

With a very few exceptions, the professional literature on female delinquency is of little help in determining how, in what ways, and to what extent that delinquency is subculturally patterned. There is little on what this delinquency actually consists of, other than that it usually involves sexual misconduct of some kind; or on the relationships of the girls to the boys and men with whom they are involved, and how these relationships, as well as the girls' relationships to other peers of both sexes, are affected by their sexual behavior; or on the contexts of other activities; or on other characteristics of the social settings within which sexual episodes occur. It is our position that the meaning and function, for the persons concerned, of any form of delinquent behavior can only be inferred from rich and detailed descriptive data about the behavior itself, about its position in a larger context of interaction, and about how it is perceived and reacted to by the actor himself and by other participants in that interactive context. These data are largely lacking for female delinquency.

In *Delinquent Boys* Cohen suggested the socially structured motivations to participation in what might be called a female parent delinquent subculture. He argues that a girl's status depends largely upon the status of the males with whom she is identified; that, in order to achieve respectability, a girl must be able to attract the "honorable" attentions of respectable and responsible males; that many girls, especially of lower socioeconomic status, have not been trained in the arts and graces and lack the material means necessary for competing successfully for such attentions; that such girls, despairing of respectable marriage and social mobility, are inclined to seek reassurance of their sense of adequacy *as girls* by abandoning their reputation for chastity, which has proven, for them, an unrewarding virtue, and by making themselves sexually available; that they gain, thereby, the assurance of male attention and male favors, albeit within transitory and unstable relationships which further lower their value on the marriage market. Like its male counterpart, this pattern represents the rejection of conventional and respectable but unattainable status goals and the disciplines which lead to them, and the substitution therefor of the satisfactions to be obtained in the immediate present with the resources presently available. The complete mechanism whereby the social structure generates this subculture is surely much more complex than this, but the argument is intended only to suggest a common core of motivation which goes far to explain the characteristic sexual content of this subculture and, indeed, of female delinquency in general.

Not only is little known about this parent subculture. With perhaps one exception, still less is known about the numerous varieties of female delinquent subcultures, except that they exist. There are gangs of girls organized for and around sexual activities; there are mixed groups of middle- and upper-middle-class boys and girls organized as sex gangs, with an emphasis on refinement, gentility, and sophistication; and there are gangs of girls strongly resembling the male hoodlum gang. At the present time little can be said, even in a descriptive way, about any of these.

It is possible to say a little more about the female drug addict subculture, on the basis of our analysis of interview material gathered in the course of the Chicago drug use study, and of material in preparation for a Master's degree thesis at the University of Chicago. The observations to be set forth here are tentative and will be more fully elaborated in a later publication.

The girls whose interviews we have read are predominantly Negro, of low social status, and located in the same type of area as that from which the male addicts characteristically come. However, some of them come from relatively respectable and well-off Negro families and there are no strikingly obvious common patterns, sequences, or problems of adjustment exhibited by all the cases. However, certain features recur with impressive frequency. Almost all of these girls have had difficulty in establishing satisfactory relationships with the other sex, although for divers reasons. A theme which runs through history after history is isolation from the main stream of normal, relaxed, boy-girl relationships, loneliness, depression, and a pathetic yearning for marriage to a stable, responsible, respectable man. These girls appear to fall prey easily to exploitative and irresponsible men, who exercise extraordinary power over them apparently because of the girls' need for male companionship and love, or a simulacrum thereof. Pregnancy, desertion, and "hustling" occur with monotonous regularity. The girl may be introduced to opiate drugs by other girls, by male companions, or in mixed groups of "fast" company. The nature of these circumstances is such that the girls often find themselves isolated, depressed, and threatened. These conditions heighten their dependence on the drug and upon social contacts which assure the completion of the cycle.

After addiction, hustling on a full time basis in order to support her habit and sometimes her lover's habit is almost invariable. During the period of addiction her range of associates is almost entirely narrowed to other addicts and prostitutes, but her relationships with even these people are likely to be tangential and incidental to the procurement of the drug, and to her profession. A vicious cycle is characteristic of all the histories we have read: addiction and prostitution lead to a further isolation from respectable society and a lowering of status; these, in turn, increase loneliness and depression and the girl's vulnerability to exploitation by men; and these, in turn, encourage continuation in or relapse into the use of drugs.

Although these girls move on the fringes of the cat culture, they do not, we think, participate fully in it. They are not "fast, noisy, aggressive cats," seeking status among other cats through their kicks and their hustle. They are not proud of their habit and their hustle is strictly business, frequently a distasteful one. Without exception, these girls express a desire for respectability, but they find it difficult to escape from the vicious circle in which they have become entrapped.

SUMMARY

It is apparent that we have barely stepped over the threshold of the study of delinquent subcultures. The purpose of this paper has been to enumerate some of the principal varieties of these subcultures, to describe or to suggest some of their important features, to speculate on their origins, to indicate the types of research and theoretical work which are most needed, and to provide some suggestive hypotheses to be tested or revised by later research.

Selection 78

The Provo Experiment in Delinquency Rehabilitation

LaMar T. Empey and Jerome Rabow

It is a sad commentary on the history of criminology and penology that scholars and practitioners in these fields have not worked together as closely as they might have. The student of the etiological and causal factors of crime and delinquency has rarely attempted to project his voice into practical penal programs. Conversely, those persons planning and administering programs for criminals and delinquents all too frequently have taken into account but little of the research and theory on the causes, operation, and structure of delinquency and crime. In addition, both groups have often tacitly ignored basic social theory and, even worse, the relevant middle-range theories.

These statements are not intended as wholesale condemnations of both groups, and certainly each criticism is more applicable the farther back in time one looks. Moreover, persons espousing strictly psychological, psychoanalytic, or psychiatrically oriented causes frequently have proposed treatments that were directly related to their theories. Occasionally these programs have been placed in actual operation. Unfortunately, their success has not been such as to cause any great swing of penological theory in their direction.

Sociologists, who represent the most firmly entrenched discipline relating to criminology and penology, have over the years offered a fairly wide range of plausible and more or less verifiable theories on crime and its treatment. These theories have appeared more acceptable to practicing penologists than has psychiatric theory and treatment but have been honored far more in the breach than the observance. This division and lack of communication and acceptance has hindered the improvement of penal treatment, to the detriment of all concerned. Under present practices, the proportion of persons who receive "treatment" for crime and delinquency (excluding traffic offenses, etc.) but who "fail," only to appear again at jail, training school, reformatory, or penitentiary, varies from 40 to 80 per cent of the total, depending on the definition of failure. In short, there is great room for improvement.

The following article is especially recommended, not just because it describes a novel delinquency treatment program—and certainly not because it presents *the* solution to all our delinquency troubles—but because it demonstrates objectively that it *is* possible to persuade communities to relate theory and practice in the treatment of delinquency and that the results can be very successful.

Despite the importance of sociological contributions to the understanding of delinquent behavior, relatively few of these contributions have been systematically utilized for purposes of rehabilitation. The reason is at least partially inherent in the sociological tradition which views sociology primarily as a research discipline. As a consequence, the rehabilitation of delinquents has been left, by default, to people who have been relatively unaware of sociological theory and its implications for treatment.

This situation has produced or perpetuated problems along two dimensions. On one dimension are the problems engendered in reformatories where authorities find themselves bound, not only by the norms of their own official system, but by the inmate system as well. They are unable to work out an effective program: (1) because the goals of the two systems are incompatible; and (2) because no one knows much about the structure and function of the inmate system and how it might be dealt with for purposes of rehabilitation. Furthermore, the crux of any treatment program has ultimately to do with the decision-making process utilized by delinquents in the community, *not* in the reformatory. Yet, the decisions which lead to success in "doing time" in the reformatory are not of the same type needed for successful community adjustment. Existing conditions may actually be more effective in cementing ties to the delinquent system than in destroying them.

The second dimension of the problem has to do with the traditional emphasis upon "individualized treatment." This emphasis stems from two sources: (1) a humanistic concern for the importance of human dignity and the need for sympathetic understanding; and (2) a widespread belief that delinquency is a psychological disease and the offender a *"sick"* person. If, however, sociologists are even partially correct regarding the causes for delinquency, these two points of view overlook the possibility that most persistent

From the *American Sociological Review*, Vol. 26 (1961), 679-696. Reprinted by permission of the American Sociological Association.

delinquents do have the support of a meaningful reference group and are not, therefore, without the emotional support and normative orientation which such a group can provide. In fact, a complete dedication to an individualistic approach poses an impasse: How can an individual who acquired delinquency from a group with which he identifies strongly be treated individually without regard to the persons or norms of the system from whom he acquired it?

A successful treatment program for such a person would require techniques not normally included in the individualized approach. It should no more be expected that dedicated delinquents can be converted to conventionality by such means than that devout Pentecostals can be converted to Catholicism by the same means. Instead, different techniques are required for dealing with the normative orientation of the delinquent's system, replacing it with new values, beliefs, and rationalizations and developing means by which he can realize conventional satisfactions, especially with respect to successful employment.

This does not suggest, of course, that such traditional means as probation for dealing with the first offender or psychotherapy for dealing with the disturbed offender can be discarded. But it does suggest the need for experimental programs more consistent with sociological theory, and more consistent with the sociological premise that most *persistent* and *habitual* offenders are active members of a delinquent social system.

This paper presents the outlines of a program —the Provo Experiment in Delinquency Rehabilitation—which is derived from sociological theory and which seeks to apply sociological principles to rehabilitation. Because of its theoretical ties, the concern of the Experiment is as much with a systematic evaluation and reformulation of treatment consistent with findings as with the administration of treatment itself. For that reason, research and evaluation are an integral part of the program. Its theoretical orientation, major assumptions, treatment system, and research design are outlined below.

THEORETICAL ORIENTATION

With regards to causation, the Provo Experiment turned to a growing body of evidence which suggests two important conclusions: (1) that the greater part of delinquent behavior is not that of individuals engaging in highly secretive deviations, but is a group phenomenon—a shared deviation which is the product of differential group experience in a particular subculture, and (2) that because most delinquents tend to be concentrated in slums or to be the children of lower class parents, their lives are characterized by learning situations which limit their access to success goals.

Attention to these two conclusions does not mean that emotional problems, or "bad" homes, can be ignored. But only occasionally do these variables lead by themselves to delinquency. In most cases where older delinquents are involved other intervening variables must operate, the most important of which is the presence of a delinquent system—one which supplies status and recognition not normally obtainable elsewhere. Whether they are members of a tight knit gang or of the amorphous structure of the "parent" delinquent subculture, habitual delinquents tend to look affectively both to their peers and to the norms of their system for meaning and orientation. Thus, although a "bad" home may have been instrumental at some early phase in the genesis of a boy's delinquency, it must be recognized that it is now other delinquent boys, not his parents, who are current sources of support and identification. Any attempts to change him, therefore, would have to view him as more than an unstable isolate without a meaningful reference group. And, instead of concentrating on changing his parental relationships, they would have to recognize the intrinsic nature of his membership in the delinquent system and direct treatment to him as a part of that system.

There is another theoretical problem. An emphasis on the importance of the delinquent system raises some question regarding the extent to which delinquents are without any positive feeling for conventional standards. Vold says that one approach to explaining delinquency ". . . operates from the basic, implicit assumption that in a delinquency area, delinquency is the normal response of the normal individual—that the non-delinquent is really the 'problem case,' the nonconformist whose behavior needs to be accounted for." This is a deterministic point of view suggesting the possibility that delinquents view conventional people as "foreigners" and conventional norms and beliefs as anathema. It implies that delinquents have been socialized entirely in a criminal system and have never internalized or encountered the blandishments of conventional society.

Actually, sociological literature suggests otherwise. It emphasizes, in general, that the sub-parts of complex society are intimately tied up with the whole, and, specifically, that delinquents are very much aware of conventional standards; that they have been socialized in an environment dominated by middle-class morality; that they have internalized the American success ideal to such a degree that they turn to illegitimate means in an effort to be successful (or, failing in that, engage in malicious, or retreatist activities); that they are profoundly ambivalent about their delinquent behavior; and that in order to cope with the claims of respectable norms upon them, they maintain a whole series of intricate rationalizations by which to "neutralize" their delinquent behavior.

This suggests that delinquents are aware of conventional structure and its expectations. In many conventional settings they can, and usually do, behave conventionally. But it also suggests that, like other people, they are motivated by the normative expectations of their own subsystem. Consequently, when in the company of other delinquent boys, they may not only feel that they have to live up to minimal delinquent expectations but to appear more delinquent than they actually are, just as people in church often feel that they have to appear more holy than they actually are.

If this is the case, the problem of rehabilitation is probably not akin to converting delinquents to ways of behavior and points of view about which they are unaware and which they have never seriously considered as realistic alternatives. Instead, the feeling of ambivalence on their parts might be an element which could be used in rehabilitation.

An important sociological hypothesis based on this assumption would be that the ambivalence of most habitual delinquents is not primarily the result of personality conflicts developed in such social *microcosms* as the family but is inherent in the structure of the societal *macrocosm*. A delinquent subsystem simply represents an alternative means for acquiring, or attempting to acquire, social and economic goals idealized by the societal system which are acquired by other people through conventional means.

If this hypothesis is accurate, delinquent ambivalence might actually be used in effecting change. A rehabilitation program might seek: (1) to make conventional and delinquent alternatives clear; (2) to lead delinquents to question the ultimate utility of delinquent alternatives; and (3) to help conventional alternatives assume some positive valence for them. It might then reduce the affective identification which they feel for the delinquent subsystem and tip the scales in the opposite direction.

MAJOR ASSUMPTIONS FOR TREATMENT

In order to relate such theoretical premises to the specific needs of treatment, the Provo Experiment adopted a series of major assumptions. They are as follows:

1. Delinquent behavior is primarily a group product and demands an approach to treatment far different from that which sees it as characteristic of a "sick," or "well-meaning" but "misguided," person.

2. An effective program must recognize the intrinsic nature of a delinquent's membership in a delinquent system and, therefore, must direct treatment to him as a part of that system.

3. Most habitual delinquents are affectively and ideologically dedicated to the delinquent system. Before they can be made amenable to change, they must be made anxious about the ultimate utility of that system for them.

4. Delinquents must be forced to deal with the conflicts which the demands of conventional and delinquent systems place upon them. The resolution of such conflicts, either for or against further law violations, must ultimately involve a community decision. For that reason, a treatment program, in order to force realistic decision-making, can be most effective if it permits continued participation in the community as well as in the treatment process.

5. Delinquent ambivalence for purposes of rehabilitation can only be utilized in a setting conducive to the free expression of feelings—both delinquent and conventional. This means that the protection and rewards provided by the treatment system for *candor* must exceed those provided either by delinquents for adherence to delinquent roles or by officials for adherence to custodial demands for "good behavior." Only in this way can delinquent individuals become aware of the extent to which other delinquents share conventional as well as delinquent aspirations and, only in this way, can they be encouraged to examine the ultimate utility of each.

6. An effective program must develop a unified and cohesive social system in which delinquents and authorities alike are devoted to one task— overcoming lawbreaking. In order to accomplish this the program must avoid two pitfalls: (a) it must avoid establishing authorities as "rejectors" and making inevitable the creation of two social systems within the program; and (b) it must avoid the institutionalization of means by which skilled offenders can evade norms and escape sanctions. The occasional imposition of negative sanctions is as necessary in this system as in any other system.

7. A treatment system will be most effective if the delinquent peer group is used as the means of perpetuating the norms and imposing the sanctions of the system. The peer group should be

seen by delinquents as the primary source of help and support. The traditional psychotherapeutic emphasis upon transference relationships is not viewed as the most vital factor in effecting change.

8. A program based on sociological theory may tend to exclude lectures, sermons, films, individual counseling, analytic psychotherapy, organized athletics, academic education, and vocational training as primary treatment techniques. It will have to concentrate, instead, on matters of another variety: changing reference group and normative orientations, utilizing ambivalent feelings resulting from the conflict of conventional and delinquent standards, and providing opportunities for recognition and achievement in conventional pursuits.

9. An effective treatment system must include rewards which are realistically meaningful to delinquents. They would include such things as peer acceptance for law-abiding behavior or the opportunity for gainful employment rather than badges, movies or furlough privileges which are designed primarily to facilitate institutional control. Rewards, therefore, must only be given for realistic and lasting changes, not for conformance to norms which concentrate upon effective custody as an end in itself.

10. Finally, in summary, a successful program must be viewed by delinquents as possessing four important characteristics: (a) a social climate in which delinquents are given the opportunity to examine and experience alternatives related to a realistic choice between delinquent or nondelinquent behavior; (b) the opportunity to declare publicly to peers and authorities a belief or disbelief that they can benefit from a change in values; (c) a type of social structure which will permit them to examine the role and legitimacy (for their purposes) of authorities in the treatment system; and (d) a type of treatment interaction which, because it places major responsibilities upon peer-group decision-making, grants status and recognition to individuals, not only for their own successful participation in the treatment interaction, but for their willingness to involve others.

THE TREATMENT SYSTEM

The Provo Program, consistent with these basic assumptions, resides in the community and does not involve permanent incarceration. Boys live at home and spend only a part of each day at Pinehills (the program center). Otherwise they are free in the community.

History and locale

The Provo Program was begun in 1956 as an "in-between" program designed specifically to help those habitual delinquents whose persistence made them candidates, in most cases, for a reformatory. It was instigated by a volunteer group of professional and lay people known as the *Citizens' Advisory Council to the Juvenile Court*. It has never had formal ties to government except through the Juvenile Court. This lack of ties has permitted considerable experimentation. Techniques have been modified to such a degree that the present program bears little resemblance to the original one. Legally, program officials are deputy probation officers appointed by the Juvenile Judge.

The cost of treatment is financed by county funds budgeted through the Juvenile Court. So near as we can estimate the cost per boy is approximately one-tenth of what it would cost if he were incarcerated in a reformatory. Research operations are financed by the Ford Foundation. Concentrated evaluation of the program is now in its second year of a six year operation. Because both the theoretical orientation and treatment techniques of the program were in developmental process until its outlines were given final form for research purposes, it is difficult to make an objective evaluation of the over-all program based on recidivism rates for previous years, especially in the absence of adequate control groups. Such an evaluation, however, is an integral part of the present research and is described below.

Relations with welfare agencies and the community, *per se*, are informal but extremely cooperative. This is due to three things: the extreme good will and guiding influence of the Juvenile Court Judge, Monroe J. Paxman, the unceasing efforts of the Citizens' Advisory Council to involve the entire county as a community, and the willingness of city and county officials, not only to overcome traditional fears regarding habitual offenders in the community, but to lend strong support to an experimental program of this type.

Community co-operation is probably enhanced by strong Mormon traditions. However, Utah County is in a period of rapid transition which began in the early days of World War II with the introduction of a large steel plant, allied industries, and an influx of non-Mormons. This trend, both in industry and population, has continued to the present time. The treatment program is located in the city of Provo but draws boys from all major communities in the county—from a string of small cities, many of which border on each other, ranging in size from four to forty thousand.

The total population from which it draws its assignees is about 110,000.

Despite the fact that Utah County is not a highly urbanized area, when compared to large metropolitan centers, the concept of a "parent" delinquent subculture has real meaning for it. While there are no clear-cut gangs, *per se*, it is surprising to observe the extent to which delinquent boys from the entire county, who have never met, know each other by reputation, go with the same girls, use the same language, or can seek each other out when they change high schools. About half of them are permanently out of school, do not participate in any regular institutional activities, and are reliant almost entirely upon the delinquent system for social acceptance and participation.

Assignees

Only habitual offenders, 15-17 years, are assigned to the program. In the absence of public facilities, they are transported to and from home each day in automobiles driven by university students. Their offenses run the usual gamut: vandalism, trouble in school, shoplifting, car theft, burglary, forgery, and so forth. Highly disturbed and psychotic boys are not assigned. The pre-sentence investigation is used to exclude these people. They constitute an extremely small minority.

Number in attendance

No more than twenty boys are assigned to the program at any one time. A large number would make difficult any attempts to establish and maintain a unified, cohesive system. This group of twenty is broken into two smaller groups, each of which operates as a separate discussion unit. When an older boy is released from one of these units, a new boy is added. This is an important feature because it serves as the means by which the culture of the system is perpetuated.

Length of attendance

No length of stay is specified. It is intimately tied to the group and its processes because a boy's release depends not only upon his own behavior, but upon the maturation processes through which his group goes. Release usually comes somewhere between four and seven months.

Nature of program

The program does not utilize any testing, gathering of case histories, or clinical diagnosis. One of its key tools, peer group interaction, is believed to provide a considerably richer source of information about boys and delinquency than do clinical methods.

The program, *per se*, is divided into two phases. Phase I is an intensive group program, utilizing work and the delinquent peer group as the principal instruments for change. During the winter, boys attend this phase three hours a day, five days a week, and all day on Saturdays. Activities include daily group discussions, hard work, and some unstructured activities in which boys are left entirely on their own. During the summer they attend an all-day program which involves work and group discussions. However, there are no practices without exceptions. For example, if a boy has a full-time job, he may be allowed to continue the job in lieu of working in the program. Other innovations occur repeatedly.

Phase II is designed to aid a boy after release from intensive treatment in Phase I. It involves two things: (1) an attempt to maintain some reference group support for a boy; and (2) community action to help him find employment. Both phases are described below.

PHASE I: INTENSIVE TREATMENT

Every attempt is made in Phase I to create a social system in which social structure, peer members, and authorities are oriented to the one task of instituting change. The more relevant to this task the system is, the greater will be its influence.

Social structure

There is little formal structure in the Provo Program. Patterns are abhorred which might make boys think that their release depends upon *refraining* from swearing, engaging in open quarrels or doing such *"positive"* things as saying, "yes sir," or "no sir." Such criteria as these play into their hands. They learn to manipulate them in developing techniques for beating a system. Consequently, other than requiring boys to appear each day, and working hard on the job, there are no formal demands. The only other daily activities are the group discussions at which attendance is optional.

The absence of formal structure helps to do more than avoid artificial criteria for release. It has the positive effect of making boys more amenable to treatment. In the absence of formal structure they are uneasy and they are not quite sure of themselves. Thus, the lack of clear-cut definitions for behavior helps to accomplish three important things: (1) It produces anxiety and turns boys towards the group as a method of resolving their anxiety; (2) It leaves boys free to define situations for themselves: leaders begin to lead, followers begin to follow, and manipulators begin to manipulate. It is these types of behavior which must be seen and analyzed if change is to take place; (3) It binds neither authorities nor the peer group to prescribed courses of action. Each is free to do whatever is needed to suit the needs of particular boys, groups, or situations.

On the other hand, the absence of formal structure obviously does not mean that there is no structure. But, that which does exist is informal and emphasizes ways of thinking and behaving which are not traditional. Perhaps the greatest difference lies in the fact that a considerable amount of power is vested in the delinquent peer group. It is the instrument by which norms are perpetuated and through which many important decisions are made. It is the primary source of pressure for change.

The peer group

Attempts to involve a boy with the peer group begin the moment he arrives. Instead of meeting with and receiving an orientation lecture from authorities, he receives no formal instructions. He is always full of such questions as, "What do I have to do to get out of this place?" or "How long do I have to stay?", but such questions as these are never answered. They are turned aside with, "I don't know," or "Why don't you find out?" Adults will not orient him in the ways that he has grown to expect, nor will they answer any of his questions. He is forced to turn to his peers. Usually, he knows someone in the program, either personally or by reputation. As he begins to associate with other boys he discovers that important informal norms do exist, the most important of which makes *inconsistency* rather than *consistency* the rule. That which is appropriate for one situation, boy, or group may not be appropriate for another. Each merits a decision as it arises.

Other norms center most heavily about the daily group discussion sessions. These sessions are patterned after the technique of "Guided Group Interaction" which was developed at Fort Knox during World War II and at Highfields. Guided

Group Interaction emphasizes the idea that only through a group and its processes can a boy work out his problems. From a peer point of view it has three main goals: (1) to question the utility of a life devoted to delinquency; (2) to suggest alternative ways for behavior; and (3) to provide recognition for a boy's personal reformation and his willingness to reform others.

Guided Group Interaction grants to the peer group a great deal of power, including that of helping to decide when each boy is ready to be released. This involves "retroflexive reformation." If a delinquent is serious in his attempts to reform others he must automatically accept the common purpose of the reformation process, identify himself closely with others engaged in it, and grant prestige to those who succeed in it. In so doing, he becomes a genuine member of the reformation group and in the process may be alienated from his previous pro-delinquent groups. Such is an ideal and long term goal. Before it can be realized for any individual he must become heavily involved with the treatment system. Such involvement does not come easy and the system must include techniques which will impel him to involvement. Efforts to avoid the development of formal structure have already been described as one technique. Group processes constitute a second technique.

Before a group will help a boy "solve his problems" it demands that he review his total delinquent history. This produces anxiety because, while he is still relatively free, it is almost inevitable that he has much more to reveal than is already known by the police or the court. In an effort to avoid such involvement he may try subterfuge. But any reluctance on his part to be honest will not be taken lightly. Norms dictate that no one in the group can be released until everyone is honest and until every boy helps to solve problems. A refusal to come clean shows a lack of trust in the group and slows down the problem-solving process. Therefore, any recalcitrant boy is faced with a real dilemma. He can either choose involvement or relentless attack by his peers. Once a boy does involve himself, however, he learns that some of his fears were unwarranted. What goes on in the group meeting is sacred and is not revealed elsewhere.

A second process for involvement lies in the use of the peer group to perpetuate the norms of the treatment system. One of the most important norms suggests that most boys in the program are candidates for a reformatory. This is shocking because even habitual delinquents do not ordinarily see themselves as serious offenders. Yet, the tradition is clear; most failures at Pinehills are sent to the Utah State Industrial School. Therefore, each boy has a major decision to make: either he makes serious attempts to change or he gets sent away.

The third process of involvement could only occur in a community program. Each boy has the tremendous problem of choosing between the demands of his delinquent peers outside the program and the demands of those within it. The usual reaction is to test the situation by continuing to identify with the former. Efforts to do this, however, and to keep out of serious trouble are usually unsuccessful. The group is a collective board on delinquency; it usually includes a member who knows the individual personally or by reputation; and it can rely on the meeting to discover many things. Thus, the group is able to use actual behavior in the community to judge the extent to which a boy is involved with the program and to judge his readiness for release. The crucial criterion for any treatment program is not what an individual does while in it, but what he does while he is *not* in it.

The fourth process involves a number of important sanctions which the group can impose if a boy refuses to become involved. It can employ familiar techniques such as ostracism or derision or it can deny him the status and recognition which come with change. Furthermore, it can use sanctions arising out of the treatment system. For example, while authorities may impose restrictions on boys in the form of extra work or incarceration in jail, the group is often permitted, and encouraged, to explore reasons for the action and to help decide what future actions should be taken. For example, a boy may be placed in jail over the week-end and told that he will be returned there each week-end thereafter until his group decides to release him. It is not uncommon for the group, after thorough discussion, to return him one or more week-ends despite his protestations. Such an occurrence would be less likely in an ordinary reformatory because of the need for inmates to maintain solidarity against the official system. However, in this setting it is possible because boys are granted the power to make important decisions affecting their entire lives. Rather than having other people do things to them, they are doing things to themselves.

The ultimate sanction possessed by the group is refusal to release a boy from the program. Such a sanction has great power because it is normative to expect that no individual will be tolerated in the program indefinitely. Pinehills is not a place where boys "do time."

Authorities

The third source of pressure towards change rests in the hands of authorities. The role of an authority in a treatment system of this type is a difficult one. On one hand, he cannot be seen as a person whom skillful delinquents or groups can manipulate. But, on the other hand, he cannot be perceived permanently as a "rejector." Everything possible, therefore, must be done by him to create an adult image which is new and different.

Initially, authorities are probably seen as "rejectors." It will be recalled that they do not go out of their way to engage in regular social amenities, to put boys at ease, or to establish one-to-one relationships with boys. Adult behavior of this type is consistent with the treatment philosophy. It attempts to have boys focus upon the peer group, not adults, as the vehicle by which questions and problems are resolved.

Second, boys learn that authorities will strongly uphold the norm which says that Pinehills is not a place for boys to "do time." If, therefore, a boy does not become involved and the group is unwilling or unable to take action, authorities will. Such action varies. It might involve requiring him to work all day without pay, placing him in jail, or putting him in a situation in which he has no role whatsoever. In the latter case he is free to wander around the Center all day but he is neither allowed to work nor given the satisfaction of answers to his questions regarding his future status.

Boys are seldom told why they are in trouble or, if they are told, solutions are not suggested. To do so would be to provide them structure by which to rationalize their behavior, hide other things they have been doing, and escape the need to change. Consequently, they are left on their own to figure out why authorities are doing what they are doing and what they must do to get out of trouble.

Situations of this type precipitate crises. Sometimes boys run away. But, whatever happens, the boy's status remains amorphous until he can come up with a solution to his dilemma. This dilemma, however, is not easily resolved.

There is no individual counseling since this would reflect heavily upon the integrity of the peer group. Consequently, he cannot resolve his problems by counseling with or pleasing adults. His only recourse is to the group. But since the group waits for him to bring up his troubles, he must involve himself with it or he cannot resolve them. Once he does, he must reveal why he is in trouble, what he has been doing to get into trouble or how he has been abusing the program.

If he refuses to become involved he may be returned to court by authorities. This latter alternative occurs rarely, since adults have more time than boys. While they can afford to wait, boys find it very difficult to "sweat out" a situation. They feel the need to resolve it.

As a result of such experiences, boys are often confused and hostile. But where such feelings might be cause for alarm elsewhere, they are welcomed at Pinehills. They are taken as a sign that a boy is not in command of the situation and is therefore amenable to change. Nevertheless, the treatment system does not leave him without an outlet for his feelings. The meeting is a place where his anger and hostility can be vented—not only against the program but against the adults who run it. But, in venting his confusion and hostility, it becomes possible for the group to analyze, not only his own behavior, but that of adults, and to determine to what end the behavior of all is leading. Initial perceptions of adults which were confusing and provoking can now be seen in a new way. The treatment system places responsibility upon a boy and his peers for changing delinquent behavior, not upon adults. Thus, adult behavior which was initially seen as rejecting can now be seen as consistent with this expectation. Boys have to look to their own resources for solutions of problems. In this way they are denied social-psychological support for "rejecting the rejectors," or for rejecting decisions demanded by the group. Furthermore, as a result of the new adult image which is pressed upon them, boys are led to examine their perceptions regarding other authorities. Boys may learn to see authorities with whom they had difficulties previously in a new, non-stereotyped fashion.

WORK AND OTHER ACTIVITIES

Any use of athletics, handicrafts, or remedial schooling involves a definition of rehabilitation goals. Are these activities actually important in changing delinquents? In the Provo Experiment they are not viewed as having an inherent value in developing non-delinquent behavior. In fact, they are viewed as detrimental because participation in them often becomes a criterion for release. On the other hand, work habits are viewed as vitally important. Previous research suggests that employment is one of the most important means of changing reference from delinquent to law-abiding groups. But, such findings simply pose the important question: How can boys be best prepared to find and hold employment?

Sociologists have noted the lack of opportunity structure for delinquents, but attention to a modification of the structure (assuming that it can be modified) as the sole approach to rehabilitation overlooks the need to prepare delinquents to utilize employment possibilities. One alternative for doing this is an education program with all its complications. The other is an immediate attack on delinquent values and work habits. The Provo Experiment chose the latter alternative. It hypothesized that an immediate attack on delinquent values, previous careers, and nocturnal habits would be more effective than an educational program. Sophisticated delinquents, who are otherwise very skillful in convincing peers and authorities of their good intentions, are often unable to work consistently. They have too long believed that only suckers work. Thus concentration is upon work habits. Boys are employed by the city and county in parks, streets, and recreation areas. Their work habits are one focus of group discussion and an important criterion for change. After release, they are encouraged to attend academic and vocational schools should they desire.

THE STARTER MECHANISM: PUTTING THE SYSTEM IN MOTION

There are both theoretical and practical considerations relative to the purposeful creation of the social structure at Pinehills and the process by which it was developed. The foregoing discussion described some of the structural elements involved and, by inference, suggested the means by which they were introduced. However, the following is presented as a means of further clarification.

The first consideration involved the necessity of establishing a structure which could pose realistically and clearly the alternatives open to habitually delinquent boys. What are these alternatives? Since in most cases delinquents are lower-class individuals who not only lack many of the social skills but who have been school failures as well, the alternatives are not great. Some may become professional criminals but this is a small minority. Therefore, most of them have two principal choices: (1) they can continue to be delinquent and expect, in most cases, to end up in prison; or (2) they can learn to live a rather marginal life in which they will be able to operate sufficiently within the law to avoid being locked up. Acceptance of the second alternative by delinquents would not mean that they would have to change their entire style of living, but it does mean that most would have to find employment and be willing to disregard delinquent behavior in favor of the drudgery of everyday living.

Until these alternatives are posed for them, and posed in a meaningful way, delinquents will not be able to make the necessary decisions regarding them. The need, therefore, was for the type of structure at Pinehills which could pose these alternatives initially without equivocation and thus force boys to consider involvement in the rehabilitative process as a realistic alternative for them.

By the time delinquents reach Pinehills they have been cajoled, threatened, lectured, and exhorted—all by a variety of people in a variety of settings: by parents, teachers, police, religious leaders, and court officials. As a consequence, most have developed a set of manipulative techniques which enable them to "neutralize" verbal admonitions by appearing to comply with them, yet refraining all the while from any real adherence. For that reason, it was concluded that *deeds,* not *words,* would be required as the chief means for posing clearly the structural alternatives open to them.

Upon arrival the first delinquents assigned to Pinehills had every reason to believe that this was another community agency for which they possessed the necessary "techniques of neutralization." It was housed in an ordinary two-story home, and authorities spent little time giving instructions or posing threats. It must have seemed, therefore, that Pinehills would not constitute a serious obstacle for which they could not find some means to avoid involvement.

The following are examples of happenings which helped to establish norms contrary to this view. After attending only one day, a rather sophisticated boy was not at home to be picked up for his second day. Instead, he left a note on his front door saying he was at the hospital visiting a sick sister. Official reaction was immediate and almost entirely opposite to what he expected. No one made any efforts to contact him. Instead, a detention order was issued by the court to the police who arrested the boy later that evening and placed him in jail. He was left there for several days without the benefit of visits from anyone and then returned to Pinehills. Even then, no one said anything to him about his absence. No one had to; he did not miss again. Furthermore, he had been instrumental in initiating the norm which says that the principal alternative to Pinehills is incarceration.

A second occurrence established this norm even more clearly. After having been at Pinehills for two months and refusing to yield to the pressures of his group, a boy asked for a rehearing in court, apparently feeling that he could manipulate the judge more successfully than he could the people

at Pinehills. His request was acted upon immediately. He was taken to jail that afternoon and a hearing arranged for the following morning. The judge committed him to the State Reformatory. Since that time there has never been another request for a rehearing. In a similar way, especially during the first year, boys who continued to get in serious trouble while at Pinehills were recalled by the court for another hearing and assigned to the reformatory. These cases became legendary examples to later boys. However, adults have never had to call attention to them; they are passed on in the peer socialization process.

Once such traditions were established, they could yet be used in another way. They became devices by which to produce the type of uncertainty characteristic of social settings in which negative sanctions should be forthcoming but do not appear. The individual is left wondering why. For example, not all boys who miss a day or two at Pinehills now are sent to jail. In some cases, nothing is said to the individual in question. He is left, instead, to wonder when, and if, he will be sent. Likewise, other boys who have been in serious trouble in the community are not always sent to the State Reformatory but may be subjected to the same kind of waiting and uncertainty. Efforts are made, however, to make it impossible for boys to predict in advance what will happen in any particular case. Even adults cannot predict this, relying on the circumstances inherent in each case. Thus, both rigidity and inconsistency are present in the system at the same time.

The same sort of structural alternatives were posed regarding work. Boys who did not work consistently on their city jobs, where they were being paid, were returned to Pinehills to work for nothing. At Pinehills, they were usually alone and had to perform such onerous tasks as scrubbing the floor, washing windows, mowing the lawn or cutting weeds. They might be left on this job for hours or weeks. The problem of being returned to work with the other boys for pay was left to them for their own resolution, usually in the group. So long as they said nothing, nothing was said to them except to assign them more work.

This type of structure posed stark but, in our opinion, realistic alternatives. It was stark and realistic because boys were still living in the community, but for the first time could sense the omnipresence of permanent incarceration. However, another type of structure less stringent was needed by which boys could realistically resolve problems and make choices. Since, as has been mentioned, peer-group decision-making was chosen as the means for problem-resolution, attention was focussed upon the daily group meetings as the primary source of information. It became the focal point of the whole treatment system.

The first group, not having any standards to guide it (except those which suggested resistance to official pressures), spent great portions of entire meetings without speaking. However, consistent with the idea that deeds, not words, count, and that a group has to resolve its own problems, the group leader refused to break the silence except at the very end of each meeting. At that time, he began standardizing one common meeting practice: he summarized what had been accomplished. Of silent meetings he simply said that nothing had been accomplished. He did point out, however, that he would be back the next day—that, in fact, he would be there a year from that day. Where would they be, still there? The problem was theirs.

When some boys could stand the silence no longer, they asked the group leader what they might talk about. Rather than making it easy for them he suggested something that could only involve them further: he suggested that someone might recite all the things he had done to get in trouble. Not completely without resources, however, boys responded by reciting only those things they had been caught for. In his summary, the leader noted this fact and suggested that whoever spoke the next time might desire to be more honest by telling all. Boys were reluctant to do this but, partly because it was an opportunity to enhance reputations and partly because they did not know what else to do, some gave honest recitations. When no official action was taken against them, two new and important norms were introduced: (1) the idea that what is said in the meeting is sacred to the meeting; and (2) that boys can afford to be candid—that, in fact, candor pays.

The subsequent recitals of delinquent activities ultimately led to a growing awareness of the ambivalence which many delinquents feel regarding their activities. In the social climate provided by the meeting some boys began to express feelings and receive support for behavior which the delinquent system with its emphasis on ideal-typical role behavior could not permit.

Eventually, the meeting reached a stage where it began to discuss the plethora of happenings which occurred daily, both at Pinehills and elsewhere in the community. These happenings, rather than impersonal, easily speculated-about material, were urged as the most productive subject matter. For example, many boys had reached the stage of trying devious rather than direct methods of missing sessions at Pinehills. They came with requests to be excused for normally laudatory activi-ties: school functions, family outings, and even religious services. But, again adults refused to take the traditional course of assuming responsibility and making decisions for boys. Boys were directed to the meeting instead. This not only shifted the responsibility to them, but provided the opportunity to develop five important norms: (1) those having to do with absences; (2) the idea that the place for problem-solving is in the meeting; (3) that everyone, not just adults, should be involved in the process; (4) that if a boy wants the meeting to talk about his problems, he has to justify them as being more important than someone else's; and (5) that any request or point of view has to be substantiated both by evidence and some relevance to the solution of delinquent problems.

It became obvious that even simple requests could be complicated. Boys found themselves using their own rationalizations on each other, often providing both humorous and eye-opening experiences. The climate became increasingly resistant to superficial requests and more conducive to the examination of pressing problems. Boys who chose to fight the system found themselves fighting peers. A stubborn boy could be a thorn in the side of the whole group.

The daily meeting summaries took on increased importance as the leader helped the group: (1) to examine what had happened each day; (2) to examine to what ends various efforts were leading —that is, to examine what various boys were doing, or not doing, and what relevance this had for themselves and the group; (3) to suggest areas of discussion which had been neglected, ignored, or purposely hidden by group members; and (4) to describe the goals of the treatment system in such a way that boys could come to recognize the meaning of group discussions as a realistic source of problem-resolution.

The structural lines associated with the meeting eventually began to define not only the type of subject matter most relevant to change, but the general means for dealing with this subject matter. However, such structure was extremely flexible, permitting a wide latitude of behavior. Great care was taken to avoid the institutionalization of clear-cut steps by which boys could escape Pinehills. Problem solving was, and still is, viewed as a process—a process not easily understood in advance, but something which develops uniquely for each new boy and each new group.

Finally, in summary, the Pinehills system, like many social systems, has some rigid prerequisites for continued membership. The broad structural outlines carefully define the limits beyond which members should not go. However, unlike most extreme authoritarian systems, there is an inner structure, associated with the meeting, which does not demand rigid conformity and which instead permits those deviations which are an honest expression of feelings.

The admission of deviations within the structural confines of the meeting helps to lower the barriers which prevent a realistic examination of their implications for the broader authoritarian structure, either at Pinehills or in society at large. Boys are able to make more realistic decisions as to which roles, conventional or delinquent, would seem to have the most utility for them.

This brief attempt to describe a complex system may have been misleading. The complexities involved are multivariate and profound. However, one important aspect of the experiment has to do with the theoretical development of, and research on, the nature of, the treatment system. Each discussion session is recorded and efforts are made to determine means by which treatment techniques might be improved, and ways in which group processes can be articulated. All would be very useful in testing theory which suggests that experience in a cohesive group is an important variable in directing or changing behavior.

PHASE II: COMMUNITY ADJUSTMENT

Phase II involves an effort to maintain reference group support and employment for a boy after intensive treatment in Phase I. After his release from Phase I he continues to meet periodically for discussions with his old group. The goal is to utilize this group in accomplishing three things: (1) acting as a check on a boy's current behavior; (2) serving as a law-abiding reference group; and (3) aiding in the solution of new problems. It seeks to continue treatment in a different and perhaps more intensive way than such traditional practices as probation or parole.

Efforts to find employment for boys are made by the Citizens' Advisory Council. If employment is found, a boy is simply informed that an employer needs someone. No efforts are taken by some well-meaning but pretentious adult to manipulate the boy's life.

These steps, along with the idea that delinquents should be permitted to make important decisions during the rehabilitative process, are consistent with structural-functional analysis which suggests that in order to eliminate existing structure, or identification with it, one must provide the necessary functional alternatives.

APPROPRIATENESS OF TECHNIQUES

Many persons express disfavor with what they consider a harsh and punitive system at Pinehills. If, however, alternatives are not great for habitual delinquents, a program which suggests otherwise is not being honest with them. Delinquents are aware that society seldom provides honors for *not* being delinquent; that, in fact, conventional alternatives for them have not always promised significantly more than delinquent alternatives. Therefore, expectations associated with the adoption of conventional alternatives should not be unrealistic.

On the other hand it should be remembered that, in terms familiar to delinquents, every effort is made at Pinehills to include as many positive experiences as possible. The following are some which seem to function:

1. Peers examine problems which are common to all.

2. There is a recurring opportunity for each individual to be the focal point of attention among peers in which his behavior and problems become the most important concern of the moment.

3. Delinquent peers articulate in front of conventional adults without constraint with regard to topic, language, or feeling.

4. Delinquents have the opportunity, for the first time in an institutional setting, to make crucial decisions about their own lives. This in itself is a change in the opportunity structure and is a means of obligating them to the treatment system. In a reformatory a boy cannot help but see the official system as doing things to him in which he has no say: locking him up, testing him, feeding him, making his decisions. Why should he feel obligated? But when some important decision-making is turned over to him, he no longer has so many grounds for rejecting the system. Rejection in a reformatory might be functional in relating him to his peers, but in this system it is not so functional.

5. Delinquents participate in a treatment system that grants status in three ways: (a) for age and experience in the treatment process—old boys have the responsibility of teaching new boys the norms of the system—; (b) for the exhibition of law-abiding behavior, not only in a minimal sense, but for actual qualitative changes in specific role behavior at Pinehills, home or with friends; and (c) for the willingness to confront other boys, in a group setting, with their delinquent behavior. (In a reformatory where he has to contend with the inmate system a boy can gain little and lose much for his willingness to be candid in front of adults about peers, but at Pinehills it is a

primary source of prestige.) The ability to confront others often reflects more about the *confronter* than it does about the *confronted*. It is an indication of the extent to which he has accepted the reformation process and identified himself with it.

6. Boys can find encouragement in a program which poses the possibility of relatively short restriction and the avoidance of incarceration.

7. The peer group is a potential source of reference group support for law-abiding behavior. Boys commonly refer to the fact that their group knows more about them than any other persons: parents or friends.

SUMMARY AND IMPLICATIONS

This paper describes an attempt to apply sociological theory to the treatment of delinquents. It concentrates not only upon treatment techniques, *per se*, but the type of social system in which these techniques must operate. The over-all treatment system it describes is like all other social systems in the sense that it specifies generalized requirements for continued membership in the system. At the same time, however, it also legitimizes the existence of a subsystem within it—the meeting—which permits the discussion and evaluation of happenings and feelings which *may* or *may not* support the over-all normative structure of the larger system.

The purposeful creation of this subsystem simply recognized what seemed to be two obvious facts: (1) that the existence of contrary normative expectations among delinquent and official members of the over-all system would ultimately result in the creation of such a subsystem anyway; and (2) that such a system, not officially recognized, would pose a greater threat, and would inhibit to a greater degree, the realization of the over-all

rehabilitative goals of the major system than would its use as a rehabilitative tool.

This subsystem receives not only official sanction but grants considerable power and freedom to delinquent members. By permitting open expressions of anger, frustration, and opposition, it removes social-psychological support for complete resistance to a realistic examination of the ultimate utility of delinquent versus conventional norms. At the same time, however, the freedom it grants is relative. So long as opposition to the demands of the larger system is contained in the meeting subsystem, such opposition is respected. But continued deviancy outside the meeting cannot be tolerated indefinitely. It must be seen as dysfunctional because the requirements of the over-all treatment system are identified with those of the total society and these requirements will ultimately predominate.

At the same time, the over-all treatment system includes elements designed to encourage and support the adoption of conventional roles. The roles it encourages and the rewards it grants, however, are peer-group oriented and concentrate mainly upon the normative expectations of the social strata from which most delinquents come: working- rather than middle-class strata. This is done on the premise that a rehabilitation program is more realistic if it attempts to change normative orientations towards lawbreaking rather than attempting (or hoping) to change an individual's entire way of life. It suggests, for example, that a change in attitudes and values toward work *per se* is more important than attempting to create an interest in the educational, occupational, and recreational goals of the middle-class.

The differences posed by this treatment system, as contrasted to many existing approaches to rehabilitation, are great. Means should be sought, therefore, in addition to this project by which its techniques and orientation can be treated as hypotheses and verified, modified, or rejected.

The following exchange of letters between Whitney H. Gordon and LaMar T. Empey and Jerome Rabow regarding the Provo Experiment appeared in the *American Sociological Review,* Vol. 27 (1962), 256-258 (footnotes added by Mr. Empey.

To the Editor:

I suspect that many of us who have read the Empey and Rabow article on "The Provo Experiment in Delinquency Rehabilitation" have been profoundly impressed by it. Rarely have we been treated to a paper of such theoretical prowess coupled with rigor of implementation; and all of it stated succinctly. It is within such a framework that I should like to raise a not unsympathetic question.

In many ways—some of them superficial and some of them not—the techniques used at Pinehills are reminiscent of those employed by the Communists in Korea on selected groups of American prisoners of war. One sees the leverage of the group being applied to the individual by way of public confessions, the demand for candor, the infinite patience and inscrutability of authority. There appears the "carrot and stick" technique along with the utilization of role disruption and social anxiety as motivating forces. Beyond that, one is reminded how systematically and thoroughly the integrity of psychological privacy is undermined.

I do not doubt that Empey and Rabow are fully aware of the parallels between their work and the efforts of the Communists in Korea.

The question which I should like to raise is the obvious one of values. In Korea we were shocked at what seemed to us the cynicism with which American was turned upon American. (We were horrified by some other social phenomena, too, which are not germane to the present discussion.) We perceived something Orwellian and "ghoulish" in the "Rectification Program." I do not wish to suggest that intellectual consistency and ethical gentility require that we dismantle such programs as Empey and Rabow's. Far, far from it. The *reductio ad absurdum* of that argument may delight that uninhibited imagination (over coffee), but our authors must face the day-to-day realities of delinquent careers.

What I should urge is that we once again return to the classic question of means and ends; that we must not hide from the larger, perhaps tragically futile, issues of social existence. Whether one is warped toward legitimate American society or legitimate Communist society is not the essential question. It would be a Koestler-like dream were Empey, Rabow and some of the rest of us to find ourselves "comrades" in a Communist rectification camp. What could we say?

I raise the question and do not propose an answer—an old but honest academic trick. Before we are caught in the position of many nuclear physicists, I should like to urge that we think through with honesty quite what we are doing and what precedents we are establishing. It would be a supreme indictment of the students of society were we not to profit *a priori* from another social group now often tortured and troubled by its awesome contribution to the modern world.

WHITNEY H. GORDON
Ball State Teachers College

To the Editor:

Professor Gordon's provocative query is best discussed in terms of the two major questions he raises: (1) the possible parallel between techniques used in the Provo Experiment and those used by the Communists in Korea; and (2) whether, as a part of the larger question of the relations of means to ends, a similarity would not rule out such experimental techniques as unethical, perhaps dangerous, precedents.

Professor Gordon is correct regarding the Provo Experiment and the Communists: there are parallels between the two programs. However, a recognition of this fact does not permit any simple conclusion as to what should be done. The reason is that, as William Sargant has pointed out, there are also parallels between Communist techniques and many other common, often traditional social practices in religion, politics, medicine, psychology and others.

Professor Gordon's second question regarding the relation of means to ends, profound as it is, does not begin to address itself to all of the tremendous complexities involved. Prior to recent times Americans were seldom aroused, on any mass basis, by the use of drugs or electric shock treatment as a means of heightening suggestibility, by the calculated down-grading (sometimes degrading) of personal identity in the Military in the interest of unquestioning obedience and *esprit de corps*, or even by the stress experienced by many college students when they encounter courses which question their basic religious, economic, and moral beliefs. Only when the techniques common to many of these practices were systematically applied by the Communists were people struck by their implications; yet they are all forms of "brain washing"—attempts to change perceptions, attitudes and behavior through emotional stress, confessions, the presentation of new alternatives, followed sometimes by analyses.

Any recognition and concern over these techniques, therefore, besides that of the relation of means to ends, would seem to require that we deal with another important question: "What are the ethical, social, and scientific consequences of *not* undertaking studies which would investigate the principles upon which such techniques operate?" Answers to this problem, because of its concern with human nature, social control, and the relation of individual to social "good," might well involve the whole of social science. They could not be determined solely upon the basis of an ethical concern for the maintenance of individual privacy. What is the precise contribution of change techniques to social solidarity, as well as to the invasion of privacy? What are important *differences* among them, as well as parallels?

The involvement of science in the investigation of problems of this type arouses minimal resistance so long as it remains abstract and withdrawn. But the problem is heightened by the development of any systematic and explicitly stated program like the Provo Experiment. It poses yet another intrusion by science into realms formerly reserved for religion, social welfare, and philosophy.

Perhaps, by using the Provo Experiment as an example, we can deal with specifics rather than generalities. A systematic examination denies easy solution.

Investigation suggests that we are dealing with a population of offenders who, although they have been reared in a society emphasizing democratic values and processes, have largely had experiences to the contrary. Currently their relationship to the community is a power relationship whose principal traditional function has been to imprison them. If one seeks other alternatives, several factors must be considered:

1. What are the consequences to both delinquents and the community if a program fails to use techniques which clarify alternatives and socialize offenders?

A failure to impel involvement by *both* authorities and delinquents in the treatment process encourages the old functional adjustment of removing the offender. The delinquent may be spared the necessity of having to change and social solidarity may be enhanced, but those in power in the community are also spared even minimal responsibility. What a multitude of ethical, practical and theoretical questions are raised by this circumstance!

2. What are alternative techniques for operating within the context of a community?

One issue that has to be faced is that the relationship between treatment personnel and delinquents is not a voluntary relationship. "Clients" in this case are much less volunteers than a two-week old draftee in the Army. Furthermore, in light of the parallels among various change techniques, it should be recognized that virtually any technique is going to involve the use of power, either seductively, in the guise of a gentle specification of alternatives and the use of positive transference relationships, or in a more direct way, perhaps as specified in our original paper. Decisions regarding this question involve not only ethics but the reality of community and delinquent life as we best understand it.

3. What are traditional techniques used by court and treatment personnel in the community? What are delinquent methods for handling them?

Most traditional treatment techniques, we believe, are rooted in middle-class perceptions and problems. As a consequence, two problems are raised:

a. They lend themselves to sometimes contradictory emphases upon: (1) one-to-one relationships which are warm and accepting; and (2) to the "correct" manipulation of language and behavior—*rehabilitation by definition*. In addition to the manifest function which these techniques serve, we suspect that they also serve the latent function of making the lives of authorities more comfortable. Tensions are avoided; everybody knows what he is supposed to do.

b. However, unlike neurotics who are often isolated and self-absorbed, delinquents, we believe, share techniques and rationalizations for dealing with these techniques. By appearing to accept the middle-class definition of any treatment situation, they can make an implicit or explicit claim on authorities to be persons of the kind expected. They can exert a moral command upon authorities to treat them in a manner that persons of that kind have a right to expect.

Unfortunately, there is nothing in such a setting to encourage responsible individuality. The cynicism it engenders only strengthens delinquent perceptions and may actually contribute to further law-breaking.

4. What is a positive treatment experience?

An ethical concern for the subjects of any program would seem to require that they be able, ultimately, to understand both the objectives of their program as well as the means by which these objectives are to be realized. It is our impression, incidentally, that the Communists were not interested in this task. One of the striking things about returning American prisoners was their confusion and apathy, their lack of a personal or collective commitment to any ideology. Thus, it is one thing to break a person down under intolerable stress and quite another to use this stress positively, not only to modify perceptions, but to permit a greater susceptibility for the examination of new alternatives, skills, and opportunities.

We hypothesize, for example, that, unless delinquents are made increasingly capable of independent, yet responsible action, through a modification of both self and environment, it will be too easy for them to resort again to the delinquent system as the most functional adjustment. Treatment in the Provo Experiment, therefore, does create stress but uses it as a means of breaking up stereotyped (often cynical) role-playing. In addition, it tries to provide opportunities by which candor and communication can lead to an exploration of new alternatives. Seen in this way, there is no reason why stress cannot be used constructively.

In contrast to the religious revival or Communist techniques which leave a person in a condition of high suggestibility, but without adequate means for understanding, our approach concentrates upon means by which a delinquent group can expand its understanding. Ideally, the group learns to function as a social microcosm, and any individual can profit from learning to deal with many of the social problems involved. Not only must group members deal with an ambiguous setting, but deal with the authoritarian demands of the delinquent system.

This approach suggests that before individuals can realize maximum benefits from treatment, they have to analyze the process problems, subgroupings, interpersonal relationships, and power structures which develop within the group. Therapy is seen as being derived both from the involvement of the members with the effective development of the group as a treatment instrument as well as with the analysis of individual problems. The ideal is to have members understand the social circumstances under which their problems developed, the whole process in which they are involved, and to have them accept some responsibility, not only for themselves, but for

the other persons who have been involved with them in the reformation process.

The long-range success of such an approach would seem to hinge upon two things:

a. The granting of some power to the group by which its members can feel that they have a stake in group decision-making.

b. The subsequent opportunity in the community (training, employment, etc.) by which to utilize any new perceptions and motivations. Increased opportunity to be conventional would seem to be imperative.

It is a matter of opinion whether individuality is really lost in this process, or whether the means used are unethical. Before making any such judgment regarding this or any other program, it would be better to have information which only systematic investigation can provide: specific delineation of the means by which changes are to be effected, the ends to which these means are directed, an understanding of the processual relation of the two, and the criterion variables by which success or failure are actually measured. At best, we have only a partial specification of these factors for any program.

LaMar T. Empey
Jerome Rabow
Brigham Young University

Selection 79

A New Theory of Delinquency and Crime
Walter C. Reckless

From earliest days man has been plagued with crime and has tried to explain it. Too frequently this multiple, nonhomogeneous behavior has been explained (unsuccessfully) by some single, monistic cause. During the Middle Ages, the cause of crime was believed to be the Devil; later it was free will, then pleasure-pain hedonism. Lombroso claimed that the sources were atavism and degeneracy. With the rise of biology, heredity was given as the cause. Interest in mental testing led to the belief that delinquents were mentally defective. Concern with slums and social environment gave rise to the theory that these were the primary causes of crime. Interest in man's psyche led to the belief that here lay the sources of evil. Ministers blame lack of religion; policemen blame lack of strong law enforcement and heavy penalties; P.T.A.'s feel that the school and parents are at fault. Physiologists blame somatotypes. As proponents of each special field approach crime from their own particular point of view, one cannot help but be reminded of the blind men and the elephant.

Much of the difficulty has been that men have sought *the* cause of crime or delinquency, failing to realize that criminal behavior, or any other behavior, is a product of multiple factors. Proof that one factor is related to delinquency is not proof that many other factors are not equally important. Moreover, factors that are of great importance in one case may be of little importance in another. No longer do competent criminologists seek to explain all delinquency and crime by any single cause. Rather, they seek to find and express theories that will explain the largest number of cases or to point out characteristics that are significantly more common among criminals than noncriminals.

Most college students have been lawbreakers at one time or another, some of them quite frequently, and all can remember situations in which they might have been serious lawbreakers but were not. Hence no college student who ponders these problems and knows a few fellow students can accept an explanation which proposes that all lawbreakers are psychotic, are mesomorphic, desire to return to the womb, are from slums, are borderline feeble-minded, suffer from *anomie*, or are from broken homes. There are, however, other reasonable and acceptable possibilities, as the following article makes clear.

The preceding selection was an analysis of a *particular* theory—that delinquent subcultures are responsible for a large proportion of delinquency and crime. Reckless presents a broad theory of the causation of crime and delinquency in the framework of an analysis of *numerous* theories, propounds his own "containment" theory which he sees as a more useful theory than the others, and very briefly presents evidence from other authors which supports his theory.

Containment theory is an explanation of conforming behavior as well as deviancy. It has two reinforcing aspects: an inner control system and an outer control system. Are there elements within the self and within the person's immediate world that enable him to hold the line against deviancy or to hue to the line of social expectations? The assumption is that strong inner and reinforcing outer containment constitutes an insulation against normative deviancy (not constitutional or psychological deviancy), that is, violation of the sociolegal conduct norms.

certain phases of delinquency subculture and organized crime. Between these two extremes in the spectrum of crime and delinquency is a very large middle range of norm violation, perhaps as big as two thirds to three quarters of officially reported cases as well as the unreported cases of delinquency and crime. Containment theory seeks to explain this large middle range of offenders. According to its place on the spectrum of delinquency and crime, one might say that it occupies the middle position.

A MIDDLE RANGE THEORY

Containment theory does not explain the entire spectrum of delinquency and crime. It does not explain crime or delinquency which emerges from strong inner pushes, such as compulsions, anxieties, phobias, hallucinations, personality disorders (including inadequate, unstable, antisocial personalities, etc.), from organic impairments such as brain damage and epilepsy, or from neurotic mechanisms (exhibitionists, peepers, fire setters, compulsive shop lifters). All told these cases are minimal. And containment theory does not explain criminal or delinquent activity which is a part of "normal" and "expected" roles and activities in families and communities, such as the criminal tribes of India, Gypsy vocations and trades (very similar to the former), begging families, and

A QUICK REVIEW OF CRIMINOLOGICAL THEORIES

Before proceeding further, it might be a good idea to see in what directions theory in criminology is pointing at present. Since the early 19th century we have had a long succession of theories, most of which have not stood the test of time. It is possible to assemble these theories into three main camps or schools: (1) biological and constitutional theory—often called the school of criminal biology—in which the mainsprings of deviancy are sought in the inherited physical and mental makeup of man; (2) psychogenic theory, in which the formation of antisocial character is

From *Federal Probation*, Vol. 25 (1961), 42-46.

traced to faulty relationships within the family in the first few years of life; and (3) sociological theory, in which the pressures and pulls of the social milieu produce delinquent and criminal behavior.

Mention should be made of some of the specific theories. The dominating theory in Europe today is still the all-inclusive one which falls into the school of criminal biology. It points to the inheritance of weaknesses or pronenesses toward crime and delinquency (plus pressure from a bad environment). Many variants of this theory have shown up in recent years: The attempt to prove inheritance of proneness through the method of studying criminal twins (Lange); the attempt to identify body-mind types (Kretschmer); the general acceptance throughout Europe in the past 25 years of several criminally-oriented types of psychopaths, based on inherited proneness (according to Kurt Schneider); the attempt to identify and explain habitual (serious) offenders as contrasted with occasional offenders or offenders of opportunity, according to early onset which in turn points to inheritance of proneness (Irwin Frey); the specification of the mesomorphic somatotype (muscular) as the type of constitution which is most usually related to delinquency (first according to William Sheldon and later to the Gluecks).

The psychogenic school probably claims August Aichhorn as its fountainhead. According to Aichhorn, faulty development in the first few years of life makes it impossible for the child to control his impulses. The child lingers on as a sort of aggrandizing infant, living in the pleasure principle and failing to develop the reality principle in life. Friedlander indicates that this faulty development in the first few years of life adds up to an antisocial character structure, incapable of handling reality properly. Redl, who is also a disciple of Aichhorn, calls attention to the failure of the child to develop a management system over his impulsivity; that is, fails to develop a good ego and super ego.

The sociologists, ever since Ferri (Italy, c. 1885), have been calling attention to bad environmental conditions. This was echoed by Bonger, who placed the blame for disproportional crime and delinquency among the proletariat on the pressures of the capitalistic system. However, the American sociologists in the twenties pointed to conditions of social or community disorganization, rather than factors related to poverty. They became engrossed with identifying the location and characteristics of high delinquency areas of the city, specifying family disruption and conflict instead of broken home, and calling attention to the modal importance of companionship in delinquency.

It was not until around 1940 that a basic American sociological theory of delinquency and criminal behavior was propounded. This was done by Sutherland and it was called differential association. According to this theory, delinquent or criminal behavior is learned as are most other kinds of behavior—learned in association with others, according to the frequency, intensity, priority, and duration of contacts. Sutherland's theory really is not basically different from the one announced by Tarde 50 years earlier, which regarded criminal behavior as a product of imitation of circulating patterns. Glaser fairly recently proposed differential identification as a substitute for differential association. One takes over the models of behavior from those (reference) groups with which one identifies. But this does not have to be a face-to-face or person-to-person identification. (One can identify with the Beatniks without having actual physical contact with them.)

Still more recently Albert Cohen, picking up the lead from Whyte's *Street-Corner Society*, contended that working class boys who turned their backs on middle class virtues and values, found the solution for their status problems in the delinquency subculture of the gang. And most recently of all is the theory propounded by Cloward and Ohlin that urban slum boys gravitate to delinquency subculture when they discover they do not have access to legitimate avenues of success.

COMMENT ON THE THEORIES

Working backward in commenting on these theories, one might say that Cloward's theory only applies to those forms of delinquency which are part and parcel of the role structure of delinquency subculture. Jackson Toby makes the estimate that this might only be 10 per cent of the whole spectrum of delinquency. Assuming that Cloward's focus is very restricted, his theory does not account for the boys who do not gravitate toward the fighting gang, the criminal gang, and the retreatist groups (drugs). It does not specify that the ones who do gravitate to the three types of subculture have internalized an awareness of inaccessibility to legitimate success goals. It does not indicate that there are degrees of participation in gangs and that delinquency involvement of some members might be nil.

Cohen's theory has somewhat more merit. Somewhere and somehow in the growing-up process, slum boys turn their backs on middle-class values and look to street-corner groups to come to their aid. But Cohen is not able to specify the boys who do or do not turn their back on middle-class virtues and opportunities and gravitate to the street corner. He does not indicate whether only some of the boys in the street corner get involved in delinquent acts, as Shaw and Thrasher did a generation ago. So we have two interesting sociological formulations here, but not much realistic applicability.

Sutherland's differential association theory was meant to be a general theory, applying to the entire spectrum of delinquency and crime, from low to high in the class structure and across the board in personality. The trouble with Sutherland's theory (as well as Tarde's and Glaser's) is that it does not explain who *does* and who *does not* take up with carriers of delinquent patterns or who internalizes and who does not internalize delinquent models of behavior.

Coming now to the contributors to theory in the psychogenic school (Aichhorn, Redl, *et al.*), one should observe that at the most they only occupy a small end of the total spectrum of delinquency and crime. It is granted that there are some individuals whose ego and super-ego development is too weak or poor to control impulses and to handle ordinary expectancies. But it is not at all clear just which children succumb to or are recipients of faulty socialization in the first few years of life. And it is not clear just which of the children, teenagers, late adolescents, and adults who are supposed to have little control over their impulse system run afoul the laws and regulations of society and those who do not.

One certainly finds it difficult to specify just exactly what the proneness is that is supposed to be the mainspring of serious, habitual, and early-starting offenders (criminal biology). It seems to be a sort of weakness in character. The evidence for the inheritance of proneness is very skimpy and most unimpressive, a sort of unreliable family-tree assessment by clinicians.

William Sheldon was able to specify the different kinds of somatotypes, much more definitely than Kretschmer was able to specify his body-mind types. A group of 200 problem youth in a Boston hostel, according to Sheldon, tended to have mesomorphic (athletic) body types along with several related forms of mental deviancy. The Gluecks discovered that among 500 delinquent and 500 nondelinquent boys the delinquents showed up very much more mesomorphic than the nondelinquents. The mesomorphs were found by the Gluecks to have a higher delinquency potential

than other body types. Associated with mesomorphy were strength, social assertiveness, uninhibited motor responses, less submissiveness to authority. While mesomorphy does not explain all of delinquent behavior in the Gluecks' sample, it is certainly associated with a large segment of it and seems to reinforce many of the mental, emotional, and family traits connected with delinquency. Future studies will have to confirm the mesomorphic potential in delinquency.

GLUECKS: 4 TO 1 CAUSAL LAW

Out of their research on 500 delinquent and 500 nondelinquent boys, the Gluecks proposed a five point causal law. According to this formulation, delinquents are distinguishable from nondelinquents (1) physically, in being essentially mesomorphic; (2) temperamentally, in being restless, impulsive, aggressive, destructive; (3) emotionally, in being hostile, defiant, resentful, assertive, nonsubmissive; (4) psychologically, in being direct, concrete learners; (5) socioculturally, in being reared by unfit parents. This might be looked upon as a 4 to 1 law: four parts individual and one part situational. Items 2, 3, and 5 were chosen from among more than 100 overlapping traits, which distinguished delinquents from nondelinquents. The use of more sophisticated statistical methods would have enabled the Gluecks to find the two or three components within this maze of overlapping items which basically differentiate the delinquents from the nondelinquents. Nevertheless, the 4 to 1 causal law still stands as one of the few formulations which is worth attempting to confirm, qualify, or disprove by more rigorous research methods in the future. The law covers most of the spectrum of juvenile delinquency as we know it in the United States, certainly insofar as the full spectrum is represented by 500 boys from Boston who had been committed by juvenile courts to state schools in Massachusetts for delinquency.

INGREDIENTS OF INNER AND OUTER CONTAINMENT

In contrast to the buck-shot approach of the Gluecks, that is shooting out in all directions to explore and discover, containment theory seeks to ferret out more specifically the inner and outer controls over normative behavior. It is attempting to get closer on the target of delinquency and crime by getting at the components which regulate conduct.

Inner containment consists mainly of self components, such as self-control, good self-concept, ego strength, well-developed superego, high frustration tolerance, high resistance to diversions, high sense of responsibility, goal orientation, ability to find substitute satisfactions, tension-reducing rationalizations, and so on. These are the inner regulators.

Outer containment represents the structural buffer in the person's immediate social world which is able to hold him within bounds. It consists of such items as a presentation of a consistent moral front to the person, institutional reinforcement of his norms, goals, and expectations, the existence of a reasonable set of social expectations, effective supervision and discipline (social controls), provision for reasonable scope of activity (including limits and responsibilities) as well as for alternatives and safety-valves, opportunity for acceptance, identity, and belongingness. Such structural ingredients help the family and other supportive groups contain the individual.

Research will have to ferret out the one or two elements in inner and outer containment which are the basic regulators of normative behavior. Undoubtedly in the lists cited above there are items which, if present, determine the existence of other items and cause most of the regulation of conduct. Likewise, research must indicate the way in which the inner and outer regulatory systems operate conjointly. How much self-strength must be present in a fluid world with very little external buffer? How much weakness in self components is an effective external buffer able to manage?

SUPPORTING RESEARCH

The research and observations so far which give support to containment theory are the following:

1. According to Albert J. Reiss,[1] as a result of a study of Chicago delinquents who failed and succeeded on probation, the relative weakness of personal and social controls accounts for most cases of delinquency. Reiss found, however, that the personal controls had more predictive efficiency than the social controls as far as recidivism was concerned.

2. Nye[2] presented evidence to the effect that trends toward delinquent behavior are related to four control factors: (a) direct control which comes from discipline, restrictions, punishments; (b) internalized control which is the inner control of conscience; (c) indirect control which is exerted by not wanting to hurt or go against the wishes of parents or other individuals with whom the person identifies, and (d) the availability of alternative means to goals. Nye contends that his social control theory should not be applied to compulsive behavior or the behavior influenced by delinquency subcultures. He feels that the more indirect control is effective, the less need for direct control; the more internalized control is effective, the less need for any other type of control.

3. Reckless and Dinitz[3] found that a favorable concept of self insulated 12-year-old boys in the slum against delinquency, including perceptions about self, companions, home, and school. A poor concept of self, including perceptions that one is likely to get into trouble, his friends are in trouble, his family and home are unsatisfactory, that he will not finish school, and so on, was associated with delinquency vulnerability in 12-year-old slum boys. Four years later, followup contact revealed that the good self concept group had pretty much held the line and the favorable direction, while the poor self concept group had gravitated in unfavorable directions, 35 percent being involved with the law three times on an average. Reckless and Dinitz look upon a good or poor self concept as an internalization of favorable or unfavorable socialization.

4. As a result of his observations on hyper-aggressive, hostile children, Redl[4] identifies 22 functions of the ego in managing life situations. He conceives of the ego as the manager in the behavior control system, while the super ego is looked upon as the system which gives the signals to the ego. Redl, as is true of Aichhorn disciples,

[1] Albert J. Reiss, Jr., "Delinquency as the Failure of Personal and Social Controls," *American Sociological Review*, 16 (1951), 196-206.

[2] F. Ivan Nye, *Family Relationships and Delinquent Behavior* (New York: John Wiley and Sons, Inc., 1958), pp. 3-4.

[3] Walter C. Reckless, Simon Dinitz, and Ellen Murray, "Self Concept as an Insulator against Delinquency," *American Sociological Review*, 21 (1956), 745; "The Self Component in Potential Delinquency and Potential Non-Delinquency," *Ibid.*, 22 (1957), 569; Simon Dinitz, Barbara Ann Kay, and Walter C. Reckless, "Group Gradients in Delinquency Potential and Achievement Score of Sixth Graders," *American Journal of Orthopsychiatry*, 28 (1958), 598-605; Frank Scarpitti *et al.*, "The 'Good' Boy in a High Delinquency Area: Four Years Later," *American Sociological Review*, 25 (1960), 555-558.

[4] Fritz Redl and David Wineman, *Children Who Hate* (Glencoe, Ill.: The Free Press of Glencoe, 1951), pp. 74-140.

recognizes, particularly at the extremes, ego shortage and ego strength as well as a sick conscience and a healthy one.

Containment theory points to the regulation of normative behavior, through resistance to deviancy as well as through direction toward legitimate social expectations. It may very well be that most of the regulation is in terms of a defense or buffer against deflection. At any rate, it appears as if inner and outer containment occupies a central or core position in between the pressures and pulls of the external environment and the inner drives or pushes. Environmental pressures may be looked upon as conditions associated with poverty or deprivation, conflict and discord, external restraint, minority group status, limited access to success in an opportunity structure. The pulls of the environment represent the distractions, attractions, temptations, patterns of deviancy, advertising, propaganda, carriers of delinquent and criminal patterns (including pushers), delinquency subculture, and so forth. The ordinary pushes are the drives, motives, frustrations, restlessness, disappointments, rebellion, hostility, feelings of inferiority, and so forth. One notices at once that Bonger as well as Cloward falls into pressure theory, while Tarde, Sutherland, and Glaser fall into pull theory.

In a vertical order, the pressures and pulls of the environment are at the top or the side of containing structure, while the pushes are below the inner containment. If the individual has a weak outer containment, the pressures and pulls will then have to be handled by the inner control system. If the outer buffer of the individual is relatively strong and effective, the individual's inner defense does not have to play such a critical role. Likewise, if the person's inner controls are not equal to the ordinary pushes, an effective outer defense may help hold him within bounds. If the inner defenses are of good working order, the outer structure does not have to come to the rescue of the person. Mention has already been made of the fact that there are some extraordinary pushes, such as compulsions, which cannot be contained. The inner and outer control system is usually not equal to the task of containing the abnormal pushes. They are uncontainable, by ordinary controls.

SEVEN TESTS OF VALIDITY

1. Containment theory is proposed as the theory of best fit for the large middle range of cases of delinquency and crime. It fits the middle range cases better than any other theory.

2. It explains crimes against the person as well as the crimes against property, that is the mine run of murder, assault, and rape, as well as theft, robbery, and burglary.

3. It represents a formulation which psychiatrists, psychologists, and sociologists, as well as practitioners, can use equally well. All of these experts look for dimensions of inner and outer strength and can specify these strengths in their terms. Differential association and/or pressure of the environment leave most psychiatrists and psychologists cold and an emphasis on push theory leaves the sociologists for the most part cold. But all of the experts can rally around inner and outer weakness and strengths.

4. Inner and outer containment can be discovered in individual case studies. Weaknesses and strengths are observable. Containment theory is one of the few theories in which the microcosm (the individual case history) mirrors the ingredients of the macrocosm (the general formulation).

5. Containment theory is a valid operational theory for treatment of offenders: for restructuring the milieu of a person or beefing up his self. The most knowledgeable probation workers, parole workers, and institutional staff are already focusing to some extent on helping the juvenile or adult offender build up ego strength, develop new goals, internalize new models of behavior. They are also working on social ties, anchors, supportive relationships, limits, and alternative opportunities in helping to refashion a new containing world for the person.

6. Containment theory is also an effective operational theory for prevention. Children with poor containment can be spotted early. Programs to help insulate vulnerable children against delinquency must operate on internalization of stronger self components and the strengthening of containing structure around the child.

7. Internal and external containment can be assessed and approximated. Its strengths and weaknesses can be specified for research. There is good promise that such assessments can be measured in a standard way.

Finally, it is probable that the theory which will best supplement containment theory in the future will be "damage theory," according to which a light to dark spectrum of damage produces maladjustment and deviancy. The problem here is to find measures to isolate the less serious and less obvious damage cases and to estimate how far into the middle range of delinquency and crime the lighter impairments go.

Selection *80*

Culture and Neurosis

Karen Horney

Neuroses and psychoses were once considered products of the individual psyche, with some biological factors possibly involved. Clinically, the person was thought of as a self-contained unit, and little psychic significance was assigned to persons, groups, culture, or society. Subsequent studies in what might be called psychiatric comparative anthropology have indicated a much closer relationship between mental disorders and sociocultural elements. The evidence points to different rates of mental disorder in different societies, socioculturally related symptoms of mental disorders, and sociocultural causal factors. In other words, psychiatrists and clinical psychologists are now giving more weight to the fact that both the mentally well and the mentally ill are a part of, not apart from, general society, with all that this means in terms of reciprocal influences.

Horney was one of the earliest psychiatrists to recognize this interaction, and her statement of the relationship between culture and neurosis is a classic one. She reports that competition and rivalry are almost invariably a part of neurotic conflicts, presenting a greater problem for the neurotic than for others. For the neurotic, competition typically leads to hostility, which in turn leads to a fear of retaliation, inhibition, and feelings of inferiority, which Horney later says may be a "recoiling from competition."

For these neurotically competitive people, says Horney, anxiety arises because they also want affection and love. A vicious circle develops, consisting of anxiety and repressed hostility which lead to a need for affection, which leads to a morbid anticipation of rejection, which leads to hostility over feeling rejected, which leads back again to anxiety, need for reassuring affection, etc. All this, says Horney, is related to the fact that ours is a competitive individualist culture and that we assume (wrongly) that failure or success results solely from personal qualities and capacities. Horney concludes that in a given society, "those persons are likely to become neurotics who have met these culturally determined difficulties in accentuated form . . . and who have not been able to solve their difficulties or have solved them only at great expense to personality."

This selection therefore represents an orientation toward mental illness as a social problem rather than as a psychological problem. Selection 81 by Faris takes a somewhat different point of view, emphasizing especially the ecological aspects of mental disorder in a large city; Faris also reports evidence of the social, as versus solely psychological, aspects of mental disorder. Selection 82 by Finestone branches off to deal with a phase of modern drug addiction—a problem that has overtones both of mental illness and of its sociocultural origin and manifestations.

In the psychoanalytic concept of neuroses a shift of emphasis has taken place: whereas originally interest was focussed on the dramatic symp-

From the *American Sociological Review*, Vol. 1 (1936), 221-230. Reprinted by permission of the American Sociological Association.

tomatic picture, it is now being realized more and more that the real source of these psychic disorders lies in character disturbances, that the symptoms are a manifest result of conflicting character traits, and that without uncovering and straightening out the neurotic character structure we cannot cure a neurosis. When analyzing these character traits, in a great many cases one is struck by the observation that, in marked contrast to the divergency of the symptomatic pictures, character difficulties invariably center around the same basic conflicts.

These similarities in the content of conflicts present a problem. They suggest, to minds open to the importance of cultural implications, the question of whether and to what extent neuroses are moulded by cultural processes in essentially the same way as "normal" character formation is determined by these influences; and, if so, how far such a concept would necessitate certain modifications in Freud's views of the relation between culture and neurosis.

In the following remarks I shall try to outline roughly some characteristics typically recurring in all our neuroses. The limitations of time will allow us to present neither data—good case histories—nor method, but only results. I shall try to select from the extremely complex and diversified observational material the essential points.

There is another difficulty in the presentation. I wish to show how these neurotic persons are trapped in a vicious circle. Unable to present in detail the factors leading up to the vicious circle, I must start rather arbitrarily with one of the outstanding features, although this in itself is already a complex product of several interrelated, developed mental factors. I start, therefore, with the problem of competition.

The problem of competition, or rivalry, appears to be a never-failing center of neurotic conflicts. How to deal with competition presents a problem for everyone in our culture; for the neurotic, however, it assumes dimensions which generally surpass actual vicissitudes. It does so in three respects:

(1) There is a constant measuring-up with others, even in situations which do not call for it. While striving to surpass others is essential for all competitive situations, the neurotic measures up even with persons who are in no way potential competitors and have no goal in common with him. The question as to who is the more intelligent, more attractive, more popular, is indiscriminately applied towards everyone.

(2) The content of neurotic ambitions is not only to accomplish something worth while, or

to be successful, but to be absolutely best of all. These ambitions, however, exist in fantasy mainly —fantasies which may or may not be conscious. The degree of awareness differs widely in different persons. The ambitions may appear in occasional flashes of fantasy only. There is never a clear realization of the powerful dramatic role these ambitions play in the neurotic's life, or of the great part they have in accounting for his behavior and mental reactions. The challenge of these ambitions is not met by adequate efforts which might lead to realization of the aims. They are in queer contrast to existing inhibitions towards work, towards assuming leadership, towards all means which would effectually secure success. There are many ways in which these fantastic ambitions influence the emotional lives of the persons concerned: by hypersensitivity to criticism, by depressions or inhibitions following failures, etc. These failures need not necessarily be real. Everything which falls short of the realization of the grandiose ambitions is felt as failure. The success of another person is felt as one's own failure.

This competitive attitude not only exists in reference to the external world, but is also internalized, and appears as a constant measuring-up to an ego-ideal. The fantastic ambitions appear on this score as excessive and rigid demands towards the self, and failure in living up to these demands produces depressions and irritations similar to those produced in competition with others.

(3) The third characteristic is the amount of hostility involved in neurotic ambition. While intense competition implicitly contains elements of hostility—the defeat of a competitor meaning victory for oneself—the reactions of neurotic persons are determined by an insatiable and irrational expectation that no one in the universe other than themselves should be intelligent, influential, attractive, or popular. They become infuriated, or feel their own endeavors condemned to futility, if someone else writes a good play or a scientific paper or plays a prominent role in society. If this attitude is strongly accentuated, one may observe in the analytical situation, for example, that these patients regard any progress made as a victory on the part of the analyst, completely disregarding the fact that progress is of vital concern to their own interests. In such situations they will disparage the analyst, betraying, by the intense hostility displayed, that they feel endangered in a position of paramount importance to themselves. They are as a rule completely unaware of the existence and intensity of this "no one but me" attitude, but one may safely assume

and eventually always uncover this attitude from reactions observable in the analytical situation, as indicated above.

This attitude easily leads to a fear of retaliation. It results in a fear of success and also in a fear of failure: "If I want to crush everyone who is successful, then I will automatically assume identical reactions in others, so that the way to success implies exposing me to the hostility of others. Furthermore: if I make any move towards this goal and fail, then I shall be crushed." Success thus becomes a peril and any possible failure becomes a danger which must at all costs be avoided. From the point of view of all these dangers it appears much safer to stay in the corner, be modest and inconspicuous. In other and more positive terms, this fear leads to a definite recoiling from any aim which implies competition. This safety device is assured by a constant, accurately working process of automatic self-checking.

This self-checking process results in inhibitions, particularly inhibitions towards work, but also towards all steps necessary to the pursuit of one's aims, such as seizing opportunities, or revealing to others that one has certain goals or capacities. This eventually results in an incapacity to stand up for one's own wishes. The peculiar nature of these inhibitions is best demonstrated by the fact that these persons may be quite capable of fighting for the needs of others or for an impersonal cause. They will, for instance, act like this:

When playing an instrument with a poor partner, they will instinctively play worse than he, although otherwise they may be very competent. When discussing a subject with someone less intelligent than themselves, they will compulsively descend below his level. They will prefer to be in the rank and file, not to be identified with the superiors, not even to get an increase in salary, rationalizing this attitude in some way. Even their dreams will be dictated by this need for reassurance. Instead of utilizing the liberty of a dream to imagine themselves in glorious situations, they will actually see themselves, in their dreams, in humble or even humiliating situations.

This self-checking process does not restrict itself to activities in the pursuit of some aim, but going beyond that, tends to undermine the self-confidence, which is a prerequisite for any accomplishment, by means of self-belittling. The function of self-belittling in this context is to eliminate oneself from any competition. In most cases these persons are not aware of actually disparaging themselves, but are aware of the results only as they feel themselves inferior to others and take for granted their own inadequacy.

The presence of these feelings of inferiority is one of the most common psychic disorders of our time and culture. Let me say a few more words about them. The genesis of inferiority feelings is not always in neurotic competition. They present complex phenomena and may be determined by various conditions. But that they do result from, and stand in the service of, a recoiling from competition, is a basic and ever-present implication. They result from a recoiling inasmuch as they are the expression of a discrepancy between high-pitched ideals and real accomplishment. The fact, however, that these painful feelings at the same time fulfill the important function of making secure the recoiling attitude itself, becomes evident through the vigor with which this position is defended when attacked. Not only will no evidence of competence or attractiveness ever convince these persons, but they may actually become scared or angered by any attempt to convince them of their positive qualities.

The surface pictures resulting from this situation may be widely divergent. Some persons appear thoroughly convinced of their unique importance and may be anxious to demonstrate their superiority on every occasion, but betray their insecurity in an excessive sensitivity to every criticism, to every dissenting opinion, or every lack of responsive admiration. Others are just as thoroughly convinced of their incompetence or unworthiness, or of being unwanted or unappreciated; yet they betray their actually great demands in that they react with open or concealed hostility to every frustration of their unacknowledged demands. Still others will waver constantly in their self-estimation between feeling themselves all-important and feeling, for instance, honestly amazed that anyone pays any attention to them.

If you have followed me thus far, I can now proceed to outline the particular vicious circle in which these persons are moving. It is important here, as in every complex neurotic picture, to recognize the vicious circle, because, if we overlook it and simplify the complexity of the processes going on by assuming a simple cause-effect relation, we either fail to get an understanding of the emotions involved, or attribute an undue importance to some one cause. As an example of this error, I might mention regarding a highly emotion-charged rivalry attitude as derived directly from rivalry with the father. Roughly, the vicious circle looks like this:

The failures, in conjunction with a feeling of weakness and defeat, lead to a feeling of envy towards all persons who are more successful, or merely more secure or better contented with life.

This envy may be manifest or it may be repressed under the pressure of the same anxiety which led to a repression of, and a recoiling from, rivalry. It may be entirely wiped out of consciousness and represented by the substitution of a blind admiration; it may be kept from awareness by a disparaging attitude towards the person concerned. Its effect, however, is apparent in the incapacity to grant to others what one has been forced to deny oneself. At any rate, no matter to what degree the envy is repressed or expressed, it implies an increase in the existing hostility against people and consequently an increase in the anxiety, which now takes the particular form of an irrational fear of the envy of others.

The irrational nature of this fear is shown in two ways: (1) it exists regardless of the presence or absence of envy in the given situation; and (2) its intensity is out of proportion to the dangers menacing from the side of the envious competitors. This irrational side of the fear of envy always remains unconscious, at least in non-psychotic persons, therefore it is never corrected by a reality-testing process, and is all the more effective in the direction of reinforcing the existing tendencies to recoil.

Consequently the feeling of own insignificance grows, the hostility against people grows, and the anxiety grows. We thus return to the beginning, because now the fantasies come up, with about this content: "I wish I were more powerful, more attractive, more intelligent than all the others, then I should be safe, and besides, I could defeat them and step on them." Thus we see an ever-increasing deviation of the ambitions towards the stringent, fantastic, and hostile.

This pyramiding process may come to a stand-still under various conditions, usually at an inordinate expense in loss of expansiveness and vitality. There is often some sort of resignation as to personal ambitions, in turn permitting the diminution of anxieties as to competition, with the inferiority feelings and inhibitions continuing.

It is now time, however, to make a reservation. It is in no way self-evident that ambition of the "no-one-but-me" type must necessarily evoke anxieties. There are persons quite capable of brushing aside or crushing everyone in the way of their ruthless pursuit of personal power. The question then is: Under what special condition is anxiety evoked in neurotically competitive people?

The answer is that they at the same time want to be loved. While most persons who pursue an asocial ambition in life care little for the affection or the opinion of others, the neurotics, although possessed by the same kind of competitiveness, simultaneously have a boundless craving for affec-

tion and appreciation. Therefore, as soon as they make any move towards self-assertion, competition, or success, they begin to dread losing the affection of others, and must automatically check their aggressive impulses. This conflict between ambition and affection is one of the gravest and most typical dilemmas of the neurotics of our time.

Why are these two incompatible strivings so frequently present in the same individual? They are related to each other in more than one way. The briefest formulation of this relationship would perhaps be that they both grow out of the same sources, namely, anxieties, and they both serve as a means of reassurance against the anxieties. Power and affection may both be safeguards. They generate each other, check each other, and reinforce each other. These interrelations can be observed most accurately within the analytic situation, but sometimes are obvious from only a casual knowledge of the life history.

In the life history may be found, for instance, an atmosphere in childhood lacking in warmth and reliability, but rife with frightening elements —battles between the parents, injustice, cruelty, oversolicitousness—generation of an increased need for affection—disappointments—development of an outspoken competitiveness—inhibition—attempts to get affection on the basis of weakness, helplessness, or suffering. We sometimes hear that a youngster has suddenly turned to ambition after an acute disappointment in his need for affection, and then given up the ambition on falling in love.

Particularly when the expansive and aggressive desires have been severely curbed in early life by a forbidding atmosphere, the excessive need for reassuring affection will play a major role. As a guiding principle for behavior this implies a yielding to the wishes or opinions of others rather than asserting one's own wishes or opinions; an over-valuation of the significance for one's own life of expressions of fondness from others, and a dependence on such expressions. And similarly, it implies an overvaluation of signs of rejection and a reacting to such signs with apprehension and defensive hostility. Here again a vicious circle begins easily and reinforces the single elements: In diagram it looks somewhat like this:

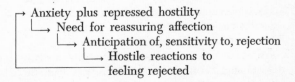

These reactions explain why emotional contact

with others that is attained on the basis of anxiety can be at best only a very shaky and easily shattered bridge between individuals, and why it always fails to bring them out of their emotional isolation. It may, however, serve to cope with anxieties and even get one through life rather smoothly, but only at the expense of growth and personality development, and only if circumstances are quite favorable.

Let us ask now, which special features in our culture may be responsible for the frequent occurrence of the neurotic structures just described?

We live in a competitive, individualistic culture. Whether the enormous economic and technical achievements of our culture were and are possible only on the basis of the competitive principle is a question for the economist or sociologist to decide. The psychologist, however, can evaluate the personal price we have paid for it.

It must be kept in mind that competition not only is a driving force in economic activities, but that it also pervades our personal life in every respect. The character of all our human relationships is moulded by a more or less outspoken competition. It is effective in the family between siblings, at school, in social relations (keeping up with the Joneses), and in love life.

In love, it may show itself in two ways: the genuine erotic wish is often overshadowed or replaced by the merely competitive goal of being the most popular, having the most dates, love letters, lovers, being seen with the most desirable man or woman. Again, it may pervade the love relationship itself. Marriage partners, for example, may be living in an endless struggle for supremacy, with or without being aware of the nature or even of the existence of this combat.

The influence on human relations of this competitiveness lies in the fact that it creates easily aroused envy towards the stronger ones, contempt for the weaker, distrust towards everyone. In consequence of all these potentially hostile tensions, the satisfaction and reassurance which one can get out of human relations are limited and the individual becomes more or less emotionally isolated. It seems that here, too, mutually reinforcing interactions take place, so far as insecurity and dissatisfaction in human relations in turn compel people to seek gratification and security in ambitious strivings, and vice versa.

Another cultural factor relevant to the structure of our neurosis lies in our attitude towards failure and success. We are inclined to attribute success to good personal qualities and capacities, such as competence, courage, enterprise. In religious terms this attitude was expressed by saying that success was due to God's grace. While these qualities

may be effective—and in certain periods, such as the pioneer days, may have represented the only conditions necessary—this ideology omits two essential facts: (1) that the possibility for success is strictly limited; even external conditions and personal qualities being equal, only a comparative few can possibly attain success; and (2) that other factors than those mentioned may play the decisive role, such as, for example, unscrupulousness or fortuitous circumstances. Inasmuch as these factors are overlooked in the general evaluation of success, failures, besides putting the person concerned in a factually disadvantageous position, are bound to reflect on his self-esteem.

The confusion involved in this situation is enhanced by a sort of double moral. Although, in fact, success meets with adoration almost without regard to the means employed in securing it, we are at the same time taught to regard modesty and an undemanding, unselfish attitude as social or religious virtues, and are rewarded for them by praise and affection. The particular difficulties which confront the individual in our culture may be summarized as follows: for the competitive struggle he needs a certain amount of available aggressiveness; at the same time, he is required to be modest, unselfish, even self-sacrificing. While the competitive life situation with the hostile tensions involved in it creates an enhanced need of security, the chances of attaining a feeling of safety in human relations—love, friendship, social contacts—are at the same time diminished. The estimation of one's personal value is all too dependent on the degree of success attained, while at the same time the possibilities for success are limited and the success itself is dependent, to a great extent, on fortuitous circumstances or on personal qualities of an asocial character.

Perhaps these sketchy comments have suggested to you the direction in which to explore the actual relationship of our culture to our personality and its neurotic deviations. Let us now consider the relation of this conception to the views of Freud on culture and neurosis.

The essence of Freud's views on this subject can be summarized, briefly, as follows: Culture is the result of a sublimation of biologically given sexual and aggressive drives—"sexual" in the extended connotation Freud has given the term. Sublimation presupposes unwitting suppression of these instinctual drives. The more complete the suppression of these drives, the higher the cultural development. As the capacity for sublimating is limited, and as the intensive suppression of primitive drives without sublimation may lead to neurosis, the growth of civilization must inevitably imply a growth of neurosis. Neuroses are the price humanity has to pay for cultural development.

The implicit theoretical presupposition underlying this train of thought is the belief in the existence of biologically determined human nature, or, more precisely, the belief that oral, anal, genital, and aggressive drives exist in all human beings in approximately equal quantities. Variations in character formation from individual to individual, as from culture to culture, are due, then, to the varying intensity of the suppression required, with the addition that this suppression can affect the different kinds of drives in varying degrees.

This viewpoint of Freud's seems actually to encounter difficulties with two groups of data. (1) Historical and anthropological findings do not support the assumption that the growth of civilization is in a direct ratio to the growth of instinct suppression. (2) Clinical experience of the kind indicated in this paper suggests that neurosis is due not simply to the quantity of suppression of one or the other instinctual drives, but rather to difficulties caused by the conflicting character of the demands which a culture imposes on its individuals. The differences in neuroses typical of different cultures may be understood to be conditioned by the amount and quality of conflicting demands within the particular culture.

In a given culture, those persons are likely to become neurotic who have met these culturally determined difficulties in accentuated form, mostly through the medium of childhood experiences; and who have not been able to solve their difficulties, or have solved them only at great expense to personality.

Selection 81

Mental Abnormality

Robert E. L. Faris

As indicated in the previous selection, one of the chief social problems in the modern world is that aspect of personal and social disorganization called *mental illness* or *mental abnormality*. Whichever term is used, we are speaking of a difference of degree, not of kind; we are concerned with a continuum, not with separate, discrete entities. Moreover, we are speaking of behavior or conditions which vary so widely that they bear little or no resemblance to each other.

The amount of mental disorder in the United States is not accurately known, but it is estimated that about one in twenty persons spends some time in a mental institution and that three times as many could benefit from formal treatment. Possibly one third of the manpower lost to the armed services has been due to mental-emotional problems. That mental illness is a matter of degree is a great hindrance in recording numbers of cases.

Psychiatrists distinguish between various degrees and types of mental illness by using the terms *psychosis* and *neurosis*. Psychosis is a relatively complete break with reality; neurosis is a less disabling illness, usually not severe enough to require hospitalization. In one sense sociologists are more concerned with neurotics, for these people remain in society, often marry, and frequently form a part of various groups. Some of them engage in criminal behavior, some become hatemongers, some become saints, some become denizens of skid row; in each case they remain a part of society and influence other people. Sociologists are not directly concerned with the diagnosis and treatment of psychotics, but they see the significance for society of, for example, one Midwestern penal institution that in 1961 had a ward of over 300 criminally insane who jointly received the services of a psychiatrist one half-day a week—on the weeks he came at all! Important also is the fact that new treatments, especially tranquilizers and improved parole systems, are successfully returning an increasing number of cases to society.

Faris points out as clearly as did Horney that abnormal behavior is, within limits, a matter of cultural relativity and that it must therefore be defined in relation to the cultural context. This "cultural relativity" may be seen, for example, in the wide range of religious behaviors in various cults and sects and denominations in America. It is not surprising that the highest rates of mental disorder in large cities are in the hotel and "hobohemia" (area of homeless men) and "skid row" locations, or that the rate progressively declines as one moves in any direction outward from the center of the city. Faris quite properly uses schizophrenia, one of the most prevalent psychoses, as his index of measurement, and the conclusions he draws seem applicable to mental disorder in general.

The human mind cannot be fully understood if it is conceived solely in terms of a physiological mechanism. The mechanism does not by itself produce the complex adaptive behavior which we recognize as human until there has been an integration which is built up in social experience and is sustained by interaction within an effective social organization. Mental normality and efficiency requires participation in organized social relations. It is to be expected, therefore, that any disorganization of a society would be reflected in some departure from mental normality among some of its members.

GENERAL NATURE OF UNCONVENTIONALITY AND MENTAL ABNORMALITY

Mental abnormality consists of behavior which is in some sense defective. It may result from any of a number of breaks in the mechanism which is necessary for efficient and orderly behavior. These breaks may be in the physiological mechanism—brain, glands, nervous system—or in the social organization. They may result from injuries or infections of various kinds, or from overprotection and isolation. The particular set of symptoms that accompanies the basic maladjustment to society is usually the product of the life-history of the individual, the unique experiences he has undergone.

The problem of precise definition of mental abnormality involves difficulties similar to those involved in the definition of crime. Normality of behavior is, within limits, a matter of cultural relativity. Just as certain actions are considered to be criminal in one culture and are approved in another, so are certain forms of behavior and thought considered normal in some areas and

abnormal in others. Furthermore, the same behavior may be normal or abnormal within our own society, depending upon the context in which it occurs. There can, then, be no universal and objective definition of insanity. It must be defined in relation to the cultural context.

For a broad but useful classification, behavior may be considered with respect to intelligibility and approval. Persons whose actions are both intelligible and approved are simply good persons, conventional and appreciated members of a community. If their actions are intelligible but not approved, they constitute breaches of custom, sins, or crimes. There may occasionally occur instances in which actions are unintelligible but valued—this is the case with the genius and the mystical leader. Finally, when actions are neither intelligible nor approved, the persons are held to be insane.

Interesting variations regarding both intelligibility and approval of certain actions may be found within our culture. Uncertainty on either of these points often leads to confusion regarding the normality of the behavior of a person. Residents of college towns, for example, are inclined to be tolerant of the public pranks that accompany hazing and the initiation activities of college fraternities. The same behavior, however, performed in distant places, away from the context of college life, is subject to being judged insane. The crucial point is often whether or not one can explain why he indulges in such actions—whether a social context is available to account for it. When a person acts as if he were either "drunk or crazy," it is with a sense of relief that his

From Robert E. L. Faris, *Social Disorganization,* Second Edition, pp. 323-382. Copyright 1955, The Ronald Press Company.

friends discover that he has in fact been consuming quantities of alcohol.

Occasionally statements that are truthful and sensible are misunderstood by persons of limited knowledge, so that an incorrect suspicion of mental abnormality is formed. During the first world war, a recruit, while undergoing the classification procedure, answered the sergeant's question regarding his occupation by stating truthfully that he was an anthropologist. Presumably the sergeant had not heard of the term, for he handed the soldier a slip which called for him to report for a special psychiatric interview.

In another instance observed by the author, an elderly man who had been for some years confined to a wheel chair was brought to a psychopathic hospital for examination. His neighbors in his home town had taken the initiative in arranging the interview because he had begun to call himself a philosopher. Having known him for all of his lifetime, the neighbors knew he was nothing of the kind and presumed that his mind was failing. What they did not realize, apparently, was that in his extensive reading, the principal occupation of his sedentary life, he had undertaken a certain amount of study of philosophical literature and had begun to feel at home in the subject. The findings of the hospital staff were that he was not insane, and he was sent home.

It is not uncommon for a person to be taken forcibly to an urban psychopathic hospital because of a solo public display of great religious zeal or frenzy. In most parts of the country this type of behavior is held to be so inappropriate that it could only be an indication of insanity. In parts of the rural South, however, particularly among members of the small and "primitive" religious sects, it is expected that religious emotions will be openly expressed, and it is often regarded as desirable that members should stand on public streets and attempt to enlighten and convert those who pass by. Such persons encounter little danger of being held for mental examination as long as they pursue this activity in the areas in which it is understood.

Boisen, in a study of prophets and other religious leaders and zealots, has shown that there are many persons who, because of their religious activities, have been held to be insane, while other persons who exhibited very similar traits and were able to gain a following became leaders and founders of sects. In some cases it appears that only the minor accidents which determine success or failure in drawing persons into a new organization were the determining factors in the fate of the would-be leader. It may be that some unbalanced fanatics living in modern cities would even have escaped commitment and become prophets if they had had the fortune to reside in regions of less sophistication.

EXTENT AND LOCATION OF MENTAL DISORDERS IN MODERN SOCIETY

Because of the indefinite borderlines of the definitions of mental abnormality, it is difficult to gather precise statistics on the prevalence of these conditions, and to make accurate comparisons covering different times and places. There has been a familiar item appearing in the press from time to time, pointing out that if the rate of increase in mental disorders continues without interruption, it will not be many decades before the entire population is insane. On the other hand, critical examination of the statistics has led to the questioning of whether these figures really prove that there is any true increase at all in the standardized rates. The figures may only show improvement in diagnoses, increases in facilities for hospitalization, and perhaps aging of the population, which allows more persons who might otherwise have died young to survive long enough to have a mental disorder. The greatest difficulty in making accurate estimates is the problem of ascertaining the number of persons who have mental disorders but who are not hospitalized or put in the care of a physician.

One of the most accurate means of stating the probable incidence of insanity in the population has been supplied by Malzberg, who has computed the expectation of mental disease in New York State by a technique similar to that used for stating the expectation of life from the life table.[1] For each year of age from one to one hundred, he presents, for males and females separately, the number developing a mental disease during the remainder of life of 1,000 alive and sane at the beginning of the age interval. At birth, the expectation for males in 1940 was 80.5, and for females 82.0. This meant that nearly one out of twelve newborn infants would develop mental disease at some time of life in New York State. This is a far higher expectation than had prevailed twenty years earlier, when figures for the same age for males and females were 48.1 and 48.2 respectively. In 1940 the expectation for males aged nine to fourteen was 85.4, slightly more than one out of 12; among older age groups the rate was progressively lower. For those males

---

[1] Benjamin Malzberg, "The Expectation of Mental Disease in New York State, 1920, 1930, 1940," in *Trends of Mental Disease* (New York: King's Crown Press, 1945), pp. 42-55.

who reached their hundredth birthday, sane, the expectation of developing a mental disease during the remaining years was only 39.2, or slightly less than one-half the expectation at birth.

Since the Malzberg study is based on figures for admissions to hospitals, it omits the unknown numbers of persons who are never committed. There is no basis for a reasonable guess concerning these, so it can only be stated that somewhat more than one out of twelve persons, as of 1940, might be expected to develop some mental abnormality during their lifetimes. This is of course an impressive figure in itself. Pollock has, in addition, made calculations concerning the economic loss resulting from this high rate of mental disease.[2] On the basis of 1931 figures for the United States as a whole, he estimates that the annual cost for hospitalization is approximately 208 millions of dollars and the annual loss of earnings 569 millions. The grand total, therefore, is about 777 millions for the cost of hospitalized cases alone. One reason for the heavy expense is that persons hospitalized for mental diseases occupy space for longer periods, on the average, than do persons hospitalized for other afflictions.

In general the hospitalization rates are higher in cities than in rural areas. Landis and Page, presenting the first-admission figures for 1933, show that for all ages the rate for urban males is the highest, after which comes the rate for urban females, and then rural males, with rural females the lowest of all.[3] The contrast is not the same, however, for each of the various classifications of disorders. The greatest contrast is found in the rates for alcoholic psychoses, which were about three and a half times as high in urban areas. General paralysis, psychopathic personality, cerebral arteriosclerosis, paranoia, senile dementia, schizophrenia, involutional melancholia, and the psychoneuroses were found to have higher urban rates, the contrast being greater in those named earlier. In the manic-depressive psychoses, throughout most of the age range the rate was highest among urban females, while in most of the same age range the next highest rates were among rural males. The urban male rates and the rural female rates were somewhat lower until the middle years of life.

RELATION OF MENTAL ABNORMALITY TO
URBAN SOCIAL DISORGANIZATION

By far the greatest and most revealing contrasts of rates of mental disorders have been found in the various sections of large industrial cities. Here the contrasts are not a matter of high rates being merely three times greater than low rates; the contrasts are on the order of ten to one or greater. Furthermore, the study of variations in urban districts whose characteristics are already well known yields far more meaningful information than does the cruder contrast between urban and rural areas.

The most intensive study of urban insanity rates has been carried on in the city of Chicago. Studies of a similar character, though of lesser scope, have been made in Providence, Milwaukee, Saint Louis, Cleveland, and other cities. These latter studies, as far as they go, confirm the findings in Chicago.

The basis of the Chicago study consisted of 34,864 cases of mental disorder admitted to four state hospitals and eight private hospitals in the Chicago region. . . . These cases were classified on the basis of the various subcommunities of the city in which the patient lived before his first admission to a hospital, and rates were computed for each area, based on the population aged fifteen and over. The lowest average annual rate in the city during this period was 48 per 100,000 population in an outlying residential area. The highest rate, more than ten times as high as the lowest, was 499, and it was that in the central business district which includes a hotel and hobo area. The next highest rate of 480 was found in an adjacent hobo and rooming-house area. The ten subcommunities with the highest rates, in fact, were all located near the center, and were hobo and rooming-house areas or Negro apartment-house areas in the most deteriorated part of the Negro districts. In general, the pattern of rates in the city area consists of a sharp concentration of high rates in the central areas and a progressive decline in all outward directions, with the lowest rates arranged along the outlying stable residential districts. Where industrial zones are located in outlying areas, as in the Lake Calumet area on the southern edge, or along the western industrial fringes, the rates are somewhat higher than in nearby residential areas.

Because of intensive research in the characteristics of the local communities in Chicago, largely carried on by the faculty and students of the Sociology Department of the University of Chicago, the conditions in these areas are quite well known. It is precisely in these areas of highest

[2] Horatio M. Pollock, *Mental Disease and Social Welfare* (Utica, N.Y.: State Hospitals Press, 1941), pp. 83-84.
[3] Carney Landis and James D. Page, *Modern Society and Mental Disease* (New York: Farrar & Rinehart, Inc., 1930), pp. 44-55.

insanity rates that other indices of social disorganization are most noticeable. In the hotel and rooming-house areas the rates of suicide, venereal infection, and family disorganization are extremely high, while in the foreign-born slum areas are concentrated the high rates of juvenile delinquency and crime. These are areas of high mobility in the population, of extreme poverty and demoralization, and of cultural heterogeneity and confusion of mores. . . .

RELATION OF SEPARATE MENTAL DISORDERS
TO URBAN CONDITIONS

Schizophrenia

While definitions of schizophrenia and descriptions of the symptoms vary in the technical literature on the subject, it can be fairly stated that the essential character of schizophrenic behavior is its unreal, dreamlike quality—an appearance of being out of touch with conventional reality—for which condition no obvious physical cause can be found. Delusions and hallucinations are common, as are inappropriate emotional states, and in many cases a progressive deterioration of intellectual capacity.

The cases of schizophrenia in the Chicago series constitute the largest single group of disorders, including 7,253 cases, or about 22 per cent of total cases of mental disorder. The distribution of these cases is quite similar to that of all types of mental disorders combined. Because of the importance of these cases in the total, this result cannot be considered surprising. The highest rate of schizophrenia, like the highest rate of all insanity, is in the central area, and the next highest rates are in the adjacent districts. The lowest rate, in an outlying area, is 14 (per 100,000 population of ages 15-64) which is less than one tenth as large as the highest rate of 150. The pattern shows the same gradation from the center outward, and the same local increases in outlying industrial districts. Rates are high both in the mobile hobo and rooming-house areas, and in the foreign-born and Negro districts. . . .

Nature of schizophrenic symptoms

Some of the traits of the schizophrenic have a resemblance to the symptoms that develop in persons who have been isolated for extended periods. These latter often develop a rich fantasy life, with inappropriate or unconventional emotions, and apparently in time also suffer deterioration of the mind. They also have, in common with the schizophrenics, a deterioration of the wish to associate with other persons—a decline in the sociability motive. The development of seclusiveness in turn contributes to further isolation where the preference of the person is a factor in social contacts.

It has been held that this trait of seclusiveness is a central aspect of the abnormality of the schizophrenic and that it may be a hereditary deficiency. It is not entirely necessary to assume a hereditary cause, however, for many persons appear to lose their preference for sociability after, and as a consequence of, a period of isolation which was not a matter of their own choice. Observation of long-term prisoners held in solitary confinement, for example, has shown that many of these, though confined against their will, nevertheless in time lose their desire for freedom and social contacts with others. Sociability is thus probably not an inborn trait, but is acquired individually in the process of interaction with other persons. Apparently it is a trait that must be continuously nourished by social intercourse to avoid deterioration of the impulse to associate with others.

In studies of early experiences in the lives of patients diagnosed as schizophrenics, it is often possible to observe clear indications of a partial social isolation, in many cases not of the person's own choosing. This isolation is essentially a restriction of the person's social world to a very small group and a deprivation of the normal intimate primary relations with persons outside of the family. Such partial isolation weakens the social adaptability of the person by depriving him of the knowledge of how to deal with other persons. His partial failures cause discouragement and further isolation, in a process which can properly be termed a vicious circle.

A special examination by the author of 101 cases of schizophrenia which, in order to avoid a bias of selection, were taken consecutively from the records of a state hospital in New England, yields useful information on the factors involved in isolation. Approximately half of the cases (53) were older persons whose friends or relatives could not be located or could not supply information about the early life of the patient. Of the remainder, where sufficient information was available about childhood experiences, the case records revealed that more than half, 27 as against 21, had been definitely sociable in childhood. These were clearly not deficient by heredity, but developed their disorder as a result of abnormal social experience. In the typical case there were three stages visible: first, a stage of normal sociability, in which the child wished and sought for companionship; second, a process of exclusion by others, accompanied by a continued effort to gain their approval and comradeship; third, acceptance of defeat, involving a change of interests away from social intercourse and the construction of a system of rationalization, developing into an interaction between the growing preference for seclusiveness and further exclusion by others in the vicious-circle process.

While apparently any of a number of fortuitous conditions may start the exclusion condition—deafness, inability to speak English, physical deformities, and the like—by far the most common condition involved is the development within the family of the traits of the "overprotected child" —the pampered, egocentric, intolerant product of too much adoration by a parent—and the inability of such a child to gain acceptance into groups of normal children. Of the 101 cases in the series examined, there were fifty-four in which the factors producing isolation were apparent, and of these, twenty-nine were unmistakably of this "spoiled child" type.

While the overprotection or pampering of children appears to be a factor in the development of schizophrenia, it is not to be supposed that this is by itself sufficient. There are many children subjected to such influences who in time outgrow their egocentric and infantile traits, usually by means of participating in the activities of children who do not grant their pampered playmates exceptional status. They learn from other children that they are not in fact more precious, able, and important than any others, but that this is only a peculiar conception that mothers have of them, as other mothers often have of their own children. But, where there are special difficulties in the way of gaining entrance into activities of other children, there are possibilities of developing the isolation process. It is in the slum areas of the city, where delinquency rates are high and where juveniles have a tradition of toughness, that children are least tolerant of the pampered and egocentric weakling who cries for his mother when frustrated. Possibly it is this fact that accounts for the greater tendency for peoples in these areas to develop schizophrenia. Elsewhere, in stable residential neighborhoods, or in suburbs, there may be a greater availability of sympathetic playmates and a higher degree of parental and neighborhood cooperation which eases the process of assimilation of the spoiled child into play groups with other children. . . .

SUMMARY

There is a general relation between the social disorganization of industrial civilization and some of the most important forms of mental abnormality. The incidence is not only greater in general in cities than in rural areas, but is by far the greatest in the parts of the large cities in which the social disorganization is most intense. The weight of the evidence is that in the central areas of the city—the hotel, hobo, rooming-house, and low-income slums populated by the foreign-born—are to be found the principal breeding grounds of insanity.

The processes do not operate in a vague general way to produce mental abnormality, but in specific ways. General paralysis, for example, has its high incidence in rooming-house areas because of the social processes which locate there the prostitution traffic and which supply the patronage which becomes subject thereby to venereal infection. Since the sources of infection are easy to locate, there is little scientific difficulty in suggesting a means of elimination of this particular disease. The obstacles, however, are political and social, and our understanding and control in these fields has not so far been sufficient to produce universal abolition of commercial prostitution. The principal barrier, and probably the last one which will be removed, is the general political corruption that exists in many large cities, permeating not merely the city administrations and police organizations, but also business interests and even a good proportion of the citizenry at large.

Alcoholic psychoses have been shown to develop in greatest frequency in those parts of the city where chronic alcoholism is greatest, and the explanation for this . . . possibly lies in the unsatisfying nature of the life available to residents of these areas, and in certain factors of culture and personality. Schizophrenia appears to grow out of a complex of family and neighborhood processes and to be complicated by confusions that exist within the culture. The neuroses seem to be related to social processes producing soft personalities which are thrown suddenly against extreme hardships of life from which they cannot withdraw, usually because of social pressure.

Some psychoses remain at present unexplained by conditions of social disorganization, although it is possible that further knowledge will in time show connections not now visible. Some have a clear-cut physiological basis that is related to sociological conditions only in the indirect manner in which are virtually all diseases, accidents, malnutrition, and the like. Since, however, those which are clearly related to the extreme disorganization of cities constitute the great majority of cases and the major burden of expense, it is a reasonable expectation that any possible stabilization of society might also bring, for the first time since careful records have been kept, a substantial reduction in the incidence of mental disorder.

Selection *82*

Cats, Kicks, and Color

Harold Finestone

The two preceding selections have dealt in a general way with mental disorders; this selection is very specific in that it deals with one particular category of a social problem related to mental illness. Drug addiction does not have a clear-cut etiology. Except for marijuana, continued use of most common drugs causes a change in the body chemistry of the user, so that when something interferes with his normal intake of the drug, he suffers "withdrawal" pains. Addiction in this sense is physiological, and physical cure can be accomplished. Unfortunately, most users have a reason for taking the drug in the first place—they use it to ease their problems and achieve euphoria. Such use sets up a psychological addiction, which is extremely difficult to cure. The addict can rarely "kick his habit," both because of the physical pain and mental travail involved and because the psychological, social, and cultural causes of his addiction usually remain untreated.

Although drug addiction has been a social problem in America for many decades, its general pattern has recently changed. The proportion of known addicts in the population has been decreasing for nearly half a century, and the characteristic user has changed. Since World War II there has been a sizable increase in the use of drugs by young people—particularly lower-class adolescents in slum areas of large cities. In fact, the United States leads the Western World both in number of juvenile and young-adult users and, despite the overall proportionate decline, in number of addicts.

The problem of drug addiction lies not so much in its effect on the user as in its social correlates. The addict's whole life must be oriented around his drug and the attainment of it in the necessary quantity. Rarely can young people support their addiction continuously from legal earnings, so they turn to theft and prostitution. The exhorbitant cost of the drug pauperizes all but a very few users, and all are exploited by the underworld, which finds the sale of drugs enormously profitable.

Most addicts do not continue to receive a real sense of euphoria from their drug; its use merely prevents the pain and discomfort which result from its absence. With each use, the addict sinks deeper into addiction. Reportedly, most persons who voluntarily enter institutions for the treatment of addiction do so not to be cured but to reduce their drug needs to a financially manageable amount. Opium derivatives, especially heroin and morphine, are very expensive; cocaine is somewhat less so; and marijuana is the cheapest, both because it is easy to obtain and because it is no more habit forming than alcohol. In Great Britain, where the use of drugs is now legal and where they are administered cheaply by any physician, drug addiction rates are very, very low compared to those in America.

In the following selection, Finestone describes in detail and then analyzes a very specific type of drug addict—the young, urban, Negro male from the slum area of Chicago. He shows how the behavior, attitudes, and values of this type of addict are all discernible and to a degree predictable—that is, the "cat" is social, his behavior is sociocultural, and he tends to follow group behavior patterns. In fact, here is an example of a delinquent (or criminal) subculture like that theorized by Cohen and Short. The patterning and uniformity of the values, attitudes, and behavior of the Negro "cat" and the generally social nature of his "kick" demonstrate the degree to which his addiction is a social, as opposed to a strictly psychological, problem.

Growing recognition that the most recent manifestation of the use of opiates in this country has been predominantly a young peoples' problem has resulted in some speculation as to the nature of this generation of drug users. Is it possible to form an accurate conception as to what "manner of man" is represented by the current species of young drug addict? Intensive interviews between 1951 and 1953 with over fifty male colored users of heroin in their late teens and early twenties selected from several of the areas of highest incidence of drug use in Chicago served to elicit from them the expression of many common attitudes, values, schemes of behavior, and general social orientation. Moreover, since there was every reason to believe that such similarities had preceded their introduction to heroin, it appeared that it was by virtue of such shared features that they had been unusually receptive to the spread of opiate use. Methodologically, their common patterns of behavior suggested the heuristic value of the construction of a social type. The task of this paper is to depict this social type, and to present a hypothetical formulation to account for the form it has taken.

No special justification appears to be necessary for concentrating in this paper on the social type of the young colored drug user. One of the distinctive properties of the distribution of drug use as a social problem, at least in Chicago, is its high degree of both spatial and racial concentration. In fact, it is a problem which in this city can be pinpointed with great accuracy as having its incidence preponderantly among the young male colored persons in a comparatively few local community areas. The following delineation of the generic characteristics of young colored drug users constitutes in many respects an ideal type. No single drug addict exemplified all of the traits to be depicted but all of them revealed several of them to a marked degree.

The young drug user was a creature of contrasts. Playing the role of the fugitive and pariah as he was inevitably forced to do, he turned up for interviews in a uniformly ragged and dirty condition. And yet he talked with an air of superiority derived from his identification with an elite group, the society of "cats." He came in wearing a non-functional tie clip attached to his sport shirt and an expensive hat as the only indications that he was concerned with his appearance and yet displayed in his conversation a highly developed sense of taste in men's clothing and a high valuation upon dressing well. He came from what were externally the drabbest, most overcrowded, and physically deteriorated sections of the city and yet discussed his pattern of living as though it were a consciously cultivated work of art.

Despite the location of his social world in the "asphalt jungle" of the "Blackbelt" he strictly eschewed the use of force and violence as a technique for achieving his ends or for the settling of problematic situations. He achieved his goals by indirection, relying, rather, on persuasion and on a repertoire of manipulative techniques. To deal with a variety of challenging situations, such as those arising out of his contacts with the police, with his past or potential victims, and with jilted "chicks," etc., he used his wits and his conversational ability. To be able to confront such contingencies with adequacy and without resort to violence was to be "cool." His idea was to get what he wanted through persuasion and ingratiation; to use the other fellow by deliberately outwitting him. Indeed, he regarded himself as immeasurably superior to the "gorilla," a person who resorted to force.

The image of himself as "operator" was projected onto the whole world about him and led to a complete scepticism as to other persons' motives. He could relate to people by outsmarting them, or through open-handed and often ruinous generosity, but his world seemed to preclude any relationship which was not part of a "scheme" or did not lend itself to an "angle." The most difficult puzzle for him to solve was the "square,"

From *Social Problems*, Vol. 5 (1957), 3-13.

the honest man. On the one hand the "square" was the hard-working plodder who lived by routine and who took honesty and the other virtues at their face value. As such he constituted the prize victim for the cat. On the other hand the cat harbored the sneaking suspicion that some squares were smarter than he, because they could enjoy all the forbidden pleasures which were his stock in trade and maintain a reputation for respectability in the bargain.

The cat had a large, colorful, and discriminating vocabulary which dealt with all phases of his experience with drugs. In addition, he never seemed to content himself with the conventional word for even the most commonplace objects. Thus he used "pad" for house, "pecks" for food, "flicks" for movies, "stick hall" for pool hall, "dig the scene" for observe, "box" for record player, "bread" for money, etc. In each instance the word he used was more concrete or earthier than the conventional word and such as to reveal an attitude of subtle ridicule towards the dignity and conventionality inherent in the common usage.

His soft convincing manner of speaking, the shocking earthiness and fancifulness of his vocabulary, together with the formidable gifts of charm and ingratiation which he deployed, all contributed to the dominant impression which the young drug user made as a person. Such traits would seem to have fitted naturally into a role which some cats had already played or aspired to play, that of the pimp. To be supported in idleness and luxury through the labors of one or more attractive "chicks" who shoplifted or engaged in prostitution or both and dutifully handed over the proceeds was one of his favorite fantasies. In contrast with the milieu of the white underworld, the pimp was not an object of opprobrium but of prestige.

The theme of the exploitation of the woman goes close to the heart of the cat's orientation to life, that is, his attitude towards work. Part of the cat's sense of superiority stems from his aristocratic disdain for work and for the subordination of self to superiors and to the repetitive daily routine entailed by work, which he regards as intolerable. The "square" is a person who toils for regular wages and who takes orders from his superiors without complaint.

In contrast with the "square," the cat gets by without working. Instead he keeps himself in "bread" by a set of ingenious variations on "begging, borrowing, or stealing." Each cat has his "hustle," and a "hustle" is any non-violent means of "making some bread" which does not require work. One of the legendary heroes of the cat is the man who is such a skillful con-man that he can sell "State Street" to his victim. Concretely, the cat is a petty thief, pickpocket, or pool shark, or is engaged in a variety of other illegal activities of the "conning" variety. A very few cats are actually living off the proceeds of their women "on the hustle."

The main purpose of life for the cat is to experience the "kick." Just as every cat takes pride in his "hustle," so every cat cultivates his "kick." A "kick" is any act tabooed by "squares" that heightens and intensifies the present moment of experience and differentiates it as much as possible from the humdrum routine of daily life. Sex in any of its conventional expressions is not a "kick" since this would not serve to distinguish the cat from the "square," but orgies of sex behavior and a dabbling in the various perversions and byways of sex pass muster as "kicks." Some "cats" are on an alcohol "kick," others on a marihuana "kick," and others on a heroin "kick." There is some interchangeability among these various "kicks" but the tendency is to select your "kick" and stay with it. Many of these young drug users, however, had progressed from the alcohol to the marihuana to the heroin "kick." Each "kick" has its own lore of appreciation and connoisseurship into which only its devotees are initiated.

In addition to his "kick" the cat sets great store on the enjoyment of music and on proper dress. To enjoy one's "kick" without a background of popular music is inconceivable. The cat's world of music has a distinctive galaxy of stars, and the brightest luminaries in his firmament are performers such as "Yardbird" (the late Charlie Parker) and disc jockeys such as Al Benson. Almost every cat is a frustrated musician who hopes some day to get his "horn" out of pawn, take lessons, and earn fame and fortune in the field of "progressive music."

The cat places a great deal of emphasis upon clothing and exercises his sartorial talents upon a skeletal base of suit, sport shirt, and hat. The suit itself must be conservative in color. Gaiety is introduced through the selection of the sport shirt and the various accessories, all so chosen and harmonized as to reveal an exquisite sense of taste. When the cat was not talking about getting his clothes out of pawn, he talked about getting them out of the cleaners. With nonchalant pride one drug user insisted that the most expensive sport shirts and hats in the city of Chicago were sold in a certain haberdashery on the South Side. The ideal cat would always appear in public impeccably dressed and be able to sport a complete change of outfit several times a day.

The cat seeks through a harmonious combination of charm, ingratiating speech, dress, music, the proper dedication to his "kick," and unrestrained generosity to make of his day to day life itself a gracious work of art. Everything is to be pleasant and everything he does and values is to contribute to a cultivated aesthetic approach to living. The "cool cat" exemplifies all of these elements in proper balance. He demonstrates his ability to "play it cool" in his unruffled manner of dealing with outsiders such as the police, and in the self-assurance with which he confronts emergencies in the society of "cats." Moreover, the "cat" feels himself to be any man's equal. He is convinced that he can go anywhere and mingle easily with anyone. For example, he rejects the type of music designated "the blues" because for him it symbolizes attitudes of submission and resignation which are repugnant and alien to his customary frame of mind.

It can be seen now why heroin use should make such a powerful appeal to the cat. It was the ultimate "kick." No substance was more profoundly tabooed by conventional middle-class society. Regular heroin use provides a sense of maximal social differentiation from the "square." The cat was at last engaged, he felt, in an activity completely beyond the comprehension of the "square." No other "kick" offered such an instantaneous intensification of the immediate moment of experience and set it apart from everyday experience in such spectacular fashion. Any words used by the cat to apply to the "kick," the experience of "being high," he applied to heroin in the superlative. It was the "greatest kick of them all."

In the formulation now to be presented the cat as a social type is viewed as a manifestation of a process of social change in which a new type of self-conception has been emerging among the adolescents of the lower socio-economic levels of the colored population in large urban centers. It is a self-conception rooted in the types of accommodation to a subordinate status achieved historically by the colored race in this country, a self-conception which has become increasingly articulated as it responded to and selected various themes from the many available to it in the milieu of the modern metropolis. Blumer's classification of social movements into general, specific, or expressive, appears to provide a useful framework for the analysis of the social type of the cat.

In terms of these categories the cat as a social type is the personal counterpart of an expressive social movement. The context for such a movement must include the broader community, which, by its policies of social segregation and discrimination, has withheld from individuals of the colored population the opportunity to achieve or to identify with status positions in the larger society. The social type of the cat is an expression of one possible type of adaptation to such blocking and frustration, in which a segment of the population turns in upon itself and attempts to develop within itself criteria for the achievement of social status and the rudiments of a satisfactory social life. Within his own isolated social world the cat attempts to give form and purpose to dispositions derived from but denied an outlet within the dominant social order.

What are these dispositions and in what sense may they be said to be derived from the dominant social order? Among the various interrelated facets of the life of the cat two themes are central, those of the "hustle" and the "kick." It is to be noted that they are in direct antithesis to two of the central values of the dominant culture, the "hustle" versus the paramount importance of the occupation for the male in our society, and the "kick" versus the importance of regulating conduct in terms of its future consequences. Thus, there appears to be a relationship of conflict between the central themes of the social type of the cat and those of the dominant social order. As a form of expressive behavior, however, the social type of the cat represents an indirect rather than a direct attack against central conventional values.

It is interesting to speculate on the reasons why a type such as the cat should emerge rather than a social movement with the objective of changing the social order. The forces coercing the selective process among colored male adolescents in the direction of expressive social movements are probably to be traced to the long tradition of accommodation to a subordinate status on the part of the Negro as well as to the social climate since the Second World War, which does not seem to have been favorable to the formation of specific social movements.

The themes of the "hustle" and "kick" in the social orientation of the cat are facts which appear to be overdetermined. For example, to grasp the meaning of the "hustle" to the cat one must understand it as a rejection of the obligation of the adult male to work. When asked for the reasons underlying his rejection of work the cat did not refer to the uncongenial and relatively unskilled and low paid jobs which, in large part, were the sole types of employment available to him. He emphasized rather that the routine of a job and the demand that he should apply himself continuously to his work task were the features that made work intolerable for him. The self-constraint required by work was construed as an unwarranted damper upon his love of spontaneity. The other undesirable element from his point of view was the authoritarian setting of most types of work with which he was familiar.

There are undoubtedly many reasons for the cat's rejection of work but the reasons he actually verbalized are particularly significant when interpreted as devices for sustaining his self-conception. The cat's feeling of superiority would be openly challenged were he to confront certain of the social realities of his situation, such as the discrimination exercised against colored persons looking for work and the fact that only the lowest status jobs are available to him. He avoided any mention of these factors which would have forced him to confront his true position in society and thus posed a threat to his carefully cherished sense of superiority.

In emphasizing as he does the importance of the "kick" the cat is attacking the value our society places upon planning for the future and the responsibility of the individual for such planning. Planning always requires some subordination and disciplining of present behavior in the interest of future rewards. The individual plans to go to college, plans for his career, plans for his family and children, etc. Such an orientation on the part of the individual is merely the personal and subjective counterpart of a stable social order and of stable social institutions, which not only permit but sanction an orderly progression of expectations with reference to others and to one's self. Where such stable institutions are absent or in the inchoate stages of development, there is little social sanction for such planning in the experience of the individual. Whatever studies are available strongly suggest that such are the conditions which tend to prevail in the lower socio-economic levels of the Negro urban community. Stable family and community organization is lacking in those areas of the city where drug use is concentrated. A social milieu which does not encourage the subordination and disciplining of present conduct in the interests of future rewards tends by default to enhance the present. The "kick" appears to be a logical culmination of this emphasis.

Accepting the emergence of the self-conception of the cat as evidence of a developing expressive social movement, we may phrase the central theoretical problem as follows: What are the distinctive and generic features of the cat's social orientation? Taking a cue from the work of Huizinga as developed in *Homo Ludens*, we propose that the generic characteristics of the social type of the cat are those of play. In what follows, Huizinga's conception of play as a distinctive type of human activity will be presented and then applied as a tool of analysis for rendering intelligible the various facets of the social orientation of the cat. It is believed that the concept of play indicates accurately the type of expressive social movement which receives its embodiment in the cat.

According to Huizinga the concept of play is a primary element of human experience and as such is not susceptible to exact definition. "The *fun* of playing resists all analysis, all logical interpretation. . . . Nevertheless it is precisely this fun-element that characterizes the essence of play." The common image of the young colored drug addict pictures him as a pitiful figure, a trapped unfortunate. There is a certain amount of truth in this image but it does not correspond to the conception which the young colored addict has of himself or to the impression that he tries to communicate to others. If it were entirely true it would be difficult to square with the fact that substantial numbers of young colored persons continue to become drug users. The cat experiences and manifests a certain zest in his mode of life which is far from self-pity. This fun element seemed to come particularly to the fore as the cat recounted his search for "kicks," the adventure of his life on the streets, and the intensity of his contest against the whole world to maintain his supply of drugs. Early in the cycle of heroin use itself there was invariably a "honeymoon" stage when the cat abandoned himself most completely to the experience of the drug. For some cats this "honeymoon" stage, in terms of their ecstatic preoccupation with the drug, was perpetual. For others it passed, but the exigencies of an insatiable habit never seemed to destroy completely the cat's sense of excitement in his way of life.

While Huizinga declines to define play, he does enumerate three characteristics which he considers to be proper to play. Each one of them when applied to the cat serves to indicate a generic feature of his social orientation.

(a) "First and foremost . . . all play is a voluntary activity." "Here we have the first main characteristic of play: that it is free, is in fact freedom." The concept of an expressive social movement assumes a social situation where existing social arrangements are frustrating and are no longer accepted as legitimate and yet where collective activity directed towards the modification of these limitations is not possible. The cat is "free" in the sense that he is a pre-eminent candidate for new forms of social organization and novel social practices. He is attempting to escape from certain features of the historical traditions of the Negro which he regards as humiliating. As an adolescent or young adult he is not fully assimilated into such social institutions as the family, school, church, or industry which may be available to him. Moreover, the social institutions which the Negroes brought with them when they migrated to the city have not as yet achieved stability or an adequate functioning relationship to the urban environment. As a Negro, and particularly as a Negro of low socio-economic status, he is excluded from many socializing experiences which adolescents in more advantaged sectors of the society take for granted. He lives in communities where the capacity of the population for effective collective action is extremely limited, and consequently there are few effective controls on his conduct besides that exercised by his peer group itself. He is fascinated by the varied "scenes" which the big city spreads out before him. Granted this setting, the cat adopts an adventurous attitude to life and is free to give his allegiance to new forms of activity.

(b) ". . . A second characteristic is closely connected with this (that is, the first characteristic of freedom), namely, that play is not 'ordinary' or 'real' life. It is rather a stepping out of 'real' life into a temporary sphere of activity with a disposition all of its own. Every child knows perfectly well that he is 'only pretending,' or that it was 'only for fun.' . . . This 'only pretending' quality of play betrays a consciousness of the inferiority of play compared with 'seriousness,' a feeling that seems to be something as primary as play itself. Nevertheless . . . the consciousness of play being 'only a pretend' does not by any means prevent it from proceeding with the utmost seriousness, with an absorption, a devotion that passes into rapture and, temporarily at least, completely abolishes that troublesome 'only' feeling."

It is implicit in the notion of an expressive social movement that, since direct collective action to modify the sources of dissatisfaction and restlessness is not possible, all such movements should appear under one guise, as forms of "escape." Persons viewing the problem of addiction from the perspective of the established social structure have been prone to make this interpretation. It is a gross oversimplification, however, as considered from the perspective of the young drug addict himself. The emergence of the self-conception of the cat is an attempt to deal with the problems of status and identity in a situation where participation in the life of the broader community is denied, but where the colored adolescent is becoming increasingly sensitive to the values, the goals, and the notions of success which obtain in the dominant social order.

"The caste pressures thus make it exceedingly difficult for an American Negro to preserve a true perspective of himself and his own group in relation to the larger white society. The increasing abstract knowledge of the world outside—of its opportunities, its rewards, its different norms of competition and cooperation—which results from the proceeding acculturation at the same time as there is increasing group isolation, only increases the tensions."

Such conditions of group isolation would appear to be fairly uniform throughout the Negro group. Although this isolation may be experienced differently at different social levels of the Negro community, certain features of the adaptations arrived at in response to this problem will tend to reveal similarities. Since the struggle for status takes place on a stage where there is acute sensitivity to the values and status criteria of the dominant white group, but where access to the means through which such values may be achieved is prohibited, the status struggle turning in on itself will assume a variety of distorted forms. Exclusion from the "serious" concerns of the broader community will result in such adaptations manifesting a strong element of "play."

Frazier in *Black Bourgeoisie* discusses the social adaptation of the Negro middle class as "The World of Make-Believe."

"The emphasis upon 'social' life or 'society' is one of the main props of the world of make-believe into which the black bourgeoisie has sought an escape from its inferiority and frustrations in American society. This world of make-believe, to be sure, is a reflection of the values of American society, but it lacks the economic basis that would give it roots in the world of reality."

In the Negro lower classes the effects of frustrations deriving from subordination to the whites may not be experienced as personally or as directly as they are by the Negro middle class, but the massive effects of residential segregation and the lack of stable social institutions and community organization are such as to reinforce strong feelings of group isolation even at the lowest levels of the society.

It is here suggested that the function performed by the emergence of the social type of the cat among Negro lower class adolescents is analogous to that performed by "The World of Make-Believe" in the Negro middle class. The development of a social type such as that of the cat is only possible in a situation where there is isolation from the broader community but great sensitivity to its goals, where the peer group pressures are extremely powerful, where institutional structures are weak, where models of success in the illegitimate world have strong appeals, where specific social movements are not possible, and where novel forms of behavior have great prestige. To give significance to his experience, the young male addict has developed the conception of a heroic figure, the "ideal cat," a person who is completely adequate to all situations, who controls his "kick" rather than letting it control him, who has a lucrative "hustle," who has no illusions as to what makes the world "tick," who is any man's equal, who basks in the admiration of his brother cats and associated "chicks," who hob-nobs with "celebs" of the musical world, and who in time himself may become a celebrity.

The cat throws himself into his way of life with a great deal of intensity but he cannot escape completely from the perspective, the judgments, and the sanctions of the dominant social order. He has to make place in his scheme of life for police, lockups, jails, and penitentiaries, to say nothing of the agonies of withdrawal distress. He is forced eventually to confront the fact that his role as a cat with its associated attitudes is largely a pose, a form of fantasy with little basis in fact. With the realization that he is addicted he comes only too well to know that he is a "junky," and he is fully aware of the conventional attitudes towards addicts as well as of the counter-rationalizations provided by his peer group. It is possible that the cat's vacillation with regard to seeking a cure for his addiction is due to a conflict of perspectives, whether to view his habit from the cat's or the dominant social order's point of view.

(c) "Play is distinct from 'ordinary' life both as to locality and duration. This is the third main characteristic of play: its secludedness, its limitedness. It is 'played out' within certain limits of time and place. It contains its own course and meaning."

It is this limited, esoteric character of heroin use which gives to the cat the feeling of belonging to an elite. It is the restricted extent of the distribution of drug use, the scheming and intrigue associated with underground "connections" through which drugs are obtained, the secret lore of the appreciation of the drug's effects, which give the cat the exhilaration of participating in a conspiracy. Contrary to popular conception most drug users were not anxious to proselyte new users. Of course, spreading the habit would have the function of increasing the possible sources of supply. But an equally strong disposition was to keep the knowledge of drug use secret, to impress and dazzle the audience with one's knowledge of being "in the know." When proselyting did occur, as in jails or lockups, it was proselyting on the part of a devotee who condescended to share with the uninitiated a highly prized practice and set of attitudes.

As he elaborates his analysis of play, Huizinga brings to the fore additional aspects of the concept which also have their apt counterpart in the way of life of the cat. For instance, as was discussed earlier, the cat's appreciation of "progressive music" is an essential part of his social orientation. About this topic Huizinga remarks, "Music, as we have hinted before, is the highest and purest expression of the *facultas ludendi.*" The cat's attitude toward music has a sacred, almost mystical quality. "Progressive music" opens doors to a type of highly valued experience which for him can be had in no other way. It is more important to him than eating and is second only to the "kick." He may have to give up his hope of dressing according to his standards but he never gives up music.

Huizinga also observes, "Many and close are the links that connect play with beauty." He refers to the "profoundly aesthetic quality of play." The aesthetic emphasis which seems so central to the style of living of the cat is a subtle elusive accent permeating his whole outlook but coming to clearest expression in a constellation of interests, the "kick," clothing, and music. And it certainly reaches a level of awareness in their language. Language is utilized by the cat with a conscious relish, with many variations and individual turns of phrase indicating the value placed upon creative expression in this medium.

It is to be noted that much of the description of the cat's attributes did not deal exclusively with elements unique to him. Many of the features mentioned are prevalent among adolescents in all reaches of the status scale. Dress, music, language, and the search for pleasure are all familiar themes of the adolescent world. For instance, in his description of the adolescent "youth culture" Talcott Parsons would appear to be presenting the generic traits of a "play-form" with particular reference to its expression in the middle class.

"It is at the point of emergence into adolescence that there first begins to develop a set of patterns and behavior phenomena which involve a highly complex combination of age grading and sex role elements. These may be referred to together as the phenomena of the 'youth culture'. . . .

"Perhaps the best single point of reference for characterizing the youth culture lies in its contrast with the dominant pattern of the adult male role. By contrast with the emphasis on responsibility in this role, the orientation of the youth culture is more or less specifically irresponsible. One of its dominant roles is "having a good time." . . . It is very definitely a rounded humanistic pattern rather than one of competence in the performance of specified functions."

Such significant similarities between this description and the themes of the social type of the cat only tend to reinforce the notion that the recent spread of heroin use was a problem of adolescence. The cat is an adolescent sharing many of the interests of his age-mates everywhere but confronted by a special set of problems of color, tradition, and identity.

The social orientation of the cat, with its emphasis on non-violence, was quite in contrast to the orientation of the smaller group of young white drug users who were interviewed in the course of this study. The latter's type of adjustment placed a heavy stress upon violence. Their crimes tended to represent direct attacks against persons and property. The general disposition they manifested was one of "nerve" and brashness rather than one of "playing it cool." They did not cultivate the amenities of language, music, or dress to nearly the same extent as the cat. Their social orientation was expressed as a direct rather than an indirect attack on the dominant values of our society. This indicates that the "youth culture" despite its generic features may vary significantly in different social settings.

In his paper, "Some Jewish Types of Personality," Louis Wirth made the following suggestive comments about the relationship between the social type and its setting.

"A detailed analysis of the crucial personality types in any given area or cultural group shows that they depend upon a set of habits and attitudes in the group for their existence and are the direct expressions of the values of the group. As the life of the group changes there appears a host of new social types, mainly outgrowths and transformations of previous patterns which have become fixed through experience."

What are some of the sources of the various elements going to make up the social type of the cat which may be sought in his traditions? The following suggestions are offered as little more than speculation at the present time. The emphasis upon non-violence on the part of the cat, upon manipulative techniques rather than overt attack, is a stress upon the indirect rather than the direct way toward one's goal. May not the cat in this emphasis be betraying his debt to the "Uncle Tom" type of adjustment, despite his wish to dissociate himself from earlier patterns of accommodation to the dominant white society? May not the "kick" itself be a cultural lineal descendant of the ecstatic moment of religious possession so dear to revivalist and store-front religion? Similarly, may not the emphasis upon the exploitation of the woman have its origin in the traditionally greater economic stability of the colored woman?

W. I. Thomas in one of his references to the problems raised by the city environment stated, "Evidently the chief problem is the young American person." In discussing the type of inquiry that would be desirable in this area he states that it should

". . . lead to a more critical discrimination between that type of disorganization in the youth which is a real but frustrated tendency to organize on a higher plane, or one more correspondent with the moving environment, and that type of disorganization which is simply the abandonment of standards. It is also along this line . . . that we shall gain light on the relation of fantastic phantasying to realistic phantasying. . . ."

Posed in this way the problem becomes one of evaluating the social type of the cat in relation to the processes of social change. This social type is difficult to judge according to the criterion suggested by Thomas. Since many of the cat's interests are merely an extreme form of the adolescent "youth culture," in part the problem becomes one of determining how functional the period of adolescence is as preparation for subsequent adult status. However, the central phases of the social orientation of the cat, the "hustle" and the "kick," do represent a kind of disorganization which indicates the abandonment of conventional standards. The young addicted cat is "going nowhere." With advancing age he cannot shed his addiction the way he can many of the other trappings of adolescence. He faces only the bleak prospect, as time goes on, of increasing demoralization. Although the plight of the young colored addict is intimately tied to the conditions and fate of his racial group, his social orientation seems to represent a dead-end type of adjustment. Just as Handlin in *The Uprooted* suggests that the first generation of immigrant peoples to our society tends to be a sacrificed generation, it may be that the unique problems of Negro migrants to our metropolitan areas will lead to a few or several sacrificed generations in the course of the tortuous process of urbanization.

The discussion of the social type of the cat leads inevitably to the issue of social control. Any attempt to intervene or modify the social processes producing the "cat" as a social type must have the objective of reducing his group isolation. For instance, because of such isolation and because of the cat's sensitivity to the gestures of his peers, the most significant role models of a given generation of cats tend to be the cats of the preceding age group. Where, in a period of rapid change, the schemes of behavior of the role models no longer correspond to the possibilities in the actual situation, it is possible for attitudes to be transmitted to a younger generation which evidence a kind of "cultural lag." Thus the condition of the labor market in Chicago is such as to suggest the existence of plentiful employment opportunities for the Negro in a variety of fields. But because such openings are not mediated to him through role models it is possible that the cat is unable to take advantage of these opportunities or of the facilities available for training for such positions.

The social type of the cat is a product of social change. The type of social orientation which it has elaborated indicates an all too acute awareness of the values of the broader social order. In an open class society where upward mobility is positively sanctioned, an awareness and sensitivity to the dominant values is the first stage in their eventual assimilation. Insofar as the social type of the cat represents a reaction to a feeling of exclusion from access to the means towards the goals of our society, all measures such as improved educational opportunities which put these means within his grasp will hasten the extinction of this social type. Just as the "hoodlum" and "gangster" types tend to disappear as the various more recently arrived white ethnic groups tend to move up in the status scale of the community, so it can confidently be expected that the cat as a social type will tend to disappear as such opportunities become more prevalent among the colored population.

Selection 83

Race Differences: The Present Position of the Problem
Otto Klineberg

The whole history of race relations has been one of repeated claims of superiority and inferiority for each of hundreds of "races." Sometimes superiority was assumed because of a purported descent from the gods, frequently because of military superiority or sheer numbers of the race, and sometimes because of a "level of civilization" as defined by those claiming superiority.

With the rise of science and the discovery of "proof" as a means of reinforcing opinion, men began to construct lengthy and complicated apologias to "prove" the superiority of their own race. Proponents of the theory of "Aryan superiority," in Western Europe and the United States, said that, in order of ascending superiority, the Negroid race was nearest the apes, then the Mongoloid, and then the Caucasoid, with the "Aryan" peoples at the top of the Caucasoid scale. Only Aryans could build civilizations alone and unaided; all great men were actual or "spiritual" Aryans; and civilizations declined and fell because the founding Aryans intermarried with their inferiors and their "mongrel" descendants were unable to maintain the original level of civilization. Such thinking was widespread in the United States, as evidenced by our many folk beliefs concerning race, by various kinds of state legislation against Orientals, Indians, and Negroes, and by our immigration laws, which the latest revision changed only in relatively minor details.

Reasonable men do not like to have their opinions remain unsupported by "evidence," so for two hundred years white men in America (nowhere else except in South Africa and Hitlerite Germany has this been true) have sought logical, biological, religious, psychological, or sociocultural bases upon which to rest their racial beliefs. Those who have not believed in racial superiority have sought evidence on the other side. To make a long story short, we have discovered numerous biological differences among the races, most of them easily discernible, but no proof that any of them—hair texture, ratio of standing to sitting height, shape of lips and ears, tendency to baldness, hair on body, skin and eye color, etc.—makes one race or the other more viable as a biological organism.

There is agreement, however, that differences in native intellect, if they could be shown, would be of real importance in proving superiority or equality. Klineberg, in the following selection, traces up to the present the history of studies of intelligence differences among races. His final conclusions are based on exhaustive study by many researchers over many years, in Europe as well as in America, and they coincide with those of the panel of international experts chosen by the United Nations, whose report is summarized in the first paragraph of the selection.

The Unesco "Statement on Race" adopts a clear and unequivocal position regarding the measurement of psychological differences between racial groups. It states:

"It is now generally recognized that intelligence tests do not in themselves enable us to differentiate safely between what is due to innate capacity and what is the result of environmental influences, training and education. Wherever it has been possible to make allowances for differences in environmental opportunities, the tests have shown essential similarity in mental characters among all human groups."

This statement was prepared and approved by a group of scholars who had long been associated with research and writing in this field, and who undoubtedly had an adequate background of information to justify their conclusions. They could not, however, within the obvious space limitations of such a statement, give more than a glimpse into that background. The purpose of the present article is to supply some of the facts which justify the position taken, and to indicate some of the recent developments which have strengthened the conviction that this is the only position which is scientifically tenable.

Before entering into details concerning the relevant research, it may be worth while to note the striking change which has occurred in the thinking of many scientists who have concerned themselves with this problem. The reasons vary, but the fact is significant. To take one example, Howard W. Odum, Professor of Sociology at the University of North Carolina, published in 1910 a volume on *Social and Mental Traits of the*

Negro, in which he expressed the definite conviction that negroes were inherently inferior to whites, and that they should be given the kind of education which was adapted to their poorer mental equipment. In 1936, Odum wrote an article on "The Errors of Sociology," published in Volume XV of the journal *Social Forces*. Among these errors Odum lists "the assumption that races are inherently different rather than group products of differentials due to the cumulative power of folk-regional and cultural environment."

In 1923 the late C. C. Brigham, Professor of Psychology at Princeton University, published *A Study of American Intelligence*, in which he reported his analysis of the results obtained through the application of intelligence tests to more than a million recruits in the American army in the first world war. Since these recruits included many immigrants and sons of immigrants, as well as negroes, Brigham compared the results obtained by various ethnic groups and found that whites were on the average superior to negroes; among the whites, North Europeans (Nordics) were superior to Central Europeans (Alpines) who in turn were superior to South Europeans (Mediterraneans). The assumption was made that the tests measured differences in native intelligence. This study of Brigham's was widely read and frequently quoted; the suggestion has even been made that it was a factor in determining the immigration policy of the United States.

Brigham himself changed his mind only a few years later about the meaning and significance of

From the *International Social Science Bulletin*, Vol. 2 (1950), 460-466. Reprinted by permission of the United Nations Educational, Scientific and Cultural Organization (UNESCO).

his analysis. As the result of a statistical study of the relationship between the various parts of the intelligence tests applied, he concluded that the method used was not scientifically sound. In an article on "Intelligence Tests of Immigrant Groups" published in the *Psychological Review* in 1930, he wrote: "As this method was used by the writer in his earlier analysis of the Army tests as applied to samples of the foreign-born in the draft, that study with its entire superstructure of racial differences collapses completely." Brigham points out also that language difficulties may also have played a part, since many of the groups tested were bilingual, or spoke their own native language much better than they did English.

After a careful survey of all the factors involved, Brigham concluded that "comparative studies of various national and racial groups may not be made with existing tests" and that "one of the most pretentious of these comparative racial studies—the writer's own—was without foundation."

One final example of a change in point of view may be of interest. Florence L. Goodenough, Professor of Psychology at the University of Minnesota, published an article in 1926 in the *Journal of Experimental Psychology* on "Racial Differences in the Intelligence of School Children." She used her own "Draw-a-Man" test, in which achievement is measured in terms of how accurately a man is drawn, without regard to the aesthetic qualities of the drawing. Since the test makes no use of language or "information," she believed it could be regarded as a test of native intelligence, independent of culture or previous experience. She reported that her groups differed in economic background, but she regarded this as irrelevant to her results. She wrote: "It seems probable, upon the whole, that inferior environment is an effect at least as much as it is a cause of inferior ability. . . . The person of low intelligence tends to gravitate to those neighbourhoods where the economic requirement is minimal. . . . His children inherit his mental characteristics." In other words, her conclusion was that there are racial differences in native ability, and that the results of the application of an intelligence test reveal the existence of such differences.

[In 1950] . . . Professor Goodenough, writing with Dale B. Harris on "Studies in the Psychology of Children's Drawings" in the *Psychological Bulletin,* reviews many of the investigations made with the "Draw-a-Man" test, and concludes that there is definite indication of the influence of culture and previous training on the results obtained. The test is not so "culture-free" as was formerly believed. Goodenough and Harris state in this article that they "would like to express the opinion that the search for a culture-free test, whether of intelligence, artistic ability, personal-social characteristics, or any other measurable trait is illusory, and that the naive assumption that the mere freedom from verbal requirements renders a test equally suitable for all groups is no longer tenable." In a footnote Goodenough states that her earlier study reporting differences among the children of immigrants to the United States "is certainly no exception to the rule. The writer hereby apologizes for it!"

These honest and courageous admissions on the part of three distinguished scholars are mentioned here because they represent in clearest form the development which has taken place in this whole field of inquiry. When the tests were first applied to representatives of different ethnic groups, it was usually in the belief that the method was capable of measuring native ability, and that the results could be so interpreted. Voices of caution and criticism were raised from the beginning, and, among psychologists at least, they were in the minority. The history of the mental testing of ethnic or racial groups may almost be described as a progressive disillusionment with tests as measures of native ability, and a gradually increasing realization of the many complex environmental factors which enter into the result.

Such factors have been described in several previous publications, and they will merely be listed at this point. They include previous schooling; socio-economic level; degree of familiarity with the language used; experience with the kinds of problems which enter into the tests; experience with tests in general; motivation, or desire to do well; rapport with the investigator; speed or tempo of activity; physical well-being; etc. Some of these factors affect one group, others another; taken together, they indicate how impossible it is to speak of a culture-free test.

One approach which was designed to avoid the above difficulties is represented by the study of very young children, presumably before they have been subjected to any influences from the social environment. This was attempted by Myrtle B. McGraw in 1931, in "A Comparative Study of a Group of Southern White and Negro Infants," published in *Genetic Psychology Monographs.* She studied white and negro infants in the first year of life, administering to them the "Baby Tests," devised by Hetzer and Wolf under the direction of Charlotte Buehler at Vienna. The results showed the white babies to be on the average definitely superior to the negro. The author concludes: "It is significant that with even the very young subjects when environmental factors are minimized the same type and approximately the same degree of superiority is evidenced on the part of the White subjects as that found among older groups."

The difficulty with this conclusion is that environmental factors, even at this early age, are by no means "minimized." The performance of an infant on the Baby Tests is markedly influenced by general physical development, which in turn depends on adequate nourishment. In this respect the negro children were definitely at a disadvantage. They came from homes that were economically inferior, and they were relatively deficient in weight. These facts are not irrelevant simply because the children are young; on the contrary, the linkage between physical and mental development should be at least as striking at the beginning of life as later.

This interpretation is supported by a more recent study of negro and white babies at New Haven, Connecticut, by B. Pasamanick, under the direction of Professor Arnold Gesell of Yale University. The results are reported in an article "A Comparative Study of the Behavioral Development of Negro Infants," published in the *Journal of Genetic Psychology* in 1946. In this study the negro infants revealed both a physical and a psychological development equal to that of the whites; the tests used showed no significant differences between the two groups. The investigator points out that as a result of the careful dietary controls introduced during the war, the negro mothers in this group received adequate nourishment, and in fact were not markedly different from the white mothers in this respect. The general economic level of the negro group had also improved as a consequence of the opportunities opened up by defence industries. These negro infants started out, physically, on equal terms with the whites. They also, in parallel fashion, showed no inferiority or retardation in psychological development. With the equating of environmental opportunities, the differences between the two groups disappeared.

This last statement is crucial to the whole problem, and is in need of considerable amplification. If it can be adequately demonstrated that the removal of environmental inequalities really brings with it the elimination of inferiorities in test performance, the issue will have been settled. It will no longer be possible to base the argument for inborn racial differences on the results of the intelligence tests. The situation of the American negro and the American Indian furnishes the most critical and at the same time the most adequate data for evaluating the point of view which is here being developed.

The American negro has been studied by means of various psychological tests in various parts of the United States. Some years ago, the writer (in *Characteristics of the American Negro,* 1944) made a survey of all the available research data, and concluded that, on the average, American negroes obtained an intelligence quotient of about 86, as compared with the norm of 100 for the general population. This points to a substantial inferiority on the part of the negro. It was at the same time striking to note the tremendous range of scores obtained by the various groups of negro children examined. One, a rural group in Tennessee, showed an average Intelligence Quotient of 58; at the other extreme, a group in Los Angeles, California, turned out to be superior to the average white population, with a score of 105. This remarkable range is in keeping with our hypothesis of environmental determination. In rural Tennessee the negroes came from an exceedingly inferior economic level of the population and attended inadequate, segregated schools. In California they suffered little discrimination, had improved their economic status and attended the same schools as did the white children.

A direct attack upon this problem was made by J. Peterson and L. H. Lanier, who in 1929 published their "Studies in the Comparative Abilities of Whites and Negroes" in *Mental Measurement Monographs.* They suggested that "a useful check on the reliability of a given race difference obtained in any locality and under any specific set of circumstances is to take what seem to be fairly representative samplings from widely different environments and to compare the various results as checks upon one another with a view to determining just which factors persistently yield differences in favour of one or the other race." With this in mind they compared negro and white boys in three different cities, Nashville (in Tennessee), Chicago and New York. The results showed that in Nashville, which is in a southern state where negroes do not have opportunities equal to those of whites, the white boys were markedly superior; in Chicago there was a slight difference in favour of the whites; in New York there were no significant differences between the two racial groups. These results are not difficult to understand if our hypothesis concerning the importance of environmental factors is correct.

The authors, however, suggest another explanation of their findings. They believe that a process of "selective migration" has occurred; that is to say, the most energetic and intelligent negroes have left the south in order to find new homes and a better life in the north. That would mean that the northern negroes did well on the tests not because they live in a superior environment, but because they were innately superior to start with. Peterson and Lanier speak of New York as showing "a selectiveness of the best genes in the negroes" as a consequence of this type of migration.

Since no conclusive evidence was presented in favour of this hypothesis of selective migration, the present writer became convinced a number of years ago that a more direct attack upon the problem was required. The results of his investigations, carried out with the co-operation of a number of advanced students at Columbia University, are presented in detail in *Negro Intelligence and Selective Migration*, published in 1935. Two principal methods were used. The first was to see whether there was any indication that those negroes who migrated were in any way superior to those who remained in their own native localities. A careful search through the school records in several southern cities, and a detailed statistical comparison of the school marks obtained by the migrants and the non-migrants respectively, showed no significant differences between the two groups. In other words, there was no evidence to indicate that those who migrated were "selected" for their superior ability.

The second approach attempted to study more directly the effect of a superior environment (in this case that of New York City) on the test scores of negro children who had come to New York from the south. If the environment exerts an influence, this should reveal itself in an improvement in test scores at least roughly proportionate to the length of time these children had lived in New York. This is precisely what the results showed. A number of different tests were applied to groups of negro boys and girls, and in general it was found that there was a close (though by no means perfect) correspondence between test scores and length of residence in New York. Those who had lived there the longest obtained on the average the best scores; those who had recently arrived from the south, the poorest. The conclusion appears clear and unequivocal. It is verified by similar studies in the case of Washington and Philadelphia (the latter study is as yet unpublished). The hypothesis is justified that as the environmental discrepancies are reduced, the differences in test results are reduced correspondingly. There is nothing to support the contention that an alternative hypothesis, like that of selective migration, is equally capable of explaining these findings.

In the case of the American Indians, the relevant material is somewhat different. In general, the test scores obtained by American Indians are inferior to those of negroes. On the average, the Indian intelligence quotient is in the neighbour-

hood of 81. This result is not difficult to explain or understand. Not only do most American Indians occupy an inferior economic position in comparison to the rest of the population, in addition, their whole background and culture are so different from that of white Americans, that it can hardly be expected that they should do equally well on tests that have been standardized on the latter group. Their relative unfamiliarity with English constitutes still another handicap; it has been demonstrated, for example, that Indian children do much better on performance tests (in which no language ability is required) than on the usual variety of linguistic tests.

On the more positive side, the late Professor T. R. Garth of the University of Denver, attempted to discover what would happen if American Indian children were placed in a superior environment. In 1935 he published in the *Psychological Bulletin* a note on the foster Indian child in the white home. He reported that a group of such foster children obtained an average intelligence quotient of 102, which is certainly a remarkable improvement over the general Indian score of 81. This result would be conclusive evidence of the effect of the environment on group differences, if it were not for the possibility that those Indian children who were living in white homes were exceptional. It may be that when white families take Indian children into their homes, they choose those who have superior intelligence. This is the hypothesis of "selection" in a different context and in another form. Professor Garth attempted to answer this criticism by testing also the brothers and sisters of these foster children; these brothers and sisters had not been taken into white homes, and were still living on the "reservation." They obtained an average intelligence quotient of only 87.5. This suggests that the superiority of the foster children is in fact due to their more favourable environmental opportunities, but the proof is not complete.

There is, however, one other line of evidence which appears to be completely convincing. It is represented by the study made by Professor J. H. Rohrer of the University of Oklahoma, "The Test Intelligence of Osage Indians" published in the *Journal of Social Psychology* in 1942. The Osage Indian children live under social and economic conditions which are quite comparable to those of the white children with whom they were compared. This is largely due to the fortunate accident that on the land which was ceded to them by the American government as a reservation, oil was later discovered. As a consequence these Indians became relatively well-to-do, and were able to create for themselves and their families living conditions far superior to those of other American Indian communities. With this fact in mind, it is illuminating to look at the results obtained by Rohrer. On one test, the Goodenough "Draw-a-Man," which is a non-language test, the white children obtained an average intelligence quotient of 103, and the Indian children 104. On a second test, which uses language, the white score was 98, the Indian 100. (These differences are so small as to be insignificant.) There can be no doubt in this case that when American Indian children have environmental opportunities comparable to those of whites, their apparent inferiority disappears completely.

Nor can this result be explained by selection. It was *after* they had been given their land that oil was discovered, they did not seek out this particular region, they exercised no real choice in the matter. They were lucky, and their good luck gave them opportunities denied to others. This is reflected not only in their economic success, but also in their success in solving the problems presented by the intelligence tests. The conclusion is inescapable that, given equal opportunities, the American Indian children perform as well as any others.

That is where the matter rests now. The net result of all the research that has been conducted in this field is that there is no scientific proof of innate racial differences in intelligence; that the obtained differences in test results are best explained in terms of factors in the social and educational environment; that as the environmental opportunities of different racial or ethnic groups become more similar, the observed differences in test results also tend to disappear.

Other approaches to the problem of psychological race differences have yielded similar conclusions. When tests of temperament or personality are used, the same considerations apply; groups differ, of course, but evidently as the result of the cultural and social influences which have played a part, and not as the result of race or biology.

The argument from the cultural contributions of a particular ethnic group to the inborn racial characteristics of that group falls down for many reasons: cultures may vary while race remains unchanged, the same culture may be found in groups of different race, what looks like a superior cultural contribution from one point of view may seem much less significant when another criterion is applied, etc. Studies of race mixture are similarly inconclusive, since individuals of mixed racial heredity cannot be shown to be different in their inborn psychological characteristics from those of "pure" race. Finally, there is no evidence that some racial groups are biologically more "primitive" or undeveloped than others.

This does not mean that heredity plays no part in the determination of behaviour. On the contrary, there is good evidence that "individuals" and "families" may be distinguished from others in terms of hereditary as well as acquired characteristics. As regards large racial groups, however, there appears to be about the same range of hereditary capacities in one group as in another. The fact that differences in behaviour between such groups obviously exist, is no proof that they exist because they are inborn.

There is ample reason, therefore, in the light of the accumulated scientific knowledge accepted by the overwhelming majority of social and biological scientists, to concur in the conclusions of the Unesco Statement on Race:

"According to present knowledge, there is no proof that the groups of mankind differ in their innate mental characteristics, whether in respect of intelligence or temperament. The scientific evidence indicates that the range of mental capacities in all ethnic groups is much the same."

Science thus ranges itself clearly and unmistakably at the side of those who maintain that any political or social action based on "racism" is completely unjustified.

Selection 84

Race Prejudice as Revealed in the Study of Racial Situations

Donald Pierson

At one time both the United States and Brazil had large slave populations, large plantations, and areas populated by more Negroes than whites. Both nations freed the slaves by federal action, Brazil later than the United States.

Despite these similarities, there is much less race prejudice in Brazil than in the United States. Because we in the United States commonly think that our way is "right" and "normal," it is especially interesting and important to note this particular "negative case" in the argument for our "normalcy"; it may even be that the racial conflicts of the United States and the Union of South Africa are actually the exceptions, not the rule.

Pierson is concerned less with describing Brazil than with stating, developing, and proving a set of related theories concerning the nature, components, and origin of prejudice. However, to illustrate and prove these theories he makes wide use of data from Brazil, thus, for the student, killing two birds with one stone. The basic theory pattern Pierson explores is that the extent of race prejudice varies with the social-cultural historical circumstances. In short, he shows that most prejudice is the result of the situation, not of inherent psychological needs.

The simplest explanation of racial, ethnic, and religious prejudice in the United States is that there are three major sources of prejudice. For some people, prejudice serves psychological needs; for others, prejudice and discrimination are tools for seeking economic, political, or social power—are thus simply means to an end; for many other persons—probably a considerable majority—prejudice and discrimination are acquired during the process of socialization while learning the other attitudes, values, and behavior patterns that make up our cultural heritage. The same factors operate in Brazil, but at quite different levels and in different ways from those in the United States. Throughout Latin America the term *negro* is used to mean a person of dark complexion, regardless of ancestry, and there is no term synonymous with our *Negro*, with all its culturally laden meanings. When a Latin sings a love song to his *negra consentida,* we know that she is a dark brunette, but we know nothing of her ancestry unless it is further stated that she is *Africana.* In the United States, failure to capitalize the word *Negro* is considered a mark of disrespect, prejudice, and discrimination, whereas in Latin America its use with a small letter seems to indicate that the word has less significance.

In analyzing the origin or causal factors of race prejudice, Pierson demonstrates that biological aversion is not a factor, since any aversion that exists is acquired through socialization. He finds ethnocentrism, the tendency to consider the values and behavior of one's own people as right and superior and those of any other people as inferior, to be a predisposing rather than a determining characteristic. Economic competition he finds to be a prerequisite to prejudice, although not necessarily a determinant of it. Most important for the growth of strong race prejudice Pierson finds to be a situation in which the members of the dominant race feel that they are under threat of displacement from an established social position—when the subordinate race seems about to claim privileges and opportunities from which they have previously been excluded. This situation clearly fits the United States in the 1950's and 1960's.

Pierson's chief theoretical contribution in the following selection is to show that prejudice is symptomatic, that it is derived from a given racial situation rather than produced by it, and that hence any attempt to reduce prejudice must be directed largely toward the situation itself and the social experiences which have produced it.

THE BRAZILIAN RACIAL SITUATION

Migrants from Europe, indigenous Indians, imported Africans, and their descendants have been

From the *International Social Science Bulletin,* Vol. 2 (1950), 467-478. Reprinted by permission of the United Nations Educational, Scientific and Cultural Organization (UNESCO).

in contact in Brazil for approximately four centuries. The racial situation which has developed is sufficiently distinct from those in certain parts of the world where a racial minority, like the United States negro or the European Jew, is (or has been) in free association with, but not accepted by, a dominant racial majority, as well as from the racial situation in India where the social order is organized around caste; it constitutes, along with perhaps the Hawaiian racial situation and certain others, a distinct type, namely, a multi-racial class society.

Although the hierarchy of occupations in Brazil still takes a decidedly pyramidal form—the white race, occupying superior status, being concentrated in the upper brackets and the darker peoples, representing inferior status, being overwhelmingly dominant in the lower brackets—each group, and especially the mixed-bloods, is now represented, to some extent at least, in all the occupational classes. The organization of Brazilian society thus tends to assume the form of a competitive order in which individuals find their places on the basis of personal competence and individual achievement rather than of racial descent.

There is no segregation, either voluntary or forced, as one finds where races have been embittered over a long period of time. Spatial distribution is largely the consequence of economic sifting. Such isolation as exists is ordinarily due to variations in educational level or, at times, to identification with elements of African or indigenous culture. For although the assimilation of the Indian and the African is far advanced, it is not yet complete.

Of peculiar significance are the facts that, with the exception of a limited number of tribes still living in the more inaccessible and undeveloped areas of Brazil, the Indian, as a racial unit, has disappeared; and that, although possibly more Africans were imported into Brazil than into any other region of the New World, the negro as a racial unit, is also disappearing. The general tendency throughout Brazilian history has been to absorb, gradually but effectively, all racial minorities into the predominantly European stock. In few places in the world has the amalgamation of peoples of divergent racial origin proceeded so continuously and on so extensive a scale.

Although the mixed-bloods are increasing, this increase appears to be at the expense of the Indian and the African and not of the European. Nor is there growing up in Brazil a relatively permanent mixed racial stock, like the Macanese in China, the Goanese in India, or the "Cape Coloured" in South Africa. Instead, the mixed-bloods appear to be gradually absorbing the non-white portions of the population, while they themselves are increasingly being incorporated into the predominantly white group.

Endogamy is far from absolute, breaking down particularly along the biological borders of the races, probably increasingly, with the passage of time and the continued rise of individuals from the lower status groups. Although colour, and especially negroid features, are still indicative of slave origin and still tend to be closely identified with low status and hence to constitute a considerable handicap to marriage into the upper classes, these characteristics lose their limiting and restrictive character as their symbolic reference is called into question by other, status-enhancing, qualities in a given individual.

Of peculiar significance is the fact that one drop of African blood does not, as in the United States (if known), class a mixed-blood as a negro. Many individuals are listed in the official statistics as "whites," and are similarly known in the community, who not only have African ancestors but actually give evidence of this descent in colour or features.

Thus the race problem, in so far as there is one, tends to be identified with the resistance which any group offers, or is thought to offer, to absorption. To individuals from all classes of the population this eventual amalgamation and assimilation of diverse racial units is a matter of pride and selfcommendation.

There are in Brazil no castes based upon race; there are only classes. These classes are still largely identified with colour, it is true, but they are classes none the less and not castes.

This does not mean that there are no social distinctions in Brazil, for distinctions are obviously common to all societies, one thing or another serving as a basis. Neither does it mean that there is no discrimination, that whites freely accept negroes in marriage, or that the negro's conception of his role is identical with his status and that he is completely satisfied with his lot. But it does mean that a man of colour may, by reason of individual merit or favourable circumstance, substantially improve his status and that this position will then be with reference not merely to the darker group whose colour he shares but to the entire community.

Since, however, a black cannot escape his colour but, on the contrary, constantly carries with him an indelible badge of low status, he tends to be catalogued by anyone meeting him for the first time as a member of the lower status group. Only as he gives evidence of other characteristics ordinarily associated with superior status, such as professional skill, educational achievement, economic competence, "gentlemanly bearing," or personal charm, is this original conception modified; and even then the fact of his being in appearance like a lower-class man remains one of the criteria of him and is undoubtedly a handicap.

It is in the light of this distinction that one perhaps best understands what at first sight appears to be discrimination on the basis of race. Since discrimination undoubtedly exists so far as the upper classes are concerned, and since to a large extent it follows colour lines, one is likely to assume a similarity to discrimination observable in South Africa or the United States and posit an automatic relationship between discrimination and race. But if attention be focused upon those "men of colour" who have risen in class and who for this reason are no longer subjected to the same discrimination as others of their fellows who have not yet risen, one sees that the relation between discrimination and race is not direct but *indirect;* that not necessarily discrimination on the basis of race, or even colour, is involved but discrimination on the basis of *class,* involving in most cases, quite expectedly, individuals of colour, owing to the concentration of the darker portion of the population for centuries in the lower status ranks.

Race has undoubtedly been a factor in Brazil in fixing classes and making them, to some extent at least, hereditary. But race as a criterion of class is increasingly breaking down, as more and more individuals of dark colour give evidence of the possession of, or the ability to achieve, other characteristics indicative of superior status. The significant fact is that a black mixed-blood *can* overcome the handicap of colour, *can* overbalance this liability by means of other assets. His social position is not fixed and rigid as it would be in a caste system. It is always subject to change.

There is in Brazil little or no race prejudice, in the sense in which that term is used in Europe, South Africa and the United States. This does not mean that there is no prejudice but that such prejudice as does exist—with the possible exception of certain areas of the south, where the arrival in comparatively recent years of immigrant peoples with alien attitudes and sentiments has perhaps modified to some extent the original Brazilian mores—is *class* rather than race prejudice. It is the kind of prejudice which one finds *inside* the ranks of the negro in the United States, among the lighter mixed-bloods.

That it is class rather than race, or even colour, prejudice is borne out by the fact that it does not exist among the lower classes and appears only as one proceeds up the social scale. This situation is thus the opposite of that in South Africa and the United States, where the most intense and implacable prejudice is to be found among the "poor whites."

It is true that the descendants of Europeans in Brazil, like all groups, are ethnocentric, and that the whites share a general feeling of the superiority of their group. Many of them are adverse to what is to them strange and bizarre behaviour as represented by such cultural survivals as *candomblé* ritual and belief. To some minds at least this behaviour is of an offensive character and may evoke deep-seated antipathies. This antagonism, however, is directed at *cultural* rather than racial variations, and tends to disappear when the negro, as he has almost entirely done, gives up his identification with African cultural forms and becomes assimilated into the predominantly white world. The antipathy does not extend, therefore, to the negro as such but rather to the *Africano,* the foreigner, who constitutes an alien cyst in the social organism.

Bearing in mind, then, the general character of the Brazilian racial situation, let us analyse the attitude of race prejudice as observed in other racial situations and see if the "negative case" of Brazil can contribute to an understanding of this phenomenon.

THE NATURE OF RACE PREJUDICE

Race prejudice, first of all, is an *attitude;* it is a tendency to act in an adverse way toward a given object: a racial group, or supposed racial group. Moreover, although obviously held in any given case by individuals, it is not an individual but a *social* attitude; it is a product of group experience and, wherever found, is a group attitude directed against another group. Each individual who holds it may stimulate both himself and others in the expression of that attitude by relating his experiences to other persons, by expressing his own feelings in their presence, by reciting racial stories or myths, as well as by observing other persons expressing in these and similar ways the same attitude so that various members of the group come to build up, to reenforce and to sustain in each other a *common* attitude.

In the second place, the attitude of race prejudice is always directed toward, and built up around, a *conceptualized* group. In other words, the object toward which the attitude is directed, and around which it is built up, is the *classification* into which the members of a group have been conceptually placed. This means that although the prejudice may be expressed against a given individual, this is accomplished only by first identifying him with the conceptualized group and then directing towards him the attitude which has been built up toward that group. In a situation in which prejudice exists against a negro, a white, or a Jew, for instance, a member of the group which holds that prejudice will first identify a given individual as *a* negro, *a* white, or *a* Jew and then be led, by reason of this identification, to direct towards him the common attitude of his group with reference to *the* negro, *the* white, or *the* Jew. If a given person can disguise his "negro-ness," whiteness, or Jewishness sufficiently to escape being classified in that category he will escape prejudice, an acomplishment which is obviously less difficult in the case of the Jew, where the variation is basically cultural and not racial, in the anthropological sense,[1] than it is where the physical differences which determine classification are more obvious.

In the third place, race prejudice, like any other attitude, when once formed, is *transmissible*. It may thus be taken over by individuals and groups whose own experience has never given rise to it. Where, for instance, parents or other close associates hold this attitude it may be passed on with other attitudes, in large measure unwittingly, to the developing child and this process may continue for generations. Or the attitude may be imported into a cultural area where historically the experiences which give rise to prejudice have never been known. An individual who, by reason of being reared in a culture where race prejudice is active or for having participated in that culture for a time as a visitor, has taken over the attitude, may carry it with him into a new group. . . .

THE COMPONENTS OF THE ATTITUDE OF PREJUDICE

The usual tendency has been to consider the attitude of prejudice as a simple or unitary attitude; that is, as if it were composed of a single feeling such as dislike or hatred, or at most of these two feelings. This conception, however, is not in keeping with the facts as observed in actual racial situations. There is no doubt that among the feelings involved in race prejudice are dislike and hatred. It is a mistake, however, to regard these feelings as the only ones, or even necessarily as the principal feelings.

The study of racial situations in which prejudice has appeared indicates that this attitude may be made up of a number of different feelings and impulses which vary in their combinations and proportions in different situations. In addition to dislike and hatred, which obviously are always present, these constituent elements may include distrust, envy, apprehension, fear, dread, resentment, possessive and sexual impulses, feelings of obligation and of guilt, as well as even destructive impulses. Some of these elements may be vividly present and hence readily identifiable, while others may be rather obscure and still others may be present without their presence being even suspected.

THE ORIGINS OF RACE PREJUDICE

The complexity of the constituent and sustaining elements in the attitude of race prejudice obviously increases the difficulty of explaining completely the social experiences which, in any particular case, have given rise to this attitude. . . .

Since it has been observed that when different races enter into contact for the first time, the existence of biological differences may evoke a certain sense of strangeness, dislike and even hostility, it has been alleged that the basis of race prejudice is an innate *biological* aversion to the members of any other race. This hypothesis, however, has never been confirmed; on the contrary, there exists considerable evidence of a negative character. Cases of first contact have been reported in which the strangeness felt merely called out curiosity, and approach and friendly relations resulted. In Brazil, there did not arise any antipathy on the part of white children toward the black *amas* who took care of them, or toward black playmates and other black associates of childhood. On the contrary, sentimental attachments between members of the different races, both young and old, many of them tenacious and persistent, have been quite common in Brazil, a situation also characteristic of the United States south. If prejudice were organic, it obviously would appear in all cases of racial contact. If, then, we discover cases in which it does not appear, the hypothesis that prejudice is instinctive is not valid.

The confusion on this point would seem to arise out of an unconscious identification of two quite distinct things: (1) instinct, and (2) custom. The

[1] When the concept "race" is used in its anthropological sense (or, more specifically, with its connotation in *Physical* Anthropology), it is merely a biological term. It refers to a population group whose members share certain physical characteristics which mark them off from other population groups and who are thus united among themselves biologically, by way of heredity. "Race" in its sociological connotation, on the other hand, may refer to any group whose members are treated by those of another group *as if* they were of a different race and who think of and act toward themselves as if they were different.

fact that race prejudice and the forms of behaviour to which it has given rise are widely distributed has led many persons to think that this attitude is instinctively derived; when, as a matter of fact, it is a *cultural trait* which in some cases has become so rooted in group habit, over so long a period of time, that the members of the group who hold it have forgotten its historical origin and tend to confuse it with innate, biological phenomena.

At the same time, the presence of "racial marks," such as rather decided variations in physical characteristics like skin colour, hair texture, body form, nasal index, lip thickness, or the prominence of the supra-orbital ridges, is an important consideration. It is significant, however, only because it increases the visibility of the members of a group and thus makes it difficult for a given individual to escape identification with that group.

Is it then possible to explain race prejudice on the basis of *cultural differences?* Studies of racial situations would seem to indicate that one of the originating circumstances is ethnocentrism, or that characteristic of all groups which is evident in a certain aversion to ways of living which seem to its members to be strange and peculiar, and in a deeply rooted feeling of the inherent superiority of one's own group and its way of life.

It would appear, however, that ethnocentrism is a *predisposing* rather than a determining characteristic. In comparatively recent times, millions of European and thousands of Asiatic immigrants, bearing with them different folk cultures, have migrated to the United States, as also to Brazil and other countries. These bearers of diverse cultures subsequently entered into such serious *biotic* competition with the native population in some places in the United States, for instance, that the native group was eventually displaced as the dominant population unit. No serious antipathy or prejudice, however, arose in any of these cases. It is true that there initially developed in most cases a certain aversion, an attitude which is reflected today in the United States in vaudeville jokes regarding the Irish, the Chinese and the Italians, for instance; but this aversion was only temporary and soon disappeared. Ethnocentrism, although an important element, does not seem to be a decisive one in the formation of race prejudice.

One might point out in this connection that although Japanese immigrants on the West Coast of the United States were more similar culturally to the native Americans than were Chinese immigrants, native Americans showed, a few decades ago, and perhaps still are showing, more prejudice toward the Japanese than toward the Chinese. It might be suggested that this greater prejudice was due to the smaller number of Japanese in comparison with the Chinese, the Americans for this reason having become more accustomed to the Chinese. But that this explanation is inadequate is suggested by the negative case of Canada where, although there are few negroes, almost no prejudice exists against them. . . .

Is it possible then to explain race prejudice on the basis of *economic competition?* . . . If this be accepted, however, one is then faced with the immediate difficulty of explaining at least one negative case. Shortly before the first world war, French Canadians with a low standard of living began to migrate into the north-eastern part of the United States where they subsequently entered into rather intense competition with native Americans. Almost no prejudice, however, subsequently arose in this case.

It is clear, nevertheless, that in certain cases where race prejudice has appeared, it has been accompanied by unaccustomed and unusually severe economic competition. Economic competition would therefore seem to be a *pre-requisite*, although not necessarily a determinant, of race prejudice.

Analyses of those racial situations in which prejudice is most pronounced would seem to indicate that of still greater significance is the development of a feeling, on the part of the members of a dominant group, that they are *under threat of displacement from an established social position;* that is, race prejudice is usually acute in those situations in which the members of a dominant group have come to fear that the members of a subordinate group are not keeping to a prescribed place of exclusion and discrimination but instead threaten effectively to claim the privileges and opportunities from which they have been excluded. This anticipated attack is sensed by the members of the dominant group as a threat to their status, security and welfare.

The circumstance which adds peculiarly to this feeling of being attacked, however, is that the two groups are living in close spatial proximity, so that the threat seems to come from an "inner enemy." The apprehension consequently has a more immediate and permanent character. The fact that the threatening group must, at least for reasons of symbiosis, be to some extent accepted, gives an anomalous and hence highly perplexing character to the feeling of apprehension and for this reason fear, and the hate which always accompanies fear, are intensified.

The greater the threat that is felt, the greater is likely to be the prejudice. The extent of this threat will be determined by such circumstances as the size of the group from which the threat is presumed to come, the degree of militancy or supposed militancy of its members, the extent of their exclusiveness, and the measure of their claims.[2]

That race prejudice has not arisen in Brazil is perhaps largely due to the fact that the whites have never at any time felt that the Indians, the negroes, or the mixed-bloods offered any serious threat to their status. The social experiences of the Brazilian past have not been those which would call out in the whites feelings of distrust, apprehension, fear, dread, resentment, or envy; nor that obscure sense of guilt which men sometimes feel toward those whom they have wronged or by whom they themselves have been wronged. . . .

Instead, the rise of lower status individuals in Brazil has always been accomplished *as individuals* and not as a group or groups; and this rise has ordinarily had in its favour those sentiments and personal attachments which primary relations tend to develop.

Although slavery existed for centuries in Brazil, it was on the whole a rather mild form of servitude, characterized especially by the natural and continuous growth of personal relations which tended to humanize the institution and undermine its formal and legal character. . . .

Manumission occurred extensively from the first days of slavery; and final emancipation came about as the culmination of a widespread and eventually irresistible popular movement which for years had dominated public thinking and action. Since abolition sentiment was not limited to any one section of Brazil but on the contrary penetrated all parts, this "struggle for consistency" in the Brazilian mores went on *inside* local communities, where it had in its favour the personal relations of persons bound together by ties of family and friendship. The slave was thus released from a servile status under circumstances which favoured the continuance of intimate personal relationships already built up.

There are in Brazil, then, no bitter memories over which the whites brood. . . . No portion of Brazilian society passed through a period of social upheaval comparable to that in the United States south during and following the American Civil War, in which a threatened reversal of the status structure of a sudden and catastrophic kind, elicited such deep-seated apprehension and fear that today, generations later, the events of that period are vividly recalled by the descendants of the whites who lived through it. There has been nothing comparable to the conquest of the American south by northern armies, the sudden release of the negro from a servile status and his abrupt elevation to positions of power; no imposition for years of onerous political control from without,

and the consequent development of feelings of resentment and bitterness which, lacking normal expression (by reason of the north's formidable power) in any form of effective aggression toward the offending object, became displaced upon the more or less helpless negro when the northern forces were withdrawn.

The widespread dispersion of Indian and negro blood in the predominantly white group . . . makes it difficult for the whites to draw sharp, clear-cut distinctions. If rigid differentiations were made between individuals entirely of European descent and those who have one or more Indian or African ancestors, the dividing line would pass through most family groups.

When race lines thus become blurred inside families, there are significant sociological effects. The natural ties, personal and familial, which ordinarily grow up between parents and offspring and between brothers, sisters and other close relatives, unite with bonds of common sentiment individuals descended from the different racial stocks and militate against any prejudicial attitudes which might arise.

In the development of this general tendency to absorb all racial minorities, the circumstances of colonial settlement played a significant role. In Brazil, unlike the United States, few European women emigrated during the first years of colonization. Until stable living conditions and a normal distribution of the sexes were achieved, the cohabitation of Portuguese men with native Indian women commonly took place. . . . These interracial unions, as in Goa and elsewhere throughout the Portuguese dominions in the East, were subsequently encouraged as a matter of policy by the Portuguese State, and the Church eventually "regularized them into Christian marriage," thereby lending religious sanction to inter-racial crossing and bringing parents and children within the control and discipline of the Church.

In Brazil, then, the traditional behaviour which originally grew up and took shape under the conditions of a racial and cultural frontier gave rise to an informal racial policy which still today underlies and gives consistency to the mores. This informal policy is perhaps best summarized in the commonly heard expression, "We Brazilians are becoming one people.". . .

It may be that the Portuguese, as certain commentators have said, are "a colour-blind people"; that is, awareness of colour and other racial differ-

---

[2] Care should be taken to distinguish between *discrimination* and *prejudice*. Although discrimination appears always to accompany prejudice, the reverse does not seem to be true.

ences has never been as pronounced with them as with certain other Europeans.

For one thing, their experiences with a darker race for several centuries were those of a conquered people with their more swarthy conquerors. The Moors, who occupied Portugal for more than five hundred years, brought in with them a superior culture and were more learned in the arts and sciences. They subsequently became the wealthy class which occupied the towns or lived in the principal castles and on the large estates. It eventually came to be considered an honour to mate with them, and such marriages often occurred, even involving members of the royal family.

The conceptualization of darker peoples which the Portuguese originally took to Brazil, then, and which has been handed on from one generation to the next, lacked that taint of inferiority which has been associated with it in certain other racial situations. Significant in this respect is the fact that the "ideal type" of femininity in Brazil has always been the *morena*, a person typically dark not only in colour of hair and eyes but also in pigmentation.

Significant also is the conceptualization of the slave and of the slave institution which the Brazilians inherited from their Portuguese ancestors and which the Portuguese took over from the Moors. Slaves on estates in the Iberian peninsula are said to have been "almost in the position of small farmers." In Mohammedan mores, there were few, if any, actions more commendable than to free slaves, such enfranchisement being urged by the Prophet as an atonement for an undeserved blow or other injustice; and, once free, no stigma attached to their previous condition.

Thus, in Brazil, the darker portion of the population and the whites have never stood over against each other as irreducible racial groups, differing not only in appearance, which is obvious, but also in kind, and fated ever to remain separate and distinct. Such inferiority as has existed has not been thought of as racial and permanent but as cultural and temporary, and already well on the way to extinction.

THE DISINTEGRATION OF PREJUDICE

The facts (1) that race prejudice is a collective attitude, (2) that it is composed of a cluster of feelings and impulses, (3) that it is always directed toward a conceptualized object, and (4) that it arises out of a social situation in which the members of a dominant group have come to feel, by reason of the serious competition offered by a subordinate group, that their status is threatened, throw light upon the means by which race prejudice is and can be broken down.

The disintegration of prejudice will probably occur in any given case only as the collective experiences which have given rise to it in that particular racial situation are themselves changed, so that the feeling that the subordinate group constitutes a threat diminishes and disappears. This may be accomplished, in the first place, by building up either one of two types of accommodation; as when, for instance, the subordinate group either retires voluntarily or is forced into a segregated position, as occurred with the Chinese on the Pacific Coast of the United States and with the Jews in medieval ghettos, so that contacts with the dominant group are appreciably diminished or even abolished; or when the subordinate group keeps steadfastly to an assigned status or to what the dominant group regards as its proper place, as eventually occurred following the Aryan invasion of India. In either case, the feeling of a threat gradually dissipates and, with it, the prejudice which it produces.

These accommodations, however, would seem to be only provisional arrangements which, today, under the conditions of intensified contact increasingly characteristic of our modern world, are difficult to maintain. A second, and more secure, means of mitigating or perhaps completely dissipating race prejudice is to alter the conceptualization which the members of the dominant group hold of the subordinate group in such a way that the latter is no longer felt to be a threat and hence to be offensive and unacceptable in the social order in question.

Rational attempts to break down prejudice have usually taken this form; that is, an effort has been made to change the conceptualization which the members of a certain group have built up of another group. In the United States, for instance, certain educational agencies, religious organizations and humanitarian groups, as well as certain individuals, have attempted to point out the inaccuracy of the prevailing concept of the negro, and the injustice, from the democratic and Christian points of view, as well as the absurdity, of prevailing conceptualizations.

Although the significance of these attempts is not to be minimized, it is questionable whether or not such rational and directed efforts produce any appreciable effect, at least in cases of pronounced prejudice, where the group conception is firmly fixed. This is due to the fact that prejudice, as has been indicated, is composed of a cluster of feelings and impulses, all of which are of an irrational character and some of which are held quite unconsciously, and which for these reasons do not change readily, even though the conceptualization involved may be shown to be injustifiable and false. Appeals directed to the intellect do not readily reach and affect basic feelings, especially those which are unconsciously held, or obscure.

Attempts to bring members of different races into contact in such a way that they come to appreciate their common human character are likely to be, and actually have been, more fruitful. When persons come to learn about each other's personal experiences so as to note in the experiences of others a similarity with their own and thus to identify themselves one with the other, adverse conceptualizations are difficult longer to maintain.

Even these efforts, however, are limited in possibility and do not readily reach and alter the more basic feelings involved in race prejudice. Any profound change is likely to emerge only out of a new body of collective experience built up either around new issues in which the racial or cultural variations in question are of little or no import; or from a significant change in the social situation such, for instance, as an extensive population shift, in which the groups in question are brought into new and different forms of interdependency.

The increasing development of the means of communication in our modern world is bringing diverse peoples and cultures more and more into contact, thus augmenting the possibilities of friction and heightening interest in race prejudice. Any attempt to deal with prejudice, however, which this heightened interest may bring must— if it hopes to be effective, even to a moderate degree—recognize that prejudice, in itself, is "symptomatic" rather than definitive; that is, that it is *derived from* a given racial situation rather than produces it; and this attempt must proceed in keeping with an analysis of the actual content of the attitude of prejudice as it exists in the given situation, as well as an analysis of the social experiences which have produced it.

Selection 85

Interethnic Marriage in Los Angeles 1948-1959
John H. Burma

Throughout the history of the United States there have been ethnic and racial minorities upon whom the majority has looked as inferior. However, a dynamic quality has characterized the discrimination and prejudice in that the objects of disrespect have varied, not only from place to place but especially from time to time. An excellent illustration are the Irish Catholics, whose social status has ranged literally from pariah to President.

By no means have only sociologists been aware of the changing character and degree of prejudice and differential treatment. Many persons have sought to measure the degree of rejection or acceptance of various ethnic groups. For adults, such attitudes may be measured, for example, by interpreting replies to questions such as "Would you accept a Negro working in your office?" Projective devices have been used with children, such as showing a picture of a white boy and a Negro boy facing each other and touching hands and asking what they are doing. Answers ("They are playing together," "The black boy is stealing something from the white boy," etc.) are interpreted as measures of attitudes. All such measuring instruments, although very useful, are less than perfect in that there may be a difference between stated attitude and actual behavior; that is, faced with a concrete situation, one does not always do what he says he would do. Actual behavior is therefore a better index to attitude than is stated expectation.

Among the many types of behavior that demonstrate an acceptance of equality between ethnic groups, none shows a deeper acceptance than that presumably whole-hearted sharing we call marriage. Mere sex relations, even over a protracted period, are often between a recognized superior and a recognized inferior and definitely are no proof of acceptance of equality. On the other hand, *marriage* in its contemporary American significance is strong evidence of the acceptance of each of the partners as equal by the other.

From such one-by-one acceptance can be drawn inferences concerning people-by-people acceptance. Colonists in New Zealand, for example, refused to intermarry with the Maori and in fact eventually hunted them like animals. Conversely, early settlers in the Hawaiian Islands accepted the upper-class natives as equals, and legal marriage occurred early and frequently. Today, the sizable extent of intermarriage between Anglos and Mexicans is an index of the increasing acceptance of each by the other. The following study of ethnic intermarriage in Los Angeles may be used in part as an index of social nearness and social acceptance as well as an index of solidarity and cohesiveness; the data are therefore significant not just per se but also for the inferences that may be drawn from them.

Since all data presented are from marriage licenses only, no measures of happiness in marriage, reasons for marriage, children, eventual divorce, acceptance by families and friends, and the like can be reported. Class, education, family background, previous geographic residence, occupation, and a host of other important related matters also are unfortunately unavailable.

Partial and incomplete studies from other states and cities indicate that in most locations, even where it is legally permissible, few if any racial intermarriages take place. Many county clerks answered the author's inquiries about the number of racial intermarriages by reporting "one or two a year," "only a very few ever," "none in the last six years," etc. Probably the only cities that rank in the same category with Los Angeles are New York, Chicago, Philadelphia, and Detroit. Even in locations with the highest rates, however, racial intermarriages, although definitely increasing, still comprise a statistically insignificant proportion of total marriages. Los Angeles County is an atypical county in regard to the number and size of the minority groups found within it, so that application of the conclusions of this study to such places as Kansas City, Phoenix, Atlanta, or Newark is not possible.

In the following selection, students should be especially careful to distinguish between absolute numbers and percentages when comparing rates of intermarriage between various ethnic groups and should avoid inferring causal relationships that the data do not clearly prove.

All major groups in the United States today—racial, religious, or ethnic—look with favor on homogeneous marriage and definite disfavor on intermarriage. Thus, all intermarriage is relatively rare. In the most extreme situations, such as New York, Los Angeles, Chicago, and Philadelphia, probably no more than one in two hundred marriages has been interethnic in the sense of involving the marriage of Negroes, Filipinos, Chinese, Japanese, or Indians with Mexicans or Anglos. At the other extreme the number is zero. Various meritorious attempts have been made to study interracial marriages on the mainland of the United States, but with a few brilliant exceptions they usually have resulted in reports valid only for a particular group in a particular city or county at a particular date. Because of the difficulty of securing data, most researchers have had to content themselves with a few years and a few dozen or a few hundred cases. Examples include studies by Baber, Barron, Catapusen, Davis and Gardner, Drake and Cayton, Golden, Klineberg, Lawrence, Risdon, McWilliams, Rogers, Schuyler, and Smith.

The present report suffers from these same difficulties, but through the special cooperation of the County Clerk of Los Angeles County and of

From *Social Forces*, December 1963, pp. 156-165. Published by the University of North Carolina Press.

the Ford Foundation, it suffers somewhat less. That is, it covers eleven consecutive years, over 375,000 total marriages and well over 3,200 mixed marriages in a county having a sizeable number of each racial group. The term "mixed marriage" as used here needs special definition immediately, for it has a special meaning: "marriage" actually refers to taking out a marriage license, not the true marriage itself, on which the gathering of data was prohibitive in both time and money. It further was found that to refer to "couples who have taken out a marriage license, but who may not have married" was impossibly wordy and cumbersome, so "married" was substituted. In Los Angeles County about five percent of marriage licenses applied for are not used within the time span of their validity, but there is no information on whether interethnic couples are more or less likely than others to let their licenses lapse. "Interethnic intermarriage" is used to mean cases in which an Anglo or Mexican married either a Negro, Filipino, Japanese, Chinese, or Indian or member of another non-European racial-ethnic group.

A number of possible theoretical hypotheses are available and will be mentioned, but this particular paper is concerned more with reporting facts and analyzing them than in deriving or proving theories, which will be done in a later paper.

The data presented here have several inherent limitations. They are based solely on marriage license applications, and such applications contain only very limited information about the persons applying for the license. Further, this study is based on three separate projects of data-gathering, which unfortunately were not always fully comparable. . . .

Until November of 1948 the laws of the state of California prohibited the legal intermarriage of whites with persons of any other race. Some intermarriages did occur through the falsification of racial data, but little is known of the number of such cases. Panunzio reports for the years 1924-33, for Los Angeles County, "some" Mexicans marrying Asiatics; seven Anglo and Japanese marriages; possibly 85 Filipino and Anglo marriages (then legal); one Chinese and Anglo; 38 Indian and Anglo or Mexican marriages; and five Negro marriages with Anglos or Mexicans. When the California miscegenation law was held unconstitutional, the earlier marriage license forms requiring a statement of race continued in use, with some registrars, at least in Los Angeles County, refusing to accept marriage licenses unless the section on race was filled out with some accuracy. By "some accuracy" is meant that the registrars looked at the words on the application, looked at the persons, and if no discrepancy readily was

observable, they accepted the application. It must be remarked that some registrars accepted applications with "races" such as "Korean," "Samoan," or "Guamanian," but in general there was considerable uniformity. As a sidelight, the author did hear a couple threaten the County Clerk with suit because he refused to accept "human race" as a satisfactory description. By observation it appeared both persons in the dispute were clearly Caucasoid.

From 1948 through 1957 this study offers no information on the intermarriage of whites and American Indians. The County Clerk's office was not interested in these marriages and did not gather these data. The author was interested, but did not have the staff to go back and recheck all the records for this single item. When more staff was available to study the licenses for 1958 and 1959, white-Indian and Indian-white marriages were included as an index of what presumably had been happening in the recent past. For the same reason divorce data also were gathered only for these final two years. No data of any kind were gathered after September 18, 1959, for on that date a new law made it illegal to ask race or color on marriage licenses.

Table 1 shows the total number of marriage licenses taken out by interracial couples for the two months of 1948 in which this was legal, and for twelve months of each succeeding year until

TABLE 1: Interracial Marriages in Los Angeles County, 1948-59

YEAR	TOTAL MARRIAGES	INTERRACIAL MARRIAGES	INTERRACIAL MARRIAGES PER 1,000 MARRIAGES
1948 (2 mo.)	5,376	28	5.2
1949	31,779	187	5.8
1950	31,915	168	5.3
1951	29,459	187	6.4
1952	30,178	171	5.7
1953	31,980	197	6.2
1954	32,095	238	7.4
1955	33,996	264	7.8
1956	36,365	268	7.4
1957	38,333	346	9.1
1958	37,700	465	12.3
1959	39,300	631*	16.1*
		3,150	

* In the 8½ months of 1959 in which race could be recorded, there were 447 intermarriages, which were prorated to 631 for twelve months and 16.1 per 1,000 per year. The twelve year total also includes this proration.

1959. For 1959, the figure is prorated for a full twelve months so that the final year will be comparable to the other years. It is to be noted that the number of interracial marriages immediately after the old law was declared unconstitutional[1] was small. Certainly there was no "rush" of interracial couples clamoring to marry, nor was there any significant increase during the next several years. During the middle years of the study an increase does become apparent, assuming very significant proportions in 1958 and 1959. Even though the numbers remain small, any rate which triples in eleven years is showing significant increase. Even at its highest the rate is small but since some seven percent of Los Angeles County population is non-white, the rate conceivably could be eight to ten times as great as it actually is. On the other hand, this is a high rate compared to most of the remainder of the nation where the rate is practically zero.

As was previously mentioned, it is quite significant that there was no rush to intermarry when intermarriage was legalized; it was not until 1954 that any sizeable increases are seen. The 1957-59 period, however, shows by far the most rapid rate of increase found in any study with which the author is familiar. The total number of marriages increased by approximately 22 percent, from 1953 to 1959; the number of intermarriages for the same period increased approximately 220 percent. As far as these data are concerned, there can be no question of the recent "snowballing" characteristic of these marriages. There is no way of determining whether this "snowball" trend is continuing, since the new law forbidding asking race on licenses effectively prevents any count. What is clear is that the intermarriage rate per 1,000 marriages in Los Angeles County is now about triple what it was in the early years of the period studied. This is a minimum count too, for it does not include marriages between American Indians and any other group, marriages between two

ethnic groups where neither is white (e.g., Chinese-Filipino), or the Mexican-Anglo or Anglo-Mexican marriages, some of which may well have included persons of primarily Indian descent.

It can be seen from Table 2 that the white and Negro groups contain more women than men, and that all other groups contain a preponderance of men. If nothing more than sheer numbers were involved, and if all men and women in each group would marry within that group if it were physically possible to do so, then white men would marry only white women and Negro men would marry only Negro women. There would be an excess of both white and Negro women, however, available to marry into other groups. All Japanese, Chinese, Filipino, Indian and Other women would marry within their respective groups, although there would be excess males in each group to marry the excess white and Negro women. According to this hypothesis the largest number of intermarriages would be Filipino-white, then Chinese-white, Other-white, Japanese-white, and Indian-white in that order. There would be no intermarriages involving white or Negro males or of females of any but these two groups, and Negro females would intermarry like white females except on a one to nine ratio. This is what Panunzio meant when he said that sex distribution was a primary factor producing or preventing intermarriage.

Observation of Table 3 indicates how fallacious is the above theory and how obvious it is that sheer numbers do not explain the incidence of intermarriage. Negro males, despite having the largest proportion of excess females, outmarry by three and three-quarter times their populational expectancy. White males, despite the excess of

---

[1] The winning argument came when two Catholics, one Negro and one white, declared that their religious freedom was hampered by the law; they could receive all the sacraments except that of marriage, which was being unconstitutionally denied them by the law.

TABLE 2:   Population of Los Angeles County, by Races, by Sex with Sex Ratios and Sex Differentials, 1960*

RACE	MALE	FEMALE	EXCESS		SEX RATIO
White	2,656,627	2,797,239	F +	140,612	95
Negro	222,731	238,815	F +	16,084	93
Japanese	38,998	38,316	M +	682	102
Chinese.............	10,836	8,450	M +	2,386	128
Filipino	7,696	4,426	M +	3,270	174
Indian..............	4,139	3,970	M +	169	104
Other...............	3,620	2,908	M +	712	128

*Adapted from U.S. Bureau of Census, U.S. Census of Population; 1960 General Population Characteristics, California. Final Report P. C. (1)-6B Table 28 (Washington, D.C.: U.S. Government Printing Office, 1961).

white females, make up over one-third of all out-marrying males.

While these data do not explain why out-marriages occur, they do make it clear that sex ratios are not very significant causal factors in such marriages. Take for example Filipino men; the figures would indicate that about one in eleven Filipino males in Los Angeles County contracted an interethnic marriage during the 1948-59 period. Even this high proportion is a great understatement, however, due to those previously and continuingly married, and those too young to marry. It is more likely that one in every three or four Filipino males marrying during this period did not marry a Filipino woman. That about two-thirds of these men married Mexican American women is not surprising in view of the color homogamy and the fact that a large number of Filipinos in the United States speak Spanish. These data bear out Panunzio's theory that when people do marry outside their own group, culture homogeneity in the main determines the selection. Filipino females, whom one would expect to be the most sought after of all groups by the Filipino

males, nevertheless out-marry proportionally far more than any other group of females. Although the data are not fully complete, these Filipino girls seem well below the average age, were mostly born in America, and are very disproportionately themselves actually Filipino-white products of mixed marriages.

As for the almost 400 Japanese females who married white men, there is no obvious explanation in the data. Once the author, in common with other sociologists interested in this field, explained the first out-marriage of Japanese girls in terms of the shortage of Japanese males due to high casualties during World War II and the marriage of Nisei soldiers to Japanese girls during the occupation of Japan. These factors may have accounted for some early intermarriages, but in no way do they shed light on the large number of these marriages during the last three years of this study, the girls being much too young to have married veterans. Since during the same period some 200 Japanese males married white females, this earlier explanation must be discarded, preferably in favor of a socio-cultural one.

TABLE 3: Percentage of Males and Females of Selected Groups, Los Angeles County, 1960; Percentage of Males and Females Intermarrying, 1948-59, and Index of Proportion of Each in the Population and Intermarriages

GROUP	MALES		FEMALES	
	PERCENT OF TOTAL POPULATION	PERCENT OF TOTAL POPULATION INTERMARRYING	PERCENT OF TOTAL POPULATION	PERCENT OF TOTAL POPULATION INTERMARRYING
White	87.51	35.98	90.61	63.98
Negro	7.33	27.60	7.73	10.12
Japanese	1.29	7.02	1.24	13.42
Chinese	.36	5.83	.27	4.94
Filipino	.31	23.95	.14	7.50

TABLE 4: Percentage of Males and Females in the Total Population, 1960, and Percentage in Total Intermarriages, for Selected Groups, Los Angeles County, 1948-59

GROUP	MALE			FEMALE		
	PERCENT IN TOTAL POPULATION	PERCENT IN INTER-MARRIAGE	INDEX	PERCENT IN TOTAL POPULATION	PERCENT IN INTER-MARRIAGE	INDEX
White	90.2	42.0	.47	90.4	58.0	.64
Negro	7.6	21.5	2.83	7.7	6.5	.84
Japanese	1.3	7.4	5.70	1.2	12.6	10.50
Chinese	.4	4.2	10.50	.3	4.4	14.66
Filipino	.3	13.7	45.67	.1	8.1	81.00
Indian	.1	3.8	38.00	.1	4.0	40.00
Other...............	.1	7.4	74.00	.1	6.4	64.00

That some 170 Chinese males married white females is arithmetically reasonable, but that nearly 150 Chinese females married white males is arithmetically so improbable that one has no alternative but to assume that other factors are involved. Although the data give no causal inferences, it is the author's opinion that assimilation, decreasing social distance, improved social status of minorities, and decreasing intolerance are likely to be found among the causal factors for all intermarrying groups. For the smaller groups not yet mentioned the samples are not large enough to draw any conclusions other than the obvious one that their intermarriages, as much as or more than the larger groups, have made significant increases in the last few years, quite possibly for the same reasons. At the very most, only about 40 percent of intermarriages could be accounted for on the basis of sex ratio imbalances.

Whatever the causal factors, Table 3 and Table 4 show that the probability that any given member of the smaller groups will intermarry is much greater than the probability that any given member of the white group will intermarry. Comparison with Table 2 shows that size of group is a much more predictive factor than sex ratio. For example, white females are found to make up 58 percent of the women intermarrying and in this sense are more likely to be involved in intermarrying than any other females. On the other hand, in Los Angeles there are far more white

females than any other group, and it is only sheer numbers which make the probability of their appearance seem high. Actually, the probability that a random white female will intermarry is far less than the probability that a random Filipino female will intermarry. For any group the formula of percent of intermarriages divided by the percent of population gives the measure of probability of intermarriage for a person within that group. For white females this index is only .64, but for Filipino females the same index is 81.00; this a Filipino female is over 125 times as likely to intermarry as is a white female.

Whether we consider the whole period or the last two years it is clear that proportionately white males, despite bulking large in total numbers, are individually the least likely to intermarry, with white women next and Negro women next. All other categories have much higher indices. No specific populational figures are available for Hawaiians or Koreans, but it is clear their rates also are high. That these variations are significant cannot be doubted when we see that for the total period, for example, the probability that a Filipino male will intermarry is almost 450 times as great as the probability of a white male intermarrying. Only among Negroes was the probability of male intermarriage significantly higher than that of female intermarriage and only among Japanese was there a consistent tendency for females to outmarry considerably more than males.

Using the supplementary and admittedly inadequate base of two years, as seen in Table 5, one observes that there were a sizeable number of white-Indian and Indian-white intermarriages (there were less than 20,000 Indians in all of California in 1950), and that there was little difference in the number of males and females intermarrying from this group. Because of the definitions used, whites were involved in 100 percent of the intermarriages counted, and 25 percent of these whites were Mexican Americans. Negroes were involved in 34 percent of the cases; Filipino Americans in 29 percent; Japanese Americans in 18 percent; Chinese Americans in 11 percent; and Other groups in 8 percent.

During the period studied there was a significant increase not only in total intermarriages but also in every individual category. Comparing the 1949-50 average with the 1958-59 average we find that while total marriages were up 21 percent, total intermarriages were up 210 percent. Marriages involving Filipinos and whites increased by 65 percent; those involving Chinese and whites increased by 122 percent; those involving Negroes and whites increased by 235 percent; those in-

TABLE 5: Intermarriage by Ethnic Classification and Sex, 1958-59

CLASSIFICATION	TOTAL NUMBER	PERCENT OF TOTAL
Negro-white	256	21.5
Filipino-white	163	13.7
White-Japanese	150	12.6
White-Filipino	96	8.1
Japanese-white	88	7.4
White-Negro	77	6.5
Hawaiian-white	63	5.3
White-Chinese	52	4.4
Chinese-white	50	4.2
White-Indian	48	4.0
White-Hawaiian	47	4.0
Indian-white	45	3.8
White-Korean	11	1.0
Korean-white	7	.6
Other	36	3.0
Total	1,189	100.1
Anglo-Mexican	1,433	
Mexican-Anglo	1,226	

volving Japanese and whites increased 525 percent; and those involving Other groups and whites increased 1840 percent. While these trends are clear, it would be dangerous to extrapolate them beyond the immediate future.

Although all data are not presented here, it has been computed that Mexican Americans are about three times more likely to outmarry than are Anglos. In the case of intermarriages involving Negro men, the incidence of Mexican American females is about 328 percent of arithmetic expectancy; with Chinese males it is about 300 percent of expectancy; with Japanese males it is about 328 percent of expectancy; and with Filipino males it is about 827 percent of expectancy.

In the cases involving white men, the incidence of Mexican American females is about 31 percent of expectancy; in the cases of Chinese females it is about 141 percent of expectancy; for Japanese females it is about 119 percent of expectancy; and for Filipino females it is about 336 percent of expectancy. The disproportionate number of Filipino and Mexican intermarriages would seem to confirm Panunzio's theory of the insignificance of cultural similarity in intermarriage. Thus, Mexican American females are more likely to intermarry than are either Anglo females or Mexican American males, and the latter are more likely to intermarry than are Anglo males. One might hypothesize on this evidence that the social distance between Mexican Americans and the other ethnic groups studied is less than between Anglos and the other ethnic groups. The 1958-59 evidence would indicate that social distance is less between Anglos and Mexican Americans than between Anglos and any of the other groups. In general one might hypothesize that the Anglos felt least social distance between themselves and Mexican Americans, then Filipinos, then Chinese, then Japanese, and felt the greatest social distance between themselves and Negroes. Dynamically, the interpretation may be made that while the social distance between whites and the other groups is decreasing in all cases, it is decreasing more rapidly between whites and Negroes and Filipinos (and about at the same rate). While this social distance hypothesis does not clash with the data (and in fact is supported by the large proportion of marriages between Mexican Americans and Filipinos), it would be a serious oversimplification to assign a monistic cause to any large social phenomenon.

One type of information which is both useful and available from marriage license applications is the age of the applicant. In order both to compare each of the groups and also to show any trends which might be occurring, the reporting is in terms of the median age for 1951-53 and for 1957-59. As a base from which to compare other groups, it should be noted that our sample of males in the white-white marriages had a median age of about 24.5 for the early period and 25 for the later period. Our sample of males in the Negro-Negro marriages had a median age of about 28 for this earlier period and about 25.5 for the later period.

The oldest group of males was in the Filipino-white marriages; for the earlier period their median age was about 41, but by the later period it had declined to about 28 which, as will be seen, is not far different from the ages of other intermarrying males during that period. We interpret this change (the largest in any group) as being due to the earlier period containing a significant number of the "wave" of Filipinos who came here 25 to 35 years ago. By the later period, most of these persons who ever were going to marry had done so, and most later marriages were by younger Filipinos who were second generation, and fewer in number. What influence, if any, a differential divorce and remarriage rate might have on ages will be explored later in this paper.

Our next oldest group of males, also significantly above the average in age, was the white males marrying Negro females. This group has a median age of 36.7 during the earlier period, which dropped to 32.8 during the later period. Also older were the Chinese males marrying white females who in the earlier period had a median age of 36.3 and of 27.7 in the later period. Like the Filipino males, it is probable that some of the differential is due to marriage of the first generation persons in the earlier period and not in the later period. The Negro males who marry white women are slightly older than the Negro-Negro average in both time periods. Anglo males who marry Japanese, Filipino, or Chinese women are about average age, and are significantly younger than Anglo males marrying Negro females. As a total group, intermarrying males are somewhat older than intramarrying males.

Intermarrying females are somewhat older than intramarrying females. For the earlier period of this study, the median age of females in white-white marriages was 23; for the later period it was 21.5 years. In Negro-Negro marriages the median ages were 27 and 23 respectively. In the first period the two oldest groups were Anglo females marrying Chinese or Filipinos and Negro females marrying Anglo males; all three were significantly beyond the median age for white brides. The Filipino girls who married Anglo men were the youngest of all—just under 23 for the earlier period and just under 22 for the later period. In the later period, all female median ages were lower, with the Anglo women marrying Negroes or Chinese being the oldest, closely followed by the Japanese women marrying Anglo men.

The groom-bride age differential in the early period for white-white marriage was 1.5 years; for Negro-Negro marriages it was 1 year. In the

later period it was 3.5 for white-white and 2.5 for Negro-Negro. In the early period the median age differential between Filipino males and their white brides was 12 years; for Anglo males with Negro brides it was 6.7 years. Even though the white brides of Chinese males were the oldest group in the early period, they were almost six years younger than their husbands. The Japanese brides who in the earlier period married white

TABLE 6:   Intermarriage by Racial Classification and Sex, 1948-59

CLASSIFICATION	1948	1949	1950	1951	1952	1953	1954	1955	1956	1957	1958	1959	TOTAL	PERCENT OF TOTAL
Negro-white	6	43	30	50	45	53	61	84	77	95	111	145	800	25.4
Negro-Anglo	4	32	19	38	33	34	52	—	—	—	93	121	426	
Negro-Mexican	2	11	11	12	12	19	9	—	—	—	18	24	118	
Filipino-white	14	74	69	69	59	50	56	53	42	63	76	87	712	22.6
Filipino-Anglo	12	39	33	37	34	31	32	—	—	—	65	56	339	
Filipino-Mexican ..	2	35	36	32	25	19	24	—	—	—	11	31	215	
White-Japanese	3	12	12	16	13	20	29	37	45	57	65	85	394	12.5
Anglo-Japanese	3	11	10	16	11	18	25	—	—	—	60	78	232	
Mexican-Japanese ..	0	1	2	0	2	2	4	—	—	—	5	7	23	
White-Negro	0	10	16	12	13	25	30	23	27	34	35	42	267	8.5
Anglo-Negro	0	10	11	10	10	16	23	—	—	—	31	34	145	
Mexican-Negro	0	0	5	2	3	9	7	—	—	—	4	8	38	
White-Filipino	0	10	9	12	11	12	14	12	22	22	41	55	220	7.0
Anglo-Filipino	0	6	4	9	9	10	12	—	—	—	33	45	128	
Mexican-Filipino ..	0	4	5	3	2	2	2	—	—	—	8	10	36	
Japanese-white	1	8	6	10	11	14	10	18	14	26	30	58	206	6.3
Japanese-Anglo	1	5	6	6	10	12	7	—	—	—	24	44	115	
Japanese-Mexican ..	0	3	0	4	1	2	3	—	—	—	6	14	33	
Chinese-white	3	19	11	9	5	8	21	12	16	17	25	25	171	5.4
Chinese-Anglo	2	11	10	6	5	7	15	—	—	—	23	23	101	
Chinese-Mexican ..	1	8	1	3	0	1	6	—	—	—	2	2	25	
White-Chinese	1	6	10	5	10	11	11	13	13	13	18	34	145	4.6
Anglo-Chinese	1	5	10	5	9	11	9	—	—	—	16	31	77	
Mexican-Chinese ..	0	1	0	0	1	0	2	—	—	—	2	3	9	
Hawaiian-white	0	0	0	0	0	1	0	0	3	7	26	37	74	2.3
White-Hawaiian.....	0	0	0	0	0	0	0	0	0	0	15	32	47	1.5
White-Korean	0	2	4	2	1	2	0	6	2	6	4	7	36	1.1
Korean-white	0	0	0	0	0	0	0	0	0	0	3	4	7	*
Other..............	0	3	1	2	3	1	6	6	7	6	18	18	71	2.2
Total	28	187	168	187	171	197	238	264	268	346	467	629	3,150	

Note: 1948 was not prorated to 12 months because no legal intermarriages took place before its last two months and 1959 was prorated to 12 months because intermarriages did continue through the remaining three and a half months of the year. Data on Mexican surnames is not available for 1955-57, so the "total" for that group represents 1948-54 plus 1958-59 with no prorating except 1959.

grooms were the only group whose median age was older than their husbands' (1.3 years). In the second period this group's median age was 1.3 years below that of their husbands', and still the nearest to equal of any group.

It would be realistic to hypothesize that some of the persons entering mixed marriages would be themselves the product of mixed marriages, and such was found to be the case. A separate study of the 1952-57 data found that marriages of persons identifiable as such (an obvious under-count since no Negro-white mixtures were in-cluded) were approximately ten percent of the total for that period. Significantly, the number increased from under seven percent for the first two years to over 12 percent for the last two years. Roughly two-thirds were intermarriages of Anglos with persons of mixed Filipino-Anglo ancestry. The remaining one-third were fairly evenly di-vided between Japanese-white, Chinese-white, and Other-white mixtures. A significant age differential also existed for this intermixed group; they were the youngest of all, and were the only group with any sizeable number of 18 year old grooms or 16-17 year old brides. The median age for the "mixed" grooms of Anglo brides was 22, the mode was only 18; the median age for Anglo grooms of "mixed" brides was 23, the mode was 18. For the "mixed" brides of Anglo grooms, the median age and mode both were 20; for the Anglo brides of "mixed" grooms the median age was 19 and the mode was 18. Should one present the hypothe-sis that "mixed" children leave their parental homes to set up their own homes earlier than is true of Anglo and Negro children, the data would not contradict such an hypothesis.

In summary as regards age: (1) for the male groups, median age decreased between the earlier and the later periods studied, but tended to remain higher than for intramarriages; (2) for the earlier period males in the Filipino-Anglo, Anglo-Negro, and Chinese-Anglo intermarriages were the oldest; Anglo males marrying Japanese or Filipino females were the youngest; (3) there was much less age range in the later period, but most inter-marrying males were two or three years older than the intramarrying males; only in Anglo-Filipino marriages was the male median lower than in Anglo-Anglo marriages; (4) for the female groups median age decreased between the earlier and the later periods, but tended to remain higher than for intramarriages; (5) in the earlier period women in the Chinese-Anglo, Anglo-Negro, and Filipino-Anglo marriages were the oldest; Filipino women marrying Anglo males were the youngest; (6) in the later period there was less age differ-ential, but with the same older and younger groups; (7) in both periods intermarrying females tended to be one to three years older than intra-marrying females; (8) the youngest of all groups were the products of mixed marriages who them-selves were intermarrying; (9) median age differen-tial between husbands and wives was significantly greater in intermarriages than in intramarriages.

Tables 5 and 6 present data concerning which ethnic groups marry which and by what sex. In each case the group written first represents the male partner in the marriage. Thus "Negro-white" is to be interpreted as Negro male marrying white female. "Korean," "Hawaiian," "Filipino" are not included as the author's analysis of race, but because they were accepted as "race" by the Los Angeles Marriage Bureau; they are repro-duced for the light they shed on intermarriage, not for their anthropological authenticity. The marked increase in 1958-59 in "other" marriages is only partly real. In analyzing the prior data the author arbitrarily assigned one ethnic group (by father's classification) to cases of mixed-parentage

TABLE 7: Previous Divorces per 1,000 for Mixed and Non-Mixed Marriages, with White-White as Index, Los Angeles County, 1958-59

CLASSIFICATION	DIVORCES PER 1,000 MARRIAGES WHITE-WHITE AS INDEX
White-Negro	158
Negro-white	146
Negro-Negro	127
Chinese-white.......	102
White-white	100
Filipino-white.......	98
Hawaiian-white	92
Anglo-Mexican	87
Mexican-Anglo	82
White-Japanese	75
White-Chinese	74
Japanese-white......	72
White-Filipino	69
White-Hawaiian.....	68
Indian-white........	53
Mexican-Mexican....	50
Filipino-Filipino.....	45
Other..............	37
Korean-Korean	37
White-Indian	34
Chinese-Chinese.....	14
Japanese-Japanese ...	13
Indian-Indian	12

persons. The authors failed to tell the persons hired to gather the 1958-59 data to do this and it was only after all data was gathered that this oversight was discovered. Thus most of the increase in "other" consists of mixed-parentage cases. The term "Mexican" refers to a Caucasian with a Mexican name, without reference to where the person was born; similarly "Anglo" is used to refer to any Caucasian who does not have a Mexican name. The form in which the author received the 1955-57 data made it impossible to determine surnames in the same fashion as 1948-54 and 1958-59. This explains incomplete tables and why the Anglo and Mexican totals do not equal the grand total for any category.

It would be nice if marriage license data could tell us whether the applicants lived happily ever after. Unfortunately, they cannot; but they can tell us whether or not the persons being married have previously been divorced. Table 7 and Table 8 present information which, in summary, shows that intermarriages involving Negroes are most likely to include previously divorced persons, the odds being about even that one of the parties has previously been divorced, and it being twice as likely that a person involved in a marriage be-

tween a white and a Negro has been married at least twice before than if the intermarriage was between any other groups. Most other intermarriages are less likely to involve divorced persons than are regular white-white marriages. Other than Negro-Negro intramarriages, all other intramarriages are very significantly less likely to include divorced persons.

In intermarriages the percentage of divorced white women by group of the groom is approximately: white 20 percent; Mexican 20 percent; Japanese 20 percent; Filipino 13 percent; Chinese 16 percent; and Negroes 40 percent.

In summary, this study indicates that in Los Angeles intermarriages are increasing significantly; the largest number of marriages include whites and Negroes, but proportionately the smaller groups intermarry tremendously more than the larger groups; some evidence of intermarriage by cultural homogamy exists; intermarried couples are on the average somewhat older than persons intramarrying, except if they themselves are the products of intermarriage; and, except for whites, in most cases there was a greater likelihood that one party had been divorced previously than in comparable intramarriages.

TABLE 8:   Percentage, by Groups, of Divorced and Never Divorced Couples, 1958-59

	INTRAMARRIAGE								
	A-A	M-M	N-N	F-F	J-J	C-C	I-I	K-K	OTHER
ND	72	82	60	86	95	94	94	88	76
D-ND	6	6	8	4	2	2	2	0	6
ND-D	7	6	10	4	2	3	2	0	11
D-D	7	3	10	4	2	0	2	5	3
EDMI	8	3	12	2	2	1	0	7	4

	INTERMARRIAGE										
	A-M	A-N	A-F	A-J	A-C	A-I	M-A	F-A	N-A	J-A	C-A	I-A
ND	70	52	72	67	69	79	75	66	50	70	59	81
D-ND	9	15	6	13	12	3	5	8	9	9	10	6
ND-D	8	2	13	12	12	5	7	12	12	11	15	6
D-D	7	10	5	4	2	8	5	3	13	4	5	3
EDMI	6	21	5	4	5	5	7	11	15	6	10	3

KEY
A—*Anglo*   ND—*No divorces*
M—*Mexican*   D-ND—*Male divorced, female not divorced*
N—*Negro*   ND-D—*Male not divorced, female divorced*
F—*Filipino*   D-D—*Both divorced*
J—*Japanese*   EDMI—*Either divorced more than once*
C—*Chinese*
I—*Indian*
K—*Korean*

Recent Research

I. Roger Yoshino

The general area of sociological study termed *social problems* presently is recognized as not being a unified area and hence little effort is spent on research in the field as a whole. Rather, following Robert Merton's suggestions concerning theories of the middle range, most present research concerns particular areas, such as crime, delinquency, mental illness, or minority-group problems. Literally dozens of other problem areas in modern society might also be properly designated as social problems. The following research summary is limited arbitrarily to a few problems, not because there are not numerous other important social problems and not because there is not voluminous recent research available but solely because of the serious limitations of space.

Some of the better known theories are differential association, delinquent subculture, and culture conflict. Among current developments in the field of criminological etiology has been a move away from such general theories toward separate theories that explain specific patterns of behavior.[1] In the area of crime, the generality does not extend beyond the fact that all criminals have deviated from the law. The feasibility of utilizing a separate theory based on arrest patterns was depicted in a recent research project conducted at a reformatory in Washington, D.C.[2] An experimental sample of offenders charged with drunkenness and assault was compared with a control sample of offenders who were incarcerated for a variety of offenses ranging from larceny to check forgery. The characteristics of the experimental group varied considerably from those of the comparison or control group. Among the differences, none from the experimental group came from slum areas with delinquent subcultures; none came from broken homes, and none had serious marital difficulties of their own; none came from homes lacking parental authority; and none lacked religious affiliation. In short, the general social milieu of offenders in the experimental group was far less criminally prone than that of offenders in the control group. While generalized theories may prove adequate for the explanation of certain crimes, separate theories provide further insight into reasons for behavior and will undoubtedly assist the social workers in the effective treatment of offenders.

Another research project that utilized behavior as the specific unit of study dealt with check forgers. Lemert[3] made a detailed study of persons who were serving sentences for check forgery in a California correctional institution. His findings accentuate the differences between check forgers and professional thieves. Check forgers were found to operate as isolates, to avoid association with criminals, and not to engage in bogus check passing on a regular basis.

What changes, if any, have taken place regarding the public's attitude toward white-collar crime? In a research project designed to isolate specifics, a sample of respondents were each given six abstracts of actual court cases involving pure foods violations.[4] Over three fourths of the respondents were in favor of severer penalties than were handed down by the courts. Furthermore, the consumers reacted to violations without regard for their own class position. This raises a question regarding Sutherland's general idea of the tolerance of white-collar crime by individuals in the same socioeconomic class as the violators. There was, however, support for the position that white-collar offenders are viewed as "lawbreakers" but not as criminals.

Observations of the past few years indicate that juvenile delinquency may be on the increase among middle-class youth.[5] It must be realized that millions of Americans who were in the lower income bracket are now economically in the middle income category. Although their income has risen, it is probable that many of these families have not yet attained middle-class values, attitudes, and behavior, and it is suggested that the children of such families, who represent a *nouveau bourgeoisie,* may account for the increased percentage of delinquency in the middle class.

Juvenile delinquency is often related to poor social environment or to association with a deviant subculture. A recent article[6] points out that delinquents do not deviate from middle-class norms, especially as these norms pertain to big money, leisure activities, and toughness. These values are subterranean or dormant in the larger society but come to the fore on vacations, in the course of a night out on the town, or during other such occasions. It is alleged that much of the delinquent's trouble is merely bad timing. When one probes beneath the façade of middle-class activities and concomitantly views delinquents as members of a leisure class, the subterranean values of the dominant society are found to be akin to the dominant values of the delinquents.

In numerous studies of social problems, theoretical ideas of social disorganization and personality deviation overlap.[7] Research devoted to the identification of the personality characteristics of juvenile delinquents' often falls into this category. A number of probationers in Los Angeles were compared with nondelinquents; with such variables as age, sex, socioeconomic status, race, and IQ closely matched.[8] This study did not provide evidence that the delinquent probationers had unique personality patterns; in fact, in one scale designed to measure the degree of hysteria symptoms, statistical data revealed that the nondelinquents were less normal than the probationers, although the scores of both experimental and control groups fell well within the range of normality. An important limitation of the study is that, for want of a practical alternative, a legal definition was used to determine the delinquent experimental group—the probationers had been apprehended for violation of the criminal law. This definition involves one of two limited assumptions: that delinquency is an attribute possessed only by those apprehended, or that those apprehended are more deviant than those who are not. If delinquency is to be used as a variable, it must be considered in terms of deviant behavior as well as the frequency of violations of the norms.

There have been a number of penetrating sociological research studies in the area of personal deviation, particularly as it pertains to mental illness. These studies emphasize the idea that becoming a mental patient is a socially structured event. In a recent study,[9] research relationship was established with both mental patient and spouse. In one type of situation, the marital partners adapted to a condition based on interpersonal isolation, emotional distance, and a minimum of explicit demands upon each other. In these cases, the wife's deviant personality did not lead to immediate changes in family life but rather to an increase in mutual withdrawal. In situations of another kind, withdrawal by the wife resulted in intense maternal concern and involvement, where the mother replaced the wife in her domestic functions. The husband withdrew to the periphery of the family system, leaving the wife and the mother in symbiotic interdependency, where there was an integration of roles involving a helpless person who needed care and a helpful one who administered help. It appeared that the collapse of such accommodation patterns between the deviant and her interpersonal world rendered the situation unmanageable and led to hospitalization.

Hollingshead and Redlich[10] compared the social class of schizophrenics with that of their fathers, and they support the thesis that social status is the independent rather than the dependent variable in mental illness. In contrast, a longitudinal study comparing the social mobility of a deviant population with a matched control group showed that deviance determines class.[11] Ex-patients of a child guidance clinic, observed after a period of thirty years, were found to have more unfavorable occupational mobility than a similar group of public school children. Severe childhood behavior problems seemed to have affected later occupational status by interfering with educational attainment. These findings support the presumptive observations by Faris and Dunham that deviance causes low social status. It seems plausible that there is a reciprocal relationship in which deviance determines class status and vice versa.

Drug addiction is considered a degraded form of deviant behavior and is generally associated with the lower socioeconomic classes. Anomalously, the United States Commissioner of Narcotics estimates that 1 in 100 physicians in comparison to 1 in 3000 lay persons is addicted to drugs. After interviews with physicians who either were or had been addicts in New York and other Eastern states, it was concluded that the established theories of deviant behavior and addiction are not adequate.[12] The theory of deviant behavior as a reflection of differences in the legitimate means of access to culturally prescribed goals does not appear to be relevant to addicted physicians, who have achieved their professional status legitimately. Nor does the theory of associational differentiation apply, since the doctors in the sample almost never associated with other addicted physicians. The traditional explanation of deviant behavior as the result of socialization in a given subculture does not provide any clues either. Research, however, suggests several combinations of underlying factors which may produce the addiction-prone physician: (a) role strain—associated with negative attitudes toward being a doctor; (b) passivity—reinforced by taking drugs; (c) omnipotence—a high self-concept and a belief that the effect of an opiate can be controlled; and (d) the varying effects of drugs on different users.

Another study report pertains to abstinence and relapse among heroin addicts.[13] In the period following physical withdrawal from heroin, the addict seeks relationship with the nonaddict society. However, the narcotic user's attempt to enact a new role that coincides with his desired self-image as an abstainer is frequently not gratified. Rather, socially disjunctive experiences based on the larger society's attitudes toward addicts force the abstainer to realign his values with those of the world of addicts. In a circular process, when addiction has been re-established, the self-recrimination engendered by remembrance of a successful period of abstinence sows the seeds of a new attempt at abstinence.

The roles forced upon the deviant in the United States make it most difficult for him to return to the nondeviant norms of society,[14] although institutionalized means are provided for a deviant to resume societal roles without a permanent stigma. Other societies consider deviance a part of the socialization process of the young—behavior that can be abandoned without much castigation. Comparative studies of those societies that allow a former deviant more ready re-entry into normal social life is an area which behooves research.

It has been stated that of all social problems there is perhaps none more unnecessary than the race problem.[15] Many of the problems and research still center around the Negro, the largest of our minority groups. As the Negro has migrated from the rural South, increased research, dealing with the problems of occupational and housing adjustment, has followed him to the North and West. One study,[16] which describes the socioeconomic status of Negroes in a Northern industrial city, shows that many of the job opportunities in an automotive production area are limited to the semiskilled operative level. The findings give strong evidence of unequal opportunities and/or differences between Negroes and whites in preparation for professional and skilled occupations. However, the data also indicate that, when educated, younger Negroes are effectively utilizing formal education in much the same manner that other minority groups did in improving their overall status.

A survey of attitudes toward Negro housing problems among white residents of Minneapolis reveals a mixture of prejudice and tolerance.[17] Fear of land value depreciation, dislike for Negroes, and the possibility of intermarriage and loss of status in the eyes of others are the major reasons given for not wanting Negroes as neighbors. On the other hand, in answer to a "loaded" question, four fifths of the white residents responded that they would not object to living in a neighborhood with one or two Negro families who keep up their homes and try to be good neighbors. The most significant findings were the inconsistencies found among expressed attitudes and those between expressed attitudes and reports of behavior. Such findings may reveal the mental dilemma which Northern white people have concerning Negroes and their relations with them.

Research conducted in New Haven, Connecticut, took up specifically the problem of residential integration and property values.[18] Although there is widespread fear among home owners that property values will depreciate when Negroes move into white neighborhoods, the facts of the study indicated otherwise. On the contrary, property values rose following Negro entry, a finding that supports similar studies carried out in California, Oregon, Kansas, Illinois, Michigan, and Pennsylvania.[19] Research shows that nonwhite entry into a neighborhood is usually associated with rising rather than with falling real estate prices and furthermore that the class of Negro entrants is generally higher than that of their white neighbors. The New Haven study, conducted in predominantly middle- and upper-class neighborhoods, differed from most previous research in depicting the low degree of Negro influx and the below average rate of turnover; that is, there was no invasion of large numbers of Negroes into any neighborhood, and apparently few white home owners decided to sell their homes on account of the nonwhite entry.

From still another point of departure, it was hypothesized that Negroes in integrated housing have more positive self-concepts than do Negroes in segregated housing. While the data did not bear out the thesis, they did show that as compared to Negroes in segregated housing, Negroes in integrated housing tend to undergo more improvement in self-concept.[20]

Negroes, especially in the lower class, are more likely than white persons to be affiliated with formal voluntary associations, inasmuch as they are not allowed to be active in much of the other organized life of American society.[21] Such inaccessibility and discrimination have led to a change in the prevailing attitude of the Negro from one of complacency to one of action. It is suggested, however, that sit-ins and other forms of protest led by middle- and upper-class Negroes are best interpreted by reference-group theory and the concept of relative deprivation.[22] The Negroes' shift from accommodation to involvement is viewed as a consequence of a shift from evaluating their social position primarily in terms of their race to evaluating it in terms of a nonmembership group. In other words, the nonmembership reference group for Negro college, business, and professional people is considered to be white persons of similar position. Data from a questionnaire administered to three Negro colleges in North Carolina confirm the thesis that the development and spread of nonviolent protest activity are less indicative of social alienation than of the Negro's identification with the white middle class.

What influence do education and religion have in the development of tolerant attitudes between peoples? Previous research indicates that the role of these institutions is not yet clearly established; however, education has been found to be negatively related,[23] while religious orthodoxy has been positively related to prejudice.[24] In an empirical study carried out in South Dakota, using the Bogardus Social Distance Scale to measure prejudice, it was found that church participation and formal education were negatively related to prejudice.[25] The data indicate that such personality variables as status concern, conservatism, and antisocial tendencies are not related to ethnic distance. Authoritarianism is the only personality factor that is positively related to prejudice. Authoritarianism and religiosity often coincide where orthodox believers have been conditioned by rigid doctrines. Formal education, which furthers understanding among peoples, diminishes prejudice regardless of the authoritarian dimension.

Much excellent research has been added to the fund of literature in the area of social problems. None of the problems included in this section are new, but the dynamics of change signals the need to continue research. Moreover, further replication of some of the findings is needed before new theories can be accepted with confidence.

References

1. Don C. Gibbons and Donald L. Garrity, "Some Suggestions for the Development of Etiological and Treatment Theory in Criminology," *Social Forces*, 38:1 (October 1959), 51-58.
2. Julian Roebuck and Ronald Johnson, "The Negro Drinker and Assault as a Criminal Type," *Crime and Delinquency*, 8:1 (January 1962), 21-33.
3. Edwin M. Lemert, "The Behavior of the Systematic Check Forger," *Social Problems*, 6:2 (Fall 1958), 141-149.
4. Donald J. Newlan, "Public Attitudes Toward a Form of White Collar Crime," *Social Problems*, 4:3 (January 1957), 228-232.
5. David Matza and Gresham M. Sykes, "Juvenile Delinquency and Subterranean Values," *American Sociological Review*, 26:5 (October 1961), 712-719.
6. Robert H. Bohlke, "Social Mobility, Stratification Inconsistency and Middle Class Delinquency," *Social Problems*, 8:4 (Spring 1961), 351-363.
7. Robert K. Merton and Robert A. Nisbet, *Contemporary Social Problems* (New York: Harcourt, Brace and World, Inc., 1961), p. 719.
8. Arthur P. Volkman, "A Matched-Group Personality Comparison of Delinquent and Nondelinquent Juveniles," *Social Problems*, 6:3 (Winter 1958-59), 238-245.
9. Harold Sampson, Sheldon L. Messinger, and Robert D. Towne, "Family Process and Becoming a Mental Patient," *The American Journal of Sociology*, 68:2 (July 1962), 88-96.

10. August B. Hollingshead and Frederick C. Redlich, *Social Class and Mental Illness* (New York: John Wiley and Sons, Inc., 1958).
11. Lee N. Robins, Harry Gyman, and Patricia O'Neal, "The Interaction of Social Class and Deviant Behavior," *American Sociological Review,* 27:4 (August 1962), 480-492.
12. Charles Winick, "Physician Narcotic Addicts," *Social Problems,* 9:2 (Fall 1961), 174-186.
13. Marsh B. Ray, "The Cycle of Abstinence and Relapse Among Heroin Addicts," *Social Problems,* 9:2 (Fall 1961), 132-140.
14. Kai T. Erikson, "Notes on the Sociology of Deviance," *Social Problems,* 9:4 (Spring 1962), 307-314.
15. Paul B. Horton and Gerald R. Leslie, *The Sociology of Social Problems,* 2nd ed. (New York: Appleton-Century-Crofts, Inc., 1960), p. 333.
16. Basil C. Zimmer, "The Adjustment of Negroes in a Northern Industrial City," *Social Problems,* 9:4 (Spring 1962), 378-386.
17. Arnold M. Rose, "Inconsistencies in Attitudes Toward Negro Housing," *Social Problems,* 8:4 (Spring 1961), 286-292.
18. Erdman Palmore and John Howe, "Residential Integration and Property Values," *Social Problems,* 10:1 (Summer 1962), 52-55.
19. Luigi Laurenti, *Property Values and Race* (Berkeley: University of California Press, 1960), pp. 8-27.
20. Ernest Works, "Residence in Integrated and Segregated Housing and Improvement in Self-Concepts of Negroes," *Sociology and Social Research,* 46:3 (April 1962), 294-301.
21. Nicholas Babchuk and Ralph Thompson, "The Voluntary Associations of Negroes," *American Sociological Review,* 27:5 (October 1962), 647-655.
22. Ruth Searles and J. Allen Williams, "Negro College Students' Participation in Sit-Ins," *Social Forces,* 40:3 (March 1962), 215-220.
23. John G. Martin and Frank R. Westie, "The Tolerant Personality," *American Sociological Review,* 24:4 (August 1959), 521-528.
24. Gordon W. Allport, *The Nature of Prejudice* (Reading, Mass.: Addison-Wesley Publishing Co., 1955), p. 444.
25. John D. Photiadis and Jeanne Biggar, "Religiosity, Education, and Ethnic Distance," *The American Journal of Sociology,* 67:6 (May 1962), 666-672.

Correlation Chart

The chart on the following pages is provided as a guide for using this volume in conjunction with the eighteen general sociology texts listed below. The boldface numbers in the left-hand column refer to the chapters of the primary texts; the numbers in the other columns indicate related readings in *Life in Society*.

Bell, Earl H., *Social Foundations of Human Behavior* (New York: Harper & Brothers, Publishers, 1961).

Berelson, Bernard, and Gary A. Steiner, *Human Behavior* (New York: Harcourt, Brace & World, Inc., 1964).

Bierstedt, Robert, *The Social Order* (New York: McGraw-Hill Book Company, Inc., 1963).

Broom, Leonard, and Philip Selznick, *Sociology*, 3rd edition (New York: Harper & Row, Publishers, 1963).

Chinoy, Ely, *Society* (New York: Random House, Inc., 1961).

Cole, William E., *Introductory Sociology* (New York: David McKay Company, Inc., 1962).

Cuber, John F., *Sociology: A Synopsis of Principles*, 5th edition (New York: Appleton-Century-Crofts, 1963).

Gouldner, Alvin W., and Helen P. Gouldner, *Modern Sociology* (New York: Harcourt, Brace & World, Inc., 1963).

Green, Arnold W., *Sociology*, 4th edition (New York: McGraw-Hill Book Company, Inc., 1965).

Horton, Paul B., and Chester L. Hunt, *Sociology* (New York: McGraw-Hill Book Company, Inc., 1964).

Johnson, Harry M., *Sociology: A Systematic Introduction* (New York: Harcourt, Brace & Company, 1960).

Lundberg, George A., Clarence C. Schrag, and Otto N. Larsen, *Sociology*, 3rd edition (New York: Harper & Row, Publishers, 1963).

Merrill, Francis E., *Society and Culture* (Englewood Cliffs, New Jersey: Prentice-Hall, Inc., 1961).

Ogburn, William F., and Meyer F. Nimkoff, *Sociology*, 4th edition (Boston: Houghton Mifflin Company, 1964).

Quinn, James A., *Sociology* (Philadelphia: J. B. Lippincott Company, 1963).

Sutherland, Robert L., Julian L. Woodward, and Milton A. Maxwell, *Introductory Sociology*, 6th edition (Philadelphia: J. B. Lippincott Company, 1961).

Toby, Jackson, *Contemporary Society* (New York: John Wiley & Sons, Inc., 1964).

Williams, Robin M., Jr., *American Society*, 2nd edition (New York: Alfred A. Knopf, Inc., 1961).

Chapter	Bell	Berelson & Steiner	Bierstedt	Broom & Selznick	Chinoy	Cole
1	1-4	1, 3, 4	1-4	1-4	1, 4	1-4
2	12-14	2	—	18, 33, 36	5-7, 18-21	83
3	7	12-14	83	5-11, 15-16, 21, 34, 80	6, 20, 83	6-7
4	5-7	—	39-41	12-14, 17-20	18-19, 32	5-6
5	8	—	5, 6	22-25	2-3, 8-11, 33, 35, 38	—
6	24, 58, 77	—	6, 11, 15, 34	66-76	25-29, 42	39-41
7	—	51-53	12-14, 32	37-38	22-24	12, 22-25
8	—	15-17, 21-25, 30-32	7, 15-17, 24	26-32	51-53	14, 51-53
9	—	23, 36-38, 60	18-21	39-41, 45-47	66-76	24, 58
10	79, 80	54-65	22-29	14, 51-53, 85	34, 83-85	42, 50
11	81, 83	66-76	38	26, 54-56	36-38, 60	—
12	45	33-35, 83-85	20	27, 57-59	42-50	54-65
13	12-21	28	51-53	27, 34-35, 83-85	60-62	32-38
14	—	30-31	42-50, 74-76	24, 77-79	63-65	18-21
15	42, 50	24, 27, 39-50, 71, 77-82	66-74	42-44, 48-50	54-56	66-76
16	36, 38	5-11	84-85	60-62	—	45-47
17	37, 60, 62	—	54-65	63-65	39-41	43-44, 48-50
18	15-17, 21, 24		8-11		12-17	28, 30-32
19	21, 77-79, 82				21, 77-82	27
20	22-25, 27-29, 43-50				4, 57	8-11
21	36, 37, 60, 62					15-17
22	26					12-14, 32
23	33-38, 84, 85					77-82
24	66-76					83-85
25	51-65					
26	30-32					
27	8-11					
28	—					
29	—					
30	—					

Chapter	Cuber	Gouldner & Gouldner	Green	Horton & Hunt	Johnson	Lundberg, Schrag & Larsen
1	1, 3-4	1-4	1-4	1, 3	1-4	1, 3-4
2	1-2	15-21	—	2, 4	15-21	72
3	—	22-25, 30-32	15-25, 66	6-7, 77	18, 23	1
4	44	7, 15-16	36-38	5	5-7, 83	22-25, 33-35
5	6-7, 42	5-6	6-7, 15	12-15	12-14, 19	5-7, 15-17
6	5, 24, 77	12-14, 18-21	5, 20, 80-81	18-21	51-53	15-21
7	—	25, 66-76	12-14	16-17, 24, 77-82	—	12-14, 18
8	12, 80	27, 83-85	16, 18, 32	22-25, 38	20	30-32, 72
9	8-11	12-14, 22-25	39-41	—	42, 49, 65	28
10	—	36-38, 60-62	68-73	51-53	60, 62	26-29, 31
11	13-14	39-50	67, 74-76	66-73	61	38
12	12	51-65	27, 34-35, 83-85	30	36-38	66-76, 84
13	15-17, 21	80-81	42-50	33-38	64-65	36-37
14	80-82	36-37, 77-82	60, 67	74-76	30, 63	39-41
15	30-31	8-11, 40	60-62	83-85	26	43-50
16	18-21, 32		30, 63-65	17, 26-29, 31	55	42
17	22-25		51-52	39-41, 45	54, 56, 59	51-53
18	23, 36-37		14, 53	42-44, 46-50	33-35, 66-68, 70-73, 84-85	54-56
19	27, 83-85		26, 54-55	8-11, 80	69, 74-76	57-59
20	39-41		56, 59	—	77-82	60-62
21	43, 45-47		57-59		17	30, 60-63
22	42-44, 48-50		16, 65		8-11	77-82
23	66-76		77-79			8-11
24	—		28-29			2
25	51-53		8-11			1
26	60-62		61-62			
27	63-65					
28	57-59					
29	54-56					
30	77-79					
31	33-38					
32	—					

Chapter	Merrill	Ogburn & Nimkoff	Quinn	Sutherland, Woodward & Maxwell	Toby	Williams
1	1, 3-4	1-3	6, 42	1-4	1, 18, 21	1, 4
2	30-38	4	49	—	2-4, 18-21, 39-41	39-40
3	23, 25	5-7, 15	43-44	5, 7, 15	5-7	5-7, 15-19, 21
4	22, 24, 38	6, 12, 83-85	1, 5-11, 15, 18-19, 81	6, 8-11	29, 39-40, 49, 60-62	14-15, 20, 51-53, 85
5	7, 15-17	—	63-65	12, 77	22, 36, 43-50	66-76
6	5-6	16, 22-23, 33-38	60-62	18-21	34, 50-51	60-62
7	6	17, 26-29	14, 51-53	12-14, 18	66-73	30, 63-65
8	12-14, 19	17, 24	54-59	36-38	12-14	57-59
9	18-21, 66-67, 70	13-14, 16-21, 25, 32	8-11, 20, 33-38	33-35	24, 77-79	54-56
10	12, 71, 80-81	5, 12, 20, 24, 76-77	39-41	22-25	80-82	16, 21, 25, 77
11	39-41	71, 80-81	25, 45-47	26-32	16-17, 30-32, 35, 52	58, 83
12	83-85	42-50	42, 44, 48, 50	25, 66-76	57-59	18, 22-29, 37, 42
13	69	39-40	66-76	83-85	63-65	59
14	66-73	24, 39-41, 53	30-32	42-47	54-56	8
15	74-76	60	12-14	39-41	37, 60-62	
16	36	25, 66-76	5, 16-17, 21, 23-24, 77-80	48-50	73-76	
17	51-53	60-62	1-2	14, 51-53	8-11, 27, 83-85	
18	54-65	30, 63-65	7-8, 11, 15, 22, 26-29	27, 57-59		
19	42-44, 48-50	—		60-65		
20	45-47	54-56, 59		80-82		
21	8-11	51-53		54-56		
22	26-29	—		8-11		
23	28, 31	8-11				
24	38	9-10, 27				
25	77-79, 82	11, 77-79				
26	1	—				
27	2					